MW01506260

Coin World Almanac

- Eighth Edition -

By the Editorial staff of Coin World

Beth Deisher
William T. Gibbs
Steve Roach
Paul Gilkes
Michele Orzano
Erik Martin
Jeff Starck
Fern Loomis

(non-Coin World staff)
David T. Alexander
Susan L. Maltby
P. Scott Rubin

Coordinating Editor
Beth Deisher

Project Editor
William T. Gibbs

Published by Amos Press Inc., P.O. Box 150, Sidney, OH 45365-0150.
www.coinworld.com; iPad app at iTunes.com

We acknowledge the many individuals, including former *Coin World* staff members, who worked on the previous editions of the *Coin World Almanac*. Without their efforts, this, the eighth edition, would have been much more difficult to complete.

The Coin World Staff

Coin World Almanac
Eighth Edition

Correspondence concerning the content of this volume should be directed to the publisher.

Copyright © 2011
by Amos Press Inc.
P.O. Box 150
Sidney, OH 45365-0150
www.coinworld.com
ISBN 10: 0-944945-60-0
ISBN 13: 978-0-944945-60-5

Table of Contents

1 Review of the News 2000 to 2011

What a time it's been!

The hobby has been witness to momentous changes in U.S. coinage and paper money in the 11 years since the last edition of the *Coin World Almanac* was published in 2000.

The decade was tumultuous, as economic forces changed the hobby, shaping it in ways both immediately obvious and more subtle but with long-term significance .

Many story lines played out through several years during the decade, with some stories still ongoing. Many of the subjects continually in the news defined the decade, from constant new coinage designs to a rising market and ever-stronger precious metal prices.

Perhaps the most noticeable change is with the coins in pocket change.

At the dawn of the decade, the idea of frequent design changes was still fresh.

After 77 years, the Washington quarter dollar shed its old design to become a constantly evolving canvas for the State quarter dollar program.

The program popularized the idea of design variety in U.S. coinage, and collectors and noncollectors alike became accustomed to looking for the next new state quarter dollar design in their pocket change.

This paved the way for special circulating designs for the Jefferson 5-cent coin, then for the Lincoln cent; even the dollar coin that had made its debut at the end of the 20th century was a target for change.

During the past decade, paper money designs also, which had suffered from stasis for decades until the mid-1990s, were increasingly changed as federal agencies responded to a very real threat from counterfeiters with access to burgeoning technology helpful to their craft. Every Federal Reserve note denomination from $5 to $100 saw a new design introduced during the decade.

Another dominant story was the fate of 1933 Saint-Gaudens gold $20 double eagle coins.

Three years after the record-setting sale of the lone example that is legal to privately own, collectors learned that 10 more examples were in existence, the fate of which has generated much media coverage.

Economic forces conspired to trigger rabid demand for bullion coins, which spilled over into the collector realm and led to the suspension of popular coin programs.

Too, the rising price of the metals in coinage increased the value of even average collector issues.

These are just some of the threads woven throughout the hobby during the past 11 years.

As 2000 loomed, few collectors could have prophesied the turbulence — and exuberance — that would result.

2000

The first year of the 2000s was marked by news, again and again, that the impossible had become reality in the numismatic world, when several unprecedented and believed-impossible errors surfaced.

Mules and other impossible realities

Coins thought impossible surfaced in circulation. Some of these coins—pieces dated 2000 and found by average collectors—sold for tens of thousands of dollars, prompting a national treasure hunt for more examples.

Some of these coins were so "impossible" that many in the hobby suspected that something was seriously amiss at the United States Mint's production facilities.

That suspicion was strengthened when a Philadelphia Mint employee was arrested for stealing routine error coins from the Mint and selling them, and when a Mint headquarters official said that one unprecedented commemorative coin error truly was impossible.

The debut of the U.S. Mint's Sacagawea dollar coin brought exciting transitional errors—a 1999-P Anthony dollar struck on a Sacagawea dollar planchet and a 2000-P Sacagawea dollar struck on an Anthony dollar planchet.

These transitional errors were soon overshadowed by the discovery of what was thought to be the United States Mint's first-known U.S. mule, a State quarter dollar obverse paired with a Sacagawea dollar reverse on a Sacagawea dollar planchet.

The first of an eventual 10 confirmed mules surfaced in Mountain Home, Ark., in an Uncirculated roll of dollars from a local bank. The quarter dollar/dollar mules, discovered in 2000, are undated and bear the P Mint mark for the Philadelphia Mint.

The Mint broke its traditional silence about error coinage, acknowledging the mules and admitting that the Mint was aware that as many as three giant bins of mules were struck. However, Mint officials said that most of the mules were caught before they were released from the Philadelphia Mint. An unknown number entered circulation, according to the Mint.

Within a few weeks of the first quarter dollar-dollar mule being reported, Sacagawea dollars struck on a Barbados dollar coin (produced at the Royal Canadian Mint) and on an outer ring of Canada's ringed-bimetallic $2 coin surfaced. These errors occurred when the Barbados coin and the Canadian ring were accidentally mixed in with Sacagawea blanks burnished by the RCM. The U.S. Mint had sought RCM help in preparing the blanks for striking.

Hobbyists learned in August that the quarter dollar/dollar mule was not the U.S. Mint's first U.S. mule. Confirmation of the new mules resulted in Professional Coin Grading Service re-examining and authenticating a previously unreported mule that it had examined but refused to authenticate earlier in 2000. This mule was a 1999 Lincoln cent/Roosevelt dime combination, having the obverse of a Lincoln cent muled with the reverse of a Roosevelt dime, struck on a cent planchet.

The cent/dime mule had been sent to PCGS for authentication earlier, but because such an error was thought impossible, the service had declined to authenticate the mule. Mint confirmation that it had struck the quarter dollar/dollar mule cast a new light on the cent/dime mule, and made authentication of the cent/dime mule possible. Because it is dated 1999, the cent/dime mule was likely struck before the quarter dollar/dollar mule.

Other errors once thought impossible surfaced in 2000.

A Maryland quarter dollar struck on a Sacagawea planchet was reported in August. Error specialists had long thought such a combination impossible because the dollar planchet was larger in diameter than the planchet normally used in striking quarter dollars. While wrong planchet errors are a well-known form of error, previous known pieces were struck on planchets that were smaller in diameter than the intended planchets (a cent can be struck on a dime planchet, for example). Hobbyists believed that the larger planchet would jam the feed mechanism, making the Maryland quarter dollar on a dollar planchet impossible.

Another coin thought impossible was a 1999-W George Washington commemorative $5 half eagle struck on a copper-nickel clad dime planchet. David Pickens, U.S. Mint associate director for numismatics, seemed to admit as much to *Coin World* during the August American Numismatic Association convention in Philadelphia. Pickens, upon viewing that coin, told *Coin World* that there was no way the coin

could have been produced or packaged at the West Point Mint under normal circumstances.

That's because no dime planchets had been used at West Point since 1996, when a special 1996-W Roosevelt dime was struck for inclusion in that year's Uncirculated Mint sets. It seemed unlikely to many that a stray dime planchet would have remained undetected within the facility for three years before being accidentally fed between dies for a commemorative gold coin.

The error coin was reportedly discovered beneath a normal example of the gold commemorative in that coin's original packaging.

The pattern of unusual errors escaping the Mint brought intense scrutiny and scorn to the institution, specifically the Philadelphia facility, but a story that broke late in the year shed some light on the situation.

According to court documents, former Philadelphia Mint coinage press operator David J. D'Angelo admitted to stealing thousands of error coins and "coin clusters" with a value between $70,000 and $120,000 over a 15-month period. He stashed the stolen coins within the Mint, intending to smuggle them out a few at a time. Court records documented at least $80,000 in sales of stolen coins by D'Angelo to collectors and Internet auctioneers.

However, D'Angelo was not linked to the production or theft of any of the spectacular errors reported throughout 2000.

1943 cent errors make news

While 2000 will long be remembered as a year when major new errors entered circulation, it will also be remembered as a time when classic error coins made headlines.

The wrong metal Lincoln cents of 1943 and 1944 are among the most familiar of error coins, even to noncollectors.

The 1943 Lincoln cent struck on a copper-alloy planchet is especially well known both inside and outside the collecting community, although the 1944 cents struck on 1943's zinc-coated steel planchets are nearly as rare and valuable as the 1943 wrong metal cents.

The record price for one of the wrong metal cents was set Feb. 6 when a 1943-S Lincoln cent struck on a copper-alloy planchet sold for $115,000 in an auction by Ira and Larry Goldberg Coins and Collectibles. Merl D. Burcham had pulled this coin from a Mint-sewn bag of 1943-S Lincoln cents in 1943, according to the Goldberg catalog.

The 1943 wrong metal cents were struck on copper-alloy planchets left over from 1942 and held in the bins used to hold and transport planchets to the coining presses. The switch to a zinc-coated steel planchet was made in 1943 so that copper normally used for the cent could be diverted to America's war effort.

Similar manufacturing methods and circumstances are believed to explain the production of the 1944

1-cent coins struck on zinc-coated steel planchets, although in the case of the Philadelphia Mint coins, the steel planchets used for the cent in 1943 were still in use, but for 1944 2-franc coins for Belgium.

The report of a new price record for one of the coins often triggers dozens of reports of "new finds," although in most cases, the happy owners actually own a normal 1943 steel cent, a 1943 steel cent plated with copper as a novelty item, or a copper-alloy cent with the date altered to 1943. Only rarely are new examples of the 1943 or 1944 wrong metal cents confirmed.

However, confirmation of a new example of 1944 steel cent occurred twice during 2000, among long-time collections.

No other wrong metal error has managed to capture the numismatic interest, or fire public imagination, in quite the same way as these two coins.

SS *Central America* treasure enters market

Collectors may long remember 2000 as the year the first gold coins and bars from the treasure recovered from the *SS Central America* entered the numismatic market.

Collectors had been waiting for a chance to acquire a piece of the *SS Central America* treasure ever since the shipwreck was found in 1988 and the first gold coins and bars were lifted to the surface.

More than a decade of legal challenges, however, prevented the salvors, the Columbus-America Discovery Group, from offering any of the gold to the numismatic market; finally, the courts awarded more than 92 percent of the gold to the salvors and the remainder to insurance companies whose predecessors had paid off claims last century.

Collectors thought they were going to get a chance to bid on the insurance companies' portion when it came to auction in December 1999, but one last legal challenge from the salvors ended that auction just hours before it was set to begin.

Portions of the treasure finally entered the numismatic market in early 2000 when a group of coin dealers led by Dwight Manley formed the California Gold Group and purchased the salvors' 92.4 percent. The deal was reportedly the largest single transaction ever in numismatics, in the $100 million range.

The group offered the first coins—525 1857-S Coronet $20 double eagles—March 1. They sold out within a few months. The remaining 1857-S double eagles were offered throughout the year. Approximately three-fourths of the 7,500 gold coins recovered at the wreck site were 1857-S Coronet double eagles, struck at the San Francisco Mint in the weeks before the gold began its ill-fated voyage.

The insurance companies' portion finally went on the auction block June 20 and 21 in a sale by Christie's, and the 250 lots brought more than $5.56 million. The auction offered federal gold coins, pioneer gold coins, gold assay bars and gold nuggets. This auction offered buyers the first chance at something other than the 1857-S double eagles recovered from the *Central America*.

Christie's offered another portion, billed as the finest quality coins and ingots and unique pieces from the treasure find and consigned by the California Gold Marketing Group, in a Dec. 14 auction. That 169-lot auction brought more than $2.21 million.

While many collectors were excited at the opportunity to acquire some of the treasure, others were angry with what they perceived to be a double standard practiced by Professional Coin Grading Service, the firm grading and encapsulating the 1857-S Coronet double eagles offered beginning in March.

The controversy began when the salvors began talking about the state of many of the coins and bars recovered, and what was being done to them to prepare them for sale.

Many of the coins and bars were encrusted with a coating of rust, limestone and other materials, the result of biological activity surrounding the wreck. However, underneath the encrustation, the surfaces of the coins were found pristine, according to the salvors. Some means had to be developed to remove the encrusted materials without affecting the surfaces of the coins and bars.

Robert Evans, the chief scientist and historian for the salvors, developed a process that he and representatives of the California Gold Group termed "curating," a term he preferred over "cleaning" because the process used did not affect the surfaces of the gold coins, according to Evans.

Collectors began criticizing PCGS for grading and slabbing these "curated" coins. Critics, many of them calling or sending Letters to the Editor to *Coin World,* claimed that the salvors, the new owners and PCGS were playing word games—that "curating" was nothing more than "cleaning."

Especially angry were those who had sent coins to PCGS for grading, only to see them returned ungraded, in "body bags" with the notation that the coins could not be graded because they had been cleaned.

Some hobbyists claimed that a double standard appeared to be in effect. Coins sent anonymously by small-time collectors were being returned ungraded because they had been cleaned, while the *Central America* coins—whose owners were known to PCGS officials—were graded and encapsulated.

Sacagawea dollar debuts amid fanfare

What happens if a new coin is released but no one cares?

That question, a twist on the proverbial tree-falling-in-a-forest riddle, may have been on the minds of collectors as a new dollar coin made its debut in 2000.

The U.S. Mint spent more than $40 million for television, radio and newspaper publicity, to beat the drum loudly and stir interest in the ballyhooed Sacagawea "Golden dollar" coin. However, the public did not exactly embrace the coin depicting the famous young Native American mother and her child.

The Sacagawea dollar is the first U.S. coin to be struck in a composition of 77 percent copper, 12 percent zinc, 7 percent manganese, 4 percent nickel alloy bonded to a copper core.

In a joint promotion with General Mills, 2000-P Sacagawea dollars were salted into every 2,500th box out of 10 million specially marked boxes across six Cheerios brand cereal products, with every 4,400th box containing a certificate redeemable for 100 Sacagawea dollars.

Another 90 million to 100 million 2000-P Sacagawea dollars were shipped in specially wrapped paper rolls of 40 coins per roll to more than 3,000 Wal-Mart retail outlets, in an unprecedented move circumventing the Federal Reserve.

More than a billion Sacagawea dollar coins were struck at the Denver and Philadelphia Mints for circulation, and the bulk of them shipped to the Federal Reserve. However, the Mint faced an uphill battle to get the American public to use the Sacagawea dollar in commerce in vending machines and over-the-counter purchases.

Though initial collector interest was keen, much of the public use occurred in select mass transit systems nationwide and U.S. Postal Service stamp-dispensing machines rather than in widespread commercial transactions.

Silver Sacagawea?

The Sacagawea dollar prompted another notable event in 2000.

The U.S. Mint was forced to delay shipment of the much anticipated 2000-S Silver Proof set, awaiting a legislative remedy to a provision that could have forced the Mint to issue a 90 percent silver Sacagawea dollar.

The Mint ultimately persuaded legislators to change the law that authorized Silver Proof sets.

The problem originated with the 1990 legislation that authorized the resumption of Silver Proof sets in 1991 (production did not begin until 1992). That legislation called for all of the coin denominations in the set legally struck for circulation, except for the Lincoln cent and Jefferson 5-cent coin, to be coined in 90 percent silver.

The requisite silver provision applied to the Roosevelt dime, Washington quarter dollar (since 1999, the five State quarters) and Kennedy half dollar. The dollar denomination was technically included in the 1990 act, but by then the Anthony dollar hadn't been struck for circulation since 1980, and not at all since 1981. However, 1999 Anthony dollars were eventually struck for circulation, pending the 2000 circulation release of the Sacagawea dollar. Separately, Proof 1999-P Anthony dollars made of copper-nickel clad were issued, but no silver versions were struck.

The U.S. Mint in 2000 faced two prospects: possibly issuing an illegal set, with a manganese-brass clad dollar, or striking a silver "golden" Sacagawea

dollar to comply with the 1990 law.

The Mint reportedly produced tens of thousands of the sets with the manganese-brass clad Sacagawea dollars before passage of the requested legislation, gambling that federal legislators would come to the rescue and amend legislation, to exempt the Sacagawea dollar from the silver provision.

Without the congressional action, the Mint would have had to cannibalize those already packaged sets to retrieve the manganese-brass clad dollars and replace them with silver ones.

The Mint got its reprieve, to the chagrin of many collectors who wanted to see sets issued with a Sacagawea silver dollar.

The legislation introduced Sept. 25 was a technical amendment to the Dollar Coin Act of 1997 that authorized the Sacagawea dollar. The House of Representatives approved it the following day and forwarded it to the Senate whose members adopted it Oct. 24 by unanimous consent. President Clinton signed the measure into law Nov. 6, and tardy shipments of the 2000-S Silver Proof sets began the same week.

Paper money design changes

The first round of redesign of Federal Reserve notes that began in 1996 was completed in 2000 with the release of redesigned Series 1999 $5 and $10 Federal Reserve notes.

As with the $20, $50 and $100, the Series 1999 $5 and $10 notes featured completely new designs, but themes that were familiar to those who use U.S. paper money.

The notes show new, larger, off-centered portraits of Abraham Lincoln (on the $5 note) and Alexander Hamilton (on the $10 note) on the face, with the backs showing new renditions of the Lincoln Memorial (on the $5 note) and Treasury Building (on the $10). The back of the $10 note provides a view of the main Treasury Building as seen from Hamilton Street. The new design eliminated the whole question about whether a more modern automobile would replace the 1920s model seen on the street outside the Treasury Building on earlier versions of $10 notes. The new Series 1999 design eliminated the view of the street altogether.

The $5 and $10 notes were not redesigned simply to change their appearance. The redesign was necessary to allow upgrading of visible anti-counterfeiting devices on all but the $1 and $2 Federal Reserve notes. For example, addition of a watermark to each note required shifting the portrait left of center.

Some of the anti-counterfeiting devices on the new $10 and $5 notes include the larger, off-center portraits; polymer security threads that glow different colors under ultraviolet light; the watermark; a low vision numeral to help those with low vision to identify the denomination; microprinting; color-shifting ink, used on the 1990s generation $10 through $100 notes but not the $5 note; and concentric fine lines appearing behind the portraits and back vignettes.

In addition to security devices the public can see, the BEP added an invisible feature to help spur development of inexpensive, pocket-size, money-reading machines for the blind.

The back of each note features a finger-wide strip printed with an ink that seems to disappear when exposed to infrared light. The strip is in a different position on each denomination and under natural light, it is impossible to tell two different green inks were used, according to Treasury officials.

Coin World began receiving reports in late May from readers who were finding the new Series 1999 $5 and $10 notes in circulation.

2001

2001 may be remembered by collectors as the year in which one of the most popular U.S. coin designs was resurrected to great acclaim.

Strong interest in American Buffalo $1

The 2001 American Buffalo commemorative silver dollar, featuring modified versions of the designs sculptor James Earle Fraser produced for the Indian Head 5-cent coin, met rabid demand from coin collectors and speculators alike.

When Congress passed legislation authorizing the coin, legislators knew they had a popular coin on their hands whose sale could raise funds to help support the Museum of the American Indian at the Smithsonian Institution's Museum of American History.

U.S. Mint officials also knew they had a popular commemorative program on their hands, but couldn't have anticipated just how popular the program would become. The entire maximum authorized mintage of 500,000 Proof and Uncirculated coins was reported sold out in a record two weeks' time.

The sellout also marked the intersection of serious demand and the then-still nascent technology of the Internet.

Many collectors were shut out completely from being able to place an order, while others, even after receiving confirmation, had their orders either canceled or reduced from the number of items originally confirmed.

Orders for the single Proof and Uncirculated dollars, two-coin sets and 50,000 limited-edition Coinage and Currency sets were accepted by the Mint by telephone, fax or mail beginning June 7. Collectors and dealers alike placed orders, in some cases multiple orders, for multiple examples of each option available, banking on the market potential of the coins.

When sales of the American Buffalo silver dollars commenced on the Mint's website beginning June 11, an arbitrary decision by the Mint's marketing hierarchy limited the number of each ordering option, whereas no limitations had been imposed when sales began June 7. The biggest complaints centered on the Mint limiting the number of Coinage and Currency sets to 20 per order and the decision to reduce orders already confirmed since June 7 to the new restriction.

As a result of the ordering debacle and the perceived number of individuals who wanted one of the cherished coins but were unable to get one, impassioned pleas came from two separate camps to Secretary of the Treasury Paul O'Neill seeking additional production to satisfy the demand.

Smithsonian officials petitioned O'Neill to permit the Mint to strike another 500,000 silver dollars under terms of a little-known provision in commemorative coin reform law that went into effect Jan. 1, 1999. The additional production was permissible if an independent marketing study could convince the Treasury secretary the demand was there.

Neither the Smithsonian's plea, nor a separate one for 250,000 more coins (possibly with a differentiating marker of a second issue) by Sen. Ben Nighthorse Campbell, R-Colo., who introduced the original American Buffalo silver dollar legislation, was approved. O'Neill cited the lack of an independent marketing study to support the claim of increased demand as his main reason for denying the requests.

Collectors had mixed reactions to the possibility of additional production. Many objected to the suggestion, saying it would threaten the future of commemorative coinage programs if collectors could never be certain that maximum mintages would be respected. Many others, including those shut out of the program, welcomed another opportunity to acquire the coins.

1933 gold $20 double eagle saga

Deadlines can be a serious motivator, especially in litigation.

On Jan. 25, 2001, four days before a case involving ownership of a 1933 Saint-Gaudens $20 gold double eagle was to go to trial, attorneys representing the U.S. Mint and British coin dealer Stephen C. Fenton reached a settlement that granted Fenton and the government equal rights to the coin. The coin had been seized Feb. 8, 1996, when the owners, including Fenton, tried to sell it in New York City to an undercover Secret Service agent.

The 1933 double eagle was the last regular-issue U.S. gold coin denomination struck by the United States Mint and was never placed into circulation. Government officials have contended for decades that the few examples that made their way into coin collections could not be legally held. The U.S. Secret Service had seized nine such coins in the 1940s and 1950s, all of which the government destroyed.

Government officials in the 1940s were aware of at least one other example in private hands. In early 1944, the United States government granted the Egyptian government an export license for an example of the coin, which Egypt King Farouk, a coin collector, had purchased from an American coin dealer. A few weeks after the license was granted, another example of the coin was announced as coming to auction. A newspaper reporter's inquiry to the Mint about the coin being sold resulted in officials examining Mint records, something that had not been done when the Farouk export license was requested. After studying records, Mint officials concluded that the coins had not been released officially and therefore could not be privately owned.

The ensuing investigation in 1944 resulted in the beginning of the seizures of the coins from collectors. The U.S. government also tried to persuade the Egyptian government to return the coin in Farouk's collection but was rebuffed. They tried again in 1954 when the Farouk coin collection was sold at auction after the king was overthrown in a military coup. The coin was removed from the 1954 auction but its whereabouts became a mystery for decades.

Fenton obtained a 1933 double eagle and more than 100 other coins from what he later identified as Farouk's collection in several private transactions in 1995.

Soon after the coin was seized in 1996, federal government attorneys commenced action alleging that the coin had been stolen from the Philadelphia Mint in the 1930s because it had not been officially issued. After initially proceeding criminally, government attorneys changed direction by commencing a civil forfeiture and declaratory judgment action seeking forfeiture of Fenton's 1933 double eagle.

Fenton's attorney, Barry H. Berke, was prepared to go to trial with extensive evidence establishing the provenance of the gold piece, claiming that this coin previously had been part of the famous collection of Egypt's King Farouk. Berke uncovered evidence that the United States Treasury Department had issued the export license for the Farouk 1933 double eagle in 1944, something that was not generally known until Berke revealed the existence of the license.

While government officials never officially acknowledged the Fenton coin to be the Farouk coin, the ensuing legal action from the 1996 seizure resulted in the government eventually conceding partial private ownership in the disputed coin. Under the settlement, what many identify as the Farouk specimen of the 1933 double eagle is the only one that may be legally held in private hands.

The coin remained in Secret Service custody until transfer to Mint custody soon after the settlement was reached. After that custody transfer it was secured at the Fort Knox Gold Bullion Depository in Kentucky.

The Secret Service had stored the coin in a government vault at the World Trade Center in New York City. That complex was destroyed by the terrorist attacks of Sept. 11.

The coin was offered at auction in 2002 (under terms agreed upon by both parties, who split the proceeds).

Two other publicly known specimens, determined to have been struck from the same pair of dies as the Fenton coin, are housed in the National Numismatic Collection at the Smithsonian Institution.

The U.S. government contends that other extant examples remain subject to confiscation, a story that would be told during much of the later part of the decade.

More SS *Central America* treasure

The sale of treasure from the 1857 shipwreck SS *Central America* was still making headlines in 2001.

The most astounding news was the $8 million that one anonymous multimillionaire paid to acquire the largest assay ingot salvaged—the 933.94-ounce ingot produced by the San Francisco assaying concern of Kellogg & Humbert and dubbed by the California Gold Marketing Group as the "Eureka" bar.

The California Gold Marketing Group had reportedly turned down an offer of $7.5 million made in January 2001 for the Eureka bar before the bar was ultimately sold to the anonymous buyer.

The bar is stamped with the serial No. 1003, the assayer stamp of Kellogg and Humbert, the weight of 933.94 ounces, the fineness at .903 fine, and its value in 1857—$17,433.57.

Marketers continued to place with collectors assay bars from Kellogg & Humbert and four other California assayers, along with pioneer and U.S. gold coins, all from the SS *Central America* cargo.

The California Gold Marketing Group melted more than 60 of the lesser-quality assay bars after having the face plates removed and refined the remaining metal to fabricate planchets for striking gold commemoratives with transfer dies made from original 1855 Kellogg & Co. $50 coin dies.

Collectors were willing to spend in the neighborhood of $5,000 to acquire Proof and Uncirculated examples of the medals, each of which contained 2.5 ounces of gold.

The commemoratives were struck daily from Aug. 20 through Sept. 12. The dates coincided with the anniversaries of the original gold cargo leaving San Francisco Bay on the SS *Sonora* to the time the SS *Central America* sank during a violent hurricane nearly 200 miles off the coast of South Carolina.

The striking of the gold commemoratives took place at The Presidio, the former military installation that overlooks the entrance to San Francisco Bay.

Some 5,000 commemoratives were sold, with a handful of well-heeled collectors purchasing pieces from each of the 24 days of production. The reverse of the each of the pieces is counterstamped with the date of striking.

Sept. 11, 2001, terrorist attacks

Every generation during the 20th century seems to have been touched by a catalytic American tragedy, and the Sept. 11, 2001, assault on the homeland stands out as the latest "where were you when?" moment.

Effects of and America's responses to the terrorist attacks on Sept. 11 included some that directly affected the coin collecting community. Among the effects, public tours and sales areas at federal money-making facilities were changed, a new location for an annual New York City coin show became necessary, and much congressional legislation was generated.

Further, the attack on the Pentagon in Arlington, Va., forced the evacuation of federal buildings in the District of Columbia, including the U.S. Mint headquarters, Treasury and Bureau of Engraving and Printing.

Within hours of the attack, coinage operations were suspended at the Mint's production facilities, and security heightened at those facilities and at the Fort Knox Gold Bullion Depository. All staff other than security personnel were reported evacuated from the facilities. Coin production was resumed with the first shifts beginning Sept. 12.

Public tours at the Philadelphia and Denver Mints were suspended and public sales outlets at both facilities for Mint numismatic products were closed on Sept. 11.

Though tours and sales resumed Sept. 12 at the Philadelphia Mint and Sept. 13 at the Denver Mint, a few weeks later officials canceled tours and closed public sales centers until further notice. The BEP's public tour and Visitor's Center Gift Shop in Washington, D.C., remained closed through the end of 2001.

The attacks on the World Trade Center in New York City also destroyed the location of the scheduled Dec. 7 to 9 New York International Numismatic Convention. The bourse in recent years had been arranged on the second-floor mezzanine that surrounded the elevators of one of the two World Trade Center towers.

A new location and new dates for the show were announced in late October— it would be in Manhattan's Waldorf-Astoria Hotel on Jan. 18 to 20, 2002.

The attacks also prompted a flurry of legislative proposals calling for commemoration of the attacks and recognition of the victims with coins or medals, but no proposal would muster enough support to become law.

Specially inscribed U.S. savings bonds went on sale Dec. 11, 2001—three months to the day after the terrorist attacks in New York, Washington, D.C., and Pennsylvania.

The Series EE savings bonds feature the words PATRIOT BOND overprinted in the upper right corner.

Then-Treasury Secretary Paul O'Neill and then-U.S. Treasurer Rosario Marin unveiled the bonds during ceremonies in the Treasury Department.

The funds raised by the bonds were not earmarked for a specific purpose but to contribute to the federal government's overall effort to fight the war on global terrorism, according to Treasury officials.

O'Neill characterized the Patriot Bonds as "an opportunity for all Americans to contribute to the government's war effort and save for their futures as well."

Although legislation authorizing similar bonds was pending before Congress at the time, the Treasury secretary issued the bonds without congressional approval, under the authority of his office.

Other stories

State quarter dollar/Sacagawea dollar coin mules continued to make news in 2001, as two more examples were discovered and authenticated. That brought the total number of known mules featuring the obverse of a State quarter dollar with the reverse of the Sacagawea dollar to 10.

Collector Tommy Bolack, who acquired six of the mules in 2000, bought the 10th example for $70,000.

Not only Sacagawea dollar error examples shaped the news in 2001.

After production of more than 1.29 billion of the Sacagawea dollars in their debut year, production fell to about one-tenth that level in 2001 as no demand materialized.

The perceived unattractiveness of the coin as it toned shortly after entering circulation did not help matters. The new alloy was prone to unattractive spotting or streaking, and color changes typically began with minimal circulation.

These effects negated the golden dollar nickname and led to speculation within the numismatic community that the Mint was conducting tests on the alloy to suspend the negative effects.

This speculation gained credence in 2001 when dollar coins with a differing luster and a darker color compared to normal circulation strike dollars entered the market.

The several hundred abnormal coins were discovered in a counting room; they eventually were bought by error specialist Mike Byers of Byers Numismatic Corp.

Byers submitted the coins to Sovereign Entities Grading Service for assessment, with the agreement that a small number of the coins would be used for testing.

Numerous tests and consultation with several error coin experts led SEGS to conclude the coins' unusual luster and color was not from some sort of coating, but instead that the coins had been subjected to some sort of experimental rinse or finish at the Mint.

Yet another controversy about finishes attracted attention in 2001.

Sacagawea dollar coin obverse designer Glenna Goodacre had been compensated for her design with $5,000 in golden dollar coins. When the coins were sold and submitted to authentication services for grading and encapsulating, debate arose over whether the coins, which exhibited a special, distinct glossy surface, had been burnished before or after their striking.

Error coin experts argued that, if the burnishing occurred post-strike, that meant the coins were cleaned and thus not eligible for grading.

The Mint disclosed that the Goodacre dollars had been washed and dried after their striking, and further investigation revealed that the washing procedure included immersion in a solution including a burnishing compound.

2002

The year 2002 is remembered for the record-setting sale of the 1933 Saint-Gaudens gold $20 double eagle that some say once belonged to Egypt's King Farouk, bringing a resolution to a case that began when the coin surfaced in 1996.

1933 Saint-Gaudens gold $20 double eagle

One of the most intriguing numismatic events conducted during 2002 was the July 30 auction in New York City of the only 1933 Saint-Gaudens $20 gold double eagle that is legal to own. The coin realized a record price of $7.59 million.

The single-lot auction, held at Sotheby's galleries in conjunction with Stack's, drew hundreds of numismatists and other luminaries eager to witness history being made.

The coin brought a hammer price of $6.6 million after less than 10 minutes of spirited bidding. The 15 percent buyer's fee was added to the total, along with a $20 Federal Reserve note to reimburse the government for officially "monetizing" the double eagle.

The coin was accompanied by a bill of sale and transfer of title specially designed and engraved by the Bureau of Engraving and Printing.

The auction closed one chapter in the coin's storied journey, but created another mystery: Who bought the coin? It seems that the only one who knows for sure is David Redden, Sotheby's senior vice president. He not only served as auctioneer for the coin, but also acted as an intermediary to maintain the winning bidder's anonymity.

The numismatic community had voiced much concern that the buyer of the Farouk coin would simply secure the coin out of the public eye, much as it had been when owned by the Egyptian monarch.

The third week of November, however, the double eagle traveled under escort by U.S. Mint security to join the extensive collection of rarities from the American Numismatic Society being placed on exhibit at the Federal Reserve Bank of New York (an exhibit still ongoing in mid 2011).

U.S. Mint activities

The U.S. Mint's primary customer is, of course, the Federal Reserve Bank, but it has a long history of reaching out to collector-customers with product pitches.

The U.S. Mint in 2002 explored uncharted territory with a wide range of numismatic products that it had previously not offered.

In 2002, the U.S. Mint struck fewer than 5 million 2002-P and 2002-D Sacagawea dollars, miniscule compared to the mintages of 1.29 billion coins in 2000 and some 110 million coins in 2001.

Following a glut of dollar coinage production in 2000 and 2001, the Federal Reserve ordered no Sacagawea dollars in 2002, so the U.S. Mint borrowed a sales tactic it had employed in marketing the State quarter dollars.

In a logical move, the Mint's Sales and Marketing Unit purchased the circulation-quality 2002 Sacagawea dollars from the Manufacturing Unit and then sold the coins directly to collectors and dealers in 2,000-coin bags and 25-coin rolls, for a premium.

Sales were so robust that the Mint struck additional quantities to fill the orders.

A similar situation arose with the 2002 Kennedy half dollars, which had experienced significant production reductions in recent years. Although the Federal Reserve ordered no half dollars from the Mint, the Mint struck circulation-quality examples and sold them to collectors and dealers at a premium.

Offering the coins direct to collectors in various options, once uncommon, is now routine.

While the Mint enjoyed an abundance of dollar and half dollar coins in 2002, a six-week shutdown of the Philadelphia Mint in the spring of 2002 helped create the lowest mintage State quarter dollar to that point.

It also evoked memories of practices from centuries ago, when shutting down the facility was an annual event because of the recurring outbreak of yellow fever in the city of Philadelphia.

The 21st century closing differed though from the shutdowns during the early years of the Mint in the late 18th and early 19th centuries.

The 2002 closing was voluntary, and the cause was not yellow fever but irregularities cited by the Occupational Safety and Health Administration.

However, similar to early shutdowns, the closings affected not only coinage production for the calendar year when the closings occurred, but production in following years as well.

On March 4, 2002, coinage production at the fourth Philadelphia Mint was suspended at the request of U.S. Mint Director Henrietta Holsman Fore, in consultation with Treasury Department officials, while steps were pursued to rectify serious health and safety violations. All of the violations were soon corrected.

The self-imposed shutdown was not without sacrifice. The closing stopped production of the 2002-P Ohio quarter dollar, which had begun only a few days before.

Less than a week's work of Ohio quarter dollar production had occurred before the coinage presses went silent.

Typically, each State quarter dollar was scheduled for a minimum of 10 weeks of production before commencement of work on the next State quarter. If demand for one of the State quarter dollars warranted, production could extend for up to 12 weeks during the course of the 10-year program.

Mint officials had expected to step up output of the 2002-P Ohio quarter dollars after reopening, so that overall production reached those of the Denver Mint, where the production schedule remained unchanged.

Circulating coinage production, which included the State quarter dollars, did not resume at the Philadelphia Mint until April 18.

Numismatic coin production, which included coins for annual Uncirculated Mint sets as well as commemoratives, resumed March 22.

The loss of six weeks of State quarter production time resulted in the 2002-P Ohio quarter dollar achieving the lowest mintage in the State quarter series to that point, with just 217.2 million coins produced.

State quarter dollars

State quarter dollars and the process involved in selecting their designs made big hobby news in 2002.

Tennessee's coin depicts a guitar, violin, sheet music and trumpet, reflecting the state's contribution of blues, folk and country music to American culture. The inscription on a banner below the instruments reads MUSICAL HERITAGE. Three stars represent Tennessee's three regions and the distinct musical styles from each.

Musically minded collectors alerted *Coin World* to a problem with the six-string guitar, which appears to have only five strings, especially on poorly struck examples of the coin.

The Ohio quarter dollar was one of several to undergo design changes between approval at state level and release, as the State quarter dollars program experienced its share of difficulties during 2002.

Ohio's coin celebrates the state's role in aviation, but a someone unidentified by U.S. Mint officials made a change to the state-approved legend.

The legend on the final rendition as used for production states BIRTHPLACE OF AVIATION PIONEERS, a departure from that on the design approved by Ohio officials. The approved legend stated BIRTHPLACE OF AVIATION. The Wright brothers lived in Dayton, Ohio, and did most of the aviation experiments at Dayton. And after the December 1903 flights in North Carolina, the Wrights conducted the rest of their flight tests near Dayton.

Additionally, the pose of the space-suited astronaut on the Mint version was changed because the original design was apparently modeled on a photo of Col. Edwin "Buzz" Aldrin Jr., a New Jersey native. Mint rules governing State quarter dollar designs prohibited using recognizable images of living individuals such as Aldrin.

Changes made by Mint officials to Indiana's 2002 State quarter dollar design did not escape criticism either.

As with Ohio, Mint officials presented Indiana with a design significantly different from that initially selected by its governor and preferred by the state's public.

The final design depicted an Indianapolis 500 style race car positioned slightly above and to the right of the center, superimposed over an outline of the state. A circle of 17 stars and two additional stars indicate that Indiana was the 19th state to enter the Union. The legend CROSSROADS OF AMERICA appears below the car.

The design Hoosier officials preferred had also depicted an Indianapolis race car superimposed over an outline of the state, but positioned slightly differently. The preferred design also depicted a basketball player, reflecting another strong state sports theme. Mint officials removed the ball player without approval from Indiana officials.

During 2002, collectors learned why previous designs did not come close to the concept illustrations submitted by states: Mint engravers received only written descriptions of design concepts for 2001 to 2003 State quarter dollars, instead of seeing any artwork sent by governors of those 15 states.

As reported in a story in the Oct. 21, 2002, issue of *Coin World,* Mint officials admitted the process for submitting designs had changed throughout the first five years of the program.

The design submission process for State quarter dollar designs changed several times for states honored from 1999 to 2003.

For the coins designed for 1999 and 2000, engravers were sent photos, children's sketches, written descriptions and actual finished designs, all provided by state officials to Mint headquarters. The engraving staff had these materials available for consultation during their phase of the design process.

The change in the overall process was made, according to Mint officials, "to avoid complications associated with historical accuracy, copyright issues and artistic rights."

For the 2001 series, some states began submitting text-only descriptions of their design concepts and, during the 2002 to 2003 series, the Mint transmitted text-only descriptions to the engravers from all the states honored in those years.

Mint officials said "because the Mint engravers were not seeing the state submissions," the "designs were rendered differently than the original submissions based on the engravers' own interpretations of the concepts."

The new process snarled the design selection process for the Missouri quarter dollar.

The design used on the coin shows three men paddling a solitary boat down a tree-lined river with the Arch of Discovery (St. Louis Arch) in the background, with the legend CORPS OF DISCOVERY 1804 2004. This final version selected by Gov. Bob Holden and Missouri first lady Lori Hauser Holden was the Mint's third rendition of the design concept, all of which differ considerably from Columbia artist Paul Jackson's original version.

The Holdens sent the top five design concepts, including Jackson's submission, to the Mint April 20. Mint officials returned revised designs to the state, created by the Mint engraving staff at the Philadelphia Mint.

The Mint's first rendition of the design featured significant differences, including the substitution of a pirogue for the canoe in the original (also placed closer to the foreground than in the original), addition of a third person to the boat's crew and omission of trees along the riverbanks on either side of the river. Later designs incorporated trees, though the rendition of the trees differed greatly from those of Jackson's original design, as did the detail of the water.

The Mint's multiple reworkings of the design submitted by Jackson resulted in an ongoing controversy. Jackson launched a public protest about changes made to his original design concept.

Coinage redesign

A movement toward sweeping coinage redesign inched forward in 2002, with collector support but congressional protest.

At the top of the U.S. Mint's wish list was the 5-cent coin, whose changes were intended to coincide in 2003 with a notable milestone.

The 5-cent coin was selected because of the role Thomas Jefferson—who is depicted on the coin—played in the Louisiana Purchase and in organizing the Corps of Discovery, which explored the new territory. The U.S. Mint Task Force on Coin Redesign recommended beginning design changes with the 5-cent coin as part of the multi-year salute during the 2004 to 2006 bicentennial of the Lewis and Clark Expedition.

The task force envisioned a new Jefferson portrait for the obverse and a new reverse design thematic of western expansion.

Mint officials expressed a desire to redesign one denomination per year, with the dime receiving a new design in 2004, the half dollar in 2005 and the cent in 2006.

Legislation for such redesign was not necessary. The secretary of the Treasury is empowered under provisions of the Mint Act of Sept. 26, 1890, to unilaterally change coin designs without congressional approval once the designs have appeared on U.S. coinage for the obligatory 25 years cited under the enabling legislation. The designs for the Jefferson 5-cent coin had been introduced in 1938.

Despite the Treasury's authority to change designs in place 25 years or longer, Congress attempted to block the 5-cent coin's redesign.

Virginia's congressional delegation was so outraged by the Mint's plan to redesign the coin, which features Virginian Jefferson and his home Monticello, that the state's Rep. Eric I. Cantor sponsored a bill that would prevent the Treasury from removing Monticello from the design.

While Congress resisted design change for the 5-cent coin, collector opinion favored a sweeping coinage redesign. The idea was greeted with enthusiasm by collectors at Mint forums throughout the year and country, and 93 percent of respondents to a *Coin World* Internet poll voted in favor of redesign.

Many of the collectors commenting on this issue expressed anger at the Virginia delegation for stopping the Mint's plans, and they noted that the 5-cent coin is a U.S. coin, not a Virginian coin.

Registry sets

U.S. coins in exceptionally high grades experienced a boom in sales, causing some collectors to wonder what was driving the rapid price increases.

One example was the $19,250 realized for a 1948-S Washington quarter dollar during a Teletrade auction.

The coin happened to be the only 1948-S Washington quarter dollar certified Mint State 68 by either Numismatic Guaranty Corp. or Professional Coin Grading Service at the time. It was certified by NGC.

Record auction prices being brought by coins "unique" to some high grade or exceedingly rare in such a high state of preservation were perceived by some to be a product of NGC and PCGS set registries.

Set registries, by definition, are listings of the finest coin sets in existence.

The owner of a given set is identified and the set is given a distinctive name. The grading company keeps track of the percentage by which a set is complete and scores its quality.

Competition for "the finest," among collectors with enough money, has always been evident, particularly in auction bidding battles. The set system, like the numerical grading system used by the services, quantifies quality and keeps tabs on sets being developed. In effect, it keeps scores.

Joint currency experiment

As 2002 dawned, so too did implementation of the largest joint currency conversion ever attempted in human history.

Overnight on Jan. 1, 2002, the euro currency became the coin of the realm for millions of people across Europe.

This sweeping transition from 12 national "legacy" currencies to one throughout the eurozone was arguably the most anticipated numismatic event in decades.

Euro coins and paper money immediately began circulating officially in 12 member nations of the European Union: Austria, Belgium, Finland, France, Germany, Greece, Ireland, Italy, Luxembourg, the Netherlands, Portugal and Spain.

Though the New Year's release date marked the first time the euro notes were available to the public, "starter kits" containing examples of the coinage were released in December, before the transition, to help people become familiar with the coinage.

The Jan. 1 date also marked the first time the currency, which had been traded on international markets for several years, would be actually used in daily transactions.

Planning was so intense that in their zeal to avoid shortages, some countries, most notably France and Germany, greatly overestimated the number of new coins needed for circulation in 2002.

The French government ordered its mint to produce 8 billion euro coins in anticipation of the switch from the franc. Only about 5 billion coins entered circulation that first year, leaving more than 3 billion surplus coins reportedly sitting in the Bank of France's vaults.

For Germany more than 17 billion euro coins were produced to replace the deutschmark, but only 10 billion of the coins entered circulation within the year.

The euro excited collectors, many of whom saw the introduction of the euro as an opportunity to collect a currency from its beginning.

Coin dealers had success with their euro offerings, with Proof sets, Mint sets and commemorative coins proving to be especially popular.

The small mintages of euros issued by non-EU countries such as Monaco, San Marino and the Vatican City caused headaches for collectors and dealers. High demand for these countries' issues sent prices on the secondary market skyrocketing above original issue price.

2003

A "missing" rarity resurfaced in 2003, leading to a historic reunion at the American Numismatic Association World's Fair of Money in Baltimore.

1913 Liberty Head 5-cent coin

The 1913 Liberty Head 5-cent coin is among the fabled fraternity of numismatic rarities and the story of how one of the five examples known became lost to the hobby community for 41 years and was rediscovered only adds to the overall legend.

Heirs and relatives of George O. Walton, a Virginia coin dealer who had died in a 1962 automobile crash, brought the coin to the Baltimore Convention Center on the morning of July 29, where experts were eagerly awaiting the chance to view the specimen.

Behind the anticipation lay a mystery. When Walton's car crashed, he was supposed to be carrying one of the five known 1913 "V nickels." A coin fitting the description was recovered from the crash scene and was among Walton's collection consigned for auction in 1963 to Stack's of New York City. However, Stack's returned the coin to the executor of Walton's estate, saying it had an altered date. The coin, mounted in a custom plastic case, was stored in an heir's closet for the next 40 years.

For more than a decade before his death Walton had displayed the coin in the specially made case at regional coin shows. Some suggested his coin was fake; others reported Walton said it was genuine but on loan from a wealthy client. Speculation about his clients led some to believe that a member of the famed R.J. Reynolds family of North Carolina may have owned it. Thus, from the mid-1960s onward, researchers dubbed the "missing 1913 Liberty Head nickel" as the "Reynolds Specimen."

On May 23, 2003, Bowers and Merena Galleries of Mandeville, La., announced a reward of $10,000 just to be first to examine and verify the "missing" 1913 coin and a guarantee of $1 million if the coin were auctioned. The announcement was carried prominently by major news outlets. Bowers and Merena was inundated by phone calls, and so were many

other dealers as well as hobby publications.

The reward was prompted by a "grand reunion" of four of the 1913 Liberty Head 5-cent coins planned for the ANA show in Baltimore.

Owners of the Legend specimen of the 1913 Liberty Head 5-cent coin announced in January of 2003 their intent to display it at the upcoming August ANA show in Baltimore. The announcement helped to persuade the owners of the other three known examples—Dwight Manley, the Smithsonian Institution, and the American Numismatic Association Money Museum—to display theirs.

The Walton heirs let it be known that they still had the piece that was the subject of speculation years ago and that they would be willing to submit it for fresh examination. It was arranged for the Walton heirs to bring their coin to Baltimore to be examined by an expert authentication panel.

The authenticators thus had what Mark Borckardt termed a once-in-a-lifetime opportunity—to compare all of the four known pieces with the suspect Walton coin at the same time.

Representing Bowers and Merena for the first examination of the Walton piece in Baltimore were Paul Montgomery, president; Borckardt, vice president; and John Dannreuther, who had brought a photo of a genuine example to the gathering.

The three concluded that the Walton piece was almost certainly genuine. Borckardt said a planchet flaw in the date area and some discoloration probably were factors in Stack's altered-date assessment. The diagnostic of the planchet flaw in the date area for this specimen was not public knowledge in 1963.

Further examination had to wait until after the four other coins arrived late that evening at the convention center under armed guard. Just after midnight, four additional authenticators—David Hall, president of Professional Coin Grading Service; Fred Weinberg, PCGS consultant; Jeff Garrett, dealer; and Larry Lee, ANA museum curator—joined the first three. All concluded that the Walton piece was indeed genuine.

The Walton coin was placed on exhibit the next day along with the four other coins. All five coins had not been together in more than 60 years.

"It pays to get a second opinion" was the headline on a *Coin World* editorial about the outcome.

SS *Republic* wreck discovered

Another sort of recovered treasure served to excite the hobby community in 2003.

In October 1865, the SS *Republic*, a passenger vessel, was blasted by a hurricane in the Atlantic Ocean. The steamship sank after its passengers and crew climbed into lifeboats and lowered themselves into the stormy seas. Still aboard the vessel as it slipped beneath the waves was a reported fortune in gold, to remain entombed until July 2003. Tampa, Fla., firm, Odyssey Marine Exploration Inc., found the wreckage after pursuing it for about a decade.

The SS *Republic* had been en route from New York to New Orleans, with a cargo that contemporary news accounts identified as $400,000 in gold specie. The gold was intended to help shore up the economy of the southern city in the aftermath of the Civil War.

After finding a wreck the Tampa firm's owners believed was the *Republic,* the company began shoring up its claims to any treasure the ship may have carried aboard when it sank. The firm's owners filed legal claims to the wreckage and its contents. And, according to a firm co-founder, they agreed to share in any profits from future sales of the coins with insurance companies that paid off claims following the 1865 sinking. (Sale of the treasure recovered from the SS *Central America* was delayed by about a decade while insurers that had paid off claims following the 1857 sinking of that vessel battled the finders of the treasure in court for ownership of the gold coins and ingots. Ultimately, the court awarded more than 90 percent of the *Central America* treasure to the finders, with the smaller portion awarded to the insurers. A legal battle is still ongoing, however.)

Recovery of the first coins from the *Republic* began in November 2003, and salvors discovered Coronet gold $20 double eagles, Coronet gold $10 eagles and Seated Liberty silver half dollars among the wreckage.

One last appearance

A stalwart of United States circulating coinage design made its last appearance in 2003.

Felix Schlag's design featuring a left-facing President Thomas Jefferson on the obverse paired with an image of Monticello on the reverse had its last hurrah, as legislation passed in 2003 called for new designs to debut on both sides of the coin in 2003, 2004 and/or 2005. (Late passage of the bill precluded any changes occurring in 2003.)

The legislation provided for the issuance of Jefferson 5-cent coins with designs reflective of the Louisiana Purchase and the exploits of the Lewis and Clark Expedition to celebrate the two bicentennials.

After expressing dissatisfaction over the design changes, the Virginia delegation to Congress secured the promise that any 2006 5-cent coins would continue to depict Jefferson on the obverse and return to showing Monticello on the reverse.

Changes in coin design process

Three separate but related events in 2003 also paved the way for changes in the way U.S. coins are designed.

Another provision of the legislation that created the new Jefferson 5-cent coin designs brought a new design review agency.

The 11-member Citizens Coinage Advisory Committee was created to replace the Citizens Commemorative Coin Advisory Committee, which had eight members, seven of whom were voting members.

The new group mirrored the earlier group in much of its structure and most duties, but the creation of the CCAC seems to have remedied complaints from some in the numismatic community about the CCCAC's lack of independence from Mint control.

The CCCAC's primary mandate was to suggest and review commemorative coin themes and designs, including the circulating State quarter dollar designs.

The CCCAC's representation included members of the numismatic community, the American Numismatic Association, collectors at large, the Mint (the Mint director for many years) and a nonvoting member from the Commission of Fine Arts.

The Mint recommended CCCAC members to the Treasury secretary. CCCAC activities were financed first by Mint appropriations by Congress and later by the Mint's Public Enterprise Fund.

The CCAC also has its members appointed by the Treasury secretary based on recommendations from the Mint through an application process. The Mint's Public Enterprise Fund also funds the CCAC.

Unlike the CCCAC, whose members chose the chairman (which was the Mint director for several years until a non-Mint member was chosen), the CCAC's chairman is appointed to a one-year term directly by the Treasury secretary.

The process of coinage design made headlines throughout the year.

In an effort to strengthen the quality of designs for U.S. coins and medals, Director of the Mint Henrietta Holsman Fore on Nov. 20 launched the U.S. Mint's Artistic Infusion Program.

The Artistic Infusion Program created a pool of 40 artists (20 college students and 20 professional artists) to create future coinage and medal designs for the U.S. Mint.

"It is the first time a pool of artists will be part of an established program to provide designs for U.S. coins and medals," Director Fore said. "We are inviting American artists to participate, because great artistry enriches our culture. Coins reflect that artistry and serve as our ambassadors when they travel throughout the world."

Artists in the program support the Mint's sculptor-engraver staff by creating two-dimensional designs. Once designs are approved, they are modeled by the sculptor-engraver staff.

At the time the program was initiated, the U.S. Mint's sculptor-engraver staff numbered four (compared to a 1980s staff of six and a chief sculptor-engraver), and each staff member was of retirement age.

In addition to the Mint's engraving staff being small in number, the abundance of new designs required for the many coinage programs, like the State quarter dollars, was taxing the sculptor-engravers.

Fore's comments about the artistry that coins can express sound similar to comments of President Theodore Roosevelt nearly a century ago as he initiated what is known as the beginning of the golden age of U.S. coinage design. That period began in 1907 with Augustus Saint-Gaudens' designs for the gold $10 and $20 coins (which Roosevelt commissioned) and ended in 1921 with the introduction of the Peace dollar.

Many collectors believe that U.S. coins lost much of their artistry as portraits began replacing images of Liberty from 1909 to just after the end of World War II. With one exception (the Franklin half dollar), the portrait designs introduced during this second phase of 20th century coinage design remained in use at the end of the 20th century.

Many collectors and others argue that today's new coinage designs (for the State quarter dollars, for example) lack the beauty and artistry of the designs from the golden age of design.

Others decry what they see as an overreliance on copying 19th and 20th century designs for re-use with current programs (for example the gold and silver American Eagles, the 2001 American Bison dollar, and the first 2004 Jefferson 5-cent coin).

In 2003, the U.S. Mint further changed the design evaluation process for the 50 State Quarters program.

Early in the year, U.S. Mint officials requested that states to be honored in 2005 and beyond submit three to five design concepts in a narrative format, instead of illustrations or formal artistic renderings.

Mint officials said the new policy would not preclude states from holding contests or in other ways getting the public involved in the design process.

The changes did not impact California's 2005 design, as state officials were in the midst of making final selections to send to Mint officials for review. West Virginia, too, was well into the design process for its State quarter dollar when the policy change was announced.

Director Fore said the changes were designed to "strengthen the program by improving communications between the U.S. Mint and the states as well as between the states and their citizens."

Though Mint officials say they had asked for only concepts at the start of the program in 1999, they did supply a design template to states. The design template naturally led to the states supplying graphics.

Mint officials said the idea behind the template was educational and a way to get children involved in creating designs. Many schoolchildren participated in design contests in various states during the program.

Under the new process, the design evaluation period for the State quarter dollars would begin 24 months before the year of issue, instead of the 18-month schedule previously used.

How individual states were to go about selecting design concepts was never specified by law.

No matter the designs and how they came to be, need for coins in circulation diminished in 2003.

A sluggish economy, economic effects of the Sept. 11, 2001, terrorist attacks, and the recycling of U.S. coins through Coinstar all furthered a downward spiral in circulation coinage demand noted since 2000.

Coinage production figures in 2003 dropped across all circulating denominations (ranging from a slight six percent decline in cent production to a 33 percent drop in 5-cent coin production). The overall demand dropped about 20 percent and reflected about a 50 to 60 percent decrease from record production figures of 28 billion coins in 2000.

If collectors had trouble finding coins in 2003, they had no trouble noticing a new generation of paper money that made its debut that year. The new designs represented the second generation of design changes since 1996.

Currency redesign

The new Series 2004 $20 Federal Reserve notes became part of United States paper money history in 2003.

The colorful notes and a multi-million dollar advertising campaign to promote them became somewhat commonplace in the weeks following the Oct. 9 official release into circulation.

The new $20 notes, featuring subtle peach, green and blue background colors, represented the first phase of the next generation of currency, commonly referred to at the Bureau of Engraving and Printing as NexGen currency.

The $20 FRNs are the most circulated high-denomination note and therefore a common target of would-be counterfeiters.

Not since the Series 1869 $10 United States note, which was nicknamed by collectors the Rainbow note for the blue, green and red hues present on its face, had U.S. paper money been so colorful.

As part of a larger five-year, $53 million advertising and marketing campaign, the notes received exposure in many venues prior to the Oct. 9 official release day.

The advertising and marketing contract covered the development of training and public education materials; outreach to cash handlers at banks, businesses and vending and transit industries; paid advertisements; and inclusion in the story lines of popular U.S. television programs.

2004

Though only temporary, the shuttering of the nation's coin and paper money collection in 2004 generated collector interest and concern (verging on outrage in some).

Nation's coin collection closes

The National Numismatic Collection has long had a home at the Smithsonian's National Museum of American History, but in 2004, the museum began renovations that forced the prized rarities into storage.

In mid-April, Smithsonian officials announced the museum would dismantle the National Numismatic Collection's "The History of Money and Medals" exhibit and the Josiah K. Lilly Collection of an almost complete run of U.S. gold coins on public display. The Lilly Collection was donated to the NNC in 1968, and other parts of the exhibits had been on display for as many as 40 years.

Aug. 1 was the last day the public could view the NNC exhibit, comprising 5,686 items in total. The items in the collection were moved to the Smithsonian's vault in a little more than two days, with the help of a volunteer team under the direction of NNC curator Richard G. Doty and museum specialist Jim Hughes.

The total public exhibit comprised some 80 cases containing coins, paper currency, medals and various items once used as money throughout the world. Those pieces joined the remainder of the collection, approximately 1.6 million items, about 450,000 coins, tokens, medals and decorations and 1.1 million pieces of paper money.

The NNC is one of the largest numismatic collections in the world and the largest in North America. Its closure was part of a long-term plan to renovate and revitalize the NMAH and its exhibition galleries.

After outcry over the exhibit closure and no plans to replace it, the museum's director expressed a commitment to exhibiting some of the collection's rare and prized coins, in addition to working to create an online "virtual" exhibit.

Before the exhibit closed, Dr. Brent D. Glass, director of the NMAH, promised that the NMAH would mount a special exhibit featuring "the real gems of the collection."

Rarities surface

As one group of national numismatic treasures went into storage, a few choice rarities unseen for decades made their triumphant return to the hobby.

2004 witnessed the return of the Lammot du Pont specimen of the 1866 Seated Liberty, No Motto silver dollar and the surfacing of the finest known 1793 Flowing Hair, Wreath, Strawberry Leaf cent.

The du Pont dollar, one of two known specimens, was unaccounted for since a robbery more than 36 years before, until a man in Maine turned it over to two numismatists at American Numismatic Rarities

LLC, Wolfeboro, N.H., in February.

The unnamed man contacted ANR in the fall of 2003 after reading a story in *Coin World* about an auction featuring the other specimen of the Seated Liberty, No Motto dollar. After subsequent telephone conversations, ANR's John J. Kraljevich concluded the man had possession of the missing du Pont coin. Kraljevich and John Pack, also of ANR, met Feb. 26 with the man at a Best Western motel in Maine, where the two numismatists examined and authenticated the coin.

The man said he had been holding the coin for about 20 years. It was in a paper envelope in a box with random medalets and other objects. The man told the ANR numismatists he had been a friend of Edwards Huntington Metcalf, a once wealthy member of a famous family. Metcalf died April 2, 2001. The man from Maine claimed Metcalf would sometimes borrow money from him and provide what he called "trinkets" as collateral for the loans. How Metcalf came to have this coin is unexplained.

ANR took possession of the coin and turned it over to an attorney for the du Pont family March 12, after which it was presented on indefinite loan to the American Numismatic Association for display in its Money Museum.

Another rarity, the Strawberry Leaf cent, is known for its trefoil, or three-lobed, leaves, on the obverse above the date. In the summer of 2004, the finest known example appeared after more than 60 years off the market.

A woman identified as the daughter of Roscoe E. Staples II entered Republic Jewelry & Collectibles in Auburn, Maine, with the coin. She told owner Dan Cunliffe that her father purchased the coin around 1941 and gave it to her mother as an anniversary gift. In August 1943, Staples was killed in action in the Pacific Theater in World War II. Apparently the widow rarely mentioned the coin while it was in her possession.

The family decided to return it to the numismatic market. It sold for $414,000, setting a since-eclipsed record for a U.S. cent. Staples is believed to have paid $2,750 for the coin when he purchased it.

Northern Marianas Islands "coins"

It wasn't so much breaking the law that caused trouble for a private issuer who struck "coins" in the name of a U.S. entity, but the subject matter of one of those "coins" that spelled the end of the short-lived coinage issue.

As a United States territory, the Commonwealth of the Northern Marianas Islands has no legal right to issue its own "coinage" or "legal tender," according to a New York court and the U.S. Mint.

David Ganz, a New York attorney and former president of the ANA, contended otherwise.

Ganz arranged a contract signed Nov. 3, 2003,

by CNMI Gov. Juan Babauta with a Wyoming firm, SoftSky Inc., which authorized the company to license private mints to produce "coins" in the name of the CNMI.

This pseudo-coinage included so called "Freedom Tower silver dollars," celebrating the tower expected to be built on the site where terrorists had destroyed the World Trade Center in New York City.

The issuance of a replica 1933 Saint-Gaudens gold $20 double eagle caught the eye of the U.S. Mint, and led SoftSky to alter its marketing language, but it was the Freedom Tower "dollars" that created much of the controversy.

On Oct. 13, 2004, upon complaints brought by New York Attorney General Eliot Spitzer, a New York court ordered that sales and advertising of the "Freedom Tower" pieces be stopped pending a further hearing.

The court followed with a permanent injunction, announced Nov. 8. The judge called the NCM promotions "deceptive" and "disingenuous," and said the piece "capitalized on the emotional and historical significance of the events of Sept. 11th. ..."

On Nov. 12, citing the permanent injunction and embarrassment to the islands, Babauta terminated the contract.

Import restrictions

2004 marked a noticeable turning point for dealers and collectors of ancient coins, who soon began to encounter import restrictions for ancient coins from Iraq.

Congress approved and President George W. Bush signed into law legislation concerning restricting importation of ancient coins from Iraq.

The provision was included in H.R. 1047, the Miscellaneous Trade and Technical Corrections Act of 2004.

The provision gave the president the authority to restrict imports of cultural property of Iraq and other items of archeological, historical, cultural, rare, scientific or religious importance illegally removed from the Iraq National Museum, the National Library of Iraq and other locations in Iraq since the war started in 2003.

Numerous hobby groups lobbied the U.S. Department of State to argue against importation restrictions on coins from Iraq, noting that no coins were stolen from the Iraq National Museum and reports of thefts at archeological sites did not focus on coins.

Early in the war, many incorrect news reports claimed museums in Iraq had been looted of antiquities and coins, but later reports indicated that the coin collection from Iraq's National Museum in Baghdad had been found intact and was safe, along with nearly all of the ancient treasures initially reported looted.

According to the hobby groups opposing the restrictions, coins made in "Greece, Turkey, Syria, Phoenicia, and Iran are found in Iraq, and coins made in Iraq are found throughout the Middle East.

It would be impossible to determine where a particular coin or even coin type was recently found and exported from Iraq," they said.

John J. Ford Jr. Collection

Though auctions began the previous year, not until 2004 did collectors begin to get a sense of the breadth and depth (and value) of the John J. Ford Jr. Collection.

By the auctions' conclusion in 2007, Ford's collection would hold the record as being the most valuable collection of numismatic items ever sold at auction, a feat made more remarkable in that the collection did not contain a single U.S. federal coin.

The New York City coin firm Stack's announced in the spring of 2003 that it had been commissioned to offer the collection over several years. Two additional auctions, offering the Ford numismatic library, to be conducted jointly by Stack's and bookseller George Kolbe, were soon announced.

Stack's called Ford "America's foremost living numismatist." He had worked as a cataloger for the firm while he was still a youngster. He later was a partner in New Netherlands Coin Co.

The historic series of auctions opened Oct. 14, 2003, when 335 lots brought nearly $5.6 million thanks to fierce bidding.

The second auction, featuring mostly early American coins and tokens, with some pioneer gold coins and ingots, was conducted May 11, and realized $6.6 million.

The third auction, conducted May 11 and 12, featured Colonial and early American paper money, and Civil War era fractional currency, realized about $3.2 million

Two separate auctions were held to dispose of Ford's numismatic library, with the June offering of the 1,000 finest items in the collection establishing a one-day record of $1.66 million.

A section of encased postage sold June 23 totaled more than $2 million, with Parts V and VI offering early American tokens and medals, and private paper money, adding about $4.4 million in an Oct. 12 auction.

In about a year, through barely one-third of the auctions, Ford's collection had reaped more than $23.4 million, presaging its headline-making quality for several more years.

Other stories

Several other large stories were actually continuations of news that began in previous years.

Collectors in 2004 were able to begin collecting the first redesigned Jefferson 5-cent coins issued as part of the Mint's Westward Journey Nickel Series.

The 2004 5-cent coins, which retained sculptor Felix Schlag's obverse portrait introduced on the denomination in 1938, were paired with two new reverses.

Collectors learned that two more redesigned 5-cent

coins to be introduced in 2005 would not only feature two new reverses, but a completely new portrait of Thomas Jefferson as well.

The Artistic Infusion Program, announced in 2003, got under way in 2004 with the selection of 18 professional artists and six student artists after the first nationwide "call for artists" late in 2003.

A second "call for artists" was issued Nov. 4, 2004, with a deadline for receipt of applications Feb. 11, 2005. Mint officials hoped to add two new professionals and 14 new students to complete the initial program goal of 20 professionals and 20 students.

Their impact was immediate.

The first assignment presented to the AIP artists, following a two-day orientation in February 2004 at the Philadelphia Mint, was executing reverse design sketches for the two 2005 Jefferson 5-cent coins.

Following the usual selection process, the winning single obverse design and both reverse designs for the 2005 Jefferson 5-cent coins were revealed to have all been submitted by AIP artists, not by Mint engravers.

U.S. paper money changes continued in 2004, with the introduction of redesigned $50 Federal Reserve notes.

The Series 2004 $50 FRN, released into circulation Sept. 28, was the second denomination in a redesign known as the next generation of currency.

The new $50 notes feature red and blue as subtle background colors. The placement of the ribbons of red ink and blue stars on the face of the new notes is meant to evoke the image of the American flag. The stars and stripes on the Series 2004 $50 FRN represent symbols of freedom.

The new notes retain the portrait of Ulysses S. Grant, Civil War general and America's 18th president, but Grant's portrait was moved up, his shoulders extending into the border. The oval and fine lines that once encased his portrait are absent.

Another new design element is a blue metallic-ink star that appears to the left of the serial number on the right-hand side of the face of the note.

The back design continues to depict a vignette of the U.S. Capitol with the addition of small numeral 50s printed in yellow ink and scattered across the back of the note.

The oval border and fine lines behind the back design's vignette on the earlier generation of notes do not appear in the new design.

2005

Can there be any doubt that no story in 2005 was larger than the U.S. Mint's announcement that it had "recovered" 10 1933 Saint-Gaudens gold $20 double eagles?

1933 Saint-Gaudens gold $20 coins surface

The population of known 1933 Saint-Gaudens gold $20 double eagles more than quadrupled in 2005, rising from three to 13, after the family of a deceased Philadelphia coin dealer turned over 10 examples to the U.S. Mint, officials revealed in August.

Numismatists long wondered whether more than three examples survived from the 445,500 coins that were struck but that officials say were never released. Evidence suggested more pieces were extant. A 1933 double eagle photograph taken in 1980 and published in a 2004 book about the coins showed an example that did not match the markings on the two coins in the Smithsonian or the Fenton coin some attributed to Farouk. Then, in 2005, solid evidence surfaced that other pieces had survived.

Mint officials announced Aug. 11, 2005, that they had "recovered" 10 more 1933 Saint-Gaudens double eagles from the descendants of Philadelphia jeweler and coin dealer Israel Switt. Switt in 1944 admitted to Secret Service agents that he sold nine 1933 double eagles to dealers. Agents in the 1940s and early 1950s then tracked down and confiscated, or their owners turned in, the nine coins Switt admitted to selling. All were melted.

According to some evidence, Israel "Izzy" Switt was purported to have handled at least 25 of the 1933 double eagles. If the figure of 25 is accurate, just 20

pieces attributed to Switt have been accounted for: the nine pieces recovered starting in 1944, the piece recovered in 1996 (which may or may not be the Farouk coin) and the 10 coins recovered in 2005. Five or more pieces could still be extant.

The recovery of the 10 1933 gold pieces increases the total of confirmed surviving examples to 13 pieces from the three previously known: two in the Smithsonian Institution's National Numismatic Collection and the coin sold in the 2002 auction.

Unlike the nine previously confiscated and melted examples, the recently recovered 10 examples will escape the melting pot, Mint officials say.

Mint officials do not consider the 10 gold pieces recovered to be coins, under government claims they were never officially released as such. The U.S. Mint views the 10 gold pieces as stolen public property belonging to the United States, and a fierce legal battle quickly broke out.

Although the 10 gold pieces are stored at the Fort Knox Gold Bullion Depository in Kentucky, Israel Switt's daughter, Joan Switt Langbord, wants them back. She retained the legal services of New York attorney Barry H. Berke, the same attorney who defended Fenton in the government's case against him, and she and her family have since waged a legal battle against the government for ownership of the coins.

Wisconsin Extra Leaves quarter dollars

A "neat" find by collector Bob Ford soon ignited a nationwide search for variants of the 2004 Wisconsin quarter dollar.

Ford, a retired teacher in Tucson, Ariz., discovered

2004-D Wisconsin quarter dollars of two different variants, each with the appearance of a mark resembling an "extra leaf" on the left side of the corn on the reverse. One of the variants has what the hobby calls an "Extra Leaf High"; another, an "Extra Leaf Low."

Though he thought they were "neat," Ford didn't think the marks were anything major, so he returned some to the bank.

That was in December 2004. Soon, a large part of the American population would be looking closely at Wisconsin quarter dollars.

Ford decided to show the oddities to Robert "Rob" Weiss, owner of a local coin shop, Old Pueblo Coin Exchange, Tucson.

Weiss and manager Ben Weinstein searched 220 2004-D Wisconsin quarter dollars in stock. They found three "High Leaf" and nine "Low Leaf" coins. Weiss sent examples to *Coin World,* which published the finds in the Jan. 10 issue.

Tool gouges were contemplated as a likely cause, but *Coin World* asked U.S. Mint officials whether any deliberate design modifications had been made. *Coin World* forwarded electronic images and stressed that the extra marks were raised on the coin. In the Jan. 24 issue, Ron Harrigal, an assistant Mint director, was quoted as saying the marks were "deep gouges in the blanks."

Did he mean die blanks, or planchets? The Mint response stood, however ambiguous. The Treasury Department's Office of Inspector General, however, did confirm in March that it was investigating the marks (the results of the investigation would not be announced for months). Some numismatic researchers were voicing suspicion that one or more Mint workers scarred the dies deliberately. Since their discovery, various numismatists have advanced theories of how the marks occurred, though none of the theories are universally embraced.

Prices for the coins soon erupted as eager collectors sought the pieces. The public learned of high prices through Associated Press reports carried in numerous local newspapers. The phenomenon received front-page treatment in *USA Today.* National radio and television networks spread the news further. All the news ignited a nationwide search for coins with "extra leaves."

Aside from a pocket of about 40 examples in west Texas, and scattered reports elsewhere, almost all the "Extra Leaf" quarter dollars found were located in the Tucson area.

Today, most U.S. coin price guides list the two variants, and at premiums still well above the coin of normal design.

Cheerios dollar

Another top news story from 2005 was further evidence that collectors might consider paying extra careful attention to coins.

Numismatist Thomas K. DeLorey had his suspicions from the outset that the reverse hub used to produce dies for striking 2000-P Sacagawea dollars included in boxes of Cheerios, as part of the Mint's promotion of the coin, was different from the hub used to manufacture dies for circulating coin production.

Confirmation establishing his suspicions as fact waited until U.S. Mint officials issued a news release acknowledging the different hubs June 17, 2005, after repeated denials of any differences.

DeLorey on Oct. 20, 1999, had attended a Chicago news conference during which Mint officials shared examples of trial pieces of the new 2000-dated dollar coins with representatives from nationwide vending machine companies.

DeLorey said he examined one of the vending machine trial coins under magnification and counted what he initially thought were 13 tail feathers on the eagle.

When DeLorey obtained Sacagawea dollars in January 2000 from a Walmart store, he compared the diagnostics of their reverses to what he had witnessed in examining the vending machine pieces and, counting 12 tail feathers on the coins obtained in circulation, concluded differences between the two existed.

DeLorey had a further hunch—he suspected that not only had the vending machine dollars been struck with dies from a different hub, it was possible that the dozen Proof 2000-W Sacagawea gold dollars launched aboard a space shuttle mission in 1999 and the Cheerios dollars may also have been produced with the same earlier reverse since those 2000-dated coins, too, were produced in 1999.

DeLorey's suspicions would later be confirmed on most accounts. Early pre-production strikes of 2000-P Sacagawea dollars struck in 1999 were indeed produced from an early hub design that was modified before regular production for the 2000 coins began.

However, all the Sacagawea dollars, that is, those struck from dies made from the earlier hub—the 5,500 Cheerios dollars and the gold Proofs—as well as all of the regular issue coins for circulation and collector sets, depict an American bald eagle with the same number of tail feathers: 12. How the feathers are formed differs in the two designs, though, and caused early confusion about the number of feathers depicted.

According to the statement from the U.S. Mint released June 17 by spokeswoman Joyce Harris, "5,500 golden dollars of a 'high detail' feather variety (12 tail feathers) were manufactured and shipped to General Mills as part of the Golden Dollar promotion in October 1999, under a detailed arrangement that they not be released until January 2000. Prior to manufacturing the coins for release to the Federal Reserve in 2000, the feather detail was softened and the center tail feather was recessed to solve a die manufacturing issue. Recessing the center tail feather gives the illusion of a 13th feather, but that was not the intent."

The differences between the two hubs are subtle, affecting only the tail feathers of the eagle, and could be easily overlooked.

The central line of the tail feather shaft is raised on the Sacagawea dollars found in the Cheerios packages and on the special gold versions, but recessed on coins struck for circulation.

The tail feathers on the Cheerios dollars also have more detail than the tail feathers on the coins struck for circulation. The changes to the design for the circulating issues were deliberate to make the tail feathers more realistic, according to the Mint.

All later Sacagawea dollars were struck from dies bearing a recessed central line on the shaft of the tail feather.

Since revelation of their distinctive reverse, examples of the dollars used in the Cheerios promotion have sold for thousands of dollars.

Presidential $1 legislation passes

One of the largest and longest-reaching stories of 2005 came right at the end.

On Dec. 13, the U.S. House of Representatives approved the Presidential $1 Coin Act of 2005, authorizing some of the most sweeping changes in circulating American coinage since the 1960s.

The legislation authorized the Presidential dollar coins, and companion First Spouse gold coins and bronze medal duplicates. In addition, the law also authorized issuing American Buffalo .9999 fine gold $50 bullion coins and four new reverse designs for the Lincoln cent in 2009. Each program is discussed in detail later in this chapter.

Raging hot market

A raging hot market continued to burn brightly in 2005.

One indicator was the number of coins that topped the $1 million mark.

That level was breached at least 14 times, for 12 individual coins, a set of coins (the fabled "King of Siam" Proof set) and even a piece of paper money. These "million dollar babies" were record-setters in a year that set records across the hobby.

The year—and the blistering hot market—began with the auctions held in conjunction with the Florida United Numismatists convention in early January, which together realized more than $80 million, doubling the previous record for a single show.

Two early Colonial American gold coins bearing the EB counterstamp of New York goldsmith Ephraim Brasher each topped $2 million in an auction conducted by Heritage Numismatic Auctions, with the only known specimen of the 1787 Brasher doubloon with the EB countermark on the eagle's breast reaching $2.99 million, including the 15 percent buyer's fee. All of the other Brasher doubloons show the countermark on one of the eagle's wings.

Steve Contursi, of Rare Coin Wholesalers, acquired the unique EB Punch on Breast doubloon, which was graded Extremely Fine 45 by Numismatic Guaranty Corporation of America. Don Kagin, from Kagin's in Tiburon, Calif., is a one-third owner in the transaction for the unique Brasher piece. He was successful in his bids on other Brasher coinage, including an NGC About Uncirculated 55 1787 New York Brasher doubloon with the Punch on Wing for $2.415 million.

A Series 1890 $1,000 Treasury note was sold Oct. 21 for $1,092,500.

The largest reported transaction of 2005 occurred Nov. 1, when Contursi bought the legendary King of Siam Proof set, in a sale Ira & Larry Goldberg Coins & Collectibles brokered. That set realized $8.5 million.

Other stories

Turmoil in Ohio politics and a national hobby organization garnered massive newsprint during 2005.

When the *Toledo Blade* revealed April 3 that Ohio coin dealer Thomas W. Noe managed two coin investment funds for the state's Bureau of Workers' Compensation, it was the first of many stories in a saga that focused national attention on the business side of the hobby and altered the shape of Buckeye politics and investment policy.

Ohio Bureau of Workers' Compensation officials gave Noe $25 million in 1998 and $25 million in 2001 to purchase rare coins. The funds were from moneys OBWC collected as workers' compensation premiums, paid in by Ohio employers. Those premiums were invested in a variety of investment options, totaling more than $18 billion, with more than 150 different managers.

Until he came under scrutiny for his management of the coin funds, Noe served on several state boards and was chairman of the federal Citizens Coinage Advisory Committee.

On April 7, the Ohio inspector general began an investigation into the investment practices of the funds. Ohio Attorney General Jim Petro then announced May 26 that the state of Ohio was pursuing civil and criminal charges against Noe, after Noe's legal counsel advised state officials that $10 million to $12 million of the funds' assets were unaccounted for.

Elsewhere, the American Numismatic Association Board of Governors' removal of a sitting governor during a closed-door session in mid-October led to the public disclosure of an ongoing dispute over naming rights to the association's museum. By year's end ANA leaders admitted they had erred in the naming rights issue but refused to reconsider the ouster of Walter J. Ostromecki Jr.

The ANA Board voted in an executive session Oct. 14 to remove Ostromecki, citing "breach of confidentiality" as the reason. Ostromecki had won election to the governing board in early July and was sworn into office July 30 in San Francisco at the conclusion of the ANA annual convention.

With the disclosure of Ostromecki's removal and

an allegation that the removed governor had divulged confidential information to an ANA member, Clifford Mishler made public nine letters, revealing an ongoing debate over ANA museum naming rights.

Mishler and Chester L. Krause, both life members and major financial contributors to the organization for years, maintained that their donations combined with that of an anonymous donor in an aggregate of $500,000 was enough to secure the naming rights of the entire museum after Edward C. Rochette, longtime executive director and former ANA president. Mishler presided at a ceremony at ANA headquarters in June during which a banner was unfurled proclaiming the museum was to be named in Rochette's honor. Shortly thereafter, without communicating with Mishler and Krause, the ANA revealed that only the main gallery of the museum was being named for Rochette. Both Krause and Mishler protested, and eventually the ANA changed its stance, after documents indicating the museum would be named by the top three donors were discovered.

The year 2005 not only witnessed the introduction into circulation of the third and fourth Jefferson 5-cent coins in the U.S. Mint's Westward Journey Nickel Series, but also the release of the designs for what the Jefferson 5-cent coin was to look like in 2006 and subsequent years.

Both of the 2005 Jefferson 5-cent coins feature the same enlarged profile facing right of the third president, designed by professional artist Joe Fitzgerald from Silver Spring, Md., a member of the Mint's Artistic Infusion Program.

The first of the 2005 Jefferson 5-cent coins features the American Bison reverse designed by artist Jamie Franki. The American Bison 5-cent coin was introduced into circulation Feb. 28.

The second of the two 2005 Jefferson 5-cent coins bears the Ocean in View design reflective of the northwestern U.S. coastline that the Lewis and Clark expedition encountered in the early 1800s. Fitzgerald executed the winning design.

Mint officials consider the 2006 Jefferson 5-cent coin to be the fifth and final coin in the Westward Journey Nickel Series even though its designs would be used each year since.

The Mint unveiled the selected 2006 reverse design during the American Numismatic Association's Anniversary Convention in San Francisco in July, and followed up Oct. 4 with the release of the selected obverse for 2006 and later. The obverse features a forward-facing visage of Jefferson based on a 19th century portrait by artist Rembrandt Peale, was designed by Franki.

Sculptor Felix Schlag's 1938 Monticello reverse for the Jefferson 5-cent coin was selected to return on the 2006 version of the denomination. However, the Mint engraving staff returned the Monticello design to its original 1938 form. Over the years, the engraving staff had made a series of modifications to the details of the design that, while retaining the overall original appearance, differed in the fine details of the structure.

2006

Collectors who were fortunate enough to view an exhibit of 10 1933 Saint-Gaudens gold $20 double eagles would likely describe that event as the largest news story of 2006.

1933 double eagles on exhibit

The coins were on display during the Aug. 16 to 19 American Numismatic Association World's Fair of Money in Denver, the first public display of the coins since they were "recovered" by the U.S. Mint in 2004.

The coins were turned over to Mint officials by the heirs of Philadelphia jeweler Israel "Izzy" Swift, as detailed in the section of this chapter dealing with the events of 2004.

It was the first time the 10 coins were removed from safekeeping at the Fort Knox Gold Bullion Depository in Kentucky.

The display, erected by ANA Money Museum curatorial staff, showed the coins suspended in a shatterproof glass window that allowed the obverse and reverse of each coin to be viewed as people passed both sides of the exhibit under the watch of U.S. Mint police.

Arrangements between the Mint and ANA representatives to bring the coins to the Denver convention solidified in days, as the Mint announced July 27.

The display came about from the intersection of a desire on the U.S. Mint's part to display the coins and a suggestion from ANA executive director Christopher Cipoletti that "the collecting community and the general public would jump at the opportunity to see some of the treasures the Mint holds like the 1933 double eagles."

Cipoletti, in Washington, D.C., to testify before Congress on coinage matters, informed government officials that the ANA would be more than willing to work with the Mint on exhibits of Mint materials.

On July 25, he received and immediately agreed to an offer from the Mint to display the coins at the ANA convention, and arrangements were finalized July 27.

The Mint provided and paid for security for the display, though the ANA provided and paid for security for the overall exhibit area. U.S. Mint police accompanied the double eagles from Fort Knox to Denver.

American Buffalo gold coins

2006 also saw the revival for the second time in five years of a classic American coin design that proved that collectors would eagerly buy any U.S. coin depicting the popular Indian Head 5-cent coin designs of James Earle Fraser. The 2006 American Buffalo 1-ounce .9999 fine gold $50 bullion coin was introduced in June and sales for a time quickly eclipsed the sales for American Eagle gold coins.

The American Buffalo gold coin is the first pure gold coin ever issued by the U.S. Mint. The Treasury secretary had the authorization to issue a .9999 fine gold coin since 1996, but had not exercised that discretion.

Mint officials in 2005 were discussing the issuance of a .9999 fine gold coin in 2006, but held off on implementing plans, after the American Buffalo gold coin provision became part of the Presidential dollar coin legislation and seemed destined for passage.

The enabling legislation for the American Buffalo gold coin specified that the coin must bear the original 1913 Indian Head, Bison on Mound 5-cent coin designs. In meeting that mandate, the Mint more faithfully recreated Fraser's original designs for the 2006 coin than it did for the 2001-P American Buffalo silver dollar, also bearing a recreation of Fraser's designs.

The fields of the American Buffalo gold coins mimic the surface texture that Fraser imparted to the Indian Head 5-cent coin.

In contrast, the 2001 commemorative coin features untextured fields. (Mint Engraver Charles E. Barber reduced the irregular, textured surface of the 5-cent coin, smoothing the surfaces and fields, when he created the Bison on Plain subtype in 1913 as a replacement for the Bison on Mound subtype.)

The proportions of the 2006 designs also more accurately reflect the original than do the 2001 recreations for the silver commemorative coin.

American Eagle anniversary sets

Not all the U.S. Mint's 2006 actions were so positively received

Collectors who ordered sets of what they believed were limited-edition releases of coins celebrating the 20th anniversary of the American Eagle coin program received a surprise when the U.S. Mint announced the individual availability of some of the coins in the sets, and in one instance, at a significantly lower price than in the set.

The Mint issued three 20th Anniversary American Eagle sets beginning Aug. 30, and they were an instant hit among collectors, with one of the sets, containing three gold coins with three different surface finishes, selling out in less than two days.

The other two sets did not sell as fast, with sellouts announced in the second week of November.

Of the three 20th Anniversary American Eagle sets offered, two were three-coin sets, each containing coins in three finishes: Proof, Uncirculated and Reverse Proof, one set offering silver American Eagles and the other featuring gold American Eagles.

A third set, the American Eagle 20th Anniversary Gold and Silver set, paired two coins, an Uncirculated American Eagle 1-ounce .9167 fine gold coin and an Uncirculated 1-ounce .999 fine silver coin, both bearing the W Mint mark of the West Point Mint. The set, limited to a release of 20,000 units, was offered at

$850 per set, with a limit of 10 sets per order.

The Uncirculated coins have a satiny finish similar to the bullion coins, except that the planchets for the Uncirculated coins are burnished, tumbled with steel pellets, before striking (the bullion coin planchets do not undergo the same burnishing). The Uncirculated coins bear a W Mint mark, while the bullion versions do not carry a Mint mark. The Mint mark had previously been reserved for the Proof American Eagles.

The regular Proof American Eagles in each set were the same coins offered for sale individually (and for the gold coin, in another set) beginning Feb. 2. The Proof coins exhibit frosted devices against mirrored fields. All bear a W Mint mark.

The Reverse Proof pieces are the first coins bearing that finish produced by the U.S. Mint. The Reverse Proof finish is the opposite of the regular Proof finish, and has the mirrored finish on the devices with the fields frosted. The silver coin bears the P Mint mark from the Philadelphia Mint. The Reverse Proof gold coin bears the W Mint mark.

The three-coin silver sets, priced at $100 each, were limited to an issue of 250,000 sets. Collectors were restricted to 10 sets per order.

The price tag of $2,610 for the three-coin gold set was not a deterrent to collectors who gobbled up the slim offering of 10,000 sets in less than 48 hours, despite a limit of 10 sets per order.

For the three-coin sets, the Reverse Proof coins created the most stir among collectors. The Uncirculated coins also stirred a lot of excitement, though not all of it positive.

Collectors ordering the three-coin sets were aware that the Proof coins in the two sets were identical to the Proof coins offered earlier. When the Proof American Eagle gold and silver coins had gone on sale in February, mintage limitations were announced with no indication that additional quantities of both coins would be offered later in the year in the 20th Anniversary sets.

While some grumbled about additional Proof American Eagle 1-ounce coins in the 20th Anniversary sets, those buying the sets did so believing that the Reverse Proof and Uncirculated coins would be available only in the limited-edition sets. The collectors were partially wrong.

On Sept. 15, Mint officials announced that its holiday catalog, to be released Sept. 28, would include offerings of single Uncirculated 2006-W American Eagle 1-ounce platinum, gold and silver coins, with the silver and gold coins identical to those in the three 20th Anniversary sets. Mint officials also announced that individual Uncirculated 2006-W half-ounce, quarter-ounce and tenth-ounce gold and platinum coins would be available, and that Uncirculated four-coin gold and platinum sets would also be offered.

Some collectors voiced the opinion that the Mint had misled them in its offering of the 20th Anniversary American Eagle program. A close examination of the language in the Mint's Aug. 21 notice for the 20th Anniversary sets revealed a statement that the Reverse Proofs would only be available in the three-coin sets. The Aug. 21 notice of the availability of the 20th Anniversary sets was silent about future availability of the Uncirculated coins. Mint officials responded to the fallout over the Uncirculated American Eagle 1-ounce gold and silver coins by stating they had never ruled out offering the Uncirculated coins as single-coin options.

Collectors who purchased the two-coin gold and silver Uncirculated set (priced at $850 per set) were especially upset upon seeing the pricing for the individual coin offerings. The single Uncirculated 1-ounce gold coin was priced at $720 and the single Uncirculated 1-ounce silver coin was offered for $19.95. The combined price of two individual coins was $110 lower than the price of the set containing the same two coins. In essence, those who bought the set were paying $110 extra for the packaging.

Coin World received telephone calls, email and traditional letters from subscribers soon after the Sept. 15 announcement, expressing their anger. Some correspondents indicated that they were contemplating returning the two-coin sets and just ordering the individual coins. Collectors also registered their displeasure on several online coin forums about the Mint's offering of individual Uncirculated American Eagles. For several consecutive weeks after the Sept. 15 announcement, the Mint's weekly sales report recorded a decline in the number of two-coin sets reported as sold, after it had appeared the sets were headed for a sellout. It is probable that some of the reversal in sales resulted from returned sets. However, by the Nov. 14 sales report, the Mint had received enough orders to reach the limit of 20,000 sets.

It is uncertain how many of the more than 1,000 two-coin sets returned to the Mint by their purchasers were returned in reaction to the later offering of the coins individually at a cheaper price. It is also unknown how many of those returning the sets bought the individual coins.

Noe case continues

The saga of embattled coin dealer Thomas W. Noe continued during 2006, as Noe pleaded guilty in a federal case to campaign finance abuse and was found guilty in a state criminal case for his management of two rare coin investment funds for the state of Ohio's Bureau of Workers' Compensation.

In the federal case, Noe pleaded guilty to funneling $45,400 to President George W. Bush's 2004 re-election campaign in 2003. Noe pleaded guilty to three counts of violating federal election laws: conspiracy, making illegal campaign contributions and making a false statement. He had been sentenced in that case on Sept. 13 and ordered to pay a $136,200 fine. Noe also received two years probation for each federal count, which he is to serve concurrently after release from prison. Noe must also serve 200 hours of community

service during probation.

Before he began serving his federal sentence, Noe faced trial on the state charges. A Lucas County, Ohio, jury found him guilty on two counts of theft, 18 counts of forgery, four counts of money laundering, four counts of tampering with records and one count of engaging in a pattern of corrupt activity in the state criminal trial. Jurors found Noe not guilty on seven counts of money laundering and four counts of tampering with records. The jury also ruled that Noe had to forfeit $3 million worth of stock in Numismatic Guaranty Corp. that he bought in the state's name. In the state case, Noe was sentenced Nov. 20 to serve 18 years in state prison, and was also ordered by Lucas County Common Pleas Judge Thomas Osowik to pay $213,000 in fines, to pay $13.7 million in restitution to the Ohio Bureau of Workers' Compensation and to pay the cost of the prosecution, estimated at $2.5 million.

Upon his conviction on state charges, Noe was immediately taken into federal custody. Noe served 23 of 27 months in federal prison for the election law violations. He was immediately transferred from the federal prison to the state prison to begin serving his 18-year state sentence.

Metals prices make news

Precious metals trended strongly upward in 2006, contributing to a buoyant coin market.

As for base metals, debate about whether to abolish the cent, a discussion now decades old, ratcheted up. Congress was told in July that production costs had begun exceeding face value not only for that lowliest of U.S. denominations, the cent, but for the 5-cent coin as well.

Testifying July 19 to a House committee, David A. Lebryk, deputy director of the Mint, said metal costs combined with three other factors—fabrication, labor and overhead, and transportation—to make the cost of circulating these two coins greater than face value. That was true even using a supply of metals purchased at earlier, lower prices; newer prevailing prices would raise the costs to about 1.4 cents for the cent and 7 cents for the 5-cent coin, he said.

Sen. Jim Kolbe, R-Ariz., had introduced legislation the day before to require rounding transactions to the nearest 5 cents, eliminating the need for the cent.

Lebryk said, however, that the greater need for 5-cent coins that would result from rounding transactions would only make the Mint's financial losses worse. The base metals used in everyday coinage were not alone in their upward movement; all metal prices were on the march in 2006.

Gold had closed at $517.70 for 2005, as silver hovered around $9 per troy ounce. A surge as the market entered February caused *Coin Dealer Newsletter* to ask, "Is it 1979 again?" Prices stood at $565.90 and $9.75 on Feb. 3.

As gold stayed about the same, silver reached a

22-year high, in excess of $10.50 an ounce, in late March.

By mid-May, both metals had advanced to their high point for the year, with gold about $700 and silver above $14. Prices tumbled from there but recovered enough that toward the end of the year the metals appeared to have reached a new plateau since the end of 2005. Gold was holding at about $600 or a little higher, while silver fluctuated in a range between $11 and $14.

2007

Perhaps no other U.S. Mint coin program in 2007 created such a frenzy, among not only collectors but also the general public, as did the Presidential dollars and the errors associated with the coins' edge lettering.

Presidential dollar coin errors

The errors generated hundreds and even thousands of dollars for the persons lucky enough to have discovered the anomalies.

The George Washington Presidential dollars entered circulation Feb. 15. Not long after, reports began filtering through the numismatic and general press that thousands of the new dollar coins were appearing in circulation and wrapped rolls without the required edge inscriptions.

The enabling legislation had required the date, E PLURIBUS UNUM and IN GOD WE TRUST to be applied to the coin's edge, allowing more room for the presidential portrait on the obverse of each respective coin and the Statue of Liberty reverse design. Mint officials assigned the Mint mark to the edge, although the legislation did not specify its location on the coins.

Mint officials developed a technique to apply incuse edge lettering for the coins, using equipment separate and apart from the coinage presses. This separation between the striking of the coin and the application of the edge inscriptions resulted in a number of different errors, including coins with no edge inscriptions, coins with multiple inscriptions and more.

U.S. Mint officials acknowledged that tens of thousands of 2007-P George Washington Presidential dollars were inadvertently shipped from the Philadelphia Mint without first having been subjected to the edge-lettering operation. These coins were dubbed "Godless dollars" because of the missing motto.

As reports of the errors spread, the Professional Coin Grading Service offered a $2,500 bounty for the first Presidential dollar to appear with a blank obverse and reverse but with the edge lettering. A separate $10,000 reward was offered for the first submission of a 2007-P or 2007-D Sacagawea dollar bearing the Presidential dollar edge lettering instead of the plain edge.

Examples of both errors did surface, both in Colorado and both products of the Denver Mint.

U.S. Mint officials quickly announced steps would be taken to avoid similar problems with the remaining Washington dollar production as well as future Presidential dollar releases.

The added steps, using color-coded coin tubs to differentiate between coin blanks, struck coins without edge lettering and those struck coins bearing edge lettering, did not work as well as U.S. Mint officials hoped, however.

Shortly after the May 17 release of the John Adams Presidential dollars, an undisclosed number of the coins surfaced with blundered edge lettering.

Errors again surfaced with the launch of the Thomas Jefferson Presidential dollars on Aug. 16. First, thousands of the coins were reported with faint edge lettering. Later, several hundred coins missing the edge lettering were reported to have surfaced in the Detroit area.

The errors and resulting embarrassment led to the development of a costly closed loop system that integrated the edge lettering equipment within the process as the final production step for the Presidential dollars. Since then, only a few plain-edge coins have been produced.

Metal prices rise, affect coinage sales

Prices for precious metals continued volatile in 2007, even to the point of disrupting the U.S. Mint's American Eagle program and other coin programs.

In 2007, the "spot" price for an ounce of gold neared its historical peak, while the spot price of platinum continued to break pricing barriers. Silver made strides as well, reaching prices not seen in about 27 years.

The volatility affected both collectible coins and bullion sales, notably prompting the U.S. Mint to halt sales of some collector versions of its bullion coins. In September and October, the Mint began suspending sales of the Proof and Uncirculated 2007-W American Eagle gold and platinum coins and American Buffalo gold coins while prices could be adjusted. Sales of the various coins were resumed gradually before the end of the year. Sales of Proof and Uncirculated American Eagle gold coins resumed Oct. 15 at prices 9 to 17 percent higher than when sales were suspended nearly a month before. Sales of the Proof and Uncirculated 2007-W American Eagle platinum coins resumed Nov. 6, at prices 6.5 percent to 9.4 percent higher than when sales were suspended.

The price of base metals also made headlines in 2007. After the production costs for the 1- and 5-cent coin rocketed past their face value in 2006, the U.S. Mint imposed a ban on melting the coins late in 2006 that took effect (after a period for public comment) in 2007.

During 2007, prices on base metals generally rose at an alarming rate into May. Copper, zinc and nickel then all began a fairly steady fall until late autumn, took a slight blip upward, then declined slightly toward the end of the year.

The overall picture was of volatility and great percentage shifts in prices over short periods of time.

The Mint announced in recent years that it was conducting a study of possible alternative coin compositions, but no specific proposals have ever emerged.

Import restrictions anger collectors

Collectors and dealers in ancient coins voiced loud opposition, but could not thwart efforts to restrict the importation of certain ancient coins from Cyprus.

The restrictions, which became effective July 16, were "unprecedented in both methodology and scope and should be a cause of great concern," one industry spokesperson said.

The restrictions were imposed at the direction of the U.S. Department of State.

Cyprus officials said the import restriction of coins was a big success for their country.

U.S. collectors have stated that ancient coins found within modern Cyprus are extremely common and have been avidly collected since the Renaissance. In addition, the cost to defend seized coins could be prohibitive, opponents to the rule say.

To restrict import of cultural artifacts, a foreign country must provide evidence that looting of culturally important sites is a problem, that legal and enforcement departments are fighting pillaging in that country and that a significant U.S. market exists for the restricted item.

Offering no explanation for the decision, State Department officials extended Cyprus' previous import restrictions for an additional five years and added coins to the memorandum of understanding that spells out the restrictions.

Restricted coins, made of gold, silver and bronze, include those produced in Cyprus from the end of the sixth century B.C. to A.D. 235.

Three organizations representing numismatists, the Ancient Coin Collectors Guild, the International Association of Professional Numismatists, and the Professional Numismatists Guild, sought an injunction against the action but were unsuccessful.

Coins establish new record prices

Several blockbuster rarities and collections established record prices in 2007.

In November, a collection of more than 1,000 United States pattern coins sold for more than $30 million in a private transaction to a collector identified only as Mr. Simpson.

Simpson's purchase more than doubled the previous record price paid for a single coin or set in a private transaction.

An anonymous purchaser on April 25 paid $5 million for the finest-known 1913 Liberty Head 5-cent coin, the second-highest amount ever paid for a single U.S. coin. The coin was once owned by consummate collector Louis E. Eliasberg Sr. It is graded Proof 66

by Professional Coin Grading Service.

Another great rarity, one of four known Proof 1804 Capped Bust gold $10 eagles, tied the Eliasberg 1913 Liberty Head 5-cent for second place, selling Sept. 26 in a private transaction for $5 million.

Albanese Rare Coins Inc., Albion, N.Y., brokered the transaction for "the King of Eagles," which broke the previous record price of $2,274,000, achieved in February 2005. The 1804 eagle was certified Proof 65 ultra cameo ★ by Numismatic Guaranty Corp., with the star designating exceptional eye appeal.

The finest-known 1907 Saint-Gaudens, Ultra High Relief, Lettered Edge, Roman Numerals gold $20 double eagle also set a record in 2007.

The coin, which has been graded Proof 69 by both Numismatic Guaranty Corp. and PCGS, was purchased in a private transaction by Certified Assets Management of Wilmington, Del., from Heritage Auction Galleries, on behalf of Heritage's client, officials announced Aug. 17.

The coin was last offered publicly in the Heritage auction of the Philip Morse collection of Saint-Gaudens double eagles in November 2005, where it realized $2,990,000, a record at the time.

In all, at least seven transactions were record-breaking, reaching more than $1 million each, four of those for $3 million or more, indicating health at the top end of the market.

Ford Collection sales complete

Collectors in 2007 witnessed the final auction of the record-breaking John J. Ford Jr. Collection.

A collection of a lifetime, it took four years of auctions to sell.

From Oct. 14, 2003, through Oct. 16, 2007, the Ford Collection was sold at public auction by Stack's in 21 different sales.

The collection set a record for a single-owner collection, especially significant considering that Ford eschewed federal U.S. coinage, and not a single lot contained regular-issued United States coinage from the U.S. Mint.

The 21 Ford coin, exonumia and currency auctions brought $56,402,744 and the two literature sales by Stack's and George Frederick Kolbe realized $1,852,604, for a total of $58,255,348—a world record for a single-owner collection.

Other stories

Sales of the inaugural 2007-W First Spouse .9999 fine gold half-ounce $10 coins started out hot, with the first two releases—the Martha Washington and Abigail Adams coins—selling out the entire 40,000-coin mintage of both in less than two hours June 19.

The sales Aug. 30 by the United States Mint of the Proof Thomas Jefferson Liberty First Spouse coins took less than two hours. The Uncirculated version did not sell out until a few weeks after launch, although Mint officials mistakenly reported a launch-day sellout.

Sales of the Proof and Uncirculated Dolley Madison First Spouse coins, launched Nov. 19, were slower than their predecessors. The drop-off in sales followed a nearly 25 percent increase in the purchase price from the first three releases following a surge in the spot price of gold.

A rare 1969-S Lincoln, Doubled Die Obverse cent discovered in an Uncirculated roll late in 2007 was certified as tied for finest known.

Michigan collector Michael Tremonti found the coin among the first of two rolls of 1969-S Lincoln cents, spotting it with his naked eye. It did not exhibit the notorious and valueless "machine doubling," but the distinctly different doubling, with two distinct sets of numbers and letters, one overlying the other, for almost all obverse design details.

In such choice condition, fresh from a bank roll, the coin was worth a strong five figures, so Tremonti desired quick confirmation, which came the next day during a visit with expert Ken Potter, who reported on the discovery in a front-page news article in the Oct. 29 issue of *Coin World*.

Subsequently, as reported in the Nov. 19 issue, Professional Coin Grading Service certified the coin as Mint State 64 red, tied for finest known to the service.

The American Numismatic Association experiences profound change in 2007.

Members elected seven newcomers to the board of governors during the 2007 national election, and the new board, in one of its first actions, placed Executive Director Christopher Cipoletti on administrative leave. He was dismissed in October

The ANA posted its fifth consecutive year of red ink with mounting legal fees amid imbroglios over Cipoletti, lawsuits with past contract workers and other upheaval. Plans for revamping bylaws and opening a museum in conjunction with the U.S. Mint, as well as election ethics violation, were also in the background for the organization in 2007.

Issuance of the Liberty Dollar, a private voluntary barter currency created by "monetary architect" Bernard von NotHaus, focused scrutiny on the business and ultimately sparked the Nov. 14, 2007, seizure by FBI and Secret Service agents of tons of the Liberty Dollar medallions in various precious metals along with copper versions.

Among the confiscated pieces were thousands bearing the portrait of one of the Republican presidential candidates, Ron Paul, with a portion of proceeds designated to support Paul's campaign.

Though sales of the pieces were launched in 1998, the FBI only began taking a serious interest in von NotHaus and the Liberty Dollar in the summer of 2005 when it began a two-year investigation into the Liberty Dollar.

In mid-September 2006, at the recommendation of federal investigators, the U.S. Mint posted an advisory on its website warning consumers that use of the Liberty Dollar as a monetary substitute constituted a federal crime.

2008

It is hard to select just a few among the stories that stood out in 2008, and compelling cases can be made for many as milestones in numismatics.

However, the unprecedented collector and investor demand for American Eagle 1-ounce .999 fine silver bullion coins from the U.S. Mint was so strong in 2008 that sales totals were more than 70 percent higher than any other year in the 23-year history of the American Eagle Bullion Coin Program to that point.

Silver American Eagle sales skyrocket

The Mint recorded sales of more than 19.5 million of the 1-ounce silver coins in 2008.

That sales established such a record was astounding, given the suspension of sales twice, for a total of nearly two months, and the imposition of sales restrictions during the last nine months of 2008.

The sales level was also achieved in the face of the U.S. Mint's inability to obtain sufficient blanks from its two vendors to meet the insatiable demand.

U.S. Mint officials indefinitely suspended sales Feb. 4 so that the West Point Mint could replenish its inventory of coins, with sales resuming March 4 before being suspended again March 19.

When sales resumed a second time April 21, authorized purchasers were faced with ordering restrictions, with coins placed in a distribution pool and allocated according to a schedule based on previous ordering patterns.

While demand was skyrocketing for the American Eagle silver bullion coins, the U.S. Mint was at the same time dealing with an inability to obtain sufficient blanks to meet its demand for the coins.

There was no shortage of physical silver, just of fabricated blanks for coins and rounds (1-ounce silver pieces issued by private firms). Blank manufacturers could not keep up with the worldwide demand from the U.S. Mint and its competitors, creating the shortage.

U.S. Mint officials also ran into difficulties with the American Eagle gold bullion coins because of blank acquisitions. Rationing of American Eagle 1-ounce gold bullion coins was implemented by the Mint Aug. 15 because of blank shortages.

On Oct. 6, authorized purchasers were notified that the U.S. Mint would focus its bullion coin production for the remainder of calendar year 2008 almost exclusively on American Eagle 1-ounce gold and silver coins.

As the supplies of gold and silver American Eagles tightened beginning early in 2008, the premiums in the marketplace for the 1-ounce coins, primarily the American Eagle gold and silver bullion coins, began to climb. As low as 17.6 percent on Aug. 13 for the American Eagle 1-ounce silver bullion coins, the premiums gyrated upward to 46.91 percent by Oct. 15 before reaching to 76.22 percent on Oct. 28.

Premiums for 1-ounce examples of the American Eagle .9167 fine gold bullion coin, American Buffalo 1-ounce .9999 fine gold bullion coin and American Eagle 1-ounce platinum bullion coin also rose with demand.

What was fueling such demand?

Precious metal prices dominate news

The spot price of gold and platinum hit record levels during calendar year 2008.

But just as quickly as the prices rose, they fell during the year.

The price of platinum skyrocketed to more than $2,200 an ounce at its peak, then plummeted to less than half its peak level.

After topping $1,000 an ounce, gold, while slipping back from its record highs by a few hundred dollars per ounce, leveled off to between $700 and a bit above $800.

The spot price of silver eclipsed the $20 an ounce mark in 2008, its highest level in decades, though still less than half the record level reached in January 1980 when the metal topped $50 an ounce. The spot price of silver fell in 2008, too, dropping below $10 an ounce.

Sales of silver and gold were especially strong all year long amid economic uncertainty striking both domestically and abroad.

Chinese counterfeits

China in 2008 was linked to discoveries of fake coins and fake "slabs," threatening an erosion of confidence in the hobby and ultimately the market itself.

That China was the source of these counterfeits was no shock to keen observers of the hobby in recent years, but the enormity of the situation certainly became evident in 2008.

Collectors learned early in the year that counterfeit examples of coin holders, or "slabs," used by grading and authentication services, had been discovered.

Numismatic Guaranty Corp. acknowledged the fake slabs with a Jan. 7 advisory. A few months later, Professional Coin Grading Service, on March 27, announced that fake examples of its slabs, too, had been discovered, specifically originating from China.

Fake coins were found in the NGC holders, which featured fake certification labels matching information found on proper labels. Collectors could not just check the validity of a certification number to determine whether the slabs were genuine.

NGC alerted collectors to several diagnostics that distinguish the fake holders from real ones, but PCGS declined to release diagnostics, since officials with the firm were concerned that doing so would "only provide specific instructions to the counterfeiters on how to improve their fakes."

PCGS officials said the counterfeit holders contained fake coins and fake certification numbers.

Chinese sellers of counterfeit coins approached U.S. collectors about marketing their products in the United States, a *Coin World* investigation confirmed.

Coin World identified a seller of fake coins and revealed the extent of the problem.

A man known by his eBay ID at that time, Jinghuashei, operated Big Tree Coin Factory, which produced more than 100,000 fake coins per month for sale around the world. The counterfeiter said he had about 100 competitors, all selling fake coins.

As long as the counterfeits date before 1949, the manufacturers are immune from Chinese laws against fakes, Jinghuashei said.

Jinghuashei branched out to offer counterfeit error coins, including broadstruck, double-struck and off-center coins, many of high quality and difficult to identify as fake.

United Kingdom coin designs

After using the same images for nearly 40 years, the United Kingdom shook up its circulating coinage designs in 2008 with the introduction of a revolutionary concept.

For the first time, individual elements of a single design were used across a range of a nation's circulating coins.

Designer Matthew Dent, a then-26-year-old artist from Wales, created the designs, which beat more than 4,000 others, including those from publicly invited artists and Royal Mint engraving staff, in a public nationwide contest begun in 2005.

Dent's designs, which he likened to a puzzle, feature different details of the Shield of the Royal Arms. Positioned correctly together, they reveal the complete shield of arms.

The Royal Arms, a symbol of the reigning monarch, has appeared in various forms on the coinage of almost every British monarch since the reign of Edward III (1327 to 1377).

Paper money discriminates

Federal paper money discriminates against blind and visually impaired individuals.

That was the ruling on May 20, 2008, when the United States Court of Appeals for the District of Columbia Circuit upheld a lower court decision that the U.S. Treasury Department failed to design, produce and issue paper money that is readily distinguishable to blind and visually impaired individuals.

The decision means possible changes for Federal Reserve notes.

The lawsuit, filed in 2002 by the American Council for the Blind and two individuals with visual impairments, Patrick Sheehan and Otis Stephens, alleged that the physical design of Federal Reserve notes violates Section 504 of the federal Vocational Rehabilitation Act.

The Bureau of Engraving and Printing estimated

that possible changes to FRNs to make the notes more distinguishable to the visually impaired would cost in excess of $200 million, depending on the specific technology employed.

The appeals court rejected arguments by the Treasury that making FRNs accessible would impose an undue burden on the government and sent the lawsuit back to U.S. District Judge James Robertson to address American Council for the Blind's request for relief.

In God We Trust moves off edge

After a spate of embarrassing errors with the edge lettering created "Godless" Presidential dollars and Sacagawea dollars in 2007, Congress voted to move the IN GOD WE TRUST motto from the edge to a more prominent location on the dollar coins.

The motto, along with the date, Mint mark and E PLURIBUS UNUM, appear incuse on the edge of 2007 and 2008 Presidential dollars.

The legislation was buried within 3,565 pages of the Consolidated Appropriations Act, 2008, H.R. 2764, which gained approval Dec. 19, 2007.

In the 2007 act, Congress left the decision about whether to place the motto on the obverse or the reverse to the discretion of the Mint. The Mint chose the obverse of the Presidential dollar for the IN GOD WE TRUST inscription because it is consistent with where it appears on other current circulating coins.

State quarter dollar program ends

As 2008 closed, the year marked the end of the popular State quarter dollar program.

The program introduced one design for each of the nations' 50 states, released five per year in the order in which the states joined the Union.

The new designs had stirred life into the hobby and introduced collecting to a whole new generation; U.S. Mint estimates claimed that some 147 million people, or slightly fewer than 1-in-2 Americans, collected the State quarter dollars.

The program earned direct profit of more than $6.1 billion for the U.S. Treasury, as collectors kept coins instead of spending them.

Sales of collector coins in numerous packaging and set options and related products also reaped financial rewards for the U.S. Mint.

The success also inspired two successor series.

Other stories

Continuing a story line from the previous year,

2009

2009 will long be remembered as the year collectors had to do without one of their favorite collector coin issues.

No Proof American Eagle silver dollars

The U.S. Mint's Oct. 6 announcement that it would not strike Proof American Eagle silver dollars and gold $50 coins for 2009 sent a shock wave

in 2008 the 110th Congress considered more than a dozen pieces of legislation that sought to reduce the production costs of 1- and 5-cent coins, which had each exceeded the face value of the coins for a time.

None of the introduced bills became law.

The debate over how to lower production costs for the cent and 5-cent coin included a request by Edmund C. Moy, director of the U.S. Mint, that Congress transfer its constitutional authority to determine coinage compositions to the executive branch, of which the Mint is a part.

Congress declined to relinquish its power to regulate coinage compositions.

Early demand for the Uncirculated 2008-W American Eagle 1-ounce silver coins spiked, upon a discovery that some examples had been struck by a reverse die bearing the design subtype of 2007. Mint officials had made some changes to the obverse and reverse designs of the American Eagle silver dollar for 2008, but a leftover 2007 die was used in the production of some of the Uncirculated 2008 dollars; none of the bullion or Proof examples was affected.

Collector John Nanney discovered the variation upon receiving an example of the Uncirculated version of the silver American Eagle coin. The Mint determined a total of some 47,000 2008-W American Eagle, Reverse of 2007 examples were struck.

A Russian gold coin rarity sold at auction in late 2008 established a world record price for a non-U.S. coin. The Russian rarity was among several new records established in 2008 for world coins.

An anonymous buyer paid £1,782,500 including the buyer's fee, or about $2,820,091 in U.S. funds, for the unique 1755 Elizabeth I gold 20-ruble pattern during a Nov. 6 auction by St. James's Auctions in association with Baldwin's. The 20-ruble pattern is graded About Uncirculated 58 by Numismatic Guaranty Corp.

The previous record price for a world coin (or non-U.S. coin) was the $1,380,000 realized for the Polish 1621 gold 100-ducat piece of Sigismund III from the Kroisos Collection, sold by Stack's in New York City on Jan. 14, 2008.

On Dec. 2, a Hadrian bronze sestertius realized the equivalent of $1.9 million U.S., a record price for an ancient coin. The coin, struck circa A.D. 135 by the Rome Mint, sold in an auction by Numismatica Genevensis in Switzerland.

through American Eagle collectors nationwide.

Anger and disbelief were common sentiments shared by many collectors, some of whom expressed their displeasure with the decision through *Coin World's* Letters to the Editor page.

The Mint buffered the reaction from collectors to its decision by noting that the Gold Bullion Coin

Act of 1985 and the Liberty Coin Act of 1985 only obligates the Mint to produce gold and silver bullion coins, but not Proof American Eagle silver and gold coins, which are geared toward collectors and sold for a greater markup, unlike the bullion coins.

Proof American Eagle .999 fine silver 1-ounce coins and American Eagle .9167 fine gold 1-ounce coins had been struck every year since 1986. Proof half-ounce gold $25 coins were first struck by the Mint in 1987 and Proof gold quarter-ounce $10 and tenth-ounce $5 coins followed in 1988.

Though the Proof American Eagle coins would return in 2009, collectors were unhappy at the prospects of having a gap in their collections.

In suspending the programs, the U.S. Mint cited the rabid demand for silver and gold bullion coins, which spilled over from the previous year. The Mint diverted blanks toward production of bullion coins instead of saving them for the Proof versions.

Gold, silver prices spur demand

Following on the heels of significantly higher prices in 2008, the demand for precious metals by investors and collectors subsided very little in 2009. As a result, the U.S. Mint found itself still struggling to keep up with collector and investor demand—and continuing to set sales records.

The spot price for gold began the year in the $800 range, but was mostly up in 2009, particularly toward the latter half of the year. Gold briefly breached the $1,000 mark in late September before settling into what proved to be a long-term stay above $1,000 beginning Oct. 1. Previously, the price for an ounce of gold had only surpassed the $1,000 level on one occasion, for a few days in mid-March 2008. By Dec. 2, 2009, the spot price of gold had achieved an all-time high of $1,212.50 before dipping again slightly.

Silver, too, saw mostly upward movement from the beginning to the end of 2009, though as the year came to a close it had not matched its recent high of $20.92 achieved March 17, 2008, or its historical high of Jan. 21, 1980, when the spot price briefly topped $50 and finished the day at $42.07.

The U.S. Mint continued to experience problems in procuring precious metals blanks, difficulties that delayed the production of many of its products. Lack of silver and gold planchets was cited in the Mint's decision to not strike Proof or Uncirculated 2009 American Eagle silver and gold coins.

The shortage of blanks also contributed to the decision to forego production of Proof fractional gold American Eagle coins as well as any fractional versions of American Buffalo coins, although the Mint did strike fractional American Eagle bullion coins late in the year.

American Eagle silver bullion coins sold at a record pace in 2009. The Mint sold more than 28.7 million American Eagle 1-ounce silver bullion coins, establishing an annual sales record.

National Numismatic Collection returns

After a nearly four-year wait, portions of America's coin collection went back on display in 2009.

The new exhibit of rarities from the National Numismatic Collection opened June 12 on the first floor of the Smithsonian Institution's Museum of American History in Washington, D.C.

The Smithsonian also in 2009 announced a partnership with the U.S. Mint that would take some of the collection's highlights out on the road, traveling to a variety of venues.

The "Stories on Money" exhibit at the Smithsonian was the museum's first fixed public display of items exclusively from the numismatic collection since the entire National Museum of American History was closed in 2005 for extensive renovations.

The new exhibit brought out 187 pieces from the more than 1.6 million numismatic items in the NNC, for a display divided into seven exhibit segments. The exhibit includes some major rarities that previously experienced little or no public display.

Among the major rarities displayed are examples of all three classes of 1804 Draped Bust dollar; the 27-millimeter 1907 Saint-Gaudens, Ultra High Relief, Roman Numerals .900 fine gold $20 double eagle that the U.S. Mint used in modeling its .9999 fine gold 2009 version; one of two 1933 Saint-Gaudens double eagles in the NNC; the two Proof 1877 gold $50 half union patterns in the collection; and an 1822 Capped Head gold $5 half eagle, one of three known.

The committed 500-square-foot exhibit space is tiny compared to the 3,000 square feet dedicated to numismatic exhibits before the 2005 closing.

After the 2005 museum closing, public displays including isolated National Numismatic Collection items were mounted at the Smithsonian Castle, and traveling exhibits were sent to numismatic conventions, including the American Numismatic Association World's Fair of Money.

That spirit of partnership was behind an Aug. 5 announcement that a joint traveling exhibit to feature items from the NNC and "heritage assets" from the U.S. Mint was expected to be readied for exhibition in 2011.

The traveling exhibit was to be staged at six to eight museums across the United States during a two- to three-year period. The specific museums were not announced. The exhibit is anticipated to fill a 2,500-square-foot area and contain items from each agency's collection.

U.S. cent breaks $1 million barrier

The first U.S. large cent to break the $1 million mark was sold at auction Sept. 6, 2009, in the first auction for large cents in the Dan Holmes Collection.

The 1795 Liberty Cap, Reeded Edge cent, cataloged as Sheldon 79 in *Penny Whimsy* by William H. Sheldon, is the finest of seven known examples. It was among the 572 lots of Early Date large cents from 1793 through 1814 sold in the Holmes Collection auction.

The coin, graded Very Good 10 by Professional Coin Grading Service, was sold at auction Sept. 6 by Ira & Larry Goldberg, Auctioneers, with McCawley & Grellman.

Holmes, of Cleveland, bought the coin in 1993 for $115,000 from New York dealer Tony Terranova.

Greg Hannigan, from Hannigan's Rare Coins in Palm Beach, Fla., won the 1795 Liberty Cap, Reeded Edge cent for $1,265,000, including the 15 percent buyer's fee. Hannigan said he purchased it on behalf of an unnamed collector, who was willing to bid higher if necessary.

The first of four auctions of the Holmes Collection brought prices realized of $15,082,577.75 Sept. 6 in Beverly Hills, Calif.

Nearly 150 copper collectors and dealers participated in the history-making auction held at the Crowne Plaza Beverly Hills hotel.

The auction included all 302 "collectible" die varieties enumerated in *Penny Whimsy*. The auction also included 52 of the 53 known "noncollectible" die varieties for the series.

Holmes' collection was assembled over 35 years, with the noncollectible portion considered the most comprehensive collection of these noncollectible varieties ever assembled.

Holmes had originally intended to begin the auction of his collection sometime in 2011, but moved up the schedule after doctors delivered the diagnosis Sept. 23, 2008, that he was afflicted with amyotrophic lateral sclerosis, also known as Lou Gehrig's disease.

The auction served as more than a simple offering of his Early Date cents, being also an occasion for fellow collectors to celebrate Holmes' life and achievements.

Banner year for Lincoln coinage

2009 provided collectors with a complete harvest of coins dedicated to Abraham Lincoln, including a commemorative silver dollar and four cents in collector and circulation versions.

The cents and silver dollar recognized the bicentennial of Lincoln's birth on Feb. 12.

Examples of the cents, under the act's provisions, were produced in copper-plated zinc for circulation, with numismatic versions, struck in Proof and for Uncirculated Mint sets, in the bronze composition used for the Lincoln cent when the coin was introduced in 1909.

The four 2009 Lincoln cents have reverse designs individually representing Lincoln's birthplace and early years in Kentucky (1809 to 1816, Early Childhood cent); and time in Indiana (1816 to 1830, Formative Years cent); in Illinois (1830 to 1861, Professional Life cent); and in Washington, D.C. (1861 to 1865, Presidency cent).

Official launch ceremonies were held for each of the cents. The ceremonies were accompanied by exchange sessions, during which those attending could purchase rolls of the new cents at face value.

Ceremonies were held Feb. 12 in Hodgenville, Ky., for the Early Childhood cent; on May 14 in Lincoln City, Ind., for the Formative Years cent; on Aug. 13 in Springfield, Ill., for the Professional Life cent; and on Nov. 12 in Washington, D.C., for the Presidency cents.

Hundreds attended each event, and the coins obtained in the exchanges were soon offered for (and sold) for significant premiums in the marketplace.

The Abraham Lincoln Bicentennial commemorative silver dollar was placed on sale starting Feb. 12. With a mintage limit of 500,000, a maximum of 450,000 coins were made available individually, with 50,000 Proof coins reserved for the limited-edition Lincoln Coin and Chronicles set, offered later in 2009.

On April 14, U.S. Mint officials reported sufficient orders had been received to constitute a sellout of the 450,000 individual coins—325,000 Proof coins and 125,000 of the Uncirculated version.

The Lincoln Coin and Chronicles set containing all four Proof 2009-S Lincoln, Bicentennial cents, along with a Proof 2009-P Lincoln, Bicentennial silver dollar, sold out all 50,000 sets the day after it became available Oct. 15.

2009 Ultra High Relief gold $20

The 2009 Saint-Gaudens, Ultra High Relief, Roman Numerals 1-ounce .9999 fine gold $20 double eagle, highly anticipated before its Jan. 22 release, drew collector attention for much of the first half of 2009.

A total of 115,178 examples were sold, totaling $112.4 million in revenue during Fiscal Year 2009. The coin was the highest revenue-generating numismatic product during 2009.

The coin was produced under authority granted by Congress to the secretary of the Treasury to issue .9999 fine gold coins without further congressional approval.

The Ultra High Relief coin was sold as a numismatic product, so its purchase price was at a significant premium over its intrinsic value. The price fluctuated during the sales period based on the average spot price of gold.

Ultra High Relief sales were responsible for 25.5 percent of total numismatic product sales revenue during FY 2009. Net income from the sale of the Ultra High Relief coins totaled $6.4 million.

Ten days before the UHR coin's 2009 release, Mint officials on Jan. 12 released a pricing structure that would be implemented for all U.S. gold and platinum coin issues, beginning with the Ultra High Relief double eagle. Under the new pricing structure, the Mint could change the price of the coin weekly to keep pace with the price of gold, and often did throughout the year.

The price of the 2009 Ultra High Relief coin when first issued was $1,189, with a household ordering limit of one coin.

The Mint adjusted order limits throughout the program. The one-coin per household limit was raised to 10 coins per household on July 27, less than two weeks before the ANA World's Fair of Money in Los Angeles.

The convention was the first occasion when collectors and dealers could order the coins and receive them at the same time. Many Mint customers took advantage of the opportunity, buying their maximum 10 coins, then flipping them for an immediate $50 to $60 per coin profit from several dealers who were buying hundreds of the coins for their inventories.

The order limit was raised to 25 coins on Aug. 31; all restrictions were lifted Sept. 21.

Other news

A severely weakened economy led to the lowest circulating coinage production in decades.

The United States Mint's largest customer is the Federal Reserve, and a glut of coinage (as people broke open piggy banks and returned coins to commerce), coupled with decreased retail demand, led to a diminished need to strike circulation coins.

The lower mintages for all circulating coins affected production of the one-year, six-coin District of Columbia and U.S. Territories quarter dollar program. The program was a follow-up to the popular and successful 10-year State quarter dollars program of 1999 to 2008.

For the new program, quarter dollars were issued commemorating the District of Columbia and the territories of the Commonwealth of Puerto Rico, Guam, American Samoa, U.S. Virgin Islands and the Commonwealth of the Northern Mariana Islands.

Mintages for the coins were well below mintages for even the lowest-mintage State quarter dollars. Some collectors voiced frustration at being unable to find any of the District of Columbia and U.S. Territories quarter dollars in circulation. Even in early 2011, some collectors have yet to find any of the 2009 quarter dollars in circulation.

The collector community struck back at the scourge of Chinese counterfeiting with educational efforts geared at reaching coin collectors who were unaware of the menace.

2010

In a year when the hobby experienced several records—including the 2010 price of gold and demand for certain coins—none may be more impressive than the world record price paid for a single coin.

Record prices for silver dollar, cent

On May 14, a 1794 Flowing Hair silver dollar sold for $7.85 million in a private transaction, breaking the previous record of $7,590,020 for the 1933 Saint-Gaudens gold $20 double eagle that sold at auction in 2002 (and still holds the record price for a coin sold at auction).

Graded Specimen 66 by Professional Coin Grading Service, it is the finest known 1794 Flowing Hair dollar and is believed by several experts to be the first silver dollar ever struck by the U.S. Mint, according to parties in the transaction.

Steven L. Contursi, president of Rare Coin Wholesalers of Irvine, Calif., sold the coin to the nonprofit Cardinal Collection Educational Foundation in Sunnyvale, Calif.

Researcher and early U.S. dollar specialist Martin Logies operates and represents the foundation and is its numismatic curator.

The private sale was brokered by Greg Roberts, president and chief executive officer of Spectrum Group International of Irvine, Calif.

Contursi has long touted the coin as the first silver dollar struck at the then-fledgling U.S. Mint, though no documentary evidence has been found to back this claim.

"There's no conclusive proof, as an attorney might say, but the circumstantial evidence is compelling," Logies said.

Approximately 2,000 silver dollars were recorded struck on a hand-turned screw press at the Mint in Philadelphia on Oct. 15, 1794, the only day of production for dollar coins that year. Of that total, 1,758 were deemed of acceptable quality and delivered.

The dollars were made from silver provided by the U.S. Mint's first director, David Rittenhouse, according to Logies.

As significant as the record sale for the 1794 Flowing Hair dollar is, two other record prices for specific U.S. coins were set during 2010.

A record $1.7 million was paid by an initially unidentified Southwestern United States businessman for the only known example of a 1943-D Lincoln cent struck at the Denver Mint on a leftover copper-alloy planchet instead of the intended zinc-coated steel. The purchaser has since been identified as Bob R. Simpson.

The purchase price represents the highest price paid not only for a Lincoln cent, but for any cent, regardless of series.

The coin, graded and encapsulated Mint State 64 brown by Professional Coin Grading Service, was sold to its new owner by Legend Numismatics from Lincroft, N.J.

Andy Skrabalak of Angel Dee's Coins and Collectibles in Woodbridge, Va., acted as agent on behalf of the bronze 1943-D Lincoln cent's former owner.

Another rarity set a record in 2010. One of five known examples of the 1913 Liberty Head 5-cent coin realized a $3.25 million bid at Heritage Auctions' Platinum Night auction during the 2010 Florida United Numismatists convention.

With the 15 percent buyer's fee, the total price paid

was $3,737,500, making the piece the most expensive 1913 Liberty Head 5-cent coin ever to sell at auction.

Known as the "Olsen specimen," it is graded Proof 64 by Numismatic Guaranty Corp and is the second finest known 1913 Liberty Head 5-cent coin. It is also known outside collecting circles for its Dec. 11, 1973, appearance in an episode of the television show *Hawaii Five-O* titled "The $100,000 Nickel."

A rare Chinese coin established a new record price for a Chinese coin sold at auction.

The 1910 Yunnan Spring dollar, graded Mint State 65 by Numismatic Guaranty Corp., realized $1,035,000, including the 15 percent buyer's fee, in Champion Hong Kong Auction's Aug. 22 sale in Hong Kong.

The coin is the first Chinese coin to sell for more than $1 million U.S., according to the firm.

Record American Eagle silver coin sales

2010 was the third year in a row that American Eagle 1-ounce .999 fine silver bullion coins sold at a frenetic pace, with sales records falling each successive year since late 2007.

The demand for silver bullion American Eagles in 2010 was unparalleled.

The United States Mint recorded sales of 34,662,500 of the American Eagle silver bullion coin during 2010, a figure 20.5 percent higher than in calendar year 2009.

A sales benchmark of 10,475,000 coins was reached in 2002, a record that held until 2008 when American Eagle silver bullion coin sales reached 19,583,500 coins. 2009 sales toppled the 2008 record, with 2009 sales totaling 28,766,500 coins.

Some of the early calendar year 2010 sales comprised both 2009 coins and 2010 coins.

2010 holds the distinction of not only breaking the single-year sales record, but also setting a record high for a monthly sales total.

The 4.26 million American Eagle silver bullion coins sold in November represented the highest monthly sales total since the American Eagle silver bullion coin program was introduced by the U.S. Mint in November 1986.

Also in 2010, United States Mint officials appeared to have solved the planchet supply problem that caused program problems in 2008 and 2009, by adding a third planchet supplier.

Return of Proof American Eagle silver dollars

Perhaps the addition of the third planchet supplier made the difference, but collectors of Proof silver American Eagle coins didn't care what machinations went into the production, just the final result.

After a forced hiatus in 2009, collectors returned to the program when sales of the Proof 2010-W American Eagle silver dollars began Nov. 19.

Earlier in the year, the increased demand that had forced suspension of the Proof version in 2009 cascaded into 2010 and threatened the issuance of Proof 2010-W American Eagle silver dollars.

However, demand lessened for American Eagle silver bullion coins in August and September, according to officials, enabling the Mint to shift some capacity to produce the numismatic versions.

Sales of the Proof 2010-W American Eagle silver dollar reached 856,356 before it was taken off sale Dec. 28.

Precious metals demand

2010 was a major year for precious metals, with gold hitting an all-time high and silver reaching a 30-year high.

Continuing economic uncertainties, both in the United States and abroad, along with low consumer confidence, turned more investors to commodities— including precious metals—as an alternative store of wealth.

On the first day of trading for the year, Jan. 4, gold opened at $1,113 an ounce (all prices are London Fix), staying in a relatively tight range until May 7, when it hit $1,202.25. On Sept. 29, gold broke a new barrier, closing at $1,307.50 and then on Nov. 9, gold shattered the $1,400 mark, closing at $1,421. Prices hovered around $1,400 an ounce in December, with gold closing the year at $1,410.

Silver had an even more dynamic year. It opened on Jan. 4 at $17.17 an ounce, dropping to $15.14 on Feb. 8. Things were relatively slow and steady until it hit $20.02 on Sept. 8. The price quickly rose to the $24.49 level on Oct. 14. Steady gains continued until a 30 year-high was reached at $30.50 on Dec. 7. Silver touched $30.70 on Dec. 30, a new high, before closing the year at $30.63.

Platinum's gains were more modest, starting the year at $1,500 an ounce and reaching $1,731 Dec. 31. Palladium showed greater gains, opening 2010 at $421 and closing on Dec. 31 at $791.

America the Beautiful series

A third circulating commemorative quarter dollar program made its debut in 2010—the America the Beautiful quarter dollar program.

President George W. Bush signed America's Beautiful National Parks Quarter Dollar Coin Act into law Dec. 23, 2008. The new law, PL 110-456, assured a successor program to the popular 50 State quarter dollars program by requiring reverse designs emblematic of a national park or other national site in each state, the District of Columbia, and each territory of the United States, on circulating quarter dollars beginning in 2010.

The new law requires the National Parks quarter dollars to be issued at a rate of five new designs per year for the next 11 years in the order in which the sites selected were established.

The total number of coins will be 56: 50 states, the District of Columbia and the five U.S. territories.

Sites were selected by the Treasury secretary after consultation with the Interior secretary and the governor or other chief executive of each state, territory and the District of Columbia.

The Treasury secretary was also given authority to order the issuance of a second series of quarter dollars commemorating a different site in each of the 56 entities at the conclusion of the first program. After the program is closed, whether after one round of coins or two rounds, the quarter dollar will be required to depict the pre-1999 George Washington portrait on the obverse (the portrait was made smaller and inscriptions were rearranged starting in 1999) and, on the reverse, a scene of Washington crossing the Delaware River to lead an attack on British forces during the Revolutionary War.

The authorizing act also approved an unprecedented version of each America the Beautiful coin—a 5-ounce .999 fine silver bullion version, also denominated as a 25-cent coin.

America the Beautiful bullion uproar

The 2010 America the Beautiful 5-ounce .999 fine silver bullion coins would prove one of the most anticipated, ballyhooed and controversial coin programs of 2010.

The obverse and reverse of the bullion coins replicate the designs employed for the 24.3-millimeter circulating quarter dollars for Hot Springs National Park, Yellowstone National Park, Yosemite National Park, Grand Canyon National Park and Mount Hood National Forest, as required under provisions of America's Beautiful National Parks Quarter Dollar Coin Act of 2008.

The controversy resulted from the Mint's decisions, in response to rising speculative presale pricing, to suspend sales on Dec. 6 (the day the sales to the Mint's network of authorized purchasers began) and then on Dec. 9 to revise the sales terms for authorized purchasers buying the coins. The speculative pricing was driven in part by smaller-than-anticipated mintages for the coins.

On Dec. 1, the U.S. Mint announced that the maximum mintage for each 2010 design would be 33,000 coins, not the 100,000 pieces per design it had announced months before.

Mint officials suspended sales on Dec. 6, shortly after the sales had begun, amid public complaints alleging secondary market price gouging. When the Mint resumed sales Dec. 10, it required the first-tier distributors to sell the coins directly to the public for a Mint-fixed profit and to limit distribution to one per household for each of the five coin designs.

The restrictions effectively prevented secondary market distributors from buying quantities of coins directly from the first-tier distributors who buy from the Mint. Some second-tier distributors had already begun advertising promotions announcing the pending availability of the coins when they learned that they would not be able to acquire the coins directly from the authorized purchasers of the coins.

Officials also announced that the Mint would offer a numismatic version, to be sold directly to the public. Collector versions of the 2010 coins went on sale individually during the first quarter of 2011.

The numismatic version of the 2010 coin were to be limited to 27,000 coins for each of the five designs. Mint officials said the coins would carry the P Mint mark of the Philadelphia Mint where both the bullion and numismatic versions were being struck, and bear a finish applied post-strike that is similar to the surface finish in use for the Mint's 3-inch bronze medals.

Paper money shown, but not circulating

Paper money collectors were teased with the release of images of a redesigned Series 2009 $100 Federal Reserve note, but intended release of the actual notes would be delayed.

On April 21, 2010, the redesigned $100 FRN was unveiled during ceremonies in Washington, D.C. During the ceremony, a release date of Feb. 10, 2011, was announced for the new note, seemingly answering the question of when the note would begin circulating.

But within six months Federal Reserve Board officials announced a delay in the planned release date because of production problems. A new release date was not announced.

BEP and Federal Reserve officials continued to work toward a new release date as they sought a solution to the problem of sporadic creasing of the paper during printing.

The redesigned $100 FRNs represent the first redesign of the denomination since 1996, when the first of the "big heads" designs were introduced.

The new design features a portrait of Benjamin Franklin with a watermark of Franklin visible from either side of the note.

In addition, the new design incorporates a blue 3-D security ribbon, an optically variable device, featuring multiple shifting images of a bell and the inscription 100. The thread is clearly visible on the face of the note.

The back of the note shows a view of the back of Independence Hall. An enlarged "100" figure in gold, added to the right of the back, is to help visually impaired individuals recognize the note's face value.

Other stories

The year 2010 saw many new designs featured on circulating U.S. coins. Among these were four new Presidential dollars, a new reverse apiece for the Lincoln cent and the Sacagawea/Native American dollar, and five new quarter dollars for the new America the Beautiful series.

Once a welcome novelty, changing and new coin designs had by 2010 become a standard expectation among U.S. coin hobbyists.

Given the abundance of collector knowledge disseminated in hobby and club publications and websites, discoveries of new varieties are notable events. Die variety collectors in 2010 were treated to three major discoveries across two highly collectible series.

Two of the varieties came within the Morgan dollar series, with two previously unknown varieties of 1878 Morgan, 7 Tail Feathers coins identified. Both represent the first new varieties reported for the date and type in more than 40 years.

The third variety, within the Capped Bust dime series, represents a new die marriage for the 1827 dime struck from previously known dies. It is the first new Capped Bust dime variety reported since the 1984 publication of the standard reference on.

Coin World celebrated a milestone anniversary, its 50th, in 2010. *Coin World* was launched in April 1960 as a weekly coin publication, which was a novel idea at the time.

In 2010, *Coin World* honored its golden anniversary, celebrating the publication's rich history with five of the year's Special Editions, each recapping a successive decade and the people, events, and coins and other numismatic collectibles that shaped the hobby and rare coin market since 1960.

In the remaining seven Special Editions, *Coin World* examined a wide range of topics in-depth, focusing on such topics as technology's effects on the hobby (January), the "Ship of Gold" (February), dollar coins (March), big and small coins (May), Boston numismatics (July), gold coins (September) and silver dollars (November). In many of these seven themed issues, various collector specialty areas were explored.

2011

The U.S. Mint's first foray into issuing giant modern silver coins continued from 2010, and dominated headlines for much of the first half of 2011.

Nine authorized purchasers offered the 2010 5-ounce silver bullion coins to the public, starting Jan. 3, and then hopeful buyers waited anxiously to learn whether their orders were accepted and whether they would ultimately secure examples of the America the Beautiful 5-ounce silver bullion coins. The coins sold out from the authorized purchasers to the buying public, whereupon many of the coins re-entered the marketplace, selling for multiples of their initial price.

Before sales of the 2011 America the Beautiful 5-ounce bullion coins opened, the U.S. Mint announced on March 9 an end to sales restrictions that had been in place for the 2010 coins. Sales of the 2011 collector and bullion coins proceeded without the rancor or clamor surrounding sales of the 2010 bullion versions.

Also in January, the Mint sold 6,422,000 silver American Eagles, a monthly sales record.

Congressional scrutiny

Collector coins, as well as those coins in circulation, received scrutiny from legislators and policy makers in 2011.

In the 112th Congress, the House Financial Services Committee, which has coinage oversight in the House of Representatives, released a report Feb. 10 that laid out broader plans to review coins and paper money more closely than in recent sessions of Congress, with such key goals as reducing the production price of U.S. coins and accessing the long-term demand for coins.

Production costs for circulating coins continue to rise, notably for the 1- and 5-cent coins, which cost 1.79 cents and 9.24 cents respectively, far above their face value, according to the U.S. Mint's 2010 annual report.

In an effort toward lowering the costs, the U.S. Mint solicited suggestions for new coinage alloys that would meet certain criteria for coinability and commerce but be cheaper than current alloys.

Backers of the movement to replace the $1 Federal Reserve Note with a $1 coin received a boost with the release March 4 of a study conducted by the Government Accountability Office on request from Congress that found a savings of $5.5 billion over 30 years if the U.S. dropped the paper $1 note for a coin. It was the fourth such report issued in 20 years, each finding the retention of the paper $1 is the chief barrier to successful adoption of a $1 coin.

Shared American Eagle production

Collectors learned in late March that the U.S. Mint planned to begin striking American Eagle silver bullion coins at the San Francisco Mint, because unprecedented demand continuing from 2010 strained capacity at the West Point Mint, where the coins have been struck exclusively since 2001. A record 34,764,500 American Eagle 1-ounce silver coins were sold in 2010, eclipsing the record from 2009 by more than 4 million coins.

Mint officials confirmed March 23 plans for the 2011 production at the San Francisco Mint, the first time since 2000 that American Eagle silver bullion coins would be produced at both facilities.

Liberty Dollar founder convicted

The trial of a man who issued private silver and gold medals and promoted using them for barter came to a close after several years of litigation.

On March 18, Bernard von NotHaus was found guilty in a federal courthouse in Statesville, N.C., on all counts involving counterfeiting, possessing and selling his own coins with intent to defraud. His attorneys immediately filed an appeal, seeking to overturn the conviction. U.S. Attorney Anne Tompkins characterized von NotHaus' actions as "a unique form of domestic terrorism."

Collectors of the private Liberty Dollars received assurance April 12 from a representative for the U.S. Attorney's Office in Charlotte, N.C., that despite the conviction, collectors could legally buy, own and sell the Liberty Dollars without fear of prosecution, as long as they did not attempt to pass them as current money.

Counterfeits from China and 9/11 medals

Counterfeits from China also came under increasing scrutiny.

Customs and Border Patrol agents in Chicago on April 20 intercepted a package with 361 counterfeit U.S. Trade dollars that were on their way to an Illinois resident who was expecting to sell the fakes through online auction site eBay.

2011 marked the 10th anniversary of the Sept. 11, 2001, terrorist attacks on America, and the legislators who successfully pushed for a 1-ounce silver medal to commemorate the event took issue with a private firm offering collectibles of its own. New York Sen. Charles Schumer and Rep. Jerrold Nadler, both Democrats, called upon the Federal Trade Commission to prevent the National Collectors Mint from selling medals depicting one of the three sites of the terrorist attacks, the World Trade Center buildings in New York City. Pieces of the medals are coated with what the issuer said is silver recovered from the site of the fallen "Twin Towers."

The politicians claim the National Collectors Mint was profiting in the millions of dollars by misleading buyers that the items were official U.S. government-issued coins and the medals had silver recovered from the WTC site. The National Collectors Mint denied misleading buyers and noted that "the silver, was in fact, recovered from the World Trade Center site. ... We have lawyers' letter and a complete chain of custody for the materials."

The United States Mint on June 20 began sales of the official, congressionally authorized 1-ounce silver medals, which have a maximum mintage of 2 million pieces. The sale price of the medals includes a $10 surcharge to raise money for the National September 11th Memorial and Museum.

Eric P. Newman celebrates 100th birthday

Numismatic author, researcher and collector Eric P. Newman marked a milestone in 2011, reaching his centennial. The St. Louis native has authored more than a dozen books, many of which are recognized as the standards for the subject, on varied topics of numismatic interest, including Colonial coins and paper money. Fellow collectors in the Rittenhouse Society honored Newman with his own medal.

Departures

Many names and institutions in the hobby said their last good-byes, figuratively and literally, during 2011.

U.S. Mint Director Edmund Moy announced his resignation, effective Jan. 9, to take a new position with a Seattle-based energy company. Moy served as the 38th director of the U.S. Mint since being sworn in Sept. 5, 2006. Director Moy famously called for a "neo-Renaissance" in American coinage design, and in that effort oversaw the launch of the 2009 Saint-Gaudens, Ultra High Relief gold $20 coin.

Director Moy wasn't the only person to leave the Mint. After 46 years in service of the U.S. government, 36 of those at the U.S. Mint, longtime sculptor-engraver John Mercanti retired Dec. 30, 2010, an announcement that made its way through the hobby in the early weeks of 2011. Mercanti is credited with dozens of coin and medal designs during his tenure, and has begun efforts to expand the collector base by educating young hobbyists.

Colonial coin expert Joseph R. Lasser and exonumia dealer Steve Tanenbaum, pillars of numismatic research and knowledge, died during 2011.

Lasser, whose generous contributions of coins, paper money and funding to the numismatic department of the Colonial Williamsburg Foundation helped that institution build a significant collection, died Jan. 17 at the age of 87.

Tanenbaum, 62, was fatally injured Feb. 11 in New York City when he was struck by a car driven by a fleeing murder suspect. Tanenbaum was an expert in Civil War tokens, Hard Times tokens, inaugural medals, merchant and transportation tokens, and many other areas of exonumia.

Firms merge

Another milestone during the year was the "disappearance" of two venerable numismatic firms, Bowers & Merena and Stacks, who announced a merger late in 2010 that took place in early 2011 as consolidation of the numismatic auction business accelerated.

Stack's was a longtime New York City family coin firm that in recent years had merged with another firm, American Numismatic Rarities (which formed after Bowers & Merena was sold several years prior). Bowers & Merena itself had experienced growth, adding Ponterio & Associates in late 2009 and early 2010.

Merger of Bowers & Merena and Stacks created the new firm Stack's Bowers Galleries, with a world coinage division called Stack's Bowers and Ponterio.

Discoveries

A previously unknown Chain cent was discovered in a Dutch auction. The 1793 Flowing Hair, Chain, America cent, purchased by a Dutch collector in a small group of coins in 1993, was offered by Theo Peters of Muntenveiling International Coin Auctioneers, Amsterdam, the Netherlands, in a Feb. 12 auction, where it realized a hammer price equivalent to $52,870 U.S.

The U.S. Mint confirmed in early February that a small number of "Frosted Freedom" 2007-W American Eagle platinum $100 coins were pre-production pieces inadvertently released. The inscription FREEDOM on the reverse was initially given a frosted finish, but after trial strikes were made, the word was given a mirrored finish for production strikes. None of the Frosted Freedom pre-production strikes was supposed to be released, but some accidentally were. U.S. Mint officials said as many as 12 of the 1-ounce coins may have been released, with 21 of each of the half-ounce $50 and quarter-ounce $25 coins also released. The coins first came to notice when a dealer announced discovery of a single example. As of early June, one example of each size had been reported.

In early 2011, a rare variety of a New Jersey copper surfaced in an eBay auction, where it realized $106,655. The 1786 copper, designated Maris 18-L by specialists, was only the second known example when it sold for $105,655.55 in a Feb. 6 auction on eBay.com, establishing a new record price for an early American coin sold through that venue.

The ninth known example of a rare variety of the 1795 Flowing Hair, Two Leaves silver half dollar surfaced in March during the ANA National Money Show in Sacramento, Calif. The Overton 101 variety was examined by expert Sheridan Downey at the show after having been bought in an auction in 2009.

A unique silver ingot from an Idaho firm surfaced in Minnesota, realizing $12,210 in a May 1 auction. The discovery bar containing more than 25 ounces of silver is reportedly the first bar struck at the Trade Dollar Mining and Milling Co. in Silver City, Idaho.

Market events

Numerous events helped shape the market during the first six months of 2011.

The Professional Numismatists Guild abandoned an expanded definition of coin doctoring that its governing board had added to its code of ethics six months earlier, and returned to the one-sentence statement long used in the code. After a heated debate during a luncheon meeting open to members and the public Jan. 5 in Tampa, Fla., the membership voted 45 to 2 to remove the expanded definition. Some PNG members suggested they were being unfairly targeted, since no complaints of coin doctoring had been filed with the PNG, and other sections of the PNG Code of Ethics address misrepresenting the quality of a coin.

Import restrictions on certain Italian coin types were announced in 2011 by the U.S. State Department and U.S. Customs. While Roman Imperial and most Roman Republic coins are not affected, many widely collected Greek coins are. Notice was published in the Jan. 19 *Federal Register,* stating that the coins are included in a Memorandum of Understanding via a designated list of archaeological materials "in response to a Diplomatic Note from the Government of Italy requesting the Designated List be amended. Coins constitute an inseparable part of the archaeological record of Italy, and, like other archaeological objects, they are vulnerable to pillage and illicit export." The effect of the import restrictions is that certain Greek "coins of Italian types" may be imported into the United States only if accompanied by either an export permit issued by Italy or other documentation indicating that the coins left Italy prior to Jan. 19, the effective date of the restriction.

Heritage Auction Galleries announced Jan. 6 that it would conduct an auction to help raise funds to create a permanent endowment for the National Numismatic Collection, which is housed in the Smithsonian's Museum of American History in Washington, D.C. Heritage officials announced the goal for the January 2012 auction is to raise more than $1 million.

The NNC, with more than 1 million numismatic items, ranks as one of the premier numismatic collections in the world, holding some of the United States' greatest numismatic treasurers. The endowment will be used to help care for the collection and provide greater access to it for both scholars and the general public. Projects planned in the immediate future include photographing the entire collection and making it available in an online catalog, producing a Web-based numismatic library, and providing additional traveling exhibits with an emphasis on offering a window into the nation's history through coinage.

A concerted effort to convince Congress to eliminate one portion of the Patient Protection and Affordable Care Act was successful, as Congress passed and President Obama signed a bill to repeal expanded IRS form 1099 reporting regulations that many, including coin dealers, found onerous. The House passed the bill March 3 and the Senate April 4. The expanded regulations under the 2010 act would have forced companies and other organizations to file 1099 forms for anyone who completed transactions of $600 or more in goods and services cumulatively within a year, creating paperwork and privacy concerns.

The rising price of precious metals rippled across the market, establishing frequent new record highs for gold (not adjusted for inflation) and lifting silver to near its historic high price during the first half of 2011. Gold closed at $1,549 an ounce June 6 on the London bullion exchange, with silver closing at $48.70 an ounce in London on April 28. Silver prices fell after that peak, but remained above $30 an ounce through mid-June.

Prices for rarities also made news, as a unique gold dinar sold by Morton & Eden Ltd. April 4 established a new record price for a non-U.S. coin sold at auction The Umayyad dinar dated A.H. 105 (circa A.D. 723 to 724) realized £3,720,000 ($6,013,156.80 U.S.), including the 20 percent buyer's fee, making it the second most expensive coin ever sold at auction. The total price is surpassed by the prices brought by two U.S. coins: the auction record is $7,590,020, paid for a 1933 Saint-Gaudens gold $20 double eagle sold in 2002 by Sotheby's; and the overall record is $7.85 million, paid for a 1794 Flowing Hair silver dollar in a private treaty sale completed May 14, 2010.

A Roman gold aurei medallion sold in an April 5 auction for about $1.4 million U.S. established what is believed to be a new record price for an ancient Roman gold coin. The circa A.D. 308 8-aureus gold medallion, issued under Maxentius, was sold by Swiss firm Numismatica Ars Classica.

2 Numismatics and Washington

The United States' official coins and paper money all have their origins in Washington, D.C., the seat of the federal government.

The U.S. Constitution grants Congress authority over U.S. coinage and paper money, with the administrative branch responsible for carrying out the will of Congress. Before either of the nation's moneymaking agencies—the United States Mint and the Bureau of Engraving and Printing, both part of the Department of Treasury—can produce new coins and paper money, Congress must pass authorizing legislation that is then signed into law by the president.

While the U.S. Mint strikes no coins in Washington, its headquarters are located in the nation's capital. The agency that prints Federal Reserve notes—the Bureau of Engraving and Printing—is also headquartered in Washington, but unlike the Mint, produces much of the nation's paper money in the capital.

Other agencies that have some legal authority over the nation's legal tender coinage and paper money—among them the Department of Treasury, the Commission of Fine Arts and the Federal Trade Commission—have their main headquarters in Washington.

This chapter provides coin collectors and dealers information they can use to influence the nation's legal tender. The government does listen to citizens and even makes changes when the calls are loud enough. The State quarter dollars program, which began in 1999, was the result of suggestions from numismatic leaders during testimony before a congressional subcommittee. New products offered by the Mint are often the result of collector requests. Armed with the information in this chapter, individuals know who to contact when they have opinions or questions on the scope of the nation's coinage and paper money.

Note: Separate chapters in this book address the Federal Reserve, the Treasury Department (and related agencies such as the U.S. Secret Service), the BEP and the U.S. Mint. Contact information for those agencies is in those chapters.

Contacting Congress

Collectors interested in numismatic legislation that may be pending before Congress or wanting to comment to legislators on numismatic issues, have many avenues open to them. Generally, collectors can contact their members of Congress to comment on such matters (tips on writing to Congress follow).

Key congressional telephone numbers/addresses

U.S. Capitol Switchboard	(202) 224-3121
Congressional Budget Office	(202) 226-2620
Congressional Record Index	(202) 512-2075
Federal Register	(202) 741-6000
Library of Congress	(202) 707-5000
Status of Senate and House legislation	(202) 225-1772

Key legislative websites

Current House Floor Proceedings	**http://clerk.house.gov/floorsummary/floor.html**
Senate Calendar of Business	**www.gpoaccess.gov/calendars/senate**
THOMAS (source for federal legislative information)	**http://thomas.loc.gov/**
General Congressional Information	**www.congress.org/**
FirstGov	**www.usa.gov/**
Senate	**www.senate.gov/**
House of Representatives	**www.house.gov/**

Senate telephone numbers

Senate Document Room	(202) 224-7701
Senate Floor Information:	
(Republican)	(202) 224-8601
(Democrat)	(202) 224-8541

Senate office buildings

Dirksen Senate Office Building, First and C Streets Northeast, Washington, DC 20510
Hart Senate Office Building, Second and C Streets Northeast, Washington, DC 20510
Russell Senate Office Building, First and C Streets Northeast, Washington, DC 20510

House of Representatives telephone numbers

House Document Room ....(202) 226-5200
House Floor Information:
  (Republican) ....(202) 225-7430
  (Democrat)..(202) 225-7400

House of Representatives office buildings

Cannon House Office Building, First Street and Independence Avenue Southeast, Washington, DC 20515
Longworth House Office Building, Independence and New Jersey Avenues Southeast, Washington, DC 20515
Rayburn House Office Building, Independence Avenue and South Capitol Street Southwest, Washington, DC 20515.

Senate Banking, Housing and Urban Affairs Committee

Bills introduced in the Senate concerning coinage and other numismatic subjects are referred to the Senate Banking, Housing and Urban Affairs Committee.

The committee is referred all such proposed legislation, messages, petitions, memorials and other matters.

Senate Banking Committee offices are located in the Dirksen Senate Office Building. Telephone (202) 224-7391, fax (202) 224-5137. Senate Banking Committee Web address: **http://banking.senate.gov/public/**.

House Financial Services Committee

Bills introduced to the House concerning coinage and other numismatic subjects are referred to the House Financial Services Committee, specifically to the Subcommittee on Domestic Monetary Policy and Technology.

Subcommittee offices are located in the Rayburn House Office Building. Telephone (202) 225-4247, fax (202) 226-0556. House Financial Services Committee Web address: **http://financialservices.house.gov/**.

Writing effective letters to Washington

Members of Congress rely on the opinions of their constituents for direction in voting on legislation. Using a letter sent via postal mail may ineffective because of security measure. Email and faxes are preferred.

Addressing your correspondence

To a senator:
The Honorable (full name)
United States Senate
Washington, DC 20510
Dear Senator (last name)

To a representative:
The Honorable (full name)
United States House of Representatives
Washington, DC 20515
Dear Representative (last name):

Tips on how to write an effective letter:

Emails are best used to contact members of Congress. Contact information can be found at **www.senate.gov** and **www.house.gov** and the same guidelines apply as in writing a traditional letter. As a matter of professional courtesy, many members of Congress will acknowledge, but not respond to, messages from individuals who are not constituents, so it is important to include a return postal mailing address when sending email.

➤ Know your Congress member's full name and spell it correctly. Incorrect spelling makes it look like you are not well-informed.

➤ Identify yourself at the head of the letter by name, mailing address, telephone number and email address (if any) to help the member's office staff reply to your letter.

➤ Be concise and be courteous.

➤ Identify the measure or bill by number when possible. Also include the name of the bill and be specific as to its content or subject.

➤ Include any reasons why you hold a certain stance on an issue. Knowing why you think the way you do is as important to the member of Congress as knowing what side of the issue you are on.

➤ If you have comments on more than one issue, separate letters will be more effective.

➤ Finally, sign your name, and follow that with your city and state. Use your voice in Congress to your best advantage.

If you have no access to an email account and can only send a traditional letter, follow these tips:

➤ Use plain stationery or personal letterhead.

➤ If you can't type the letter, use clear handwriting on ruled paper and double-space it. Use ballpoint pens rather than felt tips or pencils, as these tend to smudge. Neatness still counts.

Contacting the White House

All legislation that passes both houses of Congress is sent to the president for consideration. The president can sign the legislation into law, though legislation becomes law automatically after passage of a 10-day period after the bill is delivered to Congress. The exception to this 10-day period is commonly called a pocket veto. In a pocket veto, the president can kill a bill if it goes unsigned and Congress adjourns prior to the 10-day time limit. The president may also veto the legislation outright.

The White House is located at 1600 Pennsylvania Avenue Northwest, Washington, DC 20500. Telephone (202) 456-1111 for comments or (202) 456-1414 to reach the switchboard, or fax it at (202) 456-2461. White House Web address: **www.whitehouse.gov/**.

Checking legislation delivered to the president

All legislation that passes both houses of Congress is sent to the president for consideration. The president can sign the legislation into law, though legislation becomes law automatically after passage of a 10-day period after the bill is delivered to Congress even without a presidential signature. The exception to this 10-day period is commonly called a pocket veto. In a pocket veto, the president can kill a bill if it goes unsigned and Congress adjourns prior to the 10-day time limit. The president may also veto the legislation outright.

Collectors can check into the status of a particular piece of numismatic legislation at the following websites:

Pending Legislation..**www.whitehouse.gov/briefing-room/pending-legislation**
Signed Legislation..**www.whitehouse.gov/briefing-room/signed-legislation**
Vetoed Legislation..**www.whitehouse.gov/briefing-room/vetoed-legislation**

Federal Trade Commission

The Federal Trade Commission is located at 600 Pennsylvania Ave. N.W., Washington, DC 20580. Telephone (202) 326-2222. Web address: **www.ftc.gov/**

The Federal Trade Commission was organized as an independent administrative agency in 1951, pursuant to the Federal Trade Commission Act of 1914.

The FTC handles policy and complaints in consumer protection areas such as advertising, automobiles, children's issues, credit, diet/health/fitness, electronic commerce and the Internet, environment, franchise and business opportunities, at home business opportunities, investments, pay-per-call services, privacy, products and services, scholarships, employment and job placement, telemarketing (including numismatic telemarketers) and tobacco.

Part of the FTC's responsibility is the enforcement of the Hobby Protection Act. See Chapter 3 for details.

As an administrative agency, the commission deals with trade practices on a continuing and corrective basis. Its function is to prevent, through cease-and-desist orders and other means, those practices condemned by the law of federal trade regulation.

The FTC offers a variety of free publications to consumers. For more information about the publications, contact the FTC.

The FTC does not resolve individual consumer complaints. For consumer complaints nationwide, call toll free FTC Consumer Response Center at (877) 382-4357, or use the secure complaint form, available online at: **www.ftccomplaintassistant.gov/**.

Federal Bureau of Investigation

The headquarters of the Federal Bureau of Investigation is located at 935 Pennsylvania Ave. N.W., Washington, DC 20535-0001. Telephone (202) 324-3000, Web address **www.fbi.gov**.

The FBI is a division of the Department of Justice, headed by the attorney general. The FBI is charged with investigating all violations of federal laws with the exception of those that have been assigned by legislative enactment to some other federal agency.

The FBI's jurisdiction includes a wide range of responsibilities in the criminal, civil, and security fields. Among these are major numismatic thefts, extortion, bank robbery and interstate transportation of stolen property.

U.S. General Services Administration

The headquarters of the General Services Administration is located in the General Services Building, 18th and F streets Northwest, Washington, DC 20405. Telephone (202) 501-1231, Web address **www.gsa.gov**.

The GSA was established in 1949. It is one of three central management agencies in the federal government. (The Office of Personnel Management and the Office of Management and Budget are the others.) Essentially, GSA provides space, supplies and services to assist federal employees in their work.

To collectors, the GSA is best known for its sales of precious metals. Beginning in April 1968 and continuing through November 1970, the GSA sold silver on the market in varying finenesses and amounts.

The same law that authorized the Eisenhower dollar, signed Dec. 31, 1970, authorized the GSA to sell the 2.9 million silver dollars in the vaults of the Treasury Department.

The Carson City Mint silver dollars (most of them Morgan dollars) went on sale on a bid basis beginning Oct. 31, 1972, and continued through Oct. 31, 1973. In 1980, the GSA administered a sale of nearly 1 million Carson City silver dollars.

On Oct. 14, 1981, the GSA began weekly sales of 1.25 million troy ounces of silver from the National Defense Strategic and Critical Materials Stockpile in the form of 1,000-ounce bars.

Congress mandated the use of stockpile silver in various coins, starting with the George Washington commemorative in 1982.

Once the stockpile was deleted, Congress mandated different silver sources.

National Archives and Records Administration

The NARA main office is located at 700 Pennsylvania Ave. N.W., Washington, DC 20408. Telephone (866) 272-6272, Web address www.archives.gov.

Archives II is located at 8601 Adelphi Road, College Park, MD 20740-6001. Telephone (866) 272-6272, fax (301) 837-0483.

The Declaration of Independence, the U.S. Constitution and the Bill of Rights, as well as other exhibits depicting the history of the nation, are on display for visitors at the main National Archives Building.

Archival program

The National Archives and Records Administration is the nation's record keeper and performs a variety of functions relating to the preservation, use and disposition of the records of the U.S. government. NARA preserves and makes available for further government use and for private research the nation's records of enduring value, both textual and audiovisual.

Among its other activities are the administration of a regional network of storage-type facilities for nonarchival records, operation of the presidential library system and a government records management program, and publication of legislative, regulatory and other widely used materials.

In addition to furnishing information about the nature and extent of the records in the custody of the archivist and the conditions under which they may be used, NARA also supplies data from the records themselves. A trained reference staff is ready to aid researchers in finding and using the material desired.

Records management

NARA maintains liaison with federal agencies to improve the management and the quality of records created by the government, to facilitate prompt and orderly disposition of inactive records and to improve the usefulness of those that may be offered to the archivist for preservation.

Upon request, advice and technical assistance is given on organizing records management programs and establishing schedules and procedures for the retirement of records no longer needed currently. Evaluations of the record creation, maintenance, and disposition practices of federal agencies are made and agencies may request guidance and assistance in their paperwork problems.

Federal Records Centers

Federal Records Centers are maintained to store and service noncurrent records of federal agencies and historically valuable regional records of the National Archives of the United States.

Federal Records Centers also provide reimbursable microfilming service for federal agencies.

Publishing Laws and Presidential Documents

Federal legislation consists of both the acts of Congress and "regulations" that government agencies have issued under authority delegated by the Congress.

All current presidential proclamations and executive orders and regulations of government agencies having general applicability and legal effect are published in the *Federal Register,* which appears five times a week. At least annually, all regulations in force are published in codified form in the Code of Federal Regulations.

Presidential speeches, news conferences, messages, and other materials made public by the White House are published currently in the *Weekly Compilation of Presidential Documents* and annually in the *Public Papers of the Presidents.* Further information on federal agencies is provided in the annual *United States Government Manual.*

Presidential Libraries

The libraries preserve and describe and render reference service on presidential papers and collections, prepare documentary and descriptive publications, and exhibit historic documents and museum items.

For general information on presidential libraries, contact: Office of Presidential Libraries, National Archives at College Park, Room 2200, 8601 Adelphi Road, College Park, MD 20740-6001. Telephone (301) 837-3250, fax (301) 837-3199.

George H.W. Bush Library
1000 George Bush Drive W.
College Station, TX 77845
Telephone: (979) 691-4000
Fax: (979) 691-4050
Email: Library.Bush@nara.gov
Web: http://bushlibrary.tamu.edu/index.php

George W. Bush Library
To be located on the campus of Southern Methodist University in Dallas
Telephone: (972) 353-0545

Fax: (972) 353-0599
Email: **gwbush.library@nara.gov**
Web: **www.georgewbushlibrary.gov/**

Jimmy Carter Library
441 Freedom Parkway
Atlanta, GA 30307-1498
Telephone: (404) 865-7100
Fax: (404) 865-7102
Email: **carter.library@nara.gov**
Web: **www.jimmycarterlibrary.gov**

William J. Clinton Library
1200 President Clinton Ave.
Little Rock, AR 72201
Telephone: (501) 374-4242
Fax: (501) 244-2883
Email: **Clinton.library@nara.gov**
Web: **www.clintonlibrary.gov/**

Dwight D. Eisenhower Library
200 S.E. Fourth St.
Abilene, KS 67410-2900
Telephone: (785) 263-6700
Fax: (785) 263-6715
Email: **eisenhower.library@nara.gov**
Web: **www.eisenhower.archives.gov/**

Gerald R. Ford Library
1000 Beal Ave.
Ann Arbor, MI 48109-2114
Telephone: (734) 205-0555
Fax: (734) 205-0571
Email: **ford.library@nara.gov**
Web: **www.fordlibrarymuseum.gov/**

Gerald R. Ford Museum
303 Pearl St. N.W.
Grand Rapids, MI 49504-5353
Telephone: (616) 254-0400
Fax: (616) 254-0386
Email: **ford.museum@nara.gov**
Web: **www.fordlibrarymuseum.gov/**

Herbert Hoover Library
210 Parkside Drive, Box 488
West Branch, IA 52358-0488
Telephone: (319) 643-5301
Fax: (319) 643-5825
Email: **hoover.library@nara.gov**
Web: **http://hoover.archives.gov/**

Lyndon B. Johnson Library
2313 Red River St.
Austin, TX 78705-5702
Telephone: (512) 721-0200
Fax: (512) 721-0170
Email: **Johnson.library@nara.gov**
Web: **www.lbjlibrary.org/**

John F. Kennedy Library
Columbia Point
Boston, MA 02125-3398
Telephone: (617) 514-1600
Fax: (617) 514-1625
Email: **kennedy.library@nara.gov**
Web: **www.jfklibrary.org/**

Nixon Presidential Library, California
18001 Yorba Linda Blvd.
Yorba Linda, CA 92886
Telephone: (714) 983-9120
Fax: (714) 983-9111
Email: **nixon@nara.gov**
Web: **www.nixonlibrary.gov/**

Nixon Presidential Library, Maryland
8601 Adelphi Road
College Park, MD 20740-6001
Telephone: (301) 837-3290
Fax: (301) 837-3202
Email: **nixon@nara.gov**
Web: **www.nixonlibrary.gov/**

Ronald Reagan Library
40 Presidential Drive
Simi Valley, CA 93065-0600
Telephone: (800) 410-8354
Fax: (805) 577-9702
Email: **reagan.library@nara.gov**
Web: **www.reagan.utexas.edu/**

Franklin D. Roosevelt Library
4079 Albany Post Road
Hyde Park, NY 12538-1999
Telephone: (845) 486-7770
Fax: (845) 486-1147
Email: **roosevelt.library@nara.gov**
Web: **www.fdrlibrary.marist.edu/**

Harry S. Truman Library
500 W. U.S. Highway 24
Independence, MO 64050-1798
Telephone: (816) 268-8200
Fax: (816) 268-8295
Email: **truman.library@nara.gov**
Web: **www.trumanlibrary.org**

Reading rooms

Archives and other historical material for research purposes are available at the main National Archives Building in Washington, D.C.; at Archives II in College Park, Md.; at the Presidential Libraries; and at the national and regional Federal Records Centers. Call the main office for more information.

Publications

The National Archives has many publications of interest to the public. For a list, write the Office of the Director, Publications Division, National Archives and Records Administration, 700 Pennsylvania Ave. NW, Washington, DC 20408.

Online resources

The National Archives has been increasing its content online over the past decade. Access to Archival Databases (AAD) allows users to search more than 30 archival series records, which includes over 350 data files totaling more than 50 million unique records. It is available online at **http://aad.archives.gov/aad/**.

The Archival Research Catalog (ARC) provides more than 126,500 digitized historical documents, photographs and images that are accessible online at **www.archives.gov/research/arc/topics/**. A Web version of the *Guide to Federal Records in the National Archives of the United States* is available at **www.archives.gov/research/guide-fed-records/**, and is regularly updated to reflect new acquisitions of federal records.

Government Printing Office

The Government Printing Office is located at 732 N. Capitol St. N.W., Washington, DC 20401. Telephone (202) 512-1800, fax (202) 512-2104, email **gpo@custhelp.com**, Web address **www.gpo.gov**.

The Government Printing Office began operations in 1860. The activities of the Government Printing Office are outlined and defined in the Act of Oct. 22, 1968, as amended.

The congressional Joint Committee on Printing acts as the board of directors of the Government Printing Office. The public printer is required by law to be a practical printer versed in the art of bookbinding and is appointed by the president with the advice and consent of the Senate.

The Government Printing Office executes orders for printing and binding placed by Congress and the departments and establishments of the federal government. It furnishes blank paper, inks and similar supplies to all governmental activities on order. It prepares catalogs and distributes and sells government publications.

The *Annual Report of the Director of the Mint* and other Mint and Treasury Department publications are available from the GPO.

GPO sells through mail orders and government publications that originated in various government agencies, and administers the depository library program through which selected government publications are made available in libraries throughout the country.

Commission of Fine Arts

Commission of Fine Arts, National Building Museum, 401 F St. N.W., Suite 312, Washington, DC 20001-2728. Telephone (202) 504-2200, fax (202) 504-2195, email **cfastaff@cfa.gov**, Web address **www.cfa.gov/**.

The Commission of Fine Arts was established by Congress in 1910 "to meet the growing need for a permanent body to advise the government on matters pertaining to the arts; and particularly, to guide the architectural development of Washington so that the capital city would reflect, in stateliness and grandeur, the emergence of the United States as a world power," according to *The Commission of Fine Arts — A Brief History 1910-1995*.

The commission also advises the U.S. Mint on the design of medals and coins (both noncirculating commemorative and circulating), advises the American Battle Monuments Commission on the design of war memorials and is responsible generally for advising on questions of art when so requested by the president or committees of Congress.

The review process is generally the same for coins as for medals. United States Mint officials bring sketches of the coins and medals under review to the commission for consideration. Often, Mint officials bring more than one design for a particular coin or medal.

Commission members examine the design sketches and then make their recommendations about the best designs for the coins. They also may suggest changes to the recommended designs, such as modifications to the legends or refinements to the major design elements.

Mint officials do not always follow the recommendations of the Commission of Fine Arts. In one famous example, the commission in 1932 recommended two designs by Laura Gardin Fraser for the quarter dollar planned to commemorate the 200th birthday of George Washington. The secretary of the Treasury, however, selected two designs by another artist, although most collectors then and today believe that the original designs the commission recommended are superior to those used from 1932 through 1998.

Commission of Fine Arts meetings are normally open to the public. On occasion, however, United States Mint officials have asked that meetings be closed to the public and media in order to keep secret the coinage designs under consideration.

The commission is composed of seven members appointed by the president who serve without pay for four-year terms. Past commissioners include coin designers James E. Fraser (1915 to 1920) and Adolph Weinman (1929 to 1933).

Current members of the Commission of Fine Arts: Earl A. Powell III, chair; Pamela Nelson, vice chair; and N. Michael McKinnell, Diana Balmori, Elizabeth Plater-Zyberk, Witold Rybczynski and Edwin Schlossberg.

U.S. General Accountability Office

The U.S. General Accountability Office is located at 441 G St. NW, Washington, DC 20548. Telephone (202) 512-3000, email **contact@gao.gov**, Web address **www.gao.gov**.

The GAO is an independent, nonpartisan agency that works for Congress.

GAO is often called the "congressional watchdog" and conducts audits, surveys, investigations and evaluations of federal programs. This work is done at the request of congressional committees or members, or to fulfill GAO specifically mandated or basic legislative requirements. GAO's findings and recommendations are published as reports to congressional members or delivered as testimony to congressional committees.

The GAO makes electronic files of released reports, testimony and decisions made by the Comptroller General available daily on its website.

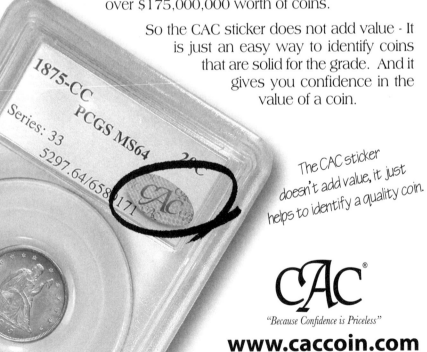

3 Numismatics and the Law

Introduction

In 1976 when the first edition of *Coin World Almanac* was published, this chapter offered a listing of recent numismatic laws and bills, statutory authority for coinage, the advisory policies of the Treasury Department, a listing of the contents of Title 18 of the Criminal Code (counterfeiting) and Title 31 (governing coinage and gold) and a listing of laws authorizing medals, all information not easily available to collectors otherwise. Now, up-to-the-minute access to numismatic legislation and law via the Internet allows collectors to quickly educate themselves in these areas. Electronic access to legislative information and law is available to anyone connected to the Internet.

On Jan. 5, 1995, the Library of Congress launched a new online public Internet system called THOMAS at **http://thomas.loc.gov**, offering free access to congressional and legislative information. The system was initiated at the request of the members of the 104th Congress. THOMAS offers the full text of all bills from the 1973-1974 93rd Congress to the present, the text of the *Congressional Record* from the 101st Congress to the present, information about how laws are made, electronic mail addresses of members of Congress and committees, and links to other government and congressional websites.

Congress divides its work among more than 200 committees, and THOMAS offers committee reports from the 104th Congress to the present.

In any given two-year congressional session, many coin and paper money related bills are introduced, but very few are ever approved and signed into law.

Electronic access is also available for the United States Code at **www.law.cornell.edu/uscode**. The site holds the Internet publications of the Legal Information Institute, a part of the Cornell Law School, and has been cited as "the most linked to web resource in the field of law." The site offers a hypertext version of the full U.S. Code and is searchable by word or section citation.

While this chapter will provide highlights of legislative and legal changes in the decade since the last edition of the *Coin World Almanac* was published in 2000, it is by no means an exhaustive reference. Readers may also wish to refer to earlier editions. The chapter also features information about laws created earlier than those recorded at THOMAS.

United States Code, Title 31

The coinage laws of the United States, for many years, were uncodified since the Act of April 2, 1792. The Coinage Act of 1873 was the first attempt to codify existing law. The Revised Statutes of 1874-1878 actually constituted the first serious revision and codification of the minting and coinage laws, and for a century that followed, these were the official versions for reference.

In March 1792, the House of Representatives debated the possible use of the portrait of the president appearing on the coinage "with an inscription which shall express the initial or first letter of his Christian or first name, and his surname at length, and the year of coinage; and upon the reverse ... the figure or representation of an eagle with the inscription "United States of America. ..." [3 Annals of Congress 1348 (1792].

What emerged as Sec. 10 of the original Mint Act was an "impression emblematic of liberty with an inscription of the word Liberty and the year of coinage."

On the reverse, precious metal coinage was required to bear the figure of an eagle in addition to UNITED STATES OF AMERICA.

This ultimately became Sec. 18 of the Coinage Act of 1873, Sec. 3517 of the revised statutes, and later, in uncodified form, was known as 31 USC 324. It is today found in 31 USC 5112.

Excerpts from United States Code, Title 31

Following are some important excerpts from U.S. Code, Title 31, "Money and Finance," as applicable to numismatics. Sections not dealing with numismatics are omitted.

Sec. 301. Department of the Treasury

(a) The Department of the Treasury is an executive department of the United States government at the seat of the Government.

(b) The head of the Department is the Secretary of the Treasury. The Secretary is appointed by the president, by and with the advice and consent of the Senate. ...

... (g) The Department shall have a seal.

Sec. 302. Treasury of the United States

The United States Government has a Treasury of the United States. The Treasury is in the Department of the Treasury.

Sec. 303. Bureau of Engraving and Printing

(a) The Bureau of Engraving and Printing is a bureau in the Department of the Treasury.

(b) The head of the Bureau is the Director of the Bureau of Engraving and Printing appointed by the Secretary of the Treasury. The Director—

(1) shall carry out duties and powers prescribed by the Secretary; and

(2) reports directly to the Secretary.

Sec. 304. Bureau of the Mint

(a) The Bureau of the Mint is a bureau in the Department of the Treasury.

(b)(1) The head of the Bureau is the Director of the Mint. The Director is appointed by the President, by and with the advice and consent of the Senate. The term of the Director is 5 years. The President may remove the Director from office. On removal, the President shall send a message to the Senate giving the reasons for removal.

(2) The Director shall carry out duties and powers prescribed by the Secretary of the Treasury.

Sec. 307. Office of the Comptroller of the Currency

The Office of the Comptroller of the Currency, established under Section 324 of the Revised Statutes (12 U.S.C. 1), is an office in the Department of the Treasury.

Sec. 308. United States Customs Service

The United States Customs Service, established under Section 1 of the Act of March 3, 1927 (19 U.S.C. 2071), is a service in the Department of the Treasury.

Sec. 312. Continuing in office

When the term of an office of the Department of the Treasury ends, the officer may continue to serve until a successor is appointed and qualified.

Administrative

Sec. 321. General authority of the Secretary

(a) The Secretary of the Treasury shall ... (3) issue warrants for money drawn on the Treasury consistent with appropriations; mint coins, engrave and print currency and security documents, and refine and assay bullion, and may strike medals; ...

(b) The Secretary may

(1) prescribe regulations to carry out the duties and powers of the Secretary;

(2) delegate duties and powers of the Secretary to another officer or employee of the Department of the Treasury; ...

Sec. 331. Reports

The Secretary of the Treasury shall submit to Congress each year an annual report. The Secretary shall report to either House of Congress in person or in writing, as required, on matters referred to the Secretary by that House of Congress.

Sec. 3301. General duties of the Secretary of the Treasury

(a) The Secretary of the Treasury shall

(1) receive and keep public money;

(2) take receipts for money paid out by the Secretary;

(3) give receipts for money deposited in the Treasury;

(4) endorse warrants for receipts for money deposited in the Treasury;

(5) submit the accounts of the Secretary to the Comptroller General every three months, or more often if required by the Comptroller General; and

(6) submit to inspection at any time by the Comptroller General of money in the possession of the Secretary.

Sec. 3327. General authority to issue checks and other drafts

The Secretary of the Treasury may issue a check or other draft on public money in the Treasury to pay an obligation of the United States Government. When the Secretary decides it is convenient to a public creditor and in the public interest, the Secretary may designate a depositary to issue a check or other draft on public money held by the depositary to pay an obligation of the government. As directed by the Secretary, each depositary shall report to the Secretary on public money paid and received by the depositary.

Monetary system

Sec. 5101. Decimal system

United States money is expressed in dollars, dimes or tenths, cents or hundredths, and mills or thousandths.

A dime is a tenth of a dollar, a cent is a hundredth of a dollar, and a mill is a thousandth of a dollar.

Sec. 5102. Standard weight

The standard troy pound of the National Institute of Standards and Technology of the Department of Commerce shall be the standard used to ensure that the weight of the United States coins conforms to specifications in Section 5112 of this title.

Sec. 5103. Legal tender

United States coins and currency (including Federal reserve notes and circulating notes of Federal reserve banks and national banks) are legal tender for all debts, public charges, taxes, and dues. Foreign gold or silver coins are not legal tender for debts.

General Authority

Sec. 5111. Minting and issuing coins, medals, and numismatic items

(a) The Secretary of the Treasury

(1) shall mint and issue coins described in Section 5112 of this title in amounts the Secretary decides are necessary to meet the needs of the United States;

(2) may prepare national medal dies and strike national and other medals if it does not interfere with regular minting operations but may not prepare private medal dies;

(3) may prepare and distribute numismatic items; and

(4) may mint coins for a foreign country if the minting does not interfere with regular minting operations, and shall prescribe a charge for minting the foreign coins equal to the cost of the minting (including labor, materials, and the use of machinery).

(b) The Department of the Treasury has a coinage metal fund and a coinage profit fund. The Secretary may use the coinage metal fund to buy metal to mint coins. The Secretary shall credit the coinage profit fund with the amount by which the nominal value of the coins minted from the metal exceeds the cost of the metal. The Secretary shall charge the coinage profit fund with waste incurred in minting coins and the cost of distributing the coins. The Secretary shall deposit in the Treasury as miscellaneous receipts excess amounts in the coinage profit fund.

(c) Procurements Relating to Coin Production.

(1) In general. The Secretary may make contracts, on conditions the Secretary decides are appropriate and are in the public interest, to acquire articles, materials, supplies, and services (including equipment, manufacturing facilities, patents, patent rights, technical knowledge, and assistance) necessary to produce the coins referred to in this title.

(2) Domestic control of coinage.

(A) Subject to subparagraph (B), in order to protect the national security through domestic control of the coinage process, the Secretary shall acquire only such articles, materials, supplies, and services (including equipment, manufacturing facilities, patents, patent rights, technical knowledge, and assistance) for the production of coins as have been produced or manufactured in the United States unless the Secretary determines it to be inconsistent with the public interest, or the cost to be unreasonable, and publishes in the Federal Register a written finding stating the basis for the determination.

(B) Subparagraph (A) shall apply only in the case of a bid or offer from a supplier the principal place of business of which is in a foreign country which does not accord to United States companies the same competitive opportunities for procurements in connection with the production of coins as it accords to domestic companies.

(3) Determination.

(A) In general. Any determination of the Secretary referred to in paragraph (2) shall not be reviewable in any administrative proceeding or court of the United States.

(B) Other rights unaffected. This paragraph does not alter or annul any right of review that arises under any provision of any law or regulation of the United States other than paragraph (2).

(4) Nothing in paragraph (2) of this subsection in any way affects the procurement by the Secretary of gold and silver for the production of coins by the United States Mint.

(d)(1) The Secretary may prohibit or limit the exportation, melting, or treatment of United States coins when the Secretary decides the prohibition or limitation is necessary to protect the coinage of the United States.

(2) A person knowingly violating an order or license issued or regulation prescribed under paragraph (1) of this subsection, shall be fined not more than $10,000, imprisoned not more than 5 years, or both.

(3) Coins exported, melted, or treated in violation of an order or license issued or regulation prescribed, and metal resulting from the melting or treatment, shall be forfeited to the United States government. ...

Sec. 5112. Denominations, specifications, and design of coins

(a) The Secretary of the Treasury may mint and issue only the following coins:

(1) a dollar coin that is 1.043 inches in diameter.

(2) a half dollar coin that is 1.205 inches in diameter and weighs 11.34 grams.

(3) a quarter dollar coin that is 0.955 inch in diameter and weighs 5.67 grams.

(4) a dime that is 0.705 inch in diameter and weighs 2.268 grams.

(5) a 5-cent coin that is 0.835 inch in diameter and weighs 5 grams.

(6) except as provided under subsection (c) of this section, a one-cent coin that is 0.75 inch in diameter and weighs 3.11 grams.

(7) A fifty dollar gold coin that is 32.7 millimeters in diameter, weighs 33.931 grams, and contains one troy ounce of fine gold.

(8) A twenty-five dollar gold coin that is 27.0 millimeters in diameter, weighs 16.966 grams, and contains one-half troy ounce of fine gold.

(9) A ten dollar gold coin that is 22.0 millimeters in diameter, weighs 8.483 grams, and contains one-fourth troy ounce of fine gold.

(10) A five dollar gold coin that is 16.5 millimeters in diameter, weighs 3.393 grams, and contains one-tenth troy ounce of fine gold.

(11) A $50 gold coin that is of an appropriate size and thickness, as determined by the Secretary, weights 1 ounce, and contains 99.99 percent pure gold.

(b) The half dollar, quarter dollar, and dime coins are clad coins with 3 layers of metal. The 2 identical outer layers are an alloy of 75 percent copper and 25 percent nickel. The inner layer is copper. The outer layers are metallurgically bonded to the inner layer and weigh at least 30 percent of the weight of the coin. The dollar coin shall be golden in color, have a distinctive edge, have tactile and visual features that make the denomination of the coin readily discernible, be minted and fabricated in the United States, and have similar metallic, anti-counterfeiting properties as United States coinage in circulation on the date of enactment of the United States $1 Coin Act of 1997. The 5-cent coin is an alloy of 75 percent copper and 25 percent nickel. In minting 5-cent coins, the Secretary shall use bars that vary not more than 2.5 percent from the percent of nickel required. Except as provided under subsection (c) of this section, the one-cent coin is an alloy of 95 percent copper and 5 percent zinc. The specifications for alloys are by weight.

(c) The Secretary may prescribe the weight and the composition of copper and zinc in the alloy of the one-cent coin that the Secretary decides are appropriate when the Secretary decides that a different weight and alloy of copper and zinc are necessary to ensure an adequate supply of one-cent coins to meet the needs of the United States.

(d)(1) United States coins have the inscription "In God We Trust". The obverse side of each coin has the inscription "Liberty". The reverse side of each coin has the inscriptions "United States of America" and "E Pluribus Unum" and a designation of the value of the coin. The design on the reverse side of the dollar, half dollar, and quarter dollar is an eagle. Subject to other provisions of this subsection, the obverse of any 5-cent coin issued after December 31, 2005, shall bear the likeness of Thomas Jefferson and the reverse of any such 5-cent coin shall bear an image of the home of Thomas Jefferson at Monticello. The Secretary of the Treasury, in consultation with the Congress, shall select appropriate designs for the obverse and reverse sides of the dollar coin. The coins have an inscription of the year of minting or issuance. However, to prevent or alleviate a shortage of a denomination, the Secretary may inscribe coins of the denomination with the year that was last inscribed on coins of the denomination.

The Secretary of the Treasury, in consultation with the Congress, shall select appropriate designs for the obverse and reverse sides of the dollar coin. The coins have an inscription of the year of minting or issuance. However, to prevent or alleviate a shortage of a denomination, the Secretary may inscribe coins of the denomination with the year that was last inscribed on coins of the denomination.

(2) The Secretary shall prepare the devices, models, hubs, and dies for coins, emblems, devices, inscriptions, and designs authorized under this chapter. The Secretary may, after consulting with the Citizens Coinage Advisory Committee and the Commission of Fine Arts, adopt and prepare new designs or models of emblems or devices that are authorized in the same way as when new coins or devices are authorized. The Secretary may change the design or die of a coin only once within 25 years of the first adoption of the design, model, hub, or die for that coin. The Secretary may procure services under Section 3109 of Title 5 in carrying out this paragraph.

(e) Notwithstanding any other provision of law, the Secretary shall mint and issue, in quantities sufficient to meet public demand, coins which:

(1) are 40.6 millimeters in diameter and weigh 31.103 grams;

(2) contain .999 fine silver;

(3) have a design—

    (A) symbolic of Liberty on the obverse side; and

    (B) of an eagle on the reverse side;

(4) have inscriptions of the year of minting or issuance, and the words "Liberty", "In God We Trust",

"United States of America", "1 Oz. Fine Silver", "E Pluribus Unum", and "One Dollar"; and

    (5) have reeded edges.

  (f) Silver coins.

    (1) Sale price.— The Secretary shall sell the coins minted under subsection (e) to the public at a price equal to the market value of the bullion at the time of sale, plus the cost of minting, marketing, and distributing such coins (including labor, materials, dies, use of machinery, and promotional and overhead expenses).

    (2) Bulk sales. The Secretary shall make bulk sales of the coins minted under subsection (e) at a reasonable discount.

    (3) Numismatic items. For purposes of section 5132(a)(1) of this title, all coins minted under subsection (e) shall be considered to be numismatic items.

  (g) For purposes of section 5132(a)(1) of this title, all coins minted under subsection (e) of this section shall be considered to be numismatic items.

  (h) The coins issued under this title shall be legal tender as provided in section 5103 of this title.

  (i) (1) Notwithstanding section 5111(a)(1) of this title, the Secretary shall mint and issue the gold coins described in paragraphs (7), (8), (9), and (10) of subsection (a) of this section, in quantities sufficient to meet public demand, and such gold coins shall—

    (A) have a design determined by the Secretary, except that the fifty dollar gold coin shall have—

      (i) on the obverse side, a design symbolic of Liberty; and

      (ii) on the reverse side, a design representing a family of eagles, with the male carrying an olive branch and flying above a nest containing a female eagle and hatchlings;

    (B) have inscriptions of the denomination, the weight of the fine gold content, the year of minting of issuance, and the words "Liberty", "In God We Trust", "United States of America", and "E Pluribus Unum"; and

    (C) have reeded edges.

    (2) (A) The Secretary shall sell the coins minted under this subsection to the public at a price equal to the market value of the bullion at the time of sale, plus the cost of minting, marketing, and distributing such coins (including labor, materials, dies, use of machinery, and promotional and overhead expenses).

    (B) The Secretary shall make bulk sales of the coins minted under this subsection at a reasonable discount.

    (3) For purposes of section 5132(a)(1) of this title, all coins minted under this subsection shall be considered to be numismatic items.

    (4) (A) Notwithstanding any other provision of law and subject to subparagraph (B), the Secretary of the Treasury may change the diameter, weight, or design of any coin minted under this subsection or the fineness of the gold in the alloy of any such coin if the Secretary determines that the specific diameter, weight, design, or fineness of gold which differs from that otherwise required by law is appropriate for such coin.

    (B) The Secretary may not mint any coin with respect to which a determination has been made by the Secretary under subparagraph (A) before the end of the 30-day period beginning on the date a notice of such determination is published in the Federal Register.

    (C) The Secretary may continue to mint and issue coins in accordance with the specifications contained in paragraphs (7), (8), (9), and (10) of subsection (a) and paragraph (1)(A) of this subsection at the same time the Secretary in minting and issuing other bullion and proof gold coins under this subsection in accordance with such program procedures and coin specifications, designs, varieties, quantities, denominations, and inscriptions as the Secretary, in the Secretary's discretion, may prescribe from time to time.

  (j) General Waiver of Procurement Regulations.—

    (1) In general.— Except as provided in paragraph (2), no provision of law governing procurement or public contracts shall be applicable to the procurement of goods or services necessary for minting, marketing, or issuing any coin authorized under paragraph (7), (8), (9), or (10) of subsection (a) or subsection (e), including any proof version of any such coin.

    (2) Equal employment opportunity.— Paragraph (1) shall not relieve any person entering into a contract with respect to any coin referred to in such paragraph from complying with any law relating to equal employment opportunity.

  (k) The Secretary may mint and issue bullion and proof platinum coins in accordance with such specifications, designs, varieties, quantities, denominations, and inscriptions as the Secretary, in the Secretary's discretion, may prescribe from time to time.

  (l) Redesign and Issuance of Quarter Dollar in Commemoration of Each of the 50 States.—

    (1) Redesign beginning in 1999.—

    (A) In general.— Notwithstanding the fourth sentence of subsection (d)(1) and subsection (d)(2), quarter dollar coins issued during the 10-year period beginning in 1999, shall have designs on the reverse side selected in accordance with this subsection which are emblematic of the 50 States.

(B) Transition provision,— notwithstanding subparagraph (A), the Secretary may continue to mint and issue quarter dollars in 1999 which bear the design in effect before the redesign required under this subsection and inscription of the year "1998" as required to ensure a smooth transition into the 10-year program under this subsection.

(C) Flexibility with regard to placement of inscriptions.— Notwithstanding subsection (d)(1), the Secretary may select a design for quarter dollars issued during the 10-year period referred to in subparagraph (A) in which—

(i) the inscription described in the second sentence of subsection (d)(1) appears on the reverse side of any such quarter dollars; and

(ii) any inscription described in the third sentence of subsection (d)(1) or the designation of the value of the coin appears on the obverse side of any such quarter dollars.

(2) Single state designs. The design on the reverse side of each quarter dollar issued during the 10-year period referred to in paragraph (1) shall be emblematic of 1 of the 50 States.

(3) Issuance of coins commemorating five states during each of the 10 years.—

(A) In general.— The designs for the quarter dollar coins issued during each year of the 10-year period referred to in paragraph (1) shall be emblematic of 5 states selected in the order in which states ratified the Constitution of the United States or were admitted into the Union, as the case may be.

(B) Number of each of 5 coin designs in each year.— Of the quarter dollar coins issued during each year of the 10-year period referred to in paragraph (1), the Secretary of the Treasury shall prescribe, on the basis of such factors as the Secretary determines to be appropriate, the number of quarter dollars which shall be issued with each of the five designs selected for each year.

(4) Selection of design. (A) In general.— Each of the 50 designs required under this subsection for quarter dollars shall be—

(i) selected by the Secretary after consultation with—

(I) the Governor of the State being commemorated, or such other state officials or group as the state may designate for such purpose; and

(II) the Commission of Fine Arts; and

(ii) reviewed by the Citizens Commemorative Coin Advisory Committee.

(B) Selection and approval process.— Designs for quarter dollars may be submitted in accordance with the design selection and approval process developed by the Secretary in the sole discretion of the Secretary.

(C) Participation.— The Secretary may include participation by State officials, artists from the States, engravers of the United States Mint, and members of the general public.

(D) Standards.— Because it is important that the Nation's coinage and currency bear dignified designs of which the citizens of the United States can be proud, the Secretary shall not select any frivolous or inappropriate design for any quarter dollar minted under this subsection.

(E) Prohibition on certain representations.— No head and shoulders portrait or bust of any person, living or dead, and no portrait of a living person may be included in the design of any quarter dollar under this subsection.

(5) Treatment as numismatic items. For purposes of sections 5134 and 5136, all coins minted under this subsection shall be considered to be numismatic items.

(6) Issuance.—

(A) Quality of coins.— The Secretary may mint and issue such number of quarter dollars of each design selected under paragraph (4) in uncirculated and proof qualities as the Secretary determines to be appropriate.

(B) Silver coins.— Notwithstanding subsection (d), the Secretary may mint and issue such number of quarter dollars of each design selected under paragraph (4) as the Secretary determines to be appropriate, with a content of 90 percent silver and 10 percent copper.

(C) Sources of bullion.— The Secretary shall obtain silver for minting coins under subparagraph (B) from available resources, including stockpiles established under the Strategic and Critical Materials Stockpiling Act.

(7) Application in event of the admission of additional states.— If any additional State is admitted into the Union before the end of the 10-year period referred to in paragraph (1), the Secretary of the Treasury may issue quarter dollar coins, in accordance with this subsection, with a design which is emblematic of such State during any 1 year of such 10-year period, in addition to the quarter dollar coins issued during such year in accordance with paragraph (3)(A).

(m) Commemorative Coin Program Restrictions.—

(1) Maximum number.— Beginning Jan. 1, 1999, the Secretary may mint and issue commemorative coins under this section during any calendar year with respect to not more than 2 commemorative coin programs.

(2) Mintage levels.—

(A) In general.— Except as provided in subparagraph (B), in carrying out any commemorative coin program, the Secretary shall mint

(i) not more than 750,000 clad half-dollar coins;

(ii) not more than 500,000 silver one-dollar coins; and

(iii) not more than 100,000 gold five-dollar or ten-dollar coins.

(B) Exception. If the Secretary determines, based on independent, market-based research conducted by a designated recipient organization of a commemorative coin program, that the mintage levels described in subparagraph (A) are not adequate to meet public demand for that commemorative coin, the Secretary may waive one or more of the requirements of subparagraph (A) with respect to that commemorative coin program.

(C) Designated recipient organization defined.— For purposes of this paragraph, the term "designated recipient organization" means any organization designated, under any provision of law, as the recipient of any surcharge imposed on the sale of any numismatic item.

(n) Redesign and Issuance of Circulating $1 Coins Honoring Each of the Presidents of the United States.—

(1) Redesign beginning in 2007.— Notwithstanding subsection (d) and in accordance with the provisions of this subsection, $1 coins issued during the period beginning January 1, 2007, and ending upon the termination of the program under paragraph (8), shall—

(A) have designs on the obverse selected in accordance with paragraph (2)(B) which are emblematic of the Presidents of the United States; and

(B) have a design on the reverse selected in accordance with paragraph (2)(A).

(2) Design requirements.— The $1 coins issued in accordance with paragraph (1)(A) shall meet the following design requirements:

(A) Coin reverse.— The design on the reverse shall bear—

(i) a likeness of the Statue of Liberty extending to the rim of the coin and large enough to provide a dramatic representation of Liberty while not being large enough to create the impression of a "2-headed" coin;

(ii) the inscription "$1"; and

(iii) the inscription "United States of America".

(B) Coin obverse.— The design on the obverse shall contain—

(i) the name and likeness of a President of the United States; and

(ii) basic information about the President, including—

(I) the dates or years of the term of office of such President; and

(II) a number indicating the order of the period of service in which the President served.

(C) Edge-incused inscriptions.—

(i) In general.— The inscription of the year of minting or issuance of the coin and the inscription "E Pluribus Unum" shall be edge-incused into the coin.

(ii) Preservation of distinctive edge.— The edge-incusing of the inscriptions under clause (i) on coins issued under this subsection shall be done in a manner that preserves the distinctive edge of the coin so that the denomination of the coin is readily discernible, including by individuals who are blind or visually impaired.

(D) Inscriptions of "liberty".— Notwithstanding the second sentence of subsection (d)(1), because the use of a design bearing the likeness of the Statue of Liberty on the reverse of the coins issued under this subsection adequately conveys the concept of Liberty, the inscription of "Liberty" shall not appear on the coins.

(E) Limitation in series to deceased presidents.— No coin issued under this subsection may bear the image of a living former or current President, or of any deceased former President during the 2-year period following the date of the death of that President.

(F) Inscription of "in god we trust".— The design on the obverse or the reverse shall bear the inscription "In God We Trust".

(3) Issuance of coins commemorating presidents.—

(A) Order of issuance.— The coins issued under this subsection commemorating Presidents of the United States shall be issued in the order of the period of service of each President, beginning with President George Washington.

(B) Treatment of period of service.—

(i) In general.— Subject to clause (ii), only 1 coin design shall be issued for a period of service for any President, no matter how many consecutive terms of office the President served.

(ii) Nonconsecutive terms.— If a President has served during 2 or more nonconsecutive periods of service, a coin shall be issued under this subsection for each such nonconsecutive period of service.

(4) Issuance of coins commemorating 4 presidents during each year of the period.—

    (A) In general.— The designs for the $1 coins issued during each year of the period referred to in paragraph (1) shall be emblematic of 4 Presidents until each President has been so honored, subject to paragraph (2)(E).

    (B) Number of 4 circulating coin designs in each year.— The Secretary shall prescribe, on the basis of such factors as the Secretary determines to be appropriate, the number of $1 coins that shall be issued with each of the designs selected for each year of the period referred to in paragraph (1).

(5) Legal tender.— The coins minted under this title shall be legal tender, as provided in section 5103.

(6) Treatment as numismatic items.— For purposes of section [1] 5134 and 5136, all coins minted under this subsection shall be considered to be numismatic items.

(7) Issuance of numismatic coins.— The Secretary may mint and issue such number of $1 coins of each design selected under this subsection in uncirculated and proof qualities as the Secretary determines to be appropriate.

(8) Termination of program.— The issuance of coins under this subsection shall terminate when each President has been so honored, subject to paragraph (2)(E), and may not be resumed except by an Act of Congress.

(9) Reversion to preceding design.— Upon the termination of the issuance of coins under this subsection, the design of all $1 coins shall revert to the so-called "Sacagawea-design" $1 coins.

  (o) First Spouse Bullion Coin Program.—

(1) In general.— During the same period described in subsection (n), the Secretary shall issue bullion coins under this subsection that are emblematic of the spouse of each such President.

(2) Specifications.— The coins issued under this subsection shall—

    (A) have the same diameter as the $1 coins described in subsection (n);

    (B) weigh 0.5 ounce; and

    (C) contain 99.99 percent pure gold.

(3) Design requirements.—

    (A) Coin obverse.— The design on the obverse of each coin issued under this subsection shall contain—

        (i) the name and likeness of a person who was a spouse of a President during the President's period of service;

        (ii) an inscription of the years during which such person was the spouse of a President during the President's period of service; and

        (iii) a number indicating the order of the period of service in which such President served.

    (B) Coin reverse.— The design on the reverse of each coin issued under this subsection shall bear—

        (i) images emblematic of the life and work of the First Spouse whose image is borne on the obverse; and

        (ii) the inscription "United States of America".

    (C) Designated denomination.— Each coin issued under this subsection shall bear, on the reverse, an inscription of the nominal denomination of the coin which shall be "$10".

    (D) Design in case of no first spouse.— In the case of any President who served without a spouse—

        (i) the image on the obverse of the bullion coin corresponding to the $1 coin relating to such President shall be an image emblematic of the concept of "Liberty"—

            (I) as represented on a United States coin issued during the period of service of such President; or

            (II) as represented, in the case of President Chester Alan Arthur, by a design incorporating the name and likeness of Alice Paul, a leading strategist in the suffrage movement, who was instrumental in gaining women the right to vote upon the adoption of the 19th amendment and thus the ability to participate in the election of future Presidents, and who was born on January 11, 1885, during the term of President Arthur; and

        (ii) the reverse of such bullion coin shall be of a design representative of themes of such President, except that in the case of the bullion coin referred to in clause (i)(II) the reverse of such coin shall be representative of the suffrage movement.

    (E) Design and coin for each spouse.— A separate coin shall be designed and issued under this section for each person who was the spouse of a President during any portion of a term of office of such President.

    (F) Inscriptions.— Each bullion coin issued under this subsection shall bear the inscription of the year of minting or issuance of the coin and such other inscriptions as the Secretary may determine to be appropriate.

(4) Sale of bullion coins.— Each bullion coin issued under this subsection shall be sold by the Secretary at a price that is equal to or greater than the sum of—

(A) the face value of the coins; and

(B) the cost of designing and issuing the coins (including labor, materials, dies, use of machinery, overhead expenses, marketing, and shipping).

(5) Issuance of coins commemorating first spouses.—

(A) In general.— The bullion coins issued under this subsection with respect to any spouse of a President shall be issued on the same schedule as the $1 coin issued under subsection (n) with respect to each such President.

(B) Maximum number of bullion coins for each design.— The Secretary shall—

(i) prescribe, on the basis of such factors as the Secretary determines to be appropriate, the maximum number of bullion coins that shall be issued with each of the designs selected under this subsection; and

(ii) announce, before the issuance of the bullion coins of each such design, the maximum number of bullion coins of that design that will be issued.

(C) Termination of program.— No bullion coin may be issued under this subsection after the termination, in accordance with subsection (n)(8), of the $1 coin program established under subsection (n).

(6) Quality of coins.— The bullion coins minted under this Act shall be issued in both proof and uncirculated qualities.

(7) Source of gold bullion.—

(A) In general.— The Secretary shall acquire gold for the coins issued under this subsection by purchase of gold mined from natural deposits in the United States, or in a territory or possession of the United States, within 1 year after the month in which the ore from which it is derived was mined.

(B) Price of gold.— The Secretary shall pay not more than the average world price for the gold mined under subparagraph (A).

(8) Bronze medals.— The Secretary may strike and sell bronze medals that bear the likeness of the bullion coins authorized under this subsection, at a price, size, and weight, and with such inscriptions, as the Secretary determines to be appropriate.

(9) Legal tender.— The coins minted under this title shall be legal tender, as provided in section 5103.

(10) Treatment as numismatic items.— For purposes of section [1] 5134 and 5136, all coins minted under this subsection shall be considered to be numismatic items.

(p) Removal of Barriers to Circulation of $1 Coin.—

(1) Acceptance by agencies and instrumentalities.— Beginning January 1, 2006, all agencies and instrumentalities of the United States, the United States Postal Service, all nonappropriated fund instrumentalities established under title 10, United States Code, all transit systems that receive operational subsidies or any disbursement of funds from the Federal Government, such as funds from the Federal Highway Trust Fund, including the Mass Transit Account, and all entities that operate any business, including vending machines, on any premises owned by the United States or under the control of any agency or instrumentality of the United States, including the legislative and judicial branches of the Federal Government, shall take such action as may be appropriate to ensure that by the end of the 2-year period beginning on such date—

(A) any business operations conducted by any such agency, instrumentality, system, or entity that involve coins or currency will be fully capable of—

(i) accepting $1 coins in connection with such operations; and

(ii) other than vending machines that do not receive currency denominations higher than $1, dispensing $1 coins in connection with such operations; and

(B) displays signs and notices denoting such capability on the premises where coins or currency are accepted or dispensed, including on each vending machine.

(2) Publicity.— The Director of the United States Mint, shall work closely with consumer groups, media outlets, and schools to ensure an adequate amount of news coverage, and other means of increasing public awareness, of the inauguration of the Presidential $1 Coin Program established in subsection (n) to ensure that consumers know of the availability of the coin.

(3) Coordination.— The Board of Governors of the Federal Reserve System and the Secretary shall take steps to ensure that an adequate supply of $1 coins is available for commerce and collectors at such places and in such quantities as are appropriate by—

(A) consulting, to accurately gauge demand for coins and to anticipate and eliminate obstacles to the easy and efficient distribution and circulation of $1 coins as well as all other circulating coins, from time to time but no less frequently than annually, with a coin users group, which may include—

(i) representatives of merchants who would benefit from the increased usage of $1 coins;

(ii) vending machine and other coin acceptor manufacturers;

(iii) vending machine owners and operators;

(iv) transit officials;

(v) municipal parking officials;

(vi) depository institutions;

(vii) coin and currency handlers;

(viii) armored-car operators;

(ix) car wash operators; and

(x) coin collectors and dealers;

(B) submitting an annual report to the Congress containing—

(i) an assessment of the remaining obstacles to the efficient and timely circulation of coins, particularly $1 coins;

(ii) an assessment of the extent to which the goals of subparagraph (C) are being met; and

(iii) such recommendations for legislative action the Board and the Secretary may determine to be appropriate;

(C) consulting with industry representatives to encourage operators of vending machines and other automated coin-accepting devices in the United States to accept coins issued under the Presidential $1 Coin Program established under subsection (n) and any coins bearing any design in effect before the issuance of coins required under subsection (n) (including the so-called "Sacagawea-design" $1 coins), and to include notices on the machines and devices of such acceptability;

(D) ensuring that—

(i) during an introductory period, all institutions that want unmixed supplies of each newly-issued design of $1 coins minted under subsections (n) and (o) are able to obtain such unmixed supplies; and

(ii) circulating coins will be available for ordinary commerce in packaging of sizes and types appropriate for and useful to ordinary commerce, including rolled coins;

(E) working closely with any agency, instrumentality, system, or entity referred to in paragraph (1) to facilitate compliance with the requirements of such paragraph; and

(F) identifying, analyzing, and overcoming barriers to the robust circulation of $1 coins minted under subsections (n) and (o), including the use of demand prediction, improved methods of distribution and circulation, and improved public education and awareness campaigns.

(4) Bullion dealers.— The Director of the United States Mint shall take all steps necessary to ensure that a maximum number of reputable, reliable, and responsible dealers are qualified to offer for sale all bullion coins struck and issued by the United States Mint.

(5) Review of co-circulation.— At such time as the Secretary determines to be appropriate, and after consultation with the Board of Governors of the Federal Reserve System, the Secretary shall notify the Congress of its assessment of issues related to the co-circulation of any circulating $1 coin bearing any design, other than the so-called "Sacagawea-design" $1 coin, in effect before the issuance of coins required under subsection (n), including the effect of co-circulation on the acceptance and use of $1 coins, and make recommendations to the Congress for improving the circulation of $1 coins.

(q) Gold Bullion Coins.—

(1) In general.— Not later than 6 months after the date of enactment of the Presidential $1 Coin Act of 2005, the Secretary shall commence striking and issuing for sale such number of $50 gold bullion and proof coins as the Secretary may determine to be appropriate, in such quantities, as the Secretary, in the Secretary's discretion, may prescribe.

(2) Initial design.—

(A) In general.— Except as provided under subparagraph (B), the obverse and reverse of the gold bullion coins struck under this subsection during the first year of issuance shall bear the original designs by James Earle Fraser, which appear on the 5-cent coin commonly referred to as the "Buffalo nickel" or the "1913 Type 1".

(B) Variations.— The coins referred to in subparagraph (A) shall—

(i) have inscriptions of the weight of the coin and the nominal denomination of the coin incused in that portion of the design on the reverse of the coin commonly known as the "grassy mound"; and

(ii) bear such other inscriptions as the Secretary determines to be appropriate.

(3) Subsequent designs.— After the 1-year period described to in paragraph (2), the Secretary may—

(A) after consulting with the Commission of Fine Arts, and subject to the review of the Citizens Coinage Advisory Committee, change the design on the obverse or reverse of gold bullion coins struck under this subsection; and

(B) change the maximum number of coins issued in any year.

(4) Source of gold bullion.—

(A) In general.— The Secretary shall acquire gold for the coins issued under this subsection by purchase of gold mined from natural deposits in the United States, or in a territory or possession of the United States, within 1 year after the month in which the ore from which it is derived was mined.

(B) Price of gold.— The Secretary shall pay not more than the average world price for the gold mined under subparagraph (A).

(5) Sale of coins.— Each gold bullion coin issued under this subsection shall be sold for an amount the Secretary determines to be appropriate, but not less than the sum of—

(A) the market value of the bullion at the time of sale; and

(B) the cost of designing and issuing the coins, including labor, materials, dies, use of machinery, overhead expenses, marketing, and shipping.

(6) Legal tender.— The coins minted under this title shall be legal tender, as provided in section 5103.

(7) Treatment as numismatic items.— For purposes of section [1] 5134 and 5136, all coins minted under this subsection shall be considered to be numismatic items.

(8) Protective covering.—

(A) In general.— Each bullion coin having a metallic content as described in subsection (a)(11) and a design specified in paragraph (2) shall be sold in an inexpensive covering that will protect the coin from damage due to ordinary handling or storage.

(B) Design.— The protective covering required under subparagraph (A) shall be readily distinguishable from any coin packaging that may be used to protect proof coins minted and issued under this subsection.

(r) Redesign and Issuance of Circulating $1 Coins Honoring Native Americans and the Important Contributions Made by Indian Tribes and Individual Native Americans in United States History.—

(1) Redesign beginning in 2008.—

(A) In general.— Effective beginning January 1, 2008, notwithstanding subsection (d), in addition to the coins to be issued pursuant to subsection (n), and in accordance with this subsection, the Secretary shall mint and issue $1 coins that—

(i) have as the designs on the obverse the so-called "Sacagawea design"; and

(ii) have a design on the reverse selected in accordance with paragraph (2)(A), subject to paragraph (3)(A).

(B) Delayed date.— If the date of the enactment of the Native American $1 Coin Act is after August 25, 2007, subparagraph (A) shall be applied by substituting "2009" for "2008".

(2) Design requirements.— The $1 coins issued in accordance with paragraph (1) shall meet the following design requirements:

(A) Coin reverse.— The design on the reverse shall bear—

(i) images celebrating the important contributions made by Indian tribes and individual Native Americans to the development of the United States and the history of the United States;

(ii) the inscription "$1"; and

(iii) the inscription "United States of America".

(B) Coin obverse.— The design on the obverse shall—

(i) be chosen by the Secretary, after consultation with the Commission of Fine Arts and review by the Citizens Coinage Advisory Committee; and

(ii) contain the so-called "Sacagawea design" and the inscription "Liberty".

(C) Edge-incused inscriptions.—

(i) In general.— The inscription of the year of minting and issuance of the coin and the inscription "E Pluribus Unum" shall be edge-incused into the coin.

(ii) Preservation of distinctive edge.— The edge-incusing of the inscriptions under clause (i) on coins issued under this subsection shall be done in a manner that preserves the distinctive edge of the coin so that the denomination of the coin is readily discernible, including by individuals who are blind or visually impaired.

(D) Reverse design selection.— The designs selected for the reverse of the coins described under this subsection—

(i) shall be chosen by the Secretary after consultation with the Committee on Indian Affairs of the Senate, the Congressional Native American Caucus of the House of Representatives, the Commission of Fine Arts, and the National Congress of American Indians;

(ii) shall be reviewed by the Citizens Coinage Advisory Committee;

(iii) may depict individuals and events such as—

(I) the creation of Cherokee written language;

(II) the Iroquois Confederacy;

(III) Wampanoag Chief Massasoit;

(IV) the "Pueblo Revolt";

(V) Olympian Jim Thorpe;

(VI) Ely S. Parker, a general on the staff of General Ulysses S. Grant and later head of the Bureau of Indian Affairs; and

(VII) code talkers who served the United States Armed Forces during World War I and World War II; and

(iv) in the case of a design depicting the contribution of an individual Native American to the development of the United States and the history of the United States, shall not depict the individual in a size such that the coin could be considered to be a "2-headed" coin.

(E) Inscription of "in god we trust".— The design on the obverse or the reverse shall bear the inscription "In God We Trust".

(3) Issuance of coins commemorating 1 Native American event during each year.—

(A) In general.— Each design for the reverse of the $1 coins issued during each year shall be emblematic of 1 important Native American or Native American contribution each year.

(B) Issuance period.— Each $1 coin minted with a design on the reverse in accordance with this subsection for any year shall be issued during the 1-year period beginning on January 1 of that year and shall be available throughout the entire 1-year period.

(C) Order of issuance of designs.— Each coin issued under this subsection commemorating Native Americans and their contributions—

(i) shall be issued, to the maximum extent practicable, in the chronological order in which the Native Americans lived or the events occurred, until the termination of the coin program described in subsection (n); and

(ii) thereafter shall be issued in any order determined to be appropriate by the Secretary, after consultation with the Committee on Indian Affairs of the Senate, the Congressional Native American Caucus of the House of Representatives, and the National Congress of American Indians.

(4) Issuance of numismatic coins.— The Secretary may mint and issue such number of $1 coins of each design selected under this subsection in uncirculated and proof qualities as the Secretary determines to be appropriate.

(5) Quantity.— The number of $1 coins minted and issued in a year with the Sacagawea-design on the obverse shall be not less than 20 percent of the total number of $1 coins minted and issued in such year.

(s) Redesign and Issuance of Circulating Quarter Dollar Honoring the District of Columbia and Each of the Territories.—

(1) Redesign in 2009.—

(A) In general.— Notwithstanding the fourth sentence of subsection (d)(1) and subsection (d)(2) and subject to paragraph (6)(B), quarter dollar coins issued during 2009, shall have designs on the reverse side selected in accordance with this subsection which are emblematic of the District of Columbia and the territories.

(B) Flexibility with regard to placement of inscriptions.— Notwithstanding subsection (d)(1), the Secretary may select a design for quarter dollars issued during 2009 in which—

(i) the inscription described in the second sentence of subsection (d)(1) appears on the reverse side of any such quarter dollars; and

(ii) any inscription described in the third sentence of subsection (d)(1) or the designation of the value of the coin appears on the obverse side of any such quarter dollars.

(2) Single district or territory design.— The design on the reverse side of each quarter dollar issued during 2009 shall be emblematic of one of the following: The District of Columbia, the Commonwealth of Puerto Rico, Guam, American Samoa, the United States Virgin Islands, and the Commonwealth of the Northern Mariana Islands.

(3) Selection of design.—

(A) In general.— Each of the 6 designs required under this subsection for quarter dollars shall be—

(i) selected by the Secretary after consultation with—

(I) the chief executive of the District of Columbia or the territory being honored, or such other officials or group as the chief executive officer of the District of Columbia or the territory may designate for such purpose; and

(II) the Commission of Fine Arts; and

(ii) reviewed by the Citizens Coinage Advisory Committee.

(B) Selection and approval process.— Designs for quarter dollars may be submitted in accordance with the design selection and approval process developed by the Secretary in the sole discretion of the Secretary.

(C) Participation.— The Secretary may include participation by District or territorial officials, artists from the District of Columbia or the territory, engravers of the United States Mint, and members of the general public.

(D) Standards.— Because it is important that the Nation's coinage and currency bear dignified designs of which the citizens of the United States can be proud, the Secretary shall not select any frivolous or inappropriate design for any quarter dollar minted under this subsection.

(E) Prohibition on certain representations.— No head and shoulders portrait or bust of any person, living or dead, and no portrait of a living person may be included in the design of any quarter dollar under this subsection.

(4) Treatment as numismatic items.— For purposes of sections 5134 and 5136, all coins minted under this subsection shall be considered to be numismatic items.

(5) Issuance.—

(A) Quality of coins.— The Secretary may mint and issue such number of quarter dollars of each design selected under paragraph (3) in uncirculated and proof qualities as the Secretary determines to be appropriate.

(B) Silver coins.— Notwithstanding subsection (b), the Secretary may mint and issue such number of quarter dollars of each design selected under paragraph (3) as the Secretary determines to be appropriate, with a content of 90 percent silver and 10 percent copper.

(C) Timing and order of issuance.— Coins minted under this subsection honoring the District of Columbia and each of the territories shall be issued in equal sequential intervals during 2009 in the following order: the District of Columbia, the Commonwealth of Puerto Rico, Guam, American Samoa, the United States Virgin Islands, and the Commonwealth of the Northern Mariana Islands.

(6) Other provisions.—

(A) Application in event of admission as a state.— If the District of Columbia or any territory becomes a State before the end of the 10-year period referred to in subsection (l)(1), subsection (l)(7) shall apply, and this subsection shall not apply, with respect to such State.

(B) Application in event of independence.— If any territory becomes independent or otherwise ceases to be a territory or possession of the United States before quarter dollars bearing designs which are emblematic of such territory are minted pursuant to this subsection, this subsection shall cease to apply with respect to such territory.

(7) Territory defined.— For purposes of this subsection, the term "territory" means the Commonwealth of Puerto Rico, Guam, American Samoa, the United States Virgin Islands, and the Commonwealth of the Northern Mariana Islands.

(t) Redesign and Issuance of Quarter Dollars Emblematic of National Sites in Each State, the District of Columbia, and Each Territory.—

(1) Redesign beginning upon completion of prior program.—

(A) In general.— Notwithstanding the fourth sentence of subsection (d)(1) and subsection (d)(2), quarter dollars issued beginning in 2010 shall have designs on the reverse selected in accordance with this subsection which are emblematic of the national sites in the States, the District of Columbia and the territories of the United States.

(B) Flexibility with regard to placement of inscriptions.— Notwithstanding subsection (d)(1), the Secretary may select a design for quarter dollars referred to in subparagraph (A) in which—

(i) the inscription described in the second sentence of subsection (d)(1) appears on the reverse side of any such quarter dollars; and

(ii) any inscription described in the third sentence of subsection (d)(1) or the designation of the value of the coin appears on the obverse side of any such quarter dollars.

(C) Inclusion of District of Columbia, and territories.— For purposes of this subsection, the term "State" has the same meaning as in section 3(a)(3) of the Federal Deposit Insurance Act.

(2) Single site in each state.— The design on the reverse side of each quarter dollar issued during the period of issuance under this subsection shall be emblematic of 1 national site in each State.

(3) Selection of site and design.—

(A) Site.—

(i) In general.— The selection of a national park or other national site in each State to be honored with a coin under this subsection shall be made by the Secretary of the Treasury, after consultation with the Secretary of the Interior and the governor or other chief executive of each State with respect to which a coin is to be issued under this subsection, and after giving full and thoughtful consideration to national sites that are not under the jurisdiction of the Secretary of the Interior so that the national site chosen for each State shall be the most appropriate in terms of natural or historic significance.

(ii) Timing.— The selection process under clause (i) shall be completed before the end of the 270-day period beginning on the date of the enactment of the America's Beautiful National Parks Quarter Dollar Coin Act of 2008.

(B) Design.— Each of the designs required under this subsection for quarter dollars shall be—

(i) selected by the Secretary after consultation with—

(I) the Secretary of the Interior; and

(II) the Commission of Fine Arts; and

(ii) reviewed by the Citizens Coinage Advisory Committee.

(C) Selection and approval process.— Recommendations for site selections and designs for quarter dollars may be submitted in accordance with the site and design selection and approval process developed by the Secretary in the sole discretion of the Secretary.

(D) Participation in design.— The Secretary may include participation by officials of the State, artists from the State, engravers of the United States Mint, and members of the general public.

(E) Standards.— Because it is important that the Nation's coinage and currency bear dignified designs of which the citizens of the United States can be proud, the Secretary shall not select any frivolous or inappropriate design for any quarter dollar minted under this subsection.

(F) Prohibition on certain representations.— No head and shoulders portrait or bust of any person, living or dead, no portrait of a living person, and no outline or map of a State may be included in the design on the reverse of any quarter dollar under this subsection.

(4) Issuance of coins.—

(A) Order of issuance.— The quarter dollar coins issued under this subsection bearing designs of national sites shall be issued in the order in which the sites selected under paragraph (3) were first established as a national site.

(B) Rate of issuance.— The quarter dollar coins bearing designs of national sites under this subsection shall be issued at the rate of 5 new designs during each year of the period of issuance under this subsection.

(C) Number of each of 5 coin designs in each year.— Of the quarter dollar coins issued during each year of the period of issuance, the Secretary of the Treasury shall prescribe, on the basis of such factors as the Secretary determines to be appropriate, the number of quarter dollars which shall be issued with each of the designs selected for such year.

(5) Treatment as numismatic items.— For purposes of sections 5134 and 5136, all coins minted under this subsection shall be considered to be numismatic items.

(6) Issuance.—

(A) Quality of coins.— The Secretary may mint and issue such number of quarter dollars of each design selected under paragraph (3) in uncirculated and proof qualities as the Secretary determines to be appropriate.

(B) Silver coins.— Notwithstanding subsection (b), the Secretary may mint and issue such number of quarter dollars of each design selected under paragraph (3) as the Secretary determines to be appropriate, with a content of 90 percent silver and 10 percent copper.

(7) Period of issuance.—

(A) In general.— Subject to paragraph (2), the program established under this subsection shall continue in effect until a national site in each State has been honored.

(B) Second round at discretion of secretary.—

(i) Determination.— The Secretary may make a determination before the end of the 9-year period beginning when the first quarter dollar is issued under this subsection to continue the period of issuance until a second national site in each State, the District of Columbia, and each territory referred to in this subsection has been honored with a design on a quarter dollar.

(ii) Notice and report.— Within 30 days after making a determination under clause (i), the Secretary shall submit a written report on such determination to the Committee on Financial Services of the House of Representatives and the Committee on Banking, Housing, and Urban Affairs of the Senate.

(iii) Applicability of provisions.— If the Secretary makes a determination under clause (i), the provisions of this subsection applicable to site and design selection and approval, the order, timing, and conditions of issuance shall apply in like manner as the initial issuance of quarter dollars under this subsection, except that the issuance of quarter dollars pursuant to such determination bearing the first design shall commence in order immediately following the last issuance of quarter dollars under the first round.

(iv) Continuation until all states are honored.— If the Secretary makes a determination under clause (i), the program under this subsection shall continue until a second site in each State has been so honored.

(8) Designs after end of program.— Upon the completion of the coin program under this subsection, the design on—

(A) the obverse of the quarter dollar shall revert to the same design containing an image of President Washington in effect for the quarter dollar before the institution of the 50-State quarter dollar program; and

(B) notwithstanding the fourth sentence of subsection (d)(1), the reverse of the quarter dollar shall contain an image of General Washington crossing the Delaware River prior to the Battle of Trenton.

(9) National site.— For purposes of this subsection, the term "national site" means any site under the supervision, management, or conservancy of the National Park Service, the United States Forest Service, the

United States Fish and Wildlife Service, or any similar department or agency of the Federal Government, including any national park, national monument, national battlefield, national military park, national historical park, national historic site, national lakeshore, seashore, recreation area, parkway, scenic river, or trail and any site in the National Wildlife Refuge System.

(10) Application in event of independence.— If any territory becomes independent or otherwise ceases to be a territory or possession of the United States before quarter dollars bearing designs which are emblematic of such territory are minted pursuant to this subsection, this subsection shall cease to apply with respect to such territory.

(u) Silver Bullion Investment Product.—

(1) In general.— The Secretary shall strike and make available for sale such number of bullion coins as the Secretary determines to be appropriate that are exact duplicates of the quarter dollars issued under subsection (t), each of which shall—

(A) have a diameter of 3.0 inches and weigh 5.0 ounces;

(B) contain .999 fine silver;

(C) have incused into the edge the fineness and weight of the bullion coin;

(D) bear an inscription of the denomination of such coin, which shall be "quarter dollar"; and

(E) not be minted or issued by the United States Mint as so-called "fractional" bullion coins or in any size other than the size described in paragraph (A).

(2) Availability for sale.— Bullion coins minted under paragraph (1)—

(A) shall become available for sale no sooner than the first day of the calendar year in which the circulating quarter dollar of which such bullion coin is a duplicate is issued; and

(B) may only be available for sale during the year in which such circulating quarter dollar is issued.

(3) Distribution.—

(A) In general.— In addition to the authorized dealers utilized by the Secretary in distributing bullion coins and solely for purposes of distributing bullion coins issued under this subsection, the Director of the National Park Service, or the designee of the Director, may purchase numismatic items issued under this subsection, but only in units of no fewer than 1,000 at a time, and the Director, or the Director's designee, may resell or repackage such numismatic items as the Director determines to be appropriate.

(B) Resale.— The Director of the National Park Service, or the designee of the Director, may resell, at cost and without repackaging, numismatic items acquired by the Director or such designee under subparagraph (A) to any party affiliated with any national site honored by a quarter dollar under subsection (t) for repackaging and resale by such party in the same manner and to the same extent as such party would be authorized to engage in such activities under subparagraph (A) if the party were acting as the designee of the Director under such subparagraph.

Sec. 5113. Tolerances and testing of coins

(a) The Secretary of the Treasury may prescribe reasonable manufacturing tolerances for specifications in Section 5112 of this title (except for specifications that are limits) for the dollar, half dollar, quarter dollar, and dime coins. The weights of the 5-cent coin may vary not more than 0.194 gram. The weight of the one-cent coin may vary not more than 0.13 gram. Any gold coin issued under section 5112 of this title shall contain the full weight of gold stated on the coin.

(b) The Secretary shall keep a record of the kind, number, and weight of each group of coins minted and test a number of the coins separately to determine if the coins conform to the weight specified in Section 5112(a) of this title. If the coins tested do not conform, the Secretary—

(1) shall weigh each coin of the group separately and deface the coins that do not conform and cast them into bars for reminting; or

(2) may remelt the group of coins.

Sec. 5114. Engraving and printing currency and security documents

(a) Authority To Engrave and Print.—

(1) In general.— The Secretary of the Treasury shall engrave and print United States currency and bonds of the United States Government and currency and bonds of United States territories and possessions from intaglio plates on plate printing presses the Secretary selects. However, other security documents and checks may be printed by any process the Secretary selects. Engraving and printing shall be carried out within the Department of the Treasury if the Secretary decides the engraving and printing can be carried out as cheaply, perfectly, and safely as outside the Department.

(2) Engraving and printing for other governments.— The Secretary of the Treasury may produce currency, postage stamps, and other security documents for foreign governments if—

(A) the Secretary of the Treasury determines that such production will not interfere with engraving and printing needs of the United States; and

(B) the Secretary of State determines that such production would be consistent with the foreign policy of the United States.

(3) Procurement guidelines.— Articles, material, and supplies procured for use in the production of currency, postage stamps, and other security documents for foreign governments pursuant to paragraph (2) shall be treated in the same manner as articles, material, and supplies procured for public use within the United States for purposes of title III of the Act of March 3, 1933 (41 U.S.C. 10a et seq.; commonly referred to as the Buy American Act).

(b) United States currency has the inscription "In God We Trust" in a place the Secretary decides is appropriate. Only the portrait of a deceased individual may appear on United States currency and securities. The name of the individual shall be inscribed below the portrait.

(c) The Secretary may make a contract for a period of not more than 4 years to manufacture distinctive paper for United States currency and securities. To promote competition among manufacturers of the distinctive paper, the Secretary may split the award for the manufacture of the paper between the 2 bidders with the lowest prices a pound. When the Secretary decides that it is necessary to operate more than one mill to manufacture distinctive paper, the Secretary may—

(1) employ individuals temporarily at rates of pay equivalent to the rates of pay of regular employees; and

(2) charge the pay of the temporary employees to the appropriation available for manufacturing distinctive paper.

Sec. 5115. United States currency notes

(a) The Secretary of the Treasury may issue United States currency notes. The notes—

(1) are payable to bearer; and

(2) shall be in a form and in denominations of at least $1 that the Secretary prescribes.

(b) The amount of United States currency notes outstanding and in circulation

(1) may not be more than $300,000,000; and

(2) may not be held or used for a reserve.

Sec. 5116. Buying and selling gold and silver

(a)(1) With the approval of the president, the Secretary of the Treasury may—

(A) buy and sell gold in the way, in amounts, at rates, and on conditions the Secretary considers most advantageous to the public interest; and

(B) buy the gold with any direct obligations of the United States government or United States coins and currency authorized by law, or with amounts in the Treasury not otherwise appropriated.

(2) Amounts received from the purchase of gold are an asset of the general fund of the Treasury. Amounts received from the sale of gold shall be deposited by the Secretary in the general fund of the Treasury and shall be used for the sole purpose of reducing the national debt.

(3) The Secretary shall acquire gold for the coins issued under section 5112(i) of this title by purchase of gold mined from natural deposits in the United States, or in a territory or possession of the United States, within one year after the month in which the ore from which it is derived was mined. The Secretary shall pay not more than the average world price for the gold. In the absence of available supplies of such gold at the average world price, the Secretary may use gold from reserves held by the United States to mint the coins issued under section 5112(i) of this title. The Secretary shall issue such regulations as may be necessary to carry out this paragraph.

(b)(1) The Secretary may buy silver mined from natural deposits in the United States, or in a territory or possession of the United States, that is brought to a United States mint or assay office within one year after the month in which the ore from which it is derived was mined. The Secretary may use the coinage metal fund under section 5111(b) of this title to buy silver under this subsection.

(2) The Secretary may sell or use Government silver to mint coins, except silver transferred to stockpiles established under the Strategic and Critical Materials Stock Piling Act (50 U.S.C. 98 et seq.). The Secretary shall obtain the silver for the coins authorized under section 5112(e) of this title by purchase from stockpiles established under the Strategic and Critical Materials Stock Piling Act (50 U.S.C. 98 et seq.). At such time as the silver stockpile is depleted, the Secretary may obtain silver as described in paragraph (1) to mint coins authorized under section 5112(e). If it is not economically feasible to obtain such silver, the Secretary may obtain silver for coins authorized under section 5112(e) from other available sources. The secretary shall not pay more than the average world price for silver under any circumstances. As used in this paragraph, the term "average world price" means the price determined by a widely recognized commodity exchange at the time the silver is obtained by the Secretary. The Secretary shall sell silver under conditions the Secretary considers appropriate for at least $1.292929292 a fine troy ounce.

Sec. 5117. Transferring gold and gold certificates

(a) All right, title, and interest, and every claim of the Board of Governors of the Federal Reserve System, a Federal Reserve Bank, and a Federal Reserve agent, in and to gold is transferred to and vests in the United States Government to be held in the Treasury. Payment for the transferred gold is made by crediting equivalent amounts in dollars in accounts established in the Treasury under the 15th paragraph of Section 16 of the Federal Reserve Act (12 U.S.C. 467). Gold not in the possession of the Government shall be held in custody for the government and delivered on the order of the Secretary of the Treasury. The Board of Governors, Federal Reserve Banks, and Federal Reserve agents shall give instructions and take action necessary to ensure that the gold is so held and delivered.

(b) The Secretary shall issue gold certificates against gold transferred under subsection (a) of this section. The Secretary may issue gold certificates against other gold held in the Treasury. The Secretary may prescribe the form and denominations of the certificates. The amount of outstanding certificates may be not more than the value (for the purpose of issuing those certificates, of 42 and two-ninths dollars a fine troy ounce) of the gold held against gold certificates. The Secretary shall hold gold in the Treasury equal to the required dollar amount as security for gold certificates issued after January 29, 1934.

(c) With the approval of the president, the Secretary may prescribe regulations the Secretary considers necessary to carry out this section.

Sec. 5118. Gold clauses and consent to sue

(a) In this section—

(1) "gold clause" means a provision in or related to an obligation alleging to give the obligee a right to require payment in—

(A) gold;

(B) a particular United States coin or currency; or

(C) United States money measured in gold or a particular United States coin or currency.

(2) "public debt obligation" means a domestic obligation issued or guaranteed by the United States government to repay money or interest.

(b) The United States Government may not pay out any gold coin. A person lawfully holding United States coins and currency may present the coins and currency to the Secretary of the Treasury for exchange (dollar for dollar) for other United States coins and currency (other than gold and silver coins) that may be lawfully held. The Secretary shall make the exchange under regulations prescribed by the Secretary.

(c)(1) The Government withdraws its consent given to anyone to assert against the government, its agencies, or its officers, employees, or agents, a claim

(A) on a gold clause public debt obligation or interest on the obligation;

(B) for United States coins or currency; or

(C) arising out of the surrender, requisition, seizure, or acquisition of United States coins or currency, gold, or silver involving the effect or validity of a change in the metallic content of the dollar or in a regulation about the value of money.

(2) Paragraph (1) of this subsection does not apply to a proceeding in which no claim is made for payment or credit in an amount greater than the face or nominal value in dollars of public debt obligations or United States coins or currency involved in the proceeding.

(3) Except when consent is not withdrawn under this subsection, an amount appropriated for payment on public debt obligations and for United States coins and currency may be expended only dollar for dollar.

(d)(1) In this subsection, "obligation" means any obligation (except United States currency) payable in United States money.

(2) An obligation issued containing a gold clause or governed by a gold clause is discharged on payment (dollar for dollar) in United States coin or currency that is legal tender at the time of payment. This paragraph does not apply to an obligation issued after October 27, 1977.

Sec. 5119. Redemption and cancellation of currency

(a) Except to the extent authorized in regulations the Secretary of the Treasury prescribes with the approval of the president, the Secretary may not redeem United States currency (including Federal Reserve notes and circulating notes of Federal Reserve Banks and national banks) in gold. However, the Secretary shall redeem gold certificates owned by the Federal Reserve Banks at times and in amounts the Secretary decides are necessary to maintain the equal purchasing power of each kind of United States currency. When redemption in gold is authorized, the redemption may be made only in gold bullion bearing the stamp of a United States Mint or assay office in an amount equal at the time of redemption to the currency presented for redemption.

(b)(1) Except as provided in subsection (c)(1) of this section, the following are public debts bearing no interest:

(A) gold certificates issued before January 30, 1934.

(B) silver certificates.

(C) notes issued under the Act of July 14, 1890 (ch. 708, 26 Stat. 289).

(D) Federal Reserve notes for which payment was made under Section 4 of the Old Series Currency Adjustment Act.

(E) United States currency notes, including those issued under Section 1 of the Act of February 25,

1862 (ch. 33, 12 Stat. 345), the Act of July 11, 1862 (ch. 142, 12 Stat. 532), the resolution of January 17, 1863 (P.R. 9; 12 Stat. 822), Section 2 of the Act of March 3, 1863 (ch. 73, 12 Stat. 710), or Section 5115 of this title.

(2) Redemption, cancellation, and destruction of currency. — (A) The Secretary shall redeem from any currency described in paragraph (1) from the general fund of the Treasury upon presentment to the Secretary; and

(B) cancel and destroy such currency upon redemption. The Secretary shall not be required to reissue United States currency notes upon redemption.

(c)(1) The Secretary may determine the amount of the following United States currency that will not be presented for redemption because the currency has been destroyed or irretrievably lost:

(A) circulating notes of Federal Reserve Banks and national banks issued before July 1, 1929, for which the United States government has assumed liability.

(B) outstanding currency referred to in subsection (b)(1) of this section.

(2) When the Secretary makes a determination under this subsection, the Secretary shall reduce the amount of that currency outstanding by the amount the Secretary determines will not be redeemed and credit the appropriate receipt account.

(d) To provide a historical collection of United States currency, the Secretary may withhold from cancellation and destruction and transfer to a special account one piece of each design, issue, or series of each denomination of each kind of currency (including circulating notes of Federal Reserve Banks and national banks) after redemption. The Secretary may make appropriate entries in Treasury accounts because of the transfers.

Sec. 5120. Obsolete, mutilated, and worn coins and currency

(a)(1) The Secretary of the Treasury shall melt obsolete and worn United States coins withdrawn from circulation. The Secretary may use the metal from melting the coins for reminting or may sell the metal. The Secretary shall account for the following in the coinage metal fund under Section 5111(b) of this title:

(A) obsolete and worn coins and the metal from melting the coins.

(B) proceeds from the sale of the metal.

(C) losses incurred in the sale of the metal.

(D) losses incurred because of the difference between the face value of the coins melted and the coins minted from the metal.

(2) The Secretary shall reimburse the coinage metal fund for losses under paragraph (1)(C) and (D) of this subsection out of amounts in the coinage profit fund under Section 5111(b) of this title.

(b) The Secretary shall—

(1) cancel and destroy (by a secure process) obsolete, mutilated, and worn United States currency withdrawn from circulation; and

(2) dispose of the residue of the currency and notes.

(c) The Comptroller General shall audit the cancellation and destruction of United States currency and the accounting of the cancellation and destruction. Records the Comptroller General considers necessary to make an effective audit easier shall be made available to the Comptroller General.

Sec. 5121. Refining, assaying, and valuation of bullion

(a) The Secretary of the Treasury shall—

(1) melt and refine bullion;

(2) as required, assay coins, metal, and bullion;

(3) cast gold and silver bullion deposits into bars; and

(4) cast alloys into bars for minting coins.

(b) A person owning gold or silver bullion may deposit the bullion with the Secretary to be cast into fine, standard fineness, or unrefined bars weighing at least 5 troy ounces. When practicable, the Secretary shall weigh the bullion in front of the depositor. The Secretary shall give the depositor a receipt for the bullion stating the description and weight of the bullion. When the Secretary has to melt the bullion or remove base metals before the value of the bullion can be determined, the weight is the weight after the melting or removal of the metals. The Secretary may refuse a deposit of gold bullion if the deposit is less than $100 in value or the bullion is so base that it is unsuitable for the operations of the Bureau of the Mint.

(c) When the gold and silver are combined in bullion that is deposited and either the gold or silver is so little that it cannot be separated economically, the Secretary may not pay the depositor for the gold or silver that cannot be separated.

(d)(1) Under conditions prescribed by the Secretary, a person may exchange unrefined bullion for fine bars when—

(A) gold and silver are combined in the bullion in proportions that cannot be economically refined; or

(B) necessary supplies of acids cannot be procured at reasonable rates.

(2) The charge for refining in an exchange under this subsection may be not more than the charge imposed

in an exchange of unrefined bullion for refined bullion.

(e) The Secretary shall prepare bars for payment of deposits. The Secretary shall stamp each bar with a designation of the weight and fineness of the bar and a symbol the Secretary considers suitable to prevent fraudulent imitation of the bar.

Sec. 5122. Payment to depositors

(a) The Secretary of the Treasury shall determine the fineness, weight, and value of each deposit and bar under Section 5121 of this title. The value and the amount of charges under subsection (b) of this section shall be based on the fineness and weight of the bullion. The Secretary shall give the depositor a statement of the charges and the net amount of the deposit to be paid in money or bars of the same species of bullion as that deposited.

(b) The Secretary shall impose a charge equal to the average cost of material, labor, waste, and use of machinery of a United States mint or assay office for

(1) melting and refining bullion;

(2) using copper as an alloy when bullion deposited is above standard;

(3) separating gold and silver combined in the bullion; and

(4) preparing bars.

(c) The Secretary shall pay to the depositor or to a person designated by the depositor money or bars equivalent to the bullion deposited as soon as practicable after the value of the deposit is determined. If demanded, the Secretary shall pay depositors in the order in which the bullion is deposited with the Secretary. However, when there is an unavoidable delay in determining the value of a deposit, the Secretary shall pay depositors in the denominations requested by the depositors. After the depositor is paid, the bullion is the property of the United States Government.

(d) To allow the Secretary to pay depositors with as little delay as possible, the Secretary shall keep in the mints and assay offices, when possible, money and bullion the Secretary decides are convenient and necessary.

Sec. 5131. Organization

(a) The United States Mint has—

(1) a United States Mint at Philadelphia, Pennsylvania.

(2) a United States Mint at Denver, Colorado.

(3) a United States Mint at West Point, New York.

(4) a United States Mint at San Francisco, California.

(b) The Secretary of the Treasury shall carry out duties and powers related to refining and assaying bullion, minting coins, striking medals, and numismatic items at the mints. However, until the Secretary decides that the mints are adequate for minting and striking an ample supply of coins and medals, the Secretary may use any facility of the United States Mint to mint coins and strike medals and to store coins and medals.

(d) Laws on mints, officers and employees of mints, and punishment of offenses related to Mints and minting coins apply to assay offices, as applicable.

Sec. 5132. Administrative

(a)(1) Except as provided in this chapter, the Secretary of the Treasury shall deposit in the Treasury as miscellaneous receipts amounts the Secretary receives from the operations of the United States Mint. Expenditures made from appropriated funds which are subsequently determined to be properly chargeable to the Numismatic Public Enterprise Fund established by section 5134 shall be reimbursed by such Fund to the appropriation. The Secretary shall annually sell to the public, directly and by mail, sets of uncirculated and proof coins minted under paragraphs (1) through (6) of section 5112 (a) of this title, and shall solicit such sales through the use of the customer list of the United States Mint. Except with respect to amounts deposited in the Numismatic Public Enterprise Fund in accordance with section 5134, the Secretary may not use amounts the Secretary receives from profits on minting coins or from charges on gold or silver bullion under section 5122 to pay officers and employees.

(2) (A) In addition to the coins described in paragraph (1), the Secretary shall sell annually to the public directly and by mail, sets of proof coins minted under paragraphs (1) through (6) of section 5112 (a).

(B) Notwithstanding any other provision of law, for purposes of this paragraph—

(i) the coins described in paragraphs (2) through (4) of section 5112 (a) shall be made of an alloy of 90 percent silver and 10 percent copper; and

(ii) all coins minted under this paragraph shall have a mint mark indicating the place of manufacture.

(C) All coins minted under this paragraph shall be considered to be—

(i) numismatic items for purposes of paragraph (1) and section 5111 (a)(3); and

(ii) legal tender, as provided in section 5103.

(D) The Secretary shall obtain silver for coins minted under this paragraph by purchase from stockpiles established under the Strategic and Critical Materials Stock Piling Act (50 U.S.C. 98 et seq.). At such time as the silver stockpile is depleted, the Secretary shall obtain silver for such coins by purchase of silver mined from natural deposits in the United States or in a territory or possession of the United States not more than 1 year following the month in which the ore from which it is derived was mined. The Secretary shall pay not more than the average world price for such silver. The Secretary may issue such regulations as may be necessary to carry out this subparagraph.

(3) Not more than $54,208,000 may be appropriated to the Secretary for the fiscal year ending on September 30, 1993, to pay costs of the mints. Not more than $965,000 of amounts appropriated pursuant to the preceding sentence shall remain available until expended for research and development.

(b) To the extent the Secretary decides is necessary, the Secretary may use amounts received from depositors for refining bullion and the proceeds from the sale of byproducts (including spent acids from surplus bullion recovered in refining processes) to pay the costs of refining the bullion (including labor, material, waste, and loss on the sale of sweeps). The Secretary may not use amounts appropriated for the mints to pay those costs.

(c) The Secretary shall make an annual report at the end of each fiscal year on the operation of the United States Mint.

Sec. 5133. Settlement of accounts

(a) The Secretary of the Treasury shall—

(1) charge the superintendent of each mint with the amount in weight of standard metal of bullion the superintendent receives from the Secretary;

(2) credit each superintendent with the amount in weight of coins, clippings, and other bullion the superintendent returns to the Secretary; and

(3) charge separately to each superintendent, who shall account for, copper to be used in the alloy of gold and silver bullion.

(b) Settlement of Accounts.—

(1) In general.— At least once each year, the Secretary of the Treasury shall settle the accounts of the superintendents of the mints.

(2) Procedure.— At any settlement under this subsection, the superintendent shall—

(A) return to the Secretary any coin, clipping, or other bullion in the possession of the superintendent; and

(B) present the Secretary with a statement of bullion received and returned since the last settlement (including any bullion returned for settlement).

(3) Audit.— The Secretary shall—

(A) audit the accounts of each superintendent; and

(B) allow each superintendent the waste of precious metals that the Secretary determines is necessary—

(i) for refining and minting (within the limitations which the Secretary shall prescribe); and

(ii) for casting fine gold and silver bars (within the limit prescribed for refining), except that any waste allowance under this clause may not apply to deposit operations.

(c) After settlement, the Secretary shall compare the amount of gold and silver bullion and coins on hand with the total liabilities of the mints. The Secretary also shall make a statement of the ordinary expense account.

(d) The Secretary shall procure for each mint a series of standard weights corresponding to the standard troy pound of the National Institute of Standards and Technology of the Department of Commerce. The series shall include a one pound weight and multiples and subdivisions of one pound from .01 grain to 25 pounds. At least once a year, the Secretary shall test the weights normally used in transactions at the mints against the standard weights.

Sec. 5134. Numismatic Public Enterprise Fund

(a) Definitions.— For purposes of this section—

(1) Fund.— The term "Fund" means the Numismatic Public Enterprise Fund.

(2) Mint.— The term "Mint" means the United States Mint.

(3) Numismatic item.— The term "numismatic item" means any medal, proof coin, uncirculated coin, bullion coin, or other coin specifically designated by statute as a numismatic item, including products and accessories related to any such medal, coin, or item.

(4) Numismatic operations and programs.— The term "numismatic operations and programs"—

(A) means the activities concerning, and assets utilized in, the production, administration, sale, and management of numismatic items and the Numismatic Public Enterprise Fund; and

(B) includes capital, personnel salaries, functions relating to operations, marketing, distribution, promotion, advertising, and official reception and representation, the acquisition or replacement of equipment, and the renovation or modernization of facilities (other than the construction or acquisition of new buildings).

(5) Secretary.— The term "Secretary" means the Secretary of the Treasury.

(b) Establishment of Fund.— There is hereby established in the Treasury of the United States a revolving Numismatic Public Enterprise Fund consisting of amounts deposited in the fund under subsection (c)(2) of this section or section 221(b) of the United States Mint Reauthorization and Reform Act of 1992 which shall be available to the Secretary for numismatic operations and programs of the United States Mint without fiscal year limitation.

(c) Operations of the Fund.—

(1) Payment of expenses.— Any expense incurred by the Secretary for numismatic operations and programs which the Secretary determines, in the Secretary's sole discretion, to be ordinary and reasonable incidents of the numismatic business shall be paid out of the Fund, including any expense incurred pursuant to any obligation or other commitment of Mint numismatic operations and programs which was entered into before the beginning of fiscal year 1993.

(2) Deposit of receipts.— All receipts from numismatic operations and programs shall be deposited into the Fund, including amounts attributable to any surcharge imposed with respect to the sale of any numismatic item.

(3) Transfer of seigniorage.— The Secretary shall transfer monthly from the Fund to the general fund of the Treasury an amount equal to the total amount on the seigniorage of numismatic items sold since the date of any preceding transfer.

(4) Transfer of excess amounts to the treasury.—

(A) In general.— At such times as the Secretary determines to be appropriate, the Secretary shall transfer any amount in the Fund which the Secretary determines to be in excess of the amount required by the Fund to the Treasury for deposit as miscellaneous receipts.

(B) Report to congress.— The Secretary shall submit an annual report to the Congress containing—

(i) a statement of the total amount transferred to the Treasury pursuant to subparagraph (A) during the period covered by the report;

(ii) a statement of the amount by which the amount on deposit in the Fund at the end of the period covered by the report exceeds the estimated operating costs of the Fund for the 1-year period beginning at the end of such period; and

(iii) an explanation of the specific purposes for which such excess amounts are being retained in the Fund.

(d) Budget Treatment.—

(1) In general.— The Secretary shall prepare budgets for the Fund, and estimates and statements of financial condition of the Fund in accordance with the requirements of section 9103 which shall be submitted to the President for inclusion in the budget submitted under section 1105.

(2) Inclusion in annual report.— Statements of the financial condition of the Fund shall be included in the Secretary's annual report on the operation of the Mint.

(3) Treatment as wholly owned government corporation for certain purposes.— Section 9104 shall apply to the Fund to the same extent such section applies to wholly owned Government corporations.

(e) Financial Statements, Audits, and Reports.—

(1) Annual financial statement required.— By the end of each calendar year, the Secretary shall prepare an annual financial statement of the Fund for the fiscal year which ends during such calendar year.

(2) Contents of financial statement.— Each statement prepared pursuant to paragraph (1) shall, at a minimum, contain—

(A) the overall financial position (including assets and liabilities) of the Fund as of the end of the fiscal year;

(B) the results of the numismatic operations and programs of the Fund during the fiscal year;

(C) the cash flows or the changes in financial position of the Fund;

(D) a reconciliation of the financial statement to the budget reports of the Fund; and

(E) a supplemental schedule detailing -

(i) the costs and expenses for the production, for the marketing, and for the distribution of each denomination of circulating coins produced by the Mint during the fiscal year and the per-unit cost of producing, of marketing, and of distributing each denomination of such coins; and

(ii) the gross revenue derived from the sales of each such denomination of coins.

(3) Annual audits.—

(A) In general.— Each annual financial statement prepared under paragraph (1) shall be audited—

(i) by—

(I) an independent external auditor; or

(II) the Inspector General of the Department of the Treasury, as designated by the Secretary; and

(ii) in accordance with the generally accepted Government auditing standards issued by the

Comptroller General of the United States.

       (B) Auditor's report required.— The auditor designated to audit any financial statement of the Fund pursuant to subparagraph (A) shall submit a report—

              (i) to the Secretary by March 31 of the year beginning after the end of the fiscal year covered by such financial statement; and

              (ii) containing the auditor's opinion on—

                     (I) the financial statement of the Fund;

                     (II) the internal accounting and administrative controls and accounting systems of the Fund; and

                     (III) the Fund's compliance with applicable laws and regulations.

       (4) Annual report on fund.—

       (A) Report required.— By April 30 of each year, the Secretary shall submit a report on the Fund for the most recently completed fiscal year to the President, the Congress, and the Director of the Office of Management and Budget.

       (B) Contents of annual report.— The annual report required under subparagraph (A) for any fiscal year shall include—

              (i) the financial statement prepared under paragraph (1) for such fiscal year;

              (ii) the audit report submitted to the Secretary pursuant to paragraph (3)(B) for such fiscal year;

              (iii) a description of activities carried out during such fiscal year;

              (iv) a summary of information relating to numismatic operations and programs contained in the reports on systems on internal accounting and administrative controls and accounting systems submitted to the President and the Congress under section 3512(c);

              (v) a summary of the corrective actions taken with respect to material weaknesses relating to numismatic operations and programs identified in the reports prepared under section 3512(c);

              (vi) any other information the Secretary considers appropriate to fully inform the Congress concerning the financial management of the Fund; and

              (vii) a statement of the total amount of excess funds transferred to the Treasury.

       (5) Marketing report.—

       (A) Report required for 10 years.— For each fiscal year beginning before fiscal year 2003, the Secretary shall submit an annual report on all marketing activities and expenses of the Fund to the Congress before the end of the 3-month period beginning at the end of such fiscal year.

       (B) Contents of report.— The report submitted pursuant to subparagraph (A) shall contain a detailed description of—

              (i) the sources of income including surcharges; and

              (ii) expenses incurred for manufacturing, materials, overhead, packaging, marketing, and shipping.

    (f) Conditions on Payment of Surcharges to Recipient Organizations.—

       (1) Payment of surcharges.—

       (A) In general.— Notwithstanding any other provision of law, no amount derived from the proceeds of any surcharge imposed on the sale of any numismatic item shall be paid from the fund to any designated recipient organization unless—

              (i) all numismatic operation and program costs allocatable to the program under which such numismatic item is produced and sold have been recovered; and

              (ii) the designated recipient organization submits an audited financial statement that demonstrates, to the satisfaction of the Secretary, that, with respect to all projects or purposes for which the proceeds of such surcharge may be used, the organization has raised funds from private sources for such projects and purposes in an amount that is equal to or greater than the total amount of the proceeds of such surcharge derived from the sale of such numismatic item.

       (B) Unpaid amounts.— If any amount derived from the proceeds of any surcharge imposed on the sale of any numismatic item that may otherwise be paid from the fund, under any provision of law relating to such numismatic item, to any designated recipient organization remains unpaid to such organization solely by reason of the matching fund requirement contained in subparagraph (A)(ii) after the end of the 2-year period beginning on the later of—

              (i) the last day any such numismatic item is issued by the Secretary; or

              (ii) the date of the enactment of the American 5-Cent Coin Design Continuity Act of 2003, such unpaid amount shall be deposited in the Treasury as miscellaneous receipts.

       (2) Annual audits.—

       (A) Annual audits of recipients required.— Each designated recipient organization that receives any payment from the fund of any amount derived from the proceeds of any surcharge imposed on the sale of any numismatic item shall provide, as a condition for receiving any such amount, for an annual audit, in accordance with generally accepted government auditing standards by an independent public accountant selected by the organization, of all such payments to the organization beginning in the first fiscal year of the organization in which any such amount is received and continuing until all amounts received by such organization from the fund with respect to such surcharges are fully expended or placed in trust.

(B) Minimum requirements for annual audits.— At a minimum, each audit of a designated recipient organization pursuant to subparagraph (A) shall report—

(i) the amount of payments received by the designated recipient organization from the fund (!1) during the fiscal year of the organization for which the audit is conducted that are derived from the proceeds of any surcharge imposed on the sale of any numismatic item;

(ii) the amount expended by the designated recipient organization from the proceeds of such surcharges during the fiscal year of the organization for which the audit is conducted; and

(iii) whether all expenditures by the designated recipient organization during the fiscal year of the organization for which the audit is conducted from the proceeds of such surcharges were for authorized purposes.

(C) Responsibility of organization to account for expenditures of surcharges.— Each designated recipient organization that receives any payment from the fund of any amount derived from the proceeds of any surcharge imposed on the sale of any numismatic item shall take appropriate steps, as a condition for receiving any such payment, to ensure that the receipt of the payment and the expenditure of the proceeds of such surcharge by the organization in each fiscal year of the organization can be accounted for separately from all other revenues and expenditures of the organization.

(D) Submission of audit report.— Not later than 90 days after the end of any fiscal year of a designated recipient organization for which an audit is required under subparagraph (A), the organization shall—

(i) submit a copy of the report to the Secretary of the Treasury; and

(ii) make a copy of the report available to the public.

(E) Use of surcharges for audits.— Any designated recipient organization that receives any payment from the fund of any amount derived from the proceeds of any surcharge imposed on the sale of any numismatic item may use the amount received to pay the cost of an audit required under subparagraph (A).

(F) Waiver of paragraph.— The Secretary of the Treasury may waive the application of any subparagraph of this paragraph to any designated recipient organization for any fiscal year after taking into account the amount of surcharges that such organization received or expended during such year.

(G) Nonapplicability to federal entities.— This paragraph shall not apply to any Federal agency or department or any independent establishment in the executive branch that receives any payment from the fund of any amount derived from the proceeds of any surcharge imposed on the sale of any numismatic item.

(H) Availability of books and records.— An organization that receives any payment from the fund of any amount derived from the proceeds of any surcharge imposed on the sale of any numismatic item shall provide, as a condition for receiving any such payment, to the Inspector General of the Department of the Treasury or the Comptroller General of the United States, upon the request of such Inspector General or the Comptroller General, all books, records, and work papers belonging to or used by the organization, or by any independent public accountant who audited the organization in accordance with subparagraph (A), which may relate to the receipt or expenditure of any such amount by the organization.

(3) Use of agents or attorneys to influence commemorative coin legislation.— No portion of any payment from the fund to any designated recipient organization of any amount derived from the proceeds of any surcharge imposed on the sale of any numismatic item may be used, directly or indirectly, by the organization to compensate any agent or attorney for services rendered to support or influence in any way legislative action of the Congress relating to such numismatic item.

(4) Designated recipient organization defined.— For purposes of this subsection, the term "designated recipient organization" means any organization designated, under any provision of law, as the recipient of any surcharge imposed on the sale of any numismatic item.

(g) Quarterly Financial Reports.—

(1) In general.— Not later than the 30th day of each month following each calendar quarter through and including the final period of sales with respect to any commemorative coin program authorized on or after the date of enactment of the Treasury, Postal Service, and General Government Appropriations Act, 1997, the Mint shall submit to the Congress a quarterly financial report in accordance with this subsection.

(2) Requirements.— Each report submitted under paragraph (1) shall include, with respect to the calendar quarter at issue—

(A) a detailed financial statement, prepared in accordance with generally accepted accounting principles, that includes financial information specific to that quarter, as well as cumulative financial information relating to the entire program;

        (B) a detailed accounting of—

                (i) all costs relating to marketing efforts;

                (ii) all funds projected for marketing use;

                (iii) all costs for employee travel relating to the promotion of commemorative coin programs;

                (iv) all numismatic items minted, sold, not sold, and rejected during the production process; and

                (v) the costs of melting down all rejected and unsold products;

        (C) adequate market-based research for all commemorative coin programs; and

        (D) a description of the efforts of the Mint in keeping the sale price of numismatic items as low as practicable.

Sec. 5135. Citizens Coinage Advisory Committee

    (a) Establishment.—

        (1) In general.— There is hereby established the Citizens Coinage Advisory Committee (in this section referred to as the "Advisory Committee") to advise the Secretary of the Treasury on the selection of themes and designs for coins.

        (2) Oversight of advisory committee.— The Advisory Committee shall be subject to the authority of the Secretary of the Treasury (hereafter in this section referred to as the "Secretary").

    (b) Membership.—

        (1) Appointment.— The Advisory Committee shall consist of 11 members appointed by the Secretary as follows:

        (A) Seven persons appointed by the Secretary—

                (i) one of whom shall be appointed from among individuals who are specially qualified to serve on the Advisory Committee by virtue of their education, training, or experience as a nationally or internationally recognized curator in the United States of a numismatic collection;

                (ii) one of whom shall be appointed from among individuals who are specially qualified to serve on the Advisory Committee by virtue of their experience in the medallic arts or sculpture;

                (iii) one of whom shall be appointed from among individuals who are specially qualified to serve on the Advisory Committee by virtue of their education, training, or experience in American history;

                (iv) one of whom shall be appointed from among individuals who are specially qualified to serve on the Advisory Committee by virtue of their education, training, or experience in numismatics; and

                (v) three of whom shall be appointed from among individuals who can represent the interests of the general public in the coinage of the United States.

        (B) Four persons appointed by the Secretary on the basis of the recommendations of the following officials who shall make the selection for such recommendation from among citizens who are specially qualified to serve on the Advisory Committee by virtue of their education, training, or experience:

                (i) One person recommended by the Speaker of the House of Representatives.

                (ii) One person recommended by the minority leader of the House of Representatives.

                (iii) One person recommended by the majority leader of the Senate.

                (iv) One person recommended by the minority leader of the Senate.

        (2) Terms.—

        (A) In general.— Except as provided in subparagraph (B), members of the Advisory Committee shall be appointed for a term of 4 years.

        (B) Terms of initial appointees.— As designated by the Secretary at the time of appointment, of the members first appointed—

                (i) four of the members appointed under paragraph (1)(A) shall be appointed for a term of 4 years;

                (ii) the four members appointed under paragraph (1)(B) shall be appointed for a term of 3 years; and

                (iii) three of the members appointed under paragraph (1)(A) shall be appointed for a term of 2 years.

        (3) Preservation of public advisory status.— No individual may be appointed to the Advisory Committee while serving as an officer or employee of the Federal Government.

        (4) Continuation of service.— Each appointed member may continue to serve for up to 6 months after the expiration of the term of office to which such member was appointed until a successor has been appointed.

        (5) Vacancy and removal.—

        (A) In general.— Any vacancy on the Advisory Committee shall be filled in the manner in which the original appointment was made.

(B) Removal.— Advisory Committee members shall serve at the discretion of the Secretary and may be removed at any time for good cause.

(6) Chairperson.— The Chairperson of the Advisory Committee shall be appointed for a term of 1 year by the Secretary from among the members of the Advisory Committee.

(7) Pay and expenses.— Members of the Advisory Committee shall serve without pay for such service but each member of the Advisory Committee shall be reimbursed from the United States Mint Public Enterprise Fund for travel, lodging, meals, and incidental expenses incurred in connection with attendance of such members at meetings of the Advisory Committee in the same amounts and under the same conditions as employees of the United States Mint who engage in official travel, as determined by the Secretary.

(8) Meetings.—

(A) In general.— The Advisory Committee shall meet at the call of the Secretary, the chairperson, or a majority of the members, but not less frequently than twice annually.

(B) Open meetings.— Each meeting of the Advisory Committee shall be open to the public.

(C) Prior notice of meetings.— Timely notice of each meeting of the Advisory Committee shall be published in the Federal Register, and timely notice of each meeting shall be made to trade publications and publications of general circulation.

(9) Quorum.— Seven members of the Advisory Committee shall constitute a quorum.

(c) Duties of the Advisory Committee.— The duties of the Advisory Committee are as follows:

(1) Advising the Secretary of the Treasury on any theme or design proposals relating to circulating coinage, bullion coinage, congressional gold medals and national and other medals produced by the Secretary of the Treasury in accordance with section 5111 of title 31, United States Code.

(2) Advising the Secretary of the Treasury with regard to—

(A) the events, persons, or places that the Advisory Committee recommends be commemorated by the issuance of commemorative coins in each of the 5 calendar years succeeding the year in which a commemorative coin designation is made;

(B) the mintage level for any commemorative coin recommended under subparagraph (A); and

(C) the proposed designs for commemorative coins.

(d) Expenses.— The expenses of the Advisory Committee that the Secretary of the Treasury determines to be reasonable and appropriate shall be paid by the Secretary from the United States Mint Public Enterprise Fund.

(e) Administrative Support, Technical Services, and Advice.— Upon the request of the Advisory Committee, or as necessary for the Advisory Committee to carry out the responsibilities of the Advisory Committee under this section, the Director of the United States Mint shall provide to the Advisory Committee the administrative support, technical services, and advice that the Secretary of the Treasury determines to be reasonable and appropriate.

(f) Consultation Authority.— In carrying out the duties of the Advisory Committee under this section, the Advisory Committee may consult with the Commission of Fine Arts.

(g) Annual Report.—

(1) Required.— Not later than September 30 of each year, the Advisory Committee shall submit a report to the Secretary, the Committee on Financial Services of the House of Representatives and the Committee on Banking, Housing, and Urban Affairs of the Senate. Should circumstances arise in which the Advisory Committee cannot meet the September 30 deadline in any year, the Secretary shall advise the Chairpersons of the Committee on Financial Services of the House of Representatives and the Committee on Banking, Housing, and Urban Affairs of the Senate of the reasons for such delay and the date on which the submission of the report is anticipated.

(2) Contents.— The report required by paragraph (1) shall describe the activities of the Advisory Committee during the preceding year and the reports and recommendations made by the Advisory Committee to the Secretary of the Treasury.

(h) Federal Advisory Committee Act Does Not Apply.— Subject to the requirements of subsection (b)(8), the Federal Advisory Committee Act shall not apply with respect to the Committee.

Sec. 5136. United States Mint Public Enterprise Fund

There shall be established in the Treasury of the United States, a United States Mint Public Enterprise Fund (the "Fund") for fiscal year 1996 and hereafter: Provided, That all receipts from Mint operations and programs, including the production and sale of numismatic items, the production and sale of circulating coinage, the protection of Government assets, and gifts and bequests of property, real or personal shall be deposited into the Fund and shall be available without fiscal year limitations: Provided further, That all expenses incurred by the Secretary of the Treasury for operations and programs of the United States Mint that the Secretary of the Treasury determines, in the Secretary's sole discretion, to be ordinary and reasonable incidents of Mint operations and programs, and any expense incurred pursuant to any obligation or other commitment of Mint operations and programs that was entered into before the establishment of the Fund, shall be paid out of the Fund: Provided further, That not to exceed 6.2415 percent of the nominal value of the coins minted, shall be paid out of the Fund for the circulating coin operations and programs in fiscal year 1996 for those operations and programs previously provided for by appropriation: Provided further, That the Secretary of the Treasury may borrow such funds from the General Fund as may be necessary to meet existing liabilities and obligations incurred prior to the receipt of revenues into the Fund: Provided further, That the General Fund shall be reimbursed for such funds by the Fund within one year of the date of the loan: Provided further, That the Fund may retain receipts from the Federal Reserve System from the sale of circulating coins at face value for deposit into the Fund (retention of receipts is for the circulating operations and programs): Provided further, That the Secretary of the Treasury shall transfer to the Fund all assets and liabilities of the Mint operations and programs, including all Numismatic Public Enterprise Fund assets and liabilities, all receivables, unpaid obligations and unobligated balances from the Mint's appropriation, the Coinage Profit Fund, and the Coinage Metal Fund, and the land and buildings of the Philadelphia Mint, Denver Mint, and the Fort Knox Bullion Depository: Provided further, That the Numismatic Public Enterprise Fund, the Coinage Profit Fund and the Coinage Metal Fund shall cease to exist as separate funds as their activities[1] and functions are subsumed under and subject to the Fund, and the requirements of 31 USC 5134 (c)(4), (c)(5)(B), and (d) and (e) 2 of the Numismatic Public Enterprise Fund shall apply to the Fund: Provided further, That at such times as the Secretary of the Treasury determines appropriate, but not less than annually, any amount in the Fund that is determined to be in excess of the amount required by the Fund shall be transferred to the Treasury for deposit as miscellaneous receipts: Provided further, That the term "Mint operations and programs" means

(1) the activities concerning, and assets utilized in, the production, administration, distribution, marketing, purchase, sale, and management of coinage, numismatic items, the protection and safeguarding of Mint assets and those non-Mint assets in the custody of the Mint, and the Fund; and

(2) includes capital, personnel salaries and compensation, functions relating to operations, marketing, distribution, promotion, advertising, official reception and representation, the acquisition or replacement of equipment, the renovation or modernization of facilities, and the construction or acquisition of new buildings: Provided further, That the term "numismatic item" includes any medal, proof coin, uncirculated coin, bullion coin, numismatic collectible, other monetary issuances and products and accessories related to any such medal or coin: Provided further, That provisions of law governing procurement or public contracts shall not be applicable to the procurement of goods or services necessary for carrying out Mint programs and operations.

Sec. 5141. Operation of the Bureau of Engraving and Printing

(a) The Secretary of the Treasury shall prepare and submit to the President an annual business-type budget for the Bureau of Engraving and Printing. ...

Sec. 5142. Bureau of Engraving and Printing Fund

(a) The Department of the Treasury has a Bureau of Engraving and Printing Fund. Amounts—

(1) in the Fund are available to operate the Bureau of Engraving and Printing;

(2) in the Fund remain available until expended; and

(3) may be appropriated to the Fund.

(b) The Fund consists of

(1) property and physical assets (except building and land) acquired by the Bureau;

(2) all amounts received by the Bureau; and

(3) proceeds from the disposition of property and assets acquired by the Fund.

(c) The capital of the Fund consists of—

(1) amounts appropriated to the Fund;

(2) physical assets of the Bureau (except buildings and land) as of the close of business June 30, 1951; and

(3) all payments made after June 30, 1974, under section 5143 of this title at prices adjusted to permit buying capital equipment and to provide future working capital.

(d) The Secretary shall deposit each fiscal year, in the Treasury as miscellaneous receipts, amounts accruing to the Fund in the prior fiscal year that the Secretary decides are in excess of the needs of the Fund. However, the Secretary may use the excess amounts to restore capital of the Fund reduced by the difference between the charges for services of the Bureau and the cost of providing those services.

(e) The Secretary shall maintain a special deposit account in the Treasury for the Fund. The Secretary shall credit the account with amounts appropriated to the Fund and receipts of the Bureau without depositing the receipts in the Treasury as miscellaneous receipts.

Sec. 5143. Payment for services

The Secretary of the Treasury shall impose charges for Bureau of Engraving and Printing services the Secretary provides to an agency or to a foreign government under section 5114. The charges shall be in amounts the Secretary considers adequate to cover the costs of the services (including administrative and other costs related to providing the services). The agency shall pay promptly bills submitted by the Secretary, and the Secretary shall take such action, in coordination with the Secretary of State, as may be appropriate to ensure prompt payment by a foreign government of any invoice or statement of account submitted by the Secretary with respect to services rendered under section 5114.

Sec. 5144. Providing impressions of portraits and vignettes

The Secretary of the Treasury may provide impressions from an engraved portrait or vignette in the possession of the Bureau of Engraving and Printing. An impression shall be provided—

(1) at the request of—

(A) a member of Congress;

(B) a head of an agency;

(C) an art association; or

(D) a library; and

(2) for a charge and under conditions the Secretary decides are necessary to protect the public interest.

Other legal and legislative issues

South African Krugerrand

The South African Krugerrand was the world's best selling gold bullion coin until anti-apartheid movements in the mid-1980s began. Congress was moving toward a ban on the importation of the coins when President Ronald Reagan stepped in and issued Executive Order 12535 on Oct. 1, 1985 (50 Fed. Reg. 40325), which banned future importation of the coin. (For more information about this action, refer to Volume 31 of the Code of Federal Regulations, Sec. 545.101.) The ban is no longer in effect.

American Eagle gold, silver and platinum bullion coins

In late 1985, the United States introduced the world to the American Eagle gold bullion coins. The Gold Bullion Coin Act of 1985 authorized four .9167 fine gold coins: a $50 coin containing one ounce of pure gold, a $25 half-ounce coin, a $10 quarter-ounce coin and a $5 tenth-ounce coin.

The reverse design, by Dallas sculptor Miley Busiek, depicts a family of American eagles. The design was used on the reverses of all four denominations.

In 1986, a 1-ounce silver American Eagle one dollar face value bullion coin was authorized (Title 31, Sec. 5112). It features a design on the obverse modified from the Walking Liberty half dollar of 1916 to 1947, and the reverse shows a heraldic eagle and shield.

American Eagle platinum bullion coins were authorized by Congress in 1996 and first issued in 1997. They are of .9995 purity and are struck in four denominations: a $100 coin containing one ounce of platinum, a $50 half-ounce coin, a $25 quarter-ounce coin and a $10 tenth-ounce coin.

The 1-ounce platinum coin displays the highest face value ($100) ever to appear on a U.S. coin.

American Buffalo .9999 fine bullion gold coins

American Buffalo .9999 fine 24-karat gold coins were authorized by Public Law 109-145, signed into law Dec. 22, 2005. The design utilizes James Earle Fraser's design for the Indian Head 5-cent piece, more popularly known as the Buffalo nickel, produced from 1913 to 1938.

The American Buffalo gold bullion coins are the first .9999 fine gold coins struck by the United States Mint. They were first struck in 2006 as a $50 1-ounce coin, and in 2008 fractional American Buffalo coins of half-ounce, quarter ounce and tenth ounce sizes, in denominations of $25, $10 and $5 respectively, were produced.

Collectibles in retirement accounts

The Taxpayer Relief Act of 1997 (Public Law 105-34) was signed into law by President Clinton in August 1997 and allows certain bullion coins and bars as qualified investments in Individual Retirement Accounts (IRAs). Before the signing of this legislation, only gold and silver American Eagles were qualified precious metals IRA investments. The legislation amended Section 408(m) of the Internal Revenue Code and applies to taxable years beginning after Dec. 31, 1997.

While American Eagle bullion coins can be included as part of an IRA portfolio, American Buffalo gold coins may not. American Eagle 1-ounce silver bullion coins are currently the only silver coins allowed in an IRA.

Readers should consult with a tax attorney or certified public accountant for legal advice on this issue.

Executive orders

Executive Orders Relating to Coins (March 4, 1921, to date)

The executive order is an order issued by the president which, when constitutionally permitted, has the full force of law. For example, the president has the authority to proclaim "National Coin Week," either of his own volition (as President Nixon did in 1974) or at the request of Congress (as President Reagan did in 1983). Below follows a brief listing of the use of executive orders in the coin field from the Harding administration (March 4, 1921) to the present.

The use has been sparing, and certain orders with

respect to occupied countries during World War II have been omitted.

The largest single use relates to gold and silver, and is simply presented for historic interest. The abbreviations used in the *Congressional Information Service Index to Presidential Executive Orders and Proclamations* include: PR, for Presidential Proclamation, and EO, for Executive Order. No designation means it was an Administrative Order.

The fact that the annual Assay Commission has its membership designated by an executive order in 1926 does not mean that the order was subsequently followed.

Annual Assay Commission, 1926-
Membership designation
1926-08-9
Coin Week, National, proclamation
1974-PR-4286; 1983-PR-5027
Commission of Fine Arts functions expansion
1921-EO-3524
Gold Coin, bullion, and currency transactions, restrictions established
1933-EO-6260
Holding abroad by persons subject to U.S. jurisdiction, prohibition with exception for licensed coin collectors
1962-EO-11037
Revision
1934-EO-6556; 1960-EO-10896; 1961-EO-10905
Revocation
1974-EO-11825
Gold dollar weight established
1934-PR-2072
Silver and silver coins importation and transportation regulations revision
1935-24-1
Silver coinage suspension until Dec. 31, 1937, previously extracted silver minting authorization
1937-24-1
Silver coinage suspension until Dec. 31, 1938, previously extracted silver minting authorization
1938-24-2
Silver mined from U.S. natural deposits, coinage mints receipt and addition to U.S. monetary stocks regulations extension
1938-PR-2317
Silver purchase for U.S. mints, delivery requirement and procedure established
1934-EO-6814
Silver withdrawal from monetary use, suspension of free silver sales and use in coinage
1961-21-20

Gold ownership

In 1933, Americans were prohibited from private gold ownership with certain exemptions (among the exemptions were rare and unusual gold coins). The right to own gold without restrictions was not restored until Dec. 31, 1974.

Following are extracts from the Order of the Acting Secretary of the Treasury, Henry Morgenthau Jr., requiring the delivery of gold coin bullion and gold certificates to the Treasurer of the United States, followed by Executive Order 6260, relating to the hoarding, export and earmarking of gold coin, bullion, or currency, issued by President Franklin Delano Roosevelt Aug. 28, 1933. Those form the substantive basis for gold prohibition regulations.

Gold coin turn-in order of the Secretary of the Treasury

Requiring the Delivery of Gold Coin, Gold Bullion, and Gold Certificates to the Treasurer of the United States

WHEREAS Section 11 of the Federal Reserve Act of December 23, 1913, as amended ... provides ...

"Whenever in the judgment of the Secretary of the Treasury such action is necessary to protect the currency system of the United States, the Secretary of the Treasury, in his discretion, may require any or all individuals, partnerships, association and corporations to pay and deliver to the Treasurer of the United States any or all gold coin, gold bullion, and gold certificates owned by such individuals, partnerships, associations and corporations. Upon receipt of such gold coin, gold bullion or gold certificates, the Secretary of the Treasury shall pay therefor an equivalent amount of any other form of coin or currency coined or issued under the laws of the United States. ...

WHEREAS in my judgment such action is necessary to protect the currency system of the United States;

NOW, THEREFORE, I, HENRY MORGENTHAU, JR., ACTING SECRETARY of the TREASURY, do hereby require every person subject to the jurisdiction of the United States forthwith to pay and deliver to the Treasurer of the United States all gold coin, gold bullion, and gold certificates situated in the United States, owned by such person, except as follows:

A. Gold bullion owned by a person now holding such gold under a license heretofore granted by or under authority of the Secretary of the Treasury, pursuant to the Executive Order of August 23, 1933, Relating to the Hoarding, Export, and Earmarking of Gold Coin, Bullion, or Currency and to Transactions in Foreign Exchange;

B. Gold coin having a recognized special value to collectors or rare and unusual coin (but not including quarter eagles, otherwise known as $2.50 pieces);

C. Unmelted scrap gold and gold sweepings in an amount not exceeding in the aggregate $100 belonging to any one person; . . .

D. Gold coin, gold bullion, and gold certificates owned by a Federal reserve bank or the Reconstruction Finance Corporation; and

E. Gold bullion and foreign gold coin now situated in the Philippine Islands, American Samoa, Guam, Hawaii, Panama Canal Zone, Puerto Rico, or the Virgin Islands of the United States, owned by a person not domiciled or doing business in the continental United States.

Section 2. Delivery. The gold coin, gold bullion, and gold certificates herein required to be paid and delivered to the Treasurer of the United States shall be delivered by placing the same forthwith in the custody of a Federal reserve bank or branch or a bank member of the Federal Reserve System for the account of the United States. ...

Section 3. Payment and Reimbursement of Costs. Upon receipt of the confirmation signed and delivered as required under Section 2, the Secretary of the Treasury will pay for the gold coin, gold bullion, and gold certificates placed in custody for the account of the United States in accordance with Section 2, and equivalent amount of any form of coin or currency coined or issued under the laws of the United States designated by the Secretary of the Treasury. ...

Section 4. Definitions. As used in this Order, the term "person" means any individual, partnership, association, or corporation; the term "United States" means the United States and any place subject to the jurisdiction thereof; the term "continental United States" means the States of the United States, the District of Columbia, and the Territory of Alaska; the term "gold coin" means any coin containing gold, including foreign gold coin; and the term "gold bullion" means any gold which has been put through a process of smelting or refining that is in such form that its value depends upon the gold content and not upon the form, but does not include gold coin or metals containing less than five troy ounces of fine gold per short ton.

Section 5. Any individual, partnership, association, or corporation failing to comply with any requirement hereof or of any rules or regulations issued by the Secretary of the Treasury hereunder shall be subject to the penalty provided in Section 11(n) of the Federal Reserve Act, as amended.

This order may be modified or revoked at any time.

H. Morgenthau, Jr., Acting Secretary of the Treasury.
APPROVED: Franklin D. Roosevelt
THE WHITE HOUSE
December 28, 1933

Executive Order [No. 6260] August 28, 1933

Relating to the Hoarding, Export, and Earmarking of Gold Coin, Bullion, or Currency and to Transactions in Foreign Exchange:

By virtue of the authority vested in me by section 5(b) of the act of October 6, 1917, as amended by section 2 of the act of March 9, 1933, entitled "An act to provide relief in the existing national emergency in banking and for other purposes," I, FRANKLIN D. ROOSEVELT, PRESIDENT of the UNITED STATES OF AMERICA, do declare that a period of national emergency exists, and by virtue of said authority and of all other authority vested in me, do hereby prescribe the following provisions for the investigation and regulation of the hoarding, earmarking, and export of gold coin, gold bullion, and gold certificates by any person within the United States or any place subject to the jurisdiction thereof; and for the investigation and regulation of transactions in foreign exchange and transfers of credit and the export and withdrawal of currency from the United States or any place subject to the jurisdiction thereof by any person within the United States or any place subject to the jurisdiction thereof. ...

Section 3. Returns. Within 15 days from the date of this order every person in possession of and every person owning gold coin, gold bullion, or gold certificates shall make under oath and file as hereinafter provided a return to the Secretary of the Treasury containing true and complete information relative thereto, including the name and address of the person making the return; the kind and amount of such coin, bullion, or certificates

held and the location thereof; if held for another, the capacity in which held and the person for whom held, together with the post-office address of such person; and the nature of the transaction requiring the holding of such coin, bullion, or certificates and a statement explaining why such transaction cannot be carried out by the use of currency other than gold certificates; provided that no returns are required to be filed with respect to—
(a) Gold coin, gold bullion, and gold certificates in an amount not exceeding in the aggregate $100 belonging to any one person; (b) Gold coin having a recognized special value to collectors of rare and unusual coin; (c) Gold coin, gold bullion, and gold certificates acquired or held under a license heretofore granted by or under authority of the Secretary of the Treasury; and (d) Gold coin, gold bullion, and gold certificates owned by Federal Reserve banks. ...

Section 4. Acquisition of gold coin and gold bullion. No person other than a Federal Reserve bank shall after the date of this order acquire in the United States any gold coin, gold bullion, or gold certificates except under license therefor issued pursuant to this Executive order. ...

The Secretary of the Treasury, subject to such further regulations as he may prescribe, shall issue licenses authorizing the acquisition of —
(a) Gold coin or gold bullion which the Secretary is satisfied is required for a necessary and lawful transaction for which currency other than gold certificates cannot be used, by an applicant who establishes that since March 9, 1933, he has surrendered an equal amount of gold coin, gold bullion, or gold certificates to a banking institution in the continental United States or to the Treasurer of the United States; (b) Gold coin or gold bullion which the Secretary is satisfied is required by an applicant who holds a license to export such an amount of gold coin or gold bullion issued under subdivisions (c) or (d) of section 66 hereof, and (c) Gold bullion which the Secretary, or such agency as he may designate, is satisfied is required for legitimate and customary use in industry, profession, or art by an applicant regularly engaged in such industry, profession, or art, or in the business of furnishing gold therefor. Licenses issued pursuant to this section shall authorize the holder to acquire gold coin and gold bullion only from the sources specified by the Secretary of the Treasury in regulations issued hereunder.

Section 5. Holding of gold coin, gold bullion, and gold certificates. After 30 days from the date of this order no person shall hold in his possession or retain any interest, legal or equitable in any gold coin, gold bullion, or gold certificates situated in the United States. ...

Section 9. The Secretary of the Treasury is hereby authorized and empowered to issue such regulations as he may deem necessary to carry out the purposes of this order. Such regulations may provide for the detention in the United States of any gold coin, gold bullion, or gold certificates sought to be transported beyond the limits of the continental United States, pending an investigation to determine if such coin, bullion, or certificates are held or are to be acquired in violation of the provisions of this Executive order. Licenses and permits granted in accordance with the provisions of this order and the regulations prescribed hereunder, may be issued through such officers or agencies as the Secretary may designate.

Section 10. Whoever willfully violates any provision of this Executive order or of any license, order, rule, or regulation issued or prescribed hereunder, shall, upon conviction, be fined not more than $10,000, or, if a natural person, may be imprisoned for not more than 10 years, or both; and any officer, director, or agent of any corporation who knowingly participates in such violation may be punished by a like fine, imprisonment, or both.

Section 11. The Executive orders of April 5, 1933, forbidding the hoarding of gold coin, gold bullion, and gold certificates, and April 20, 1933, relating to foreign exchange and the earmarking and export of gold coin or bullion or currency, respectively, are hereby revoked. ...

FRANKLIN D. ROOSEVELT.
THE WHITE HOUSE,
August 28, 1933

United States Code, Title 18

Title 18 of the United States Code governs "crimes and criminal procedure," and several sections relate to currency mutilation, debasement of coinage, counterfeiting and other criminal offenses. What follows are extracts of Title 18. Title 18 has been enacted as positive law. This means that unlike many other sections of the United States Code, which merely evidence what the law is, Title 18 is itself the law of the land. The same is applicable to Title 31.

Presidential seal

A section of Title 18 not outlined below gives the president of the United States authority to change regulations governing the seals of the president and vice president.

On May 28, 1976, President Ford, by authority of this section of the Title, amended subsection (b) of section 1 of Executive Order No. 11649 to read that the presidential and vice presidential seals may be used "in encyclopedias, dictionaries, books, journals, pamphlets, periodicals or magazines incident to a description or history of seals, coats of arms, heraldry, or the Presidency or Vice Presidency."

Chapter 17 coins and currency

Sec. 331. Mutilation, diminution, and falsification of coins.

Whoever fraudulently alters, defaces, mutilates, impairs, diminishes, falsifies, scales, or lightens any of the coins coined at the Mints of the United States, or any foreign coins which are by law made current or are in actual use or circulation as money within the United States; or

Whoever fraudulently possesses, passes, utters, publishes, or sells, or attempts to pass, utter, publish, or sell, or brings into the United States, any such coin, knowing the same to be altered, defaced, mutilated, impaired, diminished, falsified, scaled, or lightened—

Shall be fined under this title or imprisoned not more than five years, or both.

Sec. 332. Debasement of coins; alteration of official scales, or embezzlement of metals.

If any of the gold or silver coins struck or coined at any of the Mints of the United States shall be debased, or made worse as to the proportion of fine gold or fine silver therein contained, or shall be of less weight or value than the same ought to be, pursuant to law, or if any of the scales or weights used at any of the Mints or assay offices of the United States shall be defaced, altered, increased, or diminished through the fault or connivance of any officer or person employed at the said Mints or assay offices, with a fraudulent intent; or if any such officer or person shall embezzle any of the metals at any time committed to his charge for the purpose of being coined, or any of the coins struck or coined at the said Mints, or any medals, coins, or other moneys of said Mints or assay offices at any time committed to his charge, or of which he may have assumed the charge, every such officer or person who commits any of the said offenses shall be fined or imprisoned not more than ten years, or both.

Sec. 333. Mutilation of national bank obligations.

Whoever mutilates, cuts, defaces, disfigures, or perforates, or unites or cements together, or does any other thing to any bank bill, draft, note, or other evidence of debt issued by any national banking association, or Federal Reserve bank, or the Federal Reserve System, with intent to render such bank bill, draft, note, or other evidence of debt unfit to be reissued, shall be or imprisoned not more than six months, or both.

Sec. 334. Issuance of Federal Reserve or national bank notes.

Whoever, being a Federal Reserve Agent, or an agent or employee of such Federal Reserve Agent, or of the Board of Governors of the Federal Reserve System, issues or puts in circulation any Federal Reserve notes, without complying with or in violation of the provisions of law regulating the issuance and circulation of such Federal Reserve notes; or

Whoever, being an officer acting under the provisions of Chapter 2 of Title 12, countersigns or delivers to any national banking association, or to any other company or person, any circulating notes contemplated by that chapter except in strict accordance with its provisions,

Shall be fined or imprisoned not more than five years, or both.

Sec. 335. Circulation of obligations of expired corporations.

Whoever, being a director, officer, or agent of a corporation created by Act of Congress, the charter of which has expired, or trustee thereof, or an agent of such trustee, or a person having in his possession or under his control the property of such corporation for the purpose of paying or redeeming its notes and obligations, knowingly issues, reissues, or utters as money, or in any other way knowingly puts in circulation any bill, note, check, draft, or other security purporting to have been made by any such corporation, or by any officer thereof, or purporting to have been made under authority derived therefrom, shall be fined or imprisoned not more than five years, or both.

Sec. 336. Issuance of circulating obligations of less than $1.

Whoever makes, issues, circulates, or pays out any note, check, memorandum, token, or other obligation for a less sum than $1, intended to circulate as money or to be received or used in lieu of lawful money of the United States, shall be fined or imprisoned not more than six months, or both.

Sec. 337. Coins as security for loans.

Whoever lends or borrows money or credit upon the security of such coins of the United States as the Secretary of the Treasury may from time to time designate by proclamation published in the Federal Register, during any period designated in such a proclamation, shall be fined or imprisoned not more than one year, or both.

Chapter 25 counterfeiting and forgery

Sec. 471. Obligations or securities of United States.

Whoever, with intent to defraud, falsely makes, forges, counterfeits, or alters any obligation or other security of the United States, shall be fined or imprisoned not more than 20 years, or both.

Sec. 472. Uttering counterfeit obligations or securities.

Whoever, with intent to defraud, passes, utters, publishes, or sells, or attempts to pass, utter, publish, or sell, or with like intent brings into the United States or keeps in possession or conceals any falsely made, forged, counterfeited, or altered obligation or other security of the United States, shall be or imprisoned not more than 20 years, or both.

Sec. 473. Dealing in counterfeit obligations or securities.

Whoever buys, sells, exchanges, transfers, receives, or delivers any false, forged, counterfeited, or altered obligation or other security of the United States, with the intent that the same be passed, published, or used as true and genuine, shall be fined or imprisoned not more than 20 years, or both.

Sec. 474. Plates or stones for counterfeiting obligations or securities.

(a)Whoever, having control, custody, or possession of any plate, stone, or other thing, or any part thereof, from which has been printed, or which may be prepared by direction of the Secretary of the Treasury for the purpose of printing, any obligation or other security of the United States, uses such plate, stone, or other thing, or any part thereof, or knowingly suffers the same to be used for the purpose of printing any such or similar obligation or other security, or any part thereof, except as may be printed for the use of the United States by order of the proper officer thereof; or

Whoever makes or executes any plate, stone, or other thing in the likeness of any plate designated for the printing of such obligation or other security; or

Whoever sells any such plate, stone, or other thing, or brings into the United States any such plate, stone, or other thing, except under the direction of the Secretary of the Treasury or other proper officer, or with any other intent, in either case, than that such plate, stone, or other thing be used for the printing of the obligations or other securities of the United States; or

Whoever has in his control, custody, or possession any plate, stone, or other thing in any manner made after or in the similitude of any plate, stone, or other thing, from which any such obligation or other security has been printed, with intent to use such plate, stone, or other thing, or to suffer the same to be used in forging or counterfeiting any such obligation or other security, or any part thereof; or

Whoever has in his possession or custody, except under authority from the Secretary of the Treasury or other proper officer, any obligation or other security made or executed, in whole or in part, after the similitude of any obligation or other security issued under the authority of the United States, with intent to sell or otherwise use the same; or

Whoever prints, photographs, or in any other manner makes or executes any engraving, photograph, print, or impression in the likeness of any such obligation or other security, or any part thereof, or sells any such engraving, photograph, print, or impression, except to the United States, or brings into the United States, any such engraving, photograph, print, or impression, except by direction of some proper officer of the United States; is guilty of a class B felony.

(b) For purposes of this section, the terms "plate", "stone", "thing", or "other thing" includes any electronic method used for the acquisition, recording, retrieval, transmission, or reproduction of any obligation or other security, unless such use is authorized by the Secretary of the Treasury. The Secretary shall establish a system (pursuant to section 504) to ensure that the legitimate use of such electronic methods and retention of such reproductions by businesses, hobbyists, press and others shall not be unduly restricted.

Sec. 474A. Deterrents to counterfeiting obligations and securities.

(a) Whoever has in his control or possession, after a distinctive paper has been adopted by the Secretary of the Treasury for the obligations and other securities of the United States, any similar paper adapted to the making of any such obligation or other security, except under the authority of the Secretary of the Treasury, is guilty of a class B felony.

(b) Whoever has in his control or possession, after a distinctive counterfeit deterrent has been adopted by the Secretary of the Treasury for the obligations and other securities of the United States by publication in the Federal Register, any essentially identical feature or device adapted to the making of any such obligation or security, except under the authority of the Secretary of the Treasury, is guilty of a class B felony.

(c) As used in this section—

(1) the term "distinctive paper" includes any distinctive medium of which currency is made, whether of wood pulp, rag, plastic substrate, or other natural or artificial fibers or materials; and

(2) the term "distinctive counterfeit deterrent" includes any ink, watermark, seal, security thread, optically variable device, or other feature or device;

(A) in which the United States has an exclusive property interest; or

(B) which is not otherwise in commercial use or in the public domain and which the Secretary designates as being necessary in preventing the counterfeiting of obligations or other securities of the United States.

Sec. 475. Imitating obligations or securities; advertisements.

Whoever designs, engraves, prints, makes, or executes, or utters, issues, distributes, circulates, or uses any business or professional card, notice, placard, circular, handbill, or advertisement in the likeness or similitude of any obligation or security of the United States issued under or authorized by any Act of Congress or writes, prints, or otherwise impresses upon or attaches to any such instrument, obligation, or security, or any coin of the United States, any business or professional card, notice, or advertisement, or any notice or advertisement whatever, shall be fined under this title. Nothing in this section applies to evidence of postage payment approved by the United States Postal Service.

Sec. 476. Taking impressions of tools used for obligations or securities.

Whoever, without authority from the United States, takes, procures, or makes an impression, stamp, analog, digital, or electronic image, or imprint of, from or by the use of any tool, implement, instrument, or thing used or fitted or intended to be used in printing, stamping, or impressing, or in making other tools, implements, instruments, or things to be used or fitted or intended to be used in printing, stamping, or impressing any obligation or other security of the United States, shall be fined under this title or imprisoned not more than 25 years, or both.

Sec. 477. Possessing or selling impressions of tools used for obligations or securities.

Whoever, with intent to defraud, possesses, keeps, safeguards, or controls, without authority from the United States, any imprint, stamp, analog, digital, or electronic image, or impression, taken or made upon any substance or material whatsoever, of any tool, implement, instrument or thing, used, fitted or intended to be used, for any of the purposes mentioned in section 476 of this title; or

Whoever, with intent to defraud, sells, gives, or delivers any such imprint, stamp, analog, digital, or electronic image, or impression to any other person—

Shall be fined under this title or imprisoned not more than 25 years, or both.

Sec. 478. Foreign obligations or securities.

Whoever, within the United States, with intent to defraud, falsely makes, alters, forges, or counterfeits any bond, certificate, obligation, or other security of any foreign government, purporting to be or in imitation of any such security issued under the authority of such foreign government, or any Treasury note, bill, or promise to pay, lawfully issued by such foreign government and intended to circulate as money, shall be fined or imprisoned not more than 20 years, or both.

Sec. 479. Uttering counterfeit foreign obligations or securities.

Whoever, within the United States, knowingly and with intent to defraud, utters, passes, or puts off, in payment or negotiation, any false, forged, or counterfeited bond, certificate, obligation, security, Treasury note, bill, or promise to pay, mentioned in Section 478 of this title, whether or not the same was made, altered, forged, or counterfeited within the United States, shall be fined or imprisoned not more than 20 years, or both.

Sec. 480. Possessing counterfeit foreign obligations or securities.

Whoever, within the United States, knowingly and with intent to defraud, possesses or delivers any false, forged, or counterfeit bond, certificate, obligation, security, treasury note, bill, promise to pay, bank note, or bill issued by a bank or corporation of any foreign country, shall be fined or imprisoned not more than 20 years, or both.

Sec. 481. Plates, stones, or analog, digital, or electronic images for counterfeiting foreign obligation securities.

Whoever, within the United States except by lawful authority, controls, holds, or possesses any plate, stone, or other thing, or any part thereof, from which has been printed or may be printed any counterfeit note, bond, obligation, or other security, in whole or in part, of any foreign government, bank, or corporation, or uses such plate, stone, or other thing, or knowingly permits or suffers the same to be used in counterfeiting such foreign obligations, or any part thereof; or

Whoever, except by lawful authority, makes or engraves any plate, stone, or other thing in the likeness or similitude of any plate, stone, or other thing designated for the printing of the genuine issues of the obligations of any foreign government, bank, or corporation; or

Whoever, with intent to defraud, makes, executes, acquires, scans, captures, records, receives, transmits, reproduces, sells, or has in such person's control, custody, or possession, an analog, digital, or electronic image of any bond, certificate, obligation, or other security of any foreign government, or of any treasury note, bill, or promise to pay, lawfully issued by such foreign government and intended to circulate as money; or

Whoever, except by lawful authority, prints, photographs, or makes, executes, or sells any engraving, photograph, print, or impression in the likeness of any genuine note, bond, obligation, or other security, or any part thereof, of any foreign government, bank, or corporation; or

Whoever brings into the United States any counterfeit plate, stone, or other thing, engraving, photograph, print, or other impressions of the notes, bonds, obligations, or other securities of any foreign government, bank, or corporation—

Shall be fined under this title or imprisoned not more than 25 years, or both.

Sec. 482. Foreign bank notes.

Whoever, within the United States, with intent to defraud, falsely makes, alters, forges, or counterfeits any bank note or bill issued by a bank or corporation of any foreign country, and intended by the law or usage of such foreign country to circulate as money, such bank or corporation being authorized by the laws of such country, shall be fined or imprisoned not more than 20 years, or both.

Sec. 483. Uttering counterfeit foreign bank notes.

Whoever, within the United States, utters, passes, puts off, or tenders in payment, with intent to defraud, any such false, forged, altered, or counterfeited bank note or bill, mentioned in section 482 of this title, knowing the same to be so false, forged, altered, and counterfeited, whether or not the same was made, forged, altered, or counterfeited within the United States, shall be fined or imprisoned not more than 20 years, or both.

Sec. 484. Connecting parts of different notes.

Whoever so places or connects together different parts of two or more notes, bills, or other genuine instruments issued under the authority of the United States, or by any foreign government, or corporation, as to produce one instrument, with intent to defraud, shall be guilty of forgery in the same manner as if the parts to put together were falsely made or forged, and shall be fined or imprisoned not more than 10 years, or both.

Sec. 485. Coins or bars.

Whoever falsely makes, forges, or counterfeits any coin or bar in resemblance or similitude of any coin of a denomination higher than 5 cents or any gold or silver bar coined or stamped at any Mint or assay office of the United States, or in resemblance or similitude of any foreign gold or silver coin current in the United States or in actual use and circulation as money within the United States; or

Whoever passes, utters, publishes, sells, possesses, or brings into the United States any false, forged, or counterfeit coin or bar, knowing the same to be false, forged, or counterfeit, with intent to defraud any body politic or corporate, or any person, or attempts the commission of any offense described in this paragraph— Shall be fined or imprisoned not more than fifteen years, or both.

Sec. 486. Uttering coins of gold, silver or other metal.

Whoever, except as authorized by law, makes or utters or passes, or attempts to utter or pass, any coins of gold or silver or other metal, or alloys of metals, intended for use as current money, whether in the resemblance of coins of the United States or of foreign countries, or of original design, shall be fined or imprisoned not more than five years, or both.

Sec. 487. Making or possessing counterfeit dies for coins.

Whoever, without lawful authority, makes any die, hub, or mold, or any part thereof, either of steel or plaster, or any other substance, in likeness or similitude, as to the design or the inscription thereon, of any die, hub, or mold designated for the coining or making of any of the genuine gold, silver, nickel, bronze, copper, or other coins coined at the Mints of the United States; or

Whoever, without lawful authority, possesses any such die, hub, or mold, or any part thereof, or permits the same to be used for or in aid of the counterfeiting of any such coins of the United States— Shall be fined or imprisoned not more than fifteen years, or both.

Sec. 488. Making or possessing counterfeit dies for foreign coins.

Whoever, within the United States, without lawful authority, makes any die, hub, or mold, or any part thereof, either of steel or of plaster, or of any other substance, in the likeness or similitude, as to the design or the inscription thereon, of any die, hub, or mold designated for the coining of the genuine coin of any foreign government; or

Whoever, without lawful authority, possesses any such die, hub, or mold, or any part thereof, or conceals, or knowingly suffers the same to be used for the counterfeiting of any foreign coin—Shall be fined or imprisoned not more than five years, or both.

Sec. 489. Making or possessing likeness of coins.

Whoever, within the United States, makes or brings therein from any foreign country, or possesses with intent to sell, give away, or in any other manner uses the same, except under authority of the Secretary of the Treasury or other proper officer of the United States, any token, disk, or device in the likeness or similitude as to design, color, or the inscription thereon of any of the coins of the United States or of any foreign country issued as money, either under the authority of the United States or under the authority of any foreign government shall be fined under this title.

Sec. 490. Minor coins.

Whoever falsely makes, forges, or counterfeits any coin in the resemblance or similitude of any of the one-cent and 5-cent coins minted at the mints of the United States; or

Whoever passes, utters, publishes, or sells, or brings into the United States, or possesses any such false, forged, or counterfeited coin, with intent to defraud any person, shall be fined or imprisoned not more than three years, or both.

Sec. 491. Tokens or paper used as money.

(a) Whoever, being 18 years of age or over, not lawfully authorized, makes, issues, or passes any coin, card, token, or device in metal, or its compounds, intended to be used as money, or whoever, being 18 years of age or over, with intent to defraud, makes, utters, inserts, or uses any card, token, slug, disk, device, paper, or other thing similar in size and shape to any of the lawful coins or other currency of the United States or any coin or other currency not legal tender in the United States, to procure anything of value, or the use or enjoyment of any property or service from any automatic merchandise vending machine, postage-stamp machine, turnstile, fare box, coinbox telephone, parking meter or other lawful receptacle, depository, or contrivance designed to receive or to be operated by lawful coins or other currency of the United States, shall be fined under this title, or imprisoned not more than one year, or both.

(b) Whoever manufactures, sells, offers, or advertises for sale, or exposes or keeps with intent to furnish or sell any token, slug, disk, device, paper, or other thing similar in size and shape to any of the lawful coins or other currency of the United States, or any token, disk, paper, or other device issued or authorized in connection with rationing or food and fiber distribution by any agency of the United States, with knowledge or reason to believe that such tokens, slugs, disks, devices, papers, or other things are intended to be used unlawfully or fraudulently to procure anything of value, or the use or enjoyment of any property or service from any automatic merchandise vending machine, postage-stamp machine, turnstile, fare box, coinbox telephone, parking meter, or other lawful receptacle, depository, or contrivance designed to receive or to be operated by lawful coins or other currency of the United States shall be fined under this title or imprisoned not more than one year, or both.

Nothing contained in this section shall create immunity from criminal prosecution under the laws of any State, Commonwealth of Puerto Rico, territory, possession, or the District of Columbia.

(c) "Knowledge or reason to believe", within the meaning of paragraph (b) of this section, may be shown by proof that any law-enforcement officer has, prior to the commission of the offense with which the defendant is charged, informed the defendant that tokens, slugs, disks, or other devices of the kind manufactured, sold, offered, or advertised for sale by him or exposed or kept with intent to furnish or sell, are being used unlawfully or fraudulently to operate certain specified automatic merchandise vending machines, postage-stamp machines, turnstiles, fare boxes, coin-box telephones, parking meters, or other receptacles, depositories, or contrivances, designed to receive or to be operated by lawful coins of the United States.

Sec. 492. Forfeiture of counterfeit paraphernalia.

All counterfeits of any coins or obligations or other securities of the United States or of any foreign government, or any articles, devices, and other things made, possessed, or used in violation of this chapter or of sections 331–333, 335, 336, 642 or 1720, of this title, or any material or apparatus used or fitted or intended to be used, in the making of such counterfeits, articles, devices or things, found in the possession of any person without authority from the Secretary of the Treasury or other proper officer, shall be forfeited to the United States.

Whoever, having the custody or control of any such counterfeits, material, apparatus, articles, devices, or other things, fails or refuses to surrender possession thereof upon request by any authorized agent of the Treasury Department, or other proper officer, shall be fined under this title or imprisoned not more than one year, or both.

Whenever, except as hereinafter in this section provided, any person interested in any article, device, or other thing, or material or apparatus seized under this section files with the Secretary of the Treasury, before the disposition thereof, a petition for the remission or mitigation of such forfeiture, the Secretary of the Treasury, if he finds that such forfeiture was incurred without willful negligence or without any intention on the part of the petitioner to violate the law, or finds the existence of such mitigating circumstances as to justify the remission or the mitigation of such forfeiture, may remit or mitigate the same upon such terms and conditions as he deems reasonable and just.

If the seizure involves offenses other than offenses against the coinage, currency, obligations or securities of the United States or any foreign government, the petition for the remission or mitigation of forfeiture shall be referred to the Attorney General, who may remit or mitigate the forfeiture upon such terms as he deems reasonable and just.

Sec. 504. Printing and filming of United States and foreign obligations and securities.

Notwithstanding any other provision of this chapter, the following are permitted:

(1) The printing, publishing, or importation, or the making or importation of the necessary plates for such printing or publishing, of illustrations of—

(A) postage stamps of the United States,

(B) revenue stamps of the United States,

(C) any other obligation or other security of the United States, and

(D) postage stamps, revenue stamps, notes, bonds, and any other obligation or other security of any foreign government, bank, or corporation.

Illustrations permitted by the foregoing provisions of this section shall be made in accordance with the following conditions—

(i) all illustrations shall be in black and white, except that illustrations of postage stamps issued by the United States or by any foreign government, and stamps issued under the Migratory Hunting Stamp Act of 1934 may be in color;

(ii) all illustrations (including illustrations of uncanceled postage stamps in color) shall be of a size less than three-fourths or more than one and one-half, in linear dimension, of each part of any matter so illustrated which is covered by subparagraph (A), (B), (C), or (D) of this paragraph, except that black and white illustrations of postage and revenue stamps issued by the United States or by any foreign government and colored illustrations of canceled postage stamps issued by the United States may be in the exact linear dimension in which the stamps were issued; and

(iii) the negatives and plates used in making the illustrations shall be destroyed after their final use in accordance with this section.

The Secretary of the Treasury shall prescribe regulations to permit color illustrations of such currency of the United States as the Secretary determines may be appropriate for such purposes.

(2) The provisions of this section shall not permit the reproduction of illustrations of obligations or other securities, by or through electronic methods used for the acquisition, recording, retrieval, transmission, or reproduction of any obligation or other security, unless such use is authorized by the Secretary of the Treasury. The Secretary shall establish a system to ensure that the legitimate use of such electronic methods and retention of such reproductions by businesses, hobbyists, press or others shall not be unduly restricted.

(3) The making or importation of motion-picture films, microfilms, or slides, for projection upon a screen or for use in telecasting, of postage and revenue stamps and other obligations and securities of the United States, and postage and revenue stamps, notes, bonds, and other obligations or securities of any foreign government, bank, or corporation. No prints or other reproductions shall be made from such films or slides, except for the purposes of paragraph (1), without the permission of the Secretary of the Treasury.

For the purposes of this section the term "postage stamp" includes postage meter stamps.

Hobby Protection Act

The legal effect of government on numismatics is not limited to laws. The "Hobby Protection Act," passed by Congress, became effective with the passage of regulations by the Federal Trade Commission (16 CFR part 304). See section in this chapter under Federal Trade Commission for more information.

Freedom of Information Act

Collectors can make use of the Freedom of Information Act when doing research on the U.S. Mint, Bureau of Engraving and Printing, the U.S. Department of Treasury, or other governmental agencies.

Known as 5 U.S.C. 552, the act requires agencies to maintain and make available for public inspection and copying, current indexes providing identifying information for the public as to any matter issued, adopted or promulgated after July 4, 1967, and required to be made available or published. There are certain exceptions.

Material that is not yet in the National Archives is accessible under the FOIA. All administrative agencies of the government are liable (except for certain specific exceptions) to comply with requests. There may be charges for the information requested, designed to reflect its actual cost, and (usually) it must be requested with specificity.

The Treasury Department's Internet site offers information about filing a FOIA request, procedures required in each individual agency within the Treasury Department as well as the addresses and telephone numbers of FOIA officers in each agency. Individual agencies offer an electronic reading room as well as a FOIA Frequently Asked Questions section.

The Treasury's FOIA site can be accessed at **www. treasury.gov/FOIA**.

Each agency is required to separately state and publish in the Federal Register the procedures it will follow. Each agency is required to make a determination within 10 days of receipt (Saturdays, Sundays and public holidays excepted) whether or not it will reply, and, if an appeal is taken, determine that within 20 days. If an agency improperly withholds documents, attorney's fees and other litigation costs may possibly be assessed against the government.

Several types of documents are specifically exempt from disclosure: Properly classified material; limited kinds of purely internal matters; matters exempt from disclosure by other statutes; trade secrets or commercial or financial information obtained from a person and privileged or confidential; internal agency communications that represent the deliberative, pre-decisional process, attorney work product, or attorney-client records; information that would be a clearly unwarranted invasion of personal privacy; law enforcement records to the extent that one of six specific harms could result from disclosure; bank examination records; and oil well and similar information.

Selected coinage laws 1791 to 1989

Below is a selected list of coinage legislation acted on by Congress from the 1791 Joint Resolution that authorized creation of a Mint through commemorative coins of 1990. The list is incomplete in that it does not include every enacted bill pertaining to coinage. Coinage legislation becoming law after 1989 is reviewed in the following section.

The listing offers the date of passage (either when approved by the president or when a veto was overridden by the Senate and House), followed by the chapter in the session laws or, if approved after 1959, the public law number is listed. The first two digits of each public law number indicate which Congress passed the law, while the digits following the dash indicate the number of the law enacted. The last notation is a number signifying in which volume of the Statutes at Large the complete text of the law is found.

J. Res. No. 3, March 3, 1791, 1 Stat. 225	Joint Resolution to authorize a Mint for the United States.
April 2, 1792, ch. 16, 1 Stat. 246.	Original Mint Act.
May 8, 1792, ch. 39, 1 Stat. 283.	Authorization for purchase of copper for cents and half cents.
Jan. 14, 1793, ch. 2, 1 Stat. 299.	Changes weight of copper cent and half cent.
Feb. 9, 1793, ch. 5, 1 Stat. 300.	Legal status of foreign coins in U.S.
March 3, 1795, ch. 47, 1 Stat. 439.	Permits president to reduce weight of copper coinage and allows seigniorage.
Feb. 1, 1798, ch. 11, 1 Stat. 539.	Legal status of foreign coins in U.S.
May 14, 1800, ch. 70, 2 Stat. 86.	Extension of Mint location at Philadelphia for two years.
March 3, 1801, ch. 21, 2 Stat. 111.	Further extension of Mint location at Philadelphia.
April 10, 1806, ch. 22, 2 Stat. 374.	Legal status of foreign coins in U.S.
March 3, 1819, ch. 97, 3 Stat. 525.	Continues in force legal tender values of foreign coin in U.S.
May 19, 1828, ch. 67, 4 Stat. 277.	Continuation of Mint at Philadelphia until otherwise provided by law.
June 28, 1834, ch. 96, 4 Stat. 700.	Reduces weight of foreign gold coins (revaluation of the dollar).
March 3, 1835, ch. 39, 4 Stat. 774.	Authorizes establishment of Branch Mints.
Jan. 18, 1837, ch. 3, 5 Stat. 136.	Coinage Act of 1837, codification repealing all prior inconsistent laws.
April 22, 1864, ch. 64, 13 Stat. 54.	Two-cent coin created.
Feb. 12, 1873, ch. 131, 17 Stat. 424.	Coinage Act of 1873 (codification).
Jan. 29, 1874, ch. 19, 18 Stat. 6, 31 U.S.C. Sec. 5111(a)(4).	Permits U.S. Mint to strike coins for foreign governments.
June 20, 1874, ch. 320, 18 Stat. 97.	Re-establishes New Orleans as a Branch Mint.
Jan. 14, 1875, ch. 15, 18 Stat. 296.	Resumption of specie payment authorized.
March 3, 1875, ch. 143, 18 Stat. 478.	Creation of 20-cent coin.
April 17, 1876, ch. 63, 19 Stat. 33.	Use of silver coin to redeem fractional currency permitted.
Feb. 28, 1878, ch. 20, 20 Stat. 25.	Bland-Allison Act, reauthorization of standard silver dollar.
May 2, 1878, ch. 79, 20 Stat. 47	Prohibits further coining of 20-cent coin.
June 9, 1879, ch. 12, 21 Stat. 8, now part of 31 U.S.C. Sec. 5103.	Limits legal tender status of silver coins.
March 3, 1887, ch. 396. 24 Stat. 634.	Trade dollar eliminated.
July 14, 1890, ch. 708, 26 Stat. 289.	Silver purchase act, discontinuance of dollar coinage.
Sept. 26, 1890, ch. 944, 26 Stat. 484, 31 U.S.C. Sec. 5112.	Prohibits design changes more often than once in 25 years.
Sept. 26, 1890, ch. 945, 26 Stat. 485.	Discontinues gold $3 and $1 coins, copper-nickel 3-cent coin.
Nov. 1, 1893, ch. 8, 28 Stat. 4	Bimetallism. Formerly 31 USC 311.
June 4, 1897, ch. 2, 30 Stat. 27.	Recoinage of noncurrent gold and silver coin authorized by appropriation.
March 14, 1900, ch. 41, 31 Stat. 45.	Gold Standard Act of 1900.
Aug. 23, 1912, ch. 350, 37 Stat. 384.	Redefines duties of superintendents of the Mints and New York Assay Office.
Aug. 28, 1933, EO 6260.	Recall of gold coins.
Jan. 30, 1934, ch. 6, 48 Stat. 337.	Gold Reserve Act of 1934, effectively ending gold coinage.
Dec. 18, 1942, ch. 767, 56 Stat. 1064.	War Powers Act of 1942 (authorizes compositional change in cent, creation of a 3-cent coin).
Sept. 5, 1962, Public Law 87-643, 76 Stat. 440.	Compositional change eliminating tin.
Aug. 20, 1963, Public Law 88-102, 77 Stat. 129.	Permits appropriations for new Philadelphia Mint, subsequently Denver Mint.
Dec. 30, 1963, Public Law 88-256,	Authorizes Kennedy half dollar 77 Stat. 843.
Sept. 3, 1964, Public Law 88-580	Authorizes "date freeze" on coinage.
July 23, 1965, Public Law 89-81	The Coinage Act of 1965, authorizes clad coinage, silver-clad half dollars.
June 24, 1967, Public Law 90-29	Restores Mint marks to coinage.

Dec. 31, 1970, Public Law 91-607	Authorizes Eisenhower dollar; ends silver in half dollar; directs transfer of Carson City silver dollars to General Services Administration
Oct. 6, 1972, Public Law 92-463	Federal Advisory Committee Act of 1972; effectively abolished Assay Commission as of Jan. 4, 1975. (See Public Law 96-209.)
Sept. 21, 1973, Public Law 93-110	Set gold value at $42.22 per ounce. Legalizes private gold ownership when Treasury secretary determines it to be in the national interest. (See Public Law 93-373.)
Oct. 18, 1973, Public Law 93-127	Authorizes Bicentennial coinage; new reverse for quarter dollar, half dollar and dollar, authorizes dual-date obverse, and silver-copper clad collector coins
Nov. 29, 1973, Public Law 93-167	Hobby Protection Act.
Dec. 11, 1973, Public Law 93-179	American Revolution Bicentennial Administration created as successor to Bicentennial Commission.
Aug. 14, 1974, Public Law 93-373	Legalizes private gold ownership, Dec. 31, 1974.
Oct. 11, 1974, Public Law 93-441	Authorizes compositional change in 1-cent coin under certain prescribed circumstances, by either lowering the copper content or permitting a new composition other than copper-zinc. Authorizes date changes for Bicentennial coins; also authorizes transfer of 10 percent of Eisenhower dollar sales to Eisenhower College.
Dec. 26, 1974, Public Law 93-541	Amends Bicentennial legislation to allow simultaneous production of Bicentennial coins and regular-dated (1974) coins.
Dec. 17, 1974, Public Law 93-554	Releases funds to Eisenhower College from Public Law 93-441.
Oct. 10, 1978, Public Law 95-447	Authorizes Anthony dollar.
March 7, 1979, Public Law 96-2	Authorizes Carson City Mint silver dollar sale (final disposal).
March 14, 1980, Public Law 96-209	Abolishes position of Assay Commissioner.
Dec. 23, 1981, Public Law 97-104	George Washington commemorative half dollar authorized.
July 22, 1982, Public Law 97-220	Olympic commemorative coin legislation.
Sept. 13, 1982, Public Law 97-258	Revision of Title 31, U.S. Code (codification).
Nov. 14, 1983, Public Law 98-151	Directs Treasury secretary to produce Uncirculated coin sets.
July 9, 1985, Public Law 99-61	Statue of Liberty-Ellis Island Commemorative Coin Act.
July 9, 1985, Public Law 99-61	Liberty Coin Act— Silver Dollar Liberty Coin.
Dec. 17, 1985, Public Law 99-185	Gold Bullion Coin Act of 1985.
Oct. 11, 1986, Public Law 99-514	Tax Reform Act of 1986 (bullion coins with IRAs).
Oct. 29, 1986, Public Law 99-582	Bicentennial of Constitution commemorative coins.
Nov. 7, 1986, Public Law 99-631	Ban importation of Soviet gold coins, 22 USC sec. 5100.
Oct. 28, 1987, Public Law 100-141	Olympic Commemorative Coin Act of 1988.
Aug. 1, 1988, Public Law 100-378	Bicentennial of U.S. Congress Commemorative Coin Act.
Oct 3, 1988, Public Law 100-467	Dwight D. Eisenhower Commemorative Coin Act of 1988.
Nov. 11, 1988, Public Law 100-647	Prohibition on collectibles not to include State coins.
Nov. 17, 1988, Public Law 100-673	Authorizes Bicentennial of the U.S. Congress commemorative coins.
Nov. 18, 1989, Public Law 100-696	Uses of commemorative coin surcharges.
June 9, 1989, Public Law 101-36	Authorizes first-strike ceremony for the Bicentennial of the Congress Commemorative Coins at U.S. Capitol.

Recent numismatic legislation

The legislative processes leading to the laws next listed, some of those enacted from 1990 to 2010 that relate to coins, can be briefly described, as follows:

Congress meets for a two-year period commencing in the early January of odd-numbered years. Elections take place in even-numbered years, with presidential elections every other term. Each meeting of Congress is divided into two sessions.

When a coin-related bill is introduced in the House, it is referred to the House Committee on Banking and Financial Services, and then to a subcommittee, usu-ally the Subcommittee on Domestic and International Monetary Policy.

The Senate Committee on Banking, Housing and Urban Affairs considers numismatic legislation that has been introduced in the Senate.

Since passage of the Bland-Allison Act of 1878 (which created the Morgan dollar) over the veto of President Hayes, no numismatic-related bill has been passed over the veto of an incumbent president. (Some commemorative coin bills were vetoed between 1928 and 1960; Congress sustained all vetoes.)

Coin legislation of interest that has become law since 1990 is presented here, listed by year of issue and official title, with the denomination of the coins authorized, legislative purpose, date of signing by the president and Public Law number.

Laws dealing with national medals are listed in a later section. Bills that did not become law are not listed.

1991 Mount Rushmore 50th Anniversary
Authorized copper-nickel clad half dollar, silver dollar and gold $5 coin. Signed into law July 16, 1990 (Public Law 101-332). Amended Sept. 29, 1994, by Public Law 103-328, to allow Mount Rushmore officials to tap $6 million from surcharges that were originally specified to be paid to the government for reduction of the national debt.

1991 Korean War Memorial
Authorized silver dollar to commemorate Korean War veterans. Signed into law Oct. 31, 1990 (Public Law 101-495).

1991 USO 50th Anniversary
Authorized silver dollar to commemorate United Service Organizations. Signed into law Oct. 2, 1990 (Public Law 101-404).

1992 Olympics
Authorized copper-nickel clad half dollar, silver dollar and gold $5 coin to commemorate 1992 Olympic Games. Signed into law Oct. 3, 1990 (Public Law 101-406).

1992 White House Bicentennial
Authorized silver dollar to mark the bicentennial of the laying of the cornerstone of the White House. Signed into law May 13, 1992 (Public Law 102-281).

1992 Christopher Columbus Quincentenary
Authorized copper-nickel clad half dollar, silver dollar and gold $5 coin. Marks the 500th anniversary of Columbus' first voyage to the New World. Signed into law May 13, 1992 (Public Law 102-281).

1993 Bill of Rights/James Madison
Authorized silver half dollar, silver dollar and gold $5 coin to commemorate the Bill of Rights and its author, James Madison. Signed into law May 13, 1992 (Public Law 102-281).

1994 World Cup USA
Authorized copper-nickel clad half dollar, silver dollar and gold $5 coin to commemorate the first World Cup soccer games held in the United States. Signed into law May 13, 1992 (Public Law 102-281).

1991-1995 World War II 50th Anniversary
Authorized copper-nickel clad half dollar, silver dollar and gold $5 coin in commemoration of the 50th anniversary of American involvement in World War II. Signed into law Oct. 14, 1992 (Public Law 102-414).

1743-1993 Thomas Jefferson 250th Anniversary
Authorized silver dollar to celebrate the 250th birthday of Thomas Jefferson. Signed into law Dec. 14, 1993 (Public Law 103-186).

1994 Prisoner of War
Authorized silver dollar to commemorate American POWs. Signed into law Dec. 14, 1993 (Public Law 103-186).

1994 Vietnam Veterans Memorial
Authorized silver dollar to mark the 10th anniversary of the Vietnam Veterans memorial. Signed into law Dec. 14, 1993 (Public Law 103-186).

1994 Women in Military Service
Authorized silver dollar to honor American women serving in the military. Signed into law Dec. 14, 1993 (Public Law 103-186).

1994 U.S. Capitol Bicentennial
Authorized silver dollar to commemorate the 200th anniversary of the building of the U.S. Capitol. Signed into law Dec. 14, 1993 (Public Law 103-186).

1995 Civil War Battlefields
Authorized clad half dollar, silver dollar and gold $5 coin to commemorate Civil War battlefields. Signed into law Oct. 5, 1992 (Public Law 102-379).

1995 Special Olympics World Games
Authorized silver dollar to commemorate the Special Olympics. Signed into law Sept. 29, 1994 (Public Law 103-328).

1995-1996 Games of the XXVI Olympiad, Atlanta
Authorized four copper-nickel clad half dollars, eight silver dollars and four gold $5 coins to commemorate the 1996 Olympic Games in Atlanta.

This law included as a separate title the 1992 Mint Reform law. The reform law authorized a numismatic enterprise fund, authorized the Citizens Commemorative Coin Advisory Committee and granted the Treasury secretary authority to make certain changes to the American Eagle gold bullion coins without seeking congressional approval (for example, to produce a .9999 fine gold version of the American Eagle).

Signed into law Oct. 6, 1992 (Public Law 102-390). Law was amended to adjust mintages on Dec. 26, 1995 (Public Law 104-74).

1996 National Community Service

Authorized silver dollar to honor those involved in National Community Service. Signed into law Sept. 29, 1994 (Public Law 103-328).

1996 Smithsonian 150th Anniversary

Authorized silver dollar and gold $5 to celebrate the 150th anniversary of the founding of the Smithsonian Institution. Signed into law Jan. 10, 1996 (Public Law 104-96).

1996 U.S. Commemorative Coin Act

Approved specific commemorative coin reforms:

➤ Requires the Mint to recover expenses before payment of surcharges.

➤ Requires recipient organization to submit an audited financial statement that verifies that the organization has raised funds from private sources in an amount equal to or greater than the maximum amount of surcharges the organization may receive from the sale of the coins.

➤ Requires annual audits of the organization after it begins receiving surcharge payments from the Mint. The audits would be required until all of the surcharge funds are expended.

➤ Sets minimum requirements for the annual audits.

➤ Requires accounting of the surcharge moneys separate from all other revenues and expenditures of the recipient organization.

➤ Requires the recipient organization to provide its books and records relating to expenditure of surcharges to the Treasury's inspector general or the comptroller general.

➤ Prohibits surcharge moneys derived from sale of the coins from being used to lobby Congress on numismatic legislation.

Signed into law Sept. 30, 1996 (Title 31 Sec. 5112)

1997 United States Botanic Garden

Authorized silver dollar to honor the national Botanic Garden in Washington, D.C. Signed into law Sept. 29, 1994 (Public Law 103-328).

1997 Franklin Delano Roosevelt

Authorized gold $5 coin to honor dedication of Franklin Delano Roosevelt Memorial. Signed into law Oct. 20, 1996 (Public Law 104-329).

1997 Jackie Robinson

Authorized silver dollar and gold $5 coin to honor Jackie Robinson as first African-American to play in Major League Baseball. Signed into law Oct. 20, 1996 (Public Law 104-329).

1997 National Law Enforcement Officers Memorial

Authorized silver dollar to honor law enforcement officers. Signed into law Oct. 20, 1996 Public Law 104-329).

1998 30th anniversary of the death of Robert F. Kennedy

Authorized silver dollar to commemorate the 1968 assassination of Attorney General Robert F. Kennedy. Signed into law Sept. 29, 1994 (Public Law 103-328).

1998 Black Revolutionary War Patriots

Authorized silver dollar to honor African-Americans who fought in the Revolutionary War. Signed into law Oct. 20, 1996 (Public Law 104-329).

1999-2008 50 States Commemorative Circulating Quarters

Authorized production of circulating commemorative quarter dollars with reverse design honoring each state. Signed into law on Dec. 1, 1997 (Public Law 105-124).

1999 150th Anniversary of the death of Dolley Madison

Authorized silver dollar to honor first lady Dolley Madison. Signed into law Oct. 20, 1996 (Public Law 104-329).

1999 Bicentennial of the death of George Washington

Authorized $5 gold coin to commemorate the death of George Washington in 1799. Signed into law Oct. 20, 1996 (Public Law 104-329).

1999 125th Anniversary of Yellowstone National Park

Authorized silver dollar to commemorate the first national park. Signed into law Oct. 20, 1996 (Public Law 104-329).

2000 United States $1 Coin Act

Authorized a gold-colored dollar to be struck for circulation as a replacement for the Anthony dollar. Signed into law Dec. 1, 1997 (Public Law 105-124).

2000 Bicentennial of the Library of Congress
Authorized silver dollar and either a gold $5 coin or gold-platinum bimetallic $10 coin to commemorate the 200th anniversary of the founding the Library of Congress. Signed into law Oct. 19, 1998 (Public Law 105-268).

2000 Leif Ericson Millennium
Authorized silver dollars to be struck on behalf of Iceland and the United States. Signed into law Dec. 6, 1999 (Public Law 106-126).

2001 Capitol Visitor Center
Authorized copper-nickel clad half dollar, gold $5 coin and gold-platinum ringed bimetallic $10 coin to mark the first convening of Congress. Signed into law Dec. 6, 1999 (Public Law 106-126).

2001 American Buffalo
Authorized silver dollar to commemorate the opening of the Museum of the American Indian of the Smithsonian Institution. Signed into law Oct. 27, 2002 (Public Law 106-375)

2002 Bicentennial of the U.S. Military Academy at West Point
Authorized silver dollar to commemorate West Point. Signed into law Sept. 29, 1994 (Public Law 103-328).

2002 Winter Olympic Games
Authorized silver dollar and gold $5 coin to honor the participation of American athletes in the 2010 Olympic Winter games in Salt Lake City, Utah. Signed into law Nov. 6, 2000 (Public Law 106-435).

2003 Centennial of First Flight
Authorized copper-nickel clad half dollar, silver dollar and $10 gold coin to commemorate the first controlled, heavier-than-air powered flight of the Wright Brothers in 1903. Signed into law Dec. 1, 1997 (Public Law 105-124).

2003-2005 5-cent coin designs
Authorized new reverse designs for the obverse and reverse of the 5-cent coin for coins issued in 2003, 2004 and 2005 in recognition of the bicentennial of the Louisiana Purchase and the expedition of Meriwether Lewis and William Clark. Also established the Citizens Coinage Advisory Committee. Signed into law April 23, 2003 (Public Law 108-15). A technical amendment allowed the U.S. Mint to issue, after Dec. 31, 2005, numismatic items that contain 5-cent coins minted in the years 2004 and 2005. Signed into law June 15, 2006 (Public Law 109-230).

2004 Thomas Edison
Authorized silver dollar to commemorate the many accomplishments of inventor Thomas Edison. Signed into law Oct. 31, 1998 (Public Law 105-331). A law to extend the date for surcharge payments was signed on Feb. 8, 2007 (Public Law 110-3).

2004 Lewis and Clark Expedition
Authorized silver dollars to commemorate the bicentennial of the Meriwether Lewis and William Clark expedition. Signed into law Dec. 6, 1999 (Public Law 106-126). It was amended to change surcharge recipients on June 15, 2006 (Public Law 109-232).

2005 John Marshall
Authorized silver dollars honoring John Marshall, chief justice of the United States from 1801 to 1835. Signed into law Aug. 6, 2004 (Public Law 108-290).

2005 Marine Corps 230th Anniversary
Authorized silver dollars commemorating the 230th anniversary of the U.S. Marine Corps and to support construction of the Marine Corps Heritage Center. Signed into law Aug. 6, 2004 (Public Law 108-291).

2005 Presidential $1 Coin Act
Authorized production of dollar coins in commemoration of each of the past presidents of the United States to improve circulation of the dollar coin, to create the new First Spouse Bullion Coin Program, and to provide for American Buffalo .9999 fine gold bullion coins. Signed into law Dec. 22, 2005 (Public Law 109-145).

2006 Benjamin Franklin
Authorized two silver dollars, one with a younger Franklin image and one with an older Franklin image, honoring the 300th anniversary of Franklin's birth in 2006. Signed into law Dec. 21, 2004 (Public Law 108-464).

2006 Old San Francisco Mint
Authorized production of $5 gold coins and silver dollars in commemoration of the Old Mint at San Francisco, otherwise known as the "Granite Lady." Signed into law June 15, 2006 (Public Law 109-230).

2007 Jamestown 400th Anniversary
Authorized the production of silver dollars and $5 gold coins to honor the founding of the colony at Jamestown, Va., the first permanent English colony in America. Signed into law Aug. 6, 2004 (Public Law 108-289). A technical amendment affecting surcharge distribution was signed into law on Oct. 29, 2009 (Public Law 111-96, Section 8).

2007 Little Rock Central High School Desegregation
Authorized production of silver dollars honoring the 50th anniversary of the desegregation of Little Rock

Central High School in Little Rock, Ark. Signed into law Dec. 22, 2005 (Public Law 109-146).

2007 Dollar Inscriptions and Territory quarter dollars

Reversing the placement of the inscription "In God We Trust" on the Presidential and Native American dollar coins from the edge to the obverse or reverse, and providing for the redesign and issuance of circulating quarter dollars honoring the District of Columbia and each of the U.S. territories. Signed into law Dec. 26, 2007 (Public Law 110-161).

2008 America's Beautiful National Parks quarter dollars

Authorized a program for circulating quarter dollar coins that are emblematic of a national park or other national site in each State, the District of Columbia, and each territory of the United States. Signed into law Dec. 23, 2008 (Public Law 110-456).

2008 American Bald Eagle

Authorized production of copper-nickel clad half dollars, silver dollars and gold $5 coins to celebrate the recovery of the bald eagle, the national living symbol of freedom. Signed into law Dec. 23, 2004 (Public Law 108-486).

2008 Native American $1 Coin

Authorized the production of dollar coins in commemoration of Native Americans and the important contributions made by Indian tribes and individual Native Americans to the development of the United States and the history of the United States. Signed into law Sept. 20, 2007 (Public Law 110-82). A technical amendment signed into law Feb. 29, 2008, allowed for the continued minting and issuance of certain dollar coins in 2008. (Public Law 110-192).

2009 Louis Braille

Authorized production of silver dollars to honor Louis Braille, who invented the Braille method for reading and writing by the blind. Signed into law July 27, 2006 (Public Law 109-247).

2009 Abraham Lincoln

Authorized production of silver dollars for the 200th anniversary of the birth of Abraham Lincoln. Signed into law Sept. 27, 2006 (Public Law 109-285).

2010 American Veterans Disabled for Life

Authorized production of silver dollars in commemoration of veterans who became disabled for life while serving in the Armed Forces of the United States. Signed into law July 17, 2008 (Public Law 110-277).

2010 Boy Scouts of America Centennial

Authorized silver dollars commemorating the 100th anniversary of the Boy Scouts of America. Signed into law Oct. 8, 2008 (Public Law 110-363).

2010 Coin Modernization, Oversight and Continuity Act

Gives the secretary of the Treasury and the U.S. Mint the authority to research and develop alternative compositions for circulating coins and to report findings to Congress.

It also provides for technical corrections to existing coin law including allowing changing the technical specifications of the America the Beautiful Silver Bullion Coins and enabling the U.S. Mint to produce Proof American Eagle bullion coins. Signed into law Dec. 14, 2010 (Public Law 111-302).

2010 American Eagle Palladium Bullion Coin

Authorizes the production of palladium bullion coins to provide affordable opportunities for investments in precious metals, though production is contingent on the completion of a market study. The $25 coins will contain 1 troy ounce of .9995 fine palladium. Signed into law Dec. 14, 2010 (Public Law 111-303).

2011 United States Army

Authorized copper-nickel clad half dollars, silver dollars and gold $5 coins in recognition and celebration of the establishment of the United States Army in 1775 and to honor the American soldier of both today and yesterday. Signed into law Dec. 1, 2008 (Public Law 110-450).

2011 Medal of Honor

Authorized silver dollars and gold $5 coins in celebration of the founding of the Medal of Honor in 1861. Signed into law Nov. 6, 2009 (Public Law 111-91).

2012 National Infantry Museum and Soldier Center

Authorized production of silver dollars in commemoration of the legacy of the United States Army Infantry and the establishment of the National Infantry Museum and Soldier Center. Signed into law Oct. 8, 2008 (Public Law 110-357).

2012 Star Spangled Banner

Authorized production of silver dollars and gold $5 coins to celebrate the 200th anniversary of the writing of the Star-Spangled Banner. Signed into law Aug. 16, 2010 (Public Law 111-232).

2013 Girl Scouts of the USA

Authorized production of silver dollars in commemoration of the 100th anniversary of the establishment of the Girl Scouts of the United States of America. Signed into law Oct. 29, 2009 (Public Law 111-86).

2013 5-Star Generals

Authorized copper-nickel clad half dollars, silver dollars and gold $5 coins in recognition and celebration of attendance and graduation from the Command and General Staff College of Gens. George C. Marshall, Douglas MacArthur, Dwight D. Eisenhower, Henry "Hap" Arnold and Omar N. Bradley, all of whom were five-star generals. Signed into law Oct. 8, 2010 (Public Law 111-262).

2014 Civil Rights Act of 1964

Authorized production of silver dollars in commemoration of the 50th anniversary of the enactment of the Civil Rights Act of 1964. Signed into law Dec. 2, 2008 (Public Law 110-451).

Laws authorizing medals, 1874 to 2010

Issuance of national Mint medals is governed by section 3551 of the Revised Statutes, and codified in section 368 of Title 31 of the U.S. Code. Regular production of medals began under Treasury Department authority in 1856, according to the Annual Report of the Director of the Mint for 1873, and when the nation's coinage legislation was codified in that same year, a clause was written into the law to permit continuance of the practice provided that the dies for the medals were of national character, produced at the Philadelphia Mint, executed by the chief engraver, and used without interference with the regular coinage operations.

The legislative origins of national Mint medals can be traced to Sec. 52 of the Coinage Act of 1873; prior to the enactment of this general coinage statute, national Mint medals had been struck under departmental authority only (HR Executive Document No. 42, 43rd Congress, 1st Session 471 (1873)).

Laws enacted by Congress are cited either by their volume and page number in the Statutes at Large, or by the public or private law number.

1874 to 1900

Public Law No. 71 (Extract), approved June 20, 1874. Lifesaving medals of the first and second class.

Public Law No. 109 (Extract) 45th Congress, approved June 18, 1878. Secretary of the Treasury is hereby authorized to bestow the life-saving medal of the second class on certain people.

Public Law No. 67 (Extract) 47th Congress, approved May 4, 1882. Authorizing the gold and silver life-saving medal.

Public Law No. 217 (Extract) 47th Congress, approved Aug. 7, 1882. To replace life-saving medals that have been stolen from parties upon whom they have been bestowed.

Public Res. No. 51, 54th Congress, approved May 2, 1896. Relative to the Medal of Honor authorized by the Acts of July 12, 1862, and March 3, 1863.

Act of Aug. 5, 1892, ch. 381 sec. 3, 27 Stat. 389. Authorizing striking of 50,000 bronze medals for the World's Columbian Exposition.

Public Res. No. 27, 55th Congress, approved May 4, 1898. Relative to the Medal of Honor authorized by the Acts of Dec. 21, 1861, and July 16, 1862.

Public Res. No. 38, 55th Congress, approved June 3, 1898. Authorizing the secretary of the navy to present a sword of honor to Commodore George Dewey, and to cause to be struck bronze medals commemorating the Battle of Manila Bay, and to distribute such medals to the officers and men of the ships of the Asiatic Squadron of the United States.

1901 to 1920

Public Res. No. 17, 56th Congress, approved March 3, 1901. Authorizing the secretary of the navy to cause bronze medals to be struck and distributed to certain officers and men who participated in the war with Spain.

Public Law No. 155, 56th Congress, approved March 3, 1901. An act for the reward of enlisted men of the Navy or Marine Corps.

Public Law No. 192, 57th Congress, approved June 28, 1902. Directing the secretary of the Treasury to bestow medals upon 1st Lt. David H. Jarvis, 2nd Lt. Ellsworth P. Bertholf, and Samuel J. Call, surgeon, all of the Revenue-Cutter Service.

Public Res. No. 23, 58th Congress, approved April 15, 1904. Authorizing issuance of duplicate medals where the originals have been lost or destroyed through no fault of the beneficiary.

Act of April 13, 1904, ch. 1253, sec. 6, 33 Stat. 178. Authorizing medals to be struck for the Lewis and Clark Centennial Exposition.

Public Law No. 149 (Extract) 58th Congress, approved April 23, 1904. The furnishing of a national trophy and medals and other prizes to be provided annually under regulations prescribed by the secretary of war.

Public Law No. 264, 58th Congress, approved April 28, 1904. Making appropriations for national trophy and medals for rifle contests.

Public Law No. 360, 59th Congress, approved June 29, 1906. An act providing medals for certain persons.

Public Res. No. 8, 59th Congress, approved January 27, 1907. Authorizing the secretary of war to award the Medal of Honor to Roe Reisinger.

Public Res. No. 17, 59th Congress, approved February 27, 1907. Relating to the holders of the Medals of Honor.

Public Res. No. 42, 62nd Congress, approved July 6, 1912. Conveying the thanks of Congress to Capt. Arthur Henry Rostron and his officers and crew of the steamship *Carpathia* of the Cunard Line for the rescuing of 704 lives from the wreck of the steamship *Titanic* in the North Atlantic Ocean.

Public Law No. 271 (extract) 63rd Congress, approved March 3, 1915. Preparing a Medal of Honor to be awarded to any officer of the Navy, Marine Corps or Coast Guard who shall have distinguished himself in battle or displayed extraordinary heroism in the line of his profession.

Public Law No. 56, 64th Congress, approved April 27, 1916. Establishing the Army and Navy Medal of Honor Roll.

Public Law No. 85 (extract) 64th Congress, approved June 3, 1916. Investigation concerning Medals of Honor.

Public Law No. 193 (extract) 65th Congress, approved July 9, 1918. The furnishing of a national trophy and medals for rifle contests.

Public Law No. 253, 65th Congress, approved Feb. 4, 1919. To provide for the award of Medals of Honor, Distinguished Service Medals and Navy Crosses.

Public Law No. 125, 66th Congress, approved Jan. 24, 1920. Appropriations for Medal of Honor, Distinguished Service Crosses, and Distinguished Service Medals.

Public Law No. 215 (extract) 66th Congress, approved June 5, 1920. To present to the city of Verdun, France, a suitable memorial medal or tablet.

1921-1929

Public Law No. 388, 66th Congress, approved March 4, 1921. Authorizing bestowal upon the unknown, unidentified British soldier buried in Westminster Abbey and unknown, unidentified French soldier buried in the Arc de Triomphe of the Medal of Honor.

Public Law No. 67, 67th Congress, approved Aug. 24, 1921. Authorizing bestowal upon the unknown, unidentified American to be buried in the Memorial Amphitheater of the National Cemetery at Arlington, Va., the Medal of Honor and the Distinguished Service Cross.

Public Res. No. 23, 67th Congress, approved Oct. 12, 1921. For the bestowal of the Medal of Honor upon an unknown, unidentified Italian soldier buried in the National Monument to Victor Emmanuel II, in Rome.

Public Law No. 190, 67th Congress, approved April 7, 1922. To extend the limitations of time upon the issuance of Medals of Honor, Distinguished Service Crosses, and Distinguished Service Medals to persons who served in the Army of the United States during the world war.

Public Law No. 438, 67th Congress, approved Feb. 24, 1923. To prohibit the unauthorized wearing, manufacture, or sale of medals and badges awarded by the War Department.

Public Law No. 470, 68th Congress, approved Feb. 25, 1925. To recognize and reward the accomplishment of the world flyers.

Public Law No. 524, 68th Congress, approved March 2, 1925. To authorize the secretary of the Treasury to prepare a medal with appropriate emblems and inscriptions commemorative of the Norse-American Centennial.

Public Law No. 466 (extract) 69th Congress, approved July 2, 1926. Authorizing the president to present, but not in the name of Congress, a medal to be known as the Soldiers Medal.

Public Law No. 538, 69th Congress, approved Jan. 5, 1927. Providing for the promotion of Lt. Commander Richard E. Byrd, United States Navy, retired, and awarding to him a Medal of Honor.

Public Law No. 539, 69th Congress, approved Jan. 5, 1927. Providing for the promotion of Floyd Bennett, aviation pilot, United States Navy, and awarding to him a Medal of Honor.

Public Law No. 1, 70th Congress, approved Dec. 14, 1927. Authorizing the president of the United States to present in the name of Congress a Medal of Honor to Col. Charles A. Lindbergh.

Public Law No. 288, 70th Congress, approved April 21, 1928. To amend the Act of Feb. 24, 1923, an act to prohibit the unauthorized wearing, manufacture, or sale of medals and badges awarded by the War Department.

Public Law No. 341, 70th Congress, approved May 2, 1928. To authorize the president to present the Distinguished Flying Cross to Col. Francesco de Pinedo, Dieudonne Costes, Joseph LeBrix, Ehrenfried Günther Freiherr von Hünefeld, James C. FitzMaurice and Hermann Koehl.

Public Res. No. 39, 70th Congress, approved May 4, 1928. To provide for the coinage of a medal in commemoration of the achievements of Col. Charles A. Lindbergh.

Public Law No. 369, 70th Congress, approved May 12, 1928. To provide for the gratuitous issue of service medals and similar devices.

Public Law No. 515 (extract) 70th Congress, approved May 26, 1928. That all recommendations for decorations by the United States of America shall be considered before the proper board.

Public Law No. 557, 70th Congress, approved May 28, 1928. An act to amend the Defense Act.

Public Res. No. 66, 70th Congress, approved May 29, 1928. To provide for the striking of a medal commemorative of the achievements of Thomas A. Edison.

Private Law No. 287, 70th Congress, approved May 29, 1928. Awarding a gold medal to Lincoln Ellsworth.

Public Law No. 1024, 70th Congress, approved March 4, 1929. To provide for the recognition for meritorious service by members of the police and fire departments of the District of Columbia.

1930 to 1935

Public Res. No. 75, 71st Congress, approved May 23, 1930. Authorizing the presentation of medals to the officers and men of the Byrd Antarctic expedition.

Public Law No. 324, 71st Congress, approved June 9, 1930. An act waiving the limiting period of two years in Executive Order No. 4576 to enable the board of awards of the Navy Department to consider recommendations of the award of the Distinguished Flying Cross to members of the Alaskan Aerial Survey Expedition.

Public Law No. 661, 71st Congress, approved Feb. 14, 1931. An act for the award of the Air-mail Flyer's Medal of Honor.

Public Law No. 694, 71st Congress, approved Feb. 20, 1931. Authorizing the manufacturing of a medal in commemoration of the 150th anniversary of the surrender of Lord Cornwallis at Yorktown, Va., and of the establishment of the independence of the United States.

Public Res. No. 31, 72nd Congress, approved July 2, 1932. Authorizing the president of the United States to present the Distinguished Flying Cross to Amelia Earhart Putnam.

Private Law No. 237, 72nd Congress, approved March 1, 1933. Authorizing the president to make a posthumous award of a distinguished-flying cross to Glenn H. Curtiss, deceased, and to present the same to Lua Curtiss, mother of the said Glenn H. Curtiss, deceased.

Public Law No. 114, 73rd Congress, approved March 5, 1934. An act to award the Distinguished Service Cross to former holders of the certificate of merit.

Public Law No. 223, 73rd Congress, approved May 14, 1934. Act to amend the act authorizing the issuance of the Spanish War Service Medal.

Private Law No. 2, 73rd Congress, approved June 18, 1934. Authorizing the president of the United States to present the Distinguished Flying Cross to Emory B. Bronte.

Private Law No. 8, 74th Congress, approved March 21, 1935. Authorizing the president of the United States to present in the name of Congress a Medal of Honor to Maj. Gen. Adolphus Washington Greely.

Public Law No. 31, 74th Congress, approved April 10, 1935. Authorizing the president to present Distinguished Flying Crosses to Air Marshal Italo Balbo and Gen. Aldo Pellegrini, of the Royal Italian Air Force.

Public Law No. 43, 74th Congress, approved April 25, 1935. Authorizing personnel of the naval service to whom a commemorative or special medal has been awarded to wear in lieu thereof a miniature facsimile of such medal and a ribbon symbolic of the award.

Public Law No. 61, 74th Congress, approved May 15, 1935. To give proper recognition to the distinguished services of Colonel William L. Keller.

Public Law No. 398, 74th Congress, approved Aug. 29, 1935. To authorize the transfer of a certain military reservation to the Department of the Interior.

1936-1940

Public Law No. 523, 74th Congress, approved April 17, 1936. Authorizing the president to present the Distinguished Service Medal to Commander Percy Todd, British Navy, and the Navy Cross to Lt. Commander Charles A. DeW. Kitcat, British Navy.

Public Res. No. 103, 74th Congress, approved June 4, 1936. Authorizing the president of the United States to award posthumously a Distinguished Service Medal to Maj. Gen. Clarence Ransom Edwards.

Private Res. No. 5, 74th Congress, approved June 20, 1936. Authorizing the president to present the Navy Cross to J. Harold Arnold.

Private Law No. 727, 74th Congress, approved June 29, 1936. Authorizing the president to present a gold medal to George M. Cohan.

Public Res. No. 98, 74th Congress, approved June 30, 1936. Authorizing the presentation of silver medals to the personnel of the second Byrd Antarctic expedition.

Private Law No. 165, 75th Congress, approved June 18, 1937. Awarding a Navy Cross to John W. Thomason and Robert Slover.

Private Law No. 329, 75th Congress, approved Aug. 23, 1937. To authorize the award of a decoration for distinguished service to Acors Rathbun Thompson.

Public Law No. 581, 75th Congress, approved June 7, 1938. Authorizing the president to present the Distinguished Service Medal to Rear Adm. Reginal Vesey Holt, British Navy, and to Capt. George Eric Maxia O'Donnell, British Navy, and the Navy Cross to Vice Adm. Lewis Gonne Eyre Crabbe, British Navy, and to Lt. Commander Harry Douglas Barlow, British Navy.

Private Res. No. 2, 76th Congress, approved July 15, 1939. Providing for consideration of a recommendation for decoration of Sgt. Fred W. Stockham, deceased.

Private Law No. 115, 76th Congress, approved July 28, 1939. Authorizing the president to present a Distinguished Service Medal to Rear Adm. Harry Ervin Yarnell, United States Navy.

Private Law No. 214, 76th Congress, approved Aug. 7, 1939. To provide for the presentation of a medal to Howard Hughes in recognition of his achievements in advancing the science of aviation.

Private Law No. 235, 76th Congress, approved Aug. 10, 1939. To provide for the presentation of a medal to Reverend Francis X. Quinn in recognition of his valor in saving the lives of two of his fellow citizens.

Private Res. No. 5, 76th Congress, approved April 30, 1940. To authorize the president to present the Distinguished Flying Cross to Frank W. Seifert and Lt. Virgil Hine, deceased.

Public Law No. 507, 76th Congress, approved May 13, 1940. To authorize the striking of an appropriate medal in commemoration of the 300th anniversary of the establishment of Greenwich, Conn., as a town.

Private Law No. 378, 76th Congress, approved June 15, 1940. Authorizing the president to present the Navy Cross to Capt. Frank N. Roberts, United States Army.

1941-1945

Private Law No. 128, 77th Congress, approved July 22, 1941. Authorizing the Secretary of the Navy Expeditionary Medal to certain Army and civilian personnel.

Public Law No. 322, 77th Congress, approved Nov. 21, 1941. Authorizing the procurement and issue of an Army of Occupation of Germany Medal for each person who served in Germany or Austria-Hungary during the period of occupation.

Public Law No. 524, 77th Congress, approved April 11, 1942. To provide decorations for outstanding conduct or service by persons serving in the American Merchant Marine.

Public Law No. 671, 77th Congress, approved July 20, 1942. To authorize officers and enlisted men of the Armed Forces of the United States to accept decorations, orders, medals and emblems tendered them by governments of co-belligerent nations or other American republics and to create the decorations to be known as the "Legion of Merit" and the "Medal for Merit."

Public Law No. 702, 77th Congress, approved Aug. 7, 1942. To amend the Act approved Feb. 4, 1919, so as to change the conditions for the award of medals.

Public Law No. 805, 77th Congress, approved Dec. 15, 1942. To amend the Act of Jan. 24, 1920, so as to authorize the award of a Silver Star to certain persons serving with the Army of the United States.

Public Law No. 811, 77th Congress, approved Dec. 17, 1942. To authorize the president to confer decorations and medals upon units of, or persons serving with, the military forces of co-belligerent nations.

Public Law No. 52, 78th Congress, approved May 10, 1943. To provide for the issuance of devices in recognition of the services of merchant sailors.

Private Law No. 106, 78th Congress, approved Oct. 23, 1943. Authorizing the president to present, in the name of Congress, a Distinguished Service Cross to George F. Thompson.

Private Law No. 166, 78th Congress, approved Jan. 28, 1944. To provide for the presentation of silver medals to certain members of the Peary Polar Expedition of 1908 to 1909.

Private Law No. 203, 78th Congress, approved Feb. 22, 1944. Authorizing the president to present, in the name of Congress, a Distinguished Service Medal to Lt. Gen. Thomas Holcomb, United States Marine Corps.

Private Law No. 260, 78th Congress, approved April 3, 1944. Authorizing the president to present, in the name of Congress, a Distinguished Service Medal to Adm. Chester W. Nimitz, United States Navy.

Private Law No. 1, 79th Congress, approved Feb. 28, 1945. To authorize Lewis Hobart Kenney, Charles Garner, Charles Clement Goodman and Henry Charles Robinson to accept decorations and orders tendered them by the government of the United States.

Public Law No. 112, 79th Congress, approved July 2, 1945. To authorize an award of merit for uncompensated personnel of the Selective Service System.

Public Law No. 114, 79th Congress, approved July 2, 1945. To provide for the issuance of the Mexican Border Service Medal to certain members of the Army Reserve forces on active duty in 1916 and 1917.

Public Law No. 135, 79th Congress, approved July 6, 1946. Providing for a medal for service in the Armed Forces during the present war.

Public Law No. 169, 79th Congress, approved July 31, 1945. To amend the Act of May 10, 1943.

Public Law No. 185, 79th Congress, approved Sept. 24, 1945. To provide for the presentation of medals to members of the United States Antarctic Expedition of 1939 to 1941.

1946 to 1950

Private Law No. 438, 79th Congress, approved March 22, 1946. Providing for the striking and presentation to Gen. George Marshall and Fleet Adm. Ernest King of appropriate gold medals in the name of the people of the United States.

Public Law No. 444, 79th Congress, approved June 26, 1946. To modify the time limitations governing the award of certain military and naval decorations for acts performed during the present war.

Public Law No. 631, 79th Congress, approved Aug. 7, 1946. To amend the act to provide for the issuance of devices in recognition of the services of merchant sailors.

Private Law No. 831, 79th Congress, approved Aug. 7, 1946. Authorizing the president of the United States to award a special medal to General of the Armies of the United States John J. Pershing.

Public Law No. 698, 79th Congress, approved Aug. 8, 1946. Providing for a medal for service in the Merchant Marine during the present war.

Private Law No. 884, 79th Congress, approved Aug. 8, 1946. Authorizing the president of the United States to award posthumously in the name of Congress a Medal of Honor to William Mitchell.

Public Law No. 58, 80th Congress, approved May 15, 1947. To amend the Act of July 20, 1942.

Private Law No. 35, 80th Congress, approved June 30, 1947. Authorizing the presentation of the Distinguished Flying Cross to Rear Adm. Charles E. Rosendahl, United States Navy.

Public Law 314, 80th Congress, approved Aug. 1, 1947. To amend section 1 of the Act of July 20, 1942.

Public Law No. 438, 80th Congress, approved March 9, 1948. To authorize the president to award a Medal of Honor to the unknown American who lost his life while serving overseas in the Armed Forces of the United States during the World War II.

Private Law No. 8, 81st Congress, approved March 24, 1949. To authorize certain personnel and former personnel of the naval establishment to accept certain gifts and a foreign decoration tendered by foreign governments.

Public Law No. 178, 81st Congress, approved July 20, 1949. To establish the Medal of Humane Action for award to persons serving in or with the Armed Forces of the United States participating in the current military effort to supply necessities of life to the people of Berlin.

Public Law No. 221, 81st Congress, approved Aug. 12, 1949. To provide for the coinage of a medal in recognition of the distinguished services of Vice President Alben W. Barkley.

Public Law No. 501, 81st Congress, approved May 3, 1950. To extend the time limits for the award of certain decorations.

Public Law No. 503, 81st Congress, approved May 5, 1950. To authorize the acceptance of foreign decorations for participation in the Berlin Airlift.

Public Law No. 638, 81st Congress, approved Aug. 3, 1950. Authorizing the Department of Justice of the United States to recognize and to award to outstanding courageous young Americans a medal for heroism known as the Young American Medal for Bravery.

Public Law No. 661, 81st Congress, approved Aug. 4, 1950. To amend title 18, United States Code, section 705, to protect the badge, medal, emblem and other insignia of auxiliaries to veterans organizations.

1951 to 1955

Public Law No. 117, 82nd Congress, approved Aug. 17, 1951. To protect the Girl Scouts of the United States of America in the use of emblems and badges, descriptive or designating marks, and words or phrases heretofore adopted and to clarify existing law relating thereto.

Private Law No. 504, 82nd Congress, approved March 31, 1952. To provide for the presentation of the Merchant Marine Distinguished Service Medal to Henrik Kurt Carlsen, master, steamship *Flying Enterprise.*

Private Law No. 536, 83rd Congress, approved July 16, 1954. Authorizing the president to present a gold medal to Irving Berlin.

Public Law No. 259, 84th Congress, approved Aug. 9, 1955. To authorize the issuance of commemorative medals to certain societies of which Benjamin Franklin was a member, founder or sponsor in observance of the 250th anniversary of his birth.

Public Law No. 338, 84th Congress, approved Aug. 9, 1955. To provide for the striking of medals in commemoration of the 120th anniversary of the signing of the Texas Declaration of Independence and the Battle of the Alamo, Goliad and San Jacinto in the year 1836.

1956 to 1960

Public Law No. 727, 84th Congress, approved July 18, 1956. To provide for the striking of medals in commemoration of the 100th anniversary of the birth of the late Justice Louis Dembitz Brandeis.

Public Law No. 730, 84th Congress, approved July 18, 1956. To provide for a medal to be struck and presented to each surviving veteran of the U.S. Civil War.

Public Law No. 759, 84th Congress, approved July 24, 1956. To authorize medals and decorations for outstanding and meritorious conduct and service in the United States Merchant Marine.

Public Law No. 917, 84th Congress, approved Aug. 2, 1956. To extend the time limit within which awards of certain military and naval decorations may be made.

Private Law No. 14, 85th Congress, approved May 16, 1957. To waive the limitation on the time within which a Medal of Honor may be awarded to Commander Hugh Barr Miller Jr., United States Navy.

Public Law No. 85-50, 85th Congress, approved June 13, 1957. To amend the Medals of Honor Act to authorize awards for acts of heroism involving any motor vehicle.

Public Law No. 85-251, 85th Congress, approved Aug. 31, 1957. To authorize the president to award the Medal of Honor to the unknown American who lost his life while serving overseas in the Armed Forces of the United States during the Korean conflict.

Public Law No. 85-826, 85th Congress, approved Aug. 28, 1958. To authorize the chairman of the Joint Committee on Atomic Energy to confer a medal on Rear Adm. Hyman George Rickover, United States Navy.

Public Law No. 85-879, 85th Congress, approved Sept. 2, 1958. To amend the Act of Feb. 28, 1929, to include therein the name of Roger P. Ames.

Public Law No. 86-29, 86th Congress, approved May 20, 1959. To provide for the striking of medals in commemoration of the 100th anniversary of the first significant discovery of silver in the United States, June 1859.

Public Law No. 86-65, 86th Congress, approved June 23, 1959. To provide for the striking of medals in commemoration of the 100th anniversary of the settlement of the state of Colorado and in commemoration of the establishment of the United States Air Force Academy.

Public Law No. 86-184, 86th Congress, approved Aug. 24, 1959. To provide for the striking of medals in commemoration of the 100th anniversary of the admission of West Virginia into the Union as a state.

Public Law No. 86-277, 86th Congress, approved Sept. 16, 1959. To authorize the issuance of a gold medal in honor of the late Professor Robert H. Goddard.

Public Law No. 86-393, 86th Congress, approved March 18, 1960. To provide for the striking of medals in commemoration of the 100th anniversary of the statehood of Kansas.

Public Law No. 86-394, 86th Congress, approved March 18, 1960. To provide for the striking of medals in commemoration of the 100th anniversary of the founding of the Pony Express.

Public Law No. 86-582, 86th Congress, approved July 5, 1960. To amend title 10, United States Code, to authorize the award of certain medals within two years after a determination by the secretary concerned that because of loss or inadvertence the recommendation was not processed.

Public Law No. 86-593, 86th Congress, approved July 6, 1960. To amend Title 10, United States Code, with respect to certain medals.

Public Law No. 86-600, 86th Congress, approved July 7, 1960. To provide for the presentation of a medal to persons who have served as members of a United States expedition to Antarctica.

Public Law No. 86-656, 86th Congress, approved July 14, 1960. To authorize the award posthumously of appropriate medals to Chaplain George L. Fox, Chaplain Alexander D. Goode, Chaplain Clark V. Polling and Chaplain John P. Washington.

Public Law No. 86-696, 86th Congress, approved Sept. 2, 1960. To provide for the striking of medals in commemoration of the 100th anniversary of the founding of Idaho as a territory.

Public Law No. 86-697, 86th Congress, approved Sept. 2, 1960. To provide for the striking of a medal in commemoration of Century 21 Exposition to be held in Seattle, Wash.

Public Law No. 86-747, 86th Congress, approved Sept. 13, 1960. Authorizing the president of the United States to present a gold medal to Robert Frost, a New England poet.

1961 to 1965

Public Law No. 87-21, 87th Congress, approved April 24, 1961. To provide for the striking of medals in commemoration of the 250th anniversary of the founding of Mobile, Ala.

Public Law No. 87-42, 87th Congress, approved May 27, 1961. To authorize the president to award posthumously a medal to Dr. Thomas Anthony Dooley II.

Public Law No. 87-478, 87th Congress, approved June 8, 1962. Authorizing the issuance of a gold medal to entertainer Bob Hope.

Public Law No. 87-702, 87th Congress, approved Sept. 26, 1962. To provide for the coinage of a medal in recognition of the distinguished services of Sam Rayburn, speaker of the House of Representatives.

Public Law No. 87-711, 87th Congress, approved Sept. 27, 1962. To amend Public Law No. 184, 86th Congress, an act to provide for the striking of medals in commemoration of the 100th anniversary of the admission of West Virginia into the Union as a state.

Public Law No. 87-760, 87th Congress, approved Oct. 9, 1962. Authorizing the issuance of a gold medal to General of the Army Douglas MacArthur.

Public Law No. 88-77, 87th Congress, approved July 25, 1963. To amend titles 10, 14, and 38, United States Code, with respect to the award of certain medals and the Medal of Honor Roll.

Public Law No. 88-107, 88th Congress, approved Aug. 27, 1963. To authorize the presentation of an Air Force Medal of Recognition to Maj. Gen. Benjamin D. Foulois, retired.

Public Law No. 88-143, 88th Congress, approved Oct. 16, 1963. To furnish to the Padre Junipero Serra 250th Anniversary Association medals in commemoration of the 250th anniversary of the padre's birth.

Public Law No. 88-147, 88th Congress, approved Oct. 16, 1963. To provide for the striking of medals in commemoration of the 100th anniversary of the admission of Nevada to statehood.

Public Law No. 88-184, 88th Congress, approved Nov. 20, 1963. To provide for the striking of medals in commemoration of the 150th anniversary of the statehood of Indiana.

Public Law No. 88-185, 88th Congress, approved Nov. 20, 1963. To provide for the striking of medals in commemoration of the 50th anniversary of the founding of the first union health center in the United States by the International Ladies Garment Workers Union.

Public Law No. 88-262, 88th Congress, approved Jan. 31, 1964. To provide for the striking of three different medals in commemoration of the Federal Hall National Memorial, Castle Clinton National Monument and Statue of Liberty National Monument American Museum of Immigration in New York City.

Public Law No. 88-270, 88th Congress, approved Feb. 11, 1964. To provide for the striking of medals in commemoration of the 200th anniversary of the founding of St. Louis.

Public Law No. 88-651, 88th Congress, approved Oct. 13, 1964. To amend section 560 of title 38, United States Code, to permit the payment of special pension to holders of the Medal of Honor awarded such medal for actions not involving conflict with an enemy.

1966 to 1970

Public Law No. 89-382, 89th Congress, approved March 31, 1966. To provide for the striking of medals in commemoration of the 250th anniversary of the founding of San Antonio, Texas.

Public Law No. 89-393, 89th Congress, approved April 14, 1966. To provide for the striking of medals in commemoration of the 100th anniversary of the purchase of Alaska by the United States from Russia.

Public Law No. 89-400, 89th Congress, approved April 16, 1966. To furnish to the Scranton Association Inc. medals in commemoration of the 100th anniversary of the founding of the city of Scranton, Pa.

Public Law No. 89-401, 89th Congress, approved April 16, 1966. To provide for the striking of medals in commemoration of the 75th anniversary of the founding of the American Numismatic Association.

Public Law No. 89-402, 89th Congress, approved June 24, 1966. To provide for the striking of medals in commemoration of the 100th anniversary of the founding of the United States Secret Service.

Public Law No. 89-469, 89th Congress, approved June 24, 1966. Authorizes U.S. Secret Service medal.

Public Law No. 89-527, 89th Congress, approved Aug. 5, 1966. To provide for the striking of medals to commemorate the 1,000th anniversary of the founding of Poland.

Public Law No. 89-529, 89th Congress, approved Aug. 11, 1966. To authorize the award of trophies for the recognition of special accomplishments related to the Armed Forces.

Public Law No. 89-534, 89th Congress, approved Aug. 11, 1966. To provide gold star lapel buttons for the next of kin of members of the Armed Forces who lost or lose their lives in war or as a result of Cold War incidents.

Public Law No. 89-676, 89th Congress, approved October 15, 1966. To provide for the striking of a medal in commemoration of the designation of Ellis Island as a part of the Statue of Liberty National Monument in New York City.

Public Law No. 89-679, 89th Congress, approved October 15, 1966. To provide for the striking of medals in commemoration of the 50th anniversary of the Federal Land Bank system in the United States.

Public Law No. 89-783, 89th Congress, approved Nov. 6, 1966. To provide for the striking of medals in commemoration of the United States Naval Construction Battalions (SEABEES) 25th anniversary and the United States Navy Civil Engineers Corps (CEC) 100th anniversary.

Public Law No. 90-124, 90th Congress, approved Nov. 4, 1967. To provide for the striking of medals in commemoration of the 200th anniversary of the founding of San Diego.

Public Law No. 90-125, 90th Congress, approved Nov. 4, 1967. To provide for the striking of medals in commemoration of the 300th anniversary of the explorations of Father Jacques Marquette in what is now the United States.

Public Law No. 90-127, 90th Congress, approved Nov. 4, 1967. To provide for the striking of medals in commemoration of the 50th anniversary of the founding of the American Legion.

Public Law No. 90-128, 90th Congress, approved Nov. 4, 1967. To provide for the striking of medals in commemoration of the 150th anniversary of the founding of the state of Mississippi.

Public Law No. 90-303, 90th Congress, approved May 10, 1968. To provide for the striking of medals in commemoration of the 100th anniversary of the completion of the first transcontinental railroad.

Public Law No. 90-316, 90th Congress, approved May 24, 1968. To provide for the issuance of a gold medal to the widow of Walt Disney and for the issuance of bronze medals to the California Institute of the Arts in recognition of the distinguished public service and the outstanding contributions of Walt Disney to the United States and to the world.

Public Law No. 90-528, 90th Congress, approved Sept. 28, 1968. To provide for the striking of medals in commemoration of the 200th anniversary of the founding of Dartmouth College.

Public Law No. 90-600, 90th Congress, approved Oct. 17, 1968. To provide for the striking of medals in commemoration of the 150th anniversary of the founding of the city of Memphis, Tenn.

Public Law No. 91-12, 91st Congress, approved May 7, 1969. To provide for the striking of medals in honor of the dedication of the Winston Churchill Memorial and Library at Westminster College, Fulton, Mo.

Public Law No. 91-13, 91st Congress, approved May 15, 1969. To strike a medal commemorating the founding of the American Fisheries Society.

Public Law No. 91-16, 91st Congress, approved May 28, 1969. To strike a medal in commemoration of the 300th anniversary of the founding of South Carolina.

Public Law No. 91-18, 91st Congress, approved May 28, 1969. To strike a medal in commemoration of the 150th anniversary of the founding of the city of Wichita, Kan.

Public Law No. 91-29, 91st Congress, approved June 17, 1969. To strike a medal in commemoration of the 150th anniversary of the state of Alabama.

Public Law No. 91-48, 91st Congress, approved July 22, 1969. To strike a medal in commemoration of the U.S. Diplomatic Courier Service.

Public Law 91-244, 91st Congress, approved May 9, 1970. To strike a medal in commemoration of the many contributions to the founding and early development of the state of Texas and the city of San Antonio by Jose Antonio Navarro.

Public Law 91-254, 91st Congress, approved May 14, 1970. To strike a medal in commemoration of the completion of the carvings on Stone Mountain, Ga., depicting heroes of the Confederacy.

Public Law 91-381, 91st Congress, approved Aug. 17, 1970. To strike a medal in commemoration of the 100th anniversary of the founding of Ohio Northern University.

1971 to 1975

Public Law 92-228, 92nd Congress, approved Feb. 15, 1972. To authorize Bicentennial medal production for the American Revolution Bicentennial Commission.

Public Law 92-384, 92nd Congress, approved Aug. 14, 1972. To authorize a medal for the 175th anniversary of frigate USS *Constitution.*

Public Law 93-33, 93rd Congress, approved May 14, 1973. To authorize a gold medal for Roberto Clemente.

Public Law 93-114, 93rd Congress, approved Oct. 1, 1973. To authorize the San Francisco cable car national medal.

Public Law 93-132, 93rd Congress, approved Oct. 19, 1973. To authorize a gold medal for Jim Thorpe.

Public Law 93-221, 93rd Congress, approved Dec. 23, 1973. To authorize the International Environmental Exposition national medal.

Public Law 93-227, 93rd Congress, approved Dec. 29, 1973. To authorize a medal commemorating the centennial of the admittance of the state of Colorado to the Union.

Public Law 93-309, 93rd Congress, approved June 8, 1974. To authorize a gold medal for J. Edgar Hoover.

Public Law 93-617, 93rd Congress, approved Jan. 2, 1975. Adds two years for Mint to produce Jim Thorpe, San Francisco cable car national medals.

Public Law 94-117, 94th Congress, approved Oct. 17, 1975. To authorize medals in commemoration of Army, Navy and U.S. Marines bicentennials.

Public Law 94-179, 94th Congress, approved Oct. 17, 1975. Authorizing the issuance of a gold medal to U.S. Air Force Gen. Charles E. "Chuck" Yeager (first person to fly faster than the speed of sound).

1976 to 1980

Public Law 94-257, 94th Congress, approved April 1, 1976. To authorize a medal commemorating the bicentennial of John Carroll of Carrollton, Md., signing Declaration of Independence.

Public Law 95-9, 95th Congress, approved March 8, 1977. To authorize the issuance of a gold medal to Marian Anderson.

Public Law 95-229, 95th Congress, approved Feb. 14, 1979. Capitol Historical Society medal legislation.

Public Law 95-438, 95th Congress, approved Oct. 10, 1978. Authorizing the issuance of a gold medal to Gen. Ira C. Eaker (leadership and service as aviation pioneer).

Public Law 95-560, 95th Congress, approved Nov. 1, 1978. Authorizing the issuance of a gold medal to the widow of Robert F. Kennedy.

Public Law 95-630, 95th Congress, approved Nov. 10, 1978. American Arts Gold Medallion Act.

Public Law 96-15, 96th Congress, approved May 26, 1979. Authorizing the issuance of a gold medal to John Wayne.

Public Law 96-20, 96th Congress, approved June 13, 1979. Authorizing the issuance of a gold medals to Ben Abruzzo, Maxie Anderson, Larry Newman (first successful trans-Atlantic balloon trip.)

Public Law 96-21, 96th Congress, approved June 13, 1979. Authorizing the issuance of a gold medal to Hubert H. Humphrey.

Public Law 96-138, 96th Congress, approved Dec. 12, 1979. To authorize a gold medal for U.S. Red Cross.

Public Law 96-201, 96th Congress, approved March 6, 1980. Authorizing the issuance of a gold medal to

Canadian Ambassador Kenneth Taylor (intervention in hostage situation at American Embassy in Iran).

Public Law 96-211, 96th Congress, approved March 17, 1980. Authorizing the issuance of a gold medal to Simon Wiesenthal.

Public Law 96-306, 96th Congress, approved July 8, 1980. Authorizing gold-plated medals for U.S. Olympic team because of nonparticipation in Olympic Games resulting from U.S. boycott of Moscow Games.

1981 to 1985

Public Law 97-158, 97th Congress, approved March 22, 1982. Authorizing the issuance of a gold medal to Queen Beatrix of Netherlands in commemoration of 200 years of friendship with the United States.

Public Law 97-201, 97th Congress, approved June 23, 1982. Authorizing the issuance of a gold medal to Adm. Hyman G. Rickover.

Public Law 97-246, 97th Congress, approved Aug. 26, 1982. Authorizing the issuance of gold medals for Louis L'Amour, Fred Waring and Joe Louis.

Public Law 98-136, 98th Congress, approved Oct. 24, 1983. Authorizing a medal for the Louisiana World Exposition.

Public Law 98-159, 98th Congress, approved Nov. 18, 1983. Authorizing the issuance of a gold medal for U.S. Rep. Leo Ryan (murdered in Jonestown, Guyana).

Public Law 98-172, 98th Congress, approved Nov. 29, 1983. Authorizing the issuance of a gold medal to Danny Thomas.

Public Law 98-278, 98th Congress, approved May 5, 1984. Authorizing the issuance of gold medals for Harry S. Truman, Lady Bird Johnson and Elie Wiesel.

Public Law 98-285, 98th Congress, approved May 17, 1984. Authorizing the issuance of a gold medal to Roy Wilkins.

Public Law 98-306, 98th Congress, approved May 31, 1984. Authorizing the National Medal of the Arts.

Public Law 98-566, 98th Congress, approved Oct. 30, 1984. Vietnam Veterans National Medal Act.

Public Law 98-599, 98th Congress, approved Oct. 30, 1984. Missing in Action Medal Act.

Public Law 99-86, 98th Congress, approved Aug. 9, 1985. Authorizing the issuance of a gold medal honoring George and Ira Gershwin.

1986 to 1990

Public Law 99-295, 99th Congress, approved May 12, 1986. Authorizing the Young Astronaut Program Medal Act.

Public Law 99-298, 99th Congress, approved May 13, 1986. Authorizing the issuance of a gold medal to Natan (Anatoly) Shcharansky.

Public Law 99-311, 99th Congress, approved May 20, 1986. Authorizing the issuance of a gold medal for Harry Chapin.

Public Law 99-418, 99th Congress, approved Sept. 23, 1986. Authorizing the issuance of a gold medal for Aaron Copland.

Public Law 100-210, 100th Congress, approved Dec. 24, 1987. Authorizing the issuance of a gold medal for Mary Lasker (medical research); Young Astronaut program extended to Dec. 31, 1988.

Public Law 100-269, 100th Congress, approved March 28, 1988. Congress directs Department of Defense to issue medal to former POWs.

Public Law 100-437, 100th Congress, approved Sept. 20, 1988. Authorizing the issuance of a gold medal for Jesse Owens; Young Astronaut Program extended Dec. 31, 1989.

Public Law 100-639, 100th Congress, approved Nov. 9, 1988. Authorizing the issuance of a gold medal to Andrew Wyeth.

Public Law 100-674, 100th Congress, approved Nov. 17, 1988. Congressional Award Act Amendments of 1988-Gold Medal Awards ceremony in District of Columbia.

Public Law 101-260, 101st Congress, approved March 30, 1990. Provides for striking of medals in commemoration of the bicentennial of the U.S. Coast Guard.

1991 to 1995

Public Law 102-32, 102nd Congress, approved April 23, 1991. Authorizing the issuance of a gold medal to Gen. H. Norman Schwarzkopf in recognition of his exemplary performance in coordinating the planning, strategy, and execution of U.S. combat action and his invaluable contributions to the United States and to the liberation of Kuwait.

Public Law 102-33, 102nd Congress, approved April 23, 1991. Authorizing the issuance of a gold medal to Gen. Colin L. Powell in recognition of his exemplary performance in planning and coordinating the U.S. military response to the Iraqi invasion of Kuwait.

Public Law 102-479, 102nd Congress, approved Oct. 23, 1992. Provides for striking of medals to commemorate Jefferson's birth in 1743 and the founding of the American Philosophical Society that same year.

Public Law 103-457, 103rd Congress, approved Nov. 2, 1994. Authorizing the issuance of a gold medal to Rabbi Menachem Mendel Schneerson in recognition of his outstanding and enduring contributions toward world education, morality and acts of charity.

1996 to 1999

Public Law 104-111, 104th Congress, approved Feb. 13, 1996. Authorizing the issuance of a gold medal to Ruth and Billy Graham in recognition of their outstanding and enduring contributions toward faith, morality and charity.

Public Law 105-16, 105th Congress, approved June 2, 1997. Authorizing the issuance of a gold medal to Mother Teresa of Calcutta in recognition of her outstanding and enduring contributions through humanitarian and charitable activities.

Public Law 105-51, 105th Congress, approved Oct. 6, 1997. Authorizing the issuance of a gold medal to Ecumenical Patriarch Bartholomew in recognition of his outstanding and enduring contributions toward religious understanding and peace.

Public Law 105-215, 105th Congress, approved July 29, 1998. Authorizing the issuance of a gold medal to Nelson Mandela in recognition of his lifelong dedication to the abolition of apartheid and the promotion of reconciliation among the people of the Republic of South Africa.

Public Law 105-14, 105th Congress, approved May 14, 1997. Authorizing the issuance of a gold medal for Albert "Frank" Sinatra in recognition of his outstanding and enduring contributions through his entertainment career and humanitarian activities.

Public Law 105-331, 105th Congress, approved Oct. 31, 1998. Authorizing the issuance of gold medals to Jean Brown Trickey, Carlotta Walls La Nier, Melba Patillo Beals, Terrence Roberts, Gloria Ray Karlmark, Thelma Mothershed Wair, Ernest Green, Elizabeth Eckford and Jefferson Thomas, known collectively as the "Little Rock Nine," in recognition of voluntarily subjecting themselves to racial bigotry to integrate Central High School in Little Rock, Ark., in 1957.

Public Law 105-331, 105th Congress, approved Oct. 31, 1998. Authorizing the issuance of a gold medal to Gerald and Betty Ford in recognition of their dedicated public service and outstanding humanitarian contributions to the people of the United States.

Public Law 105-371, 105th Congress, approved Nov. 12, 1998. Authorized the president to award the Medal of Honor posthumously to Theodore Roosevelt for his gallant and heroic actions in the attack on San Juan Heights, Cuba, during the Spanish-American War. A provision in the law asked the president to consult with the secretary of the Army after Army officials review their record of what happened July 1, 1898, then base their decision on the Medal of Honor award standards in place in 1898. Award presented Jan. 16, 2001, to a great-grandson.

Public Law 106-26, 106th Congress, approved May 4, 1999. Authorizing the issuance of a gold medal to Rosa Parks in recognition of her contributions to the nation.

Public Law 106-153, 106th Congress, approved Dec. 9, 1999. Authorizing the issuance of a gold medal to Theodore M. Hesburgh in recognition of his outstanding and enduring contributions to civil rights, higher education, the Catholic Church, the nation, and the global community.

2000 to 2010

Public Law 106-175, 106th Congress, approved March 3, 2000. Authorizing the issuance of a gold medal to John Cardinal O'Connor, Archbishop of New York, in recognition of his accomplishments as a priest, a chaplain and a humanitarian.

Public Law 106-225, 106th Congress, approved July 20, 2000. Authorizing the issuance of a gold medal to Charles M. Schulz in recognition of his lasting artistic contributions to the nation and the world, and for other purposes.

Public Law 106-250, 106th Congress, approved July 27, 2000. Authorizing the issuance of a gold medal to Pope John Paul II in recognition of his many and enduring contributions to peace and religious understanding, and for other purposes.

Public Law 106-251, 106th Congress, approved July 27, 2000. Authorizing the issuance of a gold medal to Ronald and Nancy Reagan in recognition of their service to the nation.

Public Law 106-554, 106th Congress, approved Dec. 15, 2000. Authorizing the issuance of gold medals to Navajo Code Talkers to express recognition by the United States and its citizens in honoring the Navajo Code Talkers, who distinguished themselves in performing a unique, highly successful communications operation that greatly assisted in saving countless lives and hastening the end of World War II in the Pacific.

Public Law 107-127, 107th Congress, approved Jan 16, 2002. Authorizing the issuance of a gold medal to Gen. Henry H. Shelton, chairman of the Joint Chiefs of Staff from October 1997 through September 2001, for his leadership in coordinating the United States and NATO's successful combat action throughout Operation Allied Force in the Balkans.

Public Law 108-60, 108th Congress, approved July 17, 2003. Authorizing the issuance of a gold medal to

Prime Minister Tony Blair of the United Kingdom for service to the United States of America.

Public Law 108-101, 108th Congress, approved Oct 29, 2003. Authorizing the issuance of a gold medal for Jackie Roosevelt Robinson, in recognition of his many contributions to the nation, and to express the sense of the Congress that there should be a national day in recognition of Jackie Robinson.

Public Law 108-162, 108th Congress, approved Dec. 6, 2003. Authorizing the issuance of a gold medal to Dr. Dorothy Height in recognition of her many contributions to the Nation as a civil rights advocate.

Public Law 108-180, 108th Congress, approved Dec. 15, 2003. Authorizing the issuance of gold medal for Reverend Joseph A. DeLaine, Harry and Eliza Briggs, and Levi Pearson in recognition of their contributions to the nation as pioneers in the effort to desegregate public schools that led directly to the landmark desegregation case of *Brown et al. v. the Board of Education of Topeka et al.*

Public Law 108-368, 108th Congress, approved Oct. 25, 2004. Authorizing the issuance of a gold medal to Reverend Dr. Martin Luther King, Jr. and Coretta Scott King in recognition of their contributions to the nation on behalf of the civil rights movement.

Public Law 109-213, 109th Congress, approved April 11, 2006. Authorizing the issuance of a gold medal for the Tuskegee Airmen, collectively, in recognition of their unique military record, which inspired revolutionary reform in the Armed Forces.

Public Law 109-287, 109th Congress, approved Sept. 27, 2006. Authorizing the issuance of a gold medal to Tenzin Gyatso, the 14th Dalai Lama, in recognition of his many enduring and outstanding contributions to peace, nonviolence, human rights and religious understanding.

Public Law 109-357, 109th Congress, approved Oct. 16, 2006. Authorizing the issuance of a gold medal to Byron Nelson in recognition of his significant contributions to the game of golf as a player, a teacher and a commentator.

Public Law 109-395, 109th Congress, approved Dec. 14, 2006. Authorizing the issuance of a gold medal to Dr. Norman E. Borlaug for his work in world agriculture to alleviate poverty and malnutrition.

Public Law 110-95, 110th Congress, approved Oct. 16, 2007. Authorizing the issuance of a gold medal to Dr. Michael Ellis DeBakey for his pioneering work in the field of cardiovascular surgery, as well as for his innovative research into this and other fields of medicine.

Public Law 110-209, 110th Congress, approved May 6, 2008. Authorizing the issuance of a gold medal to Daw Aung San Suu Kyi, in recognition of her courageous and unwavering commitment to peace, nonviolence, human rights and democracy in Burma.

Public Law 110-259, 110th Congress, approved July 1, 2008. Authorizing the posthumous issuance of a gold medal for Constantino Brumidi, in recognition of his contributions to the nation as a designer and decorator of the U.S. Capitol.

Public Law 110-260, 110th Congress, approved July 1, 2008. Authorizing the issuance of a gold medal to Edward William Brooke III, the first African American elected by popular vote to the U.S. Senate, for his unprecedented and enduring service to our Nation.

Public Law 110-413, 110th Congress, approved Oct. 10, 2008. To establish the Stephanie Tubbs Jones Gift of Life Medal for organ donors and the family of organ donors.

Public Law 110-420, 110th Congress, approved Oct. 15, 2008. Authorizing the issuance of a gold medal honoring Native American Code Talkers, in recognition of the contribution of the original 29 Navajo Marine Corps Radio Operators, known as the Navajo Code Talkers, "who distinguished themselves in performing a unique, highly successful communications operation that greatly assisted in saving countless lives and hastening the end of World War II in the Pacific."

Public Law 111-40, 111th Congress, approved July 1, 2009. Authorizing the issuance of a gold medal for Women Air Force Service Pilots of World War II, the first women in history to fly American military aircraft.

Public Law 111-44, 111th Congress, approved Aug. 7, 2009. To authorize the president, in conjunction with the 40th anniversary of the historic and first lunar landing by humans in 1969, to award gold medals on behalf of Congress to Neil A. Armstrong, the first human to walk on the moon; Edwin E. "Buzz" Aldrin Jr., the pilot of the lunar module and second person to walk on the moon; Michael Collins, the pilot of their Apollo 11 mission's command module; and, to the first American to orbit the Earth, John Herschel Glenn Jr.

Public Law 111-65, 111th Congress, approved Sept. 30, 2009. Authorizing the issuance of a gold medal to Arnold Palmer in recognition of his service to the Nation in promoting excellence and good sportsmanship in golf.

Public Law 111-221, 111th Congress, approved Aug. 6, 2010. Authorizing the issuance of silver medals in commemoration of the 10th anniversary of the Sept. 11, 2001, terrorist attacks on the United States and the establishment of the National September 11 Memorial & Museum at the World Trade Center.

Public Law 111-253, 111th Congress, approved Oct. 5, 2010. Authorizing the issuance of a gold medal to Dr. Muhammad Yunus in recognition of his contributions to the fight against global poverty.

Public Law 111-254, 111th Congress, approved Oct. 5, 2010. Authorizing the issuance of a gold medal for the 100th Infantry Battalion and the 442nd Regimental Combat Team, United States Army in recognition of their dedicated service during World War II.

Sales tax and numismatic items

In the late 1980s and early 1990s, the Industry Council for Tangible Assets (ICTA) was among those leading the fight to repeal sales taxes on numismatic and bullion coins. The following state sales tax reference guide is supplied by the Industry Council for Tangible Assets. This table is designed as a quick reference guide only.

Consult the individual state statutes for exact interpretation of state sales tax laws.

ICTA is not liable for any decisions based on the information contained herein. Collectible paper money is currently tax-exempt in the following states: Florida, Georgia, Iowa, Montana, North Dakota and South Carolina.

State	Tax Rate	Collector coins	Bullion coins	Bullion
Alabama	4%	taxed	taxed	taxed
Alaska	0%	—	—	—
Arizona	5.6%	exempt	exempt	exempt (except bullion for use in jewelry and works of art)
Arkansas	6%	taxed	taxed	taxed
California	8.25%	all categories exempt (sales of $1,500+)		
Colorado	2.9%	exempt	exempt	exempt
Connecticut	6%	exempt	exempt (sales of $1,000+)	
Delaware	0%	—	—	—
District of Columbia	5.75%	taxed	taxed	taxed
Florida	6%	exempt	exempt	exempt
Georgia	4%	exempt	exempt	exempt
Hawaii	4%	taxed	taxed	taxed
Idaho	6%	all three categories exempt (excluding bullion for use in jewelry and works of art)		
Illinois	6.25%	exempt	exempt	exempt
Indiana	7%	taxed	taxed	taxed
Iowa	6%	exempt	exempt	exempt
Kansas	6.3%	taxed	taxed	taxed
Kentucky	6%	taxed	taxed	taxed
Louisiana	4%	all three categories exempt (sales of $1,000+)		
Maine	5%	taxed	taxed	taxed
Maryland	6%	all categories exempt (sales of $1,000+)		
Massachusetts	6.25%	all categories exempt (sales of $1,000+)		
Michigan	6%	exempt	exempt	exempt
Minnesota	6.875%	taxed	taxed	taxed
Mississippi	7%	taxed	taxed	taxed
Missouri	4.225%	exempt	exempt	exempt
Montana	0%	—	—	—
Nebraska	5.5%	taxed	taxed	taxed
Nevada	6.85%	taxed	taxed	taxed
New Hampshire	0%	—	—	—
New Jersey	7%	taxed	taxed	taxed
New Mexico	5%	taxed	taxed	taxed
New York	4%	taxed	exempt	exempt (sales of $1,000+)
North Carolina	5.75%	taxed	taxed	taxed
North Dakota	5%	exempt	exempt	taxed
Ohio	5.5%	taxed	taxed	taxed
Oklahoma	4.5%	taxed	taxed	taxed
Oregon	0%	—	—	—
Pennsylvania	6%	exempt	exempt	exempt
Rhode Island	7%	exempt	exempt	exempt

State	Tax Rate	Collector coins	Bullion coins	Bullion
South Carolina	6%	exempt	exempt	exempt
South Dakota	4%	exempt	exempt	exempt
Tennessee	7%	taxed	taxed	taxed
Texas	6.25%	all categories exempt (sales of $1,000+)		
Utah	4.75%	exempt	exempt	exempt
Vermont	6%	taxed	taxed	taxed
Virginia	5%	taxed	taxed	taxed
Washington	6.5%	exempt	exempt	exempt
West Virginia	6%	taxed	taxed	taxed
Wisconsin	5%	taxed	taxed	taxed
Wyoming	4%	exempt	exempt	exempt

Source: Industry Council for Tangible Assets, (Box 1365, Severna Park, MD 21146-8365)

Regulations by governmental agencies

Governmental agencies must frequently write rules and regulations to explain the impact, and state how a particular course of action or conduct is to be carried out. As a means of internal government, comparable rules are required within each government agency or bureau.

Rules written by each of the governmental agencies must first be published in the *Federal Register,* a daily government publication. When approved, they are compiled annually into the Code of Federal Regulations (CFR). Included are all the necessary requirements for the United States Mint and the Bureau of Engraving and Printing, as well as actions that the U.S. Customs Service can take against attempted importation of counterfeit coins.

Often, it is the governmental interpretation of a statute in the CFR that is the dominant factor in enforcement, rather than the law itself. This is true, for example, in the case of the Hobby Protection Act, whose regulations promulgated by the Federal Trade Commission are the keystone of its effectiveness.

Below are reprinted in edited form selected sections from the CFR that pertain to numismatics. The volume of the CFR that the material appears in precedes the Code, while the section follows it.

Thus, 16 CFR sec. 304.1(d) would refer to Volume 16 of the Code of Federal Regulations at Section 304.1 (d).

Color Illustrations of U.S. Currency
31 CFR Part 411

In 1992 President George Bush signed legislation into Public Law 105-500, the "Counterfeit Deterrence Act of 1992," to permit the secretary of the Treasury to relax the long-standing prohibition against all but black-and-white photographs of U.S. paper money.

The Secret Service developed new regulations. On June 26, 1995, the Secret Service proposed to amend Title 31, Chapter IV of the Code of Federal Regulations by adding part 411, which would permit color images of U.S. currency.

At that time illustrations of U.S. currency were only permitted providing the illustration was in black and white, and was of a size less than three-fourths or more than one and one-half, in linear dimension, of each part illustrated, and provided the negatives and plates used in making the illustration were destroyed after their final use. Under Title 18 of the U.S. Code Sec. 504, color illustrations of U.S. currency were not permitted.

Written public comments were solicited and five were received. All those commenting questioned the need for and practicality of the requirement that the term "non-negotiable" be prominently and conspicuously placed across the center portion of any color illustration. The Secret Service later removed that portion of its proposal.

Also removed was a requirement that the positives, digitized storage medium, graphic files, magnetic medium and optical storage devices be destroyed immediately. The clause requiring destruction after their final use was substituted.

However, reproduction of foreign currency continues to be limited to black-and-white and the same size restrictions as U.S. currency. The text of the law reads as follows:

Part 411 – Color Illustrations of United States Currency

Authority: 18 U.S.C. 504; Treasury Directive Number 15-56, 58 FR 48539 (Sept. 16, 1993)

Sec. 411.1 Color illustrations authorized

(a) Notwithstanding any provision of chapter 25 of Title 18 of the U.S. Code, authority is hereby given for the printing, publishing or importation, or the making or importation of the necessary plates or items for such printing or publishing, of color illustrations of U.S. currency provided that:

(1) The illustration be of a size less than three-fourths or more than one and one-half, in linear dimension, of each part of any matter so illustrated;

(2) The illustration be one-sided; and

(3) All negatives, plates, positives, digitized storage medium, graphic files, magnetic medium, optical storage devices, and any other thing used in the making of the illustration that contain an image of the illustration or any part thereof shall be destroyed and/or deleted or erased after their final use in accordance with this section.

The rule became effective May 31, 1996, and was published in the *Federal Register* on that date.

Title 31 Sec. 92 United States Mint Operations and Procedures

Sec. 92.1 Manufacture of medals.

With the approval of the Director of the Mint, dies for medals of a national character designated by Congress may be executed at the Philadelphia Mint, and struck in such field office of the Mints and Assay Offices as the Director shall designate.

Sec. 92.2 Sale of "list" medals.

Medals on the regular Mint list, when available, are sold to the public at a charge sufficient to cover their cost, and to include mailing cost when mailed. Copies of the list of medals available for sale and their selling prices may be obtained from the Director of the Mint, Washington, DC.

Sec. 92.3 Manufacture and sale of "proof" coins.

"Proof" coins, i.e., coins prepared from blanks specially polished and struck, are made as authorized by the Director of the Mint and are sold at a price sufficient to cover their face value plus the additional expense of their manufacture and sale. Their manufacture and issuance are contingent upon the demands of regular operations. Information concerning availability and price may be obtained from the Director of the Mint, Treasury Department, Washington, DC 20220.

Sec. 92.4 Uncirculated Mint Sets.

Uncirculated Mint Sets, i.e., specially packaged coin sets containing one coin of each denomination struck at the Mints at Philadelphia and Denver, and the Assay Office at San Francisco, will be made as authorized by the Director of the Mint and will be sold at a price sufficient to cover their face value plus the additional expense of their processing and sale. Their manufacture and issuance are contingent upon demands of regular operations. Information concerning availability and price may be obtained from the Director of the Mint, Treasury Department, Washington, DC 20220.

Sec. 92.5 Procedure governing availability of Bureau of the Mint records.

(a) Regulations of the Office of the Secretary adopted. The regulations on the Disclosure of Records of the Office of the Secretary and other bureaus and offices of the Department issued under 5 U.S.C. 301 and 552 and published as Part 1 of this title, 32 FR No. 127, July 1, 1967, except for Sec. 1.7 of this title entitled "Appeal," shall govern the availability of Bureau of the Mint records.

(b) Determination of availability. The Director of the Mint delegates authority to the following Mint officials to determine, in accordance with Part 1 of this title, which of the records or information requested is available, subject to the appeal provided in Sec. 92.6: The Deputy Director of the Mint, Division Heads in the Office of the Director, and the Superintendent or Officer in Charge of the field office where the record is located.

(c) Requests for identifiable records. A written request for an identifiable record shall be addressed to the Director of the Mint, Washington, DC 20220. A request presented in person shall be made in the public reading room of the Treasury Department, 15th Street and Pennsylvania Avenue, NW, Washington, DC, or in such other office designated by the Director of the Mint.

Sec. 92.6 Appeal.

Any person denied access to records requested under Sec. 92.5 may file an appeal to the Director of the Mint within 30 days after notification of such denial. The appeal shall provide the name and address of the appellant, the identification of the record denied, and the date of the original request and its denial.

Title 31 Sec. 601 Distinctive Paper For United States Currency and Other Securities

Sec. 601.1 Notice to the public.

The Secretary of the Treasury, by authority of law, has adopted a new distinctive paper for use in printing United States currency in addition to the existing distinctive papers for use in printing United States currency and other securities.

Sec. 601.2 Description of paper.

The paper utilized in the printing of United States currency and public debt issues is cream-white bank note paper which must contain security features prescribed by the Secretary of the Treasury. All currency paper shall contain distinctive fibers, colored red and blue, incorporated in the body of the paper while in the process of manufacture and evenly distributed throughout. In addition to distinctive red and blue fibers, currency paper shall contain, for denominations prescribed by the Secretary of the Treasury, security threads embedded beneath the surface of the paper during the manufacturing process. Security threads shall contain graphics consisting of the designation "USA" and the denomination of the currency, expressed in alphabetic or numeric characters. In addition to the security thread, for the denominations prescribed by the Secretary of the Treasury, the paper will bear a watermark identical to the portrait to be printed on the paper.

Sec. 601.3 Use of paper.

The new distinctive paper shall be used for printing Federal Reserve Notes of the denominations prescribed by the Secretary of the Treasury. The use of the existing distinctive papers, the distinctive features of which consist of distinctive fibers, colored red and blue, incorporated in the body of the paper while in the process of manufacture and evenly distributed throughout, and the security thread containing graphics consisting of the designation "USA" and the denomination of the currency, will be continued for printing of any currency denomination prescribed by the Secretary of the Treasury.

Sec. 601.4 Use of paper; interest-bearing securities of the United States.

The existing distinctive papers shall be used for the printing of interest-bearing securities of the United States, and for any other printing where the use of distinctive paper is indicated.

Sec. 601.5 Penalty for unauthorized control or possession.

The Secretary of the Treasury hereby gives notice that the new distinctive paper, together with any other distinctive papers heretofore adopted for the printing of paper currency or other obligations or securities of the United States, is and will be subject to the provisions of 18 U.S.C. 474A which provides, in part, that it is against the law to possess any paper, or facsimile thereof, designated by the Secretary of the Treasury for the printing of U.S. currency or any other security of the United States, except with the permission of the Secretary or the authorized official. This crime is punishable by a fine not to exceed five thousand dollars or imprisonment for not more than fifteen years, or both.

United States Customs Service

Counterfeit Coins, Obligations and Other Securities; Illustrations or Reproduction of Coins or Stamps

19 CFR Sec. 12.48. Importation prohibited; exception to prohibition of importation; procedure.

(a) In accordance with Chapter 25, Title 18, United States Code, any token, disk, or device in the likeness or similitude of any coin of the United States or of a foreign country; counterfeits of coins in circulation in the United States; counterfeited, forged, or altered obligations or other securities of the United States or of any foreign government; or plates, dies, or other apparatus which may be used in making any of the foregoing, when brought into the United States, shall be seized, and delivered to the nearest representative of the United States Secret Service, together with a report of the facts, for appropriate disposition.

(b) In accordance with section 504 of title 18, United States Code, the printing, publishing, or importation or the making or importation of the necessary plates for such printing or publishing for philatelic, numismatic, educational, historical, or newsworthy purposes in articles, books, journals, newspapers, or albums (but not for advertising purposes, except illustrations of stamps and paper money in philatelic or numismatic advertising of legitimate numismatists and dealers in stamps or publishers of or dealers in philatelic or numismatic articles, books, journals, newspapers, or albums) of black and white illustrations of canceled and uncanceled United States postage stamps shall be permitted.

(c) The importation (but not for advertising purposes except philatelic advertising) of motion-picture films, microfilms, or slides, for projection upon a screen or for use in telecasting, of postage and revenue stamps and other obligations and securities of the United States and postage and revenue stamps, notes, bonds, and other obligations or securities of any foreign government, bank, or corporation shall be permitted.

(d) Printed matter of the character described in section 504, title 18, United States Code, containing reproductions of postage or revenue stamps, executed in accordance with any exception stated in section 504, or colored reproductions of canceled foreign postage stamps may be admitted to entry. Printed matter containing illustrations or reproductions not executed in accordance with such exceptions shall be treated as prohibited importations. If no application for exportation or assent to forfeiture and destruction is received by the port director within 30 days from the date of notification to the importer that the articles are prohibited, the articles shall be reported to the United States attorney for forfeiture.

Notwithstanding any other provision of this chapter, the following are permitted: (1) The printing, publishing, or importation, or the making or importation of the necessary plates for such printing or publishing, of illustrations of: (A) Postage stamps of the United States, (B) Revenue stamps of the United States, (C) Any other obligation or other security of the United States, and (D) Postage stamps, revenue stamps, notes, bonds, and any other obligation or other security of any foreign government, bank, or corporation, for philatelic, numismatic, educational, historical, or newsworthy purposes in articles, books, journals, newspapers, or albums (but not for advertising purposes, except illustrations of stamps and paper money in philatelic or numismatic advertising of legitimate numismatists and dealers in stamps or publishers of or dealers in philatelic or numismatic articles, books, journals, newspapers, or albums). Illustrations permitted by the foregoing provisions of this section shall be made in accordance with the following conditions (i) All illustrations shall be in black and white, except that illustrations of postage stamps issued by the United States or by any foreign government may be in color; (ii) All illustrations (including illustrations of uncanceled postage stamps in color) shall be of a size less than three-fourths or more than one and one-half, in linear dimension, of each part of any matter so illustrated which is covered by subparagraph (A), (B), (C), or (D) of this paragraph, except that black and white illustrations of postage and revenue stamps issued by the United States or by any foreign government and colored illustrations of canceled postage stamps issued by the United States may be in the exact linear dimension in which the stamps were issued; and (iii) The negatives and plates used in making the illustrations shall be destroyed after their final use in accordance with this section.

(2) The making or importation, but not for advertising purposes except philatelic advertising, of motion-picture films, microfilms, or slides, for projection upon a screen or for use in telecasting, of postage and revenue stamps and other obligations and securities of the United States, and postage and revenue stamps, notes, bonds, and other obligations or securities of any foreign government, bank, or corporation. No prints or other reproductions shall be made from such films or slides, except for the purposes of paragraph (1), without the permission of the Secretary of the Treasury.

For the purposes of this section the term postage stamp includes postage meter stamps. (18 U.S.C. 504).

Coins across borders

Dealers may wish to take the coins they plan to carry to Canada to the Customs office nearest them and register them. A copy of the form will be given to the dealers to present to U.S. Customs on their return from Canada. This will identify the coins upon returning to the United States.

Concerning coins that dealers purchase in Canada, the Customs Service has ruled that metal coins issued or specifically authorized by the government whose coinage it is, including official restrikes or exact copies authorized by the government concerned, are free of duty.

All coins imported into the United States for nonmonetary purposes (for example, for resale or numismatic purposes) are considered merchandise subject to customs entry requirements, even though they are free of duty, and must be reported and the value declared.

Counterfeit money may not be imported into Canada.

For information regarding procedures for taking rare coins or medals into Canada and returning them, collectors and dealers can write to Canada Border Services Agency, Ottawa ON, Canada, K1A 0L8, or visit the agency online at www.cbsa-asfc.gc.ca.

National import restrictions

A movement is currently under way by many countries to protect their cultural patrimony and in response, U.S. Customs and Border Protection has imposed import restrictions on certain coins of Chinese, Cyprus and Italian types. The governments of these countries requested the protections, as coins constitute an inseparable part of the archaeological record of the land and they are vulnerable to pillage and illicit export. Critics of these import restrictions cite the widespread circulation of these coins in ancient times that extended beyond any current national borders.

Italian coins

The Jan. 19, 2011, *Federal Register* contained a notice that import restrictions were extended to certain coins of Italian type.

While the importation of many classic Greek coins has been affected by these import restrictions, most Roman Republic and Imperial coins remain unrestrained.

Restricted coins Italian types can only be imported into the U.S. with an export certificate issued by the Republic of Italy or "satisfactory evidence" showing that the coins were exported from, or were outside Italy, at least 10 years prior to the importation into the United States, or that the coins were exported from or were outside of Italy before Jan. 19, 2011.

The categories of coins subject to the restrictions are as follows:

"Coins of Italian Types — A type catalogue of listed currency and coins can be found in N.K. Rutter et al. (eds.), Historia Numorum: Italy (London, 2001). Others appear in G.F. Hill Coins of Ancient Sicily (Westminster, 1903).

"1. Lumps of bronze (Aes Rude) — Irregular lumps of bronze used as an early medium of exchange in Italy from the 9th century B.C.

"2. Bronze bars (Ramo Secco and Aes Signatum) — Cast bronze bars (whole or cut) used as a media of exchange in central Italy and Etruria from the 5th century B.C.

"3. Cast coins (Aes Grave) — Cast bronze coins of Rome, Etruscan, and Italian cities from the 4th century B.C.

"4. Struck coins — Struck coins of the Roman Republic and Etruscan cities produced in gold, silver, and bronze from the 3rd century B.C. to c. 211 B.C., including the 'Romano-Campanian' coinage.

"5. Struck colonial coinage — Struck bronze coins of Roman republican and early imperial colonies and municipia in Italy, Sicily, and Sardinia from the 3rd century B.C. to c. A.D. 37.

"6. Coins of the Greek cities — Coins of the Greek cities in the southern Italian peninsula and in Sicily (Magna Graecia), cast or struck in gold, silver, and bronze, from the late 6th century B.C. to c. 200 B.C."

Chinese coins

The Chinese import restrictions cover archaeological materials representing China's heritage from the Paleolithic Period to the end of the Tang Period (A.D. 907). Under the current import restrictions, restricted artifacts must be accompanied upon entry into the United States with either a valid Chinese export certificate or certifications indicating that the coin in question left China before the effective date of the restrictions, Jan. 16, 2009.

The *Federal Register* has listed the coin types impacted as follows:

"a. Zhou Media of Exchange and Tool-shaped Coins: Early media of exchange include bronze spades, bronze knives, and cowrie shells. During the 6th century BC, flat, simplified, and standardized cast bronze versions of spades appear and these constitute China's first coins. Other coin shapes appear in bronze including knives and cowrie shells. These early coins may bear inscriptions.

"b. Later, tool-shaped coins began to be replaced by disc-shaped ones which are also cast in bronze and marked with inscriptions. These coins have a central round or square hole.

"c. Qin: In the reign of Qin Shi Huangdi (221–210 BC) the square-holed round coins become the norm. The new Qin coin is inscribed simply with its weight, expressed in two Chinese characters ban liang. These are written in small seal script and are placed symmetrically to the right and left of the central hole.

"d. Han through Sui: Inscriptions become longer, and may indicate that inscribed object is a coin, its value in relation to other coins, or its size. Later, the period of issue, name of the mint, and numerals representing dates may also appear on obverse or reverse. A new script, clerical (lishu), comes into use in the Jin.

"e. Tang: The clerical script becomes the norm until 959, when coins with regular script (kaishu) also begin to be issued."

Cypriot coins

Restrictions on the importation of Pre-Classical and Classical coins of Cypriot type were published in the *Federal Register* on July 13, 2007. Impacted are coins of Cypriot types made of gold, silver and bronze including but not limited to:

"1. Issues of the ancient kingdoms of Amathus, Kition, Kourion, Idalion, Lapethos, Marion, Paphos, Soli, and Salamis dating from the end of the 6th century B.C. to 332 B.C.

"2. Issues of the Hellenistic period, such as those of Paphos, Salamis, and Kition from 332 B.C. to c. 30 B.C.

"3. Provincial and local issues of the Roman period from c. 30 B.C. to 235 A.D. Often these have a bust or head on one side and the image of a temple (the Temple of Aphrodite at Palaipaphos) or statue (statue of Zeus Salaminios) on the other."

Treasury, Secret Service advisory policies

The following policies are interpretations the Treasury has made of various parts of the U.S. Code dealing with numismatics.

Department of the Treasury policy on metal tokens

On Sept. 2, 1983, the Mint notified the public that it was proposing to change its policy that opposed the use of metal tokens provided that certain criteria was met.

Vol. 48 Federal Register 40054. Public comment was invited and, for the most part, comments were received that were aimed at preventing the unlawful use of tokens in vending machines and other coin-operated devices. On June 21, 1984, the Mint published revised token restrictions that generally adopted the increased restrictions, but invited additional comments.

Effective July 15, 1985, final regulations were issued by the Mint. The policy reflected is intended as advice and guidance for token manufacturers and users as well as the public. It represents the views of the Treasury Department concerning measures that should minimize the possibility of violating the counterfeiting provisions of Title 18 of the United States Code. It does not prescribe mandatory specifications concerning the size, composition or any other requirements of metal tokens. These matters, however, may be the subjects of state or local regulation. What it does state is that the Treasury Department does not object to tokens that meet the restrictions set forth in the notice. It should be noted that prosecution of violations of the counterfeiting statutes is vested in the Justice Department, which assesses each claimed violation based upon the facts presented.

Restrictions on the diameter of metal tokens is the most essential means of minimizing the possibility that tokens will be unlawfully used to slug vending and other gaming machines, according to the Treasury Department.

The Treasury Department determined that restrictions on minimum weight and thickness on tokens are not necessary in view of the restrictions imposed on token diameters. The regulations that follow were published from the office of the U.S. treasurer in the mid-1980s, Katherine D. Ortega:

Conditions for Department Approval

The Department does not oppose the production or use of tokens which meet the following conditions:

1. Tokens should be clearly identified with the name and location of the establishment from which they originate on at least one side. Alternatively, tokens should contain an identifying mark or logo which clearly indicates the identity of the manufacturer.

2. Tokens should not be within the following diameter ranges (inches):

0.680 — 0.775
0.810 — 0.860
0.910 — 0.980
1.018 — 1.068
1.180 — 1.230
1.475 — 1.525

3. Tokens shall not be manufactured from a three-layered material consisting of a copper-nickel alloy clad on both sides of a pure core, nor from a copper-based material except if the total of zinc, nickel, aluminum, magnesium and other alloying materials is a least 20 percent of the token's weight. In addi-

tion, tokens shall not be manufactured from material which possesses sufficient magnetic properties so as to be accepted by a coin mechanism.

4. Establishments using these tokens shall prominently and conspicuously post signs on their premises notifying patrons that federal law prohibits the use of such tokens outside the premises for any monetary purpose whatever.

5. The issuing establishment shall not accept tokens as payment for any goods or services offered by such establishment with the exception of the specific use for which the tokens were designed.

6. The design on the token shall not resemble any current or past foreign or U.S. coinage.

The Department of Treasury believes that the observance of these restrictions will minimize the possibility of a violation of the counterfeiting statutes. The prosecution of violations of these statutes is vested with the Department of Justice which must evaluate any claimed violation on the particular facts presented.

Katherine D. Ortega, Treasurer of the United States

Coin jewelry

Most coin jewelry, including cutout coinage and engraved coinage, is legal, according to the present interpretation of Sec. 331, Title 18, United States Code, which prohibits fraudulent mutilation of coins.

Coin jewelry is not prohibited by this section in the absence of fraud and treating of the coins used to produce these novelties. Manufacture and sale of two-headed and two-tailed coins are also legal, according to the Secret Service.

This opinion is advisory and is not binding upon the Department of Justice or any U.S. attorney, however, according to the Secret Service.

An official Treasury Department statement pertaining to coin jewelry is:

"Section 331, Title 18, U.S. Code, prohibits the fraudulent alteration and mutilation of United States and foreign coins, but does not prohibit said defacement if done without fraudulent intent, or if the mutilated coins are not used fraudulently.

"The Bureau of the Mint feels that it is unfortunate that laws at this time do not specifically prohibit this undesirable and reprehensible practice.

"The Mint also has very strong feelings about disfigurement of United States coins or their use other than as a means of exchange. If the practice cannot otherwise be prevented, the Mint would strongly support legislation prohibiting this use of coins.

"Coins so withdrawn from circulation must be replaced and when practiced on a wholesale scale by many firms, an unnecessary cost and burden is imposed upon the Mint."

The U.S. Mint posts guidance on its website **www. usmint.gov/consumer/** for marketers to be aware of Mint trademarks and not to use the words "United States Mint" or "U.S. Mint" in connection with any advertisement, if its use gives the impression that the advertised product is approved, endorsed or authorized by the Mint.

The Mint also claims trademark rights to certain phrases involving its products, including the phrases "America the Beautiful" and "America the Beautiful Quarter(s)." The Mint prohibits the use of those phrases in advertising. Advertisers should contact the United States Mint before using such phrases in their advertising copy, to determine whether it violates Mint trademarks.

Coin replicas

Sec. 489, Title 18, United States Code, prohibits making, importing, possessing with intent to sell, give away or use in any manner, any token, disk or device in the likeness or similitude as to design, color or inscription of any of the coins of the United States, or of any foreign country.

This section is directed at devices which, although not strictly counterfeit coins, may be mistaken for genuine coins by unwary persons, because they approximate genuine coins in size, color, design and inscription.

However, items made to sell, give away or use in any manner that are substantially larger and heavier than any coin of the United States or any coin of a foreign country, and which do not bear any indication of value and therefore do not purport to be money, do not violate Sec. 489.

The policy of the Treasury regarding substantially enlarged replicas of coins is that any coin reproduction must be more than twice the size of a United States dollar coin, the largest United States coin when the policy was formulated. Consequently, all reproductions must be more than 3 inches in diameter.

Thickness of the item is not material, according to the Treasury.

The manufacture of a raised impression of a coin is considered to be in violation of Sec. 489, if the impression is removable; approximately the size of a genuine coin; and is sufficiently in likeness of a genuine coin to be capable of being passed off as such.

Counterfeiting laws fall under the jurisdiction of the U.S. Secret Service and the U.S. Department of Justice, and are in Chapter 25, Title 18, United States Code.

The U.S. Mint advises sellers of replicas to make it clear in advertising and marketing materials that the offered piece is a replica.

Gold-plated and colorized coins

Since the gold regulations were amended April 19, 1971, it has been legal to obtain, hold, transport, import or export any gold-plated coins.

Restrictions were imposed to prevent the diversion of coins to decorative uses during the coin shortage of the 1960s. Since all coins are now in ample supply, such restrictions became unnecessary, according to the Treasury Department.

The U.S. Mint advises those considering marketing and creating colorized or plated U.S. coins to consult with an attorney, writing: "The United States Mint may own copyright by assignment, as permitted by 17 U.S.C. § 105. In fact, the United States Mint owns copyright in several commemorative and circulating coin designs. Although the copyright symbol does not appear on the coin itself, the United States Mint generally includes the symbol on marketing materials. Copyrighted coin designs include several designs used in the 1995-1996 Olympic Commemorative Coin Program, the 1995 Civil War Battlefield Commemorative Coin Program, and the Golden Dollar (Sacagawea) coin obverse. If your company wants to use a copyrighted design, then you will need to contact [the] Deputy Chief Counsel, United States Mint, 801 9th Street, NW, Washington, DC 20220. Requests may be faxed to (202) 756-6110. The United States Mint deems any unauthorized use of a United States Mint copyrighted design to constitute copyright infringement."

Paper money reproductions

The Counterfeit Detection Act of 1992, Public Law 102-550, in Section 411 of Title 31 of the Code of Federal Regulations, permits color illustrations of U.S. currency, provided that: The illustration is of a size less than three-fourths or more than one and one-half, in linear dimension, of each part of the item illustrated, the illustration is one-sided and all negatives, plates, positives, digitized storage medium, graphic files, magnetic medium, optical storage devices, and any other thing used in the making of the illustration that contain an image of the illustration or any part thereof are destroyed and/or deleted or erased after their final use

To meet regulations, paper money art reproduction must be at least these measurements:

Fractional Currency

Actual size: sizes vary; smallest note is the 3-cent Third Issue note, measuring 39 millimeters by 64 millimeters; largest note in width is the 50-cent Third Issue, measuring 46 millimeters by 133 millimeters; deepest note is the Crawford 50-cent Fifth Issue note at 52 millimeters by 108 millimeters.

Unless exact note size is known, to comply with legal requirements illustrations should be at least 2.25 by 3.75 inches (58.5 by 96 millimeters) or smaller than 1.125 by 1.875 inches (29.25 by 48 millimeters).

Small Size Paper Money

(Federal Reserve notes, silver and gold certificates, United States notes, national bank notes, Federal Reserve Bank notes)

Actual size: 6.125 by 2.625 inches (156 by 67 millimeters).

More than one and one-half times actual size: 9.25 by 4 inches (235 by 102 millimeters).

Less than three-fourths actual size: 4.59375 by 1.96875 inches (117 by 50 millimeters).

Large Size Paper Money

Actual size: 7.5 by 3.125 inches (191 by 79 millimeters).

More than one and one-half times actual size: 11.2598 by 4.75 inches (286 by 121 millimeters).

Less than three-fourths actual size: 5.625 by 2.21875 inches (143 by 56 millimeters).

Defacing paper money

Sec. 333 of Title 18 of the U.S. Code prohibits, among other things, mutilating, cutting, defacing, disfiguring, or perforating or uniting or cementing together any national bank or Federal Reserve note with intent to render such currency unfit to be reissued.

Instances such as dollar bills embedded in jewelry, or portraits of popular persons superimposed on Federal Reserve notes as souvenirs do not usually constitute intent to render the currency unfit to be reissued, and so are not prohibited.

Coin reproductions

Photographs or printed illustrations, motion-picture films or slides of United States and foreign coins may be used for any purpose including advertising.

With few exceptions, existing law generally prohibits the manufacture, sale or use of any token, disk or device in the likeness or similitude of any coins that are issued as money.

Scrip

Congress has enacted legislation to prevent scrip certificates from circulating as or instead of lawful money. Sec. 336 of Title 18 of the U.S. Code prohibits the making, issuing, circulating, or payment out of any obligation of less than a dollar "intended to circulate as money or to be received or used in lieu of lawful money of the United States."

After analyzing the statute and the cases interpreting it, the Treasury has ruled that scrip redeemable only in merchandise and not in coin or currency, that is not negotiable and that is redeemable only at the particular store location where issued would not be in violation of the statute.

Federal Trade Commission

16 CFR Part 304 The Hobby Protection Act (53 Federal Register 38942)

On Nov. 29, 1973, Congress passed the Hobby Protection Act requiring manufacturers and importers of imitation political items to mark plainly and permanently with the calendar year the items were made. It also requires manufacturers and importers of imitation numismatic items to mark the items plainly and permanently with the word "copy."

The Act required the FTC to develop regulations regarding how the marking would be carried out. The FTC issued its Rules and Regulations in 1975 under the Hobby Protection Act. Those rules established the sizes and dimensions of the letters and numerals to be used as well as the location of the markings.

In 1988, the FTC amended section 304.6 of the Rules and Regulations under the Hobby Protection Act (16 CFR Part 304) to provide additional guidance on the minimum size of letters for the word "copy" as a proportion of the diameter of the coin reproductions—no less than 2 millimeters high, 6 millimeters wide and a minimum depth of 0.3 millimeter or one half the thickness of the reproduction, whichever is the lesser. The amendment permits use of a smaller marking to accommodate coins that are issued as miniature imitations.

FTC had discovered that if the coin were too small to comply with the minimum letter size requirements, the manufacturer or importer had to individually request from the commission a variance from those requirements. Because imitation miniature coins were becoming more common, the FTC decided to allow the word "copy" on miniature imitation coins in sizes that could be reduced proportionally with the size of the item.

On March 25, 1997, the Federal Trade Commission published in the *Federal Register* a request for written public comments concerning the rules and regulations under the Hobby Protection Act.

The request was part of the FTC's systematic review of all its current regulations and guides. The comments were limited to the overall costs, benefits and regulatory and economic impact of the Hobby Protection Act, especially with an eye to the impact on small businesses. The FTC asked for comments on 21 separate issues.

The American Numismatic Association, Casino Chips and Gaming Tokens Collectors Club and *Coin World* filed formal statements asking the FTC to continue protecting consumers by maintaining the Hobby Protection Act. The FTC received more than 1,000 comments on the rules and regulations.

According to the FTC, the comments "uniformly supported the continuing need for the rules and noted that the rules have been successful in protecting consumers from those who would try to pass off reproductions as originals."

FTC officials also indicated that the comments "indicated that the rules do not impose significant burdens or costs on firms subject to the rules."

Some of the comments received were related to products not covered by the Act, such as replicas of antiques and collectibles being offered as genuine.

The FTC decided not to expand the rules to include these items based on the "Act's limited scope, the existence of other state and federal laws that provide remedies for these problems, and the availability of resources that educate and warn collectors on how to distinguish originals from reproductions."

In July 1998, the Federal Trade Commission unanimously voted to retain in its present form the rules and regulations. The decision was published in the July 7, 1998, issue of the *Federal Register.*

Copies of the full text of the *Federal Register* notice are available from the FTC website at **www.ftc.gov** and also from the FTC's Consumer Response Center, Room 130, Sixth Street and Pennsylvania Avenue Northwest, Washington, DC 20580, or by telephoning (202) 382-4357 or TDD for the hearing-impaired at (866) 653-4261. To find out the latest news as it is announced, call the FTC NewsPhone recording at (202) 326-2710.

Commission of Fine Arts

The Commission of Fine Arts was established by the Act of May 17, 1910. Since then, it has frequently been called upon by the United States Congress to make determinations with respect to coin and medal designs.

A portion of the enabling act, now codified in Title 40 of the United States Code, follows:

40 US Code, Sec. 9101. Commission of Fine Arts

A permanent Commission of Fine Arts is created to be composed of seven well-qualified judges of the fine arts, who shall be appointed by the President, and shall serve for a period of four years each, and until their successors are appointed and qualified. The president shall have authority to fill all vacancies.

The Commission of Fine Arts advises on:

(1) the location of statues, fountains, and monuments in the public squares, streets, and parks in the District of Columbia;

(2) the selection of models for statues, fountains, and monuments erected under the authority of the Federal Government;

(3) the selection of artists to carry out clause (2); and

(4) questions of art generally when required to do so by the President or a committee of Congress.

(Among the commission's responsibilities is the review of all commemorative coin and congressional medal designs.)

Citizens Commemorative Coin Advisory Committee

The Citizens Commemorative Coin Advisory Committee was established as part of the United States Mint Reauthorization and Reform Act of 1992 (signed into law Oct. 6, 1992 Public Law 102-390). The seven-member committee was appointed by the secretary of the Treasury on Nov. 15, 1993.

The committee was abolished on April 23, 2003, with the passage of Public Law 108-15, which established the Citizens Coinage Advisory Committee.

The law mandated that the CCCAC shall "designate annually the events, persons, or places that the Advisory Committee recommends be commemorated by the issuance of commemorative coin in each of the five calendar years succeeding the year in which such designation is made; make recommendations with respect to the mintage level for any commemorative coin recommended and; submit a report to the Congress containing a description of the events, persons, or places which the committee recommends be commemorated by a coin, the mintage level recommended for any such commemorative coin, and the Committee's reasons for such recommendations."

The first members appointed included U.S. Mint Director Philip N. Diehl, who assumed the position of chairman with approval of other committee members, David L. Ganz, Elvira Clain-Stefanelli, Reed Hawn, Elsie Sterling Howard, Danny Hoffman and Thomas V. Shockley III.

The CCCAC developed criteria for evaluating commemorative coin subject selection after reviewing public comments actively solicited through the general and numismatic press; through a public forum on July 30, 1994, at the American Numismatic Association's annual convention; and through direct contact with committee members who made themselves available to the public by telephone, fax and mail.

The CCCAC determined that the nation's coinage should be a permanent reflection of its values and culture. The committee committed itself to themes and designs that "represent the noblest values and achievements of the nation, recognizing the widest variety of contributions to our history and culture. A primary goal of the committee [was] to ensure that commemorative themes and designs meet the highest standards for artistic excellence," according to the CCCAC's first report to Congress in 1994.

To meet those goals the committee decided that:

Historical persons, places, events and themes to be commemorated should have an enduring effect on the nation's history or culture. Their significance should be national or international in scope. Several themes were considered inappropriate for commemoration: state or regional anniversaries with little or no national significance; local institutions such as governments, universities, and public and private schools; commercial enterprises and products; and organizations, individuals, and themes principally sectarian in nature.

No living person should be honored by commemoration on U.S. coins.

Events to be commemorated should have national or international significance and draw participation from across America or around the world.

Commemorative coins should be issued in the appropriate year of commemoration.

Historical events should generally be considered for commemoration on important or significant anniversaries.

Commemorative themes and designs should not be considered if one treating the same subject has been issued in the past 10 years. Commemorative coinage designs should reflect traditional American coin iconography as well as contemporary developments in the arts.

Designs should be determined in consultation with sponsoring organizations but should not be determined by legislation.

Commemorative coinage should not be required to contain logos and emblems of non-governmental organizations as part of the design.

Coins should be dated in the year of their issuance.

Legislation authorizing the production of coins should be enacted no less than nine months before the date on which the coins may first be available to the public.

The CCCAC issued its first report to Congress in November 1994. In August 1994, the committee sent a letter to then Senate Banking chairman Donald W. Riegle, Jr., and Joseph P. Kennedy II, chairman of the House Banking subcommittee in charge of coinage issues, expressing concern over the proliferation of commemorative coin programs and pending legislation. Thirteen programs had been approved for the years 1994 to 2002. The committee stated in its 1994 report to Congress that the "public is telling the Congress and the CCCAC, and the Mint's falling sales are reinforcing the message, that the commemorative coin market is saturated."

The CCCAC recommended that future commemorative coin programs be limited to silver dollars with maximum mintages of not more than 500,000 and copper-nickel clad half dollars with maximum mintages of 750,000. If a commemorative program has a special significance, a gold $5 coin could be added and the CCCAC recommended that the mintage be kept at 100,000.

Another significant part of its 1994 report was the CCCAC's endorsement of a circulating commemorative coin. The committee observed that coinage "is a tangible way to touch the lives of every American. Circulating coinage promotes our national ideals, builds awareness and pride in our history, and informs millions of foreign visitors who use U.S. coins."

The CCCAC recommended that Congress authorize the secretary of the treasury to issue a circulating commemorative coin, and allow the secretary to select either the quarter dollar or a higher denomination. In addition, the secretary would be given the authority to determine when to issue such a coin and an appropriate design.

Eventually Congress did approve the 50 States Circulating Commemorative Coin program introduced by Rep. Michael N. Castle, R-Del. President Clinton signed the bill Dec. 1, 1997, and it became Public Law 105-124.

Citizens Coinage Advisory Committee

The CCAC was established by Act of Congress in 2003 to:

➤ Advise the secretary of the Treasury on any theme or design proposals relating to circulating coinage, bullion coinage, Congressional Gold Medals, and national and other medals.

➤ Advise the secretary of the Treasury with regard to the events, persons, or places to be commemorated by the issuance of commemorative coins in each of the five calendar years succeeding the year in which a commemorative coin designation is made.

➤ Make recommendations with respect to the mintage level for any commemorative coin recommended.

The CCAC submits a letter to the Secretary of the Treasury after each public meeting with the minutes of the meeting.

The various seats on the panel are filled by individuals representing specific elements of the American population or holding special knowledge in certain areas.

Its current members are:

Michael A. Ross, 2010 to 2014, specially qualified in American history

Donald Scarinci, 2008 to 2012, person recommended by Senate Majority Leader

Heidi Wastweet, 2010 to 2014, specially qualified in sculpture or medallic arts

Vacant, recommended by the speaker of the House

Gary Marks, 2007 to 2011, representative of general public

Arthur Houghton, 2007 to 2011, specially qualified in numismatic curation

Michael Brown, 2007 to 2011, recommended by Senate minority leader

Vacant, specially qualified in numismatics

Dr. Doreen Bolger, 2009 to 2013, representative of general public

Michael Olson, 2009 to 2013, person recommended by House minority leader

Erik N. Jansen, 2011 to 2015, representative of general public

In its first report for the fiscal year 2003 ending Sept. 23, 2003, the committee recommended themes and designs for the new 5-cent coins to be issued in 2003, 2004 and 2005 celebrating the bicentennials of the Louisiana Purchase and the expedition by Meriwether Lewis and William Clark.

The committee approved 10 commemorative themes for the years 2005 through 2009:

2005	Secretariat	35th Anniversary of birth of the famous race horse
	American Railway	175th anniversary of first American built railroad train
2006	San Francisco Mint	100th anniversary of 1906 earthquake
	Benjamin Franklin	300th anniversary of birth
2007	Jamestown	400th anniversary of America's first permanent English settlement
	Augustus Saint-Gaudens	100th anniversary of $20 gold high-relief coin
2008	American Numismatic Society	150th anniversary
	Model "T" Ford	100th anniversary
2009	Abraham Lincoln	200th anniversary of Lincoln's birth
	Norman Rockwell	115th anniversary of Rockwell's birth

In its report for fiscal year 2004, the committee approved commemorative themes for the years 2006 through 2010, replacing its recommendation for a 2007 Augustus Saint-Gaudens program with a dollar honoring the 250th anniversary of Alexander Hamilton's birth, and changing the 2008 programs to the 150th anniversary of Theodore Roosevelt's birth and the 50th anniversary of the first American satellite.

The committee kept the 2009 Lincoln recommendation, and dropped the Normal Rockwell program. It added for 2010 support for a silver dollar commemorating the 150th anniversary of the Pony Express.

In its fiscal year 2005 report, the committee recommended portraying presidents on circulating commemorative dollar coins and to use multiple cent designs honoring the bicentennial of Lincoln's birth in 2009.

The committee also recommended the 150th anniversary of the birth of Theodore Roosevelt and the 50th anniversary of NASA and Jet Propulsion Laboratory as commemorative programs for 2008, despite the American Bald Eagle Recovery program already enacted for 2008.

The CCAC removed its support for a silver dollar commemorative honoring the 200th anniversary of Lincoln's birth in 2009, replacing it with programs recognizing the 200th anniversary of the Birth of Louis Braille and the 200th anniversary of Robert Fulton's steamboat patent.

Regarding 2010 programs, the CCAC kept its support for the 150th anniversary of the Pony Express, adding the 50th anniversary of the Echo communications satellite to the subject to create a joint commemorative celebrating the evolution of American communication technology. The CCAC also voiced support for a silver dollar honoring American Veterans Disabled for Life.

Finally, the fiscal year 2005 report recommended a bullion coin or medal series showcasing advanced design techniques. "These could include colorized medals, laser etching, selective gold-plating, holograms, enamel paint, gold cameo inserts, holographic colors, or bi-metallic outer rings. The technique of colorizing would be ideal to bring the natural beauty of the Autumn Foliage in New England, the Northern Lights of Alaska, the Big Sky Country in the North West, and the Cherry Blossoms of Washington D.C."

In its fiscal year 2006 report, the CCAC continued to recommend circulating commemoratives and added a recommendation for a 2011 commemorative program recognizing the 50th Anniversary of the Peace Corps.

For the fiscal year 2007, the committee expressed its support for U.S. Mint Director Edmund C. Moy's call for a "Neo-Renaissance" in American coin design, and added support for the development of a five-year circulating "Liberty" commemorative series starting in 2010.

"Each year, one denomination could be issued with an image representing Liberty, alongside the regular design for that denomination. The series could begin with a Liberty half-dollar issued alongside the Kennedy half-dollar during the year 2010, followed by a Liberty quarter issued alongside the Washington quarter in 2011, a Liberty dime issued alongside the Roosevelt dime in 2012, a Liberty 5-cent coin (nickel) issued alongside the Jefferson nickel in 2013, and a Liberty cent issued alongside the Lincoln cent in 2014. With these five new coins, each issued for a single year, America's coinage would present a series of new, artistic images representing one of America's core values."

For commemorative programs, the committee provided support to a 2011 silver dollar honoring the 200th anniversary of the Birth of Harriet Beecher Stowe, who wrote *Uncle Tom's Cabin*. It added 2012 program recommendations for a silver dollar to raise funds for the National Fallen Firefighters Memorial on the grounds of the National Fire Academy in Emmitsburg, Md., and a silver dollar for the 200th anniversary of the Battle between USS *Constitution* and the HMS *Guerriere.*

In its report for fiscal year 2008, the committee continued to support Mint Director Moy's vision for improved coinage designs, as well as the America's Beautiful National Park Quarter Dollar program which began in 2010. The committee moved its proposed "Liberty" series starting date to 2011.

The CCAC added two programs to its list of recommended commemorative programs for 2013: coins honoring the 50th anniversary of Dr. Martin Luther King's "I Have a Dream" Speech and silver dollars for the 100th anniversary of the 17th Amendment to the Constitution, which mandated that U.S. senators be elected by the people rather than through appointment by state legislators.

The CCAC suggested in its fiscal year 2009 annual report that the American Eagle silver bullion coins could be redesigned in 2011 "in light of the 25-year design change statute and the lapse of production of collector varieties in 2009." No Proof American Eagle silver bullion coins were produced in 2009.

By 2010, the CCAC cut the number of commemorative coins it asked Congress to approve, hoping that fewer requests would have greater impact on Capitol Hill. The committee agreed to give high priority to its suggestions for a 2012 coin to mark the bicentennial of the Star-Spangled Banner and a 2013 coin to mark the 50th anniversary of Dr. Martin Luther King's "I Have a Dream" speech. The CCAC dropped proposals for its 2012 USS *Constitution* and 2013 17th Amendment programs.

During a June 28, 2010, meeting in Colorado Springs, Colo., the CCAC voted to establish "a visual definition of design excellence," intended to serve as a benchmark to inspire those who design U.S. coins to be innovative and creative. It was the first project of a five-member subcommittee formed earlier that year by the CCAC.

On Jan. 19, 2011, the CCAC released a 62-page report based on the subcommittee's findings, *A Blueprint for Advancing Artistic Creativity and Excellence in United States Coins and Medals,* recommending the creating of a Coin and Medal Design Division within the U.S. Mint to help improve the quality and originality of U.S. coin and medal designs.

The report recommended removing all responsibility for artistic design from the U.S. Mint's Sales and Marketing Department and that the Mint's Design Working Group be abolished. The report urged artists creating designs for the Mint "to pursue original interpretative designs. They should use symbolism, allegory and abstraction rather than rely primarily on realistic or literal depictions of design themes." The report asked artists to consider the size of the coin in preparing designs and to "simplify designs whenever possible."

At the same Jan. 19 meeting, the members discussed preparing its 2010 annual report, renewing its recommendation for a dollar honoring fallen firefighters, date of issuance moved from 2012 to 2014, and recommended silver dollars in 2015 honoring the Battle of New Orleans, final battle of the War of 1812, and honoring the 150th anniversary of the United States Constitution's 13th Amendment abolishing slavery.

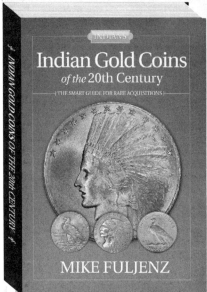

4 The Treasury

While the Treasury Department's chief role is being the executive agency responsible for promoting economic prosperity and ensuring the financial security of the United States, collectors are most interested in two Treasury agencies: the United States Mint, which produces the nation's coinage, and the Bureau of Engraving and Printing, which prints Federal Reserve notes.

Several other agencies once part of the Treasury Department with collector connections, however, have been transferred to a new cabinet level department. The Sept. 11, 2001, terrorist attacks against the United States set into motion a comprehensive reorganization of the federal government that included the establishment of Department of Homeland Security.

Effective in 2003, U.S. Customs and Border Protection and the U.S. Secret Service were removed as bureaus within the Treasury Department and transferred to the Department of Homeland Security.

The U.S. Secret Service (**www.secretservice.gov**) is empowered to investigate the counterfeiting of U.S. coins, paper money and other financial documents.

United States Customs is now known as U.S. Customs and Border Protection (online at **www.cbp.gov**). It is discussed in the *Coin World Almanac* because of its responsibility for regulating foreign imports, which include certain coins as well as antiquities and other foreign financial instruments.

For the purposes of continuity, since past editions of the *Coin World Almanac* covered the Secret Service and U.S. Customs within "The Treasury" chapter, this chapter of the *2011 Coin World Almanac* continues to carry information about both agencies despite their shift to Homeland Security.

History of the Treasury Department

Even before the signing of the Declaration of Independence, the Continental Congress provided by resolution on Feb. 17, 1776, "that a committee of five be appointed for superintending the Treasury." During the first session of the Constitutional Congress, a law "to establish the Treasury Department" was enacted on Sept. 2, 1789. This enactment occurred only six months after the Constitution became the basic law of the land on March 4, 1789.

For several years, Philadelphia was the temporary capital of the nation. When plans to move the seat of government to the District of Columbia were made, they included recommendations for construction of a Treasury building. This building, located on the east side of the site of the present building, was completed in 1799 and occupied in 1800 by the 69 employees of Treasury, seven employees (total employment) of the State Department and some personnel of the Navy Department.

This first building was partially destroyed by fire in 1801. Repaired, it continued to house Treasury personnel until 1814, when a fire set by the British as a spectacle for an invading army destroyed the building.

Following withdrawal of the British forces, prompt authority was granted for a new Treasury Building. Again the Treasury fell victim to a fire when the second structure and most of its contents were destroyed in the early morning of March 31, 1833. An investigation authorized by President Jackson led to the arrest of two brothers who were charged with setting the fire to destroy certain papers that would prove fraudulent conduct by persons engaged as Treasury agents. One brother was finally acquitted after four trials because of the statute of limitations, while the other was convicted and sentenced to 10 years in prison.

Apparently the department was without a home of its own for years following the 1833 fire. On July 4, 1836, Congress authorized the construction of a "fireproof building of such dimensions as may be required for the present and future accommodations" of the Treasury Department. Perhaps the building when completed in 1842 was an imposing structure at the time, but it fell far short of providing accommodations for the future. Having cost less than $700,000, the building, which is now only a part of the east wing of the existing structure, contained 150 rooms.

It was necessary in a few years to enlarge the building, and Congress in March of 1855 granted authority to extend the building. Construction of what is now the south wing was begun in July 1855 and completed in September 1861. The Civil War more or less interrupted further construction, but by 1864 construction on the west wing had been completed up to the line of the present north facade.

The department continued to grow, and the government building housing the Department of State was removed from the north area of the site to make room for the north wing, which was completed in 1869.

On its way up

Thus, more than a third of a century after construction began, the Treasury Building became the structure originally intended. The building as it is today is estimated to have cost approximately $8 million.

One result of its expansion was a violation of the original plan for the city—to leave unobstructed the view from the White House to the Capitol.

Because early planning had the entire official city facing the canal that at one time ran through downtown Washington where the mall is now located, the south entrances of both the White House and the Treasury Building are the historical front entrances of the buildings. However, as the city grew, the north entrance of the White House became its front entrance; and many people think of the 15th Street entrance to the Treasury as its main entrance, perhaps because it is the easiest to enter since the other three entrances have long flights of stone steps.

The stone used in the south, west and north wings was quarried on Dix Island, near Rockland, Maine, and transported in sailing vessels. The facades are adorned by monolithic columns of the Ionic order, each 36 feet tall, each costing $5,000 and weighing 30 tons. Thirty-four of these pillars are situated on the 15th Street side of the building, 30 of them forming a colonnade 341 feet long. This colonnade has for many years provided viewing space for inaugural parades and other state functions. Eighteen columns are on the west side and 10 each on the north and south sides.

A statue of Alexander Hamilton, first secretary of the Treasury, is located on the south patio of the building, while a statue of Albert Gallatin, fourth secretary of the Treasury, who served as secretary for the longest period of time, 1801 to 1814, is located on the north patio. The grounds of the building—rose gardens at the north and south ends, and grass, magnolia trees and other plants gracing the west side—add much to the beauty of the building.

The interior, although it has been altered many times, reminds one that this is an old building. The deeply worn stone steps leading to all floors show the many years they were used before elevators were installed. Until 1959, even the elevators were nearly collector's items, one having been installed in 1898. Since 1959, all elevators have been replaced by automatic, self-operating cars. Signs of the early heating devices in the form of fireplaces still can be found, some of which can still be used. The building was originally lighted by oil lamps, and the sanitary accommodations were just as primitive.

Offices for 10 percent

The Treasury Building is used primarily for executive offices, the secretary of the Treasury occupying a suite on the third floor. Despite its size, the building can today accommodate only about 10 percent of all Treasury personnel located in Washington, D.C. More than 20 other buildings house Treasury employees, and it is necessary to rent additional space to meet all needs.

Fifteen vaults are located in the basement, ranging in size from 10 feet by 16 feet to 50 feet by 90 feet. According to the Treasury, "Today money is not stored in the Treasury Building and vaults are no longer used." At one time most of the nation's gold and silver bullion was stored in the vaults, but bulk quantities of bullion are no longer located in the Main Treasury Building.

The large Cash Room at the north end of the building was often used for special occasions, its first such use being the March 4, 1869, inaugural ball for President Grant's first inauguration. However, its daily use was as a check-cashing facility and it operated well into the early 1970s. Treasury officials then determined the cost of clerical and security personnel could no longer be justified and the room was closed June 30, 1976.

After a brief period of renovation, the Cash Room was reopened for special events, and was used for example, for the presentation by Treasury officials of a $24 million check to the Statue of Liberty/Ellis Island renovation fund.

In early 1987, the Cash Room was closed for a total floor-to-ceiling renovation. The reopening of the Cash Room headlined the Treasury's 200th birthday celebration in September 1989.

On June 26, 1996, the Cash Room was heavily damaged when fire spread through the north wing. Renovations were again undertaken. A special Treasury Historical Association (a body described further later) committee began planning in late 1997 for a special fund-raising project that began in July 1998. The THA sought financial support from industry firms and individuals to restore the gold-leaf work in the ceiling of the Cash Room and the North Wing corner domes in the Treasury Building. While emergency congressional appropriations were provided to repair the damage to these areas caused by the rooftop fire, the funds raised by this THA project complemented the appropriations in order to bring the North Wing into its original brilliance and grandeur. THA raised $200,000 of private funding for this project. By 2011, the Treasury's website could state, "The striking marble Cash Room sparkles again today as it did on the night of Ulysses S. Grant's inaugural reception in 1869."

Certain sections of the Treasury Building, specifically fifth floor offices, are being renovated and modernized under the Treasury Building and Annex Repair and Restoration Program (TBARR). Fundraising, with the assistance of the Treasury Historical Association, began in 2007 for the multi-year restoration project.

Beginning with the 1989 Treasury Bicentennial celebration, public tours of historical areas of the building were instituted, with variations over time in the procedure scheduling such tours. Currently, for security reasons, all visitors must provide name, date of birth and Social Security number, since clearance must be granted by the U.S. Secret Service.

Hour-long tours of the Main Treasury Building, located at 1500 Pennsylvania Ave. N.W., in Washington, D.C., are available by advanced reservation through the visitor's congressional offices.

The first stop on the tour is the Salmon P. Chase Suite, one of the restored historic rooms on the third floor that served as the offices for Chase, who served as Secretary of the Treasury during the Civil War.

The next stop on the tour is the Secretary's Conference Room and Diplomatic Reception Room. The conference room is located directly across the hall from the Secretary's Office and next door to the Diplomatic Reception Room.

The final stop on the third floor is the Andrew Johnson Suite, location of the restored office used by President Johnson as his temporary White House immediately following the assassination of Abraham Lincoln in 1865.

On the second floor is the Burglar-proof Vault, with its restored decorative cast iron wall. Built in 1864, the wall lining was composed of metal balls sandwiched between three steel plates that were intended to prevent a burglar from penetrating the vault. It is now part of the office of the Treasurer of the United States.

The historic marble Cash Room on the second floor is the final stop on the tour. It is still used for special functions and meetings. For example, on Jan. 17, 2011, Treasury Secretary Timothy F. Geithner chaired a Financial Stability Oversight Council (FSOC) meeting in the Cash Room. For more information on tours and reservations, visit the main Treasury website at **www.treasury.gov/**.

Please note that this is not the tour for seeing the production of United States paper money. To see paper currency production, you need to tour either the main Bureau of Engraving and Printing in Washington, D.C., at 14th and C streets S.W., telephone (202) 874-3019, or the Fort Worth Satellite Printing Facility, 9000 Blue Mound Road, Fort Worth, TX 76131, telephone (817) 231-4000 or toll free (866) 865-1194.

Admission to the Treasury Building is free. Check **www.treasury.gov** for tour information. The BEP and Main Treasury Building are closed for all federal holidays and the week between Christmas and New Year's Day.

Among the many interesting architectural features of the Main Treasury Building are the unique stairways that appear somehow to be suspended in mid-air. Actually the steps are cut-worked granite and marble blocks cantilevered from structural walls, partially supported by the arch action of the steps.

The stairwell underwent major restoration work during 2010, with preservation work continuing into 2011.

The fifth floor, which was formerly the attic, was renovated for office space in 1910.

It is also interesting to note that the name of the building was not made a permanent part of the structure until 1958, more than 100 years after Treasury was built.

THE TREASURY DEPARTMENT is cut into the facade above the south entrance as well as above the 15th Street Northwest entrance.

Treasury souvenirs

The Treasury no longer maintains an exhibit hall but information about the Treasury as well as the Mint and other Washington, D.C., area attractions is available at the Washington DC Visitor Information Center, 1300 Pennsylvania Ave. NW, Washington, DC 20004, telephone (866) 324-7386. Internet information and links to other Washington tourist sites and landmarks are available at **www.house.gov/house/tour_dc.html.**

Top officials

In addition to the secretary of the Treasury and his top staff, the Main Treasury Building houses the top officials of the office of the treasurer of the United States and the office of the assistant secretary for international affairs. Other important activities of the department, such as the United States Mint, Internal Revenue Service, Bureau of Engraving and Printing, the Savings Bonds Division, Bureau of the Public Debt, Comptroller of the Currency and the Bureau of Accounts, are housed in nearby buildings.

So are the two agencies now part of the Department of Homeland Security—U.S. Customs and Border Protection and the U.S. Secret Service.

Among the activities that once were a part of the Treasury Department and are now parts of other organizations are the Postal Service, until 1829; the General Land Office (now the Interior Department); some of the activities that later were assigned to the Departments of Commerce and Labor in 1903; and some of the major functions now assigned to the General Accounting Office. Other activities included those now performed by the Public Health Service of the Department of Health, Education, and Welfare; the Public Buildings Service (formerly the Supervising Architect) and the Federal Supply Service (formerly the Procurement Division) of the General Services Administration; the Bureau of the Budget; the United States Coast Guard (now a part of the Department of Transportation); and the Bureau of Narcotics (now the Bureau of Narcotics and Dangerous Drugs of the Department of Justice).

Location for history

In this building were developed the ideas for organizations such as the International Monetary Fund and the International Bank for Reconstruction and Development, and more recently the Inter-American Development Bank and the Asian Development Bank. Also in this building, plans were made for the Lend-Lease program of World War II, and for expediting the building of the United States Air Corps s the U.S. Air Force was known in World War II.

The Treasury Department building has been the locale of a number of interesting events, one of the earliest involving President Andrew Jackson who, during the laying of the cornerstone, placed therein a satin-lined case containing a golden lock of hair from the infant daughter of his confidential adviser and secretary, who was Mrs. Jackson's nephew. This girl, Mary Emily Donelson, was later employed in the Treasury. Today the location of that cornerstone is inaccessible because of the extension of the outer limits of the building.

President Andrew Johnson used one of the Treasury offices on the present third floor as his office immediately following the assassination of President Abraham Lincoln, to allow Mrs. Lincoln time to move from the White House unhurried. A picture of a Cabinet meeting held in that room testifies to this unusual arrangement.

During World War II, a tunnel connected the White House to the Treasury. There was in the basement a furnished shelter area for the president of the United States in case he was unable to avoid enemy attack any other way. During this period the basement of the Treasury would also have served as a refuge for the entire cabinet, had that been necessary.

As recently as the early 1940s, some of the offices contained important historical documents—among them the Louisiana Purchase, one of George Washington's travel account books and files containing notes from President Lincoln. These have been turned over to the National Archives and other organizations for preservation.

The First Baptist Church of Washington, D.C., held its first meeting in the building in July 1801, and intermittently has held commemorative meetings on the south steps. These steps were used during World War II for massive bond rallies in which entertainment celebrities participated to sell war bonds to finance the nation's war effort. They have also been used for inaugurating community chest and other drives.

Treasury Historical Association

To help preserve the Treasury Building itself, an organization called the Treasury Historical Association was formed Dec. 13, 1973.

Although the Treasury Historical Association was chartered as an "in-house" organization, with memberships open to present and former Treasury employees, members of the public interested in the maintenance and preservation of this important federal landmark are invited to join the association also.

Applications for membership and requests for bro-

chures illustrating available THA souvenirs should be mailed to: Treasury Historical Association, Box 28118, Washington, DC 20338-8118. The telephone number is (202) 298-0550. The Internet address is **www.treasuryhistoricalassn.org**.

Membership fees are tax-deductible.

Four levels of membership are offered:

➤ General, dues of $20 per year or $50 for three years

➤ Supporting, dues of $60 per year

➤ Patron, dues of $120 per year

➤ Life Donor, $1,500 or more, one time; payment arrangements available in three equal installments within a calendar year, if desired by member

Members at all levels receive discounts on THA commemorative products, free publications and invitations to THA-sponsored lectures.

Time capsule

Early in 1976, as part of the Treasury Department's celebration of the Bicentennial, Secretary of the Treasury William E. Simon approved the establishment of a time capsule, which was dedicated in a ceremony on Sept. 8, 1976, and to be opened by the secretary of the Treasury in the tricentennial year. The capsule is to serve as a symbol to Americans living in the 21st century of 20th century Americans' faith in the nation's future.

Treasury officials were asked to prepare messages for inclusion in the capsule, to be read by their counterparts in 2076. These messages address the key issues facing each office or bureau so that future generations of Americans might have a clearer perspective of the concerns of their bicentennial predecessors. A message from President Gerald Ford is included in the contents of the capsule, along with various Bicentennial medals, a $2 bill signed by U.S. Treasurer Francine I. Neff and Secretary Simon, and other contemporary memorabilia. The container itself remained unsealed until the end of the year so that other mementos of the Bicentennial celebration could be included.

The capsule, which measures 40 inches in height, 36 inches at the base, and 30 inches at the top, was designed by the Department's Graphics Branch and was to stand on display in the Main Treasury Building for 100 years. Its four sides are made of reinforced concrete 3 inches thick. The Treasury seal and the numerals "2076" are displayed on one side of the container. An airtight inner chamber preserves the contents of the capsule.

Twenty-four words are inscribed on the capsule's dedication plaque:

"America's greatest resource is the vibrant heritage of a free people. May we have the wisdom and the vision to nourish this birthright forever." — *William E. Simon*

The words form the keystone of Treasury Secretary William E. Simon's message to his counterpart in 2076 and serve as a message of hope and confidence to all Americans who will be celebrating the 300th anniversary of the United States.

According to the current THA chairman, Thomas P. O'Malley, "The time capsule is located in the public corridor on the first floor of the Treasury Building, where the east wing and the west wing intersect. It is in a free-standing three-dimensional trapezoid-shaped receptacle.

It is under the jurisdiction of the curator of the Treasury Building, Richard Cote.

Secretaries of the Treasury

President	Secretaries	Term
Washington	Alexander Hamilton, New York	Sept. 11, 1789, to Jan. 31, 1795
	Oliver Wolcott, Connecticut	Feb. 3, 1795, to March 3, 1797
Adams, John	Oliver Wolcott, Connecticut	March 4, 1797, to Dec. 31, 1800
	Samuel Dexter, Massachusetts	Jan. 1, 1801, to March 3, 1801
Jefferson	Samuel Dexter, Massachusetts	March 4, 1801, to May 13, 1801
	Albert Gallatin, Pennsylvania	May 14, 1801, to March 3, 1809
Madison	Albert Gallatin, Pennsylvania	March 4, 1809, to Feb. 8, 1814
	George W. Campbell, Tennessee	Feb. 9, 1814, to Oct. 5, 1814
	Alexander J. Dallas, Pennsylvania	Oct. 6, 1814, to Oct. 21, 1816
	William H. Crawford, Georgia	Oct. 22, 1816, to March 3, 1817
Monroe	William H. Crawford, Georgia	March 4, 1817, to March 6, 1825
Adams, J.Q.	Richard Rush, Pennsylvania	March 7, 1825, to March 5, 1829
Jackson	Samuel D. Ingham, Pennsylvania	March 6, 1829, to June 20, 1831
	Louis McLane, Delaware	Aug. 8, 1831, to May 28, 1833
	William J. Duane, Pennsylvania	May 29, 1833, to Sept. 22, 1833
	Roger B. Taney, Maryland	Sept. 23, 1833, to June 25, 1834
	Levi Woodbury, New Hampshire	July 1, 1834, to March 3, 1837
Van Buren	Levi Woodbury, New Hampshire	March 4, 1837, to March 3, 1841
Harrison, W.H.	Thomas Ewing, Ohio	March 6, 1841, to April 4, 1841
Tyler	Thomas Ewing, Ohio	April 5, 1841, to Sept. 11, 1841
	Walter Forward, Pennsylvania	Sept. 13, 1841, to March 1, 1843
	John C. Spencer, New York	March 8, 1843, to May 2, 1844
	George M. Bibb, Kentucky	July 4, 1844, to March 4, 1845
Polk	George M. Bibb, Kentucky	March 5, 1845, to March 7, 1845
	Robert J. Walker, Mississippi	March 8, 1845, to March 5, 1849
Taylor	Wm. M. Meredith, Pennsylvania	March 8, 1849, to July 9, 1850
Fillmore	Wm. M. Meredith, Pennsylvania	July 10, 1850, to July 22, 1850
	Thomas Corwin, Ohio	July 23, 1850, to March 6, 1853
Pierce	James Guthrie, Kentucky	March 7, 1853, to March 6, 1857
Buchanan	Howell Cobb, Georgia	March 7, 1857, to Dec. 8, 1860
	Philip F. Thomas, Maryland	Dec. 12, 1860, to Jan. 14, 1861
	John A. Dix, New York	Jan. 15, 1861, to March 6, 1861
Lincoln	Salmon P. Chase, Ohio	March 7, 1861, to June 30, 1864
	Wm. P. Fessenden, Maine	July 5, 1864, to March 3, 1865
	Hugh McCulloch, Indiana	March 9, 1865, to April 15, 1865
Johnson, A.	Hugh McCulloch, Indiana	April 16, 1865, to March 3, 1869
Grant	Geo. S. Boutwell, Massachusetts	March 12, 1869, to March 16, 1873
	Wm. A. Richardson, Massachusetts	March 17, 1873, to June 3, 1874
	Benjamin H. Bristow, Kentucky	June 4, 1874, to June 20, 1876
Grant	Lot M. Morrill, Maine	June 7, 1876, to March 3, 1877
Hayes	Lot M. Morrill, Maine	March 4, 1877, to March 9, 1877
Hayes	John Sherman, Ohio	March 10, 1877, to March 3, 1881
Garfield	William Windom, Minnesota	March 8, 1881, to Sept. 19, 1881
Arthur	William Windom, Minnesota	Sept. 20, 1881, to Nov. 13, 1881
	Charles J. Folger, New York	Nov. 14, 1881, to Sept. 4, 1884
	Walter Q. Gresham, Indiana	Sept. 25, 1884, to Oct. 30, 1884
	Hugh McCulloch, Indiana	Oct. 31, 1884, to March 3, 1885
Cleveland	Hugh McCulloch, Indiana	March 4, 1885, to March 7, 1885
	Daniel Manning, New York	March 8, 1885, to March 31, 1887
	Charles S. Fairchild, New York	April 1, 1887, to March 3, 1889

President	Secretaries	Term
Harrison, B.	Charles S. Fairchild, New York	March 4, 1889, to March 6, 1889
	William Windom, Minnesota	March 7, 1889, to Jan. 29, 1891
	Charles Foster, Ohio	Feb. 25, 1891, to March 3, 1893
Cleveland	Charles Foster, Ohio	March 4, 1893, to March 6, 1893
	John G. Carlisle, Kentucky	March 7, 1893, to March 3, 1897
McKinley	John G. Carlisle, Kentucky	March 4, 1897, to March 5, 1897
	Lyman J. Gage, Illinois	March 6, 1897, to Sept. 14, 1901
Roosevelt, T.	Lyman J. Gage, Illinois	Sept. 15, 1901, to Jan. 31, 1902
	L.M. Shaw, Iowa	Feb. 1, 1902, to March 3, 1907
	G.B. Cortelyou, New York	March 4, 1907, to March 7, 1909
Taft	Franklin MacVeagh, Illinois	March 8, 1909, to March 5, 1913
Wilson	W.G. McAdoo, New York	March 6, 1913, to Dec. 15, 1918
	Carter Glass, Virginia	Dec. 16, 1918, to Feb. 1, 1920
	David F. Houston, Missouri	Feb. 2, 1920, to March 3, 1921
Harding	Andrew W. Mellon, Pennsylvania	March 4, 1921, to Aug. 2, 1923
Coolidge	Andrew W. Mellon, Pennsylvania	Aug. 3, 1923, to March 3, 1929
Hoover	Andrew W. Mellon, Pennsylvania	March 4, 1929, to Feb. 12, 1932
	Ogden L. Mills, New York	Feb. 13, 1932, to March 4, 1933
Roosevelt, F.D.	William H. Woodin, New York	March 5, 1933, to Dec. 31, 1933
	Henry Morgenthau, Jr., New York	Jan. 1, 1934, to April 12, 1945
Truman	Henry Morgenthau, Jr., New York	April 13, 1945, to July 22, 1945
	Fred M. Vinson, Kentucky	July 23, 1945, to June 23, 1946
	John W. Snyder, Missouri	June 25, 1946, to Jan. 20, 1953
Eisenhower	George M. Humphrey, Ohio	Jan. 21, 1953, to July 29, 1957
	Robert B. Anderson, Connecticut	July 29, 1957, to Jan. 20, 1961
Kennedy	Douglas Dillon, New Jersey	Jan. 21, 1961, to Nov. 22, 1963
Johnson, L.B.	Douglas Dillon, New Jersey	Nov. 23, 1963, to April 1, 1965
	Henry H. Fowler, Virginia	April 1, 1965, to Dec. 20, 1968
	Joseph W. Barr, Indiana	Dec. 21, 1968, to Jan. 20, 1969
Nixon	David M. Kennedy, Utah	Jan. 22, 1969, to Feb. 10, 1971
	John B. Connally, Texas	Feb. 11, 1971, to June 12, 1972
	George P. Shultz, Illinois	June 12, 1971, to May 7, 1974
	William E. Simon, New Jersey	May 8, 1974, to Aug. 9, 1974
Ford	William E. Simon, New Jersey	Aug. 10, 1974, to Jan. 20, 1977
Carter	W. Michael Blumenthal, Michigan	Jan. 23, 1977, to Aug. 4, 1979
	G. William Miller, Rhode Island	Aug. 7, 1979, to Jan. 20, 1981
Reagan	Donald T. Regan, Massachusetts	Jan. 22, 1981, to Feb. 2, 1985
	James A. Baker III, Texas	Feb. 3, 1985, to Aug. 17, 1988
	Nicholas F. Brady, New Jersey	Sept. 14, 1988, to Jan. 20, 1989
Bush, G.H.W.	Nicholas F. Brady, New Jersey	Jan. 20, 1989, to Jan. 17, 1993
Clinton	Lloyd Bentsen, Texas	Jan. 20, 1993, to Dec. 22, 1994
	Robert E. Rubin, New York	Jan. 10, 1995, to July 1, 1999
	Lawrence E. Summers, Massachusetts	July 2, 1999, to Jan. 20, 2001
Bush, G.W.	Paul H. O'Neill, Pennsylvania	Jan. 30, 2001, to Dec. 31, 2002
	John W. Snow, Virginia	Feb. 3, 2003, to June 29, 2006
	Henry M. Paulson Jr., Illinois	July 10, 2006, to Jan. 20, 2009
Obama, Barack	Timothy F. Geithner, New York	Jan. 26, 2009, to present

Treasurers of the United States

Treasurer	Term
Michael Hillegas, Pennsylvania	July 29, 1775, to Sept. 11, 1789
Samuel Meredith, Pennsylvania	Sept. 11, 1789, to Oct. 31, 1801
Thomas T. Tucker, South Carolina	Dec. 1, 1801, to May 2, 1828
William Clark, Pennsylvania	June 4, 1828, to May 31, 1829
John Campbell, Virginia	May 26, 1829, to July 20, 1839
William Selden, Virginia	July 22, 1839, to Nov. 23, 1850
John Sloan, Ohio	Nov. 27, 1850, to April 6, 1852
Samuel Casey, Kentucky	April 4, 1853, to Dec. 22, 1859

Treasurer	Term
William C. Price, Missouri	Feb. 28, 1860, to March 21, 1861
F.E. Spinner, New York	March 16, 1861, to June 30, 1875
John C. New, Indiana	June 30, 1875, to July 1, 1876
A.U. Wyman, Wisconsin	July 1, 1876, to June 30, 1877
James Gilfillan, Connecticut	July 1, 1877, to March 31, 1883
A.U. Wyman, Wisconsin	April 1, 1883, to April 30, 1885
Conrad N. Jordan, New York	May 1, 1885, to May 23, 1887
James W. Hyatt, Connecticut	May 24, 1887, to May 10, 1889
J.N. Huston, Indiana	May 11, 1889, to April 24, 1891
Enos H. Nebecker, Indiana	April 25, 1891, to May 31, 1893
D.N. Morgan, Connecticut	June 1, 1893, to June 30, 1897
Ellis H. Roberts, New York	July 1, 1897, to June 30, 1905
Charles H. Treat, New York	July 1, 1905, to Oct. 30, 1909
Lee McClung, Tennessee	Nov. 1, 1909, to Nov. 21, 1912
Carmi A. Thompson, Ohio	Nov. 22, 1912, to March 31, 1913
John Burke, North Dakota	April 1, 1913, to Jan. 5, 1921
Frank White, North Dakota	May 2, 1921, to May 1, 1928
H.T. Tate, Tennessee	May 31, 1928, to Jan. 17, 1929
W.O. Woods, Kansas	Jan. 18, 1929, to May 31, 1933
W.A. Julian, Ohio	June 1, 1933, to May 29, 1949
Georgia Neese Clark, Kansas	June 21, 1949, to Jan. 27, 1953
Ivy Baker Priest, Utah	Jan. 28, 1953, to Jan. 29, 1961
Elizabeth Rudel Smith, California	Jan. 30, 1961, to April 13, 1962
Kathryn O'Hay Granahan, Pennsylvania	Jan. 3, 1963, to Nov. 20, 1966
Dorothy Andrews Elston Kabis, Delaware	May 8, 1969, to July 3, 1971
Romana Acosta Banuelos, California	Dec. 17, 1971, to Feb. 15, 1974
Francine Irving Neff, New Mexico	June 21, 1974, to Jan. 19, 1977
Azie Taylor Morton, Texas	Sept. 12, 1977, to Jan. 20, 1981
Angela Buchanan, Maryland	Jan. 21, 1981, to July 1, 1983
Katherine Davalos Ortega, New Mexico	Sept. 23, 1983, to June 30, 1989
Catalina Vasquez Villalpando, Texas	Dec. 11, 1989, to Jan. 20, 1993
Mary Ellen Withrow, Ohio	March 1, 1994, to Jan. 20, 2001
Rosario Marin, California	Aug. 16, 2001, to June 30, 2003
Anna Escobedo Cabral, California	Jan. 19, 2005, to May 18, 2009
Rosa Gumataotao Rios, California	Aug. 6, 2009, to present

Treasury officials

Department of the Treasury
1500 Pennsylvania Ave. N.W., Washington, DC 20220
General information: (202) 622-2000
Fax: (202) 622-6415
Web address: **www.treasury.gov**

Secretary of the Treasury	Timothy F. Geithner
Chief of Staff to Secretary of the Treasury	Mark A. Patterson
Deputy Secretary of the Treasury	Neal S. Wolin
Treasurer of the United States	Rosa Gumataotao Rios
Director (acting), United States Mint	Richard A. Peterson
Director, Bureau of Engraving and Printing	Larry R. Felix
Comptroller of the Currency	John Walsh (acting)
General Counsel	George W. Madison
Under Secretary (Terrorism and Financial Intelligence)	Stuart A. Levey
Assistant Secretary (Economic Policy)	Vacant
Assistant Secretary (Financial Institutions)	Vacant
Assistant Secretary (Intelligence and Analysis)	Leslie Ireland
Assistant Secretary (Terrorist Financing)	Vacant
Assistant Secretary (Financial Stability)	Timothy Massad
Assistance Secretary (Legislative Affairs)	Kim N. Wallace

Assistant Secretary (Management; Chief Financial Officer
and Chief Performance Officer) .... Daniel Tangherlini
Under Secretary (International Affairs) .... Lael Brainard
Assistant Secretary (International Finance) .... Charles Collyns
Assistant Secretary (International Markets and Development) .... Marisa Lago
Assistant Secretary (Tax Policy) .... Michael Mundaca
Director (acting), Bureau of Alcohol, Tobacco, Firearms,
and Explosives (Department of Homeland Security) .... Kenneth E. Melson
Commissioner (acting), U.S. Customs Service and Border
Protection (Department of Homeland Security) .... Jayson P. Ahern
Commissioner, Internal Revenue Service .... Douglas H. Shulman
Commissioner, Bureau of the Public Debt .... Van Zeck
Director, U.S. Secret Service (Department of Homeland Security) ...... Mark J. Sullivan
Inspector General .... Eric M. Thorson
Director, U.S. Savings Bonds Division .... Rosa Gumataotao Rios

Treasury Department seal

The seal of the Treasury Department is older than the United States government. The Continental Congress in 1778 appointed a Committee of Finance, or Board of Treasury, and John Witherspoon, Gouverneur Morris and Richard Henry Lee were authorized to design a Treasury seal. The earliest example of the seal is found on papers dated 1782. When the U.S. government was established in 1789, the Continental Treasury seal design was continued in use.

In 1849, the Treasury needed to replace the physically worn seal device used in impressing official documents and ordered Edward Stabler to make a facsimile. Apparently, Stabler carried out his orders with reservations, for his seal shows differences from the original; but they are so minute that a casual observer would not notice them.

The seal of the Department of the Treasury, with further updates since Stabler's time, is overprinted on the face of each note printed by the United States.

On Jan. 29, 1968, a revision of the official seal was approved. The new seal has an inscription in English, the department of the treasury. This inscription replaces the earlier Latin legend thesaur. amer. septent. sigil., an abbreviation said to represent "Thesauri Americae Septentrionalis Sigillum," translated as "The Seal of the Treasury of North America." The new seal bears the date 1789, recording the year of the department's creation.

The arms on the seal depict balance scales, representing the scales of justice; a key, the emblem of official authority; and a chevron with 13 stars for the original states.

Function of the Treasury Department

The Department of the Treasury performs four basic functions: formulating and recommending financial, tax and fiscal policies; serving as a financial agent for the U.S. government; law enforcement; and manufacturing coins and paper money.

Pursuant to the Sept. 11, 2001, terrorist attacks, the Department of the Treasury added an Office of Terrorism and Financial Intelligence (TFI) which develops and implements U.S. government strategies to combat terrorist financing domestically and internationally. TFI also develops and implements the National Money Laundering Strategy as well as other policies and programs to fight financial crime.

According to the Department of the Treasury website, www.treasury.gov, the treasury department is organized into two major components – offices, which are primarily responsible for the formulation of policy and management of the department as a whole; and bureaus, which make up 98 percent of the department, and which are responsible for carrying out the specific operations assigned to the department.

The offices (www.treasury.gov/offices) represent Domestic Finance, Economic Policy, General Counsel, International Affairs, Management/Chief Financial Officer, Public Affairs, Tax Policy, Terrorism and Financial Intelligence, Treasurer of the United States, Office of Thrift Supervision, and the U.S. Mint.

The bureaus (www.treasury.gov/bureaus) represent the Alcohol and Tobacco Tax and Trade Bureau; the Bureau of Engraving and Printing; Bureau of the Public Debt; the Community Development Financial Institution; Financial Crimes Enforcement Network; the Financial Management Service; Inspector General; the Treasury Inspector General for Tax Administration; the Internal Revenue Service (the largest bureau); and the Office of the Comptroller of the Currency.

Office of the Secretary

The secretary of the Treasury, as a major policy adviser to the president, has primary responsibility for formulating and recommending domestic and international financial, economic and tax policy; participating in the formulation of broad fiscal policies that have general significance for the economy;

and managing the public debt. The secretary also oversees the activities of the department in carrying out its major law enforcement responsibility; in serving as the financial agent for the U.S. government; and in manufacturing coins, paper money and other products for customer agencies.

Office of the Comptroller of the Currency

The office of the comptroller of the currency was created by an act of Congress approved Feb. 25, 1863, as an integral part of the national banking system.

The comptroller, as the administrator of national banks, is responsible for the execution of laws relating to national banks and promulgates rules and regulations governing the operations of all national banks. Approval of the comptroller is required for the organization of new national banks, conversion of state-chartered banks into national banks, consolidations or mergers of banks where the surviving institution is a national bank, and the establishment of branches by national banks.

The office of the comptroller exercises general supervision over the operations of national banks, including trust activities and overseas operations. Each bank is examined periodically through a nationwide staff of bank examiners under the immediate supervision of deputy comptrollers and regional administrators.

In addition to chartering, regulating and supervising all national banks, the Office of the Comptroller of the Currency also supervises the federal branches and agencies of foreign banks. The OCC has four district offices plus an office in London to supervise the international activities of national banks.

The OCC is headed by the comptroller, who is appointed by the president, with the advice and consent of the Senate, for a five-year term. The comptroller also serves as a director of the Federal Deposit Insurance Corp.

The OCC's nationwide staff of examiners conducts on-site reviews of national banks and provides sustained supervision of bank operations. The agency issues rules, legal interpretations and corporate decisions concerning banking, bank investments, bank community development activities and other aspects of bank operations.

National bank examiners supervise domestic and international activities of national banks and perform corporate analyses. Examiners analyze a bank's loan and investment portfolios, funds management, capital, earnings, liquidity, sensitivity to market risk, and compliance with consumer banking laws. They review the banks' internal controls, internal and external audit, and compliance with law. They also evaluate bank management's ability to identify and control risk.

In regulating national banks, the OCC has the power to:

➤ Examine the banks.

➤ Approve or deny applications for new charters, branches, capital, or other changes in corporate or banking structure.

➤ Take supervisory actions against banks that do not comply with laws and regulations or that otherwise engage in unsound banking practices. The agency can remove officers and directors, negotiate agreements to change banking practices, and issue cease and desist orders as well as civil money penalties.

➤ Issue rules and regulations governing bank investments, lending, and other practices.

For further information, contact the OCC Customer Assistance Group, 1301 McKinney St., Suite 3450, Houston TX 77010. The toll-free telephone number is (800) 613-6743. Visit online at **www.occ.treas.gov**.

General correspondence can be sent to: Comptroller of the Currency, Administrator of National Banks, Washington, DC 20219, or via email directed to the office at **publicaffairs3@occ.treas.gov**.

United States Mint

801 Ninth St. N.W.
Washington, DC 20220
Telephone: (202) 354-7222 (Public Affairs)
Telephone: (202) 354-7200 (Mint Director's Office)
Web address: **www.usmint.gov**

The Mint of the United States was established by act of Congress April 2, 1792. The Bureau of the Mint was established by act of Congress Feb. 12, 1873. Mint Director Donna Pope changed the name of the agency to the United States Mint on Jan. 25, 1984.

The functions of the U.S. Mint are the production of coins, circulating, commemorative and bullion; the manufacture and sale of medals of a national character; the manufacture and sale of Proof and Uncirculated coin sets and other numismatic items; and the custody, processing and movement of bullion. The Mint acquires and disburses gold, silver and platinum for authorized purposes, and directs the distribution of coins from the Mints to the Federal Reserve Banks and branches.

To order Mint products, contact the Mint's contracted order processing and fulfillment vendor, Pitney-Bowes Government Solutions, by regular mail at Customer Service Center, United States Mint, 2799 Reeves Road, Plainfield, IN 46168, telephone (800) 872-6468. Hearing and speech-impaired customers with TTY equipment may call (888) 321-6468 to order products.

U.S. Customs and Border Protection
(now part of Department of Homeland Security)

1300 Pennsylvania Ave. N.W.
Washington, DC 20229
Telephone: (202) 344-1770
Web address: **www.cbp.gov**

U.S. Customs and Border Protection was created as the U.S. Customs Service by the act of March 3,

1927. Authority for the collection of customs revenue was established by the second, third and fifth acts of the first Congress in 1789.

CBP engages in activities for the collection and protection of the revenue; the prevention of fraud and smuggling; and the processing and regulation of people, carriers, cargo and mail into and out of the United States; and performs a variety of functions for other government agencies in safeguarding agriculture, business, health, security and related consumer interests. Collectors and dealers should be aware that Customs enforces restrictions placed on the import of certain coins from other nations (see Chapter 3).

In addition to enforcing federal restrictions suppressing traffic in illegal importation of restricted coins, CBP is active in enforcing laws against trafficking in illegal narcotics (in conjunction with the Drug Enforcement Administration and in cooperation with foreign governments); in enforcing munitions control in cargo theft prevention; in enforcing regulations affecting articles in international trade where parallel regulations control domestic articles (such as copyright, trademark and patent restrictions regulated domestically by the Patent Office or the Copyright Office; and special marking provisions for wool, fur and textile products, controlled domestically by the Federal Trade Commission); and in enforcing regulations related to dumping.

CBP enforces certain environmental protection programs for other agencies, such as enforcing the prohibition on discharge of refuse and oil into or upon coastal navigable waters of the United States (for the U.S. Coast Guard) as outlined in the Oil Pollution Act; enforcing laws and regulations regarding wild animals and birds of endangered species and those injurious to community health, plant and animal life, as well as other agriculture and plant quarantine regulations concerning animals, poultry and animal byproducts; and ensuring that imported vehicles and equipment conform to safety and emission standards required under the National Traffic and Motor Vehicle Safety Act of 1966 and the Clean Air Act.

CBP headquarters is located in Washington, D.C. CBP is decentralized and most of its personnel are stationed throughout the country and overseas, where its operational functions are performed.

The 50 states, plus the Virgin Islands and Puerto Rico, are divided into seven Customs Regions. Contained within these regions are 46 subordinate district offices, under which are approximately 300 ports of entry combined.

United States Secret Service
(now under the Department of Homeland Security)
950 H St. N.W.
Washington, DC 20223
Telephone: (202) 406-5708
Web address: **www.secretservice.gov**
The responsibilities and jurisdiction of the United

States Secret Service are prescribed by law in Title 18, United States Code, Section 3056.

The Secret Service has a dual function: protection and investigation.

The Secret Service Division was created on July 5, 1865, in Washington, D.C., to suppress counterfeit currency. The division's first chief, William P. Wood, was sworn in by Secretary of the Treasury Hugh McCulloch. In 1867, Secret Service responsibilities were broadened to include "detecting persons perpetrating frauds against the government." This appropriation resulted in investigations into the Ku Klux Klan, nonconforming distillers, smugglers, mail robbers, land frauds, and a number of other infractions against the federal laws.

In 1870, Secret Service headquarters were moved to New York, only to return in 1874 to Washington, D.C.

In 1877 Congress passed an act prohibiting the counterfeiting of any coin, gold or silver bar, with the Secret Service made responsible for the act's enforcement.

The Secret Service was officially acknowledged as a distinct organization within the Treasury Department in 1883.

In 1894, the Secret Service began informal part-time protection of President Grover Cleveland.

After the assassination, in 1901, of President William McKinley at the Pan-American International Exposition in Buffalo, N.Y., Congress directed the Secret Service to protect the President of the United States. Protection remains a key mission of the United States Secret Service.

According to the Secret Service website, today the Secret Service is authorized to protect:

➤ the president, the vice president (or other individuals next in order of succession to the Office of the President), the president-elect and vice president-elect

➤ the immediate families of the above individuals

➤ former presidents and their spouses, except when the spouse remarries. In 1997, congressional legislation became effective limiting Secret Service protection to former presidents for a period of not more than 10 years from the date the former president leaves office. Before the 1997 amendment, Secret Service protection was accorded former presidents and their spouses for their lifetimes.

➤ children of former presidents until age 16

➤ visiting heads of foreign states or governments and their spouses traveling with them, other distinguished foreign visitors to the United States, and official representatives of the United States performing special missions abroad

➤ major presidential and vice presidential candidates, and their spouses within 120 days of a general presidential election

➤ other individuals as designated per executive order of the president

➤ national special security events, when designated as such by the secretary of the Department of Homeland Security

The Secret Service is also authorized to detect and arrest any person committing any offense against the laws of the United States relating to coins, currency and other obligations and securities of the United States and of foreign governments; detect and arrest any person violating any of the provisions of sections 508, 509 and 871 of Title 18 of the United States Code; execute warrants issued under the authority of the United States; carry firearms; and perform such other functions and duties by law.

Bureau of Engraving and Printing (Headquarters)

14th and C streets S.W.
Washington, DC 20228
Telephone: (877) 874-4114
Telephone: (202) 874-8888
Public Tours: (866) 874-2330, toll-free
Web address: **www.moneyfactory.com**

The bureau operates on basic authorities conferred by the acts of July 11, 1862, March 3, 1877, June 4, 1897, and additional authorities that are still in force, contained in past appropriations made to the bureau for work to be undertaken. A working capital fund of $3,250,000 was established in accordance with the provisions of Section 2 of the Act of Aug. 4, 1950, which placed the bureau on a completely reimbursable basis. The BEP is headed by a director appointed by the secretary of the Treasury.

The Bureau of Engraving and Printing designs, engraves and prints all major items of financial character issued by the U.S. government. It produces paper currency; Treasury bonds, bills, notes, and certificates; postage, revenue and certain customs stamps. Printing operations are conducted at facilities in Washington, D.C., and Fort Worth, Texas.

Office of the Treasurer

Department of the Treasury
1500 Pennsylvania Ave. N.W.
Room 2134
Washington, DC 20220
Telephone: (202) 622-2000
Web address: **www.treasury.gov/about/ organizational-structure/offices/Pages/ Office-of-the-Treasurer.aspx**

The office of the treasurer is the only office within the Treasury Department older than the department itself.

The office of the treasurer of the United States was originally created by the act of Sept. 6, 1777, for the purpose of receiving, holding and paying out the public moneys for the federal government. However, most of those responsibilities of the office were transferred to the Bureau of Government Financial Operations with its creation Feb. 1, 1974.

The treasurer is responsible for reviewing and endorsing U.S. currency and represents the secretary of the Treasury and undersecretary for monetary affairs as a major spokesman in communicating and coordinating departmental programs and policies.

During the Reagan administration, the office of treasurer was upgraded to include the responsibilities of direct oversight of the United States Mint, the Bureau of Engraving and Printing and the United States Savings Bond program, and serving on the secretary's senior staff.

In 1993, the Savings Bonds Division was abolished and their functions and employees were put under the supervision of the Bureau of Public Debt in an effort to streamline the federal government.

5 The United States Mint

The Act of April 2, 1792, provided for gold, silver and copper coinage and also created a federal Mint in the city of Philadelphia, which was then the nation's capital. Upon the Mint's founding, President Washington placed the operation under the supervision of the secretary of state, where it remained until 1799 when it was made an independent agency reporting directly to the president. In practice, the Treasury Department began to exercise loose oversight, a practice that continued until formalization of responsibilities in 1873.

As the nation's population spread out across the continent and the need for coinage increased, Congress authorized a series of production facilities formally designated as Branch Mints, beginning with the Act of March 3, 1835, with a superintendent appointed to be in charge at each facility (each Branch Mint is discussed in detail in this chapter). The Act of Feb. 13, 1837, placed all business of the Branch Mints under the control and regulation of the director of the Mint in Philadelphia.

Researcher Don Taxay quotes Treasury Secretary George S. Boutwell in 1869 as referring to the Mints and assay offices as "nominally in the charge of the Treasury Department." There was not, however, "by authority of law, any person in the Department who, by virtue of his office, is supposed to be informed upon the subject, and none upon whom the Secretary of the Treasury can officially rely for information as to the management of this important branch of the Government business."

That changed when the Act of Feb. 12, 1873, made the Mint a bureau of the Treasury Department. The director was still appointed by the president, for a five-year term, but the bureau was placed "under the general direction of the Secretary of the Treasury," who of course was also appointed by the president.

Under the 1873 act, the director was given "the general supervision of all mints and assay offices." He was to report to the secretary. The secretary was to "appoint the number of clerks, classified according to law, necessary to discharge the duties of said Bureau."

The headquarters of this new bureau were established in Washington. Previously, directors had operated from the main Mint at Philadelphia. For the first time, in 1873 a superintendent was appointed at the Philadelphia Mint with the same responsibilities as the superintendents of the other facilities (previously,

the director exercised the duties of superintendent at the Philadelphia Mint). Also under the 1873 act, the Branch Mint era ended, with each of the four production facilities then in operation formally designated as a "United States Mint at [name of Mint]."

Today, the director of the Mint is appointed by the president, with the advice and consent of the U.S. Senate. The director is responsible for coinage production and the distribution of coins to and among the Federal Reserve Banks and branches, which in turn release them, as required, to commercial banks.

In addition, the Mint maintains physical custody of Treasury stocks of gold and silver and moves, places into storage and releases these metals from custody for such purposes as authorized.

On a reimbursable basis, the U.S. Mint manufactures and sells medals of a national character, produces Proof and Uncirculated coin sets for sale to collectors, and strikes bullion and commemorative coinage for sale to the public.

The director administers the Philadelphia, Denver, San Francisco and West Point Mints, and the gold bullion depository in Fort Knox, Ky. The director of the Mint and the director's staff administer Mint service activities from Mint headquarters in Washington, D.C.

The director makes annual reports to the secretary of the Treasury concerning Mint operations for the fiscal year, which runs Oct. 1 to Sept. 30. The information published in the annual report has changed over the years. The report generally discusses the year's highlights of coinage production, collector programs and improvements to Mint processes and facilities.

Beginning with fiscal year 1981, the Mint reports released are greatly abbreviated compared to those issued prior to 1981. A Mint report, generally released before June of the following calendar year, no longer goes into great detail reporting production figures. The Mint no longer releases actual mintage figures for commemorative and bullion coin programs, just sales figures.

The latest *Annual Report of the Director of the Mint*, giving complete Mint statistics and a report of Mint activities for the fiscal year which ended Sept. 30, 2009, is available from the United States Mint, Office of Corporate Communication, by telephone at (202) 354-7211, or online at **www.usmint.gov**.

The main offices of the Mint are located in Washington, D.C., in an eight-story complex at 801 Ninth St. N.W. that houses Mint headquarters, a Mint sales center and additional retail space.

The Mint moved from Judiciary Square, 633 Third Ave. N.W., its previous headquarters since 1985, between October 1999 and early 2000.

Questions concerning the purchase of collector coins sold by the Mint should be directed in writing to Customer Service Center, United States Mint, 2799 Reeves Road, Plainfield, IN 46168, or by telephone to the Customer Service Center at (800) 872-6468.

The Mint and its Washington officials may be contacted by writing to the United States Mint, Department of the Treasury, 801 Ninth St. N.W., Washington, DC 20220. The telephone number for the director's office in Washington is (202) 354-7200. For general information, telephone the Office of Public Affairs at (202) 354-7222 in Washington.

Mint website

The Mint maintains a website, **www.usmint.gov**. Recognizing the marketing and communications potential of the World Wide Web, the Mint launched its website in mid-1998.

The website allows customers to access information and images concerning program launches and product availability; developments within coin programs such as the America the Beautiful quarter dollar program and the Presidential dollars program; accessibility to news releases and coin images of existing and new products; commemorative and bullion coin statistics; and Mint medals.

Special links in several of these sections provide updated information on sales. For American Eagle bullion coins, monthly sales statistics are included for Uncirculated gold, silver and platinum coins.

Information available includes Mint history, the meaning of Mint marks, frequently asked questions, how coins are made, monthly cumulative circulating coinage production statistics, coin specifications, and how to arrange tours at either the Philadelphia Mint or Denver Mint.

Customers can order products directly from the United States Mint's website with a credit card by using a number of secure server options.

Many of the United States Mint's products are available through a subscription option offered at the website, with each new issue shipped to customers as the product is released.

Mint officials

Office of the Director

Director (acting)	Richard Peterson
Deputy director	Richard Peterson
Director of Public Affairs	Thomas Jurkowsky
Director, Office of Legislative Affairs	Cliff Northrup
Counsel to the Mint	Daniel P. Shaver
Chief Financial Officer	Patricia M. Greiner
Chief Strategy Officer	Mike Stojsavljevich
Executive Secretary	Eric Anderson
Associate director of Sales and Marketing	B.B. Craig
Assistant director for Division of External Relations and Communications	Cynthia Meals Vitelli
Assistant director of Division of Customer Operations	Dufour Woolfley
Director of $1 Coin Programs	Patrick M. McAfee
Associate director of Manufacturing	Vacant
Chief, New Product Design, Research and Development	Ronald E. Harrigal
Senior Advisor and Chief, Quality Division	George Shue
Chief Engraver, Engraving and Design Division	Vacant
Assistant Director for Protection/Chief, U.S. Mint Police	Dennis O'Connor

Mint facilities

Mint headquarters
801 Ninth St. N.W.
Washington, DC 20220
Philadelphia Mint
Fifth Street at Independence Mall
Philadelphia, PA 19106
Marc Landry, plant manager
Denver Mint
Colfax and Delaware streets

Denver, CO 80204
David Croft, plant manager
San Francisco Mint
155 Hermann St.
San Francisco, CA 94102
Larry Eckerman, plant manager
United States Bullion Depository
Fort Knox, KY 40121
Bert Barnes, officer in charge

West Point Mint
West Point, NY 10996
Ellen McCullom, plant manager

Customer Service Center
United States Mint
2799 Reeves Road
Plainfield, IN 46168

Present Mint institutions

Philadelphia Mint

The Act passed on April 2, 1792, established the United States Mint. As a result, a plot of ground was purchased in Philadelphia, located on the east side of Seventh Street, below Arch Street.

This was the first public building to be erected by the government of the United States. For 40 years, the federal government continued to use the building on Seventh Street as the national Mint.

Guards are essential to the Mint's elaborate security system. In the past, as now, security precautions were very important. In 1793, the sum of $3 was paid for a watchdog to protect the Mint. The first dog, named Nero, was reportedly a savage one and accompanied the watchman on his hourly rounds.

The watchman, armed with a dirk and pistol, in making his rounds would ring a bell at regular intervals in order that the populace of Philadelphia might know that the Mint was still safe. Food for the dog was considered an essential expense of the Mint, the same as hay and other food was considered essential for the horses that provided power for operating the Mint machinery in those days.

On July 4, 1829, construction began for a new Mint, on the northwest corner of Chestnut and Juniper streets. The facility was built at a cost of $291,000. This building was used as the Philadelphia Mint for more than 70 years.

The third Philadelphia Mint building, on Spring Garden Street between 16th and 17th streets, built in 1900, covered a ground area of 58,000 square feet. The exterior of the building was of Maine granite and faced a street on each of the four sides. The main entrance was on Spring Garden Street.

The front portion of the building rose three stories above the basement and terraces. The rear portion was one story lower than the front, but owing to the slope of the ground the basement was almost entirely above ground, which gave three clear stories to this portion also. The lobby, reached by the Spring Garden Street entrance, was finished with strongly veined Italian marble walls and vaulted mosaic ceilings. Mosaics illustrating the ancient methods and processes of coinage formed the panels. These mosaics formed one of the most beautiful and expressive features in the building. The ceilings were covered with a solid mosaic of gold – each unit being a piece of glass backed with gold.

These beautiful mosaics make a link between the third Philadelphia Mint and its replacement, dedicated at its official opening Aug. 14, 1969. The third Mint served the nation for more than 65 years, but

the growth of the country made demands that could no longer be handled by the then-outmoded facilities. After the completion of the fourth Philadelphia Mint, the mosaics were painstakingly removed and reinstalled in the new facility. There they are a prime attraction for the Mint's thousands of visitors.

Groundbreaking ceremonies held Sept. 17, 1965, launched construction of the fourth Philadelphia Mint, nearly three times the size of the Spring Garden Street facility. The building has a pink granite facade and bronze-tinted glass, and covers more than five acres of ground, approximately three city blocks. The main entrance plaza and lobby, facing Fifth Street at Independence Mall, overlooks the original site. Offices, production divisions and public areas occupy more than 500,000 square feet of space.

The new Mint was designed for an annual production capability of 2 billion coins on a five-day, 40-hour week, or a total capacity of about 8 billion coins per year on a 24-hour day, seven-day week basis.

Facilities originally included melting, casting, rolling and annealing facilities, cladding lines to produce clad strip for composite coins, and the coining areas. However, the Mint began shutting cladding operations down during fiscal year 1982, and officially shut down the facilities in fiscal 1983, relying instead totally on private sector producers of coinage strip from which blanks for all circulating coin denominations from 5-cent and above are punched. A private sector vendor supplies ready-to-strike cent planchets.

The Philadelphia Mint began upgrading its coin production operations in the 1990s with the addition of a number of high-speed presses to either supplement or replace machinery that had been in operation for decades. The most recent significant addition is a new press installed in 2010 intended to strike the America the Beautiful 3-inch 5-ounce silver bullion coins. The GMP 1000 coin and medal embossing press, manufactured by Gräbener Pressensysteme GmbH & Co. KG, was installed in the basement of the Philadelphia Mint. Construction began in the basement to accommodate the Gräbener press during the summer of 2009.

The multi-ton press is hydraulically supported atop a 4-foot-deep, concrete-lined pit equipped with sensors to detect any equipment failure, as well as any possible infiltration of water, since the Philadelphia Mint is located close to the Delaware River.

The press has a rating showing its capacity to strike with up to 1,000 metric tons per square inch. Gräbener's GMP 1000 press is rated as capable of striking pieces with a maximum diameter of 85 millimeters (3.346 inches), but it can be adjusted to accept a diameter up to 120 millimeters (4.724 inches) depending on blank composition. The press can be adjusted to register from 20 to 40 strokes per minute.

Circa 2005 to 2006, the engraving staff at the Philadelphia Mint was introduced to digital sculpturing of coin designs from which coinage dies would eventually be produced. Members of the engraving staff are using either traditional methods, digital sculpturing on computers, or a combination of both (see U.S. Coins chapter, "How Coins Are Made" section, for details). Much of the actual circulating coinage production operation at the Philadelphia Mint can be viewed from a glass-enclosed elevated gallery designed to accommodate 2,500 visitors an hour.

However, after terrorist attacks against the United States on Sept. 11, 2001, tour access was restricted. Check the link on the U.S. Mint's website at **http://usmint.gov/mint_tours/** for specific information.

The numismatic room on the mezzanine contains Mint relics, historic coins and medals.

A sales counter is maintained where Mint medals, coin sets and certain Mint publications may be purchased. It is operated by an independent outside company, Delaware North Services, which operates other sales centers and concession services at federal tourist locations across the country.

Denver Mint

Gold was first discovered in 1858 in what is now the state of Colorado, on the Platte River, near the city of Denver. For a time, mining in Colorado was chiefly from placer claims, which were deposited by water currents in riverbeds. Lode gold was found, however, near present Central City, Colo., on May 6, 1859, and other discoveries followed.

When the California Gold Rush of 1849 lost its impetus with the declining production of mines in California, miners turned their attention to Denver City where, within a few years, a small village of cottonwood log cabins began to emerge. This town became an "outfitting" point for miners. Recognizing a need for a circulating medium, much as necessity is the mother of invention, several firms in Colorado organized themselves as private mints. They melted raw gold in the form of dust and nuggets, all of which contained an appreciable amount of silver, and formed it into what are now known as Pikes Peak coins. These were much like some of the gold coins struck privately in California some years previously.

Congress, in January 1862, received a proposal from the Treasury Department that a Branch Mint be established at Denver for gold coinage. As indicative of the need, they were informed that in the two preceding years the private mint of Clark, Gruber and Co. had turned out gold coins to the extent of $120,000. The government bought the Clark-Gruber facility in the fall of 1862, for the sum of $25,000.

In the early days of Denver, when Indian raids were anticipated, the Mint building was used as a place of refuge for women and children, it being the town's most substantial structure. "The hostility of the Indian tribes along the routes ..." was one of the reasons given by the director of the Mint for the Denver plant not being able to assume its position as a Branch Mint.

The Denver facility opened its doors in September 1863 as an Assay Office. Its activities were restricted to melting and stamping bullion brought in by miners without refining. Under the regulations that were prescribed, the plant was to accomplish this task "within a day or an hour" after it was received. The bars were to be stamped as to the "fineness" (amount of gold and silver contained) and weight. Also stamped on the bars was a device bearing the American eagle and around it the inscription U.S. BRANCH MINT, DENVER.

By 1867 the miners had exhausted, to a large extent, the rich beds of placer gold appearing in the streams. The Assay Office at Denver had little business while miners turned their attention to "lode" mining and uncovered underground veins of ores having a high percentage of gold and silver. It was found, however, that to crush and pulverize these ores and to extract the precious metals required complicated apparatus and skilled labor, as well as rail transportation, all of which were largely lacking.

Disappointed that the Union Pacific Railroad passed the city to the north, a group of Colorado citizens banded together. Through their enterprise a rail line was built in 1870 that connected Denver with Cheyenne, Wyo., tying them in with the economic life of the nation, from coast to coast.

In the late 19th century Colorado experienced the effect of an acceleration in silver mining because of government purchasing programs.

When the programs were terminated, the abrupt reduction in silver output was offset by the rise of the great gold camp at Cripple Creek, Colo.

The Clark-Gruber facility, which the government had used continuously, began to deteriorate and in 1877 was reported as being so dilapidated as to be considered unsafe.

Still, the facility remained in place.

Hopes for a Denver Mint facility were again kindled when on Feb. 20, 1895, Congress provided for the establishment of a United States Mint at Denver for the coinage of gold and silver. A $500,000 appropriation provided that, until it could become a Mint in accordance with law, it would have to operate as an Assay Office.

On April 22, 1896, a site was purchased at a cost of about $60,000. In the meantime, the deposit activity at the Denver Mint stepped up considerably. The sources of the deposits were principally the mines of Arizona, New Mexico, Colorado and Utah. In 1895, the aggregate value of gold and silver deposited annually was in excess of $5.6 million.

Moving day into the new Mint took place on Sept.

1, 1904, when the Mint transferred its operations from the historic Clark-Gruber building at 16th and Market streets to the Renaissance structure at West Colfax and Evans streets.

Coinage organization began with the naming of officials for the superintendency and various departments on Oct. 15, 1904. Earlier it had been the practice for Denver to send its bullion deposits to Philadelphia for parting and refining. Bullion shipments to Philadelphia ceased Dec. 31, 1904.

The new structure, viewed from the street, provided two stories above ground. Actually, it had five floors. It was 175 feet long and 100 feet wide.

The stone facing of the building is Colorado granite, up to and including the water table. The Arkins granite between the water table and the cornice was procured in Maine. Tennessee marble forms the window trimmings, and the marble used in the interior finish was obtained in Vermont.

The decorations of the main corridor on the first floor, the mezzanine floor and the second floor were completed in 1909 under the direction of John Gibson, a member of an old Philadelphia firm.

This firm also furnished the three mural paintings in the area above the cornice inside the main vestibule. They are the work of an Italian named Vincent Adriente who worked under the supervision of the celebrated mural artist Edwin Howland Blashfield, of New York City.

The paintings are purely symbolic and typify Commerce, Mining and Manufacturing.

The Great Seal of the United States, in the form of a large metal casting, was placed in the center of the vestibule floor. By the summer of 1961 this seal had worn so smooth it was considered unsafe and was replaced by a mosaic replica.

The Denver Mint was equipped with all the latest methods and machinery, the coinage apparatus having been built at the Philadelphia Mint where a large part of the machinery used by the Mints was made.

In its first year of operation the coining room turned out gold coin valued at $23.8 million, and subsidiary coin, half dollars, quarter dollars and dimes, amounting to $3.2 million.

By Act of Congress, the Bureau of the Mint has had authority since 1874 to strike coins for friendly foreign governments. In 1906 the Denver Mint started its first production of foreign coinage—4.8 million gold 5-peso coins for the government of Mexico.

The Mint Act of 1873, which codified all existing Mint laws, had restricted the manufacture of 5-cent coins and cents to the United States Mint at Philadelphia. At the time that act was passed few if any of these coins were in use in the West, although by legislation in 1906 Congress gave recognition to the fact that they were then in circulation all over the country. The secretary of the Treasury was then authorized to direct the coinage of 5-cent coins and cents at any of the Mints. Minor coinage started at the Denver Mint

in 1911. The production of cents that year amounted to 12.6 million pieces.

It had always been the practice in the United States to conduct refineries in conjunction with coinage operations, thus enabling the facilities to receive crude bullion. The installation of a refinery at the Denver Mint in 1906 was itself as momentous as its commencement of coinage. In its first six months of operations the new Denver refinery turned out refined gold and silver valued at $32 million. Operating through the years, it contributed substantially to the total output of refined gold and silver of the Mint.

In 1937, an addition was made to the Denver Mint, covering an area of approximately 6,000 square feet and consisting of a basement and two stories. The old building was remodeled. Ten coining presses, with backup equipment, were installed.

In October 1945, ground was broken for a three-story addition measuring 161 feet long by 96 feet wide. The cost of this addition was more than $1.5 million. The new wing was built to house modern "brass mill" melting and rolling equipment.

The rolling system and equipment, designed by one of the foremost rolling mill engineering firms in the nation, was engineered to process a bronze coinage ingot weighing 420 pounds.

Out of consideration for an interested public, a visitor's balcony was constructed in each of the first two floors, suspended under the 24-foot ceilings, from which spectators may look down on money-making operations.

As coinage demands grew in the late 1960s and into 1970, Mint Director Mary Brooks began to explore the possibility of building a new Denver Mint. Although present Mint facilities were keeping up with the public's demand for coins, she believed by 1980 those facilities would be outdated.

After a series of congressional hearings and conferences, Congress voted July 3, 1971, to allocate $1.5 million to purchase a site for a new Denver Mint. Officials of the Bureau of the Mint shopped for land.

Two sites were chosen, the South Platte River basin and the Clayton Trust property in the Park Hill section of Denver. The first site was abandoned when the Burlington Northern Railroad stuck to its plans to install mainline tracks adjacent to the area. Brooks announced on July 16, 1974, the new Mint would be built on the Park Hill site, which was acquired. Construction was set to begin in the fall of 1975 or early 1976 with a completion date around 1980. The new Mint was to be designed to produce 10.7 billion coins annually and possibly up to 16 billion.

A House bill to provide funds for the new Denver Mint was introduced March 26, 1975. It passed the House Sept. 19, 1975, and went to the Senate Public Works Committee Sept. 22, 1975. In an unusual procedure, Assistant Secretary of the Treasury David Macdonald and Frank H. MacDonald, deputy director of the Mint, testified at an executive session of the

Public Works Committee. Witnesses are not normally called into an executive session.

If passed, the bill would have authorized an increase of $60 million that could be appropriated to the Treasury Department for the construction of Mint facilities. The bill would have raised the total authorized by Congress since 1963 for Mint construction to $105 million.

On Feb. 27, 1976, Mint and Treasury officials testified in support of the Denver Mint legislation before the Senate Banking, Housing and Urban Affairs committee.

At one point, Mint officials considered the purchase of an empty tire manufacturing plant in Littleton, Colo., as a potential site for the Denver Mint. However, the plant was sold in March 1976 to a tire firm. Rep. William Armstrong, R-Colo., said moving the Mint to suburban Littleton would save the Bureau of the Mint about $20 million. Rep. Pat Schroeder, D-Colo., opposed the Littleton move, and advocated the continued use of the present Mint downtown in Denver, and expansion of the Philadelphia Mint.

At this point, Sen. William Proxmire, D-Wis., chairman of the Senate Banking committee, directed a General Accounting Office examination of all Bureau of the Mint facilities to determine total-picture needs.

The GAO advised against the construction of a new Mint in Denver, primarily because of the 1-cent coin's then-dubious future in the U.S. coinage lineup. The GAO report criticized Treasury Department estimates of future coinage demands.

The proposed phase-out of the cent, which accounted for more than 70 percent of the production at the nation's Mint facilities, diminished the need for construction of a new coinage facility at that time, the GAO report said.

The report proposed several alternatives, including upgrading current production capacity and modifying production strategies to meet the short-term needs.

The report concluded with the recommendation that the Treasury secretary require the Bureau of the Mint to make a comprehensive study of the various options for increasing production within its present facilities.

On March 7, 1976, during budgetary hearings before the House Appropriations Subcommittee, Acting Mint Director MacDonald told representatives the Bureau management was "totally in disagreement with" the GAO report regarding the Denver Mint. He characterized the report as being full of things that "seem like cheap shots like how we can put coinage presses in the restrooms."

Bureau of the Mint officials abandoned their plans for a new Denver Mint in the Nixon administration and sold the Park Hill site to an Alaskan firm on Jan. 19, 1984, for $3,351,356.05.

Expansion of the present Denver facility was approved and construction began in late May 1984.

Mint Director Donna Pope reported that the expansion would be done in two phases. Phase one would comprise construction of an expanded south dock for all material deliveries and coin shipments, roadway approaches and departures from the south dock. Also part of the first phase was a two-story building addition on the west side to provide for storage and processing of coinage materials on the ground floor, and secured storage in the basement for coins. The second phase included the relocation and installation of production equipment, support facilities for increased coin production and utilities systems.

Improvement of the facilities continued under Superintendent Cynthia Grassby Baker. While the Mint's technology staff worked to install high-speed coinage presses and automated material handling systems, Baker directed the refurbishing of the building's historical decor. Some controversy erupted in 1989 when plans for a new visitors' entrance drew fire from architectural critics who claimed the addition did not fit with the building's classic style.

The new visitors' entrance was dedicated on Sept. 9, 1991, with 15 exhibits on loan from the United Bank of Denver on such areas as pioneering, trade and money. Visitors entering the public entrance to the Denver Mint are treated to a monetary history of yesteryear as they enter the realm of today's coin production for general circulation and for collectors.

After the terrorist attacks against the United States on Sept. 11, 2001, tour access was restricted for several years by reservations through congressional representatives. Check the link on the U.S. Mint's website at **http://usmint.gov/mint_tours/** for specific information on current restrictions, if any.

Mint officials began their efforts in 1991 to secure the necessary appropriations for a new die shop at the Denver Mint to augment the die production facility associated at the Philadelphia Mint. Die production had always been limited to the Philadelphia facility. The Philadelphia Mint also houses the engraving staff. The thought behind building a second die shop was not only to increase die production capacity and ensure faster production and distribution of coins for Western states, but also to have a die shop at the ready in case the die shop at Philadelphia would be compromised for any reason.

Groundbreaking for the die shop to be attached to the Denver Mint was Sept. 22, 1994. The die shop officially opened for business on May 13, 1996. The master die production remains at the Philadelphia Mint, with the subsequent stages—working hubs and working dies—completed at Denver.

The Philadelphia Mint's die shop also prepares all dies for the West Point Mint. Working hubs and working dies used for coins to be struck at the San Francisco Mint are executed at the Denver Mint's die shop. The San Francisco Mint completes the final polishing to flat surfaces of working coin dies and laser frosts all raised design elements for Proof coin dies.

The die production equipment installed at the Denver Mint was greatly advanced over that used at the Philadelphia Mint. One of the biggest changes was the production of dies using a single impression from a working hub instead of multiple hubbing impressions like those needed at the Philadelphia Mint.

As the 1990s ended, die-production equipment had been installed at the Philadelphia Mint, resulting in it abandoning multiple hubbing operations for circulating denominations. A multiple-hubbing process requires additional procedures between impressions to soften the steel and receive the next impression to bring up details. With the single-hubbing process, only one impression into the die steel from a working hub is necessary for the working dies. The single hubbing procedure is reportedly employed to eliminate the possibility of doubled die coins.

The addition of the die shop boosted the U.S. Mint's die production capabilities by 50 percent. The Denver die shop supplies the San Francisco Mint with working dies after receiving master dies from the Philadelphia Mint.

During the 1990s, the Denver Mint also added a large number of high-speed presses, some to augment and others to replace older coin presses.

The high-speed presses strike coins with a single pair of dies oriented horizontally, with the capability of 700 to 750 coins per minute.

This compares to the quad presses with four pairs of dies able to produce up to 200 coins per minute per pair of dies.

San Francisco Mint and Assay Office

The discovery of gold at Coloma (Sutter's Mill) by John Marshall, in 1848, was the world-echoing event that contributed to the recommendation by President Millard Fillmore in 1850 that a Branch Mint be established in California. Gold being mined in the hills had grown from a trickle to a deluge too heavy for facilities at the distant Philadelphia Mint to handle and much time was consumed in transporting the precious metal on its hazardous journey.

The coinage situation in the West was in a chaotic state. Many different kinds of coins circulated—French louis d'ors, Dutch guilders, Indian rupees, Mexican reales, English shillings, as well as American pieces—but even so, there was a scarcity; and gold dust, while acceptable, was not a convenient medium of exchange.

To remedy the difficulty, private mints sprang up that converted the gold into coins, but this was not the permanent solution to the problem.

The San Francisco Branch Mint was authorized by the Act of Congress approved July 3, 1852, and the coins produced there gradually replaced the miscellaneous assortment in circulation. The Mint commenced receiving deposits on April 3, 1854. Between April and December 1854 it coined $4,084,207, all in gold pieces.

Operations were conducted in a small building on Commercial Street, just 60 feet square. According to the *Report of the Secretary of the Treasury on the state of the Finances* for 1866, "It is almost impossible to conceive how so much work can be well done, and so much business transacted safely, in so small a space. The entrance to the business office is up a steep pair of stairs and through a dark hall rendered unwholesome by the fumes of acids, and uncomfortable by the noise of machinery and the heat of the engine. The apartments of the different officers and the desks of the clerks are cramped and inconvenient, and the vaults depend for their safety chiefly upon the presence of well-tried watchmen."

About 10 years after operations commenced, the suggestion was made in the 1866 *Report of the Secretary of the Treasury on the state of the Finances* that there be purchased "a suitable site upon which should be speedily erected a mint building creditable to the Government, and commensurate with the wants of the great mineral districts of the Pacific Coast." It was not until 1872 to 1873, however, that such a building was completed and the work of fitting up the necessary machinery, fixtures and apparatus was begun. The new Mint at Fifth and Mission was occupied in the summer of 1874, and was one of the best-appointed Mints in the world.

The work of the San Francisco Mint was interrupted by the great earthquake of April 18, 1906. The structure and its contents were saved from the resultant fire by intelligent and courageous work on the part of the superintendent and employees, but as the fuel used for its melting, annealing and assaying operations was city gas, the destruction of the gas works made a discontinuance of operations necessary. The Mint, by reason of the destruction of the federal subtreasury and all of the banks of the city, became the only financial institution able to do business in the city and the agency through which all remittances to and from the city and disbursements within the city were made.

The Mint became the depository and treasury for the relief fund, and its superintendent, Frank A. Leach, had many new and very important responsibilities suddenly thrust upon him, all of which were borne with fidelity and ability.

The steadily increasing coinage demands of the nation following the Great Depression made mandatory the enlargement of minting facilities. In the summer of 1937, San Francisco Mint personnel made another move, this time into an imposing three-story marble edifice some distance from the principal business district where the 1874 building was located. The approximately 33,000 square feet of space in the 1937 structure housed the most modern facilities of the day and new equipment to replace worn and obsolete machinery. (See the section dealing with former Mint facilities for the history of the Old San Francisco Mint at Fifth and Mission since coin operations there were ended.)

The newest San Francisco Mint went into operation in 1937, striking U.S. coins of all denominations, plus coins for the Philippine Islands in 1944 and 1945, as World War II came to a close. In most years, the San Francisco mintages of U.S. coins lagged behind those of the Philadelphia and Denver Mints, although for some denominations, in some years, San Francisco Mint totals were slightly higher than the Denver facility's mintages.

Meanwhile, in the decade following the end of World War II, the Philadelphia and Denver Mints were being improved. It was believed that these two expanded facilities would be adequate to meet the nation's coin demand for some time to come. Therefore, in March 1955, coinage operations at the San Francisco Mint were discontinued.

The equipment was removed and most of the building was remodeled for occupancy by other agencies of the government. The Mint retained only a small area for the conduct of assay functions, including receipts of gold and silver deposits.

A profound change in the classification of the 1937 Mint structure came in the mid-1960s when it once again became an operating minting facility. During the fall of 1963, it became apparent that a coin shortage was spreading nationally, and by July 1964, emergency measures had been adopted to relieve the situation. One of these measures was the utilization of space in the 1937 San Francisco Mint building (designated the San Francisco Assay Office since approval of a law July 11, 1962, until it regained Mint status March 31, 1988). The Treasury Department reacquired and once again adapted the space to the making of coins.

With the additional equipment secured from the Department of Defense, the San Francisco Assay Office first began producing 1-cent and 5-cent coin planchets and took on annealing and upsetting operations also, thus lessening the load at the Denver Mint and allowing the Denver facility more leeway for the other manufacturing functions.

The finished planchets were then shipped to Denver for the final stamping process. This enabled the making of many more coins at the Denver Mint than would ordinarily have been possible. Reactivation of coining operations at the San Francisco Assay Office was authorized by the Coinage Act of 1965, approved by President Johnson July 23, and on Sept. 1 the presses began turning out the first coins struck there since coinage was discontinued 10 years before.

In 1968, the San Francisco Assay Office assumed production of all Proof coinage; not until 1983 and 1984 with the Olympic coinage program were U.S. Proof coins intended for public purchase struck at another Mint facility.

From 1968 to 1974, only some of the circulation-strike coinage bore the San Francisco Mint mark. Since 1974, only the Anthony dollars of 1979 to 1981 struck at the San Francisco facility have borne the S

Mint mark, except for Proof coinage. The San Francisco facility has not struck coinage for circulation since 1983 when it struck more than 180 million 1983 Lincoln cents without Mint marks.

The San Francisco Mint specializes in the production of Proof coins, and for a number of years the Uncirculated and Proof versions of the silver American Eagle bullion coin. It also finishes Proof dies prior to coinage.

West Point Bullion Depository, West Point Mint

Formerly the West Point Silver Bullion Depository, in New York, the West Point Mint serves as a fourth Mint of the United States, in addition to its status as the main storehouse of the nation's silver and the holder of a portion of the government's gold supply.

The Treasury Department's Financial Management Service website at **www.fms.treas.gov/gold/current. html** provides a monthly gold report listing where all the Treasury gold holdings reside at any given time.

The depository was completed at a cost of about $500,000 and occupied in 1938. It is a rectangular, windowless, one-story, concrete building, 170 feet by 256 feet, situated on a four-acre tract of land formerly a part of the West Point Military Reservation.

The building is located within 500 feet of the Old Storm King Highway, Route 218, near West Point's "Old North Gate."

Offices and guardrooms are on the first floor and mezzanine, at the front of the building, with entrance through a vestibule. Light and air for this section are obtained through skylights. The remainder of the structure is under a solid composition roof. A vertical-lift steel door in the center of the front affords passage for bullion trucks.

With this door closed, complete isolation is provided for loading operations. To the rear of the loading platform are rolling steel doors and checking rooms through which the storage vault is reached.

A master vault door and an emergency door guard a series of vault compartments. The master vault door is equipped with a time lock, and is of drill-proof and flameproof metal. A 9-foot steel fence surrounds the building, with a steel gate controlled by guards to regulate the entrance and departure of persons and vehicles. The outside walls are of reinforced concrete. An inside corridor connects the four turrets or watchtowers at the corners, where sentries may observe the terrain in all directions.

The depository's outside walls may be placed under floodlight.

Gold from the New York Assay Office began to arrive at the West Point Bullion Depository Nov. 8, 1981, with the last shipment from the NYAO arriving Aug. 12, 1982. During that time, 25 convoys using 133 tractor-trailers transferred 193,782 gold bars weighing from 5 ounces to 125 pounds each. The total gross weight transferred was about 2,318 tons. Law enforcement officials cooperating in the move included U.S. Secret Service special agents, New York and New Jersey state police, and local law enforcement agencies. The U.S. Army assisted in security on arrival at the Depository.

Permission to use the depository facilities to coin money was granted in the law providing for the Bicentennial coinage, signed Oct. 18, 1973.

The section reads: "Until the Secretary of the Treasury determines that the Mints of the United States are adequate for the production of ample supplies of coins and medals, any facility of the Bureau of the Mint may be used for the manufacture and storage of medals and coins."

Mint Director Mary Brooks announced in mid-1974 that some of the older Mint presses were being installed at the West Point facility to produce coins and medals. Twenty dual coin presses, some retired from the Philadelphia Mint, were installed. Ten began operations in November 1974, and the others began operations in early 1975.

Following the end of the Bicentennial program, the West Point facility continued to produce cents on its coin presses with no Mint mark. In late 1976, it began test-striking quarter dollars.

In 1975 and again in May 1977 it also produced bronze 1-centesimo coins for Panama. The last circulating U.S. coins struck at the West Point facility were 400,000 1986 Lincoln cents, all indistinguishable from the Philadelphia Mint cents.

At first, no West Point-struck coins bore Mint marks. That changed on Sept. 13, 1983, when the ceremonial first 1984 Olympic gold $10 eagles were struck, each bearing a W Mint mark.

All of the American Arts Gold Medallions were also struck at the West Point facility.

At the debut of the American Eagle gold and silver bullion coin program in the fall of 1986, the West Point facility took on a major role in bullion coin production. The facility struck its first American Eagle gold coins in 1986 and its first American Eagle silver bullion coins in 1989. The facility has been the sole producer of gold bullion coins since 2005, including all of the American Buffalo gold coins.

Public Law 100-274, approved March 31, 1988, gave official Mint status to the West Point coining facility, along with the San Francisco Mint. Since 1988, much though not all of the nation's gold bullion and commemorative coins has been struck at the West Point Mint. Many other commemorative coins have been struck at the West Point Mint as well.

In 1995, as part of the 10th Anniversary set marking 10 years of the American Eagle coin program, a Proof 1995-W American Eagle silver dollar was included in 30,125 sets also containing the four Proof American Eagle gold coins for the year.

In 1996, to mark the 50th anniversary of the introduction of the Roosevelt dime, a special Roosevelt dime was struck at the West Point Mint with the W Mint mark for inclusion in the 1996 Uncirculated set.

Already responsible for producing the Uncirculated and Proof American Eagle gold and silver coins, in June 1997 the West Point Mint added Proof American Eagle platinum coins to its repertoire. They were the first official U.S. coins struck in platinum.

The Uncirculated American Eagle bullion platinum coins were added in September 1997.

Fort Knox Gold Bullion Depository

A large amount of the monetary gold stocks of the United States is stored in the vault of the Fort Knox Gold Bullion Depository. The balance of the government's holdings is stored at the Denver Mint and the West Point Mint, with only small quantities stored at the Philadelphia Mint and the San Francisco Mint.

The Fort Knox Gold Bullion Depository was completed in December 1936 at a cost of $560,000. It is located approximately 30 miles southwest of Louisville, Ky., on a site that formerly was a part of the Fort Knox military reservation. The first gold was moved to the Depository by railroad in January 1937. That series of shipments was completed in June 1937.

The two-story basement and attic building is constructed of granite, steel and concrete; exterior dimensions measure 105 by 121 feet. Its height is 42 feet above the first floor level. Construction was under supervision of the Procurement Division of the Treasury Department, now the Public Buildings Administration of the General Services Administration. Upon completion, the Depository was placed under the jurisdiction of the director of the Mint.

Within the building is a two-level steel and concrete vault, divided into compartments. The vault door weighs more than 20 tons. No one person is entrusted with the combination. Various members of the Depository staff must separately dial combinations known only to them. The vault casing is constructed of steel plates, steel I-beams and steel cylinders laced with hoop bands and encased in concrete. The vault roof is of similar construction and is independent of the depository roof.

Between the corridor encircling the vault and the outer wall of the building is space utilized for offices, storerooms and the like.

The outer wall of the depository is of granite, lined with concrete. Included in the materials used in construction were 16,500 cubic feet of granite, 4,200 cubic yards of concrete, 750 tons of reinforcing steel and 670 tons of structural steel.

Over the marble entrance at the front of the building is the inscription "United States Depository" and the seal of the Treasury Department. Offices of the Officer in Charge and the Captain of the Guard open upon the entrance lobby. At the rear of the building is another entrance for the reception of bullion and supplies.

The building is equipped with the latest and most modern protective devices. The nearby Army post gives additional protection. The Depository is equipped with its own emergency power plant, water system and other facilities. In the basement is a pistol range for the guards.

The gold in the Depository is in the form of standard Mint bars of almost pure gold, or coin gold bars resulting from the melting of gold coins. These bars are slightly smaller than an ordinary building brick. The approximate dimensions are 7 by 3-5/8 by 1-3/4 inches.

The fine gold bars contain approximately 400 troy ounces of gold each. The avoirdupois weight is about 27.5 pounds. They are stored without wrappings in the vault compartments. When they are handled, great care is exercised to avoid abrasion of the soft metal.

The guard force, under the supervision of the Officer in Charge, is made up of men selected from various government agencies or recruited from Civil Service Registers.

Ordinarily, no visitors are allowed inside the Fort Knox Depository. Franklin D. Roosevelt visited there in 1943, the one and only time a gold vault was opened for inspection for anyone other than authorized personnel until Sept. 23, 1974. On that date, a seven-man congressional inspection team and nearly 100 reporters toured the Depository for the first public check of the nation's gold hoard.

Rep. Philip M. Crane, R-Ill., started things off when he discussed a rumor with Treasury Secretary William Simon in mid-1974 that gold was missing from the vault.

To dispel any doubts that the gold was really there, Mint Director Mary Brooks conducted the Fort Knox inspection.

A special audit followed the tour, conducted by the General Accounting Office and the Treasury. Congress has since provided for continuing audits by the Bureau of the Mint.

The United States Mint is audited annually by the Department of Treasury Office of Inspector General. These independent audits are conducted in accordance with Government Auditing Standards, issued by the Comptroller General of the United States.

The most recent report OIG-11-004 "Audit of the United States Mint's Schedule of Custodial Deep Storage Gold and Silver Reserves as of September 30, 2010 and 2009," dated Oct. 21, 2010, reported an unrestricted opinion on the custodial schedule (i.e., gold and silver inventory).

In addition, the audit disclosed no material weaknesses and no instances of reportable noncompliance with laws and regulations.

The audit reports are available at the website **www. treasury.gov/about/organizational-structure/ig/ Pages/audit_reports_index.aspx**.

Secretary of the Treasury W. Michael Blumenthal paid his first visit to the Depository in July 1977, accompanied by Undersecretary of the Treasury Bette B. Anderson. This was the first visit to Fort Knox by a Secretary of the Treasury since John W. Snyder paid a call in 1947. Director of the Mint Donna Pope paid a visit to the Depository in the summer of 1981.

The Fort Knox facility is also home to 12 2000-W Sacagawea .9167 fine gold dollars that were struck by the U.S. Mint in 1999 without congressional approval. They were among 39 Proof gold examples the Mint struck, but the remaining 27 examples were melted.

The 22-karat Sacagawea dollars were produced on the same 27-millimeter, .9167 fine gold planchets as are used to produce American Eagle half-ounce gold coins. Manganese-brass clad Sacagawea dollars struck for circulation are 26.3 millimeters in diameter.

The 12 remaining gold Proofs were placed aboard the space shuttle *Columbia* in July 1999 for a five-day mission in space, with plans by then Mint Director Philip N. Diehl to place the coins on loan for public display in museums around the country, with additional coins to be struck for collectors.

However, as soon as the shuttle returned to Earth, the coins were whisked away and secured in a vault at Mint headquarters before later being moved at an undisclosed date for safekeeping at the Philadelphia Mint. Congressional leaders put the lid on any more unauthorized gold Proof Sacagawea dollar production.

In 2001, U.S. Mint Director Henrietta Holsman Fore directed that the 12 coins be removed from the Philadelphia Mint and transferred to Fort Knox.

The coins were temporarily removed by U.S. Mint officials for public display at the 2007 World's Fair of Money in Milwaukee before being returned to Fort Knox.

In 2004, the 12 coins were joined by 10 1933 Saint-Gaudens gold $20 double eagles that U.S. Mint officials reported in September 2004 had been "recovered."

The coins, found in a Philadelphia bank vault in 2003 by the daughter of the late Philadelphia jeweler and coin dealer Israel Swift, were turned over to the Mint for authentication, but were confiscated as being illegal to own.

The ownership of the coins is the subject on ongoing litigation by Swift's heirs.

All 10 double eagles were publicly displayed by the U.S. Mint during the American Numismatic Association's 2006 World's Fair of Money in Denver.

Former Mint institutions

Charlotte, North Carolina

The discovery of gold in the southern Appalachian Mountains and the unearthing of large quantities of the precious metal presented a major problem for prospectors in that region of the nation in the 1820s.

Miners, once they had recovered the gold, were faced with a long trip to the Philadelphia Mint to have their finds smelted and struck into gold coins. The infant industry soon sought relief from Washington, D.C. When the federal government did not meet demands for a local Mint, a German immigrant named Christian Bechtler established a private mint at Rutherfordton, N.C., in 1831.

Seeing a potentially large supply of gold being diverted away from government control inspired Congress to authorize the Charlotte Mint in 1835.

The building and equipment were budgeted at $50,000, but the costs overran this figure and the opponents of a Branch Mint tried to use the expense to stop the construction. The Charlotte Mint opened on Dec. 4, 1837, for the assaying and processing of gold, but no coins were struck until March 27, 1837.

Like the Dahlonega Mint in Georgia, the Charlotte facility struck only gold coins. Its production was limited to $5 half eagles, $2.50 quarter eagles and dollars, with a more even distribution of the three than at the Dahlonega Mint.

A fire damaged the building on the night of July 27, 1844, resulting in a halt to production for a year and a half, until 1846. The fire has been attributed to a burglar who was either careless or malicious.

The Branch Mints were considered by the Philadelphia Mint to be poor stepsisters, and they consequently received the worst equipment. Worn-out presses received repairs when they should have received a decent burial, and rusted reverse dies unfit for duty at the Philadelphia Mint were Mint-marked and shipped south. One redeeming feature of this practice is that it is hard to convincingly alter a Philadelphia Mint coin to one from a scarcer Mint, because the resulting fake will be literally too good to be true.

During the 1850s, production at the Charlotte Mint became increasingly irregular, as the local gold supplies dried up and weren't replaced by California bullion. Half eagles were the only denomination consistently struck during this decade.

Throughout the entire period of federal control, the Charlotte Mint struck a total of $5,059,188 worth of gold coins. This compares with $4,084,773 worth of gold coins struck at the San Francisco Mint in 1854 alone, and $18,008,300 struck there the following year. The Charlotte Mint struck 5,992 half eagles in 1861 before it was seized by the Confederate forces on April 20, and 887 pieces afterward.

A quantity of bullion remained uncoined, either because of technical difficulties or because the bullion value of the gold was greater than the face value of the coins that could have been made from it.

It is a tribute to the dedication of bureaucrats everywhere that somebody in the then Confederate Mint in October 1861 sent to the Philadelphia Mint 12 half eagles that had been struck under the federal government in early 1861 and had been set aside for assay purposes. Millions of dollars' worth of federal property had been seized by the Confederacy, and yet somebody was more concerned with the integrity of the Charlotte Mint than the Confederate Treasury.

Throughout the remainder of the Civil War the building was used for office space by the Confederate armed forces. After the war officials of the Union army occupied it for a while, and eventually it was restored to the status of an Assay Office.

In 1935, one century after the authorization of the Mint, it was decided to tear the building down to make room for a new post office building. A local citizens' group purchased the materials and reconstructed the building on a new site, where it now serves as an art museum.

The Mint Museum Randolph is located at 2730 Randolph Road in Charlotte. The museum can be contacted by phone at (704) 337-2000, or visit online at **www.mintmuseum.org/**.

New Orleans, Louisiana

The Act of Congress approved March 3, 1835, established a Branch Mint at New Orleans. The mayor and city council offered to deed to the United States government a portion of ground bounded by Esplanade, Barracks Street and Bayou Road, which was surrounded by a moat and formerly known as old Fort St. Charles.

"On the 19th of June 1835 the municipal authorities of the city of New Orleans conveyed to the United States, ... a certain piece ... of land situated in the City of New Orleans, known as 'Jackson Square,' immediately fronting the river Mississippi, for the express purpose of erecting thereon a branch of the Mint of the United States. ..."

By this liberal and patriotic act, the United States became possessed of one of the most valuable squares of ground in the city, without any cost to the government. The value, at the time of the donation, has been estimated at a little less than $500,000.

In consideration for deeding this ground it was agreed that a building should be erected thereon for minting purposes, and should it happen in the future that this Mint facility cease to operate, the title of the property would revert back to the city.

The New Orleans Mint building was erected under the supervision of William Strickland, the architect who drew the plans. The cornerstone of the original building, an edifice 280 feet long and three stories high, was laid in September 1835. Due to sickness and other delays, the work was not completed until 1838; operations commenced March 8, 1838. The first coinage consisted of dimes, in the sum of $40,242.00; this was the total coinage for 1838.

The New Orleans Mint suspended operations in 1839, from July 1 until Nov. 30, because of an outbreak of yellow fever that is said to have been one of the worst scourges the city has ever known.

At the beginning, the machinery used for minting purposes was run by hand; the first steam boiler and steam press were not used at the New Orleans Mint until 1845. Coinage operations continued until Jan. 31, 1861, when the Mint was taken over by the state of Louisiana, but all operations carried on with the same officers who had functioned under the United States. On March 31, it was again taken over, this time by the Confederate States of America, in whose custody it continued until it was closed on May 31 of that year. According to old records, more than $200,000 in bullion was in the vaults at that time, which was coined by the Confederate forces, and a good portion of the machinery was later taken from the Mint by the Confederates and transferred to various gun factories in the state.

Following recapture of the city May 1, 1862, Dr. M.F. Bonzano, melter and refiner at the New Orleans Mint, returned to that city from the North, whence he had gone during the war, and took possession of the Mint and its property acting under orders of Secretary of the Treasury Salmon P. Chase.

During the war much of the machinery had been damaged and otherwise rendered ineffective by disuse and other causes incident to the war. Extensive repairs, besides additional machinery, were required before coinage operations could be resumed.

In 1874, John Jay Knox, then deputy comptroller of the currency, said that it was not probable that coinage would ever again be necessary at the New Orleans Mint and that the Philadelphia Mint had sufficient capacity for all coinage requirements. However, after a period of inactivity, the New Orleans Mint reopened its doors Oct. 23, 1876, as an Assay Office.

Because the provisions of the original land grant were not being followed, and no coins were being manufactured, the United States marshal, a Mr. Packard, proposed on July 28, 1876, that the New Orleans Mint be seized for the state of Louisiana, on the grounds that it was not being used as a Mint. No action was taken, however, for the Mint continued in the capacity of an Assay Office until 1879, when coinage operations were resumed.

In connection with the reopening of the New Orleans Mint, the Annual Report of the Director of the Mint for 1878 contains the following:

"The Act of Congress making appropriation for the Mint at New Orleans provided that no expenditure of money should be made for that Mint until the city should release all title and claim and all conditions of forfeiture to the lands or premises upon which the Mint is located, and negotiations looking to that effect were entered into with the city authorities, which resulted in the square of ground being deeded in fee-simple to the government."

In the early days, the officers were housed in the Mint, and an old record book contains an entry to the effect that "Dr. Bonzano moved his residence from the Mint to his plantation. ..."

In 1884, all persons still maintaining living quarters in the building were informed by the director that they must move out by Aug. 1 of that year.

Coinage operations continued uninterrupted from 1879 to 1909, at which time they were discontinued because it was felt that facilities at the more modern Denver and San Francisco Mints were adequate to handle the demand. From 1909 to 1919, the building was used exclusively as an Assay Office.

The Veterans Bureau was granted permission to occupy a portion of the space, remaining for one year, during 1919. Beginning in 1922, the Veterans Bureau Dispensary was housed in the Mint and continued there for a number of years.

The building was vacated June 30, 1931, and the Assay Office activities transferred to space in the New Orleans Customhouse, where operations were continued until June 30, 1942, when they ceased for good.

In 1966, the federal government presented the Mint building to Louisiana with the understanding that the state would provide face-lifting funds, and renovation work would be completed in 10 years.

The Louisiana legislature faced a deadline in 1976 on the proposed appropriation of $3.5 million to the state's museum board for the restoration of the New Orleans Mint.

In 1976, the state was given four more years of grace by the federal government in which to renovate the Old Mint.

Meanwhile, in April 1976 a numismatic exhibit sponsored by the Orleans Token and Medal Society was installed in the Old Mint, which was opened to the public on an extended basis by the New Orleans Bicentennial Commission.

A set of "O" Mint coins represented the first of several exhibits planned by OTAMS on both concurrent and alternating bases.

State plans to renovate the New Orleans Mint, however, came to a temporary halt on May 27, 1976, because of a Louisiana state supreme court ruling that tidelands revenues received from the federal government could not be used at this time. The Louisiana state museum board had counted on this funding to develop the Mint restoration.

Exactly one year later on May 27, 1977, Gov. Edwin W. Edwards of Louisiana told state legislators he agreed to support amendments to bond bills to provide the full $3.5 million necessary to restore the Old Mint in New Orleans.

Plans for the restoration called for leasing part of the space in the New Orleans Mint for private business, such as curio shops and restaurants, developing an area for media presentations for tourists, plus creating an auditorium and museum library on the third floor of the building.

Gov. Edwards signed the capital outlay bill, which included funds for the Mint restoration, into law July 14. The bill was divided into cash and bond portions and included other construction projects besides the Mint restoration.

The restoration process began in 1977, with the majority of the work being done in 1979. The interior and exterior of the building were restored to their mid-1850s appearance, and a new roof was erected.

The third floor of the Mint houses the Louisiana Historical Center, including the museum's 40,000-volume library concerning the history of Louisiana. Also on the third floor is the Amistad Research Center, a 2-million volume library about minorities in the United States.

Additional details on the center can be found at **http://lsm.crt.state.la.us/collections/hcenter.htm**.

While Louisiana state budget cuts in 1989 threatened to close the doors of the museum, state officials were able to work through the crisis. To help ease the financial burden from reduced state funding and help support future museum programs, the Louisiana Museum Foundation established an endowment fund in 1995.

A more intense threat to the facility was Hurricane Katrina, which battered the Louisiana coast from Aug. 27 to 29, 2005. The Old Mint building was severely damaged; its copper roof was torn off, allowing the wind and rain to damage some of the items in the various collections.

While only a small number of items were damaged, the threat of mold required the evacuation over the next eight months of artifacts from the damaged areas to a 20,000-square-foot facility in Baton Rouge. It took two years and more than $5 million to repair the hurricane damage.

Among the exhibits on display in the 71,000-square-foot facility at the time of the hurricane was a display focused on New Orleans Mint operations. The exhibit, "Gold and Silver Coinage of the New Orleans Branch Mint," incorporated tools and artifacts associated with the production facility's coiners along with official Mint documents and records.

Also on display was a small coinage press reported to have been acquired from the Mint and later owned by New Orleans Mardi Gras doubloon manufacturer Alvin Sharpe. Part of the exhibit was devoted to counterfeiting, and included an 1857 half dollar counterfeiting device.

The museum has also displayed, through a loan from collector Robert LeNeve from Boynton Beach, Fla., the unique 1861-O Seated Liberty half dollar. The museum has also displayed a type collection of New Orleans Mint silver coins.

On Oct. 16, 2007, the Louisiana State Museum reopened the Old Mint for the first time since Hurricane Katrina with the exhibit, "Gold." After nearly three months, the exhibit moved on to museums in Denver, Chicago and Atlanta for similar exhibition, before returning to the New Orleans museum.

The exhibit includes dozens of natural gold specimens, including a 108-pound boulder containing more than 22 pounds of crystalline gold, more than 100 cultural objects and hundreds of gold bars and coins. The exhibit also includes a gold treasure box recovered from a 1715 shipwreck off the coast of Florida, an 18-karat gold baby rattle, and a few of the millions of coins minted at the New Orleans Mint when it was in operation between 1838 and 1909.

Among other major exhibits was a 2008 exhibit, "Treasures of Napoléon," that included the earliest known letter in his hand; the valise that brought him the signed Louisiana Purchase documents from America; the sword that proclaimed him emperor in the coronation ceremony at Notre Dame in Paris; his camp bed from the Battle of Wagram; his personal map of the French Empire (1812); the clothes he wore soon before his death; one of his legendary hats, which Napoléon wore during the battle at Essling in 1809; and in his own hand, the first will he wrote during his final, lonely exile on the desolate island of St. Helena.

The museum continues to flourish today.

Dahlonega, Georgia

The Dahlonega Mint was established to accommodate the gold miners of northern Georgia and to help the Charlotte Mint compete with the private Bechtler Mint doing business in North Carolina. The facility began accepting bullion for receipt and began assay of bullion on Feb. 12, 1838, and struck its first coinage on April 21, 1838.

The area of northern Georgia had been a part of the Cherokee nation, but it was obtained in 1830 in exchange for lands in Oklahoma. The name of the town is taken from the Indian word Tah-lon-e-ka, which means "yellow metal."

The Indians and the white men had found gold in small quantities in this area for many years, but the first large strike did not occur until the 1820s. The exact year is uncertain, but several colorful tales describe the first major find.

The most popular story is that a running deer kicked up a nugget that was spotted by the pursuing hunter. History does not record the name of the hunter or the fate of the deer.

Throughout its existence the Dahlonega Mint struck gold coins exclusively. The most common denomination produced was the half eagle, with only token coinages of $2.50 quarter eagles and dollars.

In 1854, the Dahlonega Mint produced its only issue of gold $3 coins. Presumably this denomination was less popular in the South than it was in the North, as the New Orleans Mint also struck it in just this first year, and the Charlotte Mint never did. Only 1,120 pieces were struck at the Dahlonega Mint.

Although all Dahlonega Mint gold coins bear the name of the United States of America, this legend did not always apply. In 1861 the Confederate States of America confiscated all federal property within its boundaries, including the three Branch Mints in the South. The Dahlonega Mint was placed under the management of the governor of Georgia.

Unlike at the New Orleans Mint, little bullion was

on hand at the Dahlonega and Charlotte Mints at the commencement of hostilities.

The Dahlonega Mint is thought to have contained $13,345 worth of uncoined gold when it was seized on April 8, 1861, but the official records were never recovered after the Civil War.

The small quantity of 1861-D Indian Head dollars in existence must have been struck under either Confederate or Georgian authority, as the U.S. Mint Report lists no dollars for this date and Mint. It is thought that a number of 1861-D Coronet half eagles may also have been produced, and poorly struck pieces are often attributed to this alleged striking. As the Dahlonega Mint did produce half eagles under federal auspices that year, and as it had never been known for its fine workmanship, it is impossible to state with certainty who produced any particular piece.

The small amount of bullion remaining on hand after the facility was seized was not struck into coins for a number of reasons, mainly because of technical problems and the lack of die-making facilities. Late in the war the Dahlonega Mint served as a temporary repository for the Confederate Treasury, before the city was overrun.

The Dahlonega and Charlotte Mints were considered by many to have been redundant ever since the opening of the San Francisco Mint, and proposals to close them were made even before the Civil War. The Dahlonega Mint never reopened after the war, and its building was donated to the state of Georgia for educational purposes.

The structure was reopened as the main building of North Georgia College in 1873, but it was destroyed by fire in 1878. Price Memorial Hall was built on its foundation the following year and occupied in 1880. It stands today as the administration building for North Georgia College and State University.

At one time, Price Memorial Hall housed a complete set of Dahlonega Mint gold coins, assembled by H.A. Alexander, an Atlanta lawyer. The 52-coin set included one of each date for each gold coin denomination—$1, $2.50 quarter eagle, $3 and $5 half eagle—struck between 1839 and 1861, noninclusive, and includes Small Date and Large Date varieties where applicable.

The set was donated in November 1952 by Alexander to the state of Georgia, with Gov. Herman E. Talmadge accepting the donation on behalf of the state. The set was temporarily stored for several weeks in the office of Secretary of State Ben W. Fortson Jr. in the state Capitol in Atlanta until an exhibit area could be established at Price Memorial Hall.

The collection, which was insured for $5,000, was stolen on March 30, 1963, and never recovered despite intense investigative efforts by multiple agencies, including the FBI and the Georgia Bureau of Investigation.

In November 1971, the college, then known as North Georgia College, commissioned a Gainesville, Ga., coin dealer to buy a complete replacement set of Dahlonega Mint gold coins.

The coins were purchased for a total of $35,000 from Stack's in New York.

The college received the replacement coins on Dec. 8, 1972, but they were not put on display until May 5, 1973. The coins remained on display in Price Memorial Hall until some time in 1994, when they were moved to another Georgia state-run location at the Dahlonega Courthouse Gold Museum while Price Memorial Hall underwent renovations, according to museum exhibit guide Lynda Bryan.

The museum is part of the Georgia Department of Natural Resources, Division of State Parks, Recreation and Historic Sites.

Bryan said the gold coins were considered to be on temporary loan to the museum for public display until school officials were to come and retrieve the coins for return to the college. Bryan said school officials never came to pick up the coins, and state officials determined the Dahlonega Mint gold pieces would receive more public recognition remaining on exhibit at the museum.

The collection was last appraised for North Georgia College and State University on Feb. 24, 1999, for $486,950. The 1861-D Coronet gold dollar, listed only as in Uncirculated condition, "premium quality," without a numerical grade, alone was appraised in 1999 for $95,000. (Heritage Numismatic Auctions sold an 1861-D Coronet gold dollar, graded Mint State 65 by Numismatic Guaranty Corp., on Jan. 10, 2008, for $149,500.) The collection at the museum is one of only two complete sets of Dahlonega Mint gold coins on public display as of 2011, the other being exhibited at the Federal Reserve Bank of Atlanta.

The "golden heritage" of the Dahlonega area is attested to by a large plaque, erected in connection with "Project Golden Steeple," through which Price Memorial Hall's steeple was leafed with native gold donated for the purpose.

Old San Francisco Mint

After the Bureau of the Mint abandoned the 1874 Mint building in 1937, spent decades in limbo, serving various government organizations. In 1968, however, the federal government vacated the nearly century-old building, which came to be lovingly known as the "Granite Lady," and declared it surplus to government needs.

Various groups fought over the empty and deteriorating building, some wanting to demolish it, others wanting to restore and preserve it.

In the spring of 1972, President Nixon intervened to save the 1874 Mint structure at Fifth and Mission streets from its then uncertain fate. He announced the transfer of the building from the General Services Administration to the Department of the Treasury's Bureau of the Mint for restoration and continued use by the government and the enjoyment of the public.

A year later, in April 1973, the Mint's Special Coins and Medals and Computer employees were able to move their operations into the rooms in the rear of the building. The building was newly renovated and equipped to speed the processing of mail orders received from the public for the special coins and medals produced by the Mint.

On June 16, 1973, the Old San Francisco Mint was officially reopened as a public museum and working Mint facility under Mint Director Mary Brooks. The museum rooms were authentically restored to their original 1874 appearance.

A film titled *The Granite Lady* was produced as a Bicentennial project by the Bureau of the Mint that tells the story of the Old San Francisco Mint. With Mercedes McCambridge as narrator, the film features two child actors and some of the 200 Mint employees in contemporary costumes.

On Nov. 7, 1976, a VIP reception hosted by Mint Director Mary Brooks celebrated the completion of the restoration of the Old San Francisco Mint.

Brooks told the several hundred reception guests that the sale of the millions of U.S. coins and national medals financed the $4.5 million restoration of the century-old edifice.

Jan. 28, 1977, was another momentous day in the illustrious history of the Old Mint. Ceremonies at the Mint that day were held to commemorate official recognition of the Fifth and Mission streets' structure as "California Registered Historical Landmark No. 875."

A plaque unveiled that day is inscribed with the following thumbnail sketch of the role the Old Mint played in the growth of San Francisco from a tiny mission to a great metropolis:

"The Old Mint (1869), San Francisco's second, is California's only such Greek Revival structure. Due to unsurpassed productivity, it became a subtreasury in 1874. Intact after the 1906 disaster, it served as a clearing house–bank, thus aiding in the city's reconstruction. Closed in 1937: Restored 1972-76 by Mint Director Mary Brooks."

The Old San Francisco Mint continued to serve the United States Mint for a number of years, primarily as a museum, with some of its duties transferred to other facilities. Among the changes were the transfer of the Mint Data Center and consolidation of the Old San Francisco Mint with the San Francisco Mint

In June 1990, the Clifford-Kagin pioneer gold collection, which had been on display at the Old Mint for years, was removed from display during a dispute as to insurance liability.

Once the centerpiece of the Old Mint Museum was gone, discussion arose as to what the future mission of the facility would be. It was discovered that an earthquake that had struck Nevada in October 1989 and was felt in San Francisco had caused some structural damage to the Old Mint. The Old Mint was one of the only structures to survive the great San Francisco earthquake and fire of 1906, but it would not survive the temblors of the 1989 quake and the ensuing political firestorm.

It was determined more than $25 million would be needed to seismically retrofit and protect the Old Mint from future earthquake damage.

The Old Mint was ordered closed to the public on Jan. 3, 1994, by Secretary of the Treasury Lloyd Bentsen, but reopened the following day amid political and public pressure for a 90-day study period to research alternatives to the facility's closure.

Bentsen granted an additional 120-day extension on March 18, while public and private options for the Old Mint were pursued.

A 56-page report was generated recommending the facility be multi-purpose, with a museum and education thrust being foremost, along with retail options, and maintaining the facility as a national landmark regardless of use.

Legislation was introduced to allow the Old Mint to be transferred to the General Services Administration so it could qualify for federal restoration funds. On July 19, 1994, unsuccessful legislation was introduced in the Senate calling for commemorative silver dollars and half dollars to be struck and sold to help raise the necessary capital.

On Aug. 2, Secretary of the Treasury Bentsen agreed to keep the Old Mint open until the end of the year. The same day, the Senate approved legislation to help save the Old Mint.

On Aug. 24, President Clinton signed into law a measure that would allow the Old Mint to be eligible for up to $18 million in federal funds.

Despite these efforts, the Old Mint was closed Dec. 30, 1994.

On Nov. 19, 1995, Clinton signed into law legislation providing $2.6 million to the Old Mint to make safety repairs.

The building sat vacant under the jurisdiction of the Region Nine office of the General Services Administration until August 1999, when the GSA was prepared to turn over the building to the city of San Francisco.

The U.S. government formally transferred ownership of the Old San Francisco Mint to the city of San Francisco in February 2002. An 1879-S Morgan silver dollar struck at the facility was used by Mayor Willie Brown to pay the federal government the $1 needed for the city to buy the Old Mint from the federal government.

In 2005, those involved with what is known as The Mint Project began to research and identify the key stories to incorporate into The Mint Project exhibits that will be displayed throughout the 102,000 square feet covering four stories.

In 2006, the project received toward its overall development nearly $5 million in surcharges from the United States Mint's sales of 227,970 Proof and Uncirculated combined silver dollars and 61,674

Proof and Uncirculated gold $5 half eagles combined issued for the San Francisco Old Mint Centennial.

By August 2006, a schematic design of the Mint Project was completed, with the Old Mint Museum master plan completed in January 2007. By March 2007, approximately $29 million of the project's estimated $95 million development budget had been raised.

In November 2007, an 18,000-square-foot section of Jesse Street, adjacent to the Old Mint building, reopened as Mint Plaza, San Francisco's then newest downtown public space.

The offices of Mayor Gavin Newsom and Supervisor Chris Daly and the San Francisco Museum & Historical Society partnered with Martin Building Company to create Mint Plaza and ensure a seamless experience for Old Mint visitors. The Mint Project capital campaign was launched in January 2009, and continued into early 2011 to raise funds toward completion of the project.

Complete updates on the project can be found on the Old Mint link off the San Francisco Museum & Historical Society website at **www.sfhistory.org/**.

Carson City, Nevada

The bill to establish a Branch Mint in Nevada was passed on March 3, 1863. It was urged in the Senate that the heavy tax of transportation cost upon producers in Nevada, the wonderful increase of gold and silver bullion and the necessity of keeping it in the United States through coinage, were considered sufficient inducements for Congress to order the establishment of a Mint.

Secretary of the Treasury Hugh McCulloch on Dec. 27, 1865, authorized a committee of three Nevada citizens to select and approve a location for a Mint in Carson City. The committee members were Abe Curry (founder of Carson City), F. Rice and John Mills. Curry facilitated the work of the commissioners by donating an entire city block as the Mint site.

On July 18, 1866, the three commissioners received authority to proceed with the construction of the Carson City Mint. On Sept. 18, 1866, the cornerstone was dedicated and laid by the Grand Masonic Lodge of Nevada. The Mint Director's Report for 1866 carried the following item: "... This building is in rapid process of erection. It is of good size, sixty by ninety feet, of two stories, built of a good quality of sandstone, and is exceedingly well arranged. It is located upon a large and handsome lot of ground, entirely disconnected from other buildings. ...

"As the mines of Nevada are almost entirely silver, and as the exportation of silver is almost wholly in bars, there being very little demand for silver coin, it will be inexpedient to introduce machinery for coinage into this institution at present. ..."

All of 1868 and most of 1869 were spent installing machinery and fixtures and it was not until December of 1869 that the Branch Mint at Carson City was ready for business as a Mint. On Jan. 8, 1870, it was

opened for the receipt of bullion.

On Nov. 6, 1885, it was directed that the Carson City Mint be closed, except for the receipt of bullion for "parting and refining" and local purchases of silver for the standard dollar coinage.

The Carson City Mint remained closed to the receipt of deposits until Oct. 1, 1886. Under the usual provision for the Mint at Carson City in the legislative appropriation act for the year, it was reopened for deposits as an Assay Office, with an acid refinery.

The coinage department of the Carson City Mint was reopened July 1, 1889, but owing to the dilapidated condition in which the building and machinery were found, after four years of idleness, repairs and improvements to the building and overhauling and repairing of the machinery were necessary. Consequently, coinage of gold and silver was not commenced until Oct. 1, 1889.

Coinage operations continued until 1893 when, by direction of the secretary of the Treasury, they were suspended, effective June 1, and the force employed in the coiner's department dispensed with.

Upon suspension of coinage operations, the presses and other machinery used in the coining department were painted and leaded under the supervision of Charles Colburn, the retiring coiner, to prevent corrosion.

From July 1 to Nov. 14, 1898, the Carson City Mint was open to the receipt of gold and silver deposits. Following this the secretary of the Treasury ordered changing the Mint to an Assay Office, to take effect July 1, 1899, as authorized by an Act of Congress approved Feb. 24, 1899.

A steadily decreasing volume of work resulted in the final closing of the Carson City Mint. No appropriation having been provided for its maintenance, operations ceased June 30, 1933.

The property then passed out of the custody of the Bureau of the Mint but remained under government control until legislation approved May 22, 1939, authorized the sale of the property. It is now owned by the state of Nevada, and the Nevada State Museum is operated on the premises.

Contained in the museum is the original Carson City Mint dollar press. The old press was used to strike the official Nevada 1976 Bicentennial medals. The state Bicentennial commission paid approximately $29,000 to get the press into operation once again. It was built originally in the Virginia and Truckee Railroad shops in Carson City.

The press continues for automated use as a revenue source. Various medals have been struck on the press since its refurbishment.

The museum, in addition to housing the Carson City Mint dollar press, also possesses the original 1876 Nevada U.S. Centennial medal die. This was used to strike the state Bicentennial medal. Many Carson City Mint coins are on display as well, including a complete set of Carson City Mint silver dollars.

Former Assay Offices

U.S. Assay Office, St. Louis, Mo., authorized by the Act of Feb. 1, 1881; opened July 1, 1881; closed June 30, 1911.

U.S. Assay Office, Helena, Mont., authorized by the Act of May 12, 1874; commenced operations Jan. 15, 1877; closed June 30, 1933.

U.S. Assay Office, Salt Lake City, authorized by the Act of May 30, 1908; opened Feb. 1, 1909; closed June 30, 1933.

U.S. Assay Office, Deadwood, S.D., established by the Acts of June 11, 1896, and Feb. 19, 1897; opened

April 20, 1898; closed June 30, 1927.

U.S. Assay Office, Boise, Idaho, established by the Act of Feb. 19, 1869, first deposits received in March of 1872; closed June 30, 1933.

U.S. Assay Office, Seattle, Wash., authorized by the Act of May 21, 1898; first deposits of gold received July 15, 1898; closed March 31, 1955.

U.S. Assay Office, New York, N.Y., authorized by Act of March 3, 1853; commenced operation Oct. 10, 1854; closed Dec. 30, 1982.

Directors of the U.S. Mint, 1792-2011

The president of the United States, by and with the advice and consent of the U.S. Senate, appoints the director of the Mint. The length of the term of office was not fixed by law from 1792 to 1873. The Act of Feb. 12, 1873, fixed the term of the director at five years. However, there is no restriction on the reappointment of directors.

Director	Term of service
David Rittenhouse, Pennsylvania	April 1792 to June 1795
Henry William de Saussure, South Carolina	July 1795 to October 1795
Elias Boudinot, New Jersey	October 1795 to July 1805
Robert M. Patterson, Pennsylvania	January 1806 to July 1824
Samuel Moore, Pennsylvania	July 1824 to July 1835
Robert Maskell Patterson, Pennsylvania	July 1835 to July 1851
George N. Eckert, Pennsylvania	July 1851 to April 1853
Thomas M. Pettit, Pennsylvania	April 1853 to May 1853
James Ross Snowden, Pennsylvania	June 1853 to April 1861
James Pollock, Pennsylvania	May 1861 to September 1866
William Millward, Pennsylvania	October 1866 to April 1867
Henry Richard Linderman, Pennsylvania	April 1867 to April 1869
James Pollock, Pennsylvania	May 1869 to March 1873
Henry Richard Linderman, Pennsylvania	April 1873 to December 1878
Horatio C. Burchard, Illinois	February 1879 to June 1885
James P. Kimball, Pennsylvania	July 1885 to October 1889
Edward O. Leech, District of Columbia	October 1889 to May 1893
Robert E. Preston, District of Columbia	November 1893 to February 1898
George E. Roberts, Iowa	February 1898 to July 1907
Frank A. Leach, California	September 1907 to November 1909
A. Piatt Andrew, Massachusetts	November 1909 to June 1910
George E. Roberts, Iowa	July 1910 to November 1914
Robert W. Woolley, Virginia	March 1915 to July 1916
F.J.H. von Engelken, Florida	September 1916 to February 1917
Raymond T. Baker, Nevada	March 1917 to March 1922
F.E. Scobey, Ohio	March 1922 to September 1923
Robert J. Grant, Colorado	November 1923 to May 1933
Nellie Tayloe Ross, Wyoming	May 1933 to April 1953
William H. Brett, Ohio	July 1954 to January 1961
Eva Adams, Nevada	October 1961 to August 1969
Mary Brooks, Idaho	September 1969 to February 1977
Stella Hackel Sims, Vermont	November 1977 to April 1981
Donna Pope, Ohio	July 1981 to August 1991
David J. Ryder, Idaho	Sept. 3, 1993, to Nov. 24, 1993*
Philip N. Diehl, Texas	June 1994 to March 26, 2000**
Jay Johnson, Wisconsin	May 25, 2000, to August 2001
Henrietta Holsman Fore	Aug. 7, 2001, to May 2005***
Edmund C. Moy	Sept. 5, 2006, to Jan. 9, 2011****

* Ryder was first nominated on July 25, 1991, by President Bush to become Mint director. On July 9, 1992, after the Senate failed to act on the

nomination, Treasury Secretary Nicholas F. Brady named Ryder acting director. On Sept. 3, when Congress was not in session, Bush named Ryder as Mint director under a recess appointment provision.

** Diehl was named executive deputy director in September 1993. He was confirmed to his presidential appointment to a five-year term on June 24, 1994. He remained in office at the request of Secretary of the Treasury Larry Summers until his successor was to be confirmed by the U.S. Senate.

*** In the interim period between Fore's departure and Moy's assuming the directorship, then Deputy Mint Director David Lebryk served as acting Mint director, and the Mint's chief counsel, Daniel P. Shaver, served as acting deputy Mint director.

**** On Jan. 25, 2011, U.S. Treasurer Rosa "Rosie" Gumataotao Rios named Richard Peterson, the Mint's associate director for manufacturing, not only as deputy Mint director, a Civil Service position, but also as acting Mint director. Peterson will serve as acting Mint director until President Obama, a Democrat, names a replacement for Moy, who was a Bush appointee.

Mint superintendents

It was 80 years from the time David Rittenhouse took over as first director of the U.S. Mint until future directors were given an "assistant" via the office of the superintendent.

The Coinage Act of 1873 put all Mint and assay office activities under the newly organized Bureau of the Mint in the Department of the Treasury, and the director's headquarters were moved to the Treasury Building in Washington, D.C. The top officer at the Philadelphia Mint was thereafter designated as superintendent.

Legislation passed into law in October 1996 during the waning days of the congressional session eliminated nine presidentially appointed positions—the chief engraver; the four Mint superintendents (Denver, Philadelphia, West Point and San Francisco); and the four assayers (one at each of the four Mint production facilities).

The duties of chief engraver, although not titled that way, are handled by an administrator, with no artistic responsibilities. The four Mint superintendent posts are now career Civil Service positions. Under the Mint's ongoing restructuring, in the last quarter of calendar year 1999, the position of Mint superintendent was renamed plant manager.

Superintendents and their term of service, and the name of the Mint director(s) at the time of their service, were:

Philadelphia Mint

Superintendent	Term
James Pollock	Feb. 12, 1873, to 1879
Col. A. Loudon Snowden	1879 to 1885
Daniel M. Fox	1885 to 1889
Col. Oliver C. Bosbyshell	Nov. 1, 1889 to 1894
Dr. Eugene Townsend	1894 to 1895
Maj. Herman Kretz	1895 to 1898
Henry Boyer	1898 to 1902
John H. Landis	1902 to 1914
Adam M. Joyce	1914 to 1921
Freas Styer	1921 to 1934
A. Raymond Raff	1934 to 1935
Edward H. Dressel	1935 to 1953
Rae V. Biester	1953 to 1961
Michael H. Sura	1961 to 1969
Nicholas G. Theodore	1969 to 1977
Shallie M. Bey Jr.	1978 to 1981
Anthony H. Murray Jr.	1981 to July 29, 1988
John T. Martino	Oct. 16, 1989, to July 23, 1993
Augustine A. Albino	Aug. 2, 1996, to Oct. 28, 1998*
Steven Kunderewicz	Nov. 8, 1998, to Sept. 24, 2000**

Plant Manager	Term
Richard Robidoux	Sept. 24, 2000, to March 1, 2008
J. Marc Landry	March 3, 2008, to present

* Albino was appointed to the post Aug. 2, but his position did not officially become a career post until Oct. 17, 1996.
** Kunderewicz was named acting superintendent on Nov. 8, 1998. The position was renamed plant manager in late 1999 under the Mint's restructuring.

Denver

Superintendent	Term
Frank M. Downer	Oct. 15, 1904, to Aug. 29, 1913
Thomas Annear	Aug. 29, 1913, to July 1, 1921
Robert J. Grant	July 1, 1921, to Nov. 12, 1923
Frank E. Shepard	Nov. 25, 1923, to June 30, 1933

Mark A. Skinner	June 16, 1933, to Dec. 1, 1942
Moses E. Smith	April 1, 1943, to April 5, 1952
Gladys P. Morelock	Aug. 1, 1952, to Feb. 8, 1953
Alma K. Schneider	Feb. 9, 1953, to May 18, 1961
Fern V. Miller	May 19, 1961, to July 31, 1967
Marian N. Rossmiller	Aug. 1, 1967, to March 20, 1969
Betty Higby	March 21, 1969, to March 18, 1978
Evelyn Davidson	March 20, 1978, to Aug. 14, 1981
Nora Hussey	Aug. 9, 1981, to July 31, 1987
Cynthia Grassby Baker	Jan. 28, 1988, to May 5, 1989
Barbara McTurk	Oct. 12, 1989, to July 27, 1993
Raymond J. DeBroeckert	Oct. 17, 1996, to Nov. 27, 1999*
Plant Manager	**Term**
Jay Neal	Nov. 28, 1999, to January 2001**
Timothy Riley	June 3, 2001, to Nov. 11, 2006
George Shue	November 2006 to May 2007 (acting)
Larry Eckerman	May 2007 to Sept. 24, 2007 (acting)
David Croft	Sept. 24, 2007, to present

* DeBroeckert was named acting Denver Mint superintendent on July 26, 1993, pending the introduction and passage of legislation converting the presidentially appointed Mint superintendent positions to Civil Service career manager jobs. He became the first career Mint superintendent on Oct. 17, 1996.

** Denver's production manager, Judith Groshek, served as acting superintendent for several months prior to Jay Neal's Nov. 28, 1999, hiring as a plant manager, the new name for the career post as a Mint production facility's chief executive.

San Francisco

Superintendent	**Term**
Lewis Aiken Birdsall	Oct. 17, 1853, to Dec. 6, 1855
Peter J. Lott	Nov. 17, 1855, to June 4, 1857*
Charles H. Hempstead	June 19, 1857, to June 3, 1861
Robert Julius Stevens	June 4, 1861, to May 9, 1863
Robert Bunker Swain	May 21, 1863, to July 15, 1869
Oscar Hugh LaGrange	Aug. 1, 1869, to Dec. 31, 1877
Henry Lee Dodge	Jan. 1, 1878, to June 30, 1882
Edward Freeman Burton	July 1, 1882, to July 31, 1885
Israel Lawton	Aug. 1, 1885, to July 31, 1889
William Henry Dimond	Aug. 1, 1889, to July 31, 1893
John Daggett	Aug. 1, 1893, to July 31, 1897
Frank Aleamon Leach	Aug. 1, 1897, to Sept. 18, 1907
Edward Daniel Sweeney	Sept. 19, 1907, to Aug. 17, 1912
Frank Aleamon Leach	Aug. 23, 1912, to Aug. 15, 1913
Thaddeus Wilton Huff Shanahan	Aug. 16, 1913, to June 30, 1921
Michael Joseph Kelly	July 1, 1921, to June 30, 1933
Peter J. Haggerty	July 1, 1933, to Dec. 31, 1944
Neal H. Callaghan	June 1, 1945, to Nov. 4, 1947
G.B. Gillin	July 1, 1948, to Nov. 30, 1951
John P. McEnery	June 1, 1952, to Nov. 5, 1952
R.P. Buell	July 1, 1953, to June 30, 1955
A.C. Carmichael	July 1, 1955, to July 31, 1958
Officer in Charge, U.S. Assay Office	**Term**
J.R. Carr	Aug. 1, 1958, to Sept. 30, 1968
John F. Brekle	Oct. 1, 1968, to June 30, 1972
Bland T. Brockenborough	Aug. 20, 1972, to Nov. 15, 1980
Thomas H. Miller	Nov. 30, 1980, to March 31, 1988
Superintendent, U.S. Mint	**Term**
Carol Mayer Marshall	March 27, 1990, to Jan 20, 1993
Dale B. DeVries	Oct. 17, 1996, to Dec. 18, 1999**
Plant Manager	**Term**
Larry Eckerman	Dec. 19, 1999, to present

* According to Nancy Y. Oliver and Richard G. Kelly in *Superintendents of the 1st and 2nd San Francisco Mints – 16 Biographical Sketches*, the overlap of Birdsall and Lott was due to Birdsall's early resignation, his exit from the San Francisco Mint prior to his official resignation date of Dec. 6th, and Lott arriving early and performing the superintendent's duties before his official appointment date, which was most likely Dec. 7.

** DeVries was named deputy superintendent on Sept. 12, replacing acting superintendent Donald T. Butler. His formal appointment was confirmed on Oct. 17, along with that of Raymond J. DeBroeckert at Denver and Augustine A. Albino at Philadelphia.

West Point

Superintendent	Term
Clifford M. Barber	March 31, 1988, to November 1990
Bert W. Corneby	November 1990 to July 23, 1993
Bradford E. Cooper	Aug. 2, 1996, to March 1999 *
Plant Manager	**Term**
Ellen McCullom	Dec. 5, 1999, to present**

*Cooper was officially named as deputy superintendent on Aug. 2, 1996, but did not have his appointment confirmed as a career Mint superintendent until Oct. 17, 1999.

**Cooper moved to Mint headquarters in March 1999 in an administrative capacity while also assisting at the West Point Mint. Ellen McCullom was named acting superintendent in March 1999, and on Dec. 5, 1999, was named plant manager, the new title for the career post as executive of a Mint production facility.

Charlotte

Superintendent	Term
John Hill Wheeler	Jan. 19, 1837, to Aug. 15, 1841
Burgess Sidney Gaither	Aug. 15, 1841, to June 15, 1843
Green Washington Caldwell	June 15, 1843, to April 1, 1847
William Julius Alexander	April 1, 1847, to Aug. 1, 1849
James Walker Osborne	Aug. 1, 1849, to May 1853
Green Washington Caldwell	May 1853 to April 20, 1861*
Officer in Charge, U.S. Assay Office	**Term**
Dr. Isaac W. Jones	March 19, 1867, to 1869
Calvin Josiah Cowles	1869 to 1885
Robert P. Waring	1885 to 1889
Stuart Warren Cramer	1889 to 1893
W.E. Ardrey	1893 to 1897
W.S. Clanton	1897 to 1903
D. Kirby Pope	1903 to 1908
William S. Pearson	1908 to 1911
Frank Parker Drane	1911 to 1913

The Charlotte Assay Office was closed June 30, 1913.

* On April 20, 1861, the Charlotte Mint was seized by Confederate forces, who continued coining operations until May 20, 1861. The Mint was officially closed May 31, 1861. An Assay Office was authorized by an Act of the Confederate Congress approved Aug. 24, 1861, and Dr. J.H. Gibbon received appointment as assayer. In May 1862, the facility was turned over to the Confederate Navy Department. Following the war, it was reopened as a U. S. Assay Office March 19, 1867.

Carson City

Superintendent	Term
Abraham Curry	Jan. 8, 1870, to September 1870*
Henry F. Rice	September 1870 to May 1873
Frank D. Hetrich	May 1873 to August 1875
James Crawford	September 1875 to March 8, 1885
Theodore R. Hofer	(temporary superintendent) March 9, 1885, to March 17, 1885
William Garrard	March 18, 1885, to June 30, 1889
Samuel Coleman Wright	July 1, 1889, to Aug. 1, 1892
Theodore R. Hofer	Aug. 6, 1892, to May 20, 1894
Jewett W. Adams	May 20, 1894, to September 1898
Roswell K. Colcord	September 1898 to July 1, 1899

The Carson City Mint became an Assay Office effective July 1, 1899. Colcord remained as the officer-in-charge until 1911.

* Curry resigned unexpectedly to seek the Republican nomination to become Nevada's first lieutenant governor, according to Rusty Goe in *The Mint on Carson Street*. Curry lost the GOP nomination on Sept. 14, 1870, to James S. Slingerland

Dahlonega

Superintendent	Term
Joseph J. Singleton	Jan. 4, 1837, to April 10, 1841*
Paul Rossignol	April 3, 1841, to June 19, 1843*
Maj. James F. Cooper	June 19, 1843, to Oct. 1, 1849
Col. Anderson W. Redding	Oct. 1, 1849, to July 1, 1853
Julius M. Patton	July 1, 1853, to Oct. 1, 1860
George Kellogg	Oct. 1, 1860, to April 1861**

* In *The United States Branch Mint at Dahlonega, Georgia: Its History and Coinage*, author Clair Birdsall explains Rossignol was appointed Dahlonega superintendent sometime in late March or early April 1841. In an April 3, 1841, letter to U.S. Mint Director Robert Maskell Patterson, Singleton wrote that he expected Rossignol's arrival within hours. Singleton remained as superintendent until Rossignol arrived a week later.

** Birdsall writes that Kellogg submitted his resignation April 25, 1861, to be effective May 15, and expected to be renamed superintendent under Confederate control, but he never was reappointed (the facility was closed permanently shortly after his resignation).

Coiner	Term
David H. Mason	March 7, 1837, to Aug. 29, 1848
John D. Field, Jr.	Oct. 3, 1848, to Nov. 1, 1849
Robert H. Moore	Nov. 1, 1849, to May 18, 1853
John D. Field Jr.	May 18, 1853, to June 1, 1961
Assayer	**Term**
Joseph W. Farnum	March 13, 1837, to May 10, 1843
Isaac L. Todd	May 1, 1843, to Dec. 9, 1850
Mathew F. Stephenson	Dec. 9, 1850, to July 26, 1854
Isaac L. Todd	July 26, 1854, to June 1, 1861

The Dahlonega Mint was seized by Confederate forces April 8, 1861; continued in operation until May 14, 1861; and officially closed May 31, 1861. An Act of the Confederate Congress, approved Aug. 24, 1861, authorized the opening of an Assay Office and Lewis W. Quillian was appointed assayer.

New Orleans

Superintendent	Term
David Bradford	1837 to 1839
Joseph M. Kennedy	Oct. 18, 1839, to September 1850
Robert M. McAlpine	Nov. 24, 1850, to May 13, 1853
Charles Bienvenu	1853 to Dec. 31, 1857
Logan McNight	Jan. 1, 1858, to May 8, 1858
John H. Alpuente (acting)	May 8, 1858, to May 25, 1858
Howard Millspaugh (acting)	May 25, 1858, to July 9, 1858
William A. Elmore	July 9, 1858, to Jan. 30, 1861
M.F. Bonzano (assayer in charge)	1874 to 1875
M.F. Bonzano (custodian)	1875 to 1876
M.F. Bonzano (assayer in charge and superintendent)	1876 to 1877
M.F. Bonzano (assayer in charge)	1877 to 1878
Michael Hahn	June 1878 to Dec. 28, 1878
Henry S. Foote	Dec. 28, 1878, to May 19, 1880*
Martin V. Davis	June 11, 1880, to 1882**
Dr. A.W. Smyth(e)	Aug. 15, 1882, to June 24, 1885
Gabriel Montegut	June 24, 1885, to 1893***
Overton Cade	June 20, 1893, to 1898
Charles W. Boothby	August 1898 to 1902
Hugh S. Suthon	1902 to 1911
William M. Lynch	1911 to 1914
Leonard Magruder	1914 to 1932
Cecil Grey	1932 to 1933
Hugh T. Rippeto	1933 to 1941
Charles M. Miller	April 21, 1941, to June 30, 1942

* Resigned due to cancerous brain tumor
** Removed from office in June 1882 to answer criminal charges
*** Tendered his resignation in late March 1889

Chief engravers

President George Washington appointed the man who was to become the first engraver of the United States Mint—Joseph Wright.

Although Wright (1756 to 1793), a native of Bordentown, N.J., and a portrait painter, never lived to see his appointment become official, many numismatic scholars count him as the first engraver because he was the first to serve in that capacity. However, because his appointment was never official, the Mint considers his successor the first engraver. Over the years, the title used to describe the position became chief engraver and more recently, chief sculptor-engraver.

Wright was first appointed as a draughtsman and later became the first designer and diesinker at the newly formed Mint. He made the dies of a medal honoring George Washington, the bust on the obverse of which some individuals consider to be the best medallic profile likeness of Washington. Wright also made the medal honoring Maj. Henry Lee that was authorized by Congress Sept. 24, 1779. The medal was for the Battle of Paulus Hook.

Wright is also believed to have designed the Liberty Cap cent struck on the thick cent planchets between 1793 and 1795, and to have engraved the 1793 Liberty Cap cent.

However, before Wright's official appointment as engraver of the Mint could be confirmed, he died of yellow fever in September 1793. On Nov. 6, 1793, Thomas Jefferson reportedly wrote a letter suggesting that David Rittenhouse, the first director of the U.S. Mint, recommend an engraver to replace Wright.

Robert Scot

At the time of Wright's death, Henry Voigt (also spelled Voight), acting chief coiner and superintendent, filled in as engraver for a few months before a replacement was found. Voigt continued to make the dies used by the Mint until the appointment of Robert Scot. Voigt held the office of chief coiner until his death in February 1814. Voigt is credited with the nation's first coins and the production of the 1792 half dismes and Silver Center cents.

According to the Mint's records, it is believed that Rittenhouse recommended Scot to be the first official engraver. On Nov. 23, 1793, Scot received a letter from Jefferson advising him of his appointment and enclosing his commission signed by Washington.

Very little is known of Scot, except that he was sometimes confused with the Scottish bank note engraver of the same name.

What is known comes from Foster Wild Rice's book, *Antecedents of the American Bank Note Company of 1858,* which states Scot, born in England, came to Philadelphia about 1783 and engraved for Dodson's edition of *Ree's Encyclopedia* from 1794 to 1803. The length of Scot's term as engraver varies depending on which source is checked. In Frank Stewart's book, *First United States Mint,* Scot reportedly served until Nov. 1, 1823, and Leonard Forrer, in his *Biographical Dictionary of Medalists,* says Scot served until January 1824. However, it is believed that Scot died in November 1823.

William Kneass

The third man to become engraver, William Kneass (1781 to 1840), was appointed to the position Jan. 28, 1824, with a salary of $2,000 a year. Little is known about Kneass's early life or training, except that he was born in Lancaster, Pa.

Kneass became famous as an engraver in Philadelphia in 1815 with studios located on Fourth Street near Chestnut. His studio was well known as a rendezvous for many prominent Philadelphians. Most researchers say a friend, Adam Eckfeldt, the chief coiner at that time, was most responsible for his appointment. Kneass had been chiefly a plate engraver for book-work before his appointment as engraver.

During his term as engraver there were some notable changes in coinage, as in 1834 and 1838 for gold, and 1836, 1838 and 1840 for silver, although some of this work was done by Christian Gobrecht,

an assistant engraver at the Mint. Kneass is also credited with a pattern half dollar dated 1838.

Christian Gobrecht

Kneass died in office Aug. 27, 1840. His successor was his assistant, Christian Gobrecht, who, although he was engraver for only three years and eight months, left behind many mementos of his work. Gobrecht designed pattern pieces and regular-issue coins. He is probably best known for his designing of the famous silver dollars of 1836, 1838 and 1839, generally called Gobrecht dollars, although his work in medallic art is also famous.

Gobrecht was born in Hanover, Pa., in 1785 and exhibited mechanical ability and a talent for drawing and design at an early age, according to a December 1911 article in *The Numismatist.*

Gobrecht began his working years as an apprentice to a clockmaker. After spending several years in the trade he turned to engraving.

Gobrecht began small, cutting headlines for newspapers and punches for type founders. He later became a writer and seal engraver. In 1811, Gobrecht moved to Philadelphia where he continued to supply portrait plates for publishers while becoming established as an engraver and diesinker for medals.

In 1816 he began working for Murray, Draper, Fairman and Co., bank note engravers. Within 10 years he had furnished designs and models of dies to the U.S. Mint in Philadelphia.

Among his better known dies and medals at this time were the Franklin Institute medal of 1825 based on a design by Thomas Sully, and a portrait medal of Charles Wilson Peale.

Gobrecht also produced a portrait medal of Charles Carroll of Carrollton, the seal of St. Peter's Church, Philadelphia and award medals for the New England Society for the Promotion of Manufactures and the Massachusetts Charitable Merchants Association and the Seal of Pennsylvania Hospital.

In 1836, Gobrecht was appointed draughtsman and diesinker to the U.S. Mint and Kneass' assistant. After Kneass' death, Gobrecht held the position of engraver until his death July 23, 1844.

Coins Gobrecht designed include the famous dollars of 1836, 1838 and 1839 and several varieties of half dollars of that period. His obverse design of one of the dollars, with stars around a seated figure of Liberty, was retained as the regular device in 1840 (although a new reverse was selected) and was used on the dollar until 1873 when the denomination was abandoned briefly.

Although some believe that the 1836 Gobrecht dollars bearing below the base Gobrecht's name and a Latin inscription indicating he designed the coin were struck that year, other evidence suggests that the Name Below Base variety was not produced until 1858. The Name On Base variety, however, was struck in 1836, for circulation.

Gobrecht's name was removed from later versions

struck in 1838 and 1839. Many of the Gobrecht dollars are restrikes, struck about 1858. Gobrecht's obverse design was used on the half dollar, quarter dollar, dime and half dime. The Seated Liberty design type was used on the three largest denominations through 1891; the new Barber designs were adopted as replacements in 1892.

Gobrecht also produced six different subtypes of copper large cents.

James Barton Longacre

James Barton Longacre succeeded Gobrecht as engraver Sept. 6, 1844. He was born in Delaware County, Pa., in 1794 and as a young man he was an apprentice in a bookstore in Philadelphia. He later studied under George Murray of Philadelphia, who taught him engraving. Longacre did some high-class plate work before he became free of his apprenticeship in 1834. His earliest known work is in the *S.F. Bradford Encyclopedia.*

There are no records of Longacre ever serving as an assistant engraver at the U.S. Mint. He was hired specifically as the engraver. Among the coins Longacre designed are the Flying Eagle cent, Indian Head cent, the 2-cent coin, both 3-cent coins, Shield 5-cent coin, all three gold dollars, the Indian Head gold $3 coin and the Coronet double eagle.

In 1867, Longacre completely remodeled the coinage of the Republic of Chile.

Although Longacre spent 25 years as engraver, he designed only two medals.

One was the reverse of the medal awarded to Capt. Ingrahm, the obverse of which was done by P.F. Cross, one of his assistants. Longacre also designed the 1860 Assay Commission medal.

In 1928, Longacre's work was represented in the exhibition of the 100 notable American engravers held in the New York Public Library. Longacre's hiring of William Barber in 1865 as an assistant engraver paved the way for the first of two Barbers to occupy the position of engraver after Longacre's death Jan. 1, 1879.

William Barber

William Barber (1807 to 1879) was appointed engraver shortly after James B. Longacre's death and served in that post until his death Aug. 31, 1879. Although he is one of the most well-known Mint engravers who did much original work on pattern coins, he designed only two coins for circulation—the Seated Liberty 20-cent coin and the Trade dollar.

Barber produced more than 40 public and private medals. Among his most famous works are medals honoring David Rittenhouse, Jean Louis Rodolphe Agassiz and Cyrus Field. Other medallic works include medals of James Pollock, Joseph Pancoast, Dr. Henry Linderman, the Centennial medals of 1876 and the Valley Forge medal of 1877.

He also designed several Assay Commission medals, the most famous of which was his 1868 piece showing Liberty using her torch to destroy the implements of the recent Civil War. His Assay Commission medal of 1876 commemorates the 100th anniversary of America's Independence with a bust of Washington on the reverse.

Two of Barber's assistants at the time would later become chief engravers—Charles E. Barber and George T. Morgan. His son, Charles, was appointed to the position in 1880 upon the death of his father.

Charles E. Barber

Charles E. Barber (1840 to 1917) served as an assistant for 10 years before being appointed to the top engraver post. Among his designs, known as the Liberty Head or Barber design, were the half dollar that was struck from 1892 until 1915, the quarter dollar struck from 1892 until 1916 and the dime obverse struck from 1892 until 1916.

Barber designed the Liberty Head 5-cent coin struck from 1883 until 1913. He designed the 1915-S Panama-Pacific International Exposition gold $2.50 quarter eagle. Barber is also credited with the Flowing Hair Stella $4 pattern obverse, as well as the obverse of the World's Columbian Exposition half dollar with a bust of Columbus, issued in 1892 and 1893 (the reverse was done by George Morgan).

In 1905, the U.S. government sent him to study the Mints of Europe ,and as the result of his travels the medal department of the U.S. Mint improved, according to historical records. His work is visible in all the principal medals executed after 1869. His best work is seen in the medals of Presidents Garfield and Arthur; Indian Peace, Army and Marksmanship medals; and the Great Seal of the United States.

Other medals include the Metis shipwreck and John Horn medals, a medal for the International Medical Congress at Washington in 1887, one for the International Exhibition in Chicago in 1893, and President Cleveland medals. Reports conflict on whether Charles or his father designed the Assay Commission medal of 1879, honoring H.R. Linderman, a director of the Mint, and Joseph Henry, the first director of the Smithsonian Institution.

Charles Barber continued his service until his death Feb. 18, 1917. At that time, his assistant, George T. Morgan, was appointed to the position.

George T. Morgan

George T. Morgan (1845 to 1925) was 31 years old when he was appointed as an assistant engraver and worked at the Mint until his death 48 years later.

Little is known about Morgan's early life except that he was born in Birmingham, England, and attended the Birmingham Art School before he won a national scholarship to the South Kensington Art School. Morgan studied at South Kensington for two years and later studied under Wyon of the Royal Mint in London for four years.

Probably his most famous work while employed by the U.S. Mint was the Morgan dollar (called the

"Bland" dollar when it was first struck) of 1878 to 1904 and 1921. The Morgan dollar was the first U.S. coin to bear an engraver's initial (M) on both the obverse and the reverse.

The dollar was authorized by the Bland-Allison Act of Feb. 28, 1878, which provided for a minimum monthly silver coinage of 2 million and established this coin weighing 412.5 grains troy as legal tender.

The name Bland dollar is taken from the name of Rep. Richard Bland of Missouri, one of the authors of the act responsible for the Morgan dollar's minting.

Morgan designed the reverse of the 1892 World's Columbian Exposition half dollar, the obverse of the 1918 Lincoln-Illinois Centennial half dollar, and the reverse of the 1916 and 1917 McKinley Memorial gold dollar. He collaborated with Charles Barber to design the 1915-S Panama-Pacific International Exposition quarter eagle. Morgan also designed the obverse of the Coiled Hair Stella patterns.

He was also known for his portraits of the Mint's presidential series of medals. He designed presidential medals honoring Rutherford B. Hayes, Woodrow Wilson and Warren G. Harding. Collaborating with Charles Barber, he designed medals depicting Abraham Lincoln, Martin Van Buren, James Garfield, Chester Arthur, Benjamin Harrison, William McKinley, Theodore Roosevelt and William Taft. His portraits of Presidents Hayes, Cleveland and Harrison appeared on the obverse of the Assay Commission medals of 1880, 1886 and 1893.

In addition to his work at the U.S. Mint, Morgan also designed a medal of David Roberts for the Art Union Co. of London. Other private commissions include medals for Thomas Carlyle on his 80th birthday; Railway Exhibition at Chicago in 1883 (in conjunction with Barber); and Henry Bessemer, 1879 (an example in gold was presented to King Edward VII in 1906).

Morgan also designed medals honoring secretaries of the Treasury Alexander Hamilton, Daniel Manning, George Cortelyou, Franklin MacVeagh, William Gibbs McAdoo and Carter Glass. Medals created by Morgan and Barber together honoring Treasury secretaries include William Windom, John G. Carlisle, Lyman J. Gage and Leslie Shaw. He also designed four directors of the Mint medals and collaborated with Barber to design four others.

Morgan was also a life member of the Philadelphia Academy of the Fine Arts and a member of the famous Philadelphia Sketch Club.

John Ray Sinnock

When George T. Morgan died in 1925, President Calvin Coolidge appointed John R. Sinnock as chief engraver. Sinnock had served as assistant engraver and medalist beginning in 1917 before he resigned two years later.

Sinnock returned to the Mint's engraving staff in 1923 as assistant chief engraver.

Sinnock, born in Raton, N.M., in 1888, attended the Pennsylvania Museum Art School in Philadelphia. There he won the A.W. Mifflin scholarship for advanced study and traveled in Europe.

When he returned from Europe, he served as an instructor at the Pennsylvania Museum Art School for eight years and also taught art classes at Western Reserve University in Cleveland.

His appointment as assistant engraver came when he was 29 but it would be eight years before he would assume the chief engraver's duties. He worked at that job until his death May 14, 1947, at the age of 59, after an illness of several months' duration.

In his 22 years as chief engraver, Sinnock left behind many works including his best known, the redesigned Purple Heart in 1931. But probably the best known of his coin designs, and the only one still being minted today, is the Roosevelt dime, placed into circulation in 1946.

According to an interview with Sinnock shortly after the release of the coin, he said the obverse portrait of Roosevelt is a composite of two studies, sculptured in relief, which he made from life in 1933 and 1934. He also consulted photographs of Roosevelt taken shortly before his death.

One of the best known stories that circulated about the dime was the mild uproar created because of the designer's initials, "JS," at the trunk of Roosevelt's neck. Some of the public mistook the initials for those of Joseph Stalin, the Soviet Union's leader.

Sinnock was also the designer of the Franklin half dollar, which didn't appear in circulation until after his death. The Franklin half dollar was struck from 1948 until 1963. Sinnock's initials, JRS, appear under Franklin's shoulder (the R may have been added in response to the rumors over the JS on the dime).

In 1926, Sinnock designed two commemorative coins for the Sesquicentennial of American Independence celebration—the gold quarter eagle and silver half dollar. The half dollar dies were in very low relief. The commemorative $2.50 quarter eagle and half dollar were sold to help raise funds for financing the International Fair held in Philadelphia in 1926.

Sinnock also designed the reverse of the 1918 Lincoln-Illinois Centennial half dollar, while he was an assistant at the Mint. George T. Morgan designed the obverse. Sinnock also designed the Cuban 1-peso coin of 1934, the 1-lempira coin for Honduras in 1931 and a $1 pattern piece for China in 1929 that was never adopted by the Chinese.

The French government purchased a medal design by Sinnock called *Vanguard of the Nation*.

Among the most notable and nationally award-winning medals Sinnock designed were the special congressional gold medals honoring Thomas A. Edison, the Yangtze medal for Naval and Marine Corps personnel serving in 1926 to 1927 and in the Shanghai-Yangtze area in 1930 to 1932, and the Ellsworth-Admundsen-Nobile medal commemorating the flight over the North Pole of the dirigible *Norge* in 1929.

Sinnock designed four medals for the Mint's presidential series including those depicting Calvin Coolidge in 1926, Herbert Hoover in 1929, Franklin D. Roosevelt in 1935 and the obverse of the Harry S. Truman medal in 1945.

Sinnock also designed secretaries of the treasury medals for Andrew Mellon in 1931, Ogden L. Mills in 1932, William Woodin in 1933, Henry Morgenthau Jr. in 1938, Fred Vinson and John W. Snyder.

Sinnock also designed medals for two undersecretaries of the Treasury and four assistant secretaries of the treasury. Sinnock designed two medals honoring directors of the Mint, Robert J. Grant in 1931 and the obverse of the Nellie Tayloe Ross medal in 1933.

Sinnock is also credited with a congressional silver medal to honor members of the party with Adm. Robert Peary in his 1909 expedition to the North Pole, and the 1945 Navy Department medal. He designed Assay Commission medals of 1926, 1927, the obverse of 1928, 1929, 1930, 1931, 1932, 1933, 1934, 1935, 1937 and 1938.

He was a member of the National Sculpture Society, Philadelphia Sketch Club, the American Federation of Arts, Philadelphia Art Alliance and American Artists Professional League and an honorary member of the Philadelphia Water Color Club.

Gilroy Roberts

Gilroy Roberts was appointed as chief engraver July 22, 1948, but he was no stranger to the U.S. Mint. By the time he received the appointment he had worked both at the Philadelphia Mint and the Bureau of Engraving and Printing in Washington, D.C.

Roberts, who was born in Philadelphia March 5, 1905, was appointed by President Truman to head the Mint's engraving division in 1948. Roberts, whose father originally wanted him to be a musician, took his inherited artistic talents into medallic art.

He grew up in an artistic world. His father was a sculptor and Roberts' earliest sculpturing experience was with modeling clay, then woodcarving and stone sculpturing. In 1934 and 1935, Roberts attended evening art classes at Frankfort High in Philadelphia, where he studied under Paul Remy. In his spare time, he modeled and carved small sculptures for commission and for exhibit in national exhibitions.

In 1936, Roberts took and passed a competitive Civil Service examination for the position of assistant sculptor-engraver at the U.S. Mint.

Roberts was hired June 3, 1936, as Sinnock's understudy and continued in that job until Jan. 6, 1938, when he became an engraver at the Bureau of Engraving and Printing in Washington.

While serving at the BEP, Roberts became proficient in the art of note and stamp engraving.

Roberts did the portraits on a number of official revenue stamps and postage stamps, including the 3-cent Ralph Waldo Emerson stamp and the 3-cent Charles W. Elliot stamp, the 1-cent Stephen Collins Foster stamp and the 1-cent Eli Whitney stamp

in the Famous American series. During his time in Washington, Roberts studied under Eugene Weis and Heinz Warneke at the Corcoran Art School from 1939 until 1943. He returned to the Mint May 1, 1944, as an assistant engraver, where he continued the study of bas-relief with Sinnock.

Roberts' best known work is the obverse of the John F. Kennedy half dollar. Upon completion of the half dollar, Roberts placed his stylized initials, GR, on the truncated bust of the coin.

When the coin was released, rumors flew around that the initials were really a hammer and sickle – a symbol of the Soviet Union – marking the spot where the late president was shot. The Treasury Department continuously denied the rumor and eventually issued a press release, which included an enlargement of the coin showing Roberts' monogram.

Other coins designed by Roberts include the obverse and reverse of Denmark's 1944 5-krone piece; 1953 El Salvador, 50- and 25-centavo coins, obverse only; Cuba, 1 peso, obverse in 1953, and both the obverse and reverse of the 50-, 25-, 5- and 1-centavo coins in 1953; Haiti, 10- and 5-centime coins, obverse in 1958; and the Liberian $1, 50-, 25-, 10-, 5- and 1-cent obverses of 1959.

Sinnock also designed the following United States Mint list medals: presidential series, Truman reverse; portraits of Eisenhower, first and second terms; Kennedy; and Lyndon B. Johnson.

Roberts designed portraits of G.M. Humphrey and Douglas Dillon for the secretary of the Treasury medal series, and portraits of William H. Brett and Eva Adams for the director of the Mint series.

Roberts also designed several congressional medals including: Irving Berlin, 1954; Dr. Jonas Salk, 1955; Sir Winston Churchill, obverse, 1955; a medal of Ulysses S. Grant and Robert E. Lee honoring the surviving veterans of the Civil War, 1956; and Adm. Hyman George Rickover, reverse, 1958. Other medals include annual Assay Commission series of many years, obverse and reverse; Perry Navy, reverse, 1945; director of the Mint marksman, 1948; Department of the Interior award, obverse, 1948; Atomic Energy Commission medals: Enrico Fermi, 1956; Ernest Orlando Lawrence, 1960; Citation medal, 1960.

Some private commissions include: American Numismatic Society, medal of Louis C. West; Medallic Art Co. of New York, medals of William T. Louth, Julius Lauth, Frances Trees; Helen Keller Foundation, portrait of Helen Keller; Drexel Institute, medal of founder Anthony Drexel; memorial tablet of Charles T. Bach; Patriots Memorial, Valley Forge, Pa.; a series of state seals; Institute for Advanced Study, Princeton, N.J. medal of Albert Einstein; Metropolitan Life Insurance Co. portrait of F.W. Eckers; Scripps Howard Newspaper Alliance medal of Ernie Pyle.

Also included in Roberts' portfolio: a portrait of Bobby Jones for the American Golf Association; Life Golf Tournament portrait of Ben Hogan; Yeshiva

University, New York City, portrait of Albert Einstein; Radio Corporation of America medal of Gen. David Sarnoff; Woods Hole Oceanographic Institute portrait of Henry Bigelow; American Medical Association portrait of Dr. Hektoen; Montana Centennial Medal of three governors of Montana, Babcock, Toole and Edgerton; National Commemorative Society, "In God We Trust" medal and others.

His exhibitions have included the Pennsylvania Academy of Fine Arts, Philadelphia in 1930, 1934, 1945, 1946; Corcoran Gallery of Art, Washington, D.C.; National Sculpture Society in New York; Paris, France and Italy, 1961; and The Hague, Netherlands, 1963.

Roberts also lectured about U.S. coins at the American Numismatic Society in New York in 1961 and the Exchange Club in Philadelphia in 1962. Among his awards are the National Sculpture Society Bas-Relief exhibition, 1951, honorable mention. International exhibition coins and medals in Madrid, Spain, 1951, gold medal and citation.

Roberts resigned his position as chief engraver at the age of 59 on Oct. 8, 1964, when he became the first chief engraver in the history of the Mint who did not die in office.

Roberts had served as chief engraver for 16 years and had spent a total of 28 years working for the government, 26 years at the Mint and two years at the Bureau of Engraving and Printing.

Roberts resigned from the Mint under the advice of his physician, but he did not resign from the world of minting. He accepted a position as chairman of the board of General Numismatics Corp., forerunner of the Franklin Mint He later became chairman of the board emeritus and a director of the Franklin Mint.

In this capacity, Roberts was given the opportunity to travel and he personally "shopped" for the intricate machinery being installed in the Franklin Mint. His travels took him to Asia, among other places.

Roberts designed dozens of medals including the following for commemorative societies while he was with the Franklin Mint: Abba Eban, Martin Luther King, Malcom X, Mahalia Jackson, Geoffrey Chaucer, Miraculous medal, Cardinal Spellman, Saint Peter, Abraham, Eisenhower, Three Astronauts, First Step on the Moon, Joan of Arc and Sarah Bernhardt.

He also designed Franklin Mint medallic greeting cards from 1965 to 1968 as well as the Robert F. Kennedy Memorial medal and the Richard Nixon and Spiro Agnew Inauguration medal in 1973.

Other medallic series include the U.S. president's series for the White House Historical Association, the Franklin Mint's "Roberts' Birds" series of 50 silver medals, Pandora's Box, baby announcement medals for boys and girls, and a series of medals commemorating the 12 signs of the Zodiac (also made into jewelry).

Also, he designed the Franklin Mint's Bicentennial medals with portraits of 30 great Americans for 1976, a John F. Kennedy Inaugural 25th Anniversary medal in 1986 and the Encyclopaedia Britannica Award in 1986, struck by Medallic Art Co.

He also designed plates including a Liberty Tree etched in glass, Nixon and Agnew in silver and 12 signs of the Zodiac in silver as well as three-dimensional sculptures, a large sundial at the Franklin Mint museum, a Great American Eagle and four bird groups in pewter.

Roberts died on Jan. 26, 1992, at the age of 86. Many of his sculpturing tools and equipment were placed on display in an extensive exhibit at the American Numismatic Association Money Museum in Colorado Springs, Colo., beginning in 1991 under permanent loan from the Gilroy and Lillian P. Roberts Charitable Foundation.

The first items to be put on display were received by the ANA on May 4, 1989, preceding a completed loan agreement signed July 19, 1989, according to Stanley Merves, foundation trustee. Additional items were shipped to the ANA up to, and even after, Roberts' death, according to Merves.

The initial exhibit was placed on display in July 1991, according to Merves.

The exhibit remained on display until mid-2009, when the exhibit was dismantled pursuant to a 2007 decision by the Gilroy and Lillian P. Roberts Charitable Foundation to move the exhibit east to the Philadelphia area.

Some of Roberts' items formerly on display at the ANA are now on display in Philadelphia at Temple University's new Tyler School of Art building in a 160-square-foot exhibit area on the facility's first floor. The remainder of the items are in storage, according to David L. Unruh, Temple University's senior vice president for institutional advancement.

The Roberts exhibit, with items swapped out periodically, will remain on display for at least the next three years, Unruh said in the spring of 2011, until the Gilroy and Lillian P. Roberts Charitable Foundation finds a more permanent first-floor home for the material with more exhibit space allotted.

An engraving class for practicing and would-be sculptors and engravers named in his honor is part of the ANA's annual Summer Seminar. The course was introduced in 1993, but has not been offered consecutively in subsequent years.

Students who take Art of Engraving are either professional artists or art students, and are required to submit samples of their art work for assessment by a review committee. Art of Engraving is taught in a two-year sequence and is capped at six students.

In years where art of engraving has not been taught, the ANA has offered the Art of Money, a single-sequence class that is open to nonartists.

The five-day Art of Engraving class for the 2011 Summer Seminar is, as previous engraving classes, underwritten by the Gilroy and Lillian P. Roberts Charitable Foundation.

Frank Gasparro

Gilroy Roberts' successor, Frank Gasparro, was sworn in Feb. 23, 1965. He was born in Philadelphia Aug. 26, 1909, and showed his artistic talent at a young age. He attended classes at the Samuel Fleisher Art Memorial school in Philadelphia while still in grade school. At the age of 15, he began taking private lessons from Guiseppe Donato, a former foreman to the sculptor Rodin. Donato took Gasparro under his wing and when Gasparro would visit Donato's studio, the master would show him the fine points of the art.

Gasparro continued to study under Donato until 1929, even after his graduation from South Philadelphia High School. He also enrolled at the Pennsylvania Academy of Fine Arts in Philadelphia in 1928, where he studied under sculptors and medalists Charles Grafly, Walker Hancock and Albert Laessle until 1931.

Gasparro launched his professional career in 1932, at the age of 23, as a freelance sculptor working primarily in statuary art and commercial plaster models. He continued in that field until 1937 when he joined the staff of the Federal Art Administration, which was a part of the Works Progress Administration under the Roosevelt administration during the Great Depression.

Under the FAA, each artist was given a salary and allowed to work on any project; all the artists' work became the property of the government. He created sculptures that were placed in wading pools in playgrounds in the Philadelphia area, where some can still be seen.

He returned to freelance sculpturing in 1941 and then became an assistant engraver in 1942 at the U.S. Mint. On Feb. 11, 1965, President Johnson appointed Gasparro to the chief engraver's position.

During his tenure, Gasparro supervised the production of some 30,000 dies a year for all U.S. coinage and medals produced at the Philadelphia Mint. His work at the Mint included portraiture, low and high relief medals and insignia designing.

Gasparro is probably best known to coin collectors for his reverse of the Kennedy half dollar, 1964; his design and execution of the reverse of the Lincoln Memorial cent in 1959; his Eisenhower-Apollo 11 dollar introduced in 1971; and the Anthony dollar.

He also designed the Philadelphia Medal of Honor in 1955. In 1964, he won the emblem contest sponsored by the Treasury Safety Council. Foreign coins also occupied his design capabilities including the 1943 Guatemala Revenue 25 centavos, among others.

Gasparro also designed annual Assay Commission medals in 1949, 1950, 1951, 1952 and 1965. For the presidential medals series of the Mint, he designed the Eisenhower reverse in 1954 and the Kennedy reverse.

Other designs and models prepared by Gasparro at the U.S. Mint include: Federal Security Agency medal and Federal Security Agency Service Award emblem in 1951; Provost Marshal General badge, 1951; Coast Guard Commendation medal, 1952; White House Cap Device insignia, 1953; Secretary of the Treasury medal, 1953; Department of Commerce medal and emblem, 1952; Central Intelligence medal, 1953; Central Intelligence star, 1953; Central Intelligence Distinguished medal, 1955; Treasury Department Secret Service Guard Cap and Breast Badge, 1954; U.S. Secretary of the Treasury Robert B. Anderson medal; and Dr. Thomas A. Dooley III congressional medal.

Also included among his works are: the 1.3125-inch and the 2.25-inch Pony Express medals, 1960; and medals for Treasury Secretaries George M. Humphrey and Douglas Dillon. Private commissions include the Stroud Jordan medal, 1953.

Gasparro served as an instructor in sculpture at the Fleisher Art Memorial in Philadelphia and he was honored by the Italian government in 1973 with the decoration of Cavaliere Ufficiale.

In 1968, the American Numismatic Association named Gasparro the Outstanding Numismatic Sculptor of the Year. In 1969, he designed the medal for the ANA's convention. He is also credited with the Jimmy Carter medal in the Mint's presidential series as well as a congressional medal honoring Marian Anderson.

He was a member of the Society of Medalists, the French Society of the Medal and Pennsylvania Academy of the Fine Arts Fellowship board of directors.

After his retirement as chief engraver on Jan. 16, 1981, Gasparro continued his artistic work including designing a George Washington 250th anniversary commemorative medal in 1982 and President's Day Celebration medal in 1983 for Design-Pak Inc.

He also designed a number of medals for Bowers and Merena Galleries including the Virgil Brand medal in 1983, the Salute to the Olympics medal in 1984, the President Ronald Reagan official presidential inaugural medal obverse in 1984, and the Walter Mondale vice presidential medal obverse in 1984, both struck at the Franklin Mint, the Frank Gasparro medal in 1985, the Abraham Lincoln medal in 1986 and the Jefferson Davis medal in 1986.

Gasparro continued to work on additional medals, the following from Unicover Corp.: St. Francis di Assisi commemorative in 1981, Jacques Cartier in 1984, Rose Bowl in 1984, space shuttle-NASA in 1983, Babe Ruth in 1983, Migratory Bird Stamp medal in 1984, Brandenburg Gate-Berlin Anniversary in 1986, President Ronald Reagan official inaugural medal reverse in 1984 and Walter Mondale vice president medal in 1984.

In 1986, Gasparro was the designer of the American Numismatic Association anniversary convention medal and then he did several medal series for Paramount International Coin Co. including an 11-medal series for the Statue of Liberty Centennial, 1985 and 1986, and an 11-medal series to commemorate the

United States Constitution in 1987. Gasparro also designed the reverse of the 1991 Mount Rushmore Golden Anniversary commemorative silver dollar.

Nearly $5,000 was raised at an auction May 12, 1999, to benefit the rededicated Frank Gasparro Sculpture Studio at the Samuel S. Fleisher Art Memorial in Philadelphia.

The event also served as a celebration of Gasparro's 90th birthday. The former U.S. Mint Chief Sculptor-Engraver taught at the school for 45 years. In 1999, he still taught once a week at the nation's oldest and largest tuition-free art school.

The fund-raiser auction offered coins and medals designed by Gasparro. The auction proceeds and financial gifts given in honor of Gasparro went toward renovation of the studio.

The signage for the studio includes a galvano portrait of Gasparro by the late Michael Iaccoca, Gasparro's longtime friend and colleague on the Mint engraving staff.

According to a Fleisher Art Memorial spokesman in 2011, the studio continues to function as a teaching environment for aspiring sculptors.

Gasparro continued to maintain a personal studio and practice his craft with commissions to produce medallic art and sculpture up until his death.

Gasparro died at age 92 on Sept. 29, 2001, 12 days after an accidental fall at home.

A scholarship in Gasparro's name was established in 2002 at Fleisher from donations from the numismatic community.

Elizabeth Jones

Chief Sculptor-Engraver Elizabeth A.B. Jones has Italy to thank for many of the high points in her life. In part her appointment as chief engraver in 1981 can be traced back to her studies in Rome when she switched from oil painting to sculpture. That change led her to medallic art and a wide range of artistic endeavors.

Before moving to Italy, Jones graduated from Vassar College with a bachelor's degree in the History of Art in 1957. She then studied at the Art Students League in New York City until 1962. She spent the next two years studying at the Scuolo dell'Arte della Medaglia inside the Italian Mint.

There, under the guidance of the Italian Mint's paper money engraver, Jones and other students learned how to engrave in steel. She also learned how to sculpture medals, medallic art and low relief.

While still a student, she was invited to exhibit her work in the Federation Internationale de la Medaille. Shortly thereafter, her services as a translator were called upon when fellow American U.S. Mint Director Eva Adams visited the Italian Mint.

"I really hadn't been noticed by Americans until then. She asked me right then and there if I would come back and work in Philadelphia," Jones said, recalling her first meeting with the woman who was to become a good friend. "I said I had only been here

two or three years and I really want to stay. When Mr. Gasparro retired, she was on the phone to me in Washington, D.C., where I was visiting during the Christmas holidays, and told me to apply for the position." (Adams was no longer Mint director at that time.)

Jones was nominated by President Ronald Reagan July 13, 1981, confirmed by the Senate Sept. 28 and sworn in Oct. 27. She became the first woman to be named chief sculptor-engraver.

Less than six months after her nomination was confirmed, she was faced with her first major project – designing the first U.S. commemorative coin issued since 1954, to honor the 250th birthday of George Washington.

"As soon as I heard about the possibility of my doing the Washington half dollar coin, I decided instantaneously I was going to put him on a horse," she said. "He was such a famous horseman and general, often portrayed in paintings on his horse in battles, and he is also portrayed in innumerable outdoor equestrian monuments throughout the country."

In her mind, she envisioned a move away from the standard profile-type of design that Jones said is so prominent in all other medals, paintings and coins, to a younger-looking Washington astride a horse.

She had already decided on the image she wanted when, in the course of her research, she visited the portrait gallery of the Second Bank of the United States and came across an oval painting by Rembrandt Peale that depicts Washington astride a horse.

"I really was shocked. It was almost like a vision because that's just what I had in mind doing," she said.

In order to carry out her design image, Jones said she often worked weekends but admits now she was nervous and she overdrew.

"When you work too long at something, you don't see it anymore," she said, recalling her first drawings for the Washington commemorative. That may have made it all the worse for her when, after turning the sketch over to U.S. Mint Director Donna Pope for her approval, Jones was invited to a function at the Union League Club in Philadelphia.

While there, inspiration arrived in the form of a floor-to-ceiling portrait by Thomas Sully, of Washington on horseback.

"I was so inspired. I wanted to stop the original design and I asked Mrs. Pope, 'Please don't let it be published,' because I wanted to make changes but she said it was too late," Jones said. "I was sick. But I knew in my mind what I was going to do anyway with the coin. And as it turns out, the coin came out far better than the original design."

It was a different kind of atmosphere when it came time to submit designs for the 1984 Los Angeles Olympic Games, Jones said, when she and her staff of sculptor-engravers were approached to design the commemorative 1983 Olympic silver dollar. The initial designs were an attempt to move away from traditional themes.

"We did not do the discus thrower on purpose, because it had been done and re-done over and over again. But at a certain point, after [Treasury] Secretary [Donald] Regan had seen everything, he still wasn't satisfied and he said he wanted some drawings using the discus thrower," she recalled.

Jones and the other engravers submitted the discus thrower designs, which she said presented a challenge to provide a fresh, different and modern look to the "discobolus," so she employed the technique of a multiple image to convey motion. The design apparently caught the Treasury secretary's eye.

But even then Regan was still not pleased, Jones recalled, because her design displayed the Olympic rings without the stars, for the sake of simplicity and clarity of design.

"He insisted that the stars be placed with the Olympic rings as he said it was the official logo of the Los Angeles Olympic Games," she said. "That was a terrible job because the stars had to be much bigger than they should have been because of the reduction process. To me it just fouled up the whole coin because it complicated and overloaded the design."

But that disappointment faded, and two years later, Jones again felt the exhilaration of designing a successful and popular coin – the Statue of Liberty gold $5 commemorative coin. She said because the dimensions of the coin were so small, 21.59 millimeters, the design needed to be as simple and direct as possible.

"You simply have to have a bold concept when you do such a tiny coin," she said. "I didn't want to cut the Statue in half, I had seen that on some medals and I think that's a very graceless design on a small coin."

She saw the view she had in mind in a photograph used in a mail-order advertisement. Although part of Liberty's face was in the shadows, Jones used her knowledge of the structural elements of the face to reconstruct what she needed. That was just one of the times photographs, her own or someone else's, played a major part in the design process and her work in general.

"If you look at a group of different photographs of the Statue, from some angles her nose looks very Roman, in another photographs her forehead is very pronounced. She changes in many photographs, in some her face looks oval, some her chin is very square and her face is very full," Jones observed. "One photograph is never enough. When I did portraits of people, I would do the photographs myself. I would take four of five rolls of 36 frames each. I would take them from all angles, on different days and in different lights.

"Designing coins is much more difficult than designing medals. You have much more freedom in designing medals, in every aspect," she said. "I did seven different pieces for the Franklin Mint so I was used to working in low relief. But they did not

have the criteria of incredible precision that we have because they would tell me it couldn't be higher than 'such and such.' Well, that was child's play compared to making a coin in the U.S. Mint. They didn't have the problem of making thousands of dies. I imagine they could afford to throw away the die after 800 strikes where we have to get 8,000 strikes or more for the penny, for example. The design has to be compatible with long die life."

As a tribute to her artistic successes, the Scuolo dell'Arte della Medaglia in Rome hosted a retrospective exhibition of her work in September 1987. It was the first in a series of alumni retrospective exhibits planned by the school. Elvira Clain-Stefanelli, executive director of the Smithsonian's National Numismatic Collection, wrote the preface for the exhibition catalog. In addition, Jones has participated in numerous one-person shows and group exhibitions. Before her appointment as chief engraver, she completed several commemorative medals including those depicting Picasso and Wolfgang Amadeus Mozart for the Stefano Johnson Mint in Milano, Italy; Pablo Casals, International Numismatic Agency in New York City; the University of Pennsylvania Art Museum (Lucy Wharton Drexel Award, a gold medal); the Johns Hopkins University; Creighton University; silver medal of Cardinal Spellman for the American Episcopate; Salute to Israel (25th anniversary); Gloria Steinem for the Food and Agricultural series of CERES medals honoring outstanding women of the world; the Holy Year Jubileum for the Medallic Art Co.; medal for Israel's 30th anniversary for the Judaic Heritage Society; annual prize medals for St. Stephen's School, Rome; Dubai Sheraton Hotel, United Arab Emirates, including the portrait of H.E. Sheikh Rashid; Pope Paul II, for Premier Giulio Andreotti, a medal cast in solid gold as gift of the Italian Government; Nobel Prize Laureates, Stockholm, 1979; and the anniversary medal, Judaic Heritage Society in 1980.

She was awarded an honorary diploma from the Academia Brasileiro das Belas Artes in Rio de Janeiro in 1967; the Outstanding Sculptor of the Year from the American Numismatic Association in 1972; and the Louis Bennett Award from the National Sculpture Society in 1978.

Her commissioned work for the Franklin Mint includes medallic portraits of Albert Schweitzer, Susan B. Anthony, Charles Dickens, Richard Wright, Walter Reed and Gen. Campbell. She has also completed dozens of commissioned oil paintings and several pieces of commissioned jewelry.

The obverse and reverse designs for the presidential medal the Mint produced marking the first term of President Ronald Reagan are also Jones' creations.

Jones' classic obverse design for the 1988 Olympic gold $5 half eagle commemorative coin, showing Nike, the goddess of victory, is considered one of the most beautiful coin designs ever produced at the U.S.

Mint and earned Jones Coin of the Year honors. The obverse design is among 18 designs for U.S. coins or medals that appear in three-foot-high, 400-pound concrete medallions gracing the parapet of the Mint's Washington headquarters.

Jones is a member of both national and international numismatic and medallic associations including American Numismatic Association, American Medallic Sculpture Association, American Numismatic Society, Federation Internationale de la Medaille and the National Sculpture Society.

In June 1990, Jones reported that she would be leaving office in August 1990.

A cover story published in the July 11, 1990, issue of *Coin World* noted that on June 13, 1990, Jones had received a phone call from U.S. Mint Director Donna Pope informing her that the Treasury Department had accepted her resignation effective in two months. Jones had submitted her resignation to the White House in November 1988, soon after George H.W. Bush's election as president.

Jones had followed custom as a presidential appointee to submit her resignation upon a pending change in administration, even though George H.W. Bush and Reagan were both Republicans.

Jones clarified to *Coin World* in March 2011 that she thought it unusual that she was being informed by the Treasury Department that he resignation had been accepted; she said she thought notification should come from the White House. Jones finally received notification from White House officials on Dec. 3, 1990, that her services would not be needed after Dec. 13, 1990.

She is the first chief engraver not to be reappointed. Traditionally, presidential appointees tender their resignations at a change of administration; and traditionally for the position of chief engraver, that resignation was rejected.

However, Jones' resignation was accepted, more than a year and a half after it was tendered.

Michael Simon performed the administrative functions associated with the chief engraver after Jones' departure, holding the title of chief of the Engraving Division. All of the artistic duties, including those that would be the responsibility of chief engraver, were divided among the individual members of the Mint's engraving staff at the Philadelphia Mint after Jones ended her tenure. Simon retired in 2005.

The position of chief engraver was one of five presidentially appointed positions either eliminated or transformed under legislation requested by the Clinton Administration in 1993, but never introduced and passed until the closing days of the 104th Congress in the fall of 1996.

The law eliminated the chief engraver's position, along with the assayer's posts at the Mints at Denver, Philadelphia, San Francisco and West Point.

Jones sporadically continues her craft today with private commissions, producing large sculptures in New York, along with dabbling in Japanese calligraphy.

Her privately commissioned life-sized bronze bust of Henry Kissinger was unveiled in April 2003 and is on public display in the Kluge Study Center for International Affairs at the Library of Congress in Washington. Jones executed a bronze bust of former United Nations Secretary General Kofi Annan that was dedicated May 20, 2009, at Annan's alma mater, Macalester College, in St. Paul, Minn. The sculpture is on display in the institution's Institute for Global Citizenship. Annan graduated in 1961 from Macalester College with a bachelor's degree in economics.

John Mercanti

A member of the U.S. Mint's engraving staff at the Philadelphia Mint since 1974, Mercanti received a titular promotion to chief engraver from U.S. Mint Director Edmund C. Moy during a Feb. 3, 2009, press conference at the Philadelphia Mint.

Mercanti had sought the presidentially appointed chief engraver's position soon after Jones submitted her resignation in August 1990. He was nominated to the chief engraver's post in September 1990 by President George H.W. Bush. The 101st Congress, which ended in late October, chose not to act on the nomination. Mercanti was renominated by Bush on Jan. 4, 1991. Two months later, Mercanti withdrew his name from consideration in a March 21 message to the White House in which he cited personal reasons for his decision to withdraw.

In June 2006, Mercanti, a former colleague of Jones, was elevated to the new position of Supervisory Design and Master Tooling Development Specialist. In his supervisory position over design and master tooling development, Mercanti was responsible for the production of all master tooling from design through master dies and work hubs. The position is primarily responsible for overseeing the complete development of master tooling (reduction hub, master die, work hubs) from approved designs through approved trial strike; the artistic design of all new products; supervising tool makers, engravers, and other craft and trades personnel involved in the development of master tooling; and the timely delivery of reduction hubs and master dies for all recurring and new products to Philadelphia and Denver die shops.

Mercanti held those responsibilities while also monitoring technological developments that could help improve die and coin production processes.

Mercanti's 2009 appointment as chief engraver at the United States Mint was a "time-limited, temporary promotion," and the position was not the same as the presidentially appointed position of the same name abolished by Congress in 1996.

Moy gave Mercanti the title of chief engraver during a press conference at the Philadelphia Mint accompanying the unveiling of an exhibit chronicling the development of the 2009 Saint-Gaudens, Ultra High Relief, Roman Numerals gold $20 double eagle.

Although Mercanti became the 12th member of the U.S. Mint's engraving staff to hold the chief engraver's title since the U.S. Mint's establishment on April 2, 1792, he is not officially recognized as the 12th chief engraver of the Mint, according to the U.S. Mint's Office of Public Affairs.

In bestowing the title of chief engraver on Mercanti, Moy had no legal authority to restore the presidentially appointed position authorized in April 1792 (then called the engraver), thus the position was not the same as the traditional one.

In March 11, 2009, replies to questions posed Feb. 4 by *Coin World* concerning the chief engraver title, the Mint's Office of Public Affairs indicated Mercanti's "chief engraver" title represents the new title for Mercanti's then-existing position of "supervisory design and master tooling development specialist."

"The new name is a change in nomenclature only; it is not a new appointment, nor is the new name intended to confer any honor or award," according to the Mint's Office of Public Affairs.

"Because this is not a restoration of the presidentially appointed position, the current incumbent will not be recognized as the 12th Chief Engraver. The name change was occasioned by some minor refinements to the position's roles and responsibilities. The change was authorized by the Director of the United States Mint."

With the administrative change in Mercanti's title, the Office of Public Affairs indicated the position called "supervisory design and master tooling development specialist" ended.

Mercanti retired Dec. 31, 2010. Any replacement for Mercanti will be designated as chief engraver, according to U.S. Mint officials.

The engraving department at the Philadelphia Mint was overseen by Michael Simon, an administrator without engraving credentials, from the time of Jones' 1990 departure until Simon's retirement in 2005. Mercanti was supervising the engraving staff for nearly a year until he was officially designated supervisory design and master tooling specialist in May 2006.

In his supervisory position over design and master tooling development, Mercanti was responsible for the production of all master tooling from design through master dies and work hubs. The position is primarily responsible for overseeing the complete development of master tooling (reduction hub, master die, work hubs) from approved designs through approved trial strike; the artistic design of all new products; supervising tool makers, engravers, and other craft and trades personnel involved in the development of master tooling; and the timely delivery of reduction hubs and master dies for all recurring and new products to Philadelphia and Denver die shops.

2011 Mint engraving staff

Sculptor-Engravers: Donald Everhart II, Norman E. Nemeth, Charles L. Vickers

Medallic Sculptors: Joseph F. Menna, Phebe Hemphill, Jim Licaretz, Michael Gaudioso

Although the United States Mint website at **www. usmint.com** lists all members of the U.S. Mint engraving staff as sculptor-engravers, all are not.

Changes in titles for the engraving staff members were first made about 2005. Technological development in the form of more designs being "sculptured" by computer instead of by hand resulted in new members of the Mint's engraving staff being classified as medallic artists rather than sculptor-engravers. When Menna was hired in August 2005, he was hired as with the title of medallic artist, although he was both classically trained in the traditional methods of bas relief modeling and sculpturing, along with advanced digital sculpturing skills on computer. Hemphill, hired in May 2006, was designated as a medallic sculptor, although she has been additionally trained in traditional sculpturing. Licaretz, who worked for the U.S. Mint in the 1980s until 1988 as a sculptor-engraver, rejoined the engraving staff in December

2006 as a medallic sculptor. Hired in December 2009, Gaudioso joined the engraving staff with the medallic sculptor title, and possesses the same skill set as Menna and Hemphill. Menna, Hemphill, Licaretz and Gaudioso are now (as of May 2011) all called medallic artists. Everhart, Nemeth, and Vickers are the last to be designated with the title of sculptor-engraver, according to Mint officials.

Those who eventually replace them will be designated as medallic artists. Vickers joined the Mint in December 2003; Nemeth, in late 2001; and Everhart, in January 2004

The medallic artist title, according to U.S. Mint officials, better reflects the changing technology and training from the traditional methods of the sculptor-engraver of designing first on paper, and modeling in clay and plaster, from which final models would be made for die production. Designs now can be generated directly onto a computer screen, manipulated where necessary and models generated from the digital sketches. The members of the Mint's engraving staff employ elements of both in the design and die development processes.

Artistic Infusion Program

The U.S. Mint augmented its coin and medal design capabilities when on Nov. 20, 2003, it announced a nationwide competition to select up to 20 college students and up to 20 professional artists to design United States coins and medals as part of a new Artistic Infusion Program. The AIP was the brainchild of Mint Director Henrietta Holsman Fore. Fore introduced the program to supplement the design capabilities of the engraving department whose staff was being pushed to the limits with designs needed for an increasing number of coins and medals.

AIP artists are asked to submit designs for specifically assigned coins and medals. The design submissions are then considered along with those from members of the U.S. Mint's engraving staff.

An internal Mint design review team then selects which designs to allow to proceed for further review by the congressionally authorized review panels. Under the Mint policy, the two advisory panels, the Commission of Fine Arts and the Citizens Coinage Advisory Committee, do not see all of the designs generated. Finalist design submissions are reviewed by both the Commission of Fine Arts and the Citizens Coinage Advisory Committee. Designs recommended by the reviewing bodies are submitted to the Treasury secretary through the Mint for final approval.

AIP artists are paid a specified commission for each design submitted and a separate commission is paid if a design is selected for use on a coin or medal. When the AIP was introduced in 2003, the "honorarium" was $1,000 for master designers and $500 for associates per design assignment regardless of the number of designs submitted, with the same compensation level awarded for each design selected. Associate designers then were graduate level students, whereas now they are professionals new to the AIP program. In early 2009, the AIP charter was revised to include a new fee schedule for master designers and associate designers—$2,500 and $2,000, respectively, per design assignment regardless of the number of designs submitted, and $5,000 per selected design. At the same time, the student designer effort (the original associate designer classification) was terminated. The student designers had difficulty competing with the professional artists and it was determined that the Mint should consider an apprenticeship program in the future to tap into the talent of graduate-school art students.

If an approved design is the work of an AIP artist, the design is sculptured in model form by an assigned member of the U.S. Mint's engraving staff. The initials of both the AIP artist and the assigned member of the U.S. Mint's engraving staff will appear on the coin or medal.

The AIP has dropped the graduate student component from its Call for Artists, leaving master designers and associate designers. Under the current program (spring 2011) guidelines, found at **www.usmint.gov/about_the_mint/artisticInfusion/?action=about**, an associate designer is a professional artist with less than two years experience as an AIP artist or one that has just been selected for the program. A master designer is a professional artist with two years experience as an AIP associate designer.

Services offered by the Mint

The United States Mint has offered to collectors and interested noncollectors such services as Mint tours, in addition to numerous items to collect. Among these items are Proof sets, Silver Proof sets, Uncirculated Mint sets, Silver Quarter sets, bags and rolls of circulating commemorative cents and quarter dollars, Kennedy half dollars, First Day Coin Covers, First Spouse gold $10 coins and companion bronze medals; bags, rolls and boxes of Sacagawea, Native American dollars, and Presidential dollars; quarter dollar first-day covers, and bronze duplicates of national medals.

Bags and rolls of circulation quality 50 State quarter dollars were offered from 1999 through 2008, along with the six-coin District of Columbia and U.S. Territories quarter dollars in 2009. The 12-year, 56-coin America the Beautiful quarter dollar series was introduced in 2010. Coins from all three programs have been offered in various product configurations and coin finishes, including Proof, Silver Proof, Uncirculated Mint set and circulation quality.

Bags and rolls of circulation quality Sacagawea dollars were offered by the U.S. Mint from both the Denver and Philadelphia Mints from 2000 through 2008, with the coins available only as a numismatic product offering from 2002 through 2008, with none directly issued into circulation.

The Native American dollar, replacing the Sacagawea dollar, were introduced in 2009, the same year the Mint introduced its Direct Ship Program for Native American and Presidential dollars. Presidential dollars were introduced in 2007. The Native American dollar retains the Sacagawea dollar obverse, but bears a new reverse annually.

The Direct Ship Program allows customers to order, at face value with no shipping costs, $250 face value boxes containing 10 25-coin rolls of Native American dollars and specific Presidential dollars, by Presidential portrait, randomly from either the Denver or Philadelphia Mint, but not both, in each box.

Presidential dollars have been offered in various product configurations in Proof, Uncirculated Mint set and circulation-quality finishes.

Proof and Uncirculated versions of the Proof and

Uncirculated First Spouse half-ounce .999 fine gold $10 coins were introduced in 2007 with the Presidential dollar series, and include companion bronze medals.

Rolls and sets of Lincoln cents were issued by the U.S. Mint in 2009 to mark the 200th birthday of President Abraham Lincoln and the centennial anniversary of the Lincoln cent. The cents bear reverse designs representing four phases in Lincoln's life, from birth through the 16th presidency.

In 2009, the U.S. Mint issued a Saint-Gaudens, Ultra High Relief 27-millimeter, half-ounce .9999 fine gold $20 double eagle, capturing one version of sculptor Augustus Saint-Gaudens' original 1907 vision for a circulating Ultra High Relief gold coin.

Since 1982, the Mint has offered a variety of commemorative coins and since 1986, American Eagle gold and silver bullion coins (bullion coins are distributed through wholesalers, collector coins are offered directly to collectors). American Eagle platinum bullion coins were added in 1997 but none have been sold since November 2008. Proof and Uncirculated American Buffalo .9999 fine gold coins were introduced in 2006.

Burnished Uncirculated American Eagles and American Buffalo coins, bearing the W Mint mark of the West Point Mint, were introduced in 2006 and offered through 2009, but sales have since been suspended. Special American Eagle anniversary sets were issued in 2006 and 2007 with coins bearing Proof, Reverse Proof and Uncirculated finishes.

Annual offerings comprise Proof sets and sets of Uncirculated coinage (after the Mint did not produce Uncirculated Mint sets in 1982 and 1983, Congress passed a law requiring yearly sales).

Silver Proof sets were added in 1992. State Quarter Silver Proof sets were offered dated 1999 through 2008; District of Columbia and U.S. Territories Silver Quarter Proof set dated 2009 were offered; and since 2010, America the Beautiful Silver Quarter Proof sets have been offered.

National medals are offered as well.

Souvenir Mint sets—each offering the coins of a single Mint—were offered as well, from 1972 to 1998. They were available only at the Denver Mint and Philadelphia Mint, which have sales centers. The facilities no longer offer the Souvenir sets. The Souvenir Mint sets contain half of the coins from the annual Uncirculated Mint set (only those coins struck at the facility offering the sets for sale).

Persons on the Mint's customer mailing list receive order forms for all Mint products offered by mail as well as a catalog each fall. The catalog of Mint products was first issued in late 1985 and was an immediate success. To be placed on the Mint's mailing list, interested persons may write to Customer Service Center, United States Mint, 2799 Reeves Road, Plainfield, IN 46168. The Mint's customer service telephone number is (800) 872-6468.

Some items, like the Souvenir Mint sets, were offered at over-the-counter locations only and not through the mail. Other items are offered only at the Mint's website, **www.usmint.gov**. The Mint has also produced on occasion special souvenir sets of coins or medals for selected numismatic conventions, including the annual American Numismatic Association show; these, too, are not offered through the mail. The Mint in 1983 experimented with over-the-counter sales of Proof sets at certain locations to attract more noncollectors to the hobby of coin collecting. Mint over-the-counter sales outlets have continued to offer Proof sets since then.

Sales centers are located at the Denver Mint, Philadelphia Mint and at Union Station and U.S. Mint headquarters in Washington, D.C.

Mint tours

Philadelphia Mint: The United States Mint at Philadelphia is open for self-guided tours Monday through Friday from 9 a.m. to 3 p.m. Summer hours (Memorial Day through Labor Day), are Monday through Saturday, 9 a.m. to 4:30 p.m. The United States Mint is closed on federal holidays. All tours are free and self-guided; no reservations are necessary. Visitors can see actual coin production. Exhibits and audio/video stations provide information about the United States Mint and its history, coinage and current programs. The tour takes about 45 minutes. The visitors' entrance is on the corner of Fifth and Arch streets. Adults will be asked to provide government-issued photo identification for security purposes. Prospective visitors are advised to telephone (215) 408-0112 for up-to-date tour information, any time.

Visit the U.S. Mint website at **/www.usmint.gov/ mint_tours/** for detailed tour information for both the Philadelphia Mint and Denver Mint, as well as the ability to take virtual tours.

Denver Mint: Reservations are required for all tours of the United States Mint at Denver. Reservations can be scheduled through the U.S. Mint's website link at **www.usmint.gov/mint_ tours/?action=Reservation>**. A limited number of stand-by tickets are available for those without reservations. Standby tickets are available any given day on a first-come, first-served basis.

Available tickets are based on no-shows and do not guarantee a tour. Standby tickets are not always available. All tours are free of charge. Standby tickets, when available, can be picked up beginning at 7:30 a.m. at the Denver Mint's information booth which is located on Cherokee Street between 14 Avenue and Colfax Avenue.

Guided tours start on the hour and are available to be scheduled from 8 a.m. to 2 p.m. Monday through Friday (excluding federal holidays). Visitors are encouraged to submit requests as early as possible since tour availability is limited. General tour information is available at (303) 405-4761.

Tour reservations for individuals or small groups of

up to 20 people can be scheduled through the Mint's Web-based tour reservation system. Reservations are accepted up to two months in advance. Available spaces for large groups of between 21 and 50 people are based on the same online schedule spaces available to individuals and small groups.

Large group tours may be arranged by calling the Office of Public Affairs at the United States Mint, Denver, (303) 405-4759.

Group tours must be scheduled at least two weeks before the tour date requested. To schedule tours for the busy spring and summer months, calling at least six to eight weeks in advance is recommended. The maximum number of visitors in any tour is 50 people.

Those who have scheduled a tour must be at the tour entrance no later than 15 minutes before the scheduled tour time. Late arrivals will not be admitted. A virtual tour is available in a slide presentation online at **usmint.gov/mint_tours/action=VTShell**.

The San Francisco Mint, the Fort Knox Gold Bullion Depository and the West Point Mint are closed to members of the public.

Important Mint contact information
Customer Service Center
United States Mint
2799 Reeves Road
Plainfield, IN 46168
(800) 872-6468
Collectors should contact the Indiana customer service contractor to get on the Mint's mailing list or to request a list of bronze medals for sale.
The full line of Mint coins, medals and other items are for sale at the following sales centers:
Philadelphia Mint (sales center)
151 North Independence Mall East
Philadelphia, PA 19106-1886
Denver Mint (sales center)
320 W. Colfax Ave.
Denver, CO 80204
United States Mint Sales Center (Union Station)
50 Massachusetts Ave. N.E.
Washington, DC 20002
United States Mint Sales Center (Mint headquarters)
801 Ninth St. N.W.
Washington, DC 20220

Medals produced by the United States Mint

While the first medals physically struck at the federal Mint in Philadelphia were not produced until shortly after the Mint's establishment in 1792, the nation's federal medallic history began in 1776 with the congressional gold medal series, authorized by the Continental Congress to honor military commanders in the Continental Army and Navy for their victories in fighting British forces.

Because the new United States lacked the technical capacity to strike large medals, most of these first medals were produced by commission at the Paris Mint, arranged by American representatives to France during the war, including Thomas Jefferson.

Medallic recognition of American military commanders began when Congress on March 25, 1776, voted to award George Washington, then commander of the Continental Army, the first congressional gold medal for his "wise and spirited conduct" in bringing about British evacuation of Boston.

The medals authorized by the Continental Congress—11 different pieces, 10 awarded to Continental Army commanders and one to John Paul Jones of the Continental Navy—are today known as the Comitia Americana (Latin for American Congress) medals.

Original examples of these medals are among the most sought-after pieces in the U.S. medallic field.

Gold examples of each were struck for presentation to the recipient, with silver and copper examples struck for presentation to foreign diplomats and other entities. Later restrikes and copies produced in various metals also exist.

Of the Comitia Americana medals, just one piece appears to have been struck by the federal Mint at Philadelphia. According to R.W. Julian, author of the 1977 reference, *Medals of the United States Mint: The First Century 1792-1892,* the most logical candidate for the first medal struck at the United States Mint is a congressional gold medal designated by the Continental Congress for Maj. Henry Lee, for a military victory at the Battle of Paulus Hook in New Jersey on Aug. 19, 1779, although that claim as first medal boasts what Julian references as "a flawed pedigree." All other medallic honors for Revolutionary War exploits for other Continental Army and Navy officers were executed in Paris. Production of Lee's medal, however, was overlooked by the commissioners in France charged with ordering the dies and medals.

Lee applied in 1790 to Secretary of State Thomas Jefferson to have his forgotten medal produced. Jefferson, either in 1790 or 1791, according to Julian, commissioned the foremost American artist and diesinker, Joseph Wright from Philadelphia, to engrave the appropriate dies.

"Unfortunately, the dies broke in hardening and there is some question as to whether or not the gold medal was actually struck," Julian wrote.

Julian wrote it is known that Wright had finished the dies, and the breaking of the dies likely occurred circa 1793. Julian said he believes that despite the heavy cracking of the dies, more so on the reverse die, that the gold medal was actually struck and presented to Lee. The gold medal, however, cannot be traced today. According to Julian, a pair of uniface lead strikes was made; they now rest in the collection of Philadelphia's American Philosophical Society.

Julian notes there are conflicting reports on whether the original Lee gold medal was actually struck. When a die register was begun at the Mint in 1841, an entry indicated the cracked obverse die was on hand, but the cracked reverse was missing.

In 1874, uniface obverse impressions were struck for the Lee family, four silver and three bronze, although others may have been struck earlier.

Chief Engraver William Barber was directed Jan. 8, 1874, to execute a new reverse die for the Lee medal. However, as late as March 28, 1877, the original obverse was still in use, according to Julian. A new obverse was likely made within a few years of that time, according to Julian.

A congressional gold medal authorized for Gen. Horatio Gates, one of the medals comprising the Comitia Americana series and one that was originally struck in Paris, was also restruck in silver and white metal, likely tin, versions at the Philadelphia Mint. In order for family and friends of Gates to have copies of the medal, according to Julian, Aaron Burr delivered the Gates dies from France to the Mint sometime after March 4, 1801.

"When large-scale striking of Mint medals began in early 1861, these [Gates] dies were still in working condition," according to Julian.

The original Gates gold medal, struck in Paris, is in the collection of the New York Historical Society.

From the 1790s through today, the Philadelphia Mint has produced a wide range of medals, encompassing not only congressional gold medals, but also other medals authorized by Congress (not all congressionally authorized medals fall into the congressional gold medal category), medals issued to participants on the U.S. Assay Commission, Indian peace medals, presidential medals, military medals, naval medals, U.S. Mint and Treasury medals, personal medals, commemorative medals and school medals. Other medals struck at the Philadelphia Mint include agricultural, mechanical, scientific, professional, lifesaving, marksmanship, religious and fraternal medals. The Philadelphia Mint has also produced other medals that do fit into the listed categories, some of which will be discussed later.

Congressional gold medals

The United States Congress continues to this day the tradition introduced by the Continental Congress of voting to award individuals (and, at times, organizations) gold medals to recognize singular accomplishments and contributions benefitting society.

The congressional gold medal series adopted by the Continental Congress in 1776 with the Washington medal for production at the Paris Mint initially focused strictly on recognizing military achievements of Continental Army officers (plus the Navy's Jones). Although authorized by the Continental Congress in 1776, not until March 21, 1790, was Washington presented his medal, by Thomas Jefferson (who had represented American interests in France for years and who was a proponent of the Comitia Americana medal series). The original gold medal is in the collection of the Boston Public Library.

Following the ratification of the U.S. Constitution, congressional gold medals continued to recognize military and naval victories.

The first gold medal authorized by the United States Congress was awarded to Capt. Thomas Truxtun in 1800 for his gallant effort during the action between the United States frigate *Constellation* and the French ship *La Vengeance* during the undeclared naval war between the United States and France of 1798 to 1800.

Additional congressional gold medals were subsequently authorized for military officers involved with the War of 1812 and the Mexican-American War from 1846 to 1848.

Not until 1858 did the American Congress break with the tradition of honoring heroism associated with the actions of American military and naval personnel, when Dr. Frederick A. Rose, an assistant-surgeon in the British Navy, was recognized for his kindness and humanity to sick American seamen aboard the U.S. steamer *Susquehannah* when that crew was stricken with yellow fever, according to Stephen W. Stathis, section research manager for the Congressional Research Service, in *Congressional Gold Medals 1776-2009*. Stathis' report, in tracing the history of the congressional gold medal program, lists each medal authorized and the date authorizing legislation was signed into law by the president.

While some congressional gold medals since then have recognized military heroism and leadership, "in the 20th and 21st centuries, Congress continued broadened the scope of such honors to include recognition of excellence in such varied fields as the arts, athletics, aviation, diplomacy, entertainment, exploration, medicine, politics, religion, and science," according to Stathis.

Recipients in these nonmilitary categories include composer George M. Cohan, actor John Wayne, poet

Robert Frost, filmmaker Walt Disney, author Louis L'Amour, aviator Charles A. Lindberg, astronauts Neil A. Armstrong, Buzz Aldrin, Michael Collins and John Glenn, in addition to inventor Thomas A. Edison, physician and cardiovascular surgeon Dr. Michael E. DeBakey, former President Ronald Reagan and former First Lady Nancy Reagan.

Others recognized include athletes Joe Louis, Robert Clemente and Jackie Robinson, the Little Rock Nine, the Rev. Dr. Martin Luther King and Mrs. Coretta Scott King for their civil rights efforts, and Mother Teresa of Calcutta.

The recognition of Dr. Rose in 1858 also introduced the concept of honoring individuals from other nations. Of the 20th and 21st century medals, more than 30 medals were authorized for recipients outside the United States. Among recent medals, the medal authorized in 2008 for Burmese dissident and human rights activist Daw Aung San Suu Kyi has yet to be struck and presented. She was released in late 2010 by the military junta in Burma (Myanmar), after years under house arrest.

While original gold congressional medals are rarely seen on the market, collectors have ample opportunities to collect official restrikes and duplicates of many of the medals.

The Philadelphia Mint began making restrikes of the gold medals from original dies and copies from new dies in the mid-19th century, all in various metals. Congress in the 20th century would eventually recognize collector interest in the gold medals it authorized, explicitly authorizing the Mint (in authorizing legislation for each medal) to produce and sell bronze duplicates. Under this authority, duplicates of most of the 20th and 21st century 3-inch congressional gold medals have been offered by the U.S. Mint in 3-inch and 1.5-inch bronze versions.

One exception is for the 1997 congressional gold medal authorized May 14, 1997, for singer and actor Frank Sinatra. Sinatra died from a heart attack on May 14, 1998, exactly one year after President Clinton had signed the authorizing medal legislation into law. The Sinatra gold medal was sent to the White House on June 4, 1998, and presented the following day to Sinatra's daughter, Nancy Sinatra, at the Washington, D.C., offices of Rep. Jose Serrano.

It had been suggested that copyright concerns by the Sinatra family over images of the entertainer used as inspiration for the medal designs was blocking production, but Mint officials indicated that was not the case. The enabling legislation permitted, but did not mandate, that the Mint produce duplicates for sale to the public. The decision whether to produce the duplicates rested with the Treasury secretary.

After designs for the Sinatra medal had already been sketched and put into model form, dies cut and bronze trial strikes made in preparation for full production, production plans were put on hold pending the outcome of legal questions and other undisclosed

issues. Those legal questions and other undisclosed issues remain undisclosed. No bronze duplicates of the Sinatra medal were ever produced for sale to the public. Reportedly, no photographs of the finished gold medal were ever taken.

History of the U.S presidential medal series

One of the longest-running series of medals struck by the U.S. Mint is that recognizing U.S. presidents.

Many of the medals that are now included in the U.S. Mint's presidential series are copies of medals made originally for presentation to American Indian chiefs and warriors, a series known as Indian peace medals. The Spanish, French and British had all presented medals to the native inhabitants of the Americas; the British especially had produced large and magnificent silver medals, each bearing the likeness of the reigning British monarch on one side and the monarch's coat of arms on the other. The British medals were made of solid silver and were given to the Indian chiefs as marks of friendship and special recognition. They were highly prized by the Indians.

When the United States replaced the British in dealing with the Indians in the former British colonies, the new government found it necessary to continue the practice of presenting medals so as to have peaceful relations with the tribes and influence with the chiefs. The federal government, then, began the production of Indian peace medals, which became a settled and extremely important part of American Indian policy.

As early as 1787, Henry Knox, secretary of war under the Articles of Confederation, urged Congress to comply with the request of the Indians for "medals, gorgets, wrist and arm bands with the arms of the United States impressed or engraved thereon." Congress was pressed for funds, but Knox noted that the Indians would turn in their British medals, which could be melted down to produce new ones. Thomas Jefferson, as secretary of state, outlined the policy behind the distribution of medals to the Indians; he spoke of it as "an ancient custom from time immemorial." The medals, he said, "are considered as complimentary things, as marks of friendship to those who come to see us, or who do us good offices, conciliatory of their good will toward us, and not designed to produce a contrary disposition towards others. They confer no power, and seem to have taken their origin in the European practice, of giving medals or other marks of friendship to the negotiators of treaties and other diplomatic characters, or visitors of distinction."

Medals expected

Whatever the origin, the practice took firm hold in the United States. The Indians expected to receive medals, and it was impossible to conduct Indian affairs without the use of them. Thomas L. McKenney, head of the Office of Indian Affairs, in 1829 wrote to the secretary of war about the policy of distributing medals. "So important is its continuance esteemed to be," he said, "that without medals, any plan of operations among the Indians, be it what it may, is essentially enfeebled. This comes of the high value which the Indians set upon these tokens of Friendship. They are, besides this indication of the Government Friendship, badges of power to them, and trophies of renown. They will not consent to part from this ancient right, as they esteem it; and according to the value they set upon medals is the importance to the Government in having them to bestow."

The U.S. government took great pains to produce medals of real artistic merit for the Indians, according to researchers. About one of the medals, McKenney wrote: "I am certainly anxious that these medals should be as perfect in their resemblance of the original, as the artist can make them. They are intended, not for the Indians, only, but for posterity."

The medals given to the Indians bear the likeness of the president in office during the presentation, and the medals can be traced administration by administration.

Washington medals

The Washington medals are unique, both in concept and individually. The government presented a number of medals to Indian chiefs during Washington's term of office, but it did not mass-produce the medals—undoubtedly because it did not command the technical means to do so, according to multiple sources. Instead, each medal was a separate production, hand engraved on oval plates of silver, the large ones roughly 4 by 6 inches in size. On one side was engraved the figure of Washington with that of an Indian in the peaceful gesture of throwing away his tomahawk. On the reverse was an eagle bearing the crest of the United States on its breast, with an olive branch in its right talon, a sheaf of arrows in its left. The plate was bound with a silver band and provided with a loop at the top by which it could be hung around the neck of the chief. The most famous of these Washington Indian medals was the one presented to the Seneca chief, Red Jacket, in 1792. The medal of Washington in today's presidential series, however, was designed to match later Indian medals and was not made until early in the 20th century.

No medals for Indians were made while John Adams was president. Medals distributed to the chiefs during his term of office were the so-called Seasons medals, which had been produced in England during Washington's second administration. They showed scenes of a farmer sowing grain, women spinning and weaving, and domestic cattle, which were supposed to incite in the Indians a desire for white civilization. Later, a John Adams medal similar in design to other Indian peace medals was struck in order to make the later presidential series complete.

The production of Indian peace medals began to be regularized during the administration of President Thomas Jefferson. The pattern for the medals was

more or less established, although the methods of manufacture were still not quite set. Medals depicting Jefferson were ordered in three sizes—large (4 inches in diameter), medium (3 inches) and small (2 inches). The obverse and reverse of the medals were struck separately on thin silver disks, then fastened together with a silver band to form a hollow medal. The medals were struck from dies cut by a special engraver who worked directly in the steel of the die, cutting out the features that would appear in relief on the finished medal. On the obverse they bear a bust of Jefferson in profile, with a legend that reads: TH JEFFERSON PRESIDENT OF THE U.S. A.D. 1801. On the reverse are two hands clasped, one of an American military officer with a cuff showing three stripes and three buttons, the other of a native wearing a bracelet engraved with spread eagle. A crossed peace pipe and tomahawk and the words PEACE AND FRIENDSHIP complete the design.

The hollow feature of the Jefferson medals distinguishes them from later medals of similar design concept produced at the Philadelphia Mint. Apparently no press in the country at the time was powerful enough to strike the medals from solid discs of silver.

The hollow nature was a satisfactory expedient as far as the appearance of the medal was concerned, but the Indians compared them unfavorably with the heavy medals they were accustomed to receiving from the British. The Jefferson medal issued today by the Mint in the presidential series is a solid medal that follows the design of the original medals.

New design

When James Madison succeeded Jefferson in 1809, new medals had to be designed and struck. The task of ordering the medals fell to John Mason, who held the office of superintendent of Indian Trade. He turned to a friend in Philadelphia, John Vaughan, to engage an artist and to oversee the production of the medals at the Mint. Mason insisted that the hollow medals be replaced by solid ones and the Mint undertook to strike such medals. The Madison medals, like the Jefferson ones, were produced in three sizes, although the diameters – 3, 2.5 and 2 inches – differed from those of the Jefferson medals. The medals were composed of solid silver, and at the suggestion of Vaughan, the reverse had a slightly changed design. Vaughan objected to having both the wrists encuffed as they appeared on the Jefferson medals. This, he said, did not indicate the diversity of the races that were joined in the handclasp of friendship. He had the artist leave one of the arms bare, and this new design was used repeatedly until completely new designs were substituted for the reverse of the medals in the 1850s and later.

Mason also asked that the lettering on both sides of the medal be "so arranged that a small hole may be made through the medal exactly over the head of the President (so as to suspend it erect when worn by the Chiefs) without interfering with the letters." A review of these medals reveals that for some unaccountable reason this wise advice was never heeded; placement of the inscriptions on the medals was never positioned as Mason recommended.

When it was time to have medals struck for President James Monroe, both the man directing the work and the artist-engraver were new. Thomas L. McKenney had replaced John Mason as superintendent of Indian Trade and Moritz Furst was engaged in place of John Reich, who had engraved the Madison medals. The general form of the medals, nevertheless, followed the set formula. Furst prepared satisfactory likenesses of Monroe on the three sizes of the medals and the dies of the previous reverse were used again.

Furst was also engaged to make the medals of Presidents John Quincy Adams, Andrew Jackson and Martin Van Buren. These medals, like those that followed, were ordered by the head of the Indian Office (and the commissioner of Indian Affairs, after that office was created in 1832), who was the official responsible for the distribution of the medals to the chiefs. It was the custom to order 100 of each of the three sizes, although from time to time not all the medals were given out during the administration they represented. Rather than give the Indian chiefs medals of a previous administration, with the portrait of a president who was no longer in office, medals left over at the end of a president's tenure were regularly melted down to help provide the silver needed for the new medals.

As the series of medals progressed, they began to be considered as "presidential medals," quite apart from their original purpose as Indian peace medals. Franklin Peale, who became chief coiner at the Mint in 1839, believed that the Mint should be the depository of dies of all national medals, and he urged that medals missing from the presidential series (for example, one for John Adams) be supplied. He was supported by Robert M. Patterson, director of the Mint, who in 1841 suggested making a medal of President William Henry Harrison, whose term had been too short to permit making Indian medals bearing his portrait. Nothing came of the proposals at the time.

Technical advance

When it came time to prepare medals for President John Tyler, technical advances had taken some of the difficulties out of medal making. The invention in France of a "portrait lathe," a mechanical means of cutting dies, did away with the need for the special engraver to cut the dies by hand. A medallion of the president could now be modeled in wax, with the opportunity for making corrections until a suitable likeness was obtained. From this, by use of an intermediate plaster cast, a casting in fine iron was made of the medallion. With the use of the steam-powered lathe, reduced facsimiles (dies) were turned out in steel, and the lettering was then stamped in.

The new machine at the Mint was used for making the dies of the President John Tyler Indian peace medal, from a medallion modeled by Ferdinand Pettrich. It was also used for making the dies of the President James K. Polk medal from a model made by the artist John Gadsby Chapman and the dies of the President Zachary Taylor medal from a medallion sculptured by Henry Kirke Brown. The portrait lathe was adjusted to make the various sizes of the dies from the same model, so that all three sizes of these medals are identical and do not show the variations that occurred in the earlier medals, when the dies were cut individually by hand.

The next medals were again made from dies cut by engravers, who signed contracts with the commissioner of Indian Affairs to engrave the dies and strike the medals for presentation to the Indians. The two young New York artists who were engaged were Salathiel Ellis and Joseph Willson. Ellis engraved the dies for the portraits of Presidents Millard Fillmore, Franklin Pierce, James Buchanan and Abraham Lincoln, while Willson made the reverses for the medals. The old Peace and Friendship design that had been used for so many years on the reverse of the medals was now laid aside, and scenes depicting the adoption of civilization were used instead. One such design was used on the reverse of the Fillmore and Pierce medals, and another on the Buchanan and Lincoln Indian peace medals. For all of these later medals only the large and medium size were made; the small size was discontinued.

The Mint issues, as part of the presidential series, bronze copies of the medals designed for presentation to the Indians from Jefferson to Buchanan, uniformly now in the 3-inch size, although in past times the smaller sizes as well were reproduced.

With President Buchanan, however, the presidential series began to diverge from the Indian peace medal series. The Buchanan medal uses the reverse from the Fillmore and Pierce medals, instead of the one designed for it by Willson, and the Lincoln medal in the Mint presidential series is an inaugural medal, not the one designed for presentation to the chiefs.

Paquet designs

Anthony Paquet engraved the Indian peace medal for President Andrew Johnson's administration. He had begun to make the medal for presentation to Indians during Lincoln's second administration and, after Lincoln's assassination, changed the obverse to show the bust of Johnson. The reverse was a completely new design, one suggested by the commissioner of Indian Affairs to show the change from Indian culture to white civilization. This medal became part of the presidential series.

Although the presidential series for presidents following Andrew Johnson are not those made for the Indians, Indian peace medals continued to be produced for each administration through that of President Benjamin Harrison. The medal for President Ulysses S. Grant was designed by Paquet and was struck in only one size, 2.5 inches in diameter. The medals for Presidents Rutherford B. Hayes, James A. Garfield, Chester A. Arthur and Grover Cleveland were oval medals measuring 3 by 2.25 inches and on the reverse showed an Indian and a white man in a rural scene. Mint engravers Charles E. Barber and George T. Morgan designed them. For Benjamin Harrison, both an oval and a round Indian peace medal were made. Only small numbers of these later medals were struck in silver, for the Indian tribes were no longer treated as sovereign nations, and the importance of the chiefs in dealings with the U.S. government had declined.

Today, the presidential medals offered by the U.S. Mint include not only those that were originally called Indian peace medals, but also medals issued to mark a president's term in office, similar to the inaugural medals issued by official presidential inaugural committees. The Mint has produced the presidential medals for many of the presidents, with different medals issued for each term in office.

Other medal series

In additional to bronze duplicates of congressional gold medals and presidential medals, other medal series offered by the U.S. Mint include 3-inch bronze medals depicting U.S. Mint directors and Treasury secretaries.

In 1992, the U.S. Mint produced for sale to the public 3-inch and 1.5-inch bronze medals honoring the Bicentennial of the U.S. Mint. Donald Miller, a police officer at the Philadelphia Mint, provided the winning obverse design and Lauren Vaughan, secretary to the Office of Public Information at Mint headquarters in Washington, D.C., contributed the winning reverse design. Miller's and Vaughan's designs were selected from those submitted in a design competition among Mint employees.

The obverse design of the Mint bicentennial medal is based on Miller's rendition of a 1914 oil painting by John Ward Dunsmore titled *Inspecting the First Coins.* In the painting, Dunsmore depicts what might have taken place at the ceremony. First lady Martha Washington, lorgnette in hand, sits before a tray of silver coins held by Henry Voigt, credited with the nation's first coins and the production of the Washington half dismes and Silver Center cent patterns of 1792. In the distinguished group around Martha Washington are President Washington, his secretary of State, Thomas Jefferson, and Treasury Secretary and Mrs. Alexander Hamilton. Tobias Lear, private secretary to the president, watches David Rittenhouse, newly appointed Mint Director, offer a coin from the tray for the first lady's inspection. Adam Eckfeldt surveys the proceedings from his post at the coining press.

The obverse carries Miller's initials and those of former Chief Sculptor-Engraver of the United States Frank Gasparro. The artwork is based on Gasparro's design for the reverse of the 1965 Assay Commission medal, which was inspired by Miller's rendition of

John Ward Dunsmore's 1914 oil painting, *Inspecting the First Coins.*

Gasparro's design was repurposed for the 1992 Bicentennial of the Mint medal.

The reverse of the 1992 Bicentennial of the Mint medal carries Vaughan's initials, LMV, along with those of Mint Sculptor-Engraver Thomas Rogers, who executed the design. The reverse design of the medal features a collage of obverse and reverse designs, 15 designs in all, from the first U.S. cent (1792 Silver Center cent) through the 1992 Olympic gold $5 half eagle.

In 1993, Benjamin Franklin, who organized the first fire service in the American Colonies, was recognized on a congressionally authorized Proof silver medal honoring firefighters. The firefighters medal both honors Franklin as the founder of the first organized fire company in Philadelphia in 1736 and the heroic contributions of firefighters past and present. The medal measures 1.6 inches in diameter and contains 1 ounce of .999 fine silver. The medal has a plain edge. The medal was struck at the Philadelphia Mint and carries the P Mint mark on the reverse.

The Franklin/firefighters medal's obverse, featuring a frontal portrait of a bespectacled Franklin and a firefighter's helmet, was designed by Mint Sculptor-Engraver Thomas D. Rogers Sr. The reverse, depicting a firefighter carrying a just-rescued child down a ladder, was designed by Mint Sculptor-Engraver T. James Ferrell.

The centennial anniversary of the establishment in 1903 of the National Wildlife Refuge System by President Theodore Roosevelt was commemorated with a 2003 series of prooflike 1.5-inch silver and bronze medals struck at the Philadelphia Mint. The 2003 National Wildlife Refuge System Centennial Medal Series program was produced by the U.S. Mint under its general statutory authority at Title 31 of the United States Code, Section 5111, that permits the striking of national and other medals. No special congressional legislation was passed or necessary authorizing the wildlife medals.

The medals share a common obverse depicting a full-length portrait of Theodore Roosevelt standing at the edge of a mountain cliff. The four reverse designs depict a bald eagle taking flight from the treetops; two canvasback ducks in flight against a wetlands background; an elk standing on prairie grass with rocky landscape in the foreground; and a river scene featuring a leaping salmon in full side view in the foreground, with a second, smaller, salmon leaping in the background. The four reverse designs were originally submitted as obverse designs, while the common obverse was originally submitted as a reverse design.

All four medal designs were struck in silver versions. The Eagle medal only was also offered in a bronze version with no mintage ceiling. The Eagle silver medal was restricted to a mintage of 35,000 medals, while the maximum mintage and release was 25,000 apiece for the remaining three designs. All of the silver medals were sold out.

The National Wildlife Refuge System silver medals are the first U.S. Mint products produced with dies subjected to a computer-driven "laser-texturing technique," which has since replaced the previous standard "grit-blasting" technology for "frosting" Proof dies.

First Spouse medals

The same legislation that authorized the Presidential $1 Coin Series and the First Spouse $10 gold coins also included provisions for 1.3125-inch bronze First Spouse medals. The bronze medals bear the same obverse and reverse designs that appear on the gold coins, except without the statutory inscriptions and mottoes that make the gold pieces coins and not medals. The First Spouse bronze medals were introduced in 2007, the same year the Presidential $1 Coin Series and the First Spouse gold $10 coins were also introduced.

Among the medal programs still in the pre-production phase by the U.S. Mint as this book went to press in mid-2011 is one to commemorate the 10th anniversary of the Sept. 11, 2001, terrorist attacks, and the establishment of the National September 11 Memorial & Museum at the World Trade Center. The medals are authorized under the National September 11 Memorial & Museum Commemorative Medal Act, which President Barrack Obama signed into law Aug. 6, 2010 as Public Law 111-221. The Mint is authorized to strike up to 2 million silver medals in 2011 and 2012. Each medal is legislatively required to contain one ounce of pure silver. Production will be split between the Philadelphia and Denver Mints, with medals bearing the respective P and D Mint marks.

While medals and not coins, the 9/11 commemoratives are authorized by the act to be produced "in the quality comparable to proof coins" and that they "shall be considered to be numismatic items."

Design requirements for the medals mandate inclusion of the years 2001-2011 and the inscription ALWAYS REMEMBER.

The U.S. Mint has produced medals for multiple other series, including so-called dollar medals recognizing events, fairs and expositions of local, state or national importance (cataloged in *So-Called Dollars* by Harold E. Hibler and Charles V. Kappen, updated

2008 second edition, as revised and edited by Tom Hoffman, Dave Hayes, Jonathan Brecher and John Dean); half-ounce and 1-ounce American Arts Gold Medallions issued from 1980 through 1984 (and discussed in detail in the Bullion Coins chapter of this almanac), national bicentennial medals and the U.S. Capitol Historical Society's 1978 medal depicting Valley Forge, which was the first medal in a series that ended in 1991. (U.S. Capitol Historical Society medals from 1979 through 1991 were struck by Medallic Art Co.).

Currently, medals produced for sale to the public by the Mint normally are produced in bronze (90 percent copper, 10 percent zinc). They are often referred to as "list medals" because they are listed in Mint sales brochures or posted online at **www.usmint.gov**. The brochures contain photographs and descriptions of products offered (medals, easels, presentation cases, and display albums) and pricing for both mail order and over-the-counter sales.

Large medals may be up to 3 inches in diameter and require multiple strikes of the press to bring up the relief. These medals are hand-finished and individually packaged. Each large medal comes with a plastic display easel. Smaller medals, such as the 1.5-inch and 1.3125-inch "miniature" sizes, are produced on presses similar to those used for the manufacture of coins. Generally, only one strike is required for the smaller medals. Though not hand-finished like the larger medals, the miniature medals are lacquered to protect their surfaces from tarnish. The smaller medals are packaged by machine.

The Mint offers 3-inch and 1.5-inch bronze duplicates of many of the congressional gold medals, as well as 3-inch Treasury secretary and U.S. Mint director medals. Production of Treasury secretary and U.S. Mint director medals was suspended in late 2010 because of economic constraints. Medals for Edmund C. Moy, who resigned his Mint director's post effective Jan. 9, 2011, and that for the current Treasury secretary, Timothy F. Geithner, have been placed on hold.

The presidential medals, which include George Washington and Abraham Lincoln, are offered in 3-inch and 1.3125-inch versions.

Check with the U.S. Mint at **www.usmint.gov**, or call the U.S. Mint's order fulfillment center at (800) 872-6468, for further information on additional medal offerings.

Seigniorage

Seigniorage, up until the late 1990s, was calculated as the difference between the monetary value of coins and their face value. It is now considered to be the difference between a coin's face value and the cost to produce it, which includes metals acquisition and all production and delivery costs.

The seigniorage on coins, arising from the exercise of the government's monetary powers, differs from receipts coming from the public, since there is no corresponding payment on the part of another party. The Mint's sole customer for circulating coinage for distribution through commerce is the Federal Reserve.

Seigniorage is excluded from receipts and treated like borrowing as a means of financing a budget deficit, or as a supplementary amount to be applied (to reduce debt or to increase the cash in the treasury) in the years of a budget surplus.

In a historical sense, seigniorage is a charge imposed by the agency that is legally entrusted with the power to produce coins for circulation as money. The term is borrowed from the French word "seigneurage," which literally means "the right of the lord."

Indeed, the delegation of the right (or privilege) to the sovereign is a tradition that can be traced back to Roman times. In the Middle Ages, the prerogative was exercised by the governing nobles of each state – the feudal lords and kings – and it was mainly the abuse of the prerogative that caused the most famous cases of currency debasements.

In fact, up to the reign of Charles VII, the seigniorage obtained by reducing the amount of gold or silver in coins or by raising the charge for manufacturing coins was considered an important source of revenue for the French crown. It was not until 1803 that France passed laws to limit the seigniorage charge that could be imposed by the state.

The question of seigniorage in the United States goes back to the first secretary of the Treasury, Alexander Hamilton, whose views on seigniorage were generally unfavorable. Hamilton apparently preferred to have the metallic value of coins equal to their monetary value, as he believed counterfeiters would be induced to duplicate coins if the monetary value of coins exceeded the metallic value.

Thus, when Congress adopted Hamilton's coinage recommendations in 1792, the seigniorage charge was limited to one half of 1 percent of the value of bullion presented to the Mint for immediate coinage. If the person presenting bullion had to wait for delivery of the coins, there was to be no seigniorage charge at all. In practice, however, seigniorage did not actually disappear. Increased coin production after 1795 resulted in lower minting costs and the weight of some of the minor coins was reduced.

In 1800, the U.S. Mint showed a net profit of about $5,000 on coinage and in the years that followed, a small margin of seigniorage was usually realized.

During fiscal years 1934 to 1964, total silver seigniorage in the United States amounted to $1,916.2 million. Of this total, $1,172.9 million originated from the revaluation of silver bullion behind silver certificates and $743.3 million was from the production of silver coins. The seigniorage from revaluation of silver bullion was the result of increases in the price of silver during 1934 to 1964 and a law in May 1933 that permitted the Treasury to hold silver in either bullion (bar) form or coins as reserve backing for the Treasury's silver certificates in circulation. Before May 1933, the law allowed only silver dollars as reserve backing for silver certificates.

The price of silver in the New York market increased from an average price of 45 cents per troy ounce in 1933 to $1.293 in 1964. As a result, the dollar value of silver bars was required as reserve for the same amount of certificates, with the difference representing the amount of seigniorage.

The nature and composition of seigniorage after fiscal year 1964 reflect the results of changes in the law regarding coinage, as well as increases in coin production. During fiscal years 1964 to 1967, the U.S. Treasury received a total of $1,665.1 million of seigniorage. Unlike from 1934 to 1964, nearly all the seigniorage in the latter period resulted from coin production, with a relatively small amount due to revaluation.

The difference between the two periods largely reflects that in recent years the market price of silver has been as high as the monetary value of silver; consequently, no revaluation of seigniorage could be realized.

A huge jump in coin seigniorage occurred in fiscal year 1966, an increase of $530 million over fiscal year 1965. The major reason for the sharp increase reflected the enactment of the Coinage Act of 1965, which, by altering the metallic composition of half dollars, quarter dollars and dimes, drastically reduced the cost of metals used in producing coins. The bulk ($546 million) of seigniorage was the result of coining copper-nickel clad quarter dollars and dimes.

Seigniorage in Fiscal Year 2000 totaled $428 million; in FY2001, $262.6 million; in FY2002, $350.5 million; FY2003, $693.2 million; FY2004, $721.7 million; FY2005, $586.7 million; FY2006, $465 million; FY2007, $562 million; FY2008, $750 million; FY2009, $475 million; and FY2010, $388 million.

The establishment of a Mint Public Enterprise Fund in 1996 (Title 31, Section 5136, United States Code) and elimination of several individual funds for Mint operations allows the Mint to use its profits to operate without having to seek congressional appropriations. Any amount in the PEF in excess of the amount required by the fund to support Mint operations is to be transferred to the general Treasury upon direction of the Secretary of the Treasury "not less than annually."

The Assay Commission

The U.S. Assay Commission was one of the oldest institutions in the annals of American history until public participation was eliminated during the Carter administration. The original provision for this body was made in the Act of April 2, 1792, Section 18, which established the Mint and provided for a national coinage.

The duty of the Assay Commission was to test

the weight and fineness of the coins reserved by the operating Mints during the preceding calendar year, in order to assure that they conformed to their respective legal standards. During each calendar year, coins were selected at random from each Mint's coinage and shipped quarterly to the Philadelphia Mint, where they were preserved for delivery, with the selected Philadelphia coins, to the Assay Commission when it met the following February. If it appeared by such examination and test, that these coins did not differ from the standard fineness and weight by a greater quantity than allowed by law, the trial was considered and reported as satisfactory.

If, however, any greater deviation from the legal standard or weight appeared, this fact was certified to the president of the United States. And if, on a view of the circumstances of the case, he so decided, the officers implicated in the error were thenceforward disqualified from holding their respective offices.

Those coins not used for the assay test were returned to Mint stocks for circulation. They were not mutilated or marked in any manner to distinguish them from other coins. The pieces upon which assay tests were made were returned to the Mint for melting.

The Assay Commission was established by the Founding Fathers to serve as an impartial check upon the nation's coinage, additional to that routinely performed by Mint employees.

The Assay Commission met in one-day sessions at the Mint in Philadelphia, on the second Wednesday in February, as required by law. There were three ex officio members of the commission: a judge of the United States District Court for the Eastern District of Pennsylvania; the comptroller of the currency; and the assayer of the United States Assay Office at New York. The membership always included a representative of the National Bureau of Standards. The weights used by the commission were sent to the National Bureau of Standards to be calibrated before the Assay Commission meeting to assure that they conformed to the standard troy weight measure used in the Mints. The standards representative delivered them.

While no statute limited the number who could serve, both a ceiling on appropriated funds for expenses to cover the meeting and necessity that membership be divided into three small committees, assigned to the task of counting, weighing and assaying coin samples, dictated the size. Owing to the smallness of the commission, and the honor attached to service, it became customary to make very few repeat appointments in the final years.

First authorized to serve on the commission in 1837, public members had been appointed by the president continuously at least since 1874, according to available records, until 1977 when a major decision was made about the commission. The last list of appointments to the Assay Commission were made by President Gerald R. Ford in 1976.

Although outgoing Director of the Mint Mary Brooks submitted 117 names to the White House—a list from which about 25 members would by tradition have been named to the 1977 Assay Commission—President Ford's successor, Jimmy Carter, declined to name any public members to the historic body. Carter, according to numismatic researcher R.W. Julian, abolished the public part of the commission in early 1977, believing that the work of the commission did not justify the expenses involved. It is believed about 34 public members had been recommended to be named to the commission from the list of 117 presented.

Thirty-one of the original 50 1977 Assay Commission medals produced were distributed to participants, key Treasury and Mint officials and staff and to the Smithsonian Institution's Division of Numismatics and the Bureau of the Mint archives. The remaining 19 were melted. However, following public outcry over distribution of the medals, the Mint struck pewter duplicates of the medal for sale to collectors. The only distinguishing marks on the original medals are the names of the persons receiving them, engraved on the edges.

The failure of the Carter administration to name public members to the 1977 Assay Commission sent shock waves through the numismatic fraternity, which had a natural predilection for the mission of the Assay Commission and had enjoyed notable recognition among commissioners in years past. Numismatists had a natural inclination toward the tradition and mission of the Assay Commission and had readily accepted appointment to the group as a signal honor, despite being obliged to pay their own expenses. The Mint expended $2,500 annually for the event.

The last meeting of the statutory members of the Assay Commission came in 1980. No meetings were held during the Reagan administration and with the closing of the N.Y. Assay Office, the statutory members' position was eliminated.

Twenty-three years after its death, the U.S. Assay Commission faced the prospect of legislative resurrection. H.R. 3866, introduced March 8, 2000, by Rep. Steven R. Rothman, D-N.J., called for the re-establishment of the Assay Commission. Rothman's legislation stated the re-establishment was "in the national interest for the citizens of the nation and those who purchase products of the United States Mint, to know that gold, silver and platinum coinage" produced by the Mint are "of the proper size, weight and purity provided for by law."

Although the legislation inaccurately stated the Mint began producing silver, gold and platinum bullion coinage in 1977, a staff member in Rothman's office said that reference was used to cover the period from when the commission was deactivated until the present.

Rothman's bill was referred to the House Banking Subcommittee on Domestic and International Monetary Policy, where it died for lack of action.

6 Bureau of Engraving and Printing

The Bureau of Engraving and Printing came into existence Aug. 29, 1862. It is not known when the title "Bureau of Engraving and Printing" was first adopted. Early records show such names for the bureau as "Small Note Department," "Small Note Bureau," "Small Note Room," "Note Bureau," "National Note Bureau" and "First Division of the National Currency Bureau."

The creation of the BEP was an indirect consequence of the Civil War, and primarily the result of the self-confidence, courage, ingenuity and patriotism of one man—Spencer Morton Clark. It also is the result of the foresight of Salmon P. Chase (President Lincoln's first secretary of the Treasury), his confidence in Clark's ability, and his recognition of Clark's accomplishments.

President Lincoln called Congress into extra session on July 4, 1861, following the firing on Fort Sumter, the first salvo of the Civil War. At the time, the nation was on the edge of bankruptcy and hardly in condition to finance a war. During the special session of Congress, Secretary Chase recommended that Congress set up a system of taxation and one of floating loans. His scheme for borrowing included the issuance of non-interest-bearing notes that would circulate as money.

Although there was some doubt that the government had the constitutional authority to issue paper money, Congress adopted Chase's plan in the Act of July 17, 1861, and as a result the first U.S. government-issued paper money came into being. The first notes, popularly known as "demand notes" because of certain provisions of their issuance, were produced by the American Bank Note Co. and the National Bank Note Co., both of New York, under contract with the government.

One of the provisions of the new law specified that the authorized securities should be signed by the first or second comptroller, or the register of the Treasury, and countersigned by such other officers of the Treasury Department as the secretary of the Treasury cared to designate. It was soon evident that if the designated officers were to perform duties other than signing currency, the law would need to be revised.

Signatures

On Aug. 5, 19 days after enactment of the original law, President Lincoln signed a bill to change the signature requirements. Under the new law, the notes were to be signed by the treasurer of the United States and the register of the Treasury. The new legislation also provided that the Treasury secretary could designate other personnel to sign the notes for these officers. A force of 70 clerks was assigned to sign these early notes—with their own names.

With such a variety of signatures on notes, security was poor. Spencer Clark, the chief clerk of the Bureau of Construction in the department, who at the time was acting engineer in charge of the bureau, suggested to Secretary Chase that the notes be imprinted with the facsimile signatures of the required officers. He also suggested that the notes be imprinted with a copy of the Treasury seal as additional evidence of lawful issue.

The Treasury secretary approved Clark's proposal and Congress approved the act on Feb. 25, 1862. Clark was directed to procure the necessary machinery. A variation of the seal designed by Clark is still used on U.S. securities.

Clark described the original seal design as having for its interior a facsimile of the seal adopted by the Treasury Department for its documents on a ground of geometric lathe work, the exterior being composed of 34 similar points. "These points," Clark said, "were designed to be typical of the 34 states, and to simulate the appearance of the seals ordinarily affixed to public documents."

Clark was loyal to the government and gave no recognition to the rebellion then going on, and included a point in his design for each of the 11 states then in secession as well as well the states not in rebellion. He further said of his seal: "It was difficult of execution, and it was believed that counterfeiters could not readily make a successful imitation of it. So far [1864] the belief has seemed well founded, for it has not, that I am aware of, been successfully imitated."

Clark told Secretary Chase that it would be both proper and economical to print the signatures by "a peculiar process and with peculiar ink." Two presses were secured for overprinting the signatures, an operation that began in March of 1862. Early records do not explain how long this practice continued.

Automation

Notes printed by the two New York bank note companies were delivered to the Treasury for final processing and issuing. The notes were printed in sheets of four subjects and in the beginning were trimmed and separated manually by the use of shears. Approximately 70 women were employed, at a salary of $50 per month, for the trimming and separating operations.

Because of the expense and tediousness of this method, Clark gained authority to construct two machines on a trial basis, one for trimming and one for separating. The trials of Clark's machines were reported to Secretary Chase as failures and Chase gave orders to have them removed. However, Clark asked the secretary to personally check the machines, an inspection that revealed to Chase that actually the machines were quite effective. Chase rescinded his order to have them removed and directed Clark to submit plans for performing the work on machines operated by steam.

A steam engine and boilers were secured, along with necessary auxiliary equipment, and set up in the southwest room of the south wing of the basement in the main Treasury building. Presses for sealing, trimming and separating were installed. On Aug. 29, 1862, Clark commenced with one male assistant and four female operators. Chase, in a diary entry dated Sept. 13, 1862, said: "Visited Mr. Clark's sealing and trimming machines for the ones and twos and found them a perfect success."

Secretary Chase was so pleased with Clark's machines that he asked him to investigate further possibilities relating to the printing of securities. Clark's investigations determined that the government was paying enormous prices to the bank note companies for printing notes. He told Secretary Chase that he could produce the work in the department for "a comparatively small outlay, at a great saving of cost in the issues."

Chase had introduced in Congress a proposal based on Clark's report, asking for authority to engrave and print notes at the Treasury in Washington. This authority was given by the Act of July 11, 1862, and in August, little more than a month after passage of the act, Clark reported to Chase that the first engraver (James Duthie) had been hired and was progressing satisfactorily. Date of the first printing in the department is in question. A congressional report of 1864 states that printing of some public moneys was begun in the autumn of 1862, but Clark reported to Secretary Chase on Dec. 13, 1862, "no printers are yet employed." One account says plate printing in the Treasury did not begin until January 1863.

Clark had great executive talent and was very careful in his selection of skilled artists and tradesmen for the department. He submitted a list of American engravers of known reputation. Two of those named, Joseph P. Ourdan and John F.E. Prud'homme, became full-time employees in the department. Other well-known engravers, working on a piece basis, included Charles Burt, Louis Delnoce, Alfred Sealey and Archibald McLees. Joseph James P. Ourdan, father of Joseph P. Ourdan, also came to work for the

department. His son had instructed him in the art of engraving.

The bureau's first engraver, James Duthie, was a skilled etcher, and served as superintendent of engraving until 1865. Another early craftsman was Elisha Hobart, trained as an engraver, but later a transferrer. Hobart is remembered for his engraving of Sargent's painting *Landing of the Pilgrims,* on which he worked for two years.

Clark also hired George W. Casilear as an engraver, but soon afterward, Casilear was made custodian of dies and rolls. Later, Casilear became superintendent of engraving and served in that capacity, except during President Cleveland's first administration, until October 1893.

Another early engraver was Henry Gugler, hired in January 1863. A native of Germany, Gugler had been in the United States only about 10 months when hired by Clark. Gugler later founded the lithographic firm of H. Gugler and Son, Milwaukee, which became the Gugler Lithographic Co.

NorthStar Print Group acquired Gugler in 1978; Multi-Color Corp., Cincinnati, acquired NorthStar in 2005.

Fractional currency

One of the first products produced by the bureau was fractional currency, issued in place of coins during and for some 10 years after the Civil War. In all, five issues of postage and fractional currency were produced and released. The second and third were printed at the bureau. The greater part of the fourth issue was produced by a private bank note firm but the Treasury seal was applied by the plate printers at the bureau. Three different 50-cent notes were in the fourth issue and the face sides of two of these notes were printed at the bureau. Faces of the fifth issue were done at the bureau and a private firm did the work on the backs.

The third issue of 5-cent fractional currency bore a portrait of Clark and was the subject of much controversy (see Chapter 9, "Portraits on U.S. Paper Money"). The controversy reached Congress and resulted in the law that remains in effect today that the portrait of a living person shall not be used on a security of the United States (31 U.S.C. 413).

The first paper money produced at the Treasury establishment, other than fractional notes, were the compound interest notes of 1863 and 1864 and the 5 percent Treasury notes of 1863.

By 1864, the bureau had grown to a point where it employed 237 men and 288 women. In November 1864, Clark reported equipment in use as 15 transfer machines, 72 hydraulic and 96 hand presses, 14 sealing presses, six ink mills and 22 numbering machines.

Formal recognition

The first reference on record of the use of the name "Bureau of Engraving and Printing" is found in a copy of an order of July 31, 1868, placed with John R. Hoole and Sons, New York City, for an ornamental strip with that wording, for use in printing a form needed by the bureau. The first legislative recognition of the agency is found in the Act of March 3, 1869, which prohibited any work from being done "in the engraving and printing bureau for private parties."

Additional organizational recognition is found in the Act of July 11, 1896, which provides "That all business of the Bureau of Engraving and Printing shall be under the immediate control of the director of the Bureau, subject to the direction of the Secretary of the Treasury, and the director of said Bureau shall report to and be responsible directly to the Secretary of the Treasury."

The extent to which steam presses were being used in those early days of the bureau is recounted in the bureau's annual report for the fiscal year 1888, which reads: "The steam presses are now printing much more than one-third of the work at the Bureau, with a great economy of rooms, labor and expense. The cost of the printing done by them is less than $80,000. To print the same work by hand would cost $180,000."

The use of distinctively marked paper in printing paper money, limited by law to this single purpose, was early recognized as one of the prime deterrents to counterfeiting.

In 1862, Secretary Chase authorized Clark to make "investigations and experiments in reference to the manufacture of a distinctive paper in the [Treasury] building." Early suppliers of such distinctive paper were Stuart Gwynn of Boston, J.M. Wilcox and Co., Philadelphia and the Crane Paper Co. of Dalton, Mass. Crane, the latest firm contracted with, still supplies the bureau with distinctive paper and has been sole supplier of the currency paper since the late 19th century.

Although Spencer Clark made a formal recommendation for separate facilities for the printing and processing of currency a scant three years after beginning operations, it was a good many years before the bureau moved from its facilities at the main Treasury building and into its own building. Land for this purpose was purchased on June 26, 1878, from William W. Corcoran, the Washington historical figure best known as the founder of the world-famous Corcoran Gallery of Art.

A contract for the excavation for the project was awarded the following month, and the structure, designed in Romanesque style by James G. Hill, supervising architect of the Treasury, was completed in record time at a cost of $300,000. It was ready for occupancy on July 1, 1880. The bureau remained in this building until 1914 when the present headquarters was built. An annex to the bureau was completed in 1938. Officials have studied the possibility of building a new facility in the Washington area in order to incorporate machinery capable of producing notes with a variety of high-tech devices needed to combat increasingly sophisticated counterfeiting.

The Bureau today

The Bureau of Engraving and Printing is the world's largest securities manufacturing establishment. It has two facilities (Washington, D.C., and Fort Worth, Texas) and operates 24 hours a day, five days a week. The bureau designs, engraves, and prints United States paper currency and miscellaneous engraved items for federal government departments and independent agencies, and its insular possessions. White House invitations, commissions, diplomas, certificates, identification cards and liquor strip stamps are some of the miscellaneous products printed by the bureau.

The headquarters of the BEP, in Washington, D.C., is housed in two specially constructed buildings with a combined floor space of approximately 25 acres. The BEP added 288,000 square feet of additional floor space when a $15 million Western Currency Facility near Fort Worth, Texas, went into production in 1991. Ground was broken for the Fort Worth printing plant on April 25, 1987. A 140,000 square foot addition at the Fort Worth facility opened in 2004 and includes a public tour. Notes produced at the Fort Worth plant are distinguishable by a small "FW" facility mark near the face check number.

The BEP's principal product is United States paper currency. All of the currency notes now printed are Federal Reserve notes, which are issued in denominations of $1, $2, $5, $10, $20, $50, and $100.

Federal Reserve notes is the only class that can now be printed; printing of United States notes, Federal Reserve Bank notes, national bank notes, gold certificates and silver certificates has been discontinued. Some notes from each of these classes are still in public circulation or collections.

The Department of the Treasury announced on July 14, 1969, that currency in denominations of $500, $1,000, $5,000 and $10,000 would no longer be produced because of the lack of demand.

The largest denomination of currency ever printed was the $100,000 gold certificate of 1934, which features the portrait of President Wilson. This note was designed for official transactions only, and none of these notes ever circulated outside Federal Reserve Banks.

The first $2 Federal Reserve note was issued on April 13, 1976, as the latest permanent addition to the denominations of United States currency. Series 2003A $2 notes are currently being printed and issued.

Beginning in 1966, a collection of 306,275 of the BEP's "certified proofs," proofs that were produced for nearly every instrument printed by the agency, was transferred to the Smithsonian Institution's Division of Numismatics.

The transfer began when the BEP ran out of room to store the proofs, which represent all the major note types of the United States, plus such other items as Cuban silver certificates and Philippine Treasury certificates, printed for former U.S. possessions, bonds, stocks, revenue items, checks and other instruments.

How paper money is printed

To assure the best protection against counterfeiting, all U.S. paper money is primarily printed by the "line engraved," or intaglio, process, from engraved plates (additional nonintaglio printing is required for certain security and other features on the most recent generations of notes). Intaglio-printed documents are the most difficult to produce and to counterfeit. Other processes lack the fidelity of fine lines and the distinctive three-dimensional effect of raised line on paper inherent in intaglio printing. An outstanding element of protection is the portrait. The use of portraits in security designs takes full advantage of the characteristics of intaglio printing since even a slight alteration in breadth, spacing, or depth of line on the part of a counterfeiter will cause a perceptible facial change. The portraits used in the designs of securities are those of persons of historical importance. Portraits of living persons are prohibited by law.

In the intaglio process, the individual features of a chosen design are hand-tooled by highly skilled engravers who engrave in varying depths into steel with delicate steel-cutting instruments called gravers. With infinite care, each feature, such as the portrait, the vignette, the numerals, the lettering, the script, and the scroll work is hand-engraved by a different master craftsman expertly trained in his or her own particular skill.

As design-process technologies change, so does the potential for changes in the engraving and plate-making process, though specific details about any recent changes are unavailable. A BEP official in early 2011 stated: "The Bureau of Engraving and Printing continually evaluates new technology and security features to apply to the manufacture of secure U.S. currency so that it remains at the forefront of technology and offers maximum security against currency counterfeiters. Combined with years of experience in traditional methods of engraving and printing, the fusion of old and new methodologies can result in a three-dimensional design environment that incorporates innovative new technologies and security features for U.S. currency."

Whatever press is used (see next section), each sheet is forced, under extremely high pressure, into the fine engraved lines of a plate to pick up the ink. The backs of the notes are printed with green ink on one day, and the faces are printed with black ink after the ink has cured (dried).

The use of specially formulated fast-drying non-offset ink, developed in the BEP's laboratories, has eliminated the former time-consuming need for tissuing or interleaving between sheets. The inks and distinctive paper used by the BEP in the manufacture of currency are produced under specifications designed to deter counterfeiting and to assure a high-quality product.

The distinctive paper (75 percent cotton and 25 percent linen) used to produce the paper money of the United States has red and blue fibers embedded in it. A security thread, a strip of clear polyester, is embedded in the paper. The thread includes microprinting of the letters USA and the denomination of the note. Another security feature is the micro-engraved UNITED STATES OF AMERICA around the portrait. The microprinting is designed to disrupt counterfeiting by high-quality photocopiers. The redesigned Series 1996 notes feature watermarks, off-center portraits, color-changing ink and other anti-counterfeiting devices.

Types of presses used

In 2011, the BEP uses two different models of presses to print Federal Reserve notes.

Approximately 75 percent of Fiscal Year 2010's currency production was printed on Intaglio-10 presses (I-10) and 25 percent was printed on the Super Orlof Intaglio (SOI) presses. The BEP continues to print much of the paper money by the intaglio process on high-speed sheet-fed presses.

Each of the I-10 presses has four 32-note printing plates and is capable of printing 9,000 sheets per hour.

The introduction of a new generation of press starting in 2005 was in response to an evolving counterfeiting threat. The growth of computer and reprographics technology, and its widespread availability, has enabled almost anyone with access to off-the-shelf hardware and software to produce counterfeit paper money, a crime that was once the purview of crime organizers or skilled printers. Most of the design changes to U.S. paper money introduced since the mid-1990s have been in response to this threat, with frequent design changes—once unthought of—now likely, according to federal officials. The need to keep ahead of the counterfeiters has led the government to incorporate new anti-counterfeiting elements into each new generation of notes. To advance that effort, the BEP has had to introduce new printing presses with capacities unavailable on the I-10 presses.

Installation of state-of-the-art Super Orlof Intaglio printing presses began in 2005 at the BEP headquarters in Washington, D.C. The presses, made by KBA Giori Inc. in Switzerland, can produce 10,000 50-subject sheets per hour though the presses can be configured to print traditional 32-note sheets as well. Other major security note printers around the world

---

The proofs are inked impressions pulled from new printing plates and submitted to Bureau of Engraving and Printing officials for examination and approval before production of notes begins.

use the newer, super-size printing equipment. The older I-10 presses used at the BEP produce 32-subject sheets, with four notes across and eight down, from a single face or back plate.

The new SOI presses have three plates (compared to one on the current presses); a computerized ink-control system that allows for precise control of the amount of ink, thus saving a cost to the BEP; and an electronic inspection system. The SOI presses can handle intricate anti-counterfeiting devices not possible on the BEP's older presses. Both BEP production facilities, in Washington, D.C., and the Western Currency Facility in Fort Worth, Texas, have SOI presses in place.

In June 2009 the BEP began printing some Series 2006 $1 and $20 FRNs on the Super Orlof Intaglio presses at its Washington headquarters and Western Currency Facility in Fort Worth.

COPE Pak

The I-10 and SOI presses can perform only some of the steps needed to produce a finished Federal Reserve note. Overprinting and additional processing is required after the faces and backs of the sheets of notes have been produced.

In June 1985, the BEP began using a system called COPE Pak to streamline the printing, overprinting and cutting operations, as well as the parceling and shrink wrapping phases of the currency making process.

COPE Pak is an acronym for "Currency Overprinting, Processing and Packaging Equipment." Before the acquisition of the COPE Pak equipment, the overprinting, note examining and packaging operations took place in three separate areas of the BEP.

COPE Pak machines reduce the number of times employees must handle the money. The printing process for the COPE Pak machinery begins in the same way as with the previously used COPE machines.

The back of notes printed in 32-subject sheet format are printed first, and after the ink has cured for several days, the face. The sheets are then trimmed, split into two 16-subject sheets. The BEP's Washington, D.C. facility has six COPE presses; three of them are outfitted entirely with automated inspection technology and three are staffed by human examiners. The BEP's Western Currency Facility in Fort Worth, Texas, uses real time, online computer examination equipment to inspect COPE letterpress features on every note. Examiners are not assigned to the seven COPE presses at the Fort Worth plant. Pressmen are, however, responsible for the printing and processing attributes. Fort Worth COPE pressmen continue to pull sheets and straps to examine and verify printing and cutting accuracy.

No matter the inspection system used, the 16-subject sheets are then delivered to the COPE Pak machines for overprinting, examining, counting and packaging. They are fed into the equipment in two 10,000-sheet stacks.

Blowers separate the sheets and suction feet pick up one sheet at a time. Grippers then pull the sheets along the feedboard into the printing cylinders. "Two-sheet detectors," actuated by the excessive thickness of any combined sheets, tell the system to shut down when the suction heads pick up more than one sheet.

At the printing cylinders, the black Federal Reserve Bank seals and letters, plus the green Treasury seals and serial numbers, are applied to the face of the note. Sheets are then collated into stacks of 100. When a stack of 100 sheets accumulates, it is cut lengthwise and widthwise and the stacks of individual notes are fed into a paper bander.

When 10 straps of 100 notes are collated in the carousel, they pass to another paper bander. From this bander, 1,000-note packages are automatically sent on to counting stations where the contents are counted twice if necessary to ensure 100 percent accountability for all the notes processed. The counting stations are automated and the first stage counts every bundle (1,000 notes strapped together); the second counter is activated if there is a miscount. If the second count is correct the bundle proceeds through the system. If the second count is incorrect, the bundle is automatically pushed out of the production line for a manual count. If the bundle is not corrected within minutes, the system automatically stops to wait for the bundle to be reinserted.

Upon being counted, the packages are shrink wrapped and labeled. A label placed on the end of the package identifies the package by denomination, bank and the beginning and ending serial numbers.

Once the notes are inspected, they travel to a rotating carousel with 32 compartments, corresponding to each plate position number on the 32-subject printing plates.

Finally, the shrink-wrapped 1,000-note packages are collated in groups of four in a collating drum and delivered to another shrink-wrapping apparatus, making a finished "brick" of 4,000 notes, ready for shipment to the 12 Federal Reserve Banks. COPE Pak combines into a single streamlined continuum the operations of overprinting (serial numbers, Treasury seals, Federal Reserve seals and bank numbers), inspection, counting, banding and shrink-wrapping, all with automatic mechanical transfer of work from station to station.

If a mechanical problem should occur in the system, a malfunction indicator provides a digital readout, telling the operator which part is malfunctioning. This device can monitor more than 700 functions.

All currency is double overwrapped for greater protection, bar-coded to facilitate accountability and inventory control and is separable into four packages of 1,000 notes to allow easier breakdown and transfer of currency from Federal Reserve District Banks to other, smaller institutions.

Web press

A further step in the direction of advancing the

technological level of the BEP was taken when it awarded a $10.2 million contract to the Hamilton Tool Co. of Hamilton, Ohio, for the construction of a web-fed press for printing U.S. currency.

The prototype 120-foot-long Alexander Hamilton web-fed intaglio press was delivered to BEP head-quarters in Washington, D.C., in September 1991 at a cost of $12.7 million. The BEP began producing the web-fed notes in 1992. The web press only printed the $1 Federal Reserve notes for Series 1988A, 1993 and 1995.

The press used 25.5-inch wide rolls of paper 23,000 to 24,000 feet long and weighing between 950 and 970 pounds. Approximately 400 feet of paper was threaded through the machine during a press run.

The web-fed press printed both sides of the currency paper during a single pass, but not the overprinting on the face of the note. Notes printed on the web-fed press differ slightly from sheet-fed notes.

On web notes, there is a plate number in the lower-right corner of the face of the notes. On the back of the web notes, the plate number appears above the E in ONE, rather than below it as on sheet-fed notes.

The House and Senate Conference Committee on the Treasury, Postal and General Government Appropriations Act of 1997 directed the BEP to resolve performance issues with the press and submit detailed plans for use of the space currently occupied by the web press once it has been removed. According to the House appropriations subcommittee, more than $32 million was spent to "unsuccessfully develop a one-of-a-kind, three-component, web-based currency production system."

The BEP stopped printing notes on the press in late 1995 but asked for more time to consider its options before submitting a report to Congress. In late 1996 the same subcommittee ordered the BEP to immediately suspend development and implementation of the press but no report was submitted to the subcommittee.

The BEP announced on Nov. 19, 1996, that the Bureau would halt development of the press. The machine's departure from the collecting scene was much quieter than when it arrived. The BEP sold the press in 1997 for $105,000 to a lone bidder, who was described as an unidentified "private individual."

Star notes

In the event a finished note is found to be imperfect after it has been overprinted, it is replaced with a "star" note. In design, star notes are exactly like the notes they replace, but they carry an independent series of serial numbers. The star appears after the serial number in place of the suffix letter on Federal Reserve notes. The serial number of the imperfect note that was replaced is not used again in the same numbering sequence.

The average life of a $1 note is about 42 months, the average $5 bill lasts 16 months, a $10 bill typically lasts 18 months, a $20 bill lasts about 24 months, a $50 note typically lasts 55 months and a $100 bill lasts about 89 months. The size of a currency note is approximately 2.61 inches by 6.14 inches and the thickness is .0043 inch. There are 233 new notes to an inch-high stack (not compressed) and 490 equal a pound. A million notes weigh approximately a ton and occupy approximately 42 cubic feet of space (with moderate pressure).

Distribution

After paper money is printed, the BEP ships the currency to the 12 Federal Reserve Banks and its 26 branches. These agencies, in turn, distribute the money to the commercial banking system throughout the country.

Unfit currency exchange and destruction

Exchange of mutilated paper currency

Lawfully held paper currency of the United States that has been mutilated will be exchanged at its face amount if clearly more than one-half of the original whole note remains. Fragments of mutilated currency that are not clearly more than one-half of the original whole note will be exchanged at face value only if the Bureau of Government Financial Operations is satisfied that the missing portions have been totally destroyed. This judgment is based on such evidence of total destruction as is deemed necessary and is final.

No relief will be granted an account of paper currency of the United States that has been totally destroyed.

The public should address all correspondence regarding mutilated currency to the Bureau of Engraving and Printing, MCD/OFM, BEPA, Room 344A, Box 37048, Washington, DC 20013. The package should be sent registered mail and a return receipt requested. This is only for mutilated paper money.

More information about this service is available on the BEP's website **www.moneyfactory.gov**.

Destruction of unfit currency

When paper currency becomes worn and no longer fit for general use, it is withdrawn from circulation, destroyed and replaced by new notes. The worn out notes are destroyed at Federal Reserve banks and branches throughout the country, under procedures prescribed by the Department of the Treasury.

Before being destroyed, the currency is verified as to genuineness, kind, value and number of pieces. One-dollar bills make up the bulk of the currency that is retired because of unfitness.

Silver certificates, United States notes and Federal Reserve notes in all denominations below $500 that are no longer fit for use are verified and destroyed at

Federal Reserve Banks and branches throughout the country, under procedures prescribed by the Department of the Treasury.

Federal Reserve notes in denominations of $500 and above are canceled with distinctive perforations and cut in half lengthwise. The lower halves are shipped to the Department of the Treasury in Washington, D.C., where they are verified and destroyed. The upper halves are retained by the Federal Reserve Banks and destroyed after the banks are notified by the Treasury that the lower halves have been verified.

For more information about U.S. paper money in circulation, visit the Financial Management Services Website **www.fms.treas.gov** and search under that Treasury bureau's publications index for the Treasury bulletin titled "U.S. Currency and Coin Outstanding and in Circulation."

Tours of the BEP

Tours of the BEP's headquarters in Washington, D.C., and the BEP's Fort Worth, Texas, facility are available for the public to view the various operations in the manufacture of currency notes.

The BEP headquarters is located at 14th and C streets Southwest, just south of the Washington Monument and next door to the U.S. Holocaust Museum.

The public tour at the Fort Worth facility is located at the Western Currency Facility, 9000 Blue Mound Road outside Fort Worth.

Admission to each facility is free and the guided tour takes approximately 30 minutes. Obtain current information by visiting the BEP's website at **www. moneyfactory.gov**. At the end of the tour, visitors can browse in the Visitors' Center, which includes items of interest to both numismatists and philatelists.

Products sold by the BEP

The BEP offers a variety of products to the public. A full listing of products with pricing and ordering information is available on the BEP's website, at **www.moneyfactory.gov**. Here are a few of the products available.

➤ Uncut sheets of U.S. paper money: The Bureau offers uncut sheets and partial sheets of U.S. $1, $2, $5, $10, $20 and $50 Federal Reserve notes. The sheets are available in three sizes: full 32-note sheets, half sheets of 16 notes and four-note partial sheets.

➤ Souvenir cards: In 1969, the BEP began engraving and manufacturing souvenir cards in honor of special events. The souvenir cards contain engraved reproductions of various United States paper currency issues. In 2003 the BEP stopped printing souvenir cards and began offering pricier intaglio print cards. The traditional souvenir cards would sell for $6 to $7 while the individual intaglio cards were priced as much as three- to five-times more.

Each intaglio print card features reproductions of portions of U.S. paper money as well as stamps relating to the location of the show or event the intaglio print cards are honoring.

➤ Engraved and lithographed printings: The BEP also produces for sale to the public engraved and lithographed printings of presidential and chief justice portraits, building vignettes, government seals, and miscellaneous printings.

Bureau directors and terms

Spencer Morton Clark	Aug. 22, 1862, to Nov. 17, 1868
George B. McCartee	March 18, 1869, to Feb. 19, 1876
Henry C. Jewell	Feb. 21, 1876, to April 30, 1877
Edward McPherson	May 1, 1877, to Sept. 30, 1878
O.H. Irish	Oct. 1, 1878, to Jan. 27, 1883
Truman N. Burrill	March 30, 1883, to May 31, 1885
Edward O. Graves	June 1, 1885, to June 30, 1889
William M. Meredith	July 1, 1889, to June 30, 1893
Claude M. Johnson	July 1, 1893, to May 10, 1900
William M. Meredith	Nov. 23, 1900, to June 30, 1906
Thomas J. Sullivan	July 1, 1906, to May 4, 1908
Joseph E. Ralph	May 11, 1908, to Oct. 31, 1917
James L. Wilmeth	Dec. 10, 1917, to March 31, 1922
Louis A. Hill	April 1, 1922, to Feb. 14, 1924
Wallace W. Kirby	June 16, 1924, to Dec. 15, 1924
Alvin W. Hall	Dec. 22, 1924, to Dec. 15, 1954
Henry J. Holtzclaw	Dec. 16, 1954, to Oct. 8, 1967
James A. Conlon	Oct. 9, 1967, to July 1, 1977
Seymour Berry	June 30, 1978, to April 6, 1979
Harry R. Clements	July 15, 1979, to Jan. 3, 1983
Robert J. Leuver	Feb. 22, 1983, to April 1, 1988
Peter H. Daly	Aug. 26, 1988, to July 22, 1995

172 - Bureau of Engraving and Printing

Larry E. Rolufs ....July 24, 1995, to Dec. 31, 1997
Thomas A. Ferguson (interim director) ....Jan. 1, 1998, to Dec. 6, 1998
Thomas A. Ferguson ....Dec. 7, 1998, to Dec. 31, 2005
Larry R. Felix..Jan. 11, 2006, to date

7 The Federal Reserve

The Federal Reserve Bank is the United States' central bank, independent within the government yet answerable to the government because the president of the United States appoints the Fed chairman and members of the board of governors, subject to Senate approval, and because the bank is subject to congressional oversight.

A question often asked is whether the Federal Reserve Bank is a government bank or a private bank. It may be best described as a quasi-public bank that sells shares of stock to member private banks.

The Federal Reserve Bank is not a government institution, despite being subject to legislative oversight and appointments; the executive and legislative branches of the federal government have no direct say in the decisions the bank makes.

As for being a private bank, the Federal Reserve's 12 regional banks do sell shares of stocks to private member stocks, but unlike other private banks, the stock shares of the 12 regional banks may not be sold or traded, and the stocks pay fixed dividends.

As the United States' central bank, the Federal Reserve has four fundamental duties:

➤ Conducting the nation's monetary policy by influencing the money and credit conditions in the economy, in pursuit of full employment and stable prices

➤ Supervising and regulating banking institutions to ensure the safety and soundness of the nation's banking and financial system and to protect the credit rights of consumers

➤ Maintaining the stability of the financial system and containing systemic risk that may arise in financial markets

➤ Providing certain financial services to the U.S. government, to the public, to financial institutions and to foreign official institutions, thereby playing a major role in the operation of the nation's payments system

Most important of the Federal Reserve's responsibilities is monetary policy, the means by which the Fed influences the growth of money and credit in the U.S. economy.

When the supply of money grows too rapidly in relation to the economy's ability to produce goods and services, inflation may result. It is a case of too many dollars in the hands of buyers chasing the same amount of goods.

On the other hand, too little growth in the money supply can lead to such problems as recession and unemployment. As the money flow slows down, people have fewer dollars to spend for various goods and services. Businesses, in turn, receive less money for the goods and services they produce and have less to spend for the resources they use.

Through monetary policy, the Federal Reserve tries to avoid either of these extremes.

To do so, the Federal Reserve analyzes the national economy and seeks to influence growth in money and credit that will contribute to stable prices, high employment and growth in the economy.

The Fed can put more money into the economy—actually create money—by buying U.S. Treasury bonds on the open market. The Fed pays broker-dealers of the bonds for the securities. The sellers of the bonds, in turn, deposit the money in various financial institutions. While these financial institutions are required by law to keep a certain percentage of this money on reserve, they are free to loan out the remainder. (In August 2007, the Federal Reserve pumped money into the economy by buying subprime mortgages; the mortgages were a major contributing cause of the recession that started in December 2007.)

A second way in which the Federal Reserve can influence the economy is by raising or lowering the discount rate, the interest rate charged financial institutions when they borrow reserves from the Fed. Discount rate changes can be powerful signals of the direction of monetary policy.

The Federal Reserve can also have a powerful impact on the flow of money and credit by either raising or lowering reserve requirements, the percentage of their deposits that financial institutions must keep on reserve. If the Fed lowers reserve requirements, this can lead to more money being injected into the economy since it frees up funds that were previously set aside. On the other hand, if the Fed raises reserve requirements, it reduces the amount of money that institutions are free to loan out or invest. However, the Fed is cautious about changing reserve requirements and has done so only occasionally because of the dramatic impact it can have on both financial institutions and the economy.

As of December 2006, the reserve requirement was 10 percent on transaction deposits, and there were zero reserves required for time deposits (financial instruments such as certificates of deposits and interest-bearing savings deposits), according to the New York Federal Reserve Bank.

Function of the Federal Reserve System

The Federal Reserve System as it operates today consists of the board of governors in Washington; the 12 Federal Reserve Banks, their branches and other facilities situated throughout the United States; the Federal Open Market Committee; the Federal Advisory Council; the Consumer Advisory Council; the Thrift Institutions Advisory Council; and the member commercial banks, which include all national banks in the United States and any state-chartered banks that have voluntarily joined the Federal Reserve System. Some of these functions are outlined below. For more information visit the Federal Reserve's website at **www.federalreserve.gov**.

Board of Governors

Broad supervisory powers are vested in the board of governors, which has its offices in Washington. The board is composed of seven members appointed by the president of the United States by and with the advice and consent of the Senate. The chairman of the board of governors is, by executive order, a member of the National Advisory Council on International Monetary and Financial Policies.

The board determines general monetary, credit and operating policies for the Federal Reserve System as a whole and formulates the rules and regulations necessary to carry out the purposes of the Federal Reserve Act. The board's principal duties consist of exerting an influence over credit conditions and supervising the Federal Reserve Banks and member banks.

Power to influence credit conditions:

The board is given the power, within statutory limitations, to fix the requirements concerning reserves to be maintained by member banks against deposits and the power to determine the maximum rate of interest that may be paid by member banks on their time deposits (interest-bearing savings deposits) and savings deposits. Another important instrument of credit control is found in open market operations. The members of the board of governors are also members of the Federal Open Market Committee. The board of governors reviews and determines the discount rates charged by the Federal Reserve Banks on their discounts and advances. For the purpose of preventing excessive use of credit for the purchase or carrying of securities, the board is authorized to regulate the amount of credit that may be initially extended and subsequently maintained on any security (with certain exceptions).

Pursuant to the provisions of the Defense Production Act of 1950 and Executive Order 10480 of Aug. 14, 1953, the board prescribes regulations under which the Federal Reserve Banks act as fiscal agents of certain government departments and agencies in guaranteeing loans made by banks and other private financing institutions to finance contracts for the procurement of materials or services that the guaranteeing agencies consider necessary for the national defense.

Supervision of Federal Reserve Banks:

The board is authorized to make examinations of the Federal Reserve Banks, to require statements and reports from such banks, to supervise the issue and retirement of Federal Reserve notes, to require the establishment or discontinuance of branches of Federal Reserve Banks, and to exercise supervision over all relationships and transactions of those banks with foreign banks. The board of governors reviews and follows the examination and supervisory activities of the Federal Reserve Banks with a view to furthering coordination of policies and practices.

Supervision of member banks:

The board has jurisdiction over the admission of state banks and trust companies to membership in the Federal Reserve System, the termination of membership of such banks, the establishment of branches by such banks, and the approval of bank mergers and consolidations where the resulting institution will be a state member bank. It receives copies of condition reports submitted by them to the Federal Reserve Banks. It has power to examine all member banks and the affiliates of member banks and to require condition reports from them. It has authority to require periodic and other public disclosure of information with respect to an equity security of a member state bank that is held by 500 or more persons.

It establishes minimum standards with respect to installation, maintenance and operation of security devices and procedures by member state banks. It has authority to issue cease and desist orders in connection with violations of law or unsafe or unsound banking practices by member state banks and to remove directors or officers of such banks in certain circumstances. It may, in its discretion, suspend member banks from the use of the credit facilities of the Federal Reserve System for making undue use of bank credit for speculative purposes or for any other purpose inconsistent with the maintenance of sound credit conditions.

The board may grant authority to member banks to establish branches in foreign countries or dependencies or insular possessions of the United States, to invest in the stocks of banks or corporations engaged in international or foreign banking, or to invest in foreign banks. It also charters, regulates and supervises certain corporations that engage in foreign or international banking and financial activities.

The board is authorized to issue general regulations permitting interlocking relationships in certain circumstances between member banks and organizations dealing in securities or between member banks and other banks.

Other functions:

Under the Bank Holding Company Act of 1956, the Federal Reserve was given authority to approve the establishment of a bank holding company, among other authorities it has over bank holding companies. Under the Change in Bank Control Act of 1978, the board is required to review other bank acquisitions. Under the Truth in Lending Act, the board is required to prescribe regulations to assure a meaningful disclosure by lenders of credit terms so that consumers will be able to compare more readily the various credit terms available and avoid the uninformed use of credit. The act also regulates issuance of credit cards and liabilities for their unauthorized use.

Under the International Banking Act of 1978, the board has the authority to impose reserve requirements and interest rate ceilings on branches and agencies of foreign banks in the United States, to grant loans to them, to provide them access to Federal Reserve services, and to limit their interstate banking activities. The board also is the rule-making authority for the Equal Credit Opportunity Act, the Home Mortgage Disclosure Act, the Fair Credit Billing Act, and certain provisions of the Federal Trade Commission Act as they apply to banks.

Expenses:

To meet its expenses and pay the salaries of its members and its employees, the board makes semiannual assessments upon the Federal Reserve Banks in proportion to their capital stock and surplus.

Currency issue:

The Federal Reserve System has among its purposes to ensure that the economy has enough currency to meet the public's demand. Paper money and coins are put into or retired from circulation by the Federal Reserve Banks, which use depository institutions as the channel of distribution. The Federal Reserve Banks issue Federal Reserve notes. These notes are obligations of the United States and are a prior lien (a lien that is recorded prior to any other claims) upon the assets of the issuing Federal Reserve Bank. They are issued against a pledge by the Reserve Bank with the Federal Reserve agent of collateral security consisting of gold certificates, paper discounted or purchased by the bank, and direct obligations of the United States.

Other powers:

The Federal Reserve Banks are empowered to act as clearinghouses and as collecting agents for depository institutions in the collection of checks and other instruments.

They are also authorized to act as depositories and fiscal agents of the United States and to exercise other banking functions specified in the Federal Reserve Act.

They perform a number of functions concerning the issue and redemption of United States government securities.

History of the Federal Reserve System

A National Monetary Conference, appointed by Congress in 1908, sought to remedy money crises involving banks in the United States. Sen. Nelson W. Aldrich was chairman.

A recognized depression had occurred in 1907, similar to previous crises in 1837, 1857, 1871 and 1894. The National Monetary Conference was to seek a solution to mitigating or eliminating these recurring dips in the economy.

The result of their efforts was reflected in the Federal Reserve Act, signed Dec. 23, 1913, by President Woodrow Wilson. The basic purpose of the new organization was "to give the country an elastic currency, to provide facilities for discounting commercial paper and to improve supervision of banking."

Founders of the Federal Reserve System believed that the amount of currency and credit would be balanced if issued against real bills, that is, short-term, self-liquidating paper—statutorily defined at 17 CFR 260.11b-6 in section 311(b)(6)—based on commercial, industrial and agricultural transactions. Excessive changes in the domestic price level, they believed, could also be held in check if rules of the international gold standard were faithfully observed. The founders also believed that if the money and

credit system were based on real bills and gold, it would work more or less automatically; there would be no need to "manage" money. Finally, policies could be adapted closely to local conditions, and control by either politicians or Wall Street could be avoided if power were decentralized by regions.

The first decade

As the new Federal Reserve System conducted business during its early existence, the act was amended from time to time primarily in the interest of greater operating efficiency: procedures for electing directors were simplified, larger denomination Federal Reserve notes were provided, trust powers of national banks were broadened and so on.

Amendments were also passed to strengthen the financial structure of the Federal Reserve Banks. Member bank reserves were concentrated in the Federal Reserve Banks, gold was mobilized and provision was made to build up the surplus of Federal Reserve Banks. Some of these measures and the experience gained from a few years of operations enabled the Federal Reserve System to undertake successfully its job of helping to finance World War I.

After the war came inflation and sharp recession. Farmers were particularly hard hit, and changes in the act give a hint of the repercussions on the Federal Reserve System. The number of appointed members of the Federal Reserve Board was increased from five to six, and agricultural interests were given representation on the board. Not long after, the act was amended further to facilitate agricultural financing.

Although action was taken to strengthen the Federal Reserve System generally during the first decade, no major new tool of credit control was added. In 1920, it is true, the Federal Reserve Banks were given authority to impose graduated discount rates on banks that borrowed excessively, but this provision was repealed in 1923. As early as 1916 the board recommended that it be given power to raise reserve requirements in emergencies; this authority was not obtained until 17 years later.

Two early changes that at first glance seem only technical really marked a departure from the strict real-bills principle (an economic theory that when central banks loan money only for "productive" projects, the loans would not be inflationary). In 1916, Federal Reserve Banks were authorized to "make advances for periods not exceeding fifteen days to its member banks on their promissory notes secured by the deposit or pledge of bonds, notes, certificates of indebtedness, or Treasury bills of the United States," or by other securities. The change was made primarily in the interest of operating efficiency, but it actually broke the direct link, so important to founders of the Federal Reserve System, between self-liquidating transactions and the flow of credit.

The next year the relation between real bills and Federal Reserve notes was officially changed. The original act provided that notes must be matched by an equivalent amount of eligible paper. Whenever a Federal Reserve Bank had to issue notes it would get them from the Federal Reserve Agent and deposit eligible paper as collateral. In practice, however, the bank could then cancel its liability for the notes by depositing gold with the Federal Reserve Agent and taking back the eligible paper. The close relationship between real bills and Federal Reserve notes was actually broken because, in essence, notes were matched by gold in addition to eligible paper. In 1917, an amendment to the act turned practice into law by permitting the use of gold as collateral for notes.

The 'new era'

After the first decade came a period of legislative quiet, what might be called the age of "new era" complacency. Confidence in monetary policy as a solution to the economic troubles of the country rose to an all-time peak.

For several years after its organization, the Federal Reserve Board included in its annual reports a section describing legislation passed during the year and another section detailing legislation that it recommended for action. Proposed legislation in one year was likely to be reported as actual legislation

the next. Congress acted promptly on most of these recommendations during the early years of the Federal Reserve System, particularly during World War I.

In the 1920s, the situation was quite different. The section on proposed legislation did not appear in the annual reports for a number of years. No amendments were proposed or enacted for the years 1924 to 1926, and only minor changes were made in most other years. Only one of the proposed changes was enacted in 1928, none in 1929.

The board's list of recommended legislation in 1929 included items like these: permit officers of mutual savings banks to be Class B or C directors of Federal Reserve Banks, clarify the section of the act that describes procedures for counting ballots in elections of Federal Reserve Bank directors, make it a federal offense to rob a Federal Reserve Bank or member bank and so on.

All this time, pressures were building within the economy that were to show that the 1920s were not so calm as this legislative status quo might suggest.

Depression and emergency

The early 1930s were as hectic as the 1920s were placid. Within five years, the act was amended 23 times, with most of the action confined to two years—1933 and 1935.

Business activity was already well on its way downward in 1930. During that year a few minor changes were made in the act along lines recommended in the board's annual report for the year before. No amendments were made in 1931.

It was not until 1932 that the act was changed materially. In that year and the one following, the Great Depression hit the banking system hard. Banks were caught by three developments: panicky withdrawals of currency, conversion of deposits and currency into gold and declining values on which bank assets were based. The result was a severe liquidity crisis in 1932 and a banking crisis in 1933.

In this atmosphere of emergency, reluctant permission was given to temporary deviations from some of the principles on which the original act was based. The first Glass–Steagall Act, passed early in 1932, reduced further the relationship between real bills and Federal Reserve notes. Collateral requirements, first altered in 1917, were relaxed again, this time because they stood in the way of an easy-money policy. The Federal Reserve wanted to meet the public's demand for liquidity and to buy more government securities to help stimulate the economy. However, the Federal Reserve System was hamstrung by collateral requirements. Federal Reserve Banks were required to hold 100 percent collateral, in the form of eligible paper and gold, against their notes. They also had to hold gold reserves equal to 40 percent of their note liabilities and 35 percent of their deposit liabilities. Any gold used as collateral against notes could also be used as reserve against notes, but not as reserve against deposits. With the amount of commercial paper shrinking with commerce and gold disappearing into private hoards, there just was not enough to permit the necessary expansion of the money supply.

In order to break this logjam, Congress authorized Federal Reserve Banks to use government securities, in addition to eligible paper and gold, as collateral for Federal Reserve notes. The grant of authority was temporary, but after a number of extensions, it was finally made permanent in 1945.

The year 1932 also saw a further break in the link between real bills and credit. The public was seeking greater liquidity and safety by drawing out paper currency and converting to gold; the banks, in turn, sought liquidity by calling loans and selling assets on an already depressed market. A vicious spiral developed, feeding upon itself and making banks weaker and weaker. Banks could not get enough funds from Federal Reserve to break out of this spiral because they did not have enough eligible paper to discount (discounting was a standard bank practice; a bank might loan a customer $1,000 if the customer signed a note to pay the bank $1,100 at a specified future date; in effect, the bank was discounting the customer's note by the customer less than the note's value of $1,100).

So, the Glass–Steagall Act authorized Federal Reserve Banks to make loans to member banks on notes "secured to the satisfaction of such Federal Reserve Banks." However, these loans were to be made only "in exceptional and exigent circumstances," the discount rate was to be at least 1 percent higher than the regular rate, and the authority was granted only for about a year. The real-bills principle was dying, but it was dying hard. After two extensions, a significant break with the real-bills principle came with the Banking Act of 1935, which removed most of the requirement "that advances be made only in exceptional and exigent circumstances and to member banks whose other means of obtaining accommodation from Federal Reserve Banks were exhausted," according to Milton Friedman and Anna Jacobson Schwartz in *A Monetary History of the United States 1867-1960*. The 1935 act also reduced the interest rate differential to 0.5 percent and made this provision a permanent part of the act.

1933 crisis

The year 1933 was even more hectic. On March 9, five days after the new administration took office and in the midst of the banking holiday, the Emergency Banking Act of 1933 passed through the complete legislative process in a single day. E.A. Goldenweiser relates that the General Counsel of the Federal Reserve Board prepared a draft of the law in one night. Among its many provisions, the Emergency Banking Act amended the Federal Reserve Act in several respects. In an effort to make currency more readily available, Congress broadened the powers of the Federal Reserve Banks to issue Federal Reserve Bank notes. In order to facilitate access to Federal Reserve Bank credit, it liberalized the 1932 provision authorizing loans to member banks on paper previously considered ineligible, and gave the Federal Reserve Banks power to make advances to individuals, partnerships and corporations on notes secured by government obligations.

Shortly after this, Congress passed the Thomas Inflation Amendment. This law contained several measures affecting the Federal Reserve—especially provision for direct purchases of government securities from the Treasury—but actually amended the Federal Reserve Act, as such, in only one major respect. Curiously, this particular provision was anti-inflationary, not inflationary; it permitted the Federal Reserve Board to change reserve requirements if "an emergency existed by reason of credit expansion."

Up to this point, action was essentially of an emergency nature. The Banking Act of 1933, however (passed, incidentally, just about when the Depression hit bottom), undertook to deal with some of the basic causes of the situation.

In the first place, the Banking Act of 1933 struck at speculative excesses to which banks had contributed. Banks were required to divorce themselves from security affiliates and to correct certain other undesirable practices that had developed during the 1920s. Behind some of these measures were increasing doubts about the real-bills principle as a means of channeling credit into "productive" uses. Thus one provision required the Reserve Banks to keep informed as to the uses that banks were making of Federal Reserve credit so as to avoid "undue use ... for the speculative carrying of or trading in securities, real estate or commodities, or for any other purposes inconsistent with the maintenance of sound credit conditions."

Meanwhile the idea of regional autonomy was also being reassessed. Ten years earlier, Federal Reserve Banks had discovered that their open-market operations, undertaken initially to bolster earnings, had noticeable effects on the money market. So in order to coordinate their activities, they set up an informal committee. The second Glass–Steagall Act, more formally known as the Banking Act of 1933, gave statutory basis to this committee by creating the Federal Open Market Committee and authorized the Federal Reserve Board to prescribe regulations for its conduct. No member of the board was a member of the Federal Open Market Committee, however, and any Reserve Bank could still decline to go along with the committee's policies. (The Federal Open Market Committee remains an integral part of the Federal Reserve, though revisions were made involving the committee in the Banking Act of 1935 and again in 1942.)

In the case of dealings with foreign central banks, the change was more abrupt. The Federal Reserve Bank of New York, which handled the financial operations involved, had carried on most of the negotiations on foreign matters. The Banking Act of 1933 changed that, by providing that "no officer or other representative of any Federal Reserve Bank shall conduct negotiations of any kind with the officers or representatives of any foreign bank or banker without first obtaining the permission of the Federal Reserve Board."

Among the many provisions of the Banking Act designed to strengthen the banking system, perhaps the most outstanding was deposit insurance. Although this measure related only indirectly to the Federal Reserve, Congress included it in the Federal Reserve Act. It remained there after a major revision in 1935 and was not removed until 1950 when it became the subject of a separate law.

The government called in virtually all gold in 1934. Actually, most of the rules of the gold standard as a guide for monetary policy had not been honored for years, but no indication of this can be seen in the Federal Reserve Act. Even in 1934 about the only hint that something had happened was the substitution of the words "gold certificates" for the word "gold" wherever it occurred. If we were to judge by the act alone, gold would seem to occupy today essentially the same position it did in 1913.

During the same year, however, two other developments reflected a widening concept of the Federal Reserve System's responsibilities. One was the grant of authority for Federal Reserve Banks to make working capital loans to existing industrial and commercial businesses unable to get credit through usual channels. This marked a further departure from the traditional idea that the Federal Reserve Banks should be simply bankers' banks. The other development had nothing to do with the Federal Reserve Act itself, but because it introduced a new principle of credit control it deserves special mention. It was a provision of the Securities Exchange Act, which authorized the Federal Reserve Board to prescribe margins for stock purchases and sales. This was the first of the selective credit regulations and the permanent tool of policy.

Major revision

By 1935, business was on its way up again. Compared with 1933, unemployment was down by 2 million and industrial production was up 25 percent. All the time the economy was recovering from the Depression, ideas were fermenting. The result was the most comprehensive reappraisal and revision of the Federal Reserve Act in all its history.

The Banking Act of 1935 contained many important provisions that need not be discussed in detail; it clarified many sections of the Federal Reserve Act and generally strengthened the banking system. As has been mentioned, it marked a significant break with the real-bills doctrine. It also marked a further departure from the principle of regional decentralization. The organization of the Federal Reserve System as we know it dates from 1935.

The Federal Reserve Board became the board of governors of the Federal Reserve System. Congress provided terms of four years for the chairmanship and vice-chairmanship (both officials being eligible for reappointment), lengthened terms of board members from 12 to 14 years, and removed the secretary of the Treasury and the comptroller of the currency (who had been serving as ex-officio members) from the board.

The makeup of the Federal Open Market Committee was changed even more drastically. The Banking Act of 1933 had set up a committee of 12 members, one from each Federal Reserve Bank. The Banking Act of 1935 reduced representation of the Federal Reserve Banks to five individuals and included all seven members of the board of governors.

Changes in powers went in the same direction as changes in organization. Decisions of the Federal Open Market Committee were made binding on all Federal Reserve Banks. The board of governors was given power to change reserve requirements, within limits, without the necessity of declaring an emergency or securing approval of the president of the United States. Federal Reserve Banks were required to establish their discount rates every 14 days or more often if deemed necessary by the board of governors; this meant that the rate would come up for formal review and determination more frequently.

After 1935

The repairs of the early 1930s put the Federal Reserve Act in good working order. It has, in fact, weathered war and inflation, prosperity and recession without another major overhaul. But this is not to say that Federal Reserve operations have been standing still. For the most part, the Federal Reserve System has been able to adapt and update its techniques within the existing framework of the Federal Reserve Act.

The recession of 1937 to 1938 passed with no noticeable repercussions on the act. Then came Munich, Poland, Dunkirk and Pearl Harbor. Congress made several changes to facilitate war financing. It gave the Federal Reserve power to buy limited amounts of securities direct from the Treasury and exempted war-loan accounts from reserve requirements, a temporary wartime measure. To ease reserve positions, Congress reduced the gold certificate backing required against Federal Reserve notes and deposits to 25 percent. Without changing the act, the president of the United States gave the Federal Reserve selective controls over consumer credit. The purpose was to fight inflation and help divert resources to military production. This executive order expired in 1947.

After the war, the Federal Reserve continued the wartime policy of supporting the government securities market. The board of governors, concerned with the inability of the Federal Reserve System to restrain inflation and support securities prices at the same time, suggested additional powers—either new kinds of reserve requirements or an across-the-board increase in ordinary reserve requirements. Congress granted the board authority to raise requirements above regular limits in 1948. The provision was temporary, however, and expired about a year later.

When fighting broke out in Korea in the early 1950s, the Federal Reserve System was given selective controls over consumer and real estate credit. As in World War II, selective controls were instituted by executive order without changing the act. The board requested controls on a permanent, stand-by basis but Congress did not comply.

In 1951, the Federal Reserve again sharpened its tools without legislative action. It negotiated an accord with the Treasury that ended the Fed's long practice of supporting government bond interest rates. Since 1951, the Federal Reserve has remained independent and pursued a course of using open market operations to support its monetary policy goals.

Legislative changes in the act since 1953, as in the preceding 18 years, have been relatively minor. Among them was the addition of more effective regulation of bank holding companies. Certain sections regarding real estate loans by national banks were changed. In 1954, Federal Reserve Banks were permitted to pay out notes of other Reserve Banks, thus eliminating another vestige of the old idea of regional autonomy. In 1958, authority for Reserve Banks to make commercial and industrial loans under Section 13b of the Federal Reserve Act was terminated by the Small Business Investment Act, effective Aug. 21, 1959. In 1959, Congress passed legislation affecting reserve requirements. Vault cash may be counted as legal reserves, the central reserve city classification was terminated and the board was given broader authority in reclassifying banks for reserve purposes.

In 1958, though, a new problem emerged to confront the Federal Reserve System, one that had lain dormant for many years. That problem was a persistent deficit in the United States balance of payments. The United States was spending more abroad for imports, investments and military and economic aid than it received for exports of goods and services and for other transactions. One result was a substantial outflow of gold.

The Federal Reserve System reacted to this new problem on several fronts, mostly within the framework of the existing Act. In 1961, the so-called "bills only" policy of the Federal Open Market Committee was discontinued. Under "bills only," Federal Reserve System purchases and sales of securities had been confined primarily to short-term Treasury bills, but the Federal Open Market Committee now authorized the Federal Reserve to purchase securities that took longer to mature than the short-term Treasury bills.

The committee hoped "to encourage bank credit and monetary expansion while avoiding direct downward pressures on short-term interest rates and thus moderate outflows of short-term capital attracted by higher interest rates abroad."

In 1962, the Federal Open Market Committee authorized open market transactions in foreign currencies to "moderate and offset short-term pressures on the dollar in the foreign exchange markets." One technique devised by the Federal Reserve System to gain foreign funds to implement these transactions was the "swaps" arrangements first negotiated in August 1962 with several foreign central banks and with the Bank for International Settlements.

Congress also, for balance-of-payments reasons, amended the Federal Reserve Act in 1962 "to exempt for three years deposits of foreign governments and certain foreign institutions from regulation by the Board of Governors as to rates of interest that member banks may pay on time deposits," or instruments such as interest-bearing savings deposits or certificates of deposit.

Finally, in a 1963 measure unrelated to the balance of payments, the Federal Reserve Act was amended to authorize Federal Reserve System issuance of $1 and $2 Federal Reserve notes. This legislation was aimed at eliminating Treasury silver certificates of those denominations and thus making "monetary silver available for coinage."

Since 1963, several changes have been made in the way the international and domestic money system operates. In 1965, Congress passed legislation to repeal the remaining requirement for 25 percent gold backing of commercial banks' deposits at Federal Reserve banks, freeing about $5 billion of the country's gold stock for additional sale to dollar-holding foreign governments and for future growth of the domestic money supply.

That same year, the Coinage Act of 1965 was passed, eliminating most silver in United States coins. Despite these measures, the gold and silver draining out of Treasury continued at a steady, debilitating rate.

In 1967, then, President Johnson signed a bill authorizing the eventual end of the redemption of silver certificates with silver bullion, setting a June 24, 1968, deadline for their redemption. Congress removed reserve requirements for Federal Reserve notes, United States notes and Series 1890 Treasury notes in March 1968.

In 1974, the Federal Reserve System joined with the Treasury in putting into effect regulations prohibiting the export, melting or treating of the cent to help offset a cent shortage.

With the International Banking Act of 1978, the Federal Reserve Board gained the authority to impose reserve requirements and interest rate ceilings on branches and agencies of foreign banks in the United States. The act also gave the board the authority to grant loans to foreign banks in the United States and to limit interstate banking activities.

During the 1970s, double-digit inflation resulted from a rise in producer and consumer prices, soaring oil prices and a federal deficit that more than doubled.

The Federal Reserve took a number of steps, called "painful in the short term" but "successful overall in bringing double-digit inflation under control," according to **www.federalreserveeducation.org**,

Additional banking changes were made starting in the 1980s that involved the Federal Reserve.

"The Monetary Control Act of 1980 required the Fed to price its financial services competitively against private sector providers and to establish reserve requirements for all eligible financial institutions," according to federalreserveeducation.org. "The act marks the beginning of a period of modern banking industry reforms. Following its passage, interstate banking proliferated, and banks began offering interest-paying accounts and instruments to attract customers from brokerage firms. Barriers to insurance activities, however, proved more difficult to circumvent. Nonetheless, momentum for change was steady, and by 1999 the Gramm-Leach-Bliley Act was passed, in essence, overturning the Glass–Steagall Act of 1933 and allowing banks to offer a menu of financial services, including investment banking and insurance."

The nation, and the Federal Reserve, have faced multiple economic crises and challenges since the mid-1980s.

The stock market crash of Oct. 19, 1987, prompted the Federal Reserve chairman to state, "The Federal Reserve, consistent with its responsibilities as the nation's central bank, affirmed today its readiness to serve as a source of liquidity to support the economic and financial system." Following the crash, economic growth characterized the 1990s, ending finally in the short recession of 2001, which ended in November of that year.

"In response to the bursting of the 1990s stock market bubble in the early years of the decade, the Fed lowered interest rates rapidly," according to federalreserveeducation.org. "Throughout the 1990s, the Fed used monetary policy on a number of occasions including the credit crunch of the early 1990s and the Russian default on government securities to keep potential financial problems from adversely affecting the real economy. The decade was marked by generally declining inflation and the longest peacetime economic expansion in our country's history."

In the days that followed the Sept. 11, 2001, terrorist attacks, the Federal Reserve "lowered interest rates and loaned more that $45 billion to financial institutions in order to provide stability to the U.S. economy," according to federalreserveeducation.org. "By the end of September, Fed lending had returned to pre-September 11 levels and a potential liquidity crunch had been averted."

The Federal Reserve's greatest challenges since the Great Depression, however, loomed.

The rise in home ownership in the first decade of the 21st century, made possible by expanded access to credit and low mortgage rates, created a housing boom. "The housing boom got a boost from increased securitization of mortgages—a process in which mortgages were bundled together into securities that were traded in financial markets," according to federalreserveeducation.org. "Securitization of riskier mortgages expanded rapidly, including subprime mortgages made to borrowers with poor credit records."

In 2006, house prices faltered and began to slide, triggering an economic crisis that continues into 2011. Short-term loan rates began to rise and credit tightened, slowing the pace of the economy. People started spending less; businesses accelerated layoffs and froze new hirings. In December 2007, the United States entered a recession, although it was not immediately clear at that point. Major financial institutions began to fail, among them the savings and loan Washington Mutual and the investment bank Lehman Brothers in the fall of 2008, worsening the recession as the financial panic intensified.

"As short-term markets froze, the Federal Reserve expanded its own collateralized lending to financial institutions to ensure that they had access to the critical funding needed for day-to-day operations," according to federalreserveeducation.org. "In March 2008, the Federal Reserve created two programs to provide short-term secured loans to primary dealers similar to discount-window loans provided to banks. Conditions in these markets improved considerably in 2009."

Still, the crisis worsened in other areas. "The possible failure of the investment bank Bear Stearns early in 2008 carried the risk of a domino effect that would have severely disrupted financial markets," according to federalreserveeducation.org. "In order to contain the damage, the Federal Reserve provided non-recourse loans to the bank JP Morgan Chase to facilitate its purchase of certain Bear Stearns assets. Following the collapse of the investment bank Lehman Brothers, financial panic threatened to spread to several other key financial institutions, potentially leading to a cascade of failures and a meltdown of the global financial system. The Federal Reserve provided secured loans to the giant insurance company American International Group (AIG) because of its central role guaranteeing financial instruments."

The Federal Reserve also "increased the availability of one- and three-month discount-window loans to banks," according to federalreserveeducation.org.

The economic crisis resulted in the banking industry in the United States facing its worse crisis since the Great Depression, prompting extraordinary measures by the Federal Reserve. Notes federalreserveeducation.org: "In the spring of 2009, the Federal Reserve, in conjunction with other federal regulatory agencies, conducted an exhaustive and unprecedented review of the financial condition of the 19 largest U.S. banks. This included a 'stress test' that measured how well these banks could weather a bad economy over the next two years. Banks that didn't have enough of a capital cushion to protect them from loan losses under the most adverse economic scenario were required to raise new money from the private sector or accept federal government funds from the Troubled Asset Relief Program."

In addition, "In response to the economic crisis, the Federal Reserve's policy making body, the Federal Open Market Committee, slashed its target for the federal funds rate over the course of more than a year, bringing it nearly to zero by December 2008," notes federalreserveeducation.org. "This is the lowest level for federal funds in over 50 years and effectively is as low as this key rate can go. Cutting the federal funds rate helped lower the cost of borrowing for households and businesses on mortgages and other loans.

"To stimulate the economy and further lower borrowing costs, the Federal Reserve turned to unconventional policy tools. It purchased $300 billion in longer-term Treasury securities, which are used as benchmarks for a variety of longer-term interest rates, such as corporate bonds and fixed-rate mortgages. To support the housing market, the Federal Reserve authorized the purchase of $1.25 trillion in mortgage-backed securities guaranteed by agencies such as Freddie Mac and Fannie Mae and about $175 billion of mortgage agency longer-term debt. These Federal Reserve purchases have reduced mortgage interest rates, making home purchases more affordable."

Critics of the Federal Reserve

The strength wielded by the Federal Reserve, and its chairman, plus its relative freedom to control the money supply and interest rates without congressional curbs, gives it considerable power over the economy. That power has led critics of the Federal Reserve to question whether the Fed should have that much power or whether the Federal Reserve should exist at all.

Criticism has followed the Federal Reserve since its creation in 1913, with the origins of criticism to a central banking system dating to the birth of the United States. Thomas Jefferson, James Madison, and Andrew Jackson all were distrustful of a powerful central bank. Jackson's distrust of the Second Bank of the United States and the actions he took while president probably helped create the Panic of 1837, resulting in the period known as the Hard Times.

Criticism of the Federal Reserve takes many forms. Both mainstream economists and conspiracy theorists are critical of the Fed's actions and even its very existence. The criticism seems to have intensified in the 21st century; a major feature of the 2010 general election in the United States included objections to the various steps the government and the Federal Reserve took during the economic crisis that began in 2006.

A new political entity, billed as the tea party or Tea Party, sprang up during the campaigns for the 2010 election. Members of the movement generally seek smaller government, reduced federal spending and elimination of the Federal Reserve.

A prominent critic of the Federal Reserve for decades has been Rep. Ron Paul, R-Texas. A strict constitutionalist and libertarian by philosophy, and judged the most conservative member of Congress by some rankings, Paul published a book in 2009 titled *End the Fed.*

Rep. Paul, who has sought the U.S. presidency twice, gained additional power after the 2010 election placed the House of Representatives under the control of the Republican Party, whose membership now included representatives who also held allegiance to the tea party. He was named chairman of the House Financial Services Subcommittee on Domestic Monetary Policy, placing him in a position to conduct hearings on the Federal Reserve. As this book went to press in mid-2011, no such hearings had been scheduled.

Sources of information

Federal Reserve records and information may be obtained from the following sources.

Public Affairs Office

The Public Affairs Office issues press releases, speeches, testimony and other announcements to the press and the public. It also responds to inquiries from the press and the public about Federal Reserve Board meetings, availability of special announcements, testimony, speeches and statistical releases; bank holding company and other banking announcements; dates of Federal Open Market Committee (FOMC) meetings; and release dates for FOMC minutes and the Beige Book.

Contact the Public Affairs Office at (202) 452-2955 between 9:00 a.m. and 5:00 p.m., Monday through Friday.

Federal Reserve Board website

The board's website, at **www.federalreserve.gov**, contains statistics, documents, and information that originate at the board and the Federal Reserve Banks. The board's site also has direct links to the sites of each of the Federal Reserve Banks, the Federal Financial Institutions Examination Council, other federal banking regulators, and certain foreign central banks.

A search function permits custom searches for documents. The website also includes a number of links to other financial entities, including the individual Federal Reserve Banks, the Federal Deposit Insurance Corporation, the Department of the Treasury and foreign central banks.

Freedom of Information Office

The FOI Office maintains and furnishes several types of documents, including public information letters, Federal Reserve regulatory letters, comment letters on regulatory proposals, legal interpretations, administrative letters, minutes of board meetings, index of board actions, open meeting memoranda, transcripts of Federal Open Market Committee meetings and conference calls, and CRA performance evaluations.

FOIA requests may be submitted in writing to the Freedom of Information Office, Board of Governors of the Federal Reserve System, 20th Street and Constitution Avenue Northwest, Washington, DC 20551; sent by facsimile to the Freedom of Information Office, (202) 872-7565; or submitted electronically. A Federal Reserve form is available online at **www.federalreserve.gov/generalinfo/foia/ efoia/efoiaform.cfm**.

For information about the status of a FOIA request or questions about the FOIA process, contact the FOIA Service Center by calling (202) 452-3684. The FOIA Service Center is open from 9:00 a.m. to 5:00 p.m., Monday through Friday.

National Technical Information Service (NTIS)

NTIS provides several series of Federal Reserve data, generally in electronic format, including Bank Credit, Banking Reserves, Bank Structure Files, International Financial Statistics, Money Stock, Survey of Consumer Finances, selected Bank Holding Company Report Forms, and the Report of Condition and Income. Requesters may obtain the current catalog and price list of Federal Reserve data distributed by NTIS on the NTIS Banking and Financial website. The website is **www.ntis.gov.**

Requesters also may call toll free (888) 584-8332 or write to U.S. Department of Commerce, Technology Administration, National Technical Information Service, 5301 Shawnee Road, Alexandria, VA 22312.

Federal Reserve Board Governors

Ben S. Bernanke, Chairman
Janet L. Yellen, Vice Chair
Kevin M. Warsh
Elizabeth A. Duke
Daniel K. Tarullo
Sara Bloom Raskin

The president nominates the seven members of the Federal Reserve Board and they are confirmed by the Senate. A full term is 14 years. One term begins every two years, on Feb. 1 of even-numbered years. A member who serves a full term may not be reappointed. A member who completes an unexpired portion of a term may be reappointed. All terms end on their statutory date regardless of the date on which the member enters office.

The chairman and the vice chairman of the board are named by the president from among the members and are confirmed by the Senate. They serve a term of four years.

A member's term on the board is not affected by his or her status as chairman or vice chairman.

Federal Reserve Districts

Federal Reserve districts are arranged roughly geographically from east to west. See the Paper Money chapter for additional information on Federal Reserve identifiers used on Federal Reserve notes.

Boston
New York
Philadelphia
Cleveland
Richmond
Atlanta
Chicago
St. Louis
Minneapolis
Kansas City
Dallas
San Francisco

**Federal Reserve
Bank of Boston**
600 Atlantic Ave.
Boston, MA 02210-2204
(617) 973-3000
Website **www.bos.frb.org**
The Boston Fed serves the First Federal Reserve District, which encompasses the six New England states: Connecticut (excluding Fairfield County), Massachusetts, Maine, New Hampshire, Rhode Island and Vermont.

**Federal Reserve
Bank of New York**
33 Liberty St.
New York, NY 10045
(212) 720-5000 or (646) 720-5000
Website **www.newyorkfed.org**
The New York Fed has supervisory jurisdiction over the Second Federal Reserve District, which encompasses New York, the 12 northern counties of New Jersey, Fairfield County in Connecticut, Puerto Rico and the Virgin Islands. The New York Reserve Bank has one branch office in Buffalo, N.Y., which provides central banking services to the 14 western counties of the state. Additionally, two regional offices are located in Utica, N.Y., and East Rutherford, N.J.

**Federal Reserve
Bank of Philadelphia**
Ten North Independence Mall W.
Philadelphia, PA 19106-1574
(215) 574-6000
Website **www.philadelphiafed.org**
The Philadelphia Fed serves all of Pennsylvania except the extreme western portion, all of Delaware, and southern New Jersey. It has no branch offices.

**Federal Reserve
Bank of Cleveland**
1455 E. Sixth St.

Cleveland, OH 44114
(216) 579-2000
Website **www.clevelandfed.org**
The Federal Reserve Bank of Cleveland, including its branch offices in Cincinnati and Pittsburgh, and its check-processing center in Columbus, serves the Fourth Federal Reserve District, which encompasses Ohio, western Pennsylvania, eastern Kentucky, and the northern panhandle of West Virginia.

Federal Reserve Bank of Richmond
701 E. Byrd St.
Richmond, VA 23219-6105
(804) 697-8000
Website **www.richmondfed.org**
The Federal Reserve Bank of Richmond was incorporated May 18, 1914, and serves the Fifth Federal Reserve District, which consists of the District of Columbia, Maryland, Virginia, North Carolina, South Carolina and most of West Virginia. In addition to its headquarters in Richmond, Va., the Richmond Fed has branch offices in Baltimore and Charlotte, N.C., as well as two specialized check-processing centers located in Charleston, W.Va., and Columbia, S.C.

Federal Reserve Bank of Atlanta
1000 Peachtree St. N.E.
Atlanta, GA 30309-4470
(404) 498-8500
Website **www.frbatlanta.org**
Atlanta Fed staff examine banking institutions in Alabama, Florida, Georgia and parts of Louisiana, Mississippi and Tennessee—the states that make up the Sixth Federal Reserve District. It has six facilities—Atlanta, Birmingham, Jacksonville, Miami, Nashville and New Orleans.

Federal Reserve Bank of Chicago
230 S. LaSalle St.
Chicago, IL 60604
(312) 322-5322
Website **www.chicagofed.org**
The Chicago Fed serves the Seventh Federal Reserve District, an economically diverse region with strong manufacturing, service and agricultural sectors. Situated in the heart of the Midwest, the district includes all of Iowa and most of Illinois, Indiana, Michigan and Wisconsin.

Federal Reserve Bank of St. Louis
Broadway and Locust streets
St. Louis, MO 63102
(314) 444-8444
Website **www.stlouisfed.org**
The Eighth Federal Reserve District consists of all

of Arkansas and portions of Illinois, Indiana, Kentucky, Mississippi, Missouri and Tennessee and three branch offices in Little Rock, Ark., Louisville, Ky., and Memphis, Tenn.

Federal Reserve Bank of Minneapolis
90 Hennepin Ave.
Minneapolis, MN 55401
(612) 204-5000
Website **www.minneapolisfed.org**
The Minneapolis Fed, with one branch in Helena, Montana, serves the Ninth Federal Reserve District. The district encompasses Minnesota, Montana, North Dakota, South Dakota, 26 counties in northwestern Wisconsin and the Upper Peninsula of Michigan.

Federal Reserve Bank of Kansas City
1 Memorial Drive
Kansas City, MO 64198-0001
(800) 333-1010
Website **www.kansascityfed.org**
The Federal Reserve Bank of Kansas City serves depository institutions and the public in Colorado, Kansas, Nebraska, Oklahoma, Wyoming, northern New Mexico and western Missouri. Helping to take care of this large area—the Tenth Federal Reserve District—are branches located at Denver, Oklahoma City and Omaha, Neb.

Federal Reserve Bank of Dallas
2200 N. Pearl St.
Dallas, TX 75201-2272
(214) 922-6000
Website **www.dallasfed.org**
The Dallas Fed serves the Eleventh Federal Reserve District, which encompasses approximately 350,000 square miles and is composed of the state of Texas, northern Louisiana and southern New Mexico. Its branch offices are located in El Paso, Houston and San Antonio, Texas.

Federal Reserve Bank of San Francisco
101 Market St.
San Francisco, CA 94105-1579
(415) 974-2000
Website **www.frbsf.org**
The San Francisco Fed serves the Twelfth Federal Reserve District, which includes the nine Western states—Alaska, Arizona, California, Hawaii, Idaho, Nevada, Oregon, Utah, and Washington—plus Guam, American Samoa and the Northern Mariana Islands, and is the largest district, covering 1.3 million square miles, or 35 percent of the nation's area. Branch offices of the San Francisco Bank are located in Los Angeles, Portland, Salt Lake City and Seattle.

8 U.S. Paper Money

Pre-federal paper money

When the Massachusetts Bay Colony financed a military expedition to Canada in 1690 by issuing bills of credit paper money, the notes became the first authorized paper money to be issued by a government in the Western world. Other military campaigns and various public works/services were financed by other Colonies with similar bills of credit. The use of paper money spread throughout the British Colonies even though the crown placed strict limits on what paper money could be issued. Colonial governors who refused to authorize a paper money issue faced public disfavor (Colonial legislatures would sometimes withhold or reduce the governor's salary until he relented and authorized a note issue) and added to the growing public dissatisfaction with British rule. The crown's efforts to repress Colonial notes were a major contributing factor to the Revolutionary War, writes Eric P. Newman, one of the leading experts in early American paper money.

As the American Revolution began in 1775, the states also issued money to cover their governmental and military expenditures. Some of these notes carried messages freighted with propaganda, like the Maryland issue of July 25, 1775, which depicted George III trampling on the Magna Charta while setting fire to an American city and American Liberty trampling on slavery while backed by a large army.

Beginning in the middle of 1775, the Continental Congress issued paper money—Continental Currency—to pay for the initial costs of the Revolution. The Continental Congress asked the states to redeem the currency, but most states were preoccupied with the need to support their own military activities; consequently, taxes were neglected.

The English forbade the circulation of the Continental Currency in areas they occupied and attempted to undermine public confidence in it in other areas, often counterfeiting the money.

By 1780, economic circumstances had combined to reduce Continental Currency to one-fortieth of its original face value in specie, and the Continental Congress ceased printing the paper money. This early experiment with a federal paper money was such a failure that the Constitution of 1787 forbade states to issue paper money and did not grant the federal government authority to do so either. Nonetheless, paper money would begin to circulate not long after the Constitution was ratified.

The federal government loosened sanctions against paper money when it authorized the Bank of North America in 1781, which began issuing notes. Although states were constitutionally forbidden to issue their own money, a large number of state-chartered banks circumvented this problem by issuing bank notes as private entities, which were not expressly restrained by the Constitution. Maybe the most important of the early institutions was the Bank of the United States, chartered by Congress in 1791 and considered the first attempt at a national bank. A national bank was not universally embraced by the government, however, and the Bank of the United States' charter was permitted to lapse in 1811.

When the War of 1812 began, the U.S. government again found itself being forced to borrow money. In 1812, Congress began issuing Treasury notes to cover short-term loans. Five series of these notes were authorized for issue during the war, between 1812 and 1815, in denominations ranging from $3 to $1,000. The notes were not legal tender, but were receivable for all public dues and payable to public creditors. All notes under $100 were payable to the bearer on demand. The $5 notes did not bear interest.

By 1816, Congress established the Second Bank of the United States, granting the new institution a charter until 1836. The fight over the ultimately unsuccessful effort to renew the bank's charter in 1836 helped trigger a national economic crisis called the Hard Times. The crisis led the federal government to issue interest-bearing Treasury $50, $100, $500 and $1,000 notes in a series of eight acts passed between Oct. 12, 1837, and Jan. 28, 1847. None of these notes circulated as money, however. All are rare since most were redeemed for their interest.

In the meantime, state-chartered banks proliferated through the first half of the 19th century, though many of the institutions were not financially secure. Although these obsolete bank notes are commonly called "broken-bank notes," not all banks that issued this currency failed. Some of the issuers successfully liquidated and others converted into national banks.

During the period leading up to the Civil War, paper money had been produced by such diverse concerns as private banks, railroads, insurance companies, mining companies, pharmacies and other merchants.

A final series of interest-bearing Treasury notes was authorized starting with the Act of Dec. 23, 1857, in the denominations of $100, $500 and $1,000. Additional Treasury notes were issued under the Act of Dec. 17, 1860, and the Act of March 2, 1861. All of these notes are rare.

The constitutionality of the Treasury notes issued between 1812 and 1861 was an ever-present topic in Congress. Most interest-bearing notes bore interest at 5 or 6 percent and were payable after two years. A few 60-day notes, in denominations of $50 through $5,000, were issued. With few exceptions, all of the 121,000-plus notes that were issued have been redeemed and are unavailable.

The tremendous demand for currency created by the Civil War eventually exceeded the production capacities of the private banking system, and the governments of both the North and South began to print national currency. The end of currency production in the private sector was hastened in 1865 when the federal government began imposing a 10 percent tax on state-chartered bank notes, thus making it unprofitable for state banks to issue notes.

Large-size paper money

Notes issued from 1862 until 1928 were large-size notes, commonly called "horse blankets," sometimes known as "saddle blankets." Most large-size notes measure approximately 7.5 inches by 3.125 inches or 191 millimeters by 79 millimeters.

With this beginning, the United States started production of paper money that continues to this day. The government has issued many different types of notes.

Demand notes of 1861

In 1861, the United States government issued what is generally considered the first true federal paper money—demand notes, authorized by congressional acts of July 17 and Aug. 5, 1861. These notes differ from the Treasury notes of 1812 to 1861 in that they were intended to circulate. Demand notes were not originally legal tender but were later specified as such. The demand notes were made payable, on demand, by the assistant treasurer of the United States at Boston, New York, Philadelphia, St. Louis and Cincinnati.

Demand notes were issued in three denominations: $5, $10 and $20. Each note bears the first authorization date, July 17, and the date of issue, Aug. 10. The major portions of the face designs are identical to those on the later legal tender notes of the same denominations. The $5 note features a portrait of Alexander Hamilton at right and a statue of Columbia at left. Lincoln is portrayed at left on the $10 note with a woman representing Art at right. The $20 note features Liberty.

Black ink was used on the faces of the notes and green ink was used in the printing of the backs. The green ink was made from a secret formula and was difficult both to erase and to photograph—a counterfeit deterrent. The demand notes were soon nicknamed "greenbacks," a term that became so popular it was passed on through the years and is heard even today.

The demand notes bear the signatures of various employees of the Treasury Department who signed their own names for the register of the Treasury and treasurer of the United States (on some rare notes, they had to sign the words "For The" as well).

Demand notes do not carry the Treasury seal or the actual names of the register and treasurer, and are unique among federal paper money in those respects.

Legal tender and United States notes

Legal tender notes, later designated United States notes, consisted of five issues. The first issue of March 10, 1862, was produced in $5, $10, $20, $50, $100, $500 and $1,000 denominations. Issue two was confined to $1 and $2 notes, although the face design does indicate that a $3 denomination was planned, but not released. The third issue, dated March 10, 1863, was printed in the same denominations as the first issue, but changes were made to the back design.

The fourth issue consisted of Series 1869, 1875, 1878, 1880, 1907, 1917 and 1923, with all except the 1869 notes carrying the designation "United States note." The 1869 series was designated as "Treasury note." The United States introduced paper with silk threads as a deterrent to counterfeiting with the Series 1869 notes.

Denominations in the fourth issue:

1869 series, $1, $2, $5, $10, $20, $50, $100, $500 and $1,000.

1874 series, $1, $2, $50, and $500.

1875 series, $1, $2, $5, $10, $20, $50, $100 and $500.

1878 series, $1, $2, $5, $10, $20, $50, $100, $500, $1,000, $5,000 and $10,000.

1880 series, $1, $2, $5, $10, $20, $50, $100, $500 and $1,000.

1907 series, $5.

1917 series, $1 and $2.

1923 series, $1 and $10.

The fifth issue was limited to the $10 denomination.

Face designs on the first and third issues:

$5, Alexander Hamilton on lower right, with Washington Capitol statue of Columbia on left side.

$10, vignette of Lincoln, upper right, allegorical female representing Art, on left.

$20, Liberty with shield and sword.

$50, Alexander Hamilton. Different pose than on $5 note.

$100, American eagle. This was the first note to feature the American eagle.

$500, Albert Gallatin, secretary of the Treasury 1801 to 1813.

$1,000, Robert Morris, a signer of the Declaration of Independence and superintendent of finance 1781 to 1784.

Face designs on second issue:

$1, Vignette of Salmon P. Chase, secretary of the Treasury, 1861 to 1864.

$2, Capitol building and Thomas Jefferson.

The obligation on the first, second and third issues states "United States will pay the Bearer ... Dollars at the Treasury of New York."

Back designs of the first, second, third issues:

First and third issues, denominations $5 to $1,000, feature lathe-work design with two types of inscriptions, commonly called obligations.

Type one states: "This note is Legal Tender for all debts public and private, except on duties on Imports and Interest on Public Debt, and is exchangeable for U.S. Six percent Twenty Years Bonds, redeemable at the pleasure of the U. States after Five Years."

Type two states: "This note is a Legal Tender for all debts public and private, except duties on Imports and Interest on the Public Debt, and is receivable in payment for all Loans made to the United States."

The type two inscription (obligation) appears in the center of lathe-work design on the $1 and $2 notes of the second issue.

Face designs on the fourth issue:

$1, 1869 to 1917, head of Washington facing left, and Columbus sighting land.

$1, 1923, head of Washington facing right.

$2, Capitol building and vignette of Thomas Jefferson.

$5, *Pioneer Family* vignette and bust of Andrew Jackson.

$10, 1869 to 1880, Daniel Webster and presentation of Indian Princess, representing introduction of Old World to the New World. Popular name of this note is "Jackass note," so-called because the eagle on face design, when note is inverted, resembles the head of a jackass.

$10, 1923, Andrew Jackson.

$20, Alexander Hamilton and figure of Victory with shield and sword.

$50, 1869, Henry Clay and female holding statue of Mercury.

$50, 1874 to 1880, Benjamin Franklin, with figure of Liberty.

$100, Abraham Lincoln, with allegorical figure of Architecture.

$500, 1869, John Quincy Adams.

$500, 1874 to 1880, Maj. Gen. Joseph K. Mansfield.

$1,000, Dewitt Clinton, governor of New York.

$5,000, James Madison.

$10,000, Andrew Jackson.

The major portion of the face designs in the fourth issue remained the same. The obligation states "United States will pay the Bearer ... Dollars." The words "At the Treasury in New York" that appeared on the first three issues were removed and the single word "Washington" substituted for "New York" on the 1869 series and "Washington, D.C." on later issues. Stars following serial numbers on the 1869 series do not indicate replacement notes.

Back designs of the fourth issue differ from previous issues in that the words "and is receivable in payment for all Loans made to the United States" have been removed from the type two clause. Throughout the fourth issue, except on Series 1923 $1 and $10 notes, the warning against counterfeiting, which first appeared on the 1869 series, is used.

Series 1923 $1 has a plain back, unlike the ornate lathe-work of earlier issues.

Series 1923 $10 notes have lathe-work design.

Face design on the fifth issue:

Consisting of a $10 note, features a bison in center, with portraits of Lewis and Clark on sides.

Back design of the fifth issue:

Columbus standing between two pillars and two scrolls that carry the inscription found on the fourth issue.

Compound-interest Treasury notes

The congressional Acts of March 3, 1863, and June 30, 1864, authorized $10, $20, $50, $100, $500 and $1,000 compound-interest Treasury notes. They bear on the face the following inscription: "Three years after date the United States will pay the bearer ... dollars with interest at the rate of six percent compounded semi-annually." The back has "By Act of Congress, this note is legal tender for ... dollars but bears interest at six percent only at maturity as follows [table of interest]. This sum ... will be paid the holder for principal and interest at maturity of note three years from date."

These notes were issued to raise money to finance the Civil War.

Interest-bearing notes

The interest-bearing notes were the successors to the Treasury notes that were issued between 1812 and 1861 and were issued for the same purpose as the compound-interest Treasury notes, to raise money to finance the Civil War.

One- and two-year notes bearing interest at 5 percent were authorized by the Act of March 3, 1863. Three-year notes bearing 7.3 percent interest were authorized by the Acts of July 17, 1861, June 30, 1864, and March 3, 1865, and were issued at three different times. These three-year notes had five attached coupons that were detached and redeemed at six-month intervals.

The one-year notes were issued in denominations of $10 to $5,000, the two-year notes in denominations of $50 to $1,000 and the three-year notes ranged from

$50 to $5,000. All are extremely rare due to immediate redemption on the expiration date.

Currency certificates of deposit

The secretary of the Treasury was authorized to issue currency certificates of deposit by the Act of June 8, 1872. Denominations of the notes were $5,000 and $10,000. The $5,000 notes were payable on demand in U.S. notes at the place of deposit and were accepted in settlement of clearinghouse balances at the locations where deposits were made. The $10,000 notes were receivable on deposit without interest from national banking houses but were not to be included in the legal reserves.

Authorization of these large-denomination certificates was repealed March 14, 1900.

Silver certificates

Acts of Congress dated Feb. 28, 1878, and Aug. 4, 1886, authorized the large-size silver certificates. Five issues from Series 1878 to Series 1923 were released.

The first issue, Series 1878 and 1880, consisted of $10, $20, $50, $100, $500 and $1,000 denominations. The face side states that "There have been deposited with the Treasurer of the United States at Washington, D.C. payable at his office to the bearer on demand ... Silver Dollars." "Certificate of Deposit" is inscribed on the notes. All certificates of the 1878 series and one of the notes in the 1880 series are countersigned by assistant treasurers of the United States at New York and bear the signatures of Register of the Treasury G.W. Scofield and U.S. Treasurer James Gilfillan.

Face designs of the first issue:

$10, Robert Morris, signer of the Declaration of Independence and U.S. senator.

$20, Stephen Decatur, naval commander before and during War of 1812.

$50, Edward Everett, governor of Massachusetts, U.S. senator and secretary of state under President Fillmore.

$100, James Monroe, fifth president.

$500, Charles Sumner, U.S. senator and leader in the abolition of slavery.

$1,000, William L. Marcy, governor of New York, secretary of war under President Polk and secretary of state under President Pierce.

The Treasury seal on countersigned certificates of 1878 has the key in the red seal pointing to the right instead of to the left. This engraving error was corrected on the 1880 series.

The face design of Series 1878 and 1880 silver certificates has the word SILVER in large letters appearing on black scrollwork. The inscription says, "This Certificate is Receivable for Customs, Taxes, and all Public Dues and When So Received May be Reissued."

The second issue of silver certificates consists of Series 1886, 1891 and 1908. The 1886 series was printed in denominations of $1, $2, $5, $10 and $20.

The 1891 series includes these and also the denominations of $50, $100 and $1,000. Only the $10 note was issued in Series 1908. On the face of Series 1886, 1891 and 1908 notes appears the wording "This certifies that there have been deposited in the Treasury of the United States ... Silver Dollars payable to the Bearer on Demand."

Face designs of the second issue:

$1, Series 1886 and 1891, Martha Washington.

$2, Series 1886, Gen. Winfield Scott Hancock.

$2, Series 1891, William Windom, twice secretary of the Treasury.

$5, Series 1886 and 1891, Ulysses S. Grant.

$10, Series 1886 and 1908, Thomas A. Hendricks, U.S. vice president.

$20, Series 1886 and 1891, Daniel Manning, secretary of the Treasury.

$50, Series 1891, Edward Everett.

$100, Series 1891, James Monroe.

$1,000, Series 1891, William L. Marcy.

The back design of the 1886 series features green overall lathe-work. Large numbers denoting the denomination also are used. The certification is identical to that on the 1878 and 1880 series. The back design of the $5 note is unique, featuring five silver dollars with the obverse of one dated 1886.

The back designs of Series 1891 and 1908 notes feature a more open lathe-work presentation. Large numbers, and on some denominations, Roman numerals, indicate the denomination. The certification remains the same as on previous series.

The third issue of silver certificates, Series 1896, is one of the most popular and deemed by collectors as the most beautiful series ever produced by the United States. Titled the "Educational Series," the notes were designed or redesigned by Thomas F. Morris, designer and chief of the Engraving Division of the Bureau of Engraving and Printing from Nov. 1, 1893, to June 30, 1897. Other designers of this famed series were Will H. Low, $1; Edwin H. Blashfield, $2; and Walter Shirlaw, $5. Known engravers of the series were Charles Schlecht and George F.C. Smillie.

Claude M. Johnson, who was chief of the BEP, is credited with advocating the printing of more artistic and representative designs in paper money, and the original plan was to have Educational designs on all silver certificate denominations from $1 to $1,000 but only the $1, $2 and $5 notes were released. The $10 note was designed but never released, and records do not indicate that higher denominations were ever designed.

The designs never caught on with the public. Bank tellers complained that the three denominations were too much alike in appearance, making accurate counting difficult. In addition, the central design of the face of the $5 notes bore two partially nude women, and while it is debatable whether any public objections to the nudity played a role in the note's replacement, an 1897 proof of the $5 denomination exists with the two figures wearing additional clothing.

The face designs of the Educational notes:

$1, vignette titled *History Instructing Youth,* with the background featuring the Washington Monument and the Capitol building. The U.S. Constitution is shown in an open book and the names of 23 great Americans are featured in the border design.

$2, Steam and Electricity, represented by two youthful figures, being presented to Commerce and Manufacture, represented by two mature female figures. Another mature female figure, Science, is making the presentation.

$5, Electricity, represented by a winged female, is depicted as a controlling factor in world history.

The obligation to redeem the notes in silver dollars is carried on the face of all three notes.

The backs of the Educational notes feature portraits of George and Martha Washington on the $1 note, inventors Samuel Morse and Robert Fulton on the $2 note, and Gens. Ulysses Grant and Philip Sheridan on the $5.

The fourth issue, Series 1899, was released in three denominations, $1, $2 and $5. The face design of the $1 features the American eagle with portraits of Lincoln and Grant. The $2 note portrays Washington between figures representing Mechanics and Agriculture, and the $5 note features Ta-to-ka-in-yan-ka, Running Antelope, a Sioux Indian.

There is an interesting story behind the printing of the $5 note. Running Antelope was a member of the Oncpapa or Hunkpapa Sioux tribe. The portrait used on the note came from a photograph taken in 1872 for the Bureau of Ethnology. However, Running Antelope wore a headdress with three feathers that projected too high for a good image on the note. To correct the problem, an employee of the Bureau of Engraving and Printing posed wearing a warbonnet belonging to another tribe, and the headdress was cut out and superimposed on the photograph of Running Antelope. George F.C. Smillie engraved the design in November of 1899. The headdress, ironically, belonged to the Pawnee tribe, rivals of the Hunkpapa Sioux tribe of Running Antelope.

Back designs for the fourth issue were modified from those of earlier issues. The denomination is indicated by large numerals, with the Roman numeral "V" in the center design of the $5 note. The notes carry the same inscription on the backs as earlier issues have.

The fifth issue of silver certificates, Series 1923, consists of two denominations, $1 and $5. Washington is portrayed on the $1 and Lincoln on the $5. On the latter note, Lincoln is shown in the center of a circular design and therefore this note is sometimes called the "porthole" note.

Certification on the fifth issue is the same as on previous issues. However, the inscription, previously part of the back design, was moved to the face at left of the seal. The back of the $1 note in the fifth issue

features the words UNITED STATES OF AMERICA prominently in the center. The $5 note shows the front of the Great Seal of the United States and the words UNITED STATES OF AMERICA.

Refunding certificates

The U.S. government authorized refunding certificates on Feb. 26, 1879, to reduce the circulation of the "fiat" greenbacks when specie payments were resumed. The more notes that were converted to non-legal tender obligations, the less cash that the Treasury had to pay out on its paper obligations. The face design of the notes, issued in a $10 denomination only, bears the portrait of Benjamin Franklin (most probably based on the painting by James Barton Longacre, designer of the Indian Head cent and other U.S. coins as engraver of the Mint).

The 4 percent annual interest was to accumulate indefinitely. However, by 1907 the $10 note was worth $21.30 so Congress passed a law that allowed the government to stop payment on July 1 of that year.

Treasury or coin notes

The Legal Tender Act of July 14, 1890, authorized Series 1890 and 1891 Treasury notes (also called coin notes) in denominations of $1 to $1,000. The Treasury Department used these notes to purchase silver bullion. It was left to the secretary of the Treasury to decide if gold or silver would be paid out when the notes were redeemed. Redemption of the notes almost bankrupted the Treasury by 1893 and caused a major economic panic.

The face designs of the Treasury notes:

$1, Edwin M. Stanton, secretary of war 1862 to 1868.

$2, Gen. James B. McPherson, Union Army, commander of the Army of the Tennessee when he was killed at the Battle of Atlanta.

$5, Gen. George H. Thomas, nicknamed the "rock of Chicamauga."

$10, Gen. Philip H. Sheridan, commander in chief of the U.S. Army from 1884 to 1888.

$20, John Marshall, chief justice of the United States, served on Supreme Court from 1801 to 1855.

$50, William H. Seward, secretary of state from 1860 to 1869, negotiated purchase of Alaska from Russia, Series 1891 only.

$100, Adm. David Glasgow Farragut, first man to hold the rank of admiral of the U.S. Navy.

$500, Gen. William Tecumseh Sherman, commander in chief of the U.S. Army from 1869 to 1884, 1891 series only.

$1,000, Gen. George Gordon Meade, Union Army commander.

The back designs of the Treasury notes:

$1, large scrollwork ONE at center, Series 1890; obligation at center flanked by numeral 1s enclosed within oval scrollwork, obligation at bottom center, Series 1891.

$2, large scrollwork TWO at center, Series 1890;

various scrollwork elements, obligation at left, Series 1891.

$5, large scrollwork FIVE at center, Series 1890; obligation at right within scrollwork, Series 1891.

$10, large scrollwork TEN at center, Series 1890; obligation at center, flanked by TEN and X within scrollwork, Series 1891.

$20, large scrollwork TWENTY at center, Series 1890; obligation at center within oval scrollwork, TWENTY above and DOLLARS below, Series 1891.

$50, obligation at center within scrollwork, Series 1891.

$100, large scrollwork 100 with the 0s vaguely resembling watermelons, thus the nickname "Watermelon note," with ONE HUNDRED DOLLARS below, Series 1890; obligation at center within scrollwork, Series 1891.

$500, obligation at center within scalloped scrollwork, FIVE above and HUNDRED below, Series 1891 only.

$100, large scrollwork 1000 with the 0s vaguely resembling watermelons, thus the nickname "Grand Watermelon note," with ONE THOUSAND DOLLARS below, Series 1890; obligation at center bottom within curved rectangular plaque, ONE THOUSAND DOLLARS above within scrollwork, Series 1891.

National bank notes

The national bank notes were authorized by the National Currency Act of Feb. 25, 1863, and National Banking Act of June 3, 1864, and were issued by chartered banks from 1863 to 1928.

During the Civil War coins of gold and silver were hoarded and practically disappeared from circulation. The unsecured legal tender notes commonly known as "greenbacks" were not popular and not readily accepted by skeptical persons having no confidence in the government's promise to pay.

Although Secretary of the Treasury Salmon P. Chase recommended a national bank currency secured by government bonds in his financial report of December 1861, the National Currency Act was not passed until February 1863. Spencer M. Clark, chief of construction of the Treasury Department, as early as April 1862 conceived the plan to have the national banks issue their own currency. Chase endorsed the plan and directed Clark to invite artists and engravers to submit proposals and designs.

Clark had previously suggested that historic pictures be used as back designs for the "greenbacks" of 1862 claiming that these designs offered greater protection against counterfeiting. His proposed designs were not adopted for the legal tender notes, but were adopted for the national bank notes issued under Secretary of the Treasury W.P. Fessenden. Clark suggested that these designs cover the entire back of the notes, but while the designs were adopted, the size of each was reduced to allow space for denomination and legends.

National banks qualifying under terms of the act were granted 20-year charters that were renewable for 20-year periods. Banks so chartered were permitted to issue national bank notes not to exceed 90 percent of the total of the U.S. government bonds deposited with the treasurer of the United States. Many of the banks gaining federal charters had formerly been chartered by the state in which they resided; converting state charters to federal charters was a prime goal of the national bank note legislation.

Early issues will be found with the imprints of the American Bank Note Co., Continental Bank Note Co. and National Bank Note Co. These companies supplied the paper and delivered the printed notes to the Treasury. The Bureau then imprinted the Treasury number and Treasury seal.

The History of the Bureau of Engraving and Printing says: "National bank notes were printed exclusively by private contractors until September 1875. Thereafter this type of currency was partially printed by the Bureau of Engraving and Printing. Beginning in October 1877, the Bureau executed all work in connection with the printing of national currency."

Some notes will be found bearing the imprint of one of the three bank note companies in the design, and in very small type in the margin of the note, the notation: PRINTED AT THE BUREAU OF ENGRAVING AND PRINTING.

The dates appearing on national bank notes do not always indicate the date the charter was granted, nor the date the notes were issued. Nor do these dates denote the term of office of the Treasury officials whose signatures appear on the notes. Plates with the names of the U.S. treasurer and register of the Treasury were frequently used after the officials left office. The date appearing on the note is usually later than the granting of the charter. Some banks organized late in the First Charter period continued to issue Series 1875 notes until February 1902.

At the close of 1928, 13,269 banks had been chartered but many did not issue bank notes. Notes issued by banks in small communities are usually scarcer than those of large city banks. This thinking has at times been upset when a small-town bank released a stock of notes held in its reserve funds.

In addition to the engraved signatures of the two Treasury officials, national bank notes have the signatures of two bank officers, usually the president and cashier. Early issues did not carry the plate number on face or back.

The First Charter notes of $1 and $2 denominations were usually printed in sheets of three $1 notes and one $2 note. Check letters on notes so printed are A, B, and C on the $1 notes and A on the $2 note. Known exceptions to "three ones and a two" are:

The Westchester County National Bank, Peekskill, N.Y., Charter 1422; the Merchants National Bank, Bangor, Maine, Charter 1437; the City National Bank, Manchester, N.H., Charter 1530. These three banks were supplied with sheets of two $1 notes, check letters A and B, and two $2 notes, check letters A and B.

The other known exception is the First National Bank of Philadelphia, with sheets of four $1 and sheets of four $2 notes.

The word "National" appears in the title of all chartered banks with the exception of The Bank of North America, Philadelphia, which was allowed to retain the title it had used as a state bank.

To assist in sorting notes presented for redemption, a large letter is printed with the charter numbers on national bank notes for a period of about 25 years, approximately 1901 to 1925. These regional letters indicated the geographical area or region in which the issuing bank was located, and may be found on Second and Third Charter notes. Six letters were used as follows: E, Eastern Region; M, Middle States Region; N, New England Region; P, Pacific Region (including Alaska and Hawaii); S, Southern Region; and W, Western Region.

Bank charter numbers were overprinted on Series 1875 and all later series, and may also be found on some notes of the Original Series. The exact position varies on the face of the notes. These numbers on the first issue are in red with the exception of a very few banks that were supplied with notes bearing black charter numbers.

Known "Black Charters" are the $5 notes of the following banks: Merchants National Bank, Minneapolis, Minn., charter 1830; First National Bank, Central City, Colorado Territory, charter 2129; First National Bank, Red Oak, Iowa, charter 2130; National Bank, Green Lane, Pa., charter 2131; Kellogg National Bank, Green Bay, Wis., charter 2132; First National Bank, Boyertown, Pa., charter 2137; National Bank, Rochester, N.H., charter 2138; and The National Bank, Pontiac, Ill., charter 2141.

The First Charter period, Feb. 25, 1863, to July 11, 1882:

The first issue of national bank notes is known as the "Original Series." This was followed by Series 1875. These two series comprise the issue of First Charter notes and were issued in denominations of $1 to $1,000. Very few banks issued First Charter notes in denominations higher than $100.

The obligation of the issuing bank to pay appears on the face of the notes and reads: "This note is secured by Bonds of the United States, deposited with the United States Treasurer at Washington. The ... [Bank] ... will pay the Bearer on Demand ... Dollars."

Face designs of the First Charter notes:

$1, vignette titled *Concordia,* showing two maidens clasping hands before an altar of earlier times, which bears the coat of arms of the United States. The design represents the new Union brought about with the aid of Heaven and the eventual return to peace. Vignette designed by T.A. Liebler and engraved by Charles Burt.

$2, vignette *America Seated,* depicted by a maiden

unfurling the American flag. The bank serial number is at upper right and the Treasury number is at lower left in a vertical position. This design is best known as the "Lazy 2" because of the large numeral "2" that reclines on its side. The note carries the certification that bonds have been deposited with the treasurer of the United States in Washington. The design is very popular. Similar large numeral designs were previously used on obsolete currency.

$5, *Columbus Sighting Land,* showing the discoverer with some of his crew on the deck of a caravel. The scene at lower right depicts Columbus introducing America, represented by an Indian princess, to the Old World, Africa, Asia and Europe. Continental Bank Note Co. designer Fenton produced the design for engraving by Charles Burt.

$10, *Franklin and the Lightning* is the historical scene at left, representing Benjamin Franklin's experimentation with electrical energy and his assistant seated near him with a Leyden jar placed nearby. The year is marked by 1752 in the corner of the vignette. Eagle in flight bearing Liberty is shown at right, symbolizing *America Grasping the Lightning.* Alfred Jones did the engraving.

$20, *Battle of Lexington 1775*, depicted by Colonists in action and nurses attending the wounded. At right a symbolic design of *Loyalty,* a procession for the defense and preservation of the Union that is led by Columbia with flag. The design is by Felix O.C. Darley.

$50, *Washington Crossing the Delaware* before his victorious battle at Princeton is the vignette at left. *A Prayer for Victory* is depicted at right. Alfred Jones did the engraving.

$100, Powell's painting *The Battle of Lake Erie* was the inspiration for the vignette at left, which shows Commodore Perry leaving his burning ship, the USS *Lawrence.* At right, Columbia is seated with a fasces, a bundle of rods with a projecting ax handle. Inscribed are the words THE UNION and to the right MAINTAIN IT. Louis Delnoce did the engraving.

$500, *Civilization* appears on the left. At right is a nautical scene titled *Arrival of the Sirius, 1838.*

$1,000, Gen. Scott entering Mexico City is shown at left. At right the *Capitol Building, Washington, D.C.* The painting is by John Trumbull. Alfred Jones did the engraving. This note is believed to be nonexistent.

Tableau scenes are illustrated on the back designs of the notes of the First Charter period. The original murals decorated the rotunda of the Capitol Building in Washington and were the work of early American artists.

The coat of arms of the state of issue appears in the oval at left, with the exception of notes issued by banks in Arizona, New Mexico, Oklahoma and the state of Washington, on which the American eagle is shown in oval at right. A rather lengthy inscription qualifying the acceptance of the note and a warning against counterfeiting, "punishable by $1000 fine, or fifteen years' imprisonment at hard labor, or both," is also part of the back design.

The border designs are green with center illustrations in black on the backs:

$1, *Landing of the Pilgrims* in center of back design depicts one of the memorable events in United States history. It is framed by the legend. Charles Burt did the engraving.

$2, Sir Walter Raleigh, with a long-stemmed smoking pipe, demonstrates the use of tobacco brought from America. Louis Delnoce did the engraving.

$5, *The Landing of Columbus* from the well-known mural by John Vanderlyn.

$10, *DeSoto Discovering the Mississippi 1541.* The mural by W.H. Powell shows a group of Native Americans, soldiers and monks. A crucifix is being erected on the spot. Girsch did the engraving.

$20, *The Baptism of Pocahontas* at Jamestown, Va. The scene depicts Pocahontas kneeling, with John Smith and spectators, some of whom express interest and surprise. The painting is by John G. Chapman.

$50, *Embarkation of the Pilgrims,* a reproduction of Robert W. Wier's mural, which depicts the Pilgrims before departing for America, kneeling to ask the Divine blessing. W.W. Rice did the engraving.

$100, *The Signing of the Declaration of Independence,* July 4, 1776. One of John Trumbull's masterpieces, showing Washington, Jefferson, Franklin and a dignified group assembled for the acceptance and signing of the historic document. Girsch did the engraving.

$500, *The Surrender of Burgoyne.* Another mural by Trumbull, vividly portraying the surrender of the general to Gen. Horatio Gates of the American Army, at Saratoga, N.Y., Oct. 17, 1777. Girsch did the engraving.

$1,000, *Washington Resigning His Commission,* Dec. 23, 1783, at Annapolis, Md. Trumbull's mural shows the commander-in-chief presenting his resignation to the Congress. Girsch and Delnoce did the engraving.

The Second Charter period, July 12, 1882, to April 11, 1902:

First Issue: Series 1882. The well-known and very popular Brown Backs.

Second Issue: Series 1882 emergency issue, the Date Backs. Dates 1882 1908 on back. Whereas banks had previously been required to deposit United States government bonds with the treasurer, by Act of Congress, May 30, 1908, they were permitted to deposit other types of securities, thus enabling the banks to place a larger number of notes into circulation.

Third Issue: Series 1882 Denomination Backs. Denomination spelled out on back. Scarcest of the three series of 1882 nationals. Not all banks issued this series.

Face designs of the first, second and third issues:
The face designs of the three Second Charter

issues are the same as the First Charter issues, with the exception of the design on the $5 notes. The bank obligation to pay is also the same.

The face design of the $5 denomination of all three issues of 1882 is distinctly different from the higher denominations of this series or the $5 First Charter notes. A portrait of James A. Garfield, 20th president, is in oval at left, possibly used to immortalize the statesman following his assassination in 1881, the same year in which he assumed office. The design is by George W. Casilear, engraved by Alonzo C. Hatch.

Back designs of the first issue, Series 1882 Brown Backs:
"Brown Backs" is the well-known description of the First Series of Second Charter notes. The state seals are in ovals at left in the back design, as on the First Charter notes, and the American eagle is again shown in oval at right.

The striking change in the "Brown Backs" is in the center design, which prominently features the bank charter number in large numerals against a green background, surrounded by brown lathe-work design.

The legend appears in the top margin, and the rather lengthy counterfeiting warning extends across bottom of back design.

Back designs of the second issue, 1882 to 1908 Date Backs, printed in green ink:
The back designs of the Date Back notes show various persons and designs in the small oval at left, instead of the state seals as used on the Brown Backs and First Charter notes. Various subjects are shown in the oval at right. Featured are the following:

$5, Washington at left; Capitol Building, Washington, D.C., at right.

$10, William P. Fessenden at left; right, Mechanics as illustrated by seated workmen.

$20, American eagle, two different poses, left and right ovals.

$50, eagle with shield, left and right.

$100, eagle with flag at left, and with shield at right.

Back designs of the third issue, Series 1882 Denomination Backs, printed in green ink:
The center designs spell out in large letters the denomination of the notes. Vignettes in small ovals at left and right, remain the same as the Second Issue, also legend at top and the counterfeiting warning at bottom.

The Third Charter period, April 12, 1902, to April 11, 1922:

First Issue: Series 1902, Red Seals and Numbers. Notes of this issue are scarce, having been issued by comparatively few of all chartered banks. Red Seal notes were printed with only three signature combinations of Treasury officials.

Second Issue: 1902-1908, Blue Seals, Emergency Series. Dates on back. Authorized under Act of May 30, 1908, as were the Series 1882-1908 Second Charter notes. First issued in 1908 and with two exceptions discontinued in 1916. The $50 and $100 denominations were issued through 1925.

Third Issue: 1902 Blue Seals. No dates on back. First issued in 1916 and most common of the three issues of Third Charter notes. Fifteen signature combinations (federal officials) were used, the scarcest being the Jones-Woods signatures. Edward E. Jones assumed the office of register and Walter O. Woods the office of treasurer in 1929, the same year large-size notes were discontinued.

Face designs of the Third Charter notes:

The Treasury seal is at right on all denominations in the three issues. Prominent statesmen are featured in oval, at left.

$5, Benjamin Harrison, 23rd president of the United States.

$10, William McKinley, 25th president, assassinated in Buffalo, 1901.

$20, Hugh McCulloch, secretary of Treasury, 1865 to 1869 and 1884 to 1885.

$5, John Sherman, secretary of the Treasury 1877 to 1881; secretary of state 1897 to 1898.

$100, John J. Knox, comptroller of currency 1872 to 1884, later, president of the National Bank of the Republic, New York City.

Ostrander Smith designed all of the faces of the Third Charter notes. Charles Burt engraved the $20 note, all others engraved by George F.C. Smillie.

Back designs of the Third Charter notes:

$5, *Landing of the Pilgrims.*

$10, Female figure, with ships in background.

$20, Columbia and Capitol at Washington.

$50, Allegorical scene. Train and female figure at right. Railroad worker reclining at left.

$100, American eagle on shield, with two male figures.

The back design of all denominations bear a rather lengthy inscription: "This note is receivable at par in all parts of the United States in payment of all taxes and excises and all other dues to the United States except duties on imports and also for all salaries and other debts and demands owing by the United States to individuals, corporations and associations within the United States except interest on public debt."

Gold certificates

Acts of March 3, 1863, July 12, 1882, March 14, 1900, and Dec. 24, 1919, authorized the issuance of gold certificates.

Gold certificates were redeemable for gold coins at par, but because gold sold for a premium in relation to paper money prior to 1879, the earliest notes did not circulate.

The First, Second and Third Issues are considered noncollectible, having been used principally in transactions between banks with few notes surviving.

First Issue (believed issued 1865 to 1869):

Face design of American eagle on draped shield on all denominations; issued in denominations of $20, $100, $500, $1,000, $5,000 and $10,000. The $20

and $100 notes are extremely rare, with the remaining notes either unique or unknown.

Some of these issues were uniface.

Dates of issue were filled in with pen and ink.

Second Issue (hand dated 1870 or 1871):

Portrait of Thomas H. Benton at left on all denominations; issued in denominations of $100, $500, $1,000, $5,000 and $10,000. All are either unique or unknown.

Dates of issue were filled in with pen and ink.

Third Issue of Series 1875:

Portrait of Thomas H. Benton at left, issued in denominations of $100, $500, $1,000 and $10,000. The $100 note is extremely rare, with the remaining notes either unique or unknown.

Dates of issue were filled in with pen and ink.

Fourth Issue of Series 1882:

$20 to $10,000 denomination. As with the first three issues, denominations higher than $100 are extremely rare, practically unknown.

The obligation to pay in gold is on the face of the note. It reads: "This certifies that there have been deposited in the Treasury of the United States ... Dollars in Gold Coin, payable to the Bearer on Demand." This issue is indicated as "Department Series" on the face of the certificates.

Face designs of Series 1882:

$20, James A. Garfield, 20th president, assassinated six months after his inauguration in 1881. Portrait at right.

$50, Silas Wright, U.S. senator 1833 to 1844; New York governor 1845 to 1846. Portrait at left.

$100, Thomas H. Benton, U.S. senator for more than 30 years. Portrait at left.

$500, Abraham Lincoln. Portrait at left.

$1,000, Alexander Hamilton. Portrait at right.

$5,000, James Madison. Portrait at left.

$10,000, Andrew Jackson. Portrait at left.

Some notes of the 1882 series, bearing Bruce-Gilfillan signatures and a brown seal, were countersigned by Thomas C. Acton, assistant treasurer, and were payable in New York. Notes so countersigned are rare.

Back designs of Series 1882:

The American eagle in various poses is featured on the back design of all denominations of this series. There is no legend or inscription. Large Roman numerals "C" "D" and "M" in the back design indicate the $100, $500 and $1,000 denominations. UNITED STATES without OF AMERICA is used on all back designs of this series.

Fifth Issue of Series 1888:

Two denominations only: $5,000 James Madison, portrait at left. Back design: "5000" and eagle. $10,000 Andrew Jackson, portrait at left, Back design: "10000" and eagle with flag.

Sixth Issue of Series 1900:

$10,000 only. Andrew Jackson, as on Series 1888. Back design same as 1888.

Seventh Issue of Series 1905, 1906 and 1907:

$10, Series 1907. Michael Hillegas, center, U.S. treasurer 1775-1789. Large "X" Roman equivalent of "10" at left. .

$20, Series 1905, George Washington. The blending of gold, red, black and white on the face has caused this note to be known as the "Technicolor" note.

$20, Series 1906, George Washington. Gold and black face design with Roman numeral "XX." Back same as Series 1905 note.

The back designs in gold feature the Eagle side of Great Seal of the United States in different locations by denomination, the denomination and the words "United States of America." There is no legend or inscription.

Eighth Issue of Series 1907:

$1,000, Alexander Hamilton. Only denomination.

Ninth Issue of Series 1913 and 1922:

$50, Ulysses S. Grant at center. Issued with two signature combinations.

Tenth Issue of Series 1922:

$10, Michael Hillegas, same design as on Series 1907 note.

$20, George Washington, same design as on Series 1907 note

$50, Ulysses Grant, same design as on Series 1913 note

$100, Thomas H. Benton, same design as on Series 1882 note.

$500, Abraham Lincoln, same designs as on Series 1882 note.

$1,000, Alexander Hamilton, same designs as on Series 1907 notes

All Series 1922 notes bear signature combination Speelman-White.

A legend was added to the face of the notes: "This certificate is a Legal Tender in the amount thereof, in payment of all debts and dues public and private. Acts of March 14, 1900, as amended, and December 24, 1919."

The back designs in gold feature the Eagle side of the Great Seal of the United States in different locations by denomination, the denomination and the words "United States of America." There is no legend or inscription.

National gold bank notes

The national gold bank notes are gold-tinted and are extremely rare. Ten national gold banks were authorized by Congress to assuage the burden of handling the gold produced by the California Gold Rush. Nine of the banks were in California and one was in Boston. Researchers generally believe that the Kidder National Gold Bank of Boston did not circulate gold notes, though proof impressions of the national gold bank notes do exist.

Issued denominations were $5, $10, $20, $50, $100, redeemable in gold . Since the gold banks were also national banks, it was necessary for them to deposit U.S. bonds as security with the U.S. treasurer. The obligation on these notes is similar to the national bank notes except that the gold bank notes were payable in gold coin.

Designs are the same as for the First Charter national bank notes.

Federal Reserve Bank notes

The large-size Federal Reserve Bank notes were authorized by the Federal Reserve Acts of Dec. 23, 1913, and April 23, 1918. They were issued in two series in denominations of $1 to $50 and are often confused with national bank notes because they also have the inscription NATIONAL CURRENCY across the top. They have blue seals and blue serial numbers. The bank name is centered on the face.

Designs are the same no matter the series:

$1, portrait of George Washington at left on face, with large American eagle at center on back.

$2, portrait of Thomas Jefferson at left on face, vignette of 1914-era battleship on back.

$5, portrait of Abraham Lincoln on face at left, vignettes *Columbus in Sight of Land* (left) and *The Landing of the Pilgrims* (right) on the back.

$10, portrait of Andrew Jackson at left on face, with farm and factory scenes on back.

$20, portrait of Grover Cleveland at left on face, with vignettes representing land, sea and air transportation on the back.

$50, portrait of Ulysses S. Grant at left on face, allegorical figure of Panama at center between a civilian ship at left and warship at right on back.

The first issue, Series 1915, consisted of $5, $10 and $20 notes issued by the Federal Reserve Banks of Atlanta, Chicago, Kansas City and Dallas; the San Francisco Federal Reserve Bank issued only the $5 notes.

The obligation to pay the bearer is similar to that on the First Charter national bank notes, differing only slightly in wording but not in meaning.

The second issue, Series 1918, consisted of $1, $2, $5, $10, $20 and $50 notes issued by all 12 Federal Reserve Banks (though all banks did not necessarily issue all denominations).

The obligation to pay the bearer differs completely from the first issue, reading "Secured by United States Bonds or Certificates of Indebtedness or one-year gold notes."

Although Federal Reserve Bank notes are a rather recent issue, all are quite scarce. Treasury Department records show that only slightly more than $2 million is outstanding from a total issue of nearly $762 million.

Federal Reserve notes, Series 1914 and 1918

Federal Reserve Act, Dec. 23, 1913.

Series 1914, Red Seals, $5 to $100, scarce. Signatures: John Burke, treasurer of the United States; William Gibbs McAdoo, secretary of the Treasury.

Series 1914, Blue Seals, $5 to $100.

Series 1918, Blue Seals, $500 to $10,000.

Blue Seal signatures: Burke-McAdoo; Burke-Carter Glass; Burke-D.F. Houston; Frank White-A.W. Mellon.

Three types of notes bear the White-Mellon signature combination. Type one: District numeral and letter, rather large, lower left and upper right. Most common of the three types. Type two: Smaller numerals and letters of the various districts. Type three: Larger numerals and letters, slightly to the left and higher. Seals closer to center of note. Scarcest of the three types.

Unlike the Federal Reserve Bank notes, the obligation to pay is by the United States and reads: "The United States of America will pay the Bearer on Demand ... Dollars."

Face designs of Series 1914:

The portraits of presidents featured on Federal Reserve Bank notes are repeated on Federal Reserve notes on denominations $5 to $50, but are shown in center oval of the face design rather than at left without oval frame. Seal with numeral and letter of issuing bank is at left, and seal of the Treasury is at right. On the $100 Series 1914 Federal Reserve note, a portrait of Benjamin Franklin is used.

Face designs of Series 1918 all with Blue Seals:

$500, John Marshall, secretary of state and chief justice of the United States.

$1,000, Alexander Hamilton, first secretary of the Department of the Treasury.

$5,000, James Madison, fourth president of the United States.

$10,000, Salmon P. Chase, secretary of Treasury under Lincoln.

Back designs of Series 1914 and 1918, Red and Blue Seals:

$5 to $50 notes are same as back designs of the Federal Reserve Bank notes. The back design of the $100 Federal Reserve note features five allegorical figures.

Back Designs of Series 1918 Blue Seals:

Series 1918, $500, *DeSoto Discovering the Mississippi,* as on the $10 First Charter, national bank note.

Series 1918, $1,000, American eagle with flag.

Series 1918, $5,000, *Washington Resigning his Commission,* as on the $1,000 First Charter note.

Series 1918, $10,000, *Embarkation of the Pilgrims,* as on the $50 First Charter note.

The lengthy inscription in the lower border of the back design of the large-size Federal Reserve notes differs from that found on the Federal Reserve Bank notes. It stipulates that the note is payable in gold, and reads:

"This note is receivable by all national and member banks and the Federal Reserve Banks, and for all taxes, customs and other public dues. It is redeemable in gold on demand at the Treasury Department of the United States in the city of Washington, District of Columbia, or in gold or lawful money at any Federal Reserve Bank."

U.S. postage and fractional currency

In 1862, the need for small coins to make change became acute. Following the suspension of specie payments by the large Northeastern banks and the federal Treasury late the previous year, coinage became widely hoarded and commanded premium values as compared to the government greenbacks. The result of this hoarding was extreme difficulty in making change for business transactions.

Private attempts to remedy the small change shortage were ingenious but proved futile. Municipal, corporate and private scrip could not completely replace the withdrawn subsidiary silver coinage nationwide and local expedients such as John Gault's encased postage stamps were temporary measures.

The federal solution was the authorization of postage and fractional currency. Noncollectors today would probably be shocked to learn that the federal government once issued paper money in denominations of less than one dollar. Today, when some Americans are advocating the elimination of the dollar bill, it seems unlikely that Americans once could use federal paper money in denominations as small as 5 cents.

To relieve the citizenry of the "worthless paper trash" that was circulating, F.E. Spinner, treasurer of the United States, convinced Congress of the necessity for a federal, fractional currency. He proposed that the United States issue these small notes in values less than $1 and in sufficient quantities to meet the demand for small change. Congress responded with the Act of July 17, 1862, which monetized the postage and other U.S. stamps.

The immediate effect of the law was a run on the U.S. post offices to secure stamps for change. By Aug. 21, however, the first notes of the belated postage currency issue reached circulation. Privately printed, these notes bore the imprints of the contemporary 5- and 10-cent postage stamps. Jefferson appears on the 5- and 25-cent issues and Washington on the 10- and 50-cent notes. Both perforate and imperforate varieties exist.

The obligation on the back of these notes states, "Exchangeable for United States Notes by any Assistant Treasurer or designated U.S. Depositary in sums not less than five dollars. Receivable in payment of all dues to the U. [sic] States less than five Dollars."

Because of the prevalence of counterfeiting, the designs of the successive fractional note issues were changed frequently. The fractional currency, which succeeded the makeshift (and some students contend illegal) postage currency, was issued in four series under authorization of the Act of March 3, 1863, which also provided that the Treasury Department print its own notes.

The Second Issue fractional currency (first issue under the Act of March 3, 1863) consists of four notes in the same denominations as the earlier issue, but all bearing a bust of Washington in a bronze oval frame on the face.

The obligation on the back was changed to read, "Exchangeable for United States Notes by the Assistant Treasurers and designated depositaries of the U.S. in sums not less than three dollars. Receivable in payment of all dues to the United States less than five dollars except customs."

The third general issue added a 3-cent denomination, and each denomination has a different design. Washington appears on the 3-cent note; Spencer M. Clark, on the 5-cent issue; Washington, on the 10-cent bill; William Pitt Fessenden, on the 25-cent note; and either a seated figure of Justice or F.E. Spinner on the 50-cent issue. The Spinner note also exists with two distinct reverse varieties.

The fourth general issue includes only 10-, 15-, 25- and 50-cent denominations. The 10-cent note bears a bust of Liberty; Columbia appears on the 15-cent issue; Washington, on the 25-cent bill; and Lincoln, Edwin Stanton or Samuel Dexter appear on the 50-cent note.

The short fifth issue is confined to three notes: William Meredith, on the 10-cent note; Robert Walker, on the 25-cent bill; and William Crawford, on the 50 cents.

The small notes continued to circulate until the Resumption Act of Jan. 14, 1875, provided for their retirement by subsidiary silver coinage. In all, nearly $370 million worth of these small bills were issued, but most have long since been redeemed or destroyed. It is estimated that less than $5,000 face value survives and remains available to collectors.

The federal postage and fractional currency of the 19th century remains legal tender, although it is unlikely that collectors would want to spend their notes at face value, and even more unlikely that clerks in grocery stores or other places of business would recognize a Fifth Issue 10-cent note, for example, as legitimate U.S. currency.

Fractional note statistics

The summary tabulation below shows the extent and value of the five fractional note issues:

FIRST ISSUE
Aug. 21, 1862, to May 27, 1863

Denomination	Number	Value
5 cents	44,857,780	$2,242,889.00
10 cents	41,153,780	4,115,378.00
25 cents	20,902,784	5,225,696.00
50 cents	17,263,344	8,631,672.00
Totals	124,187,688	$20,215,635.00

SECOND ISSUE
Oct. 10, 1863, to Feb. 23, 1867

Denomination	Number	Value
5 cents	55,896,522	$2,794,826.10
10 cents	61,760,843	6,176,084.30
25 cents	30,593,365	7,648,341.25
50 cents	13,090,464	6,545,232.00
Totals	161,341,194	$23,164,483.65

THIRD ISSUE
Dec. 5, 1864, to Aug. 16, 1869

Denomination	Number	Value
3 cents	20,064,130	$601,923.90
5 cents	13,140,055	657,002.75
10 cents	169,761,345	16,976,134.50
15 cents (Specimen)	9,016	1,352.40
25 cents	124,572,755	31,143,188.75
50 cents	73,470,853	36,735,426.50
Totals	401,018,154	$86,115,028.80

FOURTH ISSUE
July 14, 1869, to Feb. 16, 1875

Denomination	Number	Value
10 cents	349,409,600	$34,940,960.00
15 cents	35,361,440	5,304,216.00
25 cents	235,689,024	58,922,256.00
50 cents	154,799,200	77,399,600.00
Totals	775,259,264	$176,567,032.00

FIFTH ISSUE
Feb. 26, 1874, to Feb. 15, 1876

Denomination	Number	Value
10 cents	199,899,000	$19,989,900.00
25 cents	144,368,000	36,092,000.00
50 cents	13,160,000	6,580,000.00
Totals	357,427,000	$62,661,900.00

Summary of all issues

Denomination	Number	Value
3 cents	20,064,130	$601,923.90
5 cents	113,894,357	5,694,717.85
10 cents	821,984,568	82,198,456.80
15 cents (Specimen)	9,016	1,352.40
15 cents	35,361,440	5,304,216.00
25 cents	556,125,928	139,031,482.00
50 cents	271,783,861	135,891,930.50
Totals	1,819,223,300	$368,724,079.45

Small-size paper money

The small-size notes were first issued in mid-1929, though some carry the series year designation of 1928. Issues in the small-size category comprise United States notes, silver certificates, national bank notes, Federal Reserve Bank notes, Federal Reserve notes and gold certificates.

The small-size notes measure 6.125 inches by 2.625 inches or 156 millimeters by 67 millimeters. Officials cited savings in production costs and easier handling as reasons for reducing the size of U.S. paper money.

As with large-size notes, small-size notes were issued in many different currency types. Designs were standardized by denomination, with a $10 silver certificate having the same designs as a contemporary $10 Federal Reserve note, for example, the only differences being in such details as the description of the currency type, the printed obligation, and the color of the Treasury seal and serial numbers.

Over the years, however, the number of currency types in active circulation became fewer as the government stopped issuing certain types. By the mid- to late 1960s, Federal Reserve notes became the only form of paper money printed and issued. All earlier forms of federal paper money currency remain legal tender. On occasion, individuals may find older currency types such as silver certificates and United States notes in circulation, along with the occasional Federal Reserve Bank note, as long-stored accumulations are spent.

United States notes

The $1 United States note was issued only in Series 1928. It features a portrait of Washington on the face and is the only small-size $1 note with a red seal. The inscription is printed over the seal and states: "This note is legal tender at its face value for all debts public and private except duties on imports and interest on the public debt." The note also advises that "The United States of America will pay to the bearer on demand One Dollar." On the back of the $1 note a large ONE appears with smaller letters stating ONE DOL-LAR over the larger ONE.

The $2 note, featuring a portrait of Jefferson on the face and his home, Monticello, on the back, was first printed in the Series 1928 and was discontinued in 1966. Final series year for the $2 United States note was 1963A. Jefferson and Monticello remained on the $2 issues from the beginning to the end, but some changes were made in the obligation and the Treasury seal was relocated starting with the 1953 series. On this and later issues the seal is on the right, while on earlier issues it was on the left.

The first obligation says, "This note is legal tender at its face value for all debts public and private except duties on imports and interest on the public debt." Beginning with the 1953 series the obligation reads, "This note is a legal tender at its face value for all debts public and private," and on the 1963 and 1963A series the obligation advises, "This note is legal tender for all debts public and private." The motto IN GOD WE TRUST was added to the $2 note beginning with the 1963 series, and with this same series the wording "Will pay to the bearer on demand" was removed.

The $5 note went through the same inscription and seal changes as did the $2 note. It features Lincoln on the face and the Lincoln Memorial on the back. The motto was added with the 1963 (final) series. The last delivery of $5 United States notes was in late 1967.

Benjamin Franklin is featured on the face of the $100 United States note and the back displays Independence Hall. First issued in Series 1966 (the only note to have that series year), it was the first note to use the newly redesigned Treasury seal (see Treasury chapter).

All United States notes have red seals and serial numbers.

Silver certificates

The small-size silver certificates were issued in denominations of $1, $5 and $10 and were discontinued in 1963. The early issues stated that the notes were redeemable in silver dollars on demand—a clause later changed to "In silver payable to the bearer on demand." After the change, it was possible to exchange silver certificates for silver bullion.

However, on June 24, 1967, President Johnson signed into law a bill that spelled the end of silver certificate redemption. The Treasury Department announced it would redeem the certificates until June 24, 1968, and one of the wildest "silver rushes" in American history was under way. Collectors, dealers and speculators bought all the silver certificates they could get their hands on, paying premium prices, then exchanged them for silver bullion to be sold back on the silver market.

Redemptions were made at the U.S. Assay Offices in San Francisco and in New York City. During the final days of redemption, long lines of certificate holders lined the sidewalks around the assay offices to trade notes for silver before the deadline.

For small transactions, the assay offices issued small envelopes each valued at $1, containing .77-plus ounces of fine silver in the form of crystals or pellets. For larger transactions, plastic bags of silver granules or bars of silver were used. The standard bar varied in weight from 1,000 to 1,100 ounces at $1.292929292 per fine troy ounce, raised to the next highest dollar. The exchanges had to be made in person because the assay offices were instructed not to exchange silver by mail.

It was possible, however, for the individual having large holdings of silver certificates to arrange with certain banks to perform the redemption as a goodwill gesture. Not all banks, though, were willing to perform this service. The banks that did cooperate would contact a bank in New York City or San Francisco and arrange for that bank to send an agent to purchase the silver. The purchasing agent in either of the two cities would ship the silver direct to the home bank's customer.

Although this mad rush to redeem silver certificates did deplete the numismatic stock somewhat, it also served to introduce additional persons to the hobby of numismatics, following the great amount of publicity that newspapers gave the modern-day silver rush. Silver certificates, like other issues that have been discontinued, remain legal tender.

The $1 silver certificate portrays Washington on the face side. On the Series 1928 to 1928E the Treasury seal is on the left and a large ONE is on the right. The back side is similar to that on the 1928 $1 United States note.

On the Series 1934 silver certificate the Treasury seal was moved from the left to right side and a large number 1 appears where the seal was on the left.

A third design, for Series 1935 to 1957 notes, reduces the size of the number 1 and the Treasury seal.

On the second two designs, the back features the Great Seal of the United States and a large ONE. The motto IN GOD WE TRUST was added to the back of some 1935G notes, and all of 1935H, 1957, 1957A and 1957B notes.

The $5 silver certificate portrays Lincoln on the face and the Lincoln Memorial on the back. The numeral 5 and the Treasury seal, left and right sides respectively, are larger on the 1934 through 1934D series than they are on series that followed, 1953 through 1953C.

Alexander Hamilton is featured on the face of the $10 silver certificate, with the U.S. Treasury Building on the back. On the first series, 1933, to the left of Hamilton is the Treasury seal and to the right TEN appears. The seal was placed upon the TEN for Series 1934 through 1934D, and was replaced on the left by the numeral 10. On later series $10 notes, the seal and numeral 10 are reduced in size from the previous issues.

The first $10 silver certificates stated "Ten Dollars payable in silver coin to the bearer on demand." This was changed for the 1934 through 1953B series and these notes read "Ten Dollars in silver payable to the bearer on demand."

The inscription on 1933 series $10 silver certificates says: "This certificate issued pursuant to sections of the Act of May 12, 1933, and is legal tender at its face value for all debts public and private." Later issues simply said, "This certificate is legal tender for all debts public and private."

All silver certificates have blue seals and serial numbers, with certain exceptions. Among the exceptions are the special notes printed for use during North African and European invasions of World War II. These notes have blue serial numbers and yellow seals. These North African/European invasion notes were printed in the following series and denominations: $1, 1935A; $5, 1934 and 1934A; and $10, 1934 and 1934A. For use in Hawaii and other islands during World War II, special $1 silver certificates were printed, having brown seals and serial numbers, and overprinted with HAWAII.

A special printing (experimental) of the $1 notes was included in the series year 1935A. The United States was testing the quality of currency paper and used two types of paper for the experimental issue. Some of the notes are marked with a large "R" in the lower right side of the face, and others with a large "S" in the lower right. Like the regular certificates, these notes have blue seals and numbers.

National bank notes

Small-size national bank notes were all of Series 1929, but were issued through 1935. Issued by hundreds of banks throughout the nation, all carry the signatures of the issuing bank's president and cashier, along with the signatures of the register of the treasury and the United States treasurer. Designs are similar to designs on other small-size notes of the same denomination. They were issued in denominations of $5, $10, $20, $50 and $100. All state NATIONAL CURRENCY at the top center of each note, and all have brown seals and brown serial numbers.

Two types of Series 1929 national bank notes exist. Type One features the issuing bank's charter number in black at each end of the face of the note. These notes were numbered in sheets of six notes with identical numbers on each but different prefix letters: A, B, C, D, E and F from top to bottom. The serial numbers ended with a suffix letter: A for the first 999,999 sheets, B for the second 999,999 sheets and so on.

Type One notes were issued from July 1929 to May 1933.

In 1933, a new method of numbering national bank notes was approved, effective on July 1, resulting in the Type Two notes. The charter number appears on the face of each note four times: in the same locations as on the earlier notes, and two additional charter numbers in brown ink alongside the serial numbers.

Under the new numbering system, the sheets still contained six notes each but the numbers ran consecutively from one to six on the first sheet, seven through 12 on the second sheet, and so on, with each of the first 999,999 notes having prefix letter A, and none having a suffix letter. The bank charter number preceded the serial number in the upper right corner and followed the serial number in the lower left corner of the notes.

After the numbering sequence reached 999,999 the prefix letter changed to B. This sequence progressed alphabetically with one exception—the letter O was never used.

The notes carried the issuing bank's name, city and state as well as the bold, black, charter number on both types. Also featured on both types were words stating that the notes were secured by United States bonds deposited with the treasurer of the United States of America.

Records do not reveal the number of national bank notes issued by type and denomination to the issuing banks, nor do the records of outstanding notes give reliable information about the number of unredeemed notes. National bank notes have one thing in common with all other discontinued notes—they remain legal tender of the United States.

Federal Reserve Bank notes

Only one series of small-size Federal Reserve Bank notes was issued, Series 1929. They are often confused with Federal Reserve notes or are mistaken for national bank notes.

The confusion arises in part from design similarities—in fact, plates formerly intended for national bank notes were used to print the Federal Reserve Bank notes. To further complicate matters, they are inscribed NATIONAL CURRENCY across the top as are national bank notes.

Federal Reserve Bank notes were authorized by Act of Congress March 9, 1933, to permit Federal Reserve Banks to issue currency equal to 100 percent of the face value of U.S. bonds, or 90 percent of the value of commercial paper used as collateral. The first notes were issued March 11, with the rapid response of the BEP to the new authorization only possible through the use of the slightly modified national bank note plates.

Since the plates for the national bank notes bore the titles of the issuing national banks, information not applicable to the Federal Reserve Bank notes, those titles were obscured with heavy lines, and the issuing Federal Reserve Bank governor's information was added in place of the national bank's president.

The obligation to pay the bearer is the same as it is on the national bank notes, but the words, "or by like deposit of other securities," have been added below the "United States of America" at the top of the notes.

Series 1929 FRBNs were printed in denominations of $5, $10, $20, $50 and $100. They have brown seals and brown serial numbers. Although they carry the series year of 1929, the first notes were not delivered until March 11, 1933, and the last delivery of the notes was on Dec. 21 of that same year.

Federal Reserve notes

Federal Reserve notes are authorized by the Act of Congress of Dec. 23, 1917. These notes are issued by the Federal Reserve Banks. They were originally authorized in denominations of $5, $10, $20, $50, $100, $500, $1,000, $5,000 and $10,000. The $1 and $2 denominations were authorized June 4, 1963, with the first $1 FRNs issued in 1963 and the first $2 FRNs released in 1976. The printing of Federal Reserve notes in denominations of $500 and higher was discontinued by action of the board of governors of the Federal Reserve System on June 26, 1946.

Federal Reserve notes are obligations of the United States and were secured by the deposit with Federal Reserve agents of an equivalent amount of collateral, consisting of gold certificates or gold certificate credits with the treasurer of the United States; such discounted or purchased paper as is eligible under the terms of the Federal Reserve Act as amended; and direct obligations of the United States.

Until 1968, Federal Reserve Banks were required to maintain a reserve, in gold certificates or gold certificate credits, equal to at least 25 percent of Federal Reserve notes in actual circulation. This requirement was abolished in 1968.

Federal Reserve notes have always been printed at the Bureau of Engraving and Printing, although it is not required by law. The Federal Reserve Act merely states that the comptroller of the currency, under the direction of the secretary of the Treasury, shall have the plates engraved and the notes printed. The entire expense of engraving and printing the notes is paid by the Federal Reserve Banks, and is credited to the bureau's revolving fund.

The number to be ordered is determined by the board of governors of the Federal Reserve System, but the comptroller of the currency issues the printing order. The volume of Federal Reserve currency fluctuates, so it is necessary to keep a large stock on hand before issue. This reserve stock is kept in the vaults of the bureau until it is shipped to the several banks.

The storage of these notes is not, strictly speaking, a BEP activity. The law requires that the stock be kept in the Treasury, subtreasury, or a Mint until delivered to the banks.

The packages of completed notes are delivered by the Currency Processing Division of the Bureau to the Federal Reserve vault located in each of the BEP's two production facilities, and remains under the control of the BEP until shipment is made to Federal Reserve banks. See Chapter 6 (Bureau of Engraving and Printing) for how paper money is printed.

Until the mid-1990s, Federal Reserve notes bore the same designs as appear on the same denominations of several other note types, with only minor modifications unique to the type. However, see the section "Features of current U.S. paper money" for details of major design changes introduced starting in 1996.

Bicentennial $2 notes

Federal Reserve note denominations increased by one April 13, 1976, when the Series 1976 $2 note was issued in commemoration of the American Independence Bicentennial. Treasury Secretary William Simon announced Nov. 3, 1975, that the note would be reissued bearing Thomas Jefferson's portrait as on the $2 United States note, but with a reverse depicting a scene from John Trumbull's *Signing of the Declaration of Independence.* The April 13 release date was Jefferson's birthday.

Treasury officials hoped public acceptance of the

$2 note would alleviate demand for the $1 note, thus relieving pressure on the Bureau of Engraving and Printing. The $1 note represents the bulk of the work of the BEP.

The release of the note did trigger a new collector's item—the postally canceled note. U.S. Postal Service officials agreed to permit collectors to attach stamps to the bills that were then postally canceled on April 13 as a first day issue, and later on other commemorative dates.

The $2 note never became popular in commerce in most areas of the United States, and nearly two decades passed before supplies fell to a level that required printing additional notes. In mid-1992, the Bureau of Engraving and Printing announced it would begin printing Series 1976 $2 FRNs again because its supply of uncut sheets of $2 notes had sold out.

The BEP said it would print 40,000 uncut sheets of the 32-subject $2 notes of Series 1976, because it was the last series authorized at the time, to be offered in four-, 16-, and 32-subject sheets.

Later, the Federal Reserve's supply of Series 1976 $2 notes fell below its minimum levels, forcing the Federal Reserve to order more $2 notes.

The BEP's Fort Worth, Texas, facility printed Series 1995 notes in 1996. All bear the Atlanta Federal Reserve Bank seal, although they circulated elsewhere. No Series 1995 $2 notes were printed in Washington. Production ended in October 1996 and the new notes entered circulation late that year. The BEP printed 153.6 million Series 1995 $2 notes.

In September 2006, the BEP printed 185,600,000 Series 2003A $2 notes.

Small-size currency series

Since July 10, 1929, the date the small-size currency was first put into circulation, the BEP has printed and delivered the following series of notes:

$1 silver certificates: Series 1928, 1928A, 1928B, 1928C, 1928D, 1928E, 1934, 1935, 1935A, 1935B, 1935C, 1935D, 1935E, 1935F, 1935G, 1935H, 1957, 1957A and 1957B.

$5 silver certificates: Series 1934, 1934A, 1934B, 1934C, 1934D, 1953, 1953A, 1953B and (printed but not released) 1953C.

$10 silver certificates: Series 1933, 1933A, 1934, 1934A, 1934B, 1934C, 1934D, 1953, 1953A and 1953B.

$1 United States notes: Series 1928.

$2 United States notes: Series 1928, 1928A, 1928B, 1928C, 1928D, 1928E, 1928F, 1928G, 1953, 1953A, 1953B, 1953C, 1963 and 1963A.

$5 United States notes: Series 1928, 1928A, 1928B, 1928C, 1928D, 1928E, 1928F, 1953, 1953A, 1953B, 1953C and 1963.

$10 and $20 United States notes: Series 1928 (reported but unverified).

$100 United States notes: Series 1966 and 1966A.

$1 Federal Reserve notes: Series 1963, 1963A, 1963B, 1969, 1969A, 1969B, 1969C, 1969D, 1974, 1977, 1977A, 1981, 1981A, 1985, 1988, 1988A, 1990, 1993, 1995, 1999, 2001, 2003, 2003A, 2006 and 2009.

$2 Federal Reserve notes: 1976, 1995, 2003 and 2003A.

$5 Federal Reserve notes: Series 1928, 1928A, 1928B, 1928C, 1928D, 1934, 1934A, 1934B, 1934C, 1934D, 1950, 1950A, 1950B, 1950C, 1950D, 1950E, 1963, 1963A, 1969, 1969A, 1969B, 1969C, 1974, 1977, 1977A, 1981, 1981A, 1985, 1988, 1988A, 1993, 1995, 1999, 2001, 2003, 2003A and 2006.

$10 Federal Reserve notes: Series 1928, 1928A, 1928B, 1928C, 1934, 1934A, 1934B, 1934C, 1934D, 1950, 1950A, 1950B, 1950C, 1950D, 1950E, 1963, 1963A, 1969, 1969A, 1969B, 1969C, 1974, 1977, 1977A, 1981, 1981A, 1985, 1988, 1988A, 1990, 1993, 1995, 1999, 2001, 2003, 2004A, 2006 and 2009.

$20 Federal Reserve notes: Series 1928, 1928A, 1928B, 1928C, 1934, 1934A, 1934B, 1934C, 1934D, 1950, 1950A, 1950B, 1950C, 1950D, 1950E, 1963, 1963A, 1969, 1969A, 1969B, 1969C, 1974, 1977, 1981, 1981A, 1985, 1988, 1988A, 1990, 1993, 1995, 1996, 1999, 2001, 2004, 2004A, 2006 and 2009.

$50 Federal Reserve notes: Series 1928, 1928A, 1934, 1934A, 1934B, 1934C, 1934D, 1950, 1950A, 1950B, 1950C, 1950D, 1950E, 1963A, 1969, 1969A, 1969B, 1969C, 1974, 1977, 1981, 1981A, 1985, 1988, 1988A, 1990, 1993, 1996, 2001, 2004, 2004A and 2006.

$100 Federal Reserve notes: Series 1928, 1928A, 1934, 1934A, 1934B, 1934C, 1934D, 1950, 1950A, 1950B, 1950C, 1950D, 1950E, 1963A, 1969, 1969A, 1969C, 1974, 1977, 1981, 1981A, 1985, 1988, 1990, 1993, 1996, 1999, 2001, 2003, 2003A, 2006 and 2009.

$500 Federal Reserve notes: Series 1928, 1934, 1934A, 1934B and 1934C.

$1,000 Federal Reserve notes: Series 1928, 1934, 1934A and 1934C.

$5,000 and $10,000 Federal Reserve notes: Series 1928, 1934, 1934A and 1934B.

$5, $10, $20, $50 and $100 Federal Reserve Bank notes: Series 1929.

$5, $10, $20, $50 and $100 national bank notes: Series 1929.

$10 and $20 gold certificates: Series 1928 and (printed but not released) 1928A.

$50, $500 and $5,000 gold certificates: Series 1928.

$100, $1,000 and $10,000 gold certificates: Series 1928 and (printed but not released) 1934.

$100,000 gold certificates: Series 1934.

Barr notes

Barr notes are those signed by Secretary of the Treasury Joseph W. Barr, who served from Dec. 21, 1968, to Jan. 20, 1969. Appointed to fill out the unexpired term of Henry H. Fowler, Barr was replaced as

Treasury secretary by David M. Kennedy.

Born in Vincennes, Ind., Barr had been undersecretary of the Treasury since April 1965. A former U.S. representative from Indiana, he joined the Treasury in 1961 as an assistant to the secretary.

Because Barr served such a short term as secretary of the Treasury, one month, some believed those notes signed by Barr were issued in limited numbers and would soon become rare.

However, production of Barr notes did not stop on Jan. 20, 1969, when he resigned. Not until June 4, 1969, were notes printed bearing the signature of Barr's successor.

Barr notes are not considered rare by informed paper money collectors.

The following chart shows how many Federal Reserve notes featuring Secretary Barr's signature were delivered to the Federal Reserve.

Barr note statistics

Federal Reserve District	Regular Notes	Star Notes
New York	123,040,000	3,680,000
Richmond	93,600,000	3,200,000
Chicago	91,040,000	2,400,000
Kansas City	44,800,000	None Printed
San Francisco	106,400,000	3,040,000
Total notes printed	458,880,000	12,320,000

Less spoilage: Based on past reports, spoilage is estimated at 6 percent for regular notes and 4.5 percent for star notes.

Official serial number range

District	Regular Notes		Star Notes	
New York	B57 600 001G	B80 640 000H	B48 800 001H	B52 480 000H
Richmond	E32 000 001F	E25 600 000G	E41 600 001H	E44 800 000H
Chicago	G84 480 001H	G75 520 000I	G52 640 001H	G55 040 000H
Kansas City	J19 200 001C	J64 000 000C	None printed	
San Francisco	L76 800 001F	L83 200 000G	L43 040 001H	L46 080 000H

The first delivery of notes bearing Joseph Barr's signature took place on Jan. 16, 1969 (Richmond District), and the last delivery was Nov. 12, 1969 (New York District).

Features of current U.S. paper money

Changes in the presses and the designs of notes have resulted in variations in some features and not in others. Beginning in 1996, the Bureau of Engraving and Printing began producing redesigned Federal Reserve notes all with a large, off-center portrait. The first redesigned note issued was the $100 note, followed by the $50 in 1997, the $20 in 1998, the $10 and the $5 in 2000. As of early 2011, officials say the $1 and $2 notes will not undergo the same redesign as the higher denominations.

Plate position numbers

A small capital letter and number combination that appears in various locations on the face of the notes comprises what is referred to as the plate position number. This item designates the position of the note on the 32-subject face plate from which a particular bill was printed.

Each I-10 press 32-note sheet is split into four quadrants, each having two vertical rows of four notes each. The upper left quadrant is No. 1, the lower left, No. 2; the upper right is No. 3; and the lower right, No. 4. Within the quadrant, the left four notes, from top to bottom, are A, B, C, D; the right row is E, F, G, H. Thus, a note with position number B3 would be in the upper right quadrant, left row, second note from top. An H1 note would be from the upper left quadrant, right row, fourth note from top.

The story was a little different for $1 Federal Reserve notes produced on the BEP's experimental web-fed intaglio press. Changes were made to the look of the notes because of requirements of the press. On notes printed on the web-fed press, the quadrant number and plate position letter at the upper left of the face were removed. The plate position letter at the lower right of the face side of the note also was removed, leaving only the face plate number (see the "Plate numbers" section).

On the back of the web notes, the back plate number appears above the E in ONE, rather than below it as on traditional sheet-fed notes. These web notes were printed for Series 1988A, 1993 and 1995 $1 Federal Reserve notes only.

Plate numbers

A small number on the face in various locations, dependent on the denomination, relates to the face plate from which a note was printed. This is referred to as the plate serial number. This number is assigned in sequential order at the time the plate is manufactured. It can be used to determine the number of the press plate from which a particular note was printed. The letter preceding the plate serial number is always the same as the letter in the upper left-hand corner on sheet-fed notes. The back of the note also has a back plate number, which relates the note to the back press plate, and is located to the lower right on notes printed on the sheet-fed presses.

Series date

The series date on the face of each bill, usually, signifies the year in which the design of the note was adopted or other change was made. The series does not change with each calendar year. The capital letter following the series year indicates that a minor change was authorized in a particular series.

According to the Bureau of Engraving and Printing, the series date changes when a new secretary of the Treasury is confirmed or when there is a major redesign on currency.

Few noncollectors realize this, resulting in confusion and the spread of misinformation. During 1999, *Coin World* received a number of calls from noncollectors who had heard that the Series 1996 $20 FRNs, released in 1998, were being recalled because they had been given the wrong date. The rumor was based on the false assumption that the series designation on a note is analogous to the date on a coin. The Series 1996 refers to when the design changes were approved to the $20 FRN, not to the year the notes were first printed and released.

Today, when a capital letter is added following the series year, it indicates a new U.S. treasurer has been appointed but the Treasury secretary has remained the same, and a corresponding change is made in the signature of the treasurer.

The current practice of series designation is relatively recent; the process has changed over the years.

Prior to 1974, the series date referred to the year in which the face design was adopted, according to the *Standard Handbook of Modern United States Paper Money* by Chuck O'Donnell. O'Donnell wrote that the capital letter following the series designation reflected minor change in a specific series. Minor changes then were viewed as including the introduction of the signatures of a new secretary of the treasury or treasurer.

That policy was changed when William B. Simon became secretary of the Treasury in 1974. He ordered that the series year be changed whenever a new secretary of the Treasury took office. However, that practice was not universally followed after he left office. The election of Jimmy Carter as president in 1976 resulted in a new treasurer and secretary of the treasury, and a new series designation—1977. However, when Carter's first Treasury secretary was replaced with his second secretary in 1979, the series designation became 1977A, not 1979, which would have been the case had the Simon policy been followed.

The policy of changing the series year with a new Treasury secretary and only the suffix letter with a change in treasurer became established with the Reagan administration and has been followed ever since. The authorization of new design elements in 1990 (actually implemented in 1991) and 1996 (implemented in 1996, 1997 and 1998) have resulted in changes to the series year as well.

In 2008, a new series designation oddity was revealed when redesigned $5 Federal Reserve notes were put into circulation as Series 2006. The new, more colorful notes, bearing the facsimile signatures of Treasury Secretary Henry M. Paulson Jr. and Treasurer Anna Escobedo Cabral, bore the same Series 2006 designation as the old-style notes bearing the Paulson-Cabral signature combination—despite the major design change, which would normally require a new series designation.

Paulson was sworn into office as Treasury secretary July 10, 2006, so when the first notes of the older style were introduced, they were issued with the Series 2006 designation as was traditional.

The reason the Series 2006 designation was kept for the more colorful design, resulting in the same series year date on two different designs? According to the BEP the colorful, redesigned $5 note "is considered to be in the same 'color of money series' as was the Series 2006 $10 bill; hence the 2006 designation."

The clue to determine which design style is which in a listing of Series 2006 $5 FRNs without images is in the serial numbers (see the "Serial numbers" section that follows for an explanation of the purpose of the two prefix letters). The first prefix letter for the earlier-style Series 2006 $5 notes is H and the first prefix letter on the colorized Series 2006 $5 FRNs is I.

Size of currency

Currency of the present size was first issued in July 1929, replacing the old, large (7.50 by 3.125 inches) notes. The present size of a U.S. bill is 6.14 inches by 2.61 inches, and the thickness is .0043 inch. New notes stack 233 to an inch, not compressed, and weigh 490 notes to a pound. A million notes will weigh approximately 2,000 pounds and occupy approximately 42 cubic feet of space, with moderate pressure.

Serial numbers

Serial numbers are designed to foil counterfeiters and to accommodate the large volume of notes printed by the BEP. No two notes of a class, denomination and series have the same serial number, except for error notes. Each serial number has eight numerals, plus one or two prefix letters, depending on the design style, and a suffix letter or suffix star (★).

When a new series of Federal Reserve notes is initiated, a new number sequence generally begins (although serial numbers continued from Series 1977 to 1977A). The first of the sequence is 00 000 001A, the second is 00 000 002A, the hundredth is 00 000 100A, the thousandth 00 001 000A and so on, until the number 96 000 000 A is reached, at which point the suffix letter changes to B and the numbering system starts over. The letter O is never used as a suffix letter because it could be confused with the digit 0.

Serial numbers do not advance sequentially from note to note on an individual sheet, but from sheet to sheet. On a sheet, the numbers advance 100,000 digits from note to note, since sheets are overprinted in 100,000-sheet runs. As a result, when the stacks of sheets are cut, serial numbers run sequentially through each stack of cut notes.

On United States notes and silver certificates, the first note was numbered A 00 000 001A, and continued in numerical sequence with the prefix and suffix letters remaining the same. When the number A 99 999 999A was reached, the suffix letter A was retained and the prefix letter changed alphabetically, until 25 blocks of 99 999 999 are printed, each with a different prefix letter of the alphabet from A to Z, omitting O.

On pre-1996 series notes, the serial number, with prefix and suffix letters or stars, appears in two places, once in the lower-left and once in the upper-right quadrant of all small-size notes. The letter in the Federal Reserve Bank seal is identical to the prefix letter of the serial number on pre-1996 Federal Reserve notes.

Serial numbers on Series 1996 and later $5, $10, $20, $50 and $100 Federal Reserve notes are located in the upper-left and lower-right quadrants on the face of the notes, a shift in their positions.

In addition, since redesign efforts began in 1996 each redesigned note bears two prefix letters before the serial number rather than one. The first prefix letter indicates the series year and the second prefix letter identifies the Federal Reserve district for which the note was printed. The table that follows details first prefix letter, series year and denominations, from Series 1996 through the early production of Series 2009 notes:

Noncolorful designs

Prefix	Series	Denominations
A	Series 1996	$20, $50, $100
B	Series 1999	$5, $10, $20, $100
C	Series 2001	$5, $10, $20, $50, $100
D	Series 2003	$5, $10, $100
F	Series 2003A	$5, $100
H	Series 2006	$5, $100

Colorful designs

Prefix	Series	Denominations
E	Series 2004	$20, $50
G	Series 2004A	$10, $20, $50
I	Series 2006	$5, $10, $20, $50
J	Series 2009	$10, $20, $100

Because Series 1996 notes introduced a universal Federal Reserve seal an additional letter-number combination was added below the serial number to indicate the series and Federal Reserve Bank the note was issued for. All Series 1996 notes bear letter A followed by the number designating the FR Bank. In addition, the letter-number combination on the Series 1996 $100 note is green in color while on the $50 and $20 notes from the same series the letter-number combination is printed in black.

Federal Reserve symbols

On the face of every pre-1996 series Federal Reserve note, the black seal to left of the portrait identifies the particular Federal Reserve Bank that issued the bill.

The Series 1996 redesigned notes introduced a universal Federal Reserve seal that doesn't differentiate between Federal Reserve Banks (see "Serial numbers" section).

The 12 Federal Reserve Banks (see Chapter 7), are each identifiable by a letter and a number, with the letter corresponding to the number, as follows (see Chapter 7 for more information on the Federal Reserve):

1	A	Boston
2	B	New York
3	C	Philadelphia
4	D	Cleveland
5	E	Richmond
6	F	Atlanta
7	G	Chicago
8	H	St. Louis
9	I	Minneapolis
10	J	Kansas City
11	K	Dallas
12	L	San Francisco

The Federal Reserve Bank number, which appears four times on pre-1996 notes, is repeated in the upper and lower and the left and right sections of the bill for identification purposes. These numbers are not on Series 1996 and later notes.

Great Seal of the United States

Both the obverse and the reverse of the Great Seal of the United States are reproduced on the backs of $1 bills. The Great Seal was adopted in 1782. Its obverse depicts an eagle breasted by a shield with the national colors. The eagle holds in his right talon an olive branch of 13 leaves and 13 berries, symbolic of peace. In his left talon he holds 13 arrows signifying the original Colonies' fight for liberty. A ribbon flying from the beak of the eagle is inscribed with the Latin motto, "E Pluribus Unum," which is translated "One out of many," in reference to the unity of the 13 Colonies as one government.

Over the eagle's head is a constellation of 13 five-pointed stars surrounded by a wreath of clouds.

The reverse of the seal depicts a pyramid, with the Roman numerals "MDCCLXXVI" on its base— 1776, the year of the Declaration of Independence. The pyramid represents permanence and strength. Its unfinished condition symbolizes the work to be done to continue to form a more perfect government and signifies the expectation that new states would be admitted to the Union.

The eye in the triangular glory represents an all-seeing Deity. The words "Annuit coeptis," translated as "He (God) has favored our undertakings," refer to the many interpositions the founding fathers saw of divine providence in the forming of the government. "Novus Ordo Seclorum," translated as "A new order of the ages," signifies a new American era.

In God We Trust

In October 1957, $1 silver certificates bearing the motto "In God We Trust" were first placed in circulation.

The suggestion to include the motto on U.S. paper currency was presented to the Secretary of the Treasury George W. Humphrey in November of 1953 by Matthew H. Rothert of Camden, Ark. Like the Baptist preacher who wrote to the secretary of the Treasury in 1861 suggesting mention of the Deity on U.S. coins, Rothert also directed his inquiry to the secretary of the treasury. He followed through with letters to several senators and representatives and to his personal friend, Thomas Weeks, secretary of commerce.

Rothert's idea came to him while he was attending church on a Sunday morning in Chicago. As the collection plate was passed, it occurred to him that only the coins in the plate had this motto. He then thought that since U.S. paper money has a much wider circulation abroad than U.S. coins, a message about the country's faith in God could be easily carried throughout the world if it were on United States paper currency.

The 84th Congress passed Public Law 140 and President Dwight D. Eisenhower signed it into law on July 11, 1955. The law provided, "At such times as new dies for the printing of currency are adopted in connection with the current program of the Treasury Department to increase the capacity of the presses utilized by the Bureau of Engraving and Printing, the dies shall bear, at such place or places as the secretary of the treasury may determine to be appropriate, the inscription 'In God We Trust,' and thereafter this inscription shall appear on all United States currency and coins."

The $ sign

The origin of the $ sign has been variously accounted for, with perhaps the most widely accepted explanation being that it is the result of evolution, independently in different places, of the Mexican or Spanish "P's" for pesos, or piastres, or pieces of eight. The theory, derived from a study of old manuscripts, is that the "S" gradually came to be written over the "P," developing a close equivalent to the $ mark, which eventually evolved.

The dollar sign was widely used before the adoption of the U.S. dollar in 1785.

Portraits on United States paper money

Listed by denomination

Denomination	Type of Note	Series	Portrait
3¢	Fractional currency	3rd issue	George Washington
5¢	Postage currency	1st issue	Thomas Jefferson
	Fractional currency	2nd issue	George Washington
	Fractional currency	3rd issue	Spencer M. Clark
10¢	Postage currency	1st issue	George Washington
	Fractional currency	2nd issue	George Washington
	Fractional currency	3rd issue	George Washington
	Fractional currency	5th issue	William M. Meredith
25¢	Postage currency	1st issue	Thomas Jefferson
	Fractional currency	2nd issue	George Washington
	Fractional currency	3rd issue	William P. Fessenden
	Fractional currency	4th issue	George Washington
	Fractional currency	5th issue	Robert J. Walker
50¢	Postage currency	1st issue	George Washington
	Fractional currency	2nd issue	George Washington
	Fractional currency	3rd issue	Gen. F. E. Spinner
	Fractional currency	4th issue	Abraham Lincoln; E.M. Stanton; or Samuel Dexter
	Fractional currency	5th issue	William H. Crawford
$1	Federal Reserve note	1963 to date	George Washington
	Federal Reserve Bank note	1918	George Washington
	United States note	1862	Salmon P. Chase
	United States note	1869 to 1928	George Washington
	Silver certificate	1886 to 1891	Martha Washington
	Silver certificate	1899	Lincoln & Grant

Denomination	Type of Note	Series	Portrait
$1 (continued)	Silver certificate	1923 to 1957B	George Washington
	Treasury or coin note	1890 to 1891	Edwin M. Stanton
$2	Federal Reserve Bank note	1918	Thomas Jefferson
	Federal Reserve note	1976 to 1995	Thomas Jefferson
	United States note	1862	Alexander Hamilton
	United States note	1869 to 1963A	Thomas Jefferson
	Silver certificate	1886	General Hancock
	Silver certificate	1891	William Windom
	Silver certificate	1899	George Washington
	Treasury or coin note	1890 to 1891	Gen. James McPherson
$5	Demand note	1861	Alexander Hamilton
	Federal Reserve note	1914 to date	Abraham Lincoln
	Federal Reserve Bank note	1915 to 1929	Abraham Lincoln
	United States note	1869 to 1907	Andrew Jackson
	United States note	1928 to 1963A	Abraham Lincoln
	National bank note	1882	James Garfield
	National bank note	1902	Benjamin Harrison
	National bank note	1929	Abraham Lincoln
	Silver certificate	1886	Ulysses S. Grant
	Silver certificate	1899	Running Antelope
	Silver certificate	1923 to 1953C	Abraham Lincoln
	Treasury or coin note	1890 to 1891	Gen. George Thomas
$10	Demand note	1861	Abraham Lincoln
	Compound-interest Treasury note	1863 to 1864	Salmon P. Chase
	Interest-bearing note, 3 year	1863	Salmon P. Chase
	Federal Reserve note	1914	Andrew Jackson
	Federal Reserve note	1928 to date	Alexander Hamilton
	Federal Reserve Bank note	1915 to 1918	Andrew Jackson
	Federal Reserve Bank note	1929	Alexander Hamilton
	Gold certificate	1907 to 1922	Michael Hillegas
	Gold certificate	1928	Alexander Hamilton
	United States note	1862 to 1863	Abraham Lincoln
	United States note	1869 to 1880	Daniel Webster
	United States note	1901	Lewis & Clark
	United States note	1923	Andrew Jackson
	National Bank note	1902	William McKinley
	National Bank note	1929	Alexander Hamilton
	Refunding certificate	1879	Benjamin Franklin
	Silver certificate	1878 to 1880	Robert Morris
	Silver certificate	1886 to 1908	Thomas A. Hendricks
	Silver certificate	1933 to 1953B	Alexander Hamilton
	Treasury or coin note	1890 to 1891	General Sheridan
$20	Compound-interest Treasury note	1863 to 1864	Abraham Lincoln
	Federal Reserve note	1914	Grover Cleveland
	Federal Reserve note	1928 to date	Andrew Jackson
	Federal Reserve Bank note	1915 to 1918	Grover Cleveland
	Federal Reserve Bank note	1929	Andrew Jackson

Denomination	Type of Note	Series	Portrait
$20 (continued)	Gold certificate	1882	James Garfield
	Gold certificate	1905 to 1922	George Washington
	Gold certificate	1928	Andrew Jackson
	Interest-bearing note, 1 year	1863	Abraham Lincoln
	United States note	1869 to 1880	Alexander Hamilton
	National bank note	1902	Hugh McCulloch
	National bank note	1929	Andrew Jackson
	Silver certificate	1878 to 1880	Stephen Decatur
	Silver certificate	1886 to 1891	Daniel Manning
	Treasury or coin note	1890 to 1891	John Marshall
$50	Compound-interest Treasury note	1863 to 1864	Alexander Hamilton
	Federal Reserve note	1914 to date	Ulysses S. Grant
	Federal Reserve Bank note	1918 to 1929	Ulysses S. Grant
	Gold certificate	1882	Silas Wright
	Gold certificate	1913 to 1928	Ulysses S. Grant
	Interest-bearing note, 1 year	1863	Alexander Hamilton
	United States note	1862 to 1863	Alexander Hamilton
	United States note	1869	Henry Clay
	United States note	1874 to 1880	Benjamin Franklin
	National bank note	1902	John Sherman
	National bank note	1929	Ulysses S. Grant
	Silver certificate	1878 to 1891	Edward Everett
	Treasury or coin note	1890 to 1891	William H. Seward
$100	Compound-interest Treasury note	1863 to 1864	George Washington
	Federal Reserve note	1914 to date	Benjamin Franklin
	Federal Reserve Bank note	1929	Benjamin Franklin
	Gold certificate	1875 to 1882	Thomas H. Benton
	Gold certificate	1928 to 1934	Benjamin Franklin
	Interest-bearing note, 1 year	1863	George Washington
	Interest-bearing note, 3 years	1864	General Scott
	United States note	1869 to 1880	Abraham Lincoln
	National bank note	1902	John J. Knox
	National bank note	1929	Benjamin Franklin
	Silver certificate	1878 to 1891	James Monroe
	Treasury or coin note	1890 to 1891	Commodore Farragut
$500	Federal Reserve note	1914	John Marshall
	Federal Reserve note	1928 to 1934	William McKinley
	Gold certificate	1875 to 1922	Abraham Lincoln
	Gold certificate	1928	William McKinley
	Interest-bearing note, 3 years	1864	Alexander Hamilton
	United States note	1862 to 1863	Albert Gallatin
	United States note	1869	John Quincy Adams
	United States note	1874 to 1880	Maj. Gen. Mansfield
	Silver certificate	1878 to 1880	Charles Sumner
$1,000	Federal Reserve note	1918	Alexander Hamilton
	Federal Reserve note	1928 to 1934A	Grover Cleveland
	Gold certificate	1875 to 1922	Alexander Hamilton

Denomination	Type of Note	Series	Portrait
$1,000 (continued)	Gold certificate	1928 to 1934	Grover Cleveland
	Interest-bearing note, 3 years	1863	Salmon P. Chase
	United States note	1862 to 1863	Robert Morris
	United States note	1869 to 1880	DeWitt Clinton
	Silver certificate	1878 to 1891	William L. Marcy
	Treasury or coin note	1890 to 1891	Gen. George Meade
$5,000	Federal Reserve note	1918 to 1934	James Madison
	Gold certificate	1882 to 1928	James Madison
	United States note	1878	James Madison
$10,000	Federal Reserve note	1918-1934	Salmon P. Chase
	Gold certificate	1882 to 1902	Andrew Jackson
	Gold certificate	1928 to 1934	Salmon P. Chase
	United States note	1878	Andrew Jackson
$100,000	Gold certificate	1934	Woodrow Wilson

Persons on U.S. paper money, listed by name

Adams, John Quincy (1767 to 1848). Sixth president of the United States. Born in Quincy, Mass., he served as American minister in the Netherlands, Berlin, St. Petersburg and London, as U.S. senator from 1803 to 1808 and was appointed secretary of state in 1817. Elected president in 1824, served until 1829. Elected to the House in 1831 where he served until his death in 1848.

$500 1869 United States (legal tender) note

$2 Southern Bank of Indiana, Terre Haute

Adams, Samuel (1722 to 1803). Born in Boston, he served as tax collector there from 1756 to 1764. He was elected to the Massachusetts legislature in 1765, serving until 1774. He was a leader in the agitation that led to the Boston Tea Party. Delegate to the first and second Continental Congress, he signed the Declaration of Independence. He was lieutenant governor and then governor (1794 to 1797) of Massachusetts.

$10 1862 Arkansas Treasury Warrant

Alcorn, J.L. (1816 to 1894). Born in Illinois, he moved to Kentucky. Served in Kentucky House of Representatives (1843), then in Mississippi House and Senate in 1840s and 1850s. Briefly served in Confederate Army. Became a Republican after end of Civil War. Governor of Mississippi (1870 to 1871). Served in U.S. Senate from Mississippi (1871 to 1877).

$1 1870 State of Mississippi, Jackson, Miss.

$2 1870 State of Mississippi, Jackson, Miss.

$3 1870 State of Mississippi, Jackson, Miss.

Baker, Edward Dickinson (1811 to 1861). Born in London on Feb. 24, 1811, he came to the United State in 1816, studied and practiced law in Springfield, Ill., served as state senator in 1840 and was elected to Congress in 1844. Elected to U.S. Senate from Oregon in 1860. Baker was killed in the early days of the Civil War while commanding a Union brigade; he was the only member of the U.S. Senate to die in battle during the war.

$5,000 1872 Currency Certificate of Deposit

Beauregard, Gen. P.G.T. (1818 to 1893). Pierre Gustave Toutant

de Beauregard was born near New Orleans. Graduated from West Point in 1838. He served through the Mexican War. He was superintendent of West Point at the outbreak of the Civil War; he resigned to enter the Confederate Army. He was in command at the bombardment of Fort Sumter and served at Bull Run, Shiloh and Corinth. He was manager of the Louisiana Lottery and commissioner of public works in New Orleans (1888).

$20 1863 State of Louisiana, Shreveport

Benjamin, Judah Philip (1811 to 1884). Born in St. Croix, British West Indies (some sources say St. Thomas, Virgin Islands), he entered Yale in 1825. He entered the U.S. Senate in 1852 and withdrew in 1861 to join the Confederacy. He served as attorney general, secretary of war and secretary of state in the Confederacy.

$2 Sept. 2, 1861, Confederate note

$2 June 2, 1862, Confederate note

$2 Dec. 2, 1862, Confederate note

$2 April 6, 1863, Confederate note

$2 Feb. 17, 1864, Confederate note

Bennett, Jonathan M. (1816 to 1887). Deputy sheriff of Lewis County, Va., 1836 to 1838. Mayor of Weston, Va., 1846. President of Exchange Bank of Virginia at Weston, 1853. Public account auditor of Virginia, 1857 to 1865. Democrat, member of West Virginia Senate, Ninth District, 1873 to 1875; chairman of Committee on Finance.

$5 1862 Virginia Treasury note

Benton, Thomas Hart (1782 to 1858). Served in U.S. Senate (1821 to 1851) and in the U.S. House of Representatives (1853 to 1855). He was in favor of Western development and spoke out against slavery.

$100 1863, 1882 gold certificate

Boone, Daniel (1734 to 1820). Born near Reading, Pa., in 1734, he made trips to Kentucky in 1767, 1769 to 1770. He guided settlers into Kentucky (1775) and erected a fort on the site of what is now Boonesboro. Served in Virginia legislature. After some years in Virginia he moved into what is now Missouri and secured a land grant.

$3 Clark's Exchange Bank, Springfield, Ill.

$10 Bank of Kentucky, Louisville, Ky.

$10 Bank of Louisville, Ky.

Boudinot, Elias (1740 to 1821). Born in Philadelphia. Opened law practice in Elizabethtown, N.J. Member and president of the Continental Congress. Member of U.S. Congress (1789 to 1795). Appointed director of the Mint in October 1795 by Washington and served until July 1, 1805. Trustee of Princeton (1772 to 1821). Helped found American Bible Society in 1816 and served as its first president.

$2 1858 Merchants Bank, New Bedford, Mass.

$2 1858 Delaware City Bank, Delaware City, Kan.

$2 1859 Safety Fund Bank, Boston, Mass.

$2 1861 Bank of Penn Township, Philadelphia, Pa.

$2 1861 What Cheer Bank, Providence, R.I.

$5 1863 Belvidere Bank, Belvidere, N.J.

$20 18-- Augusta, Ga., Insurance and Banking Co.

$20 1832 Bank of Darien, Ga.

$20 1857 Augusta, Ga., Insurance and Banking Co.

Brown, Joseph E. (1821 to 1894). Born in South Carolina. Lawyer and businessman. Elected to Georgia state Senate (1849), then as a state circuit judge (1855). Governor of Georgia (1861 to 1865). Later served as chief justice of Georgia Supreme Court, then in U.S. Senate (1880 to 1890).

$50 1862 The State of Georgia, Milledgeville

$100 1863 The State of Georgia, Milledgeville

Buchanan, James (1791 to 1868). Fifteenth president of the United States. Born near Mercersburg, Pa., he graduated from Dickinson College in 1809. A volunteer in the War of 1812, member of the House from 1821 to 1831, U.S. minister to Great Britain from 1853 to 1856, he was elected president in 1856 and served until 1861.

$3 1856 Fontenelle Bank, Bellevue, Neb.

$5 1852 Omaha, Neb., City Bank and Land Co.

$5 1857 Bank of Tekama, Neb.

$5 1858 Bank of the District of Columbia

$5 1859 Union Bank of Columbia, Washington, D.C.

$5 1861 Monongahela Valley Bank, McKee's Port, Pa.

$5 18-- Bank of Crawford County, Pa.

$10 North Western Bank, Ringgold, Ga.

$10 1857 New England Bank, Fairmount, Maine

$10 1857 Manufacturers Bank, Macon, Ga.

$20 Bank of Pittsylvania, Chatham, Pa.

Calhoun, John Caldwell (1782 to 1850). Born near Calhoun Mills, S.C., he graduated from Yale in 1804. A member of the House from 1811 to 1817, secretary of war (1817 to 1825), vice president from 1825 to 1832, senator (1832 to 1843), secretary of state (1844 to 1845), he championed slavery and the Southern cause in Senate debates.

$2 1860 Eastern Bank of Alabama, Eufala

$2 Bank of the State of S. Carolina, Charleston

$5 Northern Bank of Alabama, Huntsville

$5 Bank of South Carolina

$10 Bank of East Tennessee, Knoxville

$10 Northern Bank of Alabama, Huntsville

$10 1862 Manufacturers Bank, Macon, Ga.

$10 1860 Farmers and Mechanics Bank, Savannah, Ga.

$20 1860 Farmers and Mechanics Bank, Savannah, Ga.

$25 Planters Bank of Fairfield, Tenn.

$100 Confederate note, April 17, 1862

$1,000 Confederate note, Montgomery issue, 1861

Chase, Salmon Portland (1808 to 1873). Governor of Ohio, secretary of the Treasury under Lincoln (1861 to 1864), he originated national banking system. Chief justice of the United States (1864 to 1873).

$1 1862 legal tender note

$10 1863, 1864 6 percent compound interest Treasury note

$10 1863 5 percent compound interest Treasury note

$20 1861 6 percent 2-year, interest-bearing Treasury note

$1,000 1861, 1864, 1865 7.3 percent 3-year interest-bearing note

$10,000 1918, 1928, 1934 Federal Reserve note

$10,000 1928, 1934 gold certificate

Clark, Spencer M. (1810 to 1890). First chief of the National Currency Bureau, predecessor of the Bureau of Engraving and Printing, from 1862 to 1868. The one note to depict Clark is one of the more curious U.S. paper notes. An order from the Treasury Department directed an issue to honor Lewis and Clark, the famed explorers of the Northwest Territory. Instead, Spencer Clark, a $1,200-a-year chief clerk, interpreted the order to mean his image was to be placed on the note. Congress wanted to fire him, but Secretary of the Treasury Salmon P. Chase intervened and saved his job. As a direct result of this action, Congress enacted a law forbidding the likeness of any living person on any obligation of the United States.

5¢ fractional currency, third issue

Clark, William (1770 to 1838). American explorer and member of the Lewis and Clark Expedition, which in 1804, opened up the Louisiana Purchase to settlers.

$10 1901 legal tender note (nicknamed "Bison" note)

Clay, Clement C. (1819 to 1882). Born in Huntsville, Ala., he graduated from the University of Alabama in 1835, and was admitted to the bar in 1840. He was elected to the Senate in 1853 and reelected in 1861, when he was expelled for "treasonable utterances." He became a member of the Confederate Senate.

$1 1862, 1863, 1864 Confederate note

Clay, Henry (1777 to 1852). Born in Hanover County, Va., he practiced law in Lexington, Ky., and was elected to the Kentucky legislature in 1803. He acted as counsel for Aaron Burr in 1806. He was elected to the Senate in 1809, and served in the Senate and House until 1821. Reelected to the House in 1823 and served until 1825. He was secretary of state (1825 to 1829), senator (1831 to 1842), Whig candidate for president in 1832 and 1844, senator (1849 to 1852).

$1 Farmers and Millers Bank, Milwaukee

$2 American Bank, Baltimore

$2 Stonington Bank, Stonington, Conn.

$2 Shawnee Bank, Attica, Ind.

$5 Bank of Kentucky, Louisville, Ky.

$5 Farmers and Mechanics Bank, Shippensburg, Pa.

$20 City Bank of New Haven, Conn.

$50 1869 United States (legal tender) note

Clemens, Samuel Langhorne (Mark Twain) (1835 to 1910). American journalist, author, novelist, essayist and humorist writing under the pen name Mark Twain. Became acclaimed as a humorist after writing the short story "The Celebrated Jumping Frog of Calaveras County" in 1865. Best known works include *Life on the Mississippi, The Adventures of Tom Sawyer* and *Adventures of Huckleberry Finn*, the latter work considered one of the greatest pieces of American literature.

5¢, 10¢, 25¢, 50¢ Series 701 military payment certificate (unissued)

Cleveland, Stephen Grover (1837 to 1908). Twenty-second (1885 to 1889) and 24th (1893 to 1897) president of the United States, the only president to serve two nonconsecutive terms. Born in Caldwell, N.J., he was mayor of Buffalo, N.Y. (1881 to 1882), governor of New York (1883 to 1885). He was defeated by Benjamin Harrison in his bid for president in 1888.

$20 1915, 1918 Federal Reserve Bank note

$20 1914 Federal Reserve note

$1,000 1928, 1934 Federal Reserve note

$1,000 1928, 1934 gold certificate

Clinton, DeWitt (1769 to 1828). Born in Little Britain, N.Y., he graduated from Columbia College in 1786. He was elected to the Senate in 1798 and served until 1802, and again from 1806 to 1811. Elected mayor of New York in 1802; served three terms as governor of New York; chief sponsor of the Erie Canal.

$1 Franklin Bank, Jersey City, N.J.

$1,000 1869, 1878, 1880 United States (legal tender) note

Conant, Charles Arthur. A leading proponent of the Philippine National Bank, Conant is considered to be the "Father" of the United States-Philippine currency system.

1 peso 1918, 1921, 1924 Philippine national bank circulating notes

Counts, Daniel W. (1800 to 1883). Member of North Carolina House of Commons, 1831 to 1833, 1836, 1846 and 1848. Member of state Senate, 1850. State treasurer of North Carolina 1836 to 1839 and 1852 to 1863.

$5 1863 State of North Carolina, Raleigh, N.C.

$10 1863 State of North Carolina, Raleigh, N.C.

Crawford, William H. (1772 to 1834). A senator from Georgia (1807 to 1813), he also served as secretary of war under President Madison (1815 to 1816) and secretary of the Treasury (1815 to 1825).

50¢ fractional currency, fifth issue

Crittenden, John Jordan (1787 to 1863). Born near Versailles, Ky., he was a senator (1817 to 1819, 1835 to 1841, 1842 to 1848 and 1850 to 1853). He also served as attorney general (1841,

1850 to 1853) and as governor of Kentucky (1848 to 1850).

$50 Commercial Bank of Kentucky, Paducah, Ky.

Davis, Jefferson (1808 to 1889). Born in Fairfield, Ky., he was appointed to West Point in 1824 and served in the U.S. Army until 1835. He was elected to the House in 1845, resigned in 1846 to serve in the Mexican War. He was a senator (1847 to 1851), secretary of war (1853 to 1857), and again senator (1857 to 1861). Chosen president of the Confederacy Feb. 18, 1861. He fled from Richmond in 1865 and was captured and indicted for treason, but the government entered a nolle prosequi in 1868. He retired to his estate near Biloxi, Miss.

50¢ April 6, 1863, Confederate note

50¢ Feb. 17, 1864, Confederate note

$1 1862 State of Missouri, Jefferson City, Mo.

$1, $2, $3, 1862 Arkansas Treasury warrant

$50 Sept. 2, 1861, Confederate note

$50 Dec. 2, 1862, Confederate note

$50 April 6, 1863, Confederate note

$50 Feb. 17, 1864, Confederate note

$100 Missouri Defense Bond

Decatur, Stephen (1779 to 1820). Naval officer, hero of the "war" with Tripoli and War of 1812, killed in a duel with James Brown on March 20, 1820.

$20 1878, 1880 silver certificate

Dexter, Samuel (1761 to 1816). Member of House (1793 to 1795), Senate (1799 to 1800), secretary of war (1800), secretary of Treasury (1801).

50¢ fractional currency, fourth issue

Douglas, Stephen A. (1813 to 1861). Born in Brandon, Vt., he was elected to the House in 1843 and served until 1847. He was a senator (1847 to 1861), and a nominee for president in 1856.

$2 Bank of Ottawa, Ill.

$5 State Bank of Illinois, Shawneetown, Ill.

$10,000 1872, 1875 currency certificate of deposit

Edison, Thomas (1847 to 1931). Inventor, businessman and scientist. Responsible for such inventions as the incandescent light bulb, phonograph and motion picture camera, holding 1,093 U.S. patents in his name plus various foreign patents. Pioneered the electrification of the United States.

$5 Series 701 military payment certificate (unissued)

Everett, Edward (1794 to 1865). Born in Dorchester, Mass., he was appointed professor of Greek at Harvard at age 21. Elected to the House in 1824, he assumed the governorship of Massachusetts in 1835. He was U.S. minister to Great Britain and president of Harvard, and was appointed secretary of state (1852 to 1853), serving only four months. He was elected to the Senate in 1853 and served until 1854.

$50 1878, 1880, 1891 silver certificate

Farragut, David Glasgow (1801 to 1870). Born in Tennessee, he was adopted by Commodore Porter in 1808. He served on the Union side during the Civil War and captured New Orleans without bloodshed; his distinguished service during the war earned him the rank of vice admiral (1864) and admiral (1866), two ranks created specially for him by Congress.

$100 1890, 1891 Treasury note

Fessenden, William Pitt (1806 to 1869). Born in Boscawen, N.H., he was elected to the House (1841 to 1843) and Senate (1854 to 1864), and served as secretary of the Treasury (1864 to 1865). He was elected to the Senate again in 1865 and served until 1869.

25¢ fractional currency, third issue

$10 national bank note, Second Charter

Fillmore, Millard (1800 to 1874). Thirteenth president of the United States. Born at Locke, N.Y., he was a member of the House (1833 to 1835, 1837 to 1843) and vice president (1849 to 1850). He became president upon the death of Zachary Taylor (July 9, 1850) and was a presidential candidate in 1852.

$2 American Bank, Trenton, N.J.

$50 Northern Bank of Alabama, Huntsville, Ala.

Floyd, John B. (1806 to 1863). Born in Smithfield, Va., he was governor of Virginia (1849 to 1852), secretary of war (1857 to 1860). He resigned to enter Confederate services as brigadier of volunteers.

$10 1862 Virginia Treasury note

$1,000 Commonwealth of Virginia bond

Franklin, Benjamin (1706 to 1790). Born in Boston in 1706, he left there in 1723 for Philadelphia, where he was proprietor of a printing business and publisher of *The Pennsylvania Gazette* (1730 to 1748) and *Poor Richard's Almanac* (1725 to 1757). He was the Pennsylvania delegate to the Albany Congress in 1754 and a member of the second Continental Congress in 1775. He was on the committee to draft the Declaration of Independence and one of its signers.

$10 1863, 1864, 1865, 1875 national bank note, all charter periods (vignette: Franklin Drawing Electricity from the Sky)

$10 1870, 1872, 1873, 1874, 1875 national gold bank note (vignette as above)

$1 Merchants and Planters Bank, Savannah, Ga.

$1 1854 Bank of Anacastia, Washington, D.C.

$3 Bank of Manchester, Mich.

$3 Bank of Augusta, Ga.

$3 1860 Eastern Bank of Alabama, Eufala, Ala.

$3 Columbia Bank, District of Columbia

$5 Mechanics Bank, Memphis

$5 Roxbury Bank, Mass.

$10 Bank of the Republic, District of Columbia

$10 Eagle Bank of New Haven, Conn.

$10 Bank of Augusta, Ga.

$10 1879 refunding certificate

$20 South Carolina Bank

$20 Mechanics Bank, Augusta, Ga.

$20 Central Bank of Alabama, Montgomery, Ala.

$50 1874, 1875, 1878, 1880 United States (legal tender) notes

$100 1966 and all later series United States (legal tender) notes

$100 1914 and all later series Federal Reserve notes

$100 1929 Federal Reserve Bank note

$100 1929 national bank note

$100 1928, 1928A gold certificate

$1,000 Bank of the United States, Philadelphia

Fulton, Robert (1765 to 1815). Beginning his career as a painter, he later devoted himself to mechanics and engineering study. He invented the first practical steamboat, the Clermont (1807).

$2 1896 silver certificate (back)

$20 Series 701 military payment certificate (unissued)

Gallatin, Albert (1761 to 1849). Born in Geneva, Switzerland, he came to America in 1780. He was elected to the Senate in 1793 and served as secretary of the Treasury under Jefferson (1801 to 1814), and later as U.S. minister to France and Great Britain.

$500 1862, 1863 United States (legal tender) note

Garfield, James A. (1831 to 1881). Twentieth president of the United States. Born in Orange, Ohio, he served in the Ohio state Senate and later as a Civil War general. He was elected to the House (1863 to 1880) and was elected president in 1880. He was shot by Charles J. Guiteau in a Washington railroad station July 22, 1881, and died Sept. 19, 1881.

$5 national bank note, Second Charter

$20 1882 gold certificate

Grant, Ulysses S. (1822 to 1885). Eighteenth president of the United States. Born in Point Pleasant, Ohio, he graduated from West Point in 1843. He served in the Mexican War and was appointed brigadier general in 1861. He was in command at the Battle of Shiloh in the Civil War and was eventually placed in command of all Union Army forces. He received Lee's surrender at Appomattox Court House (April 9, 1865), and was promoted to the rank of general in 1866. He was elected president in 1868 and reelected in 1872.

15¢ fractional currency, fourth issue

$1 1899 silver certificate

$5 1886, 1891 silver certificate

$5 1896 silver certificate (back)

$50 1914 and all later issues Federal Reserve notes

$50 1918 Federal Reserve Bank note

$50 1929 national bank note

$50 1928 gold certificate

Hamilton, Alexander (1754 to 1804). First secretary of the Treasury. Born on island of Nevis, Leeward Islands, he studied at King's College (now Columbia University). He served through the Revolution as secretary and aide-de-camp to Washington. A member of the Continental Congress, he was secretary of the Treasury from 1789 to 1795. He was instrumental in defeating Aaron Burr for the presidency in 1801, later was killed by Burr in a duel. He planned and initiated policies establishing the national fiscal system.

$2 1862 legal tender note

$5 1861 demand note

$5 1862, 1863 legal tender

$10 1933 and all later series silver certificates

$10 1929 Federal Reserve Bank notes

$10 1928 and all later series Federal Reserve notes

$10 1929 national bank notes

$10 1928, 1928A gold certificates

$20 1869, 1875, 1878, 1880 legal tender notes

$50 1862 legal tender notes

$50 1863 6 percent compound interest treasury note

$50 5 percent interest-bearing note

$500 1861 7.3 percent three-year interest-bearing note

$1,000 1863, 1870, 1871, 1875, 1882, 1907, 1922 gold certificates

$1,000 1918 Federal Reserve note

Hancock, Gen. Winfield Scott (1824 to 1886). American Civil War general. He fought in the battles of Chancellorsville, Fredericksburg and Gettysburg and held off Pickett's charge at Gettysburg. He was defeated in his 1880 bid for president by James Garfield.

$2 1886 silver certificate

Harrison, Benjamin (1833 to 1901). Twenty-third president of the United States. He was a Civil War general, senator (1881 to 1887) and served one term as president (1889 to 1893).

$5 national bank note, Third Charter (all types)

Harrison, William H. (1773 to 1841). Ninth president of the United States. Born in Charles City County, Va., he was secretary of the Northwest Territory in 1798 and governor of the Territory of Indiana (1801 to 1813). Serving in the House (1816 to 1819) and Senate (1825 to 1828), he was elected president in 1840 but died of pneumonia a month after his inauguration.

$1 Southern Bank of Indiana, Terre Haute

Hendricks, Thomas Andrew (1819 to 1885). Vice president of the United States in 1885 under Grover Cleveland, serving for nine months. A member of the House (1851 to 1855) and Senate (1863 to 1869), he was elected governor of Indiana in 1872.

$10 1886, 1891, 1908 silver certificates

Henry, Patrick (1736 to 1799). Born in Hanover County, Va., he served in the Virginia legislature in 1765 and as a member of the Continental Congress. He was twice elected governor of Virginia, 1776 to 1779 and again 1784 to 1786.

$10 Bank of Augusta, Ga.

Hillegas, Michael (1729 to 1804). Born in Philadelphia, he was first treasurer of the United States (1775 to 1789).

$10 1907, 1922 gold certificate

Hollow Horn Bear (Matiheh'logego) (Circa 1850 to 1913). A Brulé Sioux leader during the Plains Wars. Famous as the chief who defeated Capt. William Fetterman on Dec. 21, 1866, in a battle near Fort Phil Kearny, Dakota Territory.

$10 Series 692 military payment certificate

Hunter, R.M.T. (1809 to 1887). Born in Essex County, Va., he was educated at the University of Virginia. He was elected to the House (1837 to 1843, 1845 to 1847), Senate (1847 to 1861), and was secretary of state of the Confederate States of America. He later served as treasurer of Virginia (1874 to 1880).

$10 Sept. 2, 1861, Confederate note

$10 Sept. 2, 1862, Confederate note

$10 Dec. 2, 1862, Confederate note

$10 April 6, 1863, Confederate note

$10 Feb. 17, 1864, Confederate note

$20 Sept. 2, 1862, Confederate note

Irving, Washington (1793 to 1859). American author, essayist, biographer and historian. Best known works include "The Legend of Sleepy Hollow" and "Rip Van Winkle." U.S. minister to Spain from 1842 to 1846.

$1 Series 70 military payment certificate (unissued)

Izard, Anne (? to ?). Posed for painting by Gilbert Stuart in 1794. Married William Allen Deas.

$5 Series 591 military payment certificate

Jackson, Andrew (1767 to 1845). Seventh president of the United States. Born in Waxhaw, S.C., he was a member of the House (1796 to 1797) and Senate (1797 to 1798), (1823 to 1825). He was elected president in 1828 and again in 1832. He refused to renew the charter of the Bank of the United States and withdrew government funds on deposit, ensuring the demise of that institution and opening the way for "wildcat" banking.

$1 Bank of East Tennessee, Knoxville

$1 Mechanics Bank of Memphis, Tenn.

$2 Corn Exchange Bank, Wapun, Wis.

$3 Mechanics Bank of Memphis, Tenn.

$3 Central Bank of Alabama, Montgomery, Ala.

$3 American Bank, Baltimore, Md.

$5 1862 Manufacturers Bank, Macon, Ga.

$5 Mechanics Bank, Concord, N.H.

$5 Mechanics Bank of Memphis, Tenn.

$5 Farmers and Merchants Bank, Cecil Co., Md.

$5 Bank of America, Clarksville, Tenn.

$5 Southern Bank of Tennessee, Memphis

$5 1869, 1875, 1878, 1880, 1907 United States (legal tender) note

$10 Mechanics Bank, Concord, N.H.

$10 State of Tennessee, 1875

$10 Bank of Tennessee, Nashville

$10 1923 United States (legal tender) note

$10 1914 Federal Reserve note

$10 1915, 1918 Federal Reserve Bank note

$20 1929 national bank note

$20 1928, 1928A gold certificate

$20 1928 and all later series Federal Reserve notes

$50 6 percent two-year interest-bearing Treasury note

$1,000 Confederate States of America Montgomery issue, 1861

$10,000 1878 United States (legal tender) note

$10,000 1863, 1870, 1871, 1875, 1882, 1888, 1902 gold certificate

Jackson, Claiborne Fox (1806 to 1862). Born in Fleming County, Ky. Elected to the general assembly of Missouri in 1842; named speaker of the house in 1844 and 1846. Governor of Missouri who advocated secession immediately prior to the Civil War.

$3 1862 State of Missouri, Jefferson City, Mo.

Jackson, James S. (1757 to 1806). Georgian politician of Democratic-Republican Party. Member of U.S. House of Representatives from 1789 to 1791. U.S. senator from 1793 to 1795 and 1801 to 1806. Governor of Georgia from 1798 to 1801.

$20 1836 Bank of Augusta, Ga.

Jackson, Gen. Thomas J. (1824 to 1863). Born in Clarksburg, Va., he was admitted to West Point in 1842 and graduated in 1846. He served in the Mexican War under Gen. Winfield Scott, and resigned from the Army in 1852. He entered Confederate service at the outbreak of the Civil War and gained his nickname "Stonewall" from his stand at Bull Run. He was accidentally shot by his own men at the Battle of Chancellorsville in 1863; he died shortly after being wounded.

$500 Feb. 17, 1864, Confederate note

Jefferson, Thomas (1743 to 1826). Third president of the United States. Born in Goochland, Va., he graduated from the College of William and Mary in 1762 and was admitted to the bar in 1767. A member of the Virginia House of Burgesses (1769 to 1774) and the Continental Congress (1775, 1776), he was chairman of the committee that prepared the Declaration of Independence. He wrote and presented the first draft of the Declaration to Congress on July 2, 1776. He was governor of Virginia (1779 to 1781), U.S. minister to France (1785 to 1789), secretary of state (1790 to 1793), vice president (1797 to 1801) and president (1801 to 1809).

5¢ postage currency, first issue

5¢ Jersey City, N.J.

25¢ postage currency first issue

$2 1869, 1874, 1875, 1878, 1880, 1917 and all later issues of United States (legal tender) notes

$2 1918 Federal Reserve Bank note

$2 1976, 1995 Federal Reserve note

$3 Farmers and Mechanics Bank, Milford, Del.

$5 1863 Real Estate Bank, Newport, Del.

$5 Bank of Kentucky, Louisville, Ky.

$5 Bank of Charleston, W.Va.

$5 Bank of Chester, Tenn.

$5 Monticello Bank, Va.

$10 Mechanics Bank, Concord, N.H.

$10 Monticello Bank, Va.

$20 Monticello Bank, Va.

$20 Bank of the Commonwealth, Richmond, Va.

$20 State of Louisiana, New Orleans, La.

$100 Monticello Bank, Va.

Knox, John Jay (1828 to 1892). Born in Knoxboro, N.Y. Deputy Comptroller of the Treasury (1867 to 1872). Comptroller of the currency (1872 to 1884). Helped prepare the bill that became the Coinage Act of 1873. Author of *United States Notes*.

$100 national bank note, Third Charter

Lafayette, Marie Joseph Paul Yves Roch Gilbert du Motier (1757 to 1834). Entering French military service in 1771, he left

to enter American service in the Revolutionary War in 1777 and was made major general in the Continental army. He returned to France in 1781.

$5 Southern Bank of Indiana, Terre Haute, Ind.

$5 Lafayette Bank, Massachusetts

$10 1837 Mississippi and Alabama Railroad Company, Brandon, Miss.

Lamar, Mary.

$2½ 1862 The Exchange Bank, Edwards County, Ill.

Letcher, John (1813 to 1884). American lawyer, journalist, and politician. Editor of (Shenandoah) Valley Star newspaper (1840 to 1850). Served in U.S. House (1851 to 1859). Governor of Virginia (1860 to 1864). Member of the House of Delegates in the Virginia General Assembly (1875 to 1877). Member of the Board of Visitors of the Virginia Military Institute (1866 to 1880), including serving as president of the board for 10 years.

$1 1862 Virginia Treasury note

$100 1862 Virginia Treasury note

Lewis, Meriwether (1774 to 1809). Born in Albermarle County, Va., he was private secretary to President Jefferson (1801 to 1803) and was named by him to lead an expedition to explore the Louisiana Purchase lands and selected William Clark as his partner. The Lewis and Clark Expedition (1804 to 1806) went up the Missouri River to its source, crossed the Great Divide and descended the Columbia River to the Pacific Ocean. He was governor of Louisiana from 1807 to 1809. Died under mysterious circumstances of gunshot wounds at an inn in Tennessee (debate continues whether Lewis committed suicide or was murdered).

$10 1901 United States (legal tender) note (nicknamed "Bison" note)

Lincoln, Abraham (1809 to 1865). Sixteenth president of the United States. Born in Hardin County, Ky., he moved to Indiana (1816) and to Macon County, Ill., in 1830. He studied law in his spare time from 1831 to 1837 and was elected to Illinois legislature (1834 to 1841). He was a member of the U.S. House of Representatives (1847 to 1849) and was nominated for vice president in 1856. Nominated for Senate in 1858 but lost. Elected president in 1860 and again in 1864. He was shot at Ford's Theatre by John Wilkes Booth on Good Friday, April 14, 1864, and died early the next morning.

50¢ fractional currency, fourth issue

$1 1861 Merchants Bank, Trenton, N.J.

$1 1862 Bank of Commerce, Georgetown, D.C.

$1 1862 Lincoln Bank, Clinton, N.Y.

$1 1899 silver certificate

$2 1862 Lincoln Bank, Clinton, N.Y.

$5 1923 "Porthole" silver certificate

$5 1915, 1918 Federal Reserve Bank note

$5 1914 and all later series Federal Reserve notes

$10 1861 demand note

$10 1862, 1863 legal tender note

$20 1863 6 percent compound interest Treasury note

$20 1863 5 percent interest-bearing note

$100 1869, 1875, 1878, 1880 United States (legal tender) note

$500 1863, 1870, 1871, 1882, 1922 gold certificates

Lind, Jenny (1820 to 1887). Singer known as the "Swedish Nightingale." Appearing first in theater in Die Freischutz (1838), she was a court singer (1840) and studied in Paris under Garcia (1841). She toured Germany and gained popularity in London (1847 to 1848). She retired from the operatic stage in 1849 and devoted herself to concert singing and oratorio. She was engaged to sing in America by P.T. Barnum (1850 to 1852) and toured Europe, spending her last years in England and becoming a British subject in 1859.

$1 (various written dates) Hartford Bank, Conn.

$1 (various written dates) Stock Security Bank, Danville, Ill.

Longfellow, Alice, Allegra and Edith. Daughters of Henry Wadsworth Longfellow. Featured in his poem "The Children's Hour."

$2 1861 Mechanics Bank, St. Louis

Lyon, Patrick. Grew up in Great Britain where at the age of 11 he began his mechanical studies and became a skilled blacksmith. He immigrated to Philadelphia in the United States at the age of 25 in 1793. In the summer of 1798, after fitting new locks and other fittings to the vault door of the Bank of Pennsylvania in Philadelphia, he was accused of robbing the bank (the first bank robbery in the United States) and imprisoned. In 1799 he was vindicated as being innocent and released from prison, and in 1805 won a civil suit against those who falsely accused him of the robbery. Became an early fire engine builder of considerable fame. Depicted in the famous portrait *Pat Lyon at the Forge* by John Neagle in 1826.

$1 Augusta Insurance and Banking Co., Augusta, Ga.

$3 Bank of Washtenaw, Mich.

Madison, Dolley (1768 to 1849). Dorthea (nee Payne) Madison was born in Guilford County, N.C., and married James Madison in 1794. She was a famous Washington hostess while her husband was secretary of state (1801 to 1809) and president (1809 to 1817).

$10 Pawtucket Bank, Epping, N.H.

Madison, James (1751 to 1836). Fourth president of the United States. He was born in Port Conway, Va., and graduated from Princeton in 1771. A member of the Continental Congress and Constitutional Convention in 1787 and the House (1789 to 1797), he was secretary of state under Jefferson (1801 to 1809) and president (1809 to 1817).

$5 Bank of Kentucky, Louisville, Ky.

$5,000 1878 United States (legal tender) note

$5,000 1863, 1870, 1871, 1872, 1882, 1888, 1928 gold certificates

$5,000 1918, 1928, 1934 Federal Reserve note

Manning, Daniel (1831 to 1887). Prominent New York banker. He was secretary of the Treasury under Cleveland (1885 to 1887).

$20 1886, 1891 silver certificates

Mansfield, Joseph King (1803 to 1862). Born in New Haven, Conn., he graduated from West Point in 1822, second in his class. Made his career serving in the U.S. Army, slowly receiving

promotion during peacetime. He was made brigadier general early in the Civil War and was killed at the Battle of Antietam.

$500 1873, 1875, 1878, 1880 United States (legal tender) notes

Marcy, William L. (1786 to 1857). Born in Southbridge, Mass., he graduated from Brown University. He was comptroller for the state of New York (1823 to 1829), associate justice of the New York Supreme Court (1829 to 1831), senator (1831, 1832), governor of New York (1833 to 1839), secretary of war (1845 to 1849) and secretary of state under Franklin Pierce (1853 to 1857).

$1,000 1878, 1880, 1891 silver certificates

Marion, Gen. Francis (1732 to 1795). Born in Winyah, near Georgetown, S.C., he fought in the Revolutionary War in guerrilla warfare, earning the nickname "the Swamp Fox." Under instructions to get Marion, British Gen. Sir Banastre Tarleton failed to even locate him. Finally, Marion invited Gen. Tarleton to dinner at Marion's camp after Tarleton asked for an interview under a truce flag.

$5 State of South Carolina, 1866 and 1872

$10 Sept. 2, 1861, Confederate note

$10 Bank of Kentucky, Louisville

$20 Bank of Kentucky, Louisville

$50 Bank of Kentucky, Louisville

Marshall, John (1755 to 1835). Born in Virginia, he was chief justice of the United States Supreme Court (1801 to 1835) and established the strength and power of the court.

$1 Southern Bank of Indiana, Terre Haute, Ind.

$10 Stafford Bank, Dover, N.H.

$20 1890, 1891 Treasury or coin notes

$50 Farmers Bank of Schuylkill County, Pa.

$500 1918 Federal Reserve note

Mason, James Murray (1798 to 1871). Member of the U.S. House of Representatives (1837 to 1839) and U.S. Senate (1847 until July 1861) from Virginia. Commissioner of the Confederacy to the United Kingdom and France between 1861 and 1865.

$50 1862 Virginia Treasury note

$1,000 Commonwealth of Virginia Bond

McClellan, George B. (1826 to 1885). Educated at the University of Pennsylvania (1842 to 1844). Transferred to West Point and graduated 1846, the youngest in his class. Author and railroad executive. Succeeded Winfield Scott as general of the Union Army. Unsuccessful Democratic presidential candidate 1864. Governor of New Jersey 1877 to 1881.

10¢ 1863 Searsport Bank, Frankfort, Maine

$1 1862 Chicopee Bank, Springfield, Mass.

$2 1861 Merchants Bank, Trenton, N.J.

$20 1862 Rutland County Bank, Vt.

McCullough, Hugh (1808 to 1895). Secretary of the Treasury under Lincoln (1865 to 1869) and Arthur (1884 to 1885).

$20 national bank note, Third Charter (all types)

McKinley, William (1843 to 1901). Twenty-fifth president of the United States. Born in Niles, Ohio, he served in the Civil War. He was a member of the House (1877 to 1883, 1885, 1891), governor of Ohio (1892 to 1896) and president (1897 to 1901). He was shot by Leon Czolgosz, an anarchist, in Buffalo, N.Y., Sept. 6, 1901, and died Sept. 14.

$10 national bank note, Third Charter (all types)

$500 1928 and all later series Federal Reserve notes

Meade, George Gordon (1815 to 1872). Born in Cadiz, Spain. Entered West Point Military Academy in 1831; graduated in 1835. Fought with U.S. Army against Seminole Indians before resigning to pursue a career in civil engineering. Reentered Army in 1842; he fought in war against Mexico. He was promoted from captain to brigadier general in 1861 and became a major general in 1864. Commanded Army of the Potomac from June 28, 1863, to end of Civil War.

$1,000 1890, 1891 Treasury notes

Memminger, Christopher Gustavus (1803 to 1888). Born in Germany, he came to the United States as a child. He was secretary of the Treasury of the Confederacy (1861 to 1864).

$5 and $10 Sept. 2, 1861, Confederate note

$5 Dec. 2, 1862, Confederate note

$5 April 6, 1863, Confederate note

$5 Feb. 17, 1864, Confederate note

Meredith, William Morris (1799 to 1873). Born in Philadelphia, he was secretary of the Treasury (1849 to 1850) and attorney general of Pennsylvania (1861 to 1867). Member of Whig Party.

10¢ fractional currency, fifth issue

Monroe, James (1758 to 1831). Fifth president of the United States. Born in Westmoreland County, Va., he served in the American Revolution, as a member of the Continental Congress and senator (1790 to 1794). He was minister to France (1794 to 1796), governor of Virginia (1799 to 1802), one of the negotiators of the Louisiana Purchase (1803), minister to England (1803 to 1807), secretary of state (1811 to 1817), and secretary of war (1814 to 1815). He served as president from 1817 to 1825.

$4 Bank of Monroe, Monroe, Mich.

$100 1878, 1880, 1881 silver certificate

Morris, Robert (1734 to 1806). Born in England, he came to America in 1747 and favored the Colonial cause in the Revolution. He was a member of the Continental Congress and a signer of the Declaration of Independence. He served as superintendent of finance (1781 to 1784), founded and organized the Bank of North America (1782) and was a delegate to the Constitutional convention in 1787. He served in the Senate from 1789 to 1795.

$10 Northampton Bank, Pa.

$10 1878, 1880 silver certificates

$1,000 1862, 1863 United States (legal tender) notes

$1,000 Bank of U.S. note (lower right corner)

Morse, Samuel Finley Breese (1791 to 1872). Born in Charleston, Mass., he was a portrait painter in Boston, Charleston and New York. He was founder and first president of the National Academy of Design and was a professor at New York University. He invented Morse code and the magnetic telegraph, sending the first message, "What Hath God Wrought?" on May 24, 1844.

$2 1896 silver certificate (reverse)

Moultrie, Gen. William (1730 to 1805). Born in Charleston, S.C., he was an American Revolutionary War general. He repulsed the British attack on Sullivan's Island, now Fort Moultrie, in Charleston Harbor in 1776 and served as a brigadier general in the Continental Army in 1776 and defended Charleston in 1779. He was governor of South Carolina (1785 to 1787, 1794 to 1796).

$5 1866 and 1872 State of South Carolina

Oglethorpe, James Edward (1696 to 1785). Born in London, he planned a project for colonizing unemployed men freed from debtors' prison on lands in America. He received a charter in 1732 for Colony of Georgia and accompanied the first band of emigrants there in 1733.

$5 1862 The State of Georgia, Milledgeville, Ga.

$5 Bank of Augusta, Ga.

$10 1836 Bank of Augusta, Ga.

Ouray, Chief (Arrow) (circa 1833 to 1880). Native American, chief of the Ute nation, with a Shoshonean Ute father and Athabaskan Apache mother. Negotiated with American government in 1863, 1868 and 1873 over the retention of Ute lands in southern Colorado. The town of Ouray, Colo., is named for him

$20 Series 692 military payment certificate

Penn, William (1644 to 1718). Named trustee to manage the West Jersey Colony in America, he had an important part in framing its charter in 1677. He received a grant of land from Charles II from which he founded Pennsylvania in 1681.

$1 1857 Penn Township Savings Institute, Philadelphia

$2 1856 Bank of Newark, Del.

$5 18-- Erie, Pa., Bank

$5 1820 Stephen Girard, Banker, Philadelphia

$5 1841 Towanda Bank, Pa.

$5 1859 Fort Stanwix Bank, Oneida, N.Y.

$10 1826 Bank of Pennsylvania, Philadelphia

$10 1833 Bank of Pennsylvania, Philadelphia

$20 Piscatqua Exchange Bank, Portsmouth, N.H.

$20 Farmers Bank of Schuylkill County, Pa.

Pettus, John Jones (1813 to 1867). Governor of Mississippi (less than a week in January 1854, then to a full term from 1859 to 1863). Became a fugitive after end of Civil War and refused to surrender to U.S. authorities. Died while still a fugitive.

$10 State of Mississippi

$20 State of Mississippi

$50 State of Mississippi

$100 State of Mississippi

Pewelle, A. A Pennsylvania merchant.

2¢ 1862 note of A. Pewelle, Reading, Pa.

3¢ 1862 note of A. Pewelle, Reading, Pa.

Pickens, Lucy Holcombe (1832 to 1899). Wife of Francis W. Pickens (1805 to 1869), governor of South Carolina who ordered the bombardment of Fort Sumter, triggering the Civil War.

$1 June 2, 1862, Confederate note

$100 Dec. 2, 1862, Confederate note

$100 Apr. 6, 1863, Confederate note

$100 Feb. 17, 1863, Confederate note

Pierce, Franklin (1804 to 1869). Fourteenth president of the United States. Born in Hillsboro, N.H., his father, Benjamin Pierce, fought in the Revolution. He served in the New Hampshire House, the House (1833 to 1837), and the U.S. Senate (1837 to 1843). He served as president from 1853 to 1857.

$10 Amoskeag Bank, Manchester, N.H.

Polk, Gen. Leonidas (1806 to 1864). Born in Raleigh, N.C. Attended West Point Military Academy, graduating in 1827. Resigned commission in December 1827 to enter Virginia Theological Seminary; became a bishop. Commissioned a major general in Confederate Army in 1861. Fought with the Army of the Mississippi and Army of the Tennessee in multiple battles. Killed in action June 14, 1864, at Pine Mountain in Georgia.

$50 1863 State of Louisiana, Shreveport, La.

Raleigh, Sir Walter (1552? to 1618). A favorite of Queen Elizabeth, he was granted a patent to send an expedition exploring the American coast from Florida to North Carolina in 1584 and named the coast north of Florida "Virginia." He sent settlers to occupy Roanoke Island, N.C., in 1585, but the colony failed. With the death of Queen Elizabeth in 1603, he fell out of favor with the English court and was eventually beheaded at Whitehall.

$2 original and 1875 "Lazy Deuce" First Charter national bank note (on the reverse, Sir Walter Raleigh in England, 1585, exhibiting corn and smoking tobacco from America)

Randolph, George Wythe (1818 to 1867). His father was governor of Virginia (1819 to 1822). His mother was the daughter of Thomas Jefferson. Entered the U.S. Navy as a midshipman in 1831. Studied law at the University of Virginia. He served as the Confederate States secretary of war from March 1862 to September 1863 when he was appointed envoy to France. He died at Edge Hill, Va., on April 4, 1867.

$100 Dec. 2, 1862, Confederate note

$100 April 6, 1863, Confederate note

$100 Feb. 17, 1864, Confederate note

Rector, Henry Massey (1816 to 1899). Served as U.S. marshal in Alabama, Arkansas Senate (1848 to 1850), state House of Representatives (1855 to 1859), one term on Arkansas Supreme Court. Governor of Arkansas (1861 to 1862). Served as private in state militia after leaving office.

$5 1862 Arkansas Treasury Warrant

Running Antelope (Ta-to-ka-in-yan-ka) (1821 to 1896 or 1897). Born near the Grand River in present day South Dakota. A head chief of the Hunkpapa Sioux. A close adviser to Sitting Bull during the Plains Indian Wars who advocated compromise with the whites.

$5 1899 silver certificate

Scott, Gen. Winfield (1786 to 1866). Born near Petersburg, Va., he was promoted to general-in-chief of the U.S. Army in 1841, and was defeated by Franklin Pierce in his bid for president in 1852. Would serve on active duty in U.S. Army as a general longer than any other individual. Fought in the War of 1812 and

the Mexican-American War. Despite being born in Virginia, he remained loyal to United States and was general-in-chief of Union Army at beginning of the Civil War although he was too elderly to go into battle personally. He resigned in November 1861 under political pressure.

$100 1865 interest-bearing note

$1 1861 Bank of Otego, Otego County, N.Y.

$1 Farmers and Mechanics Bank, Easton, Pa.

$2 Merchants Bank, Trenton, N.J.

$3 Beverly Bank, Beverly, N.J.

$20 Rutland County, Vt., Bank

Seward, William H. (1801 to 1872). Governor of New York (1839 to 1843) senator (1849 to 1861) and a prominent antislavery advocate. He served as secretary of state (1861 to 1869) and was responsible for the purchase of Alaska.

$50 1891 Treasury note

Shelby, Isaac (1750 to 1826). Colonel of militia in Virginia in 1780, he organized a Colonial force after the fall of Charleston and defeated the British at Kings Mountain. He served in the North Carolina legislature in 1781 and 1782 and settled in Kentucky in 1783, where he served as the first governor (1792 to 1796, 1812 to 1816). He helped defeat the British at the Battle of the Thames on Oct. 5, 1813.

$5 Bank of Kentucky, Louisville, Ky.

Sheridan, Gen. Philip Henry (1831 to 1888). Born in Albany, N.Y., he graduated from West Point in 1853 and succeeded William T. Sherman as commander in chief of the U.S. Army in 1884. He was promoted to general in 1888.

$5 1896 silver certificate (back)

$10 1890, 1891 Treasury or coin notes

Sherman, John (1823 to 1900). Born in Lancaster, Ohio, he practiced law in Mansfield and Cleveland. He served in the House (1855 to 1861) and Senate (1861 to 1877, 1881 to 1897), as secretary of the Treasury (1877 to 1881) and secretary of state (1897 to 1898). Brother of William T. Sherman (see next).

$50 national bank note, Third Charter (all types)

Sherman, William Tecumseh (1820 to 1891). Born in Lancaster, Ohio, he was brother of John Sherman and graduated from West Point in 1840. He was made brigadier general of volunteers in the Civil War (1861), served at Bull Run, under Grant at Shiloh and Corinth, and was promoted to major general in 1862. He was promoted to lieutenant general in 1866 and succeeded Grant as general and commander of the Army in 1869.

15¢ fractional currency (proof notes), fourth issue, never circulated

Spinner, Francis Elias (1802 to 1890). After serving as president of the Mohawk Valley Bank in Herkimer, N.Y., he was elected to the House (1855 to 1861) and then appointed treasurer of the United States by Lincoln (1861 to 1875). Considered the father of fractional currency.

50¢ fractional currency, third issue

Stanton, Edwin McMasters (1814 to 1869). Born in Steubenville, Ohio, he was attorney general (1860 to 1861), secretary of war (1862 to 1868). He refused to support President Johnson's policies after Lincoln's death and was dismissed in 1868. Johnson's impeachment was partially a result of Stanton's dismissal. He was appointed to the Supreme Court in 1869 but died before he could take his seat.

50¢ fractional currency, fourth issue

$1 1890, 1891 Treasury or coin notes

Stephens, Alexander Hamilton (1812 to 1883). Born near Crawfordville, Ga., he was elected to the Georgia legislature in 1834, the Senate in 1842 and the House (1843 to 1859). He served as vice president of the Confederacy (1861 to 1865). After the war he was imprisoned briefly and later elected to the Senate in 1866 but refused to take a seat. He was elected to the House in 1873 and served until 1882, and was elected governor of Georgia in 1883.

$20 1861, 1862, 1863, 1864 Confederate note

Stuyvesant, Petrus (1592 to 1672). Born in the Netherlands, he served in the Dutch army and in the employ of the Dutch West India Company. He lost his right leg in a war against the citizens of the island of St. Martin in 1644. He was appointed director-general of New Netherlands and adjacent regions in 1646 and arrived in New Amsterdam in 1647. He expelled the Swedes from Delaware in 1655 and surrendered New Netherlands to the English in 1664.

$3 St. Nicholas Bank, New York, N.Y.

Sumner, Charles (1811 to 1874). Born in Boston and graduated from Harvard Law School, he was elected to the Senate in 1852 and was an opponent of slavery. Serving in the Senate until 1874, he took a prominent part in impeachment proceedings against President Johnson and opposed Grant's reelection in 1872.

$500 1878, 1880 silver certificate

Sumter, Gen. Thomas (1734 to 1832). Born near Charlottesville, Va., he was a lieutenant-colonel of South Carolina troops during the Revolution. He was elected to the House (1789 to 1793, 1797 to 1801) and Senate (1801 to 1810).

$5 1866 and 1872 State of South Carolina

Taylor, Zachary (1784 to 1850), Twelfth president of the United States. Born in Orange County, Va., he entered the U.S. Army as a first lieutenant and spent most of his army life in the West. He defeated Santa Anna at Buena Vista in 1847, ending the war in northern Mexico. He served as president from 1849 to 1850, and died after only a year and four months in office.

$10 Southbridge Bank, Southbridge, Mass.

$20 City Bank of New Haven, Conn.

$20 Bank of Tennessee, Nashville, Tenn.

Thomas, Gen. George Henry (1816 to 1870). Born in Southampton County, Va., he graduated from West Point in 1840 and remained loyal to the Union during the Civil War. He was made brigadier general in 1861 and major general in 1862. He commanded the Army of the Cumberland in the Battle of Chattanooga and in Sherman's Atlanta campaign in 1864. He was promoted to major general in the regular army and commanded the military division of the Pacific in 1869 and 1870.

$5 1890, 1891 Treasury or coin notes

Tucker, Joseph C. (1818 to 1876). With partner Henry B. Stiles, in 1846 opened a general store, Tucker & Stiles, in Brookline, N.H., near Townsend, Mass. Also maker of lumber and wooden casks. Appointed postmaster of Brookline April 26, 1850. Served in various city offices in Brookline and four terms as a state legislator starting in 1857. Also operated a business selling West India goods and groceries in Boston starting in 1864.

3¢ July 4, 1864, Townsend Bank, Townsend, Mass.

24¢ July 16, 1862, Tucker and Stiles scrip, Townsend, Mass.

Van Buren, Martin (1782 to 1862). Eighth president of the United States. Born in Kinderhook, N.Y., he was attorney general of New York (1816 to 1819) and senator from New York (1821 to 1828), governor of New York (1829), resigning to become secretary of state (1829 to 1831). He served as vice president (1833 to 1837) and as president from 1837 to 1841.

$5 Mechanics Bank, Concord, N.H.

Vance, Zebulon (1830 to 1894). Born in Buncombe County, N.C. Lawyer, served in a North Carolina regiment during early part of Civil War. Governor of North Carolina (1862 to 1865, 1877 to 1879). Arrested by Union forces at end of the Civil War. Returned to law practice after release. Elected to U.S. Senate but prevented from serving by U.S. law addressing former rebels. Reelected as governor.

$20 1863 State of North Carolina, Raleigh, N.C.

Walker, Robert J. (1801 to 1869). After practicing law in Pittsburgh, Pa., and Natchez, Miss., he served in the Senate (1836 to 1845) and as secretary of the Treasury (1845 to 1849). He was the financial agent of the United States in Europe (1863 to 1864) and sold $250 million worth of U.S. bonds and prevented the sale of $75 million worth of Confederate bonds.

25¢ fractional currency, fifth issue

Ward, John E. (1814 to 1871). Mayor of Savannah, Ga., he was violently opposed to secession and left the South with the outbreak of the Civil War.

$10 1861 Confederate States of America note

Washington, George (1732 to 1799). First president of the United States. Born in Westmoreland County, Va., he was privately educated and gained experience as a surveyor by assisting in the survey of some Fairfax holdings in Shenandoah Valley. He was county surveyor in Culpeper County, Va. (1749). He was commissioned as district adjutant by Gov. Dinwiddie in 1752, later commissioned lieutenant colonel and sent with 150 men in 1754 to establish an outpost on the site of the present city of Pittsburgh. He served on Gen. Braddock's staff in 1755 and in the British expedition against Fort Duquesne. He was commissioned colonel and commander-in-chief of Virginia troops in 1755. He married Martha Custis in 1759 and joined the Virginia House of Burgesses the same year (1759 to 1774). He was a member of the first and second Continental Congress and was elected to command all Continental armies in 1775. He resigned his commission in 1783, but was called from retirement to preside at the Federal Convention in Philadelphia in 1787, and was chosen president of the United States under the new Constitution. He took his oath of office in New York City on April 30, 1789, and was unanimously re-elected in 1792. He declined a third term and retired from political life in 1797. He came out of retirement again to accept a commission as lieutenant general and commander-in-chief of the Army in 1798 and retained the commission until his death on Dec. 14, 1799.

3¢ fractional currency, third issue

5¢ fractional currency, second issue

10¢ postage currency, first issue

10¢ fractional currency, second and third issues

25¢ fractional currency, second and fourth issues

50¢ postage currency, first issue

50¢ fractional currency, second issues

$1 1869, 1875, 1878, 1880, 1917 and all later series United States (legal tender) notes

$1 1896, 1923 and all later series silver certificates

$1 1918 Federal Reserve Bank notes

$1 1963 and all later series Federal Reserve notes

$2 1899 silver certificates

$5 national bank notes, Second Charter (dated back and de-nomination backs, small vignette on reverse)

$10 Series 701 military payment certificate (unissued)

$20 1901, 1906, 1922 gold certificates

$100 1863 6 percent compound interest Treasury note

$100 1863 5 percent one-year interest-bearing note

$500 1861 7.4 percent three-year interest-bearing note

10-peso 1913 Philippine silver certificates

10-peso 1918, 1924, 1929, 1936, 1941 & Victory Series 66 Philippine Treasury certificates

10 peso 1921 & 1937 Philippine national circulating notes

Many Confederate and obsolete bank notes

Washington, Martha (1732 to 1802). Wife of George Washington, she was born Martha Dandridge and married Daniel Parke Custis who later died. She married George Washington Jan. 6, 1759.

$1 1886, 1896 silver certificate

$5 Belknap County Bank, N.H.

Watts, Thomas N. (1819 to 1892). Born in the Alabama Territory. Took a pro-Union stance in the 1850s but changed his position. Governor of Alabama (1863 to 1865).

$50 1864 Alabama State note

$10 1864 Alabama State note

Weaver, John.

$50 Commercial Bank of Alabama, Selma, Ala.

Webster, Daniel (1782 to 1852). Born in Salisbury, N.H., he graduated from Dartmouth in 1801 and was admitted to the bar in Boston in 1805. He was a member of the House (1813 to 1817, 1823 to 1827) and the Senate (1827 to 1841, 1845 to 1850). He served as secretary of state from 1841 to 1843 and again from 1850 to 1852. He was an unsuccessful candidate for Whig nomination for the presidency in 1852.

Military payment certificates

Military payment certificates (MPCs) were used from 1946 to 1973. Prior to that time U.S. military personnel stationed overseas were paid in Allied military currency, produced by the major Allied

$1 State Bank of Wisconsin, Milwaukee

$2 Bank of Peru, Ill.

$3 DuPage Co. Bank, Naperville, Ill.

$5 Farmers and Traders Bank, Charlestown, Ill.

$5 Shawnee Bank, Attica, Ind.

$10 1869, 1875, 1878, 1880 United States (legal tender) note (nicknamed the "Jackass" note)

$10 Thames Bank, Norwich, Conn.

$20 Bank of Kentucky, Louisville, Ky.

White, Lt. Col. Edward (1930 to 1967). Engineer, United States Air Force officer and a NASA astronaut. Graduate of West Point Military Academy in 1952. After graduation, joined U.S. Air Force rather than the U.S. Army. Became a NASA astronaut in 1962. As the pilot of Gemini 4, White became the first American to make a walk in space, on June 3, 1965, in a scene depicted on the back of military payment certificates showing him in a spacesuit. Assigned to the crew for Apollo 1, the first manned Apollo mission. Killed in a fire aboard the Apollo command capsule during a launch pad test on Jan. 27, 1967, along with two other astronauts.

5¢, 10¢, 25¢ and 50¢ Series 681 military payment certificate

Wilson, Woodrow (1856 to 1924). Twenty-eighth president of the United States. Born in Staunton, Va., he graduated from Princeton in 1879 and was admitted to the bar and practiced in Atlanta in 1882. After receiving his doctorate from Johns Hopkins in 1886, he taught history at Bryn Mawr and Wesleyan, and political science at Princeton. He was president of Princeton from 1902 to 1910, and governor of New Jersey (1911 to 1913). He was elected president in 1912 and served until 1921.

$100,000 1934 gold certificate

Windom, William (1827 to 1891). Born in Belmont, Ohio, he moved to Minnesota and became the first senator from Minnesota (1870 to 1881, 1881 to 1883) after serving in the House (1859 to 1869). He was secretary of the Treasury in 1881 and again from 1889 to 1891.

$2 1891 silver certificate

Wright, Silas (1795 to 1847). After practicing law in Canton, N.Y., he was elected to the House (1827 to 1829) and served as comptroller of New York (1829 to 1833), as senator from New York (1833 to 1844), and governor of New York (1845 to 1847).

$50 1882 gold certificate

Note: Various vignettes on national bank notes and other large-size U.S. paper money depict scenes in which historical figures appear, although the figures are not the focus of the images. Person depicted in this manner include Hernando de Soto, Sir Walter Raleigh, Pocahontas, Capt. James Smith, William Bradford, Myles Standish, many signers of the Declaration of Independence including John Hancock, Gen. John Burgoyne, Gen. Thomas Gates and Capt. Oliver Hazard Perry.

countries, or in the currency of the country in which they were stationed.

The need for this system arose out of the necessity to transact business with the local populations but without risking the loss of large amounts of U.S. currency, which could be used anywhere in the world.

Another reason for the creation of Allied military currency was the possibility that the enemy might flood an occupied territory's economy with currency to induce high inflation or order local banks to burn their money when Allied attack was imminent.

Allied military currency in the 1940s was used in countries being liberated from the Axis powers and the notes were denominated in the liberated country's currency. The local government was required to redeem it later.

Personnel were allowed to convert that foreign currency into U.S. currency as individual needs or wishes required. However, it wasn't long before the services accumulated foreign currencies far in excess of pay requirements, and the MPC system was developed to protect the services from those surpluses of foreign currencies.

After the MPC system was developed in 1946, all U.S. servicemen, U.S. government civilian employees and U.S. citizens employed by U.S. firms abroad doing business under government contracts were paid in MPCs and were prohibited from holding U.S. currency of any type.

U.S. citizens in the employ of a company of the host country were paid in the local currency. The local population was prohibited from holding any MPCs, which could be used only at U.S. facilities such as post exchanges or ship's stores. The local population was thus effectively restrained from purchasing items at the discounted PX prices, a form of black marketeering control.

If a U.S. serviceman or citizen wanted to buy something in the local civilian market, he was required to convert his MPCs into the local currency. Regulations restricted both the amount and frequency of MPC conversions.

Many of the servicemen supplemented their supply of convertible currency by doing a brisk business in cigarettes, silk or nylon stockings and candy. It was inevitable that many of the MPCs would then be found in the local economy in spite of strict controls. The usual route was through the black market established both by servicemen and by the local population. Servicemen sold items they had purchased at government-operated stores while local businessmen sold watches and jewelry to servicemen who were returning stateside.

When it was determined that an excessive amount of MPCs were in the local economy via the black market, the old series would be withdrawn and a new series issued. The conversion days (popularly known as "C-days") were unannounced and strictly controlled. All personnel would be restricted to station and only designated persons were allowed to make the exchange of new for old notes.

After C-day the old series was invalid and worthless. The only supply of MPCs available to collectors today are those MPCs that were inadvertently unredeemed by authorized holders or those illegally held by black marketers who were unable to convert their holdings.

In the 28-year history of military payment certificates 13 series were used in 21 foreign places in 17 countries. Denominations ranged from five cents to $20. The $20 MPC was issued only in Series 661, 681 and 692.

The first seven series were printed by private contractors in the United States and overprinted by the Bureau of Engraving and Printing. The overprint consisted of adding the series, serial and control numbers to the pre-printed notes. The last six series were completely printed and separated by the BEP.

The first issue, series 461, was released on Sept. 16, 1946. It was followed in order by series 471, 472, 481, 521, 541, 591, 611, 641, 651, 661, 681 and 692. Series 692, was released on Oct. 7, 1970, and was withdrawn from use in South Vietnam on March 15, 1973. Series 651 was released in South Korea on Nov. 19, 1973, ending a short but interesting and colorful era in another currency system.

How to detect counterfeit bills

As this 2011 edition of the *Coin World Almanac* was being edited, three distinct generations of Federal Reserve notes—the 1929 generation designs used for $1 and $2 notes, the Series 1996 designs with larger portraits and watermarks, and the Series 2004 generation with revised portraits and additional colors—were in circulation, each with its own set of anti-counterfeiting devices. Detailed, multimedia descriptions of the anti-counterfeiting properties of the notes are available at the Web site of the Bureau of Engraving and Printing (**http://moneyfactory.gov/**) under the "Anti-Counterfeiting" tab.

What follows is a more general explanation of how to detect counterfeit notes. In all cases, know your money by examining and becoming familiar with the bills you receive. Compare a suspected bill with a genuine one of the same denomination. Look at these features:

Portrait

Genuine: Appears lifelike and stands out distinctly from the fine screen-like background. The hairlines are distinct. The eyes should appear lifelike.

Counterfeit: Appears lifeless and the background is usually too dark. Portrait merges into the background. The hairlines are not distinct.

Treasury seal

Genuine: Saw-toothed points are even, clear and sharp.

Counterfeit: Saw-toothed points on the circumference are usually uneven, blunt and broken off.

Federal Reserve seal

Genuine: In pre-1996 series notes the letter inside the seal should conform to the prefix letter in the serial number. The Series 1996 notes and later series have a universal Federal Reserve seal that doesn't designate the individual bank for which the note was issued. A letter-number below the upper left serial number identifies the issuing Federal Reserve Bank.

Also on pre-1996 series notes the points of the seal should be clear and sharp and the letters distinct. The large letter in the center should be on a white background.

The universal Federal Reserve seal on Series 1996 and later notes should appear crisp with well-defined elements.

Border

Genuine: The fine lines are clear, distinct and unbroken.

Counterfeit: The fine lines that crisscross are not clear or distinct.

Paper

Genuine: Printed on distinctive paper with visible, interspersed red and blue fibers. The paper is a blend of 75 percent cotton and 25 percent linen, which gives it a special feel even if it has been washed.

Counterfeit: Printed on paper with no colored fibers evident, or with red and blue lines to simulate fibers. Notes printed on counterfeit paper may feel different or be whiter than genuine currency paper.

Beware of counterfeit notes printed on bleached notes of low denominations. Counterfeiters will bleach the ink from the low denomination notes and use the genuine currency paper to print higher denomination notes. Since $1 and $2 notes lack security threads and watermarks, any fakes of higher denominations printed on the genuine currency paper will lack the threads and watermarks found on genuine notes.

Serial numbers

Genuine: On pre-1996 series of notes the serial numbers should be firmly inked and evenly spaced. The prefix letter on Federal Reserve notes should match the letter in the Federal Reserve seal. On genuine Series 1996 and later notes there are two prefix letters: the first designates the series and the second corresponds to the Federal Reserve bank. There is also an additional letter-number combination directly under the serial number in the upper left corner. All Series 1996 notes bear letter A followed by the number designating the FR Bank. The first letter is the series year, the second letter is the Federal Reserve district letter. In addition the letter-number combination on the Series 1996 $100 note is green,

while on the $50 and $20 from the same series it is printed in black.

Counterfeit: Serial numbers on counterfeit notes may be unevenly spaced, out of alignment or printed too dark or too light. Sometimes the prefix letter doesn't match the letter inside the Federal Reserve seal. The same serial number may be used on multiple notes.

Security thread

A polyester thread is embedded vertically in the paper for denominations from $100 through $5. The thread has an inscription unique to the denomination. For example, when a $20 note is held to the light, a repeated USA20 appears on the thread.

The new Series 1996 and later redesigned notes added two new dimensions to the security thread— they are in a different position on different denominations and glow a different color in each denomination.

That design feature continues in the colorized denominations. For more information on the security threads and colors visit the Bureau of Engraving and Printing's Web site **www.moneyfactory.gov**.

Color-shifting ink

Used on Series 1996 and later $100, $50 and $20 and Series 1999 and later $10 Federal Reserve notes (but not the 1999 $5 notes) in the numeral in the lower right corner on the face of the note. The color appears to change from green to black and back to green when is tilted.

The Series 2009 $100 Federal Reserve notes also feature color-shifting ink, and to learn more about that redesign visit the Bureau of Engraving and Printing's Web site.

Microprinting

The UNITED STATES OF AMERICA is repeatedly printed around the border of the portrait or on the collar of the person portrayed and other places on Series 1996 and later notes. The letters are too small to read without magnification or to be reproduced distinctly on a copier machine. To learn more about the placement of this security device on various denominations, visit the Bureau of Engraving and Printing's Web site.

Enhancement device for the visually impaired

A large dark numeral on a light background appears in the lower right corner on the back of the Series 1996 $50 and $20 notes. The device is designed to make it easier for people with low vision to identify the note. All subsequent denominations, $10, $5 and $100, will include this low-vision feature.

Scrollwork

Look for very fine, crisscrossing lines that are sharp and unbroken on genuine notes. Fakes may have blurred lines or jagged, broken lines.

Signatures on U.S. paper money

Hand-written or facsimile signatures lend an aura of authority to paper money. Most U.S. paper money bears two signatures and some bears four. Only the postage currency, Second Issue fractional currency and 3-cent Third Issue fractional currency bear no signatures at all. Realizing that the signing of paper money would be a burdensome task, President Lincoln signed legislation allowing the secretary of the Treasury to delegate selected personnel to sign the first demand notes for the Treasury officials. Seventy employees were assigned to this task, signing their own names, with a handwritten "For The" before the appropriate title. Within a very short time the words "For The" were engraved into the printing plates.

Starting with the issues of 1863, the signatures of the Treasury officials were engraved directly into the plates and the words "for the" dropped into obscurity. From 1862 to 1925 the signature of the register of the Treasury appeared on all notes; after 1925 the signature of the secretary of the Treasury appears with that of the treasurer of the United States.

National bank notes, in addition to the signatures of the register and the treasurer, bear the signatures of the bank president and the bank cashier. Federal Reserve Bank notes also have two additional signatures: those of two Federal Reserve Bank officers.

The full names of the Treasury officials and their terms in office can be found in Chapter 4.

Signatures on large-size paper money

Legal tender and United States notes

Series	Denominations	Register of the Treasury	Treasurer
1862	$1, $2, $5, $10, $20, $50, $100, $500	Lucius E. Chittenden	F.E. Spinner
1863	$2, $5, $10, $20, $50, $100, $500	Lucius E. Chittenden	F.E. Spinner
1869	$1, $2, $5, $10, $20, $50, $100, $500	John Allison	F.E. Spinner
1874	$1, $2, $50, $100	John Allison	F.E. Spinner
1875	$1, $2, $5, $10, $20, $500	John Allison	John C. New
1875	$1, $2, $5, $50, $100, $500	John Allison	A.U. Wyman
1875A	$1, $2, $5, $10, $100	John Allison	John C. New
1875B	$1, $2, $5	John Allison	John C. New
1875C	$1	John Allison	John C. New
1875D	$1	John Allison	John C. New
1875E	$1	John Allison	John C. New
1878	$1, $2, $5, $10, $20, $50, $100, $500, $1,000	John Allison	James Gilfillan
1878	$2	Glenni W. Scofield	James Gilfillan
1880	$1, $2, $5, $10, $20	William S. Rosecrans	Enos H. Nebecker
1880	$1, $2, $5, $10, $20	Glenni W. Scofield	James Gilfillan
1880	$1, $2, $5, $10, $20, $50, $100	Blanche K. Bruce	James Gilfillan
1880	$1, $2, $5, $10, $20, $50, $100	William S. Rosecrans	J.N. Huston
1880	$1, $2, $5, $10, $20, $50, $100	James F. Tillman	Daniel N. Morgan
1880	$1, $5, $10, $20, $50, $100	Blanche K. Bruce	A.U. Wyman
1880	$5, $10, $20, $50, $100	Blanche K. Bruce	Elias H. Roberts
1880	$5, $10, $20, $50, $100	William S. Rosecrans	James W. Hyatt
1880	$5, $10, $20, $50, $100	William S. Rosecrans	Conrad Jordan
1880	$5, $10, $20, $50, $100, $500	Judson W. Lyons	Elias H. Roberts
1880	$20	William S. Elliott	Frank White
1880	$20	Houston B. Teehee	John Burke
1880	$20	William T. Vernon	Lee McClung
1880	$20	William T. Vernon	Charles H. Treat
1880	$500	John Allison	F.E. Spinner
1901	$10	Judson W. Lyons	Elias H. Roberts
1901	$10	Judson W. Lyons	Charles H. Treat
1901	$10	James C. Napier	Lee McClung
1901	$10	Gabe E. Parker	John Burke
1901	$10	Harley V. Speelman	Frank White
1901	$10	Houston B. Teehee	John Burke
1901	$10	William T. Vernon	Lee McClung

Legal tender and United States notes (continued)

Series	Denominations	Register of the Treasury	Treasurer
1901	$10	William T. Vernon	Charles H. Treat
1907	$5	William S. Elliott	Frank White
1907	$5	James C. Napier	Lee McClung
1907	$5	James C. Napier	Carmi A. Thompson
1907	$5	Gabe E. Parker	John Burke
1907	$5	Harley V. Speelman	Frank White
1907	$5	Houston B. Teehee	John Burke
1907	$5	William T. Vernon	Charles H. Treat
1907	$5	Walter O. Woods	Frank White
1907	$20	William T. Vernon	Lee McClung
1917	$1, $2	Harley V. Speelman	Frank White
1917	$1, $2	Houston B. Teehee	John Burke
1917	$1, $2, $5	William S. Elliott	John Burke
1923	$10	Harley V. Speelman	Frank White

National bank notes

Series	Denominations	Register of the Treasury	Treasurer
Original	$1, $2, $5, $10, $20	Noah L. Jeffries	F.E. Spinner
Original	$1, $2, $5, $10, $20, $50, $100	John Allison	F.E. Spinner
Original	$1, $2, $5, $10, $20, $50, $100	S.B. Colby	F.E. Spinner
Original	$5, $10, $20, $50, $100	Lucius E. Chittenden	F.E. Spinner
1875	$1, $2, $5, $10, $20, $50, $100	John Allison	James Gilfillan
1875	$1, $2, $5, $10, $20, $50, $100	John Allison	John C. New
1875	$1, $2, $5, $10, $20, $50, $100	John Allison	A.U. Wyman
1875	$1, $2, $5, $10, $20, $50, $100	Glenni W. Scofield	James Gilfillan
1875	$5	Blanche K. Bruce	Conrad Jordan
1875	$5	William S. Rosecrans	Conrad Jordan
1875	$5, $10, $20, $50, $100	Blanche K. Bruce	James Gilfillan
1875	$5, $10, $20, $50, $100	Blanche K. Bruce	A.U. Wyman
1875	$5, $10, $50, $100	William S. Rosecrans	J.N. Huston
1875	$10, $20, $50, $100	William S. Rosecrans	Enos H. Nebecker
1875	$10, $20, $50, $100	James F. Tillman	Daniel N. Morgan
1882 Brown Back	$5, $10, $20	Judson W. Lyons	Charles H. Treat
1882 Brown Back	$5, $10, $20, $50	William S. Rosecrans	J.N. Huston
1882 Brown Back	$5, $10, $20, $50, $100	Blanche K. Bruce	James Gilfillan
1882 Brown Back	$5, $10, $20, $50, $100	Blanche K. Bruce	Conrad Jordan
1882 Brown Back	$5, $10, $20, $50, $100	Blanche K. Bruce	Elias H. Roberts
1882 Brown Back	$5, $10, $20, $50, $100	Blanche K. Bruce	A.U. Wyman
1882 Brown Back	$5, $10, $20, $50, $100	Judson W. Lyons	Elias H. Roberts
1882 Brown Back	$5, $10, $20, $50, $100	William S. Rosecrans	James W. Hyatt
1882 Brown Back	$5, $10, $20, $50, $100	William S. Rosecrans	Conrad Jordan
1882 Brown Back	$5, $10, $20, $50, $100	William S. Rosecrans	Daniel N. Morgan
1882 Brown Back	$5, $10, $20, $50, $100	William S. Rosecrans	Enos H. Nebecker
1882 Brown Back	$5, $10, $20, $50, $100	James F. Tillman	Daniel N. Morgan
1882 Brown Back	$5, $10, $20, $50, $100	James F. Tillman	Elias H. Roberts
1882 Brown Back	$5, $10, $20, $50, $100	William T. Vernon	Charles H. Treat
1882 Date Back	$5, $10, $20	William S. Rosecrans	Daniel N. Morgan
1882 Date Back	$5, $10, $20	William T. Vernon	Lee McClung
1882 Date Back	$5, $10, $20, $50, $100	Blanche K. Bruce	Elias H. Roberts
1882 Date Back	$5, $10, $20, $50, $100	Judson W. Lyons	Elias H. Roberts
1882 Date Back	$5, $10, $20, $50, $100	James C. Napier	Lee McClung
1882 Date Back	$5, $10, $20, $50, $100	William S. Rosecrans	J.N. Huston

National bank notes (continued)

Series	Denominations	Register of the Treasury	Treasurer
1882 Date Back	$5, $10, $20, $50, $100	William S. Rosecrans	Enos H. Nebecker
1882 Date Back	$5, $10, $20, $50, $100	James F. Tillman	Daniel N. Morgan
1882 Date Back	$5, $10, $20, $50, $100	James F. Tillman	Elias H. Roberts
1882 Date Back	$5, $10, $20, $50, $100	William T. Vernon	Charles H. Treat
1882 Denomination Back	$5, $10, $20	Blanche K. Bruce	Elias H. Roberts
1882 Denomination Back	$5, $10, $20	James C. Napier	Lee McClung
1882 Denomination Back	$5, $10, $20	Houston B. Teehee	John Burke
1882 Denomination Back	$5, $10, $20	James F. Tillman	Daniel N. Morgan
1882 Denomination Back	$5, $10, $20	James F. Tillman	Elias H. Roberts
1882 Denomination Back	$5, $10, $20	William T. Vernon	Charles H. Treat
1882 Denomination Back	$5, $10, $20, $50, $100	Judson W. Lyons	Elias H. Roberts
1882 Denomination Back	$10, $20	Judson W. Lyons	Charles H. Treat
1902 Blue Seal, Date Back	$5, $10, $20, $50, $100	Judson W. Lyons	Elias H. Roberts
1902 Blue Seal, Date Back	$5, $10, $20, $50, $100	Judson W. Lyons	Charles H. Treat
1902 Blue Seal, Date Back	$5, $10, $20, $50, $100	James C. Napier	John Burke
1902 Blue Seal, Date Back	$5, $10, $20, $50, $100	James C. Napier	Lee McClung
1902 Blue Seal, Date Back	$5, $10, $20, $50, $100	James C. Napier	Carmi A. Thompson
1902 Blue Seal, Date Back	$5, $10, $20, $50, $100	Gabe E. Parker	John Burke
1902 Blue Seal, Date Back	$5, $10, $20, $50, $100	Houston B. Teehee	John Burke
1902 Blue Seal, Date Back	$5, $10, $20, $50, $100	William T. Vernon	Lee McClung
1902 Blue Seal, Date Back	$5, $10, $20, $50, $100	William T. Vernon	Charles H. Treat
1902 Blue Seal, No Date Back	$5, $10, $20	Edward E. Jones	Walter O. Woods
1902 Blue Seal, No Date Back	$5, $10, $20	Walter O. Woods	H.T. Tate
1902 Blue Seal, No Date Back	$5, $10, $20, $50	James C. Napier	John Burke
1902 Blue Seal, No Date Back	$5, $10, $20, $50	Walter O. Woods	Frank White
1902 Blue Seal, No Date Back	$5, $10, $20, $50, $100	William S. Elliott	John Burke
1902 Blue Seal, No Date Back	$5, $10, $20, $50, $100	William S. Elliott	Frank White
1902 Blue Seal, No Date Back	$5, $10, $20, $50, $100	Judson W. Lyons	Elias H. Roberts
1902 Blue Seal, No Date Back	$5, $10, $20, $50, $100	Judson W. Lyons	Charles H. Treat
1902 Blue Seal, No Date Back	$5, $10, $20, $50, $100	James C. Napier	Lee McClung
1902 Blue Seal, No Date Back	$5, $10, $20, $50, $100	James C. Napier	Carmi A. Thompson
1902 Blue Seal, No Date Back	$5, $10, $20, $50, $100	Gabe E. Parker	John Burke
1902 Blue Seal, No Date Back	$5, $10, $20, $50, $100	Harley V. Speelman	Frank White
1902 Blue Seal, No Date Back	$5, $10, $20, $50, $100	Houston B. Teehee	John Burke
1902 Blue Seal, No Date Back	$5, $10, $20, $50, $100	William T. Vernon	Lee McClung
1902 Blue Seal, No Date Back	$5, $10, $20, $50, $100	William T. Vernon	Charles H. Treat
1902 Red Seal	$5, $10, $20, $50, $100	Judson W. Lyons	Elias H. Roberts
1902 Red Seal	$5, $10, $20, $50, $100	Judson W. Lyons	Charles H. Treat
1902 Red Seal	$5, $10, $20, $50, $100	William T. Vernon	Charles H. Treat

Silver certificates

Series	Denominations	Register of the Treasury	Treasurer
1878	$10, $20, $50, $100, $500, $1,000	Glenni W. Scofield	James Gilfillan
1880	$10, $20, $50, $100, $1,000	Blanche K. Bruce	A.U. Wyman
1880	$10, $20, $50, $100, $500, $1,000	Blanche K. Bruce	James Gilfillan
1880	$10, $20, $50, $100, $500, $1,000	Glenni W. Scofield	James Gilfillan
1880	$50, $100	William S. Rosecrans	J.N. Huston
1886	$1, $2, $5, $10	William S. Rosecrans	Conrad Jordan
1886	$1, $2, $5, $10, $20	William S. Rosecrans	J.N. Huston
1886	$1, $2, $5, $10, $20	William S. Rosecrans	James W. Hyatt
1886	$1, $5, $10, $20, $50, $100	William S. Rosecrans	Enos H. Nebecker
1891	$1, $2, $5, $10, $20, $50, $100	William S. Rosecrans	Enos H. Nebecker

Silver certificates (continued)

Series	Denominations	Register of the Treasury	Treasurer
1891	$1, $2, $5, $10, $20, $50, $100, $1,000	James F. Tillman	Daniel N. Morgan
1891	$10, $20, $50	Blanche K. Bruce	Elias H. Roberts
1891	$10, $20, $50	Judson W. Lyons	Elias H. Roberts
1891	$20	Houston B. Teehee	John Burke
1891	$20, $50	Gabe E. Parker	John Burke
1891	$50	William T. Vernon	Charles H. Treat
1896	$1, $2, $5	Blanche K. Bruce	Elias H. Roberts
1896	$1, $2, $5	James F. Tillman	Daniel N. Morgan
1896	$5	Judson W. Lyons	Elias H. Roberts
1899	$1, $2, $5	William S. Elliott	John Burke
1899	$1, $2, $5	Judson W. Lyons	Elias H. Roberts
1899	$1, $2, $5	Judson W. Lyons	Charles H. Treat
1899	$1, $2, $5	James C. Napier	Lee McClung
1899	$1, $2, $5	James C. Napier	Carmi A. Thompson
1899	$1, $2, $5	Gabe E. Parker	John Burke
1899	$1, $2, $5	Harley V. Speelman	Frank White
1899	$1, $2, $5	Houston B. Teehee	John Burke
1899	$1, $2, $5	William T. Vernon	Lee McClung
1899	$1, $2, $5	William T. Vernon	Charles H. Treat
1899	$1, $5	William S. Elliott	Frank White
1908	$10	Gabe E. Parker	John Burke
1908	$10	William T. Vernon	Lee McClung
1908	$10	William T. Vernon	Charles H. Treat
1923	$1	Walter O. Woods	H.T. Tate
1923	$1	Walter O. Woods	Frank White
1923	$1, $5	Harley V. Speelman	Frank White

Gold certificates

Series	Denominations	Register of the Treasury	Treasurer
1882	$5, $100	James C. Napier	Lee McClung
1882	$20, $50, $100	Blanche K. Bruce	James Gilfillan
1882	$20, $50, $100	Blanche K. Bruce	A.U. Wyman
1882	$20, $50, $100	Judson W. Lyons	Elias H. Roberts
1882	$20, $50, $100	William S. Rosecrans	J.N. Huston
1882	$50, $100	Judson W. Lyons	Charles H. Treat
1882	$50, $100	William S. Rosecrans	James W. Hyatt
1882	$50, $100	William T. Vernon	Lee McClung
1882	$50, $100	William T. Vernon	Charles H. Treat
1882	$100	James C. Napier	John Burke
1882	$100	James C. Napier	Carmi A. Thompson
1882	$100	Gabe E. Parker	John Burke
1882	$100	Houston B. Teehee	John Burke
1905	$20	Judson W. Lyons	Elias H. Roberts
1905	$20	Judson W. Lyons	Charles H. Treat
1906	$20	James C. Napier	Lee McClung
1906	$20	James C. Napier	Carmi A. Thompson
1906	$20	Gabe E. Parker	John Burke
1906	$20	Houston B. Teehee	John Burke
1906	$20	William T. Vernon	Lee McClung
1906	$20	William T. Vernon	Charles H. Treat
1907	$10	James C. Napier	Lee McClung
1907	$10	James C. Napier	Carmi A. Thompson

Gold certificates (continued)

Series	Denominations	Register of the Treasury	Treasurer
1907	$10	Gabe E. Parker	John Burke
1907	$10	Houston B. Teehee	John Burke
1907	$10	William T. Vernon	Lee McClung
1907	$10	William T. Vernon	Charles H. Treat
1913	$50	Gabe E. Parker	John Burke
1913	$50	Houston B. Teehee	John Burke
1922	$10, $20, $50, $100	Harley V. Speelman	Frank White

Compound-interest Treasury notes

Series	Denominations	Register of the Treasury	Treasurer
All	All	Lucius E. Chittenden	F.E. Spinner
All	All	S.B. Colby	F.E. Spinner

Interest-bearing notes

Series	Denominations	Register of the Treasury	Treasurer
All	All	Lucius E. Chittenden	F.E. Spinner
All	All	S.B. Colby	F.E. Spinner

Treasury (Coin) notes

Series	Denominations	Register of the Treasury	Treasurer
1890	$1, $2, $5, $10, $20, $1,000	William S. Rosecrans	Enos H. Nebecker
1890	$1, $2, $5, $10, $100, $1,000	William S. Rosecrans	J.N. Huston
1891	$1, $2, $5, $10, $20	Blanche K. Bruce	Elias H. Roberts
1891	$1, $2, $5, $10, $20, $1,000	James F. Tillman	Daniel N. Morgan
1891	$1, $2, $5, $10, $50, $100, $1,000	William S. Rosecrans	Enos H. Nebecker
1891	$20	William S. Rosecrans	J.N. Huston
1895	$5	Judson W. Lyons	Elias H. Roberts

Refunding certificate

Series	Denominations	Register of the Treasury	Treasurer
Only	$10	Glenni W. Scofield	James Gilfillan

Fractional currency

Series	Denominations	Register of the Treasury	Treasurer
Third Issue	5¢, 10¢, 15¢, 25¢, 50¢ (Friedberg designs 181, 182, 183)	S.B. Colby	F.E. Spinner
Third Issue	5¢, 10¢, 15¢	Noah L. Jeffries	F.E. Spinner
Third Issue	15¢, 50¢ (Friedberg design type 181)	John Allison	F.E. Spinner
Third Issue	50¢ (Friedberg design type 181)	John Allison	John C. New
Fourth Issue	10¢, 15¢, 25¢, 50¢ (Friedberg designs 184, 185, 186)	John Allison	F.E. Spinner
Fifth Issue	10¢, 25¢	John Allison	F.E. Spinner
Fifth Issue	50¢	John Allison	John C. New

Federal Reserve Bank notes

Series	Denominations	Register of the Treasury	Treasurer
1918	$1, $2, $5, $10, $20	William S. Elliott	John Burke
1918	$1, $2, $5, $10, $20	Houston B. Teehee	John Burke

1914 Federal Reserve notes

Series	Denominations	Secretary	Treasurer
1914 Blue Seal	$5, $10, $20, $50, $100, $500, $1,000, $5,000, $10,000	Carter Glass	John Burke
1914 Blue Seal	$5, $10, $20, $50, $100, $500, $1,000, $5,000, $10,000	David F. Houston	John Burke
1914 Blue Seal	$5, $10, $20, $50, $100, $500, $1,000, $5,000, $10,000	William Gibbs McAdoo	John Burke
1914 Blue Seal	$5, $10, $20, $50, $100, $500, $1,000, $5,000, $10,000	Andrew W. Mellon	Frank White
1914 Red Seal	$5, $10, $20, $50	William Gibbs McAdoo	John Burke

Signatures on small-size paper money

Federal Reserve Bank notes

Series	Denominations	Register of the Treasury	Treasurer
1929	$5, $10, $20, $50, $100	Edward E. Jones	Walter O. Woods

National bank notes

Series	Denominations	Register of the Treasury	Treasurer
1929	$5, $10, $20, $50, $100	Edward E. Jones	Walter O. Woods

Gold certificates

Series	Denominations	Treasurer	Secretary
1928	$10, $20, $50, $100, $500, $1,000, $5,000, $10,000	Walter O. Woods	Andrew W. Mellon
1928	$10, $20	Walter O. Woods	Ogden L. Mills
1934	$100, $1,000, $10,000, $100,000	W.A. Julian	Henry Morgenthau Jr.

United States notes

Series	Denominations	Treasurer	Secretary
1928	$1	Walter O. Woods	William H. Woodin
1928	$2	H.T. Tate	Andrew W. Mellon
1928	$5	Walter O. Woods	Andrew W. Mellon
1928A	$2	Walter O. Woods	Andrew W. Mellon
1928A	$5	Walter O. Woods	Ogden L. Mills
1928B	$2	Walter O. Woods	Ogden L. Mills
1928B	$5	W.A. Julian	Henry Morgenthau Jr.
1928C	$2, $5	W.A. Julian	Henry Morgenthau Jr.
1928D	$2	W.A. Julian	Henry Morgenthau Jr.
1928D	$5	W.A. Julian	Fred M. Vinson
1928E	$2	W.A. Julian	Fred M. Vinson
1928E	$5	W.A. Julian	John W. Snyder
1928F	$2	W.A. Julian	John W. Snyder
1928F	$5	Georgia Neese Clark	John W. Snyder
1928G	$2	Georgia Neese Clark	John W. Snyder
1953	$2, $5	Ivy Baker Priest	George M. Humphrey
1953A	$2, $5	Ivy Baker Priest	Robert B. Anderson
1953B	$2, $5	Elizabeth Rudel Smith	Douglas Dillon
1953C	$2, $5	Kathryn O'Hay Granahan	Douglas Dillon
1963	$2, $5	Kathryn O'Hay Granahan	Douglas Dillon
1963A	$2	Kathryn O'Hay Granahan	Henry H. Fowler
1966	$100	Kathryn O'Hay Granahan	Henry H. Fowler
1966A	$100	Dorothy Andrews Elston	David M. Kennedy

Silver certificates

Series	Denominations	Treasurer	Secretary
1928	$1	H.T. Tate	Andrew W. Mellon
1928A	$1	Walter O. Woods	Andrew W. Mellon
1928B	$1	Walter O. Woods	Ogden L. Mills
1928C	$1	Walter O. Woods	William H. Woodin
1928D	$1	W.A. Julian	William H. Woodin
1928E	$1	W.A. Julian	Henry Morgenthau Jr.
1933	$10	W.A. Julian	William H. Woodin
1934	$1, $5, $10	W.A. Julian	Henry Morgenthau Jr.
1934A	$5, $10	W.A. Julian	Henry Morgenthau Jr.
1934B	$5, $10	W.A. Julian	Fred M. Vinson
1934C	$5, $10	W.A. Julian	John W. Snyder
1934D	$5, $10	Georgia Neese Clark	John W. Snyder

Silver certificates (continued)

Series	Denominations	Treasurer	Secretary
1935	$1	W.A. Julian	Henry Morgenthau Jr.
1935A	$1	W.A. Julian	Henry Morgenthau Jr.
1935B	$1	W.A. Julian	Fred M. Vinson
1935C	$1	W.A. Julian	John W. Snyder
1935D	$1	Georgia Neese Clark	John W. Snyder
1935E	$1	Ivy Baker Priest	George M. Humphrey
1935F	$1	Ivy Baker Priest	Robert B. Anderson
1935G	$1	Elizabeth Rudel Smith	Douglas Dillon
1935H	$1	Kathryn O'Hay Granahan	Douglas Dillon
1953	$5, $10	Ivy Baker Priest	George M. Humphrey
1953A	$5, $10	Ivy Baker Priest	Robert B. Anderson
1953B	$5, $10	Elizabeth Rudel Smith	Douglas Dillon
1953C	$5	Kathryn O'Hay Granahan	Douglas Dillon
1957	$1	Ivy Baker Priest	Robert B. Anderson
1957A	$1	Elizabeth Rudel Smith	Douglas Dillon
1957B	$1	Kathryn O'Hay Granahan	Douglas Dillon

Federal Reserve notes

Series	Denominations	Treasurer	Secretary
1928	$5, $10, $20	H.T. Tate	Andrew W. Mellon
1928	$50, $100, $500, $1,000, $5,000, $10,000	Walter O. Woods	Andrew W. Mellon
1928A	$5, $10, $20, $50, $100	Walter O. Woods	Andrew W. Mellon
1928B	$5, $10, $20	Walter O. Woods	Andrew W. Mellon
1928C	$5, $10, $20	Walter O. Woods	Ogden L. Mills
1928D	$5	Walter O. Woods	William H. Woodin
1934	$5, $10, $20, $50, $100, $500, $1,000, $5,000, $10,000	W.A. Julian	Henry Morgenthau Jr.
1934A	$5, $10, $20, $50, $100, $500, $1,000	W.A. Julian	Henry Morgenthau Jr.
1934B	$5, $10, $20, $50, $100	W.A. Julian	Fred M. Vinson
1934C	$5, $10, $20, $50, $100	W.A. Julian	John W. Snyder
1934D	$5, $10, $20, $50, $100	Georgia Neese Clark	John W. Snyder
1950	$5, $10, $20, $50, $100	Georgia Neese Clark	John W. Snyder
1950A	$5, $10, $20, $50, $100	Ivy Baker Priest	George M. Humphrey
1950B	$5, $10, $20, $50, $100	Ivy Baker Priest	Robert B. Anderson
1950C	$5, $10, $20, $50, $100	Elizabeth Rudel Smith	Douglas Dillon
1950D	$5, $10, $20, $50, $100	Kathryn O'Hay Granahan	Douglas Dillon
1950E	$5, $10, $20, $50, $100	Kathryn O'Hay Granahan	Henry H. Fowler
1963	$1, $5, $10, $20	Kathryn O'Hay Granahan	Douglas Dillon
1963A	$1, $5, $10, $20, $50, $100	Kathryn O'Hay Granahan	Henry H. Fowler
1963B	$1	Kathryn O'Hay Granahan	Joseph W. Barr
1969	$1, $5, $10, $20, $50, $100	Dorothy Andrews Elston	David M. Kennedy
1969A	$1	Dorothy Andrews Kabis	David M. Kennedy
1969A	$5, $10, $20, $50, $100	Dorothy Andrews Kabis	John B. Connally
1969B	$1	Dorothy Andrews Kabis	John B. Connally
1969B	$5, $10, $20, $50	Romana Acosta Banuelos	John B. Connally
1969C	$1	Romana Acosta Banuelos	John B. Connally
1969C	$5, $10, $20, $50, $100	Romana Acosta Banuelos	George P. Shultz
1969D	$1	Romana Acosta Banuelos	George P. Shultz
1974	$1, $5, $10, $20, $50, $100	Francine Irving Neff	William E. Simon
1976	$2	Francine Irving Neff	William E. Simon
1977	$1, $5, $10, $20, $50, $100	Azie Taylor Morton	W. Michael Blumenthal
1977A	$1, $5, $10	Azie Taylor Morton	G. William Miller
1981	$1, $5, $10, $20, $50, $100	Angela Buchanan	Donald T. Regan

Federal Reserve notes (continued)

Series	Denominations	Treasurer	Secretary
1981A	$1, $5, $10, $20, $50, $100	Katherine Davalos Ortega	Donald T. Regan
1985	$1, $5, $10, $20, $50, $100	Katherine Davalos Ortega	James A. Baker III
1988	$1, $5, $10, $20, $50, $100	Katherine Davalos Ortega	Nicholas F. Brady
1988A	$1, $5, $10, $20, $50, $100	Catalina Vasquez Villalpando	Nicholas F. Brady
1990	$1, $5, $10, $20, $50, $100	Catalina Vasquez Villalpando	Nicholas F. Brady
1993	$1, $5, $10, $20, $50, $100	Mary Ellen Withrow	Lloyd M. Bentsen
1995	$1, $2, $5, $10, $20	Mary Ellen Withrow	Robert E. Rubin
1996	$20, $50, $100	Mary Ellen Withrow	Robert E. Rubin
1999	$1, $5, $10	Mary Ellen Withrow	Lawrence E. Summers
2001	$1, $5, $10, $20, $50, $100	Rosario Marin	Paul H. O'Neill
2003	$1, $2, $10, $100	Rosario Marin	John W. Snow
2003A	$1, $2, $5, $100	Anna Escobedo Cabral	John W. Snow
2004	$20, $50	Rosario Marin	John W. Snow
2004A	$10, $20, $50	Anna Escobedo Cabral	John W. Snow
2006	$1, $5, $10, $20, $50, $100	Anna Escobedo Cabral	Henry W. Paulson Jr.
2009	$1, $20, $100	Rosa Gumataotao Rios	Timothy F. Geithner

Signers of U.S. paper money, by name

Name Office	Issue type Series	Denominations
Allison, John Register	United States notes	
	1869	$1, $2, $5, $10, $20, $50, $100, $500
	1874	$1, $2, $50, $100
	1875	$1, $2, $5, $10, $20, $50, $100, $500
	1875A	$1, $2, $5, $10, $100
	1875B	$1, $2, $5
	1875C	$1
	1875D	$1
	1875E	$1
	1878	$1, $2, $5, $10,$20, $50, $100, $500, $1,000
	1880	$500
	National bank notes	
	Original	$1, $2, $5, $10, $20, $50, $100
	1875	$1, $2, $5, $10, $20, $50, $100
	Fractional currency	
	Third Issue	15¢, 50¢ (Friedberg design type 181)
	Fourth Issue	10¢, 15¢, 25¢, 50¢ (all three design types)
	Fifth Issue	10¢, 25¢, 50¢
Anderson, Robert B. Secretary	United States notes	
	1953A	$2, $5
	Silver certificates	
	1935F	$1
	1953A	$5, $10
	1957	$1
	Federal Reserve notes	
	1950B	$5, $10, $20, $50, $100
Baker, James A. III Secretary	Federal Reserve notes	
	1985	$1, $5, $10, $20, $50, $100
Banuelos, Romana Acosta Treasurer	Federal Reserve notes	
	1969B	$5, $10, $20, $50
	1969C	$1, $5, $10, $20, $50, $100
	1969D	$1
Barr, Joseph W. Secretary	Federal Reserve notes	
	1963B	$1
Bentsen, Lloyd M. Secretary	Federal Reserve notes	
	1993	$1, $5, $10, $20, $50, $100

Name Office	Issue type Series	Denominations
Blumenthal, W. Michael Secretary	Federal Reserve notes 1977	$1, $5, $10, $20, $50, $100
Brady, Nicholas F. Secretary	Federal Reserve notes 1988 1988A 1990	$1, $5, $10, $20, $50, $100 $1, $5, $10, $20, $50, $100 $1, $5, $10, $20, $50, $100
Bruce, Blanche K. Register	United States notes 1880 National bank notes 1875 1882 Brown Back 1882 Date Back 1882 Denomination Back Silver certificates 1880 1891 1896 Gold certificates 1882 Treasury (coin) notes 1891	$1, $2, $5, $10, $20, $50, $100 $5, $10, $20, $50, $100 $5, $10, $20, $50, $100 $5, $10, $20, $50, $100 $5, $10, $20 $10, $20, $50, $100, $500, $1,000 $10, $20, $50 $1, $2, $5 $20, $50, $100 $1, $2, $5, $10, $20
Buchanan, Angela Treasurer	Federal Reserve notes 1981	$1, $5, $10, $20, $50, $100
Burke, John Treasurer	Federal Reserve note 1914 Blue Seal 1914 Red Seal United States notes 1880 1901 1907 1917 National bank notes 1882 Denomination Back 1902 Blue Seal, Date Back 1902 Blue Seal, No Date Back Silver certificates 1891 1899 1908 Gold certificates 1882 1906 1907 1913 Federal Reserve Bank notes 1918	$5, $10, $20, $50, $100, $500, $1,000, $5,000, $10,000 $5, $10, $20, $50 $20 $10 $5 $1, $2, $5 $5, $10, $20 $5, $10, $20, $50, $100 $5, $10, $20, $50, $100 $20, $50 $1, $2, $5 $10 $100 $20 $10 $50 $1, $2, $5, $10, $20
Cabral, Anna Escobedo Treasurer	Federal Reserve notes 2003A 2004A 2006	$1, $2, $5, $100 $10, $20, $50 $1, $5 (colorized and non-colorized), $10, $20, $50, $100
Chittenden, Lucius E. Register	Legal tender notes 1862 1863 National bank notes Original Compound-interest Treasury notes All Interest-bearing notes All	$1, $2, $5, $10, $20, $50, $100,$500 $2, $5, $10, $20, $50, $100, $500 $5, $10, $20, $50, $100 All All

Name Office	Issue type Series	Denominations
Clark, Georgia Neese Treasurer	United States notes	
	1928F	$5
	1928G	$2
	Silver certificates	
	1934D	$5, $10
	1935D	$1
	Federal Reserve notes	
	1934D	$5, $10, $20, $50, $100
	1950	$5, $10, $20, $50, $100
Colby, S.B. Register	National bank notes	
	Original	$1, $2, $5, $10, $20, $50, $100
	Compound-interest Treasury notes	
	All	All
	Interest-bearing notes	
	All	All
	Fractional currency	
	Third Issue	5¢, 10¢, 15¢, 25¢, 50¢ (all three design types)
Connally, John B. Secretary	Federal Reserve notes	
	1969A	$5, $10, $20, $50, $100
	1969B	$1, $5, $10, $20, $50
	1969C	$1
Dillon, Douglas Secretary	United States notes	
	1953B	$2, $5
	1953C	$2, $5
	1963	$2, $5
	Silver certificates	
	1935G	$1
	1935H	$1
	1953B	$5, $10
	1953C	$5
	1957A	$1
	1957B	$1
	Federal Reserve notes	
	1950C	$5, $10, $20, $50, $100
	1950D	$5, $10, $20, $50, $100
	1963	$1, $5, $10, $20
Elliott, William S. Register	United States notes	
	1907	$5
	1917	$1, $2, $5
	National bank notes	
	1902 Blue Seal, No Date Back	$5, $10, $20, $50, $100
	Silver certificates	
	1899	$1, $2, $5
	Federal Reserve Bank notes	
	1918	$1, $2, $5, $10, $20
Elston, Dorothy Andrews (see also Kabis, Dorothy Andrews) Treasurer	United States notes	
	1966A	$100
	Federal Reserve notes	
	1969	$1, $5, $10, $20, $50, $100
Fowler, Henry H. Secretary	United States notes	
	1963A	$2
	1966	$100
	Federal Reserve notes	
	1950E	$5, $10, $20, $50, $100
	1963A	$1, $5, $10, $20, $50, $100
Geithner, Timothy F. Secretary	Federal Reserve notes	
	2009	$1, $10, $20 and $100

Name Office	Issue type Series	Denominations
Gilfillan, James Treasurer	United States notes 1878 1880 National bank notes 1875 1882 Brown Back Silver certificates 1878 1880 Gold certificates 1882 Refunding certificates Only	 $1, $2, $5, $10, $20, $50, $100, $500, $1,000 $1, $2, $5, $10, $20, $50, $100 $1, $2, $5, $10, $20, $50, $100 $5, $10, $20, $50, $100 $10, $20, $50, $100, $500, $1,000 $10, $20, $50, $100, $500, $1,000 $20, $50, $100 $10
Glass, Carter Secretary	Federal Reserve note 1914 Blue Seal	 $5, $10, $20, $50, $100, $500, $1,000, $5,000, $10,000
Granahan, Kathryn O'Hay Treasurer	United States notes 1953C 1963 1963A United States notes 1966 Silver certificates 1935H 1953C 1957B Federal Reserve notes 1950D 1950E 1963 1963A 1963B	 $2, $5 $2, $5 $2 $100 $1 $5 $1 $5, $10, $20, $50, $100 $5, $10, $20, $50, $100 $1, $5, $10, $20 $1, $5, $10, $20, $50, $100 $1
Houston, David F. Secretary	Federal Reserve note 1914 Blue Seal	 $5, $10, $20, $50, $100, $500, $1,000, $5,000, $10,000
Humphrey, George M. Secretary	United States notes 1953 Silver certificates 1935E 1953 Federal Reserve notes 1950A	 $2, $5 $1 $5, $10 $5, $10, $20, $50, $100
Huston, J.N. Treasurer	United States notes 1880 National bank notes 1875 1882 Brown Back 1882 Date Back Silver certificates 1880 1886 Gold certificates 1882 Treasury (coin) notes 1890 1891	 $1, $2, $5, $10, $20, $50, $100 $5, $10, $50, $100 $5, $10, $20, $50 $5, $10, $20, $50, $100 $50, $100 $1, $2, $5, $10, $20 $20, $50, $100 $1, $2, $5, $10, $100, $1,000 $20
Hyatt, James W. Treasurer	United States notes 1880 National bank notes 1882 Brown Back Silver certificates 1886 Gold certificates 1882	 $5, $10, $20, $50, $100 $5, $10, $20, $50, $100 $1, $2, $5, $10, $20 $50, $100

Name Office	Issue type Series	Denominations
Jeffries, Noah L. Register	National bank notes Original .... Fractional currency Third Issue	$1, $2, $5, $10, $20 5¢, 10¢, 15¢, 50¢ (Types I, II)
Jones, Edward E. Register	Federal Reserve Bank notes 1929 .... National bank notes 1929 .... National bank notes 1902 Blue Seal, No Date Back	$5, $10, $20, $50, $100 $5, $10, $20, $50, $100 $5, $10, $20
Jordan, Conrad Treasurer	United States notes 1880 .... National bank notes 1875 .... 1882 Brown Back................................... Silver certificates 1886	$5, $10, $20, $50, $100 $5 $5, $10, $20, $50, $100 $1, $2, $5, $10
Julian, W.A. Treasurer	Gold certificates 1934 .... United States notes 1928B .... 1928C .... 1928D .... 1928E .... 1928F .... Silver certificates 1928D .... 1928E .... 1933 .... 1934 .... 1934A .... 1934B .... 1934C .... 1935 .... 1935A .... 1935B .... 1935C .... Federal Reserve notes 1934 .... 1934A .... 1934B 1934C	$100, $1,000, $10,000, $100,000 $5 $2, $5 $2, $5 $2, $5 $2 $1 $1 $10 $1, $5, $10 $5, $10 $5, $10 $5, $10 $1 $1 $1 $1 $5, $10, $20, $50, $100, $500, $1,000, $5,000, $10,000 $5, $10, $20, $50, $100, $500, $1,000 $5, $10, $20, $50, $100 $5, $10, $20, $50, $100
Kabis, Dorothy Andrews (see also Elston, Dorothy Andrews) Treasurer	Federal Reserve notes 1969A 1969B	$1, $5, $10, $20, $50, $100 $1
Kennedy, David M. Secretary	United States notes 1966A .... Federal Reserve notes 1969 .... 1969A	$100 $1, $5, $10, $20, $50, $100 $1
Lyons, Judson W. Register	United States notes 1880 .... 1901 .... National bank notes 1882 Brown Back................................... 1882 Date Back..................................... 1882 Denomination Back .... 1902 Blue Seal, Date Back .... 1902 Blue Seal, No Date Back .... 1902 Red Seal......................................	$5, $10, $20, $50, $100, $500 $10 $5, $10, $20, $50, $100 $5, $10, $20, $50, $100 $5, $10, $20, $50, $100 $5, $10, $20, $50, $100 $5, $10, $20, $50, $100 $5, $10, $20, $50, $100

Name Office	Issue type Series	Denominations
Lyons, Judson W. (continued)	Silver certificates	
	1891	$10, $20, $50
	1896	$5
	1899	$1, $2, $5
	Gold certificates	
	1882	$20, $50, $100
	1905	$20
	Treasury (coin) notes	
	1895	$5
Marin, Rosario Treasurer	Federal Reserve notes	
	2001	$1, $5, $10, $20, $50, $100
	2003	$1, $2, $10, $100
	2004	$20, $50
McAdoo, William Gibbs Secretary	Federal Reserve note	
	1914 Blue Seal	$5, $10, $20, $50, $100, $500, $1,000, $5,000, $10,000
	1914 Red Seal	$5, $10, $20, $50
McClung, Lee Treasurer	United States notes	
	1880	$20
	1901	$10
	1907	$5, $20
	National bank notes	
	1882 Date Back	$5, $10, $20, $50, $100
	1882 Denomination Back	$5, $10, $20
	1902 Blue Seal, Date Back	$5, $10, $20, $50, $100
	1902 Blue Seal, No Date Back	$5, $10, $20, $50, $100
	Silver certificates	
	1899	$1, $2, $5
	1908	$10
	Gold certificates	
	1882	$5, $50, $100
	1906	$20
	1907	$10
Mellon, Andrew W. Secretary	Federal Reserve note	
	1914 Blue Seal	$5, $10, $20, $50, $100, $500, $1,000, $5,000, $10,000
	Gold certificates	
	1928	$10, $20, $50, $100, $500, $1,000, $5,000, $10,000
	United States notes	
	1928	$2, $5
	1928A	$2
	Silver certificates	
	1928	$1
	1928A	$1
	Federal Reserve notes	
	1928	$5, $10, $20, $50, $100, $500, $1,000, $5,000, $10,000
	1928A	$5, $10, $20, $50, $100
	1928B	$5, $10, $20
Miller, G. William Secretary	Federal Reserve notes	
	1977A	$1, $5, $10
Mills, Ogden L. Secretary	Gold certificates	
	1928	$10, $20
	United States notes	
	1928A	$5
	1928B	$2
	Silver certificates	
	1928B	$1
	Federal Reserve notes	
	1928C	$5, $10, $20
Morgan, Daniel N. Treasurer	United States notes	
	1880	$1, $2, $5, $10, $20, $50, $100
	National bank notes	
	1875	$10, $20, $50, $100
	1882 Brown Back	$5, $10, $20, $50, $100

Name Office	Issue type Series	Denominations
Morgan, Daniel N. (continued)	1882 Date Back	$5, $10, $20, $50, $100
	1882 Denomination Back	$5, $10, $20
	Silver certificates	
	1891	$1, $2, $5, $10, $20, $50, $100, $1,000
	1896	$1, $2, $5
	Treasury (coin) notes	
	1891	$1, $2, $5, $10, $20, $1,000
Morgenthau, Henry Jr. Secretary	Gold certificates	
	1934	$100, $1,000, $10,000, $100,000
	United States notes	
	1928B	$5
	1928C	$2, $5
	1928D	$2
	Silver certificates	
	1928E	$1
	1934	$1, $5, $10
	1934A	$5, $10
	1935	$1
	1935A	$1
	Federal Reserve notes	
	1934	$5, $10, $20, $50, $100, $500, $1,000, $5,000, $10,000
	1934A	$5, $10, $20, $50, $100, $500, $1,000
Morton, Azie Taylor Treasurer	Federal Reserve notes	
	1977	$1, $5, $10, $20, $50, $100
	1977A	$1, $5, $10
Napier, James C. Register	United States notes	
	1901	$10
	1907	$5
	National bank notes	
	1882 Date Back	$5, $10, $20, $50, $100
	1882 Denomination Back	$5, $10, $20
	1902 Blue Seal, Date Back	$5, $10, $20, $50, $100
	1902 Blue Seal, No Date Back	$5, $10, $20, $50, $100
	Silver certificates	
	1899	$1, $2, $5
	Gold certificates	
	1882	$5, $100
	1906	$20
	1907	$10
Nebecker, Enos H. Treasurer	United States notes	
	1880	$1, $2, $5, $10, $20
	National bank notes	
	1875	$10, $20, $50, $100
	1882 Brown Back	$5, $10, $20, $50, $100
	1882 Date Back	$5, $10, $20, $50, $100
	Silver certificates	
	1886	$1, $5, $10, $20, $50, $100
	1891	$1, $2, $5, $10, $20, $50, $100
	Treasury (coin) notes	
	1890	$1, $2, $5, $10, $20, $1,000
	1891	$1, $2, $5, $10, $50, $100, $1,000
Neff, Francine Irving Treasurer	Federal Reserve notes	
	1974	$1, $5, $10, $20, $50, $100
	1976	$2
New, John C. Treasurer	United States notes	
	1875	$1, $2, $5, $10, $20, $500
	1875A	$1, $2, $5, $10, $100
	1875B	$1, $2, $5
	1875C	$1
	1875D	$1
	1875E	$1

Name Office	Issue type Series	Denominations
New, John C. (continued)	National bank notes	
	1875	$1, $2, $5, $10, $20, $50, $100
	Fractional currency	
	Third Issue	50¢ (Friedberg design type 181)
	Fifth Issue..	50¢
O'Neill, Paul H. Secretary	Federal Reserve notes	
	2001	$1, $5, $10, $20, $50, $100
Ortega, Katherine Davalos Treasurer	Federal Reserve notes	
	1981A..	$1, $5, $10, $20, $50, $100
	1985	$1, $5, $10, $20, $50, $100
	1988	$1, $5, $10, $20, $50, $100
Parker, Gabe E. Register	United States notes	
	1901	$10
	1907	$5
	National bank notes	
	1902 Blue Seal, Date Back	$5, $10, $20, $50, $100
	1902 Blue Seal, No Date Back	$5, $10, $20, $50, $100
	Silver certificates	
	1891	$20, $50
	1899	$1, $2, $5
	1908	$10
	Gold certificates	
	1882	$100
	1906	$20
	1907	$10
	1913	$50
Paulson Jr., Henry M. Secretary	Federal Reserve notes	
	2006	$1, $5 (colorized and noncolorized), $10, $20, $50, $100
Priest, Ivy Baker Treasurer	United States notes	
	1953	$2, $5
	1953A	$2, $5
	Silver certificates	
	1935E	$1
	1935F	$1
	1953	$5, $10
	1953A	$5, $10
	1957	$1
	Federal Reserve notes	
	1950A	$5, $10, $20, $50, $100
	1950B	$5, $10, $20, $50, $100
Regan, Donald T. Secretary	Federal Reserve notes	
	1981	$1, $5, $10, $20, $50, $100
	1981A..	$1, $5, $10, $20, $50, $100
Rios, Rosa Gumataotao Treasurer	Federal Reserve notes	
	2009	$1, $10, $20, $100
Roberts, Elias H. Treasurer	United States notes	
	1880	$5, $10, $20, $50, $100, $500
	1901	$10
	National bank notes	
	1882 Brown Back...................................	$5, $10, $20, $50, $100
	1882 Date Back.....................................	$5, $10, $20, $50, $100
	1882 Denomination Back	$5, $10, $20, $50, $100
	1902 Blue Seal, Date Back	$5, $10, $20, $50, $100
	1902 Blue Seal, No Date Back	$5, $10,$20, $50, $100
	1902 Red Seal......................................	$5, $10, $20, $50, $100
	Silver certificates	
	1891	$10, $20, $50
	1896	$1, $2, $5
	1899	$1, $2, $5

Name Office	Issue type Series	Denominations
Roberts, Elias H. (continued)	Gold certificates	
	1882	$20, $50, $100
	1905	$20
	Treasury (coin) notes	
	1891	$1, $2, $5, $10, $20
	1895	$5
Rosecrans, William S. Register	United States notes	
	1880	$1, $2, $5, $10, $20, $50, $100
	National bank notes	
	1875	$5, $10, $20, $50, $100
	1882 Brown Back	$5, $10, $20, $50, $100
	1882 Date Back	$5, $10, $20, $50, $100
	Silver certificates	
	1880	$50, $100
	1886	$1, $2, $5, $10, $20, $50, $100
	1891	$1, $2, $5, $10, $20, $50, $100
	Gold certificates	
	1882	$20, $50, $100
	Treasury (coin) notes	
	1890	$1, $2, $5, $10, $20, $100, $1,000
	1891	$1, $2, $5, $10, $20, $50, $100, $1,000
Rubin, Robert E. Secretary	Federal Reserve notes	
	1995	$1, $2, $5, $10, $20
	1996	$20, $50, $100
Scofield, Glenni W. Register	United States notes	
	1878	$2
	1880	$1, $2, $5, $10, $20
	National bank notes	
	1875	$1, $2, $5, $10, $20, $50, $100
	Silver certificates	
	1878	$10, $20, $50, $100, $500, $1,000
	1880	$10, $20, $50, $100, $500, $1,000
	Refunding certificates	
	Only	$10
Shultz, George P. Secretary	Federal Reserve notes	
	1969C	$5, $10, $20, $50, $100
	1969D	$1
Simon, William E. Secretary	Federal Reserve notes	
	1974	$1, $5, $10, $20, $50, $100
	1976	$2
Smith, Elizabeth Rudel Treasurer	United States notes	
	1953B	$2, $5
	Silver certificates	
	1935G	$1
	1953B	$5, $10
	1957A	$1
	Federal Reserve notes	
	1950C	$5, $10, $20, $50, $100
Snyder, John W. Secretary	United States notes	
	1928E	$5
	1928F	$2, $5
	1928G	$2
	Silver certificates	
	1934C	$5, $10
	1934D	$5, $10
	1935C	$1
	1935D	$1
	Federal Reserve notes	
	1934C	$5, $10, $20, $50, $100
	1934D	$5, $10, $20, $50, $100
	1950	$5, $10, $20, $50, $100

Name Office	Issue type Series	Denominations
Snow, John W. Secretary	Federal Reserve notes	
	2003	$1, $2, $10, $100
	2003A	$1, $2, $5, $100
	2004	$20, $50
	2004A	$10, $20, $50
Speelman, Harley V. Register	United States notes	
	1901	$10
	1907	$5
	1917	$1, $2
	1923	$10
	National bank notes	
	1902 Blue Seal, No Date Back	$5, $10, $20, $50, $100
	Silver certificates	
	1899	$1, $2, $5
	1923	$1, $5
	Gold certificates	
	1922	$10, $20, $50, $100
Spinner, F.E. Treasurer	Legal tender, United States notes	
	1862	$1, $2, $5, $10, $20, $50, $100, $500
	1863	$2, $5, $10, $20, $50, $100, $500
	1869	$1, $2, $5, $10, $20, $50, $100, $500
	1874	$1, $2, $50, $100
	1880	$500
	National bank notes	
	Original	$1, $2, $5, $10, $20, $50, $100
	Compound-interest Treasury notes	
	All	All
	Interest-bearing notes	
	All	All
	Fractional currency	
	Third Issue	5¢, 10¢, 15¢, 25¢, 50¢ (Friedberg design types 181, 182, 183)
	Fourth Issue	10¢, 15¢, 25¢, 50¢ (Friedberg design types 184, 185, 186)
	Fifth Issue	10¢, 25¢
Summers, Lawrence Secretary	Federal Reserve	
	1999	$1, $5, $10
Tate, H.T. Treasurer	United States notes	
	1928	$2
	Silver certificates	
	1928	$1
	Federal Reserve notes	
	1928	$5, $10, $20
	National bank notes	
	1902 Blue Seal, No Date Back	$5, $10, $20
	Silver certificates	
	1923	$1
Teehee, Houston B. Register	United States notes	
	1880	$20
	1901	$10
	1907	$5
	1917	$1, $2
	National bank notes	
	1882 Denomination Back	$5, $10, $20
	1902 Blue Seal, Date Back	$5, $10, $20, $50, $100
	1902 Blue Seal, No Date Back	$5, $10, $20, $50, $100
	Silver certificates	
	1891	$20
	1899	$1, $2, $5
	Gold certificates	
	1882	$100
	1906	$20
	1907	$10
	1913	$50

Name Office	Issue type Series	Denominations
Teehee, Houston B. (continued)	Federal Reserve Bank notes 1918	$1, $2, $5, $10, $20
Thompson, Carmi A. Treasurer	United States notes 1907	$5
	National bank notes 1902 Blue Seal, Date Back	$5, $10, $20, $50, $100
	1902 Blue Seal, No Date Back	$5, $10, $20, $50, $100
	Silver certificates 1899	$1, $2, $5
	Gold certificates 1882	$100
	1906	$20
	1907	$10
Tillman, James F. Register	United States notes 1880	$1, $2, $5, $10, $20, $50, $100
	National bank notes 1875	$10, $20, $50, $100
	1882 Brown Back	$5, $10, $20, $50, $100
	1882 Date Back	$5, $10, $20, $50, $100
	1882 Denomination Back	$5, $10, $20
	Silver certificates 1891	$1, $2, $5, $10, $20, $50, $100, $1,000
	1896	$1, $2, $5
	Treasury (coin) notes 1891	$1, $2, $5, $10, $20, $1,000
Treat, Charles H. Treasurer	United States notes 1880	$20
	1901	$10
	1907	$5
	National bank notes 1882 Brown Back	$5, $10, $20, $50, $100
	1882 Date Back	$5, $10, $20, $50, $100
	1882 Denomination Back	$5, $10, $20
	1902 Blue Seal, Date Back	$5, $10, $20, $50, $100
	1902 Blue Seal, No Date Back	$5, $10, $20, $50, $100
	1902 Red Seal	$5, $10, $20, $50, $100
	Silver certificates 1891	$50
	1899	$1, $2, $5
	1908	$10
	Gold certificates 1882	$50, $100
	1905	$20
	1906	$20
	1907	$10
Vernon, William T. Register	United States notes 1880	$20
	1901	$10
	1907	$5, $20
	National bank notes 1882 Brown Back	$5, $10, $20, $50, $100
	1882 Date Back	$5, $10, $20, $50, $100
	1882 Denomination Back	$5, $10, $20
	1902 Blue Seal, Date Back	$5, $10, $20, $50, $100
	1902 Blue Seal, No Date Back	$5, $10, $20, $50, $100
	1902 Red Seal	$5, $10, $20, $50, $100
	Silver certificates 1891	$50
	1899	$1, $2, $5
	1908	$10
	Gold certificates 1882	$50, $100

Name Office	Issue type Series	Denominations
Vernon, William T. (continued)	1906	$20
	1907	$10
Villalpando, Catalina Vasquez Treasurer	Federal Reserve notes	
	1988A	$1, $5, $10, $20, $50, 100
	1990	$1, $5, $10, $20, $50, $100
Vinson, Fred M. Secretary	United States notes	
	1928D	$5
	1928E	$2
	Silver certificates	
	1934B	$5, $10
	1935B	$1
	Federal Reserve notes	
	1934B	$5, $10, $20, $50, $100
White, Frank Treasurer	Federal Reserve note	
	1914 Blue Seal	$5, $10, $20, $50, $100, $500, $1,000, $5,000, $10,000
	United States notes	
	1880	$20
	1901	$10
	1907	$5
	1917	$1, $2
	1923	$10
	National bank notes	
	1902 Blue Seal, No Date Back	$5, $10, $20, $50, $100
	Silver certificates	
	1899	$1, $2, $5
	1923	$1, $5
	Gold certificates	
	1922	$10, $20, $50, $100
William S. Elliott Register	United States notes	
	1880	$20
Withrow, Mary Ellen Treasurer	Federal Reserve notes	
	1993	$1, $5, $10, $20, $50, $100
	1995	$1, $2, $5, $10, $20
	1996	$20, $50, $100
	1999	$1, $5, $10
Woodin, William H. Secretary	United States notes	
	1928	$1
	Silver certificates	
	1928C	$1
	1928D	$1
	1933	$10
	Federal Reserve notes	
	1928D	$5
Woods, Walter O. Register	United States notes	
	1907	$5
	National bank notes	
	1902 Blue Seal, No Date Back	$5, $10, $20, $50
	Silver certificates	
	1923	$1
Woods, Walter O. Treasurer	Gold certificates	
	1928	$10, $20, $50, $100, $500, $1,000, $5,000, $10,000
	United States notes	
	1928	$1, $5
	1928A	$2, $5
	1928B	$2
	Silver certificates	
	1928A	$1
	1928B	$1
	1928C	$1
	Federal Reserve notes	
	1928	$50, $100, $500, $1,000, $5,000, $10,000

Name Office	Issue type Series	Denominations
Woods, Walter O. (continued)	1928A	$5, $10, $20, $50, $100
	1928B	$5, $10, $20
	1928C	$5, $10, $20
	1928D	$5
	Federal Reserve Bank notes	
	1929	$5, $10, $20, $50, $100
	National bank notes	
	1929	$5, $10, $20, $50, $100
	National bank notes	
	1902 Blue Seal, No Date Back	$5, $10, $20
Wyman, A.U. Treasurer	United States notes	
	1875	$1, $2, $5, $50, $100, $500
	1880	$1, $5, $10, $20, $50, $100
	National bank notes	
	1875	$1, $2, $5, $10, $20, $50, $100
	1882 Brown Back	$5, $10, $20, $50, $100
	Silver certificates	
	1880	$10, $20, $50, $100, $1,000
	Gold certificates	
	1882	$20, $50, $100

Postal notes

U.S. postal notes offer collectors a glimpse into a little known area of American history and a bridge into paper money collecting.

During the Civil War, when coins needed to make change were in short supply, the federal government issued postage and fractional currency. These small-size notes were issued in denominations under $1. The designs for the first issue actually resembled postage stamps. Postage and fractional currency notes circulated from 1862 to 1875. They were issued in 3-, 5-, 10-, 15-, 25- and 50-cent denominations.

The need to have access to small denomination financial instruments continued after the war, and by 1882, the American Express Co. became the first firm to introduce small "notes" to be used in the mails. By 1883, 6,300 U.S. Post Offices were authorized to offer U.S. postal notes for amounts less than $5. At that time, 25 cents bought a meal and a dollar was a day's wages. The notes, printed on watermarked paper, had a three-month expiration date.

A series of articles by postal note collector and researcher Nicholas Bruyer, published in the early 1970s in the Society of Paper Money Collectors journal *Paper Money,* is often referred to as the source of information for collectors and researchers in this area.

According to Bruyer: "If the postage stamp has been honored as the forefather of fractional paper, then so must fractional currency be revered as the progenitor of the United States postal note. All three of these types of paper were used in the 19th century to bolster the circulation of coinage, which always seemed to be in short supply. Stamps, postage and fractional currency and postal notes were all transmitted through the mails for the payment of small sums. All were for the general use of the people, all payable to bearer. Yet, when the histories of paper money were written, the postal note somehow became separated from its compatriots."

These postal notes feature ornate lettering and borders. There were two columns on the right-hand side of the face of the postal notes requiring the post office to punch out the amount the note was worth. The signature of the postmaster and the location of the post office were required on the postal note. On the earliest notes, the month and year were also punched.

Postal notes are divided into five issues among three different bank note printers.

The First Issue, Second Issue and Third Issue postal notes were produced by the Homer Lee Bank Note Co. from 1883 to 1887. A vignette of Liberty, with the text FEE THREE CENTS surrounding the vignette, appears on the first issues. Variations of the design were used on the later issues.

Second Issue postal notes were smaller in size than First Issue notes and were printed on white paper instead of yellow paper. The Second Issue notes also had the addition of a cancellation star in the box in the lower right. According to Bruyer, "The box instructs the paying postmaster that he must 'Punch out this star canceling this note.' On the earlier notes of the First Issue, the only evidence on it indicating that it had been paid was the postmark of the paying office."

The Third Issue postal notes had the words ANY MONEY ORDER OFFICE added to reflect a change in law regarding redemption of the notes. Before the change, redemption of the postal note could only been done through "the postmaster of the money order office" at a special post office.

The Fourth Issue postal note was redesigned by Thomas F. Morris when his employer, the American Bank Note Co., was awarded a four-year contract to print the notes between 1887 to 1891. By the late 1880s, according to Bruyer, "Efforts by the Post Office to satisfy the demand for a cheap, convenient method of sending money through the mail seemed to be slowly losing ground. During 1888, four formal petitions were submitted to Congress by private and public parties concerning the postal note." Two of those petitions called for the abolition of the postal note while the other two requested the re-issuance of fractional currency in place of the postal note.

The Fifth Issue postal notes feature the same design as Fourth Issue except for the addition of the new printing company's name, Dunlap & Clarke Co.

of Philadelphia, whose four-year contract ran from 1891 to 1894. According to Bruyer, "Congress passed an act of Jan. 27, 1894, ordering that no more postal notes be produced, that the issuance of postal notes cease on July 1, 1894, and that a new 'limited money order' would take its place."

During its run between 1883 and 1894, according to Bruyer, 70,824,173 postal notes were issued worth $126.5 million. Less than 1,000 are known today because most were cashed and destroyed. Collectors usually collect postal notes by type, states of issue or unusual places of issue such as a temporary post office at an exhibition.

9   U.S. Coins

Coins in use in America before 1793

The first coins in circulation in non-Spanish North America were standard French and English issues used in a variety of unsuccessful colonies ranging from the St. Lawrence River to the Caribbean. The colonists were not likely to have too much specie left after they purchased their supplies for the voyage to the New World, but what was left most certainly did come along, as the travelers did not dare to leave anything of value in a land to which they were likely never to return.

With the establishment of successful colonies in the early 1600s, the colonists began to trade both with their parent companies and the Spanish colonies of the Caribbean. The trade with England was highly restricted and most English gold and silver that reached the North American shores soon returned to Europe in the form of taxes, custom duties and profit for the companies. The trade with Latin America was much less formal (due to smuggling) and provided much of the circulating coinage for the British Colonies.

Because the British Colonies could never acquire enough coinage of the homeland to fulfill their needs, they were eventually forced to produce some themselves. In 1652 the Massachusetts Bay Colony produced silver shillings, sixpence and threepence, but at a reduced weight so that the coins would not be exported. Various designs were used over a 30-year period, but the date on the coins remained at 1652 (except for the 1662 twopence). The traditional explanation is the fixed date was a ruse to hide the actual years of production since the mint was illegal. However, Philip L. Mossman (in the highly regarded *Money of the American Colonies and Confederation*) suggests the dates indicate the denominations were authorized. The shilling, sixpence and threepence were authorized in 1652, the twopence in 1662.

Seeing that there was (supposedly) a market for underweight coins in the Colonies, several speculators began issuing private tokens for export to these markets. Most of these issues were officially sanctioned in some fashion. In effect the speculators were given a license to counterfeit, in exchange for a percentage of the profits. Some of these tokens circulated and some did not, depending upon the greed of the manufacturer and how much he debased the

tokens. One of the more candid manufacturers, an American, changed the inscription of his unpopular copper threepence pieces to read VALUE ME AS YOU PLEASE.

Throughout the period of the Revolution and afterward, a large part of the supply of small change was made up of privately issued store card tokens. Most of these were made in England and were of better quality than the majority of the various state issues. Those issued by American merchants were allegedly payable at these stores, but the others were payable only at London or Liverpool or other equally distant places. These tokens circulated for several years after the establishment of the federal Mint in Philadelphia, despite an effort to recoin them into U.S. money.

The Articles of Confederation, adopted in 1778, permitted the states to issue their own coinages, with Congress fixing a uniform "standard of weights and measures." Only three of the 13 states struck coins for circulation under the Articles of Confederation: Connecticut, Massachusetts and New Jersey. Vermont, the 14th state, struck coinage before it entered the union. Private manufacturers under contract to the states produced most of the state coinages, although Massachusetts operated its own mint in 1787 and 1788. Connecticut authorized a mint, but most of its coinage was struck privately.

The U.S. Constitution, however, brought an end to the state coinage. Article 1, Section 10, Paragraph 1 of the Constitution reads, "No state shall ... coin money, emit bills of credit, make anything but gold or silver coin a tender in payment of debts." The sole right to coin money was granted to the federal government by the ratification of the Constitution in 1788 (although a loophole permitted private coinage until 1864, when the constitutional loophole was closed).

Federal coinage studies

As Congress debated various monetary plans in the 1780s and early 1790s, it took one concrete step and authorized a copper coin. At this time, 1787, the three states and Vermont were still producing copper coinage when they were joined by the federal government, still organized under the Articles of Confederation. Members of Congress, meeting in Philadelphia, recognized the need for a standard coinage and on April 21, 1787, ordered that a copper coin be produced by private contract but under federal inspection.

The resulting coins were the Fugio cents, generally acknowledged to be the first coins of the United States government. They are named for the Latin legend FUGIO ("I [Time] Fly") that appears on the coin's obverse. A sundial appears on the obverse, along with the legend MIND YOUR BUSINESS; 13 linked rings on the reverse signify the 13 states, surrounding the legends UNITED STATES and WE ARE ONE. James Jarvis, a Connecticut businessman, received a contract to strike 300 tons of the copper coins, or about 26,666,666 pieces. Jarvis began coinage of the cents in New Haven, Conn., shortly after approval by Congress, but had struck fewer than 400,000 Fugio cents by June 1, 1787, by which time coinage had ceased. The federal government voided Jarvis' contract for missing the December 1787 delivery date (the coins were not delivered until beginning in May 1788). The Fugio cents proved underweight and were unpopular with the public. Thus the federal government's first experiment in a federal coinage had failed.

Meanwhile, a federal coinage system had been under study since the early 1780s. Two plans merit attention here. Superintendent of Finance Robert Morris submitted the first to Congress Jan. 15, 1782. Assistant Financier of the Confederation Gouverneur Morris (no relation to Robert Morris) probably wrote the proposal. The Morris proposal was a complicated one, substituting the British system of pounds, shillings and pence for a decimal system based on the Spanish milled dollar. The basic unit would be worth 1/1,440 of the Spanish dollar, a sum arrived at by determining the largest common divisor by which

state currencies could be divided without a fraction. The denominations in the Nova Constellatio series, as the coins are called, would have been copper 5-unit and 8-unit pieces, plus a silver cent worth 100 units, a silver quint worth 500 units and a mark worth 1,000 units. The cumbersome nature of the Morris system, however, gained little support.

Alexander Hamilton, secretary of the Treasury, submitted the second plan to Congress, on Jan. 21, 1791. In his proposal, Hamilton recommended the basic unit be a dollar. The denominations would have been a gold $10 coin, a gold dollar, a silver dollar, a silver tenth-dollar, a copper coin valued at 100 to the dollar, and a second copper coin, valued at 200 to the dollar.

The Hamilton proposal was very similar to what Congress would approve in April 1792. Following Hamilton's proposal, Congress passed a resolution March 3, 1791, that a federal Mint be built, and President Washington in his third State of the Union speech agreed.

Then, on April 2, 1792, Congress passed a law authorizing both a federal Mint and coinage. Ten denominations of coins, more than recommended by Hamilton, were approved: in gold were a $10 eagle, a $5 half eagle and a $2.50 quarter eagle; in silver were a dollar, half dollar, quarter dollar, disme (the "s" was dropped from Mint documents in the 1830s, with the 10-cent coin finally called a dime) and half disme (equal to 5 cents); and in copper, a cent and half cent, neither of which had legal tender status.

The April 1792 act even outlined what design elements should appear on the coins (discussed later).

History of U.S. coinage

United States coinage history is a fascinating subject involving economics, politics, artistic expression, personal rivalry, technological breakthroughs, gold and silver discoveries and more. In short, the history of the country's coinage is the history of the United States.

Denominations

Since coinage began at the Philadelphia Mint in 1793, more than 20 denominations have been used as circulating, commemorative and bullion coins of the United States. In platinum, the denominations have been $100, $50, $25 and $10. In gold, the denominations have been $50 (commemorative and bullion coins only), $25 (the American Eagle bullion coin), $20, $10, $5, $3, $2.50 and $1. Among silver coins (many later changed to copper-nickel by the Coinage Act of 1965), there have been the silver dollar, the Trade dollar, the half dollar (50 cents), the quarter dollar (25 cents), 20-cent coin, dime (10 cents), half dime (5 cents) and 3-cent coin. The Mint has also struck copper-nickel 5-cent, 3-cent and 1-cent coins; a bronze 2-cent coin; cents in six different alloys; and a copper half cent.

The 1792 half disme was struck in small quantities for circulation, according to a report by George Washington, making it the first U.S. coin struck under the 1792 act. It was not struck at the Mint facility, which was still under construction, but was produced under the supervision of Mint officials at a Philadelphia business. Production of U.S. coinage began in earnest in 1793 with the production of copper half cents and cents. The Mint began striking silver half dimes, half dollars and dollars in 1794; and silver dimes and quarter dollars in 1796. Gold coinage began in 1795 with the $5 half eagle and the $10 eagle, followed by the $2.50 quarter eagle in 1796.

During the earlier years of the U.S. Mint, not all denominations were struck in all years. In 1804, coinage of the silver dollar ceased with the striking of 1803-dated coins; dollar coinage was not resumed until 1836. A few gold eagles were struck in 1804, but coinage of the $10 coin then ceased until 1838. No quarter eagles were struck from 1809 through 1820. Production of the other denominations was sporadic except for the cent; planchet shortages prevented any 1815-dated cents from being produced, although some 1816-dated pieces were struck in December 1815. (The British firm Boulton and Watt was the Mint's supplier of copper planchets; the embargo on imports from Britain during the War of 1812 included a ban of planchet shipments, and thus the Mint finally exhausted its inventory in 1814. After the end of the war, shipments were resumed, the first arriving near the end of 1815.) Otherwise the cent series has been issued without interruption since 1793.

Meanwhile, as the country's borders and population grew, the monetary system grew with them. The denominations authorized in 1792 were no longer sufficient to meet the country's monetary needs at the midpoint of the 19th century. Congress authorized a gold dollar and a gold $20 double eagle, both under the Act of March 3, 1849. A silver 3-cent coin was authorized to facilitate the purchase of 3-cent postage stamps (Act of March 3, 1851). A gold $3 coin was introduced in 1854 (Act of Feb. 21, 1853), again to help in the purchase of 3-cent stamps (in sheets of 100). A smaller, copper-nickel cent was approved in 1857, replacing the pure copper large cent. The half cent was eliminated, also in 1857.

The Civil War erupted in 1861, causing massive hoarding of coinage and the necessity of coinage substitutes like encased postage stamps, privately produced copper-alloy cent-like tokens and finally, the first federal paper money, some notes in denominations of less than $1. More changes to U.S. coins began in 1864, when the composition of the cent was changed to 95 percent copper and 5 percent tin and zinc (bronze), and when a bronze 2-cent coin was introduced (both under the Act of April 22, 1864).

A copper-nickel 3-cent coin was issued in 1865 (Act of March 3, 1865) to circulate alongside the silver 3-cent coin (which was struck in decreasing numbers until the last coins were produced in 1873). A copper-nickel 5-cent coin was introduced in 1866 (Act of May 16, 1866); the silver half dime was eliminated after 1873.

The year 1873 brought significant, unprecedented changes to the U.S. coinage system. The Act of Feb. 12, 1873, is called by numismatic historian Don Taxay "the most exhaustive [coinage act] in our history." Four denominations were abolished by the act: the 2-cent coin, the silver 3-cent coin, the half dime and the standard silver dollar. The act authorized a Trade silver dollar for use by merchants in Asia; Congress revoked the Trade dollar's legal tender status in the United States in 1876. The weights of the silver dime, quarter dollar and half dollar were increased. In addition, the act, in effect, demonetized silver and placed the United States on a gold standard.

Another new denomination was authorized under the Act of March 3, 1875—the silver 20-cent coin. The coin was struck for circulation in 1875 and 1876, setting the record for the shortest-lived denomination in U.S. coinage history. Coinage of Proof 20-cent coins continued for collectors only in 1877 and 1878.

Meanwhile, the powerful silver interests in the United States, faced with the demonetization of silver left by the 1873 act, lobbied Congress. The result of that lobbying effort, the Act of Feb. 28, 1878, reinstituted the standard silver dollar abolished by the Act of Feb. 12, 1873. The specifications were unchanged from the silver dollar of 1837 to 1873. Obverse and reverse designs created by Mint Engraver George T. Morgan were selected for the dollar, today generally called the Morgan dollar (it was originally called the Bland or Bland-Allison dollar, after the names of the members of Congress responsible for the bill). Coinage of the Morgan dollar continued through 1904. Coinage denominations in use continued unchanged through 1889, when the gold dollar, $3 coin and copper-nickel 3-cent coin were struck for the last time.

The circulating silver dollar was resurrected twice for circulation: in 1921, to continue through 1935; and in 1965, although the 1964-D Peace silver dollars struck in 1965 were all destroyed before being placed into circulation. The government had withdrawn support for the coins and wanted to ensure that none inadvertently entered circulation or collector circles. Tales that Mint employees were allowed to purchase the coins before the order canceling their distribution are apparently rumors; there is no credible, verifiable evidence that any of the coins survive. The copper-nickel clad dollar was introduced in 1971, with a design honoring President Dwight D. Eisenhower and the Apollo 11 lunar mission. A smaller dollar (the Anthony dollar) was issued briefly from 1979 to 1981 and again in 1999. A new Anthony-dollar sized dollar coin made of a manganese brass clad composition and depicting Sacagawea entered circulation in 2000 but like the coin it replaced, failed to circulate widely; production from 2002 to 2008 was for numismatic sales only. In effort to both replicate the popularity experienced for the State quarter dollars program and to encourage broader circulation of a dollar coin, a Presidential dollar program was started in 2007. The coins are struck on the same manganese-brass clad planchets used for the Sacagawea dollars. Four coins are issued annually, with all deceased presidents to be so honored (as long as the president has been dead for at least two years before the issuance of a coin depicting him). Each coin depicts one of the presidents on the obverse and a standard Statue of Liberty design on the reverse. Many of the inscriptions were moved from the obverse and reverse to the edge: the date, Mint mark and the mottoes E PLURIBUS UNUM and IN GOD WE TRUST. Slightly different configurations of edge inscription elements were used in 2007 and 2008, with the 2007 coins bearing two stops (•) and the 2008 coins, three stops. Congress, which had ordered the use of edge inscriptions, reversed itself partially in 2008 and ordered IN GOD WE TRUST moved from the edge to the obverse or reverse. Tens of thousands of error George Washington dollars were released into circulation without edge inscriptions, prompting complaints from some in the religious communities about "Godless" dollars. In addition, some felt that the religious motto deserved more prominence than its position on the edge. The motto was moved to the obverse starting in 2009 though the other edge inscriptions remain. Thirteen stars were added to take the place of the relocated motto and the "stops" were removed.

Despite the hopes of backers of the legislation creating the Presidential dollars, the coins do not circulate widely. The mintage for the George Washington coin is the highest by far, with mintages of later releases declining.

In yet another attempt at getting a dollar coin to circulate and to use circulating coins for commemorative purposes, the Sacagawea dollar was rebranded as the Native American dollar in 2009, with the retained obverse being joined by an annual commemorative reverse. The series is designed to commemorate the accomplishments and contributions of Native Americans. Although Congress intended the Native American dollars to circulate, the Federal Reserve has ordered none for circulation as of early 2011. They are only available directly from the Mint.

The standard silver dollar lives on in commemorative coinage, with dozens of different commemorative dollars struck since 1983. In addition, there is a 1-ounce silver bullion coin that bears a $1 denomination, introduced in 1986 as part of the American Eagle bullion program.

Since the Mint Act of 1875, only three new denominations have been authorized, none for circulation. A gold $50 coin was approved to commemorate the 1915 Panama-Pacific International Exposition being held in San Francisco. More than 70 years later, in 1986, the $50 denomination was revived for the American Eagle bullion program. That same legislation (Act of Dec. 17, 1986, Public Law 99-185) also approved the United States' first $25 coin, the American Eagle half-ounce gold bullion coin. A $100 denomination was given to the American Eagle 1-ounce platinum bullion coin, introduced in 1997.

The last gold denominations struck for circulation occurred in 1933, when coinage of the eagle and double eagle ceased under President Franklin Roosevelt's anti-gold executive orders. The gold quarter eagles and half eagles were last struck in 1929. All gold coins struck since 1984 have been commemorative or bullion coins.

A new, supersized version of one of the original denominations authorized in 1792 was introduced in late 2010 as part of the America the Beautiful quarter dollars program. The act authorizing the commemorative quarter dollars also ordered production of 3-inch, 5-ounce .999 fine silver bullion coins. The designs of the regular America the Beautiful quarter dollars and the larger bullion coins, also denominated a quarter dollar, are the same, though the bullion pieces have an additional inscription on the edge

identifying the bullion content of the coin.

Designs

The story behind the designs of U.S. coins is one of artistic experimentation and drone-like uniformity; of political necessity and political favoritism; of beauty tempered by the realities of the coining process.

The members of Congress who approved the U.S. monetary system created design parameters that affect new U.S. coin designs even in the 21st century, nearly 220 years after that initial legislation. The Mint Act of April 2, 1792, specified that certain design features and legends appear on the coins that were authorized. On one side of all coins was to be an impression symbolic of Liberty, plus the word LIBERTY and the year of coinage. For the silver and gold coins, an eagle and UNITED STATES OF AMERICA were to appear on the reverse. The denomination was to appear on the reverses of the half cents and cents.

For more than 115 years in the history of U.S. coinage, Liberty was portrayed by allegorical female figures, appearing either as a bust or a full-length portrait. Liberty's changing face through the years says a lot about the artistic abilities of the craftsmen employed on the Mint staff and the artists hired from outside to design certain coins. Some of the most attractive U.S. coins were designed by non-Mint employees, often in the face of opposition from a Mint engraving staff that had to worry about the practicalities of coinage production, sometimes requiring compromises affecting design relief and the placement of design elements. Beautiful designs created by Mint staff engravers never went beyond the pattern stage in favor of the uniformity that characterized U.S. designs from the mid-1830s into the early 20th century.

The changing portrait of Liberty also reveals the embodiment of the "ideal woman" by the physical standards set by the American men of the time, and men had always dominated U.S. coinage design until the 1980s. (The Mint engraving staff was exclusively male until President Reagan appointed Elizabeth Jones chief sculptor-engraver.) The first coinage portraits of Liberty are "Rubenesque." Among the most recent allegorical Liberty figures to appear on U.S. coins are the Liberty on American Eagle gold bullion coins—a reproduction of a design released in 1907, "slimmed down" to resemble the trimmer woman championed by American advertising and dietary standards in the 1980s and 1990s—and on the 2000 golden dollar coin, Liberty as portrayed by Shoshone guide Sacagawea.

The 1793 half cents and cents introduced the allegorical themes used on U.S. coins: The half cent depicts a bust of Liberty with her hair flowing free. A Liberty Cap on a pole, a familiar symbol of Liberty in the American and French revolutions of the latter 18th century, rests on her right shoulder, giving the design its name: the Liberty Cap. On the first cents of 1793, another Flowing Hair Liberty appears. Contemporary reports claimed Liberty looked frightened on the cent. The designs are somewhat crude by modern standards. However, the Liberty busts were cut directly into steel by hand. Mint technicians had no access to the modern equipment and techniques available today.

Since the Mint Act of 1792 required only the denomination to appear on the reverses of the copper coins, the Mint engravers had a free rein. The first half cents have a wreath on the reverse, a device used as late as 1958 on the reverse of the Lincoln cent in the form of two stalks of wheat. The reverse device on the first cents was used about a month. A 15-link chain meant to represent the unity of the 15 states appears on the first 1793 cents. The public believed the chain was a symbol of enslavement perceived to represent "a bad omen for Liberty." Changes in the design of both sides of the cent came rapidly; the first cent designs were used for a only a month in early 1793 before being replaced. A Wreath reverse replaced the Chain reverse, with a more refined Flowing Hair Liberty portrait created. Then the second Flowing Hair portrait was replaced with a Liberty Cap design similar to that on the half cent. Thus, three distinct cents were struck with the 1793 date: the Flowing Hair, Chain cent; the Flowing Hair, Wreath cent; and the Liberty Cap, Wreath cent.

Additional design changes were instituted for the cent in 1796, when a Draped Bust design was introduced and used through 1807. Liberty appears without a cap, her hair falling over bare shoulders. Loose drapery covers Liberty's bust. Another Liberty Head design called the Classic Head design was used on the cent from 1808 through 1814. It differs considerably from the earlier allegorical motifs, with Liberty wearing a ribbon inscribed with LIBERTY around her hair.

The Coronet design was introduced in 1816 on the large cent. This design would prove one of the most versatile of the 19th century. A variation of the Coronet design would appear on both copper coins until 1857 and on most of the gold denominations from the 1830s to the first decade of the 20th century. The design is similar on all of the coins, depicting Liberty wearing a coronet inscribed with LIBERTY.

Designs for the half cent were similar to the cent's designs, although the timetable for introduction was often different. The half cent used a Liberty Cap design until 1797, and from 1800 through 1808 a Draped Bust design was used. The Classic Head design was used on the half cent from 1809 through 1836 and the Coronet design was introduced in 1840.

The silver coins of the 18th century feature designs similar to those on the copper coins. The silver coins used a Flowing Hair design in 1794 and 1795, and in 1795 and 1796 a Draped Bust design was introduced on all silver coins. The Capped Bust design was used first for the half dollar in 1807, with the dime following in 1809, the quarter dollar in 1815 and the half dime in 1829. The eagles appearing on the reverse of the silver coins appeared in several forms, first in a Small Eagle design that some critics likened to a pigeon. A Heraldic Eagle was used on the dollar beginning in 1798, the half dollar in 1801 and the quarter dollar in 1804.

Allegorical Liberty figures with similar themes but somewhat different details were used on the early gold coins. A Capped Bust, Heraldic Eagle design was used from 1796 to 1807 for the quarter eagle, then replaced in 1808 with the one-year-only Capped Draped Bust type. The Capped Head quarter eagle was struck between 1821 to 1834. On the half eagle, the Capped Bust design was used from 1796 to 1807; the Small Eagle reverse was used from 1796 to 1798, and a Heraldic Eagle design was used from 1795 to 1807, concurrently with the Small Eagle at first. The Capped Draped Bust was used on the half eagle from 1807 to 1812, and the Capped Head, from 1813 to 1829. The Classic Head design was used briefly, from 1834 to 1838. For the $10 eagle, the Capped Bust design was used from 1795 to 1804, when production of the denomination ceased. On the reverse of the $10 coin, the Small Eagle was used from 1795 to 1797, and the Heraldic Eagle design was used from 1797 to 1804.

Several events took place in the mid-1830s that were to affect coinage designs for decades. Among them was the Act of Jan. 18, 1837, which eliminated the need for an eagle on the reverses of the half dime and dime. The other event was the resumption of coinage of the silver dollar in 1836, and the adoption of a new design that eventually would appear on six different denominations, used on some of them for more than half a century.

Production of the silver dollar resumed in 1836 with the Gobrecht dollar. The obverse depicts a Seated Liberty figure on a rock, her body draped in robes. The reverse depicts a Flying Eagle design. The Seated Liberty dollar was the first of several coins that would use a similar Flying Eagle theme.

With the creation of the Seated Liberty design, a new age of uniformity ensued on U.S. coins. The Seated Liberty obverse design was introduced on the half dime and dime in 1837, the quarter dollar in 1838 and the half dollar in 1839. Wreaths were placed on the half dime and dime in 1837; eagles appeared on the new quarter dollar and half dollar; and the dollar received a new eagle design in 1840, with the Flying Eagle replaced by an eagle similar to those on the quarter dollar and half dollar.

Gold coins, too, entered the uniform age of coin designs when the Coronet (sometimes called Liberty Head) design was introduced in 1838 for the $10 eagle, in 1839 for the $5 half eagle and in 1840 for the $2.50 quarter eagle. When the gold dollar and $20 double eagle were introduced in 1849 and 1850, respectively, the Coronet design was used for both. Like the silver coins, the gold coins would not break out of uniformity until the early 20th century, except for the dollar.

A new theme was introduced in 1854 on the gold dollar, replacing the Coronet figure. An Indian Head portrait by James B. Longacre was introduced, the first in a series of medallic tributes to Native Americans that would last until shortly before the beginning of World War II. (An American Indian theme reappeared in 2000, on the new dollar coin. The coin depicts a woman as Liberty, inspired by Sacagawea, the teen Indian guide of Lewis and Clark.)

Ironically, the first use of an Indian as a symbol of Liberty occurred even as the American movement to push the Indians into decreasingly smaller portions of the West accelerated. However, the gold dollar portrait was not a true Indian; Longacre simply placed an Indian headdress on the same Liberty figure he would use in many different versions of the design. A slightly larger, slightly different rendition of the Indian Head portrait was used beginning in 1856 on the gold dollar. The gold $3 coin depicts an Indian Head portrait by Longacre, and the reverse depicts not an eagle but a wreath.

When the large cent was abandoned in 1857 for a smaller cent (see section titled "specifications"), a Flying Eagle design was placed on the obverse (the 1856 Flying Eagle cents are patterns, struck before Congress authorized a change in composition and size). The obverse design was changed to an Indian Head design in 1859. Wreaths of various types appear on the reverses of both small cents. A Cornucopia Wreath was used on the reverse of the Flying Eagle cent. For the Indian Head cent, a Laurel Wreath reverse was used in 1859 only; that reverse was replaced in 1860 with an Oak Wreath With Shield design.

Several nonallegorical designs began to appear on U.S. coins in the 1850s. On the silver 3-cent coin, a six-point star appears as the central obverse design; the reverse depicts the Roman numeral III inside what resembles a large letter "C." Shields appear on the obverses of the 2-cent coin and the first copper-nickel 5-cent coin. The authorizing acts for all three of these coins granted broad authority to the director of the Mint and the secretary of the Treasury to select design devices (superseding earlier requirements that all coins had to depict an image of Liberty).

A Liberty Head design replaced the Shield design on the 5-cent coin in 1883. The silver dollar, abandoned in 1873 and reinstated in 1878, depicts a Liberty Head and an eagle (the coin is called the Morgan dollar). A version of the Seated Liberty design modified by William Barber was placed on the short-lived 20-cent coin of 1875 to 1878.

Coinage designs came under stricter congressional control with passage of a new law in 1890. Previously, design changes could occur at whatever frequency Mint officials determined to be appropriate. As long as the new designs met earlier requirements of law (incorporating a portrait of Liberty, for example), Mint officials could change designs whenever they

wanted to. As noted earlier, designs sometimes changed after being used only a month.

The new law, approved Sept. 26, 1890, prohibited the Mint from making design changes unless the designs had been used for at least 25 years. Congress had to authorize changes to designs in use for less than the required period.

The Seated Liberty design, used on most of the silver coins since 1836, was finally abandoned at the end of 1891. By that time, it was in use only on the dime, quarter dollar and half dollar, the other Seated Liberty denominations having been legislated out of existence or redesigned. Chief Mint Sculptor-Engraver Charles Barber replaced the Seated Liberty design in 1892 with a Liberty Head design. Barber also created a Heraldic Eagle for use on the reverse of the quarter dollar and half dollar; the reverse wreath appearing on the Seated Liberty dime was maintained on the reverse of the "Barber" dime. The Barber designs were used through mid-1916 for the dime and quarter dollar, and through 1915 for the half dollar. (Interestingly, Mint officials interpreted the December 1890 law as requiring design changes every 25 years, not permitting them. Thus they sought replacements for the Barber designs in 1916.)

The first two decades of the 20th century resulted in two major design trends for U.S. coins. One, beginning in 1907, resulted in what can be called the "Golden Age of U.S. Coin Designs." The other, beginning in 1909, was the first step away from the allegorical depictions that had characterized most U.S. coins since 1793, in favor of coinage tributes to prominent political figures from American history.

The Golden Age began with the election of Theodore Roosevelt as president of the United States. Roosevelt did more to improve the aesthetics of U.S. coins than any other politician. He invited Augustus Saint-Gaudens, the premier U.S. sculptor of the day, to create coin designs Roosevelt hoped would relive the beauty of ancient Greece. Saint-Gaudens submitted designs for the cent, $10 eagle and $20 double eagle. Roosevelt choose from the submissions the designs for the two gold coins. The $10 coin depicts an allegorical Liberty Head wearing an Indian headdress on the obverse and a Standing Eagle design on the reverse. The double eagle depicts a Striding Liberty facing the viewer on the obverse and a Flying Eagle design for the reverse.

The Mint engraving staff, led by Charles Barber, was not happy with the hiring of outside talent, even though Saint-Gaudens' double eagle design is considered by many collectors to be the finest ever portrayed on a U.S. coin. Experimental Ultra High Relief $20 patterns were struck in 1907; they are considered some of the finest U.S. coins ever produced in terms of artistic merit. The relief was lowered somewhat for first $20 coins struck for circulation, though the coins contain high relief features, which caused problems in production. The Ultra High Relief and High Relief coins required too many strikings for efficient production, so the relief was lowered again later in 1907. (Saint-Gaudens, who had been ill from cancer during the design process, was dead before his $20 designs were completed.)

The Golden Age continued in 1908, with new designs for the $2.50 quarter eagle and $5 half eagle by Bela Lyon Pratt: an American Indian on the obverse, and a Standing Eagle on the reverse. These were the first true Indians to appear on U.S. coins. What made the designs so unusual, however, was their placement on the coin. The designs were created in the oxymoronic "incused relief." Often incorrectly referred to as incused, the designs are raised, but sunken into the fields so the highest points are level with the flat fields. This design feature was criticized, with some suggesting that the "incused" portions would permit enough germs to accumulate to prove a health hazard.

In 1913, the designs for the 5-cent coin were changed. An American Indian was placed on the obverse and an American bison was placed on the reverse. The coin is known variously as the Indian Head, Bison or Buffalo 5-cent coin (also nicknamed the Buffalo nickel). The Indian design appearing on the obverse is probably the finest to be placed on a U.S. coin. Three Indians, Iron Tail, Two Moons and Chief John Tree, posed for designer James Fraser, who created a composite portrait. The model for the bison was Black Diamond.

More design changes were made in 1916, when the Barber designs for the dime and quarter dollar were replaced in mid-year.

The new dime features a Winged Liberty Head portrait on the obverse. The design is often and incorrectly called the Mercury dime; however, the artist never intended the figure to represent Mercury. The reverse depicts a fasces.

The quarter dollar design introduced in 1916 proved short lived. The Standing Liberty figure had an exposed right breast. Liberty's bare breast was covered with a coat of mail in 1917 (both subtypes of the 1917 coin exist). Although many numismatic books claim there was a hue and cry over Liberty's bare breast, no contemporary evidence exists that backs that theory. Research indicates artist Hermon A. MacNeil added the coat of chain to signify the nation's preparation to enter the war in Europe, a common allegorical theme in some of the sculptor's other contemporary artwork. The reverse depicts a Flying Eagle design; its position was modified slightly in 1917 at same time changes were made to the obverse. Interestingly, correspondence between Mint officials and designer MacNeil refer to changes in the placement of the eagle but apparently do not mention the change to Liberty. The coat of mail was added very quietly. The obverse change may have been illegal, since Congress did not authorize it as required by the 1890 law, although it did approve the changes made to the reverse of the coin.

The Walking Liberty half dollar was also introduced in 1916. The obverse depicts a Walking Liberty figure. The reverse depicts one of the most attractive eagles on a regular issue of U.S. coins.

The Peace dollar replaced the Morgan dollar in 1921, which had been briefly resurrected in 1921 (coinage had ceased after 1904). The Peace dollar commemorates the peace that followed the end of World War I. Coinage of the dollar ceased at the end of 1935 when the denomination was temporarily abandoned.

The second coinage trend to begin in the early 20th century appeared in 1909 when a portrait of Abraham Lincoln replaced the Indian Head on the cent. For the first time, a historical, nonallegorical person was depicted on a circulating coin of the United States. Lincoln's 100th birthday was celebrated in 1909. His 150th birthday in 1959 resulted in the Lincoln Memorial replacing the two stalks of wheat found on the Lincoln cents of 1909 to 1958; the Lincoln Memorial design was used through 2008. In 2009, four different reverse designs were used to commemorate stages of Lincoln's life in celebration of the bicentennial of his birth: the Childhood design, marking his youth in Kentucky; the Formative Years design, marking his life in Indiana; the Professional Life design, for Lincoln's career in Illinois; and the Presidency design, marking his last years, in the District of Columbia. A new, Union Shield design was introduced in 2010 as the coin's standard reverse (by law, the design will have to be used for at least 25 years unless Congress orders otherwise). The Victor D. Brenner portrait continues to be used on the obverse of the cent, with the design returned to its original form in 2010 in appearance if not in relief (the Mint engraving staff had modified the portrait's features over the decades).

The trend of depicting actual historic figures continued in 1932, when the Standing Liberty design on the quarter dollar was replaced with the Washington portrait on the bicentennial of Washington's birth. A portrait of Thomas Jefferson replaced the American Indian in 1938 on the 5-cent coin (the Treasury Department held a design contest). Franklin Roosevelt's portrait was placed on the dime in 1946, a year after his death (the first time a newly dead president's portrait was placed on a circulating coin). A portrait of Benjamin Franklin was placed on the half dollar in 1948, replacing the Walking Liberty designs. Franklin was replaced in turn in 1964 by a portrait of John F. Kennedy in a numismatic tribute to the assassinated president; Congress had to authorize this change since a span of 25 years had not passed.

Tributes to the newly dead continued in 1971, when a copper-nickel dollar coin was introduced bearing President Dwight D. Eisenhower's portrait on the obverse and an allegorical figure of an eagle landing on Earth's moon, commemorating the Apollo 11 moon landing.

The Bicentennial of the Declaration of Independence in 1976 brought changes to the reverses of the quarter dollar, half dollar and dollar. The reverse of the 1976 quarter dollar depicts a Revolutionary War drummer; the half dollar depicts Independence Hall in Philadelphia; and the dollar depicts the Liberty Bell superimposed over the moon. Although Mint officials avoided the word "commemorative" in their descriptions of the three coins, they are clearly commemorative in nature and should be classified thusly. The designs reverted to their original versions in 1977.

In 1979, a new copper-nickel dollar sized between the quarter dollar and half dollar was introduced, replacing the Eisenhower dollar. The new design depicts feminist Susan B. Anthony and a reduced version of the moon-landing design. Anthony was the first nonallegorical U.S. woman to appear on a circulating coin. The choice was not a popular one, since many collectors had hoped Flowing Hair Liberty, Flying Eagle designs by Chief Sculptor-Engraver Frank Gasparro would appear. Many letters from collectors focused on the supposed unattractiveness of Anthony, who was shown in her later years on the coin. However, those same writers apparently had never criticized the physical attributes of Lincoln (who, after all, was referred to as an ape by the press of his time, before he achieved martyrdom upon his assassination). Ironically, a descendant of Anthony was critical of an early version of Gasparro's Anthony portrait as too "pretty" and not at all indicative of the woman's strong character; Gasparro modified the design before it was placed on the coin. However, the coin did not circulate well, mainly because of its similarity in size to the quarter dollar (many found the two coins too close to each other in diameter) and because the dollar bill remained in production. Poor public usage of the smaller dollar resulted in none being struck for nearly two decades after 1981. The 1979 to 1980 coins were struck for circulation, and the 1981 coins were struck for collectors only. More were struck in 1999 after the vast inventory of 1979 and 1980 coins sitting in government vaults was gradually released into circulation.

The reintroduction of commemorative coins and the American Eagle bullion coins has brought renewed interest in coinage designs, and renewed controversy. Collectors and others have been critical of some of the designs on the commemorative coins. The two torchbearers on an early version of the 1984 Olympic $10 eagle were lampooned as "Dick and Jane running" by congressional members. Others, most notably the obverse of the 1986-W Statue of Liberty half eagle, designed by Chief Sculptor-Engraver Elizabeth Jones, have been praised.

When the American Eagle gold and silver coins were introduced in 1986, Treasury officials selected older designs for the obverses, matched with new designs on the reverses. The obverse of the silver dollar depicts Weinman's Walking Liberty half dollar obverse, enlarged for placement on the larger coin. A new Heraldic Eagle appears on the reverse. Changes made to the designs chosen for the gold bullion coins were controversial. Saint-Gaudens' Striding Liberty for the double eagle was chosen for the obverse, but not until Treasury Secretary James A. Baker ordered Liberty on a diet in 1986. The Mint engraver assigned to the project was ordered to reduce Liberty's apparent weight, slimming her arms and legs. Members of the Commission of Fine Arts decried the changes to what is considered a classic design. CFA members were also critical of the reverse, a Family of Eagles design by Dallas sculptor Miley Busiek. The legislation authorizing the gold coins mandated the Busiek design. Busiek had been an untiring champion of her design, which shows two adult eagles and two younger birds. She lobbied members of Congress and officials at the Treasury Department for months in a politically successful attempt to have her design placed on the bullion coins. She says the design reflects the values of the American family.

The next members of the bullion coin family, the platinum American Eagles, stay near the tried-and-true designs of the past although the renditions are new. On the obverse, John Mercanti rendered a medium close-up view of the Statue of Liberty, but deliberately thinned Liberty's lips and made other cosmetic changes. The reverse depicts a fairly realistic rendering of an eagle in flight with the sun in the background. In an interesting decision, Mint officials decided that beginning in 1998, the Proof versions of the platinum coin would depict a new reverse design every year for five years. The original reverse design remains in use on the bullion versions of the coins.

As the 1990s came to a close, the most exciting news for collectors was a decision to introduce new designs into circulation on a regular basis. For years, hobbyists and others had called for new designs on circulating coins. However, for decades, Mint officials had publicly opposed the idea, stating that to change coinage designs would cause hoarding of the old designs, thus generating a coinage shortage. However, that policy briefly changed in April 1988 when Mint Director Donna Pope, appearing before the Senate Banking Committee, reported that the Treasury had no major objections to a bill calling for the redesign of all circulating U.S. coins.

Congress had split over the redesign issue. The Senate had supported the measure for years, having passed redesign legislation more than a half dozen times. Redesign advocates found a champion in Sen. Alan Cranston, D-Calif. Cranston made the coinage redesign issue his last great issue. He retired at the end of the 102nd Congress at the end of 1992.

The House of Representatives, however, long opposed coinage redesign as unnecessary and unwanted by a majority of the American public. Again and again the House voted down redesign legislation. At one point in early 1992, it appeared as though the Senate and House had reached agreement on coinage redesign. The measure was added to an omnibus coin bill seeking a variety of commemorative coins for 1992 and beyond. However, on the day the vote was scheduled, someone on Capitol Hill began spreading the false rumor that the legislation would eliminate "In God We Trust" from U.S. coinage. The House defeated the bill because of the false rumor.

Finally, however, Congress changed its mind and authorized limited coinage redesign through the 50 States circulating commemorative quarter dollar program. Fifty new reverse designs were introduced over a 10-year period beginning in 1999 at a rate of five per year, one approximately every 10 weeks.

New designs were used on the new dollar coin introduced in January 2000. An unusual mixture of allegorical and historical themes were used, with the coin depicting an allegorical image of Sacagawea, the teenaged interpreter for the Lewis and Clark Expedition, and her baby. This design concept was selected after unprecedented public discourse on the subject on June 8 to 9, 1998, in Philadelphia. Members of the public were invited to speak before a panel empowered to recommend coinage designs for the dollar coin. Artists, coin collectors and others recommended such subjects as Eleanor Roosevelt, allegorical portraits of Liberty and other themes, with the Sacagawea-inspired theme selected by the panel. The decision was controversial, since no portrait of Sacagawea exists. (The reverse depicts an eagle.)

Additional design changes were made during the first two decades of the 21st century as circulating commemorative coin programs became something of the norm. (See the U.S. Commemoratives chapter for details.)

Specifications

The physical specifications of U.S. coins—metallic content, weights, diameters—have been ever changing. Changes were in response to increases and decreases in metal prices, public rejection of large-diameter coins, and other factors.

Even before the first copper coins were struck in 1793, their weights were reduced under the Act of May 8, 1792. The modified weights are 6.74 grams for the half cent and 13.48 grams for the cent (weights are given in grams for modern convenience; the early coinage laws specified the weights in grains). Weights for both copper coins were reduced in 1795, to 5.44 grams for the half cent and to 10.89 grams for the cent. The 1794 and 1795 silver coinage was struck in a composition of 90 percent silver and 10 percent copper, according to some sources. When additional silver denominations were added in 1796, the composition for all five coins was changed to 89.2427 percent silver and 10.7572 percent copper, until additional change came in 1836 and 1837.

Composition of the first gold coins is 91.6667 percent gold and 8.3333 percent copper and silver.

The only changes made to U.S. coins from the first decade of the 19th century to 1834 were to designs. Then, on June 28, 1834, the weight of gold coins was reduced and the alloy changed for two years to 89.9225 percent gold and 10.0775 percent copper and silver. In 1836, the gold alloy was changed again, to 90 percent gold and 10 percent copper and silver, an alloy unchanged until 1873. Changes were made to silver coins in 1836 as well, when the silver content was changed to 90 percent silver and 10 percent copper, an alloy used until the mid-1960s.

The rising price of silver resulted in a reduction in weights for the silver coins during 1853 (except for the silver dollar). Arrows were added to both sides of the dates on the reduced weight half dimes, dimes, quarter dollars and half dollars, a design feature used for 1853 and 1854. The arrows were removed in 1855 although the weights of the coins remained the same.

Major changes were made to the country's copper coinage in 1857. The half cent was eliminated and the large copper cent was replaced with a smaller cent composed of 88 percent copper and 12 percent nickel (Act of Feb. 21, 1857). Diameter of the old cent is approximately 29 millimeters; the new cent has a diameter of 19 millimeters. A bronze cent and 2-cent coin were introduced in 1864.

The weights of the Seated Liberty silver coinage were increased in 1873, and once again arrows were placed at either side of the date to signify the increased weight. Also, silver was dropped from the gold-coin alloy, which was changed to 90 percent gold and 10 percent copper.

The next major compositional changes in U.S. coins were made during World War II. At the beginning of the United States' entry into World War II, several metals used in coinage became strategically important to the war effort. The first to be affected was the 5-cent coin, which had nickel removed starting Oct. 8, 1942, when 5-cent coins in a new composition—56 percent copper, 35 percent silver and 9 percent manganese—went into production. Use of the copper-nickel alloy was resumed in 1946.

Also during the war, the cent composition was changed. First, tin was removed sometime late in 1942. Then, in 1943, a zinc-coated steel cent was introduced to conserve copper. The brass alloy of 95 percent copper and 5 percent zinc resumed in 1944 through 1946. The 95 percent copper, 5 percent tin and zinc composition resumed in 1947 and continued until late 1962 when, once again, tin was removed from the bronze alloy, returning the alloy to the same composition, called brass, used in 1944 to 1946.

The 175-year-old history of United States coinage was changed with the stroke of a pen on July 23, 1965. On that day President Lyndon Johnson signed into law the Coinage Act of 1965, representing the most sweeping changes to the U.S. coinage system since the Mint Act of 1873. The 1965 act eliminated silver in dimes and quarter dollars and reduced the silver content of the half dollars to 40 percent.

Special congressional hearings relative to the nationwide coin shortage were first held in 1964. Coin shortages had continually worsened in the decade prior to 1965 as a result of the population growth, expanding vending machine businesses, popularity of Kennedy half dollars and the worldwide silver shortage. In the face of the silver shortage, it was essential that dependence on silver for coinage be reduced. Otherwise the country would be faced with a chronic coin shortage.

As a result of studies conducted by both the Treasury and the Battelle Memorial Institute, a clad metal composed of three bonded layers of metal was selected for the new composition. Battelle tested various alloys to determine their suitability for coinage. (Battelle is a Columbus, Ohio-based company that specializes in high-tech experimentation and research.) The dimes and quarter dollars were composed of two layers of 75 percent copper and 25 percent nickel bonded to a core of pure copper. The half dollars were composed of two layers of 80 percent silver and 20 percent copper bonded to a core of approximately 20 percent silver and 80 percent copper; the entire coin is composed of 40 percent silver.

The combination of copper-nickel and copper gave the new dimes and quarter dollars the required electrical conductivity, a necessary property for vending machines. The copper-nickel surfaces also continued the traditional silvery color of the coins.

The legal weights of the coins were affected by the change in alloy. The new dime weight is 2.27 grams, the quarter dollar weighs 5.67 grams and the 40 percent silver half dollar weighs 11.5 grams. With the elimination of silver from half dollars in 1971 and the introduction of a copper-nickel clad version, the weight was changed to 11.34 grams. The cladding of all coins constitutes approximately 30 percent of the coin by weight.

In an effort to maximize coin production during the transition to the new alloys, 1964-dated silver coins were struck into 1965. The Coinage Act of 1965 also made it mandatory that clad coins be dated no earlier than 1965. All clad coins actually made in 1965 bear that date. The first copper-nickel clad dimes were struck in late December 1965 and were released March 8, 1966. The first copper-nickel clad quarter dollars were struck Aug. 23, 1965, and released Nov. 1, 1965. The first silver-clad half dollars were released March 8, 1966, but were struck starting Dec. 30, 1965. The 1965 date was retained until July 31, 1966, when the date was changed to 1966. Normal dating resumed Jan. 1, 1967.

Another great compositional change to U.S. circulating coinage came in mid-1982, when the brass cent was replaced with a cent of nearly pure zinc, plated with a thin layer of pure copper to retain its copper appearance, in reaction to rising copper prices.

When the American Eagle bullion coins were introduced in 1986, some numismatists were critical of the .9167 gold content, a composition they deemed "nontraditional"; there was some preference for a .900 gold content. However, the chosen composition is virtually identical to the alloy first used for U.S. gold coins, from 1795 to 1834. A new silver composition was introduced with the production of the .999 fine silver American Eagle dollar.

The Treasury secretary now has authority under a change in the law in 1992 to change the composition of the American Eagle gold coin without seeking congressional approval. The 2009 Saint-Gaudens, Ultra High Relief $20 gold double eagle, composed of .9999 fine gold, was issued under this authority. The American Buffalo .9999 fine gold bullion coins were ordered into production by Congress, however.

The platinum American Eagle bullion coins, introduced in 1997, are .9995 fine.

Mint officials experimented with ringed-bimetallic pieces in early 1993. The coins—consisting of an outer ring of one metal bonded to an inner ring of another, different-colored metal—are being used in circulation by many countries.

The introduction of the 2000 "golden" dollar depicting Sacagawea resulted in another new alloy. U.S. Mint officials selected a composition that has two outer layers composed of manganese-bronze (77 percent copper, 12 percent zinc, 7 manganese and 4 percent nickel) bonded to an inner core of pure copper. Overall, the total composition is 88.5 percent copper, 6 percent zinc, 3.5 percent manganese and 2 percent nickel. The same alloy is used in the Presidential dollars and Native American dollars.

The American Eagle 1-ounce .999 fine silver bullion coin was joined in 2010 by the America the Beautiful 5-ounce .9999 fine silver bullion coin. The America the Beautiful 5-ounce coin is 3 inches in diameter and is both the heaviest and largest-diameter U.S. coin ever issued.

Pioneer gold coins

The pioneer gold issues in the United States are an interesting series born of private enterprise and pioneer necessity. Most were produced privately and legally, since the Constitution prohibited states but not individuals from striking gold coins. "Pioneer" is a better adjective to describe the gold coins than "private gold" and "territorial gold." Some of the coins in California were struck by the U.S. Assayer, and thus are of federal issue and are not true private issues; some of the gold coins were struck in states, not U.S. territories, thus "territorial" is incorrect for many of the issues. "Pioneer" describes the spirit in which the coins were struck: as necessity issues, brought about by the inability of the federal government to provide sufficient quantities of coinage in areas of the country newly opened to settlement.

The region in which they were made can best classify the pioneer gold coins: the southern Appalachians, the western Rockies (including Utah, which was much larger as a territory than as a state) and Colorado. The scarcity of these coins is primarily due to their often having an intrinsic value less than the face value. The coins were often unaccepted and eventually were melted.

The first significant gold mines in the United States were in the mountainous backwoods of North Carolina and Georgia. Transporting the gold overland to the Philadelphia Mint was slow and dangerous, whereas shipping it around Cape Hatteras was fast but expensive and not without risk. As the miners wished to have the convenience of coined gold without the expense of shipping the raw gold to the Philadelphia Mint, two private mints were established in 1830 and 1831.

Templeton Reid at Gainesville, Ga., opened the first mint. Probably because he had no competition, he charged a high fee for processing the bullion into coins. A large quantity of gold was handled during this first and only year, but most of it was eventually melted down as were regular U.S. gold coins, due to the prevailing price ratio of gold to silver. He was forced out of business amid charges that he had debased the coins.

The following year the Bechtler family opened a second mint, at Rutherfordton in southwestern North Carolina. For years the company produced coins equal in value to regular U.S. gold, although little of it circulated, this time because the bullion value of the gold was greater than the face value of the coins. This situation improved after 1834 (ultimately the coinage was accepted), and new weight coins were temporarily marked with the date Aug. 1, 1834. The founder of the firm died in 1842, and his son and nephew carried on the business until 1852, but by then their standards of quality had declined and they could no longer compete with the two federal Branch Mints opened in Georgia and North Carolina.

While it was difficult to go from northern Georgia to Philadelphia in 1849, it was virtually impossible to get there from California. The quickest route from San Francisco to Philadelphia or New Orleans was by ship to Mexico or Central America and then overland to a second ship for the voyage north. Although the situation clearly called for a Branch Mint in California, one was not officially opened until 1854. In the meantime more than a dozen companies were engaged at various times in the production of gold coins.

A relic of this shipping route is the SS *Central America,* lost during an 1857 hurricane in the Atlantic Ocean with as much as 21 tons of California gold. Remains of the wreck were located off the South Carolina coast in 1989. Early in the salvage of the gold treasure carried by the steamship, several discovery pieces of pioneer gold were found. As the full cargo was recovered and cataloged, many chapters of this colorful history of American numismatics were rewritten as researchers gained new insights from studying the many gold ingots recovered.

The most popular pioneer gold coins struck for circulation from California gold were the $5 and $10 issues, as these were needed for use in daily commerce. Later, $20 coins and $50 slugs were made for use in large business dealings, this being an era when the value of a check was dependent not only upon the solvency of the issuer but of the bank as well.

In addition to the questionable coins from the do-it-yourself mints, legal tender coins were struck by either the U.S. Assayer or the U.S. Assay Office. The first of these were octagonal $50 coins (officially called ingots) struck by the firm of Moffat & Co. but bearing both the legend UNITED STATES OF AMERICA and the name and title of AUGUSTUS HUMBERT, UNITED STATES ASSAYER OF GOLD, CALIFORNIA, dated 1851 or 1852. Eagles and double eagles were produced in 1852 before the Moffat & Co. firm dissolved.

The U.S. Assay Office contract was taken over by a new private firm that was called the United States Assay Office of Gold. This semi-official Mint produced eagles, double eagles and $50 ingots until December 1853, at which time its facilities were closed for reorganization as the official San Francisco Mint. Because the new official Mint could not at first produce coins as fast as the old semi-official one, several private companies opened to compete with the new federal Mint through 1854 and 1855.

In addition to the shortage of large denomination coins there was always a shortage of small change for use in retail stores. Several small, anonymous companies therefore produced gold dollars, half dollars and even quarter dollars using a number of different designs. These fractional coins were struck from 1852 to 1882; it has been suggested that the later strikes were never intended for circulation but were merely souvenirs of California. Federal law in 1864 had forbid private coinage of any sort and some manufacturers of these pieces were prosecuted for counterfeiting after the 1864 law went into effect.

A number of eagles and half eagles were struck in Oregon in 1849, despite the objections of the new territorial governor. Presumably his orders eventually prevailed, as the issue was not repeated.

The Mormon government issued $2.50, $5, $10 and $20 coins in 1849, as well as half eagles in 1850 and 1860. This last issue was made of Colorado gold from the Pikes Peak area. Most of the early issues of Mormon gold did not receive widespread acceptance, as they were underweight by as much as 15 percent.

The last period of "legal" pioneer gold coins (i.e., issued before 1864), was the Pikes Peak gold rush of 1860 to 1861. Only three major firms produced coins in these two years, although several unverified patterns are known. It is interesting to note that in 1862 the largest of these companies, Clark, Gruber and Co., sold its equipment to the government, which intended to open a Branch Mint in Denver. The specie hoarding of the Civil War presumably doomed this project, and a Denver Mint did not open until 1906.

Other pioneer gold issues are known for Alaska and the northwestern states, but they were primarily made as souvenirs and did not circulate as coinage.

Just like regular coins, pioneer gold coins were subject to Gresham's Law. Those that were of full weight and value or better were hoarded and probably melted, while those that were undervalued were spent as soon as possible to avoid getting stuck with the coin.

U.S.-Philippine coinage

By David T. Alexander

David T. Alexander is a frequent contributor to Coin World *and author of the monthly column "The Research Desk." He is a longtime cataloger for Stack's and the new firm Stack's Bowers Galleries*

Before the United States

American collectors are often surprised to learn of a series of bronze, copper-nickel and silver coins struck between 1903 and 1945, unknown to them and boldly inscribed UNITED STATES OF AMERICA, bearing the American eagle and shield.

A clue to many collectors' ignorance of this interesting series is the name FILIPINAS also inscribed on the coins, the Spanish name of the vast archipelago of the Philippines, governed by the United States from the late 1890s until 1946.

The Philippines became American after Commodore George Dewey's spectacular victory over the enemy fleet at Manila Bay during the Spanish American War. The islands were the United States' largest "colonial" possession and the only one for which the United States issued a distinctive coinage.

Unlike Puerto Rico, annexed directly by the United States, or Cuba, which became an independent republic in 1902, the Philippines formed a unique territory governed by a civil administration appointed from Washington. Uncertain what to do with this vast domain and forced to fight a bloody war to retain it against the army of Gen. Emilio Aquinaldo, the United States finally decided to rule the islands while preparing them for eventual independence.

Civil government was established under Gov. Gen. William Howard Taft in 1903 and the Philippine Commission established a new coinage for the islands. In circulation as the American era opened were silver and gold coins of the prior Spanish rulers.

More plentiful were the popular Mexican silver 8-real coins and pesos, preferred trade coins of China and the Far East. Many Filipinos could also recall the countermarked Mexican and Latin American silver coins that circulated under Spanish rules and crude copper coins struck early in the 19th century.

Banking expert Charles Arthur Conant was sent to the islands in 1901 to solve the coinage question was. He decided that simply adopting regular American coins would be impractical. U.S. silver coins did not relate to the popular Mexican pesos and their denominations would not fit the low standard of living of many Filipinos.

Monetary system

Created instead was a gold-based Philippine peso divided into 100 centavos. Two of the new pesos would equal one U.S. dollar. No gold coins were struck, but .900 fine silver coins were: a peso weighing 416 grains or 26.9 grams; a 50-centavo coin (208 grains or 13.47 grams); a 20-centavo coin (83.1 grains, 5.26 grams); and a 10-centavo coin (41.15 grains, 2.66 grams). Minor coins were the copper-nickel 5-centavo piece, bronze centavo and half centavo.

Designs of the new coins had to express the sovereignty of the United States while asserting a distinctive Philippine character. Achieving this synthesis were the designs by the greatest Philippine sculptor-medalist, Melicio Figueroa. A native of Iloilo who had studied art on a royal scholarship in Spain, Figueroa was also a patriot who signed the first Philippine (Malosos) Republic's constitution.

Figueroa's minor coins feature a seated worker at an anvil; silver coins feature a graceful standing lady striking the anvil with a hammer, modeled by the artist's daughter Blanca. In the background is the smoking cone of the Mayon volcano, a unique Philippine touch for the new coins. Denominations appear in English above the figures, the Spanish form of the islands' name FILIPINAS below.

All reverses feature America's Stars and Stripes shield and spread-winged eagle with legend UNITED STATES OF AMERICA. The date appears below flanked by two dots; coins with a Mint mark bear it below the left dot. These designs appeared on the first coins struck in 1903 and continued until the Commonwealth was established in 1935.

Alas for Conant's well-laid plans, world silver values rose just as the new Philippine coins came into circulation. The result was a vast outflow of Mexican silver from the islands. During 1905 the beautiful new Philippine silver coins were worth 13 percent more as silver bullion than their face values. They disappeared despite punitive laws forbidding their export and melting.

Only a drastic reduction of silver content could save the day and in 1907 the United States released a second series of silver coins headed by a reduced-size peso struck in .800 silver, weighing 308.64 grains (19.99 grams). The three smaller denominations were reduced to .750 fine. This standard lasted until the last U.S.-Philippine coins were struck after World War II.

The Philadelphia Mint struck the bronze centavo and half centavo from 1903 to 1908. After the 500-mintage all-Proof coinage of half centavos of 1906 and 1908 this unpopular coin was abolished. From 1908 to 1920 the bronze centavo was struck only at the San Francisco Mint with the S Mint mark.

The Philadelphia Mint struck the first large-diameter copper-nickel 5-centavo coins from 1903 to 1908; the 1916 to 1919 coins were made in San Francisco. No 1907 base metal coins were struck. A major rarity is the 1919-S 5-centavo coin struck with the reverse die of the silver 20 centavos (a mule). Unlike the normal reverse, the mule's shield fills more of the field and the eagle's wings nearly reach the dentils around its edge.

Silver coins included the 10-centavo coins of 1903 to 1908, made at the Philadelphia Mint, with the San Francisco Mint coins appearing in 1903, 1907, 1908 to 1919 with the S Mint mark. The 20-centavo coin was also struck at the Philadelphia Mint from 1903 to 1908; San Francisco Mint coins of the dates 1903, 1905 and 1908 to 1919 followed. The 50-centavo coins of 1903 to 1908 again appeared from the Philadelphia Mint; San Francisco Mint dates are somewhat scattered: 1903, 1904, 1905, 1907, 1908, 1909 and 1917 to 1919.

Silver pesos of 1903 to 1908 were struck at the Philadelphia facility; San Francisco Mint large-sized pesos bear the dates 1903 to 1906. Only two Philadelphia Mint small-sized pesos are known dated 1907, and an all-Proof issue of 500 coins was struck dated 1908.

The peso coinage of 1907 through 1911 and 1921 was struck at the San Francisco Mint. Most silver pesos ended up in bank vaults as backing for silver certificates, paper money redeemable in silver similar to that issued in the United States.

The Philadelphia Mint struck 2,558 Proof sets of the new Philippine coins dated 1903; 1,355 sets in 1904; only 471 sets in 1905; and 500 sets in 1906 and 1908. These sets sold poorly at the time and few pristine examples survive today. All are still undervalued in terms of real scarcity.

Manila Mint

The American administrators realized that a Mint in the islands would free the Philippines from trans-Pacific shipment of coins. U.S. Mint engineer Clifford Hewitt was sent to Manila and supervised creation of a modern Mint in the old Intendencia Building, inaugurated in July 1920.

Commemorating the opening of the Manila Mint were crown-sized medals portraying President Woodrow Wilson and presenting a modified Assay Commission medal reverse of Columbia instructing a child in modern coining. Five were struck in gold, but only one survives, a Satin Proof believed unique. Silver and bronze examples are eagerly collected as so-called dollar medals.

The new Manila Mint (using the M Mint mark) went into production with centavo coins of 1920 to 22, and 1925 through 1936. The 5-centavo coin was struck at the new Mint from 1920 to 1921, and 1925 to 1928. Small-sized 5-centavo coins were dated 1930 to 1932 and 1934 to 1935. The 10-centavo coins from the facility bore the dates 1920 to 1921, 1929 and 1934.

Twenty-centavo coins were only struck at the Manila Mint in 1929 and only in 1920 did the M Mint mark appear on the 50-centavo coins. Another rare mule exists, combining the Standing Lady of the 20-centavo coin with a 1928/7 overdate 5-centavo reverse. Here the shield is far smaller than normal. This mule is about five times more common than the very rare 1918-S 5-centavo/20-centavo mule.

The Commonwealth of the Philippines was established in 1935 in transition to full independence, promised for 1946. The new Commonwealth emblem placed a smaller American eagle atop a tall shield bearing three stars representing the main island groups and the castle and sword-bearing sea lion from the coat of arms of Manila.

Sizes and alloys continued unchanged, the legend UNITED STATES OF AMERICA appeared, and the obverses remained the same as those of earlier issues. All bore the M Mint mark until 1941. Centavo coins were struck in 1937 through 1941; 5-, 10- and 20-centavo coins appeared only in 1937, 1938 and 1941.

The Commonwealth's birth was commemorated by three silver coins designed by Ambrosio Morales of the National University. Silver pesos of two obverse types were struck bearing the bust of Commonwealth President Manuel Quezon y Molina. His portrait was conjoined with the bust of U.S. President Franklin D. Roosevelt on one type, and with that of High Commissioner Frank Murphy on the other. Murphy faced Quezon on the single type of commemorative 50 centavos. Only 10,000 were struck of each peso and 20,000 of the 50 centavos. Planned to lure profits from the U.S. commemorative coin craze then raging, these three Philippine commemoratives sold dismally at time of issue, and are very scarce today.

World War II crashed into the Philippines Dec. 8, 1941, as Japanese air attacks on island targets followed the earlier assault on Pearl Harbor. Dangerously unprepared, the Philippines were quickly overwhelmed by invading Japanese forces, despite the heroic resistance of Fil-American forces on the strategic Bataan peninsula and island of Corregidor.

Gen. Douglas MacArthur escaped with President Quezon, but the islands had to endure a savage occupation until MacArthur's return to Leyte in October 1944 and the piecemeal reconquest of the archipelago. The country was devastated, and Manila ranked just behind Warsaw as the most thoroughly destroyed capital city of the war.

Between December 1941 and late 1944, two authorities demanded Filipino loyalty: the exiled Commonwealth of President Quezon; and the agencies set up under the Japanese occupation—the Philippine Executive Commission and post-1943 Republic of the Philippines led by Jose Paciano Laurel.

Laurel's short-lived republic issued three collectible medals but little else of numismatic interest. Issued in the name of the Commonwealth was a flood of Philippine guerrilla currency for the many units that continued to battle the Japanese after the surrender of Corregidor.

A major casualty of war was Philippine coinage, much of it confiscated and melted by the Japanese. Plunged in deep water off Corregidor was the Commonwealth silver reserve—hundreds of thousands of pesos preserved from the Japanese, if not from saltwater corrosion.

President Sergio Osmena led the returning Commonwealth, since Quezon had died of tuberculosis during 1944. Osmena's task was nearly hopeless, compounded of wartime destruction, shortages of staff, money and equipment. Inflation had ruined the economy, and the president faced the potent hostility of pro-consul MacArthur as well as the task of ferreting out alleged collaborators.

Under these circumstances the Philadelphia, Denver and San Francisco Mints struck vast amounts of pre-war type Commonwealth coins. From the masses of Uncirculated coins reposing in American coin dealers' junk boxes in the 1950s and 1960s, many of these seemed to have returned to the United States.

The San Francisco Mint struck about 52 million 1944 bronze centavos, and 14 million 1944 and almost 73 million 1945 5-centavo coins of an alloy that substituted zinc for some of the war-precious nickel. The only regular-design Commonwealth silver 50-centavo coins ever struck were the 19 million 1944-S coins

and the 18 million 1945-S coins of the same Mint.

The Denver Mint's contributions included the 31.5 million 1944-D 10-centavo coins of the usual .750 fine silver and 137 million 1945-D coins. Also struck were 28.5 million 1944-D 20-centavo coins and 82.8 million 1945-D coins. Most fascinating is the apparently rare 1944-D/S 20-centavo coins, believed an example of wartime making-do with valuable die steel.

Shattered by war, hampered by internal disorder, the Philippines found economic reconstruction frustrated by a miserly U.S. Congress that spent more on defeated enemies than on America's own battered ward.

Independence

Nonetheless, the Philippines became an independent republic on July 4, 1946. Its subsequent political story is one of growing instability and violence, reaching its nadir in the long and phosphorescently corrupt dictatorship of Ferdinand E. Marcos.

Between 1945 and 1958 only two coins appeared: the .750 silver peso and 50-centavo coin, both designed by Laura Gardin Fraser and honoring Gen. Douglas MacArthur as defender and liberator of the Philippines. Created like the 1935 Commonwealth commemoratives with an eye on U.S. collectors, these low-relief coins were an even greater disappointment on the numismatic market.

Although issued after the U.S. connection officially ended, these two coins are of major U.S. interest.

All in all, the U.S.-Philippine coinage should exert a strong attraction to American collectors. As a series it is reasonably short, generally low-priced but offers a real challenge for those for whom date and Mint collecting may have grown stale.

Current coins

Lincoln cent

When the Lincoln cent made its initial appearance in 1909, it marked a radical departure from accepted styling, introducing as it did for the first time a portrait coin in the regular series. A strong feeling had prevailed against the use of portraits on the coins of the country but public sentiment stemming from the 100th anniversary celebration of Abraham Lincoln's birthday proved stronger than the long-standing prejudice.

The only person invited to participate in the formulation of the new design was Victor David Brenner. President Theodore Roosevelt was so impressed with the talents of this outstanding sculptor that Brenner was singled out by the president for the commission.

The likeness of Lincoln on the obverse is an adaptation of a plaque Brenner executed several years prior that had come to the attention of President Roosevelt. In addition to prescribed elements—LIBERTY and the date—the motto IN GOD WE TRUST appeared for the first time on an U.S. cent. Of interest is that the

Congress passed the Act of March 3, 1865, authorizing the use of this expression on U.S. coins during Lincoln's tenure of office.

A study of three models for the reverse resulted in the approval of a very simple design bearing two stalks of wheat in memorial style. Between these, in the center of the coin, are the denomination and UNITED STATES OF AMERICA, while curving around the upper border is E PLURIBUS UNUM.

Even though no legislation was required for a new design, approval of the Treasury secretary was necessary. Franklin MacVeagh gave his approval July 14, 1909, and not quite three weeks later, on Aug. 2, the new cent was released to the public.

The original model bore Brenner's last name. Prior to issuance, however, the initials V.D.B. were substituted on the lower reverse because Mint officials felt the name was too prominent. After the coin was released, the newspaper *Washington Star* on Aug. 2, 1909, asked about the initials, with other newspapers soon quoting unnamed sources claiming the initials were either illegal advertising for Brenner or were not supposed to be on the coin (both allegations were false). As newspapers continued to create controversy where none should really have existed (U.S. coins had borne designer's initials for decades with little or no public awareness), Treasury officials decided to try to put a halt to the news coverage. Production of the coin was suspended Aug. 5 to allow officials to decide what to do with the initials. Because the coin was in great demand and because making a change in size of the initials or placing them elsewhere on the coin would have required halting production for a longer period of time than desirable, the decision was made to eliminate the initials entirely, a simple change to the master hub. Examples of the cents without the initials were struck a week after production was suspended. They were restored in 1918, in minute form on Lincoln's shoulder, where they can still be found.

More cents are produced than any other denomination, which makes the Lincoln cent a familiar item. In its life span this little coin has weathered two world wars, one of which was to change it materially. Metals play a vital part in any war effort. At the beginning of World War II the cent was composed of 95 percent copper and 5 percent tin and zinc. These metals were denied the Mint for the duration of the emergency, making it necessary to seek a substitute. After much deliberation, even including consideration of plastics, zinc-coated steel was chosen as the best in a limited range of suitable materials.

Production of this wartime cent was provided for in the act approved Dec. 18, 1942, which also set as the expiration date of the authority Dec. 31, 1946. Low-grade carbon steel formed the base, to which zinc plating .005 inch thick was deposited on each side electrolytically as a rust preventative. The same size was maintained but the weight was reduced from the standard 48 grains to 42 grains, due to the use of a lighter alloy. Operations commenced Feb. 27, 1943, and by Dec. 31 of that year the three Mints had struck an almost record-breaking number of cents, with the total reaching 1,093,838,670 coins. The copper released was enough to meet the combined needs of two cruisers, two destroyers, 1,243 B-17 Flying Fortresses, 120 field guns and 120 howitzers; or enough for 1.25 million shells for the U.S. big field guns.

On Jan. 1, 1944, the Mints were able to adopt a modified alloy, the supply being partially derived from expended shell casings that when melted furnished a composition similar to the original but with only a faint trace of tin; the 6 grains dropped from the total weight were restored. The original alloy was resumed in 1947.

On Feb. 12, 1959, a revised reverse was introduced as a part of the 150th anniversary celebration of the Great Emancipator's birth. No formal competition was held. Frank Gasparro, then assistant sculptor-engraver at the Philadelphia Mint, prepared the winning entry, selected from a group of 23 models the engraving staff at the Mint had been asked to present for consideration. Again, only the Treasury secretary's approval was necessary to make the change because the design had been in force for more than the required 25 years.

The imposing marble Lincoln Memorial in Washington, D.C., provides the central motif; the legends E PLURIBUS UNUM and UNITED STATES OF AMERICA form the rest of the design, together with the denomination. Gasparro's initials, F.G., appear on the right near the shrubbery.

The composition of the smallest U.S. denomination was changed again in 1962. Mint officials felt that deletion of the tin content would have no adverse effect upon the wearing qualities of the coin, whereas, the manufacturing advantages to be gained with the alloy stabilized at 95 percent copper and 5 percent zinc would be of much benefit. Congressional authority for this modification is contained in the Act of Sept. 5, 1962.

As the price of copper rose along with the demand for cents, a resolution was introduced Dec. 7, 1973, giving the Treasury secretary power to change the 1-cent alloy.

Mint officials tested several compositions during 1973, finally settling on aluminum. In fact, 1,579,324 1974-dated aluminum cents were struck in 1973 as experimental pieces. The Mint also used 1974-dated Lincoln cent dies to strike bronze-clad steel cents, a fact not known until 1994 when a former Pennsylvania steel worker sent an example to *Coin World*. In fact, the Treasury Department's official report on the 1973 and 1974 testing specifically denies that Lincoln cent dies were used to strike anything other than aluminum trial pieces. However, Mint officials in 1994 admitted the Treasury report was wrong. In addition, the Mint struck 66 1975-dated aluminum cents, a fact not known to the coin collecting hobby until revealed in a *Coin World* news story in 1996.

A few examples of each 1974-dated experimental piece survive.

The steelworker obtained several bronze-clad steel pieces in 1974 at the Alan Wood Steel Co. Mint officials had brought bags of the experimental pieces to the foundry to be melted and destroyed. A single bag of the bronze-clad cents broke open as it was being dumped down a chute leading to a furnace. The worker managed to grab several examples before guards were able to gather the remaining specimens and dump them into the furnace. Some five to eight examples are thought to survive, some in burned condition.

Most of the aluminum trial pieces were melted as well, although a few examples given to congressional members and staff disappeared. One coin is housed in the National Numismatic Collection of the Smithsonian Institution, donated by a congressional staff member. In 2005, an example surfaced in private hands, first graded by Independent Coin Grading as About

Uncirculated 58 and then a few months later graded by the Professional Coin Grading Service as Mint State 62. The aluminum cent reportedly had been retrieved by a U.S. Capitol police officer after being dropped by a member of the U.S. House of Representatives following a hearing concerning changing the composition of the cent because of rising copper prices. The representative reportedly told the guard to keep the coin.

A 2009 investigation conducted by the Treasury Department's Office of Inspector General into a report that an Illinois toll-booth operator who died in the spring of 2008 had been in possession of three of the prototypes since 1974 turned up no examples.

Several of the 1975 aluminum cents, sent to top Treasury officials for examination, may be missing as well.

Treasury officials consider all such trial pieces illegal to own. The steelworker who has several bronze-clad steel examples remains anonymous, as does the owner of the aluminum cent graded by PCGS. However, at least one unstruck planchet intended for the aluminum cent has been sold at public auction without Treasury intervention.

Neither experimental piece was approved for circulation. Authorizing legislation met opposition from the vending machine industry and the medical profession, and when the price of copper took a downhill turn, Mint Director Mary Brooks announced aluminum cents would not be necessary. There was no change in the 1-cent alloy.

In a report made public in September 1976, the Research Triangle Institute recommended that cent production be terminated by 1980, due to increasing costs of manufacturing the cent and the poor circulation of the coin. However, in making the study public the Mint said that it did not endorse the recommendations of the report, nor did it plan to adopt the recommendations at that time. Others have continued to press for the elimination of the cent in the 21st century but little support has been shown in Congress for such action.

Production costs for the cent have been a problem since the 1970s when less expensive alternative compositions were first considered. Action was taken in 1981. Feeling the pressure of rising copper prices again, Mint officials decided to switch to a new alloy composed of a core of 99.2 zinc and 0.8 percent copper plated by pure copper (total composition, 97.5 percent zinc, 2.5 percent copper), to be introduced in 1982. Both the old alloy and new alloy were produced during the year at all minting facilities striking cents. Copper and brass producers sued the federal government, claiming the Treasury Secretary did not have the authority to alter the composition despite the 1973 resolution. A federal judge ruled against the producers, however, and the cent has remained composed of copper-plated zinc.

However, rising metals and production costs for the cent have exceeded its face value for years, mostly recently ranging from a low of $0.0142 per cent to a high of $0.0179 per coin during the period from Fiscal Year 2007 to FY2010. In March 2011, Mint officials asked for public comment on possible alternative compositions. Whether compositional changes in the cent might be implemented in the near future was uncertain as this book went to press.

In addition to two rounds of composition changes since the 1960s, the Lincoln cent has undergone design changes to the reverse as well. In 2009, in celebration of the bicentennial of the birth of Abraham Lincoln and the centennial of the introduction of the Lincoln cent, four commemorative reverses were used, each marking a different period in Lincoln's life: Lincoln's birthplace and early years in Kentucky (1809 to 1816, Early Childhood cent); his time in Indiana (1816 to 1830, Formative Years cent); his time in Illinois (1830 to 1861, Professional Life cent); and his last years Washington, D.C. (1861 to 1865, Presidency cent).

The first of the four 2009 cents—the Lincoln, Early Childhood cent—features a depiction of the historical reproduction of the log cabin in which Lincoln was born. The inscription UNITED STATES OF AMERICA appears at the top of the design with E PLURIBUS UNUM positioned directly below the cabin. The birth date of 1809 appears below the motto. The denomination ONE CENT curves along the bottom. It was designed by AIP Master Designer Richard Masters and sculptured by U.S. Mint Medallic Artist Jim Licaretz. Their initials appear at the left and right, respectively.

The 2009 Lincoln, Formative Years cent is the second cent. It depicts a young Lincoln educating himself while working as a rail splitter in Indiana. The inscription UNITED STATES OF AMERICA appears at the top, in a smaller size than on the Childhood cent. The denomination ONE CENT appears in two straight lines to the left of the image of Lincoln, with E PLURIBUS UNUM at the bottom of the design. The design was created and sculptured by U.S. Mint Sculptor-Engraver Charles L. Vickers. His initials appear at lower right, at about the 4 o'clock position, adjacent to the end of the log.

The third cent covers Lincoln's public and political life in Illinois. It depicts the young professional Abraham Lincoln in front of the State Capitol in Springfield, Ill. UNITED STATES OF AMERICA appears at the top, with ONE CENT curving in one line at the bottom and E PLURIBUS UNUM directly below the state Capitol and to the right of Lincoln's ankles and feet (the word UNUM appears on a separate line, below the E PLURIBUS). It was designed by Joel Iskowitz, a master designer with the U.S. Mint's Artistic Infusion Program, and sculptured by U.S. Mint Sculptor-Engraver Donald Everhart II. Iskowitz's initials appear at the lower left, Everhart's initials at the lower right.

The reverse of the fourth cent for the year bears a

design thematic of Lincoln's presidential years. The design presents the half-finished dome of the United States Capitol, with UNITED STATES OF AMERICA at the top (the word "of" appears lowercase, while the remaining letters of the inscription, and indeed all of the letters of same inscription on the three other coins are all caps; the explanation for the difference was called "artistic license"). The motto E PLURIBUS UNUM curves along the bottom, with ONE CENT appearing in a straight line just above the motto. It was designed by AIP Master Designer Susan Gamble and sculptured by U.S. Mint Medallic Sculptor Joseph F. Menna. Their initials appear to the lower left and right, respectively.

A new, Union Shield reverse design was introduced in 2010, authorized under the same act that authorized the commemorative designs for 2009. Under the terms of the act, the new reverse design was to convey Lincoln's binding together the severed states at the end of the Civil War.

The Commission of Fine Arts reviewed 18 proposed designs for the 2010 cent on April 16, 2009; the panel recommended a design featuring 13 stalks of wheat bound together with a single band to symbolize the United States as "one nation." Days later, however, Mint officials withdrew that design as "it was inappropriately similar to a 1920s era German pfennig," according to a Mint spokesman. The Citizens Coinage Advisory Committee reviewed the remaining 17 designs April 28 and gave a less than enthusiastic endorsement to a design for the cent that featured a federal shield carrying the motto E PLURIBUS UNUM across the top and bearing a scroll with the letters ONE CENT. Treasury officials agreed with the CCAC's choice and selected that design for the coin.

The Union Shield reverse was designed by Lyndall Bass, an associate designer with the U.S. Mint's Artistic Infusion Program. The design sculptor for the design is U.S. Mint Medallic Sculptor Joseph F. Menna. Both Bass and Menna have their initials appear on the reverse.

The 13 vertical stripes of the shield represent the states joined in one compact union to support the federal government, represented by the horizontal bar above. The Union shield, which dates back to the 1780s, was a widely used icon in the North during the Civil War. According to the Mint, the shield device is featured throughout the halls of the U.S. Capitol Building on frescoes designed by Constantino Brumidi, artist of the Capitol during Lincoln's presidency.

The ONE CENT is raised on the scroll, making it the highest point on the coin.

In addition to preparing the new reverse design for the cent in 2010, the Mint engraving staff in 2009 also worked on the Lincoln portrait. Abraham Lincoln's portrait as executed for the obverse of the 2010 Lincoln cent is strikingly close to sculptor Victor D. Brenner's original plaster model for the 1909 Lincoln

cent for an excellent reason. Brenner's original plaster model was used as a template for the modified 2010 version.

According to a U.S. Mint spokesman, the 2010 Lincoln cent obverse represents a modern, modified version of Brenner's original 1909 Lincoln cent obverse. As part of the die production process, the Mint engraving staff made a plaster model from the original 1909 galvano, according to the Mint, and then scanned the plaster model into a computer for digital modification.

Over the years, Mint engravers had modified the Lincoln portrait, lowering the relief and making cosmetic changes, especially to Lincoln's hair and beard.

Under the 1890 law, the Union Shield design will have to appear on the reverse of the cent for at least 25 years before Treasury officials can replace it with another design. Given the uncertainty over the cent's future and the possibility, however slim, that the denomination might be eliminated, it is possible that these will be the last design changes to the cent.

Jefferson 5-cent coin

The Jefferson 5-cent coin was released to the public Nov. 15, 1938, after a national contest for the obverse and reverse designs.

Felix Schlag of Chicago designed the coin. Schlag was born in Frankfurt, Germany, in September 1891. He began his art studies in the Munich Academy in Germany and became an American citizen in 1929.

The obverse of the coin carries a profile of Thomas Jefferson. The reverse bears a likeness of Monticello, the president's historic home near Charlottesville, Va.

President Franklin D. Roosevelt was personally interested in the design of the Jefferson 5-cent coin. It was a result of his suggestion that the sculptor altered his original design so as to emphasize certain architectural features, particularly the two wings of the building at Monticello. Schlag's original reverse design depicted an oblique view of Jefferson's home that was completely different both in rendition and style.

Although the law did not then require that the phrase IN GOD WE TRUST appear on the coin, it was placed there at the request of the Director of the Mint. This was the first time this motto had appeared on the United States 5-cent coin since 1883.

The design did not bear Schlag's initials. The failure of the sculptor to "sign" his work is said to have been because he did not know he could. All other current issues of United States coins bear the initials of their sculptors. In the years following the release of the coin, there was considerable interest nationally and particularly on the part of the Michigan congressional delegation, to place on the Jefferson coin the initials of the sculptor, Felix Schlag. (Schlag died in Owosso, Mich., March 9, 1974. He was 82.)

Placing the initials on the coin was an administrative decision by the secretary of the Treasury, at the request of Assistant Secretary Robert A. Wallace and

Mint Director Eva B. Adams. The initials appear on the 5-cent pieces dated 1966 and subsequent issues.

As with the Lincoln cent, the composition of the Jefferson 5-cent coin was changed during World War II, with nickel removed from the composition in its entirety, though the original composition was used for part of 1942. The alternative alloy of 56 percent copper, 35 percent silver and 9 percent manganese was used through 1945.

The designs of the Jefferson 5-cent coin remained static from 1938 to 2003, though Mint engravers tweaked the two designs over the years. In 2004 and 2005, however, four commemorative reverse designs were used in celebration of the bicentennial of the Louisiana Purchase and the Lewis and Clark Expedition into the new American territories. In addition, a one-year portrait of Jefferson was used in 2005 and yet another new portrait was introduced in 2006.

The first 2004 reverse, called the Indian Peace or Indian Peace Medal design, celebrated the bicentennial of the Louisiana Purchase with a design based on the Jefferson Indian peace medal Lewis and Clark distributed to native leaders. The design depicts a pair of hands shaking in friendship, one with the uniform sleeve of an American military officer and the other with a metal bracelet of a Native American. Above the hands are a crossed tomahawk and peace pipe. The inscription UNITED STATES OF AMERICA appears curved along the top of the coin, with LOUISIANA PURCHASE curving below those words and the date of the purchase, 1803, below that second inscription. The motto E PLURIBUS UNUM appears in two straight lines below the hands, with FIVE CENTS curving along the bottom. U.S. Mint Sculptor-Engraver Norman E. Nemeth designed the coin, based on the original 1803 design by Mint Assistant Engraver John Reich. Nemeth's initials appear below the Indian's wrist.

The second 2004 design is called the Keelboat design. It depicts an angled view of the keelboat with full sail that transported the Lewis and Clark expedition members and supplies for part of the journey in search of a northwest passage to the Pacific Ocean. It was the largest of three marine vessels used on the expedition. Capts. Meriwether Lewis and William Clark are in full uniform in the bow. Other members of the expedition use long poles to help propel the keelboat against the river's current. The inscriptions UNITED STATES OF AMERICA and E PLURIBUS UNUM curve in two lines at the top, above the boat. Below the boat is LEWIS & CLARK in a single straight line, with FIVE CENTS curving along the bottom. The reverse design of the Keelboat 5-cent coin was the work of Mint Sculptor Engraver Al Maletsky (who completed the engraving before his Dec. 31, 2003, retirement). His initials appear just below the lower right portion of the main design element.

Both 2004 coins retained the Schlag obverse portrait of Jefferson.

The Mint introduced a new Jefferson portrait in 2005 and two more commemorative reverses. The new portrait was an off-center, right-facing portrayal of Jefferson, the portrait abutting the slightly higher rim at the left side of the obverse. The motto IN GOD WE TRUST curves along the rim from the 12 o'clock to 3 o'clock positions. The word LIBERTY appears in Jefferson's handwriting in front of his lips, to the right, with the Mint mark directly below. The date 2005 appears curved at the 5 o'clock position. U.S. Mint AIP artist Joe Fitzgerald of Silver Spring, Md., designed the obverse. U.S. Mint Sculptor-Engraver Don Everhart executed the obverse design. Their initials appear on Jefferson's neckcloth.

The first of the year's special reverses depicted a plains bison, one of the many animal species Lewis and Clark Expedition members saw during their journeys. The American Bison design, also known as the Bison design, shows a male bison facing right and standing on what appears to be elevated ground. The inscription UNITED STATES OF AMERICA appears curved along the top of the coin, with E PLURIBUS UNUM appearing in three straight lines below the bison and with FIVE CENTS curving along the bottom. Artist Jamie Franki of Concord, N.C., designed the American Bison image. Nemeth executed the coin's reverse. Both of their initials appear on the coin.

The second reverse, designed by Fitzgerald, depicted the Pacific Ocean as Meriwether Lewis and William Clark (and their Corps of Discovery) saw it 200 years ago. A quote from Clark's journal, OCEAN IN VIEW! O! THE JOY!, appears on the land, though the passage in the journal reads mistakenly recorded, "Ocian in view! O! The Joy" when the men actually had found an estuary of the Columbia River. Fitzgerald wanted to use the quote, misspelling and all, but the Mint forced its change. "The Mint said that 'if we have a misspelled word, we'll have to hire someone to man the phones,'" Fitzgerald said. The remaining inscriptions all appear along the rim, starting at 9 o'clock and reading clockwise are: E PLURIBUS UNUM · UNITED STATES OF AMERICA. At the bottom, starting at 8 o'clock and reading counter clockwise are: LEWIS & CLARK 1805 · FIVE CENTS ·.

In September 2006, Mint officials announced that Fitzgerald had not obtained permission to use a professional photograph he employed as his inspiration for the Ocean in View reverse design. The Mint issued a press release Sept. 8 announcing that a photograph taken by Astoria, Ore., photographer Andrew E. Cier was being credited by the Mint as being the basis for Fitzgerald's winning coin design. Cier took the photograph of a rocky, Western coastline. It captures what Capt. William Clark might have seen upon reaching Western waters as one of the leaders of the Lewis and Clark Expedition. Fitzgerald said of the incident: "This is the first time I've used a photograph that wasn't my own. The Mint didn't give us a lot of time to turn this thing around where we could have taken our own. The Mint hasn't made up its mind about what they are going to do. I feel terrible about it. That's resulted in a few sleepless nights."

He continued: "The photographer should get proper credit. It's a beautiful photo and a beautiful coin. It would be a shame if it didn't turn out to be a beautiful experience for everyone involved."

For the 2006 Jefferson 5-cent coin, the Mint introduced yet another Jefferson portrait on the obverse and, as required by Congress, a depiction of Monticello on the reverse.

The Mint chose a three-quarters facing portrait of Jefferson, offset to the left, by Jamie Franki. The motto IN GOD WE TRUST curves along the rim from the 12 o'clock to 4 o'clock positions. The word LIBERTY appears in Jefferson's handwriting below and to the right of Jefferson's chin, with the date and Mint mark in lines below that inscription. Donna Weaver of the Mint engraving staff executed the design. Both of their initials appear within Jefferson's clothing.

For the reverse, the Mint offered the CFA and CCAC a number of new renditions of Monticello along with the Schlag design used from 1938 to 2003. In the end, the Mint chose to return to the Schlag design, and returned the fine design details that had been removed over the years. Schlag's initials were added to the reverse for the first time, appearing to the lower right of Monticello.

Both designs will have to be used on the coin for at least 25 years unless Congress chooses to order a change.

As for the future of the denomination, changes to its composition may be in the offing. The 5-cent coin, like the cent, has cost more than its face value to produce for years. It cost $0.0924 to make one 5-cent coin in FY 2010. Also as with the cent, Mint officials in March 2011 asked for public comment on alternative compositions for the denomination.

Roosevelt dime

The Roosevelt dime in 2011 holds the distinction of being the only current circulating coin that has not been redesigned or used for a circulating commemorative program since its inception.

Almost immediately after President Franklin D. Roosevelt's death in the spring of 1945, letters came to the Treasury Department from all over the country in advocacy of his portrait being placed on a coin of the United States. The dime was most frequently suggested by reason of his having been identified with that coin through the March of Dimes drives for the Infantile Paralysis Fund. Roosevelt suffered from polio, which he contracted as an adult.

The Winged Liberty Head design having been in use for more than the required time, Treasury officials acceded to public sentiment and placed the likeness of President Roosevelt on the 10-cent coin. The new Roosevelt dime was released Jan. 30, 1946, the late president's birthday.

The obverse bears a portrait of Roosevelt, facing left and LIBERTY to his left. In the left field is IN GOD WE TRUST and in the lower right field the date.

On the reverse, in the center, is a torch with an olive branch on the left and an oak branch on the right. Around the border is UNITED STATES OF AMERICA with one dime below and across the lower field is E PLURIBUS UNUM.

The designer was John R. Sinnock, at that time the Mint's chief engraver. His initials, JS, appear near the point of Roosevelt's bust. Not long after the coin entered circulation, rumors surfaced that Sinnock's initials stood for Joseph Stalin, the Soviet Union's ruthless leader. When Sinnock's designs appeared on the Franklin half dollar starting in 1948, his middle initial was used in his signature, JRS, possibly to prevent any future rumors about whose initials appear on the coin.

Washington quarter dollar

The Washington quarter dollar replaced the Standing Liberty quarter dollar in 1932. The Standing Liberty designs had not been issued for the 25 years required by law, thereby making an act of Congress necessary to issue the Washington quarter dollar. Congress passed the authorization act March 4, 1931.

John Flanagan, a noted New York sculptor, designed the coin. His work was chosen from approximately 100 models that were submitted. The Treasury Department worked in close cooperation with the Commission of Fine Arts in selecting the design. However, the commission did not agree with the Treasury Department on the final selection, but as law gives the secretary of the Treasury the right to the final selection, the work of Flanagan was chosen over the commission's objections. The first coins were issued for general circulation Aug. 1, 1932.

The obverse depicts a left-facing portrait of Washington based on the famed 1785 bust by sculptor Jean-Antoine Houdon. The word LIBERTY curves along the top, with the date below and the motto IN GOD WE TRUST at the left in two lines. The Mint mark, if any, appeared to the right of Washington's queue on the coins of 1968 to 1998, moved there from the reverse. Flanagan's initials appear along the truncation of the bust.

The reverse depicts an eagle holding a bundle of arrows, with two olive branches below. The inscription UNITED STATES OF AMERICA appears curved along the top, with E PLURIBUS UNUM crowded in two lines between the eagle's head and the nation's name. The denomination QUARTER DOLLAR appears at the bottom. On coins struck from 1932 to 1965, the Mint mark, if any, appears below the intersection of the two olive branches.

The Washington quarter dollar was issued in 1932 to commemorate the 200th birthday of the nation's first president, though Mint officials did not consider it a "special coin," or commemorative. The Washington quarter dollar, however, would become the canvas for four circulating commemorative programs: in 1975 and 1976, from 1999 to 2008, in 2009, and the ongoing program introduced in 2010.

The 1975 to 1976 version of the coin bears the dual dates 1776-1976 and a special reverse commemorating the Bicentennial of the Declaration of Independence (no 1975-dated quarter dollars were issued). The Bicentennial reverse depicts a Colonial drummer, with a flaming torch encircled by 13 stars in the field to the drummer's left. E PLURIBUS UNUM is positioned to the left of the drummer's arm. It was designed by Jack L. Ahr, whose initials JLA appear below the drummer's left arm.

The commemorative usage of the coin since 1999 has resulted in major design changes for the Washington quarter dollar.

A distinctly different obverse first issued in 1999 features the same portrait of Washington as on the 1932 to 1998 coins, but reduced by 10 percent to make space for additional legends moved from the reverse. UNITED STATES OF AMERICA is moved from the reverse to above the smaller Washington portrait, with QUARTER DOLLAR located below the bust instead of the date. IN GOD WE TRUST is relocated on the obverse to the right of Washington's queue. LIBERTY is now located to the left of Washington's neck, below his chin. This version bears Flanagan's initials as well as the WC initials of William Cousins, the Mint engraver who redesigned the obverse. This obverse appears with all three circulating commemorative program, and in 2010, has details restored that had been lost from the original Washington portrait. Over the years, the Mint engraving staff had changed the detail in Washington's hair, giving Washington's wig a much different look than on the original 1932 coin.

Regarding the reverse designs, too many have been used since 1999 to describe each in detail here. A later section of this chapter presents basic information about each of the 1999 to 2011 designs.

The Mint has used a similar template for all three commemorative programs. At the top appears the name of the state or territory for the first two programs, and the name of the park or other site for the America the Beautiful program (the state name appears incused in the broad border on this latter series).

For the State quarter dollars program, the date of the state's admittance to the Union appears just below the state name, while the issue date is at the bottom, just above E PLURIBUS UNUM, which curves at the bottom. For the similar 2009 program, the motto E PLURIBUS UNUM and date of issue appear curving along the bottom. For the America the Beautiful program, all of the statutory inscriptions appear incused in the aforementioned broad border, with the issue date centered at the bottom and E PLURIBUS UNUM to the lower right. Central designs and commemorative inscriptions differ by issue.

At the conclusion of the America the Beautiful program, the obverse is to be returned to its original pre-1999 form, with the reverse to depict a scene from Washington's daring crossing of the Delaware River for a Christmas attack on British forces during the War for Independence. That scene is seen on the 1999 New Jersey quarter dollar, although that particular rendition is not mandated for the future coins.

Kennedy half dollar

The assassination of John Fitzgerald Kennedy on Nov. 22, 1963, resulted in such an outpouring of public sentiment that President Lyndon Johnson, on Dec. 10, 1963, sent to Congress a request for legislation to authorize the Treasury Department to mint new half dollars bearing the likeness of his predecessor. Congressional authorization was required because the Franklin half dollar.

Congress gave its overwhelming approval to the president's recommendation and on Dec. 30, 1963, Public Law No. 88-256 was enacted directing the Mint to proceed with the production of the new design. The first of the Kennedy half dollars for general circulation purposes were struck at the Mints in Philadelphia and Denver on Feb. 11, 1964. The half dollar was selected because this would add another presidential portrait to a coin of regular issue.

In the center of the obverse, or face of the coin, is a strong but simple bust of the late president. Above, and around the border is LIBERTY. Just below the bust is IN GOD WE TRUST. The date is at the bottom around the border. Gilroy Roberts designed the obverse; he was then chief engraver of the U.S. Mint. His initials appear along the bottom of Kennedy's neck.

The original reverse depicts the presidential coat of arms. It is the central part of the presidential seal. UNITED STATES OF AMERICA appears above, around the border, and the denomination, HALF DOLLAR, is located along the bottom border. Other requirements already incorporated in the coat of arms are the eagle, and E PLURIBUS UNUM, which appears on the ribbon above the eagle's head. Frank Gasparro, then a Mint assistant engraver, designed the reverse. Gasparro's initials F.G. appear at the lower right edge of the shield.

Initial distribution of the coin took place on March 24, 1964, in the usual manner, when 26 million were released by the Mints directly to the Federal Reserve Banks and branches for simultaneous distribution through the commercial banking system.

As with the quarter dollar and dollar, a special Bicentennial reverse was used in 1975 and 1976. It depicts Independence Hall in Philadelphia. Seth G. Huntington designed this reverse.

The Kennedy half dollar has not circulated widely since the 1970s. Demand has been so low that none were struck for circulation in 1970 and again in 1987; all production since 2002 has been for collector sales, not for circulation.

Anthony dollar

President Carter signed the Susan B. Anthony Dollar Act into law Oct. 10, 1978, but only after a long fight over the design. A smaller dollar coin, sized between the quarter dollar and the half dollar, was recommended by the Research Triangle Institute report in 1976. The same report recommended that the introduction of a smaller dollar coin coincide with the elimination of the half dollar and the paper dollar equivalent.

The first design submitted for the dollar coin was an adaptation by Frank Gasparro of the Flowing Hair large cent design, with a Flying Eagle design of Gasparro's creation on the reverse. Many collectors panned the execution of the design at first, although supporters welcomed a return to more traditional, nonpartisan coinage designs. Meanwhile, in Congress in 1978, a movement toward placing feminist Susan B. Anthony's portrait on the coin was growing as the legislation for a smaller dollar advanced through both houses.

Many hobbyists lobbied against the Anthony proposal in favor of a more traditional, allegorical portrait. Ironically, Gasparro's Flowing Hair Liberty design became the darling of the hobby as support for the Anthony design grew in Congress.

The Senate passed the Anthony dollar legislation Aug. 22, 1978, without dissent; the House passed it Sept. 26 by a vote of 368 to 38. The first coins were struck at the Philadelphia Mint Dec. 13, 1978, with 1979 dates. The P Mint mark was used for the first time since the Wartime 5-cent coins of World War II. Denver strikes were produced Jan. 9, 1979, and the San Francisco Assay Office began producing circulation strikes Feb. 2, 1979.

Despite Treasury hopes to save $30 million a year by reducing demand for the $1 Federal Reserve note, the Anthony dollar never caught on with the public, which claimed the coin was too similar in size to the quarter dollar. The vending industry, which had supported the change in size but fought against a more distinctive multi-sided coin, never fully converted vending machines to accept the new, smaller dollar. The coins were produced for circulation and collectors' sets in 1979 and 1980, and only for collectors in 1981. The Mint began offering 1979 and 1980 Anthony dollars to its collector clientele in 1985, in sets and in Mint-sewn bags.

While the Anthony dollar is generally panned as a failure, demand from certain customers drained existing Treasury stocks. The United States Postal Service in March 1993 began installing 9,000 stamp-dispensing machines that use the Anthony dollar. Beginning in 1994, demand grew from several metropolitan transit agencies. All of this increased demand forced Treasury officials to begin considering a resumption of dollar coin production. Mint Director Philip N. Diehl told a House subcommittee on June 26, 1997, that the Mint could strike new Anthony dollars overnight once dies were produced (the Treasury Department had authority to strike the Anthony dollar at any time). By October 1997, Treasury officials were saying that the rate of drawdown showed stocks

would be depleted in 30 months. However, officials wanted to avoid striking additional Anthony dollars, and proposed an alternative; the result was authorization to begin striking a new, golden-colored dollar, to be released beginning in 2000 (see the next section on the Sacagawea dollar).

Despite reluctance to strike additional Anthony dollars, Mint officials prepared to do so if required before the new dollar coin could be introduced. By January 1999, Anthony dollar stocks had dropped to 62.2 million coins (stocks fell by 55 million coins in 1998 alone). Seeing that stocks could be eliminated before an all-new coin could be authorized, designed and produced, the Mint's engraving department created a model for a 1999 Anthony dollar. Production of the 1999 Anthony dollar began during the summer at the Philadelphia Mint and Denver Mints. The coins were shipped to Federal Reserve Banks in October and placed into circulation.

Sacagawea dollar

Mint officials, faced with striking more dollar coins, wanted to avoid, if at all possible, further production of the Anthony dollar. Some in Congress, too, favored a small dollar coin to replace the Anthony dollar. Other members of Congress said they would support a new dollar coin only if no effort was made to stop production of the $1 Federal Reserve note. (Other nations that have produced successful dollar-equivalent coins have withdrawn the corresponding note, forcing use of the coin to ensure the coin's success.)

During a hearing before a House subcommittee on June 26, 1997, officials from the Mint, Bureau of Engraving and Printing, Treasury and the General Accounting Office discussed the impact that introduction of a new dollar coin could have. GAO officials recommended eliminating the dollar note to overcome the "biggest hurdle" to introducing a new dollar coin, and recommended educating the public on using the dollar coin. Rep. Joseph P. Kennedy II, D-Mass., voiced that he did not like the idea of forcing the public to accept a new dollar coin.

Subcommittee Chairman Michael Castle, R-Del., promised to pursue legislation for a dollar coin, and introduced H.R. 2637, which sought a dollar coin. Castle decided to avoid the controversy over eliminating the dollar note, so his legislation did not address that point. He acknowledged, however, that withdrawing the note would enhance the chances of success for the dollar coin.

Castle held another hearing Oct. 21, 1997, during which Treasury officials reversed 17 years of policy on a dollar coin. Nancy Killefer, assistant secretary for management and chief financial officer for the Treasury Department, proposed a new dollar coin to replace the Anthony dollar. Killefer told members of the House Banking Subcommittee on Domestic and International Monetary Policy that Treasury wanted a coin with features officials hoped would encourage its use and make it distinguishable from the quarter dollar. Killefer called for a dollar coin that would be golden in color and feature a distinctive edge.

Mint Director Diehl, speaking during the same hearing, said the Mint needed 30 months of development time before a new dollar coin could be introduced into circulation, although the time could be shortened if necessary.

Congress approved a Senate amended version of Castle's bill on Nov. 13, 1997, and President Clinton signed it into law shortly thereafter.

While Congress debated the dollar coin legislation, discussion arose over who or what the coin should depict. Some wanted the coin to depict Anthony or some other woman or women of historical significance. Others wanted an allegorical image of Liberty. A strong candidate was an image of the Statue of Liberty (the choice of Rep. Castle).

Private minters, artists and collectors began working on suggested designs. Ron Landis of the Gallery Mint Museum, Eureka Springs, Ark., created several "One Concept" pieces depicting different renditions of the Statue of Liberty or a more generic Liberty figure. Another artist, Daniel Carr of Denver, published images of an Astronaut dollar design concept; he wanted the coin to reflect 21st century ideals rather than depict images similar to those used in the 18th and 19th centuries (older concepts were favored by many collectors). Some even wanted to resurrect Gasparro's abandoned Flowing Hair, Flying Eagle designs that had been superseded by the Anthony dollar designs. Still others recommended Sacagawea, the teenage Shoshone guide of the Lewis and Clark Expedition.

To address the issue, Treasury Secretary Robert Rubin appointed a panel, the Dollar Coin Advisory Committee, to examine the options and make recommendations as to what should appear on the coin. The committee met in private and then held public hearings June 8, 1998, at the Philadelphia Federal Reserve. The committee announced its recommendations during that hearing: The committee recommended the coin "depict Liberty as represented by a Native-American inspired by Sacagawea." Castle was the sole dissenter serving on the committee; he still preferred the Statue of Liberty. Castle introduced legislation, H.R. 4329, on July 24, 1998, that if it had passed, would have required the Treasury Department to depict the Statue of Liberty on the coin. The bill failed to gain support before the 105th Congress ended its session at the end of 1998. Castle's earlier legislation required a General Accounting Office study of the public's preferences for design concepts.

Rubin supported the recommendation of the panel, assuring that Sacagawea would be the primary design element concept. Mint officials invited artists to submit designs for the dollar coin. The invitation, mailed the second week of September 1998, included a requirement that the designs depict a woman of clearly Native American heritage rather than a woman of European heritage wearing Indian garb or headdress (a common practice on 19th century coins). The artists were required to submit designs by Oct. 28, 1998.

Mint officials conducted a semi-public viewing of the designs in Washington, D.C., the week of Nov. 16. The Mint placed on display 80 obverse designs and 41 reverse designs, at Casa Italiana, a small church near Mint headquarters. About 400 area numismatists, artists and historians were invited to view the designs and make comments. The Commission of Fine Arts met Nov. 20 to consider the 121 designs. Following that meeting, a Mint design selection panel narrowed the designs to six obverses and seven reverses, and placed all 13 designs on its Internet site for additional public comment. The panel considered those comments and others from focus groups before narrowing the designs further. The Commission of Fine Arts made its recommendations Dec. 17. Winning its approval was an obverse design by Glenna Goodacre, an artist living in Santa Fe, N.M. (whose most famous previous work was the bronze Vietnam Women's Memorial in Washington, D.C.).

The recommended obverse, in its original form, depicted a woman portraying Sacagawea, with her baby on her back. Goodacre located a 22-year-old Shoshone college student who modeled for her. The recommended reverse depicted an eagle standing on a rock that was inscribed with petroglyphs, and was submitted by Thomas G. Rogers Sr. of the Mint engraving staff.

The selected obverse met with criticism from members of the Lemhi-Shoshone tribe, of which Sacagawea was a member. They noted that the model was of the Shoshone-Bannock tribe, whose members, the critics said, have facial features differing from the Lemhi-Shoshone. Those same critics pointed out historical inaccuracies in the hairstyle and the lack of a cradleboard, which they said Sacagawea would have used to carry her baby.

As noted earlier in this chapter, Mint officials selected a composition of two outer layers of manganese-bronze bonded to an inner core of pure copper.

A first-strike ceremony for the dollar was conducted Nov. 18, 1999. The coins entered circulation in January 2000, first through Walmart and Sam's Club stores (partners with the Mint in a new effort by the Mint to promote use of the coin), followed by the Federal Reserve and banks. Mint officials promoted the coin as the "Golden dollar," leading some users to believe the coin contained actual gold. However, the name "Sacagawea dollar" quickly became the standard term for the coin.

Despite predictions that the distinctive color and plain edge of the Sacagawea dollar would encourage wider use in circulation, the coin repeated the experiences of the Anthony dollar. After a first-year mintage of nearly 1.29 billion coins in 2000, the mintage fell off sharply in 2001 to a bit more than 133.4 million coins. All circulation-quality coins struck since 2002 have been for collector sales; none have been struck for circulation because the Federal Reserve placed no new orders for the coin.

Starting in 2009, the Sacagawea dollar was repurposed as the Native Americana dollar (to be discussed following the Presidential dollars section).

Presidential dollars

The Presidential $1 Coin Act of 2005 added a new circulating commemorative denomination to U.S. coinage history and, not coincidentally, placed the Statue of Liberty on a circulating coin. Rep. Michael Castle, R-Del., sought again to achieve his goal of honoring the Statue of Liberty on a circulating coin when he introduced the Presidential dollar legislation on March 9, 2004. The bill also sought a companion noncirculating First Spouse gold $10 coin program, to run co-currently with the Presidential dollar program.

Castle envisioned the Presidential dollar program as a temporary replacement for the Sacagawea dollar. Castle, as reported in the section about the Sacagawea dollar, during the legislative process for that coin repeatedly tried to replace it with a Statue of Liberty dollar coin, to no avail. With the failure of the Sacagawea dollar to circulate, Castle envisioned a circulating commemorative dollar program patterned after the State quarter dollar program, which he also authored. Castle told *Coin World* March 5, 2004: "The dollar coin has a place in our marketplace; unfortunately, due to a host of issues the Sacagawea golden dollar was not the answer. It [the Presidential dollar legislation] will reinvigorate our circulating coin program in an affordable way for collectors and the public; it will be educational and fun; and it will be a winner financially for the government."

Castle said the Presidential dollar coin is "our way of addressing the issue of circulation [for the dollar coin]."

In order to make the obverse and reverse fields less cluttered, the legislation required that most of the inscriptions from the obverse and reverse be moved to the edge: the date, E PLURIBUS UNUM and IN GOD WE TRUST.

Castle tried to place the legislation on the fast track in the House. In the Senate, however, opposition arose even before the measure was sent to that body for consideration. Sens. Byron Dorgan, D-N.D., and Ben Nighthorse Campbell, R-Colo., in the Spring of 2004 sent a letter to congressional colleagues stating they wanted to block passage of H.R. 3916, Castle's bill. They specifically objected to removing Sacagawea from the coin. Campbell's father was of Northern Cheyenne descent; the Lewis and Clark Expedition first encountered Sacagawea in what would become North Dakota.

Castle's measure failed to gain passage in the 108th Congress, but he reintroduced Presidential dollar legislation on Feb. 18, 2005, in the 109th Congress. Again, Castle intended the coin program as a replacement for the Sacagawea dollar, which was still not being struck for circulation. However, by March 16, when the House Financial Services Committee approved Castle's bill, it had been modified to permit the Treasury secretary to continue production of the Sacagawea dollar or to declare the coin obsolete. (The bill was also revised to include authority to strike circulating commemorative Lincoln cents in 2009.)

The House voted 422 to 6 April 27 to pass the measure and sent the bill to the Senate. In the Senate, a different version of the Presidential dollar legislation was under consideration. That measure, in addition to seeking Presidential dollars, First Spouse gold coins, the continuation of production of Sacagawea dollars and commemorative 2009 Lincoln cents, also sought an American Buffalo .9999 fine gold bullion coin to bear the same designs used on the 1913 Indian Head, Bison on Mound 5-cent coin.

The Senate passed its version of the legislation, S. 1047, on Nov. 18, 2005, by unanimous consent and sent the measure to the House. Among the provisions was a requirement that Sacagawea dollars be produced in quantities equal to one-third of the total number of Presidential dollars produced during a calendar year. The House passed the measure without amendment Dec. 13 in a 291-to-113 roll-call vote under suspension of the rules. President George W. Bush signed the measure into law on Dec. 22.

Beginning with the release of the George Washington Presidential dollar Feb. 19, 2007 (the official federal holiday celebrating Washington's Birthday), four Presidential dollars are to be issued every year, through 2016 at least, and possibly beyond. Sitting presidents and living former presidents are ineligible to be depicted. Any former president must be deceased at least two years before becoming eligible for depiction on one of the coins.

Each coin depicts the honored president with standard placement of inscriptions: the president's name at the top, with the number of the president and years of service at the bottom (IN GOD WE TRUST was added to the obverse in 2009; see the earlier section of this book about the history of U.S. coinage designs for more detail). The reverse is standard to the series, showing a half-length Statue of Liberty from the perspective of someone below; inscriptions are UNITED STATES OF AMERICA and the denomination $1. Donald C. Everhart II designed the reverse depicting the Statue of Liberty. Many designers are credited for the obverse designs (details to appear later in this chapter). The coins bore the lettered edges as required by the authorizing legislation (the Mint also put the Mint mark on the edge though that was not required). As noted earlier, changes to the edge inscription were made starting in 2009.

For each new coin, banks may order and store the coins up to two weeks prior to the introduction so they will have supplies on hand on the release date.

However, despite Castle's confidence that the Presidential dollar program would result in broader circulation of dollar coins, the reality has been similar to the experiences of the Anthony and Sacagawea dollar programs. The highest mintage was achieved for the George Washington coin and mintages have fallen off sharply since, though not steadily.

Native American dollars

Even before the Presidential dollar could be implemented, resistance arose to the requirement that Sacagawea dollars continue be struck in addition to the Presidential dollars. The Federal Reserve did not need any additional Sacagawea dollars (it really did not need any Presidential dollars, either, but Congress had other plans). As 2007 opened, Fed officials said that any 2007 Sacagawea dollars would be placed into circulation mixed with other dollar coins.

Early in 2007, however, Congress began considering major changes to the Sacagawea dollar program. Sen. Byron L. Dorgan, D-N.D, introduced the Native American $1 Coin Act or S. 585 on Feb. 14, along with co-sponsors are James M. Inhofe, R-Okla., and Sen. Tom Harkin, D-Iowa. The legislation sought to replace the Soaring Eagle design on the reverse of the Sacagawea dollar with an annual commemorative design to celebrate the contributions of Native Americans. Dorgan said his intent in presenting the legislation was multifold—to honor Sacagawea and not build the inventory of the coins, and to honor other great American Indian leaders and contributions. Suggested reverse designs, listed in the bill, included the creation of Cherokee written language; the Iroquois Confederacy; Wampanoag Chief Massasoit; the Pueblo Revolt; Olympian Jim Thorpe; Ely S. Parker, a general on the staff of General Ulysses S. Grant and later head of the Bureau of Indian Affairs; and code talkers who served the United States Armed Forces during World War I and World War II.

The House version, H.R. 2358, was introduced by Rep. Dale Kildee, D-Mich., on May 17, 2007. The House passed the measure June 12 and sent it to the Senate. There, the spelling of the Shoshone guide's name was changed from its spelling in the House-approved version of the bill from "Sakakawea"—the spelling preferred by some native Americans—to the more widely used "Sacagawea." The Senate approved the amended House bill on Aug. 3 by unanimous consent. The house quickly took up the amended version and approved it Sept. 4 by voice vote. President Bush signed it into law Sept. 20.

The act changed the ratio of Sacagawea and President dollars the Mint must strike. Under the Presidential Dollar Act, the Mint was required to strike Sacagawea dollars in numbers equal to one-third of the total number of Presidential dollars struck in a given year. The Native American $1 Coin Act states, "The number of $1 coins minted and issued in a year with the Sacagawea-design on the obverse shall be not less than 20 percent of the total number of $1 coins minted and issued in such year."

The Native American $1 Coin Act does not mandate that the Federal Reserve order any of the Native American dollars. Since the program's introduction in 2009, the Fed has not ordered any of the coins. The Mint has struck circulation-quality coins every year and has sold them both at numismatic premiums in special packaging and at face value through its Direct Ship Program. Any Native American dollars entering circulating have probably been distributed by collectors or dealers ordering the coins through the Direct Ship program.

The edges of the Native American dollars have the same inscription as the 2009 and later Presidential dollars. The motto IN GOD WE TRUST appears on the obverse of the coin, with the date and Mint mark appearing on the edge (as does E PLURIBUS UNUM). The placement of the date and Mint mark, not displayed on the obverse as on many other coins, prompts those unfamiliar with the concept of edge inscriptions to wonder whether they have found an error coin. On the reverse, placement of the statutory inscriptions— UNITED STATES OF AMERICA and the denomination, given as $1—differs by design, and some designs have additional commemorative inscriptions.

The 2009 Native American dollar reverse features a Native American woman planting seeds in a field of corn, beans and squash, celebrating the Three Sister method of planting created by Native Americans. The 2010 reverse features an image of the Hiawatha Belt with five arrows bound together and the additional inscriptions HAUDENOSAUNEE and GREAT LAW OF PEACE. The 2011 reverse features the hands of the Supreme Sachem Ousamequin Massasoit and Governor John Carver, symbolically offering the ceremonial peace pipe after the initiation of the first formal written peace alliance between the Wampanoag tribe and the European settlers. The additional inscription is WAMPANOAG TREATY 1621.

Additional design details are found at a later section in this chapter.

History of Mint marks

A Mint mark on U.S. coins is a small letter or letters added to the design of a coin to show which Mint manufactured it. Mint marks on United States coins began with the Act of March 3, 1835, establishing the first Branch Mints: in New Orleans, Charlotte, N.C.,

and Dahlonega, Ga. The first Mint marks appeared in 1838.

When other Mint facilities were established, coins struck there bore an appropriate Mint mark. The letters used to signify the various Mints are as follows:

"C" for Charlotte, N.C. (gold coins only), 1838 to 1861.

"CC" for Carson City, Nev., 1870 to 1893.

"D" for Dahlonega, Ga. (gold coins only), 1838 to 1861.

"D" for Denver, Colo., 1906 to present.

"O" for New Orleans, La., 1838 to 1861; 1879 to 1909.

"P" for Philadelphia Mint, Pa., 1793 to present.

"S" for San Francisco, Calif., 1854 to 1955; as an Assay Office, 1968 to 1984; as a Mint, 1984 to present.

"W" for West Point, N.Y., 1984 to present.

With one four-year exception, U.S. coins struck at the Philadelphia Mint bore no Mint marks until 1979. The initial use of the "P" appears on the Jefferson, Wartime 5-cent coins, struck from 1942 to 1945 in a copper-silver-manganese alloy. The P Mint mark on these issues was designed to distinguish the silver alloy issues from regular copper-nickel 5-cent coins; during the war, silver was less important strategically than copper or nickel, the standard metals used for the 5-cent coin since its creation in 1866.

With passage of the Coinage Act of 1965, which gave the United States copper-nickel clad and silver-copper coinage, Mint marks were omitted from coins dated 1965, 1966 and 1967. The decision was designed to help alleviate a coin shortage by removing any distinction between coins struck at different facilities so collectors and speculators could not determine which were the more limited strikes.

After the San Francisco Assay Office opened in 1965 for coinage purposes (following 10 years of inactivity) no coins struck there would bear Mint marks until 1968, when they were returned to certain denominations for several years.

With the announcement Jan. 4, 1968, that Mint marks would return to coinage, Mint Director Eva B. Adams made several changes in Mint mark application. First, to achieve uniformity, she directed that all Mint marks be placed on the obverse of the coins. The Mint mark, she announced, on the cent, 5-cent coin, dime and quarter dollar would be to the right of the portraits, while on the half dollar it would appear in the center under the portrait of Kennedy.

Second, she announced Proof coin sets would be manufactured at the San Francisco Assay Office and would bear an S Mint mark. Previously, all Proof sets were produced at the Philadelphia Mint and so none of the coins had a Mint mark, except for some 1942 Jefferson 5-cent coins, made of a wartime alloy. Proof sets were discontinued altogether after 1964 because of the coin shortage and were revived in 1968.

Mint marks were again omitted from certain U.S. coins when cents were struck at the West Point Bullion Depository in 1974 and later, and when dimes were struck in at the San Francisco Assay Office in 1975.

Major changes were made in Mint mark policy beginning in 1978. Mint officials in 1978 announced that 1979 Anthony dollars struck at the Philadelphia Mint would bear the P Mint mark. The list of coins to bear the P Mint mark grew in 1980, when all other denominations but the cent struck at the Philadelphia Mint received the new Mint mark.

A new Mint mark, a "W," the eighth, was added to the U.S. inventory in September 1983, when the West Point Bullion Depository (now the West Point Mint) began striking 1984-dated $10 gold eagles commemorating the Los Angeles Olympic Games. Various collector versions of American Eagle silver, gold and platinum coins struck at the West Point Mint bear the W Mint mark (Proof, collector Uncirculated). A special 1996-W Roosevelt dime was struck at West Point to commemorate the 50th anniversary of the design's introduction. It was included at no extra charge in 1996 Uncirculated Mint sets.

Additional changes were announced in 1984 when it was reported that beginning in 1985, the Mint mark would be placed on the master die instead of the working dies for all Proof coinage. This was to forestall production of errors similar to the Proof 1983-S Roosevelt, No S dime and the 1982 Roosevelt, No P dime. Mint officials said that Mint marks would not be added to master dies for circulation-strike coinage.

However, in 1989, Mint officials acknowledged that the procedure would be phased in for circulating coinage, ending a 150-year-old tradition of individually punching Mint marks into each working die.

In 1986, Mint officials decided to add the Mint marks on all commemorative and Proof coins at the model stage. Thus, on these special collectors' coins, the Mint mark appears on all stages of models, hubs and dies.

Beginning in 1990, the Mint marks were placed on the master die for the cents and 5-cent coins, with the dimes, quarter dollars and half dollars undergoing the same transformation in 1991. This step virtually eliminated Mint mark varieties on U.S. coins, except for some controversial varieties that not all researchers accept as true varieties.

Eventually, the Mint mark was added at the modeling stage for circulating coinage.

Location of Mint marks

Half cents—All coined at Philadelphia Mint, no Mint mark.

Large cents—All coined at Philadelphia Mint, no Mint mark.

Flying Eagle cents—All coined at Philadelphia Mint, no Mint mark.

Indian cents—1908 and 1909, San Francisco Mint, S under the wreath on reverse side.

Lincoln cents—Under the date, D and S only.

Two cents—All coined at Philadelphia Mint, no Mint mark.

Three cents (copper-nickel)—All coined at Philadelphia Mint, no Mint mark.

Three cents (silver)—All but one coined at Philadelphia Mint; exception is 1851, New Orleans Mint—reverse side, at right.

Shield 5-cent coins—All coined at Philadelphia Mint, no Mint mark.

Liberty Head 5-cent coins—Most coined at Philadelphia Mint; exceptions are 1912 coins struck at Denver and San Francisco Mints, with S and D—reverse side to left of word CENTS.

Indian Head 5-cent coins—Reverse side under FIVE CENTS.

Jefferson 5-cent coins (1938 to 1964)—Reverse side at right of the building.

Jefferson 5-cent coins (1942 to 1945, copper-silver-manganese)—above dome on the reverse.

Jefferson 5-cent coins (1968 to 2004)—on obverse under Jefferson's queue.

Jefferson 5-cent coins (2005)—on obverse under LIBERTY.

Jefferson 5-cent coins (2006 to present)—on obverse under date.

Seated Liberty half dimes (1838 to 1859, 1870 to 1872)—Reverse side above the bow of the wreath.

Seated Liberty half dimes (1860 to 1869, 1872 to 1873)—Reverse side below the wreath.

Seated Liberty dimes (1838 to 1860, 1875)—Reverse side above the bow of the wreath.

Seated Liberty dimes (1860 to 1891)—Reverse side below the bow of the wreath.

Barber dimes—Reverse side below wreath.

Winged Liberty Head—Reverse to left of base of fasces.

Roosevelt (1946 to 1964)—Reverse, left of bottom of torch.

Roosevelt (1968 to present)—Obverse above date.

Twenty cents—Reverse side under the eagle.

Seated Liberty quarter dollars—Reverse side under eagle.

Standing Liberty quarter dollars—Obverse to left of date.

Washington quarter dollars (1932 to 1964)—Reverse under eagle.

Washington quarter dollars (1968 to present)—Obverse to right of Washington's queue.

Capped Bust half dollars (1838 and 1839)—Obverse above date.

Seated Liberty half dollars (1839 to 1891)—Reverse under eagle.

Barber half dollars (1892 to 1915)—Reverse under eagle.

Walking Liberty half dollar (1916 to 1917)—Obverse below IN GOD WE TRUST.

Walking Liberty half dollar (1917 to 1947)—Reverse, lower left adjacent to rock.

Franklin half dollar (1948 to 1963)—Reverse above bell beam.

Kennedy half dollar (1964)—Reverse near claw and laurel at left.

Kennedy half dollar (1968 to present)—Obverse under Kennedy portrait.

Seated Liberty dollar (1846 to 1891)—Reverse under eagle.

Trade dollar (1873 to 1878)—Reverse under inscription of fineness, weight.

Morgan dollar (1878 to 1904, 1921)—Reverse under bow of wreath.

Peace dollar (1922 to 1935)— Reverse at lower tip of the eagle's wing.

Eisenhower dollar (1971 to 1978)—Obverse above the date.

Anthony dollar (1979 to 1981, 1999)—Obverse to left of bust.

Sacagawea dollar (2000 to 2008)—Obverse, to the right of the bust, below the date.

Presidential dollars (2007 to date)—Edge, after date. Inscription may face either obverse or reverse.

Native American dollars (2009 to date)—Edge, after date. Inscription may face either obverse or reverse.

Coronet, Indian Head gold dollars (1849 to 1889)—On reverse under wreath.

Classic Head quarter eagles (1838 to 1839)—Obverse over the date

Coronet quarter eagles (1840 to 1907)—Reverse under the eagle, above denomination.

Indian Head quarter eagles (1908 to 1929)—Reverse lower left, near arrow heads.

Indian Head gold $3 coins—Reverse under the wreath.

Half eagles—Same as quarter eagles (dates vary slightly).

Coronet eagles (1841 to 1907)—Reverse under eagle.

Indian Head, No Motto eagle (1908)—Reverse above left tip of branch.

Indian Head, With Motto eagle (1908 to 1930)—Reverse at left of arrow heads.

Coronet double eagles (1850 to 1907)—Reverse under eagle.

Saint-Gaudens double eagles (1908 to 1931)—Reverse above the date.

American Eagle bullion coins—Gold, Proof, Reverse Proof, "Burnished" Uncirculated versions only, on obverse between second and third rays at right, below date. Silver, Reverse Proof, "Burnished" Uncirculated versions only, on reverse to left of eagle's tail, below branch. Platinum Proof version, 1997, on reverse, lower left between the first and second rays of the sun, and on 1998 coin lower right, behind eagle. Various locations on later dates of the Proof coins.

American Buffalo gold bullion coins (2008 to date)—Obverse below Indian's lower feathers at left.

First Spouse gold bullion coins (2007 to date)—Obverse to lower right, W Mint mark only, position slightly different for each First Spouse or Liberty design.

America the Beautiful 5-ounce silver bullion coins (2010 to date)—Obverse to right of Washington's queue, in same location as on standard America the Beautiful quarter dollars.

Dates, edge designs

Dates

The insertion of a chronological mark or word representing the date on coins was a practice known to the ancients, but carried out by them on their money in a different method from that pursued by more modern sovereigns. The date on a coin serves a very useful purpose, in that, with it on a coin, counterfeiting is made more difficult and enforcement authorities can isolate specific issues that may have been produced illegally.

In the United States, the Act of April 2, 1792, established the requirement that the date appear on U.S. coins (phrased in the legislation as "the year of the coinage"), and with few legislated exceptions, this law has remained unchanged since that time. In practice, however, using "the year of coinage" was not strictly enforced during the federal Mint's earliest years. For example, production of 1816 Coronet cents began in December 1815; the Mint had exhausted its planchet supply for cents in October 1814 and the need for cents in late 1815 was acute. The Mint got all of its cent planchets from a British supplier; the embargo on trading with Britain during the War of 1812 extended to the Mint, thus no planchets arrived at the Mint after the start of the war. Other similar examples may have occurred, but for most of the federal Mint's existence, most issues bore "the year of coinage."

A notable exception arose in the 1960s during a severe nationwide coin shortage in the 1960s. Congress passed legislation so that after the end of calendar year 1964, the Mint could still use the 1964 date on coinage. Starting in 1965, therefore, all denominations of United States coinage continued to be struck with the 1964 date.

When the Coinage Act of 1965 was passed, it became mandatory that the Mint continue to use the 1964 date on all 90 percent silver coins (half dollars, quarter dollars and dimes). Therefore, all the 90 percent silver coins that were manufactured in 1964, 1965 and 1966 bear the 1964 date. The last of the 90 percent silver quarter dollars were struck in January 1966, the last of the dimes in February 1966 and the last of the half dollars in April 1966.

The Coinage Act of 1965 also made it mandatory that the copper-nickel and silver-copper clad coins be dated not earlier than 1965. Therefore, all the clad coins actually made in 1965 bear the 1965 date, with production continued into the next calendar year. All the clad coins made through July 31, 1966, bear the 1965 date. The first clad dime was struck in December 1965, the first clad quarter dollar in August 1965 and the first clad half dollar in December 1965. In December 1965, the decision was made to change the 1964 date on the 5-cent coins and the cents to 1965, as one step in catching up on normal coin dating. From December 1965 through July 31, 1966, all cents and 5-cent coins struck bear the 1965 date. All denominations of U.S. coins minted during the period starting Aug. 1, 1966, through Dec. 31, 1966, carry the 1966 date. Commencing Jan. 1, 1967, the Mints resumed normal dating procedures.

The usual process of dating was interrupted again in December 1974, when Mint Director Mary Brooks announced the date 1974 would continue on dollars, half dollars and quarter dollars produced in the first half of 1975. The date of 1975 appeared, however, on cents, 5-cent and 10-cent coins. All dollars, half dollars and quarter dollars struck after July 4, 1975, bore the 1776-1976 Bicentennial dates. Normal dating was resumed in 1977. The Mint Director attributed the date freeze decision to the necessity of building a sufficient coin inventory to conduct business affairs of the nation.

In 1973, the Mint struck 1974-dated aluminum and bronze-clad steel cents in an experiment made necessary because of Mint worries over rising copper prices. When rising copper prices caused Mint officials to finally change the composition of the cent in 1982, the Mint began striking 1982 cents in late 1981 to build inventories. Mint officials began striking 1999-dated Washington, Delaware quarter dollars in December 1998 in order to meet expected demand in January 1999. Full-scale production of 2000-dated Sacagawea dollars began Nov. 18, 1999, at the Philadelphia Mint for a massive release during the first quarter of 2000.

Recent special coinage programs have led Mint officials to strike coins with dates of following or preceding years. Production of Olympic coinage of 1984 gold eagles and 1984 silver dollars began in 1983 to produce an inventory for collector sales in 1984. Striking of the 1986-dated Statue of Liberty commemorative coins began in late 1985, again to produce an inventory. The production of the Proof 1986-dated American Eagle gold and silver bullion coins, however, did not begin until early 1987 in order to permit the Mint to strike sufficient quantities of the bullion versions. Production of new Proof sets often begins prior to the beginning of the calendar year in which the Proof coins are dated (resulting in several instances of the Mint inadvertently shipping the next year's Proof sets to customers who ordered the current year's sets).

Edge designs

For many years, edge designs on U.S. coins were a more neglected aspect of the field of numismatics. Occasionally, differences were noted in reference books, such as the change from lettered edge to reeded edge on 1836 Capped Bust half dollars, some distinctions on early large cents and W.Q. Wolfson's discovery of the 1921 Morgan, Infrequently Reeded Edge dollars.

With the return of edge inscriptions on U.S. coins with the Presidential dollars of 2007 to date and the Native American dollars of 2009 to date, collectors and noncollectors are paying more attention to the third side of a coin.

Collectors of early U.S. coins with edge inscriptions and other edge ornamentation not applied by a collar—half cents through 1797, large cents through 1796, half dollars through 1836 and dollars trough 1803—were about the only ones who studied the edges of coins. When half cents and cents began featuring plain edges, and reeded edges applied by a close collar became standard on all silver and gold coins, collectors generally began ignoring edges unless examining the edge out of concern that a particular example might be counterfeit.

The earliest published mention of reeding counts known was in "Bristles and Barbs" in April 1965, and "Coinology" in June 1969, both in *Coin World,* the first being instigated by Wolfson's discovery published in *Coin World's* "Fair to Very Fine" column in December 1964.

"Coinology" for June 11, 1969, reported that the number of reeds on Winged Liberty Head and Roosevelt dimes varies from 104 to 118, an average of 111, so the statement was made that the number of reeds would probably vary also on all other denominations. The column also stated that "reeding counts are important in the study of any coinage and should be considered seriously." If the statement that the numbers of reeds varies in a series is true, it would make reeding less useful in studying fakes.

Both ornamented and lettered edges on coins to 1836 were made on a Castaing machine, consisting of two edge strips, one moving, the other not. Planchets were rolled between the two strips or "edge dies," pressing the edge device into the planchet before going to the coining press. Coins were then struck within an open collar slightly larger than the coin's diameter to avoid crushing the edge device.

Sometimes, either the planchets or the movable strip slipped, causing errors—repeated letters, missing letters, overlapping elements.

The same Castaing machine was used to make reeded edges up to 1836, reeds or grooves being used instead of letters. From 1836, a grooved collar or collar die, was used as it still is, with the edge receiving the reeding at the same instance as the coin is produced.

For more than half a century, the last U.S. coin struck for circulation with an edge device other than plain or reeded was the 1836 Capped Bust, Lettered Edge half dollar. That changed in 1907 with the introduction of the Indian Head gold $10 eagle and Striding Liberty gold $20 double eagle, both designed by Augustus Saint-Gaudens. The eagle had 46 raised stars, one for each state in the Union (later, 48); the double eagle, E PLURIBUS UNUM with the words of the motto separated by stars, all elements being raised. The edge devices were forming during striking by a three-part, segmented collar. After a coin was struck, the collar segments would spring apart, permitting ejection of the coin without damage to the edge devices. Production of both coins ended in 1933, bringing another end to U.S. coins with edge devices other than plain or reeded.

The Mint in 1992 during the XXV Olympiad commemorative coin program tested using an alternative edge device when it produced Uncirculated 1992-D Baseball silver dollars with the inscription XXV OLYMPIAD, alternating inverted four times. The inscription was applied post striking over a standard reeded edge.

Edge inscriptions on circulating U.S. coinage returned in 2007 with the first Presidential dollar, honoring George Washington. The sponsor of the legislation wanted to open up space on the obverse and reverse sides for larger design elements by moving the date and the two mottoes, IN GOD WE TRUST and E PLURIBUS UNUM, to the edge. When the Mint began designing the edge elements, it moved the Mint mark to the edge as well, although not a requirement.

To apply the edge devices, the Mint developed a system remarkably like that used from 1793 to 1836, though updated technologically. The coins were first struck with a plain collar, just like that used on the Sacagawea dollars, which used the same planchets. The struck coins were then transported to the edge inscription station. That equipment contains a semicircular edge die, bearing the edge devices formed by laser along a groove, and a steel wheel. Coins are fed into the entrance of the edge die and the wheel propels them along the groove. The wheel also applies the pressure needed to form the edge device.

The struck coins are fed into the edging equipment randomly. Therefore, the inscription may read "right side up" either facing the obverse or the reverse, and the inscription has no fixed starting point in relation to any specific point on obverse or reverse. Using two 2010 Andrew Johnson Presidential dollars pulled randomly from a roll for illustration, the date on one coin was at the 5:30 o'clock position when read from the obverse, while on the other the 2010 was at the 12 o'clock position when read from the obverse.

When the Native American dollars were introduced in 2009, using the same planchets as the earlier Sacagawea dollars and the Presidential dollars, they were given the same inscription as the 2009 and later Presidential dollars.

Because the edge inscribing process is a mechanical process, numerous errors have occurred (see the section on edges in the Errors chapter).

For the Proof versions of the Presidential and Native American dollars, the same edge devices are applied as appear on the circulating versions, though the method used to apply the inscriptions differs. A three-piece, segmented collar similar to that used starting in 1907 on the gold eagle and double eagle is used to form the inscriptions on the Proof coins.

A segmented collar is also used for forming the edge device on the 2010 and later Proof America the Beautiful quarter dollars. The edge device appears on one segment, with the other two segments blank.

What follows is a partial listing of the edge varieties found on U.S. coins. The listing does not include the errors found on Capped Bust half dollars, or Presidential dollars and Native American dollars since various repeated letters and numbers, overlapping edge elements and missing edge elements are often unique to an individual coin, the result of the mechanical process used.

On the earlier coins, different strips were used on Castaing machines, also, resulting in differences or varieties of ornamentation, lettering and more. Edge varieties and edge errors are two different things, as has always been true whether the edges contain letters, ornamental devices, reeding or a combination of any two or all of them.

We discuss varieties here, caused by changes in Castaing strips or collars as the case may be.

Half cents: Two leaf ornamentation in 1793; one leaf 1794 with both large and small lettering known; 1795, large letters or no letters (plain edges); 1796, plain edges only; 1797, medium and small letters, no leaf, and plain edge varieties, also a "Gripped" variety (rare); 1798 and after, plain edge only.

Large cents: 1793 vine and bars; two leaves; one leaf pointing down; one leaf pointing up (leaves accompany lettered edges); 1794, one leaf up, one leaf down; 1795, lettered edge, plain edge, reeded edge; 1796 and 1797, plain and partially gripped edges; 1798, plain and reeded edges; 1799 and thereafter, all plain edges.

Five-cent coins: 1882, normal plain edges, a few patterns known with five raised bars.

Half dimes: reeded from 1794 thereafter.

Dimes: reeded from 1796, with some changes in number of reeds from 1837 and possibly still varying through Winged Liberty Head and Roosevelt. According to the U.S. Mint in 1999, the count is 118.

Quarter dollars: Reeded from 1796 to now with probable variations over the years in number of reeds or spacing; from 1838 normal count is 119, but Walter Breen noted some 1876-CC coins with 153 reeds.

Half dollars: 1794 to 1806, lettered edge with words separated by stars, squares and circles, occasional lettering errors from slipping edge dies; 1807

to 1813, no star after dollar: 1814 to 1831, with star; 1830 and 1831, varieties with diagonal reeding between words; 1830 to 1836, star after dollar, varieties with vertical reeding between words; vertical reeding with no letters; 1837 and after, vertical reeding, with four different reeded collars used in 1837, and probably unstudied variations thereafter. The Kennedy half dollar has 150 reeds, according to the U.S. Mint in 1999.

Silver dollars: Lettered edge through 1803 with small designs separating words; 1840 to 1935, reeded edge with varieties possible. Normal is 188 reeds. Only positively known variety is a Philadelphia Mint 1921 Morgan with 154 reeds, known as 1921 Morgan, Infrequently Reeded Edge, discovered by Wolfson.

Trade dollars: Reeded edges with possibility of variations.

Eisenhower and Anthony dollars: Reeded, no studies known. According to the U.S. Mint, the Anthony dollar has 133 reeds.

Sacagawea golden dollar: Plain.

Presidential dollars: 2007, edge inscription: 2007 P [or D] E PLURIBUS UNUM • IN GOD WE TRUST •. Unknown number of error Proof 2007-S Thomas Jefferson dollars have out-of-sequence inscription elements resulting from two misplaced edge segments (not counting the stops): 2007 S / IN GOD WE TRUST / E PLURIBUS UNUM. For the four 2008 coins, an extra stop was added between the Mint mark and the first motto: 2008 P [or D] • E PLURIBUS UNUM • IN GOD WE TRUST •. 2009 and later: 2009 P [or D] ★ ★ ★ E PLURIBUS UNUM ★ ★ ★ ★ ★ ★ ★ ★ ★. One 2009 Zachary Taylor Presidential dollar is certified with a 2010-D edge inscription from Native American dollars.

Native American dollars: 2009 P [or D] ★ ★ ★ E PLURIBUS UNUM ★ ★ ★ ★ ★ ★ ★ ★ ★.

Gold dollars: Reeded edges with apparent variations between Mints and types, but not yet permanently identified.

Quarter eagles: Reeded edges from 1796; 1840 and after differ at branch Mints from P-Mint coins, the former having fewer reeds.

Three dollars: Reeded edges, with possible variations at branch Mints.

Half eagles: Same comment as gold $3 coins.

Eagles: To 1907, same comment. 1907 to 1911, 46 stars on edge; 1912 to 1933, 48 stars on edge (1912 with 46 stars possible but unknown yet).

Double eagles: To 1907, reeded edge without important variations; 1907 Roman Numerals, large letters on patterns, medium letters on regular issue; 1907 Arabic Numerals, small letters.

American Eagle: gold, silver, platinum bullion coins: reeded edges, no studies done.

America the Beautiful: 5-ounce silver bullion quarter dollars: .999 FINE SILVER 5.0 OUNCE.

Mottoes and other inscriptions

In the act establishing the Mint the devices and legends for the new coins were prescribed as follows: "Upon one side of each of the said coins there shall be an impression emblematic of liberty with an inscription of the word 'Liberty' and the year of the coinage; and upon the reverse of each of the gold and silver coins there shall be the figure or representation of an eagle, with the inscription, 'United States of America,' and upon the reverse of the copper coins there shall be an inscription which shall express the denomination of the piece."

Liberty

The word LIBERTY had appeared on most though not all U.S. coins, as required under the original 1792 act authorizing a federal Mint and coinage and by most subsequent coinage legislation. From 1851 to 1873, however, Congress gave Treasury and Mint officials greater latitude in selecting what inscriptions and devices to use on new coins, resulting in the word not being incorporated into the designs of several coins issued during that period.

The silver 3-cent coins, issued from 1851 to 1873, were the first U.S. coins to not bear LIBERTY, as permitted under the Act of March 3, 1851. The denomination was also the first U.S. coin to bear no image of Liberty. The coin's diminutive size (14 millimeters) gave the Mint's engraver little canvas for multiple legends and elaborate devices.

Shield 5-cent coins, issued 1866 to 1883, also lack the word LIBERTY and an allegorical representation of Liberty.

The Act of Feb. 12, 1873, codified U.S. coinage law. Among its many provisions was the requirement that LIBERTY appear on each coin.

In 1892, however, Congress began authorizing the production of commemorative coinage. Many of the commemorative coins issued from 1892 to 1954 lack LIBERTY, and many bear no allegorical depiction of Liberty. All 1982 and later commemorative coins, however, bear the word.

When the Presidential dollar series was authorized in 2005, the legislation permitted the omission of the word LIBERTY, with the depiction of the Statue of Liberty on the reverse of each coin considered a substitute for the missing word.

E Pluribus Unum

Two official mottoes have appeared on many of the coins of the United States, the one from almost the beginning of the national coinage, and the other since the Civil War. Neither, however, has had an uninterrupted history, nor has either been employed on all the denominations of the series.

The motto E PLURIBUS UNUM was first used on U.S. coinage in 1796, when the reverse of the quarter eagle (gold $2.50 coin) presented the main features of the Great Seal, on the scroll of which this inscription belongs. The same device was placed on certain of the silver coins in 1798, and so the motto was soon found on all the coins in the precious metals. In 1834, it was dropped from most of the gold coins to mark the change in the standard fineness of the coins. In 1837 it was dropped from the silver coins, marking the era of the Revised Mint Code.

The Act of Feb. 12, 1873, made this inscription a requirement of law upon the coins of the United States. A search will reveal, however, that it does not appear on all coins struck after 1873, and that not until much later were the provisions of this act followed in their entirety. From information contained in Mint records it would appear that officials did not consider the provisions of the law mandatory, but rather, discretionary. The motto does appear on all coins currently being manufactured.

The motto as it appears on U.S. coins means "One Out of Many," and doubtless has reference to the unity of the early states. It is said that Colonel Reed of Uxbridge, Mass., was instrumental in having it placed on the coins.

In God We Trust

From the records of the Treasury Department it appears that the first suggestion of the recognition of the Deity on the coins of the United States was contained in a letter addressed to the secretary of the Treasury, by the Rev. M.R. Watkinson, minister of the gospel, Ridleyville, Pa., dated Nov. 13, 1861.

This letter states:

"One fact touching our currency has hitherto been seriously overlooked. I mean the recognition of the Almighty God in some form in our coins.

"You are probably a Christian. What if our Republic were now shattered beyond reconstruction? Would not the antiquaries of succeeding centuries rightly reason from our past that we were a heathen nation? What I propose is that instead of the goddess of liberty we shall have next inside the 13 stars a ring inscribed with the words 'perpetual union'; within this ring the all-seeing eye, crowned with a halo; beneath this eye the American flag, bearing in its field stars equal to the number of the States united; in the folds of the bars the words 'God, liberty, law.'

"This would make a beautiful coin, to which no possible citizen could object. This would relieve us from the ignominy of heathenism. This would place us openly under the Divine protection we have personally claimed. From my heart I have felt our national shame in disowning God as not the least of our present national disasters.

"To you first I address a subject that must be agitated."

Under date of Nov. 20, 1861, the secretary of the Treasury addressed the following letter to the director of the Mint:

"Dear Sir: No nation can be strong except in the strength of God, or safe except in His defense. The trust of our people in God should be declared on our national coins.

"You will cause a device to be prepared without unnecessary delay with a motto expressing in the fewest and tersest words possible this national recognition."

It was found that the Act of Jan. 18, 1837, prescribed the mottoes and devices that should be placed upon the coins of the United States, so that nothing could be done without legislation.

In December 1863, the director of the Mint submitted to the secretary of the Treasury for approval designs for new 1-, 2-, and 3-cent coins, on which it was proposed that one of the following mottoes should appear: "Our country; our God"; "God, our Trust."

The secretary of the Treasury, in a letter to the Director of the Mint, dated Dec. 9, 1863, states:

"I approve your mottoes, only suggesting that on that with the Washington obverse the motto should begin with the word 'Our,' so as to read: 'Our God and our country.' And on that with the shield, it should be changed so as to read: 'In God We Trust.'"

An act passed April 22, 1864, changing the composition of the cent and authorizing the coinage of the 2-cent coin, the devices of which were to be fixed by the director of the Mint, with the approval of the secretary of the Treasury, and it is upon the bronze 2-cent coin that the motto IN GOD WE TRUST first appears.

The Act of March 3, 1865, provided that "in addition to the legend and devices on the gold and silver coins of the United States, it should be lawful for the director of the mint, with the approval of the Secretary of the Treasury, to cause the motto 'In God we trust' on such coins hereafter to be issued as shall admit of such legend thereon." Under this act, the motto was placed upon the double eagle, eagle and half eagle, and also upon the dollar, half dollar and quarter dollar in 1866.

The Coinage Act of Feb. 12, 1873, provided that the secretary of the Treasury could cause the motto "In God We Trust" to be inscribed on coins as space and design permitted.

When the double eagle and eagle of new design appeared in 1907, it was soon discovered that the religious motto had been omitted. In response to a general demand, Congress ordered it restored, and the Act of May 18, 1908, made mandatory its appearance on all coins upon which it had appeared before. The motto appears on all gold and silver coins struck since July 1, 1908, with the exception of Barber

dimes. It was not mandatory upon the cent and 5-cent coins, but could be placed thereon by the secretary of the Treasury, or the director of the Mint with the secretary's approval.

The issuance of the cent in 1909 honoring the centennial of the birth of Abraham Lincoln brought the motto IN GOD WE TRUST to the smallest denomination U.S. coin. This was an appropriate tribute to Lincoln, one of the most deeply spiritual presidents.

Almost another three decades would pass before the motto was carried over to the one remaining coin in the U.S. series that did not carry it, the 5-cent coin. In 1938, a design for this coin was chosen as a result of a nationwide competition. Michigan sculptor Felix Schlag created the designs selected, honoring Thomas Jefferson. The obverse design bears the motto.

The act approved July 11, 1955, makes appearance of the motto IN GOD WE TRUST mandatory upon all coins and paper money of the United States. Except for some error pieces, it has appeared on U.S. coins since that time.

Placement of the motto on one series of 21st century coinage, however, proved controversial, prompting Congress to reverse itself. The legislation authorizing the Presidential dollars ordered that both national mottoes, E PLURIBUS UNUM and IN GOD WE TRUST, be placed on the edge of the coin to create less cluttered fields on the obverse and reverse. For the circulating versions of the Presidential dollars, the edge inscription is added after striking. Thus, when 50,000 or more 2007 Presidential dollars were struck at the Philadelphia Mint but then were taken directly to the bagging station, bypassing the edge inscribing station, the coins were not given their edge inscription. Complaints arose about these "God-less dollars" in some religious quarters. In addition, complaints were raised by some that the placement of the motto on the edge made it insufficiently prominent on the coin.

Congress reacted to the complaints by reversing itself and ordering the motto moved from the edge to the obverse or reverse. Since 2009, the motto has appeared on the obverses of the Presidential dollars.

The motto's appearance on coinage has been controversial. Atheist organizations and individual atheists have sued the government in federal courts on several occasions, stating that the use of the motto on federal coinage and paper money violates the First Amendment of the U.S. Constitution. Several of these cases have been appealed to the U.S. Supreme Court, and in each suit, the motto has ultimately been ruled as constitutional.

Symbols

Eagle

The eagle was a favorite device of the United States' founding fathers before it was placed on U.S. national coinage.

It appears on the Great Seal of the United States,

which was adopted in 1782. At this time the states established their own mints and Massachusetts saw fit to place on the reverse of its coins a spread eagle with arrows and an olive branch in the claws.

When the Mint was established the devices and

legends for the new coins were prescribed. It was ordered that "upon the reverse of each of the gold and silver coins there shall be the figure or representation of an eagle." However, the act of Jan. 18, 1837, removed the legal requirement for the half dime and dime. Subsequent gold and silver coins—the silver 3-cent coin, the gold dollar and the gold $3 coin —were not required to have an eagle on the reverse.

The eagle on the reverse of the Franklin half dollar, introduced in 1948, is very small. The Liberty Bell is the most prominent device on the reverse of the Franklin half dollar, with a diminutive eagle to the right of the bell. The story that Franklin preferred the wild turkey over the bald eagle as a symbol of American pride is well known among collectors.

When designs were selected for the Bicentennial commemorative coins (struck in 1975 and 1976), three concepts were chosen that do not bear an eagle. Likewise, the requirement that the quarter dollar bear an eagle on the reverse was dropped for the 50-coin State circulating commemorative quarter dollar program from 1999 through 2008, as well as for the 2009 quarter dollar program honoring the District of Columbia and the U.S. territories, and the 2010 and later America the Beautiful quarter dollars.

An eagle appears on all American Eagle gold, silver and platinum bullion coins, although the eagle elements on some of the Proof versions of the platinum coins have been only a minor part of the designs. Starting with Proof 2009 American Eagle platinum coins, a tiny eagle privy mark appears on the coins.

Portraits

With the exception of great statesman Benjamin Franklin and great feminist Susan B. Anthony, the only individuals whose images appear on regular issue U.S. coins are U.S. presidents. The Indian used on the 5-cent coin introduced in 1913 is not the image of any individual but is a composite of several Indians studied by the designer (identified as Iron Tail, Two Moons and Chief John Tree). Likewise, the image of Sacagawea appearing on dollar coins since 2000 is based on a modern model, not on any contemporary image of Sacagawea (none exists). One of the most popular designs has been the allegorical Liberty who appears on many U.S. coins.

Use of "v" in Trust

In medieval times the letters "u" and "v" were used interchangeably. These letters were not given separate alphabetical listings in English dictionaries until about 1800. In recent times many sculptors have used the "V" in place of "U" for artistic reasons, such as, to represent the permanence and long time significance of their work. Artists who design coins may choose to spell "Trust" with a "V." All of the dollars of the Peace dollar design have this characteristic. From 1921 through 1935 the United States Mints made more than 190 million dollars of this type.

It is interesting to note that sometimes the "V" is similarly used in wording on public buildings.

Designer's initials

The custom of placing the signature of the engraver upon a coin die dates from remote antiquity. Many Greek coins, especially in the creations produced by the cities of Sicily and Magna Graecia, are signed with the initials of the artist, and in some cases his full name. The same practice prevailed generally in the European countries. There were no initials on United States coins until the gold dollar appeared in 1849 with the initial of Longacre, L, on the truncation of the bust.

In recent years, the Mint has adopted the custom of using on some coins the initials of both the designer and the engraver of the designs.

Some controversies involving designer's initials have been addressed elsewhere in this chapter.

Other symbols

Arrows were sometimes used on U.S. coins to symbolize preparedness. Olive branches or leaves are found often also. Symbolizing peace, the olive branch is the international emblem of friendship and accord. The fasces on the reverse of the Winged Liberty Head dime has a bundle of rods with protruding ax as the central device. It has been since ancient times a symbol of official authority. Also on this dime, the winged cap on the Roman style Liberty Head symbolizes freedom of thought.

The Roosevelt dime bears some representative symbols also. In the center of the reverse is a torch signifying liberty bounded by an olive branch on the left and an oak branch signifying strength and independence on the right.

The Kennedy half dollar contains much symbolism. The presidential coat of arms forms the motif for the reverse. The coat of arms depicts the American eagle holding the olive branch in his right claw and arrows in the left.

Symbolism on the coat of arms derived from the 13 original states governs the number of olive leaves, berries, arrows, stars and cloud puffs.

The upper part of the flag or shield upon the breast of the eagle represents the Congress binding the Colonies into an entity. The vertical stripes complete the motif of the flag of the United States. Each state of the United States is represented in the 50 stars that ring Frank Gasparro's reverse design on the Kennedy half dollar.

Issue dates, designers, original engravers, and models

The following table lists issue dates, designers, engravers and models or source of inspiration for all circulating U.S. coins.

Under the Design Type category, the design reference on the first line describes the obverse design. The second line describes the reverse design. For some coins, more than one reverse design was used with the same obverse design; all are listed.

It should be noted that for some early designs, researchers have debated who designed a particular coin; on occasion, some disagreement may result. The designer is the individual credited with the two-dimensional design concept, which could have been in the form of a sketch, painting, computer drawing or some other two-dimensional artistic medium. The engraver is the individual crediting with preparing the three-dimensional model, whether sculptured by hand (as from 1792 to the early 21st century) or by computer (since early in the 21st century).

The model or other source represents the inspiration for the design. Many designers have used busts and portraits by other artists as inspiration for their designs.

Half cents

Design Type	Issue Dates	Designers[1]	Original Engraver	Model or Source
Liberty Cap, Left	1793	Obv: Adam Eckfeldt	Adam Eckfeldt	Dupre's Libertas Americana medal
Wreath		Rev: Adam Eckfeldt	Adam Eckfeldt	Original design
Liberty Cap, Right, Large Head	1794	Obv: Robert Scot	Robert Scot	Similar to previous issue, but reversed
Wreath		Rev: Robert Scot	Robert Scot	Similar to previous issue
Liberty Cap, Right, Small Head	1795 to 1797	Obv: R. Scot-John Gardner	Robert Scot	Similar to previous issue
Wreath		Rev: R. Scot-John Gardner	Robert Scot	Similar to previous issue
Draped Bust	1800 to 1808	Obv: Gilbert Stuart-Scot	Robert Scot	Ann Willing Bingham (or not)
Wreath		Rev: Scot-Gardner	Robert Scot	Similar to previous issue
Classic Head	1809 to 1836	Obv: John Reich	John Reich	Unknown model
Wreath		Rev: John Reich	John Reich	Original design
Coronet	1840 to 1857	Obv: Scot-Christian Gobrecht	Christian Gobrecht	Coronet Type large cent
Wreath		Rev: John Reich-C. Gobrecht	Christian Gobrecht	Similar to previous issue

Large cents

Type	Issue Dates	Designers[1]	Original Engraver	Model or Source
Flowing Hair	1793	Obv: Henry Voigt	Henry Voigt	Unknown model
Chain		Rev: Henry Voigt	Henry Voigt	Fugio cent (?)
Flowing Hair	1793	Obv: H. Voigt-Adam Eckfeldt	Adam Eckfeldt	Similar to previous issue
Wreath		Rev: Adam Eckfeldt	Adam Eckfeldt	Original design
Liberty Cap	1793 to 1794	Obv: Joseph Wright	Joseph Wright	Dupre's Libertas Americana medal, portrait reversed
Wreath		Rev: Joseph Wright	Joseph Wright	Similar to previous issue
Liberty Cap, Modified	1794 to 1796	Obv: J. Wright-J. Gardner	Robert Scot	Similar to previous issue
Wreath		Rev: J. Wright-J. Gardner	Robert Scot	Similar to previous issue
Draped Bust	1796 to 1807	Obv: Gilbert Stuart-R. Scot	Robert Scot	Ann Willing Bingham (?)
Wreath		Rev: Joseph Wright-R. Scot	Robert Scot	Similar to previous issue
Classic Head	1808 to 1814	Obv: John Reich	John Reich	Unknown model
Wreath		Rev: John Reich	John Reich	Original design
Coronet, Matron Head	1816 to 1835	Obv: Robert Scot	Robert Scot	Unknown model
Wreath		Rev: John Reich	John Reich	Same as previous issue
Coronet, Modified Matron Head	1835 to 1839	Obv: Scot-Christian Gobrecht	Christian Gobrecht	Similar to previous issue
Wreath		Rev: John Reich	John Reich	Same as previous issue
Coronet, Braided Hair	1839 to 1857	Obv: Scot-Christian Gobrecht	Christian Gobrecht	Similar to previous issue
Wreath		Rev: Reich-Christian Gobrecht	Christian Gobrecht	Similar to previous issue

Small cents

Design Type	Issue Dates	Designers[1]	Original Engraver	Model or Source
Flying Eagle	1856 to 1858	Obv: Christian Gobrecht-James B. Longacre	James B. Longacre	Titian Peale's design for dollar reverse, c. 1836
Agricultural Wreath		Rev: James B. Longacre	James B. Longacre	Reverse of gold $1 & $3
Indian Head	1859 to 1909	Obv: James B. Longacre	James B. Longacre	Possibly Longacre's daughter Sarah
Laurel Wreath		Rev: James B. Longacre	James B. Longacre	Original design
Oak Wreath				
F and Shield		Rev: James B. Longacre	James B. Longacre	Original design

Small cents (continued)

Design Type	Issue Dates	Designers[1]	Original Engraver	Model or Source
Lincoln Head	1909 to 1958	Obv: Victor D. Brenner	Charles Barber	Brenner's plaque
Wheat Stalks		Rev: Victor D. Brenner	Charles Barber	Original design
Lincoln Head	1959 to 2008	Obv: Victor D. Brenner	Charles Barber	Same as previous issue
Lincoln Memorial		Rev: Frank Gasparro	Gilroy Roberts	Lincoln Memorial
Lincoln Head	2009	Obv: Victor D. Brenner	Charles Barber	Same as previous issue
Childhood in Kentucky		Rev: Richard Masters	Jim Licaretz	Lincoln birthplace log cabin recreation
Formative Years in Indiana		Rev: Charles L. Vickers	Charles L. Vickers	Original design
Professional Life in Illinois		Rev: Joel Iskowitz	Donald Everhart II	Original design
Presidency in Washington, D.C.		Rev: Susan Gamble	Joseph F. Menna	Original model
Lincoln Head	2010 to date	Obv: Brenner	Unnamed Mint staff	Same as previous issue
Union Shield		Rev: Lyndall Bass	Joseph F. Menna	Various 19th century shields

Two-cent coins

Design Type	Issue Dates	Designers[1]	Original Engraver	Model or Source
Shield	1864 to 1873	Obv: James B. Longacre	James B. Longacre	Original design
Wheat Wreath		Rev: James B. Longacre	James B. Longacre	Original design

Silver 3-cent coins

Design Type	Issue Dates	Designers[1]	Original Engraver	Model or Source
Star	1851 to 1873	Obv: James B. Longacre	James B. Longacre	Original design (three subtypes)
Large C		Rev: James B. Longacre	James B. Longacre	Original design (two subtypes)

Copper-nickel 3-cent coins

Design Type	Issue Dates	Designers[1]	Original Engraver	Model or Source
Coronet	1865 to 1889	Obv: James B. Longacre	James B. Longacre	Possibly Sarah Longacre
Laurel Wreath		Rev: James B. Longacre	James B. Longacre	Original design

Half dimes

Design Type	Issue Dates	Designers[1]	Original Engraver	Model or Source
Flowing Hair	1794 to 1795	Obv: Robert Scot	Robert Scot	Unknown model
Small Eagle		Rev: Robert Scot	Robert Scot	Original design
Draped Bust	1796 to 1797	Obv: Gilbert Stuart-R. Scot	Robert Scot	Ann Willing Bingham (?)
Small Eagle		Rev: R. Scot-John Eckstein (?)	Robert Scot	Similar to previous issue
Draped Bust	1800 to 1805	Obv: Gilbert Stuart-R. Scot	Robert Scot	Same as previous issue
Heraldic Eagle		Rev: Robert Scot	Robert Scot	Great Seal of the United States
Capped Bust	1829 to 1837	Obv: John Reich-W. Kneass	William Kneass	Unknown model (similar to dime by Reich)
Eagle and Shield		Rev: John Reich-W. Kneass	William Kneass	Original design (similar to dime by Reich)
Seated Liberty, No Drapery[2]	1837 to 1840	Obv: Christian Gobrecht	Christian Gobrecht	Drawing by Thomas Sully
Laurel Wreath		Rev: Christian Gobrecht	Christian Gobrecht	Original design
Seated Liberty, With Drapery	1840 to 1859	Obv: C. Gobrecht-R. Hughes	Christian Gobrecht	Similar to previous issue
Laurel Wreath		Rev: Christian Gobrecht	Christian Gobrecht	Same as previous issue
Seated Liberty, Legend	1860 to 1873	Obv: C. Gobrecht-R. Hughes-J.B. Longacre	James B. Longacre	Similar to previous issue
Cereal Wreath		Rev: James B. Longacre	James B. Longacre	Original design

Copper-nickel 5-cent coins

Design Type	Issue Dates	Designers[1]	Original Engraver	Model or Source
Shield	1866 to 1883	Obv: James B. Longacre	James B. Longacre	Original design
Stars and Rays; Stars, No Rays subtypes		Rev: James B. Longacre	James B. Longacre	Original design
Liberty Head	1883 to 1912	Obv: Charles Barber	Charles Barber	Unknown model
Cotton and Corn Wreath		Rev: Charles Barber	Charles Barber	Original design (two varieties)
Indian Head	1913 to 1938	Obv: James E. Fraser	Charles Barber	Composite of three Indians
Bison on Mound; Bison on Plain subtypes		Rev: James E. Fraser	Charles Barber	"Black Diamond," Central Park Zoo

Copper-nickel 5-cent coins (continued)

Design Type	Issue Dates	Designers[1]	Original Engraver	Model or Source
Jefferson Head Monticello	1938-2004	Obv: Felix Schlag Rev: Felix Schlag	John R. Sinnock John R. Sinnock	1789 Bust by Houdon Monticello
Jefferson Head Peace Medal Keelboat	2004	Obv: Felix Schlag Rev: Norman E. Nemeth Rev: Al Maletsky	John R. Sinnock Norman E. Nemeth Al Maletsky	1789 Bust by Houdon 1804 Indian peace medal by John Reich Historical references
Jefferson Head American Bison Ocean in View	2005	Obv: Joseph Fitzgerald Rev: Jamie Franki Rev: Joseph Fitzgerald	Donald Everhart II Norman E. Nemeth Donna Weaver	1789 Bust by Houdon Original design Photo by Andrew E. Cier
Jefferson Head Monticello (restored from 1938 version)	2006 to date	Obv: Jamie Franki Rev: Felix Schlag	Donna Weaver John Mercanti	1800 painting by Rembrandt Peale Monticello

Dimes

Design Type	Issue Dates	Designers[1]	Original Engraver	Model or Source
Draped Bust Small Eagle	1796 to 1797	Obv: Gilbert Stuart-R. Scot Rev: R. Scot-John Eckstein (?)	Robert Scot Robert Scot	Ann Willing Bingham (?) Similar to Scot's 1794 silver reverse
Draped Bust Heraldic Eagle	1798 to 1807	Obv: Gilbert Stuart-R. Scot Rev: Robert Scot	Robert Scot Robert Scot	Same as previous issue Great Seal of the United States
Capped Bust[3] Eagle and Shield	1809 to 1837	Obv: John Reich Rev: John Reich	John Reich John Reich	Unknown model Original design
Seated Liberty, No Drapery, No Stars and With Stars[2]				
Laurel Wreath	1837 to 1840	Obv: Christian Gobrecht Rev: Christian Gobrecht	Christian Gobrecht Christian Gobrecht	Drawing by Thomas Sully Original design
Seated Liberty, With Drapery				
Laurel Wreath	1840 to 1860	Obv: C. Gobrecht-Hughes Rev: Christian Gobrecht	Christian Gobrecht Christian Gobrecht	Similar to previous issue Same as previous issue
Seated Liberty, Legend Cereal Wreath	1860 to 1891	Obv: C. Gobrecht- R. Hughes-J.B. Longacre Rev: James B. Longacre	James B. Longacre James B. Longacre	Similar to previous issue Original design
Barber Cereal Wreath	1892 to 1916	Obv: Charles Barber Rev: James B. Longacre	Charles Barber James B. Longacre	French medal designs Same as previous issue
Winged Liberty Head Fasces with Axe Head, Olive Branch	1916 to 1945	Obv: Adolph A. Weinman Rev: Adolph A. Weinman	Charles Barber Charles Barber	Elsie Kachel Moll Stevens, Soldiers and Sailors War Memorial details, Baltimore Details from Baltimore War Memorial, by Weinman, 1909
Roosevelt Head Torch, with Oak and Olive Branches	1946-	Obv: John R. Sinnock Rev: John R. Sinnock	John R. Sinnock John R. Sinnock	Original design Original design

Twenty cents

Design Type	Issue Dates	Designers[1]	Original Engraver	Model or Source
Twenty cents Eagle	1875 to 1878	Obv: C. Gobrecht- R. Hughes-W. Barber Rev: William Barber	William Barber William Barber	Seated Liberty dollar Original design

Quarter dollars

Design Type	Issue Dates	Designers[1]	Original Engraver	Model or Source
Draped Bust Small Eagle	1796	Obv: Gilbert Stuart-R. Scot Rev: R. Scot-John Eckstein (?)	Robert Scot Robert Scot	Ann Willing Bingham (?) Similar to Scot's 1794 silver reverse
Draped Bust Heraldic Eagle	1804 to 1807	Obv: G. Stuart-R. Scot Rev: Scot	Robert Scot Scot	Same as previous issue Great Seal of the United States
Capped Bust[4] Eagle and Shield	1815 to 1838	Obv: Reich Rev: Reich	Reich Reich	Unknown model Original design (c. 1807)
Seated Liberty, No Drapery Eagle and Shield	1838 to 1840	Obv: Gobrecht Rev: Reich-Kneass- Gobrecht	Gobrecht Gobrecht	Drawing by Thomas Sully Similar to previous issue

Quarter dollars (continued)

Design Type	Issue Dates	Designers[1]	Original Engraver	Model or Source
Seated Liberty, With Drapery	1840 to 1891	Obv: Gobrecht-Hughes	Gobrecht	Similar to previous issue
Eagle and Shield		Rev: Reich-Kneass-Gobrecht	Gobrecht	Same as previous issue
Barber	1892 to 1916	Obv: C. Barber	C. Barber	French medal designs
Heraldic Eagle		Rev: C. Barber	C. Barber	Great Seal of the United States
Standing Liberty	1916 to 1930	Obv: Hermon A. MacNeil	C. Barber	Dora Doscher (two versions)
Flying Eagle		Rev: Hermon A. MacNeil	C. Barber	Original design (two versions)
Washington Head	1932 to 1998	Obv: John Flanagan	Sinnock	Bust by Houdon (1785)
Eagle		Rev: John Flanagan	Sinnock	Original design
Bicentennial, Independence Hall		Rev: Jack L. Ahr	Frank Gasparro	Original design
Delaware	1999	Eddy Seger, others	William C. Cousins	Caesar Rodney riding to Philadelphia, July 1776
Pennsylvania	1999	Donald Carlucci	John Mercanti	Montage including state map, Commonwealth statue by Rolan H. Perry
New Jersey	1999	None identified	Al Maletsky	Painting by Emmanuel Leutze, *Washington Crossing the Delaware*
Georgia	1999	Bill Fivaz, Caroline Leake, Susan Royal	James Ferrell	Montage including state map, peach
Connecticut	1999	Andy Jones	James Ferrell	Charter Oak
Massachusetts	2000	Two unidentified children	Thomas D. Rogers Sr.	Montage with state map, Chester French's Minuteman statue
Maryland	2000	Bill Krawczewicz	Thomas D. Rogers Sr.	Maryland State House
South Carolina	2000	None identified	Thomas D. Rogers Sr.	Montage of state map, bird, flower and tree
New Hampshire	2000	William C. Cousins	William C. Cousins	Rock formation Old Man of the Mountain
Virginia	2000	Paris Ashton	Edgar Z. Steever IV	Ships of Jamestown colonists
New York	2001	Daniel Carr	Al Maletsky	Statue of Liberty, state map
North Carolina	2001	Mary Ellen Robinson	John Mercanti	Dec. 3, 1903, photograph by John P. Daniels of Wright Brothers flight
Rhode Island	2001	Daniel Carr	Thomas D. Rogers Sr.	Sailboat *Reliance*, Pell Bridge
Vermont	2001	Sarah-Lee Terrat	James Ferrell	Maple trees tapped for sap
Kentucky	2001	None identified	James Ferrell	Home and horse with fence
Tennessee	2002	Shawn Stookey	Donna Weaver	Montage of musical instruments
Ohio	2002	None identified	Donna Weaver	Montage of state map, 1903 Wright Flyer and Apollo 11 astronaut on moon from photograph of Edwin "Buzz" Aldrin by Neil Armstrong
Louisiana	2002	None identified	John Mercanti	Montage of state map, pelican and trumpet with musical notes
Indiana	2002	Josh Harvey	Donna Weaver	Montage of state map and Indianapolis 500 race car
Mississippi	2002	None identified	Donna Weaver	Magnolia blossoms and leaves
Illinois	2003	None identified	Donna Weaver	Montage of state map, Chicago skyline and Lincoln statue
Alabama	2003	None identified	Norman E. Nemeth	Seated Helen Keller, pine branch and camellia flowers, Braille inscription
Maine	2003	Daniel Carr, Leland and Carolyn Pendleton	Donna Weaver	Pemaquid Lighthouse and schooner Victory Chimes
Missouri	2003	Paul Jackson	Al Maletsky	Saint Louis Arch with small boat carrying three men from Corps of Discovery
Arkansas	2003	Ariston Jacks	John Mercanti	Montage of diamond, mallard duck, marsh and pine trees
Michigan	2004	None identified	Donna Weaver	Map of Great Lakes with Michigan highlighted
Florida	2004	Ralph Butler	James Ferrell	Montage of palm trees, Spanish galleon and space shuttle
Texas	2004	Daniel Miller	Norman E. Nemeth	State map and Lone Star symbol
Iowa	2004	None identified	John Mercanti	Based on Grant Wood painting *Arbor Day*
Wisconsin	2004	Rose Marty	Al Maletsky	Montage of wheel of cheese, corn and cow's head

Quarter dollars (continued)

Design Type	Issue Dates	Designers[1]	Original Engraver	Model or Source
California	2005	Garrett Burke	Donald Everhart II	John Muir, Half Dome from Yosemite Valley
Minnesota	2005	None identified	Charles L. Vickers	Montage of state map, lake scene with two sport fishermen in boat, loon
Oregon	2005	Donna Weaver	Donna Weaver	Crater Lake with Wizard Island
Kansas	2005	None identified	Norman E. Nemeth	Bison and sunflowers
West Virginia	2005	None identified	John Mercanti	New River Gorge Bridge
Nevada	2006	Donald Everhart II	Donald Everhart II	Three mustang horses in full gallop
Nebraska	2006	Rick Masters	Charles L. Vickers	Chimney Rock, covered wagon
Colorado	2006	Leonard Buckley	Norman E. Nemeth	Rocky Mountains scene
South Dakota	2006	Michael Leidel	John Mercanti	Two bison in the Badlands
North Dakota	2006	Donna Weaver	Donna Weaver	Mount Rushmore by Gutzon Borglum, pheasant in flight and stalks of wheat
Montana	2007	Donna Weaver	Donald Everhart II	Cattle skull and landscape
Washington	2007	Charles L. Vickers	Charles L. Vickers	Leaping salmon and mountains
Idaho	2007	Donna Weaver	Norman E. Nemeth	Peregrine falcon and state map
Wyoming	2007	Donna Weaver	Norman E. Nemeth	State symbol of bucking horse and rider
Utah	2007	Joseph F. Menna	Joseph F. Menna	Completion of transcontinental railroad
Oklahoma	2008	Susan Gamble	Phebe Hemphill	Montage of scissor-tailed flycatcher and blossoms and stems of Indian blanket
New Mexico	2008	Donald Everhart II	Donald Everhart II	Map of state and Zuni sun symbol
Arizona	2008	Joel Iskowitz	Joseph F. Menna	Grand Canyon and desert scenes
Alaska	2008	Susan Gamble	Charles L. Vickers	Grizzly bear catching salmon
Hawaii	2008	Donald Everhart II	Donald Everhart II	Map of state with statue of Kamehameha the Great
District of Columbia	2009	Joel Iskowitz	Donald Everhart II	Duke Ellington at piano, sheet music
Puerto Rico	2009	Joseph F. Menna	Joseph F. Menna	Sentry box and hibiscus
Guam	2009	Jim Licaretz	Jim Licaretz	Outline of island, flying proa, latte stone
American Samoa	2009	Stephen Clark	Charles L. Vickers	Ava bowl, island images
U.S. Virgin Islands	2009	Joseph F. Menna	Joseph F. Menna	Islands, various island images
Northern Marina Islands	2009	Richard Masters	Phebe Hemphill	Latte stone, canoe sailing in lagoon
Hot Springs	2010	Donald Everhart II	Joseph F. Menna	Fountain, headquarters entrance
Yellowstone	2010	Donald Everhart II	Donald Everhart II	Bison bull, Old Faithful geyser
Yosemite	2010	Joseph F. Menna	Phebe Hemphill	El Capitan
Grand Canyon	2010	Phebe Hemphill	Phebe Hemphill	Granaries at Marble Canyon
Mount Hood	2010	Phebe Hemphill	Phebe Hemphill	Mount Hood, Lost Lake
Gettysburg	2011	Joel Iskowitz	Phebe Hemphill	72nd Pennsylvania Infantry Monument
Glacier	2011	Barbara Fox	Charles Vickers	Mount Reynolds, mountain goat
Olympic	2011	Susan Gamble	Michael Gaudioso	Gravel river bar of the Hoh River with a view of Mount Olympus
Vicksburg	2011	Thomas Cleveland	Joseph F. Menna	*USS Cairo* on the Yazoo River
Chickasaw	2011	Donna Weaver	Jim Licaretz	Lincoln Bridge

Half dollars

Design Type	Issue Dates	Designers[1]	Original Engraver	Model or Source
Flowing Hair Small Eagle	1794 to 1795	Obv: Robert Scot Rev: Robert Scot	Robert Scot Robert Scot	Unknown model Original design
Draped Bust Small Eagle	1796 to 1797	Obv: Gilbert Stuart-R. Scot Rev: R. Scot-John Eckstein	Robert Scot Robert Scot	Ann Willing Bingham (?) Similar to previous issue
Draped Bust Heraldic Eagle	1801 to 1807	Obv: Gilbert Stuart-R. Scot Rev: Robert Scot	Robert Scot Robert Scot	Same as previous issue Great Seal of the United States
Capped Bust[5] Eagle and Shield, 50 c.	1807 to 1836	Obv: John Reich Rev: John Reich	John Reich John Reich	Unknown model Original design
Capped Bust Eagle and Shield, 50 CENTS	1836 to 1837	Obv: John Reich-C. Gobrecht Rev: John Reich-C. Gobrecht	Christian Gobrecht Christian Gobrecht	Similar to previous issue Similar to previous issue
Capped Bust Eagle and Shield, HALF DOL.	1838 to 1839	Obv: John Reich-C. Gobrecht Rev: John Reich-C. Gobrecht	Christian Gobrecht Christian Gobrecht	Same as previous issue Similar to previous issue
Seated Liberty Eagle and Shield	1839 to 1891	Obv: Christian Gobrecht Rev: John Reich-C. Gobrecht	Christian Gobrecht Christian Gobrecht	Drawing by Thomas Sully Similar to previous issue

Half dollars (continued)

Design Type	Issue Dates	Designers[1]	Original Engraver	Model or Source
Barber Heraldic Eagle	1892 to 1915	Obv: Charles Barber Rev: Charles Barber	Charles Barber Charles Barber	French medal designs Great Seal of the United States
Walking Liberty Eagle on Mountain Crag	1916 to 1947	Obv: Adolph A. Weinman Rev: Adolph A. Weinman	Charles Barber Charles Barber	Roty's Sower design on French silver 1907 gold award medal, American Institute of Architects, by Weinman
Franklin Liberty Bell, Eagle	1948 to 1963	Obv: John R. Sinnock Rev: John R. Sinnock	Gilroy Roberts Gilroy Roberts	Bust by Houdon (1778) Sesquicentennial half
Kennedy Eagle Bicentennial, Independence Hall	1964 to date	Obv: Gilroy Roberts Rev: Frank Gasparro Rev: Seth G. Huntington	Gilroy Roberts Gilroy Roberts Frank Gasparro	U.S. Mint medal Seal of the president of the United States Independence Hall

Silver dollars, nonsilver dollars

Design Type	Issue Dates	Designers[1]	Original Engraver	Model or Source
Flowing Hair Small Eagle on Rock	1794 to 1795	Obv: Robert Scot Rev: Robert Scot	Robert Scot Robert Scot	Unknown model Original design
Draped Bust Small Eagle on Clouds	1795 to 1798	Obv: Gilbert Stuart-R. Scot Rev: R. Scot-John Eckstein (?)	Robert Scot Robert Scot	Ann Willing Bingham(?) Similar to previous issue
Draped Bust Heraldic Eagle	1798 to 1804	Obv: Gilbert Stuart-R. Scot Rev: Robert Scot	Robert Scot Robert Scot	Same as previous issue Great Seal of the United States
Seated Liberty[6] Flying Eagle	1836 to 1839	Obv: Gobrecht Rev: Gobrecht	Gobrecht Gobrecht	Drawing by Thomas Sully Drawing by Titian Peale
Seated Liberty Eagle and Shield	1840 to 1873	Obv: Gobrecht-Robert Hughes Rev: John Reich-Gobrecht	Christian Gobrecht Christian Gobrecht	Similar to pattern issue Reich's 1807 reverse for silver
Trade dollar Eagle	1873 to 1883	Obv: William Barber Rev: William Barber	William Barber William Barber	Unknown model Original design
Liberty Head Eagle and Wreath	1878 to 1921	Obv: George T. Morgan Rev: George T. Morgan	George T. Morgan George T. Morgan	Anna W. Williams Original design
Peace Eagle on Rock	1921 to 1935	Obv: Anthony DeFrancisci Rev: Anthony DeFrancisci	George T. Morgan George T. Morgan	Teresa C. DeFrancisci Original design
Eisenhower Apollo 11 Mission Bicentennial, Liberty Bell and Moon	1971 to 1978	Obv: Frank Gasparro Rev: Frank Gasparro Rev: Dennis R. Williams	Frank Gasparro Frank Gasparro Frank Gasparro	Sketch by Gasparro (1945) Mission patch by Collins, Armstrong, Aldrin Original design
Anthony Apollo 11 Mission	1979 to 1999	Obv: Frank Gasparro Rev: Frank Gasparro	Frank Gasparro Frank Gasparro	Original design, from photos Mission patch by Collins, Armstrong, Aldrin
Sacagawea Soaring Eagle	2000 to 2008	Obv: Glenna Goodacre Rev: Thomas Rogers	Glenna Goodacre Thomas Rogers	Randy'L He-dow Teton Original design
Native American Three Sisters Iroquois Confederacy Diplomacy, Treaty	2009 to date 2009 2010 2011	Obv: Glenna Goodacre Rev: Norman Nemeth Rev: Thomas Cleveland Rev: Richard Masters	Glenna Goodacre Norman Nemeth Charles L. Vickers Joseph F. Menna	Randy'L He-dow Teton Original design Original design Original design
Pres., G. Washington Statue of Liberty[11] Pres., J. Adams Pres., T. Jefferson Pres., J. Madison	2007 2007 2007 2007	Obv: Joseph Menna Rev: Thomas Rogers Obv: Joel Iskowitz Obv: Joseph Menna Obv: Joel Iskowitz	Joseph Menna Thomas Rogers Charles L. Vickers Joseph Menna Donald Everhart II	Original design, historical sources Original design Original design, historical sources Original design, historical sources Original design, historical sources
Pres., J. Monroe Pres., J.Q. Adams Pres., A. Jackson Pres., M. Van Buren	2008 2008 2008 2008	Obv: Joseph Menna Obv: Donald Everhart II Obv: Joel Iskowitz Obv: Joel Iskowitz	Joseph Menna Donald Everhart II James Licaretz Phebe Hemphill	Original design, historical sources Original design, historical sources Original design, historical sources Original design, historical sources
Pres., W.H. Harrison Pres., J. Tyler Pres., J.K. Polk Pres., Z. Taylor	2009 2009 2009 2009	Obv: Joseph Menna Obv: Phebe Hemphill Obv: Susan Gamble Obv: Donald Everhart II	Joseph Menna Phebe Hemphill Charles L. Vickers Donald Everhart II	Original design, historical sources Original design, historical sources Original design, historical sources Original design, historical sources
Pres., M. Fillmore Pres., F. Pierce Pres., J. Buchanan Pres., A. Lincoln	2010 2010 2010 2010	Obv: Donald Everhart II Obv: Susan Gamble Obv: Phebe Hemphill Obv: Donald Everhart II	Donald Everhart II Charles L. Vickers Phebe Hemphill Donald Everhart II	Original design, historical sources Original design, historical sources Original design, historical sources Original design, historical sources

Silver dollars, nonsilver dollars (continued)

Design Type	Issue Dates	Designers[1]	Original Engraver	Model or Source
Pres., A. Johnson	2011	Obv: Donald Everhart II	Donald Everhart II	Original design, historical sources
Pres., U.S. Grant	2011	Obv: Donald Everhart II	Donald Everhart II	Original design, historical sources
Pres., R.B. Hayes	2011	Obv: Donald Everhart II	Donald Everhart II	Original design, historical sources
Pres., J. Garfield	2011	Obv: Phebe Hemphill	Phebe Hemphill	Original design, historical sources

Gold dollars

Design Type	Issue Dates	Designers[1]	Original Engraver	Model or Source
Coronet	1849 to 1854	Obv: James B. Longacre	James B. Longacre	Possibly Sarah Longacre
Wreath		Rev: James B. Longacre	James B. Longacre	Original design
Indian Head[7]	1854 to 1889	Obv: James B. Longacre	James B. Longacre	Possibly Sarah Longacre
Wreath		Rev: James B. Longacre	James B. Longacre	Original design

Quarter eagles

Design Type	Issue Dates	Designers[1]	Original Engraver	Model or Source
Capped Bust	1796 to 1807	Obv: Robert Scot	Robert Scot	Martha Washington(?)
Heraldic Eagle		Rev: Robert Scot	Robert Scot	Great Seal of the United States
Capped Draped Bust	1808	Obv: John Reich	John Reich	Unknown model
Eagle with Raised Wings, and Shield		Rev: John Reich	John Reich	1789 Mott token
Capped Head[8]	1821 to 1834	Obv: John Reich-Robert Scot	Robert Scot	Similar to previous issue
Eagle with Raised Wings, and Shield		Rev: John Reich	John Reich	Same as previous issue
Classic Head	1834 to 1839	Obv: William Kneass	William Kneass	Reich's Classic Head cent
Eagle with Raised Wings, and Shield		Rev: John Reich-W. Kneass	William Kneass	Similar to previous issue
Coronet	1840 to 1907	Obv: Christian Gobrecht	Christian Gobrecht	Coronet type large cent
		Rev: John Reich-W. Kneass- Christian Gobrecht	Christian Gobrecht	Similar to previous issue
Eagle with Raised Wings, and Shield				
Indian Head	1908 to 1929	Obv: Bela Lyon Pratt	Charles Barber	Chief Thundercloud
Standing Eagle		Rev: Augustus Saint-Gaudens–Adolph A. Weinman–Henry Hering–Homer Saint-Gaudens– Bela Lyon Pratt	Charles Barber	Reverse of Indian Head $10 eagle

$3 coins

Design Type	Issue Dates	Designers[1]	Original Engraver	Model or Source
Indian Head	1854 to 1889	Obv: James B. Longacre	James B. Longacre	Possibly Sarah Longacre
Wreath		Rev: James B. Longacre	James B. Longacre	Original design

Half eagles

Design Type	Issue Dates	Designers[1]	Original Engraver	Model or Source
Capped Bust	1795 to 1798	Obv: Robert Scot	Robert Scot	Martha Washington (?)
Small Eagle		Rev: Robert Scot	Robert Scot	Original design
Capped Bust	1795 to 1807	Obv: Robert Scot	Robert Scot	Same as previous issue
Heraldic Eagle		Rev: Robert Scot	Robert Scot	Great Seal of the United States
Capped Draped Bust	1807 to 1812	Obv: John Reich	John Reich	Unknown model
Eagle with Raised Wings, and Shield		Rev: John Reich	John Reich	1789 Mott token
Capped Head[8]	1813 to 1834	Obv: John Reich-R. Scot	Robert Scot	Similar to previous issue
		Rev: John Reich	John Reich	Same as previous issue
Classic Head	1834 to 1838	Obv: William Kneass	William Kneass	Reich's Classic Head cent
Eagle with Raised Wings, and Shield		Rev: John Reich-W. Kneass	William Kneass	Similar to previous issue
Coronet Type	1839 to 1908	Obv: Christian Gobrecht	Christian Gobrecht	Coronet type large cent
Eagle with Raised Wings, and Shield		Rev: John Reich-W. Kneass- Christian Gobrecht	Christian Gobrecht	Similar to previous issue
Indian Head	1908 to 1929	Obv: Bela Lyon Pratt	Charles Barber	Photograph of Native American
Standing Eagle		Rev: Augustus Saint-Gaudens–Adolph A. Weinman–Henry Hering–Homer Saint-Gaudens– Bela Lyon Pratt	Charles Barber	Reverse of Indian Head $10 eagle

Eagles

Design Type	Issue Dates	Designers[1]	Original Engraver	Model or Source
Capped Bust	1795 to 1797	Obv: Scot	Scot	Possibly Martha Washington
Small Eagle		Rev: Scot	Scot	Original design

Eagles

Design Type	Issue Dates	Designers[1]	Original Engraver	Model or Source
Capped Bust Heraldic Eagle	1797 to 1804	Obv: Scot Rev: Scot	Scot Scot	Same as previous issue Great Seal of the United States
Coronet Type Eagle with Raised Wings, and Shield	1838 to 1907	Obv: Gobrecht Rev: Reich-Kneass-Gobrecht	Gobrecht Gobrecht	Coronet Type Large Cent $2.50, $5 Rev.
Indian Head Standing Eagle	1907 to 1933	Obv: Augustus Saint-Gaudens–Henry Hering–Homer Saint-Gaudens Charles Barber Rev: Augustus Saint-Gaudens–Adolph A. Weinman–Henry Hering–Homer Saint-Gaudens Charles Barber		Unknown model 1905 Theodore Roosevelt inaugural medal by A. Saint-Gaudens and A. Weinman

Double eagles

Design Type	Issue Dates	Designers[1]	Original Engraver	Model or Source
Liberty Head Heraldic Eagle	1849 to 1907	Obv: James B. Longacre Rev: James B. Longacre	James B. Longacre James B. Longacre	Possibly Sarah Longacre Original design
Saint-Gaudens Flying Eagle	1907 to 1933	Obv: Augustus Saint-Gaudens–Henry Hering Rev: Christian Gobrecht–James B. Longacre–Augustus Saint-Gaudens–Henry Hering	Charles Barber Charles Barber	Original design Gobrecht dollar rev., Flying Eagle cent obv.

American Eagle bullion coins

Design Type	Issue Dates	Designers[1]	Original Engraver	Model or Source
Silver bullion	1986-date	Obv: Adolph A. Weinman Rev: John Mercanti	Edgar Z. Steever IV John Mercanti	Walking Liberty half dollar Great Seal of the United States
Gold bullion	1986-date	Obv: Augustus Saint-Gaudens–Henry Hering Rev: Miley Busiek	Matthew Peloso Sherl Joseph Winter	Double eagle of 1907 to 1933[9] Original design
Platinum bullion	1997-date	Obv: John Mercanti Rev: Thomas D. Rogers Sr.		Statue of Liberty Original design[10]

Notes

1. When two or more names appear hyphenated as the designers, the first person created the design and the others modified it for artistic and/ or other reasons. Modifications of design and/or relief solely for striking purposes are not included.
2. Stars are not on the obverse of 1837 and 1838-O coins.
3. Smaller size (1828-37) engraved by Kneass.
4. Smaller size without E PLURIBUS UNUM (1831-1838) engraved by Kneass.
5. Slight modifications made in 1809 by Reich and in 1834 by Kneass.
6. All coins are patterns but some did circulate.
7. Small Head 1854-56; Large Head 1856-89.
8. Smaller size (1829-34) engraved by Kneass.
9. Saint-Gaudens' Liberty was "slimmed down" to meet modern standards of physical beauty, under the orders of Treasury Secretary James A. Baker III.
10. Reverse of bullion version unchanged. Reverse of Proof version changes each year.

How coins are made

The various coining facilities of the United States Mint are factories, whose products happen to be coinage of the realm.

Like any metal product, coins don't "just happen." A number of intricate steps must be taken, from the preparation of the raw metal used in the coins to the striking of the coins. And before the coins can be struck, dies must be produced.

For a new coin, the design process begins with design renderings by artists for the Mint, who are members of the Mint engraving staff or members of the Mint's Artistic Infusion Program. Once a design for a coin is selected from all the provided sketches, a model is created in the Engraving Department at the Philadelphia Mint.

While some engravers may chose to engrave a model using traditional methods, working in modeling clay, much of the modeling and engraving is now accomplished digitally, using scanners, computers and a computer-controlled milling machine.

In the 21st century, the United States Mint has employed several techniques in designing and model making: the traditional approach, with its origins in the 19th century and earlier, and practiced by a skilled engraver and sculptor; and a modern approach harnessing the power of scanners, computers and lasers in which computer design skills are prized.

Some of the first official comments on the changes in the Engraving Department were made in testimony given before a House subcommittee July 19, 2006, by David A. Lebryk, the deputy director of the Mint. He said: "We have introduced new technologies to improve our design capabilities. The old coin design method—a drawing by hand turned into a clay model followed by a plaster model to be traced and cut into steel—is being replaced with a digital design process—a computer drawing scanned into an engraving machine."

According to the deputy director, this scanning technique was used in making the hubs for the 2006 American Buffalo gold bullion coins, whose designs are based on the designs found on the 1913 Indian Head, Bison on Mound 5-cent coins. The original plasters for the earlier coin by James Earle Fraser were taken from Mint storage and digitally reproduced; new equipment, controlled by computer, cut a hub by laser.

The Engraving Department also used a computer system in designing the first Presidential dollar. The computer system enables Mint staff to design coins using such computer programs as Adobe Photoshop and Illustrator. Artists can create individual design element "layers." If a particular device needs to be revised, the changes can be made to that layer without the need to revise the entire design.

Whether a model is completely computer generated or modeled in clay and then scanned, the final sculpture is assembled and fine-tuned by computer. Then, the master hub is cut by a computer numerical controlled (CNC) milling machine. As of 2008, the Mint mothballed its Janvier engraving lathe, which, installed at the Philadelphia Mint in 1907, had been used ever since for engraving master hubs.

In recognition of the changes in the 21st century design techniques introduced, Mint officials have indicated the traditional terms for its staff coin and medal designers—engraver and sculptor-engraver—are becoming as obsolete as silver coins in circulation. The new name for coin and medal designers is "medallic artist." Mint medallic artists hired since 2005 and 2006 reportedly have backgrounds in computer design rather than traditional sculpturing and engraving.

Although the designing and hub production for such issues as the Presidential dollars and American Buffalo gold coins were largely done by computer, most of the coins discussed and priced in this book were struck from dies produced in the traditional manner, as least as practiced since the late 19th century and early 20th century. Under this traditional process, a sculptor-engraver following a sketch made a model in plastilene, a modeling clay substance. The model was three to 12 times the size of the actual coin, depending on the denomination.

A hard model was then generated, either in metal by an electroplating method (the model made from this method is called a galvano) or, during the last decades of the 20th century, in epoxy.

The galvano or epoxy model was then mounted on a Janvier transfer-engraving machine. This machine used a stylus to trace the exact details of the model, then reduced them through a ratio bar. At the other end of the machine, a needle-like carbide cutting tool cut the design into soft tool steel, producing a positive replica that Mint officials call a "reduction hub" and collectors call a "master hub."

Making dies and hubs

The master hub, no matter the method used to cut it, has the exact dimensions of the coin. It is then tempered and the steel hardened. The steel bar on which the master hub was engraved is trimmed and the shaft is turned to a specific shape. The master hub then is placed in a hydraulic press and slowly pressed into a blank piece of soft die steel called a "die blank," creating a negative replica called a master die.

Die blanks start as a cylindrical piece of steel with a cone-shaped face. A robotic arm loads each die blank into a polishing machine where the face of the blank is polished to a mirror-like finish. The cone shape of the face of the die blank facilitates the process of creating the design details. Design details are first formed in the center, where the metal of the die blank is the highest and thus comes into contact with the hub first.

The master hub is used to form a master die. (Using a single or master hub and die ensures that subsequent work hubs and dies are identical. Dies were made virtually by hand in the early years of the U.S. Mint, with inscriptions, dates and Mint marks punched into the work dies individually, resulting in dies that can be identified individually by the placement of the individual design elements.)

Multiple work hubs (the Mint's term) or working hubs (the hobby's term) are made from the master die in the hydraulic press in the same way as the original, master die was impressed. Work dies (those used to strike coins) are made from the work hubs in the same way. (A single master die can make multiple work hubs, each of which can be used to make multiple work dies.)

The U.S. Mint used a multiple hubbing process to make master dies, work hubs and work dies for much of its existence. The metal of the hub or die hardened before the design could be fully formed; the uncompleted die or hub had be heated to soften the metal, cooled and reinstalled in the hubbing press. Beginning in fiscal year 1986, the Philadelphia Mint began making master dies and work hubs using a single-squeeze hubbing process. The Denver Mint began making work dies using a single-squeeze press in 1996, upon the opening of a new die shop there. The Philadelphia Mint began using a single-squeeze operation for most dies in 1997. Half dollar and other larger denomination dies continued to be produced throughout 1998 on older equipment requiring multiple impressions of hub into die to fully form the image. The two Mints began producing half dollar dies in a single hubbing operation in 1999. The dies for the 1999 Anthony dollars were made on the old multiple-hubbing press and required multiple hubbings.

The final hub or die must be tempered and hardened, and the shafts are shaped on a lathe to permit their use in the presses.

The introduction of one design element to the die production process requires additional explanation. Mint marks have been added at various stages of the die-production process, depending on the era. Traditionally, beginning in the 1830s, Mint engravers placed the Mint mark by hand on each of the thousands of working dies. That is no longer the case. Mint marks on commemorative coins and Proof coins are placed at the initial modeling stage and have been since the mid- to late 1980s. For the circulating coins, beginning in 1990, the Mint began placing the Mint mark on the master die for the cent and 5-cent coin. The dime, quarter dollar and half dollar followed in 1991. Most recently, the Mint mark (if any) on a circulating coin is placed on the initial model.

All of these changes lessen the possibility of producing Mint mark errors and varieties.

Blanks and planchets

Modern U.S. coins have their beginnings in the private sector, where a number of companies process the raw metals from which coins are made, and produce some coinage blanks and planchets and all coils of strip metal the Mint purchases.

In preparing the raw metals used in coining, the coinage metals are assayed, mixed to the proper proportions, melted and formed into slabs that are heated and rolled to the correct thickness. For clad coinage, bonding operations are required to bond the two outer layers to the inner layer. The strip is then coiled and shipped to the Mint for blanking. The Mint once did all of its own metal processing, including melting, assaying and mixing different metals together to create alloys. The Mint produced its own strip metal as late as Fiscal Year 1982 at the Philadelphia Mint, but the operations were closed in Fiscal 1983.

Once coinage strip is rolled to the proper thickness, blanks are punched from it (both at the Mint and at the private suppliers, depending on the denomination). Blanks and planchets are the unstruck, circular pieces of metal that become coins when struck between the dies. Blanks and planchets represent the same product at different stages of production, although sometimes the terms "blank" and "planchet" are used interchangeably. Blanks are unfinished planchets that haven't been through all of the processing steps necessary before they can be struck into coins. Once a blank has been through all of the processing steps, it becomes a planchet and is ready to be struck.

Blanks are produced on blanking presses, which are simply punch presses similar to those found in any machine shop. They have a bank of punches (or rams) that travel downward, just barely penetrating the strip of coinage metal. The blanks are partially sheared, partially torn from the strip each time the punches make their downward cycle and pass through the strip. At this stage, the blanks have rough edges where they were torn from the strip. Most of the rough edges (or burrs) are removed during succeeding operations. The blanks at this point are slightly larger than the finished coins.

From this point onward, through the counting and bagging operations that represent the final steps before the Mint ships the coins to the Federal Reserve or other recipient, all the steps are automated. The Mint uses conveyor belts for moving blanks, planchets and coins throughout most steps of the production process, except for Native American and Presidential dollars. (The description of the processes that immediately follow are those used for the blanks intended for the cent through half dollar denominations, and were for the Sacagawea dollars. Because Native American and Presidential dollars have lettered edges, the blanks for these dollar coins undergo slightly different processes on the way to being struck; those processes will be discussed a few paragraphs later.)

Once punched from the strip, the blanks for every circulating coin but Native American and Presidential dollars must next be softened by being heated to controlled temperatures in a process called annealing. The blanks are heated in a rotating tubular furnace to about 1,500 degrees Fahrenheit, changing their crystal structure to a softer state. The annealing process prolongs the life of the coining dies by ensuring well-struck coins with lower striking pressures.

The annealing creates a grayish coloration on the planchets through oxidation, which must be removed. Following the annealing, the blanks are cooled in a "quench tank." From the tank, they are moved into a huge cylindrical tube called the whirlaway. The whirlaway is tilted at a 45-degree angle; blanks travel upward along the whirlaway toward the washer, while the excess liquid picked up in the quench tank is removed. The blanks are placed into washing machines similar to home washers, where they go through a series of cycles that soak and clean the blanks, according to the Mint. The agitation in the washing machines removes the gray oxides, tarnish, discoloration or contamination imparted during annealing. (Blanks for Native American and Presidential dollars are burnished in an extra step.)

After the blanks are removed from the washing machines, they are placed in a tube for drying, then moved to the final step that turns them into planchets. This next step is to give most blanks a slightly raised rim (or proto-rim). This is done in an upsetting mill.

The upsetting mill consists of a rotating wheel with V-shaped grooves on its edge. The grooved edge of the wheel fits into a curved section (or shoe) that has corresponding grooves. The distance between the wheel and the shoe gets progressively narrower so that, as the blank is rolled along the groove, it is compressed and a raised proto-rim is formed on both sides of the blank. This raised rim serves several purposes. It sizes and shapes the blank to lower the stress on the dies in the coining press and facilitates the formation of the rim on the coin. (Their status changes from blank to planchet with the addition of the proto-rim.)

The planchets are ready to be struck into coins.

For Native American and Presidential dollars, the annealing and upsetting steps occur at different points in the process than for blanks for the other coins. These dollar blanks receive a "hard upset"—that is, they are run through the upset mill to form the raised proto-rim without having been first softened by annealing. Mint officials indicate the hard upset for these dollar blanks is done before annealing so that the diameter of the blank does not increase during the upsetting step, which would affect application of the edge lettering after striking.

After annealing and being washed in a detergent solution and dried, the Native American and Presidential dollar coin planchets are burnished with steel pellets held inside a solution containing a brightening agent with anti-tarnishing properties. After drying, the brilliant planchets are ready to be struck on the coinage presses.

Striking the coins

Coining presses are designed for any denomination of coin. Dies and collars can be removed and new ones for a different denomination installed. Striking pressures are adjustable for the various denominations and metals. A circular piece of hardened steel forms the collar, which acts as the wall of the coining chamber. The dies impress the various designs and devices on the obverse and reverse for the coin while the collar forms the edge of the coin, flat and smooth on cents, 5-cent coins and Sacagawea/Presidential/Native American dollars, and reeded on the dime, quarter dollar and half dollar. The collar is mounted on springs that allow slight movement. (Forming Native American and Presidential dollar edges requires a separate operation, described later.)

The principal coining press used by the U.S. Mint for striking circulating coinage is made by Schuler AG, a German firm. Each Schuler press uses a single pair of dies, mounted so that the face of each die is perpendicular to the floor. Planchets are fed between the dies by a gravity-fed mechanism and stand on edge during striking. Each press can strike about 750 coins per minute.

While dies are traditionally designated as obverse or reverse, they are also assigned the technical designations of hammer die or anvil die. The anvil die is the fixed die while the hammer die is the one that moves and thus generates the force that raises the design elements on the coins during striking. Either side can be the anvil die or hammer die.

Newly struck coins fall into a trap. Frequently, while a press is in operation, the press attendant will pick up a finished coin for inspection from the trap, to catch some of the remaining varieties and errors that are still produced. The inspector examines the coin under a magnifier to search for any defects made in the die during operation. If the coin passes inspection, the press operator pulls the trap's lever, which dumps the coins onto a conveyor belt for transportation to the counting and bagging operations, except for the Native American and Presidential dollars.

When those dollars are struck, they have a plain edge. Finished, however, they bear edge inscriptions. The Mint adds these in a separate step following the striking of the coins.

The struck Native American and Presidential dollars, still with plain edges, are moved along a conveyor belt to an edge-lettering station. (The 2007 Presidential dollars were moved from the presses to the edge-inscription station in bins. Tens of thousands of George Washington dollars were released without lettered edges when the bins were moved directly from the presses to the counting-bagging station.)

At the edge-lettering equipment, the coins are vacuumed into an open cylinder that centrifugally forces each struck coin into an edge-lettering channel. On the inner side of the channel is a steel wheel spinning counterclockwise that contacts the plain edge of the struck coin. On the other side is a block of tooling steel that contains the raised edge lettering, formed by laser, in a groove that resembles a semicircle. The struck coins—traveling at the rate of 1,000 coins per minute—pass along the edge lettering segment where they are impressed with the edge inscriptions. The newly edge-lettered coins discharge into a cash box and then are transported to the counting-bagging operation.

Throughout the minting process, computers track such statistics as the productivity of each press operator, any repairs to a coining press, quantities of coins struck per press, plus installation, movement and destruction of the dies.

Once the coins reach the final station, they are counted automatically by machines, and are bagged or placed into shipping bins. The Mint now uses large "ballistic" bags rather than the traditional, smaller canvas bags used for more than a century. Counters atop the mechanism that dumps coins into the ballistic bags remove most out-of-specification coins (errors).

The ballistic bags are sealed and loaded onto pallets for shipment to the Federal Reserve Banks or the banks' contracted private money-handling firms for distribution into commerce.

Specifications of U.S. coins

Half cents

Coin/ Dates	Grams Weight	Tol.	Grains Weight	Tol	Dia. (mm)	Composition	Spec. Gravity
1793 to 1795	6.739		104.000		23.50*	Pure copper	8.92
1795 to 1837	5.443		84.000		23.50*	Pure copper	8.92
1837 to 1857	5.443	0.227	84.000	3.50	23.50*	Pure copper	8.92

Large cents

Coin/ Dates	Grams Weight	Tol.	Grains Weight	Tol	Dia. (mm)	Composition	Spec. Gravity
1793 to 1795	13.478		208.000		28.50*	Pure copper	8.92
1795 to 1837	10.886		168.000		28.50*	Pure copper	8.92
1837 to 1857	10.886	0.454	168.000	7.00	28.50*	Pure copper	8.92

Small cents

Coin/ Dates	Grams Weight	Tol.	Grains Weight	Tol	Dia. (mm)	Composition	Spec. Gravity
1856 to 1864	4.666	0.259	72.000	4.00	19.30*	88 Cu, 12 Ni	8.92
1864 to 1873	3.110	0.259	48.000	4.00	19.05	95 Cu, 5 Zn & Sn	8.84
1873 to 1942	3.110	0.130	48.000	2.00	19.05	95 Cu, 5 Zn & Sn	8.84
1943	2.689 2.754	0.130	41.500 42.500***	2.00	19.05	Zinc-plated steel	7.80
1944 to 1946	3.110	0.130	48.000	2.00	19.05	95 Cu, 5 Zn	8.83
1947 to 1962	3.110	0.130	48.000	2.00	19.05	95 Cu, 5 Zn & Sn	8.84
1962 to 1982	3.110	0.130	48.000	2.00	19.05	95 Cu, 5 Zn	8.83
1982 to date	2.500	0.100	38.581	1.54	19.05	97.5 Zn, 2.5 Cu****	7.17

Two cents

Coin/ Dates	Grams Weight	Tol.	Grains Weight	Tol	Dia. (mm)	Composition	Spec. Gravity
1864 to 1873	6.221	0.259	96.000	4.00	23.00*	95 Cu, 5 Zn & Sn	8.84

Copper-nickel 3 cents

Coin/ Dates	Grams Weight	Tol.	Grains Weight	Tol	Dia. (mm)	Composition	Spec. Gravity
1865 to 1873	1.944	0.259	30.000	4.00	17.90*	75 Cu, 25 Ni	8.92
1873 to 1889	1.944	0.130	30.000	2.00	17.90*	75 Cu, 25 Ni	8.92

Copper-nickel 5 cents

Coin/ Dates	Grams Weight	Tol.	Grains Weight	Tol	Dia. (mm)	Composition	Spec. Gravity
1866 to 1873	5.000	0.130	77.162	2.00	20.50*	75 Cu, 25 Ni	8.92
1873 to 1883	5.000	0.194	77.162	3.00	20.50*	75 Cu, 25 Ni	8.92
1883 to 1942	5.000	0.194	77.162	3.00	21.21	75 Cu, 25 Ni	8.92
1942 to 1945	5.000	0.194	77.162	3.00	21.21	56 Cu, 35 Ag, 9 Mn	9.25*
1946 to date	5.000	0.194	77.162	3.00	21.21	75 Cu, 25 Ni	8.92

Silver 3 cents

Coin/ Dates	Grams Weight	Tol.	Grains Weight	Tol	Dia. (mm)	Composition	Spec. Gravity
1851 to 1853	0.802	0.032	12.375	0.50	14.00*	750 Ag, 250 Cu	10.11
1854 to 1873	0.746	0.032	11.520	0.50	14.00*	900 Ag, 100 Cu	10.34

Half dimes

Coin/ Dates	Grams Weight	Tol.	Grains Weight	Tol	Dia. (mm)	Composition	Spec. Gravity
1794 to 1795	1.348		20.800		16.50*	900 Ag, 100 Cu	10.34
1795 to 1805	1.348		20.800		16.50*	892.427 Ag, 107.572 Cu	10.32
1829 to 1837	1.348		20.800		15.50*	892.427 Ag, 107.572 Cu	10.32
1837 to 1853	1.336	0.032	20.625	0.50	15.50*	900 Ag, 100 Cu	10.34
1853 to 1873	1.244	0.032	19.200	0.50	15.50*	900 Ag, 100 Cu	10.34

Dimes

Coin/ Dates	Grams Weight	Tol.	Grains Weight	Tol	Dia. (mm)	Composition	Spec. Gravity
1796 to 1828	2.696		41.600		18.80*	892.427 Ag, 107.572 Cu	10.32
1828 to 187	2.696		41.600		17.90*	892.427 Ag, 107.572 Cu	10.32
1837 to 1853	2.673	0.032	41.250	0.50	17.90*	900 Ag, 100 Cu	10.34
1853 to 1873	2.488	0.032	38.400	0.50	17.90*	900 Ag, 100 Cu	10.34
1873 to 1964	2.500	0.097	38.581	1.50	17.91	900 Ag, 100 Cu	10.34
1965 to date	2.268	0.091	35.000	1.40	17.91	75 Cu, 25 Ni on pure Cu	8.92

Twenty cents

Coin/ Dates	Grams Weight	Tol.	Grains Weight	Tol	Dia. (mm)	Composition	Spec. Gravity
1875 to 1878	5.000	0.097	77.162	1.50	22.50*	900 Ag, 100 Cu	10.34

Quarter dollars

Coin/ Dates	Grams Weight	Tol.	Grains Weight	Tol	Dia. (mm)	Composition	Spec. Gravity
1796 to 1828	6.739		104.000		27.00*	892.427 Ag, 107.572 Cu	10.32
1831 to 1837	6.739		104.000		24.26*	892.427 Ag, 107.572 Cu	10.32
1837 to 1853	6.682	0.065	103.125	1.00	24.26*	900 Ag, 100 Cu	10.34
1853 to 1873	6.221	0.065	96.000	1.00	24.26*	900 Ag, 100 Cu	10.34
1873 to 1947	6.250	0.097	96.452	1.50	24.26	900 Ag, 100 Cu	10.34
1947 to 1964	6.250	0.194	96.452	3.00	24.26	900 Ag, 100 Cu	10.34
1965 to date	5.670	0.227	87.500	3.50	24.26	75 Cu, 25 Ni on pure Cu	8.92
1976	5.750	0.200	88.736	3.09	24.26	40% silver clad**	9.53

Half dollars

Coin/ Dates	Grams Weight	Tol.	Grains Weight	Tol	Dia. (mm)	Composition	Spec. Gravity
1794 to 1795	13.478		208.000		32.50*	900 Ag, 100 Cu	10.34
1796 to 1836	13.478		208.000		32.50*	892.427 Ag, 107.572 Cu	10.32
1836 to 1853	13.365	0.097	206.250	1.50	30.61*	900 Ag, 100 Cu	10.34
1853 to 1873	12.441	0.097	192.000	1.50	30.61*	900 Ag, 100 Cu	10.34
1873 to 1947	12.500	0.097	192.904	1.50	30.61	900 Ag, 100 Cu	10.34
1947 to 1964	12.500	0.259	192.904	4.00	30.61	900 Ag, 100 Cu	10.34
1965 to 1970	11.500	0.400	177.472	6.17	30.61	40% silver clad**	9.53
1971 to date	11.340	0.454	175.000	7.00	30.61	75 Cu, 25 Ni on pure Cu	8.92
1976	11.500	0.400	177.472	6.17	30.61	40% silver clad**	9.53

Silver and nonsilver dollars

Coin/ Dates	Grams Weight	Tol.	Grains Weight	Tol	Dia. (mm)	Composition	Spec. Gravity
1794 to 1795	26.956		416.000		39.50*	900 Ag, 100 Cu	10.34
1796 to 1803	26.956		416.000		39.50*	892.427 Ag, 107.572 Cu	10.32
1840 to 1935	26.730	0.097	412.500	1.50	38.10	900 Ag, 100 Cu	10.34
1971 to 1978	22.680	0.907	350.000	14.00	38.10	75 Cu, 25 Ni on pure Cu	8.92
1971 to 1976	24.592	0.984	379.512	15.18	38.10	40% silver clad**	9.53
1979 to 1999	8.100	0.300	125.000	5.00	26.50	75 Cu, 25 Ni on pure Cu	8.92
2000 to date	8.100	?	87.500	?	26.50	77 Cu, 12 Zn, 7 Mn, 4 Ni on pure Cu	8.78

Trade dollars

Coin/ Dates	Grams Weight	Tol.	Grains Weight	Tol	Dia. (mm)	Composition	Spec. Gravity
1873 to 1883	27.216	0.097	420.000	1.50	38.10	900 Ag, 100 Cu	10.34

Gold dollars

Coin/ Dates	Grams Weight	Tol.	Grains Weight	Tol	Dia. (mm)	Composition	Spec. Gravity
1849 to 1854	1.672	0.016	25.800	0.25	13.00*	900 Au, 100 Cu & Ag	17.16

Gold dollars (continued)

Coin/ Dates	Grams Weight	Tol.	Grains Weight	Tol	Dia. (mm)	Composition	Spec. Gravity
1854 to 1873	1.672	0.016	25.800	0.25	14.86*	900 Au, 100 Cu & Ag	17.16
1873 to 1889	1.672	0.016	25.800	0.25	14.86*	900 Au, 100 Cu	17.16

Quarter eagles

Coin/ Dates	Grams Weight	Tol.	Grains Weight	Tol	Dia. (mm)	Composition	Spec. Gravity
1796 to 1808	4.374		67.500		20.00*	916.667 Au, 83.333 Cu& Ag	17.45
1821 to 1827	4.374		67.500		18.50*	916.667 Au, 83.333 Cu& Ag	17.45
1829 to 1834	4.374		67.500		18.20*	916.667 Au, 83.333 Cu+Ag	17.45
1834 to 1836	4.180	0.008	64.500	0.13	18.20*	899.225 Au, 100.775 Cu+Ag	17.14
1837 to 1839	4.180	0.016	64.500	0.25	18.20*	900 Au, 100 Cu+Ag	17.16
1840 to 1873	4.180	0.016	64.500	0.25	17.78*	900 Au, 100 Cu+Ag	17.16
1873 to 1929	4.180	0.016	64.500	0.25	17.78*	900 Au, 100 Cu	17.16

Three dollars

Coin/ Dates	Grams Weight	Tol.	Grains Weight	Tol	Dia. (mm)	Composition	Spec. Gravity
1854 to 1873	5.015		77.400		20.63*	900 Au, 100 Cu+Ag	17.16
1873 to 1889	5.015	0.016	77.400	0.25	20.63*	900 Au, 100 Cu	17.16

Half eagles

Coin/ Dates	Grams Weight	Tol.	Grains Weight	Tol	Dia. (mm)	Composition	Spec. Gravity
1795 to 1829	8.748		135.000		25.00*	916.667 Au, 83.333 Cu+Ag	17.45
1829 to 1834	8.748		135.000		22.50*	916.667 Au, 83.333 Cu+Ag	17.45
1834 to 1836	8.359	0.017	129.000	0.26	22.50*	899.225 Au, 100.775 Cu+Ag	17.14
1837 to 1840	8.359	0.016	129.000	0.25	22.50*	900 Au, 100 Cu+Ag	17.16
1840 to 1849	8.359	0.016	129.000	0.25	21.54*	900 Au, 100 Cu+Ag	17.16
1849 to 1873	8.359	0.032	129.000	0.50	21.54*	900 Au, 100 Cu+Ag	17.16
1873 to 1929	8.359	0.016	129.000	0.25	21.54*	900 Au, 100 Cu	17.16

Eagles

Coin/ Dates	Grams Weight	Tol.	Grains Weight	Tol	Dia. (mm)	Composition	Spec. Gravity
1795 to 1804	17.496		270.000		33.00*	916.667 Au, 83.333 Cu+Ag	17.45
1838 to 1849	16.718	0.016	258.000	0.25	27.00*	900 Au, 100 Cu+Ag	17.16
1849 to 1873	16.718	0.032	258.000	0.50	27.00*	900 Au, 100 Cu+Ag	17.16
1873 to 1933	16.718	0.032	258.000	0.50	27.00*	900 Au, 100 Cu	17.16

Double eagles

Coin/ Dates	Grams Weight	Tol.	Grains Weight	Tol	Dia. (mm)	Composition	Spec. Gravity
1850 to 1873	33.436	0.032	516.000	0.50	34.29	900 Au, 100 Cu+Ag	17.16
1873 to 1933	33.436	0.032	516.000	0.50	34.29	900 Au, 100 Cu	17.16

American Eagle bullion coins

Denomination	Grams Weight	Ounces Weight	MM Diameter	Composition	Weight in Ounces	Specific Gravity
$1 one-ounce	31.103	1.00000	40.1	.999 Ag	1.000 Ag	10.50
$5 tenth-ounce	3.393	0.10910	16.5	.9167 Au, .30 Ag, .533 Cu	0.100 Au 0.003 Ag 0.006 Cu	17.45
$10 tenth-ounce	3.112	0.10005	16.5	.9995 Pl	1.000 Pl	21.40
$10 quarter-ounce	8.483	0.27270	22	.9167 Au, .30 Ag, .533 Cu	0.250 Au 0.008 Ag 0.015 Cu	17.45
$25 quarter-ounce	7.78	0.25010	22	.9995 Pl	0.250 Pl	21.40
$25 half-ounce	16.966	0.54550	27	.9167 Au, .30 Ag, .533 Cu	0.500 Au 0.016 Ag 0.029 Cu	17.45

American Eagle bullion coins (continued)

Denomination	Grams Weight	Ounces Weight	MM Diameter	Composition	Weight in Ounces	Specific Gravity
$50 half-ounce	15.56	0.50030	27	.9995 Pl	0.500 Pl	21.40
$50 one-ounce	33.931	1.09100	32.7	.9167 Au, .30 Ag, .533 Cu	1.000 Au 0.033 Ag 0.058 Cu	17.45
$100 one-ounce	31.120	1.00050	32.7	.9995 Pl	1.000 Pl	21.40

American Buffalo gold bullion coins

Denomination	Grams Weight	Ounces Weight	MM Diameter	Composition	Weight in Ounces	Specific Gravity
$50 one-ounce	31.100	1.00000	32.70	.9999 Au	1.000 Au	19.32
$25 half-ounce	15.550	0.50000	27.00	.9999 Au	0.50 Au	19.32
$10 quarter-ounce	7.7800	0.25000	22.00	.9999 Au	0.25 Au	19.32
$5 tenth-ounce	3.1100	0.10000	16.50	.9999 Au	0.10 Au	19.32

First Spouse gold bullion coins

Denomination	Grams Weight	Ounces Weight	MM Diameter	Composition	Weight in Ounces	Specific Gravity
$10 half-ounce	15.550	0.50000	27.00	.9999 Au	0.50 Au	19.32

Saint-Gaudens, Ultra High Relief gold coin

Denomination	Grams Weight	Ounces Weight	MM Diameter	Composition	Weight in Ounces	Specific Gravity
$10 half-ounce	31.100	0.50000	27.00	.9999 Au	1.00 Au	19.32

Note: Compositions are given as dictated legally. For the earlier coinages, compositions were stated in the authorizing legislation as 900 parts silver and 100 parts copper, or 900 AG and 100 Cu. Later laws described the same composition as 90 percent silver and 10 percent copper. The alloys are the same; only the way they are described legally differs.

* Unofficial data.

** Consists of layers of .800 Ag, .200 Cu bonded to a core of .215 Ag, .785 Cu.

*** Cents struck on steel planchets produced in 1942 weigh 41.5 grains, while those struck on planchets produced later in 1943 weigh 42.5 grains.

**** Consists of a planchet composed of 99.2 percent zinc and 0.8 copper, the whole plated with pure copper.

Mintage figures
Regular issue U.S. coins

The following mintage figures are a listing of the number of non-Proof coins struck in each year and each Mint, and which theoretically were released into circulation and thereby made available to collectors. In cases where a certain number of coins in a production run were melted at the Mint, the amount is subtracted from the total or footnoted.

In many instances the figures given are reconstructions and may be inaccurate. Prior to about 1950, the generally accepted source of mintage figures was the U.S. Mint Report. Since the Mint Report for many years was simply a bookkeeper's record of how many coins were issued in a particular year, the figures given often had no relation to the actual number of coins struck. Much investigation has been done into the actual number of coins struck with each date. The following is a compilation from many sources.

A few words about Mint marks or the lack thereof: All U.S. coins were struck at the Philadelphia Mint through 1837, and except for 5-cent coins struck from 1942 to 1945, none bore the P Mint mark until 1979 and 1980. Coins not followed by a Mint mark (-D, -S, -CC, -O, -C, -W) were struck at the Philadelphia Mint unless the date is followed by a Mint mark letter enclosed within parenthesis: (P), (D), (S), (W). In these cases, production occurred at a Branch Mint and sometimes at the Philadelphia Mint, but no Mint mark appears on the coin.

This practice first occurred from 1965 to 1967, when no Mint marks were used on any U.S. coins, and during the 1970s and 1980s, when several denominations were produced at more than one facility without Mint marks (these coins cannot be distinguished from each other). For these Mint mark-less coins, production facilities are indicated by the Mint letter within parenthesis: Philadelphia (P), Denver (D), San Francisco (S) and West Point (W). See the section on Mint marks elsewhere in this chapter for more details.

When the date is followed by a hyphen and a Mint mark, that indicates that the specified Mint mark actually appears somewhere on the coin: 1999-S, 1876-CC, 1838-O.

Prior to 1860, production of Proof coins was small and no Proof mintage figures were kept. From 1860 on, Proof figures were kept for gold and silver coins only, as minor coins were considered unimportant. Beginning in 1878, records were kept for the minor Proof coins as well.

290 - U.S. Coins

Half cents

Year	Mintage
1793	35,334
1794	81,600
1795	139,690
1796	1,390
1797	127,840
1800	202,908
1802	20,266
1803	92,000
1804	1,055,312
1805	814,464
1806	356,000
1807	476,000
1808	400,000
1809	1,154,572
1810	215,000
1811[9]	63,140
1825	63,000
1826	234,000
1828	606,000
1829	487,000
1831[15]	2,200
1832	[16]154,000
1833	[16]120,000
1834	[16]141,000
1835	[16]398,000
1836[21]	0
1840-48[30]	0
1849[15]	43,364
1850	39,812
1851	147,672
1852[30]	0
1853	129,694
1854	55,358
1855	56,500
1856[15]	40,430
1857[15]	35,180

Cents

Year	Mintage
1793	[1]110,512
1794	918,521
1795	538,500
1796	[3]473,200
1797	897,510
1798	1,841,745
1799	42,540
1800	2,822,175
1801	1,362,837
1802	3,435,100
1803	3,131,691
1804	[9]96,500
1805	941,116
1806	348,000
1807	829,221
1808	1,007,000
1809	222,867
1810	1,458,500
1811	218,025
1812	1,075,500
1813	418,000
1814	357,830
1816	2,820,982
1817	3,948,400
1818	3,167,000

Cents

Year	Mintage
1819	2,671,000
1820	4,407,550
1821	389,000
1822	2,072,339
1823[9]	68,061
1824	1,193,939
1825	1,461,100
1826	1,517,425
1827	2,357,732
1828	2,260,624
1829	1,414,500
1830	1,711,500
1831	3,539,260
1832	2,362,000
1833	2,739,000
1834	1,855,100
1835	3,878,400
1836	2,111,000
1837	5,558,300
1838	6,370,200
1839	3,128,661
1840	2,462,700
1841	1,597,367
1842	2,383,390
1843	2,425,342
1844	2,398,752
1845	3,894,804
1846	4,120,800
1847	6,183,669
1848	6,415,799
1849	4,178,500
1850	4,426,844
1851	9,889,707
1852	5,063,094
1853	6,641,131
1854	4,236,156
1855	1,574,829
1856	[41]2,690,463
1857	[42]17,783,456
1858	24,600,000
1859	[44]36,400,000
1860	20,566,000
1861	10,100,000
1862	28,075,000
1863	49,840,000
1864	[57]52,973,714
1865	35,429,286
1866	9,826,500
1867	9,821,000
1868	10,266,500
1869	6,420,000
1870	5,275,000
1871	3,929,500
1872	4,042,000
1873[68]	11,676,500
1874	14,187,500
1875	13,528,000
1876	7,944,000
1877	852,500
1878	5,797,500
1879	16,228,000
1880	38,961,000
1881	39,208,000

Cents

Year	Mintage
1882	38,578,000
1883	45,591,500
1884	23,257,800
1885	11,761,594
1886	17,650,000
1887	45,223,523
1888	37,489,832
1889	48,866,025
1892	37,647,087
1893	46,640,000
1894	16,749,500
1895	38,341,574
1896	39,055,431
1897	50,464,392
1898	49,821,284
1899	53,598,000
1900	66,821,284
1901	79,609,158
1902	87,374,704
1903	85,092,703
1904	61,326,198
1905	80,717,011
1906	96,020,530
1907	108,137,143
1908	32,326,367
1908-S	1,115,000
1909	[89]115,063,470
1909-S	89 2,618,000
1910	146,798,813
1910-S	6,045,000
1911	101,176,054
1911-D	12,672,000
1911-S	4,026,000
1912	68,150,915
1912-D	10,411,000
1912-S	4,431,000
1913	76,529,504
1913-D	15,804,000
1913-S	6,101,000
1914	75,237,067
1914-D	1,193,000
1914-S	4,137,000
1915	29,090,970
1915-D	22,050,000
1915-S	4,833,000
1916	131,832,627
1916-D	35,956,000
1916-S	22,510,000
1917	196,429,785
1917-D	55,120,000
1917-S	32,620,000
1918	288,104,634
1918-D	47,830,000
1918-S	34,680,000
1919	392,021,000
1919-D	57,154,000
1919-S	139,760,000
1920	310,165,000
1920-D	49,280,000
1920-S	46,220,000
1921	39,157,000
1921-S	15,274,000
1922-D [97]	7,160,000

Cents

Year	Mintage
1923	74,723,000
1923-S	8,700,000
1924	75,178,000
1924-D	2,520,000
1924-S	11,696,000
1925	139,949,000
1925-D	22,580,000
1925-S	26,380,000
1926	157,088,000
1926-D	28,020,000
1926-S	4,550,000
1927	144,440,000
1927-D	27,170,000
1927-S	14,276,000
1928	134,116,000
1928-D	31,170,000
1928-S	17,266,000
1929	185,262,000
1929-D	41,730,000
1929-S	50,148,000
1930	157,415,000
1930-D	40,100,000
1930-S	24,286,000
1931	19,396,000
1931-D	4,480,000
1931-S	866,000
1932	9,062,000
1932-D	10,500,000
1933	14,360,000
1933-D	6,200,000
1934	219,080,000
1934-D	28,446,000
1935	245,388,000
1935-D	47,000,000
1935-S	38,702,000
1936	309,632,000
1936-D	40,620,000
1936-S	29,130,000
1937	309,170,000
1937-D	50,430,000
1937-S	34,500,000
1938	156,682,000
1938-D	20,010,000
1938-S	15,180,000
1939	316,466,000
1939-D	15,160,000
1939-S	52,070,000
1940	586,810,000
1940-D	81,390,000
1940-S	112,940,000
1941	887,018,000
1941-D	128,700,000
1941-S	92,360,000
1942	657,796,000
1942-D	206,698,000
1942-S	85,590,000
1943[102]	684,628,670
1943-D	217,660,000
1943-S	191,550,000
1944	1,435,400,000
1944-D	430,578,000
1944-S	282,760,000
1945	1,040,515,000

Cents

Year	Mintage
1945-D	226,268,000
1945-S	181,770,000
1946	991,655,000
1946-D	315,690,000
1946-S	198,100,000
1947	190,555,000
1947-D	194,750,000
1947-S	99,000,000
1948	317,570,000
1948-D	172,637,500
1948-S	81,735,000
1949	217,775,000
1949-D	153,132,500
1949-S	64,290,000
1950	272,635,000
1950-D	334,950,000
1950-S	118,505,000
1951	294,576,000
1951-D	625,355,000
1951-S	136,010,000
1952	186,765,000
1952-D	746,130,000
1952-S	137,800,004
1953	256,755,000
1953-D	700,515,000
1953-S	181,835,000
1954	71,640,050
1954-D	251,552,500
1954-S	96,190,000
1955	330,580,000
1955-D	563,257,500
1955-S	44,610,000
1956	420,745,000
1956-D	1,098,210,100
1957	282,540,000
1957-D	1,051,342,000
1958	252,525,000
1958-D	800,953,300
1959	609,715,000
1959-D	1,279,760,000
1960	586,405,000
1960-D	1,580,884,000
1961	753,345,000
1961-D	1,753,266,700
1962	606,045,000
1962-D	1,793,148,400
1963	754,110,000
1963-D	1,774,020,400
1964[104]	2,648,575,000
1964-D	3,799,071,500
1965 (P)[104]	301,470,000
1965 (S)	220,030,000
1966 (P)[104]	811,100,000
1966 (D)	991,431,200
1966 (S)	383,355,000
1967 (P)[104]	907,575,000
1967 (D)	1,327,377,100
1967 (S)	813,715,000
1968	1,707,880,970
1968-D	2,886,269,600
1968-S	258,270,001
1969	1,136,910,000

Cents

Year	Mintage
1969-D....	4,002,832,200
1969-S....	544,375,000
1970........	1,898,315,000
1970-D....	2,891,438,900
1970-S....	690,560,004
1971........	1,919,490,000
1971-D....	2,911,045,600
1971-S....	525,130,054
1972........	2,933,255,000
1972-D....	2,655,071,400
1972-S....	380,200,104
1973........	3,728,245,000
1973-D....	3,549,576,588
1973-S....	319,937,634
1974........	4,232,140,523
1974-D....	4,235,098,000
1974-S....	409,421,878
1975 (P)..	3,874,182,000
1975-D....	4,505,275,300
1975 (W)..	1,577,294,142
1976 (P)..	3,133,580,000
1976-D....	4,221,592,455
1976 (W)..	1,540,695,000
1977 (P)..	3,074,575,000
1977-D....	4,194,062,300
1977 (W)..	1,395,355,000
1978 (P)..	3,735,655,000
1978-D....	4,280,233,400
1978 (S)..	291,700,000
1978 (W)..	1,531,250,000
1979 (P)..	3,560,940,000
1979-D....	4,139,357,254
1979 (S)..	751,725,000
1979 (W)..	1,705,850,000
1980 (P)..	6,230,115,000
1980-D....	5,140,098,660
1980 (S)..	1,184,590,000
1980 (W)..	1,576,200,000
1981 (P)..	6,611,305,000
1981-D....	5,373,235,677
1981 (S)..	880,440,000
1981 (W)..	1,882,400,000
1982 (P)[114]	7,135,275,000
1982-D....	6,012,979,368
1982 (S)..	1,587,245,000
1982 (W)..	1,990,005,000
1983 (P)..	5,567,190,000
1983-D....	6,467,199,428
1983 (S)...	180,765,000
1983 (W)..	2,004,400,000
1984 (P)..	6,114,864,000
1984-D....	5,569,238,906
1984 (W)..	2,036,215,000
1985 (P)..	4,951,904,887
1985-D....	5,287,399,926
1985 (W)..	696,585,000
1986 (P)..	4,490,995,493
1986-D....	4,442,866,698
1986 (W)...	400,000
1987........	4,682,466,931
1987-D....	4,879,389,514
1988........	6,092,810,000
1988-D....	5,253,740,443
1989........	7,261,535,000
1989-D....	5,345,467,711
1990........	6,851,765,000
1990-D....	4,922,894,553
1991........	5,165,940,000
1991-D....	4,158,442,076
1992........	4,648,905,000
1992-D....	4,448,673,300
1993........	5,684,705,000
1993-D....	6,426,650,571
1994........	6,500,850,000
1994-D....	7,131,765,000
1995........	6,411,440,000
1995-D....	7,128,560,000
1996........	6,612,465,000
1996-D....	6,510,795,000
1997........	4,622,800,000
1997-D....	4,576,555,000
1998........	5,032,200,000
1998-D....	5,225,200,000
1999........	5,237,600,000
1999-D....	6,360,065,000
2000........	5,503,200,000
2000-D....	8,774,220,000
2001........	4,959,600,000
2001-D....	5,374,990,000
2002........	3,260,800,000
2002-D....	4,028,055,000
2003........	3,300,000,000
2003-D....	3,548,000,000
2004........	3,379,600,000
2004-D....	3,456,400,000
2005........	3,935,600,000
2005-D....	3,764,450,500
2006........	4,290,000,000
2006-D....	3,944,000,000
2007........	3,762,400,000
2007-D....	3,638,800,000
2008........	2,569,600,000
2008-D....	2,849,600,000
2009 Early Childhood in Kentucky	284,400,000
2009-D Early Childhood in Kentucky	350,400,000
2009 Formative Years in Indiana ..	376,000,000
2009-D Formative Years in Indiana ..	363,600,000
2009 Professional Life in Illinois....	316,000,000
2009-D Professional Life in Illinois....	336,000,000
2009 Presidency in Wash., D.C.	129,600,000
2009-D Presidency in Wash., D.C.	198,000,000
2010........	1,963,630,000
2010-D....	2,047,200,000

Two cents

Year	Mintage
1864[56]	19,847,500
1865........	13,640,000
1866........	3,177,000
1867........	2,938,750
1868........	2,803,750
1869........	1,546,500
1870........	861,250
1871........	721,250
1872........	65,000
1873[68]	[74]0

Three cents (copper-nickel)

Year	Mintage
1865........	11,382,000
1866........	4,801,000
1867........	3,915,000
1868........	3,252,000
1869........	1,604,000
1870........	1,335,000
1871........	604,000
1872........	862,000
1873[68]	1,173,000
1874........	790,000
1875........	228,000
1876........	162,000
1877........	[53]0
1878........	[53]0
1879........	38,000
1880........	21,000
1881........	1,077,000
1882........	22,200
1883........	4,000
1884........	1,700
1885........	1,000
1886........	[53]0
1887........	5,001
1888........	36,501
1889........	18,125

Three cents (silver)

Year	Mintage
1851........	5,447,400
1851-O.....	720,000
1852........	18,663,500
1853[34]	11,400,000
1854........	671,000
1855........	139,000
1856........	1,458,000
1857........	1,042,000
1858........	1,604,000
1859........	365,000
1860........	286,000
1861........	497,000
1862........	343,000
1863........	[54]21,000
1864........	[55]12,000
1865........	8,000
1866........	22,000
1867........	4,000
1868........	3,500
1869........	4,500
1870........	3,000
1871........	3,400
1872........	1,000
1873[68]	[53]0

Five cents

Year	Mintage
1866........	14,742,500
1867........	[64]30,909,500
1868........	28,817,000
1869........	16,395,000
1870........	4,806,000
1871........	561,000
1872........	6,036,000
1873[68]	4,550,000
1874........	3,538,000
1875........	2,097,000
1876........	2,530,000
1877........	[53]0
1878........	[53]0
1879........	25,900
1880........	16,000
1881........	68,800
1882........	11,473,500
1883........	[80]22,952,000
1884........	11,270,000
1885........	1,472,700
1886........	3,326,000
1887........	15,260,692
1888........	10,715,901
1889........	15,878,025
1890........	16,256,532
1891........	16,832,000
1892........	11,696,897
1893........	13,368,000
1894........	5,410,500
1895........	9,977,822
1896........	8,841,058
1897........	20,426,797
1898........	12,530,292
1899........	26,027,000
1900........	27,253,733
1901........	26,478,228
1902........	31,487,561
1903........	28,004,935
1904........	21,401,350
1905........	29,825,124
1906........	38,612,000
1907........	39,213,325
1908........	22,684,557
1909........	11,585,763
1910........	30,166,948
1911........	39,557,639
1912........	26,234,569
1912-D....	8,474,000
1912-S....	238,000
1913 90....	[91]60,849,186
1913-D.....	[919]9,493,000
1913-S.....	[913]3,314,000
1914........	20,664,463
1914-D....	3,912,000
1914-S....	3,470,000
1915........	20,986,220
1915-D....	7,569,500
1915-S....	1,505,000
1916........	63,497,466
1916-D....	13,333,000
1916-S....	11,860,000
1917........	51,424,029
1917-D.....	9,910,800
1917-S.....	4,193,000
1918........	32,086,314
1918-D....	8,362,000
1918-S....	4,882,000
1919........	60,868,000
1919-D....	8,006,000
1919-S....	7,521,000
1920........	63,093,000
1920-D....	9,418,000
1920-S....	9,689,000
1921........	10,663,000
1921-S....	1,557,000
1923........	35,715,000
1923-S....	6,142,000
1924........	21,620,000
1924-D....	5,258,000
1924-S....	1,437,000
1925........	35,565,100
1925-D....	4,450,000
1925-S....	6,256,000
1926........	44,693,000
1926-D....	5,638,000
1926-S....	970,000
1927........	37,981,000
1927-D....	5,730,000
1927-S....	3,430,000
1928........	23,411,000
1928-D....	6,436,000
1928-S....	6,936,000
1929........	36,446,000
1929-D....	8,370,000
1929-S....	7,754,000
1930........	22,849,000
1930-S....	5,435,000
1931-S....	1,200,000
1934........	20,213,003
1934-D....	7,480,000
1935........	58,264,000
1935-D....	12,092,000
1935-S....	10,300,000
1936........	118,997,000
1936-D....	24,814,000
1936-S....	14,930,000
1937........	79,480,000
1937-D....	17,826,000
1937-S....	5,635,000
1938........	19,496,000
1938-D....	[100]12,396,000
1938-S....	4,105,000
1939........	120,615,000
1939-D....	3,514,000
1939-S....	6,630,000
1940........	176,485,000
1940-D....	43,540,000
1940-S....	39,690,000
1941........	203,265,000
1941-D....	53,432,000
1941-S....	43,445,000
1942........	[101]107,662,000
1942-D....	13,938,000
1942-S....	32,900,000
1943-P....	271,165,000
1943-D.....	15,294,000

Five cents

Year	Mintage
1943-S	104,060,000
1944-P[103]	119,150,000
1944-D	32,309,000
1944-S	21,640,000
1945-P	119,408,100
1945-D	37,158,000
1945-S	58,939,000
1946	161,116,000
1946-D	45,292,200
1946-S	13,560,000
1947	95,000,000
1947-D	37,822,000
1947-S	24,720,000
1948	89,348,000
1948-D	44,734,000
1948-S	11,300,000
1949	60,652,000
1949-D	36,498,000
1949-S	9,716,000
1950	9,796,000
1950-D	2,630,030
1951	28,552,000
1951-D	20,460,000
1951-S	7,776,000
1952	63,988,000
1952-D	30,638,000
1952-S	20,572,000
1953	46,644,000
1953-D	59,878,600
1953-S	19,210,900
1954	47,684,050
1954-D	117,136,560
1954-S	29,384,000
1955	7,888,000
1955-D	74,464,100
1956	35,216,000
1956-D	67,222,640
1957	38,408,000
1957-D	136,828,900
1958	17,088,000
1958-D	168,249,120
1959	27,248,000
1959-D	160,738,240
1960	55,416,000
1960-D	192,582,180
1961	73,640,000
1961-D	229,342,760
1962	97,384,000
1962-D	280,195,720
1963	175,776,000
1963-D	276,829,460
1964[104]	1,024,672,000
1964-D	1,787,297,160
1965 (P)[104]	12,440,000
1965 (D)	82,291,380
1965 (S)	39,040,000
1966 (P)[104]	0
1966 (D)	103,546,700
1966 (S)	50,400,000
1967 (P)[104]	0
1967 (D)	75,993,800
1967 (S)	31,332,000
1968-D	91,227,880
1968-S	100,396,004
1969-D	202,807,500
1969-S	120,165,000
1970-D	515,485,380
1970-S	238,832,004
1971	106,884,000
1971-D	316,144,800
1972	202,036,000
1972-D	351,694,600
1973	384,396,000
1973-D	261,405,400
1974	601,752,000
1974-D	277,373,000
1975	181,772,000
1975-D	401,875,300
1976	367,124,000
1976-D	563,964,147
1977	585,376,000
1977-D	297,313,422
1978	391,308,000
1978-D	313,092,780
1979	463,188,000
1979-D	325,867,672
1980-P	593,004,000
1980-D	502,323,448
1981-P	657,504,000
1981-D	364,801,843
1982-P	292,355,000
1982-D	373,726,544
1983-P	561,615,000
1983-D	536,726,276
1984-P	746,769,000
1984-D	517,675,146
1985-P	647,114,962
1985-D	459,747,446
1986-P	536,883,493
1986-D	361,819,144
1987-P	371,499,481
1987-D	410,590,604
1988-P	771,360,000
1988-D	663,771,652
1989-P	898,812,000
1989-D	570,842,474
1990-P	661,636,000
1990-D	663,938,503
1991-P	614,104,000
1991-D	436,496,678
1992-P	399,552,000
1992-D	450,565,113
1993-P	412,076,000
1993-D	406,084,135
1994-P	722,160,000
1994-D	715,762,110
1995-P	774,156,000
1995-D	888,112,000
1996-P	829,332,000
1996-D	817,736,000
1997-P	470,972,000
1997-D	466,640,000
1998-P	688,292,000
1998-D	635,380,000
1999-P	1,212,000,000
1999-D	1,066,720,000
2000-P	1,842,500,000
2000-D	1,818,700,000
2001-P	1,369,590,000
2001-D	1,412,800,000
2002-P	1,187,500,000
2002-D	1,379,500,000
2003-P	1,085,500,000
2003-D	986,500,000
2004-P	1,328,000,000
2004-D	1,159,500,000
2005-P	1,412,000,000
2005-D	1,423,500,000
2006-P	1,381,000,000
2006-D	1,447,000,000
2007-P	1,047,500,000
2007-D	1,042,000,000
2008-P	413,000,000
2008-D	637,500,000
2009-P	96,500,000
2009-D	49,500,000
2010-P	260,640,000
2010-D	229,920,000

Half dimes

Year	Mintage
1794	7,756
1795	78,660
1796	10,230
1797	44,527
1800	40,000
1801	33,910
1802	13,010
1803	37,850
1805	15,600
1829	1,230,000
1830	1,240,000
1831	1,242,700
1832	965,000
1833	1,370,000
1834	1,480,000
1835	2,760,000
1836	1,900,000
1837	[23]2,276,000
1838	2,255,000
1838-O[26]	115,000
1839	1,069,150
1839-O	981,550
1840	1,344,085
1840-O	935,000
1841	1,150,000
1841-O	815,000
1842	815,000
1842-O	350,000
1843	1,165,000
1844	430,000
1844-O	220,000
1845	1,564,000
1846	27,000
1847	1,274,000
1848	668,000
1848-O	600,000
1849	1,309,000
1849-O	140,000
1850	955,000
1850-O	690,000
1851	781,000
1851-O	860,000
1852	1,000,500
1852-O	260,000
1853 34	[38]13,345,020
1853-O	[38]2,360,000
1854	5,740,000
1854-O	1,560,000
1855	1,750,000
1855-O	600,000
1856	4,880,000
1856-O	1,100,000
1857	7,280,000
1857-O	1,380,000
1858	3,500,000
1858-O	1,660,000
1859	340,000
1859-O	560,000
1860[46]	798,000
1860-O	1,060,000
1861	3,360,000
1862	1,492,000
1863	18,000
1863-S	100,000
1864	[55]48,000
1864-S	90,000
1865	13,000
1865-S	120,000
1866	10,000
1866-S	120,000
1867	8,000
1867-S	120,000
1868	88,600
1868-S	280,000
1869	208,000
1869-S	230,000
1870	535,600
1871	1,873,000
1871-S	161,000
1872	2,947,000
1872-S	837,000
1873[68]	712,000
1873-S[68]	324,000

Dimes

Year	Mintage
1796	22,135
1797	25,261
1798	27,550
1800	21,760
1801	34,640
1802	10,975
1803	33,040
1804	8,265
1805	120,780
1807	165,000
1809	51,065
1811	65,180
1814	421,500
1820	942,587
1821	1,186,512
1822	100,000
1823	440,000
1824	100,000
1825	410,000
1827	1,215,000
1828	125,000
1829	770,000
1830	510,000
1831	771,350
1832	522,500
1833	485,000
1834	635,000
1835	1,410,000
1836	1,190,000
1837	[22]1,042,000
1838	1,992,500
1838-O[26]	406,034
1839	1,053,115
1839-O	1,323,000
1840	1,358,580
1840-O	1,175,000
1841	1,622,500
1841-O	2,007,500
1842	1,887,500
1842-O	2,020,000
1843	1,370,000
1843-O	50,000
1844	72,500
1845	1,755,000
1845-O	230,000
1846	31,300
1847	245,000
1848	451,500
1849	839,000
1849-O	300,000
1850	1,931,500
1850-O	510,000
1851	1,026,500
1851-O	400,000
1852	1,535,500
1852-O	430,000
1853[34]	[37]12,173,010
1853-O[34]	[37]1,100,000
1854	4,470,000
1854-O	1,770,000
1855	2,075,000
1856	5,780,000
1856-O	1,180,000
1856-S	70,000
1857	5,580,000
1857-O	1,540,000
1858	1,540,000
1858-O	290,000
1858-S	60,000
1859	430,000
1859-O	480,000
1859-S	60,000
1860 [46]	606,000
1860-O	40,000
1860-S	140,000
1861	1,883,000
1861-S	172,500
1862	847,000
1862-S	180,750
1863	14,000

Dimes

Year	Mintage	Year	Mintage	Year	Mintage	Year	Mintage	Year	Mintage
1863-S	157,500	1893	3,340,000	1913	19,760,000	1939	67,740,000	1962	72,450,000
1864	11,000[55]	1893-O	1,760,000	1913-S	510,000	1939-D	24,394,000	1962-D	334,948,380
1864-S	230,000	1893-S	2,491,401	1914	17,360,230	1939-S	10,540,000	1963	123,650,000
1865	10,000	1894	1,330,000	1914-D	11,908,000	1940	65,350,000	1963-D	421,476,530
1865-S	175,000	1894-O	720,000	1914-S	2,100,000	1940-D	21,198,000	1964[104]	929,360,000
1866	8,000	1894-S	[81]0	1915	5,620,000	1940-S	21,560,000	1964-D	1,357,517,180
1866-S	135,000	1895	690,000	1915-S	960,000	1941	175,090,000	1965 (P)[104]	845,130,000
1867	6,000	1895-O	440,000	1916	[93]40,670,000	1941-D	45,634,000	1965 (D)	757,472,820
1867-S	140,000	1895-S	1,120,000	1916-D	[93]264,000	1941-S	43,090,000	1965 (S)	47,177,750
1868	464,000	1896	2,000,000	1916-S	[93]16,270,000	1942	205,410,000	1966 (P)[104]	622,550,000
1868-S	260,000	1896-O	610,000	1917	55,230,000	1942-D	60,740,000	1966 (D)	683,771,010
1869	256,000	1896-S	575,056	1917-D	9,402,000	1942-S	49,300,000	1966 (S)	74,151,947
1869-S	450,000	1897	10,868,533	1917-S	27,330,000	1943	191,710,000	1967 (P)[104]	1,030,110,000
1870	470,500	1897-O	666,000	1918	26,680,000	1943-D	71,949,000	1967 (D)	1,156,277,320
1870-S	50,000	1897-S	1,342,844	1918-D	22,674,800	1943-S	60,400,000	1967 (S)	57,620,000
1871	906,750	1898	16,320,000	1918-S	19,300,000	1944	231,410,000	1968	424,470,400
1871-CC	20,100	1898-O	2,130,000	1919	35,740,000	1944-D	62,224,000	1968-D	480,748,280
1871-S	320,000	1898-S	1,702,507	1919-D	9,939,000	1944-S	49,490,000	1969	145,790,000
1872	2,395,500	1899	19,580,000	1919-S	8,850,000	1945	159,130,000	1969-D	563,323,870
1872-CC	35,480	1899-O	2,650,000	1920	59,030,000	1945-D	40,245,000	1970	345,570,000
1872-S	190,000	1899-S	1,867,493	1920-D	19,171,000	1945-S	41,920,000	1970-D	754,942,100
1873[68]	[73]3,945,700	1900	17,600,000	1920-S	13,820,000	1946	255,250,000	1971	162,690,000
1873-CC[68]	[73]31,191	1900-O	2,010,000	1921	1,230,000	1946-D	61,043,500	1971-D	377,914,240
1873-S[68]	[73]455,000	1900-S	5,168,270	1921-D	1,080,000	1946-S	27,900,000	1972	431,540,000
1874	2,940,000	1901	18,859,665	1923	50,130,000	1947	121,520,000	1972-D	330,290,000
1874-CC	10,817	1901-O	5,620,000	1923-S	6,440,000	1947-D	46,835,000	1973	315,670,000
1874-S	240,000	1901-S	593,022	1924	24,010,000	1947-S	34,840,000	1973-D	455,032,426
1875	10,350,000	1902	21,380,000	1924-D	6,810,000	1948	74,950,000	1974	470,248,000
1875-CC	4,645,000	1902-O	4,500,000	1924-S	7,120,000	1948-D	52,841,000	1974-D	571,083,000
1875-S	9,070,000	1902-S	2,070,000	1925	25,610,000	1948-S	35,520,000	1975 (P)	513,682,000
1876	11,460,000	1903	19,500,000	1925-D	5,117,000	1949	30,940,000	1975-D	313,705,300
1876-CC	8,270,000	1903-O	8,180,000	1925-S	5,850,000	1949-D	26,034,000	1975 (S)	71,991,900
1876-S	10,420,000	1903-S	613,300	1926	32,160,000	1949-S	13,510,000	1976	568,760,000
1877	7,310,000	1904	14,600,357	1926-D	6,828,000	1950	50,130,114	1976-D	695,222,774
1877-CC	7,700,000	1904-S	800,000	1926-S	1,520,000	1950-D	46,803,000	1977	796,930,000
1877-S	2,340,000	1905	14,551,623	1927	28,080,000	1950-S	20,440,000	1977-D	376,607,228
1878	1,678,000	1905-O	3,400,000	1927-D	4,812,000	1951	102,880,102	1978	663,980,000
1878-CC	200,000	1905-S	6,855,199	1927-S	4,770,000	1951-D	56,529,000	1978-D	282,847,540
1879	14,000	1906	19,957,731	1928	19,480,000	1951-S	31,630,000	1979	315,440,000
1880	36,000	1906-D	4,060,000	1928-D	4,161,000	1952	99,040,093	1979-D	390,921,184
1881	24,000	1906-O	2,610,000	1928-S	7,400,000	1952-D	122,100,000	1980	735,170,000
1882	3,910,000	1906-S	3,136,640	1929	25,970,000	1952-S	44,419,500	1980-D	719,354,321
1883	7,674,673	1907	22,220,000	1929-D	5,034,000	1953	53,490,120	1981-P	676,650,000
1884	3,365,505	1907-D	4,080,000	1929-S	4,730,000	1953-D	136,433,000	1981-D	712,284,143
1884-S	564,969	1907-O	5,058,000	1930	6,770,000	1953-S	39,180,000	1982-P[115]	519,475,000
1885	2,532,497	1907-S	3,178,470	1930-S	1,843,000	1954	114,010,203	1982-D	542,713,584
1885-S	43,690	1908	10,600,000	1931	3,150,000	1954-D	106,397,000	1983-P	647,025,000
1886	6,376,684	1908-D	7,490,000	1931-D	1,260,000	1954-S	22,860,000	1983-D	730,129,224
1886-S	206,524	1908-O	1,789,000	1931-S	1,800,000	1955	12,450,181	1984-P	856,669,000
1887	11,283,229	1908-S	3,220,000	1934	24,080,000	1955-D	13,959,000	1984-D	704,803,976
1887-S	4,454,450	1909	10,240,000	1934-D	6,772,000	1955-S	18,510,000	1985-P	705,200,962
1888	5,495,655	1909-D	954,000	1935	58,830,000	1956	108,640,000	1985-D	587,979,970
1888-S	1,720,000	1909-O	2,287,000	1935-D	10,477,000	1956-D	108,015,100	1986-P	682,649,693
1889	7,380,000	1909-S	1,000,000	1935-S	15,840,000	1957	160,160,000	1986-D	473,326,974
1889-S	972,678	1910	11,520,000	1936	87,500,000	1957-D	113,354,330	1987-P	762,709,481
1890	9,910,951	1910-D	3,490,000	1936-D	16,132,000	1958	31,910,000	1987-D	653,203,402
1890-S	1,423,076	1910-S	1,240,000	1936-S	9,210,000	1958-D	136,564,600	1988-P	1,030,550,000
1891	15,310,000	1911	18,870,000	1937	56,860,000	1959	85,780,000	1988-D	962,385,488
1891-O	4,540,000	1911-D	11,209,000	1937-D	14,146,000	1959-D	164,919,790	1989-P	1,298,400,000
1891-S	3,196,116	1911-S	3,520,000	1937-S	9,740,000	1960	70,390,000	1989-D	896,535,597
1892	12,120,000	1912	19,350,000	1938	22,190,000	1960-D	200,160,400	1990-P	1,034,340,000
1892-O	3,841,700	1912-D	11,760,000	1938-D	5,537,000	1961	93,730,000	1990-D	839,995,824
1892-S	990,710	1912-S	3,420,000	1938-S	8,090,000	1961-D	209,146,550	1991-P	927,220,000

294 - U.S. Coins

Dimes

Year	Mintage
1991-D	601,241,114
1992-P	593,500,000
1992-D	616,273,932
1993-P	766,180,000
1993-D	750,110,166
1994-P	1,189,000,000
1994-D	1,303,268,110
1995-P	1,125,500,000
1995-D	1,274,890,000
1996-P	1,421,630,000
1996-D	1,400,300,000
1996-W	1,450,440
1997-P	991,640,000
1997-D	979,810,000
1998-P	1,163,000,000
1998-D	1,172,300,000
1999-P	2,164,000,000
1999-D	1,397,750,000
2000-P	1,842,500,000
2000-D	1,818,700,000
2001-P	1,369,590,000
2001-D	1,412,800,000
2002-P	1,187,500,000
2002-D	1,379,500,000
2003-P	1,085,500,000
2003-D	986,500,000
2004-P	1,328,000,000
2004-D	1,159,500,000
2005-P	1,412,000,000
2005-D	1,423,500,000
2006-P	1,381,000,000
2006-D	1,447,000,000
2007-P	1,047,500,000
2007-D	1,042,000,000
2008-P	413,000,000
2008-D	637,500,000
2009-P	96,500,000
2009-D	49,500,000
2010-P	557,000,000
2010-D	562,000,000

Twenty cents

Year	Mintage
1875	38,500
1875-CC	133,290
1875-S	1,155,000
1876	14,750
1876-CC	[76]10,000
1877	[53]0
1878	[53]0

Quarter dollars

Year	Mintage
1796	6,146
1804	6,738
1805	121,394
1806	286,424
1807	140,343
1815	89,235
1818	361,174
1819	144,000
1820	127,444
1821	216,851
1822	64,080

Quarter dollars

Year	Mintage
1823	17,800
1824	24,000
1825	148,000
1827	[14]0
1828	102,000
1831	398,000
1832	320,000
1833	156,000
1834	286,000
1835	1,952,000
1836	472,000
1837	252,400
1838	[25]832,000
1839	491,146
1840	188,127
1840-O	425,200
1841	120,000
1841-O	452,000
1842	88,000
1842-O	769,000
1843	645,600
1843-O	968,000
1844	421,200
1844-O	740,000
1845	922,000
1846	510,000
1847	734,000
1847-O	368,000
1848	146,000
1849	340,000
1849-O	16,000
1850	190,800
1850-O	396,000
1851	160,000
1851-O	88,000
1852	177,060
1852-O	96,000
1853[34]	[36]15,254,220
1853-O[34]	[36]1,332,000
1854	12,380,000
1854-O	1,484,000
1855	2,857,000
1855-O	176,000
1855-S	396,400
1856	7,264,000
1856-O	968,000
1856-S	286,000
1857	9,644,000
1857-O	1,180,000
1857-S	82,000
1858	7,368,000
1858-O	520,000
1858-S	121,000
1859	1,344,000
1859-O	260,000
1859-S	80,000
1860	804,400
1860-O	388,000
1860-S	56,000
1861	4,853,600
1861-S	96,000
1862	932,000
1862-S	67,000

Quarter dollars

Year	Mintage
1863	191,600
1864	93,600
1864-S	20,000
1865	58,800
1865-S	41,000
1866	16,800
1866-S	28,000
1867	20,000
1867-S	48,000
1868	29,400
1868-S	96,000
1869	16,000
1869-S	76,000
1870	86,400
1870-CC	8,340
1871	118,200
1871-CC	10,890
1871-S	30,900
1872	182,000
1872-CC	22,850
1872-S	83,000
1873[68]	[72]1,483,160
1873-CC[68]	[72]16,462
1873-S[68]	[72]156,000
1874	471,200
1874-S	392,000
1875	4,292,800
1875-CC	140,000
1875-S	680,000
1876	17,816,000
1876-CC	4,944,000
1876-S	8,596,000
1877	10,911,200
1877-CC	4,192,000
1877-S	8,996,000
1878	2,260,000
1878-CC	996,000
1878-S	140,000
1879	14,450
1880	13,600
1881	12,000
1882	15,200
1883	14,400
1884	8,000
1885	13,600
1886	5,000
1887	10,000
1888	10,001
1888-S	1,216,000
1889	12,000
1890	80,000
1891	3,920,000
1891-O	68,000
1891-S	2,216,000
1892	8,236,000
1892-O	2,640,000
1892-S	964,079
1893	5,444,023
1893-O	3,396,000
1893-S	1,454,535
1894	3,432,000
1894-O	2,852,000
1894-S	2,648,821

Quarter dollars

Year	Mintage
1895	4,440,000
1895-O	2,816,000
1895-S	1,764,681
1896	3,874,000
1896-O	1,484,000
1896-S	188,039
1897	8,140,000
1897-O	1,414,800
1897-S	542,229
1898	11,100,000
1898-O	1,868,000
1898-S	1,020,592
1899	12,624,000
1899-O	2,644,000
1899-S	708,000
1900	10,016,000
1900-O	3,416,000
1900-S	1,858,585
1901	8,892,000
1901-O	1,612,000
1901-S	72,664
1902	12,196,967
1902-O	4,748,000
1902-S	1,524,612
1903	9,669,309
1903-O	3,500,000
1903-S	1,036,000
1904	9,588,143
1904-O	2,456,000
1905	4,967,523
1905-O	1,230,000
1905-S	1,884,000
1906	3,655,760
1906-D	3,280,000
1906-O	2,056,000
1907	7,192,000
1907-D	2,484,000
1907-O	4,560,000
1907-S	1,360,000
1908	4,232,000
1908-D	5,788,000
1908-O	6,244,000
1908-S	784,000
1909	9,268,000
1909-D	5,114,000
1909-O	712,000
1909-S	1,348,000
1910	2,244,000
1910-D	1,500,000
1911	3,720,000
1911-D	933,600
1911-S	988,000
1912	4,400,000
1912-S	708,000
1913	484,000
1913-D	1,450,800
1913-S	40,000
1914	6,244,230
1914-D	3,046,000
1914-S	264,000
1915	3,480,000
1915-D	3,694,000
1915-S	704,000

Quarter dollars

Year	Mintage
1916	[92]1,840,000
1916-D	[96]6,540,800
1917	[95]22,620,000
1917-D	[95]7,733,600
1917-S	[95]7,504,000
1918	14,240,000
1918-D	7,380,000
1918-S	11,072,000
1919	11,324,000
1919-D	1,944,000
1919-S	1,836,000
1920	27,860,000
1920-D	3,586,400
1920-S	6,380,000
1921	1,916,000
1923	9,716,000
1923-S	1,360,000
1924	10,920,000
1924-D	3,112,000
1924-S	2,860,000
1925	12,280,000
1926	11,316,000
1926-D	1,716,000
1926-S	2,700,000
1927	11,912,000
1927-D	976,400
1927-S	396,000
1928	6,336,000
1928-D	1,627,600
1928-S	2,644,000
1929	11,140,000
1929-D	1,358,000
1929-S	1,764,000
1930	5,632,000
1930-S	1,556,000
1932	5,404,000
1932-D	436,800
1932-S	408,000
1934	31,912,052
1934-D	3,527,200
1935	32,484,000
1935-D	5,780,000
1935-S	5,660,000
1936	41,300,000
1936-D	5,374,000
1936-S	3,828,000
1937	19,696,000
1937-D	7,189,600
1937-S	1,652,000
1938	9,472,000
1938-S	2,832,000
1939	33,540,000
1939-D	7,092,000
1939-S	2,628,000
1940	35,704,000
1940-D	2,797,600
1940-S	8,244,000
1941	79,032,000
1941-D	16,714,800
1941-S	16,080,000
1942	102,096,000
1942-D	17,487,200
1942-S	19,384,000

Quarter dollars

Year	Mintage
1943	99,700,000
1943-D	16,095,600
1943-S	21,700,000
1944	104,956,000
1944-D	14,600,800
1944-S	12,560,000
1945	74,372,000
1945-D	12,341,600
1945-S	17,004,001
1946	53,436,000
1946-D	9,072,800
1946-S	4,204,000
1947	22,556,000
1947-D	15,338,400
1947-S	5,532,000
1948	35,196,000
1948-D	16,766,800
1948-S	15,960,000
1949	9,312,000
1949-D	10,068,400
1950	24,920,126
1950-D	21,075,600
1950-S	10,284,004
1951	43,448,102
1951-D	35,354,800
1951-S	9,048,000
1952	38,780,093
1952-D	49,795,200
1952-S	13,707,800
1953	18,536,120
1953-D	56,112,400
1953-S	14,016,000
1954	54,412,203
1954-D	42,305,500
1954-S	11,834,722
1955	18,180,181
1955-D	3,182,400
1956	44,144,000
1956-D	32,334,500
1957	46,532,000
1957-D	77,924,160
1958	6,360,000
1958-D	78,124,900
1959	24,384,000
1959-D	62,054,232
1960	29,164,000
1960-D	63,000,324
1961	37,036,000
1961-D	83,656,928
1962	36,156,000
1962-D	127,554,756
1963	74,316,000
1963-D	135,288,184
1964[104]	560,390,585
1964-D	704,135,528
1965 (P)[104]	1,082,216,000
1965 (D)	673,305,540
1965 (S)	61,836,000
1966 (P)[104]	404,416,000
1966 (D)	367,490,400
1966 (S)	46,933,517
1967 (P)[104]	873,524,000
1967 (D)	632,767,848

Quarter dollars

Year	Mintage
1967 (S)	17,740,000
1968	220,731,500
1968-D	101,534,000
1969	176,212,000
1969-D	114,372,000
1970	136,420,000
1970-D	417,341,364
1971	109,284,000
1971-D	258,634,428
1972	215,048,000
1972-D	311,067,732
1973	346,924,000
1973-D	232,977,400
1974[108]	801,456,000
1974-D	353,160,300
1976 (P)	809,408,016
1976-D	860,118,839
1976 (W)	376,000
1977 (P)	461,204,000
1977-D	256,524,978
1977 (W)	7,352,000
1978 (P)	500,652,000
1978-D	287,373,152
1978 (W)	20,800,000
1979 (P)	493,036,000
1979-D	489,789,780
1979 (W)	22,672,000
1980-P[112]	635,832,000
1980-D	518,327,487
1981-P	601,716,000
1981-D	575,722,833
1982-P	500,931,000
1982-D	480,042,788
1983-P	673,535,000
1983-D	617,806,446
1984-P	676,545,000
1984-D	546,483,064
1985-P	775,818,962
1985-D	519,962,888
1986-P	551,199,333
1986-D	504,298,660
1987-P	582,499,481
1987-D	655,595,696
1988-P	562,052,000
1988-D	596,810,688
1989-P	512,868,000
1989-D	896,733,858
1990-P	613,792,000
1990-D	927,638,181
1991-P	570,960,000
1991-D	630,966,693
1992-P	384,764,000
1992-D	389,777,107
1993-P	639,276,000
1993-D	645,476,128
1994-P	825,600,000
1994-D	880,034,110
1995-P	1,004,336,000
1995-D	1,103,216,000
1996-P	925,040,000
1996-D	906,868,000
1997-P	595,740,000
1997-D	599,680,000

Quarter dollars

Year	Mintage
1998-P	960,400,000
1998-D	907,000,000
1999-P DE	373,400,000
1999-D DE	401,424,000
1999-P PA	349,000,000
1999-D PA	358,332,000
1999-P NJ	363,200,000
1999-D NJ	299,028,000
1999-P GA	451,188,000
1999-D GA	488,744,000
1999-P CT	688,744,000
1999-D CT	657,880,000
2000-P MA	628,600,000
2000-D MA	535,184,000
2000-P MD	678,200,000
2000-D MD	556,532,000
2000-P SC	742,576,000
2000-D SC	566,208,000
2000-P NH	673,040,000
2000-D NH	495,976,000
2000-P VA	943,000,000
2000-D VA	651,616,000
2001-P NY	655,400,000
2001-D NY	619,640,000
2001-P NC	627,600,000
2001-D NC	427,876,000
2001-P RI.	423,000,000
2001-D RI.	447,100,000
2001-P VT	423,400,000
2001-D VT	459,404,000
2001-P KY	353,000,000
2001-D KY	370,564,000
2002-P TN	361,600,000
2002-D TN	286,468,000
2002-P OH	217,200,000
2002-D OH	414,832,000
2002-P LA	362,000,000
2002-D LA	402,204,000
2002-P IN.	362,600,000
2002-D IN.	327,200,000
2002-P MS	290,000,000
2002-D MS	289,600,000
2003-P IL.	225,800,000
2003-D IL.	237,400,000
2003-P AL	225,000,000
2003-D AL	232,400,000
2003-P ME	217,400,000
2003-D ME	231,400,000
2003-P MO	225,000,000
2003-D MO	228,200,000
2003-P AR	228,000,000
2003-D AR	229,800,000
2004-P MI	233,800,000
2004-D MI	225,800,000
2004-P FL	240,200,000
2004-D FL	241,600,000
2004-P TX	278,800,000
2004-D TX	263,000,000
2004-P IA.	213,800,000
2004-D IA.	251,400,000
2004-P WI	226,400,000
2004-D WI[118]	226,800,000

Quarter dollars

Year	Mintage
2005-P CA	257,200,000
2005-D CA	263,200,000
2005-P MN	239,600,000
2005-D MN	248,400,000
2005-P OR	316,200,000
2005-D OR	404,000,000
2005-P KS	263,400,000
2005-D KS	300,000,000
2005-P WV	365,400,000
2005-D WV	356,200,000
2006-P NV	277,000,000
2006-D NV	312,800,000
2006-P NE	318,000,000
2006-D NE	276,400,000
2006-P CO	274,800,000
2006-D CO	294,200,000
2006-P ND	305,800,000
2006-D ND	359,000,000
2006-P SD	245,000,000
2006-D SD	265,800,000
2007-P MT	257,000,000
2007-D MT	256,240,000
2007-P WA	265,200,000
2007-D WA	280,000,000
2007-P ID.	294,600,000
2007-D ID.	286,800,000
2007-P WY	243,600,000
2007-D WY	320,800,000
2007-P UT	255,000,000
2007-D UT	253,200,000
2008-P OK	222,000,000
2008-D OK	194,600,000
2008-P NM	244,200,000
2008-D NM	244,400,000
2008-P AZ	244,600,000
2008-D AZ	265,000,000
2008-P AK	251,800,000
2008-D AK	254,000,000
2008-P HI.	254,000,000
2008-D HI.	263,600,000
2009-P DC	83,600,000
2009-D DC	88,800,000
2009-P PR	53,200,000
2009-D PR	86,000,000
2009-P GU	45,000,000
2009-D GU	42,600,000
2009-P AS	42,600,000
2009-D AS	39,600,000
2009-P VI.	41,000,000
2009-D VI.	41,000,000
2009-P NMI	35,200,000
2009-D NMI	37,600,000
2010-P AR	30,600,000
2010-D AR	29,000,000
2010-P WY	33,600,000
2010-D WY	34,800,000
2010-P CA	35,200,000
2010-D CA	34,800,000
2010-P AZ	34,800,000
2010-D AZ	35,400,000
2010-P OR	34,400,000
2010-D OR	34,400,000

Half dollars

Year	Mintage
1794	23,464
1795	299,680
1796	934
1797	2,984
1801	30,289
1802	29,890
1803	188,234
1805	211,722
1806	839,576
1807	[121]1,051,576
1808	1,368,600
1809	1,405,810
1810	1,276,276
1811	1,203,644
1812	1,628,059
1813	1,241,903
1814	1,039,075
1815	47,150
1817	1,215,567
1818	1,960,322
1819	2,208,000
1820	751,122
1821	1,305,797
1822	1,559,573
1823	1,694,200
1824	3,504,954
1825	2,943,166
1826	4,004,180
1827	5,493,400
1828	3,075,200
1829	3,712,156
1830	4,764,800
1831	5,873,660
1832	4,797,000
1833	5,206,000
1834	6,412,004
1835	5,352,006
1836	[206]6,546,200
1837	3,629,820
1838	3,546,000
1838-O	[240]0
1839	[283]3,334,560
1839-O	162,976
1840	1,435,008
1840-O	855,100
1841	310,000
1841-O	401,000
1842	2,012,764
1842-O	957,000
1843	3,844,000
1843-O	2,268,000
1844	1,766,000
1844-O	2,005,000
1845	589,000
1845-O	2,094,000
1846	2,210,000
1846-O	2,304,000
1847	1,156,000
1847-O	2,584,000
1848	580,000
1848-O	3,180,000
1849	1,252,000
1849-O	2,310,000

Half dollars

Year	Mintage	Year	Mintage	Year	Mintage	Year	Mintage	Year	Mintage
1850	227,000	1875-CC	1,008,000	1905	662,000	1935-S	3,854,000	1961	8,290,000
1850-O	2,456,000	1875-S	3,200,000	1905-O	505,000	1936	12,614,000	1961-D	20,276,442
1851	200,750	1876	8,418,000	1905-S	2,494,000	1936-D	4,252,400	1962	9,714,000
1851-O	402,000	1876-CC	1,956,000	1906	2,638,000	1936-S	3,884,000	1962-D	35,473,281
1852	77,130	1876-S	4,528,000	1906-D	4,028,000	1937	9,522,000	1963	22,164,000
1852-O	144,000	1877	8,304,000	1906-O	2,446,000	1937-D	1,676,000	1963-D	67,069,292
1853[34]	[35]3,532,708	1877-CC	1,420,000	1906-S	1,740,154	1937-S	2,090,000	1964[104]	273,304,004
1853-O	[35]1,328,000	1877-S	5,356,000	1907	2,598,000	1938	4,110,000	1964-D	156,205,446
1854	2,982,000	1878	1,377,600	1907-D	3,856,000	1938-D	491,600	1965 (P)[104]	0
1854-O	5,240,000	1878-CC	62,000	1907-O	3,946,600	1939	6,812,000	1965 (D)	63,049,366
1855	759,500	1878-S	12,000	1907-S	1,250,000	1939-D	4,267,800	1965 (S)	470,000
1855-O	3,688,000	1879	4,800	1908	1,354,000	1939-S	2,552,000	1966 (P)[104]	0
1855-S	129,950	1880	8,400	1908-D	3,280,000	1940	9,156,000	1966 (D)	106,439,312
1856	938,000	1881	10,000	1908-O	5,360,000	1940-S	4,550,000	1966 (S)	284,037
1856-O	2,658,000	1882	4,400	1908-S	1,644,828	1941	24,192,000	1967 (P)[104]	0
1856-S	211,000	1883	8,000	1909	2,368,000	1941-D	11,248,400	1967 (D)	293,183,634
1857	1,988,000	1884	4,400	1909-O	925,400	1941-S	8,098,000	1967 (S)	0
1857-O	818,000	1885	5,200	1909-S	1,764,000	1942	47,818,000	1968-D	246,951,930
1857-S	158,000	1886	5,000	1910	418,000	1942-D	10,973,800	1969-D	129,881,800
1858	4,226,000	1887	5,000	1910-S	1,948,000	1942-S	12,708,000	1970-D	[105]2,150,000
1858-O	7,294,000	1888	12,001	1911	1,406,000	1943	53,190,000	1971	155,164,000
1858-S	476,000	1889	12,000	1911-D	695,080	1943-D	11,346,000	1971-D	302,097,424
1859	748,000	1890	12,000	1911-S	1,272,000	1943-S	13,450,000	1972	153,180,000
1859-O	2,834,000	1891	200,000	1912	1,550,000	1944	28,206,000	1972-D	141,890,000
1859-S	566,000	1892	934,245	1912-D	2,300,800	1944-D	9,769,000	1973	64,964,000
1860	302,700	1892-O	390,000	1912-S	1,370,000	1944-S	8,904,000	1973-D	83,171,400
1860-O	1,290,000	1892-S	1,029,028	1913	188,000	1945	31,502,000	1974	201,596,000
1860-S	472,000	1893	1,826,000	1913-D	534,000	1945-D	9,996,800	1974-D	79,066,300
1861	2,887,400	1893-O	1,389,000	1913-S	604,000	1945-S	10,156,000	1976[109,110]	234,308,000
1861-O	[52]2,532,633	1893-S	740,000	1914	124,230	1946	12,118,000	1976-D	287,565,248
1861-S	939,500	1894	1,148,000	1914-S	992,000	1946-D	2,151,000	1977	43,598,000
1862	253,000	1894-O	2,138,000	1915	138,000	1946-S	3,724,000	1977-D	31,449,106
1862-S	1,352,000	1894-S	4,048,690	1915-D	1,170,400	1947	4,094,000	1978	14,350,000
1863	503,200	1895	1,834,338	1915-S	1,604,000	1947-D	3,900,600	1978-D	13,765,799
1863-S	916,000	1895-O	1,766,000	1916	608,000	1948	3,006,814	1979	68,312,000
1864	379,100	1895-S	1,108,086	1916-D	1,014,400	1948-D	4,028,600	1979-D	15,815,422
1864-S	658,000	1896	950,000	1916-S	508,000	1949	5,614,000	1980	[112]44,134,000
1865	511,400	1896-O	924,000	1917	12,292,000	1949-D	4,120,600	1980-D	33,456,449
1865-S	675,000	1896-S	1,140,948	1917-D	[94]2,705,400	1949-S	3,744,000	1981-P	29,544,000
1866	744,900	1897	2,480,000	1917-S	[94]6,506,000	1950	7,742,123	1981-D	27,839,533
1866-S	1,054,000	1897-O	632,000	1918	6,634,000	1950-D	8,031,600	1982-P	10,819,000
1867	449,300	1897-S	933,900	1918-D	3,853,040	1951	16,802,102	1982-D	13,140,102
1867-S	1,196,000	1898	2,956,000	1918-S	10,282,000	1951-D	9,475,200	1983-P	34,139,000
1868	417,600	1898-O	874,000	1919	962,000	1951-S	13,696,000	1983-D	32,472,244
1868-S	1,160,000	1898-S	2,358,550	1919-D	1,165,000	1952	21,192,093	1984-P	26,029,000
1869	795,300	1899	5,538,000	1919-S	1,552,000	1952-D	25,395,600	1984-D	26,262,158
1869-S	656,000	1899-O	1,724,000	1920	6,372,000	1952-S	5,526,000	1985-P	18,706,962
1870	633,900	1899-S	1,686,411	1920-D	1,551,000	1953	2,668,120	1985-D	19,814,034
1870-CC	54,617	1900	4,762,000	1920-S	4,624,000	1953-D	20,900,400	1986-P	13,107,633
1870-S	1,004,000	1900-O	2,744,000	1921	246,000	1953-S	4,148,000	1986-D	15,366,145
1871	1,203,600	1900-S	2,560,322	1921-D	208,000	1954	13,188,203	1987-P	[117]0
1871-CC	153,950	1901	4,268,000	1921-S	548,000	1954-D	25,445,580	1987-D	[117]0
1871-S	2,178,000	1901-O	1,124,000	1923-S	2,178,000	1954-S	4,993,400	1988-P	13,626,000
1872	880,600	1901-S	847,044	1927-S	2,392,000	1955	2,498,181	1988-D	12,000,096
1872-CC	257,000	1902	4,922,000	1928-S	1,940,000	1956	4,032,000	1989-P	24,542,000
1872-S	580,000	1902-O	2,526,000	1929-D	1,001,200	1957	5,114,000	1989-D	23,000,216
1873 68	[71]2,616,350	1902-S	1,460,670	1929-S	1,902,000	1957-D	19,966,850	1990-P	22,278,000
1873-CC[68]	[71]337,060	1903	2,278,000	1933-S	1,786,000	1958	4,042,000	1990-D	20,096,242
1873-S[68]	[71]233,000	1903-O	2,100,000	1934	6,964,000	1958-D	23,962,412	1991-P	14,874,000
1874	2,359,600	1903-S	1,920,772	1934-D	2,361,400	1959	6,200,000	1991-D	15,054,678
1874-CC	59,000	1904	2,992,000	1934-S	3,652,000	1959-D	13,053,750	1992-P	17,628,000
1874-S	394,000	1904-O	1,117,600	1935	9,162,000	1960	6,024,000	1992-D	17,000,106
1875	6,026,800	1904-S	553,038	1935-D	3,003,800	1960-D	18,215,812	1993-P	15,510,000

Half dollars

Year	Mintage
1993-D	15,000,006
1994-P	23,718,000
1994-D	23,828,110
1995-P	26,496,000
1995-D	26,288,000
1996-P	24,442,000
1996-D	24,744,000
1997-P	20,882,000
1997-D	19,876,000
1998-P	15,646,000
1998-D	15,064,000
1999-P	8,900,000
2000-P	22,600,000
2000-D	19,466,000
2001-P	21,200,000
2001-D	19,504,000
2002-P	[120]3,100,000
2002-D	[120]2,500,000
2003-P	[120]2,500,000
2003-D	[120]2,500,000
2004-P	[120]2,900,000
2004-D	[120]2,900,000
2005-P	[120]3,800,000
2005-D	[120]3,500,000
2006-P	[120]2,400,000
2006-D	[120]2,000,000
2007-P	[120]4,100,000
2007-D	[120]4,100,000
2008-P	[120]1,700,000
2008-D	[120]1,700,000
2009-P	[120]1,900,000
2009-D	[120]1,900,000
2010-P	[120]1,800,000
2010-D	[120]1,700,000

Silver dollars

Year	Mintage
1794	1,758
1795	[2]203,033
1796	72,920
1797	7,776
1798	[6]327,536
1799	423,515
1800	220,920
1801[7]	54,454
1802[7]	41,650
1803[7]	85,634
1804	[8]0
1805	[10]0
1836	[19]1,600
1839	[19]300
1840	[29]61,005
1841	[29]173,000
1842	[29]184,618
1843	[29]165,100
1844	[29]20,000
1845	[29]24,500
1846	[29]110,600
1846-O	59,000
1847	[29]140,750
1848	[29]5,000
1849	[29]62,600
1850	[29]7,500
1850-O	40,000

Silver dollars

Year	Mintage
1851	[29]1,300
1852	[29]1,100
1853	[29]46,110
1854	33,140
1855	26,000
1856	63,500
1857	94,000
1858	[43]0
1859	256,500
1859-O	360,000
1859-S	20,000
1860	217,600
1860-O	515,000
1861	77,500
1862	11,540
1863	27,200
1864	30,700
1865	46,500
1866	48,900
1867	46,900
1868	162,100
1869	423,700
1870	415,000
1870-CC	12,462
1870-S	[67]0
1871	1,073,800
1871-CC	1,376
1872	1,105,500
1872-CC	3,150
1872-S	9,000
1873[68]	293,000
1873-CC[53]	2,300
1873-S[68]	[70]700
1878[79]	10,508,550
1878-CC	2,212,000
1878-S	9,774,000
1879	14,806,000
1879-CC	756,000
1879-O	2,887,000
1879-S	9,110,000
1880	12,600,000
1880-CC	591,000
1880-O	5,305,000
1880-S	8,900,000
1881	9,163,000
1881-CC	296,000
1881-O	5,708,000
1881-S	12,760,000
1882	11,100,000
1882-CC	1,133,000
1882-O	6,090,000
1882-S	9,250,000
1883	12,290,000
1883-CC	1,204,000
1883-O	8,725,000
1883-S	6,250,000
1884	14,070,000
1884-CC	1,136,000
1884-O	9,730,000
1884-S	3,200,000
1885	17,786,837
1885-CC	228,000
1885-O	9,185,000

Silver dollars

Year	Mintage
1885-S	1,497,000
1886	19,963,000
1886-O	10,710,000
1886-S	750,000
1887	20,290,000
1887-O	11,550,000
1887-S	1,771,000
1888	19,183,000
1888-O	12,150,000
1888-S	657,000
1889	21,726,000
1889-CC	350,000
1889-O	11,875,000
1889-S	700,000
1890	16,802,000
1890-CC	2,309,041
1890-O	10,701,000
1890-S	8,230,373
1891	8,693,556
1891-CC	1,618,000
1891-O	7,954,529
1891-S	5,296,000
1892	1,036,000
1892-CC	1,352,000
1892-O	2,744,000
1892-S	1,200,000
1893	389,000
1893-CC	677,000
1893-O	300,000
1893-S	100,000
1894	110,000
1894-O	1,723,000
1894-S	1,260,000
1895	[82]12,000
1895-O	450,000
1895-S	400,000
1896	9,976,000
1896-O	4,900,000
1896-S	5,000,000
1897	2,822,000
1897-O	4,004,000
1897-S	5,825,000
1898	5,884,000
1898-O	4,440,000
1898-S	4,102,000
1899	330,000
1899-O	12,290,000
1899-S	2,562,000
1900	8,830,000
1900-O	12,590,000
1900-S	3,540,000
1901	6,962,000
1901-O	13,320,000
1901-S	2,284,000
1902	7,994,000
1902-O	8,636,000
1902-S	1,530,000
1903	4,652,000
1903-O	4,450,000
1903-S	1,241,000
1904	2,788,000
1904-O	3,720,000
1904-S	2,304,000

Silver dollars

Year	Mintage
1921	[96]45,696,473
1921-D	[96]20,345,000
1921-S	[96]21,695,000
1922	51,737,000
1922-D	15,063,000
1922-S	17,475,000
1923	30,800,000
1923-D	6,811,000
1923-S	19,020,000
1924	11,811,000
1924-S	1,728,000
1925	10,198,000
1925-S	1,610,000
1926	1,939,000
1926-D	2,348,700
1926-S	6,980,000
1927	848,000
1927-D	1,268,900
1927-S	866,000
1928	360,649
1928-S	1,632,000
1934	954,057
1934-D	1,569,500
1934-S	1,011,000
1935	1,576,000
1935-S	1,964,000

Trade dollars

Year	Mintage
1873[68]	396,635
1873-CC[68]	124,500
1873-S[68]	703,000
1874	987,100
1874-CC	1,373,200
1874-S	2,549,000
1875	218,200
1875-CC	1,573,700
1875-S	4,487,000
1876	455,000
1876-CC	509,000
1876-S	5,227,000
1877	3,039,200
1877-CC	534,000
1877-S	9,519,000
1878	[78]0
1878-CC	97,000
1878-S	4,162,000
1879	[78]0
1880	[78]0
1881	[78]0
1882	[78]0
1883	[78]0
1884	[78]0
1885	[78]0

Eisenhower dollars

Year	Mintage
1971	47,799,000
1971-D	68,587,424
1972	75,890,000
1972-D	92,548,511
1973[107]	2,000,056
1973-D	2,000,000
1974[108]	27,366,000
1974-D	45,517,000

Eisenhower dollars

Year	Mintage
1976[110]	117,337,000
1976-D	103,228,274
1977	12,596,000
1977-D	32,983,006
1978	25,702,000
1978-D	33,012,890

Anthony dollars

Year	Mintage
1979-P[113]	360,222,000
1979-D	288,015,744
1979-S	109,576,000
1980-P	27,610,000
1980-D	41,628,708
1980-S	20,422,000
1981-P[116]	3,000,000
1981-D	3,250,000
1981-S	3,492,000
1999-P	29,592,000
1999-D	11,776,000

Sacagawea dollars

Year	Mintage
2000-P[119]	767,140,000
2000-D	518,916,000
2001-P	62,468,000
2001-D	70,939,500
2002-P	3,865,610
2002-D	3,732,000
2003-P	3,080,000
2003-D	3,080,000
2004-P	2,660,000
2004-D	2,660,000
2005-P	2,520,000
2005-D	2,520,000
2006-P	4,900,000
2006-D	2,800,000
2007-P	3,640,000
2007-D	5,740,000
2008-P	9,800,000
2008-D	14,840,000
2009-P	37,380,000
2009-D	33,880,000
2010-P	32,060,000
2010-D	48,720,000

Presidential dollars

Year	Mintage
2007-P G.W.	176,680,000
2007-D G.W.	163,680,000
2007-P J.A.	112,420,000
2007-D J.A.	112,140,000
2007-P T.J.	100,800,000
2007-D T.J.	102,810,000
2007-P J.Mad.	84,560,000
2007-D J.Mad.	87,780,000
2008-P J.Mon.	64,260,000
2008-D J.Mon.	60,230,000
2008-P J.Q.A.	57,540,000
2008-D J.Q.A.	57,720,000
2008-P A.J.	61,180,000
2008-D A.J.	61,070,000
2008-P M.V.B.	51,520,000
2008-D M.V.B.	50,960,000
2009-P W.H.H.	43,260,000

Presidential dollars

Year	Mintage
2009-D W.H.H.	55,160,000
2009-P J.T.	43,540,000
2009-D J.T.	43,540,000
2009-P J.P.	46,620,000
2009-D J.P.	41,720,000
2009-P Z.T.	41,580,000
2009-D Z.T.	36,680,000
2010-P M.F.	37,520,000
2010-D M.F.	36,960,000
2010-P F.P.	38,220,000
2010-D F.P.	38,360,000
2010-P J.B.	36,820,000
2010-D J.B.	36,540,000
2010-P A.L.	49,000,000
2010-D A.L.	48,020,000

Gold dollars

Year	Mintage
1849	688,567
1849-C	11,634
1849-D	21,588
1849-O	215,000
1850	481,953
1850-C	6,966
1850-D	8,382
1850-O	14,000
1851	3,317,671
1851-C	41,267
1851-D	9,882
1851-O	290,000
1852	2,045,351
1852-C	9,434
1852-D	6,360
1852-O	140,000
1853	4,076,051
1853-C	11,515
1853-D	6,583
1853-O	290,000
1854	[39]1,639,445
1854-D	[39]2,935
1854-S	[39]14,632
1855	758,269
1855-C	9,803
1855-D	1,811
1855-O	55,000
1856[40]	1,762,936
1856-D[40]	1,460
1856-S[40]	24,600
1857	774,789
1857-C	13,280
1857-D	3,533
1857-S	10,000
1858	117,995
1858-D	3,477
1858-S	10,000
1859	168,244
1859-C	5,235
1859-D	4,952
1859-S	15,000
1860	36,514
1860-D	1,566
1860-S	13,000
1861	527,150
1861-D	[51]0

Gold dollars

Year	Mintage
1862	1,361,365
1863	6,200
1864	5,900
1865	3,700
1866	7,100
1867	5,200
1868	10,500
1869	5,900
1870	6,300
1870-S	[66]3,000
1871	3,900
1872	3,500
1873[68]	125,100
1874	198,800
1875	400
1876	3,200
1877	3,900
1878	3,000
1879	3,000
1880	1,600
1881	7,620
1882	5,000
1883	10,800
1884	5,230
1885	11,156
1886	5,000
1887	7,500
1888	15,501
1889	28,950

Quarter eagles

Year	Mintage
1796	1,395
1797	427
1798	1,094
1802	3,035
1804	3,327
1805	1,781
1806	1,616
1807	6,812
1808	2,710
1821	6,448
1824	2,600
1825	4,434
1826	760
1827	2,800
1829	3,403
1830	4,540
1831	4,520
1832	4,400
1833	4,160
1834	[18]117,370
1835	131,402
1836	547,986
1837	45,080
1838	47,030
1838-C	7,908
1839	27,021
1839-C	18,173
1839-D	13,674
1839-O	17,781
1840	18,859
1840-C	12,838
1840-D	3,532

Quarter eagles

Year	Mintage
1840-O	33,580
1841	[31]0
1841-C	10,297
1841-D	4,164
1842	2,823
1842-C	6,737
1842-D	4,643
1842-O	19,800
1843	100,546
1843-C	26,096
1843-D	36,209
1843-O	368,002
1844	6,784
1844-C	11,622
1844-D	17,332
1845	91,051
1845-D	19,460
1845-O	4,000
1846	21,598
1846-C	4,808
1846-D	19,303
1846-O	62,000
1847	29,814
1847-C	23,226
1847-D	15,784
1847-O	124,000
1848	[32]8,886
1848-C	16,788
1848-D	13,771
1849	23,294
1849-C	10,220
1849-D	10,945
1850	252,923
1850-C	9,148
1850-D	12,148
1850-O	84,000
1851	1,372,748
1851-C	14,923
1851-D	11,264
1851-O	148,000
1852	1,159,681
1852-C	9,772
1852-D	4,078
1852-O	140,000
1853	1,404,668
1853-D	3,178
1854	596,258
1854-C	7,295
1854-D	1,760
1854-O	153,000
1854-S	246
1855	235,480
1855-C	3,677
1855-D	1,123
1856	384,240
1856-C	7,913
1856-D	874
1856-S	71,120
1857	214,130
1857-D	2,364
1857-O	34,000
1857-S	69,200

Quarter eagles

Year	Mintage
1858	47,377
1858-C	9,056
1859	39,444
1859-D	2,244
1859-S	15,200
1860	22,563
1860-C	7,469
1860-S	35,600
1861	1,272,428
1861-S	24,000
1862	98,508
1862-S	8,000
1863	[53]0
1863-S	10,800
1864	2,824
1865	1,520
1865-S	23,376
1866	3,080
1866-S	38,960
1867	3,200
1867-S	28,000
1868	3,600
1868-S	34,000
1869	4,320
1869-S	29,500
1870	4,520
1870-S	16,000
1871	5,320
1871-S	22,000
1872	3,000
1872-S	18,000
1873[68]	178,000
1873-S[68]	27,000
1874	3,920
1875	400
1875-S	11,600
1876	4,176
1876-S	5,000
1877	1,632
1877-S	35,400
1878	286,240
1878-S	178,000
1879	88,960
1879-S	43,500
1880	2,960
1881	640
1882	4,000
1883	1,920
1884	1,950
1885	800
1886	4,000
1887	6,160
1888	16,006
1889	17,600
1890	8,720
1891	10,960
1892	2,440
1893	30,000
1894	4,000
1895	6,000
1896	19,070
1897	29,768
1898	24,000

Quarter eagles

Year	Mintage
1899	27,200
1900	67,000
1901	91,100
1902	133,540
1903	201,060
1904	160,790
1905	217,800
1906	176,330
1907	336,294
1908	564,821
1909	441,760
1910	492,000
1911	704,000
1911-D	55,680
1912	616,000
1913	722,000
1914	240,000
1914-D	448,000
1915	606,000
1925-D	578,000
1926	446,000
1927	388,000
1928	416,000
1929	532,000

Three dollars

Year	Mintage
1854	138,618
1854-D	1,120
1854-O	24,000
1855	50,555
1855-S	6,600
1856	26,010
1856-S	34,500
1857	20,891
1857-S	14,000
1858	2,133
1859	15,638
1860	7,036
1860-S	[45]4,408
1861	5,959
1862	5,750
1863	5,000
1864	2,630
1865	1,140
1866	4,000
1867	2,600
1868	4,850
1869	2,500
1870	3,500
1870-S	[65]0
1871	1,300
1872	2,000
1873[68]	[69]0
1874	41,800
1875	[75]0
1876	[53]0
1877	1,468
1878	82,304
1879	3,000
1880	1,000
1881	500
1882	1,500
1883	900

Three dollars

Year	Mintage
1884	1,000
1885	800
1886	1,000
1887	6,000
1888	5,000
1889	2,300

Half eagles

Year	Mintage
1795	8,707
1796	6,196
1797	3,609
1798	[5]24,867
1799	7,451
1800	37,628
1802	53,176
1803	33,506
1804	30,475
1805	33,183
1806	64,093
1807	[11]84,093
1808	55,578
1809	33,875
1810	100,287
1811	99,581
1812	58,087
1813	95,428
1814	15,454
1815	635
1818	48,588
1819	51,723
1820	263,806
1821	34,641
1822	[13]17,796
1823	14,485
1824	17,340
1825	29,060
1826	18,069
1827	24,913
1828	28,029
1829	57,442
1830	126,351
1831	140,594
1832	157,487
1833	193,630
1834	[17]707,601
1835	371,534
1836	553,147
1837	207,121
1838	286,588
1838-C	19,145
1838-D	20,583
1839	118,143
1839-C	17,235
1839-D	18,939
1840	137,382
1840-C	19,028
1840-D	22,896
1840-O	38,700
1841	15,833
1841-C	21,511
1841-D	30,495
1841-O	50
1842	27,578

Half eagles

Year	Mintage
1842-C	27,480
1842-D	59,608
1842-O	16,400
1843	611,205
1843-C	44,353
1843-D	98,452
1843-O	101,075
1844	340,330
1844-C	23,631
1844-D	88,982
1844-O	364,600
1845	417,099
1845-D	90,629
1845-O	41,000
1846	395,942
1846-C	12,995
1846-D	80,294
1846-O	58,000
1847	915,981
1847-C	84,151
1847-D	64,405
1847-O	12,000
1848	260,775
1848-C	64,472
1848-D	47,465
1849	133,070
1849-C	64,823
1849-D	39,036
1850	64,491
1850-C	63,591
1850-D	43,984
1851	377,505
1851-C	49,176
1851-D	62,710
1851-O	41,000
1852	573,901
1852-C	72,574
1852-D	91,584
1853	305,770
1853-C	65,571
1853-D	89,678
1854	160,675
1854-C	39,283
1854-D	56,413
1854-O	46,000
1854-S	268
1855	117,098
1855-C	39,788
1855-D	22,432
1855-O	11,100
1855-S	61,000
1856	197,990
1856-C	28,457
1856-D	19,786
1856-O	10,000
1856-S	105,100
1857	98,188
1857-C	31,360
1857-D	17,046
1857-O	13,000
1857-S	87,000
1858	15,136
1858-C	38,856

Half eagles

Year	Mintage
1858-D	15,362
1858-S	18,600
1859	16,814
1859-C	31,847
1859-D	10,366
1859-S	13,220
1860	19,763
1860-C	14,813
1860-D	14,635
1860-S	21,200
1861	688,084
1861-C	[50]6,879
1861-D	1,597
1861-S	18,000
1862	4,430
1862-S	9,500
1863	2,442
1863-S	17,000
1864	4,220
1864-S	3,888
1865	1,270
1865-S	27,612
1866	6,700
1866-S	[62]43,920
1867	6,870
1867-S	29,000
1868	5,700
1868-S	52,000
1869	1,760
1869-S	31,000
1870	4,000
1870-CC	7,675
1870-S	17,000
1871	3,200
1871-CC	20,770
1871-S	25,000
1872	1,660
1872-CC	16,980
1872-S	36,400
1873[68]	112,480
1873-CC[68]	7,416
1873-S[68]	31,000
1874	3,488
1874-CC	21,198
1874-S	16,000
1875	200
1875-CC	11,828
1875-S	9,000
1876	1,432
1876-CC	6,887
1876-S	4,000
1877	1,132
1877-CC	8,680
1877-S	26,700
1878	131,720
1878-CC	9,054
1878-S	144,700
1879	301,920
1879-CC	17,281
1879-S	426,200
1880	3,166,400
1880-CC	51,017
1880-S	1,348,900

Half eagles

Year	Mintage
1881	5,708,760
1881-CC	13,886
1881-S	969,000
1882	2,514,520
1882-CC	82,817
1882-S	969,000
1883	233,400
1883-CC	12,958
1883-S	83,200
1884	191,030
1884-CC	16,402
1884-S	177,000
1885	601,440
1885-S	1,211,500
1886	388,360
1886-S	3,268,000
1887	[53]0
1887-S	1,912,000
1888	18,202
1888-S	293,900
1889	7,520
1890	4,240
1890-CC	53,800
1891	61,360
1891-CC	208,000
1892	753,480
1892-CC	82,968
1892-O	10,000
1892-S	298,400
1893	1,528,120
1893-CC	60,000
1893-O	110,000
1893-S	224,000
1894	957,880
1894-O	16,600
1894-S	55,900
1895	1,345,855
1895-S	112,000
1896	58,960
1896-S	155,400
1897	867,800
1897-S	354,000
1898	633,420
1898-S	1,397,400
1899	1,710,630
1899-S	1,545,000
1900	1,405,500
1900-S	329,000
1901	615,900
1901-S	3,648,000
1902	172,400
1902-S	939,000
1903	226,870
1903-S	1,855,000
1904	392,000
1904-S	97,000
1905	302,200
1905-S	880,700
1906	348,735
1906-D [83]	320,000
1906-S	598,000
1907	626,100
1907-D [83]	888,000

Half eagles

Year	Mintage
1908	[88]999,719
1908-D	[88]148,000
1908-S	[88]82,000
1909	627,060
1909-D	3,423,560
1909-O	34,200
1909-S	297,200
1910	604,000
1910-D	193,600
1910-S	770,200
1911	915,000
1911-D	72,500
1911-S	1,416,000
1912	790,000
1912-S	392,000
1913	916,000
1913-S	408,000
1914	247,000
1914-D	247,000
1914-S	263,000
1915	588,000
1915-S	164,000
1916-S	240,000
1929	662,000

Eagles

Year	Mintage
1795	5,583
1796	4,146
1797	[4]14,555
1798	1,742
1799	37,449
1800	5,999
1801	44,344
1803	15,017
1804	3,757
1838	7,200
1839[27]	38,248
1840	47,338
1841	63,131
1841-O	2,500
1842	81,507
1842-O	27,400
1843	75,462
1843-O	175,162
1844	6,361
1844-O	118,700
1845	26,153
1845-O	47,500
1846	20,095
1846-O	81,780
1847	862,258
1847-O	571,500
1848	145,484
1848-O	35,850
1849	653,618
1849-O	23,900
1850	291,451
1850-O	57,500
1851	176,328
1851-O	263,000
1852	263,106
1852-O	18,000
1853	201,253

300 - U.S. Coins

Eagles

Year	Mintage	Year	Mintage	Year	Mintage
1853-O	51,000	1878	73,780	1899-O	37,047
1854	54,250	1878-CC	3,244	1899-S	841,000
1854-O	52,500	1878-S	26,100	1900	293,840
1854-S	123,826	1879	384,740	1900-S	81,000
1855	121,701	1879-CC	1,762	1901	1,718,740
1855-O	18,000	1879-O	1,500	1901-O	72,041
1855-S	9,000	1879-S	224,000	1901-S	2,812,750
1856	60,490	1880	1,644,840	1902	82,400
1856-O	14,500	1880-CC	11,190	1902-S	469,500
1856-S	68,000	1880-O	9,200	1903	125,830
1857	16,606	1880-S	506,250	1903-O	112,771
1857-O	5,500	1881	3,877,220	1903-S	538,000
1857-S	26,000	1881-CC	24,015	1904	161,930
1858	2,521	1881-O	8,350	1904-O	108,950
1858-O	20,000	1881-S	970,000	1905	200,992
1858-S	11,800	1882	2,324,440	1905-S	369,250
1859	16,093	1882-CC	6,764	1906	165,420
1859-O	2,300	1882-O	10,820	1906-D	981,000
1859-S	7,000	1882-S	132,000	1906-O	86,895
1860	15,055	1883	208,700	1906-S	457,000
1860-O	11,100	1883-CC	12,000	1907	[85]1,443,305
1860-S	5,000	1883-O	800	1907-D	[85]1,030,000
1861	113,164	1883-S	38,000	1907-S	[85]210,500
1861-S	15,500	1884	76,890	1908	[87]374,870
1862	10,960	1884-CC	9,925	1908-D	[87]1,046,500
1862-S	12,500	1884-S	124,250	1908-S	[87]759,850
1863	1,218	1885	253,462	1909	184,789
1863-S	10,000	1885-S	228,000	1909-D	121,540
1864	3,530	1886	236,100	1909-S	292,350
1864-S	2,500	1886-S	826,000	1910	318,500
1865	3,980	1887	53,600	1910-D	2,356,640
1865-S	16,700	1887-S	817,000	1910-S	811,000
1866	3,750	1888	132,924	1911	505,500
1866-S	[61]20,000	1888-O	21,335	1911-D	30,100
1867	3,090	1888-S	648,700	1911-S	51,000
1867-S	9,000	1889	4,440	1912	405,000
1868	10,630	1889-S	425,400	1912-S	300,000
1868-S	13,500	1890	57,980	1913	442,000
1869	1,830	1890-CC	17,500	1913-S	66,000
1869-S	6,430	1891	91,820	1914	151,000
1870	3,990	1891-CC	103,732	1914-D	343,500
1870-CC	5,908	1892	797,480	1914-S	208,000
1870-S	8,000	1892-CC	40,000	1915	351,000
1871	1,790	1892-O	28,688	1915-S	59,000
1871-CC	8,085	1892-S	115,500	1916-S	138,500
1871-S	16,500	1893	1,840,840	1920-S	126,500
1872	1,620	1893-CC	14,000	1926	1,014,000
1872-CC	4,600	1893-O	17,000	1930-S	96,000
1872-S	17,300	1893-S	141,350	1932	4,463,000
1873[68]	800	1894	2,470,735	1933[99]	312,500
1873-CC[68]	4,543	1894-O	107,500		
1873-S[68]	12,000	1894-S	25,000		
1874	53,140	1895	567,770		
1874-CC	16,767	1895-O	98,000		
1874-S	10,000	1895-S	49,000		
1875	100	1896	76,270		
1875-CC	7,715	1896-S	123,750		
1876	687	1897	1,000,090		
1876-CC	4,696	1897-O	42,500		
1876-S	5,000	1897-S	234,750		
1877	797	1898	812,130		
1877-CC	3,332	1898-S	473,600		
1877-S	17,000	1899	1,262,219		

Double eagles

Year	Mintage	Year	Mintage	Year	Mintage
1849[33]	0	1854-S	141,468	1878-CC	13,180
1850	1,170,261	1855	364,666	1878-S	1,739,000
1850-O	141,000	1855-O	8,000	1879	207,600
1851	2,087,155	1855-S	879,675	1879-CC	10,708
1851-O	315,000	1856	329,878	1879-O	2,325
1852	2,053,026	1856-O	2,250	1879-S	1,223,800
1852-O	190,000	1856-S	1,189,780	1880	51,420
1853	1,261,326	1857	439,375	1880-S	836,000
1853-O	71,000	1857-O	30,000	1881	2,220
1854	757,899	1857-S	970,500	1881-S	727,000
1854-O	3,250	1858	211,714	1882	590
		1858-O	35,250	1882-CC	39,140
		1858-S	846,710	1882-S	1,125,000
		1859	43,597	1883	[53]0
		1859-O	9,100	1883-CC	59,962
		1859-S	636,445	1883-S	1,189,000
		1860	577,611	1884	[53]0
		1860-O	6,600	1884-CC	81,139
		1860-S	544,950	1884-S	916,000
		1861[47]	2,976,387	1885	751
		1861-O	[48]7,741	1885-CC	9,450
		1861-S	[49]768,000	1885-S	683,500
		1862	92,098	1886	1,000
		1862-S	854,173	1887	[53]0
		1863	142,760	1887-S	283,000
		1863-S	966,570	1888	226,164
		1864	204,235	1888-S	859,600
		1864-S	793,660	1889	44,070
		1865	351,175	1889-CC	30,945
		1865-S	1,042,500	1889-S	774,700
		1866[59]	698,745	1890	75,940
		1866-S	[60]842,250	1890-CC	91,209
		1867	251,015	1890-S	802,750
		1867-S	920,750	1891	1,390
		1868	98,575	1891-CC	5,000
		1868-S	837,500	1891-S	1,288,125
		1869	175,130	1892	4,430
		1869-S	686,750	1892-CC	27,265
		1870	155,150	1892-S	930,150
		1870-CC	3,789	1893	344,280
		1870-S	982,000	1893-CC	18,402
		1871	80,120	1893-S	996,175
		1871-CC	17,387	1894	1,368,940
		1871-S	928,000	1894-S	1,048,550
		1872	251,850	1895	1,114,605
		1872-CC	26,900	1895-S	1,143,500
		1872-S	780,000	1896	792,535
		1873[68]	1,709,800	1896-S	1,403,925
		1873-CC[68]	22,410	1897	1,383,175
		1873-S[68]	1,040,600	1897-S	1,470,250
		1874	366,780	1898	170,395
		1874-CC	115,000	1898-S	2,575,175
		1874-S	1,214,000	1899	1,669,300
		1875	295,720	1899-S	2,010,300
		1875-CC	111,151	1900	1,874,460
		1875-S	1,230,000	1900-S	2,459,500
		1876	583,860	1901	111,430
		1876-CC	138,441	1901-S	1,596,000
		1876-S	1,597,000	1902	31,140
		1877 77	397,650	1902-S	1,753,625
		1877-CC	42,565	1903	287,270
		1877-S	1,735,000	1903-S	954,000
		1878	543,625	1904	6,256,699

Double eagles

Year	Mintage
1904-S	5,134,175
1905	58,919
1905-S	1,813,000
1906	69,596
1906-D	620,250
1906-S	2,065,750
1907	[84]1,824,703
1907-D	[84]842,250
1907-S	[84]2,165,800
1908	[86]4,427,809
1908-D	[86]1,013,250

Double eagles

Year	Mintage
1908-S	[86]22,000
1909	161,215
1909-D	52,500
1909-S	2,774,925
1910	482,000
1910-D	429,000
1910-S	2,128,250
1911	197,250
1911-D	846,500
1911-S	775,750
1912	149,750

Double eagles

Year	Mintage
1913	168,780
1913-D	393,500
1913-S	34,000
1914	95,250
1914-D	453,000
1914-S	1,498,000
1915	152,000
1915-S	567,500
1916-S	796,000
1920	228,250
1920-S	558,000

Double eagles

Year	Mintage
1921	528,500
1922	1,375,500
1922-S	2,658,000
1923	566,000
1923-D	1,702,250
1924	4,323,500
1924-D	3,049,500
1924-S	2,927,500
1925	2,831,750
1925-D	2,938,500
1925-S	3,776,500
1926	816,750

Double eagles

Year	Mintage
1926-D	481,000
1926-S	2,041,500
1927	2,946,750
1927-D	180,000
1927-S	3,107,000
1928	8,816,000
1929	1,779,750
1930-S	74,000
1931	2,938,250
1931-D	106,500
1932	1,101,750
1933[98]	445,000

Bullion and related coins

This section features mintages/sales figures for all bullion and related coins of all finishes.

The series covered are American Eagle silver, gold and platinum bullion coins; American Buffalo gold bullion coins; First Spouse gold bullion coins; America the Beautiful 5-ounce silver bullion coins; and the 2009 Saint-Gaudens, Ultra High Relief gold $20 double eagle.

Sales figures/mintages for some 2009 and 2010 coins may not be final audited figures and therefore are subject to possible change in the future. Information used in this section was compiled in May 2011.

American Eagle 1-oz silver $1

Year	Business	Proof
1986 (S)	5,393,005	—
1986-S	—	1,446,778
1987 (S)	11,442,335	—
1987-S	—	904,732
1988 (S)	5,004,646	—
1988-S	—	557,370
1989 (S or W)	5,203,327	—
1989-S	—	617,694
1990 (S or W)	5,840,110	—
1990-S	—	695,510
1991 (S or W)	7,191,066	—
1991-S	—	511,924
1992 (S or W)	5,540,068	—
1992-S	—	498,543
1993 (S or W)	6,763,762	—
1993-P	—	405,913
1994 (S or W)	4,227,319	—
1994-P	—	372,168
1995 (S or W)	4,672,051	—
1995-P	—	438,511
1995-W	—	30,125
1996 (S or W)	3,603,386	—
1996-P	—	500,000
1997 (S or W)	4,295,004	—
1997-P	—	435,368
1998 (S or W)	4,847,549	—
1998-P	—	450,000
1999 (S or W)	7,408,640	—
1999-P	—	549,769
2000 (S or W)	9,239,132	—
2000-P	—	600,000
2001 (W)	9,001,711	—
2001-W	—	746,154
2002 (W)	10,539,026	—
2002-W	—	647,342
2003 (W)	8,495,008	—
2003-W	—	747,831
2004 (W)	8,882,754	—

American Eagle 1-oz silver $1

Year	Business	Proof
2004-W	—	813,477
2005 (W)	8,891,025	—
2005-W	—	816,663
2006 (W)	10,676,522	—
2006-W Unc.	470,000	—
2006-W Proof	—	843,602
2006-W Rev. Proof	—	250,000
2007 (W)	9,028,036	—
2007-W Unc.	711,504	—
2007-W Proof	—	821,759
2008 (W)	20,583,000	—
2008-W Unc.	513,514	—
2008-W Proof	—	713,353
2009 (W)	30,459,000	—
2009-W Unc.	0	—
2009-W Proof	—	0
2010 (W)	34,764,500	—
2010-W Proof	—	860,000

American Eagle 1/10-oz gold $5

Year	Business	Proof
1986 (W)	912,609	—
1987 (W)	580,266	—
1988 (W)	159,500	—
1988-P	—	143,881
1989 (W)	264,790	—
1989-P	—	84,647
1990 (W)	210,210	—
1990-P	—	99,349
1991 (W)	165,200	—
1991-P	—	70,334
1992 (W)	209,300	—
1992-P	—	64,874
1993 (W)	210,709	—
1993-P	—	58,649
1994 (W)	206,380	—
1994-P	—	62,849

American Eagle 1/10-oz gold $5

Year	Business	Proof
1995 (W)	223,025	—
1995-W	—	62,673
1996 (W)	401,964	—
1996-W	—	56,700
1997 (S or W)	528,515	—
1997-W	—	34,984
1998 (S or W)	1,344,520	—
1998-W	—	39,706
1999 (S or W)	2,750,338	—
1999-W	—	48,426
2000 (S or W)	569,153	—
2000-W	—	49,970
2001 (W)	269,147	—
2001-W	—	37,547
2002 (W)	230,027	—
2002-W	—	40,864
2003 (W)	245,029	—
2003-W	—	36,668
2004 (W)	250,016	—
2004-W	—	35,487
2005 (W)	300,043	—
2005-W	—	49,265
2006 (W)	285,006	—
2006-W Unc.	20,643	—
2006-W	—	47,277
2007 (W)	190,010	—
2007-W Unc.	22,501	—
2007-W	—	58,553
2008 (W)	305,000	—
2008-W Unc.	13,376	—
2008-W	—	29,155
2009 (W)	270,000	—
2009-W Unc.	0	—
2009-W	—	0
2010 (W)	435,000	—
2010-W Proof	—	12,250

American Eagle 1/4-oz gold $10

Year	Business	Proof
1986 (W)	726,031	—
1987 (W)	269,255	—
1988 (W)	49,000	—
1988-P	—	98,028
1989 (W)	81,789	—
1989-P	—	54,170
1990 (W)	41,000	—
1990-P	—	62,674
1991 (W)	36,100	—
1991-P	—	50,839
1992 (W)	59,546	—
1992-P	—	46,269
1993 (W)	71,864	—
1993-P	—	46,464
1994 (W)	72,650	—
1994-P	—	48,172
1995 (W)	83,752	—
1995-W	—	47,484
1996 (W)	60,318	—
1996-W	—	37,900
1997 (S or W)	108,805	—
1997-W	—	29,808
1998 (S or W)	309,829	—
1998-W	—	29,733
1999 (S or W)	564,232	—
1999-W	—	34,416
2000 (S or W)	128,964	—
2000-W	—	36,033
2001 (W)	71,280	—
2001-W	—	25,630
2002 (W)	62,027	—
2002-W	—	29,242
2003 (W)	74,029	—
2003-W	—	33,409
2004 (W)	72,014	—
2004-W	—	29,127
2005 (W)	72,015	—
2005-W	—	37,207

American Eagle 1/4-oz gold $10

Year	Business	Proof
2006 (W)	60,004	—
2006-W Unc.	15,188	—
2006-W	—	36,127
2007 (W)	34,004	—
2007-W Unc.	12,766	—
2007-W	—	46,189
2008 (W)	70,000	—
2008-W Unc.	9,200	—
2008-W	—	28,301
2009 (W)	110,000	—
2009-W Unc.	0	—
2009-W	—	0
2010 (W)	74,000	—
2010-W Proof	—	8,598

American Eagle 1/2-oz gold $25

Year	Business	Proof
1986 (W)	599,566	—
1987 (W)	131,255	—
1987-P	—	143,398
1988 (W)	45,000	—
1988-P	—	76,528
1989 (W)	44,829	—
1989-P	—	44,798
1990 (W)	31,000	—
1990-P	—	51,636
1991 (W)	24,100	—
1991-P	—	53,125
1992 (W)	54,404	—
1992-P	—	40,976
1993 (W)	73,324	—
1993-P	—	43,319
1994 (W)	62,400	—
1994-P	—	44,584
1995 (W)	53,474	—
1995-W	—	45,442
1996 (W)	39,287	—
1996-W	—	34,700
1997 (S or W)	79,605	—
1997-W	—	26,340
1998 (S or W)	169,029	—
1998-W	—	25,549
1999 (S or W)	263,013	—
1999-W	—	30,452
2000 (S or W)	79,287	—
2000-W	—	32,027
2001 (S or W)	48,047	—
2001-W	—	23,261
2002 (S or W)	70,027	—
2002-W	—	26,646
2003 (S or W)	79,029	—
2003-W	—	28,512
2004 (S or W)	98,040	—
2004-W	—	27,731
2005 (W)	80,023	—
2005-W	—	34,311
2006 (W)	66,005	—
2006-W Unc.	15,164	—
2006-W	—	34,322
2007 (W)	47,002	—
2007-W Unc.	11,455	—
2007-W	—	44,025
2008 (W)	61,000	—
2008-W Unc.	16,126	—
2008-W	—	27,864
2009 (W)	110,000	—
2009-W Unc.	0	—
2009-W	—	0
2010 (W)	53,000	—
2010-W Proof	—	7,486

American Eagle 1-oz gold $50

Year	Business	Proof
1986 (W)	1,362,650	—
1986-W	—	446,290
1987 (W)	1,045,500	—
1987-W	—	147,498
1988 (W)	465,500	—
1988-W	—	87,133
1989 (W)	415,790	—
1989-W	—	54,570
1990 (W)	373,210	—
1990-W	—	62,401
1991 (W)	243,100	—
1991-W	—	50,411
1992 (W)	275,000	—
1992-W	—	44,826
1993 (W)	480,192	—
1993-W	—	34,389
1994 (W)	221,663	—
1994-W	—	46,674
1995 (W)	200,636	—
1995-W	—	46,484
1996 (W)	189,148	—
1996-W	—	36,000
1997 (S or W)	664,508	—
1997-W	—	27,554
1998 (S or W)	1,468,530	—
1998-W	—	26,060
1999 (S or W)	1,505,026	—
1999-W	—	31,446
2000 (S or W)	433,319	—
2000-W	—	33,006
2001 (S or W)	143,605	—
2001-W	—	24,580
2002 (S or W)	222,029	—
2002-W	—	27,499
2003 (S or W)	416,032	—
2003-W	—	28,344
2004 (S or W)	417,019	—
2004-W	—	28,731
2005 (W)	356,555	—
2005-W	—	35,336
2006 (W)	237,510	—
2006-W Unc.	45,912	—
2006-W Proof	—	47,096
2006-W Rev. Proof	—	10,000
2007 (W)	140,016	—
2007-W Unc.	18,606	—
2007-W	—	51,810
2008 (W)	710,000	—
2008-W Unc.	12,387	—
2008-W	—	29,399
2009 (W)	1,493,000	—
2009-W Unc.	0	—
2009-W	—	0
2010 (W)	1,125,000	—
2010-W Proof	—	16,884

American Eagle 1/10-oz platinum $10

Year	Business	Proof
1997 (W)	70,250	—
1997-W	—	37,025
1998 (W)	39,525	—
1998-W	—	19,832
1999 (W)	55,955	—
1999-W	—	19,123
2000 (W)	34,027	—
2000-W	—	15,651
2001 (W)	52,017	—
2001-W	—	12,193
2002 (W)	23,005	—
2002-W	—	12,365
2003 (W)	22,007	—
2003-W	—	9,534
2004 (W)	15,010	—
2004-W	—	7,202
2005 (W)	14,013	—
2005-W	—	8,104
2006 (W)	11,001	—
2006-W Unc.	3,544	—
2006-W Proof	—	10,205
2007 (W)	13,003	—
2007-W Unc.	5,566	—
2007-W Proof	—	8,176
2008 (W)	17,000	—
2008-W Unc.	4,623	—
2008-W Proof	—	5,650
2009 (W)	0	—
2009-W Uncirculated	0	—
2009-W	—	0
2010 (W)	0	—
2010-W Proof	—	0

American Eagle 1/4-oz platinum $25

Year	Business	Proof
1997 (W)	27,100	—
1997-W	—	18,661
1998 (W)	38,887	—
1998-W	—	14,860
1999 (W)	39,734	—
1999-W	—	13,514
2000 (W)	20,054	—
2000-W	—	11,995
2001 (W)	21,815	—
2001-W	—	8,858
2002 (W)	27,405	—
2002-W	—	9,282
2003 (W)	25,207	—
2003-W	—	7,044
2004 (W)	18,010	—
2004-W	—	5,226
2005 (W)	12,013	—
2005-W	—	6,592
2006 (W)	12,001	—
2006-W Unc.	2,676	—
2006-W	—	7,813
2007 (W)	8,402	—
2007-W Unc.	3,690	—
2007-W Proof	—	6,017
2008 (W)	22,800	—
2008-W Unc.	3,894	—
2008-W Proof	—	3,891
2009 (W)	0	—
2009-W Unc.	0	—
2009-W	—	0
2010 (W)	0	—
2010-W Proof	—	0

American Eagle 1/2-oz platinum $50

Year	Business	Proof
1997 (W)	20,500	—
1997-W	—	15,463
1998 (W)	32,419	—
1998-W	—	13,821
1999 (W)	32,309	—
1999-W	—	11,098
2000 (W)	18,892	—
2000-W	—	11,049
2001 (W)	12,815	—
2001-W	—	8,268
2002 (W)	24,005	—
2002-W	—	8,772
2003 (W)	17,409	—
2003-W	—	7,131
2004 (W)	13,236	—
2004-W	—	5,095
2005 (W)	9,013	—
2005-W	—	5,942
2006 (W)	9,602	—
2006-W Unc.	2,577	—
2006-W Proof	—	7,649
2007 (W)	7,001	—
2007-W Unc.	3,635	—
2007-W Proof	—	22,873
2007-W Rev. Proof	—	16,937
2008 (W)	14,000	—
2008-W Unc.	3,415	—
2008-W Proof	—	3,654
2009 (W)	0	—
2009-W Uncirculated	0	—
2009-W	—	0
2010 (W)	0	—
2010-W Proof	—	0

American Eagle 1-oz platinum $100

Year	Business	Proof
1997 (W)	56,000	—
1997-W	—	18,000
1998 (W)	133,002	—
1998-W	—	14,203
1999 (W)	56,707	—
1999-W	—	12,351

American Eagle
1-oz platinum $100

Year	Business	Proof
2000 (W)	10,003	—
2000-W	—	12,453
2001 (W)	14,070	—
2001-W	—	8,990
2002 (W)	11,502	—
2002-W	—	9,834
2003 (W)	8,007	—
2003-W	—	8,246
2004 (W)	7,009	—
2004-W	—	6,074
2005 (W)	6,310	—
2005-W	—	6,602
2006 (W)	6,000	—
2006-W Unc.	3,068	—
2006-W Proof	—	9,152
2007 (W)	7,202	—
2007-W Unc.	4,177	—
2007-W Proof	—	8,363
2008 (W)	21,800	—
2008-W Unc.	4,063	—
2008-W Proof	—	5,030
2009 (W)	0	—
2009-W Unc.	0	—

American Eagle
1-oz platinum $100

Year	Business	Proof
2009-W	—	8,000
2010 (W)	0	—
2010-W Proof	—	10,000

American Buffalo
1-oz gold $50

Year	Business	Proof
2006 (W)	337,012	—
2006-W Proof	—	246,267
2007 (W)	136,503	—
2007-W Proof	—	58,998
2008 (W)	189,500	—
2008-W Unc.	9,074	—
2008-W Proof	—	18,863
2009 (W)	200,000	—
2009-W Unc.	0	—
2009-W Proof	—	0
2010 (W) Proof	—	49,236

American Buffalo
1/2-oz gold $25

Year	Business	Proof
2008-W Unc.	16,908	—
2008-W Proof	—	12,169

American Buffalo
1/4-oz gold $10

Year	Business	Proof
2008-W Unc.	9,949	—
2008-W Proof	—	13,125

American Buffalo
1/10-oz gold $5

Year	Business	Proof
2008-W Unc.	17,429	—
2008-W Proof	—	18,884

Ultra High Relief .9999
fine gold $20 coin

Year	Business	Proof
2009 (W)	115,178	—

First Spouse half-ounce
.9999 gold coins

Date	Unc.	Proof
2007-W		
M. Washington	17,661	19,169
2007-W A. Adams	17,142	17,149
2007-W T. Jefferson		
Liberty	19,823	19,815
2007-W		
D. Madison	11,813	17,661
2008-W E. Monroe	4,519	7,933

First Spouse half-ounce
.9999 gold coins

Date	Unc.	Proof
2008-W L. Adams	4,223	7,454
2008-W A. Jackson		
Liberty	4,281	7,454
2008-W M. Van Buren		
Liberty	3,443	6,187
2009-W A. Harrison	3,537	6,250
2009-W L. Tyler	3,152	5,163
2009-W J. Tyler	2,861	4,830
2009-W S. Polk	3,501	5,157
2009-W M. Taylor	3,430	4,787
2010-W A. Fillmore	3,489	6,120
2010-W J. Pierce	3,333	4,843
2010-W Buchanan		
Liberty	5,353	7,304
2010-W M. Lincoln	3,489	6,011

America the Beautiful
5-ounce silver

Date	Bullion	Unc.
2010 Hot Springs	33,000	27,000
2010 Yellowstone	33,000	27,000
2010 Yosemite	33,000	27,000
2010 Grand Canyon	33,000	27,000
2010 Mount Hood	33,000	27,000

Mintage notes

1. 1793 cent: Flowing Hair obverse, Chain reverse: 36,103; Flowing Hair obverse, Wreath reverse: 63,353; Liberty Cap obverse; Wreath reverse: 11,056.

2. 1795 silver dollar: Flowing Hair type: 160,295; Draft Bust type: 42,738.

3. 1796 cent: Liberty Cap: 109,825; Draped Bust: 363,375.

4. 1797 $10: Mintage includes both reverse types.

5. 1798 $5: Mint Report of 24,867 coins includes Small Eagle reverse coins dated 1798, as well as Heraldic Eagle coins dated 1795, 1797 and 1798. This mixture of mulings is the result of an emergency coinage late in 1798 after the Mint had been closed for a while due to yellow fever. Quantities struck of each are unknown and can only be a guess.

6. 1798 silver dollar: Mintage includes both reverse designs.

7. 1801, 1802, and 1803 silver dollar: All three dates were restruck in Proof in 1858 with a plain edge, using obverse dies made in 1834 to 1835 and the reverse die from the Class I 1804 dollar, which was also made in 1834. Due to the scandal caused by the private issue of 1804 dollars in 1858, these coins were not offered for sale to collectors until 1875, by which time their edges had been lettered.

8. 1804 silver dollar: Although the Mint Report lists 19,570 dollars for this year, it is assumed that they were all dated 1803. The 1804 dollars were first struck in 1834-35 for inclusion in diplomatic presentation sets. A few pieces, possibly flawed Proofs or production overruns, reached collectors via trades with the Mint or in circulation and the coin was popularized as a rarity. In 1858 the son of a Mint employee used the obverse die prepared in 1834 and a newly prepared reverse die plus a plain collar to secretly strike 1804 dollars, a few of which were sold to collectors. While the Mint had intended to do exactly the same thing with dollars dated 1801 to 1804, Mint officials were forced to cancel the project due to the public scandal over the privately issued 1804 dollars. The privately struck coins were recalled, and all were allegedly melted but one (which went to the Mint Cabinet collection). Instead, they and the plain edged 1801 to 1803 dollars were put in storage and offered for sale in 1875, by which time their edges had been mechanically lettered.

9. 1804, 1823 cent, and 1811 half cent: Counterfeits, called restrikes, exist that were made outside the Mint, using old, genuine but mismatched Mint dies.

10. 1805 silver dollar: The 321 dollars listed in the Mint Report for 1805 were older dollars that were found in deposits of Spanish-American silver and which were reissued through the Treasury. Because of this misinformation, a few coins have been altered to this date in the past.

11. 1807 $5: Capped Bust type: 32,488; Capped Draped Bust type: 51,605.

12. 1807 half dollar: Draped Bust type: 301,076; Capped Bust type: 750,500.

13. 1822 $5: Although the Mint Report says 17,796 coins were struck, only three pieces are known and it is likely that most of this mintage was from dies dated 1821.

14. 1827 quarter dollar: Although the Mint Report lists a mintage of 4,000 pieces for this year, it is likely that all of these coins were dated 1825 except for a few Proofs. Later this date was unofficially (but intentionally) restruck at the Mint using an obverse die dated 1827 and a reverse die that had been used in 1819, and that had a Square Base 2 in quarter dollar, rather than the Curled Base 2 of the original 1827.

15. 1831, 1849, 1856 and 1857 half cent: Originally struck in Proof and Uncirculated, the Proofs were restruck for collectors in later years.

16. 1832-35 half cent: The figures shown are listed in the Mint Report for 1833 to 1836 instead, but are assumed to be misplaced.

17. 1834 $5: Total of 732,169 coins struck. This includes 50,141 of the Capped Head design struck and released; 24,568 of the Capped Head struck but melted; and 657,460 of the Classic Head design (and weight), all released.

18. 1834 $2.50: Mintage includes 4,000 of the Capped Head, of which most or all were melted. It may be that all survivors are Proofs and circulated Proofs.

19. 1836, 1838, and 1839 silver dollar: Gobrecht dollars, some patterns and some intended for circulation, were struck in these years. Also, some varieties were restruck in later years, making mintage figures questionable. Versions exist with or without stars and the designer's name, some of them exceedingly scarce. The 1,600 mintage figure for 1836 represents 1,000 struck for circulation on the 1836 standard of 416 grains, and 600 pieces struck in 1837 (dated 1836) on the new standard of 412.5 grains.

20. 1836 half dollar: Mintage includes 6,545,000 Capped Bust, Lettered Edge coins and 1,200 pieces with a reeded edge and no motto E PLURIBUS UNUM. (The latter was actually a pattern of the design adopted the following year, but much of the mintage was placed into circulation.)

21. 1836 half cent: Originally struck in Proof only, this date was restruck in Proof in later years to provide collectors with examples of a coin that was listed in the Mint Report but which couldn't be found in circulation. See **16**.

22. 1837 dime: Capped Bust type: 359,500; Seated Liberty, Without Stars on obverse: 682,500.

23. 1837 half dime: Capped Bust type: 871,000; Seated Liberty, Without Stars on obverse: 1,405,000.

24. 1838-O half dollar: Twenty specimen pieces were struck to celebrate the opening of the New Orleans Mint.

25. 1838 quarter dollar: Capped Bust type: 366,000; Seated Liberty type: 466,000.

26. 1838-O dime and half dime: Both are of Seated Liberty, Without Stars design (type of 1837). 1838 Philadelphia coins have stars, as do all others through 1859.

27. 1839 $10: Includes first design head (type of 1838) and modified head (type of 1840 to 1907).

28. 1839 (P), 1839-O half dollar: Capped Bust type: (P): 1,362,160; -O: 178,976. Seated Liberty type: (P): 1,972,400. (Note: Although Christian Gobrecht's half dollar design was slightly modified during 1839 by the addition of a small drapery fold beneath the elbow, the design was never as fully modified as the other Seated Liberty denominations were in 1840. In subsequent years, individual dies would occasionally be overpolished, thus removing this small drapery fold. Coins struck from these inferior dies are sometimes referred to as having a "No Drapery design," when in fact no design change was intended or made.)

29. 1840 to 1853 silver dollar: Proof restrikes exist for all dates.

30. 1840 to 1848 and 1852 half cent: Originally struck in Proof only, all dates were restruck in Proof for sale to collectors.

31. 1841 (P) $2.50: Struck in Proof only, possibly at a later date. Unlisted in Mint Report .

32. 1848 (P) $2.50: Approximately 1,389 coins were counterstamped CAL. above the eagle to show that they were made from California gold. This was done while the coins were resting on an inverted obverse die on a worktable, which will probably show on a genuine coin with a fake counterstamp.

33. 1849 $20: One example in gold survives of a small number of trial strikes produced in December 1849. The dies were rejected, allegedly because of improper high relief, but in actuality to discredit engraver James B. Longacre in an attempt to force his removal. The attempt failed and Longacre eventually produced a second set of dies, but they were not completed until the following month and so they were dated 1850. The one known gold example is in the National Numismatic Collection at the Smithsonian Institution. All others were melted.

34. 1853 silver coinage: In early 1853, the weight of all fractional silver coins was reduced by about 7 percent, to prevent hoarding and melting. To distinguish between the old and new weights, arrows were placed on either side of the date on the half dime through half dollar, and rays were put around the eagle on the quarter and half dollar. The rays were removed after 1853, and the arrows after 1855. Much of the old silver was withdrawn from circulation and melted. The exception to all this was the silver 3-cent coin, which was decreased in weight but increased in fineness, making it intrinsically worth more than before and proportionate with the other fractional silver coins. No coins of the new weight were struck until 1854, at which time an olive branch and a cluster of arrows was added to the reverse.

35. 1853, 1853-O half dollar: All 1853 and virtually all 1853-O half dollar are of the new weight. Two or three 1853-O are known without the arrows and rays. Beware of alterations from 1858-O.

36. 1853, 1853-O quarter dollar: Without Arrows and Rays: (P): 44,200. With Arrows and Rays: (P): 15,210,020; -O: 1,332,000.

37. 1853, 1853-O dime: Without Arrows: (P): 95,000. With Arrows: (P): 12,078,010; -O: 1,100,000.

38. 1853, 1853-O half dime: Without Arrows: (P): 135,000; -O: 160,000. With Arrows: (P): 13,210,020; -O: 2,200,000.

39. 1854, 1854-D, 1854-S gold dollar: (P): Coronet 736,709; Indian (small head) 902,736. All 1854-D and -S dollars are Coronet design.

40. 1856, 1856-D, 1856-S gold dollar: All (P) and 1856-D Mint are Indian (large head); all 1856-S Mint are Indian (small head).

41. 1856 cent: More than 1,000 1856 Flying Eagle cents were struck in Proof and Uncirculated, in this and later years. As they were patterns, they are not included in the Mint Report or this figure.

42. 1857 cent: large cents: 333,456; small cents: 17,450,000.

43. 1858 silver dollar: It is estimated that 80 Proofs were struck,

some of them possibly at a later date.

44. 1859 cent: This year only, the reverse design is a Laurel Wreath without a shield. All other Indian cents (1860 to 1909) have a shield and an Oak Wreath.

45. 1860-S $3: Out of 7,000 coins struck, 2,592 pieces were not released because of short weight. They were melted in 1869 for use in other denominations.

46. 1860, 1860-O, 1860-S dime and half dime: Beginning in 1860 (with the exception of the 1860-S dime), the half dime and dime were redesigned by eliminating the stars, moving the legend UNITED STATES OF AMERICA to the obverse, and using a larger, more elaborate wreath on the reverse. A number of fabrications with the obverse of 1859 and the reverse of 1860 (thereby omitting the legend UNITED STATES OF AMERICA), were struck by order of the director of the Mint. These consist of half dimes dated 1859 or 1860, and dimes dated 1859. Although they are considered by some to be patterns, that designation is doubtful as the intentions of the director were highly questionable.

47. 1861 $20: A few trial pieces are known with a reverse as engraved by Anthony Paquet, with taller, thinner letters and a narrow rim. The design was judged unacceptable because the narrow reverse rim would not stack easily. (See 49.)

48. 1861-O $20: Mintage includes 5,000 coins struck by the USA; 9,750 by the state of Louisiana; and 2,991 by the Confederate States of America. It is impossible to prove the issuer of any given coin.

49. 1861-S $20: Mintage includes 19,250 pieces struck with the Paquet reverse and released into circulation. (See 47.) Most of these were recalled and melted during the next few years, but specie hoarding during the Civil War probably preserved a number of them until later years when the problem was forgotten.

50. 1861-C $5: Mintage includes 5,992 pieces coined by USA and 887 by CSA. It is impossible to prove the issuer.

51. 1861-D gold dollar: A small number were struck by the CSA.

52. 1861-O half dollar: Mintage includes 330,000 struck by the USA; 1,240,000 by the state of Louisiana; and 962,633 by the CSA. It is impossible to tell them apart. One obverse die is identifiable as having been used with the CSA reverse to strike four pattern coins, but there is no way of telling when that die was used with a regular reverse die or who issued the coins struck from it.

53. Struck in Proof only.

54. 1863 silver 3 cents: It is possible that all of these non-Proofs were dated 1862. Proof 1863/2 coins were struck in 1864.

55. 1864 (P) dime, half dime and silver 3 cents: These figures, like many others in the years 1861 to 1871, are highly controversial due to extraordinary bookkeeping methods used in the Mint in this era.

56. 1864 2 cents: Struck with Large and Small Motto IN GOD WE TRUST.

57. 1864 cent: Mintage comprises 13,740,000 copper-nickel and 39,233,714 bronze pieces. The bronze coins come with and without the designer's initial L, which appears on all subsequent issues. The 1864 variety With L is the scarcer.

58. 1866 coinage: It was decided to add the motto IN GOD WE TRUST to the reverse of all double eagles, eagles, half eagles, silver dollars, half dollars and quarter dollars beginning in 1866. Early in the year, before the new reverse dies had arrived, the San Francisco Mint produced $20, $10, $5 and half dollar coins without the motto. These are regular issue coins and are not patterns or errors. They are not to be confused with a peculiar set of Philadelphia Mint silver coins without motto, consisting of two dollars, one half dollar and one quarter dollar, which was clandestinely struck inside (but not by) the Mint for sale to a collector. A three-piece set containing the unique quarter dollar and half dollar and one of the two known silver dollars was stolen from the Willis H. du Pont collection in 1967. The quarter dollar was recovered and returned to du Pont in December 1999. The other coins were recovered separately in 2004. Beware of regular coins with motto or Mint mark removed.

59. 1866, 1866-S $20: When the reverse of the double eagle was altered to include the motto there a few minor changes were also made in the scrollwork, the most prominent being the change in the shield from flat-sided to curved. Check any alleged 1866-S No Motto $20 for this feature.

60. 1866-S $20: Includes 120,000 No Motto coins.

61. 1866-S $10: Includes 8,500 No Motto coins.

62. 1866-S $5: Includes 9,000 No Motto coins.

63. 1866-S half dollar: Includes 60,000 No Motto coins.

64. 1867 copper-nickel 5 cents: Struck with rays on reverse (type of 1866) and without rays (type of 1868 to 1883).

65. 1870-S $3: Not included in the Mint Report, supposedly one piece was struck for inclusion in the cornerstone of the new San Francisco Mint. One piece is known in a private collection, and the present whereabouts of the cornerstone piece is unknown. It is possible there is only one piece.

66. 1870-S gold dollar: 2,000 coins were struck without a Mint mark. It is unknown if they were melted and recoined or released as is and included in the Mint Report figure of 3,000 coins.

67. 1870-S silver dollar: Eleven are known in collections. Not listed in the annual Mint Report. The first official evidence of their production was found in March 2004 in the form of a San Francisco Mint warrant from the second quarter of 1870, found in archives. That warrant recorded the coins that had been struck for placement in the cornerstone of the second San Francisco Mint, which was under construction. Among the coins made for the cornerstone was an 1870-S Seated Liberty dollar. The newly produced warrant was the first record discovered confirming production of the 1870-S Seated Liberty half dime and 1870-S Indian Head gold $3 coin, each of which is known by a single example in collections. The warrant also records production of an 1870-S Seated Liberty quarter dollar, which is unknown in any collection but that is presumably in the lost cornerstone of the San Francisco Mint.

68. 1873 coinage: Early in the year, a relatively closed style of 3 was used in the date on all denominations. In response to complaints that the 3 looked like an 8, a new, more open 3 was introduced. Most types were struck with both styles, except for those that were created or discontinued by the Coinage Act of Feb. 12, 1873. This law created the Trade dollar and eliminated the standard silver dollar, the silver 5-cent coin and 3-cent coin, and the 2-cent coin. The weight of the dime, quarter dollar and half dollar were slightly increased, and the heavier coins were marked with arrows for the remainder of 1873 and all of 1874.

69. 1873 $3: Struck in Proof only, later restruck in Proof more than once.

70. 1873-S silver dollar: Presumably all were melted at the Mint after production of standard silver dollars was suspended. None are known.

71. 1873, 1873-CC, 1873-S half dollar: Without Arrows: (P): 801,200; CC: 122,500; S: 5,000. With Arrows: (P) 1,815,150; CC: 214,560; S: 228,000. (Note: The 1873-S Seated Liberty, Without Arrows half dollar is unknown in any condition in any collection. Presumably, they were all melted with the 1873-S silver dollars. Beware of any regular 1873-S with the arrows removed. The difference in weight between the two issues is insignificant, and useless in checking a suspected altered coin.)

72. 1873, 1873-CC, 1873-S quarter dollar: Without Arrows: (P): 212,000; -CC: 4,000. With Arrows: (P): 1,271,160; -CC: 12,462; -S: 156,000.

73. 1873, 1873-CC, 1873-S dime: Without Arrows: (P): 1,568,000; -CC: 12,400. With Arrows: (P): 2,377,700; -CC: 18,791; -S: 455,000. (Note: One 1873-CC Without Arrows known, all others presumably were melted.)

74. 1873 2 cents: Originally struck in Proof only early in 1873 with a Closed 3. Later restruck in Proof with an Open 3.

75. 1875 $3: Struck in Proof only, later restruck in Proof.

76. 1876-CC 20 cents: Virtually all remelted at the Mint. A few escaped, possibly as souvenirs given to visitors. Fewer than 20 are known today.

77. 1877 $20: In this year the master hubs were redesigned slightly, raising the head and changing TWENTY D. to TWENTY DOLLARS.

78. 1878, 1879 to 1885 Trade dollar: The (P) Mint Trade dollars from 1878 to 1883 were struck and sold in Proof only. Person or persons unknown struck 10 1884 and five 1885 coins in Proof in the Mint for private distribution. They are not listed in the Mint Report.

79. 1878 silver dollar: Three slightly different designs were used for both the obverse and reverse of this date, including some dies with the second designs impressed over the first. All 1878-CC and 1878-S are from the second designs. Most 1879 to 1904 dollars are of the third design, except for some second design reverses on 1879-S and 1880-CC coins. New, slightly different master hubs were prepared for 1921.

80. 1883 copper-nickel 5 cents: Shield type: 1,451,500; Liberty Head, No CENTS on reverse: 5,474,300; Liberty Head, With CENTS on reverse: 16,026,200.

81. 1894-S dime: The superintendent of the San Francisco Mint made 24 Proof strikings to coin remaining silver from melted coins of older designs. Nine can be traced today.

82. 1895 silver dollar: Apparently virtually all circulation strike coins were never issued and were probably melted in the great silver melt of 1918. Beware of altered dates and removed Mint marks.

83. 1906-D and 1907-D $5: These were, of course, struck at the Denver Mint. The Coronet half eagle is the only design that was struck at both the Dahlonega and Denver Mints.

84. 1907, 1907-D, 1907-S $20: Coronet: 1,451,786 (P) Mint and all -D and -S Mint coins. Saint-Gaudens type: 11,250 High Relief, Roman Numeral date coins and 361,667 lower-relief, Arabic date coins. A few Extremely High Relief patterns were also made.

85. 1907, 1907-D, 1907-S $10: Coronet: 1,203,899 (P) Mint and all -D and -S Mint coins. Indian Head type: 239,406.

86. 1908, 1908-D, 1908-S $20: Without motto IN GOD WE TRUST: (type of 1907) (P): 4,271,551; -D: 663,750. With motto: (type of 1909 to 1933) (P): 156,258; -D: 349,500; -S: 22,000.

87. 1908, 1908-D, 1908-S $10: Without motto IN GOD WE TRUST: (type of 1907) (P): 33,500; -D: 210,000. With motto: (type of 1909 to 1933) (P): 341,370; -D: 836,500; S: 59,850.

88. 1908, 1908-D, 1908-S $5: Coronet: 421,874 P-Mint coins. Indian Head: 577,845 P-Mint and all D and S-Mint coins.

89. 1909, 1909-S cent: Indian Head : (P): 14,368,470; -S: 309,000. Lincoln Head with designer's initials V.D.B.: (P): 27,994,580; -S: 484,000. Lincoln Head without V.D.B.: (P): 72,700,420; -S: 1,825,000.

90. 1913 Liberty Head copper-nickel 5 cents: Person or persons unknown struck five unauthorized pieces, using Mint machinery and dies. One of the five examples was missing to the numismatic community from 1962 to 2003. (See also **91.**)

91. 1913, 1913-D, 1913-S Indian Head copper-nickel 5 cents: Subtype with the bison standing on a solid mound: (P): 3 0,992,000; -D: 5,337,000; -S: 2,105,000. Subtype with the Bison on Plain, with the base of the mound recessed so as to protect the Mint mark and FIVE CENTS: (P): 29,857,186; -D: 4,156,000; -S: 1,209,000.

92. 1916, 1916-D quarter dollar: Barber Head type: 1,788,000 (P) Mint and all -D Mint. Standing Liberty type: 52,000 (P) Mint.

93. 1916, 1916-D, 1916-S dime: Barber Head type: 18,490,000; -S: 5,820,000. Winged Liberty Head type: (P): 22,180,080; -D: 264,000; -S: 10,45 0,000.

94. 1917-D, 1917-S half dollar: With Mint mark on obverse (type of 1916): -D: 765,400; -S: 952,000. On reverse (type of 1918 to 1947): -D: 1,940,000; -S: 5,554,000.

95. 1917, 1917-D, 1917-S quarter dollar: Type of 1916, with partially nude figure: (P): 8,740,000; -D: 1,509,200; -S: 1,952,000. Type of 1918, with fully clothed figure, and rearranged stars and eagle higher on reverse: (P): 13,880,000; -D: 6,224,400; -S: 5,552,000.

96. 1921, 1921-D, 1921-S silver dollar: Morgan type: 44,690,000 (P) Mint and all -D and -S Mints. Peace type: 1,006,473 (P) Mint. The 1921 Peace dollars (and a very few Proof 1922 dollars), are of a higher relief than the 1922 to 1935 dollars.

97. 1922-D, No D cent: No cents were struck in Philadelphia in 1922. Some 1922-D cents are found with the Mint mark missing or weak due to obstructed dies. Only Die Pair 2, with weak obverse and strong reverse, carries the high premiums. Coins from other die pairs bring lesser premiums. Beware of altered coins.

98. 1933 $20: Federal officials generally consider the coin illegal for private ownership, with one exception. Thirteen survivors identified. Two reside in the National Numismatic Collection at the Smithsonian Institution. Another surfaced in 1996 in private hands and was confiscated by Treasury officials, but a legal case over ownership ended with the government agreeing to allow it to be auctioned for private ownership; it sold for $7,590,000 in July 2002. Ten more surfaced in 2004 in private hands and have been subject of a legal case to determine ownership; they remain in Mint possession at press time for this edition (2011). A photograph is known of a possible 14th example.

99. 1933 $10: Very few of these were issued, perhaps several dozens known. Beware of counterfeits.

100. 1938-D copper-nickel 5 cents: Indian Head: 7,020,000. Jefferson: 5,376,000.

101. 1942 to 1945 (P), -P, -D, -S 5 cents: To conserve nickel during the war, the composition of the 5-cent coin was changed to a 56 percent copper, 35 percent silver, and 9 percent manganese alloy. Coins of this alloy were marked with a large Mint mark over the dome of

Monticello, including those from Philadelphia. They consist of some 1942-P, all 1942-S, and all 1943 to 1945 coins. The 1942 Philadelphia Mint coins were made both in compositions, as follows: copper-nickel: 49,789,000; wartime alloy: 57,873,000. Many wartime alloy 5-cent coins have been melted for their silver content.

102. 1943, 1943-D, 1943-S cent: All 1943 cents were made of zinc-coated steel. A few 1943 bronze and 1944 steel cents were made by accident or deliberately (authenticated as of May 2011: 14 Philadelphia Mint coins, six San Francisco Mint coins and one Denver Mint coin). Many fakes of these have been produced. Test any suspected off-metal 1943 or 1944 cent with a magnet to see if it has been plated, and check the date for alterations. Cents struck on steel planchets produced in 1942 weigh 41.5 grains, while those struck on planchets produced later in 1943 weigh 42.5 grains.

103. 1944 copper-nickel 5 cents: Coins without a Mint mark are counterfeits made for circulation, as are any 1923-D or 1930-D dimes. Not all counterfeits are of rare dates, meant to sell at high prices. Some were meant to circulate.

104. 1964 to 1967 coinage: All 1965- to 1967-dated coins were made without Mint marks. Many coins dated 1964 to 1966 were struck in later years.

105. 1970-D half dollar: Struck only for inclusion in Mint sets. Not a regular issue.

106. S-Mint clad dollars: Struck only for sale to collectors. Struck in 40 percent clad silver in 1971 and 1972 in Proof and Uncirculated for individual sale. Beginning in 1973, a copper-nickel clad dollar was added to the Proof sets.

107. 1973, 1973-D copper-nickel dollar: Struck only for inclusion in Uncirculated Mint sets. Not a regular issue coin. 1,769,258 Mint sets were sold. 439,899 excess dollars melted, presumably of near-equal distribution. 21,641 coins were kept for possible replacement of defective sets and may have been melted.

108. 1974-dated dollars, half dollars and quarter dollars: Includes coins struck in calendar years 1974 and 1975.

109. 1975-dated dollars, half dollars and quarter dollars: Absolutely none struck. 1975 Proof and Mint sets contain Bicentennial dollars, half dollars and quarter dollars.

110. 1976-dated dollars, half dollars and quarter dollars: Includes coins struck in calendar years 1975 and 1976.

111. 1976-S dollars, half dollars and quarter dollars: Includes copper-nickel clad Proofs sold in 1975 and 1976 in six-piece Proof sets,

and 40 percent silver clad Proof and Uncirculated coins of which 15 million pieces of each denomination were struck.

112. P Mint mark: The P Mint mark, placed on the 1979 Anthony dollar, was added to all 1980 denominations from the Philadelphia Mint except for the cent.

113. Anthony dollar: The Anthony design was introduced, replacing the larger Eisenhower dollar. All Philadelphia Mint dollars have a P Mint mark.

114. 1982 cent: The composition of the cent changed from 95 percent copper, 5 percent zinc to 97.5 percent zinc, 2.5 percent copper (composed of a planchet of 99.2 percent zinc, 0.8 percent copper, plated with pure copper). Some 1982 cents were struck in late 1981.

115. 1982 No-P dimes: Some 1982 dimes were released without a Mint mark, although dimes have been Mint marked since 1980. Distribution of the coins, many found in the Sandusky, Ohio, area indicates they were from Philadelphia.

116. Anthony dollars: Anthony dollars were sold only in three-coin sets in 1981. None were released into circulation.

117. 1987 half dollar: No 1987 Kennedy half dollars were struck for circulation. They were struck only for Uncirculated sets, Proof sets and Souvenir Mint sets.

118. Small numbers of two different 2004-D Wisconsin quarter dollars were discovered in late 2004 and first publicized in *Coin World* in early 2005 that bear unusual markings dealers and collectors have labeled an "extra leaf." Each "extra leaf" appears as a curved raised area, below and to the left of the far left cornhusk on the ear of corn on the reverse. The "Extra Leaf High" variant has a simple, narrow curved line extending from the wheel of cheese to the underside of the far left cornhusk, touching both. The "Extra Leaf Low" variant has a more elaborate, more leaf-like element, the widest end extending from the lower portion of the far left cornhusk and narrowing to a point as it arcs downward until it touches the upper surface of the cheese. A Treasury Office of Inspector General report of an investigation into the variants, issued Jan. 12, 2005, stated that the "Extra Leaf High" version was created in November 2004 during the second shift at night at the Denver Mint, with some pieces caught and destroyed by Mint personnel and other pieces mixed with regular coins and released. The report did not address the "Extra Leaf Low" variant specifically. The Treasury OIG report stated the investigation yielded no evidence of criminal wrongdoing. However, many in the hobby believe that both variants were deliberately if unofficially created.

Annual Proof coinage since 1817

The following series of charts is meant to show the quantities struck of U.S. Proof coins from 1817 to the present. In years prior to 1860, when Proof mintages were small and were not recorded, an asterisk marks those issues that are known or are thought to exist. In many instances from 1860 to 1922 the figures shown are approximate, the result of incomplete records, restrikes and the melting of unsold Proofs.

From 1817 to 1859, Proof coins were made in small batches whenever a number of orders had accumulated. An appropriate pair of dies, sometimes new but often used, was polished and used to strike the required number of coins. This is why many early Proof issues may show many varieties among only a dozen or so coins known. These Proof dies were usually returned to general use, where they would result in prooflike coins until the polished surfaces wore down. Occasionally the die chosen for use was overdated.

During these early years the most popular Proof coins were the half cent and later the silver dollar. It could be that these two coins represented, respectively, the cheapest and the most impressive (from

the aspect of size) Proof coins. It could also be that the regular issues of these two coins were small, and collectors thought the Proofs would be good investments. Collecting complete Proof sets was popular from 1840 to 1848, although this fad was not revived until the late 1850s.

Beginning in 1860 the Mint produced Proof coins in quantity in anticipation of selling them, rather than producing them on demand. As a rule, a small but uniform number of Proof gold coins and a much larger but also uniform number of Proof silver coins were made. As no records were kept of the number of nonsilver minor coin Proofs issued before 1878, they are commonly assumed equal to the silver Proofs of the same year.

This assumption may be drastically wrong, as it is apparent from the 1878 figures that the minor coins were much more popular. It has been suggested that these Proof minor coins were frequently given as Christmas presents to children. If so, we can probably assume that many of these were spent as soon as possible.

Exceptions to the uniform number plan are many,

and can usually be logically explained. Coinage laws usually took effect during the middle of a year, and the new or discontinued issues would be produced for only a part of that year. Issues that were being phased out, such as gold dollars in the 1880s, were popular as investments. Others, such as the Trade dollar, continued on in Proof form after regular coinage had been suspended. In 1883, a large number of each of the three different copper-nickel 5-cent coins was produced, unlike the 1864 cents where the number of Proof coins struck was proportionate to the number of regular coins issued.

Regular production of Proofs was suspended after 1915, with the exceptions of cents and 5-cent coins in 1916 and a few Proof half dollars and dimes in 1916 and of the cent, 5-cent coin and quarter dollar in 1917. A few, perhaps as many as 25, Morgan dollars were struck in Brilliant Proof in 1921. Approximately three of each of the 1921 and 1922 Peace dollars were struck in Matte Proof. The Proof 1922 Peace dollars were of the same high relief as the 1921 Peace dollar and of a slightly different design from the 1922 business-strike Peace dollar. Any alleged 1922 Proof must match the design of a 1921 coin exactly.

The production of Proofs was resumed in 1936, with the total mintage of each coin dependent upon orders. It may be a comment upon the relative popularity of the designs that the Washington quarter dollar was the one usually ordered least. World War II brought about a second suspension of Proof coinage, but not before the wartime metal shortages created a new curiosity, the Proof 1942-P Jefferson 5-cent coin with a P Mint mark.

In 1950, the production of Proof coins was again resumed, but now the coins were available only in complete sets. From 1950 to mid-1955 the coins were packaged in individual cellophane envelopes, stapled together across the openings. This arrangement was meant to serve as a shipping device only, but many people left the coins in the package where rust from the staple could damage the coins. Beginning in mid-1955, the coins were sealed in a soft plastic "flatpack." This series of Proofs continued through 1964.

In 1965, during a coin shortage when the Mint did not have the time to produce Proof sets, the Mint instead made available to collectors "Special Mint sets." These consisted of Uncirculated coins, packaged like the Proofs of previous years. In 1966-67 a long, hard plastic holder was used instead. These three Special Mint sets were sold at $4 per set, an increase over the $2.10 price of a 1950 to 1964 Proof sets.

In 1968, when the coin shortage was over and Mint marks were returned to coins, Mint officials moved Proof set production to the San Francisco Assay Office, formerly the San Francisco Mint. Various coins had been struck at this facility since 1964 but without Mint marks, to prevent hoarding. These five-coin sets were packaged in a larger, inflexible plastic case and were issued at $5 per set.

When the Philadelphia and Denver Mints began producing copper-nickel clad Eisenhower dollars for circulation in 1971, the San Francisco Assay Office began striking silver-copper clad dollars for collectors in Proof and Uncirculated conditions. Beginning with 1973 a copper-nickel clad dollar became part of the regular Proof set. In 1979, the Anthony dollar replaced the Eisenhower dollar; it was removed from sets beginning in 1982. Special Prestige Proof sets containing an Olympic silver dollar were sold in 1983 and 1984 at $59 each. A 1986 Prestige Proof set contains the five regular coins, the Ellis Island dollar and Immigrant half dollar. Prestige Proof sets were produced most years through 1997, when production ended.

From 2005 to 2007, the U.S. Mint sold sets containing one or two commemorative coins plus the standard Proof set, but under the name United States Mint American Legacy Collection rather than the name Prestige Proof set."

The introduction of the circulating commemorative quarter dollar programs, plus the Presidential dollar program and 2009 Lincoln cent program, led Mint officials to introduce additional, denomination-specific Proof sets. Since 1999, the Mint has sold each year's quarter dollars in two different sets, one containing the coins composed of copper-nickel clad and the other set containing quarter dollars made of 90 percent silver. Four-coin Proof sets of Presidential dollars have been offered annually since 2007. In 2009, the Mint offered a set all four Lincoln, Bicentennial cents, each struck on planchets made of 95 percent copper and 5 percent zinc and tin.

How Proofs are made

"Proof" in numismatics refers to a special manufacturing process designed to result in coins of the highest quality produced especially for collectors. "Proof" is not a grade, as many beginning collectors think, although dealers, collectors and other hobbyists assign Proof coins a numerical grade such as Proof 63 or Proof 65.

Proof coins result from the same basic processes used in producing the dies and planchets used in producing business strikes for circulation (business strikes refer to the everyday coin, struck for use in circulation). However, Mint employees use special techniques in preparing the surfaces of the dies and planchets intended for Proof coins. Special presses and striking techniques are also used in the production of Proof coins.

The Proof coins (with a few exceptions) sold by the United States Mint today are Cameo Proofs. The flat fields are mirrorlike, reflective and shiny. The frosting refers to the white, textured, nonreflective finish found on the raised devices, lettering and other points in relief. Both the frosted and mirror finishes are the results of the special techniques using in preparing the dies.

While in the past a physical media was blasted at the surface of a Proof die to create the frosted effect, a computer-controlled laser beam has been used to achieve the effect in recent years. The flat fields are polished to a mirror finish to create the cameo effect.

The planchets used to strike the Proof coins also receive special treatment. The planchets are run through a burnishing process, where they are tumbled in a media of carbon steel balls, water and an alkaline soap. The process cleans and polishes the planchets. The burnished planchets are rinsed in clear water and towel-dried by hand, then go through another cleaning and hand-drying process. Compressed air is used to blow lint and dust from the planchets.

Proof coins are struck on special hand-fed presses that operate at slower speeds than the high-speed presses used for striking business strike coinage. The Proof coining presses tend to impress the design from the dies onto the planchet; the production of a business strike is a much more rapid, violent event. Each Proof coin is struck two or more times, depending on the size of the coin, the design and the composition of the metal. The multiple striking ensures that detail is brought up fully on each coin. Circulation strikes are struck only once (although some U.S. circulation strikes in the past have been struck more than once, most notably the 1907 Saint-Gaudens, High Relief double eagle).

Proof coins are then sealed into plastic capsules or plastic holders to protect their surfaces from potentially damaging environmental factors.

Although most collectors of modern U.S. Proof coins are familiar with the Frosted Proofs in vogue today, there are many other types of Proof finishes.

Some no longer used by the U.S. Mint include the Matte Proof, used in the early 20th century. The entire surface of the coin is uniformly dull or granular; the surface results from the struck coin being pickled in acid. A Satin Finish Proof coin has a matte, satiny surface; the finishing process, used in the early 20th century, is currently unknown. A Sandblast Proof is a type of Matte Proof in which the surface of the coin is sandblasted, not pickled in acid. A Roman Finish Proof was used on gold Proofs of 1909 and 1910 and is similar to the Satin Finish Proof. A Brilliant Proof is one in which the entire surface is mirrorlike; any frosted devices are accidental, found generally only on the first few strikes of the die. Brilliant Proofs were produced by the U.S. Mint until the late 1970s and early 1980s, when Mint officials began taking care to produce the Frosted Proof. A Reverse Proof finish—bearing mirrored raised devices and frosted fields—was used on 2006 American Eagle gold and silver coins. An "enhanced" Reverse Proof finish was used on 2007 American Eagle platinum coins.

Miscellaneous notes

Proof $10 eagles dated 1804 are restrikes made in 1834 and 1835, for inclusion in Proof sets to be given as diplomatic presents. The 1804 dollar was first struck at this time for this occasion, also in Proof. The 1804 dollar was restruck in Proof in the late 1850s. The Proof dollars of 1801 to 1803 were first struck at this time.

Many different Proof issues before 1880 were restruck in Proof one or more times. As with the 1873 Indian Head gold $3 coin, in some cases, more coins of the date are known than were "officially" struck.

Branch Mint Proofs

Until 1968, Branch Mint Proofs were rare. From 1968 to 1983, all Proofs were struck in San Francisco. Since 1984, Proofs have been produced in Philadelphia, Denver, San Francisco and West Point for special coin programs.

1838-O half dollar: It is thought that 20 examples were struck as souvenirs in honor of the opening of the New Orleans Mint. No regular issue coins of this date and Mint were struck, and it is possible that these were struck in 1839.

1839-O half dollar: Three or four known.

1844-O half eagle: One known, reason for issue unknown.

1844-O eagle: One known, reason for issue unknown.

1852-O eagle: Three pieces known, reason for issue unknown.

1853-O eagle: Mintage unknown, reason for issue unknown.

1854-S double eagle: One known, in the Smithsonian Institution. Struck in honor of the opening of the San Francisco Mint.

1855-S quarter dollar: One known, presumably struck to celebrate the beginning of silver coinage at the San Francisco Mint.

1855-S half dollar: Three known, same occasion as for the quarter dollar.

1856-O half dime: One known, reason for issue unknown.

1860-O half dime: Three known, reason for issue unknown.

1861-O half dollar: Three to six known, probably struck under the authority of either the state of Louisiana or the Confederate States of America.

1870-CC silver dollar: Mintage unknown, possibly struck to mark first Carson City dollar coinage.

1875-S 20 cents: Six to seven known, probably struck to celebrate the first (or last) year of this denomination at this Mint.

1879-O silver dollar: Two now known of 12 struck to celebrate the reopening of the New Orleans Mint (closed since 1861).

1882-CC silver dollar: Mintage unknown, reason for issue unknown.

1883-CC silver dollar: Mintage unknown, reason for issue unknown.

1883-O silver dollar: One now known of 12 struck for presentation to various local dignitaries. Occasion uncertain.

1884-CC silver dollar: One reported, reason for issue unknown.

1891-O quarter dollar: Two known, probably struck to celebrate the resumption of fractional silver coinage at this Mint.

1893-CC silver dollar: 12 struck for presentation to Mint officials to mark the closing of the Carson City Mint.

1894-S dime: Twenty-four struck by the San Francisco Mint, apparently to use the remaining uncoined silver recovered from melted silver coins of old designs. Approximately nine, including two circulated pieces.

1895-O half dollar: Issued to mark reopening of New Orleans Mint.

1899-S half eagle: One or two known, reason for issue unknown.

1906-D dime: Struck in honor of the opening of the Denver Mint.

1906-D eagle: Struck in honor of the opening of the Denver Mint.

1906-D double eagle: Two now known of 12 struck in honor of the opening of the Denver Mint.

1907-D double eagle: One known, possibly struck as a specimen of the last year of this design.

Proof coinage mintages to 1942

Half cents

Year	Mintage
1825	*
1826	*
1828	*
1829	*
1831	1*
1832	*
1833	*
1834	*
1835	*
1836	1*
1840	1*
1841	1*
1842	1*
1843	1*
1844	1*
1845	1*
1846	1*
1847	1*
1848	1*
1849	1*
1850	*
1851	*
1852	1*
1854	*
1855	*
1856	1*
1857	1*

Cents

Year	Mintage
1817	*
1818	*
1819	*
1820	*
1821	*
1822	*
1823	2*
1825	*
1826	*
1827	*
1828	*
1829	*
1830	*
1831	*
1832	*
1833	*
1834	*
1835	*
1836	*
1837	*
1838	*
1839	*
1840	*
1841	*
1842	*
1843	*
1844	*
1845	*
1846	*
1847	*
1848	*
1849	*
1850	*
1852	*
1854	*
1855	*
1856	3*
1857	4*
1858	*
1859	*
1860	1,000
1861	1,000
1862	550
1863	460
1864	4705
1865	500
1866	725
1867	625
1868	600
1869	600
1870	1,000
1871	960
1872	950
1873	6 1,100
1874	700
1875	700
1876	1,150
1877	7 510
1878	2,350
1879	3,200
1880	3,955
1881	3,575
1882	3,100
1883	6,609
1884	3,942
1885	3,790
1886	4,290
1887	2,960
1888	4,582
1889	3,336
1890	2,740
1891	2,350
1892	2,745
1893	2,195
1894	2,632
1895	2,062
1896	1,862
1897	1,938
1898	1,795
1899	2,031
1900	2,262
1901	1,985
1902	2,018
1903	1,790
1904	1,817
1905	2,152
1906	1,725
1907	1,475
1908	1,620
1909	8 4,793
1910	2,405
1911	1,733
1912	2,145
1913	2,848
1914	1,365
1915	1,150
1916	1,050
1917	*
1936	5,569
1937	9,320
1938	14,734
1939	13,520
1940	15,872
1941	21,100
1942	32,600

Two cents

Year	Mintage
1864	9 100
1865	500
1866	725
1867	625
1868	600
1869	600
1870	1,000
1871	960
1872	950
1873	10 1,100

Three cents (copper-nickel)

Year	Mintage
1865	400
1866	725
1867	625
1868	600
1869	600
1870	1,000
1871	960
1872	950
1873	6 1,100
1874	700
1875	700
1876	1,150
1877	5,107
1878	2,350
1879	3,200
1880	3,955
1881	3,575
1882	3,100
1883	6,609
1884	3,942
1885	3,790
1886	4,290
1887	11 2,960
1888	4,582
1889	3,436

Three cents (silver)

Year	Mintage
1851	*
1852	*
1854	*
1855	*
1856	*
1857	*
1858	*
1859	*
1860	1,000
1861	1,000
1862	550
1863	12 460
1864	470
1865	500
1866	725
1867	625
1868	600
1869	600
1870	1,000
1871	960
1872	950
1873	6 600

Five cents

Year	Mintage
1866	125
1867	13 625
1868	600
1869	600
1870	1,000
1871	960
1872	950
1873	6 1,100
1874	700
1875	700
1876	1,150
1877	7 510
1878	2,350
1879	3,200
1880	3,955
1881	3,575
1882	3,100
1883	14 17,421

Five cents

Year	Mintage
1884	3,942
1885	3,790
1886	4,290
1887	2,960
1888	4,582
1889	3,336
1890	2,740
1891	2,350
1892	2,745
1893	2,195
1894	2,632
1895	2,062
1896	1,862
1897	1,938
1898	1,795
1899	2,031
1900	2,262
1901	1,985
1902	2,018
1903	1,790
1904	1,817
1905	2,152
1906	1,725
1907	1,475
1908	1,620
1909	4,763
1910	2,405
1911	1,733
1912	2,145
1913	[15] 3,034
1914	1,275
1915	1,050
1916	600
1917	*
1936	4,420
1937	5,769
1938	19,365
1939	12,535
1940	14,158
1941	18,720
1942	[16] 57,200

Half dimes

Year	Mintage
1829	*
1830	*
1831	*
1832	*
1833	*
1834	*
1835	*
1836	*
1837	*
1838	*
1839	*
1840	*
1841	*
1842	*
1843	*
1844	*
1845	*
1846	*
1847	*
1848	*
1849	*
1850	*
1851	*
1852	*
1853	[17] *
1854	*
1855	*
1856	*
1857	*
1858	*
1859	*
1860	1,000
1861	1,000
1862	550
1863	460
1864	470
1865	500
1866	725
1867	625
1868	600
1869	600
1870	1,000
1871	960
1872	950
1873	[6] 600

Dimes

Year	Mintage
1820	*
1821	*
1822	*
1823	[2] *
1824	*
1825	*
1827	*
1828	*
1829	*
1830	*
1831	*
1832	*
1833	*
1834	*
1835	*
1836	*
1837	*
1838	*
1839	*
1840	*
1841	*
1842	*
1843	*
1844	*
1845	*
1846	*
1847	*
1848	*
1849	*
1850	*
1851	*
1852	*
1853	[17] *
1854	*
1855	*
1856	*
1857	*
1858	*
1859	*
1860	1,000
1861	1,000
1862	550
1863	460
1864	470
1865	500
1866	725
1867	625
1868	600
1869	600
1870	1,000
1871	960
1872	950
1873	[18] 1,400
1874	700
1875	700
1876	1,150
1877	510
1878	800
1879	1,100
1880	1,355
1881	975
1882	1,100
1883	1,039
1884	875
1885	930
1886	886
1887	710
1888	832
1889	711
1890	590
1891	600
1892	1,245
1893	792
1894	972
1895	880
1896	762
1897	731
1898	735
1899	846
1900	912
1901	813
1902	777
1903	755
1904	670
1905	727
1906	675
1907	575
1908	545
1909	650
1910	551
1911	543
1912	700
1913	622
1914	425
1915	450
1916	*
1936	4,130
1937	5,756
1938	8,728
1939	9,321
1940	11,827
1941	16,557
1942	22,329

Twenty cents

Year	Mintage
1875	1,200
1876	1,150
1877	510
1878	600

Quarter dollars

Year	Mintage
1818	*
1820	*
1821	*
1822	*
1823	[2] *
1824	*
1825	*
1827	[1] *
1828	*
1831	*
1832	*
1833	*
1834	*
1835	*
1836	*
1837	*
1838	*
1839	*
1840	*
1841	*
1842	*
1843	*
1844	*
1845	*
1846	*
1847	*
1848	*
1849	*
1850	*
1851	*
1852	*
1853	[17] *
1854	*
1855	*
1856	*
1857	*
1858	*
1859	*
1860	1,000
1861	1,000
1862	550
1863	460
1864	470
1865	500
1866	725
1867	625
1868	600
1869	600
1870	1,000
1871	960
1872	950
1873	[19] 1,140
1874	700
1875	700
1876	1,150
1877	510
1878	800
1879	[20] 250
1880	1,355
1881	975
1882	1,100
1883	1,039
1884	875
1885	930
1886	886
1887	710
1888	832
1889	711
1890	590
1891	600
1892	1,245
1893	792
1894	972
1895	880
1896	762
1897	731
1898	735
1899	846
1900	912
1901	813
1902	777
1903	755
1904	670
1905	727
1906	675
1907	575
1908	545
1909	650
1910	551
1911	543
1912	700
1913	613
1914	380
1915	450
1917	*
1936	3,837
1937	5,542
1938	8,045
1939	8,795
1940	11,246
1941	15,287
1942	21,123

Half dollars

Year	Mintage
1817	[21] *
1818	*
1819	*
1820	*
1821	*
1822	*
1823	*
1824	*
1825	*
1826	*

Half dollars

Year	Mintage
1827	*
1828	*
1829	*
1830	*
1831	*
1832	*
1833	[1] *
1834	[1]*
1835	[1]*
1836	[22]*
1837	*
1838	*
1839	[23] *
1840	*
1841	*
1842	*
1843	*
1844	*
1845	*
1846	*
1847	*
1848	*
1849	*
1850	*
1852	*
1853	[17] *
1854	*
1855	*
1856	*
1857	*
1858	*
1859	*
1860	1,000
1861	1,000
1862	550
1863	460
1864	470
1865	500
1866	725
1867	625
1868	600
1869	600
1870	1,000
1871	960
1872	950
1873	[24] 1,150
1874	700
1875	700
1876	1,150
1877	510
1878	800
1879	1,100
1880	1,355
1881	975
1882	1,100
1883	1,039
1884	875
1885	930
1886	886
1887	710
1888	832
1889	711
1890	590

Half dollars

Year	Mintage
1891	600
1892	1,245
1893	792
1894	972
1895	880
1896	762
1897	731
1898	735
1899	846
1900	912
1901	813
1902	777
1903	755
1904	670
1905	727
1906	675
1907	575
1908	545
1909	650
1910	551
1911	543
1912	700
1913	627
1914	380
1915	450
1916	*
1936	3,901
1937	5,728
1938	8,152
1939	8,808
1940	11,279
1941	15,412
1942	21,120

Silver dollars

Year	Mintage
1836	[25] *
1838	[25] *
1839	[25] *
1840	[1]*
1841	[1]*
1842	[1]*
1843	[1]*
1844	[1]*
1845	[1]*
1846	[1]*
1847	[1]*
1848	[1]*
1849	[1]*
1850	[1]*
1851	[1]*
1852	[1]*
1853	[26] *
1854	*
1855	*
1856	*
1857	*
1858	[27] *
1859	*
1860	1,330
1861	1,000
1862	550
1863	460
1864	470

Silver dollars

Year	Mintage
1865	500
1866	725
1867	625
1868	600
1869	600
1870	1,000
1871	960
1872	950
1873	6 600
1878	[28] 1,000
1879	1,100
1880	1,355
1881	975
1882	1,100
1883	1,039
1884	875
1885	930
1886	886
1887	710
1888	832
1889	811
1890	590
1891	650
1892	1,245
1893	792
1894	972
1895	880
1896	762
1897	731
1898	735
1899	846
1900	912
1901	813
1902	777
1903	755
1904	650
1921	*
1922	*

Trade dollars

Year	Mintage
1873	[29] 865
1874	700
1875	700
1876	1,150
1877	510
1878	900
1879	1,541
1880	1,987
1881	960
1882	1,097
1883	979
1884	[30] 10
1885	[30] 5

Gold dollars

Year	Mintage
1849	*
1854	[31] *
1855	*
1856	*
1857	*
1858	*
1859	*
1860	154

Gold dollars

Year	Mintage
1861	349
1862	35
1863	50
1864	50
1865	25
1866	30
1867	50
1868	25
1869	25
1870	35
1871	30
1872	30
1873	6 25
1874	20
1875	20
1876	45
1877	20
1878	20
1879	30
1880	36
1881	87
1882	125
1883	207
1884	1,006
1885	1,105
1886	1,016
1887	1,043
1888	1,079
1889	1,779

Quarter eagles

Year	Mintage
1821	*
1824	*
1825	*
1826	*
1827	*
1829	*
1830	*
1831	*
1832	*
1833	*
1834	[32] *
1835	*
1836	*
1837	*
1840	*
1841	[33] *
1842	*
1843	*
1844	*
1845	*
1846	*
1847	*
1848	*
1849	*
1854	*
1855	*
1856	*
1857	*
1858	*
1859	*
1860	112
1861	90

Quarter eagles

Year	Mintage
1862	35
1863	30
1864	50
1865	25
1866	30
1867	50
1868	25
1869	25
1870	35
1871	30
1872	30
1873	[6] 25
1874	20
1875	20
1876	45
1877	20
1878	20
1879	30
1880	36
1881	51
1882	67
1883	82
1884	73
1885	87
1886	88
1887	122
1888	92
1889	48
1890	93
1891	80
1892	105
1893	106
1894	122
1895	119
1896	132
1897	136
1898	165
1899	150
1900	205
1901	223
1902	193
1903	197
1904	170
1905	144
1906	160
1907	154
1908	236
1909	139
1910	682
1911	191
1912	197
1913	165
1914	117
1915	100

Three dollars

Year	Mintage
1854	*
1855	*
1856	*
1857	*
1858	*
1859	*
1860	119

Three dollars		Half eagles		Half eagles		Eagles		Double eagles	
Year	Mintage	Year	Mintage	Year	Mintage	Year	Mintage	Year	Mintage
1861	113	1841	*	1899	99	1876	45	1864	50
1862	35	1842	*	1900	230	1877	20	1865	25
1863	39	1843	*	1901	140	1878	20	1866	30
1864	50	1844	*	1902	162	1879	30	1867	50
1865	25	1845	*	1903	154	1880	36	1868	25
1866	30	1846	*	1904	136	1881	42	1869	25
1867	50	1847	*	1905	108	1882	44	1870	35
1868	25	1848	*	1906	85	1883	49	1871	30
1869	25	1855	*	1907	92	1884	45	1872	30
1870	35	1856	*	1908	[38] 167	1885	67	1873	[6] 25
1871	30	1857	*	1909	78	1886	60	1874	20
1872	30	1858	*	1910	250	1887	80	1875	20
1873	[34] 25	1859	*	1911	139	1888	72	1876	45
1874	20	1860	62	1912	144	1889	45	1877	20
1875	[1] 20	1861	66	1913	99	1890	63	1878	20
1876	45	1862	35	1914	125	1891	48	1879	30
1877	20	1863	30	1915	75	1892	72	1880	36
1878	20	1864	50	**Eagles**		1893	55	1881	61
1879	30	1865	25	Year	Mintage	1894	43	1882	59
1880	36	1866	30	1838	*	1895	56	1883	92
1881	54	1867	50	1839	[39] *	1896	78	1884	71
1882	76	1868	25	1840	*	1897	69	1885	77
1883	89	1869	25	1841	*	1898	67	1886	106
1884	106	1870	35	1842	*	1899	86	1887	121
1885	110	1871	30	1843	*	1900	120	1888	102
1886	142	1872	30	1844	*	1901	85	1889	41
1887	160	1873	[6] 25	1845	*	1902	113	1890	55
1888	291	1874	20	1846	*	1903	96	1891	52
1889	129	1875	20	1847	*	1904	108	1892	93
Half eagles		1876	45	1848	*	1905	86	1893	59
Year	Mintage	1877	20	1855	*	1906	77	1894	50
1820	*	1878	20	1856	*	1907	[40] 74	1895	51
1821	*	1879	30	1857	*	1908	[41] 116	1896	128
1823	*	1880	36	1858	*	1909	74	1897	86
1824	*	1881	42	1859	*	1910	204	1898	75
1825	[35] *	1882	48	1860	50	1911	95	1899	84
1826	*	1883	61	1861	69	1912	83	1900	124
1827	*	1884	48	1862	35	1913	71	1901	96
1828	[36] *	1885	66	1863	30	1914	50	1902	114
1829	*	1886	72	1864	50	1915	75	1903	158
1830	*	1887	87	1865	25	**Double eagles**		1904	98
1831	*	1888	94	1866	30	Year	Mintage	1905	90
1832	*	1889	45	1867	50	1849	[42] 1	1906	94
1833	*	1890	88	1868	25	1850	[43] *	1907	[44] 78
1834	[37] *	1891	53	1869	25	1856	*	1908	[41] 101
1835	*	1892	92	1870	35	1858	*	1909	67
1836	*	1893	77	1871	30	1859	*	1910	167
1837	*	1894	75	1872	30	1860	59	1911	100
1838	*	1895	81	1873	[6] 25	1861	66	1912	74
1839	*	1896	103	1874	20	1862	35	1913	58
1840	*	1897	83	1875	20	1863	30	1914	70
		1898	75					1915	50

Proof coinage sales figures 1983 to 2010

When the Mint began offering multiple Proofs starting with Prestige Proof sets in 1983, determining the total mintage/sales figures for an individual coin became more complex. From 1968 to 1982, the total mintage for the standard Proof set also represented the individual total for each denomination of Proof coin.

The following table lists individual mintages/sales figures for all Proof coins by denominations. Since Proof figures for programs such as the State quarter dollars are identical for all the designs in a given year, just one listing appears here to save space. For circulating commemorative programs for which sales differed by design, individual listings appear.

For Proof coins issued since 1983, researchers must calculate the mintage/sales figure for each individual coin by adding the total sales for each set and packaging combination in which the coins appeared.

United States Mint officials have not provided final sales figures by denomination, but the figures in the following table represent the best effort at calculating an accurate figure based on available numbers.

Sales figures/mintages for 2009 and 2010 coins may not be final audited figures and therefore may be subject to change in the future. The information in this section was compiled in May 2011.

Cents

Year	Mintage
1983-S	3,279,126
1984-S	3,065,110
1985-S	3,362,821
1986-S	3,010,497
1987-S	3,792,233
1988-S	3,262,948
1989-S	3,220,914
1990-S	3,299,559
1991-S	2,867,787
1992-S	4,176,544
1993-S	3,360,876
1994-S	3,222,140
1995-S	2,791,067
1996-S	2,920,158
1997-S	2,796,194
1998-S	2,965,503
1999-S	3,362,464
2000-S	4,062,402
2001-S	2,618,086
2002-S	3,210,674
2003-S	3,315,542
2004-S	2,965,422
2005-S	3,329,229
2006-S	3,077,280
2007-S	2,590,005
2008-S	2,199,761
2009-S Childhood in Kentucky	2,422,373
2009-S Formative Years in Indiana	2,422,373
2009-S Professional Life in Illinois	2,422,373
2009-S Presidency in Washington	2,422,373
2010-S	1,643,393

5-cent coins

Year	Mintage
1983-S	3,279,126
1984-S	3,065,110
1985-S	3,362,821
1986-S	3,010,497
1987-S	3,792,233
1988-S	3,262,948
1989-S	3,220,914
1990-S	3,299,559
1991-S	2,867,787
1992-S	4,176,544
1993-S	3,360,876
1994-S	3,222,140
1995-S	2,791,067
1996-S	2,920,158
1997-S	2,796,194
1998-S	2,965,503
1999-S	3,362,464
2000-S	4,062,402
2001-S	2,618,086
2002-S	3,210,674
2003-S	3,315,542
2004-S Peace Medal	2,965,422
2004-S Keelboat	2,965,422
2005-S American Bison	3,654,229
2005-S Ocean in View	3,654,229
2006-S	3,077,280
2007-S	2,590,005
2008-S	2,199,761
2009-S	2,172,373
2010-S	1,643,393

Dimes

Year	Mintage
1982-S	3,857,479
1983-S	3,279,126
1984-S	3,065,110
1985-S	3,362,821
1986-S	3,010,497
1987-S	3,792,233
1988-S	3,262,948
1989-S	3,220,914
1990-S	3,299,559
1991-S	2,867,787
1992-S Clad	2,858,903
90% silver	1,317,641
1993-S Clad	2,569,882
90% silver	790,994
1994-S Clad	2,443,590
90% silver	778,550
1995-S Clad	2,124,790
90% silver	666,277
1996-S Clad	2,145,077
90% silver	775,081
1997-S Clad	2,055,000
90% silver	741,194
1998-S Clad	2,086,507
90% silver	878,996
1999-S Clad	2,557,899
90% silver	804,565
2000-S Clad	3,096,981
90% silver	965,421
2001-S Clad	2,300,944
90% silver	889,697
2002-S Clad	2,321,848
90% silver	888,826
2003-S Clad	2,172,684
90% silver	1,142,858
2004-S Clad	1,789,488
90% silver	1,175,934
2005-S Clad	2,310,063
90% silver	1,019,166
2006-S Clad	2,033,734
90% silver	1,043,546
2007-S Clad	1,728,558
90% silver	861,447
2008-S Clad	1,426,868
90% silver	772,893
2009-S Clad	1,477,967
90% silver	694,406
2010-S Clad	1,643,393
90% silver	561,351

Quarter dollars

Year	Mintage
1983-S	3,279,126
1984-S	3,065,110
1985-S	3,362,821
1986-S	3,792,233
1987-S	3,792,233
1988-S	3,262,948
1989-S	3,220,914
1990-S	3,299,559
1991-S	2,867,787
1992-S Clad	2,858,903
90% silver	1,317,641
1993-S Clad	2,569,882
90% silver	790,994
1994-S Clad	2,443,590
90% silver	778,550
1995-S Clad	2,124,790
90% silver	666,277
1996-S Clad	2,145,077
90% silver	775,081
1997-S Clad	2,055,000
90% silver	741,194
1998-S Clad	2,086,507
90% silver	878,996
1999-S State Clad	3,727,857
90% silver	804,565
2000-S State Clad	4,092,784
90% silver	965,421
2001-S State Clad	3,100,680
90% silver	889,697
2002-S State Clad	3,085,940
90% silver	888,826
2003-S State Clad	3,398,191
90% silver	1,142,858
2005-S State Clad	3,291,341
90% silver	1,625,981
2006-S State Clad	2,910,530
90% silver	1,571,839
2007-S State Clad	2,401,220
90% silver	1,299,878
2008-S State Clad	2,099,306
90% silver	1,201,914
2009-S D.C. and Territories Clad	2,093,903
90% silver	980,512
2010-S Hot Springs Clad	1,365,836
90% silver	811,944
2010-S Yellowstone Clad	1,365,732
90% silver	811,944
2010-S Yosemite Clad	1,363,302
90% silver	811,944
2010-S Grand Canyon Clad	1,362,098
90% silver	811,944
2010-S Mount Hood Clad	1,347,991
90% silver	811,944

Half dollars

Year	Mintage
1983-S	3,279,126
1984-S	3,065,110
1985-S	3,362,821
1986-S	3,010,497
1987-S	3,792,233
1988-S	3,262,948
1989-S	3,220,914
1990-S	3,299,559
1991-S	2,867,787
1992-S Clad	2,858,903
90% Silver	1,317,641
1993-S Clad	2,569,882
90% Silver	790,994
1994-S Clad	2,443,590
90% Silver	778,550
1995-S Clad	2,124,790
90% Silver	666,277
1996-S Clad	2,145,077
90% silver	775,081
1997-S Clad	2,055,000
90% silver	741,194
1998-S Clad	2,086,507
90% silver	878,996
1999-S Clad	2,557,899
90% silver	804,077
2000-S Clad	3,096,981
90% silver	965,421
2001-S Clad	2,300,944
90% silver	889,697
2002-S Clad	2,321,848
90% silver	888,826
2003-S Clad	2,172,684
90% silver	1,142,858
2004-S Clad	1,789,488
90% silver	1,175,934
2005-S Clad	2,310,063
90% silver	1,019,166
2006-S Clad	2,033,734
90% silver	1,043,546
2007-S Clad	1,728,558
90% silver	861,447
2008-S Clad	1,426,868
90% silver	772,893
2009-S Clad	1,477,967
90% silver	694,406
2010-S Clad	1,082,042
90% silver	561,351

Sacagawea $1s

Year	Mintage
2000-S	4,062,402
2001-S	2,618,086
2002-S	3,210,674
2003-S	3,315,542
2004-S	2,965,422
2005-S	3,329,229
2007-S	2,590,005
2008-S	2,199,761
2009-S 3 Sisters	2,172,373
2010-S Iroquois	1,643,393

Presidential $1s

Year	Mintage
2007-S G. Washington	3,919,753
2007-S J. Adams	3,908,793
2007-S T. Jefferson	3,908,351
2007-S J. Madison	3,906,610
2008-S J. Monroe	3,080,018
2008-S J.Q. Adams	3,076,103
2008-S A. Jackson	3,072,565
2008-S M. Van Buren	3,070,685
2009-S W.H. Harrison	2,800,298
2009-S J. Tyler	2,800,298
2009-S J. Polk	2,800,298
2009-S Z. Taylor	2,800,298
2010-S M. Fillmore	2,168,571
2010-S F. Pierce	2,168,571
2010-S J. Buchanan	2,168,571
2010-S A. Lincoln	2,168,571

Proof set mintages/sales figures 1950 to 2010

Proof sets contain Proof examples of coins struck for a given year, sometimes including coins not struck for circulation. From 1936 to 1942, coins were available individually by denomination. See the introductory section for details about the various special sets and Proof set options offered since 1983. Sales figures for 2009 and 2010 sets may not be final audited figures, and could change slightly.

Year Minted	Sets Sold	Selling Price	Face Value
1950	51,386	$2.10	$0.91
1951	57,500	2.10	0.91
1952	81,980	2.10	0.91
1953	128,800	2.10	0.91
1954	233,300	2.10	0.91
1955	378,200	2.10	0.91
1956	669,384	2.10	0.91
1957	1,247,952	2.10	0.91
1958	875,652	2.10	0.91
1959	1,149,291	2.10	0.91
1960	1,691,602	2.10	[45] 0.91
1961	3,028,244	2.10	0.91
1962	3,218,019	2.10	0.91
1963	3,075,645	2.10	0.91
1964	3,950,762	2.10	0.91
Production suspended 1965, 1966, 1967 46			
1968	3,041,506	5.00	[47] 0.91
1969	2,934,631	5.00	0.91
1970	2,632,810	5.00	[48] 0.91
1971	3,220,733	5.00	[49] 0.91
1972	3,260,996	5.00	0.91
1973	2,760,339	7.00	1.91
1974	2,612,568	7.00	1.91
1975	2,845,450	7.00	[50] 1.91
1976	4,123,056	7.00	[50] 1.91
1977	3,236,798	9.00	1.91
1978	3,120,285	9.00	1.91
1979	3,677,175	9.00	[51] 1.91
1980	3,554,806	10.00	1.91
1981	4,063,083	11.00	1.91
1982	3,857,479	11.00	[52] 0.91
1983	3,138,765	11.00	[53] 0.91
1983 Prestige	140,361	59.00	[54] 1.91
1984	2,748,430	11.00	0.91
1984 Prestige	316,680	59.00	[55] 1.91
1985	3,362,821	11.00	0.91
1986	2,411,180	11.00	0.91
1986 Prestige	599,317	48.50	[56] 2.41
1987	3,356,738	11.00	0.91
1987 Prestige	435,495	45.00	[57] 1.91
1988	2,368,957	11.00	0.91
1988 Prestige	231,661	45.00	[58] 1.91
1989	3,009,107	11.00	0.91
1990	2,793,433	11.00	0.91
1990 Prestige	506,126	46.00	[59] 1.91
1991	2,610,833	11.00	0.91
1991 Prestige	256,954	55.00	[60] 2.41
1992	2,675,618	11.00/12.50	0.91
1992 Prestige	183,285	49.00/56.00	[61] 2.41
1992 Silver	1,009,586	18.00/21.00	0.91
1992 Premiere	308,055	29.50/37.00	0.91
1993	2,337,819	12.50	0.91
1993 Prestige	232,063	51.00/57.00	[62] 2.41
1993 Silver	589,712	18.00/21.00	0.91
1993 Premiere	201,282	29.00/37.00	0.91
1994	2,308,701	12.50	0.91

Year Minted	Sets Sold	Selling Price	Face Value
1994 Prestige	175,893	$49.00/$56.00	[63] $2.41
1994 Silver	636,009	18.00/21.00	0.91
1994 Premiere	149,320	29.00/37.00	0.91
1995	2,018,945	12.50	0.91
1995 Prestige	105,845	55.00/61.00	[64] 2.41
1995 Silver	537,374	18.00/21.00	0.91
1995 Premiere	128,903	29.00/37.00	0.91
1996	2,085,191	12.50	0.91
1996 Prestige	59,886	55.00/61.00	[65] 2.41
1996 Silver	623,264	18.00/21.00	0.91
1996 Premier	151,817	29.00/37.00	0.91
1997	1,975,000	12.50	0.91
1997 Prestige	80,000	44.00	[66] 1.91
1997 Silver	605,289	18.00/21.00	0.91
1997 Premier	135,905	29.00/37.00	0.91
1998	2,086,507	12.50	0.91
1998 Silver	878,996	18.00/21.00	0.91
1998 Premier	240,658	29.00/37.00	0.91
1999	2,557,899	19.95	1.91
1999 State 25¢	1,169,958	13.95	1.25
1999 Silver	804,565	31.95	1.91
2000	3,096,981	19.95	2.91
2000 State 25¢	995,803	13.95	1.25
2000 Silver	965,421	31.95	2.91
2001	2,300,944	19.95	2.91
2001 State 25¢	799,736	13.95	1.25
2001 Silver	889,697	31.95	2.91
2002	2,319,766	19.95	2.91
2002 State 25¢	764,419	13.95	1.25
2002 Silver	892,229	31.95	2.91
2003	2,172,684	19.95	2.91
2003 State 25¢	1,225,507	13.95	1.25
2003 Silver	1,142,858	31.95	2.91
2004	1,789,488	22.95	2.96
2004 State 25¢	951,196	15.95	1.25
2004 Silver	1,175,934	37.95	2.96
2004 Silver 25¢	593,852	23.95	1.25
2005	2,260,063	22.95	2.96
2005 State 25¢	981,278	15.95	1.25
2005 Silver	1,019,166	37.95	2.96
2005 Silver 25¢	606,815	23.95	1.25
2005 Legacy	46,057	135.00	[67] 4.96
2006	1,985,282	22.95	2.91
2006 State 25¢	876,796	15.95	1.25
2006 Silver	1,043,546	37.95	2.91
2006 Silver 25¢	528,293	23.95	1.25
2006 Legacy	48,452	135.	[68] 4.91
2007	1,702,116	26.95	[70] 6.91
2007 State 25¢	672,662	13.95	[70] 1.25
2007 Silver	861,447	44.95	[70] 6.91
2007 Silver 25¢	438,431	25.95	[70] 1.25
2007 Pres. $1	1,285,972	14.95	[70] 4.00
2007 Legacy	26,442	135.	[69, 70] 8.91
2008	1,405,674	26.95	[70] 6.91
2008 State 25¢	672,438	13.95	[70] 1.25
2008 Silver	772,893	44.95	[70] 6.91

Year Minted	Sets Sold	Selling Price	Face Value	Year Minted	Sets Sold	Selling Price	Face Value
2008 Silver 25¢	429,021	$25.95	[70] $1.25	2009 Pres. $1	627,925	$14.95	[70] $4.00
2008 Pres. $1	860,172	14.95	[70] 4.00	2010	1,082,042	26.95	[70] 6.91
2009	1,477,967	26.95	[70] 6.91	2010 25¢	265,949	13.95	[70] 1.25
2009 Territories 25¢	615,936	13.95	[70] 1.25	2010 Silver	561,351	44.95	[70] 6.91
2009 Silver	694,406	44.95	[70] 6.91	2010 Silver 25¢	250,393	25.95	[70] 1.25
2009 Silver 25¢	284,884	25.95	[70] 1.25	2010 Pres. $1	525,178	14.95	[70] 4.00
2009 Lincoln 1¢	200,000	7.95	0.04				

Satin Finish mintages

From 2005 to 2010, the coins found in Uncirculated Mint sets and certain other collector sets bear a Satin Finish, rather than the same finish as found on circulation quality coins. For most coins, the individual mintages are the same as for the Uncirculated Mint sets. Other coins, however, were offered in additional collector products, meaning their mintages differ. The United States Mint resumed using an Uncirculated finish on the coins in the Uncirculated Mint sets starting in 2011.

Lincoln cents

Year	Mintage
2005	1,141,895
2005-D	1,141,895
2006	915,586
2006-D	902,184
2007	895,628
2007-D	895,628
2008	745,464
2008-D	745,464
2009 Early Childhood in Kentucky	774,844
2009-D Early Childhood in Kentucky	774,844
2009 Formative Years in Indiana	774,844
2009-D Formative Years in Indiana	774,844
2009 Professional Life in Illinois	774,844
2009-D Professional Life in Illinois	774,844
2009 Presidency in Washington	774,844
2009-D Presidency in Washington	774,844
2010-P	570,100
2010-D	570,100

Jefferson 5-cent coins

Year	Mintage
2005-P American Bison	1,466,895
2005-P Ocean in View	1,466,895
2005-D American Bison	1,466,895
2005-D Ocean in View	1,466,895
2006-P	915,586
2006-D	915,586
2007-P	895,628
2007-D	895,628
2008-P	745,464
2008-D	745,464
2009-P	774,844
2009-D	774,844
2010-P	570,100
2010-D	570,100

Roosevelt dimes

Year	Mintage
2005-P	1,141,895
2005-D	1,141,895
2006-P	915,586
2006-D	915,586
2007-P	895,628
2007-D	895,628
2008-P	745,464
2008-D	745,464

Roosevelt dimes

Year	Mintage
2009-P	774,844
2009-D	774,844
2010-P	570,100
2010-D	570,100

Washington quarter dollars

Year	Mintage
2005-P California	1,141,895
2005-D California	1,141,895
2005-P Minnesota	1,141,895
2005-D Minnesota	1,141,895
2005-P Oregon	1,141,895
2005-D Oregon	1,141,895
2005-P Kansas	1,141,895
2005-D Kansas	1,141,895
2005-P West Virginia	1,141,895
2005-D West Virginia	1,141,895
2006-P Nevada	915,586
2006-D Nevada	915,586
2006-P Nebraska	915,586
2006-D Nebraska	915,586
2006-P Colorado	915,586
2006-D Colorado	915,586
2006-P North Dakota	915,586
2006-D North Dakota	915,586
2006-P South Dakota	915,586
2006-D South Dakota	915,586
2007-P Montana	895,628
2007-D Montana	895,628
2007-P Washington	895,628
2007-D Washington	895,628
2007-P Idaho	895,628
2007-D Idaho	895,628
2007-P Wyoming	895,628
2007-D Wyoming	895,628
2007-P Utah	895,628
2007-D Utah	895,628
2008-P Oklahoma	745,464
2008-D Oklahoma	745,464
2008-P New Mexico	745,464
2008-D New Mexico	745,464
2008-P Arizona	745,464
2008-D Arizona	745,464
2008-P Alaska	745,464
2008-D Alaska	745,464

Washington quarter dollars

Year	Mintage
2008-P Hawaii	745,464
2008-D Hawaii	745,464
2009-P District of Columbia	774,844
2009-D District of Columbia	774,844
2009-P Puerto Rico	774,844
2009-P Puerto Rico	774,844
2009-P Guam	774,844
2009-D Guam	774,844
2009-P American Samoa	774,844
2009-D American Samoa	774,844
2009-P U.S. Virgin Islands	774,844
2009-D U.S. Virgin Islands	774,844
2009-P Northern Marianas Islands	774,844
2009-D Northern Marianas Islands	774,844
2010-P Arkansas, Hot Springs National Park	614,248
2010-D Arkansas, Hot Springs National Park	614,248
2010-P Wyoming, Yellowstone National Park	614,144
2010-D Wyoming, Yellowstone National Park	614,144
2010-P California, Yosemite National Park	611,714
2010-D California, Yosemite National Park	611,714
2010-P Arizona, Grand Canyon National Park	610,510
2010-D Arizona, Grand Canyon National Park	610,510
2010-P Oregon, Mount Hood National Forest	596,403
2010-D Oregon, Mount Hood National Forest	596,403

Kennedy half dollars

Year	Mintage
2005-P	1,141,895
2005-D	1,141,895
2006-P	915,586
2006-D	915,586
2007-P	895,628
2007-D	895,628
2008-P	745,464
2008-D	745,464

Kennedy half dollars

Year	Mintage
2009-P	774,844
2009-D	774,844
2010-P	570,100
2010-D	570,100

Sacagawea & Native American dollars

Year	Mintage
2005-P	1,141,895
2005-D	1,141,895
2006-P	915,586
2006-D	915,586
2007-P	895,628
2007-D	895,628
2008-P	745,464
2008-D	814,420
2009-P Three Sisters	774,844
2009-D Three Sisters	774,844
2010-P Iroquois Confederacy	570,100
2010-D Iroquois Confederacy	570,100

Presidential dollars

Year	Mintage
2007-P George Washington	1,108,459
2007-D George Washington	997,045

Presidential dollars

Year	Mintage
2007-P John Adams	1,107,504
2007-D John Adams	997,045
2007-P Thomas Jefferson	1,108,173
2007-D Thomas Jefferson	997,045
2007-P James Madison	1,107,761
2007-D James Madison	997,045
2008-P James Monroe	907,179
2008-D James Monroe	821,736
2008-P John Quincy Adams	903,366
2008-D John Quincy Adams	821,736
2008-P Andrew Jackson	899,714
2008-D Andrew Jackson	821,736
2008-P Martin Van Buren	897,686
2008-D Martin Van Buren	821,736
2009-P William Henry Harrison	893,865
2009-D William Henry Harrison	893,865
2009-P John Tyler	899,249
2009-D John Tyler	899,249
2009-P James K. Polk	889,075
2009-D James K. Polk	889,075
2009-P Zachary Taylor	887,742
2009-D Zachary Taylor	887,742
2010-P Millard Fillmore	674,724
2010-D Millard Fillmore	674,724

Presidential dollars

Year	Mintage
2010-P Franklin Pierce	672,605
2010-D Franklin Pierce	672,605
2010-P James Buchanan	671,979
2010-D James Buchanan	671,979
2010-P Abraham Lincoln	677,208
2010-D Abraham Lincoln	677,208

40% silver clad dollars

Struck in San Francisco

	Uncirculated	Proof
1971	6,868,530	4,265,234
1972	2,193,056	1,811,631
1973	1,883,140	1,013,646
1974	1,900,156	1,306,579

Special Mint sets

Year Minted	Sets Sold	Selling Price	Face Value
1965	2,360,000	$4.00	$0.91
1966	2,261,58350	4.00	0.91
1967	1,863,344	4.00	0.91

Uncirculated Mint sets

For decades, Uncirculated sets contained examples of each circulation-strike coin struck within a given year. During those years, the coins in the sets were struck no differently than the regular circulation strikes. That changed late in the 20th century, when the coins were struck under stricter guidelines than the circulating coins; the coins in the sets still had an Uncirculated finish, but were generally of higher quality than the coins issued for circulation. In 2005, the Mint began using a Satin Finish on the coins in the set; that practice continued through the 2010 sets. Starting with the 2011 sets, the Mint went back to an Uncirculated finish on the coins for the sets.

The United States Mint first offered Uncirculated Mint sets, dated 1947, in 1948. Later, after the 1947 sets sold out, 1948 coinage was offered. Before 1960,

the sets were individually packaged in cardboard folders; each set contains two examples of each coin struck that year.

Beginning in 1959, sets were packaged in polyethylene packets. In 2007, the Mint switched to new packaging; the coins were placed between layers of cardboard with a plastic window for each coin. During the coin shortage of the mid-1960s, Special Mint sets were struck in lieu of Proof sets and Uncirculated sets in 1965, 1966 and 1967. Uncirculated set production resumed in 1968. No Uncirculated sets were issued in 1982 and 1983 for what Mint officials said were budget-reduction reasons. Congress passed a law in 1983, however, requiring annual sales of Uncirculated sets, which has been done every year since 1984.

Year Minted	Sets Sold	Selling Price	Face Value	Year Minted	Sets Sold	Selling Price	Face Value
1947	12,600	$4.87	$4.46	1963	606,612	$2.40	$1.82
1948	17,000	4.92	4.46	1964	1,008,108	2.40	1.82
1949	20,739	5.45	4.96	1965	2,360,000	4.00	0.91
1951	8,654	6.75	5.46	1966	2,261,583	4.00	0.91
1952	11,499	6.14	5.46	1967	1,863,344	4.00	0.91
1953	15,538	6.14	5.46	1968	2,105,128	2.50	1.33
1954	25,599	6.19	5.46	1969	1,817,392	2.50	1.33
1955	49,656	3.57	2.86	1970	2,038,134	2.50	1.33
1956	45,475	3.34	2.64	1971	2,193,396	3.50	1.83
1957	34,324	4.40	3.64	1972	2,750,000	3.50	1.83
1958	50,314	4.43	3.64	1973	1,767,691	6.00	3.83
1959	187,000	2.40	1.82	1974	1,975,981	6.00	3.83
1960	260,485	2.40	1.82	1975	1,921,488	6.00	3.82
1961	223,704	2.40	1.82	1976	1,892,513	6.00	3.82
1962	385,285	2.40	1.82	1977	2,006,869	7.00	3.82

Year Minted	Sets Sold	Selling Price	Face Value	Year Minted	Sets Sold	Selling Price	Face Value
1978	2,162,609	$7.00	$3.82	1999	1,421,625	$14.95	$3.82
1979	2,526,000	8.00	4.82	2000	1,490,160	14.95	5.82
1980	2,815,066	9.00	4.82	2001	1,113,623	14.95	5.82
1981	2,908,145	11.00	4.82	2002	1,139,388	14.95	5.82
1984	1,832,857	7.00	1.82	2003	1,001,532	14.95	5.82
1985	1,710,571	7.00	1.82	2004	842,507	16.95	5.92
1986	1,153,536	7.00	1.82	2005	1,141,895	16.95	5.92
1987	2,890,758	7.00	1.82	2006	915,586	16.95	5.82
1988	1,447,100	7.00	1.82	2007	895,628	22.95	13.82
1989	1,987,915	7.00	1.82	2007 Pres. $1, P	20,440	8.95	4.00
1990	1,809,184	7.00	1.82	2007 Pres. $1, D	13,994	8.95	4.00
1991	1,352,101	7.00	1.82	2007 Pres. $1, P&D	87,423	15.95	8.00
1992	1,500,098	7.00/8.00	1.82	2007 Unc. $1	90,171	31.95	6.00
1993	1,297,094	8.00	1.82	2008	745,464	22.95	13.82
1994	1,234,813	8.00	1.82	2008 Pres. $1, P&D	76,272	15.95	8.00
1995	1,013,559	8.00	1.82	2008 Unc. $1	68,956	31.95	6.00
1995 Deluxe	24,166	12.00	1.82	2009	[70] 774,844	27.95	14.38
1996	1,450,440	8.00	1.92	2009 Pres. $1, P&D	[70] 105,059	15.95	8.00
1997	940,047	8.00	1.82	2010	570,100	31.95	13.82
1998	1,188,487	8.00	1.82	2010 ATB 25¢, P&D	26,303	21.95	2.50
				2010 Pres. $1, P&D	95,254	18.95	8.00

Notes

Proof $10 eagles dated 1804 are restrikes made in 1834 and 1835 for inclusion in Proof sets meant to be given as diplomatic presents. The 1804 dollar was first struck at this time for this occasion, also in Proof. The 1804 dollar was restruck in Proof in the late 1850s. The Proof dollars of 1801-03 were first struck at this time.

Many different Proof issues before 1880 were restruck in Proof one or more times. As with the 1873 gold $3 coin, in some instances, more coins of a date are known than were "officially" struck.

1. (Various dates): Known to have been restruck at least once.

2. 1823 cent, dime, quarter dollar: Exists with overdate, 1823/2.

3. 1856 cent: Includes several large cents and many hundreds of Flying Eagle cent patterns. The Flying Eagle cent pattern was restruck in later years.

4. 1857 cent: Includes both small and large cents.

5. 1864 cent: Breakdown by varieties; thought to be about 300 to 350 copper-nickel and about 100 to 150 bronze coins without the designer's initial L. Bronze coins with the L are rare in Proof, possibly 20 or less struck.

6. (Most 1873 Proofs): All Proofs are the relatively Closed 3 variety.

7. 1877 minor coinages: Estimates for this year vary considerably, usually upwards. For lack of any records, the number shown is that of the silver Proofs of this year, conforming with the method used in the preceding years. These figures may be considerably low.

8. 1909 cent: Includes 2,175 Indian Head type; 420 Lincoln Head type with VDB; and 2,198 Lincoln Head without VDB on reverse.

9. 1864 2 cents: Includes Small Motto and Large Motto varieties. The Small Motto in Proof is rare.

10. 1873 2 cents: All originals have the Closed 3. It is estimated that 500 restrikes were made, all of them with an Open 3.

11. 1887 copper-nickel 3 cents: Many struck from an overdated die, 1887/6.

12. 1863 silver 3 cents: Proofs struck from an overdated die, 1863/2, were struck in 1864.

13. 1867 5 cents: Approximately 25 Proofs struck With Rays on reverse (type of 1866), and 600 Without Rays (type of 1868-83).

14. 1883 5 cents: It has been estimated that 5,419 Shield type; 5,219 Liberty Head, No CENTS; and 6,783 Liberty Head, With CENTS were struck. Other estimates exist.

15. 1913 5 cents: Does not include the five privately struck 1913 Liberty Head 5-cent coins. The Indian Head Proofs are thought to be divided into 1,520 Bison on Mound and 1,514 Bison on Plain varieties.

16. 1942 5 cents: Includes 29,600 pre-war alloy, and 27,600 wartime alloy.

17. 1853 half dollar, quarter dollar, dime, half dime. All Proofs are of the new weight, With Arrows (and Rays on the quarter dollar and half dollar).

18. 1873 dime: No Arrows, Closed 3: 600. With Arrows, Open 3: 800.

19. 1873 quarter dollar: No Arrows, Closed 3: 600. With Arrows, Open 3: 540.

20. 1879 quarter dollar: This figure is official, but may be wrong. The true number might be near or equal to 1,100.

21. 1817 half dollar: Only one Proof known, with overdate 1817/3.

22. 1836 half dollar: Includes both Lettered Edge coins and Reeded Edge patterns.

23. 1839 half dollar: Includes all three varieties, Capped Bust and Seated Liberty, With or Without Drapery.

24. 1873 half dollar: No Arrows, Closed 3: 600. With Arrows, Open 3: 550.

25. 1836, 1838, 1839 silver dollar: All are Gobrecht dollars which were struck in Proof in several different varieties, many of which were restruck in later years. Records indicate that 1,900 of the originals were struck for circulation.

26. 1853 silver dollar: All Proofs are restrikes, made 1864-5.

27. 1858 silver dollar: Estimated that 80 pieces were struck, some of them possibly at a later date.

28. 1878 silver dollar: Includes 700 of the 8 Tail Feathers variety and 300 of the 7 Tail Feathers, flat eagle breast variety. Beware of any early strike, prooflike surface Morgan dollar being sold as a Proof.

29. 1873 silver dollar: All Proofs are of the Open 3 variety.

30. 1884-85 Trade dollar: Struck in Proof in the Mint for private distribution by person or persons unknown. Not listed in the Mint Report.

31. 1854 gold dollar: Includes both Coronet and Indian Head.

32. 1834 $2.50: Includes both Capped Head and Classic Head types.

33. 1841 $2.50: Nine known, several of them circulated or otherwise impaired.

34. 1873 $3: All original Proofs are of the more Open 3 variety. There were two restrikes with the Closed 3 and one with the Open 3.

35. 1825 $5: Struck from the regular overdated dies. 1825/4, one known, and 1825/1, two known.

36. 1828 $5: Includes at least one overdate, 1828/7.

37. 1834 $5: Includes both Capped Head and Classic Head types.

38. 1908 $5: All are Indian Head type.

39. 1839 $10: Proofs are of the type of 1838, with large letters and different hair style.

40. 1907 $10: Figure shown is for Coronet coins. An unknown number of Indian Head patterns were also struck in Proof.

41. 1908 $20 and $10: All Proofs have the motto in god we trust on the reverse.

42. 1849 $20: The one known trial strike still surviving is a Proof.

43. 1850 $20: One Proof was once owned by the engraver, James B. Longacre. Whereabouts presently unknown.

44. 1907 $20: Figure shown is for Coronet coins. An unknown number of Saint-Gaudens type coins of pattern or near-pattern status were also struck in Proof.

45. 1960 cent: Includes Large Date and Small Date varieties. As in the regular issues, the Small Date is the scarcer.

46. 1966 5-cent coin: Two Proof Jefferson 5-cent coins were struck to mark the addition of designer Felix Schlag's initials, F.S., to the obverse design. At least one coin was presented to Schlag; the other may have been retained by the Mint.

47. 1968 dime: Some Proof sets contain dimes which were struck from a Proof die without a Mint mark. This was an engraver's oversight and is not a filled die. It has been unofficially estimated that only 20 specimens from this die are known. Beware of sets opened and reclosed with "processed" P-Mint coins inserted. Check the edge of the case for signs of tampering.

48. 1970 dime: Same engraver's oversight as above. Official estimate is that 2,200 sets were released with this error.

49. 1971 5 cents: Same type of error as above. Official estimate of 1,655 sets released.

50. Including Bicentennial quarters, halves and dollars.

51. 1979 Proof set: The Anthony dollar replaced the Eisenhower dollar. During latter 1979, a new, clearer Mint mark punch was used on the dies. Sets with all six coins bearing the new Mint mark command a premium.

52. 1982 Proof set: A new Mint mark punch with serifs was introduced.

53. 1983 10-cent coin: Some 1983 sets were issued with dimes missing the S Mint mark, similar to errors on 1968, 1970, 1971 and 1975 Proof coins.

54. Contains commemorative 1983-S Olympic silver dollar in addition to the regular Proof coinage.

55. Contains commemorative 1984-S Olympic silver dollar in addition to the regular Proof coinage.

56. Contains commemorative 1986-S Ellis Island dollar and Immigrant half dollar in addition to the regular Proof coinage.

57. Contains commemorative 1987-S Constitution silver dollar in addition to the regular Proof coinage.

58. Contains commemorative 1988-S Olympic silver dollar in addition to the regular Proof coinage.

59. Contains commemorative 1990-P Eisenhower silver dollar in addition to the regular Proof coinage.

60. Contains commemorative 1991-S Mount Rushmore half dollar and 1991-S Mount Rushmore silver dollar in addition to the regular Proof coinage.

61. Contains commemorative 1992-S Olympic half dollar and 1992-S Olympic silver dollar in addition to the regular Proof coinage.

62. Contains commemorative 1993-S James Madison half dollar and 1993-S James Madison silver dollar in addition to the regular Proof coinage.

63. Contains commemorative 1994-P World Cup half dollar and 1994-S World Cup silver dollar in addition to the regular Proof coinage.

64. Contains commemorative 1995-S Civil War Battlefields half dollar and 1995-S Civil War Battlefields dollar in addition to the regular Proof coinage.

65. Contains commemorative 1996-S Olympic Soccer half dollar and 1996-P Olympic Rowing dollar in addition to the regular Proof coinage.

66. Contains commemorative 1997-S Botanic Garden dollar in addition to the regular Proof coinage. Last of the Prestige Proof sets.

67. United States Mint American Legacy Collection with 2005-P Chief Justice John Marshall silver dollar and 2005-P Marine Corps 230th Anniversary silver dollar.

68. United States Mint American Legacy Collection with 2006-P Benjamin Franklin, Founding Father silver dollar and 2006-P San Francisco Old Mint silver dollar.

69. United States Mint American Legacy Collection with 2007-P Jamestown 400th Anniversary silver dollar and 2007-P Little Rock High School Desegregation 50th Anniversary silver dollar.

70. Sales figures not final as of publication.

Proof American Eagle issue prices [1]

Year	Metal	1/10 oz	1/4 oz	1/2 oz	1 oz	Set
1986	Gold	$—	$—	$—	$550.	$—
	Silver	—	—	—	21.00	
1987	Gold	—	—	295.	585.	870.
	Silver	—	—	—	23.00	—
1988	Gold	65.00	150.	295.	585.	1065.
	Silver	—	—	—	23.00	—
1989	Gold	65.00	150.	295.	585.	1065.
	Silver	—	—	—	23.00	—
1990	Gold	70.00	150.	285.	570.	999.
	Silver	—	—	—	23.00	—
1991	Gold	70.00	150.	285.	570.	999.
	Silver	—	—	—	23.00	—
1992	Gold	70.00	150.	285.	570.	999.
	Silver	—	—	—	23.00	—
1993	Gold	70.00	150.	285.	570.	999.
	Silver	—	—	—	23.00	—
1993 Philadelphia set [2]						499.
1994	Gold	70.00	150.	285.	570.	999.
	Silver	—	—	—	23.00	—
1995	Gold	70.00	150.	285.	570.	999.
	Silver	—	—	—	23.00	—
1995 10th Anniversary set [3]						999.
1996	Gold	70.00/75.00	150./159.	285./299.	570./589.	999./1025.
	Silver	—	—	—	23.00	—
1997	Gold	75.00	159.	299.	589.	1,025.
	Silver	—	—	—	23.00	—
	Platinum	99.00	199.	395.	695.	1,350.

Year	Metal	1/10 oz	1/4 oz	1/2 oz	1 oz	Set
1997 Impressions of Liberty set [4]						$1,499.
1998	Gold	70.00	150.	285.	570.	999.
	Silver	—	—	—	24.00	—
	Platinum	99.00	199.	395.	695.	1,350.
1999	Gold	70.00	150.	285.	570.	999.
	Silver	—	—	—	24.00	—
	Platinum	99.00	199.	395.	695.	1350.
2000	Gold	70.00	150.	285.	570.	999.
	Silver	—	—	—	24.00	—
	Platinum	118.	227.	405.	740.	1,375.
2001	Gold	70.00	150.	285.	570.	999.
	Silver	—	—	—	24.00	—
	Platinum	118.	227.	405.	740.	1,375.
2002	Gold	70.00	150.	285.	570.	999.
	Silver	—	—	—	24.00	—
	Platinum	118.	227.	405.	740.	1,375.
2003	Gold	85.00	165.	315.	630.	1,098.
	Silver	—	—	—	24.00	—
	Platinum	170.	329.	587.	1,073.	1,995.
2004	Gold	90.	175.	335.	675.	1,175.
	Silver	—	—	—	27.95	—
	Platinum	210.	410.	735.	1,345.	2,495.
2005	Gold	95.	190.	360.	720.	1,260.
	Silver	—	—	—	27.95	—
	Platinum	210.	410.	735.	1,345.	2,495.
2006	Gold	100.	200.	385.	770.	1,350.
		110.	220.	445.	885.	1,575.
		105.	215.	420.	NA	1,495.
	Silver	—	—	—	27.95	—
	Platinum	220.	435.	780.	1,500.	2,750.
2007	Gold	104.95	209.95	399.95	789.95	1,449.95
		116.95	239.95	459.95	NA	1,695.95
		146.95	NA	NA	NA	NA
	Silver	—	—	—	29.95	—
	Platinum	229.95	439.95	809.95	1,599.95	2,949.95
		244.95	475.95	880.95	1,740.95	3,207.95
		269.95	539.95	999.95	1,979.95	NA

Uncirculated American Eagle issue prices [26, 27, 29, 30]

Year	Metal	1/10 oz	1/4 oz	1/2 oz	1 oz	Set
2006	Gold	$85.	$190.	$375.	$720.	$1,350.
	Silver	—	—	—	19.95	—
	Platinum	180.	390.	720	1,390.	2,585.
2007	Gold	89.95	195.95	379.95	749.95	1,379.95
		99.95	219.95	424.95	831.95	1,559.95
		119.95	279.95	529.95	1,045.95	1,939.95
	Silver	—	—	—	21.95	—
	Platinum	189.95	399.95	759.95	1,489.95	1,869.95
		204.95	435.95	830.95	1,630.95	2,976.95
		229.95	499.95	949.95	2,769.95	3,479.95

Proof American Buffalo coins issue prices [29, 30]

Year	Metal	1/10 oz	1/4 oz	1/2 oz	1 oz	Set
2006	Gold	—	—	—	$800.	—

Year	Metal	1/10 oz	1/4 oz	1/2 oz	1 oz	Set
2007	Gold	—	—	—	$825.95	—
					899.95	

First Spouse coins issue prices [29, 30]

Year	Metal	1/10 oz	1/4 oz	1/2 oz	1 oz	Set
2007 Proof	Gold	—	—	—	$429.95	—
		—	—	—	529.95	—
2007 Unc.	Gold	—	—	—	410.95	—
		—	—	—	509.95	—

Note: In 2006 and 2007, Mint officials adjusted the prices of Proof American Eagle gold coins to keep pace with changes in the price of gold, as shown in the table. In 2007, adjustments in prices were made for Uncirculated American Eagle gold coins and both Proof and Uncirculated platinum coins. An especially volatile bullion market in 2008 led to multiple price changes for Proof and Uncirculated American Eagle silver, gold and platinum coins, American Buffalo gold coins and First Spouse gold coins sold as numismatic products. At times, sales of certain of these products were suspended while pricing could be adjusted, or to make planchets used in the production of these collector versions available for some of the bullion coin versions instead. These multiple prices are difficult to compile and are not listed here. Starting in 2009, in reaction to the often volatile precious metals markets, the U.S. Mint introduced a pricing system that permitted weekly price adjustments to gold and platinum coins; the Uncirculated America the Beautiful silver 5-ounce bullion coins were scheduled to added to this pricing system in 2011 as well. The prices for the coins are based on the PM fix for the respective metal on the London bullion market on Wednesday of each week. Details of the Mint's pricing schedule are found online at the Mint Web page at **http://catalog.usmint.gov/wcsstore/ConsumerDirect/images/catalog/en_US/GoldCoinGrid.pdf**.

Notes:
1. Prices are for single-coin or -set purchase only; bulk discounts may apply; in 1996, a pre-issue discount was offered on gold coins.
2. Includes tenth-, quarter-, half-ounce gold, 1-ounce silver coin and 1-ounce silver medal.
3. Includes four gold coins and one silver, all with West Point Mint mark.
4. Includes one each Proof 1-ounce platinum, gold and silver bullion coin.

Matte Finish coins

As the United States Mint began offering more and more collector coin products in the 1980s and 1990s, officials began experimenting with special finishes to enhance some of the Uncirculated commemorative coins. By the early 1990s, for example, commemorative silver dollars were given a matte surface similar in appearance to the Matte Proof coins of the early 20th century mentioned earlier. Collectors took little note of this special finish, however, because the Mint referred to it as an Uncirculated finish (even though it differed considerably from the Uncirculated finish given to coins in the standard Uncirculated Mint sets). That is, until 1994, when the special Uncirculated finish was applied to a noncommemorative denomination placed in a special limited-edition set.

Congress authorized a commemorative silver dollar celebrating the 250th anniversary of Thomas Jefferson's birth for release in 1994. The Mint offered the 1994 Jefferson silver dollar in Proof and Uncirculated versions, the latter bearing the special matte surfaces developed over the years. Mint officials also offered the dollar in a variety of purchasing options.

Among the special options was a Jefferson Coin and Currency set, which contained three monetary instruments bearing Jefferson's portrait: a 1994-P Jefferson silver dollar, a $2 Federal Reserve note and a 1994-P Jefferson 5-cent coin. While Mint officials intended to limit this set to 50,000 pieces, they forgot to specify that limit on any sales literature. Thus the Mint produced the set to order, selling 167,703 sets.

Mint officials also forgot to tell collectors that the Jefferson 5-cent coin in the set was given the same matte surfaces that had been given to the Jefferson silver dollar in the set, to give the two coins uniform finishes. A collector, however, noted the special finish and informed *Coin World* of that fact. That suddenly made the Jefferson Coin and Currency set a hot property. Jefferson 5-cent coins are collected by many collectors, a number of whom seek to acquire Proof and traditional Uncirculated examples of each date and Mint mark. As collectors and dealers began referring to the coin as having a Matte Finish, many sought examples of the special 5-cent coin to complete their collections of the denomination. Many Matte Finish 5-cent coins were probably removed from their holders for placement in whatever holders the collectors were storing their Jefferson 5-cent sets. Prices for this special 5-cent coin remain high, well over $100 in Mint State 65 to MS-67.

Three years later, Mint officials offered a second Matte Finish Jefferson 5-cent coin (although Mint officials were still not using this terminology), this one dated 1997-P and housed in the Botanic Garden Coin and Currency set (also containing a Botanic Garden silver dollar and $1 Federal Reserve note). Production of the set was limited to 25,000 sets, meaning just 25,000 Matte Finish 1997-P Jefferson 5-cent coins would be offered, making this set an even hotter property than the Jefferson sets of three years earlier.

In what became one of the most criticized offerings by the U.S. Mint in the 1990s, the Botanic Garden Coin and Currency set sold out in about a week, before many collectors even received their order forms in the mail. Dozens of irate collectors called *Coin World* to complain about being shut out of the offering because other collectors living closer to where the order form was placed into the mail had an advantage over those living farther away. Few if any of the callers (including those lucky ones receiving the sets) wanted the sets for the Botanic Garden dollar. Most wanted the extremely limited 25,000 mintage Matte Finish 1997-P Jefferson 5-cent coin for their collections. Prices for the coin in 2011 range from $200 to $700 depending on the numerical grade.

Mint officials learned from this experience, so in 1998, when it offered a Kennedy Collectors set bearing a 1998-P Robert F. Kennedy silver dollar and 1998-P John F. Kennedy half dollar, it limited sales to a specific ordering period, not to a specific number of sets. Sales totaled more than 63,000 sets. By this time, Mint officials had also accepted the terminology that had caught on in hobby circles, and noted that

the half dollar in the set had been given the special Matte Finish. The same literature also noted that the dollar in the set was an Uncirculated coin. However, it was clear to collectors that the finish was the same on both coins (which had been the intention in 1994 when the first Matte Finish 5-cent coin was produced). *Coin World* began referring to the RFK dollar a Matte Finish specimen, prompting another coin collector publication to contact Mint officials, who confirmed that the RFK had an Uncirculated surface, not a Matte Finish. *Coin World* persisted in calling both coins Matte Finish and Mint officials eventually confirmed that yes, the finish on both coins is the identical Matte Finish. (As with the Botanic Garden set, many collectors bought the coin for the Matte Finish half dollar to keep their collections complete, not for the commemorative silver dollar.)

The Matte Finish half dollars sell in a range of $200 to $300 depending on the numerical grade.

Bicentennial sets

The 1976 Bicentennial of American Independence was numismatically celebrated with changes in the reverse designs of the Washington quarter dollar, Kennedy half dollar and Eisenhower dollar. Copper-nickel versions of all three were issued for circulation and for the regular Proof set.

Collectors were offered two three-coin sets of the same coins struck in a 40 percent silver composition, in Proof and Uncirculated versions. The silver collectors' coins were first offered Nov. 15, 1974, at prices of $15 for the Proof set and $9 for the Uncirculated set. In the 12 years of sales for the two three-coin sets, from November 1974 to Dec. 31, 1986, prices for the three-coin sets were changed no fewer than five times due to rising and falling silver prices. Mint officials reduced the prices for the Proof set Jan. 19, 1975, to $12. On Sept. 20, 1979, Mint officials suspended sales of the Bicentennial Uncirculated set because

of the rising price of silver; the bullion value of the three coins in the set exceeded the Mint's price of $9. Sales of the Bicentennial Proof set were suspended in December 1979 as silver rose to even greater heights. When sales of the two Bicentennial sets were resumed in Aug. 4, 1980, the prices rose to $15 for the Uncirculated sets and $20 for the Proof sets. Falling silver prices permitted the introduction of lower prices Sept. 1, 1981: $15 for the Proof set, $12 for the Uncirculated set. In September 1982, prices for the coins dropped even lower—to $12 for the Proof set, and $9 for the Uncirculated set.

Prices maintained those levels until sales of the sets ceased: in 1985 for the Proof set, and on Dec. 31, 1986, for the Uncirculated set.

Final mintages are 3,998,621 for the Bicentennial Proof set, and 4,908,319 for the Uncirculated set.

Source: United States Mint

10 Commemoratives

Commemorative coins, noncirculating and circulating

Commemorative coins—the most colorful coinage issues struck in the United States—are pure Americana, history of a great nation frozen into metal. Commemorative coins in the United States had their start just before the turn of the 20th century.

U.S. commemorative coinage can be categorized in several ways: noncirculating and circulating, with the noncirculating issues further divided into early commemoratives (issued 1892 to 1954) and modern commemoratives (issued 1982 to date).

Noncirculating commemorative coins are issued for sale to the public at premiums, generally to raise funds for an organization or cause directly related to the commemorative theme.

Most of the 1892 to 1954 commemorative coins struck by the U.S. Mint were turned over to various celebration committees for face value, with profits going not to the federal government, but to the committees promoting the cause being commemorated on the coin. Committee officials noted that with the production of additional date and Mint mark varieties of a single issue, more sales to collectors could be generated, with additional funds raised.

All of the modern commemorative coins are sold into the marketplace by the United States Mint, with a fee attached to the price of each coin (a surcharge) given to the beneficiary organization if certain circumstances are met.

In the United States, commemorative coinage can only be authorized by Congress, under authority granted to the legislative body by the Constitution (under Section 8—Powers of Congress: "To coin Money, regulate the Value thereof, and of foreign Coin, and fix the Standard of Weights and Measures."). A common misconception is that the Mint decides what commemorative coins to issue; in reality, the Mint is responsible for designing and striking the commemorative coins, and since 1982, for selling the coins as well, but is not responsible for deciding which programs to issue.

All commemorative coins are legal tender, just as all other U.S. coins. With few exceptions, the specifications of the commemorative coins are the same as for the standard coins of the same denominations.

This chapter discusses the broad categories of commemorative coins in three separate sections.

Early commemoratives: 1892 to 1954

It may sound odd that the start of coinage for commemorative purposes in the United States, one of the richest in the world, should stem directly from dire financial straits of an exposition commission. The World's Columbian Exposition half dollars, issued in 1892 and 1893 to honor Christopher Columbus and the 400th anniversary of his first voyage to America, were the first commemorative coins struck in the United States. They were produced to help defray the expenses of the 1892 and 1893 World's Columbian Exposition in Chicago. The half dollars, struck at the Philadelphia Mint, were sold at a cost of $1. The World's Columbian Exposition was also commemorated with the 1893 Isabella quarter dollar, the United States' first commemorative 25-cent coin.

Between December 1899, when the Lafayette-Washington dollar was struck (the 1900 on the coin refers not to the date of issue, but to the year of the Paris Exposition), and 1954, when the first period of commemorative production ceased, more than 150 U.S. commemorative coins were struck. Some commemorative issues were not completely sold; of these, the balance was returned to the Mint and melted. In the case of the World's Columbian Exposition half dollar, many were just put into circulation by banks, which accounts for the circulated condition in which they are often found. For both reasons, the quantity minted for many commemorative coins is larger than the quantity available.

At first, commemorative coins were issued sporadically. The first coins were issued in 1892 and 1893, with the next commemorative not released until 1900. From 1903 to 1918, just five commemorative coin programs were authorized.

During the decade of the 1920s, however, Congress began authorizing an increasing number of commemorative coin programs, as organizations recognized that commemorative coins were a risk-free means of raising revenue for their particular cause. The Mint sold the coins to the organizations at face value, which in turn offered them to the public at premiums. If a particular coin proved a poor seller, unsold coins could be returned to the Mint for a refund or spent, even, at virtually no loss to the organization.

As a result, the number of commemorative programs authorized rose dramatically. During the 1920s, 15 commemorative coin programs were authorized. During the 1930s, 27 programs were authorized, with many of them multi-year programs. For 1936 alone, 16 different new programs were authorized; in addition, 1936-dated commemorative coins were issued for five earlier programs, including for a program that had begun in 1926.

The themes selected for the commemorative programs varied widely. At first, expos were a popular subject; of the seven programs issued from 1892 to 1918, four were for expos). The last program of that period, in 1918, commemorated the centennial of statehood for Illinois; many of the coins that would follow in the 1920s and 1930s would commemorate anniversaries of states like Missouri and communities like Providence, R.I. Of the several dozen programs issued through the 1930s, only a few could be identified as national in scope, the most prominent being the 1926 Sesquicentennial of American Independence, marking the 250th anniversary of the Declaration of Independence. A smaller number of the programs of 1892 to the end of the 1930s sought to raise funds for memorials to famous individuals.

Some of the programs were of highly questionable significance. The 1936 Cincinnati Music Center half dollar, for example, honors a nonexistent event—50 years of Cincinnati as a music center—and depicts an individual, Stephen Foster, who had little connection with the city except for a brief stay there. The program was concocted by a Cincinnati area coin dealer, who apparently benefited personally from the sale of the coins with assistance of a cooperative Congress.

In 1939, Congress took corrective action when it voted to prohibit the striking of new dates of any pre-1939 commemorative coins, although it continued to authorize new issues, though none during World War II. President Truman approved the Iowa Centennial, Booker T. Washington and Washington-Carver half dollars.

By 1954, the Treasury Department—which had had statutory control over the Mint since 1873—had enough of commemorative coin programs. It became institutional policy at Treasury to oppose all commemorative coinage programs, with the sitting president supporting that policy with a veto signature.

Truman was the last president to approve a commemorative coinage program for more than 30 years; he joined Presidents Hoover and Franklin Roosevelt in vetoing other commemorative coinage legislation. President Eisenhower, too, exercised his veto powers, killing three commemorative coin bills on Feb. 3, 1954, calling for coins celebrating the tercentennials of New York City and Northampton, Mass., and the 250th anniversary of the Louisiana Purchase.

Eisenhower outlined in a message accompanying his vetoes the same arguments used by Treasury Department officials for nearly three decades in opposing new legislation: Commemorative coins cause confusion among the public and facilitate counterfeiting; public interest in the coins had been lagging with many coins unsold and consigned to the melting pot; and the authorization of just a few commemoratives results in a "flood" of additional commemorative issues.

Congress soon stopped most efforts at issuing commemorative coinage.

Treasury opposition to commemorative coinage was so entrenched that it even opposed commemoratives to mark the 1976 Bicentennial of American Independence. Treasury and Mint officials eventually bowed to collector pressure, and congressional orders, to issue three circulating coins marking the Bicentennial. When the 1776-1976 Bicentennial quarter dollars, half dollars and dollars were issued in 1975 and 1976, however, Treasury officials carefully avoided any and all use of the word "commemorative," although clearly the coins are commemorative in nature (the Bicentennial program is covered in detail elsewhere in this book). The official policy remained as stated by Eisenhower in 1954. It was not until the administration of Ronald Reagan that the Treasury policy was abandoned.

Modern commemoratives: 1982 to date

No recognized commemorative coins were struck from 1954 to 1982. Hundreds of applications for such coins had been made through the years, but government officials were reluctant to issue new coins. Then, in 1981, Congress found a nationally acceptable event that Treasury officials did not object to: the 250th birthday of George Washington in 1982.

Legislation was introduced in the House of Representatives on May 7, 1981 (another bill had been introduced in March and a second in April), authorizing a commemorative half dollar for the Washington birthday celebration, with modifications recommended by Treasury officials (including a 10 million coin limit). A similar bill was introduced in the Senate May 18. Passage came in the House on May 19; in the Senate, the bill was approved Dec. 9. President Reagan signed the bill into law Dec. 13, 1981. The Mint offered the 1982 Washington half dollar in Proof and Uncirculated versions through Dec. 31, 1985.

Even as legislators were arguing the merits of the Washington commemorative coin legislation, others in both houses were preparing legislation for a commemorative coin series honoring the 1984 Summer Olympic Games in Los Angeles. The first legislation met with strong opposition from the collecting community, Treasury officials and Rep. Frank Annunzio,

D-Ill., chairman of the House Banking Subcommittee on Consumer Affairs and Coinage. The original Senate proposal called for 29 different coins (more when counting Proof and Uncirculated versions); it passed the Senate Dec. 9, 1981. Much of the controversy arose from the number of coins and the method in which they would be distributed. The bill called for the coins to be turned over to a private cartel, which would donate some funds to the U.S. Olympic team but keep the profits. Opponents said this was a return to the system that helped kill commemorative coin issues in 1938 and 1954.

A legislative compromise was sought. First, a 17-coin proposal was proposed in the House; again, the Senate approved this measure, but not the House. Annunzio introduced a one-coin bill, with the coins to be sold by the U.S. Mint. Eventually, Annunzio agreed to a compromise, proposing a three-coin program. His bill ultimately prevailed and President Reagan signed the bill into law July 22.

The Annunzio proposal authorized a 1984 gold $10 eagle (first commemorative of that denomination) and 1983 and 1984 silver dollars, each to be offered in Proof and Uncirculated versions. The coins were marketed by the Mint, with surcharges of $10 from the sale of each silver dollar and $50 from the sale of each gold eagle going to United States Olympic Committee, the Los Angeles Olympic Organizing Committee and other athletic organizations. The program was deemed successful by most. It raised $73,389,300 for the Olympic teams.

The Los Angeles Olympic commemorative coin program set several standards for all future programs (such as multiple denominations and finishes), the most important being the surcharges. All subsequent commemorative coins included surcharges added to their cost and donated to designated causes. In many cases, the desire to raise funds came to be the driving reason behind many commemorative coin programs rather than the desire to commemorate a worthy subject. Many collectors object to the concept of surcharges, which increase the cost of the coinage programs (and are not considered charitable donations for income tax purposes).

No 1985 commemorative coins were authorized, the only year since 1982 for which no commemorative coin program was approved. The centennial of the dedication of the Statue of Liberty in 1986 was selected as a likely popular subject for a commemorative program. The Statue of Liberty to that time had never appeared on a U.S. coin, although several foreign coins had earlier depicted the symbol of freedom and opportunity in the United States.

Congress authorized a three-coin bill, with three denominations—a 1986 gold $5 half eagle, a 1986 silver dollar and a 1986 copper-nickel clad half dollar. The act restricted production of each coin to one Mint (Annunzio was angered over the multiple Mint mark versions of the 1983 and 1984 Olympic coins,

which he believed violated the intention of the legislation). Surcharges of $35 per gold coin, $7 per silver dollar and $2 per half dollar were earmarked for the restoration of the Statue of Liberty and the immigration facilities on Ellis Island.

Like the Olympic program, the Statue of Liberty program proved successful as a fund-raising event. U.S. Treasurer Katherine D. Ortega had set a goal of $40 million in surcharges, but the Statue of Liberty program surpassed the Olympic program (in less time, with lower per-coin surcharges and fewer varieties of coins available) and raised more than $80 million in surcharges. Total sales were about $300 million. The Statue of Liberty commemorative coin program remains the leader of all U.S. commemorative programs both in terms of surcharges raised and the total number of coins sold.

The Bicentennial of the drafting of the U.S. Constitution was the subject of the 1987 commemorative series. A 1987 gold half eagle and a 1987 silver dollar carried surcharges of $35 on each gold coin and $7 on each silver dollar. Rather than being paid to a beneficiary organization, the surcharges were earmarked for retirement of the national debt.

In 1988, a gold half eagle and silver dollar were authorized honoring the participation of American athletes during the 1988 Olympic Games. The United States joined the ranks of a bevy of nonhost nations that had learned the financial lessons of Olympic commemorative coinage. Controversy erupted over the use of the Olympic rings, a protected symbol of the International Olympic Committee. Ultimately, the rings appeared on the coins, but the dollar coin was flawed by an incorrect use of the term "Olympiad."

Flush with at least moderate success and in the eyes of many collectors turning increasingly self-serving, Congress authorized a gold half eagle, silver dollar and copper-nickel half dollar to commemorate the 1989 Bicentennial of Congress (conveniently forgetting that the judicial and administrative branches of federal government also celebrated their bicentennial birthdays in 1989). The Congress Bicentennial coins established numismatic history—first-strike ceremonies were conducted on the U.S. Capitol grounds, a publicity stunt that required legislative approval, and the first time legal tender U.S. coins had been produced outside a U.S. Mint facility.

Ignoring President Eisenhower's earlier warning about a commemorative flood, Congress authorized a silver dollar commemorating—ironically—the 100th anniversary in 1990 of the birth of Dwight D. Eisenhower.

The decade of the 1990s was flooded with commemorative coin programs—27 to be exact, representing 59 new coin designs. The designs were offered on Proof and Uncirculated coins. Congress eventually adopted Mint reform legislation in 1992 and 1996 to help curb abuses and restrict (theoretically, at least) the issuance of commemorative coin programs.

The 1992 legislation established the Citizens Commemorative Coin Advisory Committee, made up of seven persons representing collectors and the general public, appointed by the Treasury secretary, to review proposed coin programs and make recommendations for commemorative themes. The CCCAC (or its successor, the Citizens Coinage Advisory Committee) did not always give its approval to programs that have been pushed through congressional channels.

The 1996 reform act limited commemorative coin programs to two a year and set maximum mintage limits (no more than 750,000 copper-nickel clad half dollars, 500,000 silver dollars and 100,000 gold $5 or $10 coins). It also required recovery of Mint expenses before payment of any surcharges to any recipient organization and an audited financial statement that verifies that the organization has raised funds from private sources equal to or greater than the maximum amount of surcharges the organization may receive from sale of numismatic items. The reform act also required certain auditing practices.

Despite the law, Congress still adopted more than the limit of two in some subsequent years. It also stretched out the time frame in which some programs would appear, resulting in some programs appearing after the anniversary they commemorated had already passed.

1991 saw three coin programs—the first being a three-coin offering honoring the 50th anniversary of the completion of Mount Rushmore. Single silver dollar programs marking the 38th anniversary of the Korean War and the 50th anniversary of the United Services Organization (USO) followed. The celebration of the 38th anniversary of the Korean War had nothing to do with that war's famous 38th Parallel; that was sheer coincidence. Instead, the desire for funding a Korean War veterans memorial drove the program.

Three programs appeared in 1992. A three-coin program—a copper-nickel clad half dollar, silver dollar and $5 gold half eagle—commemorated the 1992 Olympic Games, the third Olympic coins program since 1983-1984. The Uncirculated dollar carries incuse edge lettering, the first time edge lettering appeared on a U.S. coin since the Saint-Gaudens double eagles. The White House bicentennial was celebrated with a silver dollar, which sold out its 500,000 maximum mintage. Another three-coin program was also offered in 1992, this one to mark the 500th anniversary of Christopher Columbus' 1492 voyage to the New World.

Two three-coin programs were authorized for 1993. The World War II 50th anniversary coins were struck in 1993 but carry the dual dates of U.S. involvement—1991-1995. The coins bear no reference to the 1993 date of issue, a seemingly illegal omission. The 1993 Bill of Rights/James Madison program offered three coins, including a silver half dollar in place of the copper-nickel clad, the first silver half dollar since

the George Washington commemorative half dollar of 1982. The program also offered a silver dollar and gold $5 half eagle.

Another dual-dated coin program—a silver dollar inscribed 1743-1993 marking the 250th anniversary of Thomas Jefferson's birth—appeared in 1994, although it marked a 1993 event. Like the World War II coins, this issue bore no reference to the date of issue.

Three more programs appeared in 1994, in violation of law—a three-coin issue commemorating World Cup Soccer; three military veterans silver dollars approved under a single act, the Prisoner of War, Vietnam Veterans Memorial and Women in Military Service coins; and a silver dollar marking the Bicentennial of the U.S. Capitol.

The proliferation of multiple commemorative coin programs angered many collectors, who were upset with the some of the themes being selected, the continuation of surcharges and the expense to obtain one of every coin struck to keep their collections intact. Many asked, why couldn't Congress authorize circulating commemoratives at face value? Such requests fell on deaf ears until the mid-1990s.

Three coin programs appeared in 1995—a single silver dollar marking the Special Olympics World Games (bearing the portrait of Eunice Kennedy Shriver, the first portrait of a living individual to appear on a U.S. coin in decades); a three-coin issue to raise funds to preserve the Civil War Battlefields; and the launch of the first year of the largest (in terms of designs offered) modern U.S. commemorative coin program ever, marking the centennial of the modern Olympic Games, held in Atlanta.

The 1995 Olympic coins comprised two gold $5 coins, four silver dollars and two copper-nickel clad half dollars, each depicting a different sport or athletic venue. 1996 continued that vein with two more gold coins, four more silver dollars and two more copper-nickel clad half dollars. The Mint launched a major marketing effort to sell the Olympic coins to more than 40 nations on all seven continents. Total sales reached only a fraction of the mammoth maximum authorized mintages.

Two other 1996 programs joined the second year of the Olympic program. National Community Service was commemorated by a silver dollar. Lobbying by collectors to get a coin program whose surcharges would be used to help maintain the numismatic collection at the Smithsonian Institution was successful, resulting in a gold and silver coin issue. Collectors and the public did not respond as well as proponents had hoped, however.

The year 1997 opened with the launch of the Botanic Garden silver dollars followed by the Jackie Robinson gold and silver coins. The latter program to honor the achievements of the first African-American baseball player to play in the major leagues received congressional approval with the stipulation that the first $1 million in surcharges benefit the U.S. Botanic Garden (which, as noted, had its own commemorative program; the diversion of surcharges was the effort of a senator whose wife was closely linked to the Botanic Garden). After sales of the Jackie Robinson coins ended in July 1998, legislation was introduced and passed over Mint objections allowing sales to be reopened, an unprecedented move that angered collectors who bought the coins and anticipated low mintages. However, the law allowed sales only to the Jackie Robinson Foundation, the beneficiary of the surcharges, and not to the public. The foundation never bought any of the coins permitted by the sales extension. (Today, the Proof and Uncirculated Jackie Robinson gold $5 coins are the second most expensive of the 1982 and later commemorative coins, due to their low mintages and growing popularity with collectors.)

The 1997 issues continued with the release of a gold $5 coin in honor of Franklin Delano Roosevelt. Many collectors believed it ironic that FDR was depicted on a gold coin since the former president was responsible for signing the 1933 executive order banning ownership of many forms of gold, including many gold coins. The year ended with a silver dollar release for the National Law Enforcement Officers Memorial, which depicts a male police officer and female civilian (presumably a fallen officer's widow) pointing to a name on the memorial.

In keeping with Mint reform legislation passed, only two programs were offered in 1998—a silver dollar to support the Robert F. Kennedy Memorial and a silver dollar to recognize the sacrifices of the Black Revolutionary War Patriots.

The Kennedy silver dollar depicts the senator and assassinated presidential candidate. The bill was sponsored by Rep. Joseph P. Kennedy II, D-Mass., then chairman of the House Banking Subcommittee on Consumer Credit and Insurance, and son of Robert Kennedy. The Kennedy coin along with four other commemorative programs were included in a House-Senate conference committee report, which allowed sponsors of the various coin bills and related amendments to bypass the normal legislative process and requirements. None of the coin proposals had a hearing before either Senate or House committees and two—the RFK and West Point proposals—were not reviewed by the Citizens Commemorative Coin Advisory Committee, which was a legal requirement. A spokesperson for Kennedy's Subcommittee said the lawmakers were faced with "political pressures right now," and did not feel they could wait for the CCCAC's report, which they understood would not be available until after the session of Congress had concluded. All of the bills became law without public comment in congressional hearings.

The Black Revolutionary War Patriots silver dollar depicts Crispus Attucks, an African-American killed by British soldiers in 1770 in what became known as the Boston Massacre. The reverse depicts a portion of a memorial to black patriots of the Revolution.

Dolley Madison, a first lady to her husband, James, the fourth president, and official hostess for his predecessor, the widowed Thomas Jefferson, was recognized on a commemorative silver dollar in 1999. The piece is notable as the first U.S. commemorative coin designed by a private company, Tiffany & Co., and the first to bear a company logo in lieu of designer's initials. The obverse depicts Dolley Madison surrounded by flowers; the reverse depicts the Madison home, Montpelier.

Also in 1999, George Washington was commemoratively honored for the second time in the modern era with a gold $5 coin noting the bicentennial of his death. The coin is notable in featuring the designs by Laura Gardin Fraser recommended by the Commission of Fine Arts in 1932 Washington quarter dollar. The Fraser designs were not selected by the Treasury secretary for the 1932 coin, a decision that many collectors criticized over the years, out of the opinion that the Fraser designs were superior to Joseph Flanagan's designs selected for the quarter dollar.

A silver dollar was introduced in 1999 to mark the 125th anniversary of the founding of the nation's first national park, Yellowstone National Park. It became the first of what would be many coins, both circulating and noncirculating, to depict a bison. The animal is depicted on the reverse with the Old Faithful geyser depicted on the obverse of the silver dollar. The selection of Old Faithful and bison for the reverse of the circulating 2010 American the Beautiful quarter dollar honoring Yellowstone prompted some collectors to criticize the duplication of theme if not the artistic execution of the same design elements.

When the 1990s closed, observers reflected on the decade. Numerous pieces of legislation had been introduced to honor outstanding Americans, monuments and other themes, including a move from the United States Olympic Committee for an annual coin issue to benefit the U.S. Olympic movement (an idea vastly unpopular with most collectors, who were thus relieved that the plan was nixed). Many of the programs never succeeded; in 1996, for example, during the waning days of the 104th Congress, legislation for nearly a dozen coin programs was introduced, but none passed. Collectors were increasingly concerned about the proliferation of commemorative coin programs, many with very narrow themes that were not very appealing to a majority of collectors.

The year 2000 began with a first for U.S. coinage—a ringed bimetallic coin. A program authorizing 500,000 silver dollars and either 100,000 gold $5 coins or 200,000 gold-platinum ringed bimetallic $10 coins to mark the 200th anniversary of the Library of Congress was approved for the year 2000; the Mint chose to strike the ringed bimetallic $10 coin, which remains the sole ringed bimetallic piece struck by the U.S. Mint of any kind.

Also approved for 2000 was a Leif Ericson Millennium silver dollar, with a maximum mintage of 500,000. The Philadelphia Mint also struck a companion 1,000-kronur coin for Iceland, the first foreign coin struck by the United States Mint since the 1980s. A two-coin Proof set containing one each of the U.S. and Icelandic Ericson coin represents the only U.S. commemorative coin set to offer a foreign coin.

Recycled coin designs proved popular for the 2001 American Buffalo silver dollar, which bears modified versions of James Earle Fraser's designs for the Indian Head 5-cent coin of 1913 to 1938. The coin sold out in about two weeks, a record for any U.S. commemorative coin program since 1982. A special set containing an Uncirculated example sold out in about six days. A number of collectors were unhappy when they were unable to purchase the coins at issue price. The rapid sales prompted officials for the surcharge recipient, the Smithsonian Institution (whose new National Museum of the American Indian was designated to receive the funds), to request Congress to authorize an additional mintage. Collectors largely opposed the proposal (although some who did not get their orders into the Mint in time to get a coin may have been supportive) and Congress refused to authorize any additional production of the popular coin.

To raise funds to support a United States Capitol Visitors Center, Congress approved for 2001 the production of up to 200,000 ringed bimetallic gold and platinum $10 coins, 500,000 silver dollars and 750,000 clad half dollars. However, Congress granted the Mint to issue substitute production of up to 100,000 gold $5 coins if the ringed bimetallic coin proved not feasible; the Mint chose the gold coin over the platinum-gold piece. Lackluster sales suggested a lack of strong collector interest in the theme.

For 2002, Congress approved a silver dollar (500,000 maximum mintage) whose surcharges benefitted the West Point (Military Academy) Association of Graduates. The obverse depicts a group of students marching in formation carrying flags; the reverse depicts a helmet and sword logo.

In addition, a two-coin program was approved honoring the 2002 Salt Lake City Winter Olympics, with the surcharges going to the Salt Lake Organizing Committee for the Olympic Games and the U.S. Olympic Committee. A silver dollar and gold half eagle were issued, with the level of sales suggesting that collector support for Olympic-themed commemorative coins had cooled. Since then, Congress has not approved any new sports-themed commemorative programs.

A three-coin program received congressional approval for the year 2003 to mark the centennial of the first powered flight of the Wright Brothers. Authorized were a copper-nickel clad half dollar, a silver dollar and a gold $10 eagle. The reverses of all three coins depict the 1903 Wright Flyer in flight, a not unexpected design choice, though one that some

thought did not show much in the way of innovation.

Thomas A. Edison's invention of the light bulb was marked in 2004 with sales of up to 500,000 silver dollars. Surcharges were split among recipient organizations and sites with connections to Edison. One group, Edison Memorial Tower Corp., failed to meet the initial deadline to raise the matching sums required before release of the Mint surcharges; legislation passed in 2007 granted a six-month extension to the recipient's deadline to meet legal requirements to raise matching funds within two years of the close of the program. The recipient did eventually meet the requirements necessary to receive the surcharge funds.

Also approved for 2004 was legislation authorizing up to 500,000 silver dollars to mark the centennial of the Lewis and Clark expedition. One option that proved both popular and controversial offered the Proof silver dollar with 50,000 hand-sewn and -beaded pouches that were to be created by artisans from different tribes whose ancestors the expedition encountered. Mint officials identified the tribes who produced the pouches as: Blackfeet Tribe, Browning, Mont.; Cheyenne River Sioux Tribe, Eagle Butte, S.D.; Confederated Salish and Kootenai Tribes, Pablo, Mont.; Confederated Tribes of Grand Ronde Community of Oregon, Grand Ronde, Ore.; Confederated Tribes of Umatilla Indian Reservation, Pendleton, Ore.; Crow Tribe, Crow Agency, Mont.; Shawnee United Remnant Band of Ohio, Bellefontaine, Ohio; Shoshone-Bannock Tribes, Fort Hall, Idaho; Standing Rock Sioux Tribe, Fort Yates, N.D.; and Three Affiliated Tribes of the Fort Berthold Reservation, New Town, N.D.

The coin and pouch sets sold out, but not everyone receiving the sets was happy with the results. Complaints by some owners of the pouches included comments about the lack of detail in the design on the pouches they received, what they perceive to be shoddy workmanship and receiving multiple pouches of the same basic style crafted by the same artisan.

In addition, all of the coin-pouch sets were shipped with an advisory from the Mint to separate the Proof silver dollar and pouch for long-term storage out of concerns of the effect the pouches could have on the coins.

In 2007, the Mint offered refunds to customers sent pouches hand-crafted by members of the Shawnee Nation United Remnant Band of Ohio after Mint officials learned the tribe was not state or federally recognized. Up to 2,000 of the total 50,000 sets offered were affected.

Two commemorative programs were authorized for 2005: one with a silver dollar celebrating Chief Justice of the United States John Marshall's 1801 to 1835 term on the Supreme Court and another offering a silver dollar marking the 230th anniversary of the founding of the U.S. Marines Corps.

The Marshall silver dollar did not sell out, but

anticipation that the Marines coin would sell out in short order prompted the secretary of the Treasury to exercise an option granted under U.S. Code. The authorizing act specified a mintage of 500,000 for the Marine Corps silver dollar. In an unprecedented move announced June 2, 2005, Treasury Secretary John W. Snow exercised his statutory discretion—before the coins went on sale July 20—to increase the maximum authorized mintage for the commemorative coin program, to 600,000 coins.

Snow acted under the provisions of Title 31 of the United States Code, Section 5112(m)(2)(B), which grants the Treasury secretary the authority to waive the mintage level for commemorative coins, if he determines, based on independent, market-based research conducted by a designated recipient organization, that the mintage limit in the authorizing legislation is not adequate to meet public demand. The Marine Corps Heritage Foundation—the recipient organization for the surcharges—provided Treasury officials with results of research and a request to increase the mintage to 600,000 silver dollars. Based on this research, Snow approved a mintage limit of 600,000 silver dollars for the Marine Corps 230th Anniversary silver dollar. Final sales for the coin totaled 598,481 pieces.

Of the two programs offered in 2006, one proved to have a popular theme. The Benjamin Franklin Tercentenary program offered a Scientist silver dollar, commemorating a younger Franklin, showing the famous kite and lightning experiment he conducted in his 40s, and a Founding Father dollar, depicting Franklin the elder statesman. Both versions—offered individually and in special sets with other coins— sold out. The San Francisco Old Mint Centennial program offered a silver dollar and a gold $5 half eagle for 2006, with obverses depicting the structure famously known as the Granite Lady. The reverses held special appeal to collectors because they replicated reverse designs struck during the San Francisco Mint's career: the Morgan dollar's reverse for the commemorative silver dollar and the reverse of the Coronet gold $5 half eagle for the gold commemorative. Neither coin sold out.

The 2007 programs commemorated the 400th anniversary of the founding of the colony at Jamestown, Va., and the 50th anniversary of the Little Rock Central High School desegregation. The Jamestown program offered a silver dollar (depicting three inhabitants of the region and the ships that brought the colonists) and a gold $5 coin (depicting Capt. John Smith conversing with Powhatan, an American Indian chief on the obverse, with a structure of the colony on the reverse); neither coin sold out. The Little Rock Central High Desegregation program featured a single silver dollar depicting a scene showing the legs of the nine black high school students accompanied by an armed soldier to protect them from the angry white mobs protesting the youths' attendance at the

previously all-white school. The coin did not sell out.

For the first time since 1990, just one commemorative coin program was offered in 2008 although it was the first three-coin program since 2003. The 2008 Bald Eagle program offered a copper-nickel clad half dollar, silver dollar and gold $5 half eagle. Not surprisingly given the theme, all three coins showed bald eagles on both sides. None sold out although the silver dollar came closest with 82.7 percent of the coins selling.

Two commemorative silver dollar programs were offered for 2009, both honoring men born in 1809. The Louis Braille Bicentennial silver dollar honored the creator of a form of raised type that permits the blind to read. The obverse depicts Braille and the reverse shows a child reading a Braille book with a tactile inscription (the word "Braille," abbreviated "brl" in Braille code). The coin did not sell out. The other 2009 commemorative program, celebrating the birth of Abraham Lincoln, not surprisingly, did sell out. The program included a limited-edition Abraham Lincoln Coin and Chronicles set, which contained a Proof silver dollar, four Proof 2009-S Lincoln cents, a reproduction of the Gettysburg Address and an image of Lincoln.

Two programs were offered in 2010: the American Veterans Disabled for Life silver dollar and the Boy Scouts of America Centennial silver dollar. For some, the obverse design was controversial in that in addition to depicting a Cub Scout and Boy Scout, both males, it also showed a teenage girl in the Venturing program. Critics thought it inappropriate that a coin honoring Boy Scouts depict a girl, while supporters noted that girls had been admitted to special-interest Explorer posts since 1969, meaning girls had been part of the Boy Scouts program in at least a small way for nearly a third of the organization's existence.

Programs on tap for 2011 and later show a clear congressional preference for coins with military themes: 2011, separate programs for the U.S. Army (created in 1775) and Medal of Honor (founded in 1861), both offering silver dollars, with the Medal of Honor program also offering a gold $5 coin; 2012, Infantry silver dollar, collecting surcharges for the National Infantry Museum and Soldier Center, and the Star-Spangled Banner Bicentennial, offering a gold $5 coin and a silver dollar; 2013, Girl Scouts USA Centennial, collecting surcharges for the organization, and a program honoring five five-star generals of the U.S. Army, George C. Marshall, Douglas MacArthur, Dwight D. Eisenhower, Henry "Hap" Arnold and Omar N. Bradley, with a gold $5 coin, silver dollar and copper-nickel clad half dollar; 2014, Civil Rights silver dollar, honoring the enactment of the Civil Rights Act of 1964, with the surcharges being delivered to the United Negro College Fund to enable it to continue its work in providing scholarships to minorities and supporting several historically black colleges and universities.

Commemorative mintages and selling prices

The Mint has changed how it records "mintages" of commemorative coins. For each commemorative coin program from 1892 through 1951, the Mint recorded the actual number of coins struck (technically, the coin's "mintage") and the number of coins melted at the end of the program, resulting in the coin's "net mintage." Only the net mintage is available for the last of the early commemorative coin programs—the Booker T. Washington-George Washington Carver half dollars of 1951 to 1954.

Since 1982, the Mint has provided "sales figures," not mintages, for the commemorative coins. Mint officials have not released the actual numbers of coins struck and melted.

Coin	Number struck	Number melted	Net mintage	Original price	Designer(s)
World's Columbian Exposition half dollar					Charles E. Barber/George Morgan
1892	950,000	None	950,000	$1.00	
1893	4,052,105	2,501,700	1,550,405	$1.00	
Isabella quarter dollar					Charles E. Barber
1893	40,023	15,809	24,124	$1.00	
Lafayette-Washington silver dollar					Charles E. Barber
1900	50,026	14,000	36,026	$2.00	
Louisiana Purchase Exposition gold dollar					Charles E. Barber
1903	250,258	215,250	each type 17,375	$3.00	
Lewis and Clark Exposition gold dollar					Charles E. Barber
1904	25,028	15,003	10,025	$2.00	
1905	35,041	25,000	10,041	$2.00	
Panama-Pacific International Exposition half dollar					Charles E. Barber
1915-S	60,030	32,896	27,134	$1.00	
Panama-Pacific International Exposition gold dollar					Charles Keck
1915-S	25,034	10,034	15,000	$2.00	
Panama-Pacific Exposition quarter eagle					Charles E. Barber
1915-S	10,017	3,278	6,749	$4.00	
Panama-Pacific Exposition $50					Robert Aitken
1915-S Round	1,510	1,027	483	$100	
1915-S Octagonal	1,509	864	645	$100	
McKinley Memorial gold dollar					Charles E. Barber/George T. Morgan
1916	20,026	10,049	9,977	$3.00	
1917	10,014	14	10,000	$3.00	
Illinois Centennial half dollar					George T. Morgan/John R. Sinnock
1918	100,058	None	100,058	$1.00	
Maine Centennial half dollar					Anthony de Francisci
1920	50,028	None	50,028	$1.00	
Pilgrim Tercentenary half dollar					Cyrus E. Dallin
1920	200,112	48,000	152,112	$1.00	
1921	100,053	80,000	20,053	$1.00	
Missouri Centennial half dollar					Robert Aitken
1921 2★4	5,000	None	5,000	$1.00	
1921 No 2★4	45,028	29,600	15,428	$1.00	
Alabama Centennial half dollar					Laura Gardin Fraser
1921 2X2	6,006	None	6,006	$1.00	
1921 No 2X2	64,038	5,000	59,038	$1.00	
Grant Memorial half dollar					Laura Gardin Fraser
1922 Star	5,006	750	4,256	$1.00	
1922 No Star	95,055	27,650	67,405	$1.00	
Grant Memorial gold dollar					Laura Gardin Fraser
1922 Star	5,016	None	5,016	$3.50	
1922 No Star	5,000	None	5,000	$3.00	
Monroe Doctrine Centennial half dollar					Chester Beach
1923-S	274,077	None	274,077	$1.00	
Huguenot-Walloon Tercentenary half dollar					George T. Morgan
1924	142,080	None	142,080	$1.00	
Lexington-Concord Sesquicentennial half dollar					Chester Beach
1925	162,099	86	162,013	$1.00	

Coin	Number struck	Number melted	Net mintage	Original price	Designer(s)
Stone Mountain half dollar					Gutzon Borglum
1925	2,314,709	1,000,000	1,314,709	$1.00	
California Diamond Jubilee half dollar					Jo Mora
1925-S	150,200	63,606	86,594	$1.00	
Fort Vancouver Centennial half dollar					Laura Gardin Fraser
1925	50,028	35,034	14,994	$1.00	
American Independence Sesquicentennial half dollar					John R. Sinnock
1926	1,000,528	859,408	141,120	$1.00	
American Independence Sesquicentennial quarter eagle					John R. Sinnock
1926	200,226	154,207	46,019	$4.00	
Oregon Trail Memorial half dollar					James E. and Laura G. Fraser
1926	48,030	75	47,955	$1.00	
1926-S	100,055	17,000	83,055	$1.00	
1928	50,028	44,000	6,028	$2.00	
1933-D	5,250	242	5,008	$2.00	
1934-D	7,006	None	7,006	$2.00	
1936	10,006	None	10,006	$1.60	
1936-S	5,006	None	5,006	$1.60	
1937-D	12,008	None	12,008	$1.60	
1938	6,006	None	6,006	$6.25 for set of three	
1938-D	6,005	None	6,005	See above	
1938-S	6,006	None	6,006	See above	
1939	3,004	None	3,004	$7.50 for set of three	
1939-D	3,004	None	3,004	See above	
1939-S	3,005	None	3,005	See above	
Vermont Sesquicentennial half dollar					Charles Keck
1927	40,034	11,872	28,162	$1.00	
Hawaiian Sesquicentennial half dollar					Juliette Mae Fraser/Chester Beach
1928	10,000	None	10,000	$2.00	
Maryland Tercentenary half dollar					Hans Schuler
1934	25,015	None	25,015	$1.00	
Texas Independence Centennial					Pompeo Coppini
1934	205,113	143,650	61,463	$1.00	
1935	10,0078	12	9,996	$1.50	
1935-D	10,007	None	10,007	$1.50	
1935-S	10,008	None	10,008	$1.50	
1936	10,008	1,097	8,911	$1.50	
1936-D	10,007	968	9,039	$1.50	
1936-S	10,008	943	9,055	$1.50	
1937	8,005	1,434	6,571	$1.50	
1937-D	8,006	1,401	6,605	$1.50	
1937-S	8,007	1,370	6,637	$1.50	
1938	5,005	1,225	3,780	$2.00	
1938-D	5,005	1,230	3,775	$2.00	
1938-S	5,006	1,192	3,814	$2.00	
Daniel Boone Bicentennial half dollar					Augustus Lukeman
1934	10,007	None	10,007	$1.60	
1935	10,010	None	10,010	$1.10	
1935-D	5,005	None	5,005	$1.60	
1935-S	5,005	None	5,005	$1.60	
1935 W/1934	10,008	None	10,008	$1.10	
1935-D W/1934	2,003	None	2,003	$3.70 for two	
1935-S W/1934	2,004	None	2,004	see above	
1936	12,012	None	12,012	$1.10	
1936-D	5,005	None	5,005	$1.60	
1936-S	5,006	None	5,006	$1.60	
1937	15,010	5,200	9,810	$1.60, $7.25 set	
1937-D	7,506	5,000	2,506	$7.25 in set	
1937-S	5,006	2,500	2,506	$5.15	
1938	5,005	2,905	2,100	$6.50 for set of three	
1938-D	5,005	2,905	2,100	See above	
1938-S	5,006	2,906	2,100	See above	

Coin	Number struck	Number melted	Net mintage	Original price	Designer(s)
Connecticut Tercentenary half dollar					Henry G. Kreiss
1935	25,018	None	25,018	$1.00	
Arkansas Centennial half dollar					Edward E. Burr
1935	13,012	None	13,012	$1.00	
1935-D	5,005	None	5,005	$1.00	
1935-S	5,506	None	5,006	$1.00	
1936	10,010	350	9,660	$1.50	
1936-D	10,010	350	9,660	$1.50	
1936-S	10,012	350	9,662	$1.50	
1937	5,505	None	5,505	$8.75 for set of three	
1937-D	5,505	None	5,505	See above	
1937-S	5,506	None	5,506	See above	
1938	6,006	2,850	3,156	$8.75 for set of three	
1938-D	6,005	2,850	3,155	See above	
1938-S	6,006	2,850	3,156	See above	
1939	2,104	None	2,104	$10 for set of three	
1939-D	2,104	None	2,104	See above	
1939-S	2,105	None	2,105	See above	
Arkansas-Robinson half dollar					E.E. Burr/Henry Kreiss
1936	25,265	None	25,265	$1.85	
Hudson, N.Y., Sesquicentennial half dollar					Chester Beach
1935	10,008	None	10,008	$1.00	
California-Pacific International Expo					Robert Aitken
1935-S	250,132	180,000	70,132	$1.00	
1936-D	180,092	150,000	30,092	$1.50	
Old Spanish Trail half dollar					L.W. Hoffecker
1935	10,008	None	10,008	$2.00	
Providence, R.I., Tercentenary					John H. Benson/Abraham G. Carey
1936	20,013	None	20,013	$1.00	
1936-D	15,010	None	15,010	$1.00	
1936-S	15,011	None	15,011	$1.00	
Cleveland, Great Lakes Exposition half dollar					Brenda Putnam
1936	50,030	None	50,030	$1.50	
Wisconsin Territorial Centennial half dollar					David Parsons/Benjamin Hawkins
1936	25,015	None	25,015	$1.50	
Cincinnati Music Center half dollar					Constance Ortmayer
1936	5,005	None	5,005	$7.75 for set of three	
1936-D	5,005	None	5,005	See above	
1936-S	5,006	None	5,006	See above	
Long Island Tercentenary half dollar					Howard K. Weinmann
1936	100,053	18,227	81,826	$1.00	
York County, Maine, Tercentenary half dollar					Walter H. Rich
1936	25,015	None	25,015	$1.50	
Bridgeport, Conn., Centennial half dollar					Henry G. Kreiss
1936	25,015	None	25,015	$2.00	
Lynchburg, Va., Sesquicentennial half dollar					Charles Keck
1936	20,013	None	20,013	$1.00	
Elgin, Ill., Centennial half dollar					Trygve Rovelstad
1936	25,015	5,000	20,015	$1.50	
Albany, N.Y., half dollar					Gertrude K. Lathrop
1936	25,013	7,342	17,671	$2.00	
San Francisco-Oakland Bay Bridge half dollar					Jacques Schnier
1936-S	100,055	28,631	71,424	$1.50	
Columbia, S.C., Sesquicentennial half dollar					A. Wolfe Davidson
1936	9,007	None	9,007	$6.45 for set of three	
1936-D	8,009	None	8,009	See above	
1936-S	8,007	None	8,007	See above	

Coin	Number struck	Number melted	Net mintage	Original price	Designer(s)
Delaware Tercentenary half dollar					Carl L. Schmitz
1936	25,015	4,022	20,993	$1.75	
Battle of Gettysburg half dollar					Frank Vittor
1936	50,028	23,100	26,928	$1.65	
Norfolk, Va., Bicentennial half dollar					William M. Simpson/Marjorie E. Simpson
1936	25,013	8,077	16,936	$1.50	
Roanoke Island, N.C., half dollar					William M. Simpson
1937	50,030	21,000	29,030	$1.65	
Battle of Antietam half dollar					William M. Simpson
1937	50,028	32,000	18,028	$1.65	
New Rochelle, N.Y., half dollar					Gertrude K. Lathrop
1938	25,015	9,749	15,266	$2.00	
Iowa Statehood Centennial half dollar					Adam Pietz
1946	100,057	None	100,057	$2.50/$3.00	
Booker T. Washington half dollar					Isaac S. Hathaway
1946	1,000,546	?	?	$1.00	
1946-D	200,113	?	?	$1.50	
1946-S	500,279	?	?	$1.00	
1947	100,017	?	?	$6.00 for set of three	
1947-D	100,017	?	?	See above	
1947-S	100,017	?	?	See above	
1948	20,005	12,000	8,005	$7.50 for set of three	
1948-D	20,005	12,000	8,005	See above	
1948-S	20,005	12,000	8,005	See above	
1949	12,004	6,000	6,004	$8.50 for set of three	
1949-D	12,004	6,000	6,004	See above	
1949-S	12,004	6,000	6,004	See above	
1950	12,004	6,000	6,004	$8.50 for set of three	
1950-D	12,004	6,000	6,004	See above	
1950-S	512,091	?	?	See above	
1951	510,082	?	?	$3 each or $10 for set of three	
1951-D	12,004	5,000	7,004	See above	
1951-S	12,004	5,000	7,004	See above	
Booker T. Washington/George Washington Carver					Isaac S. Hathaway
1951	?	?	110,018	$10 for set of three	
1951-D	?	?	10,004	See above	
1951-S	?	?	10,004	See above	
1952	?	?	2,006,292	$10 for set of three	
1952-D	?	?	8,006	See above	
1952-S	?	?	8,006	See above	
1953	?	?	8,003	$10 for set of three	
1953-D	?	?	8,003	See above	
1953-S	?	?	108,020	See above	
1954	?	?	12,006	$10 for set of three	
1954-D	?	?	12,006	See above	
1954-S	?	?	122,024	See above	

Coin	Mintage	Pre-issue/regular price	Designer(s)
George Washington half dollar			Elizabeth Jones
1982-D Uncirculated	2,210,458	$8.50/$101	
1982-S Proof	4,894,044	$10/$121	
Los Angeles Olympic Games silver dollar			Elizabeth Jones
1983-P Uncirculated	294,543	$28 or $89[2] for set of three from all 3 Mints	
1983-D Uncirculated	174,014	See above	
1983-S Uncirculated	174,014	See above	
1983-S Proof	1,577,025	$24.95[2]	
1984-P Uncirculated	217,954	$28 or $89[2] for set of three from all 3 Mints	
1984-D Uncirculated	116,675	See above	
1984-S Uncirculated	116,675	See above	
1984-S Proof	1,801,210	$322	

Coin	Mintage	Pre-issue/regular price	Designer(s)
Los Angeles Olympic Games gold eagle			James Peed/John Mercanti
1984-P Proof	33,309	$352[2]	
1984-D Proof	34,533	$352[2]	
1984-S Proof	48,551	$352[2]	
1984-W Proof	381,085	$352[2]	
1984-W Uncirculated	75,886	$339[2]	
Statue of Liberty, Immigrant half dollar			Edgar Steever/Sherl Winter
1986-D Uncirculated	928,008	$5/$63	
1986-S Proof	6,925,627	$6.50/$7.50[3]	
Statue of Liberty, Ellis Island dollar			John Mercanti/Matthew Peloso
1986-P Uncirculated	723,635	$20.50/$22[3]	
1986-S Proof	6,414,638	$22.50/$24[3]	
Statue of Liberty half eagle			Elizabeth Jones
1986-W Uncirculated	95,248	$160/$165[3]	
1986-W Proof	404,013	$170/$175[3]	
Constitution Bicentennial silver dollar			Patricia L. Verani
1987-P Uncirculated	451,629	$22.50/$26[3]	
1987-S Proof	2,747,116	$24/$28[3]	
Constitution Bicentennial half eagle			Marcel Jovine
1987-W Uncirculated	214,225	$195/$215[3]	
1987-W Proof	651,659	$200/$225[3]	
1988 Olympic Games silver dollar			Patricia L. Verani/Sherl J. Winter
1988-D Uncirculated	191,368	$22/$27[3]	
1988-S Proof	1,359,366	$23/$29[3]	
1988 Olympic Games gold half eagle			Elizabeth Jones/Marcel Jovine
1988-W Uncirculated	62,913	$200/$225[3]	
1988-W Proof	281,465	$205/$235[3]	
Congress Bicentennial half dollar			Patricia L. Verani/William Woodward
1989-D Uncirculated	163,753	$5/$6[3]	
1989-S Proof	767,897	$7/$8[3]	
Congress Bicentennial silver dollar			William Woodward
1989-D Uncirculated	135,203	$23/$26[3]	
1989-S Proof	762,198	$25/$29[3]	
Congress Bicentennial half eagle			John Mercanti
1989-W Uncirculated	46,899	$185/$200[3]	
1989-W Proof	164,690	$195/$215[3]	
Eisenhower Birth Centennial silver dollar			John Mercanti/Marcel Jovine
1990-W Uncirculated	241,669	$23/$26[3]	
1990-P Proof	1,144,461	$25/$29[3]	
Mount Rushmore 50th Anniversary half dollar			Marcel Jovine/James Ferrell
1991-D Uncirculated	172,754	$6/$7[3]	
1991-S Proof	753,257	$8.50/$9.50[3]	
Mount Rushmore 50th Anniversary silver dollar			Marika Somogyi/Frank Gasparro
1991-P Uncirculated	133,139	$23/$26[3]	
1991-S Proof	738,419	$28/$31[3]	
Mount Rushmore 50th Anniversary half eagle			John Mercanti/Robert Lamb
1991-W Uncirculated	31,959	$185/$210[3]	
1991-W Proof	111,991	$195/$225[3]	
Korean War Memorial silver dollar			John Mercanti/James Ferrell
1991-D Uncirculated	213,049	$23/$26[3]	
1991-P Proof	618,488	$28/$31[3]	
USO 50th Anniversary silver dollar			Robert Lamb/John Mercanti
1991-D Uncirculated	124,958	$23/$26[3]	
1991-S Proof	321,275	$28/$31[3]	
1992 Olympics copper-nickel clad half dollar			William Cousins/Steven Bieda
1992-P Uncirculated	161,607	$6/$7.50[3]	
1992-S Proof	519,645	$8.50/$9.50[3]	

Coin	Mintage	Pre-issue/regular price	Designer(s)
1992 Olympics silver dollar			John R. Deecken/Marcel Jovine
1992-D Uncirculated	187,552	$24/$29[3]	
1992-S Proof	504,505	$28/$32[3]	
1992 Olympic gold half eagle			Jim Sharpe/James Peed
1992-W Uncirculated	27,732	$185/$215[3]	
1992-W Proof	77,313	$195/$230[3]	
White House Bicentennial silver dollar			Edgar Z. Steever/Chester Y. Martin
1992-D Uncirculated	123,803	$23/$28[3]	
1992-W Proof	375,851	$28/$32[3]	
Columbus Quincentenary copper-nickel clad half dollar			T. James Ferrell
1992-D Uncirculated	135,702	$6.50/$7.50[3]	
1992-S Proof	390,154	$8.50/$9.50[3]	
Columbus Quincentenary silver dollar			John M. Mercanti/Thomas D. Rogers Sr.
1992-D Uncirculated	106,949	$23/$28[3]	
1992-P Proof	385,241	$27/$31[3]	
Columbus Quincentenary half eagle			T. James Ferrell/Thomas D. Rogers Sr.
1992-W Uncirculated	24,329	$180/$210[3]	
1992-W Proof	79,730	$190/$225[3]	
Bill of Rights/Madison silver half dollar			T. James Ferrell/Dean E. McMullen
1993-W Uncirculated	193,346	$9.75/$11.50[3]	
1993-S Proof	586,315	$12.50/$13.50[3]	
Bill of Rights/Madison silver dollar			William Krawczewicz/Dean E. McMullen
1993-D Uncirculated	98,383	$22/$27[3]	
1993-S Proof	534,001	$25/$29[3]	
Bill of Rights/Madison gold $5 half eagle			Scott R. Blazek/Joseph D. Pena
1993-W Uncirculated	23,266	$175/$205[3]	
1993-W Proof	78,651	$185/$220[3]	
World War II 50th Anniversary copper-nickel clad half dollar			George Klauba/Bill J. Leftwich
1991-1995-P Uncirculated (1993[4])	197,072	$8/$9[3]	
1991-1995-S Proof (1993[4])	317,396	$9/$10[3]	
World War II 50th Anniversary silver dollar			Thomas D. Rogers Sr.
1991-1995-D Uncirculated (1993[4])	107,240	$23/$28[3]	
1991-1995-W Proof (1993[4])	342,041	$27/$31[3]	
World War II 50th Anniversary gold $5 half eagle			Charles J. Madsen/Edward S. Fisher
1991-1995-W Uncirculated (1993[4])	23,672	$170/$200[3]	
1991-1995-W Proof (1993[4])	67,026	$185/$220[3]	
Thomas Jefferson 250th Anniversary silver dollar			T. James Ferrell
1743-1993-P Uncirculated (1994[5])	266,927	$27/$32[3]	
1743-1993-S Proof (1994[5])	332,891	$31/$35[3]	
World Cup Soccer copper-nickel clad half dollar			Richard T. LaRoche/Dean E. McMullen
1994-D Uncirculated	168,208	$8.75/$9.50[3]	
1994-P Proof	609,354	$9.75/$10.50[3]	
World Cup Soccer silver dollar			Dean E. McMullen
1994-D Uncirculated	81,524	$23/$28[3]	
1994-S Proof	577,090	$27/$31[3]	
World Cup Soccer gold $5 half eagle			William Krawczewicz/Dean E. McMullen
1994-W Uncirculated	22,447	$170/$200[3]	
1994-W Proof	89,614	$185/$220[3]	
Prisoner of War silver dollar			Tom Nielsen and Alfred Maletsky/Edgar Z. Steever
1994-W Uncirculated	54,790	$27/$32[3]	
1994-P Proof	220,100	$31/$35[3]	
Vietnam Veterans Memorial silver dollar			John Mercanti/Thomas D. Rogers Sr.
1994-W Uncirculated	57,317	$27/$32[3]	
1994-P Proof	226,262	$31/$35[3]	
Women in Military Service silver dollar			T. James Ferrell/Thomas D. Rogers Sr.
1994-W Uncirculated	53,054	$27/$32[3]	
1994-P Proof	213,201	$31/$35[3]	

Coin	Mintage	Pre-issue/regular price	Designer(s)
U.S. Capitol Bicentennial silver dollar			**William C. Cousins/John Mercanti**
1994-D Uncirculated	68,332	$32/$37[3]	
1994-S Proof	279,579	$36/$40[3]	
Civil War Battlefields copper-nickel clad half dollar			**Don Troiani/T. James Ferrell**
1995-D Uncirculated	113,045	$9.50/$10.25[3]	
1995-S Proof	326,801	$10.75/$11.75[3]	
Civil War Battlefields silver dollar			**Don Troiani/John Mercanti**
1995-P Uncirculated	51,612	$27/$29[3]	
1995-S Proof	327,686	$30/$34[3]	
Civil War Battlefields gold half eagle			**Don Troiani/Alfred Maletsky**
1995-W Uncirculated	12,623	$180/$190[3]	
1995-W Proof	54,915	$195/$225[3]	
Special Olympics World Games silver dollar			**J. Wyeth and T.J. Ferrell/T.D. Rogers Sr.**
1995-W Uncirculated	89,298	$29/$31[3,6]	
1995-P Proof	352,449	$31/$35[3,6]	
Games of the XXVI Olympiad, Atlanta copper-nickel clad half dollar			**Clint Hansen/T. James Ferrell**
1995-S Basketball Uncirculated	169,527	$10.50/$11.50[7]	
1995-S Basketball Proof	170,733	$11.50/$12.50[7]	
Games of the XXVI Olympiad, Atlanta copper-nickel clad half dollar			**Edgar Z. Steever/T. James Ferrell**
1995-S Baseball Uncirculated	164,759	$10.50/$11.50[7]	
1995-S Baseball Proof	119,396	$11.50/$12.50[7]	
Games of the XXVI Olympiad, Atlanta silver dollar			**Jim Sharpe/William Krawczewicz**
1995-D Gymnastics Uncirculated	43,003	$27.95/$31.95[7]	
1995-S Gymnastics Proof	185,158	$30.95/$34.95[7]	
Games of the XXVI Olympiad, Atlanta silver dollar			**John Mercanti/William Krawczewicz**
1995-D Cycling Uncirculated	20,122	$27.95/$31.95[7]	
1995-S Cycling Proof	127,465	$30.95/$34.95[7]	
Games of the XXVI Olympiad, Atlanta silver dollar			**John Mercanti/William Krawczewicz**
1995-D Track & Field Uncirculated	25,425	$27.95/$31.95[7]	
1995-S Track & Field Proof	143,304	$30.95/$34.95[7]	
Games of the XXVI Olympiad, Atlanta silver dollar			**Jim Sharpe/William Krawczewicz**
1995-D Paralympic, blind runner Uncirculated	29,015	$27.95/$31.95[7]	
1995-S Paralympic, blind runner Proof	139,831	$30.95/$34.95[8]	
Games of the XXVI Olympiad, Atlanta gold half eagle			**Frank Gasparro**
1995-W Torch Runner gold Uncirculated	14,817	$229/$249[7]	
1995-W Torch Runner gold Proof	57,870	$239/$259[7]	
Games of the XXVI Olympiad, Atlanta gold half eagle			**Marcel Jovine/Frank Gasparro**
1995-W Atlanta Stadium gold Uncirculated	10,710	$229/$249[7]	
1995-W Atlanta Stadium gold Proof	43,399	$239/$259[7]	
Games of the XXVI Olympiad, Atlanta clad half dollar			**William Krawczewicz/Malcolm Farley**
1996-S Swimming clad Uncirculated	50,077	$10.50/$11.50[7]	
1996-S Swimming clad Proof	114,890	$11.50/$12.50[7]	
Games of the XXVI Olympiad, Atlanta copper-nickel clad half dollar			**Clint Hansen/Malcolm Farley**
1996-S Soccer clad Uncirculated	53,176	$10.50/$11.50[7]	
1996-S Soccer clad Proof	123,860	$11.50/$12.50[7]	
Games of the XXVI Olympiad, Atlanta silver dollar			**Jim Sharpe/Thomas D. Rogers Sr.**
1996-D Tennis Uncirculated	16,693	$27.95/$31.95[7]	
1996-S Tennis Proof	93,880	$30.95/$34.95[7]	
Games of the XXVI Olympiad, Atlanta silver dollar			**Bart Forbes/Thomas D. Rogers Sr.**
1996-D Rowing Uncirculated	16,921	$27.95/$31.95[7]	
1996-S Rowing Proof	155,543	$30.95/$34.95[7]	
Games of the XXVI Olympiad, Atlanta silver dollar			**Calvin Massey/Thomas D. Rogers Sr.**
1996-D High Jump Uncirculated	16,485	$27.95/$31.95[7]	
1996-S High Jump Proof	127,173	$30.95/$34.95[7]	
Games of the XXVI Olympiad, Atlanta silver dollar			**Jim Sharpe/Thomas D. Rogers Sr.**
1996-D Paralympic, wheelchair athlete Unc.	15,325[7]	$27.95/$31.95[7]	
1996-S Paralympic, wheelchair athlete Proof	86,352	$30.95/$34.95[7]	

Coin	Mintage	Pre-issue/regular price	Designer(s)
Games of the XXVI Olympiad, Atlanta gold half eagle			Frank Gasparro/William Krawczewicz
1996-W Olympic Flame brazier Uncirculated	9,453	$229/$249[7]	
1996-W Olympic Flame brazier Proof	38,871	$239/$259[7]	
Games of the XXVI Olympiad, Atlanta gold half eagle			Patricia L. Verani/William Krawczewicz
1996-W Flag Bearer Uncirculated	9,397	$229/$249[8]	
1996-W Flag Bearer Proof	33,214	$239/$259[8]	
National Community Service silver dollar			Thomas D. Rogers Sr./William C. Cousins
1996-P Uncirculated	23,463	$30/$32[3]	
1996-S Proof	100,749	$33/$37[3]	
Smithsonian 150th Anniversary silver dollar			Thomas D. Rogers Sr./John Mercanti
1996-P Uncirculated	31,320	$30/$32[3]	
1996-S Proof	129,152	$33/$37[3]	
Smithsonian 150th Anniversary gold half eagle			Alfred Maletsky/T. James Ferrell
1996-W Uncirculated	9,068	$180/$205[3]	
1996-W Proof	21,772	$195/$225[3]	
Botanic Garden silver dollar			Edgar Z. Steever IV/William C. Cousins
1997-P Uncirculated	83,505	$30/32[3]	
1997-P Proof	269,843	$33/37[3]	
Jackie Robinson 50th Anniversary silver dollar			Alfred Maletsky/T. James Ferrell
1997-S Uncirculated	30,180	$30/32[3]	
1997-S Proof	110,002	$33/37[3]	
Jackie Robinson 50th Anniversary gold half eagle			William C. Cousins/James Peed
1997-W Uncirculated	5,174	$180/205[3]	
1997-W Proof	24,072	$195/225[3]	
Franklin D. Roosevelt Memorial gold half eagle			T. James Ferrell/James Peed
1997-W Uncirculated	29,417	$180/205[3]	
1997-W Proof	11,887	$195/225[3]	
National Law Enforcement Officers Memorial silver dollar			Alfred Maletsky
1997-P Uncirculated	28,575	$30/32[3]	
1997-P Proof	110,428	$33/37[3]	
Robert F. Kennedy Memorial silver dollar			Thomas D. Rogers Sr./James Peed
1998-S Uncirculated	106,422	$30/32[3]	
1998-S Proof	99,020	$33/37[3]	
Black Revolutionary War Patriots Memorial silver dollar			John Mercanti/Ed Dwight
1998-S Uncirculated	37,210	$30/32[3]	
1998-S Proof	75,070	$33/37[3]	
Dolley Madison silver dollar			Tiffany & Co.
1999-P Uncirculated	89,104	$30/32[3]	
1999-P Proof	224,403	$33/37[3]	
George Washington Death Bicentennial gold half eagle			Laura Gardin Fraser[9]
1999-W Uncirculated	22,511	$30/32[3]	
1999-W Proof	41,693	$32/37[3]	
Yellowstone National Park 125th Anniversary silver dollar			Edgar Z. Steever IV/William C. Cousins
1999-P Uncirculated	23,614	$30/32[3]	
1999-P Proof	128,646	$32/37[3]	
Library of Congress Bicentennial silver dollar			Thomas D. Rogers Sr./John Mercanti
2000-W Uncirculated	52,771	$30/32[3]	
2000-W Proof	196,900	$32/37[3]	
Library of Congress Bicentennial bimetallic $10 eagle			John Mercanti/Thomas D. Rogers Sr.
2000-P Uncirculated	6,683	$30/32[3]	
2000-P Proof	27,167	$32/37[3]	
Leif Ericson Millennium silver dollar			John Mercanti/T. James Ferrell
2000-P Uncirculated	28,150	$30./32.[3]	
2000-P Proof	144,748	$32./37.[3]	
Capitol Visitor Center copper-nickel clad half dollar			Dean McMullen/Alex Shagin and Marcel Jovine
2001-P Uncirculated	79,670	$8.75/9.75, $7.75/8.50 [3, 6]	
2001-P Proof	77,240	$11.25/12., $10.75/11.50[3]	

Coin	Mintage	Pre-issue/regular price	Designer(s)
Capitol Visitor Center silver dollar			Marika Somogyi/John Mercanti
2001-P Uncirculated	35,500	$30./32., $27./29.[3]	
2001-P Proof	141,425	$33./37., $29./33.[3]	
Capitol Visitor Center gold $5 half eagle			Elizabeth Jones
2001-W Uncirculated	6,750	$180./205., $175./200.[3]	
2001-W Proof	26,815	$195./225., $177./207.[3]	
American Buffalo silver dollar			James Earle Fraser
2001-D Uncirculated	227,080	$30./32.[3]	
2001-P Proof	272,785	$33./37.[3]	
U.S. Military Academy Bicentennial silver dollar			T. James Ferrell/John Mercanti
2002-W Uncirculated	103,201	$30./32.[3]	
2002-W Proof	288,293	$33./37.[3]	
Salt Lake City Olympic Games silver dollar			John Mercanti/Donna Weaver
2002-P Uncirculated	40,257	$30./32.[3]	
2002-P Proof	166,864	$33./37.[3]	
Salt Lake City Olympic Games gold $5 half eagle			Donna Weaver/Norman E. Nemeth
2002-W Uncirculated	10,585	$180./205.[3]	
2002-W Proof	32,877	$195./225.[3]	
First Flight Centennial copper-nickel clad half dollar			John Mercanti/Donna Weaver
2003-P Uncirculated	57,122	$9.75/10.75[3]	
2003-P Proof	109,710	$12.50/13.50[3]	
First Flight Centennial silver dollar			T. James Ferrell/ Norman E. Nemeth
2003-P Uncirculated	53,533	$31./33.[3]	
2003-P Proof	190,240	$33./37.[3]	
First Flight Centennial gold $10 eagle			Donna Weaver
2003-W Uncirculated	10,009	$340./365.[3]	
2003-W Proof	21,676	$350./375.[3]	
Thomas Alva Edison silver dollar			Donna Weaver/John Mercanti
2004-P Uncirculated	92,150	$31./33.[3]	
2004-P Proof	211,055	$33./37.[3]	
Lewis and Clark Expedition Bicentennial silver dollar			Donna Weaver
2004-P Uncirculated	142,015	$33./35.[3]	
2004-P Proof	351,989	$35./39.[3]	
Chief Justice John Marshall silver dollar			John Mercanti/Donna Weaver
2005-P Uncirculated	67,096	$33./35.[3]	
2005-P Proof	196,753	$35./39.[3]	
Marine Corps 230th Anniversary silver dollar			Norman E. Nemeth/Charles L. Vickers
2005-P Uncirculated	49,671	$33./35.[3]	
2005-P Proof	548,810	$35./39.[3]	
Benjamin Franklin Tercentenary, Scientist silver dollar			Norman E. Nemeth/Charles L. Vickers
2006-P Uncirculated	111,956	$33./35.[3]	
2006-P Proof	137,808	$35./39.[3]	
Benjamin Franklin Tercentenary, Founding Father silver dollar			Donald Everhart II/ Donna Weaver
2006-P Uncirculated	64,014	$33./35.[3]	
2006-P Proof	184,489	$35./39.[3]	
San Francisco Old Mint silver dollar			Sherl Joseph Winter/George T. Morgan
2006-S Uncirculated	65,609	$33./35.[3]	
2006-S Proof	255,700	$35./39.[3]	
San Francisco Old Mint gold $5 half eagle			Charles L. Vickers/Various
2006-S Uncirculated	16,149	$220./245.[3]	
2006-S Proof	41,517	$230./255.[3]	
Jamestown 400th Anniversary silver dollar			Donna Weaver/Susan Gamble
2007-P Uncirculated	79,801	$33./35.[3]	
2007-P Proof	258,802	$35./39.[3]	
Jamestown 400th Anniversary gold $5 half eagle			John Mercanti/Susan Gamble
2007-W Uncirculated	18,843	$220./245.[3]	
2007-W Proof	47,050	$230./255.[3]	

Coin	Mintage	Pre-issue/regular price	Designer(s)
Little Rock Central High School Desegregation silver dollar			Richard Masters/ Don Everhart
2007-P Uncirculated	66,093	$33./35.[3]	
2007-P Proof	124,678	$35./39.[3]	
Bald Eagle copper-nickel clad half dollar			Susan Gamble/Donna Weaver
2008-S Uncirculated	120,180	$7.95/8.95[3]	
2008-S Proof	220,577	$9.95/10.95[3]	
Bald Eagle silver dollar			Joel Iskowitz/James Licaretz
2008-P Uncirculated	119,204	$35.95/37.95[3]	
2008-P Proof	294,601	$39.95/43.95[3]	
Bald Eagle gold $5 half eagle			Susan Gamble/Don Everhart
2008-W Uncirculated	15,009	$284.95/309.95[3]	
2008-W Proof	59,269	$294.95/319.95[3]	
Abraham Lincoln Birth Bicentennial silver dollar			Justin Kunz/Phebe Hemphill
2009-P Uncirculated	125,000	$31.95/33.95[3]	
2009-P Proof	325,000	$37.95/41.95[3]	
Louis Braille Birth Bicentennial silver dollar			Joel Iskowitz/Susan Gamble
2009-P Uncirculated	82,639	$31.95/33.95[3]	
2009-P Proof	135,325	$31.95/33.95[3]	
Boy Scouts of America Centennial silver dollar			Donna Weaver/James Licaretz
2010-P Uncirculated	105,000	$33.95/35.95[3]	
2010-P Proof	245,000	$39.95/43.95[3]	
American Veterans Disabled for Life silver dollar			Donald Everhart II/Thomas Cleveland
2010-W Uncirculated	65,250	$33.95/35.95[3]	
2010-W Proof	153,208	$39.95/43.95[3]	

Footnotes

1. Prices for 1982 George Washington half dollar are for 1982 and 1983 to 1985.

2. Prices for 1983 and 1884 Olympic coins in some cases are first prices charged and do not reflect higher prices charged later.

3. Prices since 1986 are pre-issue/regular issue of single coins only. Most modern commemorative programs have offered various packaging options and combinations.

4. Although produced and sold in 1993, none of these coins actually carries the year of issue in its legends, in apparent violation of law. The anniversary dates 1991-1995 refer to the 50th anniversaries of the beginning and ending of United States involvement in World War II. More clearly, it would have been stated "1941-1991/1945-1995."

5. Although produced and sold in 1994, the coin does not carry the year of issue in its legends, in apparent violation of law. 1743 is the year of Jefferson's birth; 1993 is the 250th anniversary of that date.

6. The Special Olympics World Games silver dollar and Capitol Visitor Center coins were offered "encapsulated only" without the usual presentation case. The case option was also available, at a slightly higher price. Prices given here show all four prices: pre-issue and regular, with and without packaging.

7. Price options for individual coins. The coins were offered on a subscription basis from Dec. 2, 1994, through Feb. 3, 1995. The coins were then to be released four at a time—one gold, two silver, one copper-nickel clad—in February 1995, July 1995, January 1996 and sometime in the spring of 1996. Pre-issue prices and options were to be offered during the first few weeks of each release.

Commemorative coin sets, 1982 to 2010

While the U.S. Mint has offered all commemorative coins issued since 1982 individually, it has also offered commemorative coins in various kinds of sets. What follows is a compilation of all official U.S. coin sets containing one or more commemorative coins. Sets are listed by program in a consistent manner: the type of set, its contents, the number of sets sold and its pre-issue and regular prices. Commemorative coins are identified by date and Mint (and design, if necessary), with compositional information provided. For Prestige Proof set listings, the first coins (limited to one or two pieces) are the commemoratives, following by a brief description of the other coins contained within the set. Certain commemorative sets contained collectibles other than coins; those contents are also identified as fully as possible.

Sales figures provided are as accurate as possible, but may differ slightly from figures published in other unofficial sources for several reasons. United States Mint officials have not always provided final, audited sales figures by options for the various commemorative coin programs. For some programs, the sales totals reported represent those figures provided by the Mint after the close of a program but before final auditing was completed (generally, the differences in final sales and final audited sales are slight).

For multiple Young Collector's Editions or limited edition sets reported as sold out, we provide the maximum number available (usually 50,000); final, audited sales may be slightly smaller due to returns and other sales cancellations.

Multiple sources were use in compiling this list.

Coin	Mintage	Pre-issue/regular price	Designer(s)
1983–1984 Los Angeles Summer Olympics		**Number Sold**	**Issue Price**
Three-coin Uncirculated dollar set, 1983: 1983-P, 1983-D, 1983-S silver $1s		174,014	$89.00/$100
Three-coin Uncirculated silver and gold set, 1983 and 1984: 1983-P $1, 1984-P $1; 1984-W gold $10		29,974	$395
Six-coin silver $1 and gold $10 set, 1983 and 1984: Uncirculated 1983-P, 1983-S, 1984-P, 1984-S silver $1s; Uncirculated 1984-W and Proof 1984-P gold $10, housed in cherry wood box		8,926	$805
Three-coin Proof silver $1 and gold $10 set, 1983 and 1984: 1983-S, 1984-S $1s; 1984-W $10		260,083	$352/$416
Three-coin Coliseum Proof set, 1983 and 1984: 1983-S, 1984-S $1s; 1984-S $10; sold at the Olympic Games		4,000	?
Two-coin Proof dollar set, 1983 and 1984: 1983-S, 1984-S $1s		386,809	$48.00/$58.00
Three-coin Uncirculated dollar set, 1984: 1984-P, 1984-D, 1984-S silver $1s		116,675	$89.00/$100
1983 Prestige Proof set: 1983-S silver $1; regular Proof 1983-S coins, 1¢ to 50¢		140,361	$59.00
1984 Prestige Proof set: 1984-S silver $1; regular Proof 1984-S coins, 1¢ to 50¢		316,680	$59.00
Philatelic-numismatic combination: Proof 1983-S $1, housed in cacheted envelope, postmarked June 28, 1983, at the Benjamin Franklin Station, Philadelphia, and sold over the counter there		290	$35.18
1986 Statue of Liberty		**Number Sold**	**Issue Price**
Two-coin Uncirculated set: 1986-D copper-nickel clad 50¢, 1986-P silver $1		172,033	$25.50/$28.00
Three-coin Uncirculated set: 1986-D 50¢, 1986-P $1, 1986-W $5		49,406	$165/$193
Two-coin Proof set: 1986-S copper-nickel clad 50¢, 1986-S silver $1		3,510,776	$29.00/$31.50
Three-coin Proof set: 1986-S copper-nickel clad 50¢, 1986-S silver $1, 1986-W gold $5		343,345	$175/$206.50
Six-coin Uncirculated and Proof set: one of each coin		39,101	$375/$439.50
1986 Prestige Proof set: 1986-S 50¢, $1; regular Proof 1986-S coins, 1¢ to 50¢		599,317	$48.50
1987 Constitution Bicentennial		**Number Sold**	**Issue Price**
Two-coin Uncirculated set: 1987-P silver $1, 1987-W gold $5		79,688	$217/$240
Two-coin Proof set: 1987-S silver $1, 1987-W gold $5		443,75	$220/$250
Four-coin Uncirculated and Proof set: one of each coin in a mahogany wood case		89,258	$465/$525
1987 Prestige Proof set: 1987-S silver dollar, regular Proof 1987-S coins, 1¢ to 50¢		435,495	$41.00/$45.00
1988 Seoul Winter Olympics		**Number Sold**	**Issue Price**
Two-coin Uncirculated set: 1988-D silver $1, 1988-W gold $5		38,971	$220/$250
Two-coin Proof set: 1988-S silver $1, 1988-W gold $5		225,534	$225/$260
Four-coin Uncirculated and Proof set: one of each coin in a special case		13,313	$485/$550
1988 Prestige Proof set: 1988-S silver $1; regular Proof 1988-S coins, 1¢ to 50¢		231,661	$41.00/$45.00
1989 Congress Bicentennial		**Number Sold**	**Issue Price**
Two-coin Uncirculated set: 1989-D silver 50¢, 1989-D silver $1		57,054	$27.00/$29.50
Three-coin Uncirculated set: 1989-D silver 50¢, 1989-D silver dollar, 1989-W gold $5		15,940	$205/$225
Two-coin Proof set: 1989-S silver 50¢, 1989-S silver $1		269,550	$31.50/$34.00
Three-coin Proof set: 1989-S silver 50¢, 1989-S silver $1, 1989-W gold $5		110,796	$220/$245
Six-coin Uncirculated and Proof set: one of each coin in cherrywood case		24,967	$435/$480
1989 Prestige Proof set: 1989-S silver 50¢, $1; regular Proof 1989-S coins, 1¢ to 50¢		211,807	$49.00/$52.00
1990 Dwight D. Eisenhower Centennial		**Number Sold**	**Issue Price**
1990 Prestige Proof set: 1990-P silver $1; regular Proof 1990-S coins, 1¢ to 50¢		506,126	$46.00
1991 Mount Rushmore		**Number Sold**	**Issue Price**
Two-coin Uncirculated set: 1991-D copper-nickel clad 50¢, 1991-P silver $1		65,410	$27.00/$30.00
Three-coin Uncirculated set: 1991-D copper-nickel clad 50¢, 1991-P silver $1, 1991-W gold $5		10,051	$210/$235
Two-coin Proof set: 1991-S copper-nickel clad 50¢, 1991-S silver $1		250,348	$35.00/$38.00
Three-coin Proof set: 1991-S 50¢, 1991-S $1, 1991-W gold $5		70,474	$225/$255
Six-coin Uncirculated and Proof set: one of each coin		18,039	$445/$490
1991 Prestige Proof set: 1991-S 50¢, 1991 $1; regular Proof 1991-S coins, 1¢ to 50¢		256,954	$49.00/55.00
1992 Christopher Columbus Quincentennial		**Number Sold**	**Issue Price**
Two-coin Uncirculated set: 1992-D copper-nickel clad 50¢, 1992-D silver $1		56,676	$27.00/$32.00
Three-coin Uncirculated set: 1992-D 50¢, 1992-D $1, 1992-W $5		8,972	$205/$230
Two-coin Proof set: 1992-S 50¢, 1992-P $1		226,351	$34.00/$38.00
Three-coin Proof set: 1992-S 50¢, 1992-P $1, 1992-W $5		55,867	$220/$250
Six-coin Uncirculated and Proof set: one of each coin		12,489	$445/$495
1992 XXV Olympiad		**Number Sold**	**Issue Price**
Two-coin Uncirculated set: 1992-P 50¢, 1992-D $1		83,408	$28.00/$33.00
Three-coin Uncirculated set: 1992-P 50¢, 1992-D $1, 1992-W $5		9,724	$210/$235
Two-coin Proof set: 1992-S copper-nickel clad 50¢, 1992-S silver $1		168,234	$35.00/$39.00
Three-coin Proof set: 1992-S 50¢, 1992-S $1, 1992-W gold $5		47,408	$225/$255
Six-coin Uncirculated and Proof set: one of each		15,246	$445/$495
1992 Prestige Proof set: 1992-S 50¢, 1992-S $1; regular Proof 1992-S coins, 1¢ to 50¢		183,285	$49.00/$56.00
1993 Bill of Rights/James Madison		**Number Sold**	**Issue Price**
Two-coin Uncirculated set: 1993-W silver 50¢, 1993-D silver $1		50,766	$31.00/$36.00
Three-coin Uncirculated set: 1993-W 50¢, 1993-D $1, 1993-W gold $5		7,947	$205/$230

Coin	Mintage	Pre-issue/regular price	Designer(s)
1993 Bill of Rights/James Madison (continued)		**Number Sold**	**Issue Price**
Two-coin Proof set: 1993-S 50¢, 1993-S silver $1		168,081	$35.00/$39.00
Three-coin Proof set: 1993-S 50¢, 1993-S $1, 1993-W $5		49,617	$214/$245
Six-coin Uncirculated and Proof set: one of each coin		10,819	$445/$495
Young Collector's Edition set: Uncirculated 1993-W 50¢ in special educational packaging		53,806	$9.75/$11.50
Coin and medal set: Uncirculated 1993-W 50¢; bronze James Madison presidential medal		49,782	$13.50/$14.50
Coin and stamp set: Proof 1993-S 50¢; 1989 25-cent Drafting of the Bill of Rights U.S. stamp (first offered to customers whose orders for Young Collector's Edition and coin and medal set could not be filled due to sellouts)		49,926	$14.50
1993 Prestige Proof set: 1993-S 50¢, 1993-S $1; regular Proof 1993-S coins, 1¢ to 50¢		232,063	$51.00/$57.00
1993 World War II (anniversary dates 1991-1995 but no date of issue on coin; released in 1993)		**Number Sold**	**Issue Price**
Two-coin Uncirculated set: 1993-P copper-nickel clad 50¢, 1993-D silver $1		48,804	$28.00/$32.00
Three-coin Uncirculated set: 1993-P 50¢, 1993-D $1, 1993-W gold $5		9,707	$195/$220
Two-coin Proof set: 1993-P 50¢, 1993-W $1		200,457	$34.00/$38.00
Three-coin Proof set: 1993-P 50¢, 1993-W $1, 1993-W $5		46,950	$215/$245
Six-coin set: one of each coin		10,236	$435/$485
Young Collector's Edition set: 1993-P 50¢ in special packaging		46,849	$9.50/$11.50
Victory set: Uncirculated 1993-D $1; 1993 French World War II commemorative silver 1-franc coin		?	$69.95
Victory medal set: Uncirculated 1993-P 50¢; reproduction of World War II Victory Medal		49,781	$11.50/$13.50
Three-country silver set: Proof 1993-W $1, 1994 British D-Day invasion anniversary 50-pence coin, 1993 French D-Day anniversary silver 1-franc coin, sold by British Royal Mint through arrangement with U.S. Mint and Monnaie de Paris		?	$145
Three-country gold set: Proof 1993-W $5, 1994 British D-Day invasion anniversary 50-pence coin, 1993 French D-Day anniversary silver 1-franc coin, sold by British Royal Mint through arrangement with U.S. Mint and Monnaie de Paris		?	$1,350
1993 Thomas Jefferson (released in 1994)		**Number Sold**	**Issue Price**
Three-piece set: 1993-P silver $1; Matte Finish 1994-P 5¢; Series 1976 $2 note		167,703	$34.00/$39.00
1994 World Cup Soccer		**Number Sold**	**Issue Price**
Two-coin Uncirculated set: 1994-D copper-nickel clad 50¢, 1994-D silver $1		30,464	$28.00/$32.00
Three-coin Uncirculated set: 1994-D 50¢, 1994-D $1, 1994-W gold $5		7,149	$195/$220
Two-coin Proof set: 1994-P 50¢, 1994-S $1		148,295	$34.00/$38.00
Three-coin Proof set: 1994-P 50¢, 1994-S $1, 1994-W $5		54,681	$215/$245
Six-coin set: one of each coin		12,000	$435/$485
Young Collector's Edition: Uncirculated 1994-D 50¢ in special packaging		49,999	$10.50/$12.00
Special Edition set: Proof 1994-P 50¢, 1994-S $1 in special packaging		43,106	$33.00/$37.00
1994 Prestige Proof set: Proof 1994-P 50¢, 1994-S $1; regular Proof 1994-S coins, 1¢ to 50¢, five pieces		175,893	$49./56.00
One-coin Host City Venue Packages: Proof 1994-P 50¢; packaging with panoramic portrait of the host city skyline along with facts about the city and stadium, team highlights, past champions and a match schedule and scorecard, housed in a compact disc type plastic holder; packaging different for each host city:			
Boston		1,167	$17.00
Chicago		1,423	$17.00
Dallas		1,267	$17.00
Detroit		1,565	$17.00
Los Angeles		1,255	$17.00
New York		1,347	$17.00
Orlando		1,162	$17.00
San Francisco		1,161	$17.00
Washington, D.C.		2,116	$17.00
Two-coin Host City Venue Packages: Proof 1994-P 50¢, 1994-S $1; packaging with panoramic portrait of the host city skyline along with facts about the city and stadium, team highlights, past champions and a match schedule and scorecard, housed in a compact disc type plastic holder; packaging different for each host city:			
Boston		1,132	$42.00
Chicago		1,340	$42.00
Dallas		1,180	$42.00
Detroit		2,301	$42.00
Los Angeles		1,544	$42.00
New York		1,657	$42.00
Orlando		1,638	$42.00
San Francisco		1,295	$42.00
Washington, D.C.		1,873	$42.00
Striker Commemorative Coin set: Proof 1994-P 50¢, 1994-S $1, in packaging with information about World Cup and an image of Striker, the World Cup mascot		5,198	$37.00
Victory Ribbon half dollar set: Uncirculated 1994-D 50¢ mounted in a nickel-plated bezel and suspended from a red-white-and-blue ribbon for presentation		1,542	$15.00
Victory Ribbon dollar set: Uncirculated 1994-D $1 mounted in a nickel-plated bezel and suspended from a red-white-and-blue ribbon for presentation		751	$36.00

1994 World Cup Soccer (continued)

	Number Sold	Issue Price
Money clip, half dollar: Uncirculated 1994-D 50¢ mounted in a nickel-plated money clip	1,628	$17.00
Money clip, dollar: Uncirculated 1994-D $1 mounted in a nickel-plated money clip	1,595	$38.00
Key chain, half dollar: Uncirculated 1994-D 50¢ mounted in a nickel-plated key chain	1,242	$16.00
Key chain, dollar: Uncirculated 1994-D $1 mounted in a nickel-plated key chain	2,332	$37.00

1994 U.S. Veterans

	Number Sold	Issue Price
Three-coin Uncirculated set: 1994-W POW, Vietnam, Women in Military silver $1s	42,684	$75.00/$87.00
Three-coin Proof set: 1994-P POW, Vietnam, Women in Military silver $1s	190,811	$79.00/$91.00

1995 Civil War Battlefield Preservation

	Number Sold	Issue Price
Two-coin Uncirculated set: 1995-S copper-nickel clad 50¢, 1995-P silver $1	22,647	$33.00/$36.00
Three-coin Uncirculated set: 1995-S 50¢, 1995-P $1, 1995-W gold $5	5,126	$205/$230
Two-coin Proof set: 1995-S 50¢, 1995-S $1	97,961	$38.00/$43.00
Three-coin Proof set: 1995-S 50¢, 1995-S $1, 1995-W $5	24,538	$225/$255
Six-coin Uncirculated and Proof set: one of each coin	5,509	$455/$490
Prestige Proof set: Proof 1995-S 50¢, 1995-S $1; regular Proof set, 1¢ to 50¢, five pieces	107,112	$55.00/$61.00
Young Collector's Edition: 1995-S 50¢ in special packaging	51,947	$11.50/$12.50
Two-coin Union set: Proof 1995-S 50¢, 1995-S $1; housed in faux Union box photo album	30,398	$49.00/$55.00
Three-coin Union set: Proof 1995-S 50¢, 1995-S $1, 1995-W $5; housed in faux Union box photo album	18,649	$240/$265
Proof $5 and framed print	159	?
Proof $1 and framed print	392	?
Proof 50¢ and framed print	334	?
Proof $5 and print—bugler	9	?
Proof $1 and print—wooden soldier	27	?
Proof 50¢ and print—drummer boy	44	?
Proof three-coin and three framed prints	279	?
Uncirculated 50¢ wrist watch	1,755	?
Uncirculated $1 pocket watch	828	?
Uncirculated 50¢ money clip	6,172	?

1995 Special Olympics

	Number Sold	Issue Price
Two-coin Proof set: 1995-P Special Olympics silver $1, 1995-S Kennedy copper-nickel clad 50¢	2,887	$38.00

1995–1996 Atlanta Summer Olympics

	Number Sold	Issue Price
Four-coin Proof set: 1995-S Basketball copper-nickel clad 50¢, 1995-P Gymnastics, Paralympics silver $1s, 1995-W Torch Bearer gold $5	18,889	$300/$325
Four-coin Uncirculated set: 1995-S Basketball 50¢, 1995-D Gymnastics, Paralympics $1s, 1995-W Torch Bearer $5	3,623	$285/$308
Two-coin Proof set: 1995-P Gymnastics, Paralympics $1s	35,484	$59.95/$66.95
Young Collector's Edition: Uncirculated 1995-S Basketball 50¢ in special packaging	49,395	$11.95/$13.95
Young Collector's Edition: Uncirculated 1995-S Baseball 50¢ in special packaging	50,533	$11.95/$13.95
Young Collector's Edition: Uncirculated 1996-S Swimming 50¢ in special packaging	26,119	$11.95/$13.95
Young Collector's Edition: Uncirculated 1996-S Soccer 50¢ in special packaging	29,762	$11.95/$13.95
Sixteen-coin Proof set by subscription: one of each coin in a cherrywood display case with the Great Seal of the United States laser-engraved on the top, discounted 7% from individual pre-issue prices	385	$1,162
Eight-coin Proof set by subscription: one of each silver $1 in a Georgia green leather-bound display case with silver-tone trim, discounted 7% from individual pre-issue prices	4,187	$237
32-coin Uncirculated and Proof set by subscription: one of each coin in a cherrywood display case with the Great Seal of the United States laser-engraved on the top, discounted 7% from individual pre-issue prices	160	$2,261
1996 Prestige Proof set: 1996-S Soccer 50¢; 1996-P Rowing $1; regular Proof 1996-S coins, 1¢ to 50¢	59,455	$55.00/$61.00
X-canceled die: Obverse die for Proof 1995-W Torch Runner gold $5	8	$49.00
X-canceled die: Obverse die for Proof 1995-W Atlanta Stadium gold $5	39	$49.00
X-canceled die: Reverse die for Proof 1995-W gold $5 (standard Eagle design)	39	$49.00
X-canceled die: Obverse die for Uncirculated 1995-W Torch Runner gold $5	19	$49.00
X-canceled die: Obverse die for Uncirculated 1995-W Atlanta Stadium gold $5	17	$49.00
X-canceled die: Reverse die for Uncirculated 1995-W gold $5 (standard Eagle design)	33	$49.00
X-canceled die: Obverse die for Proof 1995-P Blind Runner silver $1	205	$49.00
X-canceled die: Obverse die for Proof 1995-P Gymnastics silver $1	186	$49.00
X-canceled die: Obverse die for Proof 1995-P Cycling silver $1	207	$49.00
X-canceled die: Obverse die for Proof 1995-P Track and Field silver $1	220	$49.00
X-canceled die: Reverse die for Proof 1995-P silver $1 (standard Clasped Hands design)	375	$49.00
X-canceled die: Obverse die for Proof 1996-W Olympic Cauldron gold $5	60	$49.00
X-canceled die: Obverse die for Proof 1996-W Flag Bearer gold $5	30	$49.00
X-canceled die: Reverse die for Proof 1996-W gold $5 (standard Atlanta Centennial Olympic Games logo)	78	$49.00
X-canceled die: Obverse die for Uncirculated 1996-W Olympic Cauldron gold $5	13	$49.00
X-canceled die: Obverse die for Uncirculated 1996-W Flag Bearer gold $5	13	$49.00

1995–1996 Atlanta Summer Olympics (continued)	Number Sold	Issue Price
X-canceled die: Reverse die for Uncirculated 1996-W gold $5 (standard Atlanta Centennial Olympic Games logo)	19	$49.00
X-canceled die: Obverse die for Proof 1996-P Wheelchair silver $1	135	$49.00
X-canceled die: Obverse die for Proof 1996-P Tennis silver $1	145	$49.00
X-canceled die: Obverse die for Proof 1996-P Rowing silver $1	143	$49.00
X-canceled die: Obverse die for Proof 1996-P High Jump silver $1	217	$49.00
X-canceled die: Reverse die for Proof 1996-P silver $1 (standard Atlanta Centennial Olympic Games logo design)	632	$49.00
Jesse Owens Medal / Uncirculated 1995 Olympic silver $1	839	?
Jesse Owens Medal / Proof 1995 Olympic silver $1	641	?

1996 National Community Service	Number Sold	Issue Price
Coin and stamp set: Proof 1996-S silver $1; 1940 3¢ Saint-Gaudens stamp	24,811	$40.00/$45.00

1996 Smithsonian Institution 150th Anniversary	Number Sold	Issue Price
Two-coin Proof set: 1996-P silver $1, 1996-W gold $5	12,647	$217/$240
Four-coin Uncirculated and Proof set: one of each coin	4,918	$440/$475
Young Collector's Edition: Proof 1996-P $1 in special packaging	14,976	$35.00/$40.00
Uncirculated gold $5 pendant	470	?
Uncirculated gold $5 pendant with chain	801	?
Uncirculated silver $1 pocket watch	39	?
Uncirculated gold $5 pendant	6	?
Uncirculated gold $5 pendant in box with chain	4	?
Uncirculated silver $1 money clip	74	?

1997 U.S. Botanic Garden	Number Sold	Issue Price
Coinage and Currency set: Uncirculated 1997-P silver $1; Matte Finish 1997-P 5¢; Series 1995 $1 note	24,931	$36.00/$41.00
Prestige Proof set: Proof 1997-P $1; regular Proof set, 1¢ to 50¢, five pieces	80,000	$44.00/$48.00

1997 Jackie Robinson	Number Sold	Issue Price
Two-Proof set: 1997-S silver $1, 1997-W gold $5	7,239	$217/$240
Four-coin Uncirculated and Proof set: one of each coin	3,563	$425/$460
Legacy set: Proof 1997-W $5; reproduction of a Topps 1952 Robinson baseball card; 50th anniversary lapel pin	10,271	$311/$425

1997 Franklin D. Roosevelt	Number Sold	Issue Price
Two-coin Uncirculated and Proof set: one each 1997-W gold $5	8,725	$350/$399
Lapel pin with Proof $5 in a 14-karat gold reeded bezel	224	$250/$275
Pendant with Proof $5 in a 14-karat gold reeded bezel	659	$240/$270
Pendant/chain with Proof $5 in a 14-karat gold reeded bezel and with a 14-karat 18-inch, mirror-box chain	665	$365/$390
Proof $5 in granite	97	?
Proof $5 leather stamp set	384	?

1997 National Law Enforcement Officers Memorial	Number Sold	Issue Price
Insignia set: Proof 1997-P silver $1; lapel pin; patch	19,045	$55.00
Sterling silver money clip with Uncirculated silver $1	3,439	$59.00

1998 Robert F. Kennedy	Number Sold	Issue Price
Two-coin Collector Set: Uncirculated 1998-S silver $1; Matte Finish 1998-S John F. Kennedy 50¢	64,141	$59.95
Two-coin Uncirculated and Proof set: one each 1998-S silver $1	29,326	$59.95/$64.95

1998 Black Revolutionary War Patriots	Number Sold	Issue Price
Two-coin Uncirculated and Proof set: one each 1998-S silver $1	17,170	$59.95/$64.95
Young Collector's Edition: Uncirculated 1998-S $1 in special informative packaging	9,062	$37.00/$40.00
Black Revolutionary War Patriots set: Proof 1998-S $1; four stamps	6,648	$79.00/$84.00

1999 Dolley Madison	Number Sold	Issue Price
Two-coin Uncirculated and Proof set: one each 1999-P silver $1	66,156	$59.95/$64.95

1999 George Washington Death Bicentennial	Number Sold	Issue Price
Two-coin Uncirculated and Proof set: one each 1999-W gold $5	17,412	$350/$399

1999 Yellowstone National Park	Number Sold	Issue Price
Two-coin Uncirculated and Proof set: 2000-P, 2000-S silver $1s	58,949	$59.95/$64.95

2000 Leif Ericson Millennium	Number Sold	Issue Price
Two-piece set: Proof 2000-P silver $1; Proof 2000 Icelandic silver 1,000-kronur coin	86,136	$63.00/$68.00

2001 American Buffalo	Number Sold	Issue Price
Two-coin Uncirculated and Proof set: 2001-D, 2001-P silver $1s	120,705	$59.95
Coinage and Currency set: Uncirculated 2001-D $1; face plate print, 1899 $5 silver certificate 1987 Red Cloud 10¢ stamp; 2001 Bison 21¢ stamp	49,963	$54.95

2001 U.S. Capitol Visitor Center	Number Sold	Issue Price
Three-coin Proof set: 2001-P copper-nickel clad 50¢; 2001-P silver $1; 2001-W gold $5	21,532	$250.00
Uncirculated Clad Collector set: Uncirculated clad 50¢ with historical information	31,256	$16.50/$17.50

	Number Sold	Issue Price
2002 Salt Lake City Winter Olympic Games		
Two-coin Proof set: 2002-P silver $1, 2002-W gold $5	19,122	$210.00/$235.00
Four-coin Uncirculated and Proof set: one of each coin	4,869	$440.00/$475.00
2004 Thomas A. Edison		
Thomas Alva Edison Collectors set: Uncirculated 2004-P silver $1; display case with working light bulb replica	24,370	$49.95
2004 Lewis and Clark Bicentennial		
Coin and Pouch set: Proof 2004-P silver $1; hand-sewn pouch by artisans	48,835	$120.00
Coinage and Currency set: Uncirculated 2004-P $1; Uncirculated 2004-D Sacagawea $1; two Uncirculated 2004-D Westward Journey 5¢s; uniface replica of face of 1901 $10 United States note (Bison note); silver-plated bronze 1801 1.3125-inch Jefferson Indian peace medal replica; three Lewis and Clark Expedition stamps; two educational booklets	49,934	$90.00
2005 Chief Justice John Marshall		
Coin and Chronicles set: Uncirculated 2005-P silver $1s; intaglio print; educational booklet	18,065	$59.95
American Legacy Collection: Proof 2009-P Marshall $1; Proof U.S. Marines Corps 2009-P silver $1; one each regular Proof 2005-S coins, 1¢ to $1, 11 pieces	48,057	$135.00
2005 Marine Corps 230th Anniversary		
Marine Coin and Stamp set: Uncirculated 2005-P $1; uncanceled 1945 3¢ Iwo Jima stamp	50,000	$40.00
American Legacy Collection: See John Marshall listing		
2006 Benjamin Franklin Tercentenary		
Coin and Chronicles set: Uncirculated 2006-P Scientist silver $1; four stamps; *Poor Richard's Almanack* reprint; intaglio print honoring Franklin's contribution to the drafting of the Declaration of Independence	50,000	$65.00
American Legacy Collection: Proof 2006-P Founding Father silver $1; Proof 2006-S San Francisco Old Mint silver $1; regular Proof 2006-S coins, 1¢ to $1	48,452	$135.00
2006 San Francisco Old Mint Centennial		
American Legacy Collection: See Benjamin Franklin listing		
2007 Little Rock Central High School Desegregation		
Little Rock Coin & Medal set: Proof 2007-P $1; bronze Little Rock Nine congressional 1.5-inch medal	24,925	$40.00
American Legacy Collection: Proof 2007-P Little Rock silver $1; 2007-P Jamestown Tercentenary silver $1; regular Proof 2007-S coins, 1¢ to Presidential and Sacagawea $1s, 14 pieces	26,442	$135.00
2007 Jamestown Tercentenary		
American Legacy Collection: see Little Rock listing		
2008 Bald Eagle		
Three-coin Proof set: 2008-S copper-nickel clad 50¢; 2008-P silver $1; 2008-W gold $5	24,719	$369.95
Bald Eagle Coin and Medal set: Uncirculated 2008-P $1; bronze Bald Eagle medal, National Wildlife Refuge System Centennial	26,918	$44.95
Young Collector set: Uncirculated 2008-S 50¢; "Mint Kids" educational adventure materials	22,439	$14.95
American Legacy set: Proof 2008-P $1; regular Proof 2008-S coins, 1¢ to $1, 14 pieces	21,194	$100.00
2009 Louis Braille Bicentennial		
Education Set: Uncirculated 2009-P silver $1 in tri-fold binder with educational material and readable Braille	11,411	$44.95
Uncirculated silver dollar in easy-open capsule (coin removable for feeling tactile features)	23,746	$31.95/ $33.95
2009 Abraham Lincoln Bicentennial		
Abraham Lincoln Coin and Chronicles set: Proof 2009-S silver dollar; four Proof 2009-S cents; Gettysburg Address reproduction; Abraham Lincoln image with signature reproduction	49,984	$55.95

Modern commemorative surcharges

Since the 1983-1984 program commemorating the 1984 Los Angeles Summer Olympics Games, a surcharge has been added to the price of each commemorative coin, initially with the funds raised given to the entity or entities named in the authorizing legislation. In 1996, legislation reformed the payout of surcharges, after the Mint experienced a loss on several poorly received programs but still had to pay all the surcharges raised to the recipient organization.

The reform act, among other provisions, required recovery of Mint expenses before payment of any surcharges to any recipient organization and an audited financial statement that verifies that the organization has raised funds from private sources equal to or greater than the maximum amount of surcharges the organization may receive from sale of numismatic items. The reform act also required certain auditing practices.

Since implementation of the reform act, the Mint has withheld surcharges when a program has failed to meet expenses or the designated recipient failed to meet the requirements of the law.

Many collectors view commemorative coin surcharges as an undesirable burden on the collecting community, with the desire to raise funding for a member of Congress' favored project being considered more important than the national relevance of the commemorative coin program theme.

Program Year/ Commemorative Program Legislation	Authorizing Legislation/Date	Surcharges Collected	Surcharges Paid	Beneficiary
1982: George Washington Commemorative Coin Act Surcharges @ $0 (silver 50¢)	**PL 97-104** 12/31/81	$0	$0	
1984: Olympic Commemorative Coin (1984 Los Angeles Summer Olympic Games) Surcharges @ $50 (gold $10), $10 (silver $1)	**PL 97-220** 7/22/82	$73,461,280	$73,461,280	1) United States Olympic Committee (50% of surcharges collected) and 2) Los Angeles Olympic Organizing Committee (50% of surcharges collected)
1986: Statue of Liberty-Ellis Island Commemorative Coin Act/Liberty Coin Act Surcharges @ $35 (gold $5), $7 (silver $1), $2 (50¢) 7/9/85	**PL 99-61**	$83,149,316	$83,149,316	Statue of Liberty – Ellis Island Foundation
1987: Bicentennial of the Constitution Coins and Medals Act Surcharges @ $35 (gold $5), $7 (silver $1)	**PL 99-582** 10/29/86	$52,744,860	$52,744,860	Surcharges deposited in Treasury to reduce the national debt
1988: 1988 Olympic Commemorative Coin Act Surcharges @ $35 (gold $5), $7 (silver $1)	**PL 100-141** 10/28/87	$22,908,368	$22,908,368	Surcharges paid to the United States Olympic Committee
1989: Bicentennial of the United States Congress Commemorative Coin Act Surcharges @ $35 (gold $5), $7 (silver $1), $1 (copper-nickel clad 50¢)	**PL 100-673** 11/17/88	$14,619,072	$14,619,072	Surcharges paid to The Capitol Preservation Fund (50%) and Treasury to reduce the national debt (50%)
1990: Dwight David Eisenhower Commemorative Coin Act of 1988 Surcharges @ $7 (silver $1)	**PL 100-467** 10/3/88	$9,702,910	$9,702,910	All surcharges to Treasury to reduce the national debt
1991: Mount Rushmore Commemorative Coin Act Surcharges @ $35 (gold $5), $7 (silver $1), $1 (copper-nickel clad 50¢)	**PL 101-332** 7/16/90	$12,065,167	$12,065,167	1) Federal Treasury – 50% to reduce the national debt and 2) Mount Rushmore National Memorial Society of Black Hills – 50% to improve, enlarge & renovate the Mount Rushmore Memorial
1991: Korean War Veterans Memorial Thirty-Eighth Anniversary Commemorative Coin Act Surcharges @ $7 (silver $1)	**PL 101-495** 10/31/90	$5,820,759	$5,820,759	Surcharges deposited to Korean War Veterans Memorial Fund
1991: United Service Organization's 50th Anniversary Commemorative Coin Act Surcharges @ $7 (silver $1)	**PL 101-404** 1/2/90	$3,123,631	$3,123,631	1) USO Programs – 50% to fund programs and 2) 50% transferred to the general fund to reduce the national debt
1992: 1992 Olympic Commemorative Coin Act Surcharges @ $35 (gold $5), $7 (silver $1), $1 (50¢) 10/3/90	**PL 101-406**	$9,202,226	$9,202,226	All surcharges paid to the U.S. Olympic Committee
1992: 1992 White House Commemorative Coin Act Surcharges @ $10 (silver $1)	**PL 102-281** 5/13/92	$4,996,540	$4,996,540	White House Endowment Fund
1992: Christopher Columbus Quincentenary Coin Act Surcharges @ $35 (gold) $7, (silver $1), $1 (copper-nickel clad 50¢)	**PL 102-281** 5/13/92	$7,613,251	$7,613,251	Christopher Columbus Fellowship Foundation to establish the Christopher Columbus Fellowship Program
1993: James Madison-Bill of Rights Commemorative Coin Act Surcharges @ $30 (gold $5), $6 (silver $1), $3 (silver 50¢)	**PL 102-281** 5/13/92	$9,190,797	$9,190,797	James Madison Memorial Fellowship Trust Fund

Program Year/ Commemorative Program Legislation	Authorizing Legislation/Date	Surcharges Collected	Surcharges Paid	Beneficiary
1993: World War II 50th Anniversary Commemorative Coins Act	**PL 102-414**			Battle of Normandy Foundation – 1st $3 million; American Battle Monuments Commission next $7 million; excess surcharges over $10 million – 30% to the Battle of Normandy Foundation and 70% to the American Battle Monuments Commission
Surcharges @ $35 (gold $5), $8 (silver $1), $2 (copper-nickel clad 50¢)	10/14/92	$7,797,614	$7,797,614	
1994: World Cup USA 1994 Commemorative Coin Act	**PL 102-281**			World Cup USA 1994 Inc. (the organizing committee)
Surcharges @ $35 (gold $5), $7 (silver $1), $1 (50¢)	5/13/92	$9,309,995	$9,309,995	
1994: Jefferson Commemorative Coin Act of 1993	**PL 103-186**			Jefferson Endowment Fund (1st $5,000,000) and the Corporation for Jefferson's Poplar Forest (over $5,000,000)
Surcharges @ $10 (silver $1)	12/14/93	$5,998,180	$5,998,180	
1994: United States Veterans Commemorative Coin Act of 1993 **– Prisoner-of-War Commemorative Coin** **– Vietnam Veterans Memorial Commemorative Coin** **– Women in Military Service for America Memorial Commemorative Coin**	**PL 103-186**			Prisoner of War Surcharges to 1) Secretary of the Interior, 2) Andersonville POW Museum Endowment Fund, 3) Secretary of Veterans Affairs. Vietnam Veterans Surcharges to Vietnam Veterans Memorial Fund and Women in Military Surcharges to Women in Military Service for America Memorial Foundation Inc.
Surcharges @ $10 (silver $1, three coins) Note: No surcharges collected on 36,120 coins purchased by Women in Military Service for America	12/14/93	$8,393,210	$8,393,210	
1994: Bicentennial of the United States Capitol Commemorative Coin Act	**PL 103-186**			Capitol Preservation Fund
Surcharges @ $15 (silver $1)	12/14/93	$5,218,665	$5,218,665	
1995/96: Atlanta Centennial Olympic Games Commemorative Coin Act	**PL 102-390**			Atlanta Committee for the Olympic Games and the United States Olympic Committee
Surcharges @ $50 (gold $5), $10 (silver $1), $3 (copper-nickel clad 50¢)	10/6/92	$26,202,754	$26,202,754	
1995: Civil War Battlefield Commemorative Coin Act of 1992	**PL 102-379**			Civil War Battlefield Foundation
Surcharges @ $35 (gold $5), $7 (silver $1), $2 (copper-nickel 50¢)		$5,909,649	$5,909,649	
1995: 1995 Special Olympic World Games	**PL 103-328**			1995 Special Olympics World Games Organizing Committee Inc.
Surcharges @ $10 (silver $1)	9/29/94	$4,410,650	$4,410,650	
1996: National Community Service Commemorative Coins	**PL 103-328**			National Community Service Trust
Surcharges @ $10 (silver $1)	9/29/94	$1,250,430	$1,250,430	
1996: Smithsonian Institution Sesquicentennial Commemorative Coin Act of 1995	**PL 104-96**			Smithsonian Institute
Surcharges @ $35 (gold $5), $10 (silver $1)	1/10/96	$2,683,220	$2,683,220	
1997: United States Botanic Garden Commemorative Coins	**PL 103-328**			National Fund for the United States Botanic Garden
Surcharges @ $10 (silver $1) from Botanic coins	9/29/94	$2,481,760	$2,481,760	
Surcharges @ $10 from Jackie Robinson coins [a]		$1,000,000	$1,000,000	
Total		$3,481,760	$3,481,760	
1997: United States Commemorative Coin Act of 1996: Franklin Delano Roosevelt	**PL 104-329**			Franklin Delano Roosevelt Memorial Commission
Surcharges @ $35 (gold $5)	10/20/96	$1,447,880	$1,447,880	
1997: United States Commemorative Coin Act of 1996: Jackie Robinson	**PL 104-329**			National Fund for the United States Botanic Garden (for 1st 100,000 silver coins sold) and the Jackie Robinson Foundation
Surcharges @ $35 (gold $5), $10 (silver $1)	10/20/96	$2,425,430	$2,425,430	
Surcharges transferred to the Botanic Garden Program [a]		($1,000,000)	($1,000,000)	
Total		$1,425,430	$1,425,430	

Program Year/ Commemorative Program Legislation	Authorizing Legislation/Date	Surcharges Collected	Surcharges Paid	Beneficiary
1997: United States Commemorative Coin Act of 1996: National Law Enforcement Officers Memorial Surcharges @ $10 (silver $1)	PL 104-329 10/20/96	$1,390,030	$1,390,030	Secretary of the Interior/ National Law Enforcement Officers Memorial Maintenance Fund
1997: Robert F. Kennedy Memorial Commemorative Coins Surcharges @ $10 (silver $1)	PL 103-328 9/29/94	$2,054,420	$2,054,420	Robert F. Kennedy Memorial
1998: United States Commemorative Coin Act of 1996: Black Revolutionary War Patriots Surcharges @ $10 (silver $1)	PL 104-329 10/20/96	$1,122,800	$902,758 [b]	Black Revolutionary War Patriots Foundation
1999: United States Commemorative Coin Act of 1996: Dolley Madison Surcharges @ $10 (silver $1)	PL 104-329 10/20/96	$3,135,070	$3,135,070	National Trust for Historic Preservation
1999: United States Commemorative Coin Act of 1996: George Washington Surcharges @ $35 (gold $5)	PL 104-329 10/20/96	$2,247,140	$2,247,140	Mount Vernon Ladies' Association
1999: United States Commemorative Coin Act of 1996: Yellowstone National Park Surcharges @ $10 (silver $1)	PL 104-329 10/20/96	$2,701,580	$2,701,580	National Park Foundation (50%) and Yellowstone National Park (50%)
2000: Library of Congress Bicentennial Commemorative Coin Act of 1998 Surcharges @ $50 (bimetallic $10), $5 (silver $1)	PL 105-268 10/19/98	$2,994,135	$2,994,135	Library of Congress Trust Fund Board
2000: Leif Ericson Millennium Commemorative Coin Surcharges @ $10 (silver $1)	PL 106-126 12/6/99	$1,728,980 $1,020,830 $2,749,810	$1,728,980 $1,020,830 [c] $2,749,810	Liefur Eiriksson Foundation Central Bank of Iceland
2001: Capitol Visitor Center Commemorative Coin Surcharges @ $35 (gold $5), $10 (silver $1), $3 (50¢)	PL 106-126 12/6/99	$3,527,542	$3,527,542	Capitol Preservation Fund
2001: National Museum of the American Indian Commemorative Coin Act of 2000 or American Buffalo Coin Commemorative Coin Act of 2000 Surcharges @ $10 (silver $1)	PL 106-375 10/27/00	$5,000,000	$5,000,000	National Museum of the American Indian/ Smithsonian Institution
2002: 2002 Winter Olympic Commemorative Coin Act Surcharges @ $35 (gold $5) $10 (silver $1) (Program ended 12/31/02)	PL 106-435 11/6/00	$3,592,380	$3,592,380	Salt Lake Organizing Committee for the Olympic Winter Games of 2002
2002: United States Military Academy Bicentennial Commemorative Coins Surcharges @ $10 (silver $1) (Program ended March 16, 2003)	PL 103-328 9/29/94	$3,914,940	$3,914,940	Association of Graduates U.S. Military Academy
2003: First Flight Commemorative Coins Surcharges @ $10 (silver $1)	PL 105-124 12/1/97	$3,713,537	$3,713,537	First Flight Foundation
2004: Thomas Alva Edison Commemorative Coin Act Surcharges @ $10 (silver $1)	PL 105-331 10/31/98	$3,032,050	$3,033,160	1) Museum Of Arts and History (1/8), 2) Edison Birthplace Association Inc (1/8), 3) National Park Service (1/8), 4) Edison Plaza Museum (1/8), 5) Edison Winter Home and Museum (1/8), 6) Edison Institute/Greenfield Village(1/8), 7) Edison Memorial Tower (1/8) and 8) Hall of Electrical History/ Schenectady Museum Association (1/8)

348 - Commemoratives

Program Year/ Commemorative Program Legislation	Authorizing Legislation/Date	Surcharges Collected	Surcharges Paid	Beneficiary
2004: Lewis and Clark Expedition Bicentennial Commemorative Coins Surcharges @ $10 (silver $1)	PL 106-126 12/6/99	$4,940,040	$4,940,040	National Lewis and Clark Bicentennial Council (2/3) and National Park Service (1/3)
2005: John Marshall Commemorative Coin Act Surcharges @ $10 (silver $1)	PL 108-290 8/6/04	$2,638,490	$2,638,490.00	Supreme Court Historical Society
2005: Marine Corps 230th Anniversary Commemorative Coin Act Surcharges @ $10 (silver $1)	PL 108-291 8/6/04	$5,984,810	$5,984,810	Marine Corps Heritage Foundation
2006: Benjamin Franklin Commemorative Coin Act Surcharges @ $10 (silver $1)	PL 108-464 12/21/04	$4,982,670	$4,982,670	The Franklin Institute
2006: San Francisco Old Mint Commemorative Coin Act Surcharges @ $10 (silver $1)	PL 109-230 6/15/06	$4,746,880	$4,746,880	San Francisco Museum and Historical Society
2007: Jamestown 400th Anniversary Commemorative Coin Act of 2004 Surcharges @ $35 (gold $5), $10 (silver $1)	PL 108-289, amended by PL 111-86 8/6/04	$5,692,285	$5,692,285	Jamestown-Yorktown Foundation of the Common- wealth of Virginia 50%. Other 50% split 1) The Secretary the Interior (1/3), 2) The Association for the Preservation of Virginia Antiquities (1/3) and 3) The Jamestown-Yorktown Foundation of the Common- wealth of Virginia (1/3)
2007: Little Rock Central High School Desegregation 50th Anniversary Commemorative Coin Act Surcharges @ $10 (silver $1)	PL 109-146 12/22/05	$1,907,710	$1,907,710	The Secretary of the Interior
2008: American Bald Eagle Recovery and National Emblem Commemorative Coin Act Surcharges @ $35 (gold $5), $10 (silver $1), $3 (50¢)	PL 108-486 12/23/04	$7,760,051	$7,760,051	The American Eagle Foundation of Tennessee
2009: Abraham Lincoln Commemorative Coin Act Surcharges @ $10 (silver $1)	PL 109-285 9/27/06	$4,999,340	$0	Abraham Lincoln Bicentennial Commission
2009: Louis Braille Bicentennial – Braille Library Commemorative Coin Act Surcharges @ $10 (silver $1)	PL 109-247 7/27/06	$2,217,090	$2,217,090	National Federation of the Blind
2010: Boy Scouts of American Centennial Commemorative Coin Act Surcharges @ $10 (silver $1)	PL 110-363 	$3,499,830	$3,499,830	National Boy Scouts of America Foundation
2010: American Veterans Disabled for Life Commemorative Coin Act Surcharges @ $10 (silver $1)	PL 110-277 	$2,810,710	$2,810,710	Disabled Veterans' LIFE Memorial Foundation
2011: United States Army Commemorative Coin Act of 2008 Program Ongoing as of June 20, 2011 Surcharges @ $35 (gold) $10 (silver) $5 (clad)	PL 110-450 12/1/08	$2,372,465	$0	Army Historical Foundation
2011: Medal of Honor Commemorative Coin Act of 2009 Program Ongoing as of June 20, 2011 Surcharges @ $35 (gold) $10 (silver)	PL 111-91 11/6/09	$0	$0	Congressional Medal of Honor Foundation
Grand Total		**$487,855,419**	**$480,264,682**	

Note: Public Law 104-208 requires beneficiary organizations to meet certain requirements (raising private funds and being audited).
   The United States Mint is also required to assure itself that all costs will be recovered prior to distributing surcharges.
a) Public Law 104-329 required that the surcharges from the first 100,000 silver Jackie Robinson Program coins sold be transferred to the National Fund for the United States Botanic Garden Program.
b) Black Patriots - Benefits reduced by the amount of program loss.
c) Leif Ericson - Proceeds from the sale of Iceland coins went to the Central Bank of Iceland.

Circulating commemoratives: 1976, 1999 to date

When Congress began issuing commemorative coinage at the end of the 19th century, the coins were not intended to circulate, although unsold coins were placed into circulation by the organizations selling the coins for several programs when the coins did not sell as well as anticipated.

Starting in the early 20th century, the Mint began issuing circulating coins that were first released on significant anniversaries related to the coins' subjects. Circulating coins honoring Abraham Lincoln and George Washington were introduced on significant birthdays of the men depicted on the coins (100 years for Lincoln in 1909, 200 years for Washington in 1932), but these coins were intended as permanent replacements for the old designs and are not considered true circulating commemoratives. The coins bear no commemorative inscriptions. When the Washington quarter dollar was authorized, officials specifically noted that the coin was not to be considered a "special coin"—a Mint phrase used to describe commemorative coins—in any way.

Until the 1976 Bicentennial of American Independence, the Mint never issued a true circulating commemorative coinage. The nation simply had no tradition of doing so.

The idea for a special circulating coinage commemorating the Bicentennial was discussed as early as a decade before the Bicentennial, first in the coin collecting community. The idea gained additional support with the creation in 1966 of the American Revolution Bicentennial Commission, which was created to advise the government on the celebration of the signing of the Declaration of Independence. A provision in the law authorizing the commission required it to report its recommendations, including the possibility of issuing commemorative coins.

The coin community got a chance to advance the idea of a special coinage through heavy representation on the Coins and Medals Advisory Panel, a panel of the ARBC that was formed in 1970 (coin collectors, dealers, club officials and hobby periodical editors served on the panel). The panel's official report recommended changing all six circulating denominations, cent through dollar, and issuing a single noncirculating commemorative coin unique in design and composition.

Mint Director Mary Brooks was the public voice for the Treasury Department's official opposition to a circulating Bicentennial coinage and any noncirculating commemorative coins. Brooks testified before the panel, sharing the Treasury Department's reasons for opposition: commemorative coins "do not serve as a medium of exchange, are not readily available and recognizable to the public, invade the production capacities of the Mint and … have been the subject [in the past] of hoarding and profiteering. In short, commemorative coins tend to defeat the purpose of the coinage system."

Treasury opposition did not keep collectors from continuing to lobby for "special coins," especially as the nation's 200th birthday got nearer. By the early 1970s, collectors' wish lists had grown: Bicentennial designs on all circulating coins, plus noncirculating commemoratives, including a gold coin. Treasury officials opposed all such recognition of the Bicentennial. Brooks noted that the Mint would produce the coins if and only if Congress intervened and required special coinage in commemoration of the event, which she did not recommend. Early during the discussions, Brooks did suggest it might be appropriate to place some sort of recognition of the Bicentennial on the packaging for the Mint's 1976 sets rather make any changes to the coins.

However, by November 1972, as collectors' lobbying efforts intensified, Treasury officials agreed to add the date 1776 to all 1976 coins—a concession that still fell well below the collector community's expectations.

The legislative branch of government, however, listened more closely to the collector electorate and rejected Treasury's do-nothing attitude. Members of Congress in January 1973 began introducing legislation proposing Bicentennial coinage. As the number of Bicentennial coin bills grew, Treasury officials, realizing that Congress was likely to authorize some sort of coinage over their objections, decided to support a modest plan: changing the reverses of the half dollar and dollar. Collectors, however, complained that the Treasury's do-little proposal fell short of what they believed the nation should do in recognition of the Bicentennial (neither the dollar nor the half dollar circulated widely, meaning that few individuals would ever see the two coins in circulation). Treasury officials relented a little more in July 1973, agreeing to support legislation that would include the quarter dollar in the redesign effort. Finally, in October 1973, the modest, three-coin Bicentennial coinage bill became law.

Even after Congress approved the Bicentennial coins, Treasury officials avoided describing the coins as "commemorative coins" since Treasury steadfastly opposed all commemorative coinage (and, of course, no special noncirculating commemorative coins were authorized for the event, unlike for the 1926 Sesquicentennial). Nonetheless, the Bicentennial coins are circulating commemoratives—they commemorate a specific event in American history and were issued for only a limited time. Production of the Bicentennial coins began in 1975 with the 1776-1976 date used for both the 1975 and 1976 production.

Despite Mint worries about hoarding of the new designs, no coinage shortages developed. The Bicentennial quarter dollars can still be found in circulation occasionally, and the two higher denominations can be found in bank rolls at some banks.

After the Bicentennial coin program ended, coinage redesign and circulating commemorative coins again became a nonissue. As far as Treasury officials were concerned, it was not going to happen again.

State quarter dollars

As seen in the section of this chapter dealing with noncirculating commemorative coins, Treasury officials finally dropped opposition to noncirculating commemoratives in the early 1980s, with a new series of coins issued beginning in 1982. A decade after that program started, a circulating commemorative coin program in Canada drew the attention of the U.S. collector community.

Royal Canadian Mint officials embraced a circulating commemorative coin program to celebrate that nation's 125th anniversary of confederation in 1992. The RCM placed a commemorative design on the circulating dollar coin and issued 12 commemorative 25-cent coins, each bearing a design commemorating a Canadian province or territory, one issued every month from January to December during the centennial year.

The program proved popular, and not only in Canada. Collectors in the United States awaited each new Canada 125 25-cent coin as eagerly as collectors did in Canada. American collectors also began calling for a similar program in the United States—50 circulating commemorative coins, one for each state. Within a year, of the Canadian program's introduction, leaders within the U.S. numismatic community began promoting the idea of circulating commemorative U.S. coins available at face value as an alternative to pricey noncirculating commemorative coins bearing surcharges given to beneficiary agencies.

In 1993, the Citizens Commemorative Coinage Advisory Committee was formed to advise the government on commemorative issues. At the first meeting of the CCCAC, on Dec. 14, 1993, one of the panel members, David L. Ganz—a longtime collector and then president of the American Numismatic Association—proposed a circulating commemorative coin. The suggestion was met with opposition from other panel members, some of whom thought Ganz was attempting to exceed the panel's mandate (Ganz believed his proposal was well within the mandate). A persistent Ganz, however, gradually won the support of the panel's chair, U.S. Mint Director Philip Diehl, to include as a part of the CCCAC's December 1994 annual report to Congress a recommendation that the Treasury secretary receive authorization to issue a circulating commemorative coin in a denomination of a quarter dollar or higher. Not long after the report was published, Ganz and other hobby leaders gained an opportunity to make their pitch before an influential member of Congress in a public forum.

During the mid-1990s, hobby leaders were becoming increasingly concerned that the noncirculating commemorative coinage program was repeating the mistakes of the 1930s that led eventually to a hiatus in commemorative production from 1954 to 1982 (see the earlier section of this chapter). In July 1995, the House Coinage Subcommittee, chaired by Rep. Michael Castle, R-Del., conducted a hearing addressing the noncirculating commemorative coinage program, with testimony heard from a number of hobby leaders. At one point during the hearing, veteran New York City coin dealer Harvey Stack, one of the most vocal opponents of the excesses of the noncirculating commemorative program, recommended a series of circulating coins honoring the first 13 states in the Union, followed by the release every year or two of new coins commemorating the other states as they came into the Union.

Castle embraced the idea (it did not hurt that he represented Delaware, the first state, which would place it at the head of the list were such a program to be enacted). In a response to a question from Castle, Ganz, who also testified at the hearing, seized the opportunity to push his proposal and recommended the quarter dollar be the vehicle for a circulating commemorative coin program. Castle did more than pay lip service to the idea, though; he introduced legislation, H.R. 3793, on July 11, 1996, calling for such a program.

Passage of a State quarter dollars program, however, proved to be a bit complicated.

Castle's bill passed the House of Representatives by voice vote at 5:13 p.m. on Sept. 4, 1996, and was referred to the Senate. However, before the Senate would act on Castle's bill, the unrelated H.R. 1776, the Black Revolutionary War Patriots Commemorative Coin Act, was amended in the Senate with six other noncirculating commemorative coin programs, a section reforming the CCCAC and a section ordering a Treasury study to determine whether a State quarter dollars program should be implemented, with the Treasury secretary given the authority to implement the program should the results of the survey be positive. The Senate passed the amended H.R. 1776 by unanimous consent on Oct. 3; the House passed the measure by unanimous consent at 2:23 p.m. the next day. President Clinton signed the act into law on Oct. 20 (Public Law 104-329).

According to Ganz, the Treasury study ordered in Public Law 104-329 was intended to kill any chance of a State quarter dollars program. Although Diehl as Mint director supported such a program, political appointees in the Treasury Department did not. The Treasury study's results, however, rather than shutting the door to a program, would open the door.

The feasibility study, which had to be reported to Congress by Aug. 1, 1997, included a national telephone survey to determine potential public acceptance of the program. According to the *Mint's 50 State Quarters Report: 10 Years of Honoring Our Nation's History and Heritage*, published in 2009, 51 percent of those polled "were favorable to the program," 38 percent showed indifference and 11 percent were unfavorable. "Younger demographic groups and households with children had the highest approval ratings," according to the report. Another question in the survey, however, received a response that might have surprised Treasury officials. "About 74 percent of the respondents said there was an almost certain, very likely, good or fair possibility they would save the quarters," according to the report.

Projecting survey responses to the adult U.S. population, the study estimated that "98 million people would be interested in saving one or more full sets of state quarter coins," the report states.

The study also examined revenue and cost implications. The survey estimated a "range of approximately $2.6 billion to $5.1 billion in added seigniorage directly attributable to the program," the report states.

As for the program's potential impact on production and distribution, the study identified various approaches to meet an anticipated increase in demand for quarter dollars during the life of the program, and indicated the "program would have minimal, if any, effect on distribution systems."

The study also reviewed public awareness and education issues, and explored the design selection process.

With the study's results largely favorable to the program, Treasury Secretary Robert E. Rubin could have implemented the State quarter dollars program under the authority granted him by P.L. 104-329. Instead, Rubin opted to defer the implementation decision to Congress, thus requiring new legislation.

With the 105th Congress in session starting in 1997, Castle introduced new legislation seeking State quarter dollars in the House (H.R. 2414) on Sept. 5, 1997. Sen. John H. Chafee, R-R.I., introduced a Senate version, the S. 1228, on Sept. 26, 1997. The House passed H.R. 2414 at 6:57 p.m. on Sept. 23, 1997, by a vote of 413 to 6. The House bill sat in the Senate, though S. 1228 moved forward with two major amendments—one approving a circulating dollar coin (what eventually became the Sacagawea dollar) and another seeking the noncirculating First Flight Centennial commemorative coins, celebrating the 100th anniversary of the Wright brothers' December 1903 flights at Kitty Hawk, N.C. The amended S. 1228 passed the Senate by unanimous consent on Nov. 9, 1997; the same bill passed the House at 10:03 p.m. on Nov. 13. President Clinton signed the bill into law on Dec. 1 (Public Law 105-124).

The law's passage on Dec. 1, 1997, left insufficient time to implement the State quarter dollars program in 1998. During 1998, Mint officials developed plans for the program: They developed a design selection process and criteria for what represented acceptable and unacceptable designs. They took steps to ensure sufficient numbers of the coins could be produced and placed into circulation to meet collector demand and to cause no coin shortages. They also began developing marketing plans and collector products incorporating the State quarter dollars.

Developing design criteria and a design selection process was an essential step in 1998. The basic process involved both state and federal officials making decisions about which designs would appear on the coins. Each state's governor was responsible for submitting design concepts/themes/narratives to the Mint well in advance of the coin's scheduled release. The Mint was responsible for executing the design suggestions into more refined form for formal consideration and eventually coining.

The Mint's official *50 State Quarters Report: 10 Years of Honoring Our Nation's History and Heritage* (available at **www.usmint.gov/downloads/ mint_programs/50sqReport.pdf**) detailed the basic process in place during the course of the program:

"Each governor was to provide the United States Mint three to five design concepts or themes representative of the state. Individual governors determined the process for identifying concepts within their state. The United States Mint would then review submitted concepts for appropriateness. From approved concepts, the United States Mint developed candidate designs and provided them to the Treasury Secretary for review and approval. The [Commission of Fine Arts] and [Citizens Commemorative Coin Advisory Committee] would also review and consult on candidate designs at that time. The United States Mint returned designs approved by the Treasury Secretary to the states. Each governor determined a process for recommending his or her state's final design from the approved candidate designs. Once chosen, the state returned its final design recommendation to the United States Mint, which forwarded it to the Department of the Treasury for the Secretary's final approval."

To ensure the designs submitted fell within Mint guidelines and were technically feasible, i.e., could be struck in mass production, all of the designs underwent scrutiny by many individuals at the Mint. The Mint director, Mint legal counsel, the Office of Sales and Marketing, and the Office of Manufacturing all reviewed the original quarter dollar artwork submitted by the governors. Design renderings by Mint engraving staff were also reviewed by both the Commission of Fine Arts and the Citizens Commemorative Coin Advisory Committee.

Among the general guidelines sent to the states were details about what was acceptable and what was unacceptable in terms of designs, as repeated in the official *50 State Quarters Report:*

➤ Designs should maintain a dignity befitting the Nation's coinage.

➤ Designs should have broad appeal to the state's citizens and avoid controversial subjects or symbols likely to offend.

➤ Suitable subject matter include state landmarks (natural and man-made), landscapes, historically significant buildings, symbols of state resources or industries, official state flora and fauna, state icons and outlines of the state.

➤ State flags and seals are not suitable for inclusion in designs.

➤ As stated in the authorizing legislation, the design should promote the diffusion of knowledge of the state, its history and geography, and the rich diversity of our national heritage.

➤ Priority consideration will be given to designs that are enduring representations of the state.

➤ Inappropriate design concepts include logos or depictions of specific commercial, private, educational, civic, religious, sports or other organizations whose membership or ownership is not universal.

The Mint engraving staff worked on the designs most of the time. However, in October 1999, Mint officials invited 14 artists outside the Mint to submit designs for the 2001 State quarter dollars. The artists came from a group of 20 who submitted designs for the new dollar coin launched in 2000. Mint officials said that the design competition was a pilot program to supplement the engravers and the engraving staff.

During the course of the program, the Mint revised the design selection process, both for what it requested from the states and what it sent the engraving staff. In response to questions from *Coin World,* Mint officials in the fall of 2002 said: "For the 1999 to 2000 series, we transmitted to our engravers photographs and sketches submitted by the states as 'design concepts,' which included incidental explanatory language (such as captions) to clarify design elements. During the 2001 series, some states began submitting text-only descriptions of their design concepts and, during the 2002 to 2003 series, the United States Mint transmitted text-only descriptions to the engravers from all the states honored in those years."

A few of the changes to the procedure were implemented in 2002. In a February 2002 letter to the five governors whose states were to be honored in 2004, Mint Director Henrietta Holsman Fore asked governors to "identify, by a process of your state's choosing, three to five different coin designs that are emblematic" of that state. Fore asked that those designs be sent to the Mint by June 24, 2002. The Mint expected to send final "design candidates" to the governors by early November. The governors had to return their final selection to the Mint by early January 2003. Mint officials also say for the 2004 designs it had resumed "its practice of transmitting [to the engravers] photographs, sketches and other visual depictions of design concepts from the states with a text description."

Mint officials say their 2002 request to the governors to submit actual designs was a departure from the previous policy of asking them for design concepts or themes. Mint officials said that the change was in response to complaints from several states already honored with State quarter dollars about changes made to designs submitted to the Mint. Many of the state design selection committees took the final design concepts they'd selected and had local artists render the concepts into finished designs. When the Mint engravers made changes to what the states considered were the final designs, controversy often erupted.

For example, several Maine designs were radically different in execution from the versions sent by the states, although the themes were the same. On one, the version provided by the Mint featured a prominent, distinctly shaped mountain in Maine rendered unidentifiable. On another, a famous lighthouse appeared on a rocky promontory unlike the facility's real location, and a specific three-masted ship became a two-masted vessel.

The letter also indicated that Mint officials had advanced the time line for notification to state governors concerning design concept submissions; it was now set at 22 months before the issuance of the coin. Previously, governors were notified 18 months before the issuance of that state's coin to begin the design process.

In producing the 2003 State quarter dollar designs, the Mint's sculptor-engravers "were instructed to create original, coinable and appropriate designs based on the concepts the state communicated." The idea of ensuring a submitted design, concept or theme was coinable introduced state officials to concepts they had probably never considered before unless those officials were coin collectors and thus likely more educated on the topic. Sometimes, changes to design submissions made to make a design workable in coin form drew questions from state officials about why certain changes had been made. Mint officials said when that happened, the governor or his/her staff was "contacted and every effort [was] made to amend the design to render it coinable."

According to Mint officials, defining "coinability" is difficult because "many elements, such as obverse/ reverse balance and metal flow, may be different for each design."

The Mint eventually supplied states a list of factors it considers when determining whether a design is coinable:

"It must be able to be produced in sufficient quantity to meet demand.

"All designs must fit into the design template.

"Designs must be analyzed with respect to the obverse design. Areas where a large amount of metal movement is expected must be located near the center of the coin. Less metal movement is possible near the border of the coin.

"Symmetrical, centered designs work best. Alignment must look correct to the naked eye.

"Avoid layering images more than two deep.

"Small pointed items, such as stars, should be kept to a minimum, especially toward the edge of the coin. The points are hard to fill adequately.

"Lines should have body (rounded, preferably) from beginning to end, not fade into the background or end in long thin points.

"Avoid narrow lines such as sun rays.

"Avoid incused lettering or design."

At the mid-point of the program's duration, Mint officials made the final and most drastic changes to the design process. According to *50 State Quarters Report,* "In 2003, the United States Mint solicited feedback from numismatic and artistic communities, state officials, historians, educators and the general public on the 50 State Quarters Design Evaluation and Selection Process. Responses indicated that, while stakeholders widely accepted the process, they desired improved communications among the United States Mint and the states and general public. Stakeholders also requested that the Design Evaluation Process place greater emphasis on educational value, historical accuracy and artistic beauty. The United States Mint revised the process accordingly, and then-Secretary John W. Snow approved the changes on March 11, 2003."

The revised design evaluation process took effect beginning in 2004, herein reprinted from *50 State Quarters Report:*

➤ Stage 1—The United States Mint initiated the formal state design process by contacting the state governor approximately 24 months prior to the beginning of the year in which the state was honored. The governor, or other state officials or group the state designated, appointed an individual to serve as the state's liaison to the United States Mint for the 50 State Quarters Program.

➤ Stage 2—The state conducted a concept selection process as determined by the state. The state provided the United States Mint three to five different concepts or themes emblematic of the state. Each concept or theme was to be in a narrative format, explaining why the concept was emblematic of the state and what the concept represented to the state's citizens.

➤ Stage 3—Based on narratives, the United States Mint produced original artwork representing the concepts, focusing on aesthetic beauty, historical accuracy, appropriateness and coinability.

➤ Stage 4—The United States Mint contacted the state to collaborate on the artwork. The state would appoint a historian, or other responsible official or expert, to participate in this collaboration and ensure historical accuracy and proper state representation. The United States Mint refined the artwork before forwarding it to advisory bodies.

➤ Stage 5—The CCAC and CFA reviewed candidate designs and made recommendations for revisions. The United States Mint then revised candidate designs to address any recommendations.

➤ Stage 6—The United States Mint presented candidate designs to the Secretary of the Treasury for review and approval.

➤ Stage 7—The United States Mint returned all Secretary-approved candidate designs to the state.

➤ Stage 8—From among the approved designs, the state recommended the final design through a process determined by the state and within a time frame specified by the United States Mint.

➤ Stage 9—The United States Mint presented the state's recommended design to the Treasury Secretary for final approval.

According to *50 State Quarters Report:* "The new process required states to submit design concepts in narrative formats. States had previously presented concepts in various forms, including artistic renderings without narrative justifications. The United States Mint Sculptor-Engravers encountered problems translating some of these concepts into original artwork. Concepts submitted as sketches or polished artworks were often too intricate for sculptor-engravers to recreate on the coin medium. Concepts transmitted in verbal or written formats sometimes failed to adequately convey the submitter's intent. By requiring states to submit concepts in narrative formats explaining the design's emblematic value, the new process enabled United States Mint Sculptor-Engravers and artists to better render appropriate and aesthetically pleasing designs. State historians assisted sculptor-engravers and artists to ensure renderings were historically accurate. Each state was given an opportunity to evaluate candidate designs before they were made public. States were not afforded this opportunity under the original process in which designs were publicized during CFA and CCCAC or [Citizens Coinage Advisory Committee] review. If states were unhappy with candidate designs, the United States Mint would have to revise or create new designs, delaying final design selection and approval. Early and frequent state involvement prevented such problems in the new process. While revisions extended the Design Evaluation Process from 18 months to 24 months, they improved communication between the United States Mint and key stakeholders, and enhanced the Program's educational, historic and artistic value."

The process implemented in 2004 remained in effect for the remainder of the program.

Throughout the design process, most states solicited public input on designs for their quarter dollars, with many states conducted public votes. According to 50 State Quarters Report, "An estimated 3.5 million people participated in the design process for their state quarter either through concept submission or voting."

New profits, and a change in philosophy

The popularity and profit of the State quarter dollars program birthed a changed philosophy at the United States Mint: Coinage redesign is good, especially for the bottom line. As many as 140 million individuals, many of whom had previously shown little interest in collecting coins, collected the new quarter dollars, eagerly awaiting each newest release. Collectors all over the country grew used to the refrain from others: "Do you have the new quarter yet?" Mint officials, who earlier had worried that coin shortages might result from the widespread hoarding or collecting that any new designs might encourage, found that no such shortages arose, despite hundreds of millions of State quarter dollars being pulled from circulation and held in collections. Mint officials also appreciated the profits they derived from the program, and not only from sales of collector versions of the coins.

The Mint derives revenue from sales of circulating coins to the Federal Reserve Bank. Every quarter dollar pulled from circulation represents profit to the Mint since it must be replaced through additional Federal Reserve orders.

The State quarter dollars program resulted in a significant, immediate rise in revenue for the Mint. In Fiscal Year 1998, the last year for the old-style Washington quarter dollar, the Mint's revenues from sales of quarter dollars to the Federal Reserve totaled $419.3 million. In FY2000, quarter dollar revenues totaled more than $1.5 billion.

Total circulating revenue for the 10-year program was $8,607,000,000; total seigniorage (profit) was $6,255,000,000 during the same period.

For the numismatic State quarter dollars program, the Mint generated $470.1 million in revenue and $136.2 million in earnings and seigniorage from the sale of related products (Proof sets of several types, Uncirculated Mint sets, first-day covers, spoons bearing the coins and more).

The additional revenue and growth in popularity of collecting coins from circulation led Mint officials to begin looking at other denominations to serve as platforms for circulating commemorative coin programs. In April 2002, the Mint director told collectors at a forum in Ohio that the Mint was considering changing the designs of the Jefferson 5-cent coin in 2003 to reflect the bicentennial of the Louisiana Purchase and the Lewis and Clark Expedition. The comments were met with strong collector support and Mint officials were poised to change the designs of the 5-cent coin in 2003. In a reversal of positions as compared to the 1970s and 1990s, opposition arose in Congress in June 2002, from the Virginia delegation when it heard of the Mint's plans. (Jefferson was a native Virginian, and Monticello, depicted on the 5-cent coin, is located within the state and a popular destination for tourists; having two icons of the state depicted on the 5-cent coin was seen as a badge of honor.) Virginian legislators introduced legislation in 2002 that would permit the redesign of the 5-cent coin from 2003 through 2005 to commemorate the two bicentennials, but would also require that Jefferson and Monticello appear on the coin from 2006 onward. The bill did not become law in that Congress, but a new version did pass in the next Congress. It became law in April 2003.

Because of the lateness in the bill's passage, Mint officials did not have enough time to change the designs of the 5-cent coin in 2003. But in 2004, Mint officials introduced two new reverses on the coin: The first celebrated the bicentennial of the Louisiana Purchase with a design based on the Jefferson Indian peace medal Lewis and Clark distributed to native leaders; and the second depicted the larger boat the expedition used along the Missouri River for a portion of the journey. Both coins retained the existing obverse portrait of Jefferson.

The Mint introduced a new Jefferson portrait in 2005 and two more commemorative reverses. The new portrait was an off-center, right-facing portrayal of Jefferson, the portrait abutting the slightly higher rim at the left side of the obverse. The first of the year's special reverses depicted a plains bison, one of the many animal species Lewis and Clark Expedition members saw during their journeys. The second reverse depicted a scene of the Pacific Ocean coastline to represent the end of the westward journey of Lewis and Clark.

The Mint marketed the series as the Westward Journey Nickel program. All four 2004 and 2005 circulating commemorative Jefferson 5-cent coins proved popular. As with the State quarter dollars, many Americans awaited the release into circulation of each new commemorative Jefferson, Westward Journey 5-cent coin.

In 2006, the Mint introduced another new Jefferson portrait. The new portrait, still used today, depicts Jefferson facing the viewer. For the reverse, Mint officials considered a number of new renditions of Monticello, but in the end reverted to the original design introduced in 1938. However, a Mint engraver did restore to the design all of the detail that the Mint engraving staff had removed from the coin over the decades, resulting in a sharper, crisper design than had been used in years.

With coinage redesign and circulating commemoratives now embraced by collectors, Treasury and Mint officials and members of Congress, two other denominations were singled out for change: the cent and the dollar. The same 2005 act approved changes to both coins.

With the State quarter dollars program nearing its December 2008 end, its creator, Rep. Castle, began looking for a similar coin program—one that would pump multiple new coin designs into circulation every year, and both promote coin collecting and continue a concept that the State quarter dollars represented: coinage as history lessons. Castle conceived of depicting every U.S. president on a circulating dollar coin, struck on the same manganese-brass clad planchets used for the Sacagawea dollars. He predicted that not only would the program be embraced by collectors, it would encourage wider circulation of a dollar coin. (Collectors knew better; historically, dollar coins have never circulated widely in the

United States.) Others in Congress, looking to the 200th anniversary of the birth of Abraham Lincoln in 2009, started promoting new designs for a circulating Lincoln cent. Both measures became part of the Presidential $1 Coin Act of 2005 (the act also authorized the American Buffalo .9999 fine gold bullion coins). After passage in the Senate as S. 1047 in late November 2005, the House approved the measure Dec. 13 in a 291 to 113 roll-call vote under suspension of the rules. President George W. Bush signed the measure into law Dec. 22, 2005.

Presidential dollars

Beginning with the release of the George Washington Presidential dollar Feb. 19, 2007 (the official federal holiday celebrating Washington's Birthday), four Presidential dollars will be issued every year through 2016 at least, and possibly beyond. Sitting presidents and living former presidents are ineligible to be depicted. Any former president must be deceased at least two years before being eligible for depiction on one of the coins.

Each coin depicts the honored president with standard placement of inscriptions: the president's name at the top, with the number of the president and years of service at the bottom (an additional inscription was added in 2009). The reverse is standard to the series, showing a half-length Statue of Liberty from the perspective of someone below; inscriptions are UNITED STATES OF AMERICA and the denomination $1. For the eight 2007 and 2008 Presidential dollars, all of the remaining inscriptions were placed on the edge; Congress had ordered the date, IN GOD WE TRUST and E PLURIBUS UNUM be placed on the edge to make space for larger, more dramatic designs on the faces, and Mint officials elected to place the Mint mark there as well. Controversy arose, however, over the placement of IN GOD WE TRUST on the edge. According to Snopes.com (a website that addresses urban myths), in February 2007 an email began circulating urging that the Presidential dollars be boycotted because the IN GOD WE TRUST motto had been omitted; Snopes. com was unable to identify who had originated the email, which spread nationwide. Then, during the first year of production the Philadelphia Mint struck 50,000 or more George Washington dollars without the edge inscription (see chapter on errors for more details on how this occurred), as well as much smaller numbers of John Adams and Thomas Jefferson dollars, prompting broad media coverage of what some were calling "Godless dollars." Congress responded to pressure from certain religious circles and ordered that the motto be moved to the obverse or reverse. The Mint moved the motto to the obverse for the 2009 coins, shifting the presidential inscription at the bottom counter-clockwise to make space.

While the boycott urged in the email may have played little or no role, by mid-2008 it had become clear that the Presidential dollar program had not resulted in the wide circulation of dollar coins in commerce. Many collectors in letters to *Coin World* and in comments made online suggested that few if any collectors had ever received one of the coins in change, although many of the same collectors had made efforts to spend the coins. The failure of the coin to circulate had the same affect on mintages as it did for the earlier Anthony and Sacagawea programs: The mintages for the Presidential dollars (like the Anthony and Sacagawea coins) have generally fallen since the production of the Washington coin, which remains the record holder for highest mintage.

As of May 2011, each new Presidential dollar was ceremoniously released at a launch event conducted at a site with a connection to the honored president.

Lincoln Bicentennial cents

Congress in 2000 authorized the formation of the Abraham Lincoln Bicentennial Commission, to guide the government in its celebration of the birth of Abraham Lincoln in 2009.

The commission's newly formed Advisory Committee of Lincoln experts gathered Feb. 10 and 11, 2003, at the Library of Congress in Washington, D.C., to begin discussions of how best to celebrate the anniversary, including, possibly, through coinage.

"At this early stage," the commission's executive director, Michael Bishop, told *Coin World* in February 2003, "the legislation that created the commission requires that we look at the possibility of doing a commemorative coin or bicentennial 'penny.' We are very interested in doing both.

"In preliminary ideas for the 'penny,' it's likely that the profile would not change, even for the year, but the reverse might feature different scenes from Lincoln's life or various Lincoln sites throughout the country." A series of three or four reverse designs could be done in the course of the year, he said. "There have been some suggestions about changing the color, just for the bicentennial year, but at this stage such discussion is theoretical," he said.

"We've had two meetings with officials of the U.S. Mint in order to discuss the process by which such changes are made, including three or more designs. There seemed to be a generally positive response among the people with whom we met. They seemed very willing to work with us."

To fulfill the commission's eventual recommendations of commemorating the bicentennial on the reverse of the Lincoln cent in 2009, authorizing legislation, the Abraham Lincoln Bicentennial 1-cent Coin Redesign Act was introduced in 2004. The legislation proposed that the reverse of the cent "bear four different designs each representing a different aspect of the life of Abraham Lincoln, such as—his birth and early childhood in Kentucky; his formative years in Indiana; his professional life in Illinois; and his presidency in Washington, D.C." Under the proposal, Lincoln cents with a new reverse design would be issued every three months during 2009. The reverse design on Lincoln cents issued after

Dec. 31, 2009, was to bear "an image emblematic of President Lincoln's preservation of the United States of America as a single and united country," according to the legislation.

That measure failed to become law before the conclusion of the 108th Congress, but similar legislation was introduced in the 109th Congress. Authority for the 2009 Lincoln, Bicentennial cents was not granted in stand-alone legislation, however, as noted earlier.

The measure authorized four different circulating commemorative cents to be struck, each depicting the same four themes sought in the failed 2004 legislation: Lincoln's birthplace and early years in Kentucky (1809 to 1816, Early Childhood cent); his time in Indiana (1816 to 1830, Formative Years cent); his time in Illinois (1830 to 1861, Professional Life cent); and his last years Washington, D.C. (1861 to 1865, Presidency cent).

In late 2007, as the Mint began releasing finalist designs under consideration for the four coins, an email campaign was begun expressing outrage. The email contained images of some of the reverse designs, with the text claiming that the American Civil Liberties Union and "other similar groups" had succeeded in having the motto IN GOD WE TRUST omitted from the new reverse designs as part of a campaign to eliminate all references to God and religion in society. As with the similar email campaign at the start of the Presidential dollars program, there was no truth to the email; the motto IN GOD WE TRUST has been in the same location on the obverse of the Lincoln cent since 1909.

The first 2009 Lincoln cent—the Early Childhood coin, commemorating Lincoln's birth and youth in Kentucky—was placed into circulation Feb. 12, 2009, on the 200th birthday of Abraham Lincoln. The coin depicts a lob cabin representative of Lincoln's birthplace. A ceremony was held at Larue High School in Hodgenville, Ky., not far from the site of the Lincoln birthplace, concluding with a cent exchange. Individuals were afforded an opportunity to acquire rolls of the cents, and after officials determined they had enough coins on hand to meet the demand of those present, individuals were permitted to acquire $25 boxes of rolled cents at face value. Some persons at the event immediately offered participants sizeable profits for their rolls and boxes of cents.

Similar exchanges were conducted Feb. 12 at three locations in Washington, D.C.: Mint headquarters, the Mint sales counter at Union Station, and on Capitol Hill. The Mint also began selling two-roll sets of the cents, one roll each from the Denver and Philadelphia Mints, for $8.95 plus $4.95 shipping and handling. Collectors who had been unable to participate in the Feb. 12 cent exchanges and who were unwilling to the pay the high premium the Mint was charging for the cents waited to find them in circulation, and waited, and waited some more. Meanwhile, prices for the rolls of cents acquired at the Feb. 12 exchanges and

from the Mint at a premium began climbing.

When the Mint announced that the second 2009 Lincoln cent—commemorating Lincoln's Formative Years—would be released May 14 at Lincoln State Park in Lincoln City, Ind., many predicted, accurately, that the venue would be packed with collectors and dealers wanting the cents. People began lining up at the exchange site well before dawn, hours before the 10 a.m. ceremony, with rainy skies still dark. When the gates were opened, participants were handed a notice that banned secondary market sales of the coins on park grounds without acquisition of a license (and no licenses were granted).

Several coin firms sent multiple representatives to the event to acquire the maximum number of rolls available (six rolls per pass through the line), and at least one firm gained permission from the owners of a nearby private residence to set up shop, where they were ready to buy the coins from collectors, paying each a profit for the coins. The line to acquire the coins stretched a half mile or so at times, but eventually everyone was able to get the coins. Rolls of the cents immediately began selling on eBay for huge premiums, starting at more than $100 for a 50-cent roll. Prices fell as more cents from the May 14 event entered the marketplace and some of the fervor subsided.

Cent exchanges for the second design were also held at the Mint headquarters and Union Station sites in Washington, and another exchange was held on Capitol Hill May 15. The Mint also offered two-roll sets of the cents beginning May 14 at the same $8.95 charge as for the first release.

As with the first cent, the second cent trickled into circulation very slowly. Again, collectors expressed their frustration and displeasure at being unable to find the coins.

The third 2009 Lincoln cent—honoring Lincoln's Professional Life in Illinois—was released Aug. 13 in Springfield, Ill., where Lincoln practiced law. The ceremony and distribution of the cent were both conducted at the Old State Capitol in Springfield.

The Aug. 13 crowd, estimated at 2,000 to 2,500 people, began to form at the east side entrance to the Old State Capitol property beginning a little after 10 p.m. Central Time Aug. 12—just short of 12 hours before the 10 a.m. Aug. 13 ceremony. The roll exchange, handled by Chase Bank located across the street and to the northeast side of the Old State Capitol property, began seconds after the end of the official program, which lasted approximately a half hour. As with the first two coin exchanges, rolls of the Professional Life cent immediately began selling at premiums in the secondary market.

The fourth launch ceremony, for the cent commemorating Lincoln's presidency, had been anticipated by Mint officials as likely to draw the largest crowds, given its location in Washington, D.C. The 10 a.m. ceremony Nov. 12 for the cent reflecting

Abraham Lincoln's presidency was scheduled be held at sculptor Henry Merwin Shrady's Ulysses S. Grant Memorial at the base of the west side of the U.S. Capitol, which faces the Washington Mall. A cent exchange was scheduled to be conducted there in addition to exchanges at U.S. Mint sales outlets at Union Station, 50 Massachusetts Ave. N.E. and the first floor of U.S. Mint headquarters at 801 Ninth Ave. N.W., also beginning at 10 a.m.

However, on the morning of the Nov. 12 event, a steady rain spawned by a spin-off storm from Hurricane Ida kept the crowd at the Capitol ceremony to approximately 150 people. Crowds appeared to be larger at the two indoor locations where the other cent exchanges were conducted.

Some collectors not able to attend the four ceremonies and unwilling to pay premiums for the coins had difficulty adding them to their collections. As each new design was introduced, reports of the 2009 Lincoln cents being found in circulation began trickling in, but it was clear that many collectors were frustrated in their efforts to find the cents at face value at their local banks.

Why the difficulty in finding the coins in circulation? The severe economic recession that spread nationwide had a direct effect on coinage circulation in the United States. Coins began flooding back to banks and to the Federal Reserve, whose vaults became clogged with coins. The Fed began ordering vastly fewer new coins from the Mint than it had in 2008 before the recession grabbed the economy by the neck and wouldn't let go. What new coins were being struck, including the 2009 Lincoln cents, apparently sat in vaults longer than new cents had rested before 2009. Also, Mint and Federal Reserve officials made no special provisions for local banks to order the 2009 cents by design. Even those banks willing to special order the cents from the Federal Reserve were unable to acquire them for customers. Many collectors became increasingly upset that they could not find the cents in circulation, blaming the Mint, the Federal Reserve, dealers and anyone else they could scapegoat.

The Mint also offered various collector versions of the four cents. The authorizing act required that numismatic versions—those struck for use in Proof and Uncirculated Mint sets—be composed of the same 95 percent copper, 5 percent tin and zinc alloy used for the cent in 1909. Tin had been removed from the composition in 1962, and a switch to a copper-plated zinc composition was introduced in 1982. Collectors thus had 16 different cents to obtain: Philadelphia Mint and Denver Mint versions of each design struck for circulation, totaling eight coins; four different Proof versions, one of each design; and four different Satin Finish versions from the Uncirculated Mint set, again one of each design.

When the 2010 Lincoln cent was introduced, it bore a new Union Shield reverse and a revitalized version of Victor David Brenner's 1909 portrait, which had been much modified over the years by the Mint engraving staff.

The 2009 Lincoln cent program, however, did not close out the Mint's circulating commemorative coin programs. Congress has approved two other multi-year, circulating commemorative coin programs, one making its debut in 2009 (though, as will be shown, only barely circulating) and the other in 2010.

District of Columbia and U.S. Territories quarter dollars

A second circulating commemorative quarter dollar program made its one-year appearance in 2009: the District of Columbia and U.S. Territories quarter dollars.

Supporters of the District of Columbia-Territories quarter dollar program had long sought the same level of coinage recognition as given to the states, though the measure never gained much support until the final effort was made. The member of the U.S. House of Representatives representing the District of Columbia introduced legislation seeking such coins five times before one of the measures became law. The successful legislation became a part of an omnibus spending bill, the Consolidated Appropriations Act of 2008, H.R. 2764. It passed the House on June 22, 2007; was passed in the Senate with an amendment on Sept. 6, 2007; went through the process of resolving the House and Senate versions starting Dec. 17 before final approval Dec. 19; and became Public Law 110-161 with President George W. Bush's signature on Dec. 26, 2007.

The act authorized coins for, in the order of issuance: District of Columbia, Puerto Rico, Guam, American Samoa, U.S. Virgin Islands and Northern Mariana Islands.

The design evaluation process used for the State quarter dollars program was continued for the 2009 program.

The District of Columbia and U.S. Territories quarter dollars did not seem to generate the same level of collector interest as the State quarter dollars program. Some of the lower interest might be attributable to collector "burnout," but it could also be attributed to substantially lower mintages and another factor that made it much more difficult to find the 2009 coins in circulation for many. State quarter dollar mintages peaked in 2000 with more than 6.4 billion coins struck, attributable to a strong economy and resultant demand for coinage in circulation. Mintages fell and rose from 2001 to 2008, with the lowest level reached in 2003 when 2.28 billion quarter dollars were struck. A worsening economy resulted in lower commercial demand for coinage; the 2008 quarter dollar total was nearly 2.44 billion coins, with the 2009 total being about a quarter of the 2008 total at 533.92 million coins. Additionally, obtaining the 2009 coins from banks or circulation was also made more difficult because the Mint and Federal Reserve abandoned the collector-friendly policy in place during the State quarter dollars program of allowing banks to order each new coin for a specific period of time. Banks could not order the 2009 coins by design; the Federal Reserve filled orders for quarter dollars in 2009 by shipping whatever coins were on hand with no special effort to ship the 2009 coins. Collectors in regions where local supplies of quarter dollars were adequate to meet commercial demand had difficulty finding the 2009 coins. Even in early 2011, some collectors have never found a 2009 quarter dollar in circulation.

Native American dollars

With the introduction of the Presidential dollar in 2007, advocates of the Sacagawea dollar decided to promote the coin as a circulating commemorative and maybe boost its use in circulation. The Sacagawea dollar was introduced in 2000 with a series high mintage of 1,286,056,000 coins and grand hopes that it would circulate more widely than the Anthony dollar. However, as was the case two decades earlier with the release of the Anthony dollar in 1979, as well as with the Presidential dollars, released after the introduction of the Sacagawea dollar, the Sacagawea dollar failed to circulate widely. The mintage in 2001 dropped to 133,407,500 coins. The two-year total mintage was more than sufficient to meet commercial needs for the rest of the decade and into the next, so the Federal Reserve did not order any Sacagawea dollars from the Mint from 2002 to 2008. All circulation-quality production was limited to the number of coins needed for numismatic sales, with the coins sold by the Mint directly to the public at a premium above their face value. Mintages from 2002 to 2008 totaled well below 8 million pieces every year.

In an effort to reinvigorate the Sacagawea dollar, it was reimagined as a circulating commemorative coin platform starting in 2009. Under the Native American $1 Coin Act, passed in 2007, the Mint annually will issue a Sacagawea, Native American dollar (no end date has been given for this program in the authorizing legislation). Each year, the Native American dollar is given a new reverse design emblematic of an American Indian or tribal contribution to society, replacing the traditional Soaring Eagle reverse. In addition, the enabling act ordered changes to both the obverse and edge of the Sacagawea dollar in its Native American form. The date and Mint mark were ordered moved from the obverse to the edge, along with the motto E PLURIBUS UNUM from the Soaring Eagle reverse. The edge, previously smooth, now bears the same incused edge inscription used on the 2009 and later Presidential dollars.

In 2009, a Three Sisters design was selected, representing a Native American method of planting corn, beans and squash. The 2010 design commemorates the Haudenosaunee, also known as the Iroquois Confederacy, with the theme of "Government—The Great Tree of Peace," depicting the Hiawatha Belt with five arrows bound together. The theme of 2011 coin is "Diplomacy, Treaties with Tribal Nations," marking the first formal written peace alliance between the Wampanoag tribe and the European settlers.

A provision in the Native American $1 Coin Act states, "The number of $1 coins minted and issued in a year with the Sacagawea-design on the obverse shall be not less than 20 percent of the total number of $1 coins minted and issued in such year." That percentage is derived from the number of Presidential dollars struck.

However, the Federal Reserve was not a supporter of the Native American dollar program and as of early 2011 has ordered none of the coins for use in circulation. Production of circulation-quality Native American dollars has been limited to numismatic sales and to distribution via the Mint's Direct Ship Program. (The U.S. Mint introduced the Direct Ship Program in June 2008 to help circulation of Presidential dollar coins for coins dated 2007 and 2008, and extended the program in 2009 for the Native American dollars. The program allows customers to place orders, at face value, for $250 face value boxes containing 10 rolls, with the Mint absorbing the shipping costs. The boxes contain either Denver Mint coins or Philadelphia Mint coins, but customers cannot designate from which Mint they want the coins to fill the order.)

The only Native American dollars entering circulation are probably being released by individuals or individual banks acquiring the coins through the Direct Ship Program.

America the Beautiful quarter dollars program

A new circulating quarter dollar program designed to celebrate national parks, national forests, national military parks and other similar sites in all 50 states, the District of Columbia and the five U.S. territories (56 sites and coins total) made its debut in 2010.

The new America the Beautiful quarter dollar program, as it is called, is all about natural beauty and history. During the 11-year course of the program (or 22 years, if the secretary of Treasury executes an option permitting a second 11-year series), each coin will depict a scene reflecting a national park, national forest, national battlefield or other national site. The coins will be issued in the order in which the selected site was federally recognized. Like the State quarter dollars program, five coins will be released annually. What is unclear in 2011 is whether the new coins will prove as popular with the public as the State quarter dollars. The answer may depend on two factors: the economy and how the coins are released into circulation.

The America the Beautiful quarter dollar program was the creation of Rep. Castle, the chief sponsor of the legislation authorizing both the State quarter dollar and Presidential dollar coin programs. With the conclusion of the State quarters program in sight at the end of 2008 and Mint officials gearing up for the one-year District of Columbia and U.S. Territories coin program in 2009, Castle sought what he perceived as the natural continuation of both programs.

Castle introduced the America's Beautiful National Parks Quarter Dollar Coin Act of 2008 on June 4, 2008. In many areas, H.R. 6184 mirrored the earlier State quarters legislation, though expanded from the start to also authorize coins honoring the District of Columbia and the five U.S. territories—the Commonwealth of Puerto Rico, Guam, American Samoa, the Commonwealth of the Northern Mariana Islands and the United States Virgin Islands. The Mint would be granted authority to continue to use certain inscriptions on the obverse of the coins rather than on the reverse, just as permission had been granted in 2007 when the State quarter dollars were approved; that provision meant the Mint could continue to use all statutory inscriptions on the obverse in order to make space on the reverse for the special commemorative inscriptions. The design selection process outlined in the legislation closely followed both the final design process used in the State quarter dollars program and the restrictions against certain types of designs mirrored the restrictions in the State quarters program. But the new legislation had one difference that was literally huge.

A provision in the legislation called for 3-inch, 5-ounce .999 fine silver bullion coin versions of the regular coins. Large-size silver bullion pieces are not a new concept. Canada issued a Maple Leaf 10-ounce silver bullion coin in 1998, and private firms have issued bullion pieces in multiples of an ounce for years. However, the United States Mint had never made such a piece before the America the Beautiful program.

The bill called for the 5-ounce bullion coins to bear the same designs as the regular coins. Although they will carry a bullion value that at a silver price of $34 an ounce equals about $170, the coins are denominated as quarter dollars. These quarters, however, not only will dwarf every quarter dollar ever struck, they will be larger than any coin or pattern piece ever struck by the U.S. Mint. The coins will bear an edge inscription stating the bullion content of each piece (the only inscription difference from the regular quarter dollars). The 5-ounce bullion coins will be sold through the same network of authorized purchasers that sells the Mint's American Eagle and American Buffalo bullion coins and by national parks and other related sites.

The coins are huge. Each America the Beautiful bullion coin will have a diameter of 3 inches and weigh 5 troy ounces; those specifications were dictated by the legislation. In contrast, the largest-diameter coin in widespread circulation today—the quarter dollar—is 0.96 inch in size, less than a third the diameter of the new bullion coins. It takes nearly 28 copper-nickel clad quarter dollars to match the weight of a single America the Beautiful 5-ounce silver bullion coin. The provision seeking the 5-ounce silver bullion coins was not universally embraced in the collector community.

The America's Beautiful National Parks Quarter Dollar bill moved very quickly along the legislative path in the House of Representatives. The House Committee on Financial Services passed legislation June 25, 2008, just a few weeks after the measure had been introduced. The full House approved the measure July 9 with a vote of 419-0. The Senate passed the measure Dec. 8, 2008. President Bush signed it into law Dec 23, 2008 (Public Law 110-456).

The legislation also takes the guesswork out of what designs will go on the quarter dollar once the program ends (whether the series extends over 11 years or 22 years). Once the program ends, the obverse design is to return to the image of George Washington used in 1998 and the reverse is to depict an image of Washington crossing the Delaware River prior to the battle of Trenton, N.J. That scene is depicted on the 1999 New Jersey State quarter dollar.

With passage of the legislation at the end of 2008, the next step was the selection of the 56 sites (see accompanying table) by the 270-day deadline mandated in the bill. The secretary of the Treasury had until Sept. 19, 2009, to select the 56 sites. Equally important, the Mint had only a few months in which to create designs for the first five coins to be issued in 2010, during the program's initial year. Following the requirements set forth in the authorizing act for the new quarter dollar program, officials at the national and state/territorial levels worked at devising the list. The list was publicly released Sept. 9, 2009, 10 days ahead of the deadline.

Maybe the biggest surprise about the 56 sites was that the first site to be recognized—Hot Springs National Park in Arkansas—is not the nation's first national park. It is, however, the first nationally protected site. The Hot Springs Reservation came under federal protection in legislation passed by Congress on April 20, 1832, becoming the nation's first nationally protected area. Arkansas was still a territory at the time. It became the 25th state on June 15, 1836.

The sites selected for the 56 coins are national parks, national forests, national military parks, national historical parks, national historic sites, a national recreation area, several national monuments, wildlife refuges, a national scenic roadway, a national scenic waterway, national lakeshores, a national seashore, a national wilderness area and a national preserve. While a few sites have been depicted on U.S. coins previously—Yellowstone National Park on Wyoming's coin and the Statue of Liberty/Ellis Island for New Jersey—most have never been commemorated on any federally issued coin or medal.

As noted, the Mint engraving staff did not have much time to prepare designs for the first five coins.

Mint officials are following a seven-step design selection process, paraphrased as follows:

Step 1: The United States Mint will initiate the formal design process for each national site as identified by the order of the official list approved by the secretary of the Treasury. ... Designs will be processed at a rate of five per year.

Step 2: The U.S. Mint will contact the head of the federal entity responsible for the supervision, management or conservancy of each national site. The Mint will ask the federal entity's head to appoint a knowledgeable federal official to serve as its liaison for the national site (e.g., national park superintendent, national forest supervisor, federal preservation officer). The liaison will assist the Mint by identifying source materials for candidate designs.

Step 3: Based on the source materials, the Mint will produce three to five candidate designs focusing on aesthetic beauty, historical accuracy, authenticity, appropriateness and coinability.

Step 4: The United States Mint will consult with the federal liaison to ensure the historical accuracy, authenticity and overall composition of each candidate design to ensure it appropriately represents the site.

Step 5: Final candidate designs will be submitted to the secretary of the interior, the chief executive of the host jurisdiction (state/District of Columbia/territory), the Commission of Fine Arts and the Citizens Coinage Advisory Committee for review and comment. The U.S. Mint may make changes to address any concerns or recommendations resulting from this review process.

Step 6: The director of the United States Mint will make a final recommendation to the secretary of the Treasury, after considering all relevant factors, including the comments and recommendations of the secretary of the interior, the chief executive, the CFA, the CCAC and the federal entity responsible for the supervision, management, or conservancy of each national site.

Step 7: The secretary of the Treasury will make the final design selection.

Well before any sites were selected for the America the Beautiful quarter dollar program and before any designs were being prepared, members of the coin collector community and, most importantly, the Citizens Coinage Advisory Committee, began conducting a campaign to replace the portrait of George Washington on the obverse of the coin with one of Theodore Roosevelt.

The idea had been floated for several years. The Editorial in the June 23, 2008, issue of *Coin World* had recommended replacing Washington's portrait with one of the president that most people connect with the National Parks System. "President Theodore Roosevelt's visionary leadership in conservation and creation of national parks during his administration makes him the ideal candidate to occupy the obverse of quarters issued under this program," wrote *Coin World* Editor Beth Deisher. During the months that followed, support for the idea grew in the coin community, with one individual embracing the suggestion also in a position to take action. At the CCAC's

Jan. 27, 2009, meeting in Washington, one of the panel's members, Richard J. Meier of Rockford, Ill., described his desire to personally lobby for the idea.

Meier had outlined his idea in a "Guest Commentary" published in the Jan. 19, 2009, issue of *Coin World*, published Jan. 5. (At the time, most in the hobby were calling the series the National Parks quarters, even though many of the sites to be honored with the coins are not national parks.)

"If the State quarter dollar series is any indication, the National Parks series will be every bit as popular with the general populace. Certainly the State quarters, plus the quarter dollars for the 2009 District of Columbia and U.S. Territories program, have engaged a whole new generation of collectors, since the entire series is compelling and can be acquired at face value!" Meier wrote.

"However, I believe there is one component still missing from Rep. Michael Castle's proposal, and there's still time to rectify it. Namely, I think the time has come to change the obverse of the quarter dollar for the duration of National Parks series.

"The president who deserves to grace the obverse of the National Parks series, in my opinion, is Theodore Roosevelt.

"President Roosevelt was known as the naturalist and conservationist who set aside millions of acres of land for national parks and forests. He has never been featured on a circulating coin, yet he and the National Parks Service go hand-in-hand.

"According to my research, under the watch of our 26th president 150 national forests, five national parks, 18 national monuments, four national game preserves and 21 reclamation projects were set aside for the benefit of generations to come. Roosevelt successfully gained federal protection for about 230 million acres.

"In addition, he appreciated artistic coinage, saying that the redesign of American coins was his 'pet baby.' As evidence of this, it was Roosevelt who personally commissioned the world-renowned sculptor Augustus Saint-Gaudens to create new designs, such as we see on the famous gold $20 coin, ..." Meier wrote.

"Although I am not in a position of decision-making, I would urge Rep. Castle and Congress to give my proposal their consideration. President Theodore Roosevelt is the most deserving person to be represented on our nation's 25-cent piece during the time that the national parks are featured on the reverse of that denomination. His representation on the obverse of the quarter will educate the public to understand the pioneering importance that this president gave to ecology, conservation and the greening of America. The National Parks system, and all Americans in turn, arguably owe him a greater debt of gratitude for his ecological commitment than to any other president. Therefore, may his image duly grace the obverse of the soon-to-be-realized National Parks quarter!"

As reported in *Coin World's* Feb. 16, 2009, issue, several of the other CCAC members voiced strong support for Meier's idea as soon as he aired it at the Jan. 27 meeting. Mint officials at the meeting were less enthused about the idea.

Donald Scarinci, a New Jersey lawyer who sits on the panel, wondered whether the idea should be suggested to Treasury Secretary Timothy F. Geithner, who had been sworn into office the previous day. "The worst case scenario he could do is say he doesn't have time to deal with it," Scarinci said. Geithner became the nation's chief financial officer with an economy in ruins, a banking industry in crisis and plummeting employment.

Mint officials at the January meeting seemed to be surprised at Meier's suggestion, but the idea swiftly shot through the committee, as reported in the Feb. 16 *Coin World.* "We're here to give advice," said Scarinci, seeking to assure Mint officials. "There's no harm in passing a resolution."

Mint staff advisers to the CCAC suggested the committee move a little slower. After all, Geithner had been in office less than 24 hours and Mint officials said they didn't know how he might view the issue.

In addition, the U.S. Mint's legal counsel, Greg Weinman, said the Mint is not keen on the committee acting on new issues, as reported in *Coin World.* Weinman said the Mint preferred that the CCAC stick to reviewing Mint-approved coin designs and outlining new coin proposals in the committee's annual report, he said, as the panel is federally empowered to do. Weinman said that advising the Treasury secretary on what might be considered for the quarter dollar's obverse is "somewhat a gray area," the Feb. 16, 2009, *Coin World* reported.

At the meeting, Weinman acknowledged that the authorizing act did not specify what design should appear on the obverse of the coin, prompting the committee to move forward with a resolution, though not before Michael Brown, a former Mint staff member who sits on the CCAC, cautioned that he could envision "the ladies of Mount Vernon with pitchforks in hand" being infuriated by the idea. All eight CCAC members voted unanimously for Meier's idea by voice vote.

The proposal found support from some in the coin collecting community. "Bravo to members of the Citizens Coinage Advisory Committee for voicing their opinions and refusing to be browbeaten into silence by the U.S. Mint's bureaucrats," Deisher wrote in the Feb. 16 issue. She noted that since publication of the June 23, 2008, Editorial, "Many collectors have communicated with *Coin World* ... supporting the idea of TR's portrait on the obverse of the National Parks quarters."

At the CCAC's Sept. 22 meeting in which the panel reviewed the 2010 reverse designs, committee members berated Mint officials for not placing a portrait of Roosevelt on the coins. In response, Mint officials at the meeting told the committee that nothing happened to the CCAC's recommendations. They reported that Geithner never acted on it one way or the other and no member of Congress introduced legislation on the idea. As a result Mint officials told the CCAC they decided it was best to keep Washington on the quarter dollar and showed a computerized "enhanced" version of John Flanagan's 1932 portrait of Washington, which is smaller than the artist's original. The design uses the same template as the State quarter dollars Washington obverse, although the portrait was modified using computer scans of Flanagan's original model, still held in the Mint archives. The portrait had been otherwise modified over the years, especially in the detailing of Washington's hair. CCAC members praised the work done to restore Flanagan's original portrait but voiced disappointment in the rejection of Roosevelt.

Finally, at the CCAC's Nov. 12 meeting, the committee retreated from the Roosevelt initiative. Panel members discussed instead recommending full debate on creating a new obverse design for the denomination but also acknowledged that removing Washington from the coin and replacing him with a different subject such as Roosevelt or a representation of Liberty was a lost cause.

Concurrent with preparing designs for the 2010 coins, Mint officials moved forward to implement the silver bullion coin provision in the authorizing act. The production of the pieces would prove difficult.

The authorizing act was very specific; the diameter of the 5-ounce silver bullion coins had to be 3 inches. That requirement did not permit the Mint to experiment with diameters and thicknesses that would provide the best results in production. The restrictions in the act gave Mint technicians trouble.

During a Feb. 10, 2010, Mint forum in Springfield, Ill., the night before the release of the new Union Shield reverse for the Lincoln cent, Mint Director Edmund C. Moy reported that the 5-ounce silver bullion coin program was in trouble. One problem, he said, was that the required specifications create a very thin coin that is actually bendable by hand. Two, Mint technicians had difficulties placing the weight and fineness incuse on the edge. Because of the coin's thinness, applying the inscription was causing the edge to crumple on the trial strikes, Moy said at the forum.

Early trial strikes for the 5-ounce coins were produced on a press typically used for making large medals, but that press could not be used for regular production of the bullion coins, according to the Mint. "The press tonnage required to achieve acceptable relief on the 5-ounce, 3-inch diameter dimensions required that the Mint purchase a new press," a Mint official said. "The existing press that could achieve the required tonnage is older, of low output, and requires modification to support the 3-inch, 5-ounce bullion coin. We anticipate output in excess of 1 million coins per year, although output still needs to be confirmed with a pre-production trial strike run," according to the official.

To implement the bullion coin program, the Mint purchased a German-made GMP 1000 coin and medal embossing press from Gräbener Pressensysteme GmbH & Co. KG for the program. A U.S. Mint technical team visited Gräbener's facility from Dec. 14 to 17, 2009, to witness the operation of the press prior to its packing and shipping to the U.S. Mint. During the four-day visit, approximately 90 experimental pieces were struck with "nonsense" dies (bearing designs that simulate but do not replicate any designs found on U.S. coins) to demonstrate the press' capabilities. The .999 fine silver 5-ounce, 3-inch planchets for the experimental strikes were supplied by Sunshine Minting Inc., located in Coeur d'Alene, Idaho. The press was installed at the Philadelphia Mint. Additional testing was carried out during the spring and summer of 2010 although Mint officials released few details of the experiments.

Finally, in December 2010, Mint officials announced details of the 2010 America the Beautiful bullion coin program: mintage of each 2010 coin would be limited to 33,000 pieces (Mint officials earlier estimated a mintage of 100,000 pieces per coin), with the Mint warning authorized purchasers against charging overly high secondary market premiums for the bullion coins. Sales to the authorized purchasers were to begin Dec. 6. (The Mint also announced a collector version to bear a different finish than the bullion coins and the P Mint mark, with the mintage limited to 27,000 pieces per coin; sales of these coins were to be delayed until 2011.) Even before the authorized purchasers could begin placing orders, one authorized purchaser, American Precious Metals Exchange in Oklahoma City, Okla., pre-sold 1,000 sets from its anticipated Dec. 6 allocation of 3,000 in less than 24 hours Dec. 3. During this initial period of sales, the sets were offered by APMEX at $1,395 per set to customers who expressed an interest in purchasing sets before the release date. Secondary market prices on eBay immediately rose to many multiples of the Mint's issue price (less than $900 per five-coin set). Angry collectors immediately flooded the Mint with telephone calls and email complaining about the high primary and secondary prices, leading Mint officials to halt all sales to the authorized purchasers on Dec. 6, just a few hours after sales had begun. On Dec. 10, the Mint released new restrictions for the authorized purchasers: they could sell the coins only to the public, not to secondary market retailers (the normal customers of the authorized purchasers); the authorized purchasers were also banned from selling sets to their employees and relatives; the firms could not take more than a 10 percent profit over the cost of coin acquisition from the Mint; and sales were limited to one coin of each design per household.

Ultimately, nine authorized distributions agreed to the Mint's restrictions and participated in the program. When the authorized distributors began selling the coins, prices were less than $900. Some collectors claimed that one or more of the firms violated the terms of the agreement by selling the coins to other dealers rather than to the public; Mint officials said they were aware of the complaints and were monitoring the situation, but took no public action.

On March 9, 2011, Mint officials announced that mintages for the 2011 bullion coins would "substantially higher" than for the 2010 issues, and that as a result, all of the 2010 restrictions on sales would be lifted. First though, any participating authorized purchaser had to certify that it had sold all of the 2010 coins it had acquired through the program in compliance with the earlier restrictions.

As for the circulating versions of the America the Beautiful quarter dollars, some collectors are having trouble finding them in circulation. While the originator of the legislation, Rep. Castle, and other supporters had hoped that the America the Beautiful quarter dollar program would be as successful in generating profits and attracting collector interest as the State quarters series, early evidence suggests several serious impediments may deny that level of success.

The most important impediment, probably, is the much smaller mintages for the America the Beautiful quarter dollars when compared to the State quarter mintages. The economic recession that began in December 2007 is resulting in much reduced demand for all denominations of coinage, including quarter dollars. The 2009 mintages for many U.S. coins, especially the 5-cent coin and dime, were at 40-year lows. Whereas mintages for the State quarter dollars totaled hundreds of million of pieces for each release, mintages for the 2009 District of Columbia and U.S. Territories coins were well below 100 million pieces for each release. Mintages for the 2010 America the Beautiful quarter dollars ranged from a low of 68.4 million to a high of 70.2 million coins. With Federal Reserve inventories of quarter dollars high, any orders for the coins from the Fed and resulting mintages seem unlikely to rise in the near future. Rep. Castle, during a House subcommittee hearing on July 20, 2010, expressed surprise and disappointment when told by Mint and Federal Reserve officials present at the hearing that orders for the coins were well below the levels for the State quarters series.

The reduced number of coins, as might be expected, makes it harder for individuals to find the coins in circulation. Many people are having trouble finding the coins in circulation for another reason. Federal Reserve officials are not permitting banks to order examples of each new America the Beautiful quarter dollar as it is released, unlike the Fed's policy during the State quarters program. Orders for quarter dollars are filled with whatever coins are in inventory. Individuals who during the State quarters program could go to their local bank every few months and obtain rolls of the newest coin can no longer do so in most regions of the country.

When the last edition of the *Coin World Almanac* was published in 2000, the State quarter dollars program was in its second year only and none of the other programs addressed here were even being discussed seriously. The 11 years that have passed since 2000 have witnessed an explosion of circulating commemorative coins, with new designs now scheduled through the early part of the third decade of this century. Whether any of the programs in effect in 2011 will be as popular as that first series remains unanswered.

America the Beautiful quarter dollar sites

Year	Jurisdiction	Site	Date Formed
2010	Arkansas	Hot Springs National Park	4/20/1832
	Wyoming	Yellowstone National Park	3/1/1872
	California	Yosemite National Park	10/1/1890
	Arizona	Grand Canyon National Park	2/20/1893
	Oregon	Mount Hood National Forest	9/28/1893
2011	Pennsylvania	Gettysburg National Military Park	2/11/1895
	Montana	Glacier National Park	2/22/1897
	Washington	Olympic National Park	2/22/1897
	Mississippi	Vicksburg National Military Park	2/21/1899
	Oklahoma	Chickasaw National Recreation Area	7/1/1902
2012	Puerto Rico	El Yunque National Forest	1/17/1903
	New Mexico	Chaco Culture National Historical Park	3/11/1907
	Maine	Acadia National Park	7/8/1916
	Hawaii	Hawai'i Volcanoes National Park	8/1/1916
	Alaska	Denali National Park	2/26/1917
2013	New Hampshire	White Mountain National Forest	5/16/1918
	Ohio	Perry's Victory and International Peace Memorial	3/3/1919
	Nevada	Great Basin National Park	1/24/1922
	Maryland	Fort McHenry National Monument and Historic Shrine	3/3/1925
	South Dakota	Mount Rushmore National Memorial	3/3/1925
2014	Tennessee	Great Smoky Mountains National Park	5/22/1926
	Virginia	Shenandoah National Park	5/22/1926
	Utah	Arches National Park	4/12/1929
	Colorado	Great Sand Dunes National Park	3/17/1932
	Florida	Everglades National Park	5/30/1934
2015	Nebraska	Homestead National Monument of America	3/19/1936
	Louisiana	Kisatchie National Forest	6/3/1936
	North Carolina	Blue Ridge Parkway	6/30/1936
	Delaware	Bombay Hook National Wildlife Refuge	6/22/1937
	New York	Saratoga National Historical Park	6/1/1938
2016	Illinois	Shawnee National Forest	9/6/1939
	Kentucky	Cumberland Gap National Historical Park	6/11/1940

Year	Jurisdiction	Site	Date Formed
2016	West Virginia	Harpers Ferry National Historical Park	6/30/1944
	North Dakota	Theodore Roosevelt National Park	2/25/1946
	South Carolina	Fort Moultrie (Fort Sumter National Monument)	4/28/1948
2017	Iowa	Effigy Mounds National Monument	10/25/1949
	District of Columbia	Frederick Douglass National Historic Site	9/5/1962
	Missouri	Ozark National Scenic Riverways	8/27/1964
	New Jersey	Ellis Island National Monument (Statue of Liberty)	5/11/1965
	Indiana	George Rogers Clark National Historical Park	7/23/1966
2018	Michigan	Pictured Rocks National Lakeshore	10/15/1966
	Wisconsin	Apostle Islands National Lakeshore	9/26/1970
	Minnesota	Voyageurs National Park	1/8/1971
	Georgia	Cumberland Island National Seashore	10/23/1972
	Rhode Island	Block Island National Wildlife Refuge	4/12/1973
2019	Massachusetts	Lowell National Historical Park	6/5/1978
	Northern Mariana Islands	American Memorial Park	8/18/1978
	Guam	War in the Pacific National Historical Park	8/18/1978
	Texas	San Antonio Missions National Historical Park	11/10/1978
	Idaho	Frank Church River of No Return Wilderness	7/23/1980
2020	American Samoa	National Park of American Samoa	10/31/1988
	Connecticut	Weir Farm National Historic Site	10/31/1990
	U.S. Virgin Islands	Salt River Bay National Historical Park and Ecological Preserve	2/24/1992
	Vermont	Marsh-Billings-Rockefeller National Historical Park	8/26/1992
	Kansas	Tallgrass Prairie National Preserve	11/12/1996
2021	Alabama	Tuskegee Airmen National Historic Site	11/6/1998

11 Errors

Error coins and paper money

Most collectors and noncollectors who check the coins or notes in their change eventually will encounter pieces that look different, for lack of a better term. The coins may be missing details like a Mint mark or part of an inscription. On other coins, some design elements may be blurry or even appear doubled. Other coins may be in a different color than normal, thinner than usual or otherwise deviate from the norm in appearance or physical standards. Notes may bear an extra inked impression, sometimes in mirror form (reading backwards) and sometimes reading normally. The overprinted seals and serial numbers may be mispositioned or even upside down or printed on the back of the note rather than on the note's face.

Individuals finding such odd coins may have found error coins or die varieties, or coins from a later die state or coins representing a die stage. Alternatively, they might have encountered coins that have been damaged or have otherwise changed while in circulation, or that were deliberately altered. Similarly, people finding unusual notes may have found an error note.

This chapter delves into error coins and notes and related items. Coins are discussed first, with notes discussed later. The discussion of coins includes a review of die states and die stages.

Coins

An error or variety coin deviates from the norm as a result of a mishap in the minting processes; in effect, it represents a substandard product of the agency that produced it. Some collectors, however, instead of rejecting these substandard coins, prefer these items over normal coins.

An *error coin* is one that deviates from the norm because of an accident, mistake or mishap at any stage of the minting processes.

A *die variety* represents a coin produced by a die that differs—from the moment of the die's production—from all other dies for the same denomination, design type or subtype, date and Mint mark. The definitions for specific kinds of die varieties that follow should make this concept easier to understand. Among the 20th century coins considered "varieties" are such coins as the 1955, 1972 and 1995 Lincoln, Doubled Die Obverse cents. Die varieties are encountered less frequently in the 21st century because of modernization of die production processes.

While some classify die varieties as errors, not all die varieties were produced by mistake. The scarcity of die steel in the late 18th century and early 19th century led Mint officials to practices their 21st century counterparts would reject. For example, a die with one date (1798) might be repunched with another date (1800); (1800/798 Draped Bust cents actually exist!). Such coins are a form of die variety called "overdates," and while it is possible that some overdates occurred by mistake, most of the early overdated dies likely were created deliberately.

Deliberate die varieties were produced as recently as 55 years ago. With the temporary closing of the San Francisco Mint beginning in 1955, reverse dies stamped with the San Francisco Mint's S Mint mark purposely were restamped with the D Mint mark of the Denver Mint after the California facility was closed. The dies with the over Mint marks were placed into use at the Denver Mint and used to strike a series of 1955-D/S Jefferson 5-cent coins.

A *die state* simply represents a specific period within a die's use, marked by the presence or absence of wear or abrasion on the die. Dies wear as they strike coins; the wear will appear on the coins they strike.

A *die stage* represents a period within a die's life marked by something other than wear or abrasion. Many examples are detailed in the listings that follow.

Although it sometimes may seem that the Mint produces inordinate amounts of error coins, the number of errors produced is relatively small compared to the total number of pieces released. Those small numbers in part account for the values collectors place on error numismatic material. The Mint constantly tries to improve quality and therefore reduce the number of errors.

The Mint uses precise planchet delivery systems and automated quality checkers on its presses, which reduces the potential number of striking errors.

Die varieties have been virtually eliminated since

the 1990s. Mint marks now exist as a design element of the original model rather than being added by hand to each working die, eliminating an entire class of error-variety forever (halting the production of repunched Mint mark varieties and any variability of Mint mark placement). Also, the Mint introduced new single-impression hubbing presses that transfer the design of a working hub to a working die in one impression. While doubled die varieties continue to be produced under this new method of die production, the degree of doubling is minor and pales in comparison to the doubling on classic doubled die varieties.

Of course, values for error and variety coins depend on the same factors affecting normal numismatic merchandise: supply, demand and condition. Obviously, errors and varieties are in very short supply when compared to total mintages. However, error and variety collectors represent a fraction of the total number of collectors, which can keep prices down for some items.

Rare does not necessarily mean great value. Many error and variety coins, struck in small quantities, are available for a few dollars. Even errors that are considered unique are often available for only several dollars. Unfortunately, many persons not familiar with errors, including some dealers, place unrealistically high values on common error coins.

Some pieces, however, sustain high values. Some varieties, such as the 1955 Lincoln, Doubled Die Obverse cent and the 1972 Lincoln, Doubled Die Obverse cents, "cross over" and become popular with general collectors because of publicity and dealer promotion. Because demand is higher for a fixed supply, values are correspondingly higher for those coins. Extraordinary planchet errors (1943 Lincoln cents struck on copper-alloy planchets, for example), die errors (the double-denomination mules) and striking errors (off-center silver dollars and gold $20 double eagles) can bring extraordinary prices as well.

Error coins can be found in circulation, unlike many other collectors' items. Some collectors go to banks and obtain large quantities of coins to search through; coins not bearing errors are returned to the bank. Many errors or varieties, particularly of the minor classification, can be discovered simply by going through pocket change.

Error and variety coins

The minting of a coin is a manufacturing process, and should be fully understood by anyone interested in collecting and studying error coins. Many forms of alteration and damage received outside the Mint resemble certain types of errors, but none precisely duplicates a genuine Mint error. Collectors who understand the minting process should be better able to distinguish between errors and damage or alteration than collectors who have never studied the manufacturing process.

The causes of error coins is discussed in the section that follows. The section is split into four parts—planchet errors, die errors, striking errors and edge errors—followed by definitions of several common forms of alteration and damage.

Planchet errors are the result of defective or improper planchets. Die errors are produced due to a mishap involving the die or hub, in the production of the die, its installation in a coining press or its maintenance during use. Striking errors are created during the moment the planchet becomes a coin—the strike. Edge errors—a category not part of this chapter in the last edition of this *Almanac* when it was published in 2000—involve problems with the edge inscriptions on coins like Presidential and Native American dollars and America the Beautiful 5-ounce silver quarter dollar bullion coins.

Planchet errors

alloy errors: All U.S. coins are produced from alloyed metals, mixed when molten to strict specifications. If mixed incorrectly, the metals may cool in nonhomogeneous form, with streaks of different metals appearing on the surface of the coin.

brass-plated cent: A post-1982 error is the brass-plated cent. Zinc planchets are plated with copper to form a copper-plated zinc planchet. Zinc planchets sometimes remain within the plating tanks and dissolve, contaminating the plating solution (electrolyte), adding their zinc content to the copper, thus forming brass. Subsequent planchets are plated with brass instead of pure copper. When new, brass-plated cents are a different color than copper-plated cents, although both can tone and become difficult to distinguish.

broken, damaged planchets: Planchets are subject to various sorts of damage, including cracks (not to be confused with die cracks), holes and major breaks. Coins have been known to break into two or more pieces after striking due to major internal flaws (see laminations for a related form of planchet error).

bubbled plating: The copper plating on a copper-plated zinc cent can be marred by raised bubbles, caused by trapped gas between the cent's core and the copper plating. Some bubbles may "burst" to expose the gray zinc metal beneath the plating.

fragments, scrap struck: Small pieces of coinage metal—fragments and scrap left over from the blanking process—sometimes fall between the dies and are struck. Fragments must be struck on both sides and weigh less than 25 percent of a normal coin's weight to qualify as a struck fragment. Planchet scrap is generally larger than a fragment, and usually has straight or curved edges as a result of the blanking process.

improperly annealed planchets: Improperly annealed planchets occur when copper-nickel alloy planchets are annealed (heated) without a protective atmosphere or for a prolonged time, or both. The improper annealing results in a migration of copper and nickel to the surface of the planchets. Since the copper is the predominate metal in a copper-nickel alloy (75 percent copper to 25 percent nickel for planchets for 5-cent coins, for example), the diffusion of copper to the surface will be significantly greater than the diffusion of nickel, giving the coins a copper color where there should be none. Pieces subjected to this improper annealing feature a partial or complete coating of copper, sometimes darkened because of oxidation. When the process generates a distinct layer of copper on the coin's surface with a high degree of oxidation, the metal is brittle and can break off in places, according to Mint officials. This form of error was formerly called by the terms "sintered planchet" and "copper wash" before Mint officials confirmed how the migration of copper occurred.

incomplete planchet or clip: An incomplete planchet or clip results from a mishap in the blanking process. If the planchet strip does not advance far enough after a bank of punches rams through the sheet of metal, producing planchets, the punches come down and overlap the holes where the planchets were already punched out. Where the overlapping takes place, a curved area appears to be missing from the planchet. The word "clip," commonly used, suggests a piece of a full planchet was cut off, which is not the case. Clipping refers to the ancient process of cutting small pieces of metal from the edges of precious metals coins for the bullion. The word "clip," though, is widely accepted throughout the error hobby as another term for incomplete planchet.

Most incomplete planchet errors have an area of weakness known as the Blakesley effect. The area of the rim 180 degrees opposite the clip is weak or nonexistent since the rim-making process in the upset mill is negated by the clip. The lack of pressure in the upset mill at the area of the clip permits metal to flow away from the rim, which results in improper formation of the rim across from the clip.

incomplete punch: This occurs when the punches do not completely cut out a planchet, but leave the impression of a groove that looks like a circle. If the strip advances improperly, planchets that overlap the incomplete punch will bear the curved groove. The groove remains visible after the coin is struck.

laminations: During the preparation of the planchet strip, foreign materials—grease, dirt, oil, slag or gas—may become trapped just below the surface of the metal. Coins struck from this strip later may begin to flake and peel since adhesion is poor in the location of the trapped material. Jefferson 5-cent coins made during World War II are particularly susceptible to lamination, due to the metals used during the war metal emergency.

plating breaks: The copper plating on the Lincoln copper-plated zinc cents introduced in 1982 is thin. At times, the copper plating may be stretched to the breaking point during striking. These breaks are sometimes seen along the curve of a D Mint mark on a Denver Mint coin or along the tops or bottoms of letters adjacent to the rim. Any breaks in the copper can expose the zinc core to the elements; that generally results in corrosion at the breaks.

split planchets: Planchets can split due to deep internal laminations, or in the case of clad coinage, because of poor adhesion of the copper-nickel outer layers to the copper core. Planchets may split before or after striking. Those splitting before generally exhibit weak details due to lack of metal to fill the dies, while those split afterwards usually depict full detailing. On nonclad coins, the inner portion of the split shows parallel striations typical of the interior structure of coinage metal.

thick and thin planchets: Planchets of the wrong thickness are produced from strip that was not rolled properly. Too little pressure can result in planchet stock that is too thick; too much can result in a thin planchet. If the rollers are out of alignment on one side, a tapered planchet—one that is thicker on one side than the other—is created.

unplated planchets: Unplated planchets became possible in 1982 with the introduction of the copper-plated zinc cent. The zinc-copper alloy planchets are plated after they are punched from the strip, but some planchets miss the plating process. Coins struck on the unplated planchets are gray white in color. Beware of cents that have had their plating removed after leaving the Mint or that have been replated with zinc.

wrong metal, planchet, stock: A wrong metal error is a coin struck on a planchet intended for a different denomination of a different composition. This includes 5-cent pieces struck on cent planchets, cents struck on dime planchets, and higher denominations struck on cent and 5-cent planchets. Planchets generally must be of a size equal to or smaller than the intended planchet. A 5-cent planchet, for example, would not fit between the dies of the smaller cent. However, some Washington quarter dollars struck on slightly larger golden dollar planchets are known.

A wrong planchet error is a coin struck on a planchet of the correct composition, but the wrong denomination. These include quarter dollars struck on dime planchets, half dollars struck on quarter and dime planchets, and dollars struck on other clad planchets.

A wrong stock error occurs when clad coinage strip rolled to the thickness of one denomination is fed into the blanking press of another denomination; the diameter is correct, but the thickness is greater or less than normal. The most common appears to be quarter dollars struck on planchet stock intended for dimes.

A fourth, rarer form is the double denomination. It occurs when a coin is struck on a previously struck coin, such as a cent struck over a dime. Since the U.S. Mint has struck coins for foreign governments, it is possible to find in circulation U.S. coins struck on planchets intended for foreign coins, as well as coins struck on previously struck foreign coins.

Another rare type of wrong metal error is the transitional error. It occurs as the composition of a coin series changes. Some 1965 coins are known struck on silver planchets of 1964 composition, while some 1964 coins were struck on clad planchets (1964 coins were struck through 1965, with planchets for both types of coins available side by side). A 1999 Anthony dollar is known on a Sacagawea dollar planchet.

Die errors, varieties, states, stages

abrasion doubling: Dies that have been heavily abraded may appear to have doubled or overlapping letters or numerals, resulting from abrasion occurring inside the incused areas of the design. The "doubling" is commonly found between the letters of the inscriptions and numerals of the date. The "doubling" of the second 5 in the date on the "Poorman's Double Die" 1955 Lincoln cent is a result of abrasion doubling (it is not a doubled die). Regarded by many as a die stage, but also falls into the category of die state.

BIE: The term commonly used for minor errors affecting the letters of the word LIBERTY on Lincoln cents. A small break or chip in the die between the letters, especially BE, often resembles the letter I, hence the BIE designation. A form of die stage.

clashed dies: When during the striking process two dies come together without a planchet between them, the dies clash (come into direct contact). Depending on the force with which the dies come together and the designs, a portion of the obverse design is transferred to the reverse, and a portion of the reverse is transferred to the obverse. Coins struck from the clashed dies will show signs of the transferred designs (called clash marks). Although the cause of this type of error occurs during the striking process, the die is affected, so it is considered a die error. A form of die stage.

broken collar: The collar, the surrounding ring of steel that contains outward metal flow and forms the edge device, can break. Coins struck from a broken collar show a raised area on the edge, resulting from coinage metal flowing into the break in the collar during striking.

cuds: A cud is a type of major die break. It occurs when the die breaks at the rim and a piece of the die falls out of the press. The metal of coins struck from the damaged die flows up into the missing area, resulting in a raised blob of metal bearing no image. The side of the coin opposite the cud is weak and indistinct. This is because metal flows along the path of least resistance and will travel into the broken area and not the recesses of the other die. A retained cud occurs when the die breaks at the rim, but the piece does not fall out. Coins struck from these dies show the break, but also depict the image inside the break. To qualify as a cud, the break must be adjacent to the rim; die breaks separated from the rim are not cuds.

design mule: The result of dies for two different design types of the same denomination being used to strike a coin. The only known example on a U.S. coin is a 1959-D Lincoln cent struck with the 1958-style Wheat Heads reverse rather than the 1959-style Lincoln Memorial reverse. The Secret Service has not determined this coin to be counterfeit, although grading services have been reluctant to authenticate the coin and some die variety specialists are skeptical of its authenticity. A convicted and imprisoned counterfeiter-murderer claims to have made this piece, although he has offered no proof of his claims and many are skeptical of his claims. Design mules exist for the coins of other countries.

die breaks, chips, cracks, gouges, scratches: Damage to a die that creates a recess in its surface will become a raised area on a struck coin. A die break may or may not result in a portion of the die falling out (see cud). A die crack appears as a line of raised metal on the surface of the coin. A die chip occurs when a tiny bit of the die breaks away, and looks like a small raised lump on the surface of the coin. Die gouges and scratches generally occur when a foreign object such as a tool scores the surface of the die or the die was overpolished with a wire brush. All are die stages.

double-denomination mule: The result of dies for two different denominations being used to strike a coin. The only known double-denomination U.S. mules to escape the Mint were struck from a Washington quarter dollar obverse die and Sacagawea dollar reverse die, on a Sacagawea dollar planchet; from a 1995-D Lincoln cent obverse die and Roosevelt dime reverse die, on a cent planchet; from a 1995 Lincoln cent obverse die and Roosevelt dime reverse die, on a dime planchet; and from a 1999 cent obverse die and dime reverse die, on a cent planchet. They are similar in concept to the design mules (dissimilar dies being used to strike a coin). Authentic U.S. double-denomination mules are extremely expensive coins, bringing five-figure prices.

doubled dies: When multiple impressions of hub into die are required during the hubbing and die making process, a misalignment between hub and partially completed die can occur, resulting in overlapping, multiple images on the die for most classes of doubled dies. Die doubling appears as rounded, raised design elements, with furrows or valleys between the duplicated raised images. At the corners of the overlapping images, distinct "notches" appear on coins (at least, on most classes of doubled dies).

Specialists have identified eight classes of doubled dies. The classes are distinguished by the method in which the doubling was created: misalignment between hub and partially completed die along several axes; distortion to a hub or die that results in overlapping images; use of hubs of two different designs including differences in the size of dates or different dates; and more.

Doubled dies survived the switch from a double-hubbing process to a single-hubbing system, though under the new process the severity of the doubling is much less than on classic doubled dies of the past. Die doubling on single-squeeze hubbing presses is believed to occur when the hub and conical die blank are not perfectly aligned horizontally. If the hub is tilted slightly, for example, it can "snap" into its intended alignment after making its first contact with the die blank. The tilted hub can form a slight impression at the center of the die with the first contact before snapping into position, researchers believe. When the hub snaps into the proper position, it forms the stronger design element over the slightly out of position element formed during the first contact of hub and die.

engraving errors: Engraving errors were common on the dies of the 18th and 19th centuries, but are less common on modern dies. On the earlier dies, numerals and letters were often repunched to strengthen the design; punched in upside down or otherwise out of alignment; and sometimes, wrong letters or numbers were punched into the die. On more modern dies, engraving errors include the use of the wrong size Mint mark and Mint marks placed too close to design elements or too far from their intended locations. Other engraving errors, discussed in separate sections, include overdates and repunched and over Mint marks.

filled dies: The Mint is a factory and, like most metal-working factories, has its share of dirt, grease and other lubricants, and metal filings. Various combinations of these materials can form a sludge that can coat the surface of a die's face and fill the recessed areas of the die, preventing the metal of a coin planchet from flowing into the incused areas. The coating of sludge results in weak designs or missing design details. A filled die is one of the most common types of error coin and rarely brings a premium unless a major portion of the coin's design has been obstructed or the nature of the filled die is unusual.

intentional die abrasion: Mint employees use an abrasive on dies to extend the die's working life and to remove such things as clash marks, die scratches, dirt and grease. If the die is abraded too much, details may be erased, or small raised lines may appear on the coins. Most errors with intentional abrasion have

little value, but exceptions exist: the 1937-D Indian Head, Three-Legged Bison 5-cent coin, on which one of the bison's forelegs was mostly removed by an abrasive; and the 1922-D Lincoln, No D, Strong Reverse Die cent, with the D Mint mark erased from the die.

misplaced dates: A misplaced date is a relatively recently studied die variety. Researchers have discovered numerous coins with numbers from the date punched well away from the region of the die where the date was punched. For example, coins have been found with a number or numbers punched into the dentils along the rim or into a major design element. While theories abound, no one is sure whether this punching was accidental or deliberate. Premiums vary; refer to specialist books.

misplaced Mint marks: Until the 1990s, a Mint mark was punched into an individual working die, of which hundreds or thousands were produced and used to strike coins during the year. Since the placement of the Mint mark via a punch and mallet was done entirely by hand, the position of the mark could differ on each coin. While the diesinker aimed for a specific point on the die, sometimes the aim was off, occasionally so badly that the Mint mark touched another design element, like a numeral in the date on a Lincoln cent. Producing this class of die variety on a U.S. coin is no longer possible.

missing Mint marks: Some coins that should have Mint marks do not. While in most cases the cause of the missing Mint mark is a filled die (thus temporary, and worth very little), sometimes the Mint mark was not punched into the die, creating a die variety. A series of missing Mint mark errors occurred on coins placed into Proof sets, from 1968 to 1990; all carry substantial premiums. Another valuable example is the 1982 Roosevelt dime without Mint mark. The 1982 dime, too, carries a strong premium. New collectors should remember that many normal, older coins lack Mint marks, as do all Lincoln cents struck at the Philadelphia Mint.

overdates: When one or more numerals in the date are engraved, sunk or hubbed over a different numeral or numerals, both the original date and the second date can be seen. Examples include the 1799/8 Draped Bust cent, 1814/3 Capped Draped Bust gold $5 half eagle, the 1943/2-P Jefferson 5-cent coin and the 1942/1 Winged Liberty Head dime. Another overdate occurs when two dies with the same date, but of different varieties, are used. Prime examples of this are the 1960 Lincoln, Large Date Over Small Date cents. The hubbed overdates are also Class III doubled dies.

over Mint marks: A form of multiple Mint mark, but when punches of two different Mints are used. Examples include the 1944-D/S Lincoln cent and the 1938-D/S Jefferson 5-cent coin. Many examples probably were made deliberately when unused dies for one Mint were transferred to another Mint for use.

repunched Mint marks: For most of U.S. Mint history, Mint marks were punched into each individual working die by hand with mallet and punch. Several blows to the punch were needed to properly sink the Mint mark into the die. If the punch was not properly placed after the first blow, multiple images could result. Beginning in 1986 with collector coins and later with circulating coinage, the Mint added the Mint mark at the master die stage. Later, the Mint mark was added at the initial model stage. The changes to when the Mint mark is added to the design have completely eliminated Mint mark varieties.

rotated dies: Most U.S. coins have obverse and reverse sides oriented so each appears upright as the coin is turned on a horizontal axis. Alignment between the two is 180 degrees. Dies aligned at anything other than 180 degrees are considered rotated. Mint employees consider coins reflecting die rotation of 5 degrees or less to be within tolerance levels.

special die polishing errors: Dies intended for the production of Proof and other collector coins generally undergo special processing that when performed improperly can result in errors. Examples include a Proof 2007-S John Adams dollar with frosting that was supposed to precisely overlie the peripheral letters that is instead rotated slightly relative to those letters.

trails: Some coins possess tendrils or filaments, sometimes called "trails," extending from the edges of multiple design elements. Die trials are not fully understood by researchers. Some specialists consider the trails a form of doubled dies, but others consider the evidence for this theory weak. Another theory suggests a combination of thermal expansion and elastic recoil during the hubbing operation forms the tendrils. Yet another theory considers the trails a form of die deformation, possibly resulting from the contraction of the die metal as it cools in the aftermath of hubbing, producing creases in the die face that follow the grain of the metal crystallites.

worn dies: Dies have a set life, based on the hardness of the coinage metal being struck and the striking pressures involved. When a die wears beyond a certain point, details around the rim tend to flow into the rim, while other details weaken. The surface of the die becomes scarred, as though it was very heavily polished. Worn die errors rarely have collector value.

Striking errors

bonded planchets: If planchets are fed between a pair of dies and are struck but not ejected, a mass of coins may form, several pieces bonded to each other. Some examples have contained between 30 and 40 coins bonded into a single mass. Few such pieces escape the minting facilities. Those that do can bring high prices when sold.

broadstrikes: If the surrounding collar is pushed below the surface of the lower die during the moment of striking, the metal of the coin being struck is free to expand beyond the confines of the die. The design of the coin is normal at center, but as it nears the periphery, becomes distorted resulting from the uncontrolled spread of metal.

brockage and capped die strikes: If a newly struck coin sticks to the surface of one of the dies, it acts as a die itself—called a die cap—and produces images on succeeding coins. The image produced by any die is the direct opposite on a coin, and brockages are no different. Since the image is raised on the coin adhering to the die, the image on the brockage is incused and reversed—a true mirror image. The first brockage strikes, perfect mirror images and undistorted, are most prized. As additional coins are struck from the capped die, the die cap begins to spread and become thinner under the pressures of striking, distorting its image, with the transferred designs on newly struck coins becoming increasingly distorted as well.

At some point (after just a few strikes), as the die cap becomes more distorted, the coins struck cease to be brockages and become capped die strikes. While a brockage image is undistorted or relatively so, images on capped die strikes are increasingly malformed. Although the image is still recognizable, the design expands, producing an image that can be several times the actual size of a normal image. Finally, the die cap breaks off or is pounded so thin it ceases to affect succeeding strikes.

Sometimes, the die caps fall off early and in a relatively undistorted state. Die caps resemble bottle caps, with the metal wrapping around the surface of the die. Die caps are very rare and collectible, much more so than capped die strikes.

chain strikes: When two planchets are struck side-by-side with the same die pair, a chain strike pair is formed. The two coins will form a tight junction at the point of contact, which occurs between the dies.

double, multiple strikes: A double strike can occur when a coin is struck more than once after failing to be ejected following the initial strike. If the coin rotates slightly between strikes, but remains inside the collar, two images will appear on both sides of the coin. The first strike will be almost totally obliterated by the second strike, and the first strike will be flattened and have almost no relief. Sometimes, a struck coin will flip and fall upside down onto the surface of the die; thus, the second strike has an obverse image obliterating the original reverse, and a reverse image flattening the first obverse image.

If the coin falls partially outside the dies after the first strike, the second image is only partial. The partial second strike obliterates the original image beneath it, but the rest of the first strike is undistorted, except in the immediate vicinity of the second strike.

indented errors: An indented error is a coin struck with another coin or planchet lying partially on its surface. The area covered by the planchet does not come into contact with the die, and thus is blank if indented by a planchet, or shows a partial brockage if indented by a struck coin. The most desirable of the indented errors are larger coins with the indentation of a smaller planchet centered on one side.

machine, mechanical, strike doubling: A form of doubling occurring as a result of light secondary contact between a newly-struck coin and the die, but not the result of a double strike (i.e., a second complete cycle of the coining press). The most commonly accepted cause is a certain looseness of the die assembly or other parts in the press. Specialists recognize two types of machine doubling: push doubling and slide doubling.

Push doubling results when the die bounces following impact, shifts to the side and lands lightly on the just-struck coin. Push doubling leaves flat, marginal shelving along the edge of the design element and rounded doubling on interior design elements. Slide doubling occurs when the die shifts laterally without a bounce. The die drags itself through the newly formed design elements, smearing them. Some coins show a combination of push and slide doubling. Certain coins bear machine doubled elements that defy easy explanation.

Some authorities do not consider machine doubling an error, but believe it to be a form of Mint-caused damage since it occurs immediately after the strike. Other authorities disagree with that position. Minor examples do not carry a premium, though extreme examples are attractive and worth premiums.

off-center coins: If a planchet lies partially outside of the dies during the striking, it receives an off-center strike. Each coin struck off center is unique but, because large numbers are available, can be very inexpensive in the lower denominations. Off-center coins with dates are more valuable than coins without dates. Generally, on dated coins, the greater the off-center strike, the more it is worth. Some collectors collect off-center coins by their "clock" positions. Hold the coin with portrait upright and look for the direction the strike lies. If it is at 90 degrees, the strike is at 3 o'clock; if it lies at 270 degrees, the strike is at 9 o'clock.

partial collar: Often known as "railroad rim" errors, the edge, not the rim, is the portion of the coin affected. It occurs when the collar is pushed somewhat below the surface of the lower die, so that one portion of the coin is free to expand beyond the confines of the collar, while the other portion is restrained. On coins struck from a reeded collar, partial reeding exists on the area restrained by the collar. The error gets the nickname railroad rim from its appearance—the coin, viewed edge-on, resembles the wheel from a railroad car.

saddle strike: A saddle strike may resemble a double strike, but is the result of having a planchet fall partially between two pairs of dies on a multi-die press. Saddle strikes have two partial images and an expanse of unstruck planchet between the struck areas.

struck-through errors: Filled-die errors and indented coins are both forms of struck-through errors, which occur when foreign objects or substances fall between die and planchet during striking. In addition to the grease of a filled-die error and the planchet of an indented error, pieces of cloth, metal fragments, wire, slivers of reeding, wire bristles (from wire brushes used to clean dies, resembling staples), die covers and other objects. Sometimes, an incused letter or number of a die will fill up with grease, which solidifies under constant pressure. If the blob of grease—shaped like a letter or number—drops out of the die, it may be struck into the surface of the coin, leaving the impression of the affected letter or number. A particularly collectible form of struck-through errors is one with the foreign object still embedded into the surface of the coin.

uniface errors: If two planchets fall between the same dies at the same time, one side of each will be prevented from coming into contact with the dies. One side of each will have a normal image, while the other side—facing the other planchet—will be blank. Uniface errors can also occur on indented coins.

weak strikes: Weak strikes often resemble coins struck from grease-filled dies, but can be distinguished. They occur either when the press has been turned off—it tends to cycle through several strikings, each with less pressure than the previous—or when the press is being set up by the operators who test the placement of the dies at lower coining pressures. On reeded coins, weak strikes generally have poorly formed reeding (it is strong on filled dies). Depending on the pressure used, the image may be only slightly weak, or practically non-existent, or any stage in between.

Edge errors

Beginning in 2007, a third form of edge device was reintroduced on circulating U.S. coinage, the inscribed edge, to join the more familiar plain and reeded edges. Inscribed edge devices were used on several denominations of late 18th and early 19th century coins, the last being the 1836 Capped Bust, Lettered Edge half dollar. The gold $10 eagles and $20 doubled eagles of 1907 to 1933 had character-based edge devices: 48 raised stars on the eagle's edge and the motto E PLURIBUS UNUM with the words divided by stars on the double eagle. After 1933, all U.S. coins struck for circulation had either a plain edge or a reeded edge. That changed when the Presidential dollars were released into circulation starting in 2007 and Native American dollars in 2009.

For Presidential and Native American dollars, the edge inscription reads correctly when facing the obverse on some pieces, while on others, the edge inscription reads correctly when facing the reverse. Some finders wonder whether one type of edge device is an error. In reality, neither is an error. The edge devices on the circulating Presidential dollars and Native American dollars are applied after the obverse and reverse are struck; the coins are struck with a plain collar. The coins are then transported to a separate piece of equipment that applies the edge inscription. The struck coins are fed into the edge-inscribing equipment randomly, so the inscription can face either the obverse or the reverse. In addition, the edge inscription's starting point in relation to obverse and reverse design elements is also random.

However, edge errors and varieties have occurred. Not long after the first 2007 George Washington Presidential dollars were released into circulation in February 2007, collectors, dealers and the general public began reporting numerous edge errors. The motto IN GOD WE TRUST, date, Mint mark and motto E PLURIBUS UNUM appear on the edges of the 2007 to 2008 Presidential dollars, or should (the motto IN GOD WE TRUST was moved to the obverse of the Presidential dollars starting in 2009).

Some Washington dollar coins and later pieces lack the edge lettering. Tens of thousands of Washington dollars from the Philadelphia Mint and smaller numbers from the Denver Mint and of later designs from both Mints were struck and shipped to the counting and bagging stations without being fed into the edge-lettering equipment.

Numerous other edge errors/variations were discovered as well. One type involves multiplied edge inscriptions (apparently from a coin's being fed into the edge-lettering equipment more than once), with either partially or completely duplicated edge inscriptions found, some coins having the duplicate inscriptions in the opposite up and down orientation to each other. Another edge error involves improper spacing between individual elements of the inscription. Faint edge inscriptions are encountered.

Some pieces bear slightly raised stars, letters or numerals interspersed among the regular edge inscription elements or elsewhere on the coins. These are an interesting form of contact mark (a form of damage formerly called a bag mark). While typical contact marks are nothing more than gouges in a coin's surfaces resulting from contact with other coins, the contact marks formed by the elements of an inscribed edge can have distinct shapes. For example, if the point on a dollar coin's edge containing a star strikes another coin (obverse, reverse or edge), the incused star on the edge can form a raised star, just like a die would form a star.

An interesting error involving the edge occurred when a number of unstruck planchets were edge lettered but not struck between obverse and reverse dies. These pieces are blank on their faces but bear lettered edges; they were found in rolls of Washington dollars.

An entirely new form of edge error was discovered in early 2010. A collector found a 2009 Zachary Taylor Presidential dollar bearing a 2010-D Presidential dollar edge device. The coin was found in a roll of what should have been all 2010-D Millard Fillmore dollars, acquired through the U.S. Mint's Direct Ship Program. Apparently a 2009 Taylor dollar missed the edge inscribing step near the end of 2009 Presidential dollar production at the Denver Mint, was held somewhere in the dollar production line, and then became mixed in with the new Fillmore dollars being struck and given the 2010 edge inscription. When U.S. Mint officials learned of the error, they recalled all unsold Fillmore dollars struck at the Denver Mint to search them for similar errors. Just one piece has been found by a collector. Mint officials have not revealed whether other examples were discovered during their search of the recalled coins.

Another edge error type occurred when some Proof 2007-S Thomas Jefferson Presidential dollars were found with elements of the edge inscriptions out of sequence. Proof coins are struck with three-piece segmented collars that form the edge inscriptions at the time of striking. Mint workers created the Jefferson dollars with out-of-sequence inscriptions by installing the individual collar segments in the wrong order. On the error coins, the motto IN GOD WE TRUST on the edge is followed by the motto E PLURIBUS UNUM.

Altered and damaged coins

A coin is subjected to a variety of abuses once it leaves the safety of the U.S. Mint. It can receive unintentional damage during normal use that alters the appearance of the coin. Intentional alteration can change the appearance even more drastically, whether the coin was altered by someone just experimenting or by someone who deliberately planned to change the appearance of a coin to deceive a collector or buyer.

To the informed, damaged and altered coins do not resemble Mint errors. The minting process leaves definite signatures on the surfaces of a coin that cannot be duplicated inadvertently in circulation or in the workshop of the coin alterer. The uninformed, however, sometimes mistake damaged or altered coins for Mint errors.

Altered and damaged coins have no numismatic value. Some coins offered via eBay auctions and described as errors are nothing more than damaged coins, although the sellers may offer such pieces incorrectly described because of a lack of the specialized knowledge necessary for a complete understanding of errors and varieties rather than because of some baser motive.

A good place to begin to learn about the minting process is the section titled "How U.S. coins are made," in the U.S. Coins chapter of the *Coin World Almanac*. Several books about error coins are available from Amos Advantage (**www.amosadvantage.com**) or from coin dealers and bookstores. Most have sections about the production of U.S. coins, and how to distinguish between errors and altered or damaged coins. Joining an error coin club is a good idea as well (see the listing for the Combined Organizations of Numismatic Error Collectors of America in Chapter 21).

Education is important. The following descriptions are of damaged and altered coins most likely to cause confusion for a nonspecialist in error coins.

acid-treated coins: Coins that have been soaked in an acid solution or have had acid poured over them are thinner than unaltered coins. The thinness of the acid-treated coin depends on the strength of the acid and the duration of the treatment. Some will be so thin the edge will be sharp and knife-like. The acid-treated coin will still have visible design elements, though the designs will be somewhat weakened (the longer the treatment, the weaker the design). Coins that have had acid poured over them may exhibit channels where the acid flowed. If more acid flows over one area, it may be thinner than another area that had less contact with the acid.

added Mint mark: A coin with an added Mint mark is a form of alteration made deliberately to defraud a buyer. The most common form of added Mint mark is one that has been cut from a common coin and added to the Philadelphia version of a rarer coin. Close examination of this kind of added Mint mark will show a sharp line between the field and the Mint mark; metal flow lines found ascending from the field onto the Mint mark on an unaltered coin are generally not present on this form of alteration.

Another form of added Mint mark technique involves drilling a small hole from the edge of a coin to the point where the Mint mark would be found if the coin had one. A special tool with a small, Mint mark-shaped form is inserted into the hole. Pressure is applied to the Mint mark form from the inside, forcing the surface of the metal to raise in the shape of the Mint mark. Flow lines may be found on this type of alteration. To detect, examine the edge below the Mint mark carefully for any signs of damage left by drilling the hole.

A crude form of added Mint mark is formed by cutting the shape of the Mint mark directly into the surface of a coin. The knife marks are generally clear.

Few added Mint marks of this type escape identification.

glue: The application of a thin layer of transparent glue to the surface of a coin can cause a very deceptive appearance. The design is visible through the glue, and the hardened glue often resembles raised metal. Sometimes, the person altering the coin will press another coin into the wet glue, and let it dry. Once dry, the coins are pried apart and the glue remaining on one coin will have incused, mirror image details from the other coin. Most glues can be dissolved with clear acetone, an ingredient used in fingernail polish removers. The acetone can then be rinsed off of the coin. This may remove the glue.

hammered edge: Often, coins will be found with a diameter slightly smaller than normal and a high, thick rim. This is done by placing the coin on its edge and hammering away at it. On coins with reeded edges, the reeding is often beaten smooth.

knife cuts: Sometimes an individual will cut lines into the surface of a coin with a heavy blade such as a knife. A trench is formed with metal displaced from the trench rising up from the surface to form a raised line parallel to the trench. It not carefully examined, the raised line can be misinterpreted as a die crack.

lucky piece coin/encased coin: Most persons have seen lucky piece coins, generally cents, which are embedded in a surrounding aluminum holder that has advertising or other writing on it. Force is required to squeeze the coin into the hole in the middle of the holder. Generally, the edge is distorted and made somewhat concave; if removed from the holder, the odd appearance of the edge can fool the untrained eye. The legends on the holder are generally stamped into the metal at the same time that the coin is forced into the hole. If the stamping dies overlap the coin, some of the legend can be stamped onto the coin. Again, if removed from the holder, the raised lettering can appear to be an original portion of the design.

1943 copper cents: America's entry into World War II required sacrifice from all aspects of manufacturing, including the U.S. Mint. Copper was a critical war commodity; little could be spared for cent coinage. Extensive testing in 1942 resulted in a zinc-coated steel cent that was produced in 1943 only. Between 20 and 25 examples of copper-alloy 1943 cents are confirmed, struck on planchets remaining from 1942 coinage. Thousands of collectors believe they own one of the pieces; however, many thousands of steel cents were privately plated with copper as souvenirs. They can easily be distinguished from genuine 1943 copper cents by applying a magnet. A magnet will attract a steel cent but not a genuine copper cent. Lack of magnetic properties does not mean the coin is genuine, however.

Compare the 3 in the date of a genuine 1943 steel cent to the 3 on a suspected 1943 copper cent. If the tail of the 3 does not extend the same distance, the coin is probably an altered 1948 cent (the alterer cuts away the left half of the 8). Struck-counterfeit 1943 copper cents exist as well, so any coins passing all of the above tests should be sent to one of the several authentication services for professional evaluation.

sandwich coin: Two or more coins are placed in a stack and pressure is applied, squeezing the coins together. Design elements will transfer from one coin to the other, creating a false double-struck coin. Unlike a genuine double strike, however, the additional image will be incused and reversed. Most sandwich coins will be distorted as a result of the pressure applied by the vise. (The term "sandwich coin" was also used in the mid-1960s to describe the then new clad coinage.)

slanted digits: Certain coins, in particular the Lincoln cent, can be damaged by parts in an automatic coin wrapping machine in such a way that the date resembles an overdate error. Feed fingers in the wrapping machine scrape across the surface of the cent, shoving the metal in the last digit to one side. A slight image of the last digit remains, with the displaced metal sitting above. On some examples, the displaced metal may resemble the numeral 1 sitting over the ghost of another numeral.

Texas coins: Coins with diameters slightly greater than normal and with proportionally larger designs cannot be struck under the conditions in use at the U.S. Mint. Nicknamed a "Texas" coin (for large), the altered pieces are produced by placing the coin between two pieces of leather and striking them with a hammer. The leather somehow causes the entire design to expand—not just the diameter. Some distortion is usually present, though it may be slight.

wood-blocked coin: Coins that have strongly flattened features, plus peripheral lettering and numbers that extend into a flattened rim, have probably been placed between two blocks of wood and struck with a hammer.

Paper money errors

The production processes necessary to produce U.S. paper money are, like the minting sequence, subject to various forms of failure that can lead to error notes. Similarities do not end there. An understanding of the paper money production processes is essential for any serious collector of paper money errors since many notes can mimic errors. The ink on U.S. paper money can be altered after the notes enter circulation, both accidentally and deliberately; some forms of alteration may resemble errors. Other forms of alteration are possible, too.

The causes of paper money errors are discussed in the next section, followed by a discussion of the most commonly seen forms of altered and damaged notes.

The error note section is presented in three sections: first and second printing errors, overprinting errors, and fold and cutting errors.

The basic production sequence is the first, or back printing, followed by the second, or face printing (depending on the generation of note, multiple printing steps may be required on each side). Initial trimming and cutting is next, followed by the application of the overprinting and additional trimming steps.

First and second printing errors

blanket impression (offset printing): Called blanket impression by BEP personnel (hobbyists used to call these notes "offset errors"), this is probably the most common type of printing error. A blanket impression is a mirror-image ink impression on the wrong side of a note; a reversed image of the face design could appear on the back, or a reversed image of the back design could appear on the face. Although it may appear that the wayward ink has bled through the paper, that does not occur. Blanket impressions occur during one of the printing processes. Sheets of currency paper pass between two huge rotating cylinders, one containing inked printing plates (plate cylinder) and the second (the blanket or impression cylinder) having a flexible surface (or blanket) that impresses the paper into the ink-filled intaglio lines of the plates. If the intervening paper is torn or folded, a portion of the inked printing plates may come into direct contact with the impression cylinder. The impression cylinder picks up ink from the plate cylinder and deposits it on the next dozen or so sheets, on the side opposite the side being printed. The image is reversed because the ink

on the surface of the impression cylinder is normally oriented (the printing plates have a mirror image). Blanket impressions may affect an entire side or just a small portion of the design. Overprinting blanket impressions are known, but are much rarer than first and second printing blanket impressions. The cause is the same. The use of the term blanket impression is technically more accurate than offset printing.

board breaks: A board break occurs when a depression is created in the surface of an impression cylinder that is partially broken. Because the impression cylinder is subject to a great amount of pressure, areas of the cylinder may break and fall away. The paper opposite the depression is not forced into the ink-filled intaglio lines of the printing plate, and therefore a white, unprinted area appears on an otherwise normal note. Board breaks generally affect small areas, though larger breaks are known. The shape of a break is irregular and even jagged and can be found on numerous consecutive notes.

double denominations: Considered the ultimate in error notes, a double-denomination note has face and back printings for two different denominations, like a $5 face opposite a $10 back. The back printing, since it is first, is the correct denomination. The error occurs when a uniface sheet is fed into the wrong press for its face printing, picking up a denomination different from what is on the back. All such notes are rare, are very collectible and sell for high prices.

engraving errors: The Bureau of Engraving and Printing has a virtually spotless record involving engraving errors on U.S. paper money. Two examples stand out: Series 1981A and Series 1985 $1 Federal Reserve notes were printed with back check number 129 engraved below and to the left of the O in ONE rather than below and to the right of the E in ONE. Series 1995 $1 FRNs were printed at the Fort Worth, Texas, BEP facility bearing a smaller-than-normal back check number 295; normally, the back check number on Fort Worth notes is larger than those used on notes printed at the Washington, D.C., facility (in order to qualify as this error, the series designation must be 1995, the note must bear the FW facility mark on the face and the back check number must be 295).

incomplete printing: Any portion or all of the back or face printings may be missing from a note. If two sheets ride through a press stuck together, one sheet does not come into contact with the printing plates. This can occur during the second printing step, which means the note will have a back printing (done first), but no face printing; or, can occur during the back printing, which means the note will have no back image, but will have a face printing. Those with no face printing are visually more spectacular, since the black and green overprinting is applied over a white, blank face. Improperly or incompletely inked plates can also cause an incomplete printing, with usually only a portion of the design missing. Folded or torn sheets or scrap paper falling between a portion of the sheet and the printing plate can also cause partial or complete failure to print note surfaces. If an uninked plate comes in contact with the paper, an impression of the uninked design can be seen.

ink smears (sly wipes): Called sly wipes by BEP personnel, ink smears occur when the surface of the inked printing plate is not properly wiped before printing to remove excess ink from the surface of the plate. Older presses were wiped by an automatically-fed roll of coarse paper, while more modern presses use a "water-wipe" system that sprays a solution of water and caustic soda over the plate to wash away excess ink. On the note, an ink smear is just that—a smear of ink, black (on the face) or green (on the back), obscuring a portion of the design of the note. The smear occurs at the same instant the note is printed, and is not applied afterward. Beware of ink applied to the surface of a note after it reaches circulation. The value of each error note is directly related to the size of the smear.

inverted printings: Occurs when a sheet with a back printing is rotated 180 degrees and fed into a press for the second printing. The face is upside down in relation to the back. Often incorrectly called an "inverted reverse," "inverted face" is the technically correct term.

multiple printings: Multiple printing errors can occur if a sheet of currency paper is inadvertently fed through an intaglio printing press more than once. The entire image may be doubled or can be extremely blurred. A multiple printing error can also occur if the press stops in the middle of a printing pass and the partially printed sheet is deliberately fed into a press again to restart it. In this case the note may have one complete printing and a partial second printing. A rarer form is for the second image to be upside down relative to the first image. Both face and back can have a doubled printing. Plate check numbers are rarely the same.

off-register printing: Occurs when a currency sheet is fed into the press improperly aligned for one pass. The ink is deposited out of register relative to the printing on the opposite side. Later, during cutting that separates individual notes, the cuts may be made through the unaligned image, so that one side of the note looks off-center. Notes with the face off-register generally have the overprinting in the correct location for the note, but not in relation to the face image.

printed through foreign matter: Foreign matter, generally a scrap of paper, can stick to the surface of the finished note thus causing an incomplete printing. The note may appear normal to a casual viewer, but the shape of the scrap material should be visible. If the scrap is gently lifted, an unprinted area the same size and shape as the foreign matter will appear on the note. Notes with the foreign matter remaining attached are more collectible than notes where the scrap is missing, leaving only the incomplete printing. However, they are rarely encountered in circulation.

transposed currency stock: This is a fairly recent addition to the types of paper money errors encountered today. Beginning with the Series 1990 $100 FRN, a polymer thread was added to the currency paper before printing. The security thread bears repeating numerals, representing the denomination and the initials USA. Beginning with the Series 1996 $100 FRNs a watermark matching the portrait was added. These two additions require the paper be inserted into the press correctly. Sheets of currency paper are notched to indicate the denomination and insertion direction. If the stack of sheets is incorrectly marked or the notch is missing or incorrectly "read" the design will be in the wrong position regarding the security strip and watermark. Two types of errors can result: If the paper is flipped from one side to the other before the initial insertion in the press or if the paper is rotated from bottom to top. Both errors are hard to detect until the note is held up to a light source.

Overprinting errors

double overprints: These occur much in the same way that a doubled first and second printing error occurs. The half sheet of currency paper is fed through the Currency Overprinting and Processing Equipment twice, picking up one complete overprint and a second partial or complete overprint.

inverted overprints: When a half sheet of currency paper is rotated 180 degrees before being fed into the COPE press, the overprint is applied upside down on the face. A major epidemic of inverted overprints occurred in 1976 and 1977, resulting in hundreds of such notes being released. So many were released that it was possible to collect a complete, 12-note Federal Reserve District set of $1 inverts of the same series date.

misaligned overprint: Half sheets must be properly aligned for the overprinting to be perfectly located. If a half sheet is fed into the COPE press off center, the overprint will be misaligned in one or more directions. A small degree of latitude is permitted before a misaligned overprint error becomes collectible; generally, the overprint needs to be touching a portion of the second printing design to carry a premium. Do not confuse these with off-register notes, which appear similar but are the result of an error during the first or second printing steps.

mismatched serial numbers, letters: Several mishaps can cause the prefix or suffix letters or numbers in the serial numbers on an individual note to be mismatched. The five digits on the far right of the serial number wheels decrease automatically (serial numbers are printed from the highest number to the lowest), but the three digits at the left and the prefix and suffix letters must be changed manually. A digit in the automatically turning wheels can stick in one position, or the person resetting the manual numbers or letters, or the automatic numerals at the beginning of a press run, can make a mistake and set the wrong digit. Any number or letter can be mismatched, and a simple comparison of the left serial number and right serial number will reveal the mismatched digit.

missing and incomplete overprints: Missing and incomplete overprints may occur when scrap falls between the overprint wheels and the currency half sheet, or due to a fold or tear in the paper. Since the green overprint is applied before the black overprint (only seconds apart), one color can be normal and the other missing or incomplete. This can happen if the mishap occurs before the second overprinting step.

obstructed overprints: If a piece of foreign matter or paper obstructs the area of a note being overprinted, the note will not be printed in that area. Notes with the overprint on a piece of scrap that is still attached are more collectible than notes where the scrap has fallen off. A unique note of this type had the overprint printed through a Band-Aid brand bandage backing that remained attached to the note.

overprint on back: If a currency half sheet is turned over so the back faces the overprinting wheels, the overprint is applied on the back. Because the overprint is missing from the face, the blank areas of the face printing remain unprinted.

partially turned digit: If one of the digits in the serial number wheel fails to decrease properly, a partial digit may appear on the overprint. Sometimes, the digit sticks in the partially turned position and a series of notes is overprinted with the partial digit.

same serial numbers: If all the digits in a serial number wheel fail to decrease, a series of notes bearing the same serial number may be printed. To be collectible, at least two notes with the identical serial numbers must be saved. The notes must be from the same series date, have identical prefix and suffix letters, and must be the same denomination.

wrong stock note: If a sheet of currency of one denomination with both first and second printings is mixed in with sheets of another denomination, the overprint for the wrong denomination is applied to the wayward sheet. Since the location of the overprint differs for each denomination, it may appear to be misaligned on the note. These notes are collectible only if the immediately preceding and succeeding notes of the different denomination are saved. Otherwise, the error note is visually indistinguishable from a misaligned overprint note in appearance.

Fold and cutting errors

Fold and cutting errors cannot be categorized as neatly as the two other major types of paper money errors, since each fold and cutting error is unique. The large sheets of paper used to print U.S. paper money notes are prone to folding at any time during the production process: first printing, second printing, trimming or overprinting.

Small folds extending vertically from note edge to edge are called gutter folds. They can affect the back, face or both sides, depending on when the fold took place. Folds at the corners can obscure a portion of the design of either side or the overprint. When unfolded, a portion of one side may appear on the other side. Major folds can drastically alter the appearance of the note, leaving huge unprinted areas and areas where a portion of one side is printed over the other side, or where a portion of the overprint is placed on the back.

If the fold remains closed during the several cutting and trimming stages, then extraneous paper may exist along one or several edges. Some fold and cutting errors are so large that when unfolded, a portion of another note above, below or beside the main note remains attached.

Values of fold and cutting errors depend on size of the folded area, complexity of the fold, appearance, and general numismatic factors, including supply and demand, and condition of the error note.

Altered and damaged notes

Paper and ink are much more fragile media than the coinage alloys found in pocket change today and thus exhibit different types of damage. Notes are also subject to both accidental and deliberate alteration, the latter to either deceive a collector or cashier, or as a lark.

Education about the production processes necessary to make paper money is as important to the paper money collector as knowledge about minting techniques is to the coin collector. Several general books are available about paper money that cover paper money production processes.

The following descriptions are of that left the BEP in perfect condition but were later altered and damaged by someone unknown person or persons. Some were altered deliberately and are intended by their alterers to deceive other individuals. Other notes bear random damage or changes that could lead some finders to misinterpret the damage as a type of error or experimental printing.

added ink smears: Smeared ink other than the black and two greens used on modern U.S. paper money was almost certainly added after the note left the BEP; some green and blacks could also have been added. No easy method distinguishes between an ink smear placed on the note at the BEP and one added afterward if no color difference is obvious. This is where experience and knowledge play a hand in distinguishing between an error note and one that was damaged or altered.

altered denomination: Persons altering the denomination of a note prey on the public's ignorance about whose portraits appear on paper money denominations, and the fact—shown by government studies—that a majority of persons never examine notes passing through their hands to determine whether they are authentic. The most common method of altering the denomination is to cut several corners bearing the denomination from several notes, and glue four corners to a note of a lower denomination. Some alterers cut the denominational legend from the bottom of a note and glue that in place over the lower denomination. This is not a numismatic type of alteration, but is used to deceive persons handling large quantities of money.

bank teller stamps: Tellers in banks and other persons who handle large sums of money often stamp the band surrounding a stack with an inked seal of some sort. The stamp often has a date or other numbers on it. If the stamp is placed over the edge of the band onto the top note, untrained persons may believe the ink appearing on the note is a part of the original printing. Banks also mark stacks of bills with ink, most often pink in color, which can bleed onto the notes.

erased ink: The ink used in printing U.S. paper money is erasable like any other ink on paper. Note

alterers can use a soft eraser to remove any portion of the face or back design, or the overprint. Erasers wielded skillfully can recreate missing overprints, board breaks, notes printed through scrap and related printing errors. However, use of an eraser generally damages the fibers of the paper beneath the erased ink. Close examination, particularly through a magnifying glass or microscope, may reveal the broken fibers.

political messages: Paper money is an excellent medium to spread political messages among the public. The most popular message seems to be a rubber stamp inked onto a note, reading "This note is not legal tender." This stamp is probably used by individuals who believe paper money unbacked by gold or silver is illegal, and who advocate a return to specie currency. Other political messages have been seen as well.

random stamps: Sometimes a Federal Reserve note is found in circulation with random stamps of flowers, symbols, initials or other markings. *Coin World* has received inquiries from callers who have found the notes and wonder if they were from an experimental printing. These stamps appear to be the work of individuals who lack other means of self-expression.

VIP photographs: Novelty notes with the photograph of a Hollywood celebrity, entertainer, politician or other "newsworthy" person pasted over the center vignette are sold by a number of firms. The BEP has never issued a note bearing a portrait of King Kong, or even Elvis Presley, but private companies have offered such altered notes.

water-wipe ink fading: The BEP began using water-wipe presses—using a caustic soda solution instead of dry paper to clean excess ink from the plates—in the early 1980s. To do so, the Bureau reformulated the ink to not break down under the solution. Later BEP officials found that after the notes circulated, the ink on the back faded very quickly, particularly if the note became wet. It was necessary to again reformulate the ink, and the problem appears to have been corrected.

"Where's George?" notes: In 1999 a Boston man, Hank Eskin, created a website to track the movements of Federal Reserve notes in commerce. The website, **www.wheresgeorge.com**, asks the question "Where's George?" as in the portrait of George Washington depicted on $1 FRNs, though any denomination can be tracked.

The basic premise of the website is to track the geographic path these notes take as they are used in commerce. Users register their first name and email address and then enter the denomination, series and serial number along with their current ZIP code. Users can also enter a short note about where they found the note and provide any other information they want.

Users are encouraged to write the website's URL on the edge of the note so those who come across the note will know where to look for information about the note's trek around the country. The site tracks the exact time and date notes are entered on the registry, the city and state, the travel time, the distance in miles and the average speed.

In 2001 Eskin launched a "Where's Willy?" website to track Canadian paper money—**www.whereswilly.com**.

The Willy in the website refers to Sir Wilfrid Laurier, the first French-Canadian prime minister, who served from 1896 to 1911. His portrait is on the $5 Canadian note. "Where's Willy?" website users register their first name and email address and then enter the denomination (from $5 to $100), series (from 1969 to the present) and serial number along with their current Canadian Postal code or U.S. ZIP code. Users can also enter a short note about where they found the note and provide any other information they want.

wrong-color backs: The green ink on the back of U.S. paper money is made of blue and yellow pigments. When exposed to an acidic atmosphere the yellow pigment is sometimes destroyed, leaving only the blue. When exposed to an alkali, such as the bleach in detergent when a note is washed, the blue pigment may be destroyed, leaving the yellow pigment. Blue back and yellow back notes deceive many noncollectors who have difficulty believing that one of the pigments can disappear and leave the design and paper unaffected. The back design remains the same, but is in either blue or yellow ink. An altered yellow back note should not be confused with non-altered gold certificates, which normally have a yellow-gold back.

12 A Numismatic Chronology

The purpose of this chronology is to present in a simple and easy-to-scan form the bare outlines of numismatic history, with greater emphasis on more recent events.

United States of America

BRITISH COLONIES

1652—Nominal date on "NE" (New England), Willow, Oak and Pine Tree coinage of Massachusetts.

1658—Proprietary coinage of Lord Baltimore issued for circulation in Maryland Colony.

1681—Mark Newby arrives in New Jersey with "St. Patrick" halfpence tokens, probably struck in Dublin in 1673. They become lawful money May 8, 1682.

1690—Dec. 10, Massachusetts Bay Colony issues paper currency to pay for military expenses.

1737 to 1739—Dr. Samuel Higley strikes coppers near Granby, Conn., with the legend I AM GOOD COPPER VALUE ME AS YOU PLEASE.

UNITED STATES

1775—May 10, United Colonies of America, in Congress at Philadelphia authorizes $3 million in Continental Currency.

1777—Feb. 20, Continental Congress tables resolution to establish a mint for the coining of gold, silver and copper.

1781 to 1786—Several resolutions considered to establish a mint. Oct. 16, 1786, Congress asked to remove legal tender status from all foreign copper and to limit the value of state copper.

1785—July 6, Continental Congress approves resolution, "Resolved, that the money unit of the United States of America be one dollar. Resolved, that the smallest coin be a copper, of which 200 shall pass for one dollar."

1787—Fugio cents struck by private contractor, first coins authorized by the United States.

1792—Act of Congress to establish Mint, April 2. Same act authorizes eagle, half eagle, quarter eagle, silver dollar, half dollar, quarter dollar, disme, half disme, cent, half cent. David Rittenhouse appointed director of the Mint. U.S. Mint building erected, first U.S. government structure. Half disme (silver 5-cent coin or half dime) is first coin struck under Constitution. First metal purchased by Mint for coinage purposes—6 pounds of copper.

1793—Cents and half cents struck for first time

for general circulation. Albion Cox appointed as first assayer. Joseph Wright named first Mint engraver, Henry Voigt first chief coiner.

1794—Silver dollars, half dollars and half dimes struck for circulation.

1795—Gold half eagles and eagles struck for first time. Mint placed under Department of Treasury control informally instead of Department of State. E PLURIBUS UNUM used on U.S. coins.

1796—Quarter eagles, quarter dollars and dimes struck for first time for circulation.

1804—First U.S. virgin gold received at Mint, valued at $11,000, from Cabarrus County, N.C.

1816—Steam engine installed at Philadelphia Mint.

1817—Proof coins struck at U.S. Mint.

1829—July 4, cornerstone laid for Mint at corner of Chestnut and Juniper streets, Philadelphia.

1835—Act of March 3 establishes Mints in New Orleans, La.; Dahlonega, Ga.; and Charlotte, N.C.

1836—Steam coinage presses introduced in U.S. Mint.

1837—Charlotte Mint opened, John H. Wheeler superintendent. Seated Liberty dimes and half dimes issued from Philadelphia Mint.

1838—Branch Mints open in New Orleans and Dahlonega. U.S. Mint establishes "Cabinet of Coins."

1848—Gold discovered in California; California gold deposited at Mint. Total of 1,389 special quarter eagles with CAL. stamp on reverse struck from some of the California gold.

1849—First gold dollars for circulation minted. Gold dollar and double eagle authorized by Act of Congress March 3. Pattern double eagle struck.

1850—Gold double eagle of this year first U.S. coin to bear initials of designer. First double eagles released for circulation.

1851—Silver 3-cent coin released; first coin with limited legal tender value. Authorized March 3.

1852—Act of Congress, July 3, establishes San Francisco Mint.

1853—Reduced weight silver coins issued. Gold $3 coin authorized Feb. 21. Act of Congress authorizes Assay Office in New York.

1854—First coins issued by San Francisco Mint. First gold $3 coins minted. Silver 3-cent coins, .900 fine, issued. New York Assay Office established at 30-32 Wall St.

1857—Foreign coins demonetized. First small cents issued as replacements for large cents; new cents bearing Longacre's Flying Eagle/Wreath designs.

1858—American Numismatic Society formed. Numismatic and Antiquarian Society of Philadelphia organized. Proof sets offered.

1859—Longacre's Indian Head cent introduced.

1861—Demand notes authorized July 17 and Aug. 5. Specie payments suspended Dec. 21.

1862—Government issues legal tender notes beginning March 10. Denver Mint established April 21; superintendent appointed; Mint serves as assay office until 1906, when coins first issued from new facility. Postage currency commences July 17.

1863—National bank notes authorized; gold certificates first authorized. Branch Mint authorized in Territory of Nevada March 3; Civil War would delay construction, opening of facility at Carson City. First deposit of gold at Denver Mint Sept. 24. Fractional currency authorized March 3. Large private outpouring of tokens to relieve coin shortage.

1864—Motto IN GOD WE TRUST appears on coins for first time, on the 2-cent coin (denomination authorized April 22). Cent first of that denomination to bear initial of designer. Bronze cents authorized; private tokens banned.

1865—Copper-nickel 3-cent coin authorized April 3.

1866—Motto IN GOD WE TRUST appears on regular silver coin for first time. Shield 5-cent coins (first copper-nickel 5-cent coins) struck May 16.

1867—Carson City Mint erected. Sandstone used from Nevada State Prison quarry. Cost: $300,000.

1869—Carson City Mint opens July 1.

1870—Carson City Mint issues coins. Act of Congress establishes Boise City, Idaho, assay office.

1873—Mint made a bureau of Treasury Department. E PLURIBUS UNUM and IN GOD WE TRUST prescribed for coinage by statute. Director of the Mint's office moved to Washington, D.C. James Pollock, formerly director of the Mint, becomes first superintendent of the Philadelphia Mint under the reorganization. Trade dollars issued, authorized Feb. 12. Standard silver dollar discontinued, bimetallism effectively ended.

1875—20-cent coins issued; authorized March 3. Resumption Act of Jan. 14 provides for immediate retirement of fractional currency with subsidiary silver and redemption of greenbacks on and after Jan. 1, 1879.

1878—Large-size silver certificates authorized Feb. 28.

1879—Specie payments resumed Jan. 1; greenbacks and gold at par.

1887—Trade dollar demonetized.

1888—*The Numismatist* first issued; Dr. George F. Heath editor.

1891—American Numismatic Association organized.

1892—First U.S. commemorative coin issued—World's Columbian Exposition half dollar.

1893—Queen Isabella is the first foreign sovereign to appear on U.S. coinage (on commemorative quarter dollar for World's Columbian Exposition).

1899—George Washington portrayed for first time on U.S. coin, on Lafayette dollar. Struck in December with date of 1900.

1900—June 1, enactment of legislation for the mintage of commemorative coins. Under Gold Standard Act of 1900, U.S. goes off bimetallism standard.

1903—First U.S. commemorative gold coins, Louisiana Purchase Exposition dollars, struck.

1906—First coins from Denver Mint struck.

1907—Saint-Gaudens eagles and double eagles first struck.

1908—First coins not of precious metal struck at a Mint other than the Philadelphia facility, the 1908-S Indian Head cent.

1909—First portrait of actual person, Lincoln, on coin for general circulation.

1912—American Numismatic Association chartered by Congress.

1913—Federal Reserve Act becomes law, authorizes issuance of Federal Reserve notes. Indian Head 5-cent coin minted.

1915—Panama-Pacific International Exposition coins first commemoratives to carry the mottoes IN GOD WE TRUST and E PLURIBUS UNUM.

1921—Review of coin and medal designs placed under jurisdiction of Commission of Fine Arts. Thomas E. Kilby portrayed on Alabama Centennial half dollar, first living person identified on a U.S. coin. Peace silver dollar designed by Anthony De Francisci struck in December.

1924—Julius Guttag starts National Coin Week.

1929—First small-size paper money issued.

1932—George Washington portrayed on U.S. coins (quarter dollars) of regular issue for first time.

1933—Act issued suspending the minting of gold coins; Treasury calls in circulating gold coins from banks and other large holdings. Last U.S. gold coins (eagle and double eagle) struck for circulation.

1936—Peak year for U.S. commemorative coinage programs: 34 coins issued for 21 different programs. Negative reaction would result in drastically fewer programs during the next few years, and a cessation of all programs from 1939 through 1945 and from 1955 to 1981.

1938—First large-scale design competition for Jefferson 5-cent coin.

1942—World War II alteration of 5-cent coin composition includes Mint mark P designating Philadelphia for first time.

1943—Zinc-coated steel cents issued during World War II. A few cents are struck on copper alloy planchets at all three Mints.

1946—Roosevelt dime issued.

1948—Franklin half dollar issued.

1955—IN GOD WE TRUST made mandatory on all U.S. coins and paper money. Transition to motto on paper money took until the 1960s to be complete as old plates were discarded and replaced with new plates bearing the motto.

1961—Office of Domestic Gold and Silver Operations created; Leland Howard first director.

1962—Tin removed from 1-cent coin.

1963—First $1 Federal Reserve notes issued.

1964—Date 1964 frozen on coinage. Kennedy half dollars struck.

1965—Coinage Act of 1965: copper-nickel clad composition for dimes and quarter dollars replaces silver; half dollar clad in reduced silver content alloy. Joint Commission on Coinage established. Proof and Mint set sales suspended, replaced by Special Mint Sets.

1966—Initials of Felix Schlag placed on Jefferson 5-cent coin.

1967—$2 United States note discontinued by Treasury.

1968—U.S. Proof coins resumed. Silver certificates cease to be redeemed for silver, General Services Administration begins selling silver on the market. Gold backing removed from paper money.

1969—New Philadelphia Mint dedicated. 1969 Kennedy half dollars become last silver U.S. coins struck for circulation.

1970—No half dollars struck for circulation; production limited to coins for Proof and Uncirculated Mint sets.

1971—Mint begins production of silverless Kennedy half dollars, at Denver Mint. First Eisenhower dollar struck March 31. Technicians install new Currency Overprinting and Processing Equipment at the Bureau of Engraving and Printing. First dollar devaluation.

1972—President approves transfer of Old San Francisco Mint building to Treasury for restoration as Mint working facility and museum. ANA Certification Service opens in Washington with Charles Hoskins as director.

1973—Second dollar devaluation. President Nixon signs bill providing for Bicentennial coinage, Oct. 31, with production to begin in 1975. Hobby Protection Act becomes law Dec. 12.

1974—First Proof Bicentennial 40 percent silver trial strikes produced at the Philadelphia Mint without Mint marks; possibly three sets made, one of which may have been destroyed and two remain unaccounted for. President Ford signs bill ending restrictions on U.S. citizens' ownership of gold, as of Dec. 31, 1974.

1975—First of the nation's Bicentennial coins roll off the presses in the Mints, both copper-nickel clad copper and 40 percent silver, Uncirculated and Proof.

1976—After extended hearings, reports and studies, the $2 note returns, first small-size Federal Reserve note version, bearing Trumbull's *Signing of the Declaration of Independence* on the back.

1977—Pre-Bicentennial designs resumed. Citizen-members barred from U.S. Assay Commission.

1979—First Anthony dollars issued for circulation.

1980—Mint accepts orders for American Arts Gold Medallions, first gold pieces struck by the Mint for the United States in almost half a century.

1981—Section 314-b of the Economic Recovery Act restricts use of collectibles in IRA and Keogh retirement plans. Anthony dollar production limited to collector sets, then ceases due to lack of public acceptance.

1982—Mint strikes silver commemorative half dollar marking the 250th anniversary of George Washington's birth, ushering in a second generation of commemorative coins. Copper-plated zinc cents introduced; last brass cents struck.

1983—U.S. Mint begins striking 1983 and 1984 Olympic commemorative coinage, using a W Mint mark on the 1984 gold eagle produced at West Point Bullion Depository. Discovery of 1982 Roosevelt, No P dime focuses widespread public attention on hobby.

1984—Mint releases 1984 Olympic $10 eagle, first U.S. gold coin struck since 1933. Public attention focuses on hobby as media reports discovery of 1983 Doubled Die cent. U.S. Mint resumes sales of Uncirculated Mint sets.

1985—President Reagan signs an executive order banning importation of South African Krugerrands effective Oct. 11. A pre-issue discount offering by the U.S. Mint in December results in complete sellout of 1986 Statue of Liberty gold half eagle $5 commemorative coins. U.S. Mint offers 1986 Ellis Island silver dollar and Immigrant copper-nickel half dollar at pre-issue discount prices. Silver and gold bullion coins authorized by separate legislation.

1986—American Eagle gold bullion coins issued in October, followed by release in November of American Eagle silver bullion dollar. Treasury officials approve incorporating new anti-counterfeiting devices into Federal Reserve notes in future. Fort Worth, Texas, selected as site of Bureau of Engraving and Printing's Western printing plant. Columbus America Discovery Group locates wreckage of SS *Central America,* which sank in the Atlantic Ocean in September 1857 carrying tons of gold bars and coins from California.

1987—U.S. Constitution Bicentennial commemorative coins produced.

1988—Olympic Games commemorative coin program marketed.

1989—Three United States Proof error coins to be offered at auction are seized after Mint technicians determined them to be illegally obtained error coins and thus U.S. Mint property. Congress Bicentennial commemorative coin program marketed. The Secret Service makes its largest seizure of counterfeit United States Federal Reserve notes produced on a color laser photocopier. Coinage production at the San Francisco Mint is halted for more than 24 hours following the Oct. 17 earthquake. Recovery of gold at SS *Central America* wreck site begins.

1990—Satellite Bureau of Engraving and Printing facility opens in Fort Worth, Texas. Mint plans to eliminate the practice of placing Mint marks on each individual working die by hand over the next several years; Mint marks will be added at the master die stage. Eisenhower Centennial commemorative silver dollar marketed. Judge awards gold recovered at wreck site of SS *Central America* to the finders and not the insurers who paid claims after the 1857 sinking.

1991—Nevada State Museum opens a facility at the former Carson City Mint building. Security thread and microprinting added to Federal Reserve notes as anti-counterfeiting devices. The United States ban on South African Krugerrand coins is lifted. The BEP opens its Fort Worth facility and adds an FW facility mark to notes printed there. An influx of counterfeit U.S. gold coins follows the end of the Gulf War. Salomon Brothers financial survey drops coins. Three commemorative coin programs marketed: Mount Rushmore, Korean War Memorial and United Services Organization 50th Anniversary. Court begins to hear appeal in SS *Central America* gold ruling.

1992—Establishment of the Citizens Commemorative Coin Advisory Committee. The BEP begins sales of uncut Federal Reserve notes and use of experimental web-fed press. Three commemorative coin programs marketed: 1992 Olympics, White House Bicentennial, Columbus Quincentenary. Appeals court awards all of the gold from the SS *Central America* to the insurers, overturning lower court ruling.

1993—Prepaid telephone cards gain interest momentarily, then decline as a collectible. Cohen specimen of the 1804 Draped Bust silver dollar, stolen in 1967, recovered in Switzerland. Two commemorative coin programs marketed: Bill of Rights/James Madison and World War II 50th Anniversary, the latter without a date of issue (thus seemingly illegal under U.S. law). Columbus America Discovery Group appeals to Supreme Court to overturn ruling granting SS *Central America* gold to insurers, but Supreme Court refuses the appeal and remands case to lower court; District Court awards 10 percent of the recovered gold to insurers, 90 percent to finders; treasure salvors appeal decision.

1994—Special Matte Finish Uncirculated 5-cent coins resembling Proofs appear in some commemorative coin sets. Bekaa Valley (Lebanon) counterfeits of U.S. paper money become a major concern. All

gold coin production transferred to West Point Mint (though some gold coins would later be produced at other facilities). The Old San Francisco Mint Museum closes. Denver Mint produces 1 billion coins in a month for the first time. The first Internet coin newsgroup makes debut. Federal Reserve monetizes 3,000 stolen test notes that entered circulation. Six commemorative coin programs marketed: World Cup Soccer, Prisoner of War, Vietnam Veterans Memorial, Women in Military Service, U.S. Capitol Bicentennial and Thomas Jefferson 250th anniversary (the latter commemorating a 1993 anniversary and lacking a year of issue, thus seemingly illegal).

1995—Lincoln, Doubled Die Obverse cents draw interest to coin collecting. U.S. Mint contracts to sell Olympic commemoratives in China. Three commemorative coin programs marketed: Civil War Battlefields, Special Olympics (a silver dollar bearing the portrait of founder Eunice Kennedy Shriver, then still living) and Atlanta Centennial Olympic Games. Ruling by District Court in 1993 awarding 90 percent of the gold from SS *Central America* to the finders is upheld by Court of Appeals; insurers appeal to Supreme Court, which refuses the appeal.

1996—New generation Federal Reserve notes released at a rate of one denomination per year with microprinting, watermarks and other security devices, plus new designs for the first time since 1929; new $100 notes issued first. The Secret Service seizes, as illegal to own, a 1933 Saint-Gaudens $20 double eagle from a London coin dealer, in a sting operation in the United States. The Eliasberg specimen of the 1913 Liberty Head 5-cent coin sells for a record $1.485 million at auction. Four commemorative coin programs marketed: Atlanta Olympic Games, National Community Service, Franklin Delano Roosevelt Memorial and Smithsonian Institution 150th Anniversary. District Court judge awards 92.4 percent of gold recovered from the SS *Central America* to the finders, 7.6 percent to the insurers.

1997—Platinum American Eagle coins marketed. Matte Finish Jefferson 5-cent coins in the Botanic Garden commemorative sets generate interest and price speculation among collectors. The BEP prints $4.6 million in $100 FRNs with watermark and security thread positions reversed. New-style $50 FRNs released. The Eliasberg 1804 Draped Bust silver dollar sells at public auction for a record $1.815 million. Three commemorative coin programs marketed: Botanic Garden, National Law Enforcement Officers Memorial and Jackie Robinson.

1998—New-style $20 FRNs released. Two commemorative coin programs marketed: Robert F. Kennedy and Black Revolutionary War Patriots.

1999—Mint launches a 10-year, 50-coin program of circulating quarter dollar coins to honor each state. Nov. 18, Mint strikes first Sacagawea dollars for 2000 release. Three commemorative coin programs marketed: Dolley Madison, George Washington Death

Bicentennial and Yellowstone National Park. Effort by insurers to sell their 7.6 percent of the gold from the SS *Central America* in December is halted by court order on request of Columbus America Discovery Group.

2000—Sacagawea dollars distributed beginning in January, first as prizes in Cheerios and as change at Wal-Mart and Sam's Clubs stores, then through banks (coins in the Cheerios promotion would later be identified as a prototype design; most distinctive differences between Cheerios and circulation issues are found on eagle's tail feathers on reverse). Congress questions Mint authority to issue a 22-karat gold version of the Sacagawea dollar with a $5 denomination (Mint delays decision for a year, then abandons plan). New design $5 and $10 notes issued in May. Consortium of dealers purchases the SS *Central America* gold held by the Columbus America Discovery Group for an undisclosed price estimated at millions of dollars; some items are sold before an Appeals Court halts any remaining sales by the Columbus America Discovery Group at the request of the insurers who hold 7.6 percent of the gold; injunction against sale of insurers' portion of the gold is lifted and sale is held in December; legal battle between finders and insurers ends.

2001—U.S. government grants private ownership rights to an example of a 1933 Saint-Gaudens gold $20 double eagle believed to have been part of the legendary collection formed by Egyptian King Farouk, freeing the coin to be auctioned in 2002. Ten "mule" error coins pairing State quarter dollar obverse with Sacagawea dollar reverse surface. Strong demand for 2001 American Buffalo commemorative silver dollar creates rapid sellout after sales begin June 7. Anonymous purchaser pays $8 million for 933.94-ounce gold bar recovered from the shipwreck SS *Central America.* Terrorist attacks of Sept. 11 cripple nation's banking and financial infrastructure; U.S. Mints and BEP facilities temporarily close; Stack's auction on that day and next, Bowers and Merena auction a few days later both postponed; location of annual New York International Numismatic Convention in December among facilities destroyed at World Trade Center.

2002—Sale at auction of King Farouk specimen of Saint-Gaudens gold $20 double eagle on July 30 establishes new record price for a single coin ($7,590,000, plus $20 to U.S. Mint for "monetization" of the coin). Legislative movements to memorialize Sept. 11, 2001, terror attacks fall short. Six-week shutdown of Philadelphia Mint after Occupational Safety and Health Administration finds irregularities leads to lowest mintages for State quarter dollars at that point in the popular program.

2003—A long-lost 1913 Liberty Head 5-cent coin surfaces in the family of coin dealer George Walton and is authenticated by a panel of experts at the ANA World's Fair of Money in Baltimore. The U.S. Mint announces the Artistic Infusion Program, seeking a new artistry for U.S. coin designs. Citizens Coinage Advisory Committee replaces Citizens Commemorative Coin Advisory Committee in weighing in on new U.S. coinage and medal designs. Odyssey Marine Exploration, Tampa, Fla., recovers the 1865 shipwreck of the SS *Republic,* which was laden with a fortune in gold when it sank off the coast of Georgia during a hurricane. Colorful Series 2004 $20 Federal Reserve notes debut, the first in the NexGen series of redesigned U.S. paper money intended to resist counterfeiting. The first auction is held of the unprecedented and unrivaled John J. Ford Jr., collection, which will eventually require 21 auctions over several years.

2004—The Westward Journey 5-cent coins make their debut, offering four new reverse designs over two years. The Du Pont specimen of the 1866 Seated Liberty, No Motto silver dollar is recovered decades after it was stolen in a brazen 1967 heist. Import restrictions on Iraqi coinage announced. Series 2004 $50 FRNs enter circulation, continuing trend to add color to U.S. paper money in efforts to outpace counterfeiters. Smithsonian's National Museum of American History closes down the nation's coin and paper money collection while the exhibit space undergoes renovations.

2005—2004-D Wisconsin quarter dollar "Leaf" variations gain notice among hobby community early in the year. Westward Journey 5¢ series continues with two more reverse designs. Numerous U.S. coins shatter $1 million barrier, notably the 1787 Brasher doubloon with the EB countermark on the eagle's breast, which realized $2.99 million. 2000-P Sacagawea dollar prototype design from "Cheerios" promotion is confirmed. Marine Corps commemorative silver dollar sells out, even after mintage is bumped up to 600,000 coins. Ohio coin dealer Thomas Noe under scrutiny for management of investment funds for the Ohio Bureau of Workers' Compensation. Ten more examples of the 1933 Saint-Gaudens gold $20 double eagles surface after family of late Philadelphia coin dealer Israel Swift seeks confirmation of authenticity. Turmoil roils the ranks of the ANA, as the board of governors ousts a member amid a museum naming rights controversy. Sweeping legislation late in the year creates a Presidential dollar coin program with related First Spouse gold coins and bronze medals, an American Buffalo .9999 fine gold $50 bullion coin program and delineates four commemorative designs for the Lincoln cent in 2009.

2006—U.S. Mint places 10 "recovered" 1933 Saint-Gaudens $20 gold double eagles on display during ANA World's Fair of Money in Denver. U.S. Mint unveils designs for 2007 Presidential $1 coin program. Collectors express anger after U.S. Mint offers individual examples of some 20th Anniversary American Eagle bullion coins originally promised as being available only in limited edition sets. American

Buffalo program debuts to wide acclaim, as sales of the 1-ounce coin bearing the popular design cut into sales of the American Eagle 1-ounce gold coin. Jefferson 5-cent coin sports new "facing forward" image of the third U.S. president on the obverse.

2007—Presidential dollars debut with gigantic mintage figures that soon drop precipitously; demand is spurred by error examples that missed the edge lettering process. After 21 auctions held between October 2003 and October 2007, sales of the John J. Ford Jr. Collection total $58 million, a record price for a single-owner collection; not a single lot contained regular-issue United States coins issued by the U.S. Mint. Import restrictions for ancient coinage take effect, an unprecedented clampdown on the trade of numismatic items. ANA Executive Director Christopher Cipoletti placed on administrative leave by newly installed board of governors after election demanding change. A Michigan collector discovers a rare 1969-S Lincoln, Doubled Die Obverse, cent. An anonymous collector pays $5 million for the finest-known 1913 Liberty Head 5-cent coin, then the second-highest amount ever paid for a U.S. coin.

2008—United States Appeals Court for the Federal District of Columbia Circuit upholds a lower court decision that U.S. paper money is discriminatory against blind and visually impaired individuals. Counterfeiting of U.S. coins in China gains scrutiny from the hobby community when it learns the scale and quality of fake U.S. coins being produced. U.S. Mint strikes some examples of Uncirculated 2008-W American Eagle silver dollars with reverse die used for the 2007 coins. Release of 2008 Hawaii 25-cent coin marks end of the popular, 10-year State quarter dollar program, which the U.S. Mint claimed was collected by 140 million Americans. U.S. Mint Director Edmund Moy announces plans to issue a modified example of the Ultra-High Relief Saint-Gaudens $20 gold double eagle coin. Amid a shaky economy, demand for American Eagle silver bullion coins intensifies to record levels that the U.S. Mint is unable to acquire sufficient blanks to meet. Prices of gold and platinum reach record heights, as demand for precious metals soars amid global economic instability.

2009—The District of Columbia and Territories 25-cent coin program honors each of six entities affiliated with the United States. Four different Lincoln cents highlight different periods of the 16th president's life and legacy. The Native American dollar program honors the accomplishments and contributions of America's first peoples with annually changing designs on the reverse of the Sacagawea dollar. Record low demand for circulation coinage, the by-product of a weak economy, leads to the lowest overall mintage levels in years. Smithsonian Institution's National Museum of American History reopens the National Numismatic Collection. U.S. Mint announces the 56 sites to be honored in the America the Beautiful 25-cent coin program, beginning in 2010. Collectors express outrage when the U.S. Mint belatedly announces that it will not issue Proof 2009-W American Eagle coins. The 2009 Ultra-High Relief $20 gold double eagle debuts to positive reviews, strong demand. Bullion coin sales spike as precious metals demand intensifies.

2010—America the Beautiful circulating 25-cent coin program debuts, but the coins are rarely encountered as demand for circulating coins remains low. Release of companion America the Beautiful 5-ounce .999 fine silver coins is delayed several months and prices erupt when coins are finally issued. New record price established for a single U.S. coin, the $7.85 million paid for a 1794 Flowing Hair silver dollar graded Specimen 66 by Professional Coin Grading Service. U.S. Mint establishes sales record of nearly 35 million 1-ounce silver American Eagle $1 bullion coins. BEP unveils Series 2009 $100 Federal Reserve Note intended for release in early 2011, but late in 2010 announce that technical challenges will delay that launch. Price of gold vaults to new record highs, breaking $1,400 an ounce as world economic uncertainty continues. Proof American Eagle silver dollars excite collectors when they are again offered for sale after a one-year hiatus.

2011—Sales of America the Beautiful 5-ounce .999 fine silver bullion coins continue to make hobby headlines. Sales of privately made medals marking the 10th anniversary of the Sept. 11, 2011, terrorist attacks draw scrutiny from the sponsors of legislation calling for the U.S. Mint to strike and sell medals commemorating the anniversary. Certain coins of Italian types are including in new import restrictions imposed by the U.S. State Department and the U.S. Customs and Border Protection. Price of gold continues to set records, with silver nearing its former record. American Eagle bullion coin sales continue to be strong.

Canada

1670—First regal French silver 5- and 15-sol "Gloriam regni tui dicenti" coinage of Louis XIV, copper 2 deniers.

1717—Copper 6, 12 deniers, Louis XV.

1721 to 1722—Copper 9-denier colonial coinage.

1728—Billon marque, half marque enter circulation.

1813—"Holey dollar," cut and counterstamped Spanish dollars issued by the governor of Prince Edward Island.

1815—Magdalen Island token penny of Sir Isaac Coffin.

1823—Nova Scotia copper half-penny token introduces types issued through 1840.

1837 to 1852—Bank and bouquet copper token coinages, Upper Canada, Quebec.

1843—New Brunswick tokens.

1856—Arbutus copper Nova Scotia tokens of Victoria.

1858—Silver 5-, 10-, 20-cent coins, bronze cent struck for Canada bearing the young head of Victoria.

1861—Decimal bronze cent, half cent, New Brunswick.

1862—Silver 5-, 10-, 20-cent coins, New Brunswick; gold $10, $20 coins, British Columbia.

1865—Bronze cent, silver 5-, 10-, 20-cent coins, gold $2, Newfoundland.

1870—New Confederation silver coinage of Canada.

1871—Prince Edward Island bronze cent, English inscription obverse.

1876—Large bronze cent introduced of Canadian Confederation type.

1911—Pattern dollar for Canada, George V, DEI GRATIA omitted on first coins of George V's reign.

1912—Normal inscriptions resumed, new gold $5 and $10 Canadian coins join sovereigns of British type, minted 1908-C to 1919-C.

1920—Small bronze cent replaces older large cent.

1922—Pure nickel round 5-cent coin replaces small silver 5 cents.

1935—Silver Jubilee of the reign of King George V sees silver dollar finally introduced.

1937—New coins of George VI, first wholly redesigned reverses.

1938—Small bronze cent introduced in Newfoundland.

1942—Tombac brass replaces nickel in Canadian 5-cent coin, struck on a 12-sided planchet.

1943—Canada first to issue coinage with international telegraphic code dots and dashes, "We win when we work willingly" around rim on the reverse of tombac Victory 5-cent coin.

1944—Chrome-plated steel 5-cent coin, Victory reverse.

1946—Nickel 5-cent coin resumed, 12-sided.

1947—Last Newfoundland coins.

1951—First commemorative in 5-cent denomination marks anniversary of the isolation of nickel as a recognized element.

1967—Centenary of Confederation, completely redesigned coinage, bronze cent through gold $20. Gold coin cannot be sold in the United States due to U.S. legal restrictions on private ownership of gold.

1968—Pure nickel replaces silver in Canadian coinage; 50-cent and the dollar coins are reduced in size as well.

1971—British Columbia centenary sees reintroduction of large-size silver dollar as a commemorative, along with regular issue small pure nickel dollar.

1976—Joining the 28 silver $5 and $10 Olympic coins are two new gold $100 coins, struck in .5833 fine for sale as Uncirculated; .9166 fine in Proof.

1977—Silver Jubilee silver dollar, gold $100 coin of Elizabeth II. New, reduced diameter bronze cent announced by Royal Canadian Mint. The new 16.05-millimeter cent will be smaller than the existing 10-cent coin.

1979—Smaller bust of Queen Elizabeth II adopted on cent. Maple Leaf 1-ounce .999 fine gold bullion coin issued for first time.

1980—Cent reduced in weight.

1981—RCM begins manufacture of seven-piece Proof sets.

1982—Cent depicts smaller bust and becomes 12-sided coin. The 5-cent coin is changed to copper-nickel composition. Paper money adopted with raised-print Braille for the blind. Fineness of gold Maple Leaf coins increased to .9999 fine.

1984—Canadian flax content in paper money replaced with U.S. cotton.

1986—Royal Canadian Mint introduces Maple Leaf half-ounce gold coin.

1987—Smaller size dollar coin struck to replace dollar bill. The mysterious disappearance of a pair of master dies for Canada's new smaller Voyageur aureate-nickel dollar forces the Canadian Parliament to approve a new reverse design depicting a common loon.

1988—Royal Canadian Mint officials label as counterfeit a 1981 coin struck from the muled dies of a gold $100 coin and 50-cent coins. Silver and platinum bullion Maple Leaf coins join gold bullion coins of Canada.

1990—Platinum composition commemorative coins introduced. Canada issues its first gold $200 commemorative coin and its first gold on silver $20 commemoratives.

1992—Landmark Canada 125 circulating commemorative series of 12 25-cent coins and a dollar coin proves to be successful.

1996—Ringed bimetal $2 coin is introduced into circulation with precious metal versions made for collectors.

1997—A Maple Leaf $50 coin is issued guaranteed at $310 in U.S. dollars. Of 30,000 struck, 20,884 are returned when the price of gold falls.

1998—W Mint mark for Winnipeg appears on Canadian coins for the first time, although limited to Proof pieces. A $15 gold on silver commemorative coin is produced for collectors.

1999—"Create a Cents-ation" program calls for designs for two new series of circulating 25-cent commemoratives. More than 30,000 entries submitted and 12 coins issued, one each month, celebrating Canada's history, in first series. Two mules lacking the year date are issued in the series, for September's and November's releases.

2000—"Create a Cents-ation" program garners 30,000 submissions for 12 circulating 25-cent commemoratives celebrating Canada's future, which are released one per month throughout the year. Another mule surfaces, pairing the obverse of the February coin release with the obverse of a medal design.

2001—First paper money in the "Canadian Journey" series of notes, denominated $10, is released. A Canadian 25-cent coin mule that is dated 1992 on the obverse and 1993 on the reverse is authenticated.

2002—Circulation coins bear dual dates of 1952-2002 marking the 50th anniversary of Queen Elizabeth II's accession to the throne.

2003—Susanna Blunt effigy of Queen Elizabeth II debuts. RCM auctions a unique undated gold dollar marking Queen Elizabeth II's accession to the throne, raising $62,600 for charity. First Canadian .9999 fine silver dollar issued.

2004—Remembrance Day Poppy 25-cent coin is first colored circulating commemorative coin in the world.

2005—Circulating commemorative 5-cent coin celebrates 60th anniversary of victory in World War II. Three circulating commemorative 25-cent coins honor Alberta and Saskatchewan centennials and Year of the Veteran. Test examples of .99999 fine gold Maple Leaf coins sold via lottery system to select RCM customers.

2006—Copper-plated zinc planchets are used to strike limited quantities of cents struck by dies intended for copper-plated steel planchets, and multiply plated steel planchets are inadvertently used with dies intended to strike copper-plated zinc cents. One-year design honors 10th anniversary of $2 coin.

2007—RCM announces a massive coin program to celebrate the 2010 Vancouver Winter Olympic Games; the program includes 20 different circulating commemorative coins, 18 of them 25-cent coins and the other two dollar coins. Program also includes first kilo-sized Canadian coins, denominated $250 (silver) and $2,500 (gold). First ever Olympic-themed silver and gold bullion coins issued late in the year, with a 2008 date. Two mule 25-cent coins issued, pairing the wrong obverses with designs honoring the Paralympic sport of Wheelchair Curling and the Olympic sport of Alpine Skiing. Largest world gold coin, the Maple Leaf 100-kilogram .99999 fine gold $1 million coin, released to ignite interest in the Maple Leaf 1-ounce .99999 fine gold $200 coins, a new series for the RCM.

2008—Ottawa Mint celebrates centennial of operation. Desjardins Group releases report calling 1-cent coin "pointless."

2009—Variety on Men's Hockey Olympic Moments 25-cent coin excites collectors. A months-long investigation finds that 17,514 ounces of gold discovered to be "missing" in October 2008 was the result of improper record-keeping and not a physical loss of gold.

2010—New Wildlife .9999 fine silver Maple Leaf dollar coins, dated 2011, released in September, inaugurates a new series with animal designs. Mule error 10-cent coin features different finishes, identifying a change in the way Specimen coins are struck (the obverse side has a 2009 finish, the reverse side bears a 2010 finish). Senate Finance Committee calls for withdrawal of 1-cent coin.

Mexico

1521—Following Cortez's capture of Tenochtitlan, now Mexico City, the territory was organized as a Spanish possession. The Aztec Indians were found using cacao bean and beaten copper "hoe money" in daily commerce.

1536—The Mexico City Mint, oldest in the New World, begins coinage of silver in quarter and half reales, 1-, 2-, 3- and 4-real denominations. An issue of copper 2- and 4-maravedi coins was an unsuccessful experiment, which saw hundreds of the coins thrown into Lake Texcoco.

1556—The reign of King Philip II saw the introduction of the 8-real crown, to be struck in various designs through 1897, becoming a world coin of international circulation and universally admired reliability. The early versions of the silver coins became known as "cobs," from a Spanish expression "cabo de barra": cut from a bar. Their weight was all-important, the actual shape of any one coin a matter of indifference.

1665—Gold coinage began in Mexico during Charles II's reign.

1732—Fully round coins struck within a collar. These are known to Spanish collectors as "dos mundos" or "two worlds" type from the crowned hemispheres on the reverse; English-speaking collectors know them as the "Pillar dollar." Ancestor of the U.S. dollar.

1772—Portrait 8-reale coin struck for King Charles III.

1808—Following Ferdinand VII's ouster by Napoleon's brother Joseph, Mexican loyalists, as others would throughout the Spanish empire, rally to Ferdinand and begin striking coins with his portrait at Mexico and a dozen new mints.

1811—The revolt of Father Morelos sees a variety of cast and struck crude emergency coins, beginning a complex era of loyalist and revolutionary coinages.

1814—Copper coins in denominations of quarter real and half real struck, to replace private tokens and provide small change.

1822—Following the independence of Mexico under liberator Augustin de Iturbide, imperial coinage began in Augustin's new Mexican empire, bearing the eagle of Aztec legend, seated on a nopal cactus.

1823—Following the overthrow of the empire, a republic was proclaimed, the beginning of a century of turbulence, misrule and civil struggle. A profile hook-necked eagle killing a serpent replaces Iturbide's crowned eagle on the 8-real coin.

1824 to 1897—Coinage of uniform Liberty Cap silver 8-real pesos and minor coinage.

1829—Copper national coinage in quarter-real denominations. Copper issues of individual states had begun in 1824.

1841—The first pattern decimal 1-centavo coin struck but not adopted.

1863—San Luis Potosi strikes silver decimal 5- and 10-centavo coins.

1864—The Congress of Notables invites Archduke Maximilian of Austria to ascend the throne of a second Mexican empire during the French intervention of Napoleon III. A decimal centavo in copper was issued by the imperial government.

1866 to 1867—Imperial silver coinage of 5-, 10- and 50-centavo denominations struck in 1866, the Maximilian peso in 1866 and 1867. The emperor was captured and ordered shot by President Benito Juarez.

1869—A republican copper centavo placed in circulation, although the silver coins were still being struck in real denominations.

1869 to 1873—Balance type coin with value expressed as 1 peso; some decimal minor coins as well.

1870—Balance type gold coinage, 1-peso through 20-peso denominations.

1882—Copper-nickel briefly introduced in 1-, 2- and 5-centavo denominations.

1898—The 8-real denomination finally abandoned in favor of a new Liberty Cap peso.

1899—A new small size bronze centavo is introduced.

1905—A major monetary reform adopts the gold standard and introduces a new coinage in bronze, silver and gold, bearing a facing eagle and inscription ESTADOS UNIDOS MEXICANOS.

1910—Last of the large-size pesos, called the Caballito type from the equestrian Liberty on the obverse, introduced.

1918—Size of the peso, weight and fineness reduced. New issue is .800 fine, succeeded by a similar coin of .720 fineness in 1920. This was the start of a gradual disappearance of silver in the coinage in this and other denominations.

1936—Copper-nickel 5- and 10-centavo coins issued.

1942—Portrait and other scenic views placed on 5- and 20-centavo coins, beginning a trend toward greater variety of design for all coins.

1947—Morelos peso issued, .500 fine silver. The succeeding pesos drop to .100 fine by 1957.

1950—A commemorative 5-peso coin marking the completion of the southeastern railway continues a modern commemorative series (that began in 1921) that still continues. The sizes of all coins are now reduced, and .300 fine 25- and 50-centavo, 1-peso coins are struck.

1954 to 1955—Brass and bronze 5-, 10-, 20- and

50-centavo minor coins join the brass centavo in circulation; .720 fine silver 5-peso coin and .900 fine silver 10-peso coin make their debut.

1964—Copper-nickel, smaller 25-centavo and 50-centavo coins replace bronze pieces.

1968—A .720 fine silver 25-peso coin introduced.

1970—Bronze coinage reduced further in size; copper-nickel adopted for the 1-peso coin, with a new copper-nickel 5-peso coin planned for 1971. All reverses redesigned to bear an outline-form archaic Aztec treatment of the profile Mexican eagle.

1974—New small-size copper-nickel 20-centavo coin portrays revolutionary leader Madero, continuing trend toward smaller coins.

1976—Plans are announced for a .720 fine silver 100-peso coin, designed to stimulate the silver mining industry.

1977—Numismatic excitement high as tiny copper-nickel 10-centavo coins dated 1974, 1975 and 1976 are released; seven-sided copper-nickel 10-peso coins dated 1974, 1975 and 1976 appear; 1977-dated silver 100-peso coins are struck and released.

1980—Design of Aztec dragon adopted for 5-peso coin's reverse. Copper-nickel composition commences for 20-peso coin production.

1981—Gold bullion coins in weights of quarter-, half-, and 1-ounce pure gold, .900 fine, issued.

1982—Devaluation of peso, to 50-to-1 U.S. dollar, then to 100-to-1 U.S. dollar, takes place due to high inflation. Fifty-peso coins issued in copper-nickel.

1983—Design of Olmec culture adopted on new bronze 20-centavo coin. Design of Palenque (Maya city state) adopted on reverse of new steel 50-centavo coin.

1984—Libertad composed of .999 fine silver dated 1982 released, replacing Onza .925 fine silver trade coin.

1985—Mexico Mint becomes an autonomous institution.

1987—500-peso coin replaces note in circulation.

1987—Onza platinum bullion coins introduced.

1989—Inflationary 50,000-peso note issued.

1991—Unwieldy coinage system is revamped, with older coins withdrawn to simplify the system and new coins issued for 1992.

1992—Pre-Columbian civilizations are the subject of a new gold and silver commemorative coinage program.

1993—A currency reform ushers in new coins and notes including silver composition ringed bimetal coins.

1996—Additional denomination Libertad coins are added to the silver bullion series. Precious metal is quietly removed from the composition specifications for circulating ringed bimetal coins at the time of a currency reform.

1998—Coin manufacture is transferred to the Mint at San Luis Potosi from the Legaria plant in Mexico City.

1999—Millennium silver commemoratives celebrate Peace, the Environment, History and Culture.

2000—Two-year Uncirculated .999 fine silver 5-peso coin series celebrates Endangered species; four coins are released in 2000 and six coins in 2001.

2002—First kilogram silver coin issued, as part of the Mexican Libertad bullion series.

2003—Launch of circulating ringed bimetallic 100-peso program honoring each of 32 Mexican states and the Federal District, released in reverse alphabetical order (by the then-official Spanish alphabet), through 2005; coins show the state coat of arms. Companion Proof .999 fine silver 10-peso and ringed-bimetallic Proof .999 fine silver/.999 fine gold 100-peso versions are also issued.

2005—Commemorative ringed-bimetallic 100-peso coins celebrate the 80th anniversary of the Banco de Mexico, the centennial of the Monetary Reform of 1905, the 400th anniversary of publication of *Don Quixote* and the 470th anniversary of the Casa de Moneda. A second State series, highlighting culture and tourism of each of 32 states and the Federal District, begins and runs in alphabetical order

through 2007. Companion Proof .999 fine silver 10-peso and ringed-bimetallic Proof .999 fine silver/.999 fine gold 100-peso versions are also issued.

2006—Mexico issues its first polymer paper money, a 50-peso note that is introduced in November as part of a redesigned series. Commemorative .999 fine silver 5-peso and .999 fine gold 25-peso coins celebrate 2006 World Cup in Germany.

2007—New 20-peso polymer bank note is the second note in the new family of notes

2008—Two ringed-bimetallic 5-peso coin series introduced in a program of periodic coin releases in lead up to the bicentennial of independence and centennial of revolution anniversaries in 2010.

2009—Smaller, lighter 10- and 20-centavo coins released to save Mexico money. A 50-centavo coin is announced but not released for more than a year.

2010—Proof .999 fine silver 10- and 20-peso coins, 100-peso and 200-peso bank notes celebrate anniversaries of independence and revolution; Proof and Brilliant Uncirculated .900 fine gold 200-peso coins join the program, honoring the bicentennial of independence.

Central America

BRITISH HONDURAS, BELIZE

1864—Decimal system adopted.

1871—Private quarter-real tokens issued by importer John Jex.

1885—Copper cents introduce a new decimal colonial coinage, the first in this hemisphere south of Canada in the British colonial holdings.

1894—Silver coinage, 5 cents to 50 cents, begun.

1914—Medium-size bronze cent appears.

1946—Last silver coinage of British Honduras.

1954—Cent further reduced in size, scalloped edge used after 1956.

1973—Premier George Price engineers sudden name change of the colony to Belize after the name of the former capital, traditional coin designs modified to reflect the change.

1974—New coinage, first change in designs since 1894 announced, after name of the colony, under internal self-government, is changed to Belize. Franklin Mint strikes all-new series featuring Belize coat of arms and birds of Belize, denominations expressed in words. Traditional designs with royal portrait continued after loyalists protest over new Bird coin designs. Introduction of $1, $5 and $10 coins in Bird series.

1975—Bird series continued with numerical values on reverse, royal types continued as well.

1978—First silver and copper-nickel $25 coins, and gold $250 coin produced.

1981—World Food Day coins issued, part of international series.

1990—Dollar coin replaces note in circulation.

1998—Redemption halted of 1984 commemorative gold foil notes.

2003—New series of bank notes features enhanced security devices.

COSTA RICA

1831—Central American type coins struck, CR Mint mark.

1841—Star countermark applied to foreign coins in circulation.

1845—Woman's head and tree reverse countermarks on old Spanish 2-real coins.

1846—One-real and 2-real coin dies used to validate colonial cob coins still in active circulation.

1850—Decimal silver, expressed in fractions to agree with old real coinage value.

1865—Decimal copper-nickel and silver coins.

1896—New currency unit, the colon of 100 centimos.

1935—Issues of the Banco Internacional in copper-nickel.

1937—Banco Nacional takes over coinage responsibilities.

1954—Banco Central stainless steel coinage, first in the hemisphere.

1974—Gold, silver Conservation coinage released.

1975—Pure nickel 5-, 10- and 20-colon coins, first circulating commemoratives, issued.

1979—The 5-centimo coin is changed to a brass composition.

1982—Aluminum adopted as new composition for 10- and 25-centimo coins; stainless steel for the 50-centimo coin and 1- and 2-colon coins.

1996—1995-dated coins released as part of a currency reform.

2005—Aluminum 5- and 10-colon coins make

debut, lighter than earlier brass examples.

2010—New bank note series unveiled with all new designs and enhanced security features, with one note, denominated 20,000 colones, released late in the year.

EL SALVADOR

1828—Provisional coins and countermarked issues.

1889—Copper-nickel 1-centavo coin with Morazon portrait.

1892—Decimal peso-centavo silver coinage.

1909—Short-lived copper quarter-real coin struck and quickly recalled.

1925—Commemorative silver and gold coins for the fifth centenary of San Salvador in new unit, the colon.

1943—Large silver 25-centavo coin struck during World War II nickel shortage.

1953—Small-size silver 25-centavo coin equal to a U.S. dime is issued.

1970—Copper-nickel coins replace silver coins in circulation.

1974—Nickel-brass coinage includes 3-centavo coin last issued in 1915.

1975—Nickel-clad steel composition introduced for 5-, 10- and 25-centavo coins.

1976—Brass 1-centavo coin produced.

1977—Copper-nickel 5-, 10- and 50-centavo coins increased in thickness from 2 millimeters to 1.65 millimeters.

1984—Copper-nickel 1-colon piece introduced as regular issue coin.

1996—Central Bank considers then decides against "dollarization" (adoption of U.S. dollar in circulation).

1998—200- and 500-colon notes issued as inflation advances.

Early 2000s—After earlier rejection, process of dollarization, replacing the colon with the U.S. dollar, takes place early in the decade.

GUATEMALA

1824—Guatemala Mint strikes coinage of Central American Federation.

1829—Provisional coinage of 1 real, federation type with ESTADO DE GUATEMALA.

1859—Beginning of President Rafael Carrera's standardized real-peso coinage.

1869—Attempt at decimal peso of 100 centimos; a 25-centimo coin is struck, public reacts negatively.

1870—Decimal peso of 100 centavos decreed, abandoned the following year.

1881—Another decimalization attempt, four denominations struck, in copper and silver. Copper centavo overstruck on the 1871 issue.

1912—Last national coinage in real denominations, a copper-nickel coin first struck in 1900, as the economy begins floundering.

1915—Copper provisional coinage.

1923—Amid a collapse of the currency, aluminum-bronze 1- and 5-peso coins issued.

1926—Thorough overhaul of the Guatemalan finances sees introduction of the gold and silver quetzal of 100 centavos.

1943—President Jorge Ubico causes an international incident by issuing a new 25-centavo coin to mark inauguration of the national palace, with a map reverse showing British Honduras as a part of Guatemala.

1965—Silver coinage replaced with copper-nickel-zinc coinage.

1994—Paper money redesign prompted to thwart counterfeiters.

2001—Dollarization takes effect, allowing usage of U.S. currency.

2007—Nation issues polymer 1-quetzal note, its first polymer bank note.

2010—200-quetzal note is new, higher denomination of paper money.

HONDURAS

1823—Coins of Spanish royalist and Mexican imperial type struck at Tegucigalpa Mint, presumably to suit all factions.

1832—Provisional Central American type coinage in base silver and copper.

1871—Republican silver decimal coinage.

1879-1920—Great coinage chaos, old dies of every type used to strike copper centavo coins.

1931—New coinage of the lempira, equal to 100 centavos.

1967—Copper-nickel coinage replaces silver.

2000—Commemorative 20-lempira note marks 50th anniversary of Central Bank, new millennium.

2010—The 20-lempira note is nation's first polymer bank note.

NICARAGUA

1825—Provisional silver of Central American Federation type.

1878—First regular coinage, copper-nickel centavo.

1880—Silver decimal coins, 1 peso of 100 centavos.

1912—Overhaul of coinage introduces the silver córdoba of 100 centavos, copper-nickel coinage replaces silver coinage in 1939.

1943—Brass shell-case alloy replaces copper-nickel composition in three denominations.

1965—Central Bank becomes bank of issue.

1967—Famed Nicaragua-born Spanish language poet and writer Ruben Dario honored on gold 50-cordoba coin.

1974—Aluminum 5- and 10-centavo coins in Food and Agriculture Organization series join the range of coins in circulation.

1980—One-year issue of copper-nickel 5-córdoba coins.

1981—FAO international issues, with 1-, 10- and

25-centavo coins in aluminum.

1982—Nickel-clad steel 50-centavo coin replaces former copper-nickel coin.

1990—Issues inflationary 100,000-córdoba note.

1992—Córdoba oro name changed to córdoba.

1994—Four centavo-denomination coins replace small-denomination notes in circulation.

2008—Nation's first circulating 10-córdoba coin, dated 2007, enters circulation and honors national hero Andrés Castro.

2009—Central Bank of Nicaragua issues new 10-, 20- and 200-córdoba notes composed of polymer, and new cotton 50- and 100-córdoba note. The 200-córdoba note represents a new denomination.

2010—Commemorative 50-córdoba note marks central bank's 50th anniversary.

PANAMA

1904—First coinage, highlighted by tiny 2½-centesimo coin (nicknamed a "pill") and huge half-balboa coin.

1930—Silver coins in U.S. sizes, weights issued.

1931—First silver balboa issued.

1966—Copper-nickel clad coinage of U.S. type replaces smaller silver coins in circulation.

1971—A new denomination, 20 balboas, issued in silver, first as a commemorative for the 150th anniversary of Central American independence, then as what the government of Panama has described as a regular issue.

1975—Franklin Mint strikes all-new portrait coinage including a 5-balboa coin, 2½-centesimo coin ("pill") in new designs.

1975—First gold coinage, struck by Franklin Mint.

1976—Franklin Mint produces platinum 150-balboa coin with Bolivar portrait.

1979—Production begins of .980 fine platinum 200-balboa coin, containing 0.2994 ounce of pure platinum.

1981—Production begins of .500 fine gold 50-balboa coin, containing 0.0861 ounce of pure gold.

1988—Economic crisis and cash shortage forces circulation of earlier commemorative silver coins.

1996—Panama "dollarizes" its currency. Balboa becomes a commemorative denomination.

South America

ARGENTINA

1813—United Provinces of Rio de la Plata coinage with radiant sun, in real and sol denominations.

1822—Province of Buenos Aires and other chaotic provincial coinages.

1838—Confederated Argentine Republic coins.

1881—Modern unified bronze, silver and gold coinage of the republic decreed.

1896—Copper-nickel coinage becomes general coin in circulation until 1942.

1952—Copper-nickel-clad steel coinage issued, first in hemisphere.

1970—New coinage, 100 old pesos equal one new.

1974—Inflation's advance leads to reappearance of small-size aluminum-bronze 1-peso coin.

1983—Aluminum composition adopted for 10- and 50-centavo coins.

1985—Introduces austral currency in an effort to stop inflation.

1986—Notgeld-type paper "provincial bonds" appear as small change in circulation.

1987—Retires peso notes, replaces them with austral denominations.

1989—Strike at Mint causes paper money shortage.

1990—Issues inflationary 10,000-austral note.

1992—Currency reform devalues the australes at 10,000 to the peso.

1994—Ringed-bimetallic 1-peso coin replaces a note of the same denomination.

1999—Central Bank considers, then holds off on "dollarization."

2007—Circulating commemorative copper-nickel 2-peso coin marks 25th anniversary of the 1982 invasion of the Falkland Islands by Argentinian forces.

2010—Five circulating commemorative ringed bimetallic 1-peso coins celebrate bicentennial of Argentina's May Revolution.

BOLIVIA

1573—Potosi Mint established on the fabulous "hill of silver."

1827—Republican silver sol coinage, gold scudo coinage.

1864—Introduction of decimal boliviano of 100 centavos.

1883—First copper-nickel 5-, 10-centavo coins.

1893—Copper-nickel "caduceus" coins, a type in use through the 1940s.

1951—Introduction of bronze bolivianos.

1965—Introduction of copper and nickel-clad coinage.

1977—A .925 fine silver 200-peso-boliviano coin is issued as part of the international issue for the International Year of the Child.

1984—Inflationary 100,000-peso notes issued.

1986—New note series introduced.

1987—First circulating coins since 1980 struck as the pesos bolivianos is replaced with the boliviano in a currency reform.

1991—Ibero-American commemorative coin series begins. First coins struck for circulation since 1987.

1995—First coins struck for circulation since 1991.

1997—First coins struck for circulation since 1995. Composition of 10-centavo coin changed from copper-clad steel to stainless steel.

1998—Commemorative 50-boliviano coin honoring 450th anniversary of La Paz is issued.

2010—Designs of circulating coins changed to reflect nation's new proper name (Multinational State of Bolivia).

BRAZIL

1822—Independent imperial coins of Dom Pedro I.

1831—Dom Pedro II, types of earlier reign.

1853—Modern imperial silver coinage.

1867 to 1868—Portrait silver and copper introduced.

1871—Nickel minor coins introduced.

1889—Republic declared, monetary instability advances.

1900—400th anniversary commemorative 4,000-real coin features discoverer Pedro Alvares Cabral.

1922—First centenary of independence sees beginning of a series of national commemoratives, continuing through the next decade.

1942—President Getulio Vargas decrees new coinage, the cruzeiro of 100 centavos. Minor coins continue to bear his portrait; 1-, 2- and 5-cruzeiro coins bear a remarkably detailed relief map of Brazil.

1956—Aluminum coins introduced as runaway inflation begins its inroads.

1967—After years of financial chaos, the military government decrees a coinage reform, introducing the heavy cruzeiro, equal to 1,000 old cruzeiros. New coinage is composed of stainless steel and pure nickel.

1972—Reintroduction of commemoratives in nickel, silver and gold to mark the 150th anniversary of Brazilian independence.

1975—Silver 10-cruzeiro coin marks anniversary of Central Bank, leads to accusations of favoritism in distribution and Mint director's ouster.

1980—Manufacture begins of stainless steel 5- and 10-cruzeiro coins.

1981—Manufacture begins of stainless steel 20-cruzeiro coin.

1986—Cruzado currency introduced in an attempt to slow inflation.

1989—Cruzado coins and notes are demonetized due to inflation, replaced by cruzado novo.

1990—The cruzado novo is replaced with the cruzeiro in a currency reform.

1993—The cruzeiro is replaced at a ratio of 1,000 cruzeiro to one cruzeiro real due to inflation.

1994—Currency reform replaces the cruzeiros reals with the real at 2,750-to-1 ratio. Release of notes without a reference to God draws complaints.

1997—Counterfeiters launder notes, removing ink, to reuse paper for higher denominations.

2000—Bank issues commemorative 10-real note marking 500th anniversary of nation's discovery.

2005—Circulating commemorative 1-real coin honors 40th anniversary of bank's founding.

2010—Larger, redesigned 50- and 100-real bank notes, first notes in new series, issued.

BRITISH GUIANA

1809—Coins of George III, Dutch guilder unit.

1816—More finely struck guilder coinage.

1891—Silver 4 pence struck for "British Guiana-British West Indies"; the English type 4 pence had been in circulation as the equivalent of the quarter guilder during the reign of William IV and Victoria.

1967—Decimal coinage of 1 dollar divided into 100 cents, issued by the new Bank of Guyana.

1970—Copper-nickel dollar portrays slave insurrection leader Cuffy as Guyana joins FAO coin program.

1976—All new coinage portrays historical figures, wildlife of Guyana.

1996—All notes below $20 are withdrawn and replaced with coins.

CHILE

1749—Santiago Mint created.

1817—Chile Independiente coinage of republic.

1851—Decimal peso of 100 centavos introduced.

1895—Condor standing on mountain peak coinage, designed by French engraver Louis-Oscar Roty; standard design of fluctuating fineness, weight and size through 1941.

1920—Subsidiary coinage in copper-nickel, retaining Roty design.

1942—Bronze peso and minor coins, Bernardo O'Higgins portrait type.

1954—Aluminum coinage; inflation advances.

1960—Introduction of new escudo of 100 centesimos, valued at 1,000 old pesos.

1971—Rapid inflation of the escudo after election of Marxist President Allende.

1975—New peso introduced valued at 1,000 escudos.

1978—New aluminum-bronze 1-peso and 50-centavo coins issued.

1996—2,000-peso note created to mediate 1,000- and 5,000-peso coins.

1999—Inflation leads to 20,000-peso note.

2000—Ringed bimetallic 500-peso coin bears new circulating coin denomination.

2001—New ringed bimetallic 100-peso coin makes debut.

2004—New 2,000-peso note is nation's first polymer issue.

2009—Central Bank announces new bank note series, to be released periodically into 2011.

COLOMBIA

1627—Santa Fe de Bogota Mint authorized, operated sporadically.

1729—Popayan Mint established, few coins initially struck.

1758—Popayan in regular production.

1811—Cartagena royal coinage.

1815—Independent coinage of Nueva Granada.

1820—Name Colombia first appears on coins, soon replaced by combinations and variations on the old name Nueva Granada.

1862—United States of Colombia copper, copper-nickel, silver and gold decimal coinage.

1886—Republic of Colombia established as the official title of the country.

1892—Columbus portrait 50-centavo coin issued for anniversary of New World's "discovery."

1907—Copper-nickel "paper money" 1-, 2- and 5-peso pieces introduced to withdraw depreciated paper currency.

1917—Centavo denominations replace the paper money coinage introduced in 1907.

1930—Last regular gold coinage.

1953—Last regular silver coin, 20-centavo piece, issued.

1968—First 20th century commemorative coin marks Eucharistic Congress.

1969—Nickel-clad steel coins introduced.

1977—New denomination, 2-peso coin, appears.

1978—Design changes on 100- and 500-peso oro notes.

1979—New 20-centavo coin the size of 25-centavo piece of the 1920s is released.

1980—Newly designed 5-, 500- and 750-peso coins are released.

1981—A 30,000-peso coin is issued.

1987—An inflationary 5,000-peso note is issued.

1993 to 1994—The 200- and 500-peso notes are replaced with coins of the same denominations.

1996—The 5,000- and 10,000-peso notes are demonetized due to a major theft.

2000—A 50,000-peso bank note represents a new higher denomination.

2005—Size of 1,000- and 2,000-peso bank notes reduced.

2010—A 2,000-peso bank note with Braille is issued.

DUTCH GUIANA-SURINAME

1762—Copper duit of the Society of Suriname.

1962—Autonomous coinage of Juliana issued; Suriname now self-governing as a part of the kingdom of the Netherlands.

1976—Gold, silver coins mark Independence anniversary.

2004—Guilder replaced with dollar, new series of bank notes issued; old coins circulate at exchange rate of 1 to 100 (100 guilder cents equal to 1 dollar).

ECUADOR

1824—Royalist Cuzco Mint established.

1836—After emergence from union in Great Colombia, republic of Ecuador coins are issued.

1858—Brief experiment with Latin Monetary Union coins, 5-franco piece struck.

1872—Decimal sucre of 100 centavos adopted.

1927—Small-size sucre introduced.

1937—Nickel sucre and minor coins.

1964—Nickel-clad steel coinage are issued.

1980—New 5- and 20-sucre notes are produced.

1988—High-denomination notes released due to inflation.

1995—Ringed-bimetallic circulating coins introduced.

1997—The 1,000-sucre note is replaced with a coin.

2000—U.S. currency officially becomes legal tender throughout Ecuador in September 2000.

FRENCH GUIANA

1780—Billon 2 sous of Louis XVI.

1718—Billon 10 centimes, Louis XVIII.

1846—Billon 10 centimes, Louis-Philippe.

PARAGUAY

1845—First coinage, a copper twelfth real with lion seated before a pole crowned with a liberty cap.

1870—After devastating wars with its neighbors, Paraguay issued first decimal coinage: copper 1-, 2- and 4-centesimo pieces.

1889—Nation's only crown-sized silver peso issued.

1925—Copper-nickel small pesos and multiples contribute to gradual decay of the coinage.

1944—New aluminum-bronze coins in new currency based on 100 centimos to 1 guarani.

1953—Scalloped-edge aluminum bronze centimo issue.

1968—President Alfredo Stroessner issues commemorative coins for the centenary of the war of the triple alliance against Paraguay, waged by Brazil, Argentina and Uruguay in the 19th century.

1973—Veritable flood of German-struck commemorative "coins" begins in honor of Olympics, popes, world leaders, Indian cultures and other unrelated matters.

1974—Stainless steel regular coinage, of 1- through 50-guarani denominations, honors heroes of Paraguayan history.

1977—Notes are replaced with stainless steel 1-, 5-, 10- and 50-guarani coins.

1998—A coin replaces the 500-guarani note.

2003—Commemorative 1-guarani coin celebrates 60th anniversary of denomination.

2009—New 2,000-guarani note is nation's first polymer issue.

PATAGONIA

1874—Fantasy 2-centavo copper coin struck by eccentric Frenchman "Orlie-Antoine I," self-proclaimed "king of Araucania and Patagonia." Silver pesos appear years later, products of a Berlin coin dealer.

1889—The adventurer Julius Popper strikes gold coin-weights in the name of the "Company of the gold-washers of the south."

PERU

1568—Lima Mint first established, coinage sporadic.

1684—More or less regular coinage at Lima Mint.

1822—Republican 8-real coin struck at Lima Mint.

1824—Republican 8-real coins systematically restruck with Spanish crown by Royalists.

1825—Regular republican coinage in real denominations.

1855—Decimal silver sol of 100 centavos introduced.

1880—Brief Latin Monetary Union style coinage of silver pesetas and 5-peseta coins at Lima Mint.

1898—The gold libra, or pound, first struck.

1918—A distinctive 5-, 10- and 20-centavo copper-nickel coinage introduced with the obverse date spelled out in words.

1935—Central Reserve Bank of Peru begins coinage emissions in bank note style with legend "... will pay to the bearer one half sol ..."

1942—Brass alloy replaces copper-nickel alloy in minor coins.

1966—New, unified design brass coinage, reduced sizes. Silver commemorative 20-sol coinage for the naval combat with Spain in 1866 begins a continuing commemorative series in various denominations of silver.

1971—Copper-nickel and silver coins for 150th anniversary of Peruvian independence recall earlier struggle of a would-be liberator, the Indian Tupac Amaru.

1975—New, tiny brass sol and half sol mark inflationary trend.

1986—Government purchases precious metals with hard assets to avoid creditor embargoes.

1990—Issues inflationary 100,000-inti note.

1991—Intis currency is converted to nuevo sol at 1 million to 1 in a currency reform.

1995—Braille and ringed-bimetallic coins released.

2005—Aluminum 1-centavo coins released.

2007—Adopts aluminum for 5-centavo coins.

2010—Circulating commemorative Wealth and Pride 1-nuevo-sol coin series begins. Newly designed 2- and 5-nuevo-sol coins enter circulation.

URUGUAY

1840—Copper decimal coinage in centesimo denominations introduced.

1844—Silver peso fuerte struck during historic siege of Montevideo.

1877 to 1895—Silver peso-centesimo coinage.

1901-51—Radiant sun centesimo coins in copper-nickel and copper.

1930—French-designed coins and notes for the centenary of independence.

1953—Artigas-portrait centesimo coinage introduced at the outbreak of a steadily worsening inflationary spiral.

1969—Radiant sun of earliest coinage reappears

on aluminum bronze 1-, 5- and 10-peso coins. Spectacularly modernistic silver 1,000-peso crown struck to mark the U.N. Food and Agriculture Organization's worldwide coin plan.

1975—Monetary reform attempts to halt inflation. New peso introduced, exchanged for 1,000 old pesos. The 150th anniversary of the struggle for independence is marked by new 5-peso coin.

1981—Coins of 2 new pesos in copper-nickel-zinc, 5 new pesos in copper-nickel-aluminum and 10 new pesos of copper-nickel released. Largest coin denomination ever issued in the country, a 5,000 new pesos of silver, issued as a commemorative.

1993—Peso uruguayo coins and notes are introduced in a currency reform, old "nuevo pesos" are exchanged at a ratio of 1,000-to-1.

2000—Ringed-bimetallic 10-peso-uruguayo coin makes debut.

2003—A 2,000-peso-uruguayo note is a new, higher denomination. 5-peso-uruguayo coin debuts.

2010—The 50-centésimo coins are withdrawn from circulation.

2011—New series of coins and paper money announced.

VENEZUELA

1802—Royal coinage at Caracas.

1817—First coinage by independence forces at the start of a long struggle.

1843—After leaving the union of Great Colombia, the first distinctive Venezuela coinage of copper quarter-, half- and 1-centavo denominations issued.

1858—Handsome French-designed real coinage struck.

1873—Brief issue of centavo-venezolano coinage.

1879—Latin Monetary Union coinage, 100 centimos to 1 bolivar, equal to the French franc, issued. Gold and silver coinage with Bolivar portrait struck.

1965—Last silver bolivar issued, nickel 1- and 2-bolivar coin and pure nickel 25- and 50-centimo coins introduced.

1973—Large 10-bolivar commemorative coin issued for centenary of the national coinage with a portrait of liberator Simon Bolivar.

1977—Nickel composition coins depict denominations in larger numerals to stop confusion with silver issues of earlier years.

1990—Small-denomination emergency notes issued.

1998—Casa de la Moneda de Venezuela Mint built in Maracay.

2008—Amid rampant inflation, nation redenominates currency, issuing new coins and paper money.

The Caribbean Islands

BAHAMAS

1806—Half penny of George III struck for the Bahamas.

1966—New decimal coinage replaces British coins

in use; Bahamas dollar of 100 cents, coins in nickel-brass, copper-nickel, pure nickel and silver, from 1 cent to $5.

1971—New name, Commonwealth of the Bahamas, adopted, begins appearing on coinage.

1973—Independence greeted by new coin types and a silver $10 coin.

1974-1987—Series of large gold coins, 72 millimeters (almost 3 inches) in diameter, sold as noncirculating legal tender to collectors.

1978—Central bank discontinues acceptance of large quantities of gold coins for redemption.

1992—First commemorative note is issued.

1995—Color-enhanced commemorative coins are issued by the Valcambi S.A. Mint.

2006—New design for 1-cent coin introduced.

2007—New design for 10-cent coin introduced.

BARBADOS

1788—Pineapple penny, copper, with African crowned with Prince of Wales' plume on obverse.

1792—Similar penny and additional half penny with colony's badge, the British king as Neptune in a marine car drawn by sea horses.

1973—New coinage and notes introduced.

1995—Production ends of dollar note.

1998—First commemorative note issued.

2003—Commemorative coins honor 375th anniversary of Bridgetown, the capital city.

2007—Commemorative coins honor cricket players.

BERMUDA

1616—Sommer Islands "Hogge money" issued for the new British colony on Bermuda.

1793—Half penny of George III issued for Bermuda.

1959—Silver 5-shilling crown struck, bearing a map of the island group.

1970—Decimal coinage in bronze and copper-nickel, 100 cents to one dollar, issued.

1984—J. David Gibbons appointed chairman of the Bermuda Monetary Authority.

1992—Bermuda issues its first commemorative note.

1996—Triangular-shaped commemorative coins are struck for collectors.

2006—Two-year commemorative shipwreck coin series begins.

2009—Bermuda launches redesigned bank notes.

BRITISH CARIBBEAN TERRITORIES, EASTERN GROUP

1955—Decimal coins in bronze and copper-nickel released for Barbados, British Guiana, Windward Isles, Leeward Isles and Trinidad-Tobago.

BRITISH COLONIES

1820 to 1822—Anchor money, silver fractions of a Spanish dollar in one-sixteenth, used in the West Indian colonies. Many cut and counterstamped coins in this same region.

CUBA

1870—Revolutionary provisional coinage, five centavos to one peso struck, probably at the Potosi, Bolivia, Mint.

1897—"Souvenir" silver peso struck in the United States to dramatize Cuban independence aspirations.

1898—Revolutionary committee issues coin similar to souvenir peso with denomination ONE PESO.

1915—During the period of peak prosperity and booming economic speculation later recalled as the "dance of the millions" a full range of copper-nickel, silver and gold Cuban coinage is created. Silver 20- and 40-centavo coins struck to accommodate Spanish peseta denominations of equivalent value still circulating.

1934—Following the overthrow of the first Cuban dictator, Gen. Gerardo Machado, the new silver peso struck is dubbed the "A.B.C." type for the secret society that led in Machado's overthrow.

1951—Melting of millions of A.B.C. pesos, held as reserve backing for Cuban silver certificates, for their bullion content creates a modern rarity.

1952—Silver commemorative coins struck for the 50th anniversary of the republic.

1953—Commemorative coinage for the centenary of Jose Marti, Cuba's national hero, includes 25-centavo and 50-centavo coins for the first time.

1962—The Kremnica Mint in Czechoslovakia strikes copper-nickel coins for the new Communist regime of Fidel Castro in 20- and 40-centavo denominations.

1975—Silver 5-, 10-peso coins announced marking 15th anniversary of the communization of the island's banking system.

1994—Pesos convertibles coins, notes issued to visitors in exchange for hard currency.

1995—Color-enhanced collector coins released.

1997—Bank notes issued by the newly established Banco Central de Cuba.

CURACAO AND NETHERLANDS ANTILLES

1821—Silver real introduced.

1900—Dutch denominations begin to circulate with a silver quarter guilder.

1944—U.S. Mints strike Dutch denominations with Curacao inscription during World War II for exiled Queen Wilhelmina.

1952—New coinage, still of older Dutch type for self-governing Netherlands Antilles, including Curacao, Aruba, Bonaire, Saba and Sankt Maarten.

1970—Wholly redesigned Netherlands Antilles coinage, pure nickel replacing silver in higher denominations.

2010—Governmental separation of countries, but no new coins issued as of mid-2011.

DANISH WEST INDIES

1708—Gold ducat of King Frederik IV struck for Danish West India Company.

1740—Copper and silver skilling coinage with royal monogram and ship reverse begin their long circulation.

1816—Small base silver 2-, 10- and 20-skilling coins with royal arms introduced.

1859—Base silver decimal coins of 100 cents to one daler introduced under King Frederik VII.

1904—Multiple good silver, nickel, bronze and gold coinage of Christian IX, based on a 20 cents equaling one franc equaling 100 bits standard.

1913—Last Danish coin, bronze cent of Christian X. Islands sold to the United States in 1917, whereupon their name was changed to the United States Virgin Islands.

DOMINICAN REPUBLIC

1844—Revolt against Haiti sees issue of a brass quarter real.

1877—Brass and small copper-nickel coinage during a period of great unrest.

1891—Latin Monetary Union coinage of the silver franco of 100 centesimos.

1897—Base silver peso of 100 centavos issued.

1937—Restoration of national financial independence after foreign tutelage and U.S. occupation, as new bronze, copper-nickel and silver coinage on American standard enters circulation.

1955—The 25th anniversary of the Trujillo dictatorship marked by the first gold coin struck in the hemisphere officially in accord with the U.S. official value of $35 per ounce; face value 30 pesos.

1967—Copper-nickel replaces silver in circulation.

1969—Copper-nickel peso marks 125th anniversary of 1844 revolt against Haitian occupiers.

1972—Silver crown-sized peso returns as commemorative issue, 25th anniversary of Central Bank.

1974—Gold 30-peso coin returns for 12th Central American and Caribbean Games in greatly reduced size, reflecting rise in gold prices.

1975—Historic 10-real crown of 16th century recalled on silver 10-peso coin marking the first coin struck in Hispaniola.

1995—Watermarks and other anti-counterfeiting security devices are added to notes.

1999 to 2000—New bank notes released.

2007—A 200-peso bank note is new denomination.

2010—A 20-peso polymer bank note makes debut; nation's first polymer note.

EAST CARIBBEAN

1970—Crown-sized circulation-quality copper-nickel and Proof silver $4 coins released to commemorate the inauguration of the Caribbean Development Bank. Antigua, Barbados, St. Kitts, Dominica, Grenada, Montserrat, St. Lucia and St. Vincent all represented with new coat of arms obverses.

1972—Cayman Islands coinage of decimal type.

1989—Antigua issues commemorative legal tender notes made of precious metals. East Caribbean States changes composition of dollar from aluminum-bronze to copper-nickel; shape changed from round to decagon.

1993—New $5, $10, $20, $50 and $100 notes issued in October.

1994—New $5, $10, $20, $50 and $100 notes issued in December; designs modified for easier readability.

1998—New $100 note with additional security features issued in February.

2008—Circulating commemorative dollar marks Caribbean Development Bank's 25th anniversary.

FRENCH COLONIES

1717—Six- and 12-denier bronze coins of Louis XV designed for colonial commerce.

1721—Bronze 9-denier coin added.

1740—Billon 12-denier coin struck.

1767—Bronze 12-denier coin struck.

1758—Billon "sou marque" issued, which is to see extended circulation all over the West Indies, where it becomes familiar as the "black dog."

1825—King Charles X strikes yellow bronze 5- and 10-centime coins for the colonies.

1839 to 1844—Louis-Philippe continues colonial bronze coinage.

1897—Martinique creates copper-nickel 50-centime and 1-franc coinage, a type secured by precious metal deposited in the colonial treasury. Issued also in 1922.

1903—Similar promissory coinage in copper-nickel created for Guadeloupe.

HAITI

1802—Silver escalin denominations struck for the French Republic under the self-governing colony of Governor-General Toussaint l'Ouverture.

1807—President Henry Christophe creates a decimal currency, one gourde equals 100 centimes.

1814—Republic in southern Haiti issues base decimal coinage in denominations interchangeable with the Spanish American real.

1828—Copper coinage of fasces type begun by President J.P. Boyer, ruler of the whole island of Hispaniola.

1850—Imperial coinage of former President Faustin Soulouque, now emperor Faustin I.

1863—Reformed copper coinage of restored republic, President Fabre Geffrard.

1881—Silver gourde coinage of Latin Monetary Union fineness and weight, but not denomination, issued by President Salomon.

1904—President Nord Alexis begins copper-nickel coinage in sizes still current into the 1990s.

1968—Haiti joins FAO coinage program. Haiti markets Proof sets through Paramount to raise foreign income.

1972 to 1978—Commemoratives in gold and silver marketed to U.S. celebrate "Indian Chiefs of North America" and other themes.

1983 to 1989—Currency reform under "Baby Doc" Duvalier includes new notes composed of tyvek, DuPont fiber.

1996—In the wake of revolt and occupation, Haiti issues new coins. The 5-, 20- and 50-centime coins and 1- and 2-gourde coins meet the needs of improved commerce. A 100-gourde note is introduced.

2004—Wholesale redesign of nation's paper money.

2006—A 1,000-gourde bank note is new higher denomination.

JAMAICA

1869—Copper-nickel farthing, half penny and penny introduced.

1937—Alloy of coins changed to nickel-brass.

1969—Decimal coinage after five years of independence within British Commonwealth.

1972—Commemorative silver $10 coin celebrating 10 years of independence issued.

1990—Composition of dollar coin changed from copper-nickel to nickel-brass.

1993—Dollar coin's composition changed to brass-plated steel for two years.

1994—Dollar composition changed to nickel-clad steel; shape changed to seven-sided from round.

1996—$1, $2 and $5 notes are phased out in favor of the circulating $1 and $5 coins.

2000—Ringed-bimetallic $20 coin replaces bank note of same denomination.

2008—Bob Marley coins, dated 1995, released.

2009—2008-dated coins honoring Olympian Usain Bolt and other runners released. A $5,000 note makes debut as new highest denomination paper money. Seven-sided dollar and scallop-shaped $5 coins are replaced with round coins.

PUERTO RICO*

1895—Silver peso worth five Spanish pesetas

introduced by the colonial power.

1896—Silver minor coins introduced.

1902—With the island now under U.S. control, the First National Bank of Porto Rico issues Series 1902 national bank notes. All are rare today.

2009—Puerto Rico's quarter dollar in the six-coin District of Columbia and U.S. Territories quarter dollars program is released throughout the United States and Puerto Rico.

* Note: U.S. coinage and currency has been used in Puerto Rico for more than 100 years.

TRINIDAD AND TOBAGO

1964—Trinidad dollar established on par with the Eastern Caribbean dollar.

1969—Copper-nickel dollar struck for FAO coin plan.

1976—Newly formed Republic of Trinidad and Tobago issues first coinage. Coinage continues sporadically from late 1970s through 1990s.

1985—Undated series of notes introduced ($1, $5, $10, $20 and $100).

1994—Ten-dollar coin celebrating 30th anniversary of Central Bank first commemorative since 1984.

1995—Commemorative dollar coin celebrates 50th anniversary of United Nation's FAO.

2006—Commemorative coins celebrates Soca Warriors' entry in World Cup soccer tournament.

WINDWARD ISLES

1731—Silver 6-, 12-sol coins issued by Louis XV.

Europe

ALBANIA

1926—Albania commences coinage, 100 qindar ari equals one franka ari.

1947—Zinc first coinage of communist Albania replaces Italian occupation coinage in aluminum-bronze, stainless steel, silver.

1964—New communist Albanian coins in aluminum, a gift of China, issued.

1968—Gold 50-leke coin issued.

1988—Commemorative 50-leke coin depicting trains exiting tunnel on either side issued; tunnel is actually a hole in the coin.

1991 to 1992—Olympic commemoratives issued.

1993—Commemorative 200-leke note issued Feb. 10, 1993, celebrating 80 years of independence.

1994—New 200-, 500- and 1,000-leke notes introduced.

1996—New 200-, 500- and 1,000-leke notes introduced.

2005—Circulating commemorative 50-leke Albanian Antiquity coin, dated 2003, released.

2008—New higher denomination 2,000-leke notes introduced.

AUSTRIA

1857—Austrian empire adopts new florin silver coinage, one florin equals 100 kreuzer.

1892—New Austro-Hungarian standard of coinage; 100 heller (Hungarian 100 filler) to one silver corona (German krone, Hungarian korona).

1924—After a disastrous inflation, new Austrian coinage adopted, 100 groschen equals one schilling.

1946—Austria resumes schilling coinage interrupted by the Nazi Anschluss.

1955—Start of the long run of Austrian modern commemoratives.

1959—Aluminum-bronze composition introduced for circulating 50-groschen and 1-schilling coins; replaces aluminum.

1968—Silver 5-schilling coin changed to copper-nickel alloy in mid-year.

1974—Silver 10-schilling coin changed to copper-nickel alloy.

1975—Austria fixes upon 100-schilling denomination for silver commemoratives.

1976—Gold 1,000-schilling coin marks Austria's millenary; first new gold type issued in country since 1938.

1980—Austria introduces a gold-colored 20-schilling coin.

1985—Austria bars South African Krugerrand importation.

1986—New 50-schilling note issued.

1988—New 20-schilling note (dated 1986) introduced.

1989—Austrian Mint transfers from government to private ownership. Austria begins marketing gold bullion Vienna Philharmonic coins.

1993—Series of 500-schilling commemorative coins honoring regions of Austria begins.

1996—Austria issues circulating ringed bimetal 50-schilling coin.

1997—Latent image security device appears on Austria 50-schilling coin. New 500-schilling note introduced in October (dated Jan. 1, 1997).

1998—Austria and Luxembourg are among countries pledging to join the European Union monetary union. Austria begins striking euro coinage for release in 2002.

2002—Austria drops the schilling and adopts the euro currency on Jan. 1, as 300 million people in 12 nations across Europe replace their legacy currencies with a joint currency.

2003—Austria becomes the first nation to use niobium for coins.

2004—Giant 1,000-ounce €100,000 gold Philharmonic coin, nicknamed "Big Phil," marks 15th anniversary of bullion program.

2008—Philharmonic 1-ounce silver coin, denominated €1.5, makes debut amid record demand for bullion coins.

2011—Rising price of silver keeps sales from beginning for circulating versions of silver €5 coins at face-value, then Austrian Mint decides to melt those struck and to strike no further issues.

BELARUS

1991—Leaves Soviet Union during breakup, becomes founding member of Commonwealth of Independent States in December.

1992—Russian rubles lose legal tender status Nov. 10 (later restored).

1994—Russian rubles lose legal tender status again Nov. 8, 1994, with new notes of Belarus serving as currency.

1996—First commemorative coinage introduced.

1997—First notes (50,000-ruble and 100,000-ruble denominations) introduced.

1998—First 500,000-ruble note introduced Dec. 1, 1998.

1999—First 1 million-ruble note introduced April 30, 1999. Five-million-ruble note reported in circulation in September 1999.

2001—Commemorative 20-ruble note marks 10th anniversary of National Bank of the Republic of Belarus. Series of 10 different commemorative bank notes celebrate the new millennium.

2004 to 2005—Numerous commemorative coins celebrate 60th anniversary of liberation from Nazis, victims of World War II and victory.

2010—Commemorative 20,000-ruble bank note marks 20th anniversary of National Bank of the Republic of Belarus.

BELGIUM

1790—The historic coinage of the then Austrian Netherlands is interrupted by the rebellion coinage in copper, silver and gold.

1815—Necessity copper coinage in the name of Napoleon, later Louis XVIII, in Anvers, Antwerp.

1831—After a period of unhappy union with the Netherlands, an independent kingdom of Belgium is proclaimed; Leopold of Saxe-Coburg-Gotha becomes "Leopold premier," a double-meaning title (he is both the first Leopold and the first king of the new kingdom).

1832—The first coins are issued, a copper 10-centime piece and a silver 5-franc piece, the latter bearing Leopold's laureate head.

1834—Gold 20- and 40-franc patterns struck.

1848—Beginning of new, bare head coinage in silver, first gold coinage issued.

1860—Copper-nickel 20-centime coins struck.

1901—Holed copper-nickel coinage under Leopold II issued in 5-, 10-centime denominations; 25-centime coin added in 1908.

1915—Zinc 5-, 10- and 25-centime coinage issued under the German occupation. In addition, a necessity coinage, or Belgian notgeld, composed of iron with unusual brass-plated obverse, copper-plated reverse, is issued in occupied Ghent.

1918—Zinc 50-centime coin struck with central hole.

1922—In the post-war period of financial uncertainty, pure nickel 50-centime and 1- and 2-franc coins are struck, inscribed "good for [denomination]" to temporarily replace paper money, as in France, Italy, Luxembourg and Romania in this adjustment period.

1930—In an attempt to replace lower value paper money, a pure nickel coinage of 5-, 10- and 20-franc denominations is begun, with a new additional denomination of the belga, which is equal to 5 francs.

1935—A silver 50-franc coin is struck to mark the centenary of Belgian railroads, with a regular issue in this denomination appearing in 1939.

1941—Introduction of zinc minor coins under the German occupation, 5-, 10- and 25-centime pieces and 1- and 5-franc coins eventually struck.

1944—Allied armies entering Belgium issue zinc-coated steel 2-franc coins struck on the planchets also used for the U.S. 1943 Lincoln zinc-coated steel cent.

1948—Following liberation, a new coinage is begun, highlighted by a 100-franc piece with the busts of the nation's four kings.

1951—Baudouin I becomes king after a confused era of collaborationist charges against Leopold III. A new and innovative coinage is gradually created, including silver 50-franc commemoratives in 1958 and 1960; and a copper-nickel 10-franc coins in 1969, uniquely without obverse inscription around the king's head.

1976—Silver commemorative 250-franc coins in

separate French and Flemish types honors 25th anniversary of King Baudouin I.

1979—New coins replace minor denomination circulating notes.

1980—The 150th anniversary 25-franc coin is struck, design determined by competition.

1981—The 25-centime denomination is abolished.

1987—Commemorative ecu coin subject to Value Added Tax in France and Great Britain.

1989-1990—Several ecu-denomination "coins" marketed to collectors in anticipation of European Monetary Union.

1994—Deflation causes replacement of the 5,000-franc note with a 2,000-franc note. Coinage depicting new king, Albert II, introduced.

1995—New 200-franc note introduced.

1997—New 1,000-franc note introduced April 24, 1997. New 10,000-franc note introduced June 19, 1997.

1998—Belgium officially agrees to participate in common currency union of the European Union. New 500-franc note introduced April 16, 1998.

2002—Belgium drops the franc and adopts the euro currency on Jan. 1, 2002, as 300 million people in 12 nations across Europe replace their legacy currencies with a joint currency.

2005—Nation's first circulating commemorative €2 coin marks the Benelux (Belgium and Luxembourg) economic union.

BOSNIA-HERZEGOVINA

1992—Following breakup of Yugoslavia, Bosnia-Herzegovina introduces currency system of 1 dinara equal to 100 para. German marks in wide use.

1993—Commemorative series introduced, including dinosaur series (part of Preserve Planet Earth program).

1996—Olympic commemorative coins introduced.

1998—Konvertiblina-marka notes, in 1-konvertiblina-marka to 200-konvertiblina-marka denominations, introduced in June 1998.

2000—New 1- and 2-konvertiblina-marka coins introduced July 31, 2000.

2003—50-fening notes withdrawn March 31, 2003.

2006—50-fening coin introduced Jan. 5, 2006.

2009—1-konvertiblina-marka notes removed from circulation March 31, 2009.

2010—5-konvertiblina-marka notes removed from circulation March 31, 2010.

BULGARIA

1881—Bulgarian coinage, on a system of one lev equals 100 stotinki, issued under Prince Alexander I. Romania becomes a kingdom.

1951—Communist Peoples Republic Bulgarian coinage begins.

1962—Bulgarian monetary reform.

1963—First new Bulgarian commemoratives.

1974—Sporadic production of 5-stotinka coin resumes; the coins are struck in 1974, 1979, 1980, 1988, 1989 and 1990.

1977—Circulating 50-stotinka coin commemorates University Games at Sofia.

1988—Commemorative coins honoring Summer Games marketed.

1990—Last coins of communist government produced.

1992—First circulating coins for the Republic of Bulgaria. Stotinki denominations depict lion, lev denominations depict Madara horseman. Olympic commemoratives marketed. New 200-lev note introduced.

1993—New 500-lev note introduced.

1994—World Cup Soccer commemorative coins marketed. New 1,000- and 2,000-lev notes introduced.

1995-1996—Olympic commemorative coins marketed. New 5- and 10-lev notes introduced in 1996.

1997—Composition of 20-lev coin changed from copper-nickel to brass, diameter reduced. Twenty-lev denomination introduced.

1998—5,000-leva coin with European Community ecu symbol marketed.

1999—Monetary reform introduced July 1, 1999, with 1 new lev equal to 1,000 old leva. New 1- and 2-lev notes introduced under new system.

2002—Ringed bimetallic 1-lev coin makes debut.

2005—2,000-lev commemorative bank note marks national bank's 120th anniversary.

2007—Commemorative 1.95583-lev coin celebrates Bulgaria's accession to European Union in 2007.

2008—Designs for eventual euro coins selected in national contest.

CROATIA

1941—Independent state of Croatia in former Yugoslavia issues a single zinc 2-kuna coin on standard of 100 banica equals one kuna.

1993—Again independent (Croatia was part of Yugoslavia from 1947 to 1991), Croatia issues a new circulating coinage and notes.

1994—Currency system of 1 kuna equals 1,000 Croatian dinara introduced.

1995—Two-kuna FAO coin depicting tuna issued. Same basic design as issued with different legends in 1993.

1997—Ringed bimetallic 25-kuna coin commemorates Danube border region.

2000—Circulating commemorative 25-kuna coin celebrates Millennium.

2002—Circulating commemorative 25-kuna coin marks 10th anniversary of nation's international recognition.

2004—Commemorative 10-kuna note honors 10th anniversary of the reintroduction of the kuna currency. Circulating commemorative 25-kuna coin celebrates EU membership candidacy.

2010—Circulating commemorative 25-kuna coin highlights European Bank meeting in Zagreb.

CZECH REPUBLIC

1993—New Czech Republic issues circulating coinage in haleru and koruna denominations. New notes introduced in koruna denominations.

1994—Commemorative 200-korun coins honor various subjects, including 50th anniversary of D-Day invasion of occupied Europe. New 20-korun notes introduced April 20, 1994.

1995—Gold commemorative series honoring historic coins produced.

1996—New 2,000-korun note introduced Oct. 1, 1996.

1999—New 5,000-korun note with improved security devices introduced Sept. 8, 1999.

2001—Series 1993 1,000- and 5,000-korun notes lose legal tender status June 31, 2001.

2003—The 10- and 20-heller coins lose legal tender status Oct. 31, 2003.

2007—Series 1993 50-, 100-, 200- and 500-korun notes lose legal tender status Jan. 31, 2007.

2008—The 20-korun note and 50-heller coin withdrawn Aug. 31, 2008.

CZECHOSLOVAKIA

1921—Czecho-Slovakia begins coinage, 100 haleru equals one koruna.

1947—Czechoslovakia introduces new reduced size coins of prewar design.

1953—Czechoslovak monetary reform brings new types and designs.

1961—First coins of the Socialist Republic struck.

1964—First 10-korun commemorative coins issued.

1965—First 25-korun commemorative coins issued.

1968—First 50-korun commemorative coins issued.

1970—Czechoslovakia silver commemoratives launch new series.

1978—Composition of 50-haleru coin changed to copper-nickel from bronze (last struck in 1971).

1981—First 500-korun commemorative coin introduced (death of Ludovit Stur).

1988—Last 500-korun commemorative coins struck.

1990—Last coins struck as Czechoslovakia.

1991—Newly formed Czech and Slovak Federal Republic issues circulating coinage.

1993—Czech Republic and Slovakia split, each issuing their own independent currencies.

DENMARK

1537—Crown-sized gulden in silver of King Christian III.

1541—Silver 1-mark coin issued.

1563—Klippe emergency coinage of the Seven Years War issued.

1564—Square gold gulden or krone minted.

1572—Silver speciedaler struck by Frederik II.

1591—Heavy gold Portugaloser struck by Christian IV.

1602—Copper coinage of 2 pennings, Christian IV.

1608—Silver double speciedaler, liondaler and gold sovereign minted.

1644—First coinage with Hebrew inscription and Latin combination, translating to English as "Jehovah the just judge."

1655—Goldkrone struck under Frederik III.

1659—Commemorative double krone issued with hand from clouds hacking a Swedish arm reaching for Denmark's crown.

1670—Silver speciedaler struck to mark the death of Frederik III and the accession of Christian V, beginning a long series of such coinages.

1688—Gold coinage with view of the fortress of Christiansborg in Guinea.

1708—A 2-ducat coin is struck for the Danish West India Company.

1771—Trade piaster struck in imitation of the Spanish Pillar dollar, with circular Danish and Norwegian arms replacing the two globes.

1808—Serious inflation leads to using silver and copper, including the copper roof from the church of Our Lady in Copenhagen, in dwindling-sized coins.

1813—National Bank tokens struck in copper.

1854—Last speciedaler of Frederik VII, silver rigsdalers form currency.

1873—New Scandinavia coinage of 100 øre to the silver krone, Christian IX.

1888—First commemorative under the new system, the 25th year of the reign.

1920—Copper-nickel 10- and 25-øre coins replace silver, a consequence of the post-war economic crunch.

1941—Zinc minor coinage under the German occupation, 1, 10 and 25-øre pieces; aluminum 2 and 5-øre coins.

1960—Copper-nickel replaces aluminum-bronze for the 1-krone coin; issuance of a new 5-krone regular issue is begun in the same metal. A silver 5-krone coin marking the silver wedding anniversary of the royal couple begins another series.

1967—Silver 10-krone commemoratives begin with wedding coins of Princess Margrethe and Princess Benedikte.

1973—New coinage of Queen Margrethe II includes copper-clad steel 5-øre piece.

1976—New Mint construction begins.

1980—Ten-kroner coin and 20-krone note introduced.

1989—Devalues 5- and 10-øre coins.

1990—Circulates 5-krone coin.

1993—Debit card use reduces use of domestic coinage.

1995—Commemorative 20-krone coin marks 1,000 years of Danish coinage.

1997—Series 1997 notes introduced Sept. 12, 1997.

1999—Series 1997 50-krone note introduced May 7, 1999.

2001—New portraits of Queen Margrethe make debut on the 10- and 20-krone coins.

2008—25-øre coin loses legal tender status Oct. 1, 2008.

2009—Series 2009 50-krone note introduced Aug. 11, 2009, the first release in a design overhaul for the nation's bank notes.

2010—Series 2009 100-krone note makes debut May 4, and 200-krone note released Oct. 19.

2011—New portrait of the queen used for commemorative coins in 2010 debuts on circulating 10- and 20-krone coins.

ENGLAND

500 to 575—Beginning of Anglo-Saxon silver sceat coinage.

circa 765—Beginning of silver penny coinage, kingdoms of Kent, Mercia, etc.

circa 786—Pennies of kings of Wessex, later kings of all England.

885—Beginning of Viking coinages in England.

1257—Experimental gold penny of Henry III, worth 20 silver pennies.

1278—Introduction of silver groat, 4 pence; silver half penny and farthing.

1344—Introduction of gold florin, half and quarter florin; noble and parts.

1465—Rose noble introduced in gold, 120 grains valued at 10 shillings. Former gold noble replaced with angel of 80 grains.

1485—Reign of Henry VII, which saw a gold sovereign of 20 shillings and the silver testoon, or shilling.

1543—Start of the systematic debasement of the English coinage by Henry VIII.

1561—First attempt at milled, machine-struck coinage by French engraver Eloye Mestrelle, during reign of Elizabeth I; three-half pence and three-farthing coins introduced.

1601—Silver coinage restored to full fineness, pre-Henry VIII debasement.

1604—Gold unite introduced, lighter weight gold pound.

1613—Harrington farthings, licensed copper coinage, first such in England.

1631—Nicholas Briot actively seeks milled coinage.

1649—Commonwealth coinage, English inscriptions.

1648 to 1672—Seventeenth century token issues, in absence of official copper coins, proliferate.

1660—Restoration of Charles II, last hammered coinage.

1662—Milled coinage officially adopted.

1695—Great Silver Recoinage begins, removal of worn and clipped coinage from circulation.

1797—"Cartwheel" twopence and penny, both produced on steam machinery, issued.

1804—Bank of England dollar, overstruck on Spanish 8-real coins.

1811—Bank of England 3-shilling, 18-pence, 9-pence token issued.

1816—Complete recoinage, token silver, new gold sovereign, half-sovereign.

1860—Copper penny, half penny and farthing replaced by bronze coinage.

1920—Silver coinage reduced to .500 fine, new quaternary alloy.

1925—End of regular gold coinage.

1937—New 12-sided threepence in nickel-bronze introduced.

1947—Silver replaced by copper-nickel, small threepence discontinued.

1956—Farthing discontinued.

1967—Half penny discontinued.

1968—First decimal denominations introduced alongside pre-decimal coins.

1971—Full decimalization, 100 new pence to one pound.

1972—Crown returns as 25 new pence for anniversary of royal wedding. New coin is twice the size of 50 new pence.

1977—British public, collectors greet Silver Jubilee crowns and medals with record enthusiasm.

1978—Liberalized policy on gold coin importation.

1979—Sir Christopher Wren is portrayed on new £50 note. Royal Mint weathers a strike by workers for one week in October.

1980—Sixpence ceases to be legal tender on June 30.

1981—Wedding of Prince Charles and Lady Diana Spencer is marked with commemorative crowns.

1982—Value Added Tax is added to all sales of coins more than 100 years old. A new 20-pence coin is introduced. Coins drop the NEW PENCE legend.

1984—Half penny production ceases. £1 note ceases production and is replaced by £1 coin already in circulation.

1986—£2 coin introduced as a commemorative issue.

1987— Britannia gold bullion coins introduced.

1987—Security threads introduced into £5 and £10 notes.

1988—Withdrawal of legal tender status of £1 note.

1989—Commemorative £5 coin celebrates 500th anniversary of gold sovereign.

1990—Size reduction of notes and coins begins.

1991—Reduced-size notes with devices for sight-impaired introduced.

1993—New £20 note introduced in series.

1994—Circulating 50-pence commemorative coin celebrates 50th anniversary of D-Day invasion of occupied Europe. New £50 note introduced.

1996—First commemorative notes are issued.

1997—Ringed-bimetallic circulating £2 and smaller diameter 50-pence coins introduced.

1998—New Rank-Broadley portrait depicting an aging Queen Elizabeth II replaces previous portrait.

1999—Commemorative coin depicting Diana,

Princess of Wales, marketed; becomes very popular worldwide. New £20 note issued June 22, 1999.

2000—Commemorative coin honoring the 100th birthday of Queen Mother Elizabeth produced.

2001—Centennial death anniversary of Queen Victoria subject of £5 coin.

2002—Queen mother dies, honored with £5 coin. £5 coin marks Queen Elizabeth II's Golden Jubilee.

2003—£5 coin highlights 50th anniversary of Queen Elizabeth II's coronation.

2005—200th anniversary of Battle of Trafalger, Adm. Lord Horatio Nelson's death, commemorated with £5 coins.

2006—£5 coin marks Queen Elizabeth II's 80th birthday.

2007—Adam Smith replaces Sir Edward Elgar on back of new £20 note. £5 coin honors Queen Elizabeth II and Prince Philip's 60th wedding anniversary.

2008—Complete redesign of six circulating coin designs unveiled, begin entering circulation. Prince Charles' 60th birthday honored with £5 coin.

2009—Royal Mint announces ambitious coin program to mark 2012 London Olympic and Paralympic Games, including 29 circulating 50-pence coins bearing designs submitted via public contest.

2010—£50 note honoring Matthew Boulton and James Watt debuts.

2011—Multiple commemorative coins issued for wedding of Prince William and Catherine Middleton.

ESTONIA

1922—Estonian mark coins introduced.

1929—Monetary reform (100 senti equals 1 kroon) results in new coins.

1931—Five- and 10-sent coins struck.

1934—Two-sent coin struck.

1935—Twenty-sent coin struck.

1936—Fifty-sent coin struck. Last coins struck before Estonia is forced into the Soviet Union at the start of World War II.

1991—New independent republic issues first coinage in sent and kroon denominations.

1992—First commemorative coins of new republic. New 1-, 2-, 5-, 10-, 25-, 100- and 500-kroon notes introduced June 20, 1992.

1994—New 50-kroon notes introduced Oct. 10, 1994.

1995—New 500-kroon notes introduced.

1997—Composition of 20-sent coin changed from brass to nickel-plated steel. New 5-, 10- and 500-kroon notes introduced July 1, 1997.

1998—Composition of 1-kroon coin changed from copper-nickel to brass.

1999—A 10-litas commemorative coin celebrating 10th anniversary of Baltic peoples calling for independence from Soviet Union is issued. Same coin circulates in all three Baltic nations. New 100-kroon notes introduced May 30, 1999, with a holographic stripe at left face.

2008—Circulating commemorative 1-kroon coin,

10-kroon note, celebrate nation's 90th anniversary.

2011—Becomes 17th nation to adopt the euro, replacing the kroon with joint currency on Jan. 1, 2011.

FINLAND

1860—After groundwork by Minister of Finance J.V. Snellman, the grand duchy of Finland, under the rule of the Russian czar, adopts its own coinage of the Finnish markkaa of 100 pennia.

1917—Following the overthrow of the czar, uncrowned double eagles appear on the Finnish coinage.

1918—A single copper 5-penni coin with communist emblems is issued by the Red forces during the civil war. Normalized coinage of the new republic begins.

1926—Only gold coinage of modern Finland, 200-, 100-markka pieces.

1928—Aluminum-bronze 5, 10-markka pieces.

1931—Aluminum-bronze 20-markka piece.

1941—Holed 5-, 10-penni wartime issue.

1943—Iron wartime issues, 25-, 50-penni coins, 1-markka coin.

1951-52—The XV Olympic Games in Helsinki marked by a silver 500-markka coin.

1952—New aluminum-bronze, iron post war coinage.

1960—Silver 1,000-markka coin honors minister Snellman, founder of the coinage.

1963—Coinage reform, one new markka equals 100 old.

1967—First silver 10-markka coin honors 50th anniversary of independence. Currency devalued.

1969—Aluminum replaces the bronze 1 penni of the reform currency. Aluminum penni; copper-nickel 1 markka.

1972—Aluminum-bronze 5-markka coin issued.

1977—Aluminum 5-penni coin issued.

1979—Production of penni ceases.

1983—Aluminum 10-penni coin issued.

1984—Braille added to 10-marka note to aid the blind.

1988—New mint facility built at Vantaa.

1990—A report leads to a revampment of the entire domestic coinage system.

1991—New security devices are used on a new generation of notes.

1993—A Nordic Currency Union with Sweden and Norway is considered. The Mint of Finland is privatized. New 20-markka notes have hologram, part of series introduced in 1991.

1997—Bank of Finland reports indicate electronic money has undermined circulating coins.

1998—Finland officially agrees to participate in European Union currency union.

2002—Finland drops the markka and adopts the euro currency on Jan. 1.

2004—Launch of first circulating commemorative €2 coin, marking expansion of the European Union.

2010—Begins circulating commemorative €5 coin series honoring provinces.

FRANCE

(Since accession of Hugh Capet)

956—Hugh Capet, Duke of France, issues silver denier and billon obole, which were to become standard coins in succeeding reigns.

987—Hugh Capet becomes king, continues denier coinage.

1226—Louis IX (St. Louis) strikes gold coins: ecu d'or (also called denier d'or a l'ecu), l'angel d'or and the royal d'or. Silver coinage reform sees introduction of gros tournois, valued at 12 denier old coinage. The once fine silver denier is lapsing into a billon coinage.

1285—Phillip the Fair creates petite royal d'or.

1303—Adds chaise d'or. The term "d'or" indicates gold; first word describes the coin's obverse design, in this case the king on the royal throne, "chaise."

1328—Phillip of Valois adds parisis d'or; pavillon d'or. All of these medieval gold issues are named for their designs.

1350—John the Good introduces the mouton d'or, with the lamb of God.

1360—Adds the franc a cheval, with figure of the king charging on horseback, in silver.

1396—After one of France's first excursions into adventure in Italy, French-style coins in Genoese denominations are struck in the Genoa Mint.

1413—Billon grossus added to French coinage by Charles VI.

1417—Heaume d'or shows king in armor and helmet.

1421—Salut d'or added to gold denominations.

(After 1415, English King Henry V struck French-style coinage during his war in France.)

1436—Charles VII introduces gold ecu de la couronne.

1461—Louis XI, the "Spider king," creates billon douzain and billon liard. The liard, originally valued at three denier, became a familiar copper coin in later years.

1483—Charles VIII introduces the billon hardi.

1494—Further military intervention in Italy sees coins struck in the name of King Charles VII struck in 10 Italian Mint cities, from Pisa to Naples.

1513—Louis XII introduces circulating portrait coins, the silver teston and half teston.

1515—The reign of Francois I sees pattern portrait coin in many denominations, circulating silver testons of several designs, as well as billon hardi "black money" coinage.

1550—Henri II introduces gold portrait Henri d'or.

1560—Franco-Scots coinage issued during brief reign of Francois II, husband of Mary, Queen of Scots; gros d'argent, silver coin with its half and its quarter.

1568—First decimal denominations introduced alongside decimal coins.

1576—Reign of Henri III, cut short by assassination in France's troubled period, sees portrait silver piefort of the franc.

1594—Henri IV enters Paris after civil strife, sets path for stability and French unity. Earlier coin types become increasingly standardized.

1640—French gold becomes fixed as louis d'or and multiples under Louis XIII.

1641—Louis d'argent or louis blanc, the silver crown of 60 sols known abroad as the ecu, is introduced. French coinage is now essentially fixed in general pattern of issue until the great revolution.

1642—French invasion of Spanish Catalonia extends Louis XIII's coin types to the County of Barcelona.

1643—Louis XIV, whose long reign consolidated royal power and fixed the coinage in the general Louis d'or-silver ecu system. French culture, language and influence become all pervading because of Louis' splendor, his military campaigns and the magnificence of his court at Versailles.

1685—The heavy ecu carambole is introduced for use in occupied Flanders; the coin is valued at 80 sols, rather than the 60 or the regular ecu.

1717—Louis XV's reign sees the first coinage for the French colonies in general, the 12- and 9-denier coppers of 1717 and 1721; as well as specialized coin for the Antilles and French India.

1774—Louis XVI, last of the pre-Revolutionary rulers of France. First period coinage follows closely that of his predecessors.

1791—Following the revolution, a brief "constitutional period" precedes the reign of terror and the republic. The constitutional coinage begins in 1791; the new title "king of the French" and value of six livres are distinguishing marks. Copper and brass coins are struck, partly from looted church bells.

1793—Following execution of Louis XVI, first republican coinage of France is released, followed by a rapid inflation of the increasingly useless assignat paper currency, ostensibly guaranteed by a blanket mortgage of the national domain.

1795—Franc adopted as the chief unit of a decimal coinage, made up of 100 centimes or 10 decimes.

1803—First portrait coins of Napoleon Bonaparte, first consul of the republic issued: silver quarter- and half-, 1-, 2- and 5-franc coins, gold 20- and 40-franc pieces.

1804—Beginning of imperial coinage of Napoleon I, lasting until the "hundred days" coins of 1815.

1808—Bronze 5-centime, billon 10-centime coins introduced; Napoleon emperor.

1814-15—Restoration of the house of Bourbon, retention of the franc coinage.

1830—Under Louis Philippe, the royal arms on the reverse is replaced by value in wreath. Propaganda coins of pretender Henri V appear, 1831, joined later by coins of Napoleon II, bearing date "1816."

1848—Second republic sees massive issues of

medals, jetons and a large pattern coinage before prince president, Louis-Napoleon replaces the government, then becomes an authoritarian ruler in 1851.

1852 to 1870—Second empire of Napoleon III. Copper 1-, 2-, 5- and 10-centime coins join regular silver coinage, gold 50- and 100-franc coins replace the top value 40-franc pieces of earlier issues.

1870 to 1940—Third republic maintained the Latin Monetary Union standards, established as an international standard by Napoleon III in 1867 until the general collapse of European currencies after World War I.

1903—Nickel 25-centime coinage introduced.

1904—Similar 25-centime coin prepared with 22 sides in an attempt to reduce danger of confusion with 1-franc piece.

1914—Holed nickel Lindauer type coins begun, continued in various metal through 1946.

1933—Small Bazor type 5-franc coin in nickel, quickly withdrawn due to extensive counterfeiting.

1940—French defeat in World War II leads to Parliament calling aged Marshal Philippe Petain, hero of Verdun in World War I, to head the new French state.

1941—First coins of Vichy France.

1945—Fourth French republic begins.

1950—Currency reform, new aluminum-bronze and copper-nickel coinage.

1958—Fifth republic of Gen. Charles de Gaulle.

1960—New "heavy franc," equal to 100 old francs, introduced.

1965—Crown-sized coinage resumed with a revival of the Dupre design of Hercules, the republic and justice, first used in 1795.

1970—Silver abandoned in 5-franc coins.

1974—New 50-franc crown to supplant silver 10-franc coin; new abstract map 10-franc coin in base metal to be prepared for active circulation.

1979—The 2-franc coin is reinstated.

1982—Nation's first commemorative coin issued.

1986—Commemorative coins honor centennial of the Statue of Liberty in New York Harbor.

1987—Platinum, palladium, silver and silver piefort coins honor Lafayette.

1987—Two-month-old 10-franc coin is withdrawn due to similarity to half franc.

1988—Ringed-bimetallic 10-franc coin introduced.

1992—World's first ringed-trimetallic coin (20-franc denomination) issued.

1993—Cotton-based, smaller 50-franc note introduced, depicting author Antoine de Saint-Exupery and his literary creation, "The Little Prince," and an airplane.

1995—Two security threads used in new note series. New 500-franc note introduced in March.

1996—New 200-franc note introduced Oct. 29.

1997—New 100-franc note introduced Dec. 15.

1998—Monnaie de Paris strikes the eurozone's first European Union euro coin.

2001—Issues "ultime franc," wave-shaped coin designed by famous designer Philippe Starck.

2002—France drops the franc and adopts the euro currency on Jan. 1.

2004—Issues first kilogram-sized gold coin, denominated €500.

2007—Announces three-year series of circulating gold and silver Sower coins.

2010—Issues circulating €10 coin series honoring each of France's departments, in a program similar to the United States' State quarter dollar program.

GERMANY

1554—Imperial decree establishes the fine Cologne mark as coinage measure, a weight of silver weighing 233.855 grams.

1618 to 1623—"Kipper and wipper" period of debasement, inflation and the proliferation of mints resulting in monetary chaos.

1690—Leipzig Convention established standard of 12 taler to the fine mark.

1747—Austria abandons 1690 standard, adopts a lesser standard of 13-1/3 talers to the fine mark.

1750—Prussia adopts "Graumann standard," 14 talers to the fine mark.

1753—Austria and Bavaria announce "conventionstaler," 10 to the fine mark, a standard adopted by most German states.

1806—Abolition of Holy Roman Empire and resulting monetary disorganization.

1809—Kronentalers appear in Bavaria, similar to earlier issues in the former Austrian Netherlands, 9.08 to the fine mark.

1837—Bavaria leads south-central German states at the Munich Convention to adopt the gulden as the standard coinage unit, equal to 24½ gulden to the fine mark, or two gulden to one taler. Saxony leads Thuringian states into Dresden Convention, adopting the Graumann standard of 14 taler to the fine mark, the system already in use by Prussia and seven other states.

1838—Dresden and Munich groups agree on an integrated standard of 14 taler equaling one Cologne fine mark equaling 24½ gulden; two taler equaling 3½ gulden.

1857—Monetary union based on "zollpfund," metric pound of 500 grams or half-kilogram, equal to 30 vereinstaler; gold coinage of one krone and half krone established at 50 kronen to the zollpfund.

1873—Unification of coinage in the new German empire; silver and gold coinage, bronze subsidiary coins on a new one mark to 100 pfennig standard. Surviving vereinstaler to circulate as 3-mark coin.

1890—First colonial coins issued, for the German East Africa Company.

1894 to 1895—Bird of Paradise coins issued by the German New Guinea Company.

1904—New German East Africa coinage under Imperial administration introduced.

1908—Beginning of 3-mark coinage, commemorative issues under same decree.

1909—Copper-nickel coins on Mexican peso standard issued for German treaty port of Kiautschou.

1915—World War I iron minor coinage begins.

1916—Coins struck for emergency use in German East Africa.

1918—State authorized notgeld in Braunschweig begins flood of such necessity coins and notes.

1923—Catastrophic inflation, ending in new rentenmark currency reform.

1924—Adoption of the reichsmark.

1925—Commemorative 3- and 5-mark series begins.

1936—First coins bearing Nazi swastika introduced.

1945—"Denazified" zinc coins under Allied occupation.

1948—Monetary reform in western occupation zones; aluminum coins in east zone.

1948—West German currency reform sparks the Soviet blockade of Berlin. East Germany issues its first post-World War II currency.

1949—Bank Deutscher Laender begins issuing coins in west.

1950—Bronze and brass-clad steel coinage of the German Federal Republic, copper-nickel 50-pfennig coin, issued.

1951—Silver 5-deutsche-mark coin in circulation in Western zones. Copper-nickel 2-mark coin causes confusion among users, sees one year of striking.

1952—Silver 5-deutsche-mark coin honoring Nuremberg's Germanisches Museum begins long, distinguished series of Federal Republic commemoratives.

1952—West Germany begins prolific commemorative coin program for collectors.

1954—Independent currency of Saarland issued.

1956—First coinage bearing the title of the German Democratic Republic (East Germany), supplants earlier issues inscribed merely "Germany."

1966—First commemoratives of the German Democratic Republic; ambitious commemorative coin program begun to raise hard currency.

1969—"Magnimat" (copper-nickel clad nickel) 2-deutsche-mark coin with Adenauer portraits enters circulation in Federal Republic.

1972—Tons of recycled silver used in series of 10-deutsche-mark coins honoring the XX Olympiad, first issue with improper legend "In Germany," rather than the Olympic non-national "In Muenchen."

1975—"Magnimat" material introduced for 5-deutsche-mark coin. Only silver coins still issued in Federal Republic are commemoratives.

1986—Point-of-sale system cashless economy experimented with in Munich and in West Berlin.

1990—Plans for reunification of East and West Germany promise currency compromises. East German currency is withdrawn at midnight June 30 and replaced with West German marks.

1991—New 5- and 20-deutsche-mark notes introduced.

1997—Optical security device added to German notes following laundering of lower-denomination notes by counterfeiters to print higher denominations using the same paper.

1998—Germany officially agrees to join the European Union currency union.

2002—Germany drops the mark and adopts the euro currency on Jan. 1.

2003—Release of first group of collector coins in multi-year series commemorating the FIFA World Cup contest, which the nation is hosting in 2006.

2006—Circulating commemorative €2 coins series begins, honoring each state in the nation.

2011—Silver content reduced in collector €10 coins, dropping weight from 18 grams to 16 grams and reducing the fineness, from .925 fine to .625 fine. Later, silver content removed from circulating versions altogether, but retained it for collector version.

GREECE

1828—Coinage of independent Greece resumes, one phoenix equals 100 lepta; coins struck on the island of Aegina, where ancient Greek coinage began about 700 B.C.

1954—First Greek postwar coinage in aluminum and copper-nickel bears King Paul's likeness.

1966—Royal Greek coins of Constantine II issued.

1971—Greek royal arms of exiled King Constantine II replaced by symbol of ex-colonels' junta on nation's coins.

1973—New republican Greek coins of the junta issued.

1975—Redesigned Greek coins of post-junta era.

1979—First 10,000-drachma coin introduced; commemorates Common Market membership.

1981—New denominations of 2,500 and 5,000 drachmai introduced.

1982—More denominations changed from drachmai to drachmes measurements beginning this year.

1985—New coin denomination, 1,000 drachmes, introduced.

1990—New coin denomination, 20,000 drachmes, introduced.

1991—Commemorative coins celebrate Mediterranean Games.

1993—Commemorative 500-drachma coin celebrates 2,500 years of democracy.

1995—New 10,000-drachma note introduced March 7, 1995.

1996—Commemorative 1,000-drachma coins celebrate Olympic Centennial Games, depict participants in ancient Olympics. New 200-drachma note introduced Nov. 4.

1998—New 5,000-drachma note introduced July 1.

2001—Receives approval to adopt the euro in 2002, with the initial group of eurozone members.

2002—Greece drops the drachma and adopts the euro currency on Jan. 1.

2004—Issues first circulating commemorative €2 coin in the European Union; coin honors the 2004 Olympic Games held in Athens.

2010—Financial crisis threatens the euro in Greece.

GREENLAND

1922—Cryolite Mining and Trading Company copper-nickel tokens struck at the Copenhagen Mint in Denmark.

1926—Royal coinage in copper-nickel and aluminum-bronze.

1944—Brass 5-krone coin of 1926 design struck at Philadelphia Mint during the German occupation of Denmark.

1957—Aluminum-bronze 1-krone coin struck with crowned polar bear coat of arms for the Royal Greenland Company.

1960—Same design struck in copper-nickel.

2006—Government votes to issue nation-specific bank notes of Danish krone.

2009—Vote to issue nation-specific bank notes fails, delaying introduction of the paper money (no notes as of May 2011).

HUNGARY

1702—Coinage of the "Malcontents Revolt" of Ferenc II Rakoczy of Hungary. Unsuccessful bid for independence sees unusual "rolled" coins in bronze.

1848—Kossuth rebellion sees coins with Hungarian inscriptions.

1868—Following the compromise with Austria, Hungary begins distinctive coinage, one forint equals 100 krajczar.

1892—New Austro-Hungarian standard of coinage; 100 heller (Hungarian 100 filler) to one silver corona, (German krone, Hungarian korona).

1926—Hungary adopts new coinage, 100 filler equals one pengo, "pengo" an adaptation of the term meaning "clinking."

1945 to 1946—Inflation and communist takeovers in Romania and Hungary begin.

1946—New Hungarian forint currency replaces pengo, which had experienced the worst inflation in history.

1949—Soviet-style emblem replaces Kossuth arms of Hungary on Peoples Republic issues.

1967—Beginning of present-day system of Hungarian commemoratives. Ten- and 20-filler and 1-forint coins reduced in size.

1970—The 2-forint coin's composition is changed from copper-nickel-zinc to brass.

1971—The 5-forint coin's composition is changed from copper-nickel to nickel.

1981—FAO version of 10-forint coin issued.

1983—FAO versions of 20-filler, 5-forint and 10-forint coins issued. The 10-forint coin's composition is changed from nickel to aluminum-bronze.

1985—FAO version of 20-forint coin struck.

1989—Last coins struck under communist control.

1990—First coins struck as a republic; filler and forint denominations issued.

1994—Hungary Mint Co. opens in Budapest.

1996—Ringed-bimetallic 100-forint coin issued.

1997—New 10,000-forint note introduced.

1998—New 200-, 500- 1,000- and 2,000-forint notes introduced at different dates during year.

1999—New 5,000-forint note issued.

2000—New 2,000-forint note honors 1,000 years of the Hungarian state.

2004—Joins European Union in largest historical accession to date. Issues silver and gold coins to mark the event.

2006—New 500-forint note marks 50th anniversary of Revolution of 1956.

2008—Central bank withdraws 1- and 2-forint coins because they are too costly to make.

2009—A 200-forint coin is issued June 15, replacing bank note of same denomination, which is withdrawn Nov. 15.

ICELAND

1926—Bronze, copper-nickel coinage issued under Iceland's King Christian X; 100 aurar to one krona.

1930—The millenary of Iceland's parliament, the Althing, is marked by commemorative coinage in silver and bronze.

1940—London Mint strikes bronze and copper-nickel of 1926 type without Mint mark during the German occupation of Denmark.

1942—Zinc wartime coinage struck.

1946—First bronze, aluminum-bronze coins of the republic issued.

1958—Nickel-brass replaces aluminum-bronze.

1961—A gold 500-krona coin is struck, commemorating Icelandic intellectual leader Jon Sigurdsson.

1967—Copper-nickel 10-krona coin introduced.

1968—Copper-nickel 50-krona coin marks 50th anniversary of sovereignty.

1969—Nickel-brass 50-aurar coin, copper-nickel 5-krona coin introduced.

1970—Aluminum 10-aurar coin, regular issue copper-nickel 50-krona coin struck.

1974—Silver and gold coinage commemorates the 1,100th anniversary of Iceland's settlement.

1976—The composition of the 1-krona coin is changed from nickel-brass to aluminum.

1981—Marine designs introduced on all circulating coinage.

1984—Ten-krona denomination introduced. Struck sporadically since.

1987—Fifty-krona denomination introduced. Struck sporadically since.

1989—Composition of krona changed from copper-nickel to nickel-coated steel.

1993—Ten- and 50-krona notes replaced with coins.

1995—Intermediate denomination 2,000-krona note issued. New coin denomination, 100 kronur, introduced.

1996—Composition of 5- and 10-krona coins changed from copper-nickel to nickel-clad steel.

1999—United States and Iceland agree to joint commemorative coins to celebrate the discovery of America by Leif Ericson, for release in 2000.

2003—Updates design for 5,000-krona note.

2004—Updates design for 1,000-krona note.

2005—Updates design for 500-krona note.

IRELAND

circa 995—Sihtric, Norse king of Dublin, issues first silver pennies, imitations of Aethelraed II types struck in England.

circa 1185—Anglo-Irish coinage begins in the name of John, Lord of Ireland, son of Henry II of England.

circa 1204—"Triangle coinage" of John as King of England, Lord of Ireland.

1461—Silver groat introduced by Edward IV.

1536—The Irish harp first appears on Irish coins, during the reign of Henry VIII.

1553—Shilling appears under Mary I.

1646—The only two gold coins to be struck in Ireland, a pistole and double pistole, are issued as part of the "Inchiquin money" issue, which began in 1642.

circa 1670—"St. Patrick" copper farthings and half pennies in circulation. Many of these will appear with Mark Newby in Colonial New Jersey in 1681.

1689—Brass emergency "gun money," with some denominations dated by the month as well as the year, issued by exiled King James II, during an attempt to regain the British throne.

1728 to 1736—Widespread issue of private copper tokens.

1760—Voce populi tokens appear, privately issued, later transported in some numbers to the American Colonies.

1804—Bank of Ireland tokens begin with 6-shilling crown.

1823—Last Anglo-Irish coinage, George IV penny and half penny.

1928—Percy Metcalfe designs new national coinage, eight new reverses with a uniform Irish Free State obverse featuring the harp. Irish Free State Currency Commission notes replace private bank issues in that nation.

1966—First commemorative, silver 10-shilling coin, marks 50th anniversary of Easter Rising.

1969—First two decimal coins enter circulation.

1970—New seven-sided decimal 50-pence coin struck with design of former farthing.

1971—Decimalization completed.

1977—First Irish Mint since 1691 opened by Central Bank at Sandyford, Co. Dublin.

1980—£20 notes are reduced in size by one-third.

1990—A £1 coin replaces note.

1993-1997—New series of bank notes introduced.

1994—First Trust Bank in Belfast joins note-issuing entities.

1999—Ireland chooses traditional harp, used on past coinage, for its euro coinage reverse.

2000—Circulating commemorative £1 coin celebrates the millennium.

2002—Ireland drops the pound and adopts the euro currency on Jan. 1.

2004—Marks European Union expansion with commemorative coins.

2009—Silver, gold collector coins feature Ploughman bank note designs.

ITALY

569—Anonymous gold solidi of the dukes of Beneventum issued.

650—Anonymous one-third solidus of Lucca issued.

772—Papal coinage begins under Adrian I.

934—Fatimid Arab gold coinage of Palermo, Sicily.

1197—Frederick II strikes gold quarter augustales, in the style of the ancient Roman coinages.

1252—Florence issues the famed florin, which soon becomes a widely imitated world gold trade coin, with its standing Christ and lily reverse.

1280—Doge Giovanni Dandolo issues the first of the famous Venetian gold ducat series, with the figure of the doge kneeling before Christ.

1495—French coinage in Naples; gold zecchino struck by the republic of Pisa.

1523—Coinage designs by Benevenuto Cellini for Pope Clement VII.

1749—Charles of Spain produces coinage as King of the Two Sicilies.

1768—Venice strikes new bust type tallero in silver.

1799—Turin Mint strikes coins for Piedmont Republic after the house of Savoy retreats to Sardinia.

1807—Napoleonic coinage for the new kingdom of Italy, 100 centesimi to the silver lira, forerunner of later united Italian coinage.

1861—After the Florence Mint strikes a commemorative 5-lira coin on the occasion of his proclamation as king of Italy, Victor Emmanuel II begins the definitive unified Italian coinage, struck at Turin, Naples, and later Milan and Rome.

1870—Last papal coinage struck at the Rome Mint until 1929; Italian coinage commences at this mint.

1900—Numismatist Victor Emmanuel III becomes king upon the murder of his father Umberto I. Victor Emmanuel III is to spend a lifetime in the compilation of the *Corpus Nummorum Italicorum,* the exhaustive catalog of all coins ever struck in Italy.

1929—Following the Treaty of the Lateran, papal coinage is resumed as the state of the Vatican City is created.

1943—After King Victor Emmanuel III brings about the overthrow of Mussolini and fascism, the last regularly issued coins of the kingdom of Italy are issued.

1946—Following the referendum of June, the new Italian republic issues a new aluminum 1-, 2-, 5- and

10-lira coinage. Millions are struck; most disappear from circulation immediately, to reappear as the stuffing of Swiss-produced cloth covered buttons.

1951—New small-size aluminum coins are struck as the financial erosion of Italy under the republic continues.

1972—The tiny republic of San Marino resumes Italian-style coinage in "annual series."

1974—A nationwide coin shortage, caused by massive inflation, sees Italians reduced to using candy, tea bags, telephone tokens and even facial tissue as coin substitutes. Import-export limits are established on the lira due to inflation and loss of capital within the country. Stainless steel 100-lira coin honors radio inventor Marconi, replacing silver 500-lira coin originally proposed.

1986—"New lira" denominations introduced, dropping the last three zeros as a reaction to inflation.

1990—New 1,000-lira note introduced Dec. 27, 1990.

1991—New 2,000-lira note introduced July 8.

1992—Fiscal guerrilla warfare currency of the Northern League for Lombardy and Venice issued. New 50,000-lira note introduced Dec. 7.

1994—New 100,000-lira note introduced Dec. 12.

1997—New 500,000-lira note introduced in mid-1997.

1998—Italy officially agrees to join the European Union currency union.

2002—Italy drops the lira and adopts the euro currency on Jan. 1.

2004—Issues nation's first circulating commemorative €2 coin, marking World Food Program.

LATVIA

1922—Latvian coinage of 100 santimu equals one lats begun.

1925—Two-lats denomination introduced.

1929—Five-lats denomination introduced.

1939—Last coins issued before nation is forced into the Soviet Union during World War II. Few enter circulation.

1992—First coins issued by new republic; lats and santims denominations.

1993—First commemoratives of new government; celebrate 75th anniversary of declaration of independence from from Russia. New 5-, 10- and 20-lats notes introduced at various dates during year.

1994—New 50- and 100-lats notes introduced May 2, 1994.

1998—First two 10-lats coins in a planned eight-coin set commemorating Latvia in the 19th and 20th centuries introduced. New 200-lats note issued July 20, 1998.

1999—A 10-lats commemorative coin celebrating 10th anniversary of Baltic peoples calling for independence from Soviet Union is issued. Same coin circulates in all three Baltic nations. New 5,000-lats note introduced.

2001—Begins lengthy series of circulating 1-lats

coins with changing designs and limited mintages.

2004—Latvia joins European Union May 1, 2004, in largest expansion in EU history; commemorative coin celebrates accession. Under national currency, first coin using niobium issued.

2006—Winning designs unveiled for national side of euro coinage for future issue, delayed as of 2011 by financial concerns.

2008—Coins mark 90th anniversary of statehood.

LITHUANIA

1925—First coins issued after independence from Russia.

1936—Last noncommemorative coins struck before Lithuania is forced into the Soviet Union at beginning of World War II.

1938—Ten-litas coin commemorates 20th anniversary of independence.

1991—First coins struck by the new republic, in centas and litas denominations. Obverses depict traditional mounted knight.

1993—First commemorative coins issued by republic. New 5-, 50- and 100-litas notes introduced Dec. 10, 1993.

1994—Defunct talonas-denominated notes recycled into toilet paper. New litas-denominated notes introduced on different dates throughout year.

1995—The 50-litas denomination is introduced as a commemorative coin.

1997—New 10-, 20- and 200-litas notes introduced in November and December.

1998—New 50-litas note introduced Dec. 14, 1998.

1999—Three low-denomination notes replaced with coins, in 1-, 2- and 5-litas denominations; the two higher denominations are ringed bimetal coins. A 10-litas commemorative coin celebrating 10th anniversary of Baltic peoples calling for independence from Soviet Union is issued. Same coin circulates in all three Baltic nations.

2000—Collector coins mark millennium, 10th anniversary of nation's Independence. New 500-litas bank note issued, highest denomination paper money.

2004—Lithuania joins the European Union, announces designs for future euro coins.

2006—Inflation delays planned Jan. 1, 2007, adoption of euro, puts adoption on hold until at least 2013.

LUXEMBOURG

1795—Cast copper siege coins issued by the Austrian defenders against the French invaders.

1854—In personal union with the Netherlands' King Willem III, Grand Duke of Luxembourg, a copper coinage of 2½, 5 and 10 centimes is begun.

1890—Following the death of Willem III, his daughter is prevented from becoming Luxembourg's ruler by the Salic Law; the succession goes to the elderly Adolphe of Orange-Nassau, ruling duke of Nassau, Germany, who had been deposed from that position in 1866.

1915—Zinc coinage issued under the German occupation, holed types.

1918—Iron occupation coins enter circulation.

1924—Pure nickel "bon pour" (good for) coinage of 1-, 2-franc denominations, issued.

1939—Moselle-Frankisch name "Letzeburg" appears on the coinage.

1946—After liberation from a second German occupation, a commemorative coin set comprising silver 20-, 50- and 100-franc denominations celebrates the 600th anniversary of the medieval warrior-king John the Blind.

1963—The millenary of Luxembourg sees the striking of a commemorative silver 250-franc coin; only after striking is it discovered that the coinage laws do not provide for this denomination.

1978—Country courts world gold trade by removing 100 percent added gold tax.

1986—Legal tender Golden Lion 1-ounce gold bullion coin issued. First circulating 5-franc coins struck since 1981.

1987—First circulating 50-franc coins struck, made of nickel; denomination last used in 1946 as a silver commemorative.

1988—Compositions changed for circulating 1- and 5-franc coins.

1990—First circulating 20-franc coins struck since 1983.

1992—Medallic ecu gold and silver pieces struck to commemorate European Parliament.

1993—New 5,000-franc note introduced with April 1993 series date.

1998—Luxembourg officially agrees to join the European Union currency union.

2002—Luxembourg drops the franc and adopts the euro currency on Jan. 1.

2009—Issues first €5 coin with niobium center.

MACEDONIA

1993—Following breakup of Yugoslavia, first coinage of new Republic of Macedonia introduced, in deni denominations. Notes in "new dinari" denominations introduced.

1995—FAO version of 5-denar coin introduced.

1996—Notes dated Sept. 6, 1998, introduced by National Bank of the Republic of Macedonia as replacements for "new denari" notes of 1993. Undated gold coin commemorating fifth anniversary of independence introduced.

2008—Introduces 20-, 50-denar circulation coins.

MOLDOVA

1993—Following breakup of Soviet Union, new Republic of Moldova introduces coinage in ban denominations.

1992—New notes depicting former King Stefan cel Mare introduced in leu denominations.

1994—New 10-leu notes introduced.

1996—Commemorative 100-leu coins celebrate fifth anniversary of Moldovian independence and its

first participation in Olympic Games.

2001—Commemorative coins honor nation's 10th anniversary of independence.

2010—New 10-, 20-leu bank notes enters circulation.

MONTENEGRO

1906—Montenegro begins coinage, 100 para to one perper.

1910—Montenegro declared a kingdom, commemorative gold issued.

2002—Though neither a European Union nor eurozone member, begins using euro coins, since the nation was previously using German marks.

NETHERLANDS

750—Gold triens of Duurstede issued, among earliest recognizable coinages in what is to become the Netherlands.

1200 to 1576—Separate provincial coinages of the several provinces that came together to produce the modern Dutch nation. The denominations would include the gold mouton d'or and the gold florin.

1576—The United Provinces coinage begins, soon to be more or less standardized to familiar gold ducats, silver ducatoons or rijders, and a number of smaller silver and copper coins, generally bearing a Mint mark or coat of arms identifying the provincial mint at which the coins were struck.

1818—Following the elevation of the last stadholder as King Willem I of the new kingdom of the Netherlands, a decimal coinage of 100 cents to the gulden is begun; the largest silver coin is the 3-gulden piece.

1819—Regular gold coinage begins with the 10-gulden piece.

1840—The crown size 2½-gulden coin replaces the older 3-gulden piece as the largest silver coin in circulation.

1933—Last portrait gold coinage issued.

1941—Zinc minor coins struck by German occupiers.

1948—All new bronze and pure nickel coinage introduced after the liberation.

1954—The silver gulden reappears in smaller size than earlier coinage.

1959—The silver "rijksdaalder" or 2½-gulden coin in silver is reintroduced.

1960—The gold ducat of the old United Provinces is again struck as a trade coin.

1980—First coinage produced for Beatrix as queen.

1982—One-cent coin abolished March 31. New designs issued for circulating coinage.

1988—A 2-ducat gold trade coin is introduced; similar in design to trade ducat.

1989—Silver ducat trade coin introduced.

1990—Netherlands Mint is privatized. A computer-designed commemorative Four Queens 50-gulden coin demonstrates new visual techniques.

1991—New visual techniques used on 50-gulden

silver wedding anniversary commemorative.

1994—First two in a series of silver trade ducats commemorating the seven provinces of Netherlands issued.

1997—Fire at the Utrecht Mint disrupts Proof coin production. Cotton fiber used to make 10-gulden notes.

1998—Netherlands formally agrees to join the European Union currency union. The Netherlands Mint begins striking euro coinage Dec. 12. Officials decide that euro coinage struck in 1999, 2000 and 2001 will bear the year of production, not the year of issue (2002, when all euro coins and notes are set to be released).

2002—Netherlands drops the gulden and adopts the euro currency on Jan. 1.

NORWAY

995—First Norway penning coinage struck for Olav Tryggvason.

1020—About this date, Ethelred's Long Cross coinage copied in Norway.

1080—Byzantine influence appears on Norwegian coin iconography.

1103—No identified coinage is struck during the 12th and part of the 13th centuries.

1319—Regency period of King Magnus Eriksson of Sweden begins, including a monetary reform between the two countries.

1387—Norway passes to control of Danish kingdom, with unified coinage beginning.

1526—Metal shortage causes reduction in purity of silver coins.

1546—Silver crown-size gulden of Christian III.

1628—Mint established in Christiania (now Oslo).

1660—Gold ducat issued by Frederik III.

1687—Kongsberg Mint opens, now known as Royal Norwegian Mint.

1695—Kongsberg Mint becomes only mint for Norway. Thor Mohlen paper notes introduced.

1704—First "reisedaler" or travel daler, specially struck to pay expenses of Danish king Frederik IV's trips to his Norwegian domain

1872—Scandinavian kingdoms align their currency in the Scandinavian Monetary Union.

1875—First regular issue krone coins struck.

1906—After achieving independence, Norway and its new king, Haakon VII, mark the occasion with a commemorative 2-krone coin.

1940—Debased coinage follows Nazi German occupation of Norway.

1942—London Mint strikes nickel-brass coinage for the use of the government in exile in the Faroe Islands. Regular coinage resumes after end of war.

1958—Completely redesigned coinage with bird and animal reverses issued under new King Olav V.

1962—Royal Norwegian Mint becomes part of the Norges Bank.

1972—Last 1- and 2-øre coins struck.

1982—Last 5- and 25-øre coins struck.

1983—Circulating 10-krone coin introduced.

1991—First in an annual series of coins commemorating the 1994 Olympic Games is introduced.

1992—Last 10-øre coin struck. First coins to depict King Harald V struck.

1994—Russia withdraws Spitzbergen coins following protest by Norway. First 20-krone coins struck for circulation.

1996—New coins are introduced ahead of timetable due to confusion with older issues being replaced.

1997—New 50- and 100-krone notes introduced.

1999—New 500-krone note introduced.

2001—A 1,000-krone note makes debut, shows Edvard Munch.

2003—Begins three-year commemorative coin series marking centennial of dissolution of a union between Norway and Sweden in 1905.

POLAND

1917—Iron fenigow coins from embryonic kingdom of Poland, first Polish coinage since the 1850s.

1923—Poland consolidates several monetary systems into system with 100 groszy equaling one zloty.

1939—Last coinage struck by Poland before World War II.

1949—Polish coinage resumed, minus royal crown on the white eagle, in the name of the Polish Republic.

1958—Polish Peoples Republic title appears on coins.

1964—Polish commemorative series begun.

1966—Poland begins issue to collectors of limited runs of pattern "Proba" coins, rejected designs for commemoratives.

1972—Last 5-groszy coins struck. Commemorative 50-zloty coinage series begins.

1973—Circulating 20-zloty coinage series begins. Denomination used frequently as a commemorative.

1980—Poland begins a Kings of Poland coin series.

1986—Eagle appearing on coinage is redesigned.

1990—Poland issues note with crowned eagle of the republic following the fall of the communist regime. First coinage issued after fall of communists.

1994—Communist era notes withdrawn in Poland. New Warsaw Mint opens in Poland. Ringed-bimetallic 2-zloty coin introduced.

1995—New Polish currency system includes ringed bimetal coins. First in a series of commemorative coins struck in various denominations. New notes issued in January and June with March 1, 1994, date.

2004—Joins the European Union, marks event with commemorative coins.

2005—Begins series of circulating commemorative Historical Cities 2-zloty coins.

2006—Nation's first circulating commemorative bank note, denominated 50 zlotych, honors anniversary of Pope John Paul II's election to the papacy.

2008—Circulating commemorative 10-zloty bank note honors 90th anniversary of the Restoration of Independence.

PORTUGAL

1641—Coinage of Joao IV, the restorer of Portuguese independence, issue in silver and copper.

1656—Gold coinage resumed under Alfonso VI.

1683—Finely styled coinage of Pedro II issued.

1686—Countermarking of earlier Portuguese coinages.

1722—Portrait coinage introduced by Joao V, gold only. These pieces were a favorite overseas, where they were dubbed "Joes."

1898—Commemorative silver 200-, 500- and 1,000-reis coins mark the fourth centenary of Vasco da Gama's discovery of the sea route to India.

1900—First copper-nickel 50- and 100-reis coinage issue.

1908—Following the assassination of Carlos I and Crown Prince Luis Felipe, Manoel II becomes king; Latin titles resumed on the coinage.

1927—Nickel-bronze escudo coinage under Antonio da Oliveira Salazar's New State.

1932—Silver 2½-, 5- and 10-escudo coins introduced.

1953—The 25th anniversary of Salazar's financial reforms is marked by a new silver 20-escudo coin.

1978—The first circulating coin since 1974 military coup, a new denomination, 25-escudo piece, appears.

1981—The government releases 1977-dated copper-nickel coins.

1988—Unveils first platinum and palladium commemorative coins.

1990—Ringed-bimetallic 100-escudo coin replaces note.

1991—Ringed-bimetallic 200-escudo coin enters circulation.

1996—Gold and silver clad commemorative coin issued. New 1,000-, 2,000-, 5,000- and 10,000-escudo notes introduced.

1997—New 500-escudo note introduced Sept. 17, 1997.

1998—Portugal formally agrees to join the European Union currency union.

2002—Portugal drops the escudo and adopts the Euro currency on Jan. 1.

ROMANIA

1867—First coinage of autonomous Romania, in copper.

1947—Royal reform coinage of Romania's Michael I enters circulation.

1948—First communist coins of the Romanian Peoples Republic.

1952—Monetary reform (100 bani equals 1 leu) results in new coinage.

1966—Romania issues new coinage in the name of the Romania Socialist Republic. Coinage struck sporadically.

1990—First coins (10-leu denomination) struck under auspices of National Bank of Romania; first for the new republic, which took over government after fall of communist regime.

1991—First 20-, 50- and 100-leu coins introduced into circulation.

1992—Additional denominations issued by National Bank of Romania (1 leu, 5 lei).

1994—New 10,000-leu notes introduced.

1995—FAO coins issued.

1995-1996—Commemoratives issued to celebrate Olympic Centennial Games in Atlanta. New 50,000-leu note introduced.

1998—Commemorative coins celebrate Winter Olympic Games in Nagano and World Cup Soccer championship in France. New 5,000- and 100,000-leu notes introduced.

1999—New 2,000- and 10,000-leu notes introduced.

2001—New 1,000-leu coin introduced.

2005—Romani undergoes redenomination July 1, 2005, dropping four zeroes from inflated currency.

2007—Nation joins the European Union, issues commemorative coins for event.

2010—Issues first circulating commemorative 50-ban coin, to mark aviation anniversary.

RUSSIA

1704—First modern ruble of Peter the Great replaces archaic issues.

1764—Distinctive Siberian copper coinage, Catherine the Great.

1834—First modern commemorative coin, ruble, Czar Alexander I memorial.

1828—Beginning of world's first regular platinum coinage, 3-, 6- and 12-ruble pieces, ending in 1845.

1921—New coinage of the Russian Soviet Federated Socialist Republic.

1923—First Soviet gold coin struck: gold 10-ruble chervonetz.

1924—Coinage begins in the name of the Union of Soviet Socialist Republics.

1961—"New ruble" currency reform.

1988—Issues palladium commemorative coins for Christian millennium.

1989—Introduces Ballerina palladium bullion coins.

1991—Collapse of the Soviet Union ushers in new currencies for Armenia, Azerbaijan, Belarus, Estonia, Georgia, Kazakhstan, Kyrgyzstan, Latvia, Lithuania, Moldova, Russia, Tadzhikistan, Turkmenistan, Ukraine and Uzbekistan.

1993—Commonwealth of Independent States common currency gains limited acceptance in former Soviet republics. Emergency and nationalistic currencies appear. Russia issues ringed-bimetallic coins. New commemoratives announced.

1996—Issues first kilogram gold coin, denominated 10,000 rubles.

1998—Russian currency reform replaces the ruble with the new ruble at a ratio of 1,000-to-1. New notes introduced under new system. Commemoratives continue.

1999—Ruble continues to slide as economic woes are unabated, falls from nine to the U.S. dollar to 12 to the U.S. dollar in one day, Sept. 16.

2005—Russian Federation series of ringed-bimetallic 10-ruble coins, honoring 86 constituents, begins.

2006—Inauguration of bullion program with quarter-ounce gold "St. George the Victorious" 50-ruble coin.

2008—Issue of first 3,000-gram gold coin, denominated 25,000 rubles. Bullion program expands to include 1-ounce silver 3-ruble coin. Brass-plated steel 10-ruble coin replaces bank note of same denomination.

2010—First 5-kilogram coin, denominated 50,000 rubles, is issued. Wide-ranging 2014 Winter Olympic Games commemorative coin program announced.

SCOTLAND

1124—Silver pennies of King David I issued.

1249—Silver half penny and farthing introduced by King Alexander III.

1329—David II introduces silver groat, half groat.

1460—Billon plack, half plack of James III issued, first copper, "black money."

1513—James V, billon bawbee (sixpence) and divisions.

1542—Reign of Mary sees many coinage innovations and types based on the royal marriages in Scotland and abroad.

1603—James VI, as James I of Great Britain, France and Ireland, introduces 60-shilling crown of English design, first Scots-English interchangeable coin type.

1706—Ten-shilling and 5-shilling Scots coinage, last of the distinctively Scottish coins under Queen Anne.

1937—Scottish crest reappears on British coinage as a tribute to the queen, the former Lady Elizabeth Bowes-Lyon.

1968—Scots thistle appears on new decimal 5-pence coin.

1984—Great Britain's £1 coin features Scotland.

1990—Two of the three private banks issuing £1 notes cease their issues.

2000—Royal Bank of Scotland issues commemorative £20 note for queen mother's birth centennial. Clydesdale Bank marks millennium with £20 note.

2002—£5 note from Royal Bank of Scotland marks 50th anniversary of queen's accession to the throne.

2004—Royal Bank of Scotland honors St. Andrews' golf club with £5 note.

2005—Royal Bank of Scotland issues £5 note celebrating U.S. golfer Jack Nicklaus.

2006—Commonwealth Games feature on Clydesdale Bank commemorative £10 note.

2007—Clydesdale Bank £20 note honors Robert the Bruce.

2009—Clydesdale Bank issues redesigned series of bank notes with designs celebrating Scotland's heritage, people and culture.

SERBIA

1867—Prince Michael, Obrenovich III, issues Serbian copper coins.

1882—Milan I, king of Serbia, issues first gold coins.

2003—Federal Republic of Yugoslavia becomes Serbia and Montenegro, issues own coins, bank notes.

2006—Nation establishes independence, begins issuing new series of coins and paper money. Commemorative coins celebrate 150th anniversary of the birth of Nikola Tesla.

2007—Withdraws 50-para coin beginning Oct. 1.

2009—Copper-nickel-zinc 1-, 2- and 5-dinar coins that were issued Dec. 15, 2000, by the National Bank of Yugoslavia cease to be legal tender Jan. 1 (withdrawal began in the second half of 2008). Lighter copper-plated steel 1- and 2-dinar coins enter circulation.

SLOVAKIA

1939—Independent Slovakia begins coinage, 100 halierov equal one koruna.

1945—Last coinage as autonomous republic issued before merger with Czech Republic.

1993—First coinage issued as independent republic following breakup of Czechoslovakia, in halier and koruna denominations. First new notes introduced.

1994—Koruna composition is changed to a bronze-clad steel alloy, after one year as an aluminum-bronze piece.

1995—New 500-koruna note introduced in September; new 5,000-koruna note issued in May.

1996—Composition of 50-halier coin changed from aluminum to copper-plated steel.

1999—New 5,000-koruna note with enhanced security devices introduced.

2001—Triangular-shaped trimetallic coin (silver, gold and platinum) marks new millennium.

2003—10- and 20-halier coins stripped of legal tender status Dec. 31.

2004—Joins European Union, issues commemorative coins to celebrate the event.

2005—Designs for euro coins selected in series of contests during the year.

2009—Adopts euro currency Jan. 1, 2009, becoming the 16th nation to use the euro.

SLOVENIA

1990—Token issues introduced in variety of denominations, some overstruck on Yugoslavian 1990 10-para coins.

1991—Following breakup of Yugoslavia, currency system introduced on Oct. 8. First commemorative coinage introduced; celebrates first anniversary of independence.

1992—First circulating coinage of independent

Republic of Slovenia, in stotinov and tolar denominations. Obverses show numerical representations of denominations; reverses show fauna. New notes dated Jan. 15, 1992, introduced.

1993—First 5-tolar commemorative coinage struck. New 1,000- and 5,000-tolar notes dated June 1, 1993, introduced.

1994—New 10,000-tolar note dated June 28, 1994, introduced.

1996—Commem series celebrate fifth anniversary of independence and Olympic Games.

1997—New 5,000-tolar notes dated Oct. 8, 1997, introduced.

2000—Copper-nickel 10-tolar coin debuts.

2001—100-, 1,000- and 10,000-tolar notes overprinted to mark national bank's 10th anniversary.

2003—Copper-nickel 20- and 50-tolar coins debut. 100-, 1,000- and 10,000-tolar notes overprinted to mark future accession to European Union.

2004—Joins European Union May 1, 2004.

2005—Designs for euro coinage unveiled.

2007—Adopts euro, becoming 15th nation to join eurozone, and first from group that joined the EU in 2004.

SPAIN

711—Muslim invasion marked by a gold solidus dated A.H. 93 begins a long and complex Moorish coinage in Spain, which continues until the 15th century.

814—Carolingian coinage in Barcelona, silver dinero of Louis the Pious.

874—Independent coinage of the Counts of Barcelona begins with a silver dinero of Wilfredo.

1035—Kingdom of Leon coinage begins with silver dinero of Fernando I.

1063—Kingdom of Aragon's coinage initiated by Sancho I Ramirez.

1065—Kingdom of Castile coinage begun with dinero and obol coins of Alfonso VI.

1157—Gold maravedi with Latin inscriptions of Fernando II of Leon.

1469—Fernando V and Isabel, coinage gradually stabilizing around copper maravedi, silver real and gold excelente.

1492—Last Moorish stronghold, Granada, falls to Fernando and Isabel; gold 20 excelentes struck, probably to commemorate the final victory of the reconquest.

1636—Vast monetary confusion during the reign of Felipe IV, extensive and repeated revaluation of copper coinage by countermarking.

1809—French occupation coinage introduces "en Barcelona" peseta, struck in three silver denominations and one gold denomination, which provided important future direction for Spain's monetary development.

1825—Emancipation of the Spanish colonies in South and Central America complete, as Potosi Mint (in present day Bolivia) strikes the last Spanish style silver 8-real coins.

1869—The provisional government announces adoption of the peseta, on the standard of the Latin Monetary Union, divided into 100 centimos.

1933—First coinage of the second Spanish Republic.

1937—Civil War causes a proliferation of local and regional emergency coinage and notes, Vienna Mint strikes first coins for Francisco Franco's Nationalist government.

1966—Continued growth and prosperity marked by issue of silver 100-peseta coin.

1976—Royal portrait appears on Spanish coinage, new royal arms on 5-, 50-peseta coins. Copper-nickel 100-peseta piece introduced, all coins with star date 1976, authorization date 1975.

1978—Observation of first National Coin Week.

1982—A 2-peseta coin is introduced; struck only in 1982 and 1984. Composition of peseta changed from aluminum-bronze to aluminum.

1989—Composition of 5-peseta coin changed from copper-nickel to aluminum-bronze.

1990—Nickel-bronze 25-peseta coin with center hole introduced with Olympic Games themes. Later issues commemorate other topics.

1993—New 2,000- and 5,000-peseta notes introduced.

1994—Optical variable security device appears on commemorative coins. First commemorative notes issued.

1995—New 2,000- and 10,000-peseta notes introduced.

1998—Spain agrees to participate in the European Union currency union.

2002—Spain drops the peseta and adopts the euro currency on Jan. 1.

2005—Issues first circulating commemorative €2 coin, honoring Don Quixote's 400th anniversary.

2011—Financial crisis threatens the euro in Spain.

SWEDEN

995—Nordic coinage along English and Byzantine lines struck at Hedeby Mint.

999—First Swedish coinage, King Olof Skotkonung, issued.

circa 1150—"Penningar" bracteate coinage.

1478—First dated Swedish coins, ortug and half ortug, issued.

1521—Reign of Gustaf Vasa, founder of a new dynasty for independent Sweden.

1556—Square klippe silver øre coinage.

1568—Gold gulden of Erik XIV, Hebrew name "Jehovah" out of clouds on reverse.

1598—Jehovah-name silver coinage, under regent Karl.

1624—Square klippe emergency copper coinage.

1644—Massive copper "plate money" issues begin, valued in equivalence to the silver coins drained out of the kingdom to redeem fortresses held by the Danes.

1835—Skilling banco token copper coinage.

1856—Decimal copper half-, 1-, 2- and 5-øre coins of Oscar I.

1861—Decimal silver øre coins of Karl XV in style of Oscar's 1855 coinage, alongside the earlier issue of riksdalers riksmynt, struck until 1873.

1868—International currency gold coinage of Karl XV, one carolin equals 10 francs.

1906—Following the independence of Norway, the royal motto on the coinage becomes "Sweden's Welfare," rather than "Welfare of the Brother Peoples."

1917—Iron is adopted for World War I 1-, 2- and 5-øre.

1942—New low-silver coinage, iron reappears in the lowest three values.

1952—New ultra-modern designs on the coinage of Gustaf VI Adolf, first modernistic royal portrait in the world.

1981—The 5-øre coin is issued in brass.

1986—Swedish Mint becomes a subsidiary of the national bank.

1991—A 10-krona coin replaces note of the same denomination. New 20-krona note introduced.

1992—The 10,000-krona note is demonetized due to inadequate security devices.

1994—Austria, Finland, Sweden and Norway consider a currency union.

1996—New 50-krona note introduced.

1997—New 20-krona note introduced.

2000—Circulating commemorative 1-krona coin celebrates millennium.

2001—New design for 1- and 10-krona coins debut. Commemoratives honor centennial of Nobel Prize.

2002—Commemorative coins for Stockholm's 2,000th anniversary of founding.

2003—Public referendum to join eurozone fails.

2005—Commemorative 100-krona note marks 250th anniversary of founding of Tumba Bruk bank note paper mill.

2006—Series 1992 20-krona, Series 1986 100-krona and Series 1989 500-krona notes become invalid Jan. 1, 2006.

2009—Circulating commemorative 1-krona coin marks link between Sweden and Finland.

2010—50-øre coin no longer legal tender after Sept. 30. Commemorative coins honor wedding of Crown Princess Victoria to Daniel Wesling.

SWITZERLAND

1799 to 1800—Billon batzen-denominated and silver batzen-denominated coinage struck by Helvetian Republic.

1850—First coinage of Swiss Confederation, struck on a system of 100 rappen to 1 franc.

1883—First 20-franc gold coin struck.

1922—Last of the gold 10-franc coins struck.

1932—Nickel composition used for 5- and 10-rappen coins instead of copper-nickel through 1939 and in 1941 for the 5-rappen coin only.

1936—Commemorative 5-franc coinage begins.

1939—Composition of 20-rappen coin changed from nickel to copper-nickel.

1940—Copper-nickel composition resumed for 5- and 10-rappen coins, except for 1941 5-rappen coin (no 1941 10-rappen pieces were struck).

1942—Zinc composition replaced bronze for 1- and 2-rappen coins.

1946—Bronze composition resumed for 1- and 2-rappen coins.

1948—New designs introduced for 1- and 2-rappen coins to replace those used since 1850.

1949—Last of the gold 20-franc coins struck.

1955—Gold 25- and 50-franc denominations introduced. Both also struck in 1958 and 1959. Pieces unavailable in commercial channels.

1963—Last silver 5-franc commemorative coins struck.

1968—Composition of half-, 1-, 2- and 5-franc coins changed from .835 fine silver to copper-nickel.

1974—First copper-nickel 5-franc commemorative coins struck.

1981—Aluminum-brass replaces copper-nickel for 5-rappen coin.

1986—Bullion nonlegal tender Helvetias minted in Switzerland.

1991—First silver 20-franc commemorative coins struck. A 250-franc commemorative coin is struck to celebrate 700 years of Swiss confederation.

1995—New generation security devices appear on notes of Switzerland.

1996 to 1998—Additional note denominations issued with new designs and security devices.

2000—Series 1976 bank notes withdrawn May 1. Commemorative coins honor 2,000 years of Christianity.

2001—Gold 50-franc coin commemorates honors children's literature character Heidi.

2004—Ringed-bimetallic 10-franc, gold 50-franc coins depict Matterhorn.

UKRAINE

1992—After voting for independence from the Soviet Union in December 1991, Ukraine introduces first independent coinage in kopiyka and hryvnia denominations.

1995—First commemorative coins introduced.

1996—First Olympic Games commemorative coins introduced. First notes introduced in hryvnia denominations with 1992 and 1994 dates (1-, 2-, 5-, 10-, 20-, 50- and 100-hryvnia denominations).

1997—New notes issued with 1994 and 1995 dates (2-, 5-, 10- and 20-hryvnia denominations).

2003—Release of new note series, issued periodically through 2007, begins with 20-hryvnia note.

2005—Circulating 1-hryvnia coin marks 50th anniversary of World War II's end.

2009—2-hryvnia coin honors aviation pioneer Igor Sikorsky.

2010—Circulating 1-hryvnia coin marks 65th anniversary of World War II's end.

YUGOSLAVIA

1920—Yugoslavia created, adopts Serbian standard, 100 para equals one dinara.

1945 to 1946—Post-war coinage struck.

1953—New aluminum coins for Peoples Federated Yugoslav Republic.

1963—Socialist Federated Yugoslav coinage begins.

1968—Denomination of 100 dinara used for first time; used through 1990 in a variety of compositions for commemoratives.

1976—FAO version of 1-dinar coin issued.

1979—Yugoslavia ceases legal tender status of 1965-dated 5-, 10- and 50-dinar notes.

1990—Yugoslavia issues inflationary 1 million-dinar notes.

1991—Yugoslavia disintegrates into several separate and currency-issuing nations (Bosnia-Herzegovina, Croatia, Macedonia, Montenegro, Serbia and Slovenia).

1992—New Federal Republic of Yugoslavia (formed by Montenegro and Serbia; not everyone recognizes the republic) introduces coinage.

1993-1994—Additional coinage denominations introduced.

1994—New notes introduced at different times during year with date March 3.

1996—Introduction of 50-new-dinar note on July 31.

1997—Introduction of 100-new-dinar note, June 9.

2003 to date—See Serbia for history of coins and paper money.

British Colonies

CHANNEL ISLANDS, JERSEY

1834—French currency replaced with currency of British type in Jersey.

1841—First of the new coins issued, copper 1/13-, 1/26-, 1/52-shilling denominations.

1866—Bronze coins, smaller sizes, issued in similar denominations as issued in 1841.

1877—Conversion to standard United Kingdom denominations, still uniquely stated as 1/12, 1/24, 1/48 shillings.

1949—The liberation from German occupation in 1945 is commemorated by a bronze 1/12-shilling piece.

1966—The conquest of England by the Duke of Normandy (Jersey was a part of Normandy), is commemorated by three commemorative coins, including the first regal 5-shilling copper-nickel crown.

1968—First decimal coins appear.

1971—Decimal range completed, half new penny to 50 new pence.

1995—Jersey issues its first commemorative note.

1997—Jersey issues a ringed-bimetallic £2 coin.

2007—Jersey issues redesigned bank notes.

CYPRUS

1879—Copper piastre coinage of Victoria, first coins for the island since the medieval kingdom under the Lusignan rulers and the Venetians.

1901—Silver coinage begun, with a modified Jubilee Head portrait of Victoria used only on the Cyprus coinage.

1928—Crown sized 45-piastre coin commemorates 50 years of British rule.

1934—Copper-nickel scalloped 1-, half-piastre coins issued.

1947—Piastre denominations replaced by shilling types in copper-nickel.

1955—Decimalization, new system introduced of 1,000 mils equal to one Cyprus pound.

1963—Republic of Cyprus decimal coins issued.

1970—First crown issued after independence, copper-nickel 500-mil coin for the FAO coin program.

1984—Mil coin denominations replaced by nickel-brass 1-, 2-, 5-, 10- and 20 cent coins, and aluminum half cent.

1994—Coins replace 500-mil and 50-cent notes.

2004—Country joins European Union May 1, 2004.

2008—Pound replaced with euro Jan. 1, event marked with commemorative coin.

GIBRALTAR

1802 to 1820—Private copper token coinage in circulation.

1841—Copper 1-, 2-quart regal coins of Victoria.

1842—Half-quart coin completes roster of Gibraltar coinage, which ends in 1861.

1967—Copper-nickel crown issued.

1971—Famed Barbary ape appears on new crown of 25 new pence, start of ongoing crown series.

1975—Issues first gold coin.

1980—Annual Christmas commemorative coin issue begins.

1988—Circulating domestic legal tender coins introduced.

1990—Diameter of 5-pence coin reduced.

1991—Annual gold royal coin series depicting dogs begins. Pobjoy Mint issues gold and silver ecu coins for circulation, following with a platinum coin in 1995.

1996—Hologram appears on commemorative ecu coin. Color-enhanced commemorative crown issued.

1997—Gold on silver commemorative coins released.

2000—Gibraltar commemorates millennium with £5 note.

2004—New series of coins, commemorative £20 note celebrate tercentenary of British Gibraltar.

2009—New 50-pence coin marks 700th anniversary of the Devotion to Our Lady of Europe.

2010—Announces bank note redesign, beginning with £10 and £50 notes. Issues £5 coin describing Queen Elizabeth II as Queen of Gibraltar.

2011—Three final notes in redesign, denominated £5, £20 and £100, slated for release early in year.

GUERNSEY

1830—Distinctive copper coinage of 1- and 4-double denominations, relics of the medieval double tournois, still money of account until 1921.

1834—Eight doubles added to series.

1864—Bronze replaces copper.

1956—Redesigned bronze coins and new scalloped 3 pence.

1966—Round-cornered square copper-nickel 10-shilling Norman Conquest commemorative coin with portrait of William, Duke of Normandy.

1968—Decimal coinage begins, full range of bronze and copper-nickel complete by 1971.

1977—"New" dropped from pence denomination coins.

1985—First £2 commemorative coin introduced.

1991—Smaller £5 notes issued.

1997—Downsized 50-pence coins issued to keep in line with coins of Great Britain.

2000—New £5 note marks new millennium.

IONIAN ISLANDS

1819—Copper obol coinage under British colonial rule.

1834—Silver 30-lepta coinage.

ISLE OF MAN

1709—Cast copper penny, half penny introduced by the Earl of Derby.

1721—Struck coppers of similar type.

1798—Cartwheel type regal coppers.

1811—Silver and copper private bank tokens issued during small change famine caused by the Napoleonic wars.

1839—Manx coinage on sterling system begins under Victoria.

1894—Jewelry firm founded that becomes the private Pobjoy Mint in 1965.

1966—Private Pobjoy Mint begins contract production of commemorative coins.

1971—Decimal coinage struck under contract by the Pobjoy Mint.

1983—Plastic notes introduced into circulation.

1984—Isle of Man enters world bullion market with introduction of Angel gold coin.

1990—Pobjoy Mint introduces "pearl black" coin finish.

1996—Hologram security device used on platinum Noble coins.

2001—Harry Potter coins issued.

LUNDY

1929—Worldwide numismatic stir follows the actions of Martin Coles Harman, Lundy's owner, in issuing his own bronze coins, 1- and half-puffin pieces, named for the seabirds, which breed on the island. Hauled into the Devonshire court, he was fined £5 for violating the Coinage Act of 1870.

MALTA

1521—Gold coinage of Philippe Villiers, grand master of the Order of St. John of Jerusalem, formerly based in the kingdom of Jerusalem and later on the island of Rhodes.

1553—Copper piccioli coinage under grand master Claude de la Sengle.

1566—The great Grand Master Jean de la Valette begins bronze grano coinage (followed by the tari types in 1567) with reverse inscription "not bronze but faith."

1723—First crown-sized silver coin, the 2-scudo coin of Antonio Manoel de Vilhena.

1798—Last coinage of the Order under Grand Master Ferdinand Hompesch; Malta conquered by Napoleon's forces, the Order withdraws, eventually relocates in Rome.

1798 to 1800—Siege of Malta, ingot necessity coinage under French general Vaubois.

1866—The British colonial government issues a distinctive third-farthing coin to approximate old grani coins, along with earlier British type third-farthings already in circulation.

1902—Edward VII third-farthing coin issued.

1913—Last Malta third-farthing issued under George V.

1961—The Sovereign Military Order of Malta, long domiciled in Rome, resumes a symbolic coinage struck by a small mint set up in the palace in Rome.

1972—After attaining independence from Britain in 1964, a new decimal coinage of 1,000 mils or 100 cents to one Malta pound is begun.

2004—Malta joins European Union May 1, 2004.

2008—The pound dropped, euro adopted.

MAURITIUS AND REUNION

1779—Billon coinage of Louis XVI, Isles de France and Bourbon.

1810—Silver 10-livre crown for the Iles de France (Mauritius) and Bonaparte, (earlier Ile de Bourbon, still later the colony of Reunion).

1816—Ile de Bourbon billon 10-centime coin of Louis XVIII issued.

1822—Base silver 50- and 25-sou coins issued by the Mauritius treasury.

1877—Decimal silver and bronze Victorian coinage, 100 cents to the Mauritius rupee.

1896—French Reunion nickel 1-franc, 50-centime coins issued.

1934—First Mauritius silver 1-rupee coin issued.

1939—Beginning of separate rupee-cent coinage for Seychelles.

1948—Aluminum colonial 1-, 2-franc coins issued for French Reunion.

1955—Aluminum-bronze higher denominations in Reunion.

1971—Independence coinage of Mauritius, crown-sized 10-rupee coin bears the extinct dodo bird.

1972—Aluminum FAO minor coins, new copper-nickel seven-sided 5-rupee coins join Seychelles coinage.

1976—Independent coinage of Seychelles portrays President Mancham.

2005—500-rupee note is new, higher denomination in current bank note series.

ST. HELENA

1821—Copper half penny struck by the East India Company.

1974—Crown-sized copper-nickel 25-pence coin marks the anniversary of the East India Company royal charter.

1977—Silver jubilee of Queen Elizabeth II commemorated by issuance of crowns for St. Helena and dependency, Tristan da Cunha.

India, Southeast Asia and related areas

(Countries arranged by region)

BURMA/MYANMAR

1852—Silver peacock rupee coinage of King Mindon Min issued.

1865—Peacock copper quarter anna struck.

1866—Gold lion coinage issued.

1878—Copper quarter anna of the last king, Thibaw.

1949—Copper-nickel and pure nickel rupee standard coinage issued by newly independent Burma.

1952—Decimal rupee of 100 pyas adopted.

1966—Aluminum coinage with portrait of Gen. Aung San, founder of the republic.

1983—FAO 10-pyas coin issued in international series.

1990—Nation renamed Myanmar.

1993—Foreign exchange certificates required for use by foreign visitors.

1998—Singapore Mint strikes commemorative coins with an ultraviolet security device.

2004—Updated series of bank notes issued.

CAMBODIA

1846—Gold rooster-obverse fuang struck by King Ong Harizak.

1847—Silver pagoda quarter- and 1-tical coins issued.

1860—Franc standard coinage of King Norodom I, bronze 5-centime through silver 4-franc coins issued, along with a trade dollar or piastre equal to the Mexican peso.

1953—Aluminum three-coin set issued after the restoration of independence, 10-, 20- and 50-centime denominations.

1959—Similar coins issued in denominations of 100 sen to 1 riel.

1975—Controversy is aroused by the release through a numismatic distributor of gold 50,000-riel coins authorized by the now-vanished Lon Nol regime; dispute centered on the terms "legal tender" and "face value," another argument was raised over the "rate of exchange" for the worthless currency of a vanished government.

1981—Moneyless economy experimented with by Kmer Rouge government.

1987—Notes return to use.

1994—Undated circulation coins return to use.

2001—New 100-, 5,000-, 10,000-, and 50,000-riel bank notes issued as part of new series.

2008—New 2,000- and 20,000-riel notes issued as part of new series.

CEYLON/SRI LANKA

1747 to 1793—Silver, tin, lead and copper coinage of the Netherlands East India Company issued.

1801—First English coinage issued for Ceylon, crude dump types with Dutch denominations.

1802—Modern, machine-struck copper coinage introduced.

1815—Copper stuiver-denomination coins and pattern silver rix dollar struck.

1823—Countermarked Arcot rupee and quarter rupee released to circulation.

1830—Reign of William IV sees circulation of British type half-farthing and silver quarter-pence pieces in Ceylon.

1870—Decimal rupee adopted, 100 cents to one rupee; copper coinage struck.

1892—First silver decimal coinage, 50-, 25- and 10-cent denominations.

1909—Square copper-nickel 5-cent coin introduced.

1943—Wartime nickel-brass 50-, 25-cent coins issued.

1957—First distinctive Ceylon independent coins, Buddhist commemorative issue.

1963—Full range of decimal coins, aluminum, nickel-brass and copper-nickel, struck.

1972—First coinage with new national designation, Sri Lanka, struck.

1988—Circulating coinage ceases in favor of notes.

1998—Ringed-bimetallic 10-rupee coin introduced.

2006—Series 2005 2,000-rupee bank note joins paper money series.

2009—Commemorative 1,000-rupee note marks "ushering of peace and prosperity in Sri Lanka," the end of war with the Tamil Tigers.

2011—Announces release of new series of bank notes, including a 5,000-rupee note, a new higher denomination.

COLONIAL INDOCHINA

1875—Old French 1-centime coins, holed, are

released to circulation, valued at 1 sapeque, for the new colony of Cochin China.

1879—Square-holed 2-sapeque coinage in bronze joins a large bronze centime and silver 10-, 20- and 50-centime denominations and a pattern trade dollar, the piastre, issued with inscription "French Cochin China."

1885—Similar coinage is introduced for the whole of French Indochina, which now includes Cambodia, Annam, Tonkin and Laos.

1896—Smaller, holed 1 centime adopted.

1931—New Liberty Head piastre issued.

1935—Lindauer-designed bronze half centime introduced.

1938—Holed nickel-bronze 5-centime coin issued.

1939—Pure nickel and copper-nickel 10-, 20-centime coins struck.

1940—Following the collapse of France, locally produced zinc 1-centime coins are issued, followed by several aluminum denominations.

1945—Returning over Vietnamese protest, the French issue aluminum and copper-nickel coins of pre-war design.

1947—The last French issue is released, a copper-nickel 1 piastre struck in the name of the stillborn Indochinese Federation.

INDIA

1000 to 1300—Gold coinage of Chola.

1193—Coins of Sultan Muhammad, Delhi.

1302—Royal gold coinage of Bengal.

1495—First Portuguese colonial gold under Manoel I, Goa.

1540—Unusual but distinctive octagonal coinage issued in Assam.

1556—Innovative coinage of the great Mughal ruler Akbar introduced.

1600—Portcullis silver coinage of Elizabeth I of England enters India to compete with Spanish silver reales.

1671—Silver 1, 2 speciedalers struck for the Danish East India Company.

1672—First British silver coins struck at Bombay, a city given by the King of Portugal as a wedding gift to King Charles II.

1700—Beginning of the Muslim type coinage of the nizams of Hyderabad.

1724—Dutch East India Company coinage issued in Cochin.

1735—British United East India Company silver and lead coinage of Bombay issued.

1750—Gold mohar coinage issued in Nepal.

1765—East India Company coinage begins in Bengal, similarly in Bombay.

1791—Modern, machine-struck copper coinage produced by Matthew Boulton for East India Company for use in Bombay.

1794—Machine-struck copper for Calcutta issued.

1803—Modern copper East India Company struck for Madras.

1824—Modern copper East India Company pice coinage struck for Bengal.

1833—First all-India coinage by East India Company, in 1/12-anna, half-pice, quarter-anna and half-anna denominations. These denominations become the standard through decimalization in 1957.

1835—All-India silver portrait coinage, gold mohur coins of "William IIII, king," issued.

1840—First portrait coinage of Victoria by East India Company issued.

1846—Last coinage of Danish India, issued for Tranquebar.

1862—Following the great Indian mutiny of 1857 and demise of the East India Company, direct rule by Britain sees first all-India "Victoria Queen" silver, copper coinage issued.

1871—Modern machine-struck Portuguese colonial copper issued at Goa.

1877—Portrait coins of "Victoria Empress" issued.

1901—Gateway coinage introduced in Hyderabad.

1919—An attempt is made to replace smaller silver coinage with copper-nickel 8-, 4-, 2-anna pieces. The 8-anna coin, or half-rupee, is at once extensively counterfeited.

1945—Rajkot state strikes last state gold coin, 1 mohur.

1947—Pure nickel rupee, half-rupee and quarter rupee coins issued, tiger reverse.

1950—First coinage of independent India.

1957—Decimalization introduces a rupee of 100 naya paisa.

1964—Subsidiary coinage now called simply paisa; first aluminum coin issued, and first commemorative rupee, half rupee honor Jawaharlal Nehru.

1969—Undated Gandhi commemoratives introduced as silver 10-rupee coins.

1974 to 1975—Trend toward larger commemoratives, in 20-, 50-rupee denominations; copper-nickel and aluminum small denominations begin to multiply.

1978—High-value notes of 1,000, 5,000 and 10,000 rupees demonetized to curb corruption.

1987—Delhi Mint closes, new mint at Noida opens.

1997—New mint opens at Charlapally, other mints are modernized and new note presses installed due to a paper currency shortage.

1998—Rumors of note withdrawals cause panic.

2000—New 1,000-rupee bank note makes debut.

2005—Reserve Bank reminds retailers, banks to accept small change, says there is no coin shortage.

2006—Stainless steel begins to replace copper-nickel for 2-, 5-rupee coins.

2011—Announces plans to withdraw 25-paise coins from circulation after June 30.

LAOS

1952—Set of three holed aluminum coins, 10-, 20- and 50-centime denominations, issued.

1955—Kip is introduced at par to the Indochinese piastre.

1976—Monetary reform ushers in the Lao liberation kip.

1980—Currency reform replaces the liberation kip with new kip at a ratio of 100-to-one.

2002—10,000- and 20-000-kip bank notes, new higher denominations, make debut.

2006—Bank note series extended to include higher, 50,000-kip denomination.

2010—A 100,000-kip note, silver and gold coins celebrate 35th anniversary of Lao National Day.

PAKISTAN, BANGLADESH

1948—First coinage of the government of Pakistan.

1961—Beginning of decimalization, 100 pice, later paisa, to one rupee.

1964—English legends omitted on Pakistani coinage.

1969—Copper-nickel replaces pure nickel in the higher denominations.

1972—Bangladesh taka is established on par with the Pakistan rupee.

1997—Pakistan issues a circulating commemorative 50-rupee coin and a commemorative note.

2006—The 10-, 1,000- and 5,000-rupee bank notes sport new designs.

2007—New designs for 100-, 500-rupee bank notes.

2008—The 5- and 50-rupee bank notes feature new designs. Aluminum replaces bronze for 1-rupee coins, nickel-brass introduced for 2-rupee coins.

2009—A 10-rupee coin celebrates China's 60th anniversary.

THAILAND

1767—Silver bullet money introduced by liberator-king Taksin.

1782—Bangkok dynasty introduces bullet coins struck with central ridge from two hammer blow striking.

1851—Paper notes introduced.

1860—Modern silver tical coinage of King Phra Chom Klao, Mongkut.

1876—Portrait silver coins of King Phra Maha Chulalongkorn, undated.

1902—Dates appear on the silver portrait coinage.

1939—New national designation, "Muang Thai," or "land of the Thai," officially adopted in place of the former Siam.

1961—The first Thai commemorative coin marks the world tour of the royal couple.

1963—The first recent crown-sized silver coin issued to mark the king's 36th birthday, 20-baht denomination.

1969—First commemorative notes mark the opening of the Thai Banknote Printing Works.

1970—Large silver 50-baht coin commemorates the 20th anniversary of the World Buddhist Fellowship.

1972—New polygonal 5-baht copper-nickel coin released.

1976—Silver 100-, 150-baht commemorative coins joined by copper-nickel 1 baht coin, beginning of a flood of modern commemoratives.

1978—Demonetization of 5-baht coin caused by counterfeiting.

1988—Ringed-bimetallic 10-baht coins enter circulation.

1996—Plastic notes introduced.

2005—A 2-baht coin debuts, struck at Royal Canadian Mint in Winnipeg.

2006—Commemorative 60-baht note celebrating King Bhumibol Adulyadej's 60 years on the throne is nation's first polymer issue.

2007—Uncut sheet containing single 1-, 5-, and 10-baht notes marks king's 80th birthday.

2008—Royal Canadian Mint's plated technology employed to issue new 25- and 50-satang coins.

VIETNAM

The early coins of Vietnam resemble those of China, the square holed circular cash coins, which were cast under the Le dynasty until 1789; by the Tayson rebels in southern Vietnam; and by the Nguyen dynasty established by Nguyen Anh in 1802. The ingots and circular Vietnam issues are not considered true coins.

980—First coins of Vietnam issued.

1044—Domestic coinage ceases after this date.

1205—Tran Dynasty reintroduces domestic coinage.

1406—Ming emperors of China issue coins for Vietnam.

1750—Trinh clan captures copper mines and begins production of copper coins after this date.

1802—Cast square-holed copper and zinc dong coinage begins under Emperor Gia-Long.

1832—First European-style coins issued.

1883—Proclamation of a French protectorate ends independence of Vietnam, which already had lost Cochin-China between 1862 and 1867.

1884—Coinage of the heroic nationalist emperor Ham-Nghi.

1889 to 1926—Vietnam, its central region of Annam theoretically sovereign under French protection, continues to issue coins through the reign of emperor Bao Dai, 1926 to 1945.

1945—Following emperor's abdication, the Communist-led Viet-Minh follow his earlier declaration of independence from France. The first aluminum 20-xu coin is released.

1946—Aluminum 5-hao and 1-dong coins, bronze 2-dong coins struck, the latter two with Ho Chi Minh's portrait.

1953—The state of Vietnam, with ex-emperor Bao Dai at its head, issues three aluminum coins, 10-, 20- and 50-xu denominations.

1959—Currency reform in North Vietnam.

1960—After the deposition of Bao Dai, the new Republic of Vietnam issues an aluminum 50-su coin and copper-nickel 1-dong coin with the portrait of president Ngo Dinh-diem.

1964—Following the murder of Ngo Dinh-diem, republican coins with rice plant obverse are issued in copper-nickel.

1968—Nickel-clad steel coinage released.

1971—An aluminum 1-dong coin issued in connection with the United Nation's FAO coin program.

1975—Forcible unification of South and North Vietnam as a newly united communist state.

1978—Vietnam dong replaces currency of the north and south following reunification.

1996—Color-enhanced noncirculating legal tender commemorative coins released.

2001—Nation's first polymer note, denominated 50 dong, marks national bank's 50th anniversary. New 100,000-dong bank note highest denomination.

2003—200-, 1,000- and 5,000-dong coins issued. New 500,000-dong bank note highest denomination.

2004—New 500- and 2,000-dong coins, dated 2003, debut April 1.

Near East, Africa

(Countries arranged by regions)

ISLAMIC COINAGES, NEAR EAST, NORTH AFRICA, RELATED AREAS

630 to 720—Anonymous one-third solidus coinages of the Caliphs.

660 to 750—Gold dinar coinage of the Umayyad caliphs of Damascus.

750 to 1517—Coinage of the Abbasid caliphs of Baghdad.

969 to 1173—Coinage of Egypt's Fatimid caliphs.

756 to 1024—Renewal of Umayyad coin types in Muslim Cordoba, Spain, by a refugee of the Umayyad house.

1040 to 1308—Seljuk Turkish empire coinage, Asia Minor and neighboring areas.

1056 to 1147—Coins of Spain's Almoravid Muslim rulers.

1130 to 1269—Almohad rulers, another splinter group of North African origin in Spain. Saracenic bezant gold coinage of the Crusaders' Latin Kingdom of Jerusalem issued, types of Muslim derivation.

1192 to 1300—Coinage of shahs of Afghanistan.

1259—Last Jerusalem bezants of Latin Kingdom under Conrad and Conradin.

1451—Ottoman gold sequins of Muhammad II.

1502—Gold Ashrafis of Persian shah Ismail I.

1600—Gold of sultans of Morocco.

1773—Last coins of the khanate of Crim, Crimea, in South Russia.

1786—Modern round gold coin struck at Madrid Mint in Spain for Morocco.

1855—Distinctive coinage issued in Tunisia.

1876—Modernization of Persian coinage under Shah Nasrud-Din.

1882—Round silver machine-struck coins of Morocco's Hasan I.

1885—Sudan coins of the Mahdi, Muhammad Ahmad.

1887—Coins of the khalifa Abdullahi, the mahdi's successor.

1891—Start of modern Afghan coinage under Amir Abd ur-Rahman.

1893—Modern copper coinage in Morocco.

1894—Coppers of Fessul bin Turkee, Imam of Muscat and Oman.

1904—Independent Yemen coinage of imam Yahya bin Muhammad Hamid ad-Din.

1916—First coins of Egypt of sultan Hussein Kamil.

1920—Last coins of Ottoman Turkey under Muhammad VI. Fuad, sultan of Egypt, issues his silver coins.

1922—First Turkish republic coinage. Fuad now king in Egypt.

1923—Hejaz coinage in bronze, silver and gold of Hussein ibn Ali.

1924—First coinage of the state of Great Lebanon, French mandate.

1925—Provisional coins of Abdul Aziz ibn as-Saud at occupied Mecca Mint. Reza Shah proclaimed ruler in Persia, solar year adopted.

1927—Distinctive Hebrew, English, Arabic coinage issued in Britain's Palestine Mandate, first coins to bear abbreviated name, "Land of Israel." Gold pahlavi adopted by Reza Shah in Persia.

1931—First coinage in Iraq under King Faisal I.

1934—Latin alphabet, western dates only adopted for Turkish coinage.

1937—First coins of the Kingdom of Saudi Arabia.

1940—Modern copper-nickel coinage in Muscat and Oman under Sultan Sa'id bin Taimur.

1947—Coinage of the independent Syrian republic.

1949—First coinage of the Hashemite Kingdom of the Jordan (coinage inscription changed from OF THE JORDAN to OF JORDAN in 1955). French-type coinage in Algeria.

1952—Republic of Lebanon independent coinage; also kingdom of Libya.

1954—Egyptian republic coinage.

1956—King Muhammad V strikes Moroccan 500-franc coin after French protectorate is abolished. New coinage of Independent Sudan.

1958—United Arab Republic established, union of Egypt (UAR coins, 1958) and Syria (separate UAR coins, 1959).

1959—Following the murder of King Faisal II, Republic of Iraq coinage begins. Turkey introduces stainless steel coinage.

1960—Maldive Islands introduce new larin-rupee coinage. First distinctive republican Tunisia coinage in aluminum, aluminum-bronze.

1961—Kuwait strikes first independent coinage.

1962—Following breakup of United Arab Republic (comprising Syria and Egypt from 1958 to 1961, Egypt singly until 1971), Syrian Arab Republic strikes first coinage.

1963—Under Egyptian tutelage, Yemen Arab Republic begins coinage in the territory it is able to hold during continuing war with Imam's government.

1964—First independent coins of Algeria, federation of South Arabia.

1965—Coinage of oil-rich Bahrain, 1,000 fils to one dinar.

1966—Qatar and Dubai coinage issued, 100 dirham to one ryal.

1970—New Oman coinage based on Saudi ryal of 1,000 baizah.

1971—Following bloody revolution, "Democratic Yemen" coinage is struck for the former Federation of South Arabia. United Arab Republic (Egypt) adopts name, "Arab Republic of Egypt."

1972—Proclamation of loose union followed by identical eagle on coinage of Egypt, Libya and Syria.

1973—Coinage of United Arab Emirates in Arabian gulf, former Trucial States, including Abu Dhabi, Dubai, Sharjah, Ajman, Umm al-Qaiwain, Fujairah and Ras al-Khaimah. One dirham equals 100 fils; 1,000 fils equals one dinar.

1976—Iran adopts new imperial calendar, year 2535 on new coins.

1978—Democratic Republic of Afghanistan issues commemorative coins to raise funds.

1979—Iranian currency no longer depicts monarch after overthrow of Pahlavi dynasty.

1990—Turkey files suit in United States seeking return of ancient coins allegedly smuggled out of Turkey.

1991—Inflation and counterfeiting of local currency in Iraq after defeat in the Gulf War.

1993—Algeria issues its first ringed-bimetallic coin.

1994—Kuwait issues all new notes, some in plastic, due to massive thefts by Iraq during the Gulf War.

1995—Iran issues its first ringed-bimetallic coins. Arab Sahara Democratic Republic in Morocco issues commemorative coins to raise funds.

1996—Maldives replaces 2-rufiyaa coins with a note.

1997—Libyan notes processed to remove ink, with paper reused to counterfeit German notes. Algeria replaces the 100-dinar note with a coin.

1998—Jordan issues its first ringed-bimetallic coin.

1999—Hoard of ancient coins illegally removed from Turkey returned.

2002—Morroco's new half-dirham coin honors telecommunications, 1-dirham coin shows new king.

2003—Ringed-bimetallic 200- and 500-franc coins introduced in West African States.

2004—Iran issues new smaller 50- and 100-rial coins. Plated steel 5-, 10- and 20-ouguiya coins released in Mauritania.

2005—Iraq issues 25-, 50- and 100-dinar coins dated 2004, which prove unpopular and are later withdrawn. Turkey redenominates currency, dropping six zeroes off inflationary lira.

2006—New series of Central African States coins, including 2-franc piece, a new coin denomination.

2007—Iran's new 50,000-rial bank note featuring atomic symbols gains notice in Western media. New Sudanese pound bank note series debuts. Saudi Arabia redesigns bank note series.

2008—Egypt issues plated-steel 10-, 25- and 50-piastre coins.

2009—Iran issues three new coin denominations, 250, 500 and 1,000 rials. Turkey redenominates currency again, with new designs on notes and coins. Commemorative 1-, 5- and 10-dinar notes mark 32nd anniversary of proclamation of people's power in Libya.

2010—Yemen releases first 250-rial bank note.

ISRAEL

1948—Israel, only weeks old, strikes provisional aluminum 25-mil coins.

1949—Israel issues new 1,000 prutah to Israel pound coinage. Tenth anniversary of the independence of Israel sees beginning of commemorative coinage with release of copper-nickel 1-pound, silver 5-pound coins.

1960—New Israeli coinage of 100 agora to one pound issued.

1985—Devalued Israeli sheqel coins issued in changeover to new sheqel monetary system.

1988—Introduces 20-new-sheqel note.

1992—Issuance of 200-new-sheqel note dated 1991.

1995—Ringed-bimetallic 10-new-sheqel coin introduced to replace a note.

1996—A 20-new-sheqel commemorative coin honors assassinated Prime Minister Yitzhak Rabin.

1998—Fiftieth anniversary of founding of Israel commemorated on various coins.

1999—Israel issues medal commemorating the late King Hussein of Jordan, the nation's first medal depicting a leader of another country. Several new notes introduced: 20, 50, 100 and 200 new sheqalim.

2007—Israel launches new circulating coin, denominated 2 new Israeli sheqalim.

2008—New bank note 20 new Israeli sheqalim, marks nation's 60th anniversary; is nation's first polymer note.

2009—New series of bank notes announced, proposed honorees criticized, proposal shelved.

2010—New series of bank notes announced.

SUB-SAHARAN AFRICA, ISLANDS

300 to 850—Coinage of the kingdom of Axum, ancestor of Ethiopia.

1755—Mozambique Portuguese gold coins.

1762—Angola Portuguese silver coins.

1791—Decimal coins for freed slave colony of Sierra Leone, Lion on Rock type.

1797—"Free trade to Africa by order of Parliament" coins of the Gold Coast, Ackey denominations.

1815—Missionary coins of Griqua Town, South Africa.

1833—American Colonization Society issues copper 1-cent coin for Liberia.

1842—Silver onca ingot-coinage issue for Maria II for Mozambique.

1847—Copper coins issued for republic of Liberia.

1874—Thomas Francois Burgers gold staatspond, first official coin in South Africa (old South African Republic, the Transvaal).

1881—Sultanate of Zanzibar issues gold, silver and copper riyal coins.

1883—French West African tokens issued in brass 10-, 5-, 1-centime denominations.

1887—Holed copper, unholed silver coinage of the Independent State of the Congo under personal rule of the king of the Belgians, Leopold II, issued.

1888—Coins of the Imperial East Africa Company issued at Mombassa, rupee denominations.

1890—Comoro Islands sultan's coinage, franc standard; first copper of the new German East Africa Company.

1891—First Italian tallero for Eritrea.

1892—Coins depicting President S.J.P. Kruger issued in the restored South African Republic, minted in Berlin, Germany and Pretoria, South Africa.

1893—German East Africa silver coinage, company administration.

1894—Modern Ethiopian coinage in silver and copper under Menelik II.

1896—First regular issue silver coinage in Liberia.

1897—British East Africa pice-rupee standard.

1902—Last independent South African Republic coinage, the "Veld pond" at Pilgrim's Rest, Transvaal.

1904—New German East Africa coinage under the administration of the German Foreign Office.

1906—British East Africa aluminum cent, silver 25-, 50-cent coins issued. First regular issue aluminum coinage in the world.

1907—Aluminum 1/10 penny issued for British West Africa-Nigeria.

1909—Belgian Congo's first coins issued under Belgian rule, rather than personal rule by Leopold II. Italian Somalia coinage begins on besa-rupia standard.

1913—Silver and copper-nickel coinage issued for British West Africa-Nigeria.

1916—Emergency coinage in the defense territory of German East Africa under Gen. Paulus von Lettow-Vorbeck. The Tabora Railway shops produce both brass and copper 20- and 5-heller pieces as well as a 15-rupien gold coin.

1918—Italian Eritrea issues a "tallero veneto" in imitation of the standard Maria Theresia taler.

1920—Large franc denominations in copper-nickel issued in the Belgian Congo.

1921—Following hoarding of silver coins for jewelry purposes, brass coins replace silver in British West Africa.

1923—Pretoria Mint reopens to strike a full range of coins for the Union of South Africa (established 1910).

1929—Modern Portuguese coins issued for Sao Tome e Principe, islands in the gulf of Guinea.

1930—New Portuguese coinage issued for Cape Verde Islands.

1931—New bronze, nickel coinage issued of Haile Selassie I of Ethiopia.

1932—New Southern Rhodesia coins issued.

1933—Modern coinage for Portuguese Guinea issued.

1935—Portuguese Mozambique introduces new silver standardized coins, adding copper-nickel and bronze pieces in 1936, beginning a long colonial coin standard that was to permeate the rest of Portuguese colonial history.

1942 to 1943—Coinage of the Free French in various African colonies, led by French Equatorial Africa under Governor General Felix Eboue.

1943—Pretoria, South Africa, Mint strikes coinage for Belgian Congo for exile government.

1944—New Ethiopian coinage in bronze and silver under restored emperor.

1946—Portuguese Guinea marks fifth centenary of discovery with standard type commemorative coins.

1948—Standardized Angola Portuguese colonial coinage. French empire begins coinage explosion of standard-obverse Bazor type coins in many African, Indian and Pacific ocean colonies; initial types are 1- and 2-franc coins in aluminum, aluminum-bronze and nickel added in 1960s in surviving colonies such as the Comoro islands.

1950—Italian trusteeship coinage for Somalia issued, 100 centesimi to one somalo.

1954—Last coins of Southern Rhodesia.

1955—Federation of Rhodesia and Nyasaland coins issued.

1958—Independent Ghana sets type for African coinages with new sterling-type coins portraying the "Osagyefo" Dr. Kwame Nkrumah.

1959—Coinage begins for former French Guinea, Federation of Nigeria. New unified coinage of the Equatorial African States begins.

1960—New coins for independent Cameroon, emission bank of Rwanda and Burundi; long-independent Liberia issues new bronze, copper-nickel and silver sets.

1961—South Africa decimal coins, 100 cents (in Afrikaans, "sent") to one rand; Katanga, Mali and the unified coinage of the West African States begins.

1964—French colonial coins of the Comoro become the first to depict a living fossil, the famed coelacanth; new independence coins in East Africa, Zambia, Rhodesia, Sierra Leone and Malawi.

1965—Malagasy republic coins in Madagascar introduces stainless steel to Africa; Ghana decimal coins; South Africa, new, smaller bronze, nickel and silver rand-cent/sent coins.

1966—Coins of Gambia, Kenya, Botswana, Tanzania and Uganda struck.

1967—Somali republic begins coinage. Congo issues coinage on a standard of new 100 makuta to one zaire. South Africa introduces Krugerrand gold coin and enters bullion coin market.

1968—Zambia, former Northern Rhodesia, begins decimal coinage.

1969—Ill-fated, short-lived aluminum coins of republic of Biafra issued during the epic struggles of the Nigerian assault on the Ibos. New coins issued for the republic of Equatorial Guinea, formerly Spanish.

1970—Rhodesian decimalization.

1971—After breakup of the Equatorial African States unified currency, production begins of the new nickel 100-franc coins of Gabon, Central African Republic, Popular Republic of the Congo and Chad; decimal coins in Malawi, 100 tambala to one kwacha; decimalization in Gambia, 100 bututs to one dalasi; nickel coins introduced in place of silver in Portuguese colonies.

1973—Decimalization in Nigeria, 100 kobo to one naira; new Mauritania coinage of five khoum to one ouguiya.

1974—New decimal coins for Swaziland.

1975—Dissolution of the Portuguese empire leads to new currencies in Guinea-Bissau, Angola, Sao Tome and Mozambique.

1978—Madagascar Democratic Republic issues 10- and 20-ariary coins at five francs to the ariary. Ugandan notes drop design depicting Idi Amin.

1979—South African circulating coinage design is changed.

1980—Zimbabwe issues six denominations of coins, first issue for country. South Africa issues tenth-ounce, quarter-ounce and half-ounce Krugerrands.

1981—South Africa introduces metal-plastic

threads into the fabric of its paper money.

1985—Many countries, including the United States, ban importation of South African Krugerrand as a protest against policy of racial segregation.

1989—Inflation causes Zaire coins to vanish from circulation. South African Reserve Bank gains control of the Mint. South Africa releases nine denominations of circulating coinage in three colors or series (red series, yellow series, white series), made of a core of either steel or copper plated with different metals or alloys to give each series a distinctive color.

1990—Angola introduces new note designs.

1991—United States lifts its ban on South African Krugerrand coins.

1993—Namibia releases its first domestic currency.

1995—Angola changes the kwanza to the novo kwanza.

1996—Private entities begin issuing bank notes in war-torn Somalia.

1998—Francs congalaise replace zaire following a civil war in the Democratic Republic of Congo (formerly Zaire).

1999—South Africa announces new push to market gold Krugerrands.

2000 to 2011—Zimbabwe experiences hyperinflation during much of the decade, leading to increasingly higher denominations of paper money that is virtually worthless as soon as it is printed.

2002—South Africa stops minting 1-, 2-cent coins because of cost and lack of circulation.

2003—Kenya introduces new 40-shilling coin.

2004—To combat counterfeiting, South Africa issues new 5-rand coin.

2007—Ghana redenominates currency July 1. Nigeria issues redesigned 1-naira and 50-kobo coins and bank notes, and 2-naira coin, a new denomination.

2008—New 5-rand coin from South Africa honors Nelson Mandela's 90th birthday.

2009—Botswana launches new bank note series.

2010—Ethiopia issues ringed-bimetallic 1-birr coin.

Asia

(Countries arranged by region)

CHINA

B.C.

circa 1200—First spade coins, bronze "pu" types.

480—Ming Tao sword coinage, bronze.

circa 220—Pan Liang half-ounce coins, circular with square hole, Ch'in Dynasty.

118—Wu Ch'u coinage of Han Dynasty.

A.D.

7—Usurper Wang Mang issues knife type coins, gold-inlaid inscriptions.

618—Kai Yuan circular coins with square holes;

T'ang dynasty sets pattern for centuries of square-holed coinage that ends only after the new republic is in power, 1911. Japan, Korea and Vietnam will begin use of similar coins several centuries later.

circa 1280—Paper money issued under Mongol Yuan dynasty, inflation and counterfeiting rampant.

1837—Manchu army issues circular "god of longevity" dollar for Taiwan.

1851—T'ai P'ing rebellion coins of the "Great kingdom of Heavenly Peace" and multiple-cash brass coins of Ch'ing (Manchu) Hsien Feng emperor issued.

1861—Round silver dollars of Fukien province issued.

1889—Modernization of Canton Mint. Kwangtung province sees famed "dragon dollars" and subsidiary coinage begin about 1890, soon copied in all China.

1912—First republican coinage, "memento" dollars, issued.

1928—Kweichow province strikes first coin to show automobile in commemoration of the first motor road in the province.

1932—Standard national dollar in silver, famed "birds over junk — rising sun" type modified to show the sailing junk only in the next year.

1936—New, nonsilver coinage in bronze and pure nickel.

1937—Japan begins full-scale invasion, Chiang Kai-Shek holds out amid civil war caused by communists, continuing inflation.

1949—After defeat of Japan, communist takeover proceeds amid bitter war. San Francisco Mint restrikes millions of 1898-dated Mexican pesos for Chiang to pay his troops after inflationary collapse of the national currency.

1949—Nationalist government of Chiang Kai-Shek resumes coinage on Taiwan (Formosa).

1955—First aluminum coinage of the communist People's Republic of China.

1979—Peoples Republic issues its first gold coin.

1980—Peoples Republic introduces its first copper-zinc coinage.

1982—China Mint issues Panda gold bullion coins.

1987— Panda gold bullion coins carry Mint mark for first time.

1991—Platinum composition collector coins struck.

1993—Ringed-bimetallic Panda coins introduced.

1994—Foreign exchange certificates ordered withdrawn.

1997—Hong Kong becomes a special administrative territory of the People's Republic of China with its own separate monetary system.

2006—Commemorative coin program begins, celebrating 2008 Summer Olympic Games in Beijing; includes 10-kilogram gold 100,000-yuan coin.

2008—Circulating commemorative 10-yuan bank note marks Olympics.

2010—Mintage increased for 2011-dated 1-ounce silver Panda 10-yuan coins because of strong demand.

JAPAN

A.D. 708—First coins of native Japanese type cast, Wado Kaichin coinage made of copper mined in Musashi province under empress Genmyo. This is the first of 12 early coins called "dynastic sen."

765 to 950—Rest of dynastic coinage, from Mannen Tsuho through Kengen Saiho in 958.

1584—Mumei Obankin issued under warlord Toyotomi Hideyoshi.

1593—First "Eiraku sen," Japanese copies of China's Ming dynasty Yung Le cash coins cast, rapidly take over Japan's internal commerce.

1599—Tokugawa Ieyasu establishes Kinza Mint for gold coins, Ginza Mint for silver.

1626 to 1862—Kanei Tsuho cash type coinage.

1832—Debased gold and silver coins issued in inflationary period.

1835—Oval cast copper Tempo Tsuho coinage begun.

1853—Commodore Matthew Perry and his "black ships" begin opening Japan after 200 years of isolation. Japanese gold flows out of country.

1870—Osaka Mint goes into operation, striking modern gold, silver and copper circular coins. New monetary system introduced of one yen equal to 100 sen along American lines.

1889—Copper-nickel introduced for 5-sen coins.

1938—Aluminum wartime coinage.

1944—Coinage in tin and porcelain.

1945—Clay "toka" coinage planned, blocked by production bottlenecks, at war's ending.

1946—Coinage reform under Allied occupation, brass 50 sen.

1948—Coin inscriptions now read left to right.

1955—Pure nickel and silver coins introduced.

1964—Tokyo Olympic Games commemoratives see return of silver crown, 1,000-yen piece; first use of Western dates since pattern yen of 1873.

1976—Copper-nickel 100-yen coin marks emperor's 50th year, fourth commemorative in this metal and denomination.

1982—The 500-yen note is replaced with a copper-nickel 500-yen coin.

1984—10,000-yen notes released due to inflation.

1986—Commemorative coins issued and sold by lottery system, marking 60th year of reign of Emperor Hirohito.

1990—Police investigate a large number of possibly fake gold 100,000-yen coins.

1993—Additional security devices added to paper money to prevent counterfeiting.

1999—New 500-yen coin introduced to thwart counterfeiters.

2000—New commemorative 2,000-yen note for World Economic Council meeting in August.

2008—Nine-year series begins, honoring each of nation's 47 prefectures with circulating, collector coins.

KOREA

996—Kon Won cast cash-type coinage of King Song Jong.

1100—Heavy cast cash coin production.

circa 1400—New coinage of Yi dynasty, Sip Chon issues begun.

1625—Cho Son cast coins.

1633—First stabilized currency, Sang Pyong coins, often called "Yop Chon," issued well into the 19th century.

1885—Pattern for round, modern coinage of Korea introduced by Paul Georg von Mollendorf, Mint director from Germany, on a yang-mun standard.

1886—Pattern warn-mun coins in copper, tin and gilt copper.

1892—Actual coinage of modern round pieces on 100 fun-one yang, soon overcome by a flood of officially struck and counterfeit quarter-yang nickels.

1899—Russian coinage types, 100 chon to one won, prepared, some issued in 1901.

1905—Definitive Phoenix coinage on chon-won standard begun.

1910—Korean coinage ends with annexation to Japan.

1959—Following liberation, communist invasion and war, coinage resumes on hwan standard.

1966—Overthrow of Syngman Rhee government, new won coinage begins.

1975—The 30th year of the restoration of Korea's sovereignty and independence is marked by a copper-nickel commemorative 100-won coin of South Korea.

1989—South Korea melts unsold 1988 Olympic commemorative coins.

1995—Color-enhanced commemorative coins issued for collectors by North Korea.

2009—South Korea launches 50,000-won bank note, first in nation to feature a historical female and final in redesigned series that began in 2006.

Pacific Region

(Countries arranged alphabetically; some grouped by region)

AUSTRALIA

1813—"Holey dollar," pierced and counterstamped Spanish dollar, issued in New South Wales.

1852—Adelaide Assay Office gold pounds, ingots struck.

1853—Fort Philip gold coinage.

1855—Sydney Mint opens.

1871—British style gold coins.

1872—Melbourne Mint opens as branch of British Royal Mint.

1899—Perth Mint opens.

1910—First distinctive Australian silver coins of Edward VII.

1911—Bronze penny, half penny issued.

1927—First Australian commemorative coin, Canberra florin.

1937—Complete redesign of the coinage, first crown issued.

1942—Some World War II coins struck at U.S. Mint facilities.

1965—Royal Australian Mint opens, first mint in Australian not a branch of British Royal Mint.

1966—Decimal coinage introduced on a system of 100 cents to the Australian dollar, including a silver 50-cent coin.

1969—Polygonal copper-nickel 50-cent coin joins minor copper-nickel and bronze coins.

1970—First decimal commemorative celebrates Capt. James Cook's voyages.

1980—Currency futures market opens. Commencement of coining Koala gold $200 coin.

1984—Dollar coin replaces dollar note in circulation.

1986—Proof 1987 Nugget gold bullion coins issued to preview gold bullion.

1987—Nugget silver and platinum bullion coins issued by the Perth Mint following the Gold Corporation Act of 1987.

1988—Plastic $10 Bicentennial commemorative note introduced.

1989—Koala platinum bullion coins introduced.

1993—Perth Mint refurbished.

1994—Ringed-bimetallic $5 coin released.

1995—Palladium Emu bullion coin introduced.

1996—Note Printing Australia and UCB Films PLC form joint venture company to market plastic notes.

1998—Pad printing process for color enhancement used to produce Olympic coins issued jointly by Royal Australian Mint and Perth Mint.

1999—Series of coins issued to commemorate 2000 Sydney Olympic Games.

2000—Mule error $1 coin struck on 10-cent coin planchet.

2001—Circulating 20- and 50-cent coin series honor each Australian state, mark centennial of federation.

2009—Royal Australian Mint undergoes $65 million refurbishment.

BRITISH MALAYA, BRITISH EAST INDIES

1783—East India Company coins issued for Fort Marlboro, Sumatra, during Napoleonic wars.

1787—East India Company coins for Pulu Penang, cent-rupee standard.

1811 to 1815—East India Company coins for occupied Java.

1841—Sir James Brooke's Sarawak copper kapang issued.

1845—First coins issued for the Straits Settlements under East India Company; 1862, name changed to "India-Straits."

1863—Copper coinage issued for Raj of Sarawak.

1863—Beginning of British Hong Kong coinage.

1866—Hong Kong Mint dollars issued.

1882—British North Borneo Company coinage begun.

1892—Sarawak issues world's only holed portrait coin, 1 cent with portrait of Sir Charles Brooke, rajah.

1903—Straits Settlements dollar struck.

1907—Straits dollar reduced in size.

1935—Nickel alloys appear in Hong Kong coinage, replacing silver.

1939—New coinage issued under the Commissioners of Currency, Malaya.

1953—Coinage bears name Malaya and British Borneo.

1960—New copper-nickel Hong Kong dollar issued.

1967—New separate coinages issued for Malaysia, Brunei and Singapore.

1980—Singapore substitutes pure nickel for silver in $10 coins. Hong Kong Commodities Exchange begins gold futures trading.

1989—Hong Kong demonetizes 5-cent coins.

1991—Malaysia replaces 1-ringgit note with a coin.

1990—Plastic notes enter circulation in Singapore.

1995—Singapore Mint applies a latent image to gold coins.

1998—Malaysia demonetizes its two highest-denomination notes to curb currency speculation.

2007—Overprinted polymer $20 note marks 40th anniversary of currency exchange with Brunei.

COOK ISLANDS

1970—Commemorative dollar begins decimal coinage.

1996—New Zealand coins and notes replace many local issues.

2006—With coinage changes in New Zealand, Cook Island withdraws 10-, 20- and 50-cent coins, and New Zealand coins of these denominations circulate in their place.

FIJI

1934—Sterling-standard coinage of George V, half penny through florin.

1942—Some World War II coinage struck at U.S. Mints.

1969—Decimal coinage, 100 cents to $1, issued.

2008—Stops issuing 1- and 2-cent coins.

2009—Issues smaller, lighter 5-, 10- and 50-cent coins.

HAWAII

1847—Copper cent issued by King Kamehameha III.

1883—Silver dime through dollar coinage of King Kalakaua I issued.

1900—First of five national banks chartered; banks issue large-size and small-size national bank notes.

1942—U.S. paper money issued with special overprint of HAWAII, with use initially limited to the islands. Overprint would prevent hostile forces from using the notes in case of invasion. Restrictions on use elsewhere lifted in 1944.

MALAYA AND EAST INDIES AREA

896—Hindu coinage issued in Java.

1297—Gold coins of the sultans of Acheh, Sumatra.

1601—Dordrecht, Netherlands, strikes first trade dollar of 8-real value for the United Amsterdam Company, forerunner of Vereenigde Oost-Indische

Compagnie's (Dutch East India Company) "VOC" coins soon to follow.

1645—First VOC silver coins, first coins to bear VOC monogram, issued; withdrawn in 1647.

1686—First Batavia gold ducats appear.

1726—First VOC copper coins issued.

1728—Silver ducatoons of the United East India Company issued.

1786—Silver 3-gulden crowns issued.

1799—Batavian Republic coinage issued for the Indies.

1807—Indies coins of Louis Napoleon, King of Holland, issued.

1814—First coins of kingdom of the Netherlands for the Indies issued.

1913—Copper-nickel 5 cents, first new type in decades, introduced.

1936—Holed type bronze 1 cent issued.

1943—Aluminum and tin alloy Japanese occupation coinage issued.

1945—Last Dutch coinage for the Indies.

1949—Aluminum French colonial coinage for New Caledonia, French Oceania, issued.

1951—First coins of independent Indonesia.

1962—Distinctive Indonesian coins issued for Riau islands and New Guinea, "West Irian."

1966—Silver 100-franc crown struck by the Paris Mint for New Hebrides, jointly administered with the British.

1967—New pure nickel coinage issued: for New Caledonia, 10-, 20-, 50-franc pieces; for New Hebrides, 10-, 20-franc coins; 10- and 20- and 50-franc coins for French Polynesia.

1970—Nickel-brass 1-, 2- and 5-franc coins issued for New Hebrides.

1972—First of continuing coinage for French-administered islands by Overseas Emission Institute.

1975—Gold-on-silver coin of Solomon Islands repudiated by island government.

1977—Regular minor coinage for Solomons struck by Britain's Royal Mint.

1981—New Hebrides becomes Vanuata; issues new national currency, the vatu.

2011—1- and 2-vatu coins withdrawn after March 31, 2011.

MARSHALL ISLANDS

1986—United States, which had administered rule over Marshall Islands since end of World War II, announces Oct. 1 that the islands are to be considered a separate nation. U.S. dollar remains in circulation. New government commissions coinage, primarily for collector sale elsewhere. Themes during the 1980s, 1990s and 2000s were generally of nonlocal subjects, including Elvis Presley, the Wright Brothers, James Dean and the Ford Mustang.

NEW GUINEA

1894 to 1895—Coinage of the German New Guinea Company, 100 pfennig to 1 neu-Guinea mark.

1929—Pattern coinage for the Territory of New Guinea struck.

1935—Regular coinage begins on sterling system.

1975—New decimal coinage, 100 toea to 1 kina.

1989—Gold rush stimulates local economy.

2005—Reduces size of 1-kina coin.

2007—1- and 2-toea coins stripped of legal tender status April 19.

2008—50-toea coin is first circulating outside of Canada to sport color. Larger 1-kina coins withdrawn.

NEW ZEALAND

1933—First distinctive New Zealand coins, silver threepence to halfcrown.

1935—Waitangi commemorative crown struck.

1940—Bronze coinage of penny, half penny.

1947—Copper-nickel replaces silver in coinage.

1949—Crown commemorates aborted royal visit.

1967—Decimal coinage, 100 cents to one New Zealand dollar, commemorative dollar series begun.

1982—A new portrait of Queen Elizabeth II is adopted on notes.

1989—Stops production of 1- and 2-cent coins.

1993—$1, $2 notes replaced with coins.

1994—Ringed-bimetallic 50-cent coin enters circulation.

1997—Vending machines fail to accept new $2 coin due to a manufacturing error.

1999—Plastic composition notes introduced.

2003—Collector coins celebrate *Lord of the Rings,* which was filmed in New Zealand.

2006—Withdrawal of 5-, 10-, 20- and 50-cent coins, issues smaller and lighter 10-, 20- and 50-cent coins.

PHILIPPINES

1803—Crude copper quarto coinage for Spanish King Charles IV.

1833—Counterstamped pesos of the New World in circulation.

1861—Distinctive centavo-peso coinage of gold, Isabel II.

1864—Silver denominations struck.

1897—Only peso struck for Philippines of Spanish type, Alfonso XIII.

1903—Centavo-peso coins under U.S. sovereignty introduced.

1907—Reduced size silver coinage to halt export and melting of larger coins.

1936—Establishment of the Commonwealth of the Philippines, three commemoratives.

1937—Coinage of the Commonwealth of the Philippines.

1944—"Victory" note is first commemorative paper money for the Philippines.

1947—Restoration of the republic commemorated by MacArthur peso, half-peso coins.

1958—First minor coinage of the republic.

1961—Jose Rizal commemorative coins begin an ongoing series.

1967—All new coinage with Tagalog or Filipino inscriptions, 100 sentimos to one piso.

1975—Redesign of coinage introduces square sentimo, scalloped 5-sentimo piece and 5-piso coin in pure nickel, and silver 25- and 50-piso pieces, the latter in Proof sets. This set was partially struck for the Philippines by mints in four different countries—in the United States, Canada, Britain and West Germany.

1978—Establishment of the Bangko Sentral ng Pilipinas Mint.

1983—Piso devalued.

1984—1982-dated Reagan-Marcos commemorative appears in numismatic market, unannounced officially as released. Piso devalued by President Marcos due to flight of capital.

1986—Future commemorative coin production contracted with Pobjoy Mint rather than the Franklin Mint.

1997—New coinage includes some new metal compositions.

1998—Issues 8.5-inch by 14-inch 100,000-piso commemorative note.

TONGA

1967—Decimal coinage of 100 seniti to one pa'anga, depicting portrait of late Queen Salote Tupou III.

1967—Coronation coinage of new King Taufa'ahau Tupou IV begins commemorative coin series.

1977—Ingot-shaped coin issued.

TUVALU

1976—Formerly known as the Ellice Islands, Tuvalu opens its coinage history with a seven-coin set in bronze and copper-nickel, 1 cent through $1 denominations, featuring wildlife and sea life of this Pacific region.

2001—A 1,000-piso note, a new denomination, debuts.

2002—A 200-piso note, a new denomination, debuts.

2005—New 100-piso note features misspelling of the Philippine president's name.

2010—New series of bank notes announced, with coin redesign also promised.

WESTERN SAMOA

1967—Decimal coins of 100 sene to one tala introduced.

1969—Commemorative tala series begins with Robert Louis Stevenson coin.

1988—American Samoa retracts legal tender status of America's Cup commemorative coins.

1990—Issues polymer 2-tala note, the world's third nation to use plastic for "paper" money.

1998—Issues one piece of a three-part commemorative coin (the other two parts issued by Cook Islands and Fiji), semi-circular in shape, that when joined to the two other pieces, creates a circular coin with a center hole, to be filled by a special medal.

2008—Releases new series of bank notes.

13 World Coins and Paper Money

World Coin Collecting

From the viewpoint of a collector in the United States, world numismatics includes all coins and notes produced in other countries. The study of world numismatics can reach back to the invention of coinage in about 650 B.C. and forward to the future of money. It opens doors to the Greeks and Romans and to the knights of the crusades. World numismatics touches on the samurai of Japan and the rajas of India. It sheds light on the pirates of the Spanish Main and the artists of the Renaissance.

It even illuminates some aspects of American numismatics that many collectors never notice. Until 1857, the gold and silver coins of Spain, England and other countries were legal tender in the United States. Popular American coins such as the Barber series and the Walking Liberty half dollar were copied almost directly from the circulating coins of France. From 1874 until the mid-1980s, the U.S. Mint struck coins for foreign governments, with billions struck in the years of World War II.

Sooner or later someone shows you (or gives you) a foreign coin or note. Or perhaps you become curious about the homelands of your ancestors, and the next time you are at coin show you look for the money they would have used. You might read an article in the "World Coins" section of *Coin World*. Maybe you travel as a tourist or on business. By whatever route, you discover the broad horizon of worldwide coin collecting and numismatics.

Money from other times and places may look odd, or surprisingly familiar. You might easily understand a coin that says UNO PESO and be puzzled by another that reads EMPIRE CHERIFIEN. To a person familiar with only English or Latin-based alphabets, writing on the coin might appear indecipherable, being in Arabic, Russian or Burmese. The feel of the coin, the look of the bank note might be unusual—and compelling. You want to know more. You want to own more.

Wanting also to know more, you will acquire books that tell about the lives and times of the people who made or spent the money you collect. You might find yourself learning new languages or watching the news with keener awareness. Wanting to own more, you might join a specialty club, introduce yourself to dealers or even buy coins directly from the mints of various governments.

With the whole world and all of history since 650 B.C. open to you, in which direction do you travel? Some collectors begin with a time or place that interests them, such as imperial Rome or the crusader states of the Middle East. Others collect according to a topic, such as trains, astronomical events, flowers or buildings. Popular today are ringed-bimetallic coins, those that are made of two or more different metals bonded concentrically, with the outer ring(s) around a central hub. You could follow the life of a famous person like Marie Curie or Frederic Chopin and acquire the coins he or she might have spent in his or her travels. Some people collect coins that are not round and others collect notes that are not made of paper.

Numismatics also includes the study of tokens and medals as well as phone cards and other forms of electronic money. Some collectors seek the orders and medals of military units. Others collect checks (bank drafts), bonds and stock certificates. Bibliophiles collect books, auction catalogs and other information. Remember: Numismatics is the art and science that studies the forms and uses of money. What you collect is your decision.

How to begin collecting

Research: You cannot know what to buy, where to get it, or how much to pay for it without knowledge.

Reflect: Completeness is everything to a collector. Your goal will be more satisfying if it is both challenging and achievable.

Recognize: It is a mistake to think that someone else collecting the same theme will want to buy your collection. However, if the pieces you select are interesting and important enough in their own right—regardless of how you sort and arrange them—when you sell, you can be reasonably sure of recouping some of your investment.

Respond: The Internet makes it easier than ever for collectors in the United States to buy coins and notes from far-flung lands. You can acquire your new possessions at coin shows or from the advertisers in numismatic periodicals such as *Coin World*. You can buy from or trade with other collectors.

There is a clear difference between reading and talking about money and actually seeing it and touching it. The bargain boxes in coin shops or at the tables of dealers at coin shows are perfectly valid introductions to worldwide numismatics. You might find, for 25 cents, a worn example of a coin that you will later seek out in Proof, for a hundred times more. If you had not seen the first, you might never have known to seek the second.

The classified ads in *Coin World* frequently carry offers for "bargain lots" of coins or notes. These are necessarily the most common items, inevitably of low value, and yet, by examining them and learning about them, you will prepare yourself to make intelligent choices about items that cost a thousand times more.

Noncirculating coins

Many countries often make coins specifically for sale to collectors. Historical events of greater or lesser importance—from the first landing on the moon to the wedding anniversary of a local ruler—become the subject of coins that have no other purpose than to be exported.

Since 1950, the collector of world coins has become a target of opportunists who see the value of catering to collectors.

More than 90 nations have struck coins in conjunction with the Food and Agriculture Organization, a branch of the United Nations. Another program was the Conservation Coinage Collection, to bring attention to endangered animals.

For some collectors, the most benign abuses are the coins of small nations that commemorate events far removed from their locale. The Marshall Islands honored Elvis Presley. The Isle of Man honored the America's Cup race. The United Arab Emirates honored Vladimir Lenin and Pope Paul VI. The Caribbean nation of Niue honored tennis stars Steffi Graf and Boris Becker. Such coins rarely, if ever, circulate in the nations that issued them. The issuers produce strictly for sale to collectors, generally those living in other countries.

Some collectors who focus on 19th century U.S. type coins may take a dim view of these noncirculating coins. Even so, the coins do have their place in numismatics.

Numismatics includes the study of medals. First issued in the Renaissance, medals are perhaps more properly grouped with painting and sculpture. They are a medium for fine art. Of course, medals and coins have a lot in common. They are produced by the same or similar methods. Often, the same artists who design medals also design coins. In 1999, the shadow of a solar eclipse cut across Europe. Several nations struck coins to commemorate the event. Romania issued a noncirculating legal tender bank note. The 2,000-leu note provided a scientific schematic of the eclipse and other details that could not be presented well on a coin. Money is history you can hold in your hand. That includes commemorative money not intended for circulation.

Some people in the collector community complain that they feel exploited by noncirculating legal tender. Yet even the U.S. Mint strikes these coins. Whether you choose to buy them or not is your decision.

Mints as businesses

The global trend away from centralization of authority in general and state-run businesses in particular has continued, with the collapse of Soviet communism being only the most visible event. For example, the Austrian Mint is now a "business," a for-profit corporation whose sole shareholder is the Austrian Treasury. This is not unusual in the world of 2011. The Royal Canadian Mint operates on the same principle—and in addition it actively seeks business by striking coins for other nations. In this, it competes against Britain's Royal Mint as well against a roster of truly private businesses, such as Pobjoy Mint. Even nations that have their own mints will occasionally contract other mints to strike specific issues for them.

Member nations of the eurozone issue their own euro coins with euro obverses and their own national reverses. However, each member does not necessarily strike its own coinage, as some contract out the work to other world mints. Estonia, the latest eurozone member to join, on Jan. 1, 2011, contracted with the Mint of Finland to strikes its coins because Estonia lacked the minting facilities.

Canada

An expanding population, development of new areas and business growth were key factors in Canada's decision to issue its own money in 1858.

The early history of Canada reflects British and French interest in the northern regions of North America. While Britain won control over what became Canada as a result of war between the two world powers from 1689 to 1763, French influence remains strong (Canada's paper money has legends in French and English), especially in Quebec.

The Province of Quebec, which the British had formed from conquered French lands in 1763, was split into Upper and Lower Canada in 1791. Fifty years later, in 1841, the two Canadas became the Province of Canada. The Dominion of Canada was established in 1867, formed from New Brunswick, Nova Scotia and the Province of Canada, with the former Province of Canada split into the provinces of Ontario and Quebec. Other provinces and territories joined from 1870 to 1949, the last being Newfoundland.

Throughout much its history, Great Britain exerted certain controls over Canada. The Canadian provinces began self-government starting in 1848. Canada became an independent nation in 1931, and British control over amendments to the Canadian Constitution ended in 1982.

Throughout its history, Canada has had a fascinating array of money. A popular early Canadian "money" was the beaver pelt. As the population grew, a mixture of coinage from America, England, France, Spain and other countries came into use. This ultimately proved unsatisfactory, bringing the decision to coin a national Canadian currency.

Canada adopted a decimal system similar to the American system. All Canadian coinage from 1858 to 1907 was struck at the Royal Mint, London, or by the Heaton Mint, a private mint in Birmingham, England.

Establishing a Canadian Mint

In the closing years of the 19th century, the idea of establishing a government mint in Canada was formulated. One of the main reasons was that gold production in British Columbia and the Yukon reached unprecedented levels, and the gold was being exported to the United States.

Promoters of the plan to establish a mint believed that their plan would stabilize the price of gold. Also, government and banking reserves had always been held in gold coins of another country, or in bullion, and it was proposed that a policy of keeping reserves in domestic coinage should be inaugurated.

The subject of Canada having its own mint was taken up with the British government by W.S. Fielding, then minister of finance for the dominion. Canada had never possessed its own gold currency and authorities felt that Canadian gold coins would not be circulated to any extent outside the dominion and that even locally the demand would be limited.

It would therefore be advantageous to the dominion to be able to strike a universally accepted coin such as the sovereign. Since only the British Royal Mint or a branch of the Royal Mint could do this, it was agreed that a branch would be established in Ottawa.

On May 2, 1901, Fielding gave notice to the House of Commons of a resolution for the provision of $75,000 as an annuity for the maintenance of a branch of the British Royal Mint in Canada. Founded on this resolution, the Ottawa Mint Act was passed and received royal assent on May 23, 1901.

In negotiations with the British government, it was decided that provision be made for a coinage of 20 million pieces a year and for the refining of gold on a small scale.

Mint construction began in 1905. The building was completed and machinery installed by 1907. The Ottawa Mint Proclamation in 1907, issued under the Imperial Coinage Act of 1870, fixed Jan. 1, 1908, as the formal date of establishment of the Ottawa branch of the British Royal Mint. On Jan. 2, 1908, Governor-General Earl Grey struck the first coin.

An Act of Parliament was passed in 1931 that established the Royal Canadian Mint as a branch of the Department of Finance on Dec. 1 of that year, and the staff of the Mint was transferred from the Imperial service to the Canadian civil service.

A committee was appointed in 1968 to draft the legislation to establish the Mint as a corporate body.

Under Part X of the Government Organization Act, 1969, assented to on March 28, 1969, the RCM was established as a crown corporation on April 1, 1969.

RCM today

The Royal Canadian Mint is recognized as one of the largest and most versatile mints in the world. It is responsible for the production and supply of circulating Canadian coinage.

The Royal Canadian Mint's activities span many fields, including the design and production of coins, medals, tokens and die production. It has gained recognition throughout the industry for its advanced technology and its standards of quality.

The RCM also produces coins under contract to many different nations each year (15 on average; the RCM notes that it has produced circulation coins for more than 70 countries over the last 35 years). The RCM actively competes in the international coin market against other national and private mints, especially using the patented multi-ply plated steel technology that the Mint first used in 1999 and introduced for most circulation coins of Canada by 2002.

The RCM refinery's main function is to refine newly mined gold received from Canadian mines, much of which is made into Maple Leaf .9999 fine gold bullion coins. Subsidiary functions are to refine jewelry, scrap, placer deposits, fused metals and worn coins received from the Bank of Canada, and silver-bearing materials received from other government departments and other divisions of the Mint. A plating facility was opened at the Winnipeg Mint on April 27, 2000, and capacity for the plating facility was more than doubled, to 7,000 metric tons, within the following decade.

On May 29, 2006, the RCM inaugurated a silver refinery, and in 2007 began regularly offering gold Maple Leaf coins struck to .99999 fineness, the highest purity of gold bullion coins in the world.

Ian Bennett is president and master of the Royal Canadian Mint.

RCM facilities

The Ottawa Mint

The Royal Canadian Mint maintains its administrative offices at the Ottawa Mint in the capital city of Ottawa. The main production facility, located on Sussex Drive, is equipped with furnaces and manufacturing equipment to handle most alloys. Production includes the supply of Canada's precious metal and commemorative coins, as well as medals and numismatic products for Canada and foreign countries.

In addition, Ottawa Mint's activities include melting, rolling and refining gold and silver, and the production of planchets and tokens. The facility was shut down for a period to be modernized and was reopened for production in 1986.

The Winnipeg Mint

The formal inauguration of Canada's Winnipeg Mint in Manitoba ranked as one of the major numismatic happenings in North America in 1976.

Formally opened by Canada's Minister of Supply and Services, Jean-Pierre Goyer, on April 30, 1976, the $20 million facility is capable of producing 4.5 billion coins per year on a three-shift basis.

The Winnipeg Mint produces circulating coinage for Canada and circulating coinage for foreign countries by contract. Most numismatic coins are produced at the Ottawa Mint.

Capable of meeting Canada's coinage needs far into the future, the Winnipeg Mint's capacity is used in the production of foreign coins and blanks. Canadian officials made clear at the facility opening that Canada, a substantial factor in the world coin market in the past, intends to expand that effort, and it has done so in recent years, making billions of coins and blanks for numerous countries around the world.

Ordering Canadian coins

Collectors interested in ordering Canadian coins have the option of purchasing the coins directly from the RCM or through its extensive network of distributors around the world.

Correspondence should be directed to the Royal Canadian Mint, 320 Sussex Drive, Ottawa, Ontario, K1A 0G8, Canada. The toll-free telephone number for collectors in the United States is (800) 268-6468. The website is at **www.mint.ca**.

The National Collection

Canada's National Collection of coins and paper money is housed at the Bank of Canada, at 234 Wellington St., Ottawa, Ontario. The emphasis is on Canadian material, but selections of coins of other countries from all periods of numismatic history are also included.

The National Collection of Medals is at the Public Archives of Canada in Ottawa. All types of medals, chiefly Canadian, are kept here, and occasionally displays on a timely theme are exhibited. The National War Museum in Ottawa has an extensive collection of war medals and decorations.

The first steps toward establishing a national showplace took place in 1880 when the Dominion government purchased a Montreal numismatist's collection.

For many years, the Parliamentary Library and the Public Archives of Canada were repositories for numismatic items accumulated from gifts to the Crown and other sources. A full-time curator was appointed in 1963.

Experts say the Bank of Canada now has the largest and most complete collection of Canadian coins, tokens and paper money in existence. A sizable addition was the acquisition of the bulk of the collection of Canadian coins, tokens and paper money formed by J. Douglas Ferguson of Rock Island, Quebec, considered the most outstanding private collection of Canadian numismatic material in the world.

The Dominion's currency history spans approximately three centuries, classified by authorities as the French Colonial, the English Colonial and the post-Confederation periods. Coins and currency from each era are featured in the Bank of Canada's Numismatic Collection.

The first coins were struck for Canada in 1670 and the first paper money issued in 1675. A colorful paper money chapter was written in the late 1600s when playing cards became the first form of paper money in the Western Hemisphere. A shortage of metallic currency for French Canada forced its leaders to make money out of playing cards.

Mexico

Of all the countries in the Western Hemisphere, Mexico can safely boast one of the most colorful numismatic histories, traceable to the pre-coinage era of the Aztec and other native empires of the Americas.

Primitive money was used in exchange by local tribes and most notably by the Aztec Empire. Here copper miniature hoes and spades were used as exchange in much the same way as knife money was used in early China. Other primitive Aztec money included cocoa beans, colored beads, cowry shells, jade figures and quills filled with gold dust.

The Mixtecs used various shaped terra-cotta beads, often engraved with images. Both the Mixtecs and the Aztecs used miniature bells of copper, both with and without clappers inside.

Organized as a Spanish possession after the successful conquest initiated by Hernán Cortés, Mexico became one of the richest gold, silver and copper mining areas in history, providing a worldwide trade coinage in both gold and silver through three centuries.

The historic Mexico City Mint began production in 1536 with silver quarter-, half-, 1-, 2-, 3- and 4-real coins, issued in the name of Spain's rulers Carlos (later Holy Roman Emperor Charles V) and his mad aunt, Juana. An early copper coinage was unsuccessful, although research seems to indicate that the Indians were content to earn a few coins and then stop working until the coins were used up. This tendency, rather than any unpopularity of copper, may have led to the suspension of striking the small denominations.

The silver 8-real coin, the famed "piece of eight," saw introduction in 1556 under Spain's King Philip II, one of a series of crude, irregularly shaped "cob" coins, struck more as true weights of silver than as fully round, modern coins. This "real de a ocho" became the lineal ancestor of the U.S. silver dollar, remaining legal tender in the United States until 1857 as the "Spanish Milled dollar."

Gold coinage began in 1665 under the last of the Hapsburg kings, Charles II. The next major innovation was the perfecting of fully round "Columnario" or "Dos Mundos" coins, named for their design of two worlds symbolizing the Spanish empire, flanked by the Pillars of Hercules

These new round coins, beginning with the 1732 date, have been counterfeited extensively, particularly the early dates. The royal bust type superseded this design in 1772 under Bourbon King Charles III, with the depiction of a royal portrait (bust type) continued under Charles IV and Mexico's last Spanish ruler, Ferdinand VII.

Mexican independence was achieved in 1821. After the revolts of Fathers Hidalgo and Morelos, during a period of political uncertainty, revolutionary emergency coinages in copper and silver first appeared.

The first definitive coins of the newly independent nation were the imperial issues of Emperor Augustin I Iturbide. Here appeared the Mexican eagle, crowned, seated upon a nopal cactus, similar to the bird in the Aztec legend of the founding of Mexico City, but without the snake of later designs.

Augustin's gold and silver coins were replaced in 1823 by the first republican coinage, the Hookneck or Profile eagle types that yielded in turn to the facing eagle, used well into the 19th century. A number of mints produced uniform gold and silver coins, with small denomination copper coins issued by Mexico's states in a wide variety of designs.

The Second Empire of Emperor Maximilian saw new imperial decimal copper, silver and gold coins, again presenting a crowned eagle, supported by the Hapsburg griffins on the silver 8-real coin and gold 20-peso coin. After the overthrow and death of Maximilian, the republic was restored.

The year 1905 saw the next major overhaul of the coinage, with new sizes and designs for the only remaining Mint, in Mexico City. The silver types endured with minor changes through four decades. Gold coins first introduced in 1905 are still a regular offering on the bullion coin market, having been struck as late as 1947 for the 2-peso coin, 1948 for the 2½ peso piece, 1955 for the 5-peso coin, and 1959 for the 10- and 20-peso pieces. Bullion quarter-, half- and 1-ounce coins called "onza oro puro," each composed of .900 fine gold, were issued in 1981.

A footnote to Mexican coinage is the 1913 to 1917 emergency money, struck in a wide range of metals during the revolution that followed the long dictatorship of President Porfirio Diaz. These crude, locally struck or cast pieces are highlighted by famous coins like the Durango "Muera Huerta" or "Death to Huerta" peso, and the gold 60-peso coin of Oaxaca, today classic rarities of Mexican numismatics.

Mexico's first commemorative coins were struck in 1921 for the first centenary of independence, a silver crown-size 2-peso coin with eagle in profile, and a large and heavy 50-peso coin that was struck and restruck until 1972 and now is a gold bullion coin frequently encountered on world markets and known

familiarly as the "Centenario."

Beginning in 1947, a series of changes began for the silver content in Mexico's coinage, which ended in the adoption of bronze for all minor coins in the mid-1950s and copper-nickel after 1970. By 1977, copper-nickel 10-, 20- and 50-centavo coins and 1-, 5- and 10-peso coins were in exclusive use.

Date and design varieties on the most recent Mexican coins provide considerable interest for collectors, as have delays in releasing some denominations, such as the tiny 10-centavo piece and seven-sided 10-peso coin, known to have been struck since 1974 but only appearing years after.

Mexico's commemorative coins blossomed in the 1950s, with eight major silver types appearing, to honor railway construction, heroes of the struggle for independence and 19th and 20th century patriots. Most were produced in goodly numbers and are available at a reasonable cost.

Mexico ceased issuing the silver 25-peso coin with facing bust of President Benito Juarez after 1972, and the 100-peso piece after 1977, both of which had been struck to encourage the nation's silver mining industry. Beginning in 1982, Mexico began striking and issuing the Libertad 1-ounce silver bullion coins. Following a currency reform in 1992, ringed-bimetallic 10-, 20- and 50-new-peso coins were issued with a .925 fine silver center through 1996. The coins were withdrawn from circulation after this date and replaced with base metal coinage.

Circulating commemorative programs proliferated during the first decade of the 2000s, first with two different ringed-bimetallic 100-peso series honoring each state of Mexico from 2003 to 2005 and from 2006 to 2008. Following those successes, Mexico launched a multi-year program of circulating 5-peso coins honoring heroes of the Independence and Revolution, as the bicentennial and centennial of those events, respectively, neared in 2010.

The Uncirculated Mint Set Program began in 1977. On Oct. 6, 1983, a new branch mint was opened in the silver mining town of San Luis Potosi. Two years later, the Mexico Mint was converted into an autonomous institution having independent status under the law, with its own assets, by a presidential decree dated Dec. 26, 1985. During 1998, Casa de Moneda de Mexico moved its gold and silver manufacturing and its coin production operations from the Legaria plant in Mexico City to the Mint facility at San Luis Potosi.

Under the decree, the Mexico Mint is still the minting center of coins ordered by the Mexican Congress and authorized by the Bank of Mexico. However, the Mexico Mint can now design and produce medals for the Mexican government, commemorative medals for official or private use, bars and plaques of precious metals as authorized by the secretariat of Finance and the Bank of Mexico, and foreign coinage by order of the Mexican government or directly by the foreign government.

Contacting the Mints of the world

Many national Mints have an established online presence or are building their own websites from which they market products to the global community of collectors. It is possible to discover a Mint's website with a general search, such as "Central Bank of Iceland." It is better to know the native name ("Sedlabanki Islands") and search that instead. While the Internet offers seemingly limitless possibilities, traditional methods of communication still work just fine. There is something satisfying in writing a letter, posting it, and receiving a letter in reply—even if it does take a month or two to get that reply.

Country	Name of mint	Address
Andorra	Servei d' Emmissions	Prat de la Creu 96, 4t 4a, AD500 Andorra la Vella
Argentina	Casa de Moneda	Av. Antartida Argentina, C1104ACH, Capital Federal, Buenos Aires **www.camoar.gov.ar/INGLES/Eindex2.htm**
Australia	Royal Australian Mint	Denison Street, Deakin, A.C.T. 2600 **www.ramint.gov.au**
Australia	Perth Mint	GPO BOX M924, Perth WA 6843, Australia **www.perthmint.com.au**
Austria	Münze Österreich AG	Am. Heumarkt I, A 1030 Vienna, Österreich **www.austria-mint.com**
Belgium	Monnaie Royale de Belgique	32 Boulevard Pachéco, B-1000 Bruxelles **www.monnaieroyaledebelgique.be/**
Bermuda	Bermuda Monetary Authority	BMA House, 43 Victoria St., Hamilton HM 12, Bermuda **www.bma.bm**
Bolivia	Casa de Moneda	Calle Ayacucho s/n., Potosi, Bolivia **www.casanacionaldemoneda.org.bo**
Brazil	Casa da Moeda	Distrito Industrial de Santa Cruz, Rua René Bitten-Court, 371 Santa Cruz Rio de Janeiro-RJ, 23.565-200, Brazil **www.casadamoeda.com.br/**
Bulgaria	Bulgaria Mint Ltd.	5006 Street, Gara Iskar, 1528 Sofia **www.mint.bg**
Canada	Royal Canadian Mint	320 Sussex Drive, Ottawa, Ontario K1A 0G8 **www.mint.ca**
Chile	Casa de Moneda de Chile	Av. Portales 3586, Estación Central, Santiago **www.cmoneda.cl**
China	China Printing & Mint Bureau	**www.cbpm.cn/English/**
Colombia	Banco de la Republica	Carrera 7 No. 14-78, Bogotá D.C. **www.banrep.gov.co**
Cuba	Banco Central de Cuba	PO Box 746, Cuba 402, Municipio Habana Vieja, La Habana, Ciudad de la Habana **www.bc.gov.cu**
Czech Republic	Ceská Mincovna	U Prehrady 3204/61, 466 23 Jablonec nad Nisou **www.mint.cz**
Denmark	Royal Danish Mint	Solmarksvej 5, DK-2605 Brøndby **www.royalmint.dk**
Egypt	Central Bank of Egypt	54 Elgomhoreya Street, 11511 Cairo **www.cbe.org.eg**
European Union	European Central Bank	Kaiserstrasse 29, 60311 Frankfurt-am-Main, Germany **www.ecb.int**
Finland	Mint of Finland	P.O. Box 100, FIN-01741, Vantaa **www.suomenrahapaja.fi/eng**
France	Monnaie de Paris	11, Quai de Conti, 75270 Paris Cedex 06 **www.monaiedeparis.com**
Germany	Hamburgische Münze	Bei der Neuen Münze 19, 22145 Hamburg **www.muenzehamburg.de**
Germany	Staatliche Münze Karlsruhe	Stephanienstrasse 28 A, 76133 Karlsruhe **www.staatlichemuenzenbw.de**
Germany	Bayerisches Hauptmünzamt	Zamdorfer Strasse 92, 81677 München **www.hma.bayern.de/**

Country	Name of mint	Address
Germany	Staatliche Münze Stuttgart	Reichenhaller Strasse 58, 70372 Stuttgart **www.staatlichemuenzenbw.de**
Germany	Staatliche Münze Berlin	Ollenhauerstrasse 97, 13403 Berlin **www.muenze-berlin.de**
Greece	Bank of Greece	341 Messogion Ave., 15231 Halandri, Athens
Guatemala	Banco de Guatemala	7a. Av. 22-01, zona 1, Guatemala, CA **www.banguat.gob.gt**
Hungary	Hungarian State Mint	H-1734 Budapest, P.O.B 518., Hungary **www.penzvero.hu**
Iceland	Sedlabanki Central Bank of Iceland	Kalkofnsvegi 1, 150 Reykjavik **www.sedlabanki.is**
India	Mumbai Mint	Shahid Bhagatsingh Road, Fort, Mumbai 400 023 **www.mumbaimint.in**
Indonesia	Integrated Security Printing and System	Jl. Palatehan 4, Kebayoran Baru Blok K-V, Jakarta 12160 **www.peruri.co.id**
Iran	Central Bank of Iran	Mirdamad Blvd., NO.144, Tehran
Ireland	Central Bank of Ireland	Currency Centre, P.O. Box 61, Sandyford, Dublin 16 **www.centralbank.ie**
Israel	Bank of Israel	P.O.Box 780, 91007 Jerusalem **www.bankisrael.gov.il/firsteng.htm**
Israel	Israel Coins & Medals Corp. Ltd.	P.O. Box 2040, Nesher 36660 **www.israelmint.com**
Italy	Istituto Poligrafico e Zecca dello Stato	Via Salaria, 1027 – 00138 Roma **www.ipzs.it**
Japan	Japan Mint	Temma 1-chome, Kita-ku, Osaka 530-0043 **www.mint.go.jp/eng/index.html**
Korea, Rep. of	Korea Security Printing and Minting Corp.	146-6, Changjeon-dong, Mapo-gu, Seoul, 121-881
Latvia	Latvijas Banka	K. Valdemara Street 2A, Riga LV-1050 **www.bank.lv/en**
Lithuania	Vilnius Mint	UAB Lietuvos moneta kalykla, Eiguliu g. 4, LT – 03150 Vilnius **www.lithuanian-mint.lt/lt**
Luxembourg	Banque Centrale de Luxembourg	43, avenue Monterey, L-2163 Luxembourg **www.bcl.lu/en/index.php**
Malaysia	Bank Negara Malaysia	Jalan Dato' Onn, P.O. Box 10922, 50929, Kuala Lumpur
Malta	Central Bank of Malta	Central Bank of Malta, Pjazza Kastilja, Valletta, VLT 1060
Mexico	Casa de Moneda de México	Av. Paseo de la Reforma No. 295 - 5° piso, Col. Cuauhtémoc, C.P. 06500, Mexico DF **www.cmm.gob.mx**
Morocco	Bank Al-Maghrib	277, Avenue Mohammed V Boîte postale 445 – Rabat
Nepal	Nepal Rastra Bank	Central Office, Baluwatar, P. O. Box 73, Kathmandu, Nepal
Netherlands	Rijks Munt Utrecht	Koninklijke Nederlandse Munt, Postbus 2407, 3500 GK, Utrecht **www.knm.nl**
New Zealand	New Zealand Post	Private Bag 39990, Level 10, 7-27 Waterloo Quay, Wellington **http://stamps.nzpost.co.nz/Cultures/en-NZ/Coins**
Norway	Den Kongelige Mynt	Postboks 53, 3602 Kongsberg
Pakistan	State Bank of Pakistan	Central Directorate, I.I. Chundrigar Road, Karachi
Peru	Casa Nacional de Moneda	Jiron Junin 791, Lima 1
Philippines	Central Bank of Philippines	A. Mabini St. cor. P. Ocampo St., Malate Manila, Philippines 1004
Poland	Mint of Poland	Mennica Polska S.A., Pereca 21, 00-958 Warzawa **www.mennica.com.pl/en/main-page.html**
Portugal	Impresa Nacional — Casa da Moeda, S.A.	Av. António José de Almeida, 1000-042, Lisboa **www.incm.pt**
Romania	State Mint of Romania	str. Fabrica de Chibrituri nr. 30, 050183, Bucuresti, 5 **www.monetariastatului.ro/mint.html**
Russia	Goznak	Mytnaya str. 17, Moscow, Russia, 115162

Country	Name of mint	Address
San Marino	Azienda Autonoma di Stato Filatelico e Numismatica	Piazza Garibaldi, 5 - 47890 - Repubblica di San Marino **www.aasfn.sm**
Singapore	Singapore Mint	20 Teban Gardens Crescent, Singapore 608928 **www.singaporemint.com.sg**
Slovakia	National Bank of Slovakia	Narodna banka Slovenska, Imricha Karvasa 1, 813 25 Bratislava **www.nbs.sk**
South Africa, Republic of	South African Mint Company	Old Johannesburg Road, Gateway, Centurion **www.samint.co.za/**
Spain	Fabrica Nacional de Moneda y Timbre	Real Casa de la Moneda, Jorge Juan, 106, 28071 Madrid **www.fnmt.es**
Sudan	Sudan Mint Co. Ltd.	P.O. Box 5043, Khartoum South
Sweden	The Swedish Mint	Myntverket, Smedjegatan, Box 401, 631 06 Eskilstuna **www.myntverket.se/**
Switzerland	Swiss Federal Mint	Bernastrasse 28, CH-3003 Bern **www.swissmint.ch**
JTaiwan	Central Mint of China	No.577, Jhensing Rd., Gueishan, Taoyuan 33353, Taiwan
Ukraine	National Bank of Ukraine	9 Instytutska St., Kyiv 01601
United Kingdom	Royal Mint	Freepost NAT23496, P.O. Box 500, Llantrisant, Pontyclun, CF7 8YT **www.royalmint.com**
United Kingdom	The Birmingham Mint Ltd.	**www.birmingham-mint.com**
United Kingdom	Pobjoy Mint Ltd.	Millennia House, Bonsor Dr., Kingswood, Surrey KT20 6AY **www.pobjoy.com**
United States	United States Mint	Customer Service Center, 2799 Reeves Road, Plainfield, IN 46168 **www.usmint.gov**
Venezuela	Casa de la Moneda de Venezuela	Esquina de Mijares, Edificio Edoval, Piso 5, Parroquia Altagracia, Caracas 1010 **www.bcv.org.ve/c3/casamoneda.asp**

Foreign coin production in the United States

The U.S. Mint's involvement with the production of foreign coins lasted 109 years and began with passage of The Mint Act of Jan. 29, 1874. At one time, the U.S. Mint production facilities at San Francisco, Denver and Philadelphia produced more coins for more countries than any other nation's Mints. Today, the U.S. Mints at Denver and Philadelphia strike only U.S. coins for circulation. The last time the U.S. Mint was under contract to strike circulation coins for a foreign country was 1984.

The Mint Act of Jan. 29, 1874, authorized "for coinage to be executed at the Mints of the United States, for any foreign countries applying for the same, according to the legally prescribed standards and devices of such country, under such regulations as the Secretary of the Treasury may subscribe; and the charge for the same shall be equal to the expense thereof, including labor, materials, and use of machinery, to be fixed by the Director of the Mint, with the approval of the Secretary of the Treasury: Provided, That the manufacture of such coin shall not interfere with the required coinage of the United States."

Although U.S. Mint officials did not gain authority to strike foreign coins until 1874, the Philadelphia Mint previously struck small numbers of 1855 Peruvian gold 2-, 5-, 10- and 20-peso patterns on U.S.

Mint machinery purchased by Peru, according to some sources. Following 1875 production of Venezuelan coinage, Mint officials actively pursued coinage contracts with additional foreign governments. The Mint struck coins for the Dominican Republic in 1877 and for Colombia in 1881, 1886 and 1888. Both countries would become frequent customers of the U.S. Mint. Other nations in the Caribbean region, Central America and South America became customers in the 1890s and early 20th century.

From 1875 to 1984, the Mint at one time or another struck coins for Argentina, Australia, Bahamas, the Belgian Congo, Belgium, Bolivia, Brazil, Canada, China, Colombia, Costa Rica, Cuba, Curacao, Dominican Republic, Ecuador, Ethiopia, Fiji, France, French Indo-China, Greenland, Guatemala, Hawaii, Honduras, Israel, Liberia, Mexico, Nepal, the Netherlands, Netherlands East Indies, Nicaragua, Panama, Peru, the Philippines, Poland, El Salvador, Saudi Arabia, Siam (Thailand), South Korea, Surinam, Syria, Taiwan and Venezuela.

In 2000, the Philadelphia Mint struck a commemorative 100-kronur coin for Iceland as part of a joint U.S.-Icelandic program honoring explorer Leif Ericson's landfall in America 1,000 years earlier. A U.S. silver dollar was also issued in the same program.

Foreign coins struck by U.S. Mints

Calendar Year	Number of pieces struck	Calendar Year	Number of pieces struck	Calendar Year	Number of pieces struck
July 1, 1875-Dec. 31, 1905	155,896,973	1932	9,756,096	1960	238,400,000
1906	10,204,504	1933	15,240,000	1961	148,500,000
1907	45,253,047	1934	24,280,000	1962	256,485,000
1908	29,645,359	1935	109,600,850	1963	293,515,000
1909	11,298,981	1936	32,350,000	1964	——
1910	7,153,818	1937	26,800,000	1965	——
1911	7,794,406	1938	48,579,644	1966	7,440,000
1912	6,244,348	1939	15,725,000	1967	176,196,206
1913	7,309,258	1940	33,170,000	1968	416,088,658
1914	17,335,005	1941	208,603,500	1969	348,653,046
1915	55,485,190	1942	307,737,000	1970	483,988,392
1916	37,441,328	1943	186,682,008	1971	207,959,692
1917	25,208,497	1944	788,498,000	1972	392,723,895
1918	60,102,000	1945	1,802,376,004	1973	295,408,674
1919	100,269,195	1946	504,528,000	1974	373,293,733
1920	99,002,334	1947	277,376,094	1975	762,126,363
1921	55,094,352	1948	21,950,000	1976	562,372,000
1922	7,863,030	1949	156,687,940	1977	13,188,000
1923	4,369,000	1950	2,000,000	1978	30,846,000
1924	12,663,196	1951	25,450,000	1979	15,530,090
1925	13,461,000	1952	45,857,000	1980	19,658,000
1926	14,987,000	1953	193,673,000	1981	23,520,000
1927	3,650,000	1954	19,015,000	1982	37,788,000
1928	16,701,000	1955	67,550,000	1983	25,500,000
1929	34,980,000	1956	38,793,500	1984	45,600,000
1930	3,300,120	1957	59,264,000	**Total**	11,325,756,346
1931	4,498,020	1958	152,575,000		
		1959	129,647,000		

Source: United States Mint

World monetary units

A new world standard for abbreviations has been established, called ISO 4217. While old symbols such as $ or US$ might be understood, the official designation outside the United States for the United States dollar is USD. Similarly, the Mexican peso (which is symbolized as $ within Mexico) is the MXP.

The ISO standard is not a law and is not consistently followed by all nations. All ISO 4217 designations are three-letter codes. The first two letters generally come from the ISO 3166 standard for country abbreviations. According to ISO 3166, Canada is abbreviated CA. Therefore the Canadian dollar is CAD.

The standardization of computer interchange codes has also affected the abbreviations for fractions or divisional units. In the United States, the dollar is divided into 100 cents and old typewriters used to

have a ¢ over the 6 (shift 6). Today's keyboards place the caret ^ over the 6.

While the old cent sign ¢ is still recognized in the United States, its use is passing into history. Similarly, while the British pound still carries the traditional £, the decimalization of the currency has removed the need to abbreviate shillings and pence, since shillings so longer exist and there are 100, not 240, pence to the pound.

Finally, the consolidation of world systems means that Andorra, which is not part of the eurozone, now uses the euro because of monetary relationships with France and Spain, its surrounding neighbors. However, Andorrans see the traditional diner as a memorial to olden times, and the diner denomination is still used on collector coins.

Country	Basic unit Name	Old Symbol & ISO 4217	Fractional unit Name	Symbol or abbreviation
Afghanistan	afghani	Af, AFN	pul	
Africa, Equatorial States: Cameroon, Central African Republic, Equatorial Guinea, Chad, Congo and Gabon	Communaute Financiere Africaine franc	CFA fr, XAF	centime	
Africa, West (Monetary Union): Communaute Financiere, Benin Guinea-Bissau, Ivory Coast, Mali, Niger, Senegal, Togo, and Burkina Faso	CFA fr. XAF Africaine franc		centime	

Country	Basic unit Name	Old Symbol & ISO 4217	Fractional unit Name	Symbol or abbreviation
Albania	lek	ALL	qindarkë	
Algeria	dinar	DA, DZD	santeem	
Andorra	diner	FRF	centim	
Angola, People's Republic of	kwanza	AOA	cêntimo	
Argentina	peso	$, ARS	centavo	ctv.
Armenia	dram	AMD		
Australia	dollar	$, AUD	cent	c
Austria	euro	$, EUR	cent	
Azerbaijan	new manat	AZM, AZN	qepik	
Bahamas	dollar	B$, BSD	cent	B¢
Bahrain	dinar	BD, BHD	fils	
Bangladesh	taka	Tk, BDT	paisa	
Barbados	dollar	BDS$, BBD	cent	¢
Belarus	ruble	BYR		
Belgium	euro	F or BF, EUR	cent	
Belize	dollar	$,BZD	cent	
Bermuda	dollar	BD$, BMD	cent	
Bhutan	ngultrum	INR, BTM	chetrum	
Bolivia	boliviano	$b, BOB	centavos	
Bosnia-Hercegovina	Konvertibilna marka	BAM		
Botswana	pula	P, BWP	thebe	
Brazil	real	R, BRL	centavo	
Brunei	dollar	BND	sen	
Bulgaria	lev	BGN	stotinka	
Burundi	franc	F, BIF	centimes	
Cambodia	riel	£, KHR	sen	
Canada	dollar	$, CAD	cent	¢
Cape Verde, Republic of	escudo	$, CVE	centavo	
Eastern Caribbean States, Organization of Grenada, Montserrat and Antigua, Dominica, St. Kitts, St. Lucia, Montserrat, St. Vincent	East Caribbean dollar	E.C.$, XCD	cent	¢
Cayman Islands	dollar	$, KYD	cent	¢
Chile	peso	$, CLP	centavo	¢
China, People's Republic	yuan	RMB Y, CNY	jiao, fen	
Colombia	peso	$ or P, COP	centavo	c., ¢, Ctv.
Comoros, Republic of	franc	F, KMF	centime	
Congo (formerly Zaire)	franc congolaise	F, XAF	centime	
Cook Islands	dollar	$, NZD	cent	c
Costa Rica	colon	C or ¢, CRC	centimo	¢
Croatia	kuna	HRK	lipa	
Cuba	peso convertible peso	CUP CUC	centavo centavo convertible	
Cyprus	euro	C£, EUR	cent	
Czech Republic	koruna	Kcs, CZK	haler	h
Denmark	krone	kr., DKK	øre	
Djibouti, Republic of	franc	F, DJF	centime	
Dominica	East Caribbean dollar	E.S.$, XCD	cent	¢
Dominican Republic	peso	RD $, DOP	centavo	ctv or ¢
Ecuador	U.S. dollar	S/, USD	cent	¢
Egypt, Arab Republic of	pound	£.E.. EGP	piastre, millime	

| Country | Basic unit | | Fractional unit | |
	Name	Old Symbol & ISO 4217	Name	Symbol or abbreviation
El Salvador	U.S. dollar	C or ¢, USD	cent	¢
Equatorial Guinea	CFA franc	XAF		
Eritrea	nakfa	ERN	cent	
Estonia	euro	EUR	cent	
Ethiopia	birr	Br. $, ETB	santim	
Falkland Islands	pound	FKP	pence	
Faroes	krona	DKK	oyra	
Fiji	dollar	$, FJD	cent	¢
Finland	euro	Mk, EUR	cent	
France	euro	F, EUR	cent	
French Guadeloupe, Guiana, and Martinique	euro	F, EUR	cent	
French Polynesia: Austral, Leeward, Marquezas and Windward Isles; and Tuamotu group, Colonies Francaises du Pacifique	franc	CFP fr., XPF	centime	
Gambia, The	dalasi	D, GMD	butut	
Georgia	lari	L, GEL	tetri	
Germany	euro	DM, EUR	cent	
Ghana	cedi	NC, GHS	pesewa	
Gibraltar	pound	GIP	pence	
Greece	euro	Dr, EUR	cent	
Greenland	krone	DKK	øre	
Guatemala	quetzal	Q, GTQ	centavo	
Guernsey	pound	GGP	pence	
Guinea (Conakry)	franc	GNF	centime	
Guinea-Bissau, Republic of	CFA franc	XOF		
Guyana	dollar	G$. GYD	cent	
Haiti	gourde	G, HTG	centime	
Honduras	lempira	L., HNL	centavo	
Hong Kong	dollar	HK$, HKD	cent	
Hungary	forint	Ft., HUF	filler	
Iceland	krona	kr. or Kr, ISK.	aurar	
India	rupee	Re. (Rs.), INR	paise	
Indonesia	rupiah	Rp., IDR	sen	
Iran	rial	Rl. (Rls.), IRR	dinar	
Iraq	dinar	ID, IQD	fils	
Ireland, Republic of	euro	IR£, EUR	cent	
Isle of Man	pound	IMP	pence	
Israel	new sheqel	I£, ILS	agora	Ag.
Italy	euro	L, EUR	cent	
Jamaica	dollar	$, JMD	cent	c
Japan	yen	Y, JPY	sen	
Jersey	pound	JEP	pence	
Jordan	dinar	J.D., JOD	qirsh, piastres, fils	
Kazakhstan	tenge	KZT	tyin	
Kenya	shilling	Sh., KES	cent	
Kiribati	dollar	$, AUD	cent	
Korea, Republic of	won	W, KRW	jeon	
Kuwait	dinar	KD, KWD	fils	
Kyrgyzstan	som	KGS	tyiyn	
Laos	kip	LAK	att	

Country	Basic unit		Fractional unit	
	Name	Old Symbol & ISO 4217	Name	Symbol or abbreviation
Latvia	lat	LVL	santimi	
Lebanon	pound	L£, LBP	piastre	
Lesotho	loti	ZAR, LSL	sente, lisente	
Liberia	dollar	$, LRD	cent	
Libya	dinar	L.D., LYD	dirham	
Liechtenstein	Swiss franc	CHF	rappen	
Lithuania	litas	LTL	centas	
Luxembourg	euro	F, EUR	cent	
Macao	pataca	$, MOP	avos	
Macedonia	denars	MKD	deni	
Madagascar, Democratic Republic of	ariary	FMG, MGA	iraimbilanja	
Malawi	kwacha	K, MWK	tambala	
Malaysia	ringgit	$, MYR	sen	¢
Maldive Republic	rufiyaa	MVR	laari	I
Mali	CFA franc	MF, XOF		
Malta	euro	£M, EUR	cent	
Mauritania, Islamic Republic of	ouguiya	MRO	khoum	
Mauritius	rupee	Re, MUR	cent	
Mexico	peso	$, MXP	centavo	¢
Moldova	leu	MDL	bani	
Monaco	euro	NF, EUR	cent	
Mongolian People's Republic	tugrik	MNT	möngo	
Morocco	dirham	DH, MAD	centime	
Mozambique	new metical	$, MZN	centavo	
Myanmar (formerly Burma)	kyat	K, MMK	pya	
Namibia	dollar	$, NAD	cents	
Nepal	rupee	Re, NPR	paisa	
Netherlands	euro	F, EUR	cent	
New Caledonia	Colonies Francaises du Pacifique franc	CFP fr., XPF	centime	
New Zealand	dollar	$, NZD	cent	
Nicaragua	cordoba	C$, NIO	centavo	
Nigeria	naira	N, NGN	kobo	
Norway	krone	Kr., NOK	øre	
Oman	rial	Orl, OMR	baisa	
Pakistan	rupee	Rs, PKR	paisa	
Panama, Republic of	balboa	$, PAB	centésimo	
Papua New Guinea	kina	PGK	toea	
Paraguay	guaraní	G, PYG	céntimo	
Peru	nuevo sol	PEN	céntimo	
Philippines	piso	P, PHP	sentimo	
Poland	zloty	Zl., PLN	groszy	
Portugal	euro	$, EUR	cent	
Qatar	riyal	QDR, QAR	dirham	
Reunion	euro	Fr., EUR	cent	
Romania	new leu	n.a., ROL	bani	
Russia	ruble	R. RUB	kopek	k.
Rwanda, Republic of	franc	FRW, RWF	centime	
Saint-Pierre et Miquelon	euro	CFA fr., EUR	cent	
Samoa	tala	$, WST	sene	

Country	Basic unit Name	Old Symbol & ISO 4217	Fractional unit Name	Symbol or abbreviation
Sao Tome and Principe	dobra	Esc, STD	centimo	
San Marino	euro	£, EUR	cent	
Saudi Arabia	riyal	SR, SAR	halalah	
Seychelles	rupee	SR, SCR	cent	
Sierra Leone	leone	Le, SLL	cent	
Singapore	dollar	S$, SGD	cent	¢
Slovakia	euro	SK, EUR	cent	
Slovenia	euro	EUR	cent	
Solomon Islands	dollar	SBD	cent	
Somali Republic	shiling	Sh. So, SOS	cent	
Somaliland	shiling			
South Africa, Republic of	rand	R, ZAR	cent	
Spain	euro	Pta, EUR	cent	
Sri Lanka	rupee	Rs, LKR	cent	
St. Thomas & Prince Islands (Sao Tome)	dobra	Esc, STD	centimo	
Sudan, Republic of the	pound	SDG	piastres	
Surinam	dollar	Sf, SRD	cent	
Swaziland	lilangeni	SZL	cent	
Sweden	krona	Kr, SEK	öre	
Switzerland	franc	Fr, CHF	centime, rappen	
Syria	pound	L.S., SYP	qirsh	
Taiwan	new Taiwan dollar	NT $, TWD	cent	
Tajikistan	somoni	TJS	diram	
Tanzania, United Republic of	shilingi	Sh, TZS	senti	
Thailand	baht	B, b, THB	satang	stg.
Tokelau	New Zealand dollar	$, NZD	cent	¢
Tonga	pa'anga	T$, TOP	seniti	
Transnistria	ruble			
Trinidad and Tobago	dollar	T&T$, TTD	cent	¢
Tunisia	dinar	DT, TND	millime	M
Turkey	lira	TL., TRY	kurus	Krs.
Turkmenistan	manat	TMM	tenge	
Turks and Caicos Islands	U.S. dollar	$, USD	U.S. cent	¢
Tuvalu	Tuvalu, Australian dollar	$, TUD, AUD	Tuvalu, Australian cent	¢
Uganda	shilling	Sh., UGX	cent	
Ukraine	hryvnia	UAH	kopiyka	
United Arab Emirates	dirham	AED	fil	
United Kingdom	pound	£, GBP	pence	d.
United States of America	Dollar	$, USD	cent	¢
Uruguay	peso uruguayo	$, UYU	centésimo	
Uzbekistan	sum	UZS	tiyn	
Vanuata	vatu	VUV		
Vatican City	euro	L, EUR	cent	
Venezuela	bolivar fuerte	B, VEF	céntimo	
Vietnam	dong	VND	hào	
Yemen	rial	YER	fil	
Zambia	kwacha	K, ZMK	ngwee	n
Zimbabwe	dollar	$, ZWD	cent	

Ancient coins primer

Ancient numismatics is about the times and places of the Greeks and the Romans and their neighbors. However, that simple statement encompasses a thousand years on three continents. If you consider a town such as Naples in Italy or Alexandria in Egypt or York in England, you can assemble a collection that crosses several cultures, times, and peoples. The coin types will change, the images and metals will change, but the towns remain. The coins demonstrate the history of the town.

Most books on ancient numismatics divide the world into convenient—and arbitrary—times and places.

The coinage of ancient Greece was produced for colonies around the Mediterranean from Spain and France through Italy and Sicily to Greece itself and the Greek peoples of Asia Minor down the coast to Syria, Judaea and Alexandria in Egypt past Cyrene and ending in Carthage.

The Roman world is neatly divided into republican and imperial times, with the short imperatorial wars between the two. Most collectors who are drawn to ancients start with Roman imperial coins. They do so for many of the same reasons that collectors of American numismatics start with Lincoln cents: the coins of imperial Rome are available and affordable, and a lot has been written about them.

Parallel to the coins of Rome were the coins of the Greek cities. These are called "Greek imperial" or "Roman provincial." Peripheral to the Greeks and Romans were the other ancient peoples who struck coins, such as the Celts, the Parthians and the satraps of western India.

When the Roman emperor Theodosius died in A.D. 395, his two sons, Arcadius and Honorius, became the rulers in the East and West. The Roman Empire had been administered this way for almost 100 years. However, this time, the division was complete and the Byzantine Empire of Constantinople was born. Rome slid into anarchy, and in 476 the emperor Romulus Augustulus retired to Ravenna and the Gothic King Odoacer became the emperor of nothing. The Dark Ages had begun.

The Dark Ages ended on Christmas Day 800, when Pope Leo III crowned Charlemagne the Holy Roman Emperor. The Middle Ages were at hand. The Middle Ages ended in 1453 when the Ottoman Turks finally captured Constantinople. In the West, the invention of the printing press and the use of gunpowder coupled with the discovery of America closed the door on the medieval period.

These broad strokes hide more facts than they outline. Historically, coin collectors in Europe who were interested in "ancient" coins did not collect the coins of ancient China. That has changed. Traditionally, most collectors of "ancient" coins drew the line with the fall of Rome in 476. Today, that line has been blurred. Medieval coins are now seen as a subset of the ancient world, just as the coins of the Indo-Scythians are seen as a foreign kind of "ancient Greek" coin.

We know now that the people of Constantinople considered themselves Romans. As late as 1450, when their emperor came to Italy looking for help against the Turks, he was presented with a medal that called him the king of the Romans ("Basilion Romaion") because that had always been one of the official titles of the emperor at Constantinople.

In the past, numismatists grouped all ancient "Celtic" coins together although the Celts of the Danube basin are historically distinct from the Celts of Britain.

Traditionally, ancient coins were not popular in America. Today, that has changed. The fall of communism and competition for settlements in the Middle East, coupled with the advent of inexpensive metal detectors has brought more ancient coins to the market than were known to exist 50 years ago.

In England, a redefinition of the treasure trove law has also liberated thousands of inexpensive ancient coins for the American markets. New collectors bring new attitudes.

The origins of coinage

Who invented coins, when and why are still subjects of debate. The most likely sequence of events is that the first coins were bonus payments to mercenary soldiers hired by a self-made ruler called a "tyrant."

The western tradition of coinage begins in Lydia about the year 650 B.C. Lydia was located in what is now western Turkey. It was directly east of the Greek towns along the Ionian coast. The royal Lydian citadel town of Sardis was about 40 miles from the Greek town of Smyrna and about 100 miles northeast of the town of Ephesus.

The archaeological evidence comes from two deposits of coins and coin-like objects discovered in 1904 to 1905 by D.G. Hogarth, working under the aegis of the British Museum. Hogarth's workers found the coins at the foundation of the Temple of Artemis at Ephesus. These hoards and the associated artifacts have been examined and re-examined several times in the last 100 years. One group of coins was found in a pot and the artistic style of the pot has come under scrutiny as scholars attempt to date the site as closely as possible.

Whether coins were first struck by a Lydian or an Ionian tyrant is not certain. Within a generation or two, coins as we know them—uniform disks of metal with images and other devices stamped on them—spread across the Mediterranean world of the Greeks.

The earliest coins were a natural alloy of gold and silver called "electrum." Writing about the year 450 B.C., the Greek historian Herodotus said that the Lydians were the first to strike coins in gold and silver.

We take this to mean, literally, that they struck coins of gold and coins of silver at a time when everyone else was still using electrum. We see the silver and gold coins of Croesus of Lydia (about 550 B.C.) as being the ones to which Herodotus referred. By 500 B.C., silver was the preferred metal for coinage. Gold was used rarely and bronze did not come into common use for coins for another 100 years.

China is also a possible site as the origin of coinage. Archaeological evidence and written records from China offer strong alternatives to the easy view that the Greeks invented coins. Uniform bronze "spades" about 2 inches by 6 inches in size were known in China by 750 B.C. These spades, knives and other shapes were not functional tools, but convenient forms of bronze in the shape of familiar objects. By A.D. 100 to 200, they evolved into the cash coins that would serve China for the next 1,700 years.

Perhaps as early as 1500 B.C., the Chinese pioneered the use of cowry shells as a form of token money. The modern Chinese and Japanese kanji character for "money" derives directly from the picture for a cowry shell.

Greek coinage

To the civilized world of 500 B.C., the Greeks were a curious collection of distant tribes, thinly scattered across the mountainous coasts and islands of the west. They were barbarians with delusions of culture. By 300 B.C., the civilized world was Greek. In the words of the orator Isocrates: "The name of 'Hellene' no longer betokens a race but a way of thinking." Greek coins are the history of Greek art, Greek science and mathematics, Greek politics, and even the Greek alphabet.

As Greek art evolved from the archaic style, through the classical, to the Hellenistic, these changes affected marble statues and coins alike. Many writers believe that the Hellenistic coins of the 300s B.C. are the most beautiful ever created. The best of these come from the towns of southern Italy and Sicily. The decadrachms of Syracuse, cut by the artists Kimon and Euainetos among others, are among the most coveted coins in the world. However, stunning Hellenistic coins come from everywhere, for instance from the towns of Histaia and Chalkis on the island of Euboea. A hoard of large tetradrachms from the town of Myrina features breathtaking portraits (nominally of Apollo) in the Hellenistic style.

It is possible to collect Greek coins that have a direct relationship with Pythagoras the mathematician. Pythagoras developed a complex set of theories about how the world works. Part of this was the idea of "duals"—dark and light, hot and cold, etc. A series of coins from the towns of Kroton, Sybaris and Metapontion in southern Italy seem to display this philosophy. The images on the obverse and reverse are the same (tripod or bull or wheat stalk). One side is incuse, the other is intaglio and the two line up perfectly to make one three-dimensional presentation.

Since Pythagoras lived in southern Italy at this time, scholars attribute these coins directly to his influence.

In addition to natural science, the Greeks invented political science. As important as artistic styles and mathematics philosophies may be, the fact is that coins in general and Greek coins in particular are the artifacts of government. The first coins are identified with tyrants, self-made men on the rise, merchants who overthrew the old agricultural classes and then ran their towns like businesses. When democracies replaced tyrannies, citizens voted to pay themselves to attend the assembly. They also voted to pay themselves to serve as soldiers. Conversely, citizens who did not attend the gymnasium to stay fit for military duty had to pay a fine.

Greek coins from neighboring towns often weigh out in simple proportions and easy ratios. Two drachma from Aigina weigh as much as three from Athens, for instance—even though Aigina and Athens were constantly at odds, if not at war.

The towns of Phokaia (on the coast of Ionia) and Mytilene (on the island of Lesbos) had a long-standing treaty. They bought gold and silver, mixed it into electrum and struck "sixths" (one-sixth of a "heavy stater" or a third of a heavy drachmon) weighing about 2.5 grams. The towns took turns appointing the minter on a yearly basis. The sixths must have been sold overseas. The profit, while small, was steady. This series of coins opens a window on politics and economics. In addition, the electrum sixths of Phokaia and Mytilene intertwine two artistic themes. The coins of Mytilene are conservative, but the coins of Phokaia evolve into gems of idealized portraiture.

The "Owls" of Athens were the trade coinage of the 400s B.C. Possibly struck as early as 500 or 550 B.C., the coins with Athena and her owl were struck in the millions from 450 to 420 B.C. During this intensified mintage interval, Athens rebuilt the damage done to the town by the Persians. Citizens were paid what we would call a "negative income tax" from the town coffers and the owls paid citizens (and others) to labor on construction projects.

The coins of Corinth and her colonies typically show Pegasus, the flying horse, on the obverse. The goddess Athena in a Corinthian helmet is on the reverse. If the coin comes from Corinth, then under the horse is the letter "koppa" (or "qoph") the direct ancestor of our letter Q, an archaic Greek letter not used in the classical Greek alphabet. Archaic coins from Ionia and Italy also display these old forms and letters.

From the tyrants of Lydia, to the Hellenistic kingdoms of the heirs of Alexander, Greek coins reveal the foundation of Western civilization. Our ideas on politics, literature, philosophy, mathematics, art and more are all stamped with the images found on Greek coins. It is possible to collect coins with heroes of the *Illiad* and coins with monsters of the *Odyssey*. Mint marks show the waxing and waning of empires. You can find accurate representations of apples, pomegranates, celery, wheat, laurel and olive. You can find gods, goddesses—and their pets. Whatever motivates you to seek the best within yourself can be found in ancient Greek coins because discovering and living the best life was the essential distinguishing characteristic of Greek civilization.

Roman coinage

The long and diverse coinage of Rome developed rather late in the history of the Republic, with barter playing a key role until the expansion of the state brought Rome into contact with coin-producing Greek cities in Italy.

The development of Roman coinage mirrored the basic outlook of the Roman mind. While the Greeks sought beauty in all things, the Romans sought practicality, law and power. The first coins of Rome were the cast bronze "aes grave" bearing the image of the double-faced god Janus.

These early coins weighed a pound each and must have been cumbersome in daily use. As time went by, the bronze coinage was gradually reduced to smaller sizes. During the third century B.C., Mint towns in the Campanian plain were striking silver didrachms for Rome, and the long career of Roman coinage was under way.

Design features of Roman Republic silver included scenes from the mythical founding of the city, Romulus and Remus suckled by the she-wolf, the rape of the Sabine women, and events of the early wars.

The expanding Roman state was continually at war, making large coin issues a practical necessity to pay soldiers and purchase supplies. Therefore, Republican silver coins are relatively plentiful and inexpensive, ideal for a collector of moderate means.

Roman coins were propaganda vehicles for their day. Victories, sporting events, public buildings and political events were all commemorated in a seemingly endless procession of coin types.

The Roman Mint was under the patronage of the goddess Juno Moneta, the personification of money and financial probity. She was one of a number of personified virtues, including hope, security, joy, fertility and abundance, to name only a few of the many that were to adorn the reverses of hundreds of different coins.

Portraits of persons rather than gods were uncommon on Greek coinage until after the time of Alexander III of Macedon; they were unknown on Roman coins until the latest era of the Republic, the Imperatorial period.

In the first century B.C., portraits of living men began to adorn coins, often as a form of personal propaganda for aspiring leaders such as Pompey Magnus ("the Great"), Mark Antony and above all Gaius Julius Caesar. These imperatorial coins foreshadowed the imperial portrait coins that began with Augustus in the beginning of the Christian era.

Collectors have eagerly sought the coins of this period, largely because of their historic importance. Especially sought have been Caesar's portrait coins and the now rare issues of several of the conspirators who assassinated him. A popular (and therefore expensive) piece is the denarius of Brutus, depicting the daggers of the killing and significant inscription, the "Ides of March."

The empire struck coins for four centuries in gold, silver, orichalcum, copper and bronze. Billon, a base silver alloy, was used in provincial mints in the Near East. Generally, the gold coins, the aureus and solidus, are scarce and high priced. Silver coins are relatively inexpensive. Often, silver coins, like the gold, are in excellent condition.

This is because the basis of Roman bookkeeping was the bronze sestertius. A silver denarius was a convenient way to give or take 10 sestertii. As emperors debased the denarius, it was refused whenever possible. Daily commerce fell upon the shoulders of the sestertius. Therefore, bronze coins in higher grades are scarce today. Most are nearly smooth.

The coins of the Roman emperors are masterpieces of portraiture, especially in the early reigns. The engravers plainly sought realistic and sometimes merciless likenesses. It is doubtful that any modern dictator would tolerate the pitiless realism with which Mint engravers highlighted the gross, perverted features of Nero or the vicious vacuousness of Caligula.

One attraction of Roman coins is the historical documentation they represent. The great names of Augustus, Trajan, Hadrian or Marcus Aurelius; the names of tyrants, such as Nero, Caracalla or Heliogabalus; the record of wars, conquests, triumphs and tragedies all are brought to life by these pieces of numismatic history.

Various avenues invite for assembling a representative Roman collection. One of the most logical and popular choices is to start by seeking one coin of each emperor. With the exception of a few short-lived rulers and would-be rulers, this goal can be reached, subject to the collector's ability to wait for the right examples. The generally abundant silver mintages ease achieving this goal with silver coins, and the result is an attractive collection at moderate expense.

Collectors can thank the efficiency of the ancient mint masters for this. They worked fast to introduce new coins for any new ruler. Didius Julianus, for example, bought the throne in A.D. 193 and held it only a few months, but the mints produced 19 portrait coin types of this emperor, as well as coins portraying his wife and daughter.

Judaic coinage

Another branch of ancient coin collecting that enjoys a great popularity is the historic Judaic coinage. Coinage of Judaea goes back to the fifth century B.C. when Greek type coinage began.

The rule of the Maccabees produced a more national coinage of simple but attractive style, succeeded by the Hellenistic-Roman types of the Herodian client kings.

Perhaps the most beautiful and significant coins before the rebirth of Israel in modern history are the bronze and silver coins of the First Revolt, which ended with the Romans' destruction of Herod's Temple in A.D. 70. Their simple and harmonious designs are in strange contrast to the violence and ultimate defeat of the Revolt.

Coins of the first century's Bar-Kochba War or Second Revolt evoke a feeling of communion with this last outburst of the Jewish longing for independence and the restoration of Jerusalem and its temple. The Temple's facade and sacred instruments adorn the coins, many overstruck on contemporary Roman issues.

Byzantine coinage

The basic unit of Byzantine coinage was the gold solidus, or nomisma, the latter often struck in a characteristic cupped shape. These gold coins typically bought off barbarian invaders. Few silver pieces were in circulation; such denominations as the miliaresion and hexagram enjoyed, at best, a limited life.

The emperor Anastasius I decreed a unified bronze coinage in 498, with the actual denomination in multiple nummi expressed on each coin—K for 20, L for 30, M for 40. Byzantine bronze coins were issued in considerable quantities, and are still available at reasonable prices.

Other ancients

Historically, collectors of ancient coins tended to be people who learned to read Latin and Greek as children in school. The Celts, the Indians, the Arabs, Nubians and other ancient peoples were seen only through the screen of classical Graeco-Roman culture—when they were seen at all. Today, all of that has changed.

Among the most accessible coins today are the drachmas of the Baktrians kings and the western Indian satraps. Alexander the Great took his armies all the way to the Punjab, the "five rivers" region of northwest India. In Baktria and western India, the images and inscriptions diverge from their classical Western roots.

Similarly, the Celts offer a rich and broad field of study. Before the arrival of the Germans, Romans and others, the Celts occupied all of Europe. The Celts included the Galatians, who invaded Greek Asia Minor in the 200s B.C. and settled there, later to be Christianized, and who were cousins to the Gauls whose lands Julius Caesar found to be divided into three parts. The modern French word for Welsh is "Gallois" and the Welsh call themselves Cymry, which is to say "Cimmerian." With all of these various Celtic branches scattered through Europe, it is as impossible to own just one Celtic coin as it is to own just one Greek coin or a single Roman piece.

The Indo-Scythians, the Turkomen, Parthians and other ancient peoples all wrote their histories in their coins. Today, these fields are opening as new political realities allow the study of previously hidden artifacts.

Fakes

Many fake ancient coins can be found in the marketplace. Of course, a lot of American coins are faked, as well—so many that *Coin World* has a monthly column by Michael Fahey, "Detecting Counterfeits." At any coin show, the collector can see silver replicas of Morgan, Peace and Seated Liberty dollars that look just like the real thing, except for some small detail such as the legend ONE OUNCE where the word DOLLAR would go. Lincoln cents, Standing Liberty quarter dollars, gold coins—anything and everything American might be a fake. Yet most collectors rightfully believe that they can tell a genuine 1964 Kennedy half dollar when they see one.

It is the same with ancients. When you handle enough of them, you know them. Copies, replicas, knockoffs and fakes always fail at some level.

Generally, common coins are not subject to forgery. There are some exceptions. The Black Sea Hoard is one.

At the Augsburg Coin Fair, in November 1988, Mark Emory, working in Europe for Heritage Rare Coin Galleries, bought a hoard (possibly 1,000 pieces) of diobols, supposedly struck in Mesembria in Thrace, the site of modern Nesebur in Bulgaria. At the New York International Numismatic Convention in the first week of December 1988, Heritage sold about 300 coins to Jonathan Kern, who sold them to Classical Numismatic Auctions of Quarryville, Pa. (now called the Classical Numismatic Group in Lancaster, Pa.). CNA sent some to Martin Price the head curator for Greek coins at the British Museum. He condemned them.

Heritage insisted the coins were genuine. They hired a scientist to apply atomic absorption spectroscopy to the coins. Dr. Henry Flegler of Michigan State University declared the coins genuine.

The International Bureau for the Suppression of Counterfeit Coins in 1990 advanced the theory that the Black Sea Hoard consisted of contemporary, circulating counterfeits, truly ancient coins that were debased copies of official issues. Taking a different view, German dealer Dr. Hubert Lanz said that he identified the forgeries as the work of a man named "Slavei," a well-known modern copyist. According to Dr. Lanz, he had declined the same group that Emory later bought. As it turned out, neither assertion bore close inspection. The coins were not ancient counterfeits and Slavei denied that they were his work.

Finally, in the summer of 1993, Frank Kovacs, a dealer in ancients from San Diego went to Bulgaria, visited a museum in Sofia, purchased what were being promoted as modern replicas of Mesembrian diobols, paying $3 each, and got a receipt for them. The pieces purchased at the museum would later be die-linked to pieces from the Black Sea Hoard. In September 1993, Dr. Stanley Flegler contacted Dr. Ivan Karayotov, a museum director in Borkas, Bulgaria, who told him that the receipt offered by Kovacs was a forgery. *Coin World* then contacted Elvira Clain-Stefanelli, then the executive director of the National Numismatic Collection in the Smithsonian Institution in Washington, D.C., to translate the receipt. Clain-Stefanelli, a native of Romania, said the receipt reads "2 Mesembria copy" and "2 Apollonia copy." In October 1993, the IBSCC declared the coins to be modern counterfeits rather than ancient copies. Today, the position that the pieces from the

hoard are of modern origin is widely accepted.

All of this took four years. It involved the biggest and most visible names in numismatics and it was reported in *Coin World* and other publications. Apparently, no collector of ancients lost a dime. Heritage made good on any coins that its clients felt uncomfortable with. The coins were always suspect in the eyes of those who work with ancients on a daily basis. Only pride kept the controversy raging.

However, all across the Mediterranean world, wherever tourists look for bargains in marketplaces and bazaars, any time it is easier to make them than to find them, fake ancients will always be sold.

Bank notes and other world paper money

Not as old as coins but equally fascinating to many are bank notes and other forms of paper money. Checks, stock and bond certificates and even deposit slips and check writing machines are also collected with paper money.

Early notes

Marco Polo brought tales of paper money in circulation in China back to Italy. In 806, 400 years before Marco Polo, Emperor Hien Tsung issued certificates of deposit to merchants, who then had to carry only the paper and not the heavy metal it represented. The earliest notes known to us date from the Ming Dynasty, 1368, when notes made of mulberry bark were issued.

Emergency notes were issued during the siege of the Alhama in Spain in 1483 and in Granada, Spain, in 1490.

Bank of Stockholm notes in Sweden date from 1661, and are considered the earliest circulating bank notes in Europe. Paper money as we know it began an unbroken tradition in the American Colonies where people were long on opportunity but short on gold and silver.

Topics

With the dissolution of the communist bloc, many new nations have been launched. In addition, today few governments issue precious metal circulating coinage (and these are snapped up quickly by collectors). Paper money fills the niche once held by gold. In addition, the technology of printing and graphic reproduction has challenged governments to stay ahead of counterfeiters and forgers. Because of these trends, new issues of bank notes are now a regular occurrence.

The choices offered in topical collecting are as wide in paper money as in coins, if not wider. Collectors are successful in assembling examples of notes with bank buildings, ships, churches, animals, fruit, trees, aviation and agriculture, to name just a few. Former communist nations have put their scientists, poets and musicians on notes. So has Great Britain.

It is possible to collect only those notes with see-

through devices or those with aids to the blind built into their design.

We think of the issuance of paper money as being a natural right of the government of the nation associated with the money. In fact, in Great Britain, banks are licensed with the privilege of issuing legal tender notes and several do—which is how things used to be in the United States. If you look closely at a note from the Bank of England, you will see that it carries a copyright statement.

The paper money collector has two sources of delight not offered to coin collectors: serial numbers and signatures. One to four signatures are often found on notes, and as one of these signatures may change, endless combinations become available to the specialist.

Numbers and letters found on notes can include engraving plate numbers, serial letter combinations, issue-date changes and easiest of all, a serial number.

Housing paper money

The collector of paper money of the world experiences the same problems as the collector of notes of the United States in deciding how to store and arrange a collection.

Since notes are not as durable as coins, and folding and handling can reduce their desirability, it is important to keep the notes flat and yet in view.

Plastic sheets are made in several sizes, including 8.5 by 11 inches, with two, three or four pockets, to hold notes of varying sizes. Smaller wallet-size holders also are made, as well as single plastic pockets slightly larger than the notes to be handled.

Other useful tools for studying your notes are a magnifying glass, a ruler with millimeter readings and a good eye for color shades.

Emergency money

Siege notes, issued in times of emergency, have been mentioned already. Collectors of world notes often encounter other emergency notes, which should be reviewed.

At least a dozen countries of Europe issued emergency money in the 1914 to 1923 period of World

War I and the aftermath. In France they are called monnaies de necessite and in Germany and Austria, notgeld, emergency money. Many cities issued these; the army, railways and post offices issued others.

Collectors often separate the emergency issues from inflation issues. The latter appeared first in late 1922. By 1923 in Germany the issues reached such enormous sums that a single note might represent more than the entire indebtedness of the German people in August 1914. Even greater inflation was known in Hungary in 1946, and there are examples of spectacular inflation in recent times, notably Zimbabwe during the past decade. In some cases, governments have been known to bring out of storage notes not issued for many years and overprint them with new dates and values.

Other specialized forms of emergency money are cited as postage stamp money, encased and unencased; military payment certificates; invasion money; guerrilla issues; prisoner of war camp money; and issues from concentration and displaced persons camps.

Printers

Some government printing facilities might print bank notes for other governments. Often the name of the printer, government or private, appears on one side or the other of the note in very small letters.

Private firms that have printed notes around the world include:

American Bank Note Co., New York
British American Bank Note Co., Ottawa, Canada
Barclay and Fry Ltd., England
Blades, East & Blades Bank Note Engravers, London and Leeds, England
Bouligay & Schmidt, Mexico
Bradbury Wilkinson & Co., New Malden, Surrey, England
Calicografia e Cartevalori, Milano, Italy
Canadian Bank Note Co., Ltd., Ottawa, Canada
Charles Skipper & East, England
Chosun Textbook Printing, Co. Ltd., South Korea
Chung Hwa Book Co., China
Commonwealth Banknote Co., Melbourne, Australia
Continental Banknote Co., New York
E.A. Wright, Philadelphia, Pa.
J. Enschede & Son, Haarlem, the Netherlands
Franklin-Lee Bank Note Co., United States
Forbes Lithograph Manufacturing Co., Boston, Mass.
Homer Lee Bank Note Co., New York
Hong Kong Banknote Co., Hong Kong
Hong Kong Printing Press, Hong Kong
Giesecke & Devrient, Berlin, Leipzig & Munich, Germany
International Bank Note Co., London
Jefferies Bank Note Co., Los Angeles
Nisson & Arnold, London
Orell Fuessli, Zurich
Beijing Bureau of Engraving and Printing, Beijing, China
Perkins, Bacon & Co. Ltd., London
St. Luke's Printing Works, London
Saul Soloman & Co., Cape Town, South Africa
Security Banknote Co., New York
Shanghai Printing Co., Shanghai, China
State of California Bureau of Printing, Sacramento, Calif.
Stecher-Traung Lithograph Corp., San Francisco, Calif.
Thomas de la Rue Ltd., Basingstoke, England
Tokyo Printing Co., Tokyo
Union Printing Co., Shanghai
Union Publishers and Printers Fed. Inc., Shanghai
Waterlow & Sons Ltd., London
Waterlow Bros. & Layton Ltd., London
Watson Printing Co.
Western District Banknote Fed. Inc., Shanghai
William Brown & Co., London
W.W. Sprague & Co., Ltd., England

14 Precious Metals

Gold

Chemical symbol: Au
Atomic number: 79
Atomic weight: 196.967
Density @ 293k: 19.32 g/cm³

Gold, the precious and magical yellow metal, has been known and valued by men and women since the dawn of civilization. Egyptian, Etruscan, Assyrian and Minoan cultures all valued gold. Production of gold coinage began in Lydia (modern-day Turkey) in 700 B.C.

Early gold coinage

The first gold coins were not struck from pure gold, but from a gold and silver alloy called electrum, found in Lydia. In addition to hosting the earliest gold coins made from electrum in 700 B.C., Lydia was also the site of the first pure gold coinage, struck during the sixth century B.C. Lydia was followed in the same century by gold pieces created by Persian rulers. These were called darics, after King Darius I.

Other rulers of the ancient world, such as Philip and Alexander the Great of Macedon, as well as Lysimachus of Thrace issued widely circulating gold coins. The Romans issued gold coinage, the aurei, beginning about 83 B.C.

After the fall of Rome, the Byzantine Empire became the important outlet for gold coins. The Byzantines struck their coins in more than 10 mints throughout the empire.

The early Middle Ages saw the decline of gold coinage in the West. Monetary gold came back into use with the Crusades; the most notable example of the revival is the augustalis, issued during the 13th century by Frederick II of Hohenstaufen. In 1252, Florence issued the gold florin, followed by gold coinage issued in France, Bohemia, Hungary, the Low Countries and Spain. In 1284, Venice issued what became the most popular coin for more than 500 years, the ducat, or zecchino.

In 1343, England issued its first major gold coin, the florin, followed in 1344 by the noble. The English later struck the angel and the crown, in 1663 the guinea, and in 1816 the sovereign. Germany struck the gulden, Spain the excellente and France a variety of gold coins.

The first federal gold coins in the United States were authorized in 1792 after the Republic was formed, with the first pieces struck in 1795. Before the federal issues were authorized, a goldsmith and jeweler in New York, Ephraim Brasher, struck two different styles of gold coins in 1786 and 1787 that are the approximate equivalents of Spain's gold 8-escudo coins; the reason the Brasher doubloons (as the coins are called) were issued is unclear.

The Egyptians obtained gold from the earliest times in Nubia, a region in northeastern Africa, modern-day Sudan and Egypt. The Greeks went as far away as India, the Urals, and the mountains and rivers of Asia Minor to obtain gold. Most of the gold used in the Roman Empire came from Spain, then Hungary and Transylvania, and finally Dalmatia (located in Croatia, on the Adriatic coast) and the eastern Alps.

After the fall of the Roman Empire, gold circulation was greatly diminished in the West. From the 10th to the 15th centuries, the gold that was used came from Bohemia (part of the Czech Republic), Silesia (part of modern Poland), Transylvania and Hungary. In the 18th century Siberia and the Urals became important gold-producing regions.

The first half of the 19th century was marked by a large production of gold in Russia and by gold discoveries in the United States in Georgia, North Carolina, and finally, in 1848, the extensive finds in California. Gold production in Australia began around this time as well, followed in 1885 by finds in South Africa, and in 1897 by production in the Klondike, a gold-rich region in northwestern Canada.

Gold mining and refining

Two techniques are usually used to recover gold from its place in nature—placer mining, used to extract gold from rivers and streams; and lode mining, used to take gold out of hard rock.

Placer mining, named after the alluvial deposits (or "placers") of gold found in the beds of streams, was the most common and productive method of gold mining until the 1920s. The principle is to separate gold from river gravel by washing it with water. The gold, mixed with the river gravel, is washed through a series of sluice boxes, each containing crossbars at the bottom. As the water and gravel pass through the boxes, which are slanted downward to employ the force of gravity, the gold sinks to the bottom and lodges behind the crossbars.

An important derivative of this basic placer mining is dredging. A continuously working chain of buckets brings gravel up from the riverbed onto a ship, where it is broken, screened and washed through sluices.

Extracting gold from solid rock, or lode mining, uses the same processes common to all underground mining. Entry into the ground is gained by breaking the rock, by drilling and blasting. The gold ore is broken away from the surrounding rock in a transportable size and hauled out of the mine.

These processes of mining yield an impure gold, containing amounts of silver, copper and other metals. Two methods are most commonly used to extract gold from its metal relatives—a chemical process using chlorine, and the electrolytic process, first used in United States Mints.

In the chlorine process, the impure gold is heated until it becomes molten. Chlorine is bubbled through the molten gold, converting the silver to silver chloride, which can be skimmed off the top of the liquid solution. Unlike the electrolytic process, this chlorine method does not extract platinum from the impure gold.

The electrolytic process involves suspending plates of pure gold alternately with plates of impure gold in a cell containing a solution of gold chloride and hydrochloric acid. The impure gold plates are the anode, the pure gold plates are the cathode. Through the liquid, a current of electricity is passed from the anode plates to the cathode plates. The gold dissolves from the anodes and is precipitated on the cathodes. The other metals that were combined with the impure gold dissolve in the liquid, except the silver, which is converted into insoluble chloride and falls to the bottom of the cell. The gold that precipitates on the cathode plates is washed and melted into bars. This process yields gold that is more than .999 fine, or 99.9 percent pure.

Measure of worth

Gold is valued not only for its beauty, but also for its high resistance to corrosion, its malleability and its longevity. Gold will not readily combine with other metals. It is one of the greatest conductors of electricity.

A cubic foot of solid gold weighs about 1,200 pounds. The standard gold brick, or bullion bar, contains 1,000 troy ounces.

The purity of gold is measured in fineness, parts of gold per 1,000. Pure gold is called 24 karat. A small quantity of silver will reduce the yellowish color of gold, and with added quantities it will develop a

greenish color. Copper added will deepen the gold color. A pure white alloy is obtained by adding platinum, nickel or zinc; this is called white gold or jeweler's gold, and can also be produced by alloying yellow gold with palladium.

Rise and fall of gold standard

Because gold is durable and highly malleable, it can be hammered into almost any shape and precisely divided into any size or unit of weight. Since it can be stamped into coins of a precise weight, the values of all other goods could, in the early days of gold coinage, be measured in terms of units of gold. Eventually gold became the absolute standard of value.

Although gold is very dense, its high value compared with its weight and bulk increased the risk of its being stolen. Nevertheless, by the 16th century and even much later, some gold-holding citizens kept their fortunes of gold in their own houses. But most people eventually became accustomed to leaving their gold for safekeeping in the goldsmiths' vaults, where it was well protected. The goldsmiths would issue a receipt for the gold received.

Before long, gold-holding citizens realized it was much easier, when it came time to make a purchase or pay a debt, to simply issue an order to the goldsmith to pay over the gold to whomever they owed, rather than to transfer the gold itself. The recipient of the order, again, might find it easier to leave the gold he was to receive at the goldsmith's and in turn issue orders to the goldsmith to pay specific amounts of gold to still a third person. Thus, all these monetary transactions took place without the actual gold leaving the goldsmith's vault. This was the origin of bank notes and checks.

As this new paper money began to circulate on its own, goldsmiths discovered they could issue paper promises that exceeded the value of the gold in their vaults. Since this made the medium of exchange more abundant, trade flourished as the amount of money increased to meet its needs. When paper money became too abundant and exceeded the goods available in the market, it was withdrawn from circulation and exchanged for gold; when paper money became too scarce, gold was returned to the banks and exchanged for its paper representative.

The goldsmiths were gambling that everyone would not demand their gold at once. This was a good risk, and in nearly every country, these new banks went on expanding their credit until the amount of bank note and demand deposit liabilities, that is, the amount of paper money, was several times the amount of gold held in the banks' vaults.

For centuries this alternating appearance (when paper money was cashed in) and disappearance (when gold was exchanged for paper money) of gold was the only stabilizing factor in a radically fluctuating market. Paper notes were issued freely by goldsmiths, moneychangers, merchants and bankers. No government could control the system; gold was the only stabilizing influence on the market. As the international monetary system became more complex, more and more governments used this traditional method of balancing and stabilizing international trade and backing up domestic currency with gold.

Gold stands firm

From these origins came the gold standard. First adopted by Great Britain in 1821, it was the system under which governments issued paper money that was backed by and exchangeable for gold. The amount of money circulating in a country depended upon the amount of gold it had.

The gold standard had several advantages. Since governments couldn't legally increase the money supply without obtaining more gold, citizens were theoretically protected from politically attractive, printing-press inflation. The threat that people would demand gold for their paper tended to act as a damper on politicians.

The gold standard was also supposed to keep a nation's payments to, and receipts from, foreigners automatically in rough balance. Suppose a country bought from foreigners, or imported, more than it exported over a long period. The country would pay out much more gold than it received, which would reduce the amount of money circulating at home. A smaller money supply would, in turn, tend to reduce the prices of things the country produced. Lower prices would make the country's goods and services more attractive to both foreign and domestic buyers. This would encourage purchases by foreigners, or exports, and discourage purchase from them.

Since everyone accepted gold as a medium of exchange, the gold standard also tended to create certainty in international trade by providing a fixed pattern of exchange rates, that is, the rate or price at which the currency of one country is exchanged for currency of another country.

However, since the money supply depended on the amount of gold a country had, less money in circulation could mean less domestic business and more unemployment. In other words, the gold standard may not allow enough flexibility in the supply of money. In addition, since it provided a fixed pattern of exchange rates, the gold standard made it difficult for any nation to isolate its economy from depression or inflation in the rest of the world.

Most major nations of the world had adopted the gold standard by the 1870s. The United States was one of the last, officially adopting it in 1900.

Some countries at this time were using a close relative of the gold standard, the gold exchange standard. In this system, gold was not exported or imported at all. One country would offer to buy and sell the currency of another gold-standard country at a fixed price in the paper currency of the country making the offer. This was much cheaper than the full gold standard since the expense of transporting the gold was eliminated.

1919 and after

World War I spelled an effective end to the gold standard. War-induced inflation caused most nations to change to inconvertible currency or to restrict gold export.

At any other time the gold standard might have supplied its own automatic corrective: inflation at home would have meant that gold, in itself, was a more profitable export than goods, and a partial drain of gold abroad would thus normally have resulted in a contracted volume of money at home, making it necessary to reduce imports until a balance of trade had again been reached by an intensification of cheaper exports.

However, the expense of war caused Great Britain and other countries to spend gold profusely to buy arms from the United States.

At the end of World War I, all currencies were inflated and there was a severe shortage of gold worldwide. Most of the world's stock had gone into hiding; half of it was in the United States reserve, and the rest was in private hands. Inflation had driven the cost of gold mining up until it approached and sometimes exceeded the official price of gold. Convinced a return to the gold standard would solve the world's monetary ills, the nations of the Atlantic trading community agreed to return to the gold standard in the 1920s.

The stock market crash in 1929 killed this last effort to remain on the gold standard. In 1931, Britain went off the gold standard after using up its gold reserve in an attempt to defend its overvalued pound.

When President Franklin Roosevelt signed the Gold Reserve Act of 1934, the United States officially abandoned the gold standard. The dollar was no longer convertible to gold and gold could not be exported. The government prohibited the manufacture of gold coins, the private hoarding of gold and the use of gold as money or in lieu of money.

Rare and unusual gold coins, including those made before April 4, 1933, were exempted from delivery to the U.S. Treasury, including U.S. and foreign coins. All other gold coins, gold certificates and gold bullion were required to be turned in to the Treasury.

At the same time the secretary of the Treasury issued a public announcement that, beginning Feb. 1, 1934, the Treasury would buy all gold delivered to any U.S. Mint or any Assay Office in New York or Seattle, at the rate of $35 per fine troy ounce. An exhausted nation in the depths of a depression jumped at the offer. Wedding rings, gold plates and jewelry poured into the Treasury. By the end of 1934, gold was coming into the Philadelphia Mint at the rate of $1.5 million worth a month.

In October 1933, President Roosevelt announced he would establish a government market for gold, and on Jan. 31, 1934, he froze the price at $35 an ounce, thereby devaluing the dollar 40.94 percent. The result was a literal flood of gold pouring into the

United States from foreign countries. The onslaught of gold made the government realize it had nowhere to put it, so the gold vaults of Fort Knox, Ky., were built in 1935.

By October 1939, the United States had well over half the world's stock of gold.

Dethroning the king

With the founding of the United Nations after World War II, representatives of 44 nations met in conference at Bretton Woods, N.H., in July 1944, to form the International Monetary Fund. The IMF is a specialized agency affiliated with the United Nations, designed to stabilize international monetary exchange rates instead of the gold standard. It has no power to dictate national monetary policies.

The members of the IMF, it was decided, would all deposit quotas in the fund, only one-quarter of which had to be in gold, and the rest in their own currencies. From this fund, members could purchase with their own national currencies the gold or foreign exchange they needed.

The IMF, then, became the world's largest source of quickly available international credit. By June 1972, the 124-nation fund had provided $24.6 billion in short-term financial assistance.

Only the United States decided to keep its currency convertible at all times into gold. The United States pledged at Bretton Woods to convert foreign holdings of dollars into gold on demand at the fixed rate of $35 an ounce. The other countries could hold and count dollars as part of their reserves as if dollars were gold. Thus, the dollar became the center of the world's monetary system.

Each member of the IMF was required to maintain the dollar or gold parity ($35 an ounce) of its currency by buying its currency when the price fell to 1 percent below parity or selling if the price rose 1 percent above parity.

The London gold market reopened in 1954 after World War II had forced its close in 1939. From 1954 to 1957, the price of gold on the London market fell consistently below $35 an ounce. Private demand for gold was composed almost entirely of industrial-artistic use and hoarding in countries where savings are traditionally held in gold.

Despite the growth in industrial use of gold and that gold, at a fixed price, was cheap in comparison to other commodities, private demand generally did not absorb all newly mined gold and the gold purchased from Communist stocks during this time. Except when the monetary authorities purchased gold to maintain its price at $35 an ounce, most countries bought relatively little gold, and instead built up their dollar holdings.

The gold drain

The system ran into difficulty in 1958 when the United States saw its first significantly large balance of payments deficit. This is a name given to the excess in the amount of dollars going abroad for foreign aid, for investments, for tourist expenditures, for imports and for other payments, in comparison to the amount of dollars coming in for payments of U.S. exports to foreign countries. This meant a heavy drain on U.S. gold supply.

The balance of payments deficit persisted into 1960. Rumors began to spread in October that the United States might devalue the dollar (by raising the price of gold) to slow the gold drain. The first sharp gold panic swept the world's monetary trading centers. Under pressure from a sudden and widespread demand for gold, the market price jumped in London from $35 to $42 an ounce.

The crisis was eased temporarily as the U.S. Treasury transferred $135 million in gold to the London market, and as the Bank of England intervened as a substantial seller. This flood of gold forced the price down to $35 by the spring of 1961.

Relief was short-lived. The supply of new gold coming into the London market began to fall in mid-summer of 1961 as the two largest producers of gold, Canada and South Africa, began to add their newly mined gold to their monetary reserves. Demand for gold continued to rise, though, as the U.S. balance of payments deficit continued. The price of gold began to creep upward again.

In the autumn of 1961, the United States proposed that other nations join it to maintain the price of gold at a reasonable level. This was the birth of the London gold pool, a group formed to try to stabilize the gold market and avoid excessive swings in the price of gold that would lead to a loss of confidence in many foreign currencies.

The central banks of eight nations joined the gold pool—Belgium, France, Italy, Switzerland, the Netherlands, West Germany, the United Kingdom and the United States. Each contributed a quota to the pool, with the United States matching their combined payment. The Bank of England acted as agent for the group, given the right to draw on the pool and to sell gold if the price rose too high.

In November 1961, the first sales were made. The price of gold fell and the sales by the pool were recovered in later purchases. By February 1962, all the members of the gold pool had been repaid.

The price was temporarily under control, but the U.S. gold drain continued. To defend the dollar on foreign markets, President Lyndon Johnson signed legislation in early 1965 to drop the 25 percent requirement for gold backing of commercial banks' deposits at Federal Reserve banks. This bill freed about $5 billion of the country's remaining $15 billion gold stock for additional sale to dollar-holding foreign governments. The requirement that paper currency in circulation be backed 25 percent by gold remained.

Despite United States efforts, in 1966 and 1967 private demand began to exceed the supply of gold available at $35 an ounce. During this time, massive losses from official stocks occurred. The rate of expansion of gold production in South Africa, which had been increasing for 15 years, came to a halt in 1966. With rising production costs the outlook for a greatly increased supply of gold did not look favorable, especially at a fixed price of $35 an ounce. Greatly aggravating this drop in free world gold production in 1966 was the Soviet Union's decision to discontinue its by-then-customary gold sales.

As production of gold decreased, demand climbed, particularly from gold speculators who had entered the market in significant numbers with the gold crisis of 1960. These speculators tried to take advantage of the worsening U.S. balance of payments deficit by purchasing large amounts of gold, which they expected to increase in price.

The two-tier system

In the five months preceding March 1968, speculation absorbed nearly $3 billion in gold, almost all of which was lost by the gold pool countries, primarily the United States. Unwilling to suffer such losses in the future, the gold pool members instituted the two-tier system.

The system, outlined in a Washington meeting of the gold pool nations on March 16 and 17, 1968, set up new guidelines governing the future of gold. On one level, the price of gold was maintained at $35 an ounce. At this price, transnational governmental authorities agreed to the unlimited exchange of gold among themselves. On the second level, a free market in gold was established that could fluctuate to reflect whatever the value of gold really was. Three conditions effectively achieved this segregation:

1. An agreement among monetary authorities to trade gold among themselves at an official price of $35 an ounce.

2. Agreement to supply no more gold to private markets from official stocks.

3. Agreement to buy little or no gold from private sellers.

The concept of Special Drawing Rights (SDRs) was introduced at the March meeting and adopted later in 1969 and 1970. SDRs are a form of "paper gold" to be used in the same manner as gold, dollars or other currencies to settle debts between nations. The SDRs were distributed to members of the International Monetary Fund in proportion to their economic importance in the world economy. Designed to protect gold reserves, SDRs could be used to settle international payment deficits that would have otherwise drawn on these reserves. SDRs were given the value in gold of one U.S. dollar, which, at the official price of $35 an ounce, would buy 0.888671 gram of fine gold.

U.S. domestic policy changed to conform to the new system. The Treasury announced it would no longer purchase gold in the private market, nor would it sell gold for industrial, professional or artistic uses. Domestic producers were permitted to sell and export freely to foreign buyers as well as to authorized domestic users. Domestic consumers regularly engaged in an industry, profession or art in which gold is required were permitted to continue to import gold or to purchase gold from domestic producers.

The U.S. government also removed the remaining 25 percent gold backing from paper money in circulation, freeing another $750 million to stabilize the gold market.

The price of gold on the free-market tier began to rise. On May 17, 1968, it touched $40 an ounce on the London market. In July, however, the price fell again when the French government tried to bolster the franc and rumors spread that South Africa would be selling some of its newly mined gold on the free market. In October, the United States and other major nations in the IMF agreed to provide a mechanism for sales of newly mined gold to monetary authorities, but only when the free market price reached or fell below the official price of $35 an ounce.

Dollar devaluation

The economic crisis in the United States worsened as the balance of payments deficit persisted. Therefore, on Aug. 16, 1971, President Nixon announced the United States was freeing the dollar for devaluation against other currencies by suspending the full convertibility of foreign-held dollars into gold. This inconvertibility meant no foreign government could convert dollars into Treasury-held gold; thus, the tie between the dollar and gold was severed.

The devaluation of the dollar occurred Dec. 18, 1971, and was accomplished by raising the official price of gold from $35 to $38 an ounce. Other currencies were juggled up or down into a new pattern of exchange rates. Throughout 1972 the price of gold on the free market climbed until it leveled off in December at $61 an ounce.

Economists and monetary authorities almost unanimously regarded the 8.57 percent devaluation of the dollar as inadequate. And, since the dollar was no longer exchangeable for gold, it made little difference that the price at which the Treasury did not sell gold was raised from $35 to $38 an ounce. Another devaluation was forced, then, in February 1973. Treasury Secretary George Shultz announced that the dollar would be devalued 10 percent against SDRs (and so against gold) with the official monetary price of gold raised from $38 to $42.22 an ounce.

The price of gold on the London market took a sharp leap upward, breaking through the $100 an ounce barrier on May 14, 1973. Official stocks of gold were virtually frozen because no central bank would give up gold at the official price of $42.22 an ounce when the free market price had climbed so far above it.

The king is dead

Five and a half years after its birth, the two-tier

gold system was abandoned by central bank officials Nov. 10, 1973. The system had out-lived its usefulness since it was made when the dollar was still convertible into gold; there was no point in continuing it when the central banks of other nations could not buy gold from the U.S. Treasury with dollars, as the original agreement had allowed.

By abandoning the system the central bank officials from Belgium, West Germany, Italy, the Netherlands, Switzerland, Britain and the United States relegated gold to the status of commodity, with no special monetary status, opening the way for increased international dependence on Special Drawing Rights.

Two months later the International Monetary Fund met in Rome to finalize the demotion of gold. The IMF's Committee of Twenty decided to adopt a new world currency plan that would end all relationship between Special Drawing Rights and gold. It would be replaced by a "basket" of 14 of the world's strongest paper currencies. The value of SDRs would be based on an average value of a portfolio of these currencies, including the dollar, the British pound, French franc, West German mark, Japanese yen and a sampling of other currencies. The scheme was approved in June 1974.

The IMF Group of Ten (the United States, Britain, France, West Germany, Italy, Belgium, the Netherlands, Sweden, Canada and Japan) met in June 1974 and gave gold a new function in the monetary world. Gold stocks stored in the vaults of central banks, it was decided, could be used by economically distressed countries as security for international loans, expanding their borrowing power.

Though this was perfectly legal before, it had been economically unfeasible under the two-tier system, as no nation was ready to risk its gold as loan collateral at the official price of $42.22 when the market price was four times that. It was agreed in 1974 though, that the pledged gold could be valued at a price much closer to the free-market quote than to the official level.

President Gerald Ford signed a bill Aug. 20, 1974, lifting the 40-year-old restrictions on U.S. citizens' holding of gold. Americans, as of Dec. 31, 1974, would be permitted to buy, hold and sell gold without restriction, as they would deal in any other commodity.

After Ford signed the bill, Treasury Under Secretary Jack F. Bennett commented that the United States "might feel free to sell gold from official stocks" directly to domestic buyers. Bennett noted that unless there was such a source of gold inside the country, most of the gold purchased would have to be imported, thus further distorting the U.S. balance of payments deficit.

Gold, once the undisputed king of the international monetary system, was now reduced to the status of another commodity. Still as durable, malleable and beautiful as it always was, gold's value now rests in the hands of the gold dealers of London, Paris, Zurich and the United States.

In numismatics

U.S. gold coinage, authorized soon after the United States was formed, had been gradually phased out until the end was spelled out in 1933 when it became illegal to manufacture gold coins or to use gold as money or in lieu of money (see Gold Chronology).

With the gold acts and orders of 1933 and 1934, designed to centralize the gold reserves of the country into the hands of the government, restrictions on collecting gold coins were very stringent. The government wanted to make sure no one was "collecting" gold coins for their gold content rather than for their numismatic value; hence, all gold coins were recalled except for those "having a recognized special value to collectors of rare and unusual coin," according to the Treasury position.

A determination was made on each individual gold coin presented to the Treasury for a ruling, including gold coins made before and after 1933. The criterion for a pre-1933 coin was whether it had "recognized" special collector value on April 4, 1933. The criterion for coins struck after 1933 was whether they had "true numismatic value," based on the number issued, the purpose for which they were issued, the condition of the coin, the Mint mark if any and all other factors concerning the issue.

Foreign coins struck after 1933 and issued in large quantities, or for providing a market for gold, or simply as a money-making device, were denied entry.

These strict regulations were relaxed somewhat in 1954 when the Treasury amended the gold regulations. The amendment provided that any gold coin made before 1933 would be considered a rare gold coin. Any struck after 1933 would not be considered rare unless a specific determination to the contrary was made by the Treasury Department.

As a numismatic authority, the Treasury called on the curator of numismatics of the United States national museum, the Smithsonian Institution.

These regulations and the stricter ones made in 1933 still gave the Treasury no control over gold held outside the United States by U.S. citizens. The coin market abroad was flooded with counterfeits and restrikes of coins made before 1933, making it difficult for the Treasury to determine whether the coins held abroad were actually those ruled exempt under Treasury Department rulings.

Restrictions on U.S. citizens holding gold abroad began Jan. 14, 1961, when President Eisenhower issued an executive order prohibiting the holding of gold abroad by any persons subject to the jurisdiction of the United States. An exception was made for gold coins, again, "of recognized value to collectors of rare and unusual coin."

ODGSO is born

Before Oct. 9, 1961, the function of administering

the gold and silver regulations was assigned to the Bureau of the Mint. On that date, a Treasury Department order created the Office of Domestic Gold and Silver Operations (ODGSO) and placed it in the Office of the Undersecretary for Monetary Affairs.

The ODGSO reported directly to the deputy undersecretary for Monetary Affairs until April 1, 1969, when it was placed under the new position of assistant secretary (Economic Policy).

The primary functions of the ODGSO were to:

1. Assist in the formulation of policies regarding the control of gold.

2. Administer the Treasury gold regulations to include the issuance of licenses or other authorizations for the acquisition, possession, ownership, importation, exportation, and uses of gold for industrial, professional and artistic purposes. The office also issued licenses or other authorizations for the importation of gold coins, medals and bars of exceptional numismatic value.

3. Maintain statistical data on the production and uses of gold.

The first director of the ODGSO was Leland Howard. He retired Dec. 30, 1966, but remained as an adviser until Thomas Wolfe was named the new director in June 1967.

The new office went to work soon after its creation when President Kennedy, on July 20, 1962, proclaimed that acquiring gold coins abroad was illegal for subjects of the United States. Citizens were ordered to bring home or to dispose of any rare gold coins they held abroad by Jan. 1, 1963.

The proclamation also prohibited the importation of any rare gold coins except under licenses issued by the ODGSO.

Not all pre-1933 gold coins, then, were admissible for import any longer, a partial reinstitution of the 1933 regulations, reflecting the United States gold drain.

The ODGSO also ruled illegal the holding of mutilated gold coins, with any solder on the coin or the drilling of a hole constituting mutilation, and restrikes, which were "subject to forfeiture in the hands of purchasers, no matter how innocent."

The White House commented the action had been taken to prevent large-scale counterfeiting and restriking of rare gold coins in Europe, Argentina and India. Coin dealers reacted with a mixture of suspicion and hostility to the new ruling.

Paper money collectors received a break soon after, however. Another amendment to the gold regulations was issued allowing the holding and importation without license of U.S. gold certificates issued before Jan. 30, 1934. These certificates were issued by the government as a form of paper currency beginning in 1865 and were redeemable on demand in gold. Since it became a crime to hold gold after 1934, the certificates could no longer be cashed in after that date; the certificates themselves, indeed, were supposed to be turned in to the Treasury Department in 1934.

The government realized that many certificates were still out, in the hands of collectors, since they were no good as currency. The 1964 ruling made the possession of gold certificates legal since they posed no threat to the U.S. gold reserves.

Collectors of gold medals were informed of regulations governing their aspect of numismatics on June 26, 1964. The Treasury issued a release clarifying the acquisition of "fabricated gold."

" 'Fabricated Gold,' " the Treasury stated, "is processed or manufactured gold in any form which: a) has a gold content the value of which does not exceed 90 percent of the total domestic value of such processed or manufactured gold; and b) has in good faith, and not for the purpose of evading or enabling others to evade the provisions of the Acts, the Orders, or the Regulations in this part, been processed or manufactured for some one or more specific and customary industrial, professional or artistic uses. Hence, to qualify as a fabricated gold object an article must pass all three of the following tests:

"1. The value of the gold content may not exceed 90 percent of the total value.

"2. The article must be manufactured in good faith.

"3. The article must be for specific and customary industrial, professional or artistic uses.

"Award medals which are specially manufactured medals, presented to an individual in recognition of a worthy achievement, may be imported into the United States by the individual receiving the award, that is, the original recipient of the medal."

More regulations governing gold medals were spelled out in an Aug. 21, 1965, Treasury Department order legalizing the possession of rare gold bars:

"The Director, Office of Domestic Gold and Silver Operations, may issue or cause to be issued licenses or other authorizations, permitting the acquisition, holding, transportation and importation of gold bars which the Director is satisfied have been of recognized special value to collectors of numismatic items in all times since prior to April 5, 1933. Gold bars manufactured after Dec. 31, 1900, shall be presumed to not be of such recognized special value to collectors."

The directive continued: "The manufacture of gold medals (other than special award medals) and the plating of coins are not customary industrial, professional or artistic uses of gold within the meaning of the regulations and, accordingly, such uses of gold and the acquisition or possession of any gold medals (other than special award medals) and gold-plated coins are not authorized by the regulations or any licenses issued pursuant thereto. Without limitation the following are not deemed to be of customary industrial, professional or artistic uses of gold:

"1. The plating of any coins.

"2. The manufacture of any gold medals other than special award medals, or,

"3. The acquisition, holding, transportation, importation or exportation of any gold-plated coins or gold medals other than special award medals."

The ODGSO was called into court early in 1966 to defend its determination of "rare and unusual coin" by Stack's, one of the largest coin dealers in the United States. The dispute arose when Stack's was denied a license to import a gold coin collection from Amsterdam.

In the extensive and secret hearings, the ODGSO disclosed its criterion to determine whether a coin had "exceptional numismatic value" was the ratio between the market value of the coin and its gold bullion content. This was the first public admission by the ODGSO of how import licenses were awarded.

Stack's lost the fight Oct. 31, 1966, when the Treasury deputy undersecretary for Monetary Affairs upheld the ODGSO position and Stack's was not allowed to import the collection.

The ODGSO did rule, however, on March 21, 1966, that a set of Proof 1965 South African gold coins were of exceptional numismatic value and could be licensed for import. In 1968, though, ODGSO ruled against a request for an import license for a set of 1968 South African gold coins, taking a turnabout from its former ruling.

Regulations ease

A gradual easing of gold regulations began in 1969, after the United States and other International Monetary Fund nations set up the two-tier system for the gold market. On April 26, the Treasury announced that no more licensing would be required for pre-1934 gold coins "of legitimate issue from any nation." The change was made to remove what the Treasury called an "inconsistency" in regulations on imported pre-1934 gold coins, which generally had to have licenses, and those regularly traded within the United States.

The new ruling freed more than 250 additional gold coin issues to come into the United States. ODGSO Director Wolfe said the pre-1934 coins constituted 95 percent of all licenses.

The ban continued on importation of all gold coins struck after 1960 except for those already licensed, including: 1961, 500 kronur, Iceland; 1960, 20 pounds, Israel; 1961, 10 scudi, 5 scudi, Malta; 1960, pound and half pound, South Africa; 1961, 1962, 1963, 1964, 1965, rand and 2 rand, South Africa, all Proof; and 1961, 500 piastres, 1962, 250 piastres, Turkey.

The regulations governing coins minted after 1934 remained the same.

Early in 1970 ODGSO granted permission for the importation of one complete six-coin set of Yemen 1969 gold coins and allowed two Israel 1969 gold 100-pound Shalom coins to come into the country.

Regulations on gold medals were eased in April 1971. Licenses would be issued for the acquisition, holding, transportation and exportation of gold-plat-

ed coins or gold medals that were either antique or for public display by an institution serving the public.

The amendment also authorized the ODGSO to license foreign subsidiaries of U.S. corporations to manufacture gold medals for sale to persons not subject to the jurisdiction of the United States.

Mexican gold coins caused difficulty for the ODGSO after the office allowed importation of coins struck between 1934 and 1959. The flood of restrikes coming from Mexico caused the office to reverse its ruling three months after it was made, and place a ban on importation of all gold coins of Mexico dated since 1933.

The ruling did not stand for long. On Dec. 17, 1973, ODGSO ruled "any gold coin legally issued, dated between 1934 and 1959, may now enter the United States without the formality of applying for a license." The ruling liberated many gold coins of Mexico, Iran, 100-franc coins of Switzerland dated 1934 and 1939, a four-coin Coronation set of the United Kingdom dated 1937, and gold sovereigns of earlier years restruck in this period, as long as they were dated 1959 or earlier.

However, at the same time, all coins struck since 1960 were barred, including some for which licenses previously had been granted. So, some gold coins that had been legal were now illegal for import. Counterfeit coins and gold bullion or bars were denied passage into the United States.

President Ford's signature on the bill allowing U.S. citizens to buy, hold and sell gold without restriction ended the back and forth battle between the ODGSO and coin collectors and dealers. All gold coins (except for the 1933 double eagle; see the Chronology section for news about 1933 double eagles surfacing), as of Dec. 31, 1974, became legal for American citizens to hold, and remain so. The confusion of regulations raging since 1934 was cleared and closed. Treasury Secretary William E. Simon announced the abolition of the ODGSO in August 1975. The remaining gold responsibilities of the agency were transferred to the Treasury's assistant secretary for International Affairs.

'Gold rush'

European gold dealers, anticipating a "gold rush" by Americans after it became legal once again for them to own gold, were dismayed when this failed to come about. Indeed, the price of gold, which reached $195.25 on Dec. 27, 1974, actually slipped to $186.75 on Dec. 31, and continued to tumble, to $175.25 on Jan. 2, 1975.

Free to buy and own gold after a hiatus of more than 40 years, Americans found themselves unfamiliar with the precious metal as an investment medium. They were further assailed with the prevailing official concept that gold was a "barbarous" medium, reflecting the Keynsian philosophy that remained heavily entrenched in government circles.

The government's role in thwarting citizens' speculating in gold became apparent when Sen. William Proxmire, D-Wis., chairman of the powerful Senate Banking Committee, announced that he would introduce legislation for the sale of 25 million ounces of gold from the government stockpile in 1975.

When a previously authorized 2 million ounces of 400-ounce gold bars were offered at auction on Jan. 6, however, the market showed little interest. Only one-third of the gold offered was taken. The sale had the effect of depressing the London price of gold from $173.50 to $169.50; however, two days later it jumped back to $180.25, registering the sharpest one-day price rise on record.

General Services Administration and International Monetary Fund auctions, together with the importation of tons of gold by refugees following the fall of South Vietnam and Cambodia had a bearish effect on the market throughout 1975 and most of 1976. On July 20, the price plunged to a 31-month low of $107.75, following a second IMF auction.

Inflation heats up

The Carter election victory and the OPEC energy crunch resulted in a turn-around in the gold price and the gold market, so that by Jan. 4, 1978, the gold price registered a 2½-year high of $172.50 at the morning fix in London.

In April, Sens. Jesse Helms, R-N.C., and Barry Goldwater, R-Ariz., introduced the American Arts Gold Medallion Act of 1978 as an alternative to the mostly unsuccessful GSA auctions. Meantime, the InternationalGold Corp. (Intergold), the marketing arm of the South African gold mining industry, was aggressively marketing the Krugerrand 1-ounce bullion coin throughout the world.

Higher inflation, increasing U.S. trade deficits and a weakening dollar drove the London morning fix for gold to $223.50 by Oct. 3, 1978. Nine months later, on July 18, 1979, it was fixed at $303.85. The gold price continued to escalate through the year and into the next year, reaching a then record high of $850 on Jan. 21, 1980.

Since 1980

Today, many think of gold in economic terms as a monitor of inflation or as a commodity to purchase as a hedge against paper instruments of money. However, frenzy surrounding gold did not return to the fevered pitch of the 1973 to 1980 era, for many years. In the Reagan years, the stock market domi-

nated investment money, and the introduction of the American Eagle gold bullion coins did little to stir up the precious metals markets. Even the stock market crash of 1987 did little to restore gold to prominence.

Gold waxed and waned in value, reaching a 20-year low in 1999 when it hovered around the $250 level. The announcement by central banks around the world that they would sell off huge stockpiles of physical gold stirred the commodities exchanges for a while, and gold broke through $300 an ounce, reaching $325. However, even the threat that governments would divest their stockpiles of gold did little to sustain enthusiasm. At the height of Y2K concerns heading into the year 2000, gold went below $300.

A major factor influencing gold in the new millennium is the presence of gold exchange-traded products on the market. The first gold ETF was launched in March 2003 on the Australian Stock Exchange, and in November 2004 the SPDR Gold Trust (then under the name streetTRACKS Gold Shares) was listed on the New York Stock Exchange. The SPDR Gold Trust is currently one of the top 10 largest holders of gold in the world, and as of November 2010 it was the second largest ETF in the world. It allows investors exposure to gold without having to physically own it. As of Feb. 4, 2011, it held 39,509,197 ounces of gold in trust, with a value of more than $53 billion.

The price of gold began to rise during the 21st century, though in fits and spurts. During the last year of the 20th century, 2000, the average price of gold was $279.11. The average price fell to $271.04 in 2001. From that point on, however, the average price of gold marched steadily upward. The $800-an-ounce barrier was broken in late 2007, and in March 2008, gold broke the $1,000 an ounce barrier. As economic concerns both in the United States and around the world continued, gold continued to go up in price, closing at a high of $1,421 an ounce in the New York precious metals exchange on Nov. 9, 2010. In April 2011, gold broke through the $1,500-an-ounce barrier.

Also in the first decade of the 2000s, the U.S. Mint has made more products available for gold bullion investors including the American Buffalo .9999 fine gold coins, most popularly available as 1-ounce coins, which were made available in 2006 (see Bullion Coin chapter). In 2007, the First Spouse .9999 fine gold half-ounce $10 coins entered the marketplace and in 2009, the Mint produced a Saint-Gaudens, Ultra High Relief 1-ounce .9999 fine gold $20 double eagle.

Modern gold chronology

1782

Thomas Jefferson reports finding a lump of gold ore on the north side of the Rappahannock River in Virginia.

1792

April 2—Authorizing act issued to strike U.S.

gold eagle ($10, standard weight 270 grains, .91666 fineness), half eagle ($5, standard weight 135 grains, .91666 fineness), and quarter eagle ($2.50, standard weight 67.5 grains, .91666 fineness).

Dollar defined as a unit containing 24.75 grains of fine gold or 371.25 grains of fine silver (exchange rate between the two metals set at 15 to one).

1799

Gold discovered in Cabarrus County, North Carolina

1802

Gold discovered in South Carolina.

1821

Britain adopts the gold standard.

1827

Indians recover gold near Coker Creek, Tennessee.

1833

Samples of gold found near Georgetown, Texas.

1834

June 28—Authorizing act issued to change the standard weight of the eagle to 258 grains, .899225 fineness; the half eagle to 129 grains, .899225 fineness; and the quarter eagle to 64.5 grains, .899225 fineness.

Standard definition of dollar changed; redefined as unit containing 23.2 grains of fine gold (changed from 24.75 grains). Silver definition unchanged, remains at 371.25 grains of fine silver in one dollar. Exchange rate becomes 16 to one.

Gold mining town of Dahlonega, Ga., built.

1837

Jan. 18—Authorizing act issued to change fineness of eagle, half eagle, and quarter eagle to .900. Exchange rate becomes 15.988 to one.

1848

Jan. 24—Gold discovered by James W. Marshall, who was erecting a sawmill in partnership with Capt. John A. Sutter on the American River, a branch of the Sacramento River, near Coloma, Calif.

1849

March 3—Authorizing act issued to strike U.S. $20 gold double eagle (standard weight 516 grains, .900 fineness), and gold dollar (25.8 grains, .900 fineness).

1853

Feb. 21—Authorizing act issued to strike gold $3 coin (77.4 grains, .900 fineness).

1857

The SS *Central America* sinks in September during a hurricane off the Carolina coast with tons of gold bars and coins, many in shipment from the San Francisco Mint. Factor in Panic of 1857.

1863

March 3—Authorizing act issued to produce gold certificates.

1865

Nov. 13—First U.S. gold certificates issued.

1867

International monetary conference in Paris. Delegates vote to adopt the gold standard.

1869

Sept. 24—Financial "Black Friday" in New York, caused by an attempt by Jay Gould, financier and speculator, and James Fisk, Erie railroad magnate, to corner the gold market. Gold reached $163.50 per ounce. To bring the price down and foil the financiers' scheme, the secretary of the Treasury ordered the sale of $4 million in government gold, forcing the price down to $133 and causing a panic in the securities market.

1873

U.S. drops silver dollar from the list of coins to be struck at the Mint; effectively ends bimetallism.

1890

Sept. 26—Gold $1, $3 coins ordered discontinued.

1896

July 8—William Jennings Bryan, Democratic candidate for president, delivers his impassioned "Cross of Gold" speech at the Democratic National Convention in Chicago, calling for restoration of the bimetallic (silver and gold) standard.

1900

Bimetallism legislation repealed; Gold Standard act passed, officially placing the United States on the gold standard. Gold dollar of 25.8 grains, .900 fine becomes the unit of value; all other forms of currency maintained at parity with the gold dollar.

1902

June 28—Authorizing act issued to strike gold dollar commemorative coins (25.8 grains, .900 fineness) for the Louisiana Purchase Exposition.

1904

April 13—Authorizing act issued to strike gold dollar commemorative coins (25.8 grains, .900 fineness) for the Lewis and Clark Exposition.

1915

Jan. 16—Authorizing act issued to strike $50 (1,290 grains, .900 fineness), $1 (25.8 grains, .900 fineness) and quarter eagle (64.5 grains, .900 fineness) commemorative gold coins for the Panama-Pacific International Exposition.

1916

Feb. 23—Authorizing act issued to strike gold dollar commemorative coins (25.8 grains, .900 fineness) in honor of President William McKinley.

1925

March 3—Authorizing act issued to strike gold quarter eagle commemorative coins (64.5 grains, .900 fineness) for the Sesquicentennial Exhibition.

Nations of the Atlantic trading community agree to return to the gold standard after inflated post-World War I currency had caused its demise; Britain returns to the gold standard.

1929

Oct. 29—Stock market crash marks the end of post-World War I prosperity. Depression begins.

1931

Britain goes off the gold standard.

1933

March 2—First 1933 double eagles struck at the Philadelphia Mint (until 2010, the start of production was believed to have been March 15), two days before Franklin Roosevelt became president and before Roosevelt's order suspending gold production. The same day, a quantity of mutilated (rolled and flattened) 1932 coins was exchanged for new 1933 double eagles. The exchange of 1933 coins for 1932 coins also placed a quantity of 1933 double eagles in the Philadelphia Mint cashier's vault from which over-the-counter payout could be made.

March 6—Roosevelt makes Presidential Declaration 2039, declaring Bank Holiday and ordering that the Mint pay out no gold coins without license.

April 5—(Executive Order 6102), Aug. 28 (Executive Order 6260), Dec. 28 (Order of the Secretary of the Treasury). Government prohibits the manufacture of gold coins, private hoarding of gold and the use of gold as money or in lieu of money. Gold coins having a recognized special value to collectors of rare and unusual coin, including gold coins made before April 5, 1933, are exempted from delivery to the U.S. Treasury, including U.S. and foreign coins. All other gold coins, gold certificates and gold bullion were required to be turned in to the Treasury Department.

June 5—The United States goes off the gold standard.

1934

Jan. 31—Executive order freezes the price of gold at $35 an ounce, up from its former $20.67 an ounce, thereby devaluing the dollar 40.94 percent.

1937

Feb. 6 to March 18—1933 double eagles are sent to the refinery for melting.

1941

Smith & Son advertises 1933 double eagle available for sale in *The Numismatist.*

1942

President Roosevelt issues an executive order closing all gold mines in the United States.

1944

February—Stack's announces in an advertisement in *The Numismatist* that a 1933 double eagle will be available in the upcoming auction of the Col. James W. Flanagan Collection.

Feb. 23—B. Max Mehl sells 1933 double eagle to King Farouk of Egypt.

Feb. 25—Egypt's Royal Legation delivers 1933 double eagle to Treasury Department and asks for export license.

Feb. 29—Treasury Department issues Egyptian Royal Legation export license No. TGL-170 for 1933 double eagle.

March 11—Egyptian official retrieves 1933 double eagle from Treasury Department.

March 18—Acting Mint Director asks superintendent of Philadelphia Mint whether any 1933 double eagles had been paid out at Philadelphia Mint, citing the upcoming Stack's auction.

March 24—Secret Service agents seize 1933 double eagle from Stack's. Additional coins are seized from other dealers and collectors starting the next day, continuing until 1952. Interviews with collectors and dealers lead to identifying a Philadelphia dealer, Israel Switt, as the source for the 1933 double eagles.

March 30—Secret Service agents interview Switt, who acknowledges having sold nine examples and says he cannot recall where he obtained the coins.

July—Articles and agreements of the International Monetary Fund, a specialized agency affiliated with the United Nations, signed at Bretton Woods, N.H.

1945

Federal Reserve requirement to hold title to gold in an amount greater than or equal to 40 percent of outstanding Federal Reserve notes plus 35 percent of commercial bank deposits with Federal Reserve banks revised; requirement lowered to 25 percent of the total combined sum of Federal Reserve liabilities.

1946

Ban against gold mining lifted.

1949

September—Treasury Department drafts letter to Farouk government demanding return of 1933 double eagle, but the letter is never sent upon advice of the State Department.

1952

Aug. 21—Baltimore banker and collector Louis Eliasberg Sr. surrenders 1933 double eagle to Secret Service agents (the ninth coin recovered since March 1944).

1954

London gold market reopens after 15 years of inactivity.

Amendment to gold regulations issued; gold coins made prior to April 5, 1933, both foreign and domestic, declared to be of special value to collectors of rare and unusual coins. Gold coins made after 1933 are presumed not to be rare unless determined otherwise by the Treasury Department.

Feb. 24—Sotheby's conducts first session of Palace Collection of Egypt in Cairo, offering the numismatic collector of the disposed Farouk. The Farouk 1933 double eagle is cataloged as Lot 185 along with 16 other double eagles. The 1933 coin is withdrawn from the auction at the request of the U.S. government.

1958

United States runs a significantly large balance of payments deficit; currency of 14 nations becomes convertible for nonresidents.

1960

October—Gold panic sweeps world's monetary trading centers. Free market price of gold jumps from $29.67 to $35 an ounce in London. Consequently, eight-nation Gold Pool formed.

1961

Jan. 14—President Eisenhower issues an executive order prohibiting U.S. citizens from purchasing or holding gold abroad in any form except numismatic gold coins. Gold owned by U.S. citizens, residents and corporations abroad must be sold before June 1, 1961.

1962

July 20—President Kennedy proclaims no person subject to the jurisdiction of the United States can acquire gold coins abroad except under Treasury Department license, and no gold coins can be imported without a license. This decision prohibited ownership abroad of any kind of gold coins. Citizens were ordered to bring back to the United States or to dispose of any rare gold coins held abroad by Jan. 1, 1963.

September—Treasury Department, for the first time in 17 years, moves a large amount of gold from Fort Knox to the Treasury's Assay Office in New York City to meet foreign demand for U.S. gold bullion.

1963

Jan. 3—Treasury Secretary Dillon clarifies phrase "customary industrial, professional or artistic use" in Part 54, Title 31; adds definition reading: "Customary industrial, professional or artistic use means the use of gold in industry, profession or art, in a manner, for a purpose, in a form, and in quantities in which gold is customarily used in industry, profession or art."

June 26—Treasury Department clarifies rules on fabricated gold.

Aug. 13—Customs agents confiscate 21 gold coins from the Witte Museum's $50,000 Albert Hirschfeld collection in San Antonio, Texas, saying the coins were illegally imported.

1964

April 24—Treasury Department removes all restrictions on the acquisition or holding of gold certificates issued by the United States before Jan. 30, 1934.

Nov. 30—Monetary gold reserves drop $75 million for the week ended Nov. 25.

1965

Jan. 7—France announces its government will convert $150 million of its currency reserves into gold by buying the gold in the United States.

Jan. 13—U.S. monetary gold reserves drop $200 million in the week ended Jan. 13.

Feb. 19—Senate passes legislation to repeal requirement for 25 percent gold backing of commercial banks' deposits at Federal Reserve banks. Bill would free about $5 billion of the country's $15 billion gold stock for additional sale to dollar-holding foreign governments and for future growth of the domestic money supply.

March 4—President Johnson approves and signs legislation freeing $5 billion in U.S. gold in an effort to maintain the stability of the dollar in the world market. Leaves in effect the required 25 percent gold backing of the paper currency in circulation.

Aug. 21—Treasury Department issues order allowing the importation, transporting, holding and exportation of numismatically valued gold bars, with license. Also clarifies rules regarding gold medals and gold-plated coins.

1966

April 27—Chancellor of the exchequer announces in Parliament that Great Britain will forbid the use of gold in the making of medallions, plaques, medals and other articles. The new order also bars United Kingdom residents from holding more than four gold coins minted after 1837, except with official permission.

1967

March—Treasury reports gold stock at lowest level since 1938.

March—French government lifts restrictions on the import and export of gold, ending restrictions in effect since September 1939.

March 23—South African Proof 1966 gold coins are not admissible into the United States as collectors' items, the ODGSO rules.

June—Thomas W. Wolfe appointed acting director of ODGSO.

Aug. 2—Gold reserves reach 29-year low as gold goes into the Treasury's stabilization fund, which handles sales of U.S. gold to foreign nations.

Nov. 18—Britain devalues the pound, from $2.80 to $2.40.

Nov. 27—Dollar remains strong; Gold Pool members pledge support of the $35-an-ounce gold price.

December—United States moves almost $1 billion in gold bullion, half going to London to prevent price rise on gold.

1968

Feb. 7—Treasury reports reserves of gold have dropped to the lowest level since 1937.

Feb. 9—House Banking and Currency Committee recommends passage of administration bill to remove the 25 percent gold cover from U.S. paper money.

March 17—Treasury amends gold regulations; Treasury would no longer purchase gold in the private market, nor would it sell gold for industrial, professional or artistic uses. Domestic producers were permitted to sell and export freely to foreign buyers as well as to authorized domestic users. The amendment authorized domestic users regularly engaged in an industry, profession or art in which gold is required to import gold or to purchase gold from domestic producers within the limits of their licenses or authorization in the gold regulations.

March 17—Central Banks announce the formation of a two-tier price system for gold. Under the new plan, the price of gold would remain at $35 an ounce in transactions between cooperating governments, while it would be permitted to seek its own price in the private market.

March 20—With President Johnson's signature on the bill removing gold backing from U.S. paper money, the Treasury transfers $750 million to the Exchange Stabilization Fund. Gold prices fall on European markets.

April 7—Gold remained stable at about $37 to $38 an ounce in London.

April 16—Treasury issues new gold regulations, noting the ODGSO will accept applications for licenses submitted by persons wishing to buy and sell gold for authorized industrial, professional and artistic uses; that persons, including banks, may, without a license, buy gold for the account of persons licensed and offer storage and safekeeping services for licensed persons; and that persons holding licenses may continue to acquire newly mined gold or to import gold for authorized uses. All transactions in gold with foreign monetary authorities are prohibited.

April 19—ODGSO grants temporary permission to import a 1967 Canadian gold $20 coin so it can be displayed at the Northwest Central States Numismatic Association show.

May 2—Gold reaches a record high of $39.35 an ounce in London.

May 17—Gold tops $40 an ounce in London; pound falls to its lowest point since 1967, $2.3853.

May 30—Treasury reports gold stockpile lowest since 1936, at $10.547 billion.

July 9—Attempts by the French government to bolster the franc and rumors that South Africa would be selling some of its newly mined gold on the free market bring gold prices below $40 in London.

July—ODGSO denies a license for the importation of gold coins of South Africa dated 1968.

October—United States and other leading industrial nations in the International Monetary Fund reach an accord providing a mechanism for limited sales of newly minted gold to monetary authorities, but only when the free market price is at or below the official price of $35 an ounce.

1969

Feb. 24—Sensitive world gold market reacts to President Nixon's visit to Europe and drives the price of gold up to $46.33 in Paris.

March 5—Devaluation jitters drive gold up to $47 an ounce in Paris.

April 25—ODGSO allows import of gold coins made before 1934 without a license.

June 5—ODGSO revises medal regulations; permits licenses to be issued for the acquisition, holding, transportation and exportation of gold-plated coins or gold medals which are either antique or are for public display by an institution serving the public.

July 30—Swiss bankers confirm that South Africa is unloading sizable quantities of gold on the bullion market in Zurich.

Nov. 6—Free market gold drops to $39 an ounce in London.

Nov. 24—Gold drops to $37.90; attributed to general world monetary stability partly caused by the revaluation of the German mark.

Nov. 28—Treasury rules after Dec. 31 it will no longer be possible to deposit gold for exchange into gold bars at U.S. Mints and Assay Offices.

Dec. 2—Gold drops five cents below the International Monetary Fund ceiling of $35.35.

1970

Jan. 8—Gold reaches a 12-year low of $34.95 in London.

April 8—ODGSO grants permission for the import of one complete six-coin set of Yemen 1969 gold coins, to be donated to and become part of the permanent collection of the Smithsonian Institution.

December—Gold price up to $41.90 in New York.

1971

April 1—United Kingdom lifts all gold coin and medal restrictions; gold coin can again be freely bought, sold and held.

April 19—Treasury amends gold regulations, authorizing the director of ODGSO to license foreign subsidiaries of U.S. corporations to manufacture gold medals for sale to persons not subject to the jurisdiction of the U.S. Also removes restrictions on the gold plating of any coins and the acquisition, holding, transportation, importation, or exportation of any gold-plated coins.

July 12—Thomas Wolfe, director of the ODGSO, determines Mexican gold coins struck between 1934 and 1959 are eligible for import into the United States, with license.

July 22—Gold regulations amended, prohibiting the trading of gold in any form on commodity exchanges and the acquisition of American or foreign gold coins of any description for speculative purposes. Reaffirms existing regulations.

Aug. 15—President Nixon frees the dollar for devaluation against other currencies by cutting its tie with gold and halts the conversion of foreign-held dollars into gold.

Oct. 21—Treasury Department places a ban on importation of all gold coins of Mexico dated since 1933. Designed to prevent the importation of restrikes.

Dec. 18—President Nixon announces an 8.57 percent devaluation of the U.S. dollar. The devaluation would be accomplished by a $3 increase in the price of gold, from $35 to $38 an ounce.

1972

March 13—House postpones for a week the bill to devalue the dollar.

March 21—Dollar devaluation bill passes the House without proposed amendment to permit U.S. citizens to own gold.

March 22—Sen. Peter Dominick, R-Colo., introduces a Senate bill to allow private ownership of gold.

April 3—President Nixon signs bill to devalue the dollar.

May 8—Treasury Department formally adopts the $3 increase in the price of monetary gold to $38 an ounce.

May 17—Gold climbs to $57.75 on the London exchange.

May 29—Gold closes at $58.55 in London. Common date gold coins advancing on the average of $5 in value in two weeks.

June 6—Gold goes through $60 mark.

July—Dealer reports common-date double eagles up from $80 to $95 over a five-week period.

Aug. 2—Gold at $70 an ounce in London.

Aug. 22—Private ownership of gold endorsed by the Republican National Convention meeting in Miami.

Oct. 12—Industrial demand for gold softens, speculative pressure subsides, South Africa announces increased gold reserves; price of gold in London falls.

November—Treasury announces U.S. firms will be permitted to trade in gold futures on the new Winnipeg Commodity Exchange when it opens in mid-November, but "only to an extent consistent with their licenses."

Nov. 15—Winnipeg Commodity Exchange opens, world's first commodities market in gold futures.

Nov. 20—Gold levels off at $61 in London.

1973

January—ODGSO clarifies regulations on gold coin jewelry.

Feb. 12—Treasury Secretary George Schultz announces the dollar is devalued 10 percent; official price of gold raised to $42.22 an ounce.

Feb. 23—Gold at $95 an ounce in London, up $10 overnight.

April 1—Japanese government allows its citizens to buy, sell, hoard and own gold.

April 4—Senate OKs legislation ending ban on private ownership of gold, an amendment to the Par Value Modification Act.

May 14—Gold breaks through $100 barrier, closing at $102.50 an ounce in London.

May 29—Gold-holding amendment to Par Value Modification Act fails in the House.

June 1—Gold at $119 an ounce in London.

July 12—Senate approves free ownership of gold, an amendment to the Bicentennial coinage bill.

Aug. 14—Gold drops to $95.50 in London.

Nov. 10—Central Banks end two-tier gold system following a Berne, Switzerland, meeting. Price of gold drops to $90.

Nov. 28—Gold rallies, up to $97.25 in London.

Dec. 17—ODGSO rules any gold coin legally issued, dated between 1934 and 1959, may now enter the United States without the formality of applying for a license. Gold coins issued after 1959 assumed not to be rare.

1974

Jan. 3—Gold jumps, at $121.25 an ounce in London.

Jan. 8—Gold continues to rise, reaches $126.50.

Jan. 18—More than 750 attend a two-day symposium in New Orleans sponsored by the National Committee to Legalize Gold.

Jan. 21—Gold reaches $161.31 in the Paris Bourse. Double eagles priced at $238.

Jan. 30—Gold drops to $135 in London.

Feb. 5—G. Drake Jacobs of Aspen, Colo., files suit challenging the constitutionality of the U.S. Gold Regulations and the Trading with the Enemy Act under which the regulations were promulgated.

Feb. 10—Gold closes at $146 an ounce in London.

Feb. 21—Gold, silver, platinum and copper break all world records. Gold at $160 in London, a new world record fixing for that market.

Feb. 26—Gold crests at $188 in Paris.

March 27—Gold searches for a new floor price, settles at $174.

April 3—Gold leaps to $197 in Paris, fixed at London at a record $179.50.

May 3—Gold steady at $169 in London.

May 29—Senate approves an amendment allowing citizen ownership of gold as of Sept. 1, 1974. Amendment is attached to a bill authorizing $1.5 billion in funds to the International Development Association.

May 30—Gold jumps to $161 in London.

June 11—Treasury Secretary William E. Simon says he believes President Nixon will probably end restrictions on U.S. gold ownership by the end of the year.

June 11—Finance leaders in the Group of Ten industrial nations meet; decide to use gold stocks as security for international loans by economically distressed countries; agree that the pledge metal could be valued at a price much closer to the free-market quote than to the official level, the price determined as a result of agreement between the borrower and the lender.

June 11—Committee of Twenty of the International Monetary Fund meets, approves new scheme for valuing the Standard Drawing Rights in terms of a "basket" of currencies, including the U.S. dollar, British pound, French franc, West German mark, Japanese yen and a sampling of other currencies on international monetary markets.

June 18—House Banking and Currency Committee votes to amend the International Development Association bill with a measure to permit U.S. citizens to own gold after Dec. 31, 1974.

July 2—House passes International Development Association bill, with gold ownership amendment.

July 4—Gold prices slump to $129 an ounce in London.

July 31—House passes IDA bill with gold ownership amendment; goes to President Richard Nixon for his signature. Nixon resigns office of the presidency over Watergate scandal before he can sign the bill.

Aug. 1—Gold price at $159.40 in London.

Aug. 14—President Ford signs legislation lifting 40-year ban on U.S. citizens' holding of gold. The law will take effect at the end of December, unless the president decides to speed up the process by declaring an earlier date.

Aug. 20—ODGSO Director Wolfe says American citizens may order gold coins if coin firms are willing to place names on mailing lists in anticipation of coming legalization of holding gold by U.S. citizens.

Aug. 27—Treasury Department invites congressmen to Fort Knox Sept. 23.

Sept. 11—Rep. Philip M. Crane, R-Ill., introduces a bill prohibiting authorization by the secretary of the Treasury or the president to sell gold from the American stockpile.

Sept. 23—A seven-man congressional inspection team and nearly 100 reporters inspect the Fort Knox Bullion Depository.

Oct. 10—Several major U.S. brokerage houses announce plans to enter gold trading market at the end of 1974.

Oct. 17—ODGSO denies rumor that the Treasury is considering a Bicentennial gold coin, claiming such a coin would be illegal under current laws.

Oct. 24—Gold prices rise past $160 per ounce level, amid rumors of Middle Eastern dollar manipulations.

Oct. 24—California legislature prepares bill regulating gold dealings in post-ban days. Several coin dealers object to restrictions.

Nov. 8—Gold price hits $183 per ounce in London, leading to speculation of $200 gold by the end of the year.

Nov. 8—Federal Trade Commission requires that jewelry replicas of pioneer gold coins be marked with COPY in incuse lettering.

Nov. 8—New York Stock Exchange contemplates establishment of a gold trading center after the end of the gold ban.

Nov. 11—Gold climbs to $188.25 per ounce. Treasury secretary denies there will be a delay in the legalization of gold.

Nov. 20—Last-minute opposition to the freeing of gold sees the introduction into Congress of bills delaying gold ban lifting.

Nov. 20—Great Britain resumes striking of sovereigns for release through Bank of England.

Dec. 3—U.S. Treasury announces plans for sale of 2 million ounces of gold bullion on Jan. 6, 1975. Sale intended to ease the balance of payments deficit that would result from U.S. citizens buying gold from overseas.

Dec. 5—Federal Reserve Board Chairman Arthur Burns urges delay in lifting of gold ban, fearing that Americans will withdraw savings to buy gold.

Dec. 19—Proposal for Canadian gold Olympic coin receives unexpected endorsement from post-master general, minister responsible for Olympic coin program.

Dec. 27—Gold reaches $195.25 per ounce in London, expected to reach $200 by the end of the year.

Dec. 27—France to revalue its gold reserves to near-market level shortly after the first of the year.

Dec. 27—Philippines reported to be considering a legal tender gold coin for 1975.

Dec. 31—Striking of Panamanian gold 100-balboa coin at the private Franklin Mint in the United States marks end of U.S. gold ban.

Dec. 31—President Ford inaugural medal struck in gold for public sale, first such medal since 1933.

Dec. 31—Gold prices drop sharply in first day of legalized gold in America.

1975

Jan. 2—Gold drops to $175.25 per ounce from Dec. 31 close of $186.75, confusing metal market experts. Profit taking blamed.

Jan. 6—U.S. Treasury opens bids on 2 million ounces of gold in 400-ounce bars. Demand so small that only 753,600 ounces sold, at an average price of $165.67 per ounce. Lowest bid accepted is $153 per ounce. Treasury secretary delighted at the "failure" of the sale.

Jan. 8—London gold market jumps from $169.50 to $180 per ounce, despite the lack of interest shown in the U.S. Treasury gold sale. Gold experts unable to explain trend.

Jan. 15—Gold prices settle down near $175 per ounce level, stay there for several weeks.

Jan. 19—U.S. hobby leaders meet at American Numismatic Association round table; Mint director says that the rumors of the death of the Bicentennial gold coin are greatly exaggerated.

Jan.—Gold imports for the month of January more than double those for December. Most of increase thought to be for industrial purposes, rather than speculative.

Jan. 31—Gold closes at $176.05 per ounce.

Feb. 10—GAO audit verifies U.S. gold supplies. U.S. Mint controls called "adequate."

Feb. 19—Gold prices spurt upward to $184.50 per ounce, highest price since Jan. 2. Rumors of changes in European central bank operations blamed.

Feb. 28—Gold closes at $182 per ounce.

March—Twelve rare Adelaide Assay Office gold pounds found to be missing from the Library of New South Wales, Sydney, Australia. The genuine coins had been replaced by worthless modern replicas.

March 31—Gold closes at $176.

April 15—United Kingdom bans sale of newly minted sovereigns to U.K. residents, making them available only to overseas buyers.

April 15—U.S. Treasury announces updated gold regulations in wake of legalization.

April 15—Gold drops to $164 per ounce, several dollars below the official figure used to value French gold reserves. Speculators disappointed when France does not step in to buy gold at the unofficial "floor" price.

April 30—Gold closes at $167 per ounce.

May—Several bills introduced into U.S. House and Senate calling for a Bicentennial gold coin. Legislation receives ANA support.

May 30—U.S. Treasury announces upcoming sale of an additional half million ounces of gold on June 30.

May 30—Gold closes at $167.20 per ounce.

May—Following the fall of South Vietnam and Cambodia, tons of gold surface as refugees leave Southeast Asia.

June 2—The Treasury Department announces it will sell about a half million of its 276 million ounces of gold on hand, in bars of 250 ounces each. Gold prices on world markets fall.

June 30—The General Services Administration opens bids for the Treasury gold auction; in contrast with the Jan. 6 sale, Treasury calls interest in the June sale "substantial," with 41 successful bidders for 499,500 ounces of gold at $165.05 per ounce. Largest successful bidder is Swiss Bank Corp. of Zurich (140,000 ounces).

Aug. 11—Gold lists two-month low in London, $161.90 per ounce.

Aug. 27—Office of Domestic Gold and Silver Operations abolished; functions remaining after the lift of the gold ban are transferred to the Treasury's assistant secretary for International Affairs. J.H. Nisenson named deputy director of Gold Market Activities.

Aug. 29—The International Monetary Fund announces it will sell about $1.1 billion of its gold for the benefit of poor nations, permitting central banks to buy 25 million ounces at market-related prices. Markets begin decline.

Sept. 19—Gold plunges to year's low of $135.

Nov. 28—Charles Heim, publisher of *Heim's Investment Letter,* says outlook for gold is "negative." Price stands at $138.15 in London.

Dec. 19—The IMF Group of Ten meets in Paris, discusses possibility of reducing amount of gold to be auctioned from 25 million ounces to 17.5 million.

Dec. 31—Thomas Wolfe, former director of the Office of Domestic Gold and Silver Operations, begins a government-sponsored study of world gold and silver markets.

1976

Jan. 1—National Bicentennial medal becomes available in several metals, including three sizes in .900 fine gold. First national gold medals authorized by Congress for sale to public.

Jan. 8—Franklin Mint strikes first gold coin of the Netherlands Antilles.

Jan. 30—Gold continues to slide, closing month of January at $128.40 per ounce in New York.

Feb. 27—Gold steady for February, closing at monthly average of $130.81 per ounce in New York.

March 31—Stack's sells five gold coins from the Garrett Collection for $408,000; total auction brings more than $2.3 million.

April 21—Jesse Owens receives first gold $100 Canadian Olympic gold coin presented to an American.

April 28—International Monetary Fund anticipates beginning its gold sales in May, planning to auction off 25 million ounces over the next four years.

May 19—Australians gain the right to own, buy and sell gold.

June 2—IMF auctions 780,000 ounces of gold at a common price of $126 per ounce. The "Dutch auction" system adopted, permitting all successful bidders to receive gold at the same price. Next auction set for July 14.

July 7—Internal Revenue Service rules that trades of investment coins qualify as "like kind" exchanges and thus are not taxable transactions. The ruling involved a trade of five lots of Mexican gold 50-peso coins for six and a half lots of Austrian 100-corona coins. Since both lots were restrikes, their value depended on their gold content; thus, though the pieces differed in size and gold content, their nature was the same.

July 20—Gold plunges to 31-month low on London gold exchange, with a closing fix of $107.75, following second IMF auction.

Sept. 15—IMF sells 780,000 ounces of gold at $109.40 per ounce; market responds by moving up $2.75 to $114 per ounce.

Sept. 29—American Stock Exchange proposes to set up affiliate to trade in gold bullion options.

Oct. 27—Thomas Wolfe, former ODGSO chief, believes gold price has bottomed out and should move up in years ahead, based on increased industrial demand and other factors.

Nov. 15—Gold climbs to $139.20 on London exchange, in wake of Carter election victory; boom replaces gloom among speculators.

Oct. 1—President Ford signs Gold Labeling Act into law. The bill reduces tolerances permitted in gold products.

1977

Feb. 9—American Stock Exchange continues to promote its gold and silver commodity options program while awaiting Commodity Futures Trading Commission approval. Also plans a spot market in gold and silver.

March 15—London gold market appears to level at $140 to $150 per ounce during first weeks of March.

March 30—Gold reaches high of $153.55 per troy ounce; slips to $149.95 five days later.

April 6—Bidders pay an average of $149.18 per troy ounce in IMF gold sale. Rep. Henry S. Reuss, D-Wis., urges Treasury officials to release U.S. gold for auction to "cool" price.

April 13—South Africa revalues gold from "official" $42.40-per-ounce price to market-related price.

The move benefits the nation's gold mines by eliminating the time they must wait between receiving the "official" price and getting the difference between it and the actual selling price from the government.

April 23—Historic Reed Mine in Cabarrus County, N.C., the first gold mine in the United States, is opened to the public. Restoration includes 300 feet of original shafts.

May 11—Gold futures trading on New York's COMEX and Chicago's IMM triple in volume from the previous year, with 171,849 contracts traded in March.

June 1—Canada announces plans to strike 300,000 22-karat gold $100 coins for the Silver Jubilee of Queen Elizabeth II. IMF sells 525,000 ounces of gold at $143.32.

June 15—International Precious Metals Institute holds its first international conference at New York's World Trade Center.

June 29—North Carolina's gold rush days are recalled in three dioramas depicting the minting of gold coins at the Charlotte Mint Museum.

Oct. 10—London price of gold reaches two-year high of $157.15 per troy ounce.

Oct. 30—President Carter signs "gold clause" bill, permitting U.S. citizens to enter into contracts specifying payment in gold or in dollars based on the value of gold.

1978

Jan. 4—Gold opens at 2½-year high of $172.50 at the morning fix in the London gold market.

March 28—Weak dollar combined with energy crunch drives London gold price upward to $183.20 per troy ounce.

April 20—Treasury announces plans to sell 1.8 million troy ounces of stockpiled gold to prop up the U.S. dollar; gold responds with a price drop of more than $10.

April 20—Sen. Jesse Helms, R-N.C., and Barry Goldwater, R-Ariz., co-sponsor Gold Medallion Act of 1978 as an alternative to stockpile auctions.

Aug. 1—London's major gold merchants set the morning fix at $207.50.

Oct. 4—U.S. gold coin imports averaged 236,000 ounces during the first seven months of 1978, 76 percent ahead of the previous year's imports of these items.

Oct. 3—Gold breaks upward to $223.50 in London, as U.S. trade deficits continue to take their toll on the dollar.

1979

July 18—London gold prices shatter $300 barrier as price is fixed at $303.85.

Sept. 29—Gold sells for $400.20 in Hong Kong as world paper currencies register distress.

Sept. 29—Appropriations legislation for funding American Arts Gold Medallion program is signed by President Carter.

Dec. 12—Price of gold continues climb to $462.50 per troy ounce.

1980

Jan. 3—Gold price continues upward to $634 per troy ounce.

Jan. 21—All-time record price of $850 reached in gold trading; Comex silver trades for $50.35 per troy ounce.

April 15—Gold price slips below $500, to $495.50 per ounce.

June 16 and July 1—opening dates for ordering half-ounce American Arts Gold Medallions honoring Marian Anderson and the 1-ounce pieces commemorating artist Grant Wood.

1981

Feb. 11—Gold price continues slippage to $490 per troy ounce.

June 24—London price of gold drops off plateau, to $460 level.

July 8—Gold price falls through $400 as it is fixed in London at $397.75, the lowest price since Nov. 27, 1979; prime interest rate climbs to 20.5 percent.

Sept. 16—The U.S. Gold Commission meets to consider returning to the gold standard and other questions related to gold. Rep. Ron Paul, R-Texas, and Lewis Lehrman of New York are the only members of the 16-person commission known to favor the move.

1982

Feb. 17—Study by the Aden sisters predicts return to $850 gold by 1984; $3,600-to-$4,500 gold by 1986.

March 12—Gold price falls to $322 under pressure of high interest rates.

March 24—Reduction in prime rate bounces the gold price upward to $411.50 for the first time since Jan. 8.

1983

Jan. 18—Gold tops $500 for the first time in 22 months, as it trades at $502.50 on the New York Commodity Exchange.

Feb. 22—Gold price tumbles from $503.50 to $485.50 in a single day's trading on the Comex.

Feb. 29—J. Aron & Co. wins marketing contract for American Arts Gold Medallions; accents bullion nature of pieces by renaming them "U.S. Gold."

April 2—Designs approved for 1983 U.S. Gold, commemorating poet Robert Frost and artist Alexander Calder.

May 25—Rep. Paul introduces legislation that proposes that the International Monetary Fund sell gold at the spot price to the United States, rather than increasing the U.S. contribution to the fund.

May 31—The price of gold drops $23.90, to $412 per troy ounce on the Comex; price future is "confused" as a bill to ban Krugerrand sales is introduced in Congress.

Aug. 17—J. Aron & Co. Vice President Arnold

Reishman reports satisfaction with share U.S. Gold has carved in slow gold bullion market.

Sept. 13—The United States Mint strikes the first 1984-W Olympic gold eagle at West Point, N.Y. This is the first gold coin struck by the U.S. Mint in 50 years, and is the first to bear the W Mint mark.

1984

Jan. 9—Price of gold drops to $365.90 on the Comex in New York as the U.S. dollar gains strength against world currencies.

June 20—The U.S. Treasury terminates its U.S. Gold distribution contract with J. Aron & Co. The Treasury absorbs $2 million advertising costs, while J. Aron will reimburse $1.3 million for material on hand.

July 25—Gold plunges to an almost-two-year low of $333.50 on the Comex; experts anticipate lower price levels.

Oct. 17—A U.S. Senate and House committee declines to approve a bill that would prohibit the importation of Krugerrands and Soviet Union gold coins.

Oct. 17—A bill introduced in the final days of the 98th Congress to continue the American Arts Gold Medallion program is modified to make the issue legal tender 1-ounce gold $20 coins showing the Statue of Liberty on one side and a family of eagles on the other.

Dec. 12—U.S. Mint officials, after five weeks of telemarketing, report a "planned, smooth rise in sales of American Arts Gold Medallions."

1985

Jan. 16—Chairman Frank Annunzio of the House Consumer Affairs and Coinage subcommittee introduces legislation authorizing the sale of gold and silver coins to commemorate the Centennial of the Statue of Liberty.

Feb. 27—Jammed telephone lines for ordering American Arts Gold Medallions (U.S. Gold) result in an extension of the ordering date beyond Jan. 31.

June 19—House passes legislation that would impose immediate sanctions against South Africa, including the importation of Krugerrands.

July 3—Senate passes Statue of Liberty commemorative coin bill with an amendment calling for a 1-ounce silver bullion coin to follow the Statue of Liberty program.

July 17—Bullion dealers report the Canadian Maple Leaf is overtaking the Krugerrand in the bullion market.

July 24—The Senate passes its version of the anti-apartheid act containing a U.S. bullion coin amendment.

Aug. 14—South Africa halts release of its worldwide sales figures for Krugerrands.

Sept. 25—President Reagan issues executive order for economic sanctions against the government of South Africa and requests the Treasury Department

to report on the feasibility of minting U.S. gold bullion coins.

Oct. 11—President Reagan signs executive order banning importation of the Krugerrand.

Dec. 2—Senate passes gold bullion coin legislation.

Dec. 4—Passage by the House of gold bullion coinage legislation is blocked at the Treasury Department's request, to provide an opportunity to amend the bill to conform with Treasury recommendations

Dec. 18—House passes gold bullion coin legislation.

Dec. 17—President Reagan signs legislation authorizing the minting of four gold bullion coins—1-ounce $50, half-ounce $25, quarter-ounce $10 and tenth-ounce $5 face values—to be struck from newly mined domestic gold.

1986

March 12—Mint Director Donna Pope predicts sales of 2.2 million ounces of gold bullion coins and 4 million ounces of silver bullion coins in first year at House Appropriations subcommittee hearing.

June 11—U.S. Mint Director Donna Pope reveals all four gold bullion coins will carry a revised Augustus Saint-Gaudens double eagle Striding Liberty design on the obverse, with Texas sculptor Miley Busiek's Family of Eagles design for the reverse.

July 23—The Royal Canadian Mint reports 8 million ounces of Maple Leaf gold bullion coins have been sold since their introduction in 1979, through the end of 1985; 1985 sales increased 87.4 percent over 1984.

Aug. 13—U.S. Mint defines criteria for gold bullion coin wholesalers, who must have a net worth more than $50 million and liquid assets of $10 million. Minimum purchases of 5,000 ounces of gold, 50 million ounces of silver will be required.

Sept. 8—Though the Mint schedules its ceremonial striking of the new bullion coins for Sept. 8, sales are being delayed until Oct. 20 to permit an inventory buildup.

Sept. 9—The ban against importation of the South African Krugerrand, due to expire, is extended by President Reagan.

October—Twenty-five U.S. and foreign firms are selected by the Treasury Department to make the market for the American Eagle gold bullion coins.

Nov. 5—American Eagle gold bullion coin orders empty Mint vaults, with 558,000 ounces moving out in two days.

November—Three-week sales total for American Eagle gold coins climbs to 820,500 ounces, or 1,253,000 coins.

Nov. 26—"Eaglemania" continues: Retail premiums range from 6.7 to 16.9 percent for 1-ounce coins, 49.2 to 81.8 percent for half-ounce coins, 57.6 to 82.5 percent for the quarter ounce coins and 69.9 to 84.7 percent for the tenth-ounce.

Dec. 3—Sales of American Eagle gold coin year-end production goals set at 1.4 million 1-ounce coins,

50,000 half-ounce coins, 600,000 quarter-ounce coins and 650,000 tenth-ounce coins.

November—U.S. Mint reports that for the first time in seven weeks, demand for 1-ounce gold bullion coins fell below supply on Dec. 1. Sales of all four coins climb to 1,278,750 ounces or 1,932,000 coins.

Dec. 24—Proof 1986 American Eagle gold coin sales exceed $187 million; Proofs to be offered in some denominations in 1987.

1987

Jan. 7—Supply of all four denominations of American Eagle gold coins exceeded demand on Dec. 23 for the second week in a row. Total produced amounts to 1,607,250 ounces, or 2,675,000 coins.

Jan. 14—Mint reaches gold bullion production goals.

Jan. 14—The governor of South Dakota unveils the state's new gold South Dakota Centennial medallion.

Jan. 21—Coinage subcommittee hears Jan. 5 that eight U.S. distributors bought 34 percent of gold bullion coins; the balance was sold to 17 foreign dealers.

Feb. 6—The Nevada State Ways and Means Committee introduces a bill proposing a $16.50 fee on each ounce of gold produced by Nevada mines.

February—Belgium announces it will mint and sell gold and silver coins denominated in European Currency Units to commemorate the 30th anniversary of the European Community's founding treaty.

March 25—Great Britain announces it will enter the gold bullion coin market in 1987 with a gold "Britannia" to be issued in 1-ounce and three fractional-ounce sizes, joining similar programs operated by South Africa, Canada, the United States, Australia, the Isle of Man and China.

April 20—Worldwide sales of the Australian Nugget gold bullion coins begins.

April—Korea begins minting gold and silver coins to commemorate the 1988 Olympics.

April 30—By a vote of 5-2, Nevada's Senate Taxation Committee kills legislation for a tax on gold mined in Nevada.

May—The New York Commodities Exchange temporarily shortens trading hours to catch up on a backlog of orders for silver and gold futures.

June 16—Chicago Mercantile Exchange resumes trading gold futures after a two-year hiatus.

July 1—U.S. Mint begins production of gold and silver Bicentennial of the Constitution commemorative coins.

July—The Columbus-America Discovery Group locates the wreck of the SS *Central America,* which sank off the coast of South Carolina in 1857 with tons of gold coins and bars aboard.

Aug. 9—More than 200,000 mine workers in South Africa strike for higher wages and improved benefits; during the three-week strike, some 320,000 ounces of gold production is lost and more than 40,000 miners are fired.

Oct. 13—Britain unveils its new Britannia gold bullion coin.

Oct. 19—Dramatic crash of world stock markets sends many investors scurrying for cover in precious metals.

Dec. 14—Daily price of gold briefly exceeds $500 per ounce for the first time since February 1983.

1988

March—South Dakota exempts the state's gold and silver Bison bullion pieces from state sales taxes.

April—The Chicago Board of Trade receives Commodity Futures Trading Commission approval to begin trading 100-ounce gold futures.

July 1—Taiwan Parliament approves a proposal to eliminate the 5 percent sales tax on gold trading.

Oct. 19—Tokyo Commodity Exchange for Industry begins spot gold trading.

1989

March—The official *China Daily* newspaper reports government intentions of raising the state purchasing price of gold by almost 50 percent in an attempt to curb widespread smuggling.

April 1—Japan's 3 percent consumption tax takes effect, lowering tax on precious metal coins from 15 percent, but taking gold bullion, which was previously untaxed.

April—Turkey opens official gold market to halt gold smuggling and raise trading standards.

June 9—Governor of Texas signs bill removing 4.12 percent sales tax on gold bullion, bars, ingots and coins in transactions greater than $1,000.

June 14—U.S. Mint begins production of gold and silver coins commemorating the Bicentennial of the U.S. Congress.

Sept. 1—A New York law exempting transactions exceeding $1,000 of precious metal bars and bullion coins from a 4 percent state sales tax becomes effective; coins produced by South Africa and coins and bars not produced for investment purposes are not eligible for the exemption.

September—Salvors begin recovering gold coins and ingots from the wreck of the SS *Central America*.

September—Newmont Gold Co. announces the production of its 1 millionth ounce of gold in 1989, reportedly the first time a gold company has produced 1 million troy ounces of gold within a single year in North America.

September—Canada announces plans for series of gold, platinum and silver coins to commemorate the 10th anniversary of the Maple Leaf; Soviet Union announces platinum, palladium, gold and silver commemorative coins depicting events in Russian history; private Pobjoy Mint in the United Kingdom issues gold and silver Cat coins for Isle of Man.

Nov. 6—Pakistan lifts 30-year ban on private imports of gold to discourage smuggling.

1990

February—Svzal, a Soviet-Alaskan joint venture,

is established to develop mineral deposits and market mining technology in the Soviet Union and North America.

February—Sales of 1990 American Eagles begin as gold coins are shipped the first week of February. The Mint reports it sold 14,150 ounces of gold American Eagles in January. Sales of the 1-ounce coins at 13,000 are about 50 percent less than for the same coin in December.

March 15—The Mint reports it sold 26,000 ounces of gold American Eagles in February.

March 28—President George H.W. Bush presents a national gold medal honoring Jesse Owens to his widow.

April—American Eagle gold sales for April "stabilize" after March's sharply lower gold prices. The combined March-April sales totaled 93,000 ounces, with more gold sold in March than in April.

May 4—Mint officials announce that they will limit mintages for the Proof American Eagles by predetermining the maximum number of coins that will be produced and sold.

May—Sales of gold American Eagles for the month total 40,000 ounces.

July 16—Congress authorizes a $5 gold coin commemorating Mount Rushmore.

August—Sales of gold American Eagles for the month (70,000 ounces) are approximately triple July sales.

Sept. 25—The 1-ounce Australian Kangaroo Nugget sells out at 300,000 pieces.

Sept. 30—The Mint reports it had delivered 13,000 0.845-inch gold medals commemorating the Young Astronauts Program, and 38 3-inch gold medals.

Oct. 3—Congress authorizes a gold $5 coin commemorating the 1992 Olympic Games.

1991

Jan. 1—Canadian Goods and Services Tax takes effect. However, bullion coins such as the Canadian Maple Leaf are exempt.

Feb. 6—United States Mint's Office of Public Affairs states that 126,000 ounces of gold in the form of American Eagle coinage has been sold since beginning of the year.

April 2—A Pennsylvania coin dealer warns that U.S. service personnel may unwittingly bring back counterfeit gold upon return from duty in Operation Desert Storm after seeing at least one counterfeit coin the dealer described as "beautiful ... but counterfeit."

April 15—European Community lifts ban on the importation of the South African Krugerrand gold bullion coins as the South African government moves to end its policy of "apartheid."

May 27—Gibraltar issues a circulating gold coin intended to serve as an international currency within the 12-member European Community.

July 10—President George H.W. Bush lifts sanction against importation of South African Krugerrands to the United States.

July—Sales of gold American Eagles for the entire month down drastically. July 1990 saw 19,500 1-ounce coins sold. July 1991, though unreported by the Mint, believed to be below 2,500 1-ounce coins.

Sept. 17—A one-sentence bill is introduced in Congress to lift the U.S. ban against importation of gold coins from Russia.

Dec. 12—Announcement made that 1992 American Eagle gold bullion coins will bear the date in Arabic numbers instead of Roman numerals. Sales for the 1-ounce, half-ounce and quarter-ounce coins reach lowest yearly output since inception of program in 1986.

1992

Jan. 21—Final mintage figures for 1991 American Eagle coinage are released by the Mint. Overall, coin production for the year is the lowest since 1986.

April 21—The Industry Council for Tangible Assets gives testimony at an Internal Revenue Service hearing to encourage regulators to make a distinction between coin dealers and securities brokers for purposes of reporting requirements involving gold bullion and other tangible assets.

July 2—Florida Gov. Chiles signs into law a 6 percent sales tax that applies to sales of gold bullion. A petition is circulated among coin dealers requesting an exemption on bullion deals over $1,000.

August—A Canadian precious metals firm is awarded a three-year contract by the United States Mint for the fabrication of gold blanks for the American Eagle.

Sept. 4—Central Banks of Europe make it known that they have been selling gold in increasing volumes. Reductions in gold stockpiles are identified in Canada, United Kingdom and Austria.

December—Numerous precious metals dealers report to the press that sales of gold bullion coins have "nearly tripled" in anticipation of Bill Clinton taking office as president of the United States.

1993

February—Uruguay announces that its Banco Central del Uruguay will issue bullion coins in gaucho denominations. The 1-gaucho coin will contain 1 troy ounce of gold.

April—The United States Mint conducts a study to learn about the public's consideration of bullion and bullion-related products, including the American Eagle.

May 14—The spot price of gold suddenly springs to life and closes at $368 per ounce.

June 11—World Gold Council announces ambitious $6 million plan to promote the sale of gold bullion coins. The theme of the plan is "Liquid, Solid, Gold."

October—Announcement made that the once-banned South African Krugerrand gold bullion coin will be marketed in the United States and Europe in a "renewed" campaign, according to a spokesperson for the South African Mint Co. (Pty) Ltd. in Pretoria.

Dec. 10—Gold closes at $382.30, nearly $50 higher than the beginning of the year. American Eagle gold 1-ounce coins are poised to outsell last year's totals by 200,000 coins.

1994

February—Australia launches sales of 1994 gold, silver and platinum bullion coins in the United States. Investors may purchase gold coins in a size as large as 1 kilo or 10 ounces.

February—The United States Mint reports that the American Eagle gold coin has regained its position as the No. 1 selling investment bullion coin in the world—a position not held since 1987 shortly after the American Eagle program began.

March 8—Japan announces that it will melt about 4.25 million commemorative gold coins struck in the 1980s and 1990s to make up a revenue shortfall. The coins will be cast into ingots and sold beginning April 1.

May—Officials announce that British "escape" coins—those placed in survival kits of English soldiers during Operation Desert Storm—will be sold by the British Royal Mint. The 16,613 gold sovereigns recovered from the survival kits would be sold in late 1994.

June 21—President Clinton presents a three-coin World Cup Soccer set to Mexican President Carlos Salinas Gotari, in recognition of the introduction of direct sales of United States Mint bullion coins into Mexico.

July 21—Legislation is introduced in the U.S. Senate to expand the scope of bullion or numismatic items that can be placed into Individual Retirement Accounts.

September—War-torn Serbia (in Yugoslavia) issues a circulating gold coin in an attempt to ensure confidence in local currency system.

December—After reaching nearly half a million ounces in American Eagle 1-ounce gold coin sales in 1993, totals fell back to a more modest 221,633 1-ounce coins in 1994. On Dec. 9, 1994, gold closed at $376.50, just a few dollars less than one year ago.

1995

February—Legislation proposed by Sens. William Roth and John Breaux seeks to expand the scope of bullion-related items that can be placed in IRAs. Legislation had passed twice before in 1992 but was vetoed by President George H.W. Bush.

March—The Columbus-America Discovery group reports that there may be more gold remaining in the SS *Central America* shipwreck than the already recovered 2 tons of gold coins and bars.

April 10—Gold closes the day at $389.30 an ounce and has traded in a very narrow range for four months.

July—The U.S. Mint announces that premiums will rise on the silver American Eagle coin, but

remain the same on the gold American Eagle coins.

Oct. 3—London dealer Stephen Fenton purchases a 1933 double eagle along with other gold coins.

Oct. 16—The U.S. Supreme Court denies the appeal of a group of insurers claiming rights to more than 2 tons of gold from the 19th century shipwreck of the SS *Central America.*

Oct. 20—The use of gold in coinage dropped by 50 percent in 1994, according to a report by The Gold Institute in Washington, D.C. World usage of gold in coins in 1993 was 5 million ounces. In 1994, usage was pegged at 2.5 million ounces.

December—Republican presidential candidate Steve Forbes announces that he wants to peg the U.S. dollar to the value of gold. This procedure known as the "gold standard" ceased in the United States in 1934.

December—Gold by the ounce remains in a holding pattern for the entire year. Its price on Dec. 8 is $388.80.

1996

Feb. 8—Federal agents arrest Stephen Fenton and Jaspar "Jay" Parrino in New York City after they offer to sell agents a 1933 double eagle.

Feb. 12—The Mint reveals that sales of the 1-ounce American Eagle gold coin are the lowest—221,633 coins—since the program's inception in 1986.

Feb. 26—The Keston collection of superb U.S. Gold Coinage does very well at auction despite sagging prices for gold bullion. The collectibles market for gold continues to separate itself from the precious metals market.

March 4—Officials announce the recovery of the 1933 double eagle seized Feb. 8. The coin is pronounced genuine shortly thereafter.

April 2—Canada continues to unveil commemorative gold coins, this time the $200 face value coin commemorating the Transcontinental Landscapes. The coin is targeted for numismatists and collectors, not the bullion market.

Nov. 25—The U.S. Mint floats the idea of changing the American Eagle gold bullion coins to .9999 fine from their current .9167 fineness.

Dec. 2—Federal judge awards 92.4 percent of the salvaged gold from the shipwreck SS *Central America* to an Ohio group of investors. The bullion value of the gold alone was placed at $21 million in 1993.

Dec. 16—A Proof 1907 Saint-Gaudens double eagle sells for $825,000, a record price for a single U.S. gold coin.

1997

Jan. 27—The Mint announces that the 1-ounce American Eagle has recorded record low sales and production for the third straight year. Total mintage of the 1-ounce coin in 1996 was 189,148.

April 22—Colorado governor vetoes legislation barring sales of gold bullion coins from state sales tax. Similar battles ongoing in Florida and California.

July 21—Officials of the U.S. Mint announce that 251,000 1-ounce American Eagle gold coins have been sold through mid-year, a pace much greater than in 1996. The mid-year total was already greater than 1996's total output.

Oct. 24—Gold hits a 12-year low closing at $308.60 per ounce. Swiss National Bank reports it will possibly sell 1,400 tons of its gold holdings.

Nov. 26—Gold reaches another 12-year low, going through the psychologically important $300 barrier to close at $297.50.

1998

Feb. 23—As gold remains in record low territory, American Eagle sales at the Mint top 100,000 for the month of January, a selling pace not encountered since 1986.

May 11—Central bank sales have stopped or slowed. Gold climbs to $310 an ounce.

July 13—A Des Moines, Iowa, family wins a court ruling that they must be paid rental payments in the form of gold coins. The clause goes back to law made in 1917. The rental payment due totals $460,000.

July 20—The Mint reports a torrid pace for the sales of American Eagle bullion coins, in particular the 1-ounce coin, which had January to June sales of 508,500.

Sept. 21—Sales of the American Eagle 1-ounce coins tops 1 million for the first time since 1987. Gold closes at $270 an ounce, nearing 20-year lows.

1999

Feb. 15—The Mint reports sales of the 1-ounce American Eagle coins to be the largest since the program's inception in 1986. Total sales of the 1-ounce coins in 1998 are 1,468,530. That total is more than six times the sales of the same coins in 1996.

April 12—Officials announce that Sotheby's will auction, in the fall, the 7.6 percent portion of gold awarded to the insurers in the salvage of the shipwreck SS *Central America*.

May 17—U.S. Mint officials announce that gold American Eagles account for 60 percent of all bullion coins sold on the world markets.

May 25—In a year in which gold bullion was expected to attract buyers (in part due to Y2K concerns), the price of gold reaches a fresh 20-year low at $270.80.

June 9—Gold reaches another fresh low as it closes at $260.20.

June 21—A single U.S. gold coin, a specimen of the 1907 Saint-Gaudens, Ultra High Relief $20 double eagle, sells for $1.21 million, a record for a U.S. gold coin.

July 23—Twelve Proof 2000-W Sacagawea .9167 fine gold dollars travel into space aboard space shuttle *Columbia*, the first U.S. space mission commanded by a woman.

Aug. 11 to 15—Collectors get their first look at gold recovered from the SS *Central America*, in an exhibit at the American Numismatic Association convention in a Rosemont, Ill., a suburb of Chicago. The insurer's 7.6 percent is exhibited.

Dec. 7—A federal appeals court halts the auction of the insurers' portion of gold recovered from the SS *Central America*, just hours before the Dec. 8 to 9 sale was set to begin in New York City, angering dealers and collectors already in the city for the auction. Thomas Thompson sought the injunction; he is the mastermind behind the discovery of the wreck and the recovery of the gold.

2000

Jan. 20—Investors, the California Gold Group, announce the sale of the portion of the SS *Central America* gold owned by the Columbus-America Discovery Group (totaling 92.6 percent), and unveil much of it in California.

Feb. 7—Gold hits its high point for the year, closing at $312.70 per ounce on the London market.

Feb. 10—A $4 million dollar display of gold coins and bars salvaged from the SS *Central America*, the Ship of Gold exhibit is displayed at the Long Beach Coin and Collectibles Expo. It later makes several stops at various venues.

March—Attorneys claim the 1933 double eagle confiscated by the government in 1996 is the King Farouk coin and thus is legal to own because the government granted Farouk an export license for the coin in 1944.

March 10—U.S. Mint Director Philip N. Diehl tells *Coin World* that a planned Proof gold coin bearing the Sacagawea dollar design would be a $5 rather than $1 denomination.

May 8—Sotheby's announces that treasure retrieved from the SS *Central America* will be auctioned in New York June 20 to 21, 2000.

June 21—Sotheby's auction "Treasures from the SS Central America" realizes $5,567,815 including a Justh and Hunter bar weighing 652.84 ounces (more than 54 pounds) that realized $308,000.

Oct. 27—Gold hits its low point for the year, closing at $263.80 per ounce on the London market.

Dec. 14—169 auction lots representing the crème de la crème of the gold coins and ingots from the SS *Central America* are sold at Christie's New York for $2,214,785.

2001

Jan. 25—Out-of-court settlement is reached in the case involving the 1933 double eagle seized in 1996. Government retains ownership of the coin but agrees to authorize its private ownership, with the coin to be offered at public auction. The proceeds of the auction will be split evenly between Stephen Fenton and the government. Officials state that the settlement does not make any other extant 1933 double eagles legal to own. Days later, the coin is taken from a vault at the Secret Service office at the World Trade Center in New York City, which would later be destroyed in the terrorist attacks on Sept. 11.

April 2—Gold hits its year-low, closing at $255.95 per ounce on the London market.

Aug. 20—A "provisional mint" established in a warehouse on the grounds of The Presidio—the former U.S. Army installation in San Francisco, begins production of gold commemorative pieces struck on a former San Francisco Mint coinage press employing modified transfer dies made from original round 1855 Kellogg & Co. $50 gold coin dies.

Aug. 21—The History Channel airs a four-part mini-series *Gold!*, chronicling the history, legends and passion surrounding gold.

Sept. 17—Gold hits its year-high, closing at $293.25 per ounce on the London market.

Oct. 29—Sotheby's and Stacks offer the Dallas Bank Collection of U.S. gold coins. Assembled by Texas oilman H. Jeff Browning during the 1970s, the collection realizes $7,769,000.

Oct. 31—A Treasury Department status report states that the Treasury owns more than 261.5 million fine troy ounces of gold with a "book value" of more than $11 billion as of Oct. 31, 2001, with 94.8 percent of the total stored securely in U.S. Mint vaults.

Nov. 7—Monaco Financial LLC announced that the company had sold an 80-pound pioneer gold assay bar retrieved from the SS *Central America* for a reported $8 million.

2002

Jan. 4—Gold is at its lowest point for the year, closing on the London market at $277.75 per ounce.

Jan. 25—The U.S. Mint announces that Sotheby's and Stack's have been selected to jointly sell the Farouk-Fenton example of the 1933 Saint-Gaudens gold $20 double eagle..

Feb. 1—U.S. Mint announces that at 143,605, the mintage of the 2001 American Eagle gold bullion coin is the lowest for the 16 years the coins have been produced, beating the prior low in 1996 which was a mintage of 189,148.

Feb. 25—American Numismatic Association opens "Una and the Lion," an exhibit displaying British gold coinage through the ages.

May 31—Gold increases 17 percent over the preceding four months, closing at $326.60 per ounce, rising above the $325 per ounce threshold for the first time since Oct. 5, 1999.

June 6—The 1933 Saint-Gaudens $20 gold double eagle believed to have been once owned by King Farouk of Egypt is displayed at the Long Beach Coin, Stamp & Collectibles Expo in Long Beach, Calif.

June 24—Documents acquired by *Coin World* through a Freedom of Information request indicate that gold Proof 2000-W Sacagawea dollars struck on American Eagle half-ounce 22-karat gold planchets were produced not once as the U.S. Mint had previously reported, but at least twice.

July 30—The Farouk-Fenton 1933 Saint-Gaudens $20 double eagle sells at Sotheby's in New York City for $7,590,000, representing a world record for a coin at auction. The anonymous winning bidder also paid $20 to monetize the coin. The coin carried a pre-auction estimate of $4 to $6 million.

Dec. 27—Gold reaches its highest point for the year, closing at $349.30 an ounce on the London market.

2003

April 7—Gold is at its lowest point for the year, closing at $319.90 an ounce on the London market.

July 16—The U.S. Mint reports that the Proof 2003-W American Eagle 1-ounce gold coin has sold out as a single-coin option, after just two months of sales.

Aug. 16—Odyssey Marine Exploration Inc. officials announce that a 19th century shipwreck, said to be carrying 20,000 gold $20 double eagles, has been found at the bottom of the Atlantic Ocean at the site of an 1865 Atlantic shipwreck identified as the SS *Republic.*

Nov. 21—A unique 1854 Kellogg and Co. $20 pioneer gold coin, graded Specimen 69 by Numismatic Guaranty Corp. is displayed at the Santa Clara (Calif) Coin, Stamp & Collectibles Expo.

Nov. 30—Odyssey Marine Exploration Inc. announces that marine salvagers have recovered more than 1,600 gold and silver coins at the site of the SS *Republic.*

Dec. 5—Gold closes at $400.25 on the London futures market, marking a rise of more than 50 percent in the last three years.

Dec. 31—Gold closes the year at its highest point, reaching $416.25 per ounce on the London market.

2004

January—Heritage Galleries & Auctioneers announces that it brokered a deal for a unique set of 1872 gold pattern coins, known as the "Amazonian set," for $3.3 million.

February—The Gold Marketing Group responsible for producing 2.5-ounce gold relic pieces made from melted gold ingots from the SS *Central America* announce that the "commemorative restrikes" have sold out.

April 5—The Perth Mint in Australia displays more than 120 gold bars from around the world. The International Gold Bar Exhibition includes gold bars, nuggets, coins, jewelry and gold industrial items.

May 10—Gold reaches its year-low point, closing at $375 per ounce in the London bullion market.

September—Attorney Barry H. Berke requests meeting with United States Mint officials on behalf of his clients, three members of the Langbord family—the daughter and grandsons of Israel Switt, the Philadelphia jeweler and dealer who in 1944 acknowledged selling nine 1933 double eagles. The family turns over to Mint officials 10 1933 double eagles for authentication but does not relinquish ownership rights to the coins. The existence of the coins is kept secret by all of the parties involved.

Oct. 5—The Austrian Mint unveils the world's largest gold coin, a 1,000-ounce Vienna Philharmonic bullion coin with a face value of €100,000 and a mintage of 15 pieces.

Oct. 6—A unique Anglo-Saxon gold penny, or mancus of 30 pence, that was struck at London during the reign of Coenwulf, King of Mercia (796 to 821), sells for a record price of £230,000, or $411,400, at a London Spink's auction, setting a record for a British coin.

Oct. 14—The finest certified 1933 Indian Head gold $10 eagle, graded Mint State 66, is sold at a Stack's auction in New York City for $718,750.

Nov. 16—Monaco Financial LLC of Newport Beach, Calif., announces that it has purchased a group of 23 Coronet gold $20 double eagles recovered from the wreckage of the SS *Republic* with a retail value in excess of $2.5 million.

Nov. 22—The London spot price of $447.80 an ounce represents a 16-year high for gold, which rose 72 percent since closing at a 22-year low of $255.95 an ounce on April 2, 2001.

Dec. 2—Gold finds its year-high at $454.20 an ounce on the London bullion market.

2005

Jan. 12—Three early Colonial American gold coins bearing the EB counter stamp of New York goldsmith Ephraim Brasher bring more than $6 million during the Platinum Night auction conduced by Heritage Numismatic Auctions in conjunction with the Florida United Numismatists coin convention.

Feb. 8—Gold is at its lowest point of the year at $411.10 an ounce on the London market.

March 16—One of only two known pattern 1907 Saint-Gaudens, Ultra High Relief gold double eagles with "Edge of 1906" sells for $488,750 at a Stack's auction in New York City.

April—The U.S. Mint announces that it plans to introduce .9999 fine gold investment coins in 2006, 10 years after Congress gave the secretary of the Treasury discretion to do so.

April 18—The collection of Louis Eliasberg Sr.'s world gold and minor crown coins realizes $10,411,246 at an American Numismatic Rarities/ Spink auction in New York City.

June 2—One of the finest known 1927-D Saint Gaudens gold double eagles, graded Mint State 66, is sold in a private treaty transaction for $1.65 million.

Aug. 11—U.S. Mint officials announce that the Mint has recovered the 10 examples of the 1933 double eagles turned over to the government by the Langbord family and secured them at the Fort Knox depository. The Mint states that the coins cannot be privately owned.

Sept. 19—Gold hits $466.70 an ounce in New York, representing a 17-year high price for gold.

Dec. 12—Gold is at its high-point for the year at $536.50 an ounce on the London market.

2006

Jan. 5—Gold is at its lowest point for the year, closing at $524.75 an ounce on the London market.

May 5—U.S. Mint officials suspend sales of Proof 2006-W American Eagle gold coins due to rapidly rising bullion prices.

May 12—Gold is at its highest point for the year, closing at $725 an ounce in the London bullion market.

May 18—U.S. Mint officials raise prices for Proof 2006-W American Eagle gold coins by 10 to 16.7 percent, depending on size, in reaction to rising gold prices.

June 20—The U.S. Mint releases the 2006 American Buffalo 1-ounce .9999 fine gold $50 coin.

June 22—Proof versions of the 2006-W American Buffalo .999 fine gold $50 coin go on sale from the U.S. Mint.

Aug. 10—The first public display of 10 1933 Saint-Gaudens gold $20 double eagles "recovered" by the Mint in 2004 takes place at the American Numismatic Association World's Fair of Money in Denver.

Aug. 11—A California Moffatt $10 pioneer gold coin graded Specimen 67 brings $948,750 at an American Numismatic Rarities auction in Denver.

Aug. 31—The U.S. Mint sells out of the 10,000 three-coin gold sets celebrating the 20th anniversary of the American Eagle coin program, in slightly more than 24 hours after first making the coins available.

Sept. 14—U.S. marshals and armed private security guards remove six massive gold ingots and an 1857-S Coronet gold double eagle from a multimillion dollar display of SS *Central America* gold presented at the Long Beach Coin, Stamp & Collectibles expo.

Nov. 8—A unique 1848 gold medal awarded to Gen. Zachary Taylor for victory at Buena Vista during the Mexican War brings $460,000 at a Stack's auction in New York.

Dec. 5—The Langbord family files suit in federal court against the Treasury Department and U.S. Mint officials, seeking return of the 10 1933 Saint-Gaudens double eagles in Mint custody.

2007

Jan. 10—The London PM fix of $608.40 an ounce represents gold's low point for the year.

June 19—The entire 40,000-coin mintage of the first two 2007-W First Spouse .9999 fine gold half-ounce $10 coins—the Martha Washington and Abigail Adams coins—sells out in less than two hours.

Aug. 10—U.S. Mint displays 12 Proof 2000-W Sacagawea .9167 fine gold dollars that traveled into space aboard space shuttle *Columbia* in July 1999. The presentation at the American Numismatic Association World of Money marks the coin' first public display.

Aug. 30—The Proof Thomas Jefferson Liberty First Spouse .9999 fine gold half-ounce $10 coin sells out in less than two hours.

Sept. 21—U.S. Mint temporarily halts sales of all Proof 2007-W American Eagle gold coins because of rising gold prices, one week after suspending sales of Uncirculated 2007-W American Eagle coins for the same reason.

Nov. 2—Gold closes at $806.80 per ounce on the New York Mercantile Exchange, marking a 28-year high for gold.

Dec. 28—Gold closes on a high note at $833.75 an ounce on the London bullion market.

2008

March 14—Gold breaks the $1,000-an-ounce barrier, closing at $1,003.50 an ounce in the London bullion market.

March 17—Gold finds its high point for the year, closing at $1,011.25 an ounce in the London markets.

May 26—A Roman gold aureus of Severus Alexander, struck A.D. 223, realizes $920,000 during Ira & Larry Goldberg's auction of the Millennia Collection, setting a price record for a Roman coin.

Aug. 15—U.S. Mint officials suspend sales of American Eagle 1-ounce gold $50 bullion coins to authorized purchasers and continue to ration sales of American Eagle silver bullion coins, reacting to unprecedented demand. The Mint resumes taking orders on Aug. 25 under allocation restrictions.

Oct. 13—A Humbert $50 pioneer gold slug realizes $460,000 during Bowers and Merena's Beverly Hills Rarities Sale on Sept. 13 in Beverly Hills, Calif.

Oct. 22—U.S. Mint announces that it will start striking the 2009 Saint-Gaudens, Ultra High Relief 1-ounce .9999 fine gold $20 double eagles sometime in late November, using blanks supplied by a competing foreign mint. The coin will have the diameter of a gold $10 eagle but be twice as thick, a configuration similar to an experimental piece struck in 1907.

Oct. 24—Gold is at its lowest point of the year, closing at $712.50 an ounce in the London markets.

Nov. 6—A unique 1755 Elizabeth I gold 20-ruble Russian pattern—the largest 18th century Russian denomination—realizes £1,782,500 or $2,820,091 during an auction by St. James's Auctions in association with Baldwin's. The London auction marks a world record price for a non-U.S. coin.

Nov. 22—An 1847 Victoria Gothic, Plain Edge British gold crown pattern realized 48.4 million yen, or approximately $511,055, in a Tokyo auction.

2009

Jan. 15—Gold finds its low point for the year, closing at $810 on the London bullion market.

Jan. 22—Sales of the Saint-Gaudens, Ultra-High Relief 1-ounce .9999 fine gold $20 double eagle coin begin, but Mint officials indicate that production will depend on the Mint's ability to obtain sufficient planchets to meet demand.

June 16—U.S. Mint announced that it would not be producing any 2009 American Buffalo .9999 fine gold 1-ounce $50 bullion coins for the investor market in 2009 and that production would be restricted to the Proof version.

July 6—Mint officials announce that contrary to earlier announcement from Mint, 2009 American Buffalo 1-ounce gold coins would be produced and sold, in both bullion and Proof versions.

July 21—National Gold Exchange Inc., one of the world's largest wholesale rare coin dealers, files a Chapter 11 bankruptcy petition just days after a bank seized its inventory that was being held as collateral.

Aug. 5—The unique 1849 Coronet gold $20 double eagle pattern from the National Numismatic Collection at the Smithsonian Institution is displayed with other rarities at the American Numismatic Association World's Fair of Money in Los Angeles.

Sept. 11—After a year below $1,000 an ounce, gold finally breaks the four-digit barrier again, closing at $1,008.25 an ounce in the London markets.

Oct. 6—The U.S. Mint announces that it will not strike Proof American Eagle silver dollars and gold $50 1-ounce coins for 2009. The decision causes anger in the collector community, particularly among collectors of the Proof silver coin. The Mint had struck the two Proof American Eagle coins every year starting in 1986.

Nov. 9—Gold breaks the $1,100-an-ounce barrier, closing at $1,106.75 an ounce in the London bullion market.

Dec. 2—Gold is at its year-high, closing at $1,212.50 an ounce in the London bullion market, breaking the $1,200 barrier for the first time.

2010

Jan. 29—Gold hits its yearly low point, closing at $1,078.50 an ounce on the London bullion market.

June 25—A Canadian Maple Leaf gold $1 million coin brings "melt" value or $4,027,530 at a Vienna auction.

Aug. 10—The "Ship of Gold" California Gold Rush-era exhibit of treasure recovered from the 1857 shipwreck of the SS *Central America* is displayed at the American Numismatic Association World's Fair of Money in Boston.

Sept. 1—U.S. Mint announces that it will offer Proof 2010-W American Eagle gold coins in all four sizes.

Sept. 29—Gold breaks the $1,300-an-ounce barrier for the first time in history, closing at $1,307.50 on the London gold market.

Nov. 9—Gold hits its yearly high, closing at $1,421 an ounce on the London bullion market. This also marks the first time that gold closes above $1,400 an ounce.

2011

Jan. 6—A 1907 Indian Head, Wire Rim $10 eagle, graded Mint State 67, sells at a Heritage Auction in conjunction with the Florida United Numismatists show for $2.185 million.

April 20—Gold closes at $1,501 on the London

PM fix, breaking the $1,500-an-ounce level.

May 4—Gold closes at $1,541 an ounce on the London PM fix; prices begin falling the next two days, closing at $1,486.50 on May 6 on the London market.

May 24—Gold closes at $1,527 an ounce on the London market.

London Gold Bullion Market
Monthly Average Price 1968 to 2010
Courtesy of www.kitco.com

Year	High	Low	Average	Year	High	Low	Average
1975	$185.25	$128.75	$161.02	1993	$405.60	$326.10	$359.77
1976	$140.35	$103.50	$124.84	1994	$396.25	$369.65	$384.00
1977	$167.95	$121.00	$147.71	1995	$395.55	$372.40	$384.17
1978	$242.75	$160.90	$193.22	1996	$414.80	$367.40	$387.77
1979	$512.00	$216.85	$306.68	1997	$362.15	$283.00	$330.98
1980	$850.00	$485.75	$612.56	1998	$313.15	$273.40	$294.24
1981	$599.25	$391.25	$460.03	1999	$325.50	$254.20	$278.88
1982	$481.00	$296.75	$375.67	2000	$312.70	$263.80	$279.11
1983	$509.25	$374.50	$424.35	2001	$293.25	$255.95	$271.04
1984	$405.85	$307.50	$360.48	2002	$349.30	$277.75	$309.73
1985	$340.90	$284.25	$317.26	2003	$416.25	$319.90	$363.38
1986	$438.10	$326.30	$367.66	2004	$454.20	$375.00	$409.72
1987	$499.75	$390.00	$446.46	2005	$536.50	$411.10	$444.74
1988	$483.90	$395.30	$436.94	2006	$725.00	$524.75	$603.46
1989	$415.80	$355.75	$381.44	2007	$833.75	$608.40	$695.39
1990	$423.75	$345.85	$383.51	2008	$1,011.25	$712.50	$871.96
1991	$403.00	$344.25	$362.11	2009	$1,212.50	$810.00	$972.35
1992	$359.60	$330.25	$343.82	2010	$1,421.00	$1,078.50	$1,224.53

Silver

Chemical symbol: Ag
Atomic number: 47
Atomic weight: 107.868
Density @ 293k: 10.5 g/cm^3

Silver, a brilliant white metal, is second only to gold in malleability. It is harder than gold, has a high resistance to corrosion and is an excellent conductor of heat and electricity.

Silver was used for decorative purposes as far back as 4000 B.C., as a standard of value by 3500 B.C. and was widely used in coinage by 450 B.C.

Silver mining and refining

Most of the silver presently mined occurs in the native condition, that is, as an alloy of silver and some other metals. Most of this native silver is finely dispersed throughout other metals. Traditional mining techniques, then, are used to bring silver out of the ground.

Silver can be extracted from its ores using a variety of methods. The amalgamation process involves treating ores with water and mercury; the cyanidation process uses pulverized ore that is treated with sodium cyanide. Crude silver can be smelted, yielding a gold-silver alloy called dore.

Since gold and silver often occur together, as in forming dore, several methods are employed to separate and purify them. Electrolysis is one (see section on gold), the parting method is another. In the parting method, the dore, a very high-purity gold and silver bullion, is bathed with hot concentrated sulfuric or strong nitric acid, and the silver dissolves. Once the gold is removed, the silver is precipitated using ferrous sulfate, copper or iron.

The crime of silver

The following appeared, in large part, in a Federal Reserve Bank of San Francisco *Monthly Review* supplement, reprinted in *Coin World* in 1969. It is updated to include significant events of the 1970s through the first decade of the 21st century:

Populist orators, finding no rational explanation for the grinding deflation that racked the nation's economy before the turn of the 19th century, argued that hard times were the result of a monstrous conspiracy organized by London bankers and their Wall Street minions. When asked for evidence, these orators automatically cited the "Crime of 1873"—the (temporary) demonetization of silver.

"A crime, because it has brought tears to strong

men's eyes and hunger and pinching want to widows and orphans. A crime because it is destroying the honest yeomanry of the land, the bulwark of the nation. A crime because it has brought this once great republic to the verge of ruin, where it is now in imminent danger of tottering to its fall." (*Coin's Financial School*)

The Populists denounced this "crime" so fervently because they equated the dethronement of silver with a deliberate policy of deflation. In their eyes, the "crime" was compounded in 1900 with the formal adoption of the gold standard, and it was only partly assuaged in the 1930s with the discarding of gold as a domestic means of payment and the adoption of a silver-purchase program.

Yet, in the late 1960s when the Treasury ceased redeeming silver certificates in silver and began to mint quarter dollars and dimes out of baser metals, few observers if any suggested that the republic was on the verge of ruin. Aside from a few nostalgic editorials, the news of this final dethronement of monetary silver was confined to the financial pages.

The nation easily survived this latest episode in silver's checkered career, in large part because the turn-of-the-century monetary battles had eventually led to the enactment of the Federal Reserve Act, and thus to the institution of flexible methods of monetary control.

However, more to the point, this time it was silver's rebirth as an industrial and artistic material that contributed to its problems as a monetary metal.

Speculative excesses undoubtedly helped drive silver prices upward in the 1960s and 1970s, but a more basic reason for the upsurge was a deficit in the major sources of supply—Western mines and Treasury stockpiles—in relation to the significant increase in worldwide demand for silver. Because of its varied characteristics—silver is foremost in electrical and thermal conductivity, highest in optical reflectivity, and second only to gold in ductility—silver has gained new luster among dentists as well as debutantes, and among spacemen as well as shutterbugs, though silver's once-prominent role in photography has been greatly reduced with the transition from film photography to digital photography.

The speculation of the 1960s and 1970s was closely involved with the metal's dazzling price performance during the decade of the 1960s. The major episodes in silver's earlier monetary history, by way of contrast, were products of prolonged price declines for silver, and for everything else, in the Great Depression of the 1890s and the even greater catastrophe of the 1930s. So, just as the "Crime of '73" epitomized the earlier time of monetary troubles, the virtual repetition of that act may well typify silver's new-found period of prosperity.

Yesterday's silver

Since a major chapter in silver's long emotion-drenched monetary history ended in the 1960s, some perspective may be gained from a review of the legislative highlights. The record dates back to 1792 when the new nation set up two units of value: a gold dollar containing 24.75 grains of pure gold and a silver dollar containing 371.25 grains of pure silver.

Silver's monetary value of $1.2929 per ounce, although not defined in such terms in the law, could be derived by dividing the number of grains in an ounce (480) by the number of grains of pure silver in the silver dollar (371.25). Silver's monetary value was still measured in the same way in the 1960s but that apparently was the only sign of stability that could be found in the metal's volatile behavior.

The Founding Fathers—specifically Alexander Hamilton—had opted for a bimetallic standard, with the unit of account and all types of money kept at a constant value in terms of gold and in terms of silver. Practically, however, an alternating standard developed because of the implacable workings of Gresham's Law, the principle that bad money drives good money out of circulation. Although the relative values of the two metals at the Mint were constant by legal definition, the relative values in commodity markets fluctuated continuously, producing "bargain" prices at the Mint now for one metal and again for the other; the metal that was overvalued at the Mint consistently drove out of monetary use the metal that was undervalued for such purposes.

The original 15-1 Mint ratio of silver to gold (by weight of equivalent value) was below the market ratio existing at that time and the consequent gold outflow tended to make silver the nation's standard money until the 1830s. Gold was then revalued, however, and the resultant 16-1 Mint ratio caused a reversal of the situation and led to a disappearance of silver.

Debts and debtors

Then came the Civil War, followed by the losing 30-year battle on the part of debtor groups to maintain prices at the high wartime levels at which they had contracted their debts. The postwar price decline had developed partly because of the cessation of the war-induced demand for commodities and partly because of the sudden build-up in farm surpluses resulting from the rapid expansion of the Trans-Mississippi West—but also because of a shift in monetary policy toward contraction of the paper currency and resumption of specie payment.

The struggle of Populist farmers and other debtors to restore wartime price levels through currency inflation was led initially by the Greenbackers. That doughty group, which demanded the redemption of war bonds in paper and not in gold, suffered a crucial defeat when the administration resumed specie payments in 1879. But even before that event the inflationists had arrived at the view that they could attain their ends by injecting silver into the monetary system at an inflated ratio.

In accordance with Gresham's Law, silver at the 16-1 Mint ratio had been undervalued and had long since disappeared from circulation. In fact, such a long time had elapsed since any silver had been presented to the Mints for coinage that Congress in 1873 stopped the further minting of the standard silver dollar and thereby effectively demonetized silver. Whether deliberately or through oversight, Congress simply failed to include in a long, very detailed and technical revision of the coinage laws any provision for the continuing coinage of the standard (371.25-grain) silver dollar. Thus was the "Crime of '73" perpetrated.

No cries of outrage greeted the event at the time it occurred, since every ounce of silver was then worth $1.30. However, within three years the situation altered drastically. The price of silver dropped to $1.16 and below, on the heels of a glut occasioned by the opening of new mines in Nevada and the closing of silver markets in the new gold-standard countries of western and southern Europe.

The Populists cried conspiracy, for if silver could have been coined freely at the old 16-1 ratio the debtors could have paid their debts with the easier-to-earn silver. In order to repair the ravages of the crime, therefore, these inflationists demanded that Congress restore the free and unlimited coinage of silver at the old 16-1 ratio.

The best they could obtain, however, was the passage of the Bland-Allison Act of 1878, which required the Treasury to buy not less than $2 million of silver every month for coinage or for backing of silver certificates. However, the net increase in paper currency, which amounted to $253 million in the 1879 to 1890 period, failed to match the hopes of the backers of this legislation. The new silver certificates simply took the place of national bank notes, which were being retired in connection with the reduction of the national debt.

The price of silver dropped to 94 cents an ounce within the following decade, so the inflationists demanded that more be done. This time the best they could accomplish was the passage of the Sherman Silver Purchase Act of 1890, in a trade whereby Westerners voted for a tariff bill that they disliked while Easterners voted for a silver bill that they feared.

The Sherman Act directed the secretary of the Treasury to buy 4.5 million ounces of silver bullion—almost the entire domestic production—every month. The bullion was to be paid for through the issue of new legal-tender Treasury notes, which were to be redeemable in either gold or silver—a provision that permitted an "endless chain" of gold withdrawals in the panic of 1893.

Despite these efforts, the Sherman Act did not succeed in its purpose. It failed to raise the price of silver, and it failed to increase the amount of money in circulation and to reverse the steady decline in farm prices. (Sen. John Sherman's influence was far more lasting in the antitrust field.)

President Cleveland and other gold supporters wanted to abandon silver to its fate and to adhere formally to the gold standard. The silverites, on the other hand, continued to favor the unlimited coinage of silver and the pegging of the silver price at the traditional 16-1 ratio. For a while, Cleveland had his way; faced with the Panic of 1893 and with a substantial gold outflow that reduced the gold reserve below the tacitly recognized floor of $100 million, he forced through Congress the repeal of the Silver Purchase Act. Yet this led to his repudiation by his own party and to the mighty Populist upsurge that in 1896 brought William Jennings Bryan to the verge of the presidency.

Gold on the throne

Nonetheless, within four years the money question was no longer at the center of public controversy—in fact, was hardly in the public eye at all. Early in 1900 the victorious "goldbugs" secured the passage of an act providing that the gold dollar of 25.8 grains and .900 fine should be the unit of value and that all other forms of currency should be maintained at parity with this dollar. (Parity was to be maintained through a $150-million gold reserve that the Treasury would hold available for the redemption of paper money.) Then, later in 1900, Bryan's second defeat sealed the doom of silver as a dominant political issue.

The issue died out simply because of the long-awaited reversal of the downward trend in prices. Between 1896 (the low point) and 1914, the general price level increased 40 percent. But inflation and farm prosperity were achieved not through the Populists' chosen instrument, silver, but rather through several unexpected developments—developments related to the metal that they detested (gold) and to the center of the gold "conspiracy" that they despised (the city).

New gold discoveries in South Africa and North America, along with the development of new processes for extracting the precious metal from the ore, flooded the world with gold during these critical years. Over two decades, the amount of gold coinage increased by half, and thereby permitted a corresponding expansion of the currency supply. After 1896, therefore, the gold inflation helped bring about the happy situation that the farmers for so long had tried to win with silver. The evidence was apparent on every hand—wheat rising from 72 cents a bushel in 1896 to 98 cents a bushel in 1909, corn rising from 21 cents to 57 cents, and so on throughout a long list.

But the American city itself, and not simply the gold inflation, also saved the American farmer. Throughout that golden age, the foreign market for many of his products sharply declined. Yet, his income situation sharply improved because of the very thing that was cited as evidence of his political submergence—the great increase of the urban population. In 1890, 4.6 million American farms supplied a domestic urban population of 22 million; in 1910,

6.4 million farms supplied 42 million city-dwellers. The larger, more efficient and more mechanized farms that developed over those two decades produced an increasing part of their total produce for the home market (and less for the foreign market), under far more stable and advantageous conditions of transportation and finance than had prevailed in the past. Yet this favorable trend—labeled "From Pathos to Parity" by one historian—was achieved without any aid from the Populists' favorite weapon, silver inflation.

Silver in the 1930s

The second major development in silver's dramatic history occurred in another major period of deflation—the 1930s. Again a movement arose to halt a prolonged deflationary spiral by restoring currency values to the level at which wartime and postwar debts had been contracted. Again a remedy was proposed, in the Thomas Amendment to the Agricultural Adjustment Act of 1933, which envisioned both the printing of more paper money and unlimited coinage of silver. The amendment, in addition, authorized increased open-market purchases of government securities and a reduction in the gold content of the dollar.

The last-named of these alternatives received the most emphasis in the early New Deal days. Under the authority of the Gold Reserve Act of 1934, the value of the dollar was fixed at 59.08 percent of its formerly established (1900) value in terms of gold.

But much to the surprise of the theorists who influenced the administration's decision—theorists who posited a close relationship between the price level of commodities and the gold content of the monetary medium—the price level did not automatically respond. True enough, the wholesale price index increased somewhat in line with the general expansion of demand following the Depression low, but the increase was only about half of what the inflationists expected in view of the 41 percent reduction in the gold content of the dollar. Silver inflation, therefore, was brought forward as a supplement to the incomplete gold inflation—and as an answer to the perennial legislative demand to "do something for silver."

Since 1873, the downward trend in the price of silver had been interrupted only twice, during the silver-purchase period around 1890 and again during World War I. After the turn of the century, in fact, the market price rarely exceeded one-half the nominal Mint value.

Silver had remained in a monetary limbo with respect to new acquisitions; some was used for subsidiary coins, some circulated in the West in the form of standard silver dollars, and a roughly fixed stock of silver certificates remained as a relic of the 1890s. Thus, by the 1930s, only about 650 million ounces were in use as coin or as currency backing at the Treasury.

Government purchase

At the end of 1933, with the market price of silver standing at about 44 cents an ounce—75 percent above the Depression low—unlimited purchase of newly minted silver was initiated at $0.6464 an ounce under the authority granted by the Thomas Amendment. But inflationist pressure then brought about even further action, in the form of the Silver Purchase Act of 1934. Under its terms, the secretary of the Treasury was directed to purchase silver at home and abroad until the market price reached the traditional Mint price of $1.2929 an ounce, or until the monetary value of the Treasury's silver stock reached one-third of the monetary value of its gold stock. The support price at which purchases were made was changed on several different occasions during the ensuing dozen years; originally $0.6464, it was eventually set at $0.9050 in 1946.

Under the authority of the silver-purchase legislation of the 1930s and subsequent presidential proclamations, the Treasury acquired some 3,200 million ounces of silver—about half of it in the four-year period 1934 to 1937, and the remaining half of it in the subsequent quarter-century. A minor part (about 110 million ounces) consisted of silver that was "nationalized" in mid-1934, when the administration required nonmonetary silver to be turned in at $0.5001 per fine ounce, so as to capture the profits expected to be realized from the increased government purchase price. About 2,210 million ounces consisted of metal purchased abroad at prevailing market prices, and the remaining 830 million ounces consisted of newly minted domestic silver.

Until 1955, the Treasury support price for newly mined domestic silver was higher than the market price, so the U.S. government purchased domestic metal at the higher price while U.S. silver-using industries purchased low-priced foreign metal. However, from 1955 to late 1961, the market price approximated the support price, and silver users then began to purchase some supplies from the Treasury as well as from foreign and domestic mines.

In little more than a quarter-century, the Treasury purchased $2 billion in silver and sextupled the physical quantity used as currency or held in stockpiles. Nevertheless, the silver program during that period failed to achieve either of the objectives specified in the 1934 Silver Purchase Act: a market price equal to the monetary value of $1.2929, or a one-to-three ratio of the monetary stocks of silver and gold.

Before the 1960s and to the upsurge of world demand, market pressures failed to push prices above the $0.5001 floor. Meanwhile, the ratio of monetary silver to monetary gold stocks—both at their nominal monetary values—failed to reach the 1-3 target figure. (The ratio ranged around 1-5 in the pre-war period, then rose to 1-7 because of the early postwar gold inflow, and finally dropped to 1-4 during the following decade as gold began to flow out instead of in.) Then, when silver's supporters achieved the price upsurge they wanted, it turned out to be a mixed blessing indeed.

On its way up

Eventually, the market accomplished what a century's legislation could not do for the cause of silver price support. In the late 1950s, world consumption of silver increased about 4 percent annually, while world production rose only about 1.5 percent annually. Sales from Treasury stockpiles filled the gap—and held the price line—for almost a decade, but the depletion of stocks finally brought the process to a halt.

The first scene in a long-drawn-out final act occurred in late 1961. By that time, the worldwide industrial and coinage demand for silver approximated 300 million ounces annually, about half of which was American demand, whereas worldwide production approximated 235 million ounces annually, about one-sixth of which was from American mines. The gap had to be filled by sales from the Treasury's "free silver" stocks—that is, stocks that were not earmarked for currency backing or coinage.

The Treasury's supply of free silver had reached its peak in early 1959 at 222 million ounces. However, by the end of 1960, half that supply was gone and by late 1961, only 22 million ounces were left. There remained, however, nearly 1,700 million ounces in a bullion reserve held against the issuance of part of the nation's paper currency. About one-fourth was held against $5 and $10 silver certificates, and the remainder was used to support $1 and $2 silver certificates. The larger denominations could have been issued in the form of Federal Reserve notes, but then-existing legislation authorized only silver certificates for the smaller denominations.

The legislative stage was thus set for the beginning of the final act. In November 1961, President Kennedy wrote Treasury Secretary Dillon, "I have reached the decision that silver metal should gradually be withdrawn from our monetary reserves"—and with that, he instructed the secretary to suspend further sales of the Treasury's free silver, to suspend the use of free silver for coinage, and to obtain the silver required for coinage needs through the retirement from circulation of $5 and $10 silver certificates. By this measure, some 400 million ounces of the total reserve of 1,700 million ounces were released for coinage purposes. (Interpreting the president's statement as a Treasury withdrawal from the supply side of the market, the market responded with a 10 percent jump in price the very next day, and with a further 30 percent rise the following year.)

The next scene occurred with the passage of Public Law 88-36 (June 1963). The act repealed the Silver Purchase Act of 1934 and subsequent silver legislation, repealed the tax on transfers of interest in silver bullion, and confirmed the redeemability of silver certificates for silver dollars or bullion at the monetary value of $1.2929 an ounce. However, in particular, it authorized the issuance of Federal Reserve notes in the smaller denominations, thereby providing for the eventual elimination of silver as backing for $1 and $2 bills. The new policy, in effect, "provided for the eventual demonetization of silver except for its use in subsidiary coinage."

In congressional hearings that preceded the passage of this new law, Secretary Dillon argued that the new legislation would not mean the disappearance of the silver dollar, since the Treasury had ample supplies of "cartwheels" and other traditional coins. However, the market felt otherwise, and soon thereafter staged the dramatic epilogue to the Act of 1963—the great silver rush of 1964.

Part of the explanation was the inability of the Philadelphia and Denver Mints to keep up with the public's burgeoning demand for coin. The amount of circulating coin, which had increased roughly 50 percent in the first postwar decade, more than doubled in the following decade because of increased use for vending machines, sales taxes, school lunches, parking meters and coin telephones—and because of the insatiable demands of the growing band of coin collectors and speculators.

The Bureau of the Mint, intent on supplying the public demand for minor coin, had not minted standard silver dollars during the entire post-war periods; in fact, the last of these "cartwheels" were made in 1935. Yet, for some time, there appeared to be no problem. Out of a total supply of 485 million silver dollars, about one-third were circulating in 1950, and about two-thirds in 1960. Then the outflow increased sharply and accelerated even more in the months following the enactment of the new silver legislation.

As Treasury stocks continued to fall, at least one Treasury official began to recommend that preparations be made to resume the production of silver dollars. On Feb. 28, 1963, Mint Director Eva Adams wrote to Assistant Treasury Secretary Robert A. Wallace to recommend that funding be requested to make 100,000 new silver dollars during the first year of production—a cost she estimated at $800,000 plus the cost of the metal. Members of Congress began debating the resumption of silver dollar, with most of support coming from Western senators in whose districts silver dollars circulated widely.

By the summer of 1963, top Treasury officials had agreed with Adams that silver production should be resumed, though the decision was not universally supported in the department. In response to Adams' suggestions about design selections, Wallace ordered Adams to use the "pre-World War I" design—what collectors call the Morgan dollar.

The Denver Mint was selected as the production plant for the new dollars, and as 1963 progressed, officials and workers at the Colorado began work on the project. The assassination of President Kennedy on Nov. 22, however, led Mint officials to halt these preparations for a dollar coinage. Attention was instead directed at meeting the continuing demand for smaller silver denominations and for striking a new design half dollar honoring the martyred president.

Meanwhile, the Treasury inventory of silver dollars continued to fall in numbers. Only 28 million silver dollars were left in Treasury hands at the beginning of 1964. Many of them entered circulation by early March, and then, when the House Appropriations Committee rejected a Treasury request for authorization to begin minting these pieces again, the rush was on. In two weeks' time the Treasury shipped out more than 11 million pieces to the tradition-loving Western states—and meanwhile distributed more than 3 million pieces to a jostling, haggling crowd that besieged the Treasury building in search of choice Morgan dollars of turn-of-the century vintage.

Out of the temple

Only 2.9 million "cartwheels" were left when, in the *Wall Street Journal's* description, "Secretary Dillon drove the money changers out of his temple." Exercising the option open to him under the terms of the 1963 legislation, the secretary decreed that silver certificates thenceforth would be redeemable only in silver bullion at the monetary value of $1.2929 per ounce. Holders of silver certificates could continue to exercise their legal right to demand an amount of silver precisely equal to the silver content of a standard silver dollar, but they would be assured of getting only several slivers of metal in an envelope instead of a coin of considerable numismatic value.

Still, most observers continued to feel that silver dollars represented only a special case, and that a silver shortage was practically out of the question in the foreseeable future. In his 1963 congressional testimony, Secretary Dillon argued that, with the passage of the proposed legislation, the government's silver reserves would "assure an adequate supply of silver to meet our coinage requirements for the next 10 to 20 years." However, over the next two years alone, consumption of silver came to exceed all earlier expectations and it became readily apparent that even the Act of 1963 had failed to provide a lasting solution to the Treasury's problems.

Production of silver in the United States had fallen short of U.S. consumption consistently throughout the postwar period, but the gap began to widen appreciably after 1958. In fact, domestic production actually declined slightly from 1958 to 1963, while domestic consumption for coinage and industrial use rose sharply, from 124 to 222 million ounces. Therefore, the annual deficits increased from a sizeable 100 million ounces or so in the 1950 to 1958 period to an even more substantial 187 million ounces in 1963. Then, in 1964 the deficit jumped to 289 million ounces, as production remained level in the face of a soaring demand of 326 million ounces.

Moreover, the same type of situation existed elsewhere, as total world consumption (outside the Soviet Bloc) grew to more than 2½ times total new production. With total metal usage at 556 million ounces, the world supply deficit in 1964 amounted to 338 million ounces.

Foreign sources came to fill less and less of the U.S. deficit over the 1958 to 1963 period, because of the expanding needs for the metal abroad. At the same time, returns of lend-lease silver, which had been shipped out during World War II, dropped steadily, from a peak of 103 million ounces in 1958 to zero in 1963. In making up the growing deficiency, Treasury stocks receded by 523 million ounces in the five-year period, to 1,583 million ounces in 1963.

In 1964, moreover, foreign demand actually comprised a drain on Treasury stocks, and the United States became a net exporter of silver for the first time since the lend-lease shipments of World War II. Total exports during the year amounted to 110 million ounces, more than triple the 1963 figure, while imports declined from 64 to 55 million ounces. In meeting both this new export demand and the soaring domestic demand, Treasury stocks of the metal dropped 23 percent in 1964 alone, to 1,214 million ounces.

Hungry industries

An increase in industrial consumption of silver—mainly for use in photographic film, electronic components and storage batteries—helped to intensify the growing shortage. Industrial consumption in the United States, which had dropped from an annual average of 100 million ounces in the early 1950s to 86 million ounces in 1958, rose by more than 5 percent annually over the next five years, and then jumped 11 percent more in 1964, to 123 million ounces.

Overseas, the expansion in industrial consumption had been even more impressive, particularly in West Germany and Japan. Between 1950 and 1958, foreign industrial consumption doubled, and by 1964 it increased again by half to 163 million ounces. Thus, a shortage existed from industrial demands alone, since world industrial consumption exceeded total mine production by 71 million ounces in 1964.

The sharp upsurge in silver usage took place even in the face of a 40 percent increase in silver prices between November 1961 and June 1963. The demand for silver evidently was quite inelastic—unresponsive to an increase in price—because no known alternative equaled its high electrical and heat conductivity, resistance to corrosion and sensitivity to light.

Consumption of silver for photographic film, plates and sensitized paper—the largest single market in the United States for the metal—increased at an annual rate of about 2 percent between 1959 and 1963, and then jumped 20 percent, to 40.3 million ounces, in 1964 alone. The photographic industry's consumption would have increased even more rapidly had it not learned to economize on its supplies. By extracting silver from photographic solutions used in developing film, for example, it was able to reclaim as much as 10 million ounces in 1964.

Under the stimulus of the sharp run-up in silver prices, the photographic industry also accelerated its research aimed at the development of substitutes. In many of silver's most important applications, however, no other material could be found with silver's unique ability to record an image when exposed to light. (The only major alternative was the use of electrostatic copying methods in office equipment.) Because silver was all but indispensable to the photographic process, its use in this field tended to increase with the continued growth of the industry.

The electrical-equipment and electronics industry represented another rapidly growing outlet. Consumption of silver in these fields rose almost 50 percent between 1959 and 1964, from 20.5 to 30.3 million ounces, and, therefore, the electrical industry surpassed silverware and jewelry to become silver's second market.

Unequalled as an electrical conductor, silver's use as an electrical contact had expanded until it could be found in practically every on-off switch and electrical appliance. Silver-wire contact relays also were at the heart of most computers and almost every piece of telephone and aviation equipment. Besides, suitable substitutes were not available for applications accounting for perhaps three-fourths of the entire market—primarily voltage connections for space vehicle guidance systems, military electronic systems and the like.

Consumption in brazing alloys and solders, another rapidly growing field, expanded from 10.5 million ounces in 1959 to 15.8 ounces in 1964. During World War II the use of silver alloys as industrial joining metal gained impetus in the manufacture of shells, gun parts and ordnance. After the end of the war, silver brazing alloys became important in air-conditioning and refrigeration equipment, electrical appliances, and automobile parts—in fact, in virtually every end-product where joining or bonding was involved. An entirely new application also arose: silver-infiltrated tungsten for rocket fuels, as well as silver brazing alloys capable of withstanding heat and pressures generated at supersonic speeds. For these applications, which require high temperature soldering, substitution of other materials was completely impractical.

Consumption of silver in storage batteries, a relatively new use, almost tripled between 1959 and 1964, reaching 9 million ounces. Batteries using silver (in association with zinc or cadmium) can be recharged, and they are very useful for applications requiring high output in relation to weight, for example in spacecraft and portable tools and appliances. Because these batteries rely on the chemical reactivity of silver, the substitution of other materials again was impractical.

For all these reasons, the industrial demand for silver expanded inexorably in the early 1960s, even in the face of stable or declining demand for the metal in its more traditional uses. (Silver consumption for silverware and jewelry had actually declined, because of the rising price of sterling silver and the increas-

ing acceptance of modern design.) However, industry had to meet much of its rapidly increasing needs through the redemption of silver certificates. With each dollar exchangeable for .7734 ounce of silver, the availability of Treasury supplies held the market price at $1.2929, the level first reached in September 1963. However, because of this drain and additional withdrawals for speculative holdings and inventories, redemptions totaled 141 million ounces in 1964.

Coinage pull

Nevertheless, by far the largest drain on Treasury stocks resulted from the tremendous expansion in silver usage for coinage. The actual silver crisis might have been delayed for years had not a terrific coin shortage developed. Consumption of silver for U.S. coinage began to rise sharply in 1961 and doubled over the next two years, reaching 112 million ounces in 1963. Even with this, the demand could not be met, and the coin shortage turned critical around mid-1964.

At one time limited to relatively few geographical areas, to particular coins and to particular seasons of the year, the shortage eventually became a general problem affecting the entire economy. Merchants found it difficult and in some instances impossible to make change. Banks, unable to satisfy their customers' requests for coin, found it necessary to ration their supplies. In fact, coin rationing was instituted down the line—from the Mints, to the Federal Reserve, to the commercial banks, to the public.

A new type of entrepreneur, "the money merchant," appeared on the scene, acquiring coins by the bagful and selling them to the highest bidder. The American Bankers Association staged a "Calling All Coins" campaign, in an attempt to bring to market the large supply of coins stored in the nation's piggy banks. And one chain of food stores conceived of the idea of issuing scrip in denominations of 1, 5 and 10 cents, redeemable at the company's stores. (The chain dropped the plan when it found that it might be violating federal law.)

Some observers blamed the shortage on the growing use of some 12 million automatic coin-operated vending and service machines—ranging from parking meters and telephone pay stations to machines that dispense hot and cold drinks, sandwiches, candy, cigarettes, music and laundry and dry-cleaning services—and upon the growing coin requirements of toll roads, sales taxes and school lunches. Other observers simply traced the shortage to the burgeoning demands of a rapidly growing population and a rapidly expanding economy.

According to Treasury officials, the expansion in coin production should have been more than adequate to compensate for all these developments. From fiscal 1959 through fiscal 1964, the Mint had nearly tripled the production of coins, from 1.6 billion to 4.3 billion pieces—yet during that same period, population had increased only 8 percent, gross national product 28 percent and vending machine sales by 47 percent. Furthermore, the 48 billion coins available for circulation provided an average of 240 coins for every man, woman and child in the entire country.

The Committee on Government Operations, investigating the coin shortage, drew attention to the problem of availability as opposed to the actual supply of coins.

Large amounts had been placed in circulation, but large amounts had been withdrawn, by businessmen anxious to assure themselves of an adequate supply for the needs of trade, by the nation's 8 million to 10 million coin collectors, and by speculators, who bought up new coins by the roll, by the bag and even by the ton, in the hope of profiting from a possible increase in the price of silver or coin. Incidentally, vending industry spokesmen argued in their own defense that only about $22 million remained in their machines at any one time, although the vending machines swallowed some $3,500 million in coins every year.

As commercial banks found themselves with fewer and fewer coins, the "flowback" of coins returned to the Federal Reserve Banks had dropped sharply, from 11.4 billion coins in fiscal 1962 to only 6.7 million pieces in fiscal 1964. Deliveries of new coins from the Mint had risen, but the added supply had been more than offset by the drying up of return flows from circulation.

Coin shortage

By mid-1964, the return flow had shrunk to the point where it was less than the amount of new coins received from the Mint, whereas in more normal times the return flow was nine times as great as Mint deliveries. Consequently, the Federal Reserve Banks were unable to deliver coin on request and had to ration the limited supply.

The rise in the price of silver to $1.2929 an ounce—that is, the development of a situation where the silver dollar was worth a dollar of silver—had encouraged the run on the Treasury's depleted stock of silver dollars, as described earlier. Thus, broad new public interest in coins was stimulated when the Treasury found itself with less than 3 million silver dollars and, amidst great publicity, was forced to restrict redemption of silver certificates to bullion.

Whatever the reasons for the coin shortage, Treasury officials decided that it could be overcome only by a rapid and substantial increase in production. By flooding the economy with coins, they hoped to convince those who held them for speculative reasons that the market would soon be saturated.

The Treasury previously had planned to boost production at the existing Mint facilities gradually over time, while waiting for the completion of the new Philadelphia Mint, authorized by Congress in 1963. This new Mint was designed to have as much production capacity as the Denver and old Philadelphia Mints combined.

Events, however, forced the adoption of another approach. In mid-1964, the Treasury placed its two operating Mints on a round-the-clock seven-day-a-week intensified "crash program" in an attempt to double the annual production of coins from 4 to 8 billion in a year's time. It pushed into production all possible equipment and facilities—including the San Francisco Assay Office (which closed as the San Francisco Mint at the end of 1955 when its production facilities were deemed unnecessary), which was assigned to produce annealed planchets for 5-cent coins and cents—and also purchased metal strip for coinage from private industry. Moreover, it obtained congressional authorization to continue the 1964 date on new coins indefinitely, so that it could flood the market with 1964 coins and thus destroy the incentive for dealers and hoarders to divert such coins from normal commercial uses.

As 1964 ended, the Treasury was well along in its crash program. During that calendar year the Mint produced 5.5 billion coins, compared with 3.4 billion the year before—and in the second half of the year, it produced as many coins as in all of 1962. However, about 203 million ounces of silver were consumed during 1964's rapid upsurge of Mint production. In fact, about 73 million ounces alone went into the production of some 200 million 1964 Kennedy half dollars, which collectors, hoarders and souvenir hunters snapped up as soon as they went into circulation.

By early 1965, the director of the Mint was able to report a definite improvement in the coin situation. Businessmen were able to get through 1964, including a busy Christmas, without an actual crisis, even though consumer spending was up $26 billion (7 percent) for the year. The shortage of cents, which at one point had been critical, was completely relieved, while the shortage of 5-cent coins was almost over. Nonetheless, shortages continued in the minor silver coins, and the half dollar was not circulating at all.

At the same time, the problem of silver supplies had grown more acute. By June 1965, consumption for coinage purposes was running at a 300-million-ounce annual rate, and the Treasury's supply was down to 1,000 million ounces.

The Treasury thus faced the prospect of total depletion of its stocks within a relatively short period of time. In that event, the Mints would have had to stop coining dimes, quarter dollars and half dollars of the kind then in use. The Treasury would no longer be able to offer silver to all comers at $1.2929 an ounce. The price of the metal could rise beyond $1.3824—the point at which the silver content of these minor coins would be equal to their face value—and coins would begin to disappear from circulation. Obviously, drastic new action was required.

Silver dollar preparation resumes

Even as Treasury and Mint officials met the growing silver coinage crisis, debate continued at the Treasury Department and in Congress as to whether to resume silver dollar production. Consensus on the issue was elusive. While the two senators from Montana, where silver dollars circulated widely, championed the resumption of dollar production, funding for the coining had been removed from a House appropriations bill. The two senators reached a compromise with Treasury officials that permitted preparations to begin anew for silver dollar production. Congress funded the production July 28, 1964, with passage of the 1965 appropriations bill. President Johnson signed the measure Aug. 3.

Oddly, when the Denver Mint resumed its efforts, it prepared to strike new silver dollars of the Peace design of 1921 to 1935 and not of the old Morgan design. Why the switch was made is uncertain.

New dies began arriving at the Denver facility in October 1964 but no coins were struck immediately. Treasury approval to begin trial production of the dollars was granted in May 1965, using the 1964-dated dies. Approximately 322,394 pieces were struck. However, decisions were being made in Washington that would once and for all derail any plans to strike silver dollars routinely for release into circulation.

Demonetization of silver

The soaring industrial and coinage demand for silver and the rapid depletion of the government's silver stock forced the Treasury in May 1965, to make a momentous decision: "The world and the U.S. silver supply and production situation and outlook do not warrant continuation of the large-scale use of silver in the U.S. coinage" (*Staff Study of Silver and Coinage*).

Moreover, the Treasury argued for a once-and-for-all change; otherwise, subsidiary silver coinage undoubtedly could suffer from difficult transitional problems and from the fear of future changes in silver content.

Based on technical studies, the Treasury recommended copper-nickel clad on a copper core as the best metal for a new and permanent subsidiary coinage. This material had several desirable characteristics—ability to provide uninterrupted service as a medium of exchange; acceptability to the public in terms of weight, color, wearing qualities and operation in vending machines; ease and certainty of production; cost and availability; and compatibility with present coinage.

Copper-nickel was already the most widely used coinage material in the world. It was familiar as the basis for the American 5-cent piece, and it had circulated side by side with silver coinage in high-denomination coins in the United Kingdom. Coins of copper-nickel clad on a copper core could operate readily in vending machines without the difficulty, expense and inconvenience of modifying existing rejecters. Furthermore, the Mint had made sizeable production runs using the copper-nickel material and had not encountered any serious difficulties.

According to the Treasury, the cost of the alloy—45 cents a pound, based on 33-cent copper and

79-cent nickel—would be much less than silver at $18.81 a pound. Coinage at the projected fiscal 1965 rate would require approximately 5,355 short tons of copper and 1,785 short tons of nickel annually. In both cases, the tonnages would represent a small fractional part of total domestic consumption and could be drawn from surpluses in the strategic stockpile.

Many of these Treasury recommendations were contained in the legislation which President Johnson submitted to Congress in June 1965, and which was passed soon thereafter as Public Law 89-91, the Coinage Act of 1965. In the president's words, the legislation was designed to "ensure a stable and dignified coinage, fully adequate in quantity and in its specially designed technical characteristics to the needs of our 20th century life."

The need for this legislation was evident: "There is no dependable or likely prospect that new, economically workable sources of silver may be found that could appreciably narrow the gap between silver supply and demand. ... The one part of the demand for silver that can be reduced is governmental demand for use in coinage."

Under the Coinage Act, some 90 percent of the silver formerly used for coinage would be made available for other purposes. The new half dollar was a composite—an outside layer (80 percent silver, 20 percent copper) clad on an alloy core (21 percent silver, 79 percent copper). To the naked eye, the coin would be almost indistinguishable from the old half dollar, but it would be 40 percent instead of 90 percent silver.

The new dimes and quarter dollars, although identical in size and design to the former 90 percent silver coins, were made silverless. Each of these also was a composite—an outer layer (75 percent copper, 25 percent nickel) clad on a core of pure copper. The legislation did not call for any change in the silver dollar, but it specified that none be minted for five years, thus ending the Mint's plans to release the 322,000 odd silver dollars that had already been struck. (Eventually, all of the 1964-D Peace dollars would be melted, though persistent rumors circulate that a few survived and escaped into the marketplace, and fantasy pieces dated 1964 have been created for the collector marketplace including some struck in 2010 by a private minter.)

The government's readiness to sell silver bullion from its stocks at $1.2929 an ounce had previously provided protection against the melting of silver coins, since it effectively prevented the price of silver from rising above the face value of the coins. Now, since the Treasury intended the silver coins to circulate alongside the new coins, the act provided further protection for the silver coinage by authorizing the secretary of the Treasury to prohibit the melting, treating or export of any U.S. coin. Again, to discourage hoarding it stipulated that any .900 fine coins minted after the law's enactment would be inscribed with the date 1964.

Finally, the legislation authorized the president to establish a Joint Commission on the Coinage, a 24-man body representing the legislative and executive branches as well as the public. The commission, when convened, would be expected to make recommendations on such matters as the economy's need for coins, technological developments in metallurgy and coin-selector devices, the supply of the various metals, the future of the silver dollar and the government's future role in maintaining the price of silver.

Public opinion—as expressed in the congressional hearings that preceded the passage of the Coinage Act—was virtually unanimous in regard to the need for reducing the silver content of the nation's subsidiary coinage. Emotions ran high, however, on the question of "how much," as would be expected from the diversity of interests with a stake in silver's future.

Users and producers

Silver users, anxious to have ample supplies of the metal available at stable or declining prices, wanted silver to be eliminated from the coinage. They pointed out that total world production could fall 100 million ounces below annual industrial demand alone, so that even under the most favorable circumstances, Treasury stocks could disappear within a half-decade.

In their analysis, silver-consuming industries projected a sharp reduction worldwide in silver usage for coinage. In the United States, Mint requirements could drop perhaps 90 percent from the 1965 peak to about 30 million ounces; in other countries, coinage requirements could drop 50 percent, also to about 30 million ounces. (Most countries throughout the world had already eliminated or drastically reduced the use of silver for coinage.) However, consumers projected an increase in worldwide industrial consumption to 360 million ounces by 1970, even assuming a reduced growth rate in that segment of the market. The resultant worldwide demand, 420 million ounces annually, would substantially exceed the projected supply, which (optimistically) could be estimated at about 340 million ounces from mine production and secondary sources.

Silver producers took a somewhat different view of the future. Fearing that a sharp swing away from silver might trigger a price break, they argued for the retention of silver in the coinage to the maximum extent feasible. They claimed that the supply deficit had been abnormally inflated in 1964 by the hoarding of well more than 100 million ounces in the form of Kennedy half dollars and speculative stocks. Furthermore, they claimed because of current exploration, that world mine production could increase by one-fourth or more within several years' time. (They were right on the first count, but wrong on the second.) Thus, they argued that increased mine production along with the gradual recovery of the 1,800 million ounces of silver outstanding in coins would permit the retention of some silver in both the half dollar and the smaller denominations.

Western legislators argued that Treasury stocks would soon be depleted unless the government permitted the price of silver to rise in a free market. Moreover, they felt that the Treasury approach failed to attract increased production and thereby in effect aggravated the coin shortage. Thus, the Western governors conference in 1965 resolved "that Congress provide for retention of silver in reduced amounts in all coins now silver, that an affirmative program be adopted to increase exploration for and development of domestic silver supplies, and that silver be permitted to seek its own price in the market place."

The vending industry, with its $3.5 billion annual take in coins, wanted coins that would be "compatible" with the nation's 12 million coin-operated merchandising devices. About half of these machines tended to reject coins that lacked the correct electrical properties, and major changes in them could require several years' time and could cost perhaps $100 million. Furthermore, the industry wanted coins that would pose no inconvenience to the consuming public, which plunked 30 billion pieces into these machines annually for more than 12 billion cups of coffee, milk and soft drinks, about 4.5 billion candy bars, and numerous other goods and services.

Finally, almost every company with a material in any way suitable for coinage—from aluminum to zirconium—pressed its claim for inclusion in the new coinage.

Actually, the Coinage Act, like the new coinage, was a composite containing something for nearly everyone. For Western silver producers, silver kept at least a stake in the coinage, with the new half dollars requiring at least 15 million ounces per year. Producers were also assured a minimum of $1.25 per ounce for their silver supplies.

Silver users did not get an entirely silverless coinage, but they did get silverless dimes and quarter dollars. In addition, the continued redemption of silver certificates by the Treasury provided an effective ceiling on the price—at least for awhile. The vending industry also was well enough satisfied, because the copper-nickel and copper coins had the same electrical properties as the silver coins and worked in existing machines.

To the marketplace

Considering the persistence of the coin shortage, the release of the new coins apparently did not come a moment too soon. Despite the continued expansion in production of silver coins under the "crash program," Federal Reserve inventories of quarters had shrunk to only 15 million pieces for the entire nation before the 1965 Christmas season.

But with the help of the new Coinage Act—which authorized the reactivation of coin production at the San Francisco Assay Office, the construction of new facilities, and the acquisition of necessary metallic strip, equipment and supplies—the Mint was able to achieve an unprecedented production rate. In November 1965, the Mint released more than 230 million new clad quarter dollars, and scheduled the release of that many more pieces every single month—four times the highest production rate ever previously attained. These new coins carried the economy safely through the Christmas season without a crisis.

In early 1966, when almost 700 million new quarter dollars already were in circulation and the first new dimes and half dollars were about to be released, Assistant Treasury Secretary Wallace told a Senate subcommittee that "the supply of our most vital coins is in better shape now than in any comparable period during the last 10 years. ... There is no shortage of those coins most vital to the transaction of business." Flow-back and inventories at the Federal Reserve banks had increased in all denominations except the half dollar. However, relatively few of the latter were in circulation, despite the production of 480 million Franklin half dollars in the 1948 to 1963 period and of almost that many Kennedy halves in the following several years.

The Treasury scheduled total production for the fiscal 1965 to 1967 period at 34 billion coins—enough to provide every person in the country with 180 additional pieces. Its objective was to manufacture enough of the new clad coins to replace over a relatively brief period all of the 13 billion old dimes and quarter dollars then in circulation.

The steps taken under the new Coinage Act were successful in overcoming the nationwide coin shortage, but failed to halt the drain on the Treasury's supplies.

As 1966 advanced, in fact, the feeling grew that the Treasury might not be able to hold the line until the completion of the transition to the new coinage. The Treasury used only 54 million ounces for coinage in 1966, as against the 1965 peak of 320 million ounces, but its stocks continued to decline as both domestic and foreign industrial users increased their demands. So Treasury stocks dropped, and then dropped some more—from 1,218 million ounces in December 1964 to 804 million ounces in December 1965, and then to 594 million ounces in December 1966.

Moreover, an ominous threat existed in the form of the silver certificates that had not yet been turned in for redemption. At the end of 1966, all but 154 million of the 594 million ounces in the Treasury's holdings were earmarked for redemption of certificates.

The administration acted to meet this situation by introducing a new piece of silver legislation in March 1967. (As Public Law 90-29, it became law on June 24.) The law authorized the Treasury to write off $200 million in certificates—on the assumption that certificates of at least that amount had been lost or destroyed or were held in collections, and thus would not be turned in for redemption. In addition, it limited the time for the redemption of certificates to one year after the passage of the legislation. Any stocks then remaining, aside from 165 million ounces earmarked

for the strategic stockpile, could be sold at not less than $1.2929.

The crisis would not wait, however, as the Treasury was hit by an unprecedented flood of orders for silver bullion during the spring. (During the first half of May alone, 33 million ounces flowed out—much of it out of the country.) Thereupon, the Treasury turned for advice to the Joint Commission on the Coinage. That 24-man commission—composed of 12 members of Congress concerned with silver policies, along with four members from the executive branch and eight public members appointed by the president—had been organized under the terms of the 1965 legislation to formulate long-range coinage plans for the post-silver era. Its first meeting was held in May 1967 when it was hastily convened to make recommendations dealing with the Treasury's current dilemma.

Immediately following the commission's May 18 meeting, the Treasury moved to assure the continued availability of silver to the U.S. market by discontinuing silver sales to other than "legitimate domestic concerns" and by invoking its statutory authority to prohibit the melting or export of coins. The result was the creation of a dual market. While the dealer price in New York remained at $1.30 an ounce, silver prices on the dealer and exchange markets abroad rose sharply.

Then, as soon as the president signed the new law on June 24, the Treasury wrote off $150 million of certificates, thereby freeing 116 million ounces of previously earmarked silver stocks and raising its free stocks to 135 million ounces. Nevertheless, the spread between the unrestricted price on world markets and the Treasury price proved to be too wide to be long maintained. With the London price fluctuating around the $1.70-level in early July, producers quite naturally sold their supplies in the premium markets while industrial users turned increasingly to the Treasury for their purchases.

By mid-July, the Mint had produced more than 8 billion new dimes and quarter dollars—virtually duplicating the entire old stock of circulating silver dimes and quarter dollars—and it was minting more of these copper-nickel clad coins at a 3.1 billion annual rate. Thus the problem of transition appeared solved: Even if all other silver coins followed the silver dollars out of circulation, enough clad coins would be available in circulation and in inventory to meet the foreseeable needs of a growing economy.

At that point, following the commission's second meeting on July 14, the Treasury halted all sales of silver at the old monetary value of $1.2929 and announced that it would sell thereafter 2 million ounces a week, with the General Services Administration handling the sales at the metal's going market price. This reduction in Treasury offerings by itself would have pushed prices upward. But by an unfortunate coincidence, the next day a copper strike shut down nearly all nonferrous-metals refineries, and thereby pulled off the market, for almost nine months' time, a large part of the normal refinery supply of silver.

Prices surge

These two developments in combination created an explosive price situation. The New York price immediately jumped from the old $1.29 ceiling to $1.87 an ounce, and after a brief period of stability, it surged upward again during the international financial crises of late 1967 and 1968. In June 1968, the New York price reached $2.565 an ounce.

These rousing price developments, along with the Treasury's June 24 deadline for redemption of silver certificates, set the stage for one final silver rush. In the *Wall Street Journal's* description, "Newcomers needn't pack picks, shovels, and Klondike maps, but just have wads of paper money (silver certificates, to be specific), a future contract, and taxi fare to the nearest Federal Reserve Bank." In May and June especially, when half of the final year's redemptions occurred, long lines of people formed early each morning at the New York and San Francisco Assay Offices to make the guaranteed 0.77-ounce-per-dollar exchange. (Those with $1,300 or more first had to exchange their certificates for a receipt at the Federal Reserve Bank.)

Altogether, 77 million ounces left the Treasury's coffers during this final silver rush—roughly three times more than had been expected based on the earlier pace of redemptions. But with that transfer out of the way—and with allowances made for certain supplies earmarked either for the strategic stockpile or for the last small remnant of the silver-coinage system, the silver-copper clad Kennedy half dollar—the Treasury by late 1968 had about 250 million ounces left in bullion and coins.

The Treasury's one remaining commitment, then, was to help make up the deficiency in the nation's industrial consumption of silver—the difference between total annual consumption of roughly 50 million ounces. The deficiency was covered by the continuation of weekly GSA sales of 2 million ounces, the purpose being to maintain sales at a level that would have a neutral effect on prices.

In March 1970, the GSA reduced the number of ounces of silver at its sales to 1.5 million ounces a week. The sales were halted Nov. 10, 1970.

In any event, demonetization was in effect completed on June 24, 1968, when the right to redeem silver certificates for silver was finally terminated. The transition brought about a slight change in the composition and appearance of the nation's coins and paper currency, but it in no way affected their value as a means of payment. Silver meanwhile remained a commodity, but it was no longer money.

Silver in the West

As a major mining center, the West has always had a vital interest in the fortunes of silver. And on frequent occasions since the opening of the Comstock Lode, silver has dominated the regional as well as the national stage. The voice of silver has been heard in the halls of Congress; and the economy, the society and the politics of the West have harkened to its voice.

Prosperity has been only a fitful visitor to silver mining camps, however. Prices have fluctuated violently over the years, while the long-term trend of output and employment has been downward.

The birth of the nation's silver industry occurred in the Washoe Hills of Nevada in 1858, as thousands of miners rushed across the Sierra from the already failing placers of California's Mother Lode to stake a claim in the fabulously rich Comstock Lode. Over the next 20 years, the Comstock bonanza helped finance the Civil War, provided the foundation for a transcontinental railroad, and established San Francisco as a glittering and opulent metropolis. By the time the lode played out at the end of the century, the bonanza had yielded more than $200 million worth of silver and almost as much in gold.

However, Comstock was only one of a series of rich silver finds. In the late 1860s, there was Black Hawk Canyon (Colorado), Cottonwood Canyon (Utah), Butte (Montana) and Owyhee County (Idaho). The 1870s and 1880s saw the development of the great silver deposits at Leadville, Colo., as well as the mines in the Calico District of California.

From this series of beginnings, the Western states, as the center of U.S. mining activity, soon made the United States the world's leading silver producer. (After 1900, however, Mexico took first place.) Colorado and Montana, topping the roster of producing states in 1900, accounted at that time for 60 percent of the domestic total of about 58 million fine ounces. Utah, Idaho and Arizona were next—and then came Nevada, despite the virtual exhaustion of the Comstock.

Market manipulation

Silver market manipulations in the 1970s by the heirs of oil magnate H. Lamarr Hunt again spotlighted the white metal and resulted in a financial crisis in January 1980.

Traders on the Commodity Exchange in New York became aware in late 1973 of an anonymous source that had been taking delivery on silver contracts bought on the Comex.

An estimated 30 million ounces had been taken out of the market by mid-February of the following year, when the source of this activity was identified as Texas millionaire Nelson Bunker Hunt.

The 20 million ounces he accepted in December 1973 was the equivalent of about one year's production at Idaho's Coeur d'Alene mining district, and one source estimated the paper profits from his "squeeze" operation at $200 million in the U.S. market and $78 million in London.

Commodity brokers had already expressed concern

over Hunt's activities. Trusting that delivery will be taken on a relatively small number of contracts at any given time, brokers normally maintain only a small percentage of bullion to cover these contracts. Faced with a large demand for delivery of contracts, brokers were forced to go into the market and buy silver at the rapidly escalating market price, which had moved from $2.80 an ounce in October 1973 to $5.70 early in the second week of February 1974.

Silver traders sought congressional aid to stabilize the market, without avail, estimating that the silver holdings accumulated by Hunt and his brother, Herbert, amounted to 50 million ounces, equal to about half the 117 million ounces held by the U.S. Treasury at the time.

The Hunt brothers' efforts to corner the silver market continued until January 1980, when the price on the Comex in New York closed at just under $50. The price of silver nose-dived to $10.80 on March 27, 1980, and Hunt's broker, the New York based Bache Group, issued a call to the brothers for a $100 million margin (essentially, the fees the brothers paid to trade on the silver exchanges), which they failed to meet.

Bache Vice President Elliot J. Smith revealed that the firm met the margin call by selling the silver and that the Hunt family still owed an unspecified amount of money to the brokerage firm.

At the order of the Securities and Exchange Commission, however, trading in Bache stock was suspended in the mid-afternoon of March 27.

The Commodities Futures Trading Commission rejected a request by Bache that silver trading be closed and an administrative price be arranged for settling contracts.

CFTC Chairman James M. Stone commented that the commission's primary job is "to protect small customers and commercial users. We are not here to protect large speculators," he said.

The only grounds for suspending silver trading, according to Stone, would be if it appeared supply and demand were not the chief regulators of the marketplace. "And that has not happened," he said. He also noted that permanent position limits, which would curb the speculation in which the Hunts participated, were being investigated.

Stone said CFTC investigators were looking into several troubled brokerages—including Bache—to be sure they would not dip into other investors' funds to cover their possible losses.

A later recapitulation indicated that Hunt lost an estimated $1 billion in paper profits after the price of silver plummeted to $10.30 in four days. The squeeze left him $33 million in debt to the Bache Group; $10 million to Paine Webber, another brokerage firm; and $4 million to St. Louis broker A.G. Edwards.

His biggest debt, however, was to Engelhard Mineral & Chemical Co., with whom he had a contract to buy 19 million ounces of silver at $35 an ounce, paying $665 million for metal that was worth only a total of $270 million following the price drop.

Hunt escaped from this commitment by giving Engelhard 8.5 million ounces of silver worth $121 million, together with oil and drilling rights in Canada's Beauford Sea, which had a value of $350 million to $700 million.

It was also learned as a result of the debacle, that Hunt was a 6.5 percent owner of the Bache Group, which sustained losses of $50 million and faced an SEC investigation to determine whether the firm acted in the interest of all of its stockholders when it became involved in Hunt's silver deals.

Silver Thursday

As the full skein of financial embarrassments resulting from "Silver Thursday" was unraveled, it became apparent that ACLI Commodity Services and ContiCommodities Corp. were among those also affected by the credit they had given to the Hunts, as well as 10 banks and many other firms.

In an unprecedented move for a commodity exchange, Comex put together a revealing "Chronology of Activities of the Silver Market from September 1979 to March 1980," which detailed the extent of both individual and brokerage firm holdings in silver during this period, as well as the action taken by the exchange to increase minimum margins and limit the number of positions held by individuals, in an attempt to avoid a "squeeze" on the market.

Federal Reserve Board Chairman Paul A. Volcker subsequently encountered strong hostility when he appeared before a House committee to justify the authorization by the Federal Reserve of $1 billion in Fed loans to the Hunts to cover the brothers' losses from the collapse of the silver market.

At one time, Volcker revealed, the Texas brothers controlled two-thirds of the 170 million ounces of silver in circulation throughout the world.

A forced sale of these holdings, he argued, would not be in the interest of the brothers' creditors and would shake the entire U.S. economy.

A wide-ranging two-year investigation of the Hunt brothers by the SEC concluded in July 1982 with a citation for a minor disclosure violation.

The SEC accused Nelson Bunker and Herbert L. Hunt of failing to file reports disclosing that they had acquired more than 5 percent of the stock of Bache Group Inc.

The Hunts agreed to a consent judgment in which they promised not to violate SEC regulations in the future, but neither admitted nor denied that they had done so in the past.

The Hunts dropped a multimillion-dollar lawsuit they had filed against the SEC, in which they accused government investigators of violating federal privacy laws during the SEC's probe.

The chief victim of the silver market "squeeze" was, of course, silver itself, which until 2010 had not experienced substantial price recovery.

Coins melted

Silver's run up to the $50 per ounce mark had a major effect on the coin market. Collectors who owned "junk silver"—worn silver coins pulled from circulation in the 1960s—suddenly found themselves with an unexpected source of income. A standard silver dime, which contained 0.07 ounce of pure silver, was worth $3.50 in silver alone at $50 an ounce. Silver quarter dollars were worth $9 each in silver alone, 90 percent half dollars were worth $18 and silver dollars, $38.50 each. Even at lower levels, silver coins were worth well more than their face value and in many cases, their numismatic value.

The result was a massive melting of silver coins. Collectors and others took their silver coins, medals and ingots to coin dealers and silver refiners, and sold them for huge profits. One unfortunate offshoot was an increase in home burglaries, as burglars broke into homes seeking silver (coins, silverware) and gold. The burglary problem became so bad in some communities that local officials passed regulations regulating how pawn shops, coin dealers and other dealers in "second-hand" goods purchased and sold silver and gold merchandise, including coins. At one point, such regulations threatened the livelihood of dealers at coin shows. Dealers were required to hold any silver and gold coins they purchased at the show for a specific number of days, as well as record the identity of everyone selling them coins. Dealers were required to provide police with lists of the coins they had purchased to allow law enforcement officials an opportunity to compare those lists with inventories from home burglaries.

Even more important than the "second-hand" dealers regulations were the quantities of silver coins melted. Even 20 years later, the full extent of what was melted is not known.

Changes in silver demand

From 2000 to 2009, overall silver demand declined worldwide, from 919.1 million ounces in 2000 to 889 million ounces in 2009, according to the Silver Institute.

During the 2000 to 2009 period, demand dropped particularly dramatically in the photo-imaging industry—a field dominated by photography, X-ray and motion picture film. Photo-imaging use of silver declined from 218.3 million ounces in 2000 to 82.9 million ounces in 2009. Demand dropped each year during that time period. Much of that decline can be attributed to the increasing use of digital cameras for personal and professional photography, and abandonment of traditional film cameras.

Declines were also shown in jewelry, down from 170.6 million ounces in 2000 to 156.6 million ounces in 2009; and in silverware, from 96.4 million ounces in 2000 to 59.5 million ounces in 2009.

Use of silver in industrial applications rose and fell during same time, period: 374.2 million ounces were used in 2000; the low point for that 10-year period

was in 2001, when 335.6 million ounces were used in industrial applications, and the high point was in 2007, when 456.1 million ounces were used, before a recession began. Industrial use declined to 443.4 million ounces in 2008 and 352.2 million ounces in 2009.

Silver use in coins and medals

The one bright spot during the 10-year period starting in 2000 was the use of silver in coins and medals. In 2000, 32.1 million ounces of silver were used in coins and medals; in 2009, that total was 78.7 million ounces, which was also the peak during that 10-year period. The growth in the use of silver in coins and medals marked a resurgence of sorts after silver was abandoned in circulating coinage in the 1960s.

The growth of silver use in coins and medals was a marked departure from its use in the 1970s and early 1980s, when few silver coins of any kind were being struck. The United States Mint had returned to production of silver coins in a relatively small way in the early 1970s, when it struck silver-copper clad Eisenhower dollars, and in 1975 and 1976, when it struck Eisenhower dollars and Bicentennial quarter dollars, half dollars and dollars composed of 40 percent silver (a silver-copper clad composition), for sale to collectors.

Worldwide silver use in coinage fell to a low of 9.5 million ounces in 1981, according to the Silver Institute.

However, silver coin production in the United States took off beginning in 1982 with the return of commemorative coinage (see the Commemoratives chapter for more detail), and even more in 1986 with the production of American Eagle silver bullion coins (see chapter on Bullion Coins for more details). Silver use in coins and medals by other countries also grew.

The silver commemorative and bullion coins in production in the United States and elsewhere helped drive worldwide silver use in coins and medals to 30.4 million ounces in 1987, well above the 1981 low.

The United States Mint even resumed production of 90 percent silver Roosevelt dimes, Washington quarter dollars and Kennedy half dollars, although only for inclusion in the Silver Proof set, introduced in 1992. Sales of Silver Proof sets in addition to commemorative and bullion coin sales helped to drive worldwide use of silver in coinage to 38 million ounces in 1993. That amount rose and fell during the 1990s and 2000s as demand for silver coinage and medals rose and fell, before rising to new peaks as the end of the first decade of the 21st century neared.

Sales of American Eagle silver bullion coins are illustrative of worldwide demand for similar bullion products. In 2007, sales of American Eagle silver bullion coins totaled 9,887,000 ounces. Sales nearly doubled in 2008, to 19,538,500 ounces, driven largely by demand for silver bullion coins during the economic crisis that began that year. In 2009, the total reached 28,766,500 ounces, a record, and in 2010 a new record was set at 34,662,500 ounces of American Eagle silver bullion coins. Worldwide, for 2010, "Coins and medals fabrication rose by 28 percent to post a new record of 101.3 million ounces," according the Silver Institute.

The record demand for silver coins and medals caught some producers and mints unprepared. During 2008, as the price of silver began to increase along with demand, the U.S. Mint began having problems striking enough American Eagle silver bullion coins to meet investor demand. In 2009, the Mint did not strike Proof versions, leaving a hole in a chronology that had been unbroken since 1986. The U.S. Mint began selling Proof 2010-W American Eagle silver bullion coins late in 2010.

Also in 2010, the U.S. Mint began production of America the Beautiful 5-ounce .999 fine silver bul-lion coins denominated as quarter dollars. However, because of a late start, trouble with securing planchets and technical issues involved in striking the 3-inch diameter coins, the Mint began producing coins late in the year and limited the mintage of each of the five designs to 33,000 coins, not the 100,000 pieces per design announced months before. A numismatic version was limited to 27,000 pieces per design for the 2010 coins. The lower-than-expected mintages resulted in a robust secondary market for the bullion versions in early 2011. At press time, it was too early to tell what effect the demand for the 5-ounce silver bullion coins would have on the silver market.

As in the gold market, silver is widely held in exchange-traded funds, the largest of which is the iShares Silver Trust, which trades on the New York Stock Exchange as SLV. As of Feb. 4, 2011, it had 333,410,334 ounces of silver in trust.

Modern silver chronology

1792

April 2—Authorizing act issued to strike U.S. silver dollar (standard weight 416 grains, .89244 fine), half dollar (standard weight 208 grains, .89244 fine), quarter dollar (standard weight 104 grains, .89244 fine), dime (standard weight 41.6 grains, .89244 fine) and half disme or half dime (standard weight 20.8 grains, .89244 fine). Dollar defined as a unit containing 24.75 grains of fine gold or 371.25 grains of fine silver (exchange rate between the two metals set at 15 to 1).

1834

Standard definition of gold dollar changed to unit containing 23.2 grains of fine gold; silver unchanged at 371.25 grains. Silver-gold ratio becomes 16 to 1.

1837

Jan. 18—Authorizing act issued to change silver dollar standard weight to 412.50 grains, .900 fine; half dollar standard weight changed to 206.25 grains, .900 fine; quarter dollar changed to 103.125 grains, .900 fine; dime changed to 41.25 grains, .900 fine; half dime to 20.625 grains, .900 fine. Exchange rate becomes 15.988 to one.

1851

March 3—Authorizing act issued to strike silver 3-cent coin, standard weight 12.375 grains, .750 fine.

1853

Feb. 21—Half dollar standard weight changed to 192 grains, quarter dollar to 96 grains, dime to 38.4 grains, half dime to 19.2 grains. All remain .900 fine.

1854

Silver 3-cent coin changed to 11.52 grains, .900 fine.

1859

Silver discovered in Comstock Lode in Nevada.

1860

Decade sees silver finds in Black Hawk Canyon, Colo.; Cottonwood Canyon, Utah; Butte, Mont.; and Owyhee County, Idaho.

1873

Feb. 12—Authorizing act issued to strike Trade silver dollar, 420 grains, .900 fine. Half dollar changed to 192.9 grains, .900 fine; quarter dollar changed to 96.45 grains, .900 fine; dime changed to 38.58 grains, .900 fine. Half dime and silver 3-cent coin discontinued.

Standard silver dollar discontinued; bimetallism effectively ended.

1875

March 3—Authorizing act issued to strike silver 20-cent coin, 77.16 grains, .900 fine.

1876

July 22—Trade dollar demonetized.

1878

May 2—Twenty-cent coin discontinued.

Bland-Allison Act passed, requiring Treasury to buy not less than $2 million in silver every month for coinage or for backing silver certificates.

1887

Feb. 14—Congress authorizes redemption of unmutilated Trade dollars for six months.

March 3—Trade dollar officially discontinued.

1890

Sherman Silver Purchase Act passed, directing the secretary of the Treasury to buy 4.5 million ounces of silver bullion every month.

1896

July 8—William Jennings Bryan delivers "Cross of Gold" speech calling for a restoration of the bimetallic (silver and gold) standard.

1900

Bimetallism legislation repealed, Gold Standard Act passed, officially placing the United States on the gold standard. Gold dollar of 25.8 grains, .900 fine becomes the unit of value; all other forms of currency maintained at parity with the gold dollar.

1920

Jan. 10—Silver reaches an all-time high of $1.37 an ounce, caused by speculation and worldwide monetary devaluation.

1923

Silver reaches an all-time low of 24 cents an ounce.

1933

June 5—U.S. goes off gold standard.

Thomas Amendment to Agricultural Adjustment Act passed, authorizing unlimited coinage of silver.

1934

Silver Purchase Act passed, directing the secretary of the Treasury to purchase silver at home and abroad until the market price reaches the Mint price of $1.2929 an ounce, or until the monetary value of Treasury silver stock reaches one-third of the monetary value of its gold stock.

1935

Minting of silver dollars halted.

1961

November—President Kennedy orders secretary of the Treasury to suspend further sales of Treasury's unallocated silver, to suspend the use of free silver for coinage, and to obtain coinage silver through the retirement from circulation of $5 and $10 silver certificates. Silver begins upward price climb.

1962

Oct. 20—Silver hits 42-year high in New York, $1.22 per ounce.

1963

Feb. 28—Mint Director Eva Adams writes to Assistant Treasury Secretary Robert A. Wallace to recommend that funding be requested to make 100,000 new silver dollars during the first year of resumed production to meet demand for the coins.

March 13—Silver stands at $1.28; when it reaches $1.2929, turning silver certificates in for silver bullion becomes profitable.

June 4—Silver Purchase Act repealed; tax on transfers of interest in silver bullion repealed, $1 and $2 silver certificates to be gradually retired. Treasury is authorized to issue Federal Reserve notes in smaller denominations and is required to hold an amount of silver equal in monetary value (at $1.2929 an ounce) to the face value of all silver certificates outstanding.

July 8—Silver reaches $1.29 in New York, the numismatic melting point at which speculators could profit by converting silver certificates to silver and then selling the silver.

Dec. 30—Authorizing act issued to strike Kennedy half dollars, 90 percent silver, 10 percent copper.

1964

Jan. 29—Treasury announces silver dollars depleted from the Treasury at the rate of 700,000 per week as citizens cash in silver certificates in exchange for silver dollars.

Feb. 11—First Kennedy half dollars struck.

March 20—House Appropriations Committee refuses to give Treasury funds to strike more silver dollars.

March 23—Less than 3 million silver dollars left in the Treasury; long lines form outside the Treasury building as people wait to buy silver dollars.

March 24—First Kennedy half dollars issued.

March 26—Treasury Secretary Douglas Dillon issues an order saying citizens who want to exchange $1 silver certificates for a dollar's worth of silver will have to go to New York or San Francisco, and that the Treasury will redeem the certificates in silver bullion rather than in silver dollars.

April—Mints go on stepped-up schedule in an attempt to double the annual production of coins to ease the coin shortage. Treasury obtains permission to continue the 1964 dates on new coins indefinitely to stop hoarding.

June 17—Senate Appropriations Committee approves striking of 45 million silver dollars.

Aug. 3—President Johnson signs legislation to provide for the striking of the first silver dollars since 1935. Peace dollar design to be used.

Sept. 3—President Johnson signs a bill authorizing the secretary of the Treasury to continue using the date 1964 on all coins minted from this time on until he decides the coin shortage is over.

Sept. 17—Denver Mint receives shipment of 32 Peace dollar reverse dies from Philadelphia Mint to use in striking of new silver dollars, but the dies are found to be a corroded, pitted shape, and are destroyed.

Sept. 28—Philadelphia Mint ships new Peace dollar dies to Denver Mint. Second shipment of dies occurs on Oct. 19.

November—Government announces that no more Proof or Mint sets will be made after 1964 until the coin shortage is over.

Dec. 28—Mint Director Eva Adams says silver dollars will not be considered for striking until after the coin shortage is over.

1965

May 15—President Johnson directs the Bureau of the Mint to strike 45 million silver dollars before June 30. Denver Mint coins approximately 322,394 1964-D Peace dollar trial strikes.

May 25—Treasury announces it has decided against releasing any new silver dollars at this time, after a conference with the White House.

May 26—Denver Mint superintendent receives orders to destroy all 1964-D Peace dollar trial strikes.

May 28—Denver Mint employees mutilate all working dies for 1964-D Peace dollar.

June 3—President Johnson sends proposal to Congress calling for the elimination of silver from dimes and quarter dollars and a reduction of silver in the Kennedy half dollars; asks Congress to reopen the San Francisco Assay Office (the former Mint) for all coin processes; and for authorization to prohibit exportation, melting or treating U.S. coins.

June 11—Date of statement signed by 35 employees of the Denver Mint that they removed none of the planchets or trial strikes for the 1964-D Peace dollars; that they knew of no one who did; and that none of the planchets or dollars was in their possession.

June 24—New coinage bill passes the Senate without change.

July 14—House passes coinage bill with amendments: no Mint marks to be used on the new coins, and no Mint marks for five years; no production of silver dollars for five years; the coins are to be dated with the year of issuance or coinage unless the Treasury secretary decides this will contribute to a coin shortage; the president may enlarge the membership of the proposed Joint Commission on the Coinage to 24; and the secretary of the Treasury has standby authority to prohibit the use of coins as security on loans.

July 23—President Johnson signs the Coinage Act of 1965, providing for new dimes and quarter dollars to be three-layered "sandwich" coins with outer layers of the same copper-nickel alloy used in 5-cent coins, 75 percent copper, 25 percent nickel, and bonded to a core of pure copper; and for the silver content of the Kennedy half dollar to be reduced from 90 to 40 percent, with two outer layers of 80 percent silver and 20 percent copper, bonded to a core of 20.9 percent silver and 79.1 percent copper. Bill includes House amendments as well as Senate provisions.

Aug. 3—Mint Chief Engraver Frank Gasparro is ordered to destroy 40 pairs of partially produced Peace dollar dies held at Philadelphia Mint. Twenty-eight Peace dollars held at the Philadelphia Mint are passed through rollers before being melted.

Aug. 23—First clad coins, 25-cent coins, struck at the Philadelphia Mint; also the first coins to bear the 1965 date.

Nov. 1—Treasury releases first copper-nickel clad quarter dollars to Federal Reserve banks for circulation.

1966

March 8—Bureau of the Mint releases copper-nickel clad dimes and 40 percent silver half dollars for circulation, dated 1965.

June—Treasury Secretary Henry Fowler announces "the coin shortage is over."

July 7—Treasury Department says all U.S. coins manufactured after Aug. 1, 1966, will be dated 1966, and on Jan. 1, 1967, current annual dating of coins will be resumed.

July 12—Treasury Department announces new regulations: mutilated silver coins will be purchased at the Philadelphia and Denver Mints at approximately the going price of silver bullion.

July 26—Hearings begin on a proposal to sell the 3 million silver dollars in the Treasury Department's vaults at face value to the American Cancer Society and the American Heart Fund for resale to coin collectors at a profit. The Treasury Department voices its opposition to the bill.

Aug. 27—Royal Canadian Mint master predicts silver will disappear from Canadian coins within two years.

November—*American Metal Market* newspaper predicts silver prices will rise to between $1.50 and $1.80 an ounce in 1967.

Nov. 2—Treasury reports the silver stockpile continues to diminish, dropping by almost 3 million ounces during the five-day period from Oct. 28 to Nov. 2.

Nov. 17—Treasury reports silver stockpile down to 608.5 million ounces.

Dec. 1—Stockpile down to 601.3 million ounces.

Dec. 24—Canadian Finance Minister announces Canada will drop silver from most of its coinage, changing to nickel, in 1968. Silver is to be retained in the dollar.

1967

Jan. 3—Treasury announces its silver stockpile is at 591.9 million ounces.

March 1—Treasury reports its stockpile dropped 45 million ounces in the first two months of 1967.

March 17—Treasury Secretary Fowler asks Congress for the power to free the remaining silver held by the Treasury as backing for silver certificates.

April 10—Treasury stockpile of silver down to 524.9 million ounces.

May 18—Treasury Department immediately discontinues sales of silver to any buyers other than legitimate domestic concerns that use silver in their businesses. The Treasury also invokes its power to prohibit the melting, treatment and export of silver coins. The announcement creates a two-price system for silver; silver jumps to $1.60 an ounce in London markets.

June 2—Canada announces it is changing to the manufacture of nickel 10- and 25-cent coins.

June 5—Senate passes a measure allowing the Treasury to write off lost or destroyed silver certificates and to free for other use the silver now held against the certificates, and to allow the Bureau of the Mint to return Mint marks to U.S. coins.

June 24—President Johnson signs bill authorizing the eventual end of the redemption of silver certificates with silver bullion, and authorizing the Mint to restore Mint marks to U.S. coinage. The Treasury Department would stop redeeming silver certificates with bullion in a year. The Treasury was also given permission to begin the write-off of an obligation to hold 116 million ounces of silver against $200 million worth of silver certificates believed lost, destroyed or held by collectors.

July 14—Treasury announces it will no longer keep the price of silver at $1.2929, saying it believes enough new clad coins are in circulation to serve the nation's commerce even if all of the silver coins drop out of circulation. Silver sales from the Treasury stockpiles will now be handled by the General Services Administration and will be limited to 2 million ounces a week at the going market prices (more than $1.71 an ounce in London).

July 18—New York silver quotations reach $1.87 an ounce. Coin dealers who are buying silver certificates for redemption in silver report a booming business.

Aug. 4—GSA begins selling silver on a competitive bid basis.

Aug. 21—Silver dollars in Uncirculated and circulated bags of $1,000 offered on the New York Mercantile Exchange.

Aug. 30—New York Mercantile Exchange reports silver dollar market is brisk, with Uncirculated bags opening at $2,160 and circulated at $1,895 for $1,000 face. GSA reports about 10 million ounces of silver have been sold at its weekly sales since they began.

Oct. 12—Treasury Department announces beginning Nov. 1 silver bars issued in exchange for silver certificates will be of fineness of .996 and .998 rather than the .999 fine bars presently issued.

Oct. 13—GSA reports a sharp rise in silver prices, at $1.7715 an ounce for silver stores at West Point Bullion Depository.

Oct. 24—New record set for silver price in New York markets as a dealer pays $20,000 for a contract of 10,000 ounces on the Commodity Exchange.

Nov. 8—London reports an all-time high for silver, $1.951 per ounce.

Nov. 18—Britain devalues the pound, from $2.80 to $2.40, causing increased silver speculation and a rise in early December prices to $2.17 an ounce in New York.

Nov. 22—Treasury says it has enough silver to redeem all the silver certificates presented before the June 24, 1968, cut-off date for redemption.

Dec. 11—United States to resume selling .999 fine silver to industrial consumers.

1968

Jan. 4—First coins struck with Mint marks since those dated 1964.

Jan. 19—Silver steady in New York at $2.07 an ounce.

January—Handy & Harman Review of the Silver Market terms 1967 market "confused, unpredictable."

Feb. 2—Treasury reports it redeemed only $8 million worth of silver certificates during the first seven weeks of 1968.

March 1—Joint Commission on the Coinage recommends governmental melting of silver dimes and quarter dollars. Process in full swing soon after in the Philadelphia and Denver Mints and the San Francisco Assay Office.

March 25—GSA announces prices ranging from $2.03 to $2.13 an ounce in its sales.

April 3—Treasury reports the government has melted enough silver coins to produce 403,726.2 ounces of silver.

April 29—Coin silver derived from melted coins will be sold to industrial users, the Treasury says. Sale of .999 fine silver is suspended; the GSA will sell a million ounces of .996 fine silver to .998 fine silver each week, beginning May 3, in addition to a million ounces of .897 to .900 fine coinage silver.

June 24—Deadline for redeeming silver certificates for silver bullion. Silver certificates remain legal tender.

June 25—Total Treasury silver estimated at 482 million ounces.

July 15—Joint Commission on the Coinage meets to work out a plan for the disposition of the 2.9 million rare silver dollars still held in the Treasury vaults.

Sept. 10—GSA announces the sale of 452,000 ounces of silver to 12 firms in category B, the portion set aside for small business concerns. Handy & Harman price per ounce stands at $2.220.

Oct. 16—Silver continues month-long retreat; stands at $1.92 per ounce in London.

Oct. 31—Silver prices show inclination to firm up; New York spot price at $1.933.

Dec. 5—Joint Commission on the Coinage meets to consider a new nonsilver dollar; recommends the 2.9 million silver dollars now held by the Treasury be sold on a bid sale basis at minimum fixed prices.

Dec. 20—Treasury Secretary Fowler says Joint Commission on the Coinage has recommended minting nonsilver, copper-nickel clad half dollars to replace the existing 40 percent silver half dollar, and to make the current ban on melting silver coins permanent.

1969

Feb. 13—Silver hits a 15-month low of $1.76 per ounce on the New York and Chicago exchanges.

March 14—Spot silver at $1.79 in Chicago.

May 12—Treasury Department lifts ban on melting and exporting silver coins following meeting of Joint Commission on the Coinage. The commission also recommended minting a nonsilver half dollar and a nonsilver dollar, as well as selling the 2.9 million silver dollars remaining in the Treasury. Treasury also to reduce the amount of silver offered at its weekly auction from 2 million ounces to a quarter million.

June 17—Silver slides to $1.59 an ounce in London, the lowest price since the British devalued the pound in 1967.

July 10—Rep. James A. McClure and 146 other representatives propose the Treasury resume minting a 40 percent silver dollar with the likeness of Dwight

D. Eisenhower on it. Sen. Peter Dominick introduces a similar measure in the Senate, joined by 20 other senators.

August—Members of the Chicago Board of Trade approve the establishment of a futures market in silver, calling for trading in units of 5,000 troy ounces at not less than .999 fineness.

Sept. 9—GSA auction sets a new sales record, selling more than 14 million ounces of silver.

Sept. 22—Silver advances; spot price in New York at $1.82 an ounce, with the one-year future price moving to $2.038.

Oct. 6—Bill calling for a silverless Eisenhower dollar, a silverless half dollar and machinery for the sale of the 2.9 million silver dollars held in the Treasury fails to pass the House.

Oct. 7—Senate joint resolution introduced to mint copper-nickel Eisenhower dollar coins.

Oct. 15—Treasury reports its stock of coinage silver dropped by almost 4 million ounces during the week of Oct. 8 to 15.

Nov. 10—Wright Patman, chairman of the House Banking and Currency Committee, confirms he opposes any silver in the Eisenhower dollars.

Nov. 17—Office of Domestic Gold and Silver Operations chief Thomas Wolfe indicates GSA silver sales will probably be halted in a year.

Dec. 2—Silver prices rise in GSA sale; prices at $1.9121.

1970

Feb. 19—Mint Director Mary Brooks orders the production of 10 trial strikes using Peace dollar dies on planchets composed of 80 percent silver, 20 percent copper outer layers and 20 percent silver, 80 percent copper core, as part of testing for upcoming Eisenhower dollar production. All 10 pieces would later be destroyed.

March 4—Senate and House leaders reach a compromise agreement on a plan to mint 150 million 40 percent silver dollars and an undetermined number of copper-nickel dollar coins, all with the likeness of the late President Dwight D. Eisenhower. The conferees also agree that the Treasury will continue through Nov. 10 sales of silver at the rate of a quarter million ounces a week, and that the Office of Emergency Planning will transfer to the Mint 25.5 million ounces of surplus silver no longer needed in the nation's stockpile to be used for coinage.

March 19—Senate passes Eisenhower dollar bill; House Banking and Currency Committee chairman Wright Patman maintains his opposition to striking silver dollars.

April 9—Silver prices continue to falter, closing at season's low of $1.85.

April 29—Silver price continues to slide, closing at $1.663 an ounce in New York.

May 13—Joint Commission on the Coinage votes in favor of a silver Eisenhower dollar. Patman says he will use his influence to block House passage of the

legislation for the remainder of the year.

Spring—Last two 1964-D Peace dollar trial strikes, held at Mint headquarters in Washington, are passed through rollers and destroyed. According to Mint records, these were the last 1964-D Peace dollars in existence.

June 4—Federal Reserve Board proposes that banks stop counting silver coins they hold in their vaults as part of their reserve requirements.

June 17—Senate approves a bill to authorize further adjustments in the amount of silver certificates outstanding, and to include Federal Reserve Bank notes and national bank notes in the estimates of notes that are irretrievable as a result of being lost or in collections.

September—Senate approves the Bank Holding bill, onto which is tacked authorization to strike 150 million Eisenhower 40 percent silver dollars.

Oct. 9—*Federal Register* notes that effective Nov. 10 the U.S. Mints and Assay Offices will no longer accept deposits of silver for exchange into bars.

Nov. 10—GSA silver auctions end with the Franklin Mint buying the last silver sold by the Treasury, marking the end of the government's 194-year role in the silver market.

Nov. 24—Both the Senate and the House make concessions; passage of the Eisenhower dollar bill, tied onto revisions in the Banking Holding Company bill, draws nearer.

Dec. 8—Senate-House conferees reach agreement on the Eisenhower dollar legislation; approve coinage amendments authorizing the Mint to produce Eisenhower dollar coins in silver and copper-nickel, and half dollars in copper-nickel. Bill now goes before the Senate and House.

Dec. 18—Senate unanimously passes Eisenhower dollar legislation, following House passage the previous day.

Dec. 31—President Nixon signs Eisenhower dollar bill, marking the first dollar coin issued since 1935. The Mint is to produce over a four- or five-year period 150 million 40 percent silver coins for sale at premium prices and an undetermined number of copper-nickel clad dollars for general circulation. The bill also eliminates the 40 percent silver content from the half dollar and authorizes minting copper-nickel clad half dollars in an effort to achieve general circulation of the denomination; and authorizes the GSA to sell the 2.9 million silver dollars in the vaults of the Treasury, on a bid basis. Most of the dollars to be offered for sale are Carson City Mint coins, 90 percent silver, minted between 1878 and 1891.

1971

Jan. 25—First trial strikes for new Eisenhower dollar produced at the Philadelphia Mint.

Jan. 29—Treasury announces Eisenhower dollars of 40 percent silver will sell for $10 per coin in Proof and $3 per coin in Uncirculated. Orders will be accepted beginning July 1.

Feb. 1—Handy & Harman releases annual *Review of the Silver Market,* noting that the world silver markets were still dominated by speculators in 1970 for the fourth year in a row. The report also comments that with the end of GSA silver sales the price of silver dropped rather than climbed, contrary to expectations.

Feb. 3—Denver Mint begins producing copper-nickel half dollars.

March 31—First Eisenhower silver dollars struck at the San Francisco Assay Office.

April 1—The Royal Canadian Mint begins accepting orders for its British Columbia commemorative silver dollar.

April 1—Trading in silver coin futures begins on the New York Mercantile Exchange, with the contract covering U.S. dimes, quarter dollars and half dollars minted in 1964 or before.

May 17—West Coast Commodity Exchange begins listing U.S. silver coins as a new commodity futures contract.

May 28—New York Mercantile Exchange reflects softening silver prices; closing price slips to $1,205 for July delivery of a $1,000 face silver coin contract.

June 6—A GSA spokesman says he expects as many as 15 million bids on the silver dollars being held at the Treasury Department.

June 29—Prices drop on the New York Mercantile Exchange; $1,155 per bag of $1,000 face U.S. silver coins on July contracts.

July 2—Prices bounce back; $1,175 per bag of $1,000 face U.S. silver coins on July contracts.

Oct. 5—Silver slips to a four-and-a-half-year low, closing at $1.331 an ounce in New York.

Oct. 27—Silver closes at below $1.30 an ounce in New York.

Nov. 1—First Eisenhower dollars released for circulation.

Nov. 3—Downward trend continues; silver at $1.27 an ounce for November futures.

Dec. 6—The Treasury's 2.9 million Carson City Mint silver dollars are transferred to the U.S. bullion depository in West Point, N.Y., as a major step toward public sale of the coins in about a year.

1972

Feb. 16—San Francisco Federal Reserve Bank official William Burke notes in a *Coin World* article that many traders are now referring to silver ironically as a "semi-precious metal." He notes that from a quotation of $1.80 an ounce at the time of the last Treasury sale in November 1970, the price went down instead of up, as many had expected, reaching $1.31 an ounce in October 1971.

March 27—Trade begins on silver coin contracts in the Chicago Open Board of Trade.

April 12—Sustained price advance peaks; reaches $1.65 an ounce in New York.

May 19—Sen. Jacob K. Javits presents testimony on a bill he sponsored to authorize the Treasury secretary to make grants to Eisenhower College, Seneca

Falls, N.Y., out of proceeds from the sale of Proof Eisenhower dollars sold by the Mint.

June 8—Senate passes bill to supply 10 percent of the proceeds from the sale of Proof Eisenhower dollars to the Eisenhower College.

July 17—Silver reaches a two-year high of $1.80 in New York.

Sept. 5—Silver prices slide to $1.772 in New York.

Sept. 25—The Silver Institute Inc. sponsors an exhibition of the silver coins issued by more than 30 nations in the past 10 years for those attending the International Monetary Fund meeting in Washington, D.C.

Oct. 31—Bids open for Carson City silver dollar sale; public may submit bids for the 1882, 1883 and 1884 coins produced at the now obsolete Carson City Mint. Minimum acceptable bid placed at $30 for each coin, with bids limited to one coin of each year.

Nov. 3—Coin firm Stack's of New York calls for a Securities and Exchange Commission investigation of the GSA and its use of the terms "investment" and "investments" in its Carson City silver dollar sale brochure. SEC later declares the GSA claims are beyond the jurisdiction of the SEC.

1973

Jan. 3—GSA announces inspection of Carson City Mint dollars complete, meeting standards set for Uncirculated coins.

Jan. 17—Federal Trade Commission refuses to intervene at the request of Professional Numismatists Guild in the fight against advertising use of the term "silver dollar" for silverless coins.

Feb. 2—A total of 700,000 Carson City Mint dollars sold for $30 each.

Feb. 27—Silver continues to rise; price reaches $2.381 an ounce in London.

March 15—Sen. Jacob Javits introduces another bill to provide money from the sale of Eisenhower Proof dollars for the Eisenhower College, Seneca Falls, N.Y. Similar legislation introduced in 1972 died in the 92nd Congress.

April 17—Senate Banking, Housing and Urban Affairs committee approves bill providing $1 from the sale of each Proof Eisenhower dollar to the Eisenhower College.

April 19—Wright Patman introduces Eisenhower College bill in the House.

April 30—GSA sells 70,000 more Carson City Mint dollars, at $30 each.

May 2—Senate approves bill allocating $1 from the sale of each Eisenhower Proof silver dollar to Eisenhower College.

June 8—GSA announces it will auction 2 million ounces of reclaimed silver obtained from Defense Department projects, not part of the national stockpile. Silver coin futures drop by as much as $50 a bag.

June 20—GSA sells first of 2 million ounces of silver on a competitive bid basis, selling a total of 1,240,000 ounces.

Aug. 1—Mint Director Mary Brooks announces no 1973 copper-nickel Eisenhower dollars will be minted for general circulation.

Aug. 3—Rep. Chalmers P. Wylie introduces bill to make an outright grant of $6 million to both the Eisenhower College and the Rayburn Library.

Oct. 31—GSA closes bids on sales of Carson City Mint dollars dated 1880, 1881, and 1885; bids total $14,071,958.

Dec. 10—Royal Canadian Mint unveils first four silver coins in the Montreal Olympic commemorative series.

1974

Jan. 8—Spot silver prices reach $3.40 in New York.

Jan. 21—Silver soars to $3.97 in London.

Feb. 10—Silver futures stand at $4.815 in London.

Feb. 14—Silver at $4.427 an ounce in London.

Feb. 21—Silver breaks world price record at $5.965 in London.

April 1—GSA opens bidding for what is expected to be its last Carson City dollar sale.

April 11—Silver drops, closes at $4.27 in New York.

April 17—Silver bounces back, to $4.828 in New York for May futures.

May 3—Silver shows new strength, at $5.501 an ounce in London.

June 5—Silver Institute releases figures showing the rising price of silver in April drove 1,480,053 ounces of pre-1965 U.S. silver coins into the melting pot.

July 22—Rep. Wright Patman again introduces a bill authorizing grants from the sale of Proof Eisenhower dollars to the Eisenhower College in Seneca Falls, N.Y. The bill also gives power to the Bureau of the Mint to change the alloy and weight of the 1-cent coin. Patman's last Eisenhower College bill met defeat under a House rule technicality Aug. 3, 1973.

Aug. 3—Eisenhower College bill wins House Banking and Currency committee approval.

Aug. 21—The Pacific Commodities Exchange in San Francisco launches trading in silver futures with a new "mini-contract" for delivery of 1,000 troy ounces of silver.

Aug. 21—The GSA says there are no plans for the present about disposing of the remaining 1 million Carson City silver dollars held by the Treasury.

Sept. 11—Silver slips to $3.89 an ounce in New York. Mining stocks in both gold and silver drop.

Sept. 18—Silver falls back to $3.87 an ounce. The Silver Institute reports substantial melting of silver coins by U.S. refiners during August.

Sept. 25—House passes bill including a provision for $9 million grant to the Eisenhower College at Seneca Falls, N.Y., tapped from the proceeds of the sale of 40 percent silver Proof Eisenhower dollars.

Sept. 26—Eisenhower College bill passes Senate, goes to president for signature.

Oct. 10—Las Vegas blackjack dealer brings 1974-D Eisenhower dollar struck on 40 percent silver planchet to *Coin World* offices. U.S. Mint confirms that a quantity of copper-nickel clad dollar planchets, unfit for striking into Proofs and shipped from the San Francisco Assay Office to the Denver Mint, had accidentally included an unknown number of 40 percent silver planchets intended for Proof or Uncirculated collector coins.

Oct. 10—U.S. Bicentennial 40 percent silver coins to go on sale Nov. 15 through Jan. 31, 1975. Price of three-piece Proof sets $15, Uncirculated set $9, limit of five sets of each per customer.

Nov. 13—Presentation set of 40 percent silver Bicentennial coins presented to President Ford at White House ceremonies. Coins were struck at Philadelphia Mint and lack the S Mint mark that will appear on versions sold to the public. Current location of the set is unknown, if it survives.

Nov. 20—Senate passes appropriations bill releasing Eisenhower dollar funds for Eisenhower College and Sam Rayburn Library.

1975

Jan. 10—Royal Canadian Mint employees strike for higher wages, delaying production of third series of silver Olympic coins.

Jan. 19—U.S. Mint reduces price of three-piece, 40 percent silver Bicentennial Proof set from $15 to $12 per set. Quantity limit removed and ordering deadline extended to July 4, 1976, for Proof and Uncirculated Bicentennial sets.

Feb. 19—GSA considering new plans for the disposal of approximately 1 million Carson City Mint silver dollars left unsold in earlier sales. Coins may be put in storage for future sale.

February—Handy & Harman, precious metal dealer, releases annual review of the previous year's metal markets. Refers to 1974 as "the most chaotic period in the history of the world's silver markets."

March 2—Royal Canadian Mint strike ends. Production of silver Olympic coins to resume.

April 23—U.S. Mint begins striking 40 percent silver Bicentennial coins for release on July 4, 1975.

June 24—The newly organized Commodity Futures Trading Commission imposes new stringent regulations to protect public against fraud in transactions involving gold and silver bullion and bulk silver and gold coins. Exchange members must now file reports on silver market activities.

July 16—Silver Institute credits the 1974 increase in use of silver for coinage to the Olympic Coin Program, which put Canada in first place as a user of silver for coins.

Oct. 1—Bureau of Mines reports domestic industrial silver consumption increased 7 million ounces above the first quarter of 1975; new mine production remains unchanged.

Oct. 31—Bureau of the Mint taps more than 1 million ounces of its silver stocks between Aug. 1

and Oct. 31 to produce 40 percent silver Bicentennial coins, Bureau of Mines reports.

Dec. 17—Japanese exports of silver bullion at 219.7 metric tons during the first nine months of 1975.

1976

Feb. 11—A-Mark Coin Co., Beverly Hills, Calif., spends $7.3 million to acquire the dollar hoard of LaVere Redfield.

April 1—Indian government announces exporters of silver will be required to have a license, to be granted on a quota system. Before, India had permitted unlicensed export of silver. Prices rise in New York in response to the news.

April 12—*Wall Street Journal* reports silver experts show optimism about an increase in use of silver as the economy improves.

Aug. 26—Indian government decrees that all exports of silver be channeled through the State Trading Corporation.

Sept. 8—The House Armed Services Committee votes to reinstate the bill permitting the sale of 118 million ounces of silver from the national stockpile after silver has been eliminated from an earlier stockpile sale bill.

Oct. 2—The 94th Congress adjourns without having acted on pending legislation authorizing disposal of silver deemed in excess of stockpile objectives.

Dec. 31—Handy & Harman estimates industrial consumption of silver increased about 6 percent during 1976 to an estimated 167.5 million ounces compared to a revised figure of 157.7 million ounces in 1975.

World consumption for industrial and coinage uses combined, excluding Communist-dominated areas, amounted to about 442 million ounces, about 7 percent ahead of Handy & Harman's revised 1975 figure.

Industrial consumption rose about 8 percent over the previous year, to some 395 million ounces; consumption for coinage decreased by the same percentage to 27 million ounces, from 29.2 million ounces in 1975.

An unexpected boost was given to silver supplies in 1976 because of the demonetizing and melting of 28 million ounces of German coins.

1977

Jan. 12—The Silver Institute reports coins supplied the ingredients for 4,579,119 ounces of silver refined in the U.S. during November 1976, the second month in a row that substantial quantities of coins were supplied to refiners of .999 fine silver.

Feb. 23—Handy & Harman's 61st annual report on the silver market anticipates little change in conditions in 1977, with a somewhat higher price for the year.

March 9—Rep. Silvio Conte, R-Mass., introduces a bill to release 118 million troy ounces of silver from

the national stockpile. Experts have little expectation the bill will pass in 1977.

March 28—Silver price marches to $4.983 per troy ounce in a bid to break the $5 barrier; yields to profit taking in the next few days.

April 27—Hecla Mines' Philip Lindstrom sees silver demand growing in 1977 and higher prices in the long term.

May 1—J. Aron Commodities Corp. researchers believe inflation could carry silver to as high as $5.50 per ounce during 1977; they believe a price well above $5 will be required to free a substantial amount of silver coins for the refiners.

July 20—Coinage consumed 10 percent of the silver mined in 1976, with 180 types issued by 72 countries, according to the Silver Institute. Canada, France, Austria, the German Federal Republic and Belgium were the major producers, with the United States sixth.

July 20—Sen. James McClure, R-Idaho, introduces a bill that would set strategic stockpile objectives based on average annual import deficits. This would require a one- or two-year supply of silver for emergencies.

1978

March 8—The price of silver on the Commodity Exchange in New York gains 35 cents since March 6, to clear the $5 price barrier.

June 7—Sen. Gary Hart, D-Colo., proposes a silver stockpile sales target of 15 million ounces as a compromise between the Carter administration's request to sell 62.5 million ounces and other Western senators' opposition to any sale.

Oct. 17—Silver price climbs to $5.945 on the Comex; warehouse stocks are down by nearly 10 million ounces.

1979

Jan. 3—Silver consumption for the third quarter of 1978 (37.3 million ounces) was 5.9 million ounces, or 13.6 percent, lower than the second quarter.

Feb. 20—The price of silver climbs to a record $7.94 on the Comex, in response to political and military tensions.

May 2—Mint Director Stella Hackel says she would consider striking a silver commemorative coin for the Olympics in 1984.

July 25—Rep. Larry McDonald, D-Ga., introduces bill that would authorize the purchase of 240 million ounces of silver over the next six years, calling silver "the first of the strategic metals the world will run out of."

Aug. 8—The House is considering three silver bills: An administration request for the sale of 15 million ounces; a bill introduced by Rep. Silvio Conte, R-Mass., to sell all 139.5 million ounces in the stockpile; and the bill by Larry McDonald, to increase the stockpile by 240 million ounces.

Sept. 4—The price of silver climbs to a record

$11.02 on the Comex in New York City.

Dec. 12—Silver price on the Comex crosses $20, as it is traded for $20.08.

1980

Jan. 2—House votes to keep silver stockpile intact.

Jan. 18—Silver price soars to an all-time record of $50.35 in trading on Comex.

Jan. 28—The Chicago Board of Trade joins Comex in halting silver trading for a three-month period to stabilize prices at $33 to $36.50 level.

April 9—Silver prices tumble below $20; Hunt brothers fail to meet $100 million margin call (see main Silver narrative in this chapter for details).

May 7—Commodity Futures Trading Commission probes Hunt family's role in the "Great Silver Run-up."

May 21—The Federal Reserve approves more than $800 million in bailout loans to the Hunt family.

July 9—The Silver Institute reports the Soviet Union was the world's major silver producer in 1979, mining 49.8 million tons, 400,000 tons more than Mexico produced.

Nov. 26—The General Services Administration is accepting bids for 140,173.29 ounces of silver reclaimed by the Veterans Administration and refined by the New York Assay Office.

1981

April 1—The Reagan administration announces plans to sell 139.5 million ounces of stockpiled silver.

May 27—The Commodity Futures Trading Commission fails to pin a market manipulation "rap" on the Hunt brothers.

June 24—House subcommittee on Seapower and Strategic and Critical Materials seeks to block Reagan administration's proposal to sell stockpiled silver.

July 8—Sen. James McClure, R-Idaho, voices opposition to the sale of silver in the strategic stockpile.

Oct. 14—First General Services Administration sale of stockpiled silver draws few successful bidders.

Nov. 11—Interior Secretary James Watt joins Republican Sens. James McClure and Steven Symms and Reps. Craig and Hansen of Idaho in opposition to the silver stockpile sell-off.

Nov. 25—Idaho Sens. McClure and Symms introduce legislation to halt weekly silver stockpile sales and turn any excess silver into commemorative coins.

Dec. 9—GSA suspends Nov. 25 auction after not accepting any bids at the two previous weekly auctions.

Dec. 30—President signs Defense Appropriations Act with amendment that halts the sale of strategic silver for six months to permit a study of GSA sales and alternate disposal methods.

1982

Feb. 10—General Accounting Office calls silver bullion coin sales a viable alternative to stockpile auctions.

March 8—Spot price of silver drops to $6.85 on the Comex in New York.

May 19—Seventy-seven nations issued 180 different silver coin types during 1981, including 14 that did not issue any the previous year.

July 7—The U.S. Mint begins accepting orders for Washington commemorative silver half dollars.

July 7—The use of silver for coins and medals in the first quarter of 1982 was down 100,000 ounces from the same quarter in 1981; but the 900,000 ounces consumed was 50 percent greater than that used in the fourth quarter of the previous year.

Sept. 15—The price of silver reaches $8.465 per ounce, high for the year on the Comex on Aug. 26.

Oct. 14—The Treasury Department announces plans to strike Proof 1983 and 1984 .900 fine silver dollars together with a Proof 1984 gold coin, to commemorate the 1984 Summer Olympic Games in Los Angeles, after receiving congressional authorization. The silver coins will be struck at the San Francisco Assay Office and will bear an S Mint mark.

1983

Jan. 19—Washington commemorative half dollar sales exceed 5 million.

Feb. 16—Bureau of the Mint announces availability for future purchase of P, D and S Uncirculated 1983 and 1984 Olympic commemorative silver dollars.

Feb. 23—Secretary Watt tells silver miners that the silver stockpile disposal is still "under review" by the Interior Department.

May 18—Mint officials announce the availability of Prestige Proof sets in 1983 and 1984, each of which will contain examples of the Proof 1983-S and 1984-S Olympic commemorative dollars.

June 29—The Ad Hoc Committee for American Silver recommends that the 137.5 million ounces of silver in the stockpile be reduced to zero through the sale of silver bullion coins.

Oct. 5—A joint survey by the Ad Hoc Committee for American Silver and the Silver Institute shows strong public interest in silver bullion coins struck from stockpiled silver.

Nov. 2—Domestic silver usage during the first half of 1983, at 59 million ounces, was down 8 percent from the same period in 1982.

Dec. 14—The Treasury launches a feasibility study for marketing bullion coins struck from stockpiled silver; no action is likely before 1985.

1984

Jan. 9—Silver plummets to $7.79 as the U.S. dollar overwhelms foreign currencies.

Jan. 11—The Mint ceases Washington commemorative half dollar production.

May 16—Silver dollar specialist Wayne Miller sells his virtually complete set of Morgan and Peace dollars to professional numismatist David Hall, for a reported sum of more than $1 million.

May 23—The House Armed Services Committee recommends the sale of 10 million ounces of stockpiled silver, leaving open the possibility of minting coins from the silver.

May 30—The 1982 United States George Washington commemorative silver half dollar wins "Coin of the Year" honors in a competition sponsored by Krause Publications.

June 13—Two separate measures introduced in Congress could pave the way for Americans to buy newly minted Morgan dollars within the year. Measures fail to gain passage.

July 18—Industrial consumption of silver for the first quarter of 1984 was 30.7 million ounces, up 5 percent from a year ago, according to the Bureau of Mines.

July 25—World mints in 1983 used nearly 500,000 more ounces of silver for coinage than in 1982, with 77 countries issuing 264 coin types, according to the Silver Institute.

Aug. 22—The doubling found on numerous 1984 Olympic silver dollars is positively identified as an unusual form of strike doubling and is not the result of doubled dies, according to U.S. Mint and hobby experts.

Sept. 26—An 1804 silver dollar and 1894-S dime are among the silver rarities included in millionaire Dr. Jerry Buss' collection, to be sold soon at public auction.

Dec. 5—Mexico's new silver bullion coin, the Libertad, is selling beyond expectations, with the 1983 version released Nov. 1 and a new method of pricing due to be introduced with the release of the 1985 coin.

1985

Jan. 30—Canada plans 10 silver $20 coins and one gold $100 coin to commemorate the 1988 Olympics in Calgary.

Feb. 20—the Proof 1984-S silver dollar seems destined to be the most-purchased U.S. Olympic coin, according to Treasury Department figures.

March 13—The Centennial of Canada's National Park system is the theme of the 1985 Canadian silver dollar and $100 gold commemorative coins.

March 27—A Montreal firm purchased the only privately held example of the 1911 Canadian silver dollar for an undisclosed amount.

June 21—The Senate passes the Statue of Liberty coin program with an amendment calling for a 1-ounce silver bullion coin to follow the Statue of Liberty program.

July 9—President Reagan signs bill authorizing the striking of a 1-ounce silver bullion coin.

Oct. 16—The Republic of Korea plans a 28-coin Olympic coin program for the 1988 Summer Games in Seoul.

Oct. 30—International Numismatic Society Authentication Bureau reports receiving excellent counterfeits of the 1917-S Walking Liberty, Obverse

Mint Mark half dollar in recent weeks.

Dec. 17— President Reagan signs bill authorizing the striking of four gold bullion coins.

Dec. 25—Final sales figures for Los Angeles Olympics commemorative coins show Proof 1983-S and 1984-S silver dollars to be the big sellers.

1986

Jan. 29—Silver Users Association executive calls the failure of silver prices to move up as interest rates and the dollar weakened the "biggest surprise" of 1985.

Feb. 12—The Wayne Miller collection of Morgan and Peace dollars, sold at auction by Superior Galleries, realizes $1,109,375.

March 12—Mint Director Donna Pope tells a House Appropriations subcommittee that the Mint predicts 4 million ounces of silver bullion coins will be sold during their first year of production.

May 23—Clayton silver mine in Idaho's Coeur d'Alene district joins Hecla's Lucky Friday and Sunshine mines in closing down because of unprofitable silver prices.

June 18—Mexico releases 1986 Libertad silver coin; mintage of the 1985 date was 2,015,000 pieces. Mintages were limited to 1 million for 1982, 1983 and 1984.

June 25—Officials reveal that the silver bullion coin will feature A.A. Weinman's Walking Liberty design on the obverse and a new Heraldic Eagle design by John Mercanti on the reverse.

Aug. 20—Mint announces plans to strike Proof examples of its 1986 silver bullion coins, with Mint marks. Uncirculated strikes will carry no Mint mark.

Sept. 3—Ceremonial striking of the first silver bullion coin is tentatively set for Oct. 29 at the San Francisco Assay Office.

Oct. 29—Congress approves legislation for a .900 fine silver coin with a face value of $1 and a gold coin containing about a quarter of an ounce, to be struck to mark the Bicentennial of the U.S. Constitution.

Nov. 24—The Mint releases American Eagle silver bullion coins to 27 authorized bulk dealers and market-makers, later termed "authorized purchasers."

Dec. 3—Mint expands production of silver bullion coins from the San Francisco Assay Office to the Denver Mint, with an end-of-the-year goal of 5 million pieces.

Dec. 3—Preliminary orders for Proof 1986 silver bullion coins climb to 624,743.

Dec. 10—Sales of Proof gold bullion coins amount to $168,117,400, and Proof silver, to $18,962,055, for a total of $187,079,055.

Dec. 14—Gold and silver Proof coin sales pass $200 million mark.

1987

Jan. 14—1986 silver bullion coin production exceeds 5 million-coin goal by 96,000 pieces.

January—Banco de Mexico officially releases a Proof issue of the Libertad silver bullion coin, the first attempt by the Banco de Mexico to market a Proof coin.

February—Belgium announces it will mint and sell gold and silver coins denominated in European Currency Units to commemorate the 30th anniversary of the European Community's founding treaty.

March 11—The U.S. Mint reports the sale of 7,286,000 silver bullion coins since the program began Oct. 29; projects a need for 18 million to 24 million ounces of silver in 1987.

April—South Korea begins minting gold and silver coins to commemorate the 1988 Olympics.

April—Germany approves plans to mint silver-copper coin to commemorate 30th anniversary of the founding of the European Community.

May—The New York Commodities Exchange temporarily shortens trading hours to catch up on a backlog of orders for silver and gold futures.

July 1—U.S. Mint begins production of gold and silver Bicentennial of the Constitution commemorative coins.

September—Mexico issues 40,000 bonds—Certificados de Plata—each backed by 100 ounces of newly mined Mexican silver.

Oct. 19—Dramatic crash of world stock markets sends many investors scurrying for cover in precious metals.

1988

March—South Dakota exempts the state's Bison gold and silver bullion pieces from state sales taxes.

April—The Chicago Board of Trade receives Commodity Futures Trading Commission approval to begin trading 5,000-ounce silver futures.

June—Chicago Mercantile Exchange receives Commodity Futures Trading Commission approval to begin trading 5,000-ounce silver futures, but delays start of silver futures trading indefinitely.

July—Canada's Royal Canadian Mint announces plans to begin production of silver and platinum bullion coins.

October—U.S. Treasury's Fiscal Year 1989 appropriations bill contains provisions for selling 2.5 million ounces of its more than 400 million ounces of stockpile silver in each of the next three years.

1989

June 14—U.S. Mint begins production of gold and silver coins commemorating the Bicentennial of the U.S. Congress.

July 18—The Defense Logistics Agency sale of surplus Treasury silver brings accepted bids ranging from $5.01 to $5.08 per ounce.

August—Japan announces intentions of issuing up to 10 million silver coins to commemorate the International Garden and Greenery Exposition in 1990.

September—Canada announces plans for series of gold, platinum and silver coins to commemorate the 10th anniversary of the Maple Leaf; Soviet Union announces platinum, palladium, gold and silver commemorative coins depicting events in Russian history; Pobjoy Mint in the United Kingdom issues Cat gold and silver coins.

1990

June—The coin and antiquities collections of the Hunt brothers are sold at auction, in part to settle debts arising from their failed attempt to corner the silver market.

December—In the final hours of the 101st Congress, lawmakers approved a coinage program calling for 90 percent silver coins to be struck in Proof format of the dime, quarter dollar and half dollar.

1991

March 6—It is reported that the Mint has sold more than 1 million 1-ounce American Eagles per month for three consecutive months. Only once before did this happen since the inception of the American Eagle silver coins program in 1986.

April 4—India's role in the silver market becomes increasingly important. It is reported on this date that India imported 40 million ounces of silver during 1990, a two-fold increase from 1989. In the 1980s, India sold rather than purchased large amounts of silver.

Nov. 22—Upon the fifth anniversary of the American Eagle silver dollar program, it is announced that more than 44 million 1-ounce coins have been sold. 1991 is shaping up to be the best year for the program since 1986, on pace to sell more than 7 million 1-ounce coins.

1992

March 2—Sales of the Proof American Eagle 1-ounce silver coins reached a low point in 1991. Only 480,959 Proof 1-ounce silver coins were sold compared to nearly 1.5 million in 1986. Meanwhile, the Uncirculated 1-ounce coins reached a high of 7.2 million in 1991, the highest total since 1987.

April 21—At an IRS meeting, representatives of the Industry Council for Tangible Assets recommended reporting regulations that would require coin dealers to report silver transactions involving more than 1,000 ounces of the metal. Currently dealers are required to fill out paperwork involving silver bullion for transactions valued as low as 25 cents.

June—The U.S. Mint sets a price of $18 for the Silver Proof set. Order forms were mailed to 2.2 million customers beginning May 22. This is the first time since 1969 that the Mint has offered the Kennedy half dollar containing silver, and the first time since 1964 for the Roosevelt dime and the Washington quarter dollar.

October—An unidentified shipwreck yields 180 silver bars, 300 silver coins of Philip II of Spain and silver dinner plates and art objects. The ship is thought to have gone down in "the late 1500s and early 1600s."

1993

Jan. 18—The U.S. Mint reports sales of 1,108,000 American Eagle 1-ounce silver coins sold during December, an astonishing amount given that total production of the year was just over 5.5 million.

March 1—As part of a sweeping monetary reform in Mexico, that country's government introduces a ringed bimetallic 10-peso coin that has a silver center.

April 19—Silver industry analysts are divided on the prospects of silver as it hovers near $3.50 an ounce. Some think it could surpass $4 an ounce by mid-summer of the year; others think "it is dead in the water" as an investment.

May 24—The Industry Council for Tangible Assets pursues a ruling on "cash" reporting. Opinions about the enforcement of rules on the reporting of transactions involving circulated silver coins bags (sometimes thought to be a "cash" transaction) differ among IRS personnel nationwide.

June 7—Silver breaks the $4.50 an ounce mark, fueling speculation that the precious metal is back as a viable investment hedge against a downturn in the financial markets.

Aug. 30—The U.S. Mint reports that the American Eagle silver dollar has topped the 50 million mark, noting "the silver Eagle rapidly became the most widely traded silver coin in the world."

Dec. 23—Silver finishes the year at $4.65 an ounce, nearly $1 higher than its 1992 close of $3.66. Sales for the American Eagle 1-ounce silver coin rose from 5.54 million in 1992 to 6.76 million coins in 1993.

1994

Jan. 14—Silver breaks the $5 an ounce barrier and closes at $5.21 on Jan. 14.

March 24—Silver closes at $5.75 an ounce on the London market, a five-year high.

April—Industry observers agree that the sharp rise in the price of silver, nearly 50 cents per ounce from late February to late March, is directly related to the sharp decline in financial markets during this same period. As the stock market recovers, silver beats a retreat to $5.30 by April 15th.

June 20—The Mint reports that since the first of the year it has sold 1.45 million American Eagle silver coins, a pace far slower than 1993 sales. Volatility is apparently not good for the sale of the 1-ounce silver coins.

Oct. 24—The Mint reports that "demand for gold and silver Uncirculated American Eagle bullion coins dropped precipitously during the month of September. …" Because of "… rising metals prices and additional confidence in the stock market, there seemed to be more selling into the [precious metals] market than people buying."

Dec. 19—Officials managing the U.S. Mint's American Eagle Bullion Coin Program are looking at ways to cut costs from the production and promotion of 1-ounce silver American Eagles to avoid a suggested increase in the per coin price to authorized distributors. Since 1986, the premium has remained at $1 above the prevailing spot price.

1995

Jan. 30—Silver begins the year at well under $5 an ounce having been in the $4.65 to $4.75 area for close to two months.

Feb. 6—The number of 1994 American Eagle silver bullion coins sold by the U.S. Mint set a record low with a total of 4,227,319 coins. The total represents the first time mintage fell below 5 million coins since the program's inception in 1986.

May—A sharp drop in inventory levels of the physical metal helps silver hit a six-year high as futures contracts hit $6.16 an ounce.

June 19—Industry reporters note that silver is "finally getting scarcer, with supply falling short of demand for five consecutive years." The cumulative shortfall is 491 million ounces and most observers agree that this fundamental allowed for the sudden rise in the price of silver by the ounce.

July 10—Losses estimated between $900,000 and $1 million have forced the U.S. Mint to raise the premium on a per coin basis from $1 to $1.25 to authorized distributors. The increase went into effect on June 16.

Nov. 20—Sales of 1995-dated American Eagle 1-ounce silver coins appear to be poised to hit record lows, the second year in a row that such records will have been set.

Dec. 18—As the stock market's Dow Jones Index breaks 5,000, precious metals analysts predict "there is too much silver is around" and the market will remain static for some time. Silver closes the year at $5.25 an ounce.

1996

Jan. 1—A backlash develops over the fact that the U.S. Mint bases the price of the American Eagle silver coins on the London price of silver. Authorized dealers of the American Eagle coins say they will not purchase any more of the coins until the Mint bases pricing on the COMEX price of silver.

Feb. 19—Since mid-1985 when the U.S. Mint began using stockpiled silver for the American Eagle program, nearly 65 percent of that stockpile has been used according to Mint spokesman. Meanwhile, the price of silver by the ounce remains stable at the $5.50 level.

Aug. 28—Silver closes at $5.21.

Sept. 16—The U.S. Mint reports sales of the American Eagle silver bullion coin to be 300,000 for July and August, a record low pace.

Dec. 23—Sales of the American Eagle silver bullion coin remain on pace for a record low production. Sales of silver bullion coins around the world are sluggish.

1997

Jan. 20—The Mint announces the 1996 silver

1-ounce American Eagle coin had its lowest mintage since the launch of the program in 1986. The United States Mint on Jan. 6 projected the final 1996 mintage totals at 3.7 million coins.

Jan. 27—Analysts observe that with silver below $5 an ounce bullion coin sales should rise.

July 8—Silver closes on the London market at $4.25 an ounce. Bullion sales in the United States and around the world continue at sluggish pace.

Oct. 20—The U.S. Mint announces that sales of the American Eagle 1-ounce silver coin may set new lows. Through September, sales were 2.291 million coins, a pace slower than the 1996 lows of 3.603 million coins.

Oct. 31—Silver breaks through $5 an ounce, closing at $5.28 on Oct. 6, but falls back again to close under $5 at $4.81 on Oct. 31.

Dec. 23—Silver literally explodes to $6.20 an ounce. Analysts search for reasons saying, "physical consumption of silver is outpacing the silver mines ability to produce it and hence the rise in price."

1998

Jan. 12—The *Financial Times* in London reports that U.S. lawyers are preparing to launch a class-action suit alleging manipulation of the silver market.

Jan. 14—*Wall Street Journal* reports increased surveillance efforts by the Commodity Futures Trading Commission. Speculation abounds that much of the silver recently purchased has been shipped from U.S. warehouses to Europe to encourage price speculation.

Feb. 4—Warren Buffet announces that he has purchased approximately 130 million ounces of silver.

Feb. 5—Silver closes at $7.25 an ounce, a nine-year high going back to July 1988.

Feb. 23—The U.S. Mint reports January sales of the American Eagle 1-ounce silver coin at 460,000. Increased silver prices have resulted in increased sales of bullion related coins.

March 23—The U.S. Mint announces that Proof versions of the American Eagle 1-ounce silver coin will increase in price by $1 to keep up with the advance in the price of silver. Sales for the coin begin March 27.

June 29—Allegations of market manipulation reduce activity in the silver market. On June 11 silver closes at $5.04.

Dec. 28—Wholesalers hike the price of silver planchets needed for American Eagle 1-ounce silver coin production. The retail price to consumers advances more than 20 percent.

1999

March 15—The U.S. Mint reveals that planchet supply problems have made it difficult to fill orders for the American Eagle 1-ounce silver coin. Canadian Maple Leaf and privately produced 1-ounce silver rounds have been experiencing explosive sales the first two months of the year.

March 22—The American Eagle 1-ounce silver coin is selling for two times the spot price in light of Y2K concerns and the lack of quality planchets on which the coins can be struck.

May 10—More than 10,000 of the General Services Administration Carson City Mint silver dollars enter the market via two major coin deals.

July 19—The U.S. Mint announces American Eagle 1-ounce silver coin sales at more than 4.4 million, a figure that exceeds full-year production for three out of the past five years.

Sept. 20—A new record is set when a Texas collector pays $4.14 million for the Sultan of Muscat specimen of the famed 1804 Draped Bust silver dollar.

Sept. 27—Sales of the American Eagle silver coin remain strong. Sales, as of Aug. 31, stand at 5,756,000 coins. The spot price of silver has spent the better part of the year in a narrow trading range between $5 and $5.50 an ounce.

Dec. 20—The nearly 7.3 million 1-ounce American Eagle silver coins sold through November top every year since the inception of the silver American Eagle program except 1987. The spot price of silver hovers at $5.20 an ounce.

2000

Feb. 1—U.S. Mint officials report that the Mint sold 7,408,640 1999 American Eagle 1-ounce silver bullion coins. That figure represents a 52.8 percent increase over 1998's total of 4,847,549 coins.

Feb. 7—Silver reaches its year-high at $5.4475 per ounce on the London market.

Feb. 16—U.S. Mint officials report strong sales of the American Eagle 1-ounce silver bullion coin during January and early February. Sales totaled more than 1.4 million coins.

Feb. 24—U.S. Mint Director Philip N. Diehl tells *Coin World* that the Mint buys silver from the silver National Defense Stockpile based on the spot market price of silver on the day the metal is purchased. The Silver Institute claims that the Mint's use of silver for its annual bullion and collector coin programs threatens to deplete the stockpile by the end of 2001.

Nov. 22—U.S. Mint officials estimate that the silver in the U.S. Defense National Stockpile represents at least a year's worth of metal for annual coin programs, but the Mint is developing a plan to address future acquisition of silver for the Mint's coinage programs.

Dec. 29—Silver hits a year-low at $4.57 an ounce on the London bullion market.

2001

Jan. 19—Silver hits its year high, reaching $4.82 an ounce in the London markets.

May 4—2001 American Buffalo commemorative silver dollars first-strike ceremony is held at the Denver Mint.

Aug. 31—U.S. Mint makes 2001-S Silver Proof sets available and announces that its production will be limited to 1 million sets.

Oct. 4—U.S. Mint officials reveal that less than 15 million ounces of silver remains in its stockpile and that the Mint is developing a plan to buy silver on the market for coin programs.

Oct. 31—Armored trucks begin removing more than $200 million of gold and silver from a huge vault beneath 4 World Trade Center, part of the area damaged in the terrorist attacks of Sept. 11, 2001.

November—The November sales total of 948,000 American Eagle silver bullion coins represents the highest monthly total for calendar year 2001.

Nov. 22—Silver is at its year low, at $4.065 per ounce in the London markets.

2002

Feb. 1—Silver is at its year low, trading at $4.2467 per ounce in the London bullion market.

May 23—Legislation is introduced in the House of Representatives and Senate to allow U.S. Mint to buy silver on the open market to produce American Eagle bullion coins once the Defense National Stockpile is depleted.

June 10—U.S. Mint officials say that the Mint's supply of silver has dropped to about 25 million ounces; greater than previously estimated, but still not enough to meet the Mint's long-term demand of approximately 10 million ounces annually.

July 16—Silver reaches its year-high, trading at $5.0975 an ounce in the London bullion markets.

December—Prices for the 10-coin 2001-S Silver Proof set quadruple in the secondary market, as just 317,142 sets were produced, a sharp drop from the 965,421 sets produced in 2000.

Nov. 25—U.S. Mint authorized purchasers are informed that they must purchase two 2002 American Eagle silver bullion coins for every three 2003 coins.

December—U.S. Mint reports that December sales of 2.49 million American Eagle 1-ounce silver bullion coins is the highest year-end monthly sales total since 2,510,500 of the silver coins were sold in December 1994.

2003

Jan. 10—U.S. Mint drops restrictions on authorized purchasers to buy 2002 American Eagle silver bullion coins in orders for 2003-dated issues.

April 2—Sales of Proof 2003-W American Eagles begin. The issue eventually sells out, reaching its maximum 750,000 authorized mintage.

April 3—Silver is at its low point for the year at $4.37 an ounce in the London bullion market.

May 12—The only known Uncirculated example of the 1870-S Seated Liberty silver dollar sells at a Stack's auction for $1,092,500. Also in the auction, an 1885 Trade dollar, cataloged as Brilliant Proof, sells for $920,000.

Aug. 8—U.S. Mint officials delay shipping 10-coin 2003-S Silver Proof sets because the certificates of authenticity wrongly intimate that the dime and half dollar are copper-nickel clad and not .900 fine silver.

Dec. 31—Silver ends the year at its highest point for the year, trading at $5.965 an ounce in the London precious metals markets.

2004

Jan. 27—Odyssey Marine Explorations Inc. reports that it had recovered 2,950 gold coins and 14,230 silver coins form the wreckage of the 19th century shipwreck SS *Republic.*

Feb. 26—The Du Pont specimen of the 1866 Seated Liberty, No Motto silver dollar, one of only two known examples and unaccounted for since a 1967 robbery, is located in Maine.

March 26—The Du Pont 1866 Seated Liberty, No Motto silver dollar is displayed at the American Numismatic Association National Money Show in Portland, Ore.

April 2—Silver is at its high point for the year, trading at $8.29 an ounce in the London precious metals markets.

May 10—Just more than one month after reaching its 2004 high, silver hits its year low at $5.495 an ounce in the London markets.

Oct. 13—A New York judge orders the National Collector's Mint to suspend sales and advertising of its "2004 Freedom Tower Silver Dollar."

December—At 2,622,500, monthly sales of American Eagle bullion silver coins increased five-fold over November's levels, reaching the second-highest December total since the American Eagle coin program was launched in 1986.

2005

Jan. 4—Silver starts the year at its low point for 2005, trading at $6.39 an ounce in the London markets.

March 7—A 1894-S Barber dime graded Proof 66 sells for $1,322,500 at DLRC Auctions' sale of the Richmond Collection, Part III, in Baltimore.

March 15—U.S. Mint begins selling Proof 2005-W American Eagle silver dollars, six weeks earlier than the 2004 coins and without a maximum authorized production.

June 30—A 1794 Flowing Hair silver dollar in Mint State 64 condition realizes $1.15 million in an American Numismatic Rarities auction.

September—The Royal Canadian Mint announces that it will issue a Maple Leaf half-ounce .9999 fine silver bullion coin.

Dec. 12—Silver is at its high point for the year, at $9.225 an ounce in London.

2006

Jan. 6—Silver starts the year at its low point, trading for $8.83 an ounce in the London markets.

March 3—Silver bullion closes at $10.08 an ounce, the first time that silver has a double-digit finish since March 30, 1984, when it ended the trading day at $10.135 an ounce.

April 26—A 1792 half disme graded Specimen 67 sells for $1,322,500 at a Heritage Galleries auction held during the Central States Numismatic Society's convention in Columbus, Ohio.

May 12—Silver hits $14.94 an ounce in the London markets, its 2006 high.

May 29—The Royal Canadian Mint officially opens its new silver refinery in Ottawa, allowing it to offer in-house silver refinery services.

Aug. 30—U.S. Mint begins selling American Eagle 20th anniversary three-coin sets with silver coins in three finishes: Proof, Reverse Proof and Uncirculated (which collectors call "Burnished Uncirculated").

2007

January—U.S. Mint officials announce they are considering the concept of Proof silver versions of the Presidential dollar coins.

Jan. 9—A silver decadrachm of Athens, issued circa 467 to 465 B.C., brings $575,000 during the Triton X auction held in New York by Classical Numismatic Group. This represented a record price for an ancient Greek coin sold at public auction.

March 27—U.S. Mint begins selling Proof 2007-W American Eagle silver dollars for $29.95, $2 more than in 2006.

Aug. 21—At $11.67 an ounce, this is silver's low point for 2007 in the London bullion markets.

Nov. 7—Silver hits its high for the year, closing at $15.82 an ounce in the London markets.

2008

Feb. 4—U.S. Mint officials suspend American Eagle silver bullion coin sales because of insufficient supplies of blanks. Sales were resumed a month later.

March 17—Silver is at its high for the year, trading at $20.92 an ounce in the London bullion markets.

March 19—U.S. Mint suspends sales of American Eagle silver bullion coins again because of shortages.

April—It is discovered that an unknown number of Uncirculated 2008-W American Eagle 1-ounce silver dollars feature the reverse design of 2007. The obverse and reverse designs were slightly modified for the 2008 coins.

April 21—U.S. Mint resumes sales of American Eagle silver bullion coins, though under a rationing plan.

May 29—U.S. Mint officials continue to ration American Eagle silver bullion coins because of a supply sufficiently below unprecedented demand.

August—A quick decline in the price of silver creates a surge of retail demand from buyers, but retailers cannot build inventories at the low price levels. American Eagle silver coins are in short supply.

Aug. 20—The U.S. Mint suspends sales of Proof 2008-W American Eagle silver dollars so the blanks originally intended for the Proof program can be used in producing silver bullion coins to meet the high collector and investor demand.

Oct. 6—United States Mint decides to focus production on American Eagle 1-ounce silver and gold coins, and to end production of all other bullion coins

once their planchet supplies are exhausted.

Oct. 14—U.S. Mint raises the premium it charges authorized purchasers for American Eagle 1-ounce silver bullion coins from $1.25 to $1.40. The 15-cent increase is the first in the premium for the silver bullion coins since 1995.

Oct. 24—Silver reaches its low point for the year, closing at $8.88 an ounce in the London markets.

December—Final 2008 sales of American Eagle silver bullion coins set a record at 19,583,500 coins. Mintage for the 2008 American Eagle silver bullion coin is also a record, at 20,583,000 (2008 sales could include coins dated 2007, 2008 and 2009).

2009

Jan. 30—Silver is at its low point for the year, trading at $10.51 an ounce in the London bullion markets.

April 14—U.S. Mint officials announce a sellout of the 450,000 individual Proof and Uncirculated Abraham Lincoln Bicentennial commemorative silver dollars. The coins went on sale Feb. 12.

April 30—The Adams-Carter specimen of the Class III 1804 Draped Bust dollar realizes $2.3 million during a Heritage Auction Galleries sale in conjunction with the Central States Numismatic Society convention in Cincinnati.

July 17—Eighteen-coin 2009-S Silver Proof sets go on sale from the U.S. Mint. During the first two days of sales, 271,372 sets are sold.

Sept. 30—Sales total of American Eagle 1-ounce silver bullion coins total 20,467,500 pieces, breaking the calendar year 2008 record with three months of sales left in the year.

Oct. 6—U.S. Mint officials announce that it will not produce Proof 2009-W American Eagle silver coins for collectors due to unprecedented demand for bullion coins.

Oct. 15—The Lincoln Coin and Chronicles set containing all four Proof 2009-S Lincoln, Bicentennial cents and a Proof 2009-P Lincoln, Bicentennial silver dollar go on sale. The entire production of 50,000 sets sells out the next day.

Dec. 2—At $19.18 an ounce, silver is at its high point for the year in the London markets.

December—At 28,766,500 ounces, 2009 sales of American Eagle silver bullion coins set a record, eclipsing the 2008 record. The mintage of 2009 American Eagle silver bullion coins is also a record high, at 30,459,000.

2010

Feb. 8—Silver is at its lowest point for the year, closing at $15.14 an ounce in the London markets.

March 27—During a public forum, U.S. Mint Director Edmund C. Moy states that if the record demand for American Eagle silver bullion coins continues, no Proof 2010-W American Eagles will likely be produced.

May 14—A 1794 Flowing Hair silver dollar sells

for a reported $7.85 million in a private transaction, making it a world record price paid for a single coin.

July 31—The Mint recorded sales of 20,820,500 American Eagle silver bullion coins, pacing for a record-production for the year.

Aug. 7—A 1794 Flowing Hair silver dollar graded Mint State 64 sells for $1,207,500 at a Bowers and Merena Auction in Boston.

Nov. 19—The U.S. Mint opens sales for Proof 2010-W American Eagle silver dollars with a limit of 100 coins per household. Mint officials decide to strike and sell the Proof version after adding suppliers of the silver planchets used for the Proof and bullion versions of the coins.

Dec. 1—U.S. Mint officials announce that the maximum mintage for each 2010 America the Beautiful 5-ounce .999 fine silver bullion quarter dollar will be 33,000 coins, not the 100,000 pieces per design announced months before. In addition, the Mint will strike 27,000 Uncirculated pieces of each design with the P Mint mark of the Philadelphia Mint.

Dec. 6—The U.S. Mint suspends sales of America the Beautiful 5-ounce .999 fine silver bullion coins to authorized purchasers amid complaints of speculative presale pricing due to smaller-than-expected mintages. Sales resume Dec. 10 with restrictions on pricing, the number of coins that can be sold to each customer and to whom the coins can be sold.

Dec. 21—The U.S. Mint records sales of 34,637,500 American Eagle silver bullion coins in 2010, a record. Total mintage for 2010 American Eagle silver bullion coins is 34,764,500.

Dec. 30—Silver ends the year at its highest point, reaching $30.70 an ounce in the London markets.

2011

Jan. 4—In the first day of trading for the new year, silver closes at $30.67 an ounce in London. On the same day, the U.S. Mint announces that it has raised the price of several of its products including the 2011-S Silver Proof set, which went from a 2010 price of $56.95 to a 2011 price of $67.95.

Feb. 16—Silver closes above $30 an ounce on the London market, at $30.22.

March 7—Silver closes above $35 an ounce on the London market, at $36.60.

April 8—Silver closes above $40 an ounce on the London market, at $40.22.

April 28—In the second year of the America the Beautiful program, the U.S. Mint begins taking orders for a maximum of 126,500 each of the 2011 Gettysburg National Military Park Glacier National Park 5-ounce silver bullion coins from authorized purchasers, with none of the restrictions imposed on the purchasers for the 2010 coins.

April 28—Silver at $48.70 on the London market, about a $1 below its all-time high.

April 29—U.S. Mint opens sales of Uncirculated 2010-P Hot Springs National Park 5-ounce silver coin at a price of $279.95. Of the maximum 27,000-coin mintages, approximately 20,000 are ordered during the 12 hours of sales, with sales being placed online outnumbering sales placed by telephone at a 4-1 ratio.

May 3 to 6—Silver suffers its worst one-week slide since 1980, falling from nearly $50 an ounce to $35.28 an ounce in five days, leaving "Wall Street pros and individual investors dazed," according to the May 7 to 8 *Wall Street Journal.*

London Silver Bullion Market
Annual High, Low and Average Prices
Courtesy of www.kitco.com

Year	High	Low	Average	Year	High	Low	Average
1975	$5.225	$3.91	$4.4185	1993	$5.37	$3.545	$4.3018
1976	$5.10	$3.815	$4.3535	1994	$5.755	$4.625	$5.2873
1977	$4.96	$4.30	$4.623	1995	$6.01	$4.25	$5.1872
1978	$6.296	$4.829	$5.4009	1996	$5.79	$4.67	$5.1885
1979	$28.00	$5.961	$11.0938	1997	$6.205	$4.21	$4.8825
1980	$48.00	$10.80	$20.6316	1998	$7.31	$4.74	$5.5493
1981	$16.45	$7.95	$10.5116	1999	$5.75	$4.88	$5.2182
1982	$11.21	$4.885	$7.9473	2000	$5.4475	$4.57	$4.9506
1983	$14.745	$8.34	$11.4413	2001	$4.82	$4.065	$4.3702
1984	$10.035	$6.26	$8.1407	2002	$5.0975	$4.2476	$4.5995
1985	$6.735	$5.57	$6.1454	2003	$5.965	$4.37	$4.8758
1986	$6.195	$4.87	$5.4679	2004	$8.29	$5.495	$6.6711
1987	$10.20	$5.36	$7.0192	2005	$9.225	$6.39	$7.3164
1988	$7.99	$6.01	$6.5369	2006	$14.94	$8.83	$11.5452
1989	$6.17	$5.015	$5.494	2007	$15.82	$11.67	$13.3836
1990	$5.39	$3.93	$4.8182	2008	$20.92	$8.88	$14.9891
1991	$4.53	$3.58	$4.0407	2009	$19.18	$10.51	$14.6733
1992	$4.315	$3.63	$3.9366	2010	$30.70	$15.14	$20.1928

Platinum

Chemical symbol: Pt
Atomic number: 78
Atomic weight: 195.09
Density @ 293k: 21.45

Platinum is one of the rarest and most precious of metals. The majority of the world's supply of platinum is mined in South Africa and Russia.

Platinum's great strength, high melting point and unique catalytic properties have made it vital to industry, and its rarity and purity have created a demand for it in the jewelry industry as well.

Much stronger than gold, 1 troy ounce of platinum can be spun into a wire 2 miles long. It is all but impervious to acids; it does not tarnish; and will not melt, except at extraordinary temperatures. Moreover, as a catalyst, platinum is one of those rare elements capable of triggering a chemical reaction in another substance while remaining unchanged in the process. And, since it doesn't oxidize, platinum has been used by the National Bureau of Standards to make weights that will remain accurate forever.

Until the late 18th century, platinum was considered a nuisance. Though traces of it have been found in ancient Egyptian inlays, artisans of the time probably believed it was some form of silver. Pre-Columbian Indians forged jewelry from copper alloys, but it was the Spanish who officially reported its "discovery" in the 16th century. They found it mixed with gold and called it "platina"—little silver. Most of the time, they threw the heavy metal back into the river, to permit it to "ripen" into gold.

The only "commercial" use made of platinum at the time was in the creation of counterfeit gold pieces, which were actually platinum coated with gold. When discovered by authorities, these imitation coins were thrown into the sea.

In the early 1700s, European metallurgists began to experiment with platinum for use in industry, but the metal's high melting point—3,216 degrees Fahrenheit—proved frustrating to them. It wasn't until 1782, when scientists developed new techniques for melting platinum, that the metal became a useful material for artisans. People became interested in platinum because it has the sheen of silver, does not tarnish and its metallic bonding makes it stronger than gold. Scientists continued to experiment with the metal, and in the early 1800s they discovered that platinum has five related metals in its group—palladium, rhodium, iridium, osmium and ruthenium. These are sometimes known as the "exotic" metals, because of their super-rarity. Today, many of these related metals are mixed with platinum to create special alloys that resist melting in the 3,000- to 4,000-degree Fahrenheit temperature range.

As a jewelry metal, the platinum vogue reached its peak in the United States in the jazz age of the 1920s, the era of Jean Harlow and platinum blondes. The icy-white metal was favored for its durability and nobility. Far harder than gold, it resists the nicks and scratches of daily wear; and, unlike silver, it never has to be polished to retain its lustrous sheen.

Platinum is much stronger than gold or silver, and so it is the preferred metal for holding fine stones and weaving delicate designs. It is also heavier and is the purest of the precious jewelry metals. Most platinum is 95 percent pure, while sterling silver is 92.5 percent, and 18-karat gold is only 75 percent.

Ironically, it was platinum's unique physical and chemical properties that brought about its eclipse as the United States' premier jewelry metal in the 1940s. When World War II began, platinum was declared a strategic metal of critical importance to the national defense and its sale as a jewelry metal was critically limited. Because the sources of platinum are limited to only a few countries and it would be difficult to obtain in the event of a protracted war or other national emergency, the United States maintains platinum in the National Defense Stockpile.

The vast majority of platinum's use is as an industrial and decorative metal, with lesser use in the investment field. Platinum's use is heavily dependent on the strength of the worldwide economy, with 2009 showing declines in the autocatalyst and other industrial segments, but registering gains in demand in the jewelry and investment segments.

The greatest demand for platinum and platinum group metals (including palladium and rhodium) is from the auto industry, where the metals are used in autocatalysts. In autocatalysts, the platinum catalyst changes noxious auto fumes into carbon dioxide and water vapor. Demand in this category rises and falls with the strength of the manufacture and sales of new automobiles, falling during the recessionary period of 2008 and 2009.

Second highest demand for platinum in 2009 was from the wider industrial field. Platinum is essential in the manufacture of fertilizer, pacemakers, cancer-combating drugs, industrial rubies (used in lasers), high-grade optical glass, fiberglass and razor blades.

The metal's use in jewelry is a close third, with platinum use in jewelry in China achieving record levels in 2009.

Platinum's use as an investment metal was a distant fourth in 2009. However, "identifiable" investment demand for platinum in 2009 rose 18.9 percent from 2008 figures due to strong ETF (exchange-traded fund, traded on stock exchanges) investment, according to Johnson Matthey's *Platinum 2010* report.

In 2009, 84.5 percent of platinum was mined in South Africa (33.38 percent) and Russia (51.19 percent), with North America and Zimbabwe producing most of the balance. Another potential source of the metal is "recycled" platinum taken from catalytic converters in junked cars. The converters are removed by the wrecker and sent to a plant where the platinum is stripped off chemically. This process yields only a small amount of platinum per converter.

Canada now has a series of platinum Maple Leaf coins, Australia issues its Koala platinum coins, and the Isle of Man continues to produce the Noble in a variety of weights. Mexico has issued an "unzo platino."

The United States also sells platinum bullion coins. It began selling platinum American Eagles in 1996. However, the Mint sold no American Eagle platinum bullion coins of any size in 2009 or 2010, although it did sell Proof versions. As of May 2011, United States Mint officials had not announced a decision of the future of the American Eagle platinum bullion coin program.

London Platinum Bullion Market
Annual High, Low and Average Prices
Courtesy of www.kitco.com

Year	High	Low	Average	Year	High	Low	Average
1988	$630	$439	$531	2000	$622	$414	$544
1989	$566	$466	$512	2001	$640	$415	$529
1990	$537	$387	$472	2002	$596	$453	$539
1991	$422	$330	$376	2003	$807	$603	$691
1992	$396	$329	$359	2004	$936	$744	$845
1993	$427	$335	$376	2005	$1,012	$844	$897
1994	$437	$379	$408	2006	$1,355	$982	$1,142
1995	$478	$398	$429	2007	$1,544	$1,165	$1,303
1996	$437	$369	$400	2008	$2,273	$763	$1,574
1997	$474	$340	$394	2009	$1,494	$918	$1,203
1998	$432	$340	$374	2010	$1,786	$1,492	$1,609
1999	$455	$342	$373				

15 Bullion Coins

Bullion coins are a popular investment—and to a growing extent, collectible—medium. But just what is a bullion coin? How is it different from any other precious metal coin?

The dictionary definition of "bullion" is "uncoined precious metal of precious metal fineness," so at first glance, the term "bullion coin" seems to be contradictory. For our purposes, "bullion coin" can be defined as a noncirculating legal tender coin intended to sell for its precious metal content rather than for face value or at a collector premium.

From the earliest days of coinage to well into the 20th century, coinage was tied to the value of the metal in which it was struck. In theory, a silver or gold coin's face value (denomination) was representative of its weight.

Before the South African Krugerrand, before Canada's Maple Leaf and before the American Eagle, perhaps the world's best-known bullion coin was the Austrian taler of Empress Maria Theresa. It is widely recognized as the first bullion coin. Since the time of her death in 1780, restrikes of a 42.5-millimeter, .8333 fine silver taler dated 1780 depicting her portrait have been minted by at least 15 mints, most of them outside Austria.

The taler coin long has been accepted internationally, not only in Europe, but in areas of the world where a firm local coinage did not or does not now exist. In particular, these included southeastern Africa and the countries around and including Saudi Arabia. The Maria Theresa taler can be found with chop marks and other banker test marks, indicative of a coin that was accepted in international trade. It was not the only coin that enjoyed wide acceptance but it is by far the best known.

The U.S. Trade silver dollar, struck from 1873 to 1885, is considered a contemporary bullion coin. It is another example of a silver bullion coin used throughout the world for trade. The coin was intended for use in Asian markets but primarily in China.

As recently as the mid-1960s in the United States, 90 percent silver coinage was issued for circulation. Production of U.S. gold coinage for circulation stopped in 1933, though in reality gold coins had not widely circulated in the United States for years.

The legalization of gold ownership in the United States on Dec. 31, 1974, changed the market. From 1933 to 1974, Americans could only own gold coins considered rare and unusual. They could not own bullion coins like the Krugerrand or modern commemoratives like Canada's 1967 Centennial of Confederation $20 coin. With the elimination of all barriers to gold ownership in the United States, a worldwide market in silver and gold was developed where commodities prices change daily, and money could be made (and lost) in speculation. The stage was set for government-issued bullion coins.

Precious metals have been used in coinage since antiquity. Their durability, rarity and beauty have made silver and gold the most treasured of coinage metals.

Gold and silver's use in modern coinage is primarily in commemorative and bullion coins issued by many of the world's leading governments.

The price of gold and silver bullion coins varies with the daily price of gold and silver and they can be bought and sold around the world through organized financial markets. Bullion coins are intended for consumers interested in the intrinsic value of the metal, while commemorative coins are marketed on the basis of the potential rarity or collector appeal.

Bullion coins are issued in a variety of weights and the issuing government guarantees their purity. Unlike gold bars, gold bullion coins do not require an assay when they are bought and sold. Traditionally, a gold bullion coin is minted in quantities to meet demand and the design remains consistent from year to year.

International bullion history

The Republic of South Africa in 1967 struck 50,065 pieces of a coin called the "Krugerrand," which features the likeness of Paulus Kruger, a South African statesman. The .917 fine gold Krugerrand has a gross weight of 33.9 grams, having other metals alloyed with the gold. The Krugerrand contains a full ounce of gold.

Through 1969, South Africa struck fewer than 50,000 pieces annually. In 1970, the mintage jumped to 242,000, including for the first time 10,000 Proof versions. From 1971 to 1973, Krugerrand mintages hovered around half a million pieces, with fewer than 10,000 Proofs produced annually.

In 1974, the mintage for the bullion coin jumped to 3,180,075 pieces. This jump, which was to be sustained for the next decade, is attributable in large part to a single act—the Aug. 14, 1974, signing by President Gerald Ford of legislation lifting a 40-year ban on the ownership of gold by United States citizens, effective Dec. 31.

During the 1980s, the world economy and political conditions influenced the demand for gold bullion coins.

Intergold, as the International Gold Corp. was known in the marketplace until its reorganization in 1986 into the Gold Information Center, was the marketing arm of the South African Chamber of Mines, the semi-official consortium responsible for distribution of the Krugerrand.

Intergold established offices worldwide with the goal of educating the investing public about gold in general, bullion coins especially and Krugerrands specifically. The measure of Intergold's success can be seen in that during the early 1980s, the Krugerrand commanded as much as 80 percent of the world's gold bullion coin market.

But two factors in 1984 and 1985, beyond Intergold's influence, combined to bring down the Krugerrand as the undisputed king of bullion coins. First, the price of gold stayed relatively flat and many investors shied away from tangibles. Second, and perhaps most devastatingly, the Krugerrand became identified as a symbol of South Africa's apartheid policy of racial discrimination.

It was perhaps inevitable that, when no fewer than 10 pieces of legislation introduced in the U.S. Congress in 1985 called for some restriction on the importation of Krugerrands into the United States, President Reagan signed an executive order banning the import of Krugerrands effective Oct. 11, 1985. No restrictions were placed on Krugerrands already trading within the United States.

However, the death knell had sounded. By late 1985 and early 1986, nearly every major market for the Krugerrand had been affected by government bans or banking agreements. Krugerrands were still traded by bullion coin investors, but the net effect of the prolonged debate about the morality of South Africa's policies and the destabilizing effect of months of doubt severely dulled the coin's sheen. The Royal Canadian Mint, which had introduced its Maple Leaf .9999 fine gold bullion coin in 1979, was ready to grab the throne.

In 1984, despite growing pressures against South Africa, the Krugerrand still held about two-thirds of the gold bullion coin market worldwide. By early 1986, that distinction belonged to the Maple Leaf.

Sales of American Eagle gold bullion coins began in October 1986 and the American Eagle quickly became the world's leading gold coin. The British Britannia, Australian Nugget and other coins soon followed into the market. Some analysts predicted a 10-million-ounce-per-year market for gold bullion coins. However, they neglected to consider other changes in the financial markets.

By the end of the 1980s, the Canadian Maple Leaf had regained market dominance from the American Eagle, in large part because of demand for the pure gold Maple Leaf in the markets of Hong Kong and Japan. There the price of gold was low because of the extraordinary strength of the local currencies. But at the same time, North American and European demand for gold bullion coins declined because of the lack of inflation in the U.S. economy and the higher returns available from equity investments. As a result, overall sales of gold bullion coins in the latter part of the 1980s declined.

Market makers responded to this decline by repositioning bullion coins as both a bullion coin and a numismatic coin. In 1990, the Australian Nugget was reintroduced as the Kangaroo Nugget and its mintage was limited. The Chinese Panda was similarly marketed with limited mintages. Canada and the United States both began to rely on their Proof issues to supplement their regular marketing programs. The Krugerrand was relaunched in the United States in October 1999 with coins dated 2000. Officials of Rand Refinery Ltd., the company that issues the bullion version of the Krugerrand, said the relaunch of the coin in the United States was due to a surge in demand for gold bullion.

Silver bullion coins enjoy continued success. The American Eagle silver bullion coin, a 1-ounce pure silver dollar, is one of the world's most popular silver coins. The governments of Australia, Austria, Canada, China and Mexico issue similar coins. Demand for these affordable coins continues unabated, in part because the silver bullion coins are less expensive than gold bullion coins. Silver investment demand is centered in North America, and because of the coins' low cost in comparison to gold and platinum, a large gift market has developed, though retailers entering the second decade of the 21st century reported some resistance from casual buyers as the price of silver leapt well beyond $20 an ounce, even surpassing $48.

The market

The bullion coin market differs from the numismatic market to which many collectors are accustomed. The bullion coin market operates in a tier system structured something like a pyramid, with the issuing authority at the top. The issuing government produces and then distributes the coins in large quantity through a narrow system of large distributors. Distributors in turn sell to wholesalers, who sell to a network of retailers, who then sell to the public. There is, of course, nothing to prevent a distributor or wholesaler from also being a retailer.

At each step down on the pyramid, the field widens. Let's say, hypothetically, a government sells to 10 distributors. Each distributor sells to 10 wholesalers, for a total of 100 wholesalers. Each wholesaler then sells to 10 retailers, for a total of 1,000 retailers. The tiered distribution system is often referred to as the "pipeline."

The most important function of the distribution system is in providing a buy-back market. Bullion coins are investments; investments must have a degree of liquidity.

Governments sell coins into the pipeline but will not buy them back. Selling the bullion coins through a network of private dealers enables a ready two-way market.

Large distributors absorb buy-backs while at the same time they hedge their positions in the marketplace and hold the coins until the market turns favorable. A small dealer, such as a coin shop or local bank, would place a serious strain on its liquidity if it were compelled to buy and hold coins from an investor taking a profit. And investors would not likely purchase coins for investment that could not be resold for profit.

Legal tender

No aspect of bullion coins is quite so important or quite so difficult to explain as legal tender status. Just what, in fact, constitutes a legal tender bullion coin is the matter of no little debate and seems to change from nation to nation.

Legal tender status for a bullion coin distinguishes it, at least in the mind of the collector or investor, from the many privately issued bullion pieces on the market. It is a badge of honor and legitimacy.

As an example, the American Arts Gold Medallion series of 1980 to 1984, though issued by the Bureau of the Mint under congressional mandate, was not afforded legal tender status. The distinction between "official," which the medallions are, and "legal tender," which they are not, may seem trivial to the point of an argument of semantics. However, the investors who were expected to purchase a minimum of a million ounces of the medallions every year stayed away in droves. The program was a failure.

The American Arts Gold Medallions were designed with the investor in mind, the larger piece containing 1 ounce of fine gold and the smaller a half ounce. However, the pieces of 1980 and 1981 have a "medal-like" appearance. Obverses are portraits of the artist with the name above the bust. Reverses show a scene reminiscent of the artist with the legend AMERICAN ARTS COMMEMORATIVE SERIES and the date of issue around. The edges are plain.

In 1982 the pieces were altered to give them a more "coin-like" appearance. Reeded edges and rim beading were added. Dates were moved into the field. The legend UNITED STATES OF AMERICA was added to the obverse and ONE OUNCE GOLD or ONE HALF OUNCE GOLD was added to the reverse.

In comparison to the Krugerrand, the later American Arts Gold Medallions certainly looked like bullion coins. The Krugerrand has a reeded edge and beading. The obverse has a portrait of Paul Kruger and SUID-AFRIKA • SOUTH AFRICA; the reverse the date, and the legends KRUGERRAND and FYN GOUD 1 OUNCE FINE GOLD around a springbok design.

Marketing attempts for the sale of the American Arts Gold Medallions included the name U.S. Gold, which was given the program by J. Aron & Co., the firm that contracted in 1983 to be the prime distributor of the U.S. Mint-produced gold medallions. The public did not respond to this marketing attempt. The Mint set up a telephone ordering system that was also unsuccessful.

Maple Leaf

The Canadians did not overlook the success of the South African Krugerrand or the failure of the American Arts Gold Medallions program. The Canadians studied the U.S. experiment and did extensive market research in the United States—potentially their largest single market at start-up. The study showed that a legal tender status coin with reeded edges was what the public wanted.

The Royal Canadian Mint introduced its .999 fine gold Maple Leaf in 1979 in 1-ounce, quarter-ounce and tenth-ounce sizes. The composition was changed to .9999 fine in 1982, making the Maple Leaf the purest gold bullion coin in the world.

Production of the Maple Leaf gold bullion coins has at times consumed more than half of all the gold produced by Canadian gold mines.

In 1985 sales of the Maple Leaf reached 1.878 million ounces, an 87.4 percent increase over 1984. This amounted to a 65 percent share of the worldwide market for gold bullion investment coins in 1985. Bans on importation of the Krugerrand and other government and private sector sanctions against South Africa played a major role in driving the gold-buying public to the Maple Leaf.

In June 1986 the Maple Leaf half-ounce gold bullion coin was introduced. (Denominations assigned to the coins are $50 for the 1-ounce coin, $20 for the half-ounce coin, $10 for the quarter-ounce coin and $5 for the tenth-ounce coin.)

To try to capture some of the silver bullion coin market dominated by the United States' American Eagle silver dollar, Canada began issuing a silver Maple Leaf, and upped the ante to include a platinum series, both introduced in 1988. The original silver coin is a 1-ounce piece, though Canada has issued several different sizes over the years, often to mark special occasions.

Canada introduced a platinum Maple Leaf program in 1988, eventually offering tenth-, quarter-, half- and 1-ounce coins. Canada stopped issuing platinum bullion coins in 1999 as mintages decreased annually.

In 2007, the Royal Canadian Mint introduced Maple Leaf .9995 fine palladium 1-ounce coins, after experimental palladium strikes conducted two years prior. Palladium bullion coin production has continued since.

Canada has marketed various special bullion coins. The Canadian Timber Wolf .9999 fine silver half-ounce coin was first struck in 2006, then reintroduced in 2010 in a 1-ounce size as part of a Wildlife silver bullion coin series. Plans call for two coins to be issued each year over a three-year period.

The Royal Canadian Mint does not sell its bullion coins directly, instead offering them through a network of dealers and distributors, for a varying percentage above spot price, depending on the order size, similar to the U.S. Mint's system of distributing its American Eagle bullion coins.

The major bullion coin programs are discussed in greater detail in the section that follows.

American Eagle

The United States gold and silver bullion coin program began with the release of the American Eagle gold bullion coins on Oct. 20, 1986.

The American Eagle gold coins are produced in sizes and denominations of 1-ounce, $50; half-ounce, $25; quarter-ounce, $10; and tenth-ounce, $5.

The gold bullion coins are composed of .917 fine gold. The 1-ounce pieces are produced with guaranteed weight planchets, each containing a full ounce of gold. The fractional pieces are produced with average weight planchets.

Designs on the gold bullion coins include a modified Saint-Gaudens Striding Liberty design on the obverse and the Family of Eagles design by Dallas sculptor Miley Busiek (now Miley Frost) on the reverse.

In addition to the Uncirculated gold bullion coins, a Proof 1-ounce version was issued starting in 1986. Proof versions of fractional American Eagle gold coins (half-ounce, quarter-ounce, tenth-ounce) were offered in subsequent years.

The American Eagle 1-ounce silver bullion coin, with a $1 face value, was issued during first-strike ceremonies Oct. 29, 1986. The silver coins contain 1 troy ounce of .999 fine silver. The design has Adolph A. Weinman's Walking Liberty design on the obverse and the Heraldic Eagle design of John Mercanti on the reverse. A Proof version was also offered starting in 1986.

Originally, the American Eagle silver bullion coins were minted exclusively from silver held by the Strategic and Critical Materials Stockpile formerly maintained by the Defense Logistics Agency under the direction of the Defense National Stockpile Center (termed the "National Strategic Stockpile," for short). By the early 2000s, though, this supply of silver was running short. Congress enacted legislation in 2002 allowing the Secretary of the Treasury to purchase silver on the open market.

Authorizing legislation for the American Eagle gold coins specified that its gold must come from newly mined U.S. gold, unless it is not available. The Treasury Department used gold reserves for the program start-up and purchases gold on the open market when available in the United States and from countries that are signatories to the General Agreement on Tariffs and Trade.

Congress authorized a third American Eagle bullion coin program a decade after the silver and gold coins were introduced. On Sept. 30, 1996, President Clinton signed into the law the authorization for the U.S. Mint to begin striking platinum coins. The first American Eagle platinum coins were struck in 1997. At that time, countries including China, Russia, Australia, Isle of Man and Canada, among others, had already been striking platinum coins for many years.

The U.S. platinum coins went on sale June 6, 1997, in denominations of $10, $25, $50 and $100—the latter being the highest denomination coin ever struck by the U.S. Mint. All of the platinum coins to date have been struck at the U.S. Mint at West Point; Proof versions therefore bear the W Mint mark. Platinum coins, because of the hardness of the metal, must be struck several times in order for their designs to strike up properly.

All American Eagle silver, gold and platinum coins are sold by the U.S. Mint to a select number of authorized purchasers, who buy the bullion pieces from the Mint at the cost of the metal in each coin plus a premium, and then sell the coins to dealers and collectors at an additional premium. The Mint sells the collector versions of the coins directly to the public.

The Mint added a new type of collector American Eagle silver, gold and platinum coin to the mix when it struck Uncirculated versions bearing the W Mint mark in 2006 and sold the coins at premiums above their bullion value. The Mint termed these as "Uncirculated" coins and at the same time stopped using the word "Uncirculated" in reference to its bullion coins, which had previously always been marketed as "Uncirculated" (the bullion versions simply became "American Eagle bullion coins").

Hobbyists frequently termed these new collector Uncirculated American Eagle coins as "Burnished Uncirculated" due to their method of manufacture and to differentiate them from the previously struck Uncirculated bullion coins. Burnished Uncirculated strikes were produced from 2006 to 2008.

The American Eagle bullion coin program underwent a number of changes in 2009, most of them unwelcomed by collectors. High demand for precious metals, deriving from fears over an economic downturn in the United States and elsewhere, led to record sales for the American Eagle silver bullion coin and recent highs for the gold coin.

Since the American Eagle silver and gold programs' debut in 1986, the Mint had been required to meet the demand for the bullion versions of the coin. No such requirement existed for the collector versions.

In order to meet demand for the American Eagle gold and silver coins, the United States Mint focused its attention on the 1-ounce versions and diverted all planchets to the bullion program. This latter decision led the Mint to suspend Proof strikes in 2009 in favor of bullion-only strikes. The Mint also suspended the collector Uncirculated program. Late in 2009, the United States Mint did strike small numbers of the fractional gold bullion coins; they sold out quickly.

Many collectors of Proof American Eagle silver and gold coins were angered with the decision to suspend Proof production in 2009. Some vowed to stop collecting the Proof coins if and when the Mint resumed production. The Mint did resume when Proof strikes for the American Eagles silver and gold coins in 2010. When this book went to press, sales figures for the 2010 coins were incomplete, making it difficult to judge whether collectors had kept their vows against buying the Proof coins.

For American Eagle platinum coins, the situation in 2009 was reversed, with the Mint ceasing production of bullion and Uncirculated platinum pieces, but continuing with Proof platinum strikes. In fact, the Mint went further, discontinuing fractional platinum coins in both 2009 and 2010. As of early 2011, no American Eagle platinum bullion coins of any size had been sold since late 2008; Mint officials were noncommittal on whether the program would be resumed.

New bullion issues

The decade beginning the 2000s also saw the introduction of three new series of bullion coins and the authorization of a fourth.

The first new bullion coin program made its debut in 2006, when the Mint began striking American Buffalo 1-ounce $50 gold bullion coins under authority granted in the Presidential $1 Coin Act of 2005. These first .9999 fine gold coins of the United States have been struck by the U.S. Mint from 2006 to present. The Mint has produced bullion and collector versions of the American Buffalo gold coins: 1-ounce Proof and bullion versions every year from 2006 to 2010; and collector (Burnished) Uncirculated 1-ounce, half-ounce ($25), quarter-ounce ($10) and tenth-ounce ($5) coins in 2008 only.

All of the American Buffalo gold coins are struck at the West Point Mint, but only the collector versions bear the W Mint mark.

The second new bullion coin program was also authorized under the Presidential $1 Coin Act of 2005. Under the act, First Spouse gold $10 coins were first struck in 2007 to coincide with the Presidential dollar coin series. Though many in the hobby view them as commemorative in nature, the authorizing legislation defines them as gold bullion coins.

In 2010, in conjunction with the America the Beautiful quarter dollar program commencing that year, the U.S. Mint struck the third new program: America the Beautiful 5-ounce silver bullion coins. Though officially denominated as "quarter dollars," the 3-inch-diameter coins were intended as investment pieces. The designs of the bullion coins match the designs of the quarter dollars, though instead of the quarter's reeded edges, the 5-ounce bullion coins have smooth edges with an incused edge inscription reading .999 FINE SILVER 5.0 OUNCE.

What does the future look like for U.S. bullion coins? While silver, gold and platinum coins will likely continue to be struck, collectors can look forward to bullion coins in a new precious metal—palladium.

The American Eagle Palladium Bullion Coin Act of 2010 (H.R. 6166) was signed into law by President Barack Obama on Dec. 14, 2010. It calls for the production of a 1-ounce .9995 fine palladium coin, denominated $25. The source material is to be mined from natural deposits in the United States purchased within one year from when the ore was mined.

Production of the new bullion coins, however, is contingent on completion of a study ensuring that the coins can be produced and sold with no net cost to American taxpayers.

The coins would be struck in both Proof and Uncirculated finishes, but "the surface treatment of each year's proof or uncirculated version [must differ] in some material way from that of the preceding year."

The obverse would be a high-relief likeness of the obverse design of the Winged Liberty Head dime of 1916 to 1945. The reverse is slated to bear a high-relief version of the reverse design of the 1907 American Institute of Architects medal, along with the legally required inscriptions on both sides. The obverse and reverse designs to be duplicated on the palladium coin were originally designed by sculptor Adolph A. Weinman.

Other countries

Bullion coin programs exist in many countries.

China first issued Panda gold bullion coins in 1982, with silver Pandas introduced in 1983 and platinum Pandas released first in 1987. The Panda designs generally change with each new year's issue. The China Pandas are produced at the Shanghai and Shenyang Mints by the China Mint Company. While ostensibly bullion issues, some of the China Panda coins carry a numismatic premium associated with low mintages. The coins are legal tender but carry nominal face values.

Western Australia (one of the Australian states, having authority to issue coins) entered the gold bullion coin market in 1986 and was first in the world to produce Proof .9999 fine gold bullion coins. When the program began, each denomination depicted a different famous Australian gold nugget as a reverse design element. The designs of each were to change annually.

Western Australia revamped the program in 1989. Public opinion was that the "rocks" on the reverse made for an unattractive coin design. The program was renamed the Kangaroo Nugget, and since then, the coins feature different reverse designs of kangaroos. In 1991, Western Australia launched the Kangaroo Nugget program of 2- and 10-ounce and 1-kilogram .9999 fine gold coins to attract the large-scale precious metal investor. These heavier weight coins are produced in unlimited quantities and are intended to compete with precious metal bars. They are denominated as $200, $1,000 and $10,000, respectively. Platinum and silver bullion coins followed, called the Koala and Kookaburra, respectively.

In 1996, Australia began issuing Lunar Zodiac coins in silver and gold. The coins depict figures of the Chinese lunar new year.

The coins are each struck in the name of Australia by the Perth Mint and are legal tender under Australia's Currency Act.

Austria issues Vienna Philharmonic gold coins. Prior to 2002, the .9999 fine gold coins were struck with denominations in schillings. However, when Austria switched to the euro on Jan. 1, 2002, the denominations were changed to conform with the new monetary system. The 1-ounce gold Philharmonic, with a diameter of 37 millimeters and weight of 1 troy ounce, is denominated €100. The half-ounce gold piece (28-millimeter diameter) is denominated €50, the quarter-ounce gold (22 millimeters) €25, and the tenth-ounce gold (16 millimeters) €10. The coins are legal tender in Austria.

Austria began issuing a 1-ounce, .9999 fine silver Philharmonic coin in 2008. It has a face value of €1.5 and a diameter of 37 millimeters.

Great Britain initiated its gold bullion program in 1987 with the issue of the 1-ounce legal tender Britannia .9166 fine gold coin. Later in 1987 half-ounce, quarter-ounce and tenth-ounce coins were issued. The obverse depicts the standard crowned bust of Queen Elizabeth II facing right. The initial reverse design of a standing figure of Britannia is in flowing robes, facing left. Since the initial release, Britannia has been depicted in a variety of ways, such as standing, sitting or driving a chariot.

The Britannia did not become popular with investors as a bullion coin, but Britain's Royal Mint continues to offer it as a numismatic coin.

A £2 Britannia silver coin joined the annual Britannia gold issues beginning in 1998. The Britannia designs on the silver piece change frequently as well.

The Isle of Man bullion program was launched in 1983 with the issue of the 1-ounce platinum Noble. A tenth-ounce piece first was issued in 1984. Other weights followed: twentieth-ounce, quarter-ounce, 5-ounce and 10-ounce pieces. The coins are struck by the private Pobjoy Mint.

The Isle of Man also produces a gold bullion coinage called the Angel in sizes from the twentieth ounce to 25 ounces. Most of the Angels were struck in small quantities.

Mexico launched its Libertad bullion coin program in 1981 to compete with the bullion coins from Canada and South Africa. The Libertad came on the heels of the sterling silver (.925 silver) 1-ounce "Onza" coins of 1978 to 1980.

Three sizes of gold Libertad coins were issued when the program began in October 1981—quarter-, half- and 1-ounce coins. A twentieth-ounce size was added in 1987, and a tenth-ounce size was struck beginning in 1991. Libertad gold coins prior to 1991 had a composition of .900 gold; thereafter, the com-

position was changed to .999 fine gold.

The first Libertad 1-ounce silver coins, composed of .999 fine silver, were struck in 1982 but not released until 1984.

In 1991, fractional .999 fine silver Libertad coins were introduced, in twentieth-, tenth-, quarter- and half-ounce sizes. Two- and 5-ounce silver Libertads were first struck in 1996. The 1-kilogram silver Libertad, first issued in 2002, did not become directly available to U.S. collectors until 2003.

The reverse design of the Libertad coinage was changed in 1996, with a three-quarters view of the Angel of Liberty replacing a frontal view of the same.

Though they do not bear a denomination, all silver and gold Libertad coins have legal tender status in Mexico.

Private and state bullion pieces

Private firms produce a variety of gold and silver bullion pieces. The majority of these pieces are 1-ounce .999 fine silver round or rectangular bars, often called art bars. Some private mints produce rounds with reeded edges that have the appearance of bullion coins issued by governments. Pieces in different sizes and shapes exist, as well as similar products produced in gold. Many of these products depict artistic renderings of past coinage designs, and should not be confused with actual coinage. The pieces are neither official government bullion issues nor legal tender, and should not be confused with government bullion coin programs.

Official state bullion issues exist. California, South Dakota and Texas have issued, in the past, a variety of silver and gold bullion pieces. Many of these bullion pieces were exempt from state sales taxes. The state received a profit from the sale of these official bullion pieces.

Virginia also has authorized precious metals commemorative pieces.

In 2010 and 2011, a "Constitutional Tender" movement began gaining support in several states—most notably Utah but also in other states—as supporters sought a return to the United States Constitution's provisions in Article I, Section 10 that "No State shall … make any Thing but gold and silver Coin a Tender in Payment of Debts."

Utah's Senate voted 21 to 4 on March 9, 2011, to give preliminary approval to a bill that would recognize gold and silver coins issued by the federal government as legal tender for their precious metal value—not just their face value—in Utah. Utah Gov. Gary Herbert signed House Bill 317—the "Utah Legal Tender Act"—into law on March 25

The act also exempts the exchange of gold and silver coins from certain types of state tax liability such as state sales, income and capital-gains taxes, and calls for a committee to study and recommend alternative forms of legal tender currency for Utah.

In Montana, House Bill 513 was defeated on March 29, 2011, on a vote of 48 to 52. It would have required the state to back transactions of state business with gold and silver coins.

In North Carolina, Rep. Glen Bradley introduced House Bill 301 on March 10, 2011, which would allow the state to issue its own legal tender money backed by silver and gold.

Rep. Bradley's bill would establish a legislative commission to study a plan for an alternative state currency, noting, "In conducting its study the Committee shall consider recommendations for legislation, with respect to the need, means, and schedule for establishing such an alternative currency."

Specifications of select bullion coins

Australia

Nugget, Kangaroo, Lunar gold Denomination	Gold Fineness	Troy ounces	Weight in grams	Diameter	Edge
$100	.9999	1.00	31.162	32.10mm	Reeded
$50	.9999	0.50	15.594	25.10mm	Reeded
$25	.9999	0.25	7.807	20.10mm	Reeded
$15	.9999	0.10	3.133	16.10mm	Reeded
$5	.9999	0.05	0.050	14.10mm	Reeded
Koala platinum Denomination	**Platinum Fineness**	**Troy ounces**	**Weight in grams**	**Diameter**	**Edge**
$2,000	.9995	32.15	1001.000	75.30mm	Reeded
$1,000	.9995	10.00	311.691	60.30mm	Reeded
$200	.9995	2.00	62.313	40.60mm	Reeded
$100	.9995	1.00	31.185	32.10mm	Reeded
$50	.9995	0.50	15.605	25.10mm	Reeded
$25	.9995	0.25	7.815	20.10mm	Reeded
$15	.9995	0.10	3.137	16.10mm	Reeded
$5	.9995	0.05	1.571	14.10mm	Reeded
Kookaburra, Lunar silver Denomination	**Silver Fineness**	**Troy ounces**	**Weight in grams**	**Diameter**	**Edge**
$30	.999	32.151	1002.502	101.00mm	Reeded
$10	.999	10.000	312.347	75.50mm	Reeded
$2	.999	2.000	62.770	50.30mm	Reeded
$1	.999	1.000	31.635	40.60mm	Reeded

Austria

Philharmonic gold Denomination	Gold Fineness	Troy ounces	Weight in grams	Diameter	Edge
2,000 schillings/€100	0.9999	1.00	31.103	37.00mm	Reeded
1,000 schillings/€50	0.9999	0.50	15.552	28.00mm	Reeded
500 schillings/€25	0.9999	0.25	7.776	22.00mm	Reeded
200 schillings/€10	0.9999	0.10	3.110	16.00mm	Reeded
Philharmonic silver Denomination	**Silver Fineness**	**Troy ounces**	**Weight in grams**	**Diameter**	**Edge**
€1.50	0.999	1.00	31.103	37.00mm	Smooth

Canada

Maple Leaf gold Denomination	Gold Fineness	Troy ounces	Weight in grams	Diameter	Edge
$50	.9999	10.00	31.103	30.00mm	Reeded
$20	.9999	.50	15.551	25.00mm	Reeded
$10	.9999	.25	7.785	20.00mm	Reeded
$5	.9999	.10	3.120	16.00mm	Reeded
$1	.9999	.05	1.555	14.00mm	Reeded
Maple Leaf platinum Denomination	**Platinum Fineness**	**Troy ounces**	**Weight in grams**	**Diameter**	**Edge**
$50	.9995	1.000	31.103	30.00mm	Reeded

Canada (continued)

Maple Leaf platinum Denomination	Platinum Fineness	Troy ounces	Weight in grams	Diameter	Edge
$20	.9995	0.500	15.551	25.00mm	Reeded
$10	.9995	0.250	7.785	20.00mm	Reeded
$5	.9995	0.100	3.120	16.00mm	Reeded
$2	.9995	0.066	2.073	15.00mm	Reeded
$1	.9995	0.050	1.552	14.00mm	Reeded

Maple Leaf palladium Denomination	Palladium Fineness	Troy ounces	Weight in grams	Diameter	Edge
$50	0.9995	1.00	31.10	33.00mm	Reeded

Maple Leaf silver Denomination	Silver Fineness	Troy ounces	Weight in grams	Diameter	Edge
$5	.9999	1.00	31.03	38.00mm	Reeded

China

Panda gold Denomination	Gold Fineness	Troy ounces	Weight in grams	Diameter	Edge
1,000 yuan	.9999	12.00	373.326	70.00mm	Reeded
500 yuan	.9999	5.00	155.515	60.00mm	Reeded
100 yuan	.9999	1.00	31.103	32.05mm	Reeded
50 yuan	.9999	0.50	15.551	27.00mm	Reeded
25 yuan	.9999	0.25	7.775	21.95mm	Reeded
10 yuan	.9999	0.10	3.110	17.95mm	Reeded
5 yuan	.9999	0.05	1.555	13.92mm	Reeded

Panda platinum Denomination	Platinum Fineness	Troy ounces	Weight in grams	Diameter	Edge
100 yuan	.9995	1.00	155.500	32.00mm	Reeded
10 yuan	.9995	.050	1.555	18.00mm	Reeded

Panda silver Denomination	Silver Fineness*	Troy ounces	Weight in grams	Diameter	Edge
100 yuan	.9999	12.00	373.248	80.00mm	Reeded
50 yuan	.9999	5.00	155.520	40.00mm	Reeded
10 yuan	.9999	1.00	31.030	38.60mm	Reeded
5 yuan	.9999	0.50	15.150	33.00mm	Reeded

*Panda silver coins struck prior to 1989 were struck in .9995 fine silver.

Great Britain

Britannia gold Denomination	Gold Fineness	Troy ounces	Weight in grams	Diameter	Edge
£100	.9167	1.00	34.050	32.00mm	Reeded
£50	.9167	0.50	17.025	27.00mm	Reeded
£25	.9167	0.25	8.513	21.50mm	Reeded
£10	.9167	0.10	3.412	11.00mm	Reeded

Britannia silver Denomination	Silver Fineness	Troy ounces	Weight in grams	Diameter	Edge
£2	0.958	1.00	32.45	40.00mm	Reeded

Isle of Man

Angel gold* Denomination	Gold Fineness	Troy ounces	Weight in grams	Diameter	Edge
10 Angel	.917	10.00	339.335	63.00mm	Reeded
5 Angel	.917	5.00	169.668	50.00mm	Reeded
Angel	.9999	1.00	31.103	32.76mm	Reeded
Half Angel	.9999	0.50	15.551	27.00mm	Reeded

Isle of Man (continued)

Angel platinum Denomination	Platinum Fineness	Troy ounces	Weight in grams	Diameter	Edge
Quarter Angel	.9999	0.25	7.776	22.00mm	Reeded
Tenth Angel	.9999	0.10	3.110	16.5mm	Reeded
Twentieth Angel	.9999	0.05	1.555	15.0mm	Reeded

Noble platinum Denomination	Platinum Fineness	Troy ounces	Weight in grams	Diameter	Edge
10 Noble	.9995	10.00	311.028	63.00mm	Reeded
5 Noble	.9995	5.00	155.514	50.00mm	Reeded
Noble	.9995	1.00	31.103	32.76mm	Reeded

Noble platinum Denomination	Platinum Fineness	Troy ounces	Weight in grams	Diameter	Edge
10 Noble Half Noble	.9995	0.50	15.551	27.00mm	Reeded
Quarter Noble	.9995	0.25	7.775	22.00mm	Reeded
Tenth Noble	.9995	0.10	3.110	16.50mm	Reeded
Twentieth Noble	.9995	0.05	1.555	15.00mm	Reeded

*The Isle of Man issued .917 fine gold coins in the same denominations listed (except the 10 Angel and 5 Angel coins) until 1994 when the fineness was increased to .9999 fine. Bullion coins struck before 1994 by the Isle of Man will be slightly heavier than their .9999 fine counterparts. The coins are the same size.

Mexico

Libertad gold (1991-present) Denomination	Gold Fineness	Troy ounces	Weight in grams	Diameter	Edge
None	0.999	1.00	31.100	34.50mm	Reeded
None	0.999	0.50	15.550	29.00mm	Reeded
None	0.999	0.25	7.775	23.00mm	Reeded
None	0.999	0.10	3.110	16.00mm	Reeded
None	0.999	0.05	1.417	13.00mm	Reeded

Libertad silver Denomination	Silver Fineness	Troy ounces	Weight in grams	Diameter	Edge
None	0.999	32.15	1,000.000	110.00mm	Reeded
None	0.999	5.00	155.500	65.00mm	Reeded
None	0.999	2.00	62.200	48.00mm	Reeded
None	0.999	1.00	31.100	40.00mm	Reeded
None	0.999	0.50	15.550	33.00mm	Reeded
None	0.999	0.25	7.775	27.00mm	Reeded
None	0.999	0.10	3.110	20.00mm	Reeded
None	0.999	0.05	1.555	16.00mm	Reeded

South Africa

Krugerrand gold Denomination	Gold Fineness	Troy ounces	Weight in grams	Diameter	Edge
Krugerrand	.9167	1.00	33.930	32.70mm	Reeded
Half Krugerrand	.9167	0.50	16.970	27.00mm	Reeded
Quarter Krugerrand	.9167	0.25	8.480	22.00mm	Reeded
Tenth Krugerrand	.9167	0.10	3.390	16.50mm	Reeded

United States

American Eagle gold Denomination	Gold Fineness	Troy ounces	Weight in grams	Diameter	Edge
$50	.9167	1.00	33.93	32.70mm	Reeded
$25	.9167	0.50	16.97	27.00mm	Reeded
$10	.9167	0.25	8.48	22.00mm	Reeded
$5	.9167	0.10	3.39	16.50mm	Reeded

United States (continued)

American Buffalo gold Denomination	Gold Fineness	Troy ounces	Weight in grams	Diameter	Edge
$50	.9999	1.00	31.10	32.70mm	Reeded
$25	.9999	0.50	15.55	27.00mm	Reeded
$10	.9999	0.25	7.78	22.00mm	Reeded
$5	.9999	0.10	3.11	16.50mm	Reeded

First Spouse gold Denomination	Gold Fineness	Troy ounces	Weight in grams	Diameter	Edge
$10	.999	0.50	15.55	27.00mm	Reeded

United States

American Eagle platinum Denomination	Platinum Fineness	Troy ounces	Weight in grams	Diameter	Edge
$100	.9995	1.00	31.12	32.70mm	Reeded
$50	.9995	0.50	15.56	27.00mm	Reeded
$25	.9995	0.25	7.78	22.00mm	Reeded
$10	.9995	0.10	3.11	16.50mm	Reeded

American Eagle silver Denomination	Silver Fineness	Troy ounces	Weight in grams	Diameter	Edge
$1	.9999	1.00	31.10	40.10mm	Reeded

America the Beautiful silver Denomination	Silver Fineness	Troy ounces	Weight in grams	Diameter	Edge
25¢	.999	5.00	155.50	76.20mm	Smooth/Lettered

American Arts Gold Medallions

Year	Size	Portrait	Struck	Sold	Melted*
1980	1 ounce	Grant Wood	500,000	312,709	187,291
	half ounce	Marian Anderson	1,000,000	281,624	718,376
1981	1 ounce	Mark Twain	141,000	116,371	24,629
	half ounce	Willa Cather	200,000	97,331	102,669
1982	1 ounce	Louis Armstrong	420,000	409,098	10,902
	half ounce	Frank Lloyd Wright	360,000	348,305	11,695
1983	1 ounce	Robert Frost	500,000	390,669	109,331
	half ounce	Alexander Calder	410,000	74,571	335,429
1984	1 ounce	Helen Hayes	*35,000	33,546	**1,454
	half ounce	John Steinbeck	*35,000	32,572	**2,428

*The number melted is the number sold subtracted from the number struck. Number sold is in effect the final net mintage. Audited figures supplied by the U.S. Mint.

**The 1984 issues began with a striking of 20,000 pieces in each weight and to demand from then on, accounting for the relatively low melt figures.

16 Grading

Grading coins and paper money

No other subject has been more debated in American numismatics than grading. Since the time a dealer first asked more money for one example of a coin than for another of the same design type, date and Mint mark because one coin "graded" higher than the other, there has been controversy.

What is grading and why the controversy?

The grade of a coin (as well as of a medal, token or paper money item) represents what professional numismatist and researcher Dr. Richard Bagg aptly called its "level of preservation" in a 1977 collection of readings about grading that he co-edited. Grading controversy arises from disagreements over the grade of a coin and the sometimes enormous differences in price between two specimens of the same design type and date. For some U.S. coins, a one-point difference, or even a designation that it is a "plus" or "premium" coin for the grade, can lead to a price difference of many thousands of dollars. It is no surprise, then, that controversy exists in the area of grading.

The grade assigned a coin (in today's market, a whole number between 1 and 70) attempts to codify the amount of wear, natural mishaps, surface degradation and overall "eye appeal" displayed by a coin after leaving the coining press. The more wear and surface marks a coin displays, the less it is worth compared to another example of the same coin showing less wear and fewer blemishes.

Not all coins receive wear after being struck for circulation. Such coins are called Uncirculated or Mint State. Although two coins of the same date and design type may be technically Uncirculated, there can be a world of difference in terms of overall quality. And this difference in quality can lead to vast differences in market value.

The new collector unexposed to the intricacies of grading might show surprise at this last statement. He might think, "It seems logical a coin with fewer signs of circulation wear is worth more than one with a lot of wear. But if a coin hasn't received any wear, how can it be different from other unworn specimens of the same coin?" The answer is simple: There are graduated levels of Uncirculated coins.

Mint State, the formal term applied to coins with no wear from circulation, is currently designated by as many as 11 different whole number increments.

These increments begin at Mint State 60 and end at Mint State 70. Such factors as contact marks, luster, the strength of strike (at the time the coin received an impression from the dies at the Mint) and toning are important factors that are a part of grading Mint State coins. Whether a coin is "officially" described as Mint State 60 (an Uncirculated coin that shows problems such as impaired luster and heavy surface abrasions) or Mint State 70 (an Uncirculated coin that displays absolutely mark-free surfaces under 10x magnification and possesses a great strike) or somewhere in between is the heart of the controversy in grading.

This chapter discusses the grading of U.S. coins from a historical perspective and evolving practices in the current marketplace. The chapter also briefly delves into the grading of foreign and ancient coins and U.S. paper money.

Grading: What's involved?

Bagg, in *Grading Coins: A Collection of Readings,* co-edited in 1977 with James J. Jelinski, described the grade of a coin as its "level of preservation." It is not entirely accurate to establish grading only as "the charting of wear" on a coin, although for circulated coins it is fairly accurate. Occasionally the grade assigned a circulated coin is influenced by such factors as "nice surfaces" and "good color."

The definition of an Uncirculated coin is "a coin which has seen no circulation" according to the *Official American Numismatic Association Grading Standards for United States Coins* and the term is described as a coin with "no wear" in *Photograde: A Photographic Grading Guide for United States Coins.* Clearly, the charting of wear on such coins is irrelevant with respect to the coin's grade. However, Uncirculated coins are subject to various forms of handling that remove them from an absolutely pristine state.

A coin struck for circulation is subject to external factors affecting surface from the moment it leaves the coining press. The moment after a coin is struck it is pushed from the surface of the anvil die. The coin then falls into a bin with other coins. When the coin hits the previously struck coins lying in the bin, the portion of its surface coming into contact with the other coins can be marred. Then, as the coins are jostled on a conveyor belt, or bundled into bags, boxes or large bins for shipment, the coins will scrape, scratch and bump each other. They may experience additional scratches when being counted and rolled for distribution to banks and other commercial entities.

Contact marks

Collisions between coins (whether in a hopper, bin or bag) create a variety of surface marks known as "contact marks" or "bag marks."

A contact mark may range in severity from a light, minor disruption of the coin's surface, to a large, heavy scrape. Generally, the bigger and heavier the coin, the larger and more unsightly the contact marks because of two coins "banging" into each other.

The location of contact marks plays a major role in determining at what level of Mint State a coin is categorized. For example, marks clearly visible in the field of a coin or on the cheek, chin or forehead of a Liberty Head device, would cause a coin to be downgraded further from Mint State 70 than a coin with marks of equal severity but hidden in the curls of Liberty's hair or the wing feathers of the eagle found on the reverse of many U.S. coins.

The size of contact marks is also a factor in determining the Mint State grade of a coin. Larger marks are more distracting than smaller marks. However, a contact mark 1 millimeter long is less distracting on a large coin such as a silver dollar (diameter of 38.1 millimeters) than it is on a smaller coin such as a silver half dime (diameter of 15.5 millimeters).

The number of contact marks also plays a significant role in determining the grade level of a Mint State coin. A coin with numerous contact marks is less appealing to the eye than a coin with one or two distracting marks. The diameter of the coin plays a role here, too. A silver dollar with five contact marks scattered across its surfaces may be judged appealing; a much smaller half dime with five contact marks may be judged less appealing, since the half dime has a smaller surface area in which the marks may lay. Note the subjective nature of a word such as "eye appeal," which can be and is determined individually by the person viewing the coin.

Luster

Another important factor in the grading of Mint State coins is luster. "Luster is simply the way light reflects from the microscopic flow lines of a coin," according to ANACS grader/authenticator and *Coin World* "First Grade" columnist Michael Fahey. James L. Halperin, in *NCI Grading Guide*, defined luster as: "The brightness of a coin which results from the way in which it reflects light." A diamond's sparkle is akin to the way coin collectors talk about luster.

Luster is imparted to the surfaces of a coin at the moment of striking. The immense pressures used in the coining process create flow lines, the microscopic lines that trace the paths the metal takes while filling the crevices of the die imparting the design.

A coin with full, unimpaired luster is generally one which has a bright, shiny surface (although toning, to be discussed later, may obscure luster without being an impairment), caused by the light reflecting from the surface of the coin. When the flow lines that create the effect of luster are disturbed or removed from the surface of a coin (as is done by normal circulation), the coin may appear dullish or worn.

Cleaning a coin with a cloth or "dipping" a coin in a substance that removes a microscopic layer of the surface metal will damage the flow lines and disrupt or eliminate the luster of a coin.

A Mint State coin should show considerable luster. An Uncirculated coin without full luster should grade no higher than Mint State 63 under American Numismatic Association grading standards.

Wear versus friction

Once a coin enters the channels of commerce, it obtains circulation wear. Coins carried in a pocket rub against each other and the fabric of the clothing, creating wear. A coin is thrown into a cash register drawer where it bumps against other coins, creating more wear.

The amount of handling a coin receives translates into wear; the amount of wear determines a coin's grade for most of the 1 to 70 grading scale. High points of a design are usually the first to show wear since they are the most exposed. Then raised inscriptions and date reflect wear, and finally, the flat fields.

Circulation wear erases design details, ultimately to the point where only the slightest design features are visible to the naked eye. The separate curls of hair on the coin's portrait tend to merge, the eagle's feathers are worn away and the inscriptions seem to disappear into the fields.

Coins with only the slightest hint of wear are called About Uncirculated; the AU grade equates to the specific numbers 50, 53, 55 and 58 on the 1 to 70 system. Then, in descending order, are Extremely Fine (40, 45), Very Fine (20, 25, 30), Fine (12, 15), Very Good (8, 10), Good (4, 6), About Good (3), Fair (2), and the lowest grade, Poor (1). The higher circulated grades are divided into several levels as indicated, to denote, for example, that an Extremely Fine 45 coin is of higher quality than another legitimate Extremely Fine 40 coin. Note, also, that not all numbers between 1 and 70 are used. However, the tendency over time has been for additional numbers to gain acceptance among a majority of collectors and dealers.

Some hobbyists differentiate between circulation wear and another form of wear labeled "friction." According to Halperin in *NCI Grading Guide*, friction is "A disturbance which appears either on the high points of a coin or in the fields, as a result of that coin rubbing against other projections." It is often referred to as "cabinet friction," a term applied to the minute wear a coin receives when sliding back and forth in the drawer of a cabinet. Such cabinets (and hence the term a coin collector's "cabinet," referring to the collection itself) were used for storage by collectors of earlier generations.

Friction does disturb the luster of the coin, but it should not disturb the metal underneath. Unless the actual history of a specific specimen of a coin is known, distinguishing friction from circulation wear can be difficult.

In the modern rare coin market, one rarely sees use of the description "cabinet friction" as opposed to circulation wear. A coin either meets the particular standard under which it is being examined as Uncirculated or not, and is graded accordingly.

Strike

Strike is "The sharpness of detail which the coin had when it was Mint State," according to Halperin; Fahey defines it as "the evenness and fullness of metal-flow into all the crevices of a die."

The amount of pressure used to strike a coin controls the sharpness of strike. Design elements also affect the strike. If two large design features are centered on both sides of the same coin, there may not be enough metal to flow into every little crevice of the dies, thus leaving some details weak and ill-defined.

A coin with a sharp strike has sharp design details. For example, the curls of hair on Liberty's head are strong and distinct. The feathers on the eagle's wings and breast are clearly visible. All of the other design details, legends and elements are sharp and well defined. (For some series, softness in detail even on a strongly struck coin can be attributed to a working die whose progenitor master die was worn, such as on late 1950s Franklin half dollars.)

A coin with a weak strike has ill-defined design details. Such a coin may "look" worn from the moment it leaves the coining press. However, luster is unimpaired. Determining whether such coins are Uncirculated can be very difficult.

The strength of a coin's strike has not always been a factor in a coin's grade. The American Numismatic Association's grading standard remained a technical grading system, considering only those factors taking place after the strike, for the first 10 years. It did not include strike or eye appeal as determinants in the final grade of a coin until 1986 when it embraced 11 grades in the Mint State range. Even before the ANA's move, most collectors and dealers had begun to consider strike (and anything that affects overall eye appeal) very important when determining a coin's value in the marketplace. Therefore, today an Uncirculated coin relatively free of marks and boasting full luster may nevertheless be assigned a relatively low Mint State grade due to a very weak strike. Conversely, a coin that has a very nice strike and attractive toning may not be downgraded as severely for other flaws or blemishes. Such a balancing of the various factors of an Uncirculated coin is referred to as market grading. While some hobbyists cling to technical grading, all of the major third-party grading services today use market grading.

Toning and color

As a coin ages, the original color changes in reaction to the environment. The original red of copper coins becomes brown (or green; witness the copper of the Statue of Liberty, which once had a deep copper color). Silver coins may tone into any color of the rainbow, depending on environmental factors. Gold is a more stable metal and, even when immersed in seawater for centuries, generally shows little change in tone and color.

For the first half of the 20th century, toned coins, particularly silver coins, were judged unattractive ("That coin looks tarnished or dirty."). Silver coins were "dipped"—placed into a chemical solution that removed the toning and restored the shine by stripping away the outer layer of silver or dirt.

However, in the latter decades of the 20th century "naturally" toned coins became more acceptable and desirable. A Morgan silver dollar with rainbow toning (from its position in a roll or bag) may bring a premium due to its coloration. Proof coins from the 1840s and 1850s, though very dark in appearance at first glance, reveal under magnification excellent preservation, and such original surface examples are very much sought after in today's marketplace.

In recent years, great debate has arisen over toning (now considered a sign of originality with many collectors and dealers) and what is referred to as "artificial" toning. Though no formal definition exists for either, the term artificial toning refers to a situation in which "color" or toning is applied to or allowed to form on the surface of a coin to hide a blemish or restore the appearance of it being an original surface. A variety of "artificial toning" methods are used, but none are well documented. However, professional graders say that when a coin becomes toned in a short amount of time as opposed to during a natural aging process, often it can be detected by one who is knowledgeable of certain characteristics achieved only in "natural" toning.

Hairlines

New collectors sometimes have difficulty distinguishing hairlines from die scratches.

Die scratches are thin, raised lines on a coin, resulting from minute scratches in the surface of the die. At the moment a coin is struck, die scratches may be imparted to the coin.

A hairline is a thin scratch into the surface of a coin, most likely arriving on the surface as the result of a coin being wiped (even ever so gently wiped, as was done by early 20th century collectors). A close examination of a coin's surface using a magnifying glass should indicate whether a line on a coin is a die scratch or a hairline. Hairline scratches tend to be present in clusters whereas die scratches tend to be more random.

Hairlines, being an after-the-fact disturbance to the surface of a coin, negatively impact the grade a coin is assigned under most modern grading standards.

Die scratches, on the other hand, are perceived as something that "couldn't be helped" and therefore tend not to negatively impact the grade of a coin unless so severe to the eye appeal that they cannot be overlooked.

Adjustment marks are often found on older U.S. silver and gold coins (1792 to 1807). Planchets (unstruck coins) were individually weighed before striking. If found to be a little overweight, the excess gold or silver was filed away; the mark left by the filing is the adjustment mark.

Striking pressures often did not obliterate the adjustment marks, which may resemble a series of parallel grooves. Under ANA standards, adjustment marks do not affect the technical grade. Since the value of the coin may be affected, the market grading system takes such marks into account before assigning a graded on the 1 to 70 scale.

Grading history

Grading is one of the most debated issues in all of coin collecting. However, such debate is not new.

In one series of letters appearing in the *American Journal of Numismatics,* a coin dealer conducting an auction, the person who consigned his coins to be sold at this auction and a bidder at the auction were pitted against each other in a grading dispute. However, this series of letters ran, not in a recent issue of *AJN,* but rather in November and December 1868.

The grading of Edward Cogan, first full-time commercial coin dealer in the United States, is described by modern numismatist John W. Adams as on the "conservative end of the spectrum." Therefore, Cogan's letter to the editor of the *American Journal of Numismatics* published in the November 1868 issue is enlightening. Cogan attended the Oct. 28 to 29, 1868, auction of the collection of J. Colvin Randall, conducted in Philadelphia by Mason & Co. It was, incidentally, Ebenezer Locke Mason's first public auction.

Cogan's first letter was critical of the grading in the auction. Among the quarter dollars, he noted that "five or six of them [were] described as Proofs, without stating that they were considerably injured by circulation." Three dimes, dated 1796, 1798 and 1800, "were much over-described," Cogan said. "In regard to the Cents, I regret to say that many of them were ridiculously over-described—in the earlier dates especially," he added.

Mason was angered by Cogan's comments and penned a letter in response that appeared in the December *AJN.* He wrote that Cogan's comments were "very vague and indefinite," complaining that Cogan had failed to note some coins were described accurately. Mason adds that in regard to one 1793 Flowing Hair, Chain, AMERI. cent mentioned by Cogan as bringing the low price of $1.25, the coin was cataloged as "Poor." Mason asks, "Is that coin over-described?"

Cogan, responding in a second letter, also appear-

ing in the December issue, records a conversation he had with the consignor, J. Colvin Randall, whom he told that a 1793 cent described as Uncirculated was a "long way" from being Uncirculated. Randall replied, according to Cogan, "Why, it is Uncirculated for a 1793 cent." What Randall meant is that because the 1793 is very rare, it was OK to describe it as Uncirculated even if that was stretching the truth.

Rarity and wear

So even more than 140 years ago, grading was a subject taken very seriously by collectors and dealers. There was less standardization concerning grading terms than there is today. Today the terms are more standardized, but there are many more grades

A perusal of several issues of the *American Journal of Numismatics* in 1866 and 1867 reveals about a half dozen grading terms were in use: Good, Very Good, Fine, Very Fine, Uncirculated; in addition, Proof and nearly Proof appear.

As Cogan noted in his two letters, some catalogers in the 1860s graded not only by the amount of wear on a coin, but by its rarity. Mason even admitted, "A spot so indistinct that a microscope would scarcely make the defect observable, [on] such excessively rare coins, in this condition, were usually described as Uncirculated." Mason noted that the practice of omitting mention of such wear "had been customary with all persons cataloging collections ... on coins very nearly unique."

The practice of grading by a combination of wear and rarity was still in force at the end of the 1870s, some 11 years after the Cogan-Mason letters. In W. Elliot Woodward's Oct. 15 to 16, 1879, auction, for example, a 1796 Draped Bust quarter dollar is described as "Fair for this date." In the same auction, the cataloger says a 1799 Draped Bust cent "may be fairly called very fine for date; extremely rare."

Woodward was also using a greater number of grading terms in his auction catalogs of 1879 to 1882: Good, Very Good, Fine, Very Fine, Nearly Uncirculated, Almost Uncirculated, Uncirculated and Brilliant Uncirculated, among others.

Even today, many observers believe that an ultra rarity is sometimes given a point or two for being famous or for being pedigreed to a famous collection.

Beginnings of codification

Not until a decade later, in the 1890s, did U.S. numismatists begin to seriously consider codification of standard grading terms. Richard Bagg and James J. Jelinski cover this topic in quite some detail in their book, *Grading Coins: A Collection of Readings.* The 1977 book compiles articles from various numismatic publications, beginning with *The Numismatist* in February 1892.

A February 1892 article by J. Hopper is perhaps one of the earliest in a national publication concerning grading. In it, Hopper lists 12 grade levels: Mint Brilliant Proof, Mint Proof, Uncirculated, Extremely

Fine, Very Fine, Fine, Very Good, Good, Very Fair, Fair, Poor and Very Poor.

He defines both levels of Proof as conditions; today, most numismatists consider Proof to represent a method of manufacture and not a grade, although most will recognize that not all Proofs are equal in quality. The other level he identifies is Uncirculated, "showing no abrasion or wearing ... yet not [necessarily having] the sharp impression of the first strikes as the dies tire."

Of the lower grades, he notes that coins graded from Good and lower "are often disappointing, the terms applied misleading, until being understood, being used by dealers to describe a certain state of preservation."

In February 1913, some members of the American Numismatic Association began pressing for the ANA "to take some stand with reference to issuing some kind of statement classifying coins so that all dealers that catalogue and sell coins at auction must use the same classification."

The editor of *The Numismatist*, in the February 1913 issue, reprints a 1910 statement by ANA Secretary H.O. Granberg. The statement might have been written today except for the lack of any grades between Very Fine and Uncirculated. It is a concise and serious attempt to persuade dealers to ethically describe coins they are selling so that the buyer knows about any problems the coins may have. Granberg describes in detail eight levels of preservation: Proof, Uncirculated, Very Fine, Fine, Very Good, Good, Fair and Poor. Granberg recommends coins that have been cleaned should be noted as such, and suggests split grading for obverse and reverse where necessary.

In a departure from the catalogs of the latter half of the 19th century, Granberg recommends against grading a piece by its rarity. "Terms, such as 'good for piece' should never be used unless the reason why is stated as well," he writes.

A decade and a half later, ANA members were still calling for standardized grades. One writer in November 1927 called for standard classifications and noted that when he was younger, he had been cheated by a dealer who sent him an 1866 Shield 5-cent coin graded Fine but advertised as Uncirculated. "... I concluded this sort of establishment as too big for my schoolboy orders of three or four dollars." This statement might have been written today by a young collector.

Adding more grades

During the 1920s, a new-old grade between Very Fine and Uncirculated was being used more often—Extremely Fine. The grade had been used before, but apparently not by everyone. The lists of grades published in the ANA's journal in the first two decades of the 20th century left a huge gap between Very Fine and Uncirculated. In 1928, a writer in *The Numismatist* defined Extremely Fine: "A coin which is perfect in all details of design, except that its luster is gone or else the signs of wear show on the more exposed parts. Otherwise, the coin must show details as strong as when first struck."

However, Extremely Fine did not catch on quickly. In late 1930s the first edition of Wayte Raymond's *The Standard Catalogue of United States Coins and Tokens* was published. The hard-cover book was the "Red Book" of its day. A writer in the November 1939 issue of *The Numismatist* recommends that the *Standard Catalogue* "be the accepted authority on the classification of coins as to their condition." The *Standard Catalogue* recognized seven conditions: Proof, Uncirculated, Very Fine, Fine, Very Good, Good and Fair. Very Fine is described as "From circulation, but no signs of wear," and Fine is described as "Slightest sign of wear, but still an attractive piece."

It was not until the 17th edition, published in 1954 and dated 1954-55, that the Raymond book listed Extremely Fine as a grade. It is described as "A new coin displaying only the lightest rubbing or friction on the highest parts." Very Fine was then described as "Showing only slight evidence of circulation," and the definition for Fine was unchanged in meaning.

By then Raymond's book had some serious competition, R.S. Yeoman's "Red Book," formally titled *A Guide Book of United States Coins*. The 1954-55 *Guide Book* lists six levels of condition: Proof, Uncirculated, Very Fine, Fine, Very Good and Good. The text notes, however, that grades such as Extremely Fine and About Uncirculated "are terms frequently used to describe the degree of wear between Very Fine and Uncirculated."

Sheldon system

The greatest innovation in the grading of U.S. coins in the post-war period came, however, not in the *Standard Catalogue* or *Guide Book*, but in a book about the large cents of 1793 to 1814 first published in 1949. The title of that first edition is *Early American Cents* and its author was Dr. William H. Sheldon. Sheldon was already nationally famous, though not for his numismatic contributions. He had devised a method of physically classifying what he believed were three main types of human physiology: ectomorph, endomorph and mesomorph.

He is best known to numismatists, however, as the creator of the numerical system of grading, what some now call the Mint State system. In his 1949 *Early American Cents* (titled *Penny Whimsy* in subsequent editions), Sheldon devised a numerical grading scale of 1 to 70, with 70 representing the perfect coin and 1 representing a coin in the poorest possible condition that was still identifiable by type and date. Sheldon devised 10 basic levels of condition, several of which were divided into various sublevels; from poorest to best. Sheldon's grades were: Basal State, Fair, Very Fair, Good, Very Good, Fine, Very Fine, Extremely Fine, About Uncirculated and Mint State.

The system was designed specifically for early

large cents. When Sheldon first devised the system, which he called "quantitative grading of condition," he postulated that a Mint State 70 cent (i.e., a perfect coin) was worth 70 times the value of the same variety in Basal State 1 condition. Sheldon wrote, "For at least three grades of condition, ... there appears to be some relationship between value and conventional descriptions of condition." These levels were Fair, Good and Fine. According to Sheldon, a coin in Fair 2 condition was worth about twice a coin in Basal State 1 condition. A Good 4 coin was worth twice a Fair 2 coin. A Fine 12 coin was worth about three times a Good 4 coin.

Sheldon listed three levels of Mint State or Uncirculated: MS-60, MS-65 and MS-70.

Sheldon's system was innovative at the time, but was intended strictly for the early large cents. Soon after the book was published, changing prices made his theory of the relationship between numerical grade and value obsolete.

During the late 1950s, the grade About Uncirculated began to receive greater recognition and use. However, *The Standard Catalogue*, which ceased publication in the 1950s, never used the AU grade. Yeoman's *Guide Book* did not recognize About Uncirculated until the 1978 edition, published in 1977.

In an article published in the May 1956 issue of *The Numismatist*, Lloyd B. Gettys and Edward M. Catich attempted to define the line drawn between Uncirculated coins and those that are not. In "'AU' or 'BU'" the two illustrated with photographs the high points of wear for each U.S. coin type. In a later article, they did the same for commemorative coins.

Brown and Dunn

Another major event took place in 1958—the publishing of the first grading guide in book form. Martin R. Brown and John W. Dunn published *A Guide to the Grading of United States Coins*, a book known today as "Brown and Dunn." The first edition had no illustrations; in 1961, a revised edition was published containing a single photograph for each major design type.

Brown and Dunn recognized seven grades of U.S. coins in early editions: Good, Very Good, Fine, Very Fine, Extremely Fine, About Uncirculated and Uncirculated. The authors note that for Uncirculated coins, "there are grades." Like Sheldon who recognized three levels of Mint State, the authors recognize that not all Uncirculated coins are equal in condition. Coins that are free of marks and defects, they said, "are more desirable." The Brown and Dunn book was eventually recognized as the official grading guide of the ANA.

In the fourth edition, published in 1964, Brown and Dunn included line illustrations for each grade in each major design type, a feature all subsequent editions maintained.

Meanwhile, dealers began to use Sheldon's numerical system of 1 to 70 for other series of coins beyond

early large cents. Paramount International Coin Co. is generally credited with introducing the Mint State system to Morgan silver dollars during the late 1960s and early 1970s. Later, Paramount began "using the quantitative grading method of describing most of the lots in this sale" (May 10, 1971, mail-bid sale).

Another major movement in U.S. coin grading came in 1970 with the publication of James F. Ruddy's *Photograde*. Unlike the Brown and Dunn book, Ruddy used photographs instead of line illustrations. The book contains black-and-white photographs of every major design type in each of seven circulated grade levels: About Good, Good, Very Good, Fine, Very Fine, Extremely Fine and About Uncirculated. No photographs were used for Uncirculated coins.

Ruddy's *Photograde* was designated in 1972 as the new official grading guide of the ANA. It would be designated as such until 1977, when the ANA took a giant step forward and published its own grading guide.

ANA grading guide

As noted, members of the ANA had been calling for an official ANA grading standard almost since it was founded in 1891. The adoption of the Brown and Dunn and *Photograde* volumes as official ANA grading guides proved to be temporary measures. In 1973, ANA President Virginia Culver asked dealer Abe Kosoff to attempt to standardize grading. "Our goal was to standardize grading by defining significant degrees of wear and establishing guide lines so that the various grades may be easily identified," Kosoff wrote in the introduction to the book. "Now, after four years of effort on the part of many, there is an easy-to-use and officially approved set of standards which everyone can apply to the grading of United States coins. Now the confusion in grading caused by multiple systems and biased private opinions should be eliminated," Kosoff wrote.

The 1977 edition of *The Official ANA Grading Standards for United States Coins*, visually, appears to be a combination of Brown and Dunn, using line illustrations, and the Sheldon 1 to 70 numerical system. The first edition recognized three levels of Mint State (MS-60, MS-65 and MS-70). The circulated levels recognized were Choice About Uncirculated 55, AU-50, Choice Extremely Fine 45, EF-40, Choice Very Fine 30, VF-20, Fine 12, Very Good 8, Good 4 and About Good 3.

Two second editions were published, both with line illustrations. The first second edition, published in hard-cover in 1981, recognized two additional levels of Mint State: MS-63 and MS-67. A revised second edition was published in soft-cover in 1984.

A new, third edition of the ANA grading guide was published in April 1987. It eliminated the line illustrations and substituted black-and-white photographs. It also incorporated changes made by the ANA Board of Governors in June 1986, adopting the full 11 Mint State grades. A fourth edition was published in 1991, further refining definitions. The fifth edition published in 1996 introduced a 16-page section featuring color photographs of selected Uncirculated grades. The sixth edition, published in 2005, continued the special 16-page color section with printing on glossy paper, in which a selection of coins graded by "the leading certification services" is presented.

Grading for a fee

During the mid- to late-1970s, numismatic organizations began grading coins for a fee and providing a certificate. The International Numismatic Society Authentication Bureau began grading coins in December 1976, several months after it began authenticating coins. The INS was based in Washington, D.C.

The ANA took a major step in grading March 1, 1979, when the ANA Certification Service began grading coins for a fee and providing third-party certificates noting a grading opinion. ANACS had been founded June 22, 1972, to provide third-party opinions concerning the authenticity of a coin. Staff members would examine coins to determine whether they were genuine, counterfeit or altered.

The decision to begin grading coins for a fee was a controversial revolution for the ANA. Many collectors welcomed what they called independent, nonbiased grading opinions. Others, including dealers, questioned the grading ability and experience of ANACS staff doing the grading.

As ANACS began grading more coins, it soon became a profit center for the association. Some dealers began trading exclusively in ANACS-graded coins.

Commercial grading services

As others realized that a market existed for paid grading opinions, ANACS began receiving competition from other third-party graders. Commercial grading companies were formed, although ANACS continued to lead the pack of third-party grading services until early 1986.

In February 1986, a group of dealers formed the Professional Coin Grading Service. Like ANACS, PCGS used a modified version of Sheldon's 1 to 70 scale, with a major change. Instead of three or five levels of Mint State, PCGS introduced 11 levels: MS-60, -61, -62, -63, -64, -65, -66, -67, -68, -69 and -70. Many collectors and some dealers were outraged. No one, they claimed, could consistently and accurately distinguish single-point increments of Mint State. However, PCGS rapidly overtook ANACS to become the largest (by volume) third-party grading service.

In June 1986, the ANA Board of Governors, faced with a loss of revenue by the submission of coins to PCGS that once would have been sent to ANACS, recognized all 11 levels of Mint State, plus About Uncirculated 58, and authorized their use by ANACS.

Other commercial third-party grading companies

followed PCGS in the late 1980s. Numismatic Guaranty Corporation of America, or NGC, opened in 1987 as a prime competitor. Older existing grading services such as Numismatic Certification Institute and Accugrade were also competing for market share. Independent Coin Grading service opened in 1988 and Sovereign Entities Grading Service opened in 1989.

Encapsulated coins

Perhaps even more far-reaching—and controversial—than the use of the 11-point Mint State scale was the introduction of the encapsulated coin, or "slab." An encapsulated coin is one that, after having been graded, is encased in a sonically sealed rigid plastic holder, together with documentation of grade and authenticity. These holders are generally rectangular and popularly called "slabs."

The implication is that encapsulating a coin "freezes" its condition at the time of it being graded. This, in turn, raises the confidence of the buyer, since he can be assured that the coin inside the slab is as it is described in the documentation.

According to proponents, the slab would allow nonexperts to buy investment-type coins with a higher degree of confidence than ever before. Slabbed coins were aimed directly at inexpert investors. Many dealers professed to trading the slabbed coins "sight-unseen." That is, they would quote a price based on the description assigned by the grading service, rather than on a first-hand examination of the actual coin. Since the beginning of the 21st century more collectors and investors have chosen to include third-party graded and encapsulated coins or "slabs" in their collections and portfolios. At the same time, however, the strength of the sight-unseen market has lost some of its vibrancy. Collectors are content to buy coins in holders, but their mantra is to "buy the coin, not the slab."

PCGS introduced encapsulation in February 1986 as a "solution" to the grading controversy. Following suit in short order was NGC. By 1990 ANACS offered its own slab.

What PCGS first touted as a "solution" brought with it its own set of problems. Controversy over standards and consistency remains. The slab (not the piece of plastic, but the value of the coin associated with the number on the holder) of one service is not necessarily equal to that of another. Certain services command a premium in the market over others based on reputation of strictness or consistency.

Since grading is an opinion, different graders can reach different opinions on the grade of the same coin. Grading services have been known to assign a coin one grade upon one submission and a different grade upon another submission.

On some coin show bourses, it is possible to hear the distinctive crack of plastic slabs being broken open so that the coins inside can be removed and resubmitted in hopes of getting a more favorable grade. An effort to upgrade is known as a "crack-out."

Another problem was the mistaken belief of many that slabs give coins absolute protection from the environmental elements that cause toning. Chemicals in the atmosphere can and do permeate through the plastic. It is not unusual to find silver coins that when slabbed were bright and shiny but are beginning to tone inside the slab, within two to three years. A slab may give the coin some protection from harmful chemicals, but it does not prevent the toning process.

PCGS Grading Guide

One common complaint voiced by some hobbyists about third-party grading services was the lack of published grading standards. With the exception of ANACS when it was still a part of the American Numismatic Association (ANACS has been privately owned since 1990), none of the major grading services published their standards until 1997.

PCGS published its grading standards in book form in the fall of 1997 in *Official Guide to Coin Grading and Counterfeit Detection* by House of Collectibles, part of the Ballantine Publishing Group.

The 324-page, 14-chapter book includes an introduction to the concepts of grading—including a definition of market grading—and handling and storage, as well as details on the elements of a coin's grade.

Chapter 4 features the PCGS's grading standards from Poor 1 to Mint State 70 and Proof 50 to Proof 70. Photographs of Morgan dollars are used in the chapter to illustrate grades from About Uncirculated 58 to Poor 1.

Grading standards for individual series follow, with individual chapters focusing on copper, copper-nickel, silver and gold coins. Photos are used for the most popular series among collectors, while the standards for other series are strictly text. A section of color photos includes images of Mint State examples of popular series.

The book also contains chapters on doctored coins (coins that have been artificially enhanced) and counterfeit detection. A second edition was published in 2004, with the most significant change being the addition of better and more photographs.

In 2010 PCGS released its PCGS Photograde Online, which provides color images of most U.S. coin design series in the full range of grades from 1 to 70. It does not include a text explanation of the grades. The visual guide is also available as a free application for iPhone, iPod and iPad through the Apple store.

Amos Hobby Publishing, the publisher of *Coin World* and the *Coin World Almanac,* introduced a grading guide, *Making the Grade,* by *Coin World* editor Beth Deisher, in 2005. The spiral-bound reference was a grading guide to the 25 most widely collected U.S. coins. A second edition was published in 2008 with 50 series of coins featured.

The grading section for each series features full-color photos of the coins in a wide range of grades, plus color maps showing the high points of the design (the first areas of the coin to exhibit wear) and the areas of the design most affected by contact marks. The book provides details on where to look for wear for each series. A digital version is available via iPad.

Computer grading

Despite the rise of commercial third-party grading services in the late 1980s, consistency in grading continued to be a problem. Briefly, many thought salvation would come from the high-tech sector with computers replacing human graders. The approach was to marry computers with high-resolution video imaging systems, artificial intelligence "expert" software, and a database of codified grading standards.

Amos Press Inc., *Coin World*'s parent firm, was the first to announce interest. API contracted on Nov. 19, 1986, with Battelle Memorial Institute in Columbus, Ohio, to "determine the feasibility and practicality of using equipment to objectively grade collectible and investment grade coins." Battelle is an acknowledged leader in the scientific field in identifying, developing and applying existing or new technology to solve problems. By August 1987, Battelle scientists reported that they believed "current technology could be harnessed to objectively grade rare coins" but they cautioned that their assessment had not addressed the economic feasibility of such an undertaking.

New York entrepreneur Henry Merton joined the race in February of 1988, predicting he would be the first to introduce "objective coin grading and identification computer technology" to the marketplace. He announced that he had a patent pending and that he had joined forces with Charles Hoskins of the International Numismatic Society Authentication Bureau.

By the fall of 1988, Amos Press officials said a prototype computer coin grading system was in development and that 90 people randomly selected from the bourse at the August 1988 American Numismatic Association convention held in Cincinnati had seen a video tape and reacted positively to the analysis concept of the system.

The first company to publicly unveil a computer said to be capable of grading coins was PCGS, surprising the market by demonstrating the capabilities of its "PCGS Expert" on May 16, 1990. Two weeks later PCGS officials provided a full demonstration for more than 550 dealers and collectors attending the Long Beach Coin, Stamp & Collectibles Expo. Louis M. Crain, the developer of the software, said the computer's grading process mimicked "how a human being grades coins." David Hall said at the time that the PCGS Expert had graded more than 10,000 Morgan dollars, and that it was then set up to handle only Morgan dollars.

Amos Press purchased ANACS from the ANA in June of 1990 to gain coin grading knowledge and expertise along with a market presence to continue to pursue computerized coin grading. However, Amos Press never brought computer grading to the marketplace due to a lack of economic viability. Bruce Boyd, president of Amos Press during the 1990s, said in 2010 that after investing more than $2 million in the project, the firm's owners determined that, while technically feasible, the continuing investment was not commercially viable. Market volumes had declined and grading fees had been significantly reduced because of increasing competitive pressures. By late 1991, Amos Press made the decision to discontinue its computer grading project.

Merton's patented technology for coin grading was employed by CompuGrade, a New Orleans-based firm, when it opened for business in February 1991. However, CompuGrade shut down its computer grading operation 14 months later due to lack of sufficient submissions.

David Hall revealed in 2010 that the PCGS Expert was never actually used to grade coins. "We couldn't quite get it to duplicate what the human eye does," Hall said. He noted that while initial plans had been to eventually grade other series, PCGS attempted to use the Expert only to grade Morgan dollars because "each series had to be a separate program." He added: "The Expert could actually grade, but was limited and the mistakes were too big."

He asserted that computers—even in 2010—although much faster, would still be prone to making the same mistakes.

Computer grading was not commercially viable and as the second decade of the 21st century opened there was no evidence that a computer would in the near future replace human graders.

Grading today

In coin grading today the emphasis is on perfection or the top of the 1 to 70 grading scale, a phenomenon known as grade rarity.

Until the early 1980s, the "perfect coin" was more a dream than reality in the United States. If a perfect coin was produced in previous times, it went unrecorded and ungraded. However, the mid-1980s were revolutionary times in U.S. numismatics. Implementation of 11 increments within Mint State grading and emergence of commercial third-party grading services spurred the pursuit of grade perfection. As third-party grading blossomed, so did thoughts of collecting coins in the highest of grades.

Coincidentally, at about the same time, the United States resumed production of noncirculating commemorative coins and introduced a new line of silver and gold bullion coins dubbed American Eagles. A new chief sculptor-engraver, Elizabeth Jones, was at the helm of the Mint's engraving staff. She brought new knowledge and techniques to U.S. coinage production.

The first U.S. coin to achieve the MS-70 level as determined by third-party grading service ANACS was a 1986-W Statue of Liberty gold half eagle, which Jones designed. In 1988 when the PCGS assigned its ninth MS-70 grade, Jones' 1988-W Olympic gold half eagle was the object of perfection.

Jones said of perfection: "It is a marriage of the artist and technology. The artist has to know how to work within the limits of the technology. ..." But she also noted that producing a flawless coin goes beyond the artist. "Part of it is the die setting, the press operator, and handling of it. ... There are a lot of people involved to get a perfect coin."

Throughout the 1990s as commercial third-party grading companies competed for market share, collectors and the numismatic marketplace began to embrace the collecting of "modern" coins. In general, the point of "modern" demarcation is 1965, the point at which the U.S. government jettisoned silver from

the dimes and quarter dollars and reduced the amount of silver in the half dollars in circulation. But in the 1990s and the first decade of the 2000s, as the U.S. Mint began to strike more noncirculating commemoratives, bullion coins and "circulating commemoratives" such as the 50 State quarter dollars, Sacagawea dollar and Westward Journey 5-cent coins, these new issues began to solidify their stake on the "modern" coin market. As the second decade of the 21st century opened, MS-69 and MS-70 on the Uncirculated scale and Proof 69 and Proof 70 in Proof grades constituted the majority of grades assigned to recent modern coins, with approximately 30 percent reaching perfection (70).

Not only has the U.S. Mint improved its production technology in the last 25 years, but it has vastly improved its processes for handling and packaging numismatic or collector product lines. For example, Proof versions of silver, gold and platinum coins are individually struck and receive "white-glove" treatment from the time they are removed from the coining chamber until they are placed in special protective packaging. Similar care is taken with examples of the various circulation coins produced for Uncirculated and Proof sets sold to collectors.

The numbers of high-grade coins have grown exponentially as the market for commemorative and bullion coins has exploded with rising values for precious metals. Modern U.S. coins graded and encapsulated by the leading commercial third-party grading services as Mint State and Proof 69 and 70 are being sold not only in the traditional numismatic marketplace but on cable television shopping shows and in general interest online auction venues such as eBay.

Emphasis on attaining the highest grade possible is also at play in the classical, pre-1965 sector of the U.S. coin market.

Concern about a bias toward awarding higher grades and lack of grading consistency gave rise in 2007 to a new service, the Certified Acceptance

Corp., which for a fee reviews coins already graded and encapsulated by PCGS and NGC.

CAC affixes a distinctive green sticker to the holder of each coin that, in the firm's judgment, fully merits the grade originally assigned. Coins that qualify for a superlative rating for a given grade, based on a variety of technical and subjective tests devised by CAC founder John Albanese, command premiums of 10 to 30 percent above market value for the grade. Albanese said he focuses exclusively on PCGS- and NGC-graded coins because they tend to achieve sales prices higher than other third-party grading services.

In 2010 both PCGS and NGC moved to designate the best coins within specific grades.

PCGS launched a new grade designation that the firm's executives said would "unlock value" for 15 to 20 percent of coins within 11 current grades. Simultaneously PCGS also announced the incorporation of a new, high-tech process the firm claimed would enable PCGS to combat "gradeflation" and detect coins that have been artificially enhanced.

The new service is trademarked as PCGS Secure Plus and coins graded under the new system are encapsulated in a new holder displaying a color-shifting yellow shield on the top left of the holder and a new insert with enhanced anti-counterfeiting features. The Plus designation is expressed with a + sign next to the numerical grade and is available only in conjunction with the PCGS Secure Plus service in grades Extremely Fine 45 to Mint State 68, except for MS-60 and -61.

PCGS co-founder David Hall said the plus designation brings formal recognition to high-end coins within a particular grade that are technically superior and also addresses some significant price gaps between the one-point differentials in the 70-point scale used in the marketplace today.

Hall explained: "The reality of the marketplace is that coins considered high end for the grade are recognized by sophisticated dealers and collectors and such coins are worth a premium in the marketplace. The term 'plus' has been a part of the everyday trading and grading lingo for years. The high end for any particular grade represents the top 30 percent of the scale within a grade and I estimate that the plus designation would apply to approximately 15 percent to 20 percent of the coins within a grade."

PCGS President Don Willis said use of the plus designation would automatically "unlock value" and immediately benefit the marketplace. "If you have 100,000 coins that get the plus designation and as a result are worth on average an additional $1,000 each, you automatically add $100 million in value to the marketplace."

Numismatic Guaranty Corp. also announced that it would offer a plus designation with the + sign added to the firm's inserts for high-end grades.

NGC Chairman Mark Salzberg said: "The coin marketplace has evolved in the nearly 25 years since NGC and PCGS began certifying coins, and this is a very logical progression. We have always been conscious of the variation within grades. By providing this information on the label in the plus format, it is communicated in a simple and direct way that allows these distinctions to be readily understood."

The PCGS Secure Plus process, which is integrated into the PCGS grading system, uses lasers to digitally scan each coin to capture its distinctive characteristics. According to PCGS executives, the system will increase precision and consistency in grading, improve detection of altered coins, decrease the chance of "gradeflation," curb excessive resubmissions and help to positively identify a stolen Secure Plus coin.

The PCGS Secure Plus system in 35 seconds digitally captures a unique "fingerprint" of each coin that is then entered into a permanent data base, according to the firm. According to Willis, the PCGS Secure Plus system was developed after two years of software and hardware development and testing in partnership with Coin Secure Inc. of Palo Alto, Calif.

Willis explained: "Every coin has its own identifying characteristics. Coins are like snowflakes at the micron level; they are very different from each other. If a coin has been previously registered in our system it will be identified whenever it's again scanned by us, so duplication of coin information will be eliminated. As a result, population reports, condition census and other potentially distorted information will be much more accurate for PCGS Secure Plus coins.

"The process also can help detect if a previously registered coin has been artificially toned, dipped or processed in some other way in an effort to get a higher grade. Not since PCGS introduced encapsulated third-party grading in 1986 has such an important step been taken to protect the consumer. We believe PCGS Secure Plus will totally revolutionize the coin grading business," Willis added.

Hall said that with this system, PCGS will be able to "eliminate the payoff on that bad behavior." He also was adamant in stating that coin doctoring and gradeflation are a "bad deal for the market and for everyone," and believes eliminating or severely curbing the two will instill confidence and much greater participation in the coin market in the future.

Hall said that PCGS will continue to use three expert graders to grade each coin. The first two graders to view the coin will grade using their normal procedure. The third grader, known as the finalizer, will have access to the images and information stored in the database captured by the PCGS Secure Plus system. If the system reveals a match for a previously graded coin or detects that the coin has been altered in some way, that information will then be used to determine its grade. Coins identified as having been altered or artificially enhanced can be returned in a Genuine holder or in a body bag, without grade.

Hall revealed that internally PCGS graders have

for some time been using a 700-point scale. He said that although it is humanly impossible to consistently distinguish between a 645 and 646 grade, incorporating the PCGS Secure Plus technology will help human graders be more consistent. Those coins deemed to be 647, 648 or 649, for example, would qualify for the 64+ designation.

Hall also noted that PCGS has codified seven different levels of eye appeal, one of four grade components especially important for coins grading above Mint State or Proof 60. The seven eye appeal designations are "amazing," "positive," "above average," "neutral," "below average," "negative" and "ugly."

According to Hall, a coin exhibiting negative or below average eye appeal for the grade will not qualify for the plus grade. A brochure, which PCGS distributes to help educate the collector community, titled "Guidelines for Eye Appeal," lists the following minimum standards for eye appeal on high grades:

"MS/PR68 — Must have positive eye appeal."

"MS/PR67 — Must have above average eye appeal."

"MS/PR66 — Cannot have below average eye appeal.

"MS/PR65 — Cannot have negative eye appeal. A MS/PR65 coin can have below average luster or color (toning) if it is outstanding in every other way."

Grading ancient, world coins

Until the advent of commercial third-party grading services in the United States, grading of world coins relied exclusively on adjectival grading and some terms used varied from those used in the United States. However, aggressive marketing and the ability to reach collectors around the world via the Internet and online auctions such as eBay dramatically changed the landscape beginning around the year 2000.

While some non-U.S. based auction houses and dealer specialists continue to use adjectival grading, the use of the 1 to 70 scale—dominant among U.S. coins—is now widely used for world coins because the major U.S. grading services grade world coins.

The picture is somewhat different for ancient coins. Most auction firms and dealer specialists continue to use adjectival grading to describe the state of preservation of an ancient coin.

Two U.S. grading services offer grading for ancient coins: ANACS and a division of Numismatic Guar-

anty Corp., which is known as NGC Ancients.

ANACS has offered grading and encapsulation of ancient coins since 2008. Specialist J.P. Martin grades all ancient coins for ANACS and uses the Sheldon 1-to-70 scale. ANACS encapsulates ancient coins in its standard holder.

NGC Ancients, led by specialist David Vagi, uses an adjectival system. For circulated grades, NGC Ancients' terms describe the amount of wear a coin has received; its Uncirculated grades take into account the overall appearance of the coin to distinguish among Mint State, Choice Mint State and Gem Mint State. At its website, NGC Ancients notes that the grade is one of four components of the appearance of ancient coins that it evaluates. Others are strike, surface and style. To further explain its grading terms, NGC Ancients provides a chart at its website showing its grading levels and their Sheldon scale equivalents. NGC Ancients encapsulates ancient coins in a special holder designed for them.

Grading U.S. paper money

Few areas of numismatics have undergone as much change in the last decade as the area of grading paper money.

As the 21st century began, both collectors and dealers continued to use adjectival grading, although the number of adjectival grades commonly used was expanding. Attempts to establish a formal, hobby-wide grading system began during the 1960s and continued into the 1970s. Herbert J. Kwart published a 44-page pamphlet, *United States Paper Money Grading Standard,* in June 1984 using a numerical system; however, his system did not achieve widespread acceptance. A number of dealer-oriented paper money grading firms sprang up in the late 1990s, each offering grading specific to their interpretations.

Widely used paper money catalogs—Arthur L. and Ira S. Friedberg's *Paper Money of the United States,* Gene Hessler's *The Comprehensive Catalog of U.S. Paper Money* and Krause Publications' *Standard*

Catalog of United States Paper Money—continued to rely on adjectival grades, with minor differences in grade descriptions among the authors of the books.

The game-changer came in 2005 when the parent firms of the top two coin grading services—Professional Coin Grading Service and Numismatic Guaranty Corp.—expanded into paper currency, launching new companies dedicated exclusively to grading and authentication of U.S. and foreign paper money (PCGS Currency and Paper Money Guaranty). The two firms adapted the 1-to-70 Sheldon grading, by that time widely accepted in grading coins, for use in the grading of paper money and offering new protective holders especially designed for paper items. PCGS has since sold its PCGS Currency business to another party, though the firm retains its original name.

An overview posted at PCGS Currency's website notes that there are many "gray areas" involved in the paper money grading process. This discussion describes the recent fundamental shift that has taken place within the paper money grading:

"Paper, even of the quality used to print U.S. currency, is ultimately a fragile material that is subject to the abuses of circulation, wear, mishandling, aging, or even severe damage or destruction. Because of its pliable and fragile nature, currency has been subject to many attempts (both well-meaning and malicious) to improve notes both in appearance and grade. Some of these attempts are laudable in that otherwise unattractive and non-collectible specimens of great rarity have been restored to an appearance that makes them far more acceptable to collectors. Other attempts at 'improvement' have resulted in the effective destruction of many notes.

"In between these extremes are the gray areas, dealing with which is much more difficult. Good note restorers are sometimes capable of amazing feats, and even the best experts are sometimes hard-pressed to determine what (if any) work has been done to a note. A minor corner bend or light fold can sometimes be removed with careful and skillful work so that even the closest examination cannot reveal its previous existence. Many notes that have been lightly circulated now appear to be fully New or uncirculated, as they have been pressed or ironed out. Pinholes can be filled or closed, handling marks or finger smudges can be erased, ink marks or stains can be lightened or removed entirely, tears or splits can be closed, and virtually any problem can be attacked to improve the appearance or remove its visual signs. Sometimes, the skill with which these repairs or restorations are executed makes detection difficult or even impossible.

"The problem is not so much the existence of these gray areas, but their impact on a note's value. While purists cringe at the fact that many notes that were once About Uncirculated or even Extremely Fine are now sold as uncirculated, it boils down to fundamental economics. When a circulated note is pressed and the folds are entirely removed, it again appears 'uncirculated.' Because the market currently dictates that most notes are worth more as pressed 'uncirculated' notes than in their original state, such restoration is financially rewarded. Any time profit is available the opportunity will be exploited. If the demand remains for such pressed notes, supply will follow and restoration will continue."

The websites of PCGS Currency and Paper Money Guaranty offer detailed information about their grading standards, numerical scale, holders, population reports, guarantees and submission policies. Since these two firms dominate the paper money authentication and grading field and most paper currency sold at auction today has been graded by one or the other, collectors and investors in paper money are advised to compare the grading and services of each.

PCGS Currency, founded by PCGS parent firm Collectors Universe in 2005, was sold in February of 2009 to a new company led by its former management team of Jason W. Bradford, president, and Laura A. Kessler, vice president. The company is located in Peoria, Ill. For additional information contact the firm at (309) 222-8200 or see its website at **www.pcgscurrency.com**.

Paper Money Guaranty is one of the independent companies focused on the certification and grading of collectibles under the Certified Collectibles Group headquartered in Sarasota, Fla. For additional information contact the firm at (941) 309-1001 or toll free at (877) 764-5570, or see its website at **www.pmgnotes.com**.

While the 19th edition of *Paper Money of the United States* by Arthur L. and Ira S. Friedberg published in 2010 does not define all of the 11 grades of Mint State from 60 to 70 used by the commercial paper money grading services, it does provide numerical equivalents to the adjectival grades used in its value guide, which is especially useful for those new to the paper money field. They are reprinted below by permission:

Gem Uncirculated (Gem65): A note that is flawless, with the same freshness, crispness and bright color as when first printed. It must be perfectly centered, with full margins, and free of any marks, blemishes or traces of handling.

Choice Uncirculated (Ch63): An uncirculated note which is fresher and brighter than the norm for its particular issue. Almost as nice as Gem Uncirculated, but not quite there. Must be reasonably well centered.

Uncirculated (CU60): A note which shows no trace of circulation. It may not have perfect centering and may have one or more pinholes, counting smudges, or other evidence of improper handling, while still retaining its original crispness.

Sometimes large size notes will be encountered which are obviously uncirculated, but which may have some tiny pin holes. It was customary in the old days to spindle or pin new notes together, and that is why so many uncirculated notes may show tiny pin holes. Such imperfections do not generally impair the choice appearance of a new note, and such notes are to be regarded as being in uncirculated condition, although they generally command slightly lower prices than notes in perfect condition.

About Uncirculated (AU50): A bright, crisp note that appears new but upon close examination shows a trace of very light use, such as a corner fold or faint crease. About Uncirculated is a borderline condition, applied to a note which may not be quite uncirculated, but yet is obviously better than an average Extra Fine note. Such notes command a price only slightly below a new note and are highly desirable.

Extra Fine (EF40): A note that shows some faint evidence of circulation, although it will still be bright and retain nearly full crispness. It may have two or three minor folds or creases but no tears or stains and no discolorations.

Very Fine (VF20): A note that has been in circulation, but not actively or for long. It still retains some crispness and is still choice enough in its condition to be altogether desirable. It may show folds or creases, or some light smudges from the hands of a past generation. Sometimes, Very Fine notes are the best available in certain rare issues, and they should accordingly be cherished just as much as uncirculated notes.

Fine (F12): A fine note shows evidence of much more circulation, has lost its crispness and very fine detail, and creases are more pronounced, although the note is still not seriously soiled or stained.

Very Good (VG8): A note that has had considerable wear or circulation and may be limp, soiled or dark in appearance and even have a small tear or two on an edge.

Good (G4): A note that is badly worn, with margin or body tears, frayed margins and missing corners.

In general, discriminating collectors will not acquire Fine or worse notes because they have lost their aesthetic appeal, but this applies only to common notes. A really rare note has a ready market in even poor condition, because it may not otherwise exist, or if it is choice, will have an extremely high price commensurate with it.

Authentication and grading services

With the rise of the Internet and numismatic collectibles being sold in venues such as eBay, dozens of smaller (sometimes one-person, home-basement operations) grading services began to proliferate, often with names and acronyms similar to mainstream and long-established grading services. More than two dozens such services can be found by searching the Internet today.

Before submitting coins for encapsulation or purchasing coins already residing in holders, collectors and investors are advised to perform some basic due diligence. Considerations include whether the grading service offers a guarantee of its authentication and grading, what is the firm's longevity and reputation in the marketplace, and are the firm's graded products present in the mainstream numismatic marketplace (in auctions conducted by reputable numismatic auction firms and available from dealers in attendance at major state, regional, national, and international coin shows.)

The listing below, in alphabetical order, includes the most prominent and widely recognized grading services in the United States and Canada.

Coins

ANACS
P.O. Box 6000
Englewood, CO 80155
(800) 888-1861
www.anacs.com

Canadian Coin Certification Service
Box 1051
Saint-Basile-Le Grand, Quebec
Canada, J3N 1M5
(450) 723-1204
www.canadiancoincertification.com

Independent Coin Graders
P.O. Box 276000
Tampa, FL 33688
(877) 221-4424
www.icgcoin.com

International Coin Certification Service
2010 Yonge St.
Suite 202
Toronto, Ontario,
Canada, M4S 1Z9
(416) 488-8620

Numismatic Guaranty Corporation
P.O. Box 4776
Sarasota, FL 34230
(800) 642-2646
www.ngccoin.com

Professional Coin Grading Service
P.O. Box 9458
Newport Beach, CA 92658
(800) 447-8848
www.pcgs.com

Sovereign Entities Grading Service Inc.
P.O. Box 8129 — East Gate Center
Chattanooga, TN 37411
(888) 768-7261
www.segsgrading.com

Paper Money

Canadian Coin Certification Service
Box 1051
Saint-Basile-Le Grand, Quebec
Canada, J3N 1M5
(450) 723-1204
www.canadiancoincertification.com

PCGS Currency
P. O. Box 10470
Peoria, IL 61612-0470
(309) 222-8200
www.pcgscurrency.com

Paper Money Guaranty
P.O. Box 4755
Sarasota, FL 34230
(877) 764-5570
www.pmgnotes.com

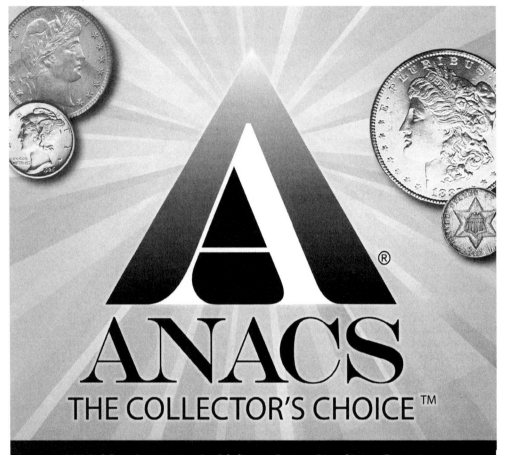

17 Counterfeit Coins

Counterfeit coins exist. That simple truth can be as frightening to a professional numismatist or long-time collector as it is to a neophyte collector, for any counterfeit coin is potentially deceptive. A hobbyist's best defense against counterfeit coins is knowledge—about the coining process, the diagnostics of specific coins and the diagnostics of counterfeits. It helps also to have a dealer who is both trustworthy and knowledgeable about counterfeit coins. Collectors may find purchasing encapsulated coins (those graded and authenticated by third-party grading services) the best protection against counterfeits, although, in recent years, counterfeiters have begun to produce counterfeit grading service slabs.

Two basic types of counterfeit coins exist. One is produced to deceive the public by passing in circulation as genuine. Counterfeits of this type have plagued the public since the first coins were produced. The second category of counterfeit is the type meant as a fraudulent numismatic item, designed to deceive the unwary collector, dealer or numismatist for illicit monetary gain.

This chapter examines counterfeit coins on a variety of levels, beginning with a basic explanation of what kinds of counterfeits exist, followed by a profile of an unabashed modern counterfeiter, a brief history of counterfeit coins and then the modern dangers of counterfeit coins and counterfeit grading service slabs, a brief consideration of the legality of owning a counterfeit collection, and finally a discussion of how to protect oneself from buying a counterfeit coin unknowingly.

The best way to learn about counterfeit coins is to examine them and compare the frauds to genuine coins of the same type and date in order to learn about the characteristics of both. The American Numismatic Association sponsors annually two five-day courses in counterfeit detection at its Summer Seminar, held in Colorado Springs, Colo. Students who attend the course have the opportunity to examine counterfeit coins (and their first cousins, altered coins) through microscopes. Genuine coins are used for comparison purposes. Details about future Summer Seminars are available by contacting the ANA at the website **www.money.org**.

If you are uncertain about the authenticity of any numismatic item, do not buy it. If the dealer refuses to send the coin to an authentication service, be wary of buying the coin. You may have to pay the authentication fee for such a coin but the fee is well worth the nominal cost, especially for a coin valued at hundreds or thousands of dollars.

Circulating or numismatic counterfeits?

Circulating counterfeit coins, also called "contemporary counterfeits," represent the earliest category of counterfeit coins. Such pieces have existed for almost as long as coins have existed, for more than 2,500 years. Some circulating counterfeits were issued to deceive users into thinking the coins were real; the issuers, who intended fraud, profited from the act of production and issuance of the fake coins. Other circulating counterfeit coins were issued from necessity when the governing authority was unable or unwilling to meet the coinage needs of a populace; such pieces are often in imitation of genuine coins, but individuals produced them to meet a local need for anything resembling coinage and of a sufficient quality to be acceptable in commerce (as will be discussed in greater detail in the historical section of this chapter, such counterfeit coins were sometimes eagerly embraced by a population having no access to official coinage).

While circulating counterfeits are virtually nonexistent in the United States in the 21st century, older circulating counterfeits are often found at archaeological sites, attesting to their wide use in circulation. Circulating counterfeit ancient coins and 19th U.S. coins can be found in dealer inventories today, labeled accurately by legitimate dealers (or not, by dealers with a looser regard for honesty). Many collectors enjoy collecting older counterfeit coins in appreciation of their historical and commercial roles. In particular, fake Capped Bust half dollars (the real ones were struck from 1807 to 1839) seem to be especially popular with collectors of the real thing.

Numismatic counterfeit coins are produced to deceive collectors, not to circulate. Coins have been collected for centuries, with the hobby becoming popular in the United States about 1858.

As collectors began studying coins and learning that some dates, Mint marked pieces and die varieties were rarer than other similar pieces and thus harder to obtain, counterfeiters began meeting the demand by making new, albeit fake, examples. Numismatic counterfeits are discussed throughout this chapter.

How counterfeits are made

Several different methods are used in making counterfeits. Counterfeits can be cast, die struck and made from genuine coins altered to mimic rarer pieces. Cast and die-struck counterfeits can either be circulating or numismatic in nature; altered coins are almost universally intended for numismatic fakery. Related pieces include replicas and electrotypes.

Cast counterfeits

Casting is "very likely the oldest method" of making counterfeit coins according to Charles M. Larson in *Numismatic Forgery*. If proper techniques are followed faithfully, the quality of a cast coin can be very high, according to Larson. Casting can also result in a crude counterfeit if the counterfeiter does not exercise care.

Producing a cast coin involves creating a mold bearing the obverse and reverse designs of the coin. Such a mold can perfectly duplicate the coin used a model for the mold. This duplication is both good and bad—the definitions of "good" and "bad" differing on whether you are the counterfeiter or the intended victim—because not only does creation of the mold perfectly duplicate all design details, it also duplicates all imperfections on the model coin, creating useful diagnostics for skilled observers who have been trained to recognize such points.

Various methods are used in creating a mold, though all generally start with a genuine coin as the model. Larson describes a sophisticated method involving the use of silicon rubber, injection wax and a special plaster, resulting in the creation of a mold that can be used in creating a cast coin. If one uses this technique, liquid rubber is poured into a mold form containing the target coin and allowed to cure; when the rubber cures, the mold is cut apart so the obverse and reverse faces are exposed. Melted wax is then injected into the reassembled rubber mold along a sprue to form a wax model. Once the wax model hardens, it can be embedded into a special, investment plaster to form the actual mold used in casting the product. Once the plaster has cured, the mold is heated so the wax melts and flows out of the sprue opening. The melting of the wax leaves a cavity inside the mold that perfectly duplicates the coin used as the original model.

Larson describes how a single mold is heated slightly to facilitate the casting of the coin, then mounted in a small centrifuge attached to a crucible containing the molten metal. When the centrifuge spins, metal is flung from the crucible along the sprue tube into the mold, forming the cast coin. When the centrifuge stops, the mold can be placed into a container of water to cool. The soaking of the water, Larson writes, will result in the plaster mold falling apart. What is left is the cast coin with an attached sprue. The sprue is cut off and the spot where it was attached to the cast coin is polished to remove traces.

A simple method of creating a mold (though rarely used for making high quality castings) uses sand. A fine casting sand is firmly packed into one half of the mold form and a coin pressed into the sand. Rods are also positioned in the sand, one leading to the coin to create a flue through which molten metal will be poured and two leading away from the coin to form air ducts for air that will displaced during the casting step. A wax sheet is positioned over the sand, coin and rods, the other half of the mold form is placed into position and more sand is poured on top of the coin. The two halves of the mold are then separated, and the coin, wax sheet and rods are removed. The separate halves of the mold are closed, now with the cavity for the coin to be cast. The whole contraption tilted so metal can be poured down the flue into the cavity while the displaced air inside the flue and cavity flows away through the air ducts. Once the metal has cooled, the cast coin can be removed.

While high-quality cast counterfeits can be difficult for new collectors to detect, cruder cast pieces can be easily identified. Many of the cruder pieces have a raised seam along the edge resulting from an imperfectly formed mold, representing where the two halves of the mold were joined together at a particular stage. Such pieces may even have a portion of the sprue still attached.

Another diagnostic of some cast coins results when a nonstandard metal is used for the fake coin—for example, a copper alloy for a gold or silver coin. Since the resulting counterfeit coin is of a different color than the real thing, the piece has to be electroplated with a metal of the correct color. Over time, the plating may wear away, exposing the original color of the metal.

Cast counterfeits continue to be made, so collectors should learn as much as they can about the various processes used and the diagnostics of each.

It should be noted that some early genuine Chinese and Indian coins were cast, but for most part, official coinages were and are all die struck.

Die-struck counterfeits

Die-struck counterfeit coins are produced much in the way all modern coins are produced at official and commercial mints.

Employing fake dies presents a number of advantages to a counterfeiter. The most obvious, of course, is that counterfeit dies allow an almost exact duplication of Mint production methods, making their detection more difficult.

Also the use of counterfeit dies allows the counterfeiter much greater latitude in his efforts. Not only can he reproduce a greater number of identical coins, he can also duplicate the rarer coins without actually being in possession of one if, for example, he uses different coins as models—for example, the obverse of a 1909-S Lincoln cent and reverse of a

1909 Lincoln, V.D.B. cent, can be used in making fake dies that, when paired, will strike counterfeits of the scarcer and more valuable 1909-S Lincoln, V.D.B. cent. The counterfeiter can create mules (unintended die pairings) at will. And error coins such as off-center strikes, rotated reverses, multiple strikes, clipped planchets, thick and thin planchets, railroad rims or partial collars and many others can be created by duplicating the very Mint procedures, or Mint equipment malfunctions, that would cause those errors inside the Mint itself.

Though a counterfeit coin's physical characteristics, and even the edges, will often faithfully reproduce the characteristics of a genuine coin, the design details and field will often reveal the origin. Logically, then, in order to detect this type of counterfeit, you must know, at the very least, the rudiments of making the fake dies.

Counterfeit dies can be made by several different methods: cutting by hand, by plating, by casting, by machine engraving and by hubbing.

Cutting a die by hand requires the counterfeiter to possess special skill sets used by engravers. For centuries, all coinage dies were made by hand engraving. While many ancient and medieval coins are of mediocre or even crude appearance, numerous ancient coins exhibit engraving of the highest artistic quality. Few individuals possess the skills to create a coin's design elements by cutting them directly into the face of a blank steel die, so this technique is rarely used by counterfeiters today. And even for an expert engraver, it is humanly impossible to exactly duplicate every detail through hand engraving.

The faces of counterfeit dies can also be produced using the electroplating method. To achieve this, Larson explains, a genuine coin is attached via a wire to the positive terminal of a weak DC electrical source (about 1 volt) and suspended in an acidic plating solution. A strip of metal, such as copper or nickel, is placed into the same solution, suspended from a wire attached to the negative terminal of the power sources, creating an anode. An electrical circuit is generated that moves molecules of metal from the strip attached to the negative terminal to the exposed face of the coin attached to the positive terminal (one side of the coin is coated in an insulating material to prevent deposits from forming on that side). Through a repetitive process, thin layers of nickel and copper can be deposited on the exposed face of the coin, forming a shell that, when thick enough, is detached from the coin to form a die face after it is fastened to a die shaft.

Dies can also be made using the same casting techniques used for making cast coins. Remember that the goal here is to create a negative copy of the coin used as the model that will then serve as a die for the striking of counterfeit coins.

Machine-engraved dies are often made by use of machines similar, if not identical, to the Contamin portrait lathes and the Janvier reducing machines used in most mints until late in the 20th century and early 21st century, when computers and lasers were introduced into the die-making process.

Using traditional 19th and 20th century die-making methods, a tracing tool follows the contours of the coin as the coin rotates about its axis. The tracing tool, through linkages, duplicates the movements of the tracing point with a cutting tool on a soft steel blank. As long as the rotation of the coin and blank remain constant—this being a one-to-one transfer step—the design being reproduced will be identical to the original. However, should the relationship change, the design details will be different. They may be wider or narrower than the original.

After the reproduction is finished the field will exhibit circular rings left by the cutting tool. A counterfeiter must polish out those rings, leading to the possibility of also removing parts of the design. On the other hand, if he doesn't do the job well enough, some of those marks may still remain on the die. So, if you spot a coin with concentric rings on its surface, you would be justified in thinking that it is a product of machine-engraved dies.

A transfer die is made by taking an original coin and forcing it into the surface of a piece of metal that when suitably hardened, can be used as a die. The design transfer can occur gradually, with the coin forced into the metal with a slowly increasing amount of force. Or the dies can also be made by impacting the coin into a soft steel blank by use of an explosive charge, a heavy press, or any other means that will impart a sudden, tremendous pressure. Impact dies can have many obvious imperfections. Large coins do not impact evenly across their surface. The impact tends to spread the coin, especially silver and copper coins that are relatively soft. This spreading results in design details that are broader than normal and, quite often, slightly doubled near the edges. Attempts to touch up the dies can be made but careful inspection will usually reveal not only the remaining defects, but also the attempt to correct those defects. Often the first clue to a coin produced from an impact die is that its design details are sharper near the center than at the edges.

No matter how counterfeit dies are made, they are then placed into a press along with a collar, and the planchets are placed between the dies to strike the counterfeit coins.

Altered coins

An altered coin is a genuine coin that has had some element changed so it resembles a rare and thus more expensive variety.

The methods of alteration are many. Thousands of 1943 Lincoln cents, produced on a steel planchet to conserve copper for the war effort, have been plated with copper to resemble very rare 1943 bronze cents. The third digit on some 1903 Liberty Head 5-cent coins has been changed into a 1 to resemble the 1913

Liberty Head 5-cent coin, a classic rarity. Mint marks have been added to many 1909 Lincoln, V.D.B. cents from the Philadelphia Mint to resemble the coin's rarer San Francisco Mint counterpart. Mint marks have been removed from many branch Mint 1895 Morgan silver dollars to "create" the scarce Philadelphia Mint version. The list is long.

Various techniques are used to create extra Mint marks. The crudest method is to simply form a Mint mark by hand using a tool to move metal around at the appropriate place until a raised Mint mark is form. It is easy to detect such Mint marks; they are rarely of the proper shape and the moving of metal around will form a scar around the fake Mint mark.

Another method is to cut a Mint mark from a common coin and to glue it into place on a Philadelphia Mint example of the same date and type. These Mint marks can be detected under close inspection: on a genuine coin, the metal from the fields shows flow lines up into the Mint mark, the result of the metal of the planchet flowing up into the recess of the die forming the Mint mark. When a Mint mark has been glued into place, no metal flow will be detected and a seam between the fields and added Mint mark should be detectable.

Another method involves drilling a hole from the edge to a point directly opposite where a Mint mark should be positioned. One jaw of a needle-nosed pliers is altered to duplicate the shape of Mint mark. The altered jaw is slid into the hole and pressure is applied, embossing the Mint mark from the inside of the coin. This technique avoids the seam found when a Mint mark is glued into place, since the Mint mark is formed from the coin's metal itself from the inside. The hole on the edge is filled and the edge polished to efface traces of the alteration (this works best on a plain edge coin, especially copper-nickel 5-cent coins). In a variation on the theme, a similar tool can be used but via a hole drilled in the face of the coin opposite the intended position of the Mint mark.

Electrotypes

An electrotype is a type of counterfeit so popular in the 19th century that even employees of the U.S. Mint produced them for sale to willing collectors who knew what they were buying. An electrotype is an inexpensive copy of what is generally a rare, expensive coin unavailable to most collectors.

Electrotypes are two thin shells of metal bearing the image of a particular coin, wrapped around a nonprecious metal planchet for inner strength. The shells are made by the same sort of electroplating process described earlier, but a wax or plaster cast of the original coin is suspended in a solution of acidic copper sulfate along with a copper anode. A weak electric current is passed through the solution, causing small copper particles from the anode to adhere to the graphite-coated cast until a thin copper shell bearing the cast's image is formed.

An electrotype can be identified fairly easily by examining the edge for signs of where the two shells were joined or by weighing the item (it will almost always be too light).

Electrotypes are considered collectible by many, particularly those produced by the U.S. Mint employees in the mid-19th century.

Replicas

The replica is a form of counterfeit generally not intentionally deceptive, but potentially so. Most replicas are not illegal, though the passage of the Hobby Protection Act of 1973 regulates modern replicas in the United States.

A replica may be a crude cast duplicate of an obsolete coin, token or medal or a high-quality struck reproduction. Replicas are intended as inexpensive souvenirs; rarely is the original intention deceptive in nature. Almost every Colonial and state coin or token has been produced in replica form, legally. Some even have the word "copy"—required by the Hobby Protection Act—"replica" or some abbreviation of either word stamped into or cast onto the coin, often on the edge. The problem arises when "copy" or "replica" is filed from the surface of a replica or perhaps filled with metal.

The Gallery Mint Museum, a private firm operating for years (it is no longer active) in Eureka Springs, Ark., produced a series of die-struck replicas of early American and U.S. mint coinage. These pieces are avidly collected because of their high quality and because they were made much in the way the original coins were made in the late 18th century and early 19th century. All pieces were properly marked with "copy," but in several cases, individuals removed the word from the replica, artificially circulated the piece and then placed the piece into the market as a genuine example of the coin. Minor differences between the original design and the replica, purposely included by the private mint's engraver, proved useful in identifying the altered replicas.

More recently, Moonlight Mint, a private mint in Denver, has produced replica pieces including a 1964-D Peace dollar, struck by dies of the minter's manufacture over genuine Peace dollars of other dates. These replica 1964-D Peace dollars do not bear "copy" and the minter insists that since no genuine examples of the trial piece survive, the word is not required. The minter strikes his replicas and various fantasy pieces of original design using a refurbished coin press once used at the Denver Mint.

Private minters in the United States are not the only firms duplicating U.S. coinage. Private mints in China have been producing what seems to be a never-ending flood of replica/counterfeit coins that have been entering the marketplace in increasing numbers. For many in the coin collecting community in the United States, these Chinese-made counterfeits represent the most dangerous trend in the hobby today. One of those private minters is profiled next.

A counterfeiter in China

In the Fujian province of the People's Republic of China late in the first decade of the 21st century, a young Chinese suburbanite plies his trade. He takes pride in providing for his wife and young son, and in the level of craftsmanship evident at his manufacturing business, called Big Tree Coin Factory. In the United States, however, he has few (public, at least) supporters in the coin collecting community, where many collectors and dealers call him by a name most consider pejorative: counterfeiter.

Liu Ciyun, owner of Big Tree Coin Factory, doesn't hide his production of coins of the United States and other countries—for more than four years he promoted it on eBay where his handle was "Jinghuashei," and he was forthright about the coins not being genuine (he stopped selling under that eBay ID in 2010 although he may continue selling directly to regular customers). On a typical day in July 2009, Jinghuashei had listed nearly 1,200 auctions of "replica" and "copied" coins, as he calls them. "I am an Ebay member from China," he stated in the auctions in his fair English. "All the coins I list are the copied coins. So each coin has 'REPLICA' mark on the surface. Please don't buy them as the original coins. I sell these copied coins only want to make your collections more perfect."

Pieces offered by the eBay seller on July 10, 2009, for example, included a U.S. 1794 Flowing Hair silver dollar made in 90 percent silver, he claimed, with a "Buy It Now" price of $49 (a genuine example in Uncirculated condition could be worth more than a million dollars); a 1909-S Lincoln, V.D.B. cent, $2.60 (value of a real coin in Mint State, $2,000 to $100,000); and an 1893-S Morgan dollar in the correct 90 percent silver composition, $35 (real, $95,000 to $800,000).

The young manufacturer was profiled in several investigative news articles published in the Dec. 1 and Dec. 8, 2008, issues of *Coin World*. For those articles, Jinghuashei told American journalist Susan Headley in late 2008 that he adheres to Chinese and U.S. laws in making "copied coins": it is legal under Chinese law to make counterfeit versions of coins dated before 1949, and the U.S. Hobby Protection Act requires replica coins, notes, tokens and like objects to be plainly and permanently marked with the word "copy."

However, *Coin World* has documented thousands of examples of Jinghuashei's selling pieces without the word "copy" (even if he marked them with "replica," he would still be in violation of U.S. law, which requires the word "copy," not "replica").

A brief history of counterfeit coins

Jinghuashei claims to have many competitors in his province: approximately 100 manufacturers of fake coins. No matter the number of businesses competing with him in Fujian, Jinghuashei and his fellow manufacturers of counterfeits have joined an age-old fraternity. Counterfeit coins and notes are as almost as old as the concept of money itself, writes Lynn Glaser in *Counterfeiting in America.*

The first coinage was produced during the seventh century B.C. in Lydia, in a region of modern-day Greece, with the concept spreading through the Greek, Asian and Roman worlds over the centuries. Counterfeit coins arose quickly, Glaser writes, "... As early as the sixth century B.C. counterfeiting had become so prevalent that the laws of Solon [an Athenian statesman and lawmaker, circa 638 B.C. to 558 B.C.] decreed death to the counterfeiter." According to the website **www.forumancientcoins.com/**, estimates of contemporary counterfeit ancient Greek silver coinage range from 2 to 5 percent of the total amount of coin in circulation.

Counterfeiters exist because many people have been willing to produce coins (and paper money) that pass as genuine. Being able to produce a medium of exchange like a coin at a fraction of the cost of the real thing and use it in commerce to buy goods and services equivalent to what a real coin of the same type can buy, can entice some, despite the risks of

being caught by authorities and punished.

The risks are great because the penalties can be harsh—fines and jail time today in the United States, with punishment much tougher in the past. "Under Constantine the Great [circa Feb. 27, 272 to May 22, 337] some counterfeiters were burned to death," Glaser writes. In 10th century England, a counterfeiter's hands could be cut off in punishment, and later under the Normans, castration and having one's eyes cut out were the proscribed punishment, according to Glaser. In the late Middle Ages in England, counterfeiting was considered high treason and was punishable by gruesome death, writes Kenneth Scott in *Counterfeiting in Colonial America*: an individual convicted of counterfeiting English coinage could be hung by the neck and then taken down while still alive; his entrails cut from his body and burned while he was still alive; and finally, he could be beheaded and his body cut into quarters.

Such barbaric punishment, however, still "proved inadequate to check the crime," Glaser writes, and capital punishment was not always imposed.

Not everyone considered counterfeit coinage bad. Glaser notes that during the two centuries following the restoration of Charles II to the English throne in 1660, the government did not provide the populace with sufficient low value coinage for use in commerce, and in 1775, the crown stopped making copper coinage altogether. Glaser writes, "During most of that time England would have found itself with no coins at all if it had not been for a large circulation of counterfeit and worn-out coins." Matthew Boulton, one of the geniuses behind the Industrial Revolution, noted in 1789 that much of the counterfeit coinage in circulation was ordered from the counterfeiters by the "lowest class of manufacturers," who paid their workers in counterfeit copper coins (36 shillings in counterfeit copper coinage, ordered at a cost of 20 shillings, could be paid out to workers at face value), cites Don Taxay in *Counterfeit, Mis-Struck and Unofficial U.S. Coins*. The populace had little choice; it really did not matter whether a particular coin was genuine or counterfeit as long as others accepted it in commerce. Boulton would become a legitimate private minter, making private copper coinage for businesses and, once the government resumed a copper coinage, striking government copper coinage under contract (he also was the chief supplier to the early U.S. Mint of copper planchets for half cents and large cents). He also revolutionized minting technology, introducing techniques that would in the 19th century make it harder to counterfeit coins.

Counterfeiting in Colonial America

The unwillingness of the English government to issue low value coinage and the willingness of counterfeiters to meet public needs followed Colonists to the British colonies in North America. The crown held all authority over coinage and was sparing in granting the Colonies authority to strike coinage. With coins largely unavailable during the early years of British colonial rule in North America, colonists had to use a variety of things as money, many of them officially sanctioned and regulated by the Colonial governments: corn, pelts, tobacco, bullets, Indian wampum and Spanish colonial coinage. As one might guess, Spanish coinage was counterfeited, but it might surprise many that even wampum was counterfeited. Despite the pleadings of the Colonies, the British crown refused to grant royal warrants for coinage.

The first coins struck in what would become the United States were produced in the Massachusetts Bay Colony beginning in 1652, during the English Civil War and the vacancy of the throne.

The Massachusetts General Court took advantage of the royal vacancy when it authorized the production of silver threepence, sixpence and shillings to take the place of substandard and counterfeit coinage in circulation in the Massachusetts Bay Colony.

Philip L. Mossman in *Money of the American Colonies and Confederation* writes, "The mint came into existence as a reaction to the lightweight, counterfeit and debased silver coins which appeared in New England quickly after the initial settlements." John Hull, master of the Massachusetts Mint, said in his diary in 1652, "Also upon occasion of much counterfeit coin brought in the country, and much

loss accuring [occurring] in that respect (and that did occasion a stoppage of trade), the General Court ordered a mint to be set up, and to coin it, bringing the sterling standard for fineness. ..."

(The Massachusetts Bay Colony's mint would strike silver coins as late as 1682, long after the Restoration. The first issues were undated, with all but one of the later issues dated 1652, probably because that was the year the coins were authorized. The only other date used was 1662, on the fourth denomination to be authorized, the twopence.)

Counterfeit Massachusetts coinage was soon in circulation. "In 1674 a Suffolk County court found John du Plisse guilty of dispersing pewter imitations" of the Massachusetts silver coins, Glaser writes. Other cases followed in Massachusetts and in other Colonies, including in New York and Pennsylvania (William Penn, upon his arrival in Philadelphia in 1682, was shocked at the amount of counterfeit coinage in circulation, according in Glaser).

Compounding the problem was the British practice of transporting to its North American colonies convicted felons, including counterfeiters, who soon set up shop in the New World. Glaser cites the arrival in 1770 in Maryland of a ship carrying felons; within days of their arrival, the *Massachusetts Gazette* was warning that the transplanted counterfeiters were already circulating fake dollars and shillings.

Counterfeiters could succeed in passing spurious coins for several reasons: One, the shortage of widespread, uniform coinage meant that the average citizen was not always familiar with what a genuine coin should look like, and two, production methods for genuine coins in circulation in the 13 Colonies did not always produce coins that were perfectly round, well struck and bearing devices that discouraged clipping (the cutting of metal from the edges of silver and gold coins; cutting a sliver or two from every silver coin one used was profitable for the clipper, who could melt the silver, cast it into bars and sell it).

After the establishment of the United States in 1776, nearly three decades passed before the new nation could address the coinage needs of its citizens; the federal Mint was not authorized until 1792. The new Mint, when it began striking coins for circulation in 1793, was capable of producing a well-struck, uniform coinage, eliminating one of the contributing factors to the easy acceptance of fakes. The techniques and machinery used at the first U.S. Mints were based on those developed by Matthew Boulton. Thomas Jefferson, who played a key role in developing the U.S. coinage system authorized in 1792, wrote in 1790 that the United States should emulate Boulton's processes, which, he noted, were superior to those used by any government at that time and made counterfeiting more difficult.

However, producing sufficient coinage to meet the needs of public commerce remained a problem; the shortfall was so great for so long that silver and gold foreign coins remained legal tender in the United States until 1857. The lack of uniformity of the coinage in circulation only encouraged the production of counterfeits that circulated side by side with the real thing. Counterfeiters did, of course, produce fake U.S. coins, and the government in the early 19th century took steps to discourage the crime. Congress, with the Act of April 21, 1806, devised the first "set of comprehensive laws and penalties for the counterfeiting of U.S. and current foreign coins," Taxay writes.

Further refinement of the minting process at the U.S. Mint in the 1830s made counterfeiting of U.S. coins even more difficult. John Leonard Riddell, a medical doctor, scientist and, beginning in 1839, melter-refiner at the New Orleans Branch Mint, wrote a book, *Monograph of the Silver Dollar, Good and Bad,* in 1845. As melter-refiner, he encountered large numbers of coins sent to the New Orleans Mint to be melted and converted into U.S. coinage. With the keen eyes of a scientist (he was one of the principal inventors of the binocular microscope and made studies of the flora and fauna of the regions in which he traveled), he described and illustrated genuine and counterfeit Mexican and other Spanish American silver dollars (8-real coins) and American half dollars he encountered in his post at the Mint. The number of counterfeit Spanish American coins cataloged by Riddell far outnumbered the number of fake U.S. half dollars, with most of the counterfeit half dollars seen dated before 1836. He attributed the soundness of the latest U.S. coins to the standardization of designs and improvements in coinage techniques introduced at the U.S. Mint in 1836. He noted that when the English and French had done the same years earlier, those governments had largely solved the age-old problem of counterfeiting with their uniform coinage: "Those coins are very rarely counterfeited." Since 1836 in the United States, "It is hence easy to detect any counterfeits dated since." He noted, "Previous to that date the dies were much more irregularly produced, and as a consequence many counterfeits, especially of the Half Dollar, have been made and put in circulation, which the ordinary observer cannot well distinguish from those which are good." The Spanish Colonial silver remained at great risk for counterfeiting, Riddell wrote, because of the lack of uniformity of dies and the outmoded methods of die production employed at the Spanish colonial mints.

Some dangerous counterfeit U.S. gold coins surfaced in the 1840s, probably struck from dies that were created from hubs that themselves had been made from genuine dies removed from the U.S. Mint. Although Mint officials denied the possibility, the evidence says otherwise, according to Taxay. Mint officials noted that the execution of these fakes were perfect, though minute inspection of the impression of the coin detected a slight softness not seen on genuine coins struck at a U.S. Mint facility. Mint officials concluded that the dies used in making these fakes had been hubbed from genuine U.S. coins, a conclusion with which Taxay disagrees. He states that making dies from hubs hubbed from a coin would have resulted in the loss of a lot more fine detail than was evident on the coins. (A number of incidents are recorded in which genuine dies escaped from the U.S. Mint in the 19th century, making it possible that some could have been used by counterfeiters.)

Counterfeiting of paper money was a greater problem than the counterfeiting of coins in much of 19th century America, even though coin forgery technically was much easier than note forgery, according to *Illegal Tender: Counterfeiting and the Secret Service in Nineteenth-Century America* by David R. Johnson. Any skilled manufacturer could make a mold of a coin and use it to cast $50 to $200 in spurious coins every week, depending on the denomination, Johnson writes. This ease of production meant many counterfeit coin mills were operated by individuals rather than organized groups, he writes. Paper money production, however, required a greater effort and thus "encouraged more complex organization." However, of benefit to the counterfeiters of notes was the widespread growth of local printers, which provided talent and opportunity.

Riddell's observations in 1845 proved prophetic. In the years leading up to the U.S. Civil War, "there was not a great flood of [counterfeit] coins in the country" due to the uniformity of U.S. coinage and the precautions taken at discouraging counterfeiting (reeded edges, uniform dies and weights, and so on), Johnson writes.

The start of the Civil War in 1861 resulted in a rapid withdrawal of coins from circulation. (Silver and gold were hoarded out of fear. When the government began issuing the first federal paper money in 1861 as means of financing the war, the paper currency depreciated in relation to gold, further encouraging those holding silver and gold coins to hoard them rather than spend them.) When specie payments were suspended in 1861 by the U.S. government, federal coinage essentially ceased to circulate even though the Mint continued to strike coins. Counterfeiting of coins was hardly a problem given that no genuine coins circulated. Counterfeiting of the new federal paper money, however, made note counterfeiting a federal problem for the first time, and in 1863, the U.S. Secret Service was founded expressly to combat counterfeiting. (Presidential protection duties became the responsibility of the Secret Service nearly 40 years and three assassinated presidents later.)

As U.S. coins began reappearing in circulation following the end of the Civil War, counterfeit pieces began reappearing as well. According to Glaser, the first piece detected was a fake gold $20 double eagle found at the Bank of England, with another one found at the New York Treasury. Counterfeit gold $5 and $10 coins also began surfacing.

At the end of the 19th century, according to Glaser,

the Secret Service assessed the state of counterfeiting in the United States: counterfeit standard silver dollars and half dollars were the preferred products of counterfeit mills in the South and Midwest, some counterfeit silver coins were made in the East (paper money was the preferred bogus medium); in the West, genuine silver and gold coins were subjected to alterations that removed some of precious metals for accumulation and melting. The counterfeiting of base-metal coins was easily done and thus was encountered more than other forms of counterfeiting, according to the Secret Service report, cited in a 1905 article in *Cosmopolitan* (the magazine was a far cry from its current incarnation as the flesh-baring journal flanking store check-out lines today). The counterfeiting of silver coins was harder to achieve, according to the report. According to Glaser, the 1905 article noted that because the Secret Service made the counterfeiting of paper money so risky, "fully ninety percent of the annual prosecutions instituted by the Service relate to making, passing or having in possession counterfeit coin," quite different from prosecution patterns today.

Counterfeiting in the 20th century

Two things can be said about the counterfeiting of U.S. coins in the 20th century: One, the appearance of circulating counterfeit coins would wane, with one notable exception in mid-century, and two, the production of numismatic counterfeits—pieces intended to deceive collectors—grew.

Gold coins did not circulate widely during the first three decades of the 20th century, as the sporadic mintages of $2.50 quarter eagles, $5 half eagles, $10 eagles and $20 double eagles show. Much of the gold that was struck would go straight into government vaults, unneeded for circulation. In March 1933, President Franklin D. Roosevelt ordered a stop to gold coin production and a complete withdrawal of gold coinage from circulation. While individuals could keep small quantities of gold coins and exemptions were made for collector coins, most gold coins had to be turned in to the government.

That did not stop counterfeiters, according to Glaser, who were actively making fake gold coins in Europe where investors could legally own gold, unlike in the United States, where many forms of gold were illegal to own until 1974.

In the United States, circulating counterfeit coins sometimes included cast Washington quarter dollars, note Virgil Hancock and Laurence Spanbauer in *Standard Catalog of United States Altered and Counterfeit Coins*. They illustrate seven different dates of cast Washington quarter dollars from the 1930s, 1940s and 1950s.

Jefferson 5-cent coins, which circulated widely, were another denomination targeted by counterfeiters, the most infamous of whom was Francis Leroy Henning.

Henning was a middle-aged mechanical engineer who in the 1950s produced fair-quality counterfeit Jefferson 5-cent coins of several dates, the most common being 1944, at a counterfeit mill in New Jersey. The Secret Service caught Henning with the help of coin collectors, who in 1954 began contacting the Secret Service about the appearance of fake Jefferson 5-cent coins in circulation in the Camden, N.J., and Philadelphia region. Sharp-eyed collectors noted that some 1944 coins lacked the large Mint mark used on the denomination from mid-1942 through the end of 1945 to denote a change of composition required by the diversion of nickel and copper, the two metals in the normal alloy, to the Allied war effort. To denote the change in composition on the genuine coins, the Mint mark was moved from its normal location to the right of the representation of Monticello to above the building's dome. The size of the Mint mark was greatly increased and a P Mint mark was used for the first time for coins struck at the Philadelphia Mint. The lack of a Mint mark above the dome on these fake 1944 coins was quickly picked out by collectors, as were imperfections in color and appearance on other dates like 1946 and 1947.

Initially, the Secret Service judged the coins to be genuine, but collectors, unconvinced, continued to press the issue, and the Secret Service, with the help of the Mint, concluded that someone had set up a counterfeit mill to produce 5-cent coins. Secret Service agents began attending coin club meetings and enlisted the assistance of collectors in tracking the spread of the coins, and sent an advisory to banks asking tellers to be on the lookout for the fake coins. Eventually, the Secret Service was led to Henning, who had a record of counterfeiting. He had been making the die-struck coins in the Camden-Philadelphia region, using dies made from sophisticated engraving equipment that impressed even Mint officials, according to Dwight H. Stuckey in *The Counterfeit 1944 Jefferson Nickel.*

Henning made at least five different dates of counterfeit Jefferson 5-cent coins—1944, the first according to Stuckey, followed by 1946, 1947, 1939 and 1953 coins, plus one other date. News accounts about the investigation led Henning to try to cover his tracks; he dumped his dies and some 200,000 fake coins into a creek. The Secret Service recovered about 14,000 of the dumped fake coins.

According to Stuckey, Henning placed about 100,000 counterfeit 5-cent coins into circulation. Stuckey notes that the Secret Service continued to receive examples of the fakes from collectors into the 1970s. The fakes were eventually melted by the Mint and the metal used in the manufacture of genuine coins. Henning was sentenced to three years in prison and fined $5,000. Today, Henning counterfeit Jefferson 5-cent coins have a small following in the collector community, where the fake 1944 coin lacking the Mint mark carries a premium.

The small mountain of counterfeit 5-cent coins

struck by Henning appears to have been the peak of circulating counterfeit production in the United States. No case of similarly large distributions of circulating counterfeits is known since.

In contrast, counterfeiting for numismatic purposes flourished in the 20th century and continues today in the 21st century.

Authenticators and other numismatists have discovered that virtually every U.S. coin with significant value, and even pieces of lesser value, has been counterfeited. Key-date coins are frequent targets of the counterfeiters, and gold coins are an especially tempting target of counterfeiters.

Counterfeiting spread worldwide during the 20th century. Hancock and Spanbauer noted that in 1969, the Middle East was a hotbed of counterfeiting activity. Two different "castes" of counterfeiter operated there, the two authenticators wrote: those who produced fakes with low gold content, and those who made sure their fakes contained the right amount of gold (the numismatic or collector value of certain fake coins made their production profitable even when the manufacturers included full gold content). In many circumstances, a skilled authenticator could describe the origin of a particular fake by recognizing the handiwork of a particular counterfeiter.

By 1979, however, counterfeiters were operating worldwide, Hancock and Spanbauer state, citing "Hong-Kong, Singapore, Lebanon, and Morocco, to list a few." Moroccan counterfeiters offered most dates of U.S. gold $3 coins at a price of $50 each; in Iran, the price for fake $3 coins was $52 each. The quality of the fakes had risen during the previous 10 years as well.

The number of counterfeit coins entering the marketplace in the 1960s and early 1970s prompted hobby leaders to take action. The American Numismatic Association Certification Service (ANACS) was formed in 1972 to combat numismatic counterfeiting with a staff of trained counterfeit detection experts who examined coins submitted by collectors and dealers for authentication.

Within a few years of its founding, ANACS began receiving a famous series of counterfeit gold U.S. coins that would become known as the "omega" fakes. ANACS kept the discovery of the "signature" secret for more than two years, until going public with the discovery in an article by ANACS Director Charles R. Hoskins in the May 1976 *The Numismatist.*

ANACS had detected what it believed were counterfeit 1882 Indian Head gold $3 coins and a 1907 Saint-Gaudens, High Relief gold $20 double eagle of high gold content and quality. Not everyone agreed with ANACS's findings.

When ANACS rejected the 1882 Indian Head gold $3 coins as counterfeit, "several collectors and dealers called and wrote ANACS to protest," Hoskins wrote. "They believed we were condemning perfectly genuine specimens of this valuable coin. Articles were published to defend the coins, and to politely suggest that the Certification Service had erred in condemning them."

Hoskins said ANACS bore the criticism until it judged that the time was right to reveal absolute proof that the coins under dispute were fake. They were "signed" by their counterfeiter. A small Greek omega symbol, Ω, could be seen inside the loop of the R in LIBERTY in the headband of the $3 coins, and inside the eagle's talons on the reverse of the double eagle. The symbol was tiny, visible only under a 30X or higher microscope. No such symbol appears on genuine U.S. coins. With the publication of the signature, the collecting community accepted that these coins were fakes of the highest quality.

The Omega counterfeiter has never been identified. Estimates are that the Omega counterfeiter produced more than 20,000 counterfeits ($3, $10 and $20 coins) that, if genuine, would be worth $300 million today. The quality is so high that some collectors, like those who collect the Henning fakes, now seek out an Omega counterfeit, and are willing to spend more than $1,000 for one for their collection.

Other counterfeit U.S. coins have been so good that collectors, dealers and authenticators accepted them as genuine for decades. In one famous recent case, several die varieties of Morgan silver dollars that were accepted as genuine for more than a century were shown to be contemporary counterfeits—every single example of them. On April 25, 2005, the Professional Coin Grading Service, a third-party authentication and grading firm, reported "grading and variety experts at PCGS have recently uncovered undeniable evidence that three of the so-called 'Micro O' Morgan varieties, the 1896-O, 1900-O, and 1902-O, are actually contemporary counterfeits, most probably struck outside the US Mint sometime in the early 20th century. This is a significant discovery and one that will certainly have an impact on Morgan dollar variety collectors."

PCGS officials explained: "After examining the group of coins, it became apparent that these Morgan dollars were not struck in the New Orleans Mint in the years indicated by their dates. In fact, they were not struck in the mint at any time. These coins are among the most deceptive copies of United States coins seen. It is probable that they date to the early part of the twentieth century, but may have been struck as late as the 1940's. They have been known to numismatists since at least the mid-1960s."

Not only is the quality of die engraving excellent on these coins, they are of high silver content (at least one coin actually has a higher concentration of silver than real Morgan dollars).

While not all counterfeit coins are of the high quality of the Omega gold coins and the three Micro O Morgan dollars identified by PCGS, professional authenticators warn that huge numbers of counterfeit collector coins are in the marketplace. The authentication services in the coin market do a good job detecting the fakes (even though some of the services previously authenticated the Micro O Morgan dollars), but collectors who buy unauthenticated key dates like 1914-D Lincoln cents and 1916-D Winged Liberty Head dimes risk buying counterfeit coins. The situation for the 1916-D Winged Liberty Head dime is so bad that the number of counterfeit examples is believed to outnumber the number of genuine coins struck by the Denver Mint in 1916.

Counterfeiting in the 21st century

If one could sum up the counterfeiting of U.S. coins today in one word, that word would be the name of a nation: China.

China is the counterfeiting center of the world, according to the International Intellectual Property Alliance, not just for coins but for a wide range of products. According to a researcher who has extensively studied Chinese counterfeits of U.S. coins, 80 percent of all counterfeit goods seized at U.S. ports by the Customs and Border Protection Agency come from China. In recent years, major news media accounts have been filled with reports of Chinese counterfeit goods, some of which are deadly: toys with high levels of lead and counterfeit food products like baby formula that sickened or killed dozens to hundreds of Chinese children, according to one researcher.

It might surprise observers in the United States that the counterfeiting of coins in China is legal as long as the coins are dated no later than 1949 (which has not stopped some counterfeiters in China from making counterfeits of current U.S. coins like the U.S. Mint's First Spouse gold $10 coins).

When counterfeit coins from China started entering the U.S. marketplace in quantity in the early 21st century, U.S. Trade dollars were especially prevalent (not a surprise; the U.S. Mint made Trade dollars not for use in domestic commerce, but for use in China, which meant a lot of genuine Trade dollars probably remain in China today to be copied by the counterfeiters).

What makes Chinese counterfeiting so dangerous is the ease with which the fakes can enter the U.S. marketplace. Online auction sites like eBay make it easy for a counterfeiter in China to sell fakes to collectors and dealers in the United States, including to some U.S. sellers who then offer the coins as genuine.

When collectors and dealers first started seeing a rise in the number of fake U.S. coins sold on eBay by sellers in China, the quality of the fake coins was often extremely poor. Coins often were crude in execution, and little attention was paid to getting the dates, designs and specifications right.

Gregory V. Dubay, a researcher of the Chinese counterfeits, has identified four levels in terms of quality of Chinese-made counterfeit coins: Level 1, close in basic design but not meeting specifications (weight, quality of strike, composition), often made from dies showing such problems as cracks, excessive polish and more; Level 2, basic coin design, not meeting specifications, fairly well executed but showing various die and striking problems; Level 3, fairly clear coin designs, with clean, crisp devices, made either of the wrong metal or debased precious metal, struck at higher pressure than the first two levels; and Level 4, "extremely well executed design and elements," well struck at high pressure, specifications matching those of the real coins including being made of 90 percent gold or silver, full weight. Dubay also warns about possible Level 5 counterfeits, which start with a genuine U.S. Mint coin that is altered to resemble a rarer piece, is further altered to correct diagnostic features, is artificially circulated and then is placed into a fake grading service slab.

According to Dubay, the quality of such fakes is increasing. *Coin World* Editor Beth Deisher helped Dubay conduct a class about the Chinese counterfeit U.S. coins at the American Numismatic Association Summer Seminar in Colorado Springs, Colo., in July 2009. The class was attended by collectors, dealers and authentication experts. The instructors displayed counterfeit coins from China as well as counterfeit dies from Chinese manufacturers (some of the Chinese businesses are happy to sell discarded dies pulled from service).

Near the end of the ANA Summer Seminar course, the instructors conducted a test with some chilling results. Exhibited were three Carson City Mint Morgan silver dollars; participants were asked to judge whether the pieces were genuine or counterfeit (two were fake, one was real). While some of the participants correctly identified the pieces, at least one top authenticator—someone with decades of experience of authenticating coins—identified one of the fake Morgan dollars as genuine. Another equally talented authenticator with decades of experience correctly identified the genuine coin, but was convinced that the two counterfeit pieces were genuine coins whose dates had been altered (which the counterfeiter who made them denies).

One of those counterfeiters, Liu Ciyun, uses genuine coins as models for making dies. Journalist Headley writes that he downloads digital information about a scanned genuine coin into a computerized coin sculpturing system via laser beam input. Headley states that Liu's system permits the creation of an extremely accurate three-dimensional model of the coin. Liu can clean up any problems on the scan using the sculpturing system before using the data in cutting a die via a laser. The laser cuts the image of the coin directly into the die steel. The same kind of system has been in use at the United States Mint for only a few years.

Liu said he uses other dies that were made at another shop.

Some of the counterfeit coins being struck in China today may be produced on presses once used by the

U.S. Mint. Fred Weinberg, an error coin specialist in California, told Headley for her *Coin World* articles that the Shanghai Mint in China (a government mint) was designed to be a replica of the third Philadelphia Mint as it looked in the early 20th century. The U.S. Mint sold some of its obsolete minting equipment to the Shanghai Mint starting in the 1920s, according to Weinberg. Other sources told Headley that the Shanghai Mint began selling off some of the equipment in the mid-1950s. While no one can confirm whether any of the Chinese private mints are using former U.S. Mint equipment, the possibility exists, according to Headley.

Liu Ciyun has produced hundreds of different dates and types of counterfeit coins, including fakes of many denominations and dates, some of rare issues and others not. He makes counterfeit "error coins."

While a manufacturer like Liu sells his products openly as "copied coins" and claims he makes no effort to sell them as genuine, most of the pieces he sends to buyers are not marked "replica" as promised.

Worse, second-hand sellers are not shy about offering counterfeit/replica/copied coins as the real thing, and that is where the danger to the collector community lies, according to some hobby leaders.

A telephone call to the *Coin World* office in early July 2009 was typical of what dealers and others in the hobby continue to report in 2011. The Michigan dealer related that a customer had just brought in U.S. coins that he had bought in a local auction for $600. All of the pieces were Chinese fakes, according to the dealer. This incident is by no means an isolated one. Knowledgeable dealers and collectors have identified counterfeit U.S. coins being sold without appropriate identification by merchants at flea markets and local auctions throughout the United States.

While the U.S. collector community is growing increasingly concerned about the counterfeiting of coins in China, the U.S. government had been silent on the issue until the spring of 2011. Coin counterfeiting is rarely addressed by the Secret Service in the 21st century, unlike in the agency's past. "The Secret Service made 29,000 arrests for counterfeiting U.S. currency in the five-year period between 2003 and 2008, according to a *Forbes Magazine* article, while making no reported arrests for owning counterfeits of collectible coins," according to the Web page found at **http://rg.ancients.info/guide/counterfeits.html**.

Fighting back

With little or no government action to combat the spread of counterfeit coins, five hobby entities in 2009 undertook a joint effort to combat the counterfeiting problem: the American Numismatic Association, the world's largest coin collectors organization; the Professional Numismatists Guild, an organization of some top coin firms in the United States; Professional Coin Grading Service, a leading authentication/grading service; Numismatic Guaranty Corp., another of the leading authentication/grading services; and the Industry Council for Tangible Assets, which represents the coin and bullion industry on government and legislative matters.

Representatives of the group met by teleconference on May 7, 2009, and then met face to face a few weeks later. According to a press statement, they agreed to a three-part strategy as a group and individually: consumer education, working to compel online auction services to be more responsive to fraudulent listings of replica coins; and the exploration of possible criminal actions by federal law enforcement agencies.

In July 2009, those who are fighting counterfeiting achieved a major success. A collector in Canada who is also a member of the Royal Canadian Mounted Police whose duties are similar to those of a U.S. Secret Service agent, took the problem of replica/counterfeit Canadian coins sold via eBay before his superiors. With the help of information provided by a private collector in Canada, the RCMP officer persuaded his superiors to approach eBay on the problem. Canada has no Hobby Protection Act, the United States' law permitting manufacture of replica coins as long as they are marked "copy." A replica Canadian coin is considered counterfeit in Canada whether or not it is marked as a copy.

Armed with much stricter laws than those in the United States, the RCMP presented a briefing to eBay officials, pointing out that the replica coins could not be legally sold in Canada. Within days of the briefing, eBay pulled all replica Canadian coins from eBay auctions, first at eBay Canada, and then from the U.S. site.

Replica/counterfeit U.S. coins continue to plague eBay and the secondary marketplace, however, with the federal government largely indifferent to the issue. In a July 20, 2010, hearing before the House Financial Services' Subcommittee on Domestic Monetary Policy that focused on coin and paper money issues, some on the panel expressed alarm over reports of a mass influx of Chinese-struck "replica" coins that are not marked with the word "copy" and are being sold in the United States as rare American coins. During the two-hour hearing, Rep. Frank Lucas, R-Okla., said that called for "aggressive" action by law enforcement agencies.

But a Secret Service official told the subcommittee that his agency did not believe counterfeit U.S. coins emanating from foreign countries pose a major criminal issue. Kenneth Jenkins, special agent in charge of the service's criminal investigative division, said it had received fewer than 100 complaints about counterfeit coins. A bigger problem, he suggested is bogus U.S. paper currency coming into the U.S. from Peru.

Another person testifying at the hearing had a much different view of the counterfeiting issue. Michael B. Clark, president of Delaware-based Diamond State Depository, a subsidiary of Dillon Gage that deals in precious metals, first addressed American Eagle silver bullion coin supply problems that were then a major concern to precious metal sellers. Then, in his written testimony, Clark struck out at the counterfeiting of rare U.S. coins by large companies in China, saying "these counterfeits will cause significant financial harm to the American public" if allowed to remain unchecked. He urged the subcommittee to have the Treasury Department's inspector general investigate "the sources and extent of such counterfeiting." Clark said the counterfeiters are producing high-quality fakes coins that often come encapsulated in fake plastic holders similar to those used by legitimate coin grading services.

Despite Clark's pleas, echoed by dealers and collectors throughout the coin collecting community, the government appeared to take no action on counterfeiting for the remainder of 2010 and into early 2011. Them, in April 2011, the situation changed.

Counterfeits seized

A full-scale investigation into counterfeit rare U.S. coins produced in China was launched in Chicago by U.S. Customs and Border Protection agents after a package containing bogus U.S. Trade dollars was seized April 20, 2011, at the International Mail Branch at O'Hare International Airport.

The 361 counterfeit coins seized were bound for a recipient at an Illinois address, who was expecting to sell the fakes online over the eBay auction site, according to Customs and Border Protection officer Brian J. Bell, who serves as the public affairs liaison in Chicago and who spoke with *Coin World* April 22.

As a result of the seizure, Bell said CBP agents stationed at international mail facilities in major U.S. cities have been notified of the seizure and to be on the lookout for similar packages.

"We've notified other facilities," Bell said. "You may start seeing more seizures coming from China [to] prevent them from entering the market. We're going to do our best to stay on top of this."

Bell said O'Hare handles direct mail flights from China.

CBP is constantly screening arriving international mail and is on the lookout for any type of contraband, counterfeit or prohibited items being shipped to the United States that can harm the community or take advantage of the unsuspecting buyer, according to the agency.

CBP officers and agriculture specialists are stationed at International Mail Facilities located throughout the country.

"Legitimate traders are being duped into buying these coins believing they are genuine," said David Murphy, CBP director of field operations in Chicago. "We strongly recommend buyers or any consumers to be aware and use caution when making these types of purchases on the Internet."

Bell said the investigation initiated by U.S. Immigration and Customs Enforcement was to look into whether the intended recipient of the intercepted package has knowingly purchased and sold similar counterfeits before on eBay or through any other venue. Bell said investigators would also be working with eBay officials to examine the eBay activity of the package's intended recipient.

Bell said that CBP had been contacted by the intended recipient about the status of his package after it did not arrive at his address when expected. Bell said the intended recipient was notified that CBP was looking into the matter and would alert him to the package's disposition. Bell said the intended recipient indicated he planned to sell the contents of the seized package on eBay.

CBP officers became suspicious when they noticed anomalies while conducting x-rays of the heavy package bound to an Illinois address from China. Bell said the intended recipient's address was in English, while the shipper's address was in Chinese.

The 361 counterfeit coins seized are dated 1873 through 1878, the years the Philadelphia, San Francisco and Carson City Mints struck Trade dollars intended for circulation.

Bell said a sample counterfeit coin was sent for analysis to CBP Laboratory and Scientific Services in Chicago where it was determined to be silver-plated brass, not .900 fine silver, although the weight was close to the weight of a genuine coin. The package was seized based on the laboratory results, Bell said.

As of June 2011, no further action had been reported in the case.

Counterfeit slabs

In 2008, several major grading services acknowledged that counterfeit versions of their slabs—the sonically sealed holders containing coins the firms have graded and authenticated—had surfaced in the marketplace.

Numismatic Guaranty Corp. was the first firm to confirm reports, in January 2008. According to an advisory posted at the NGC website at **www.ngccoin. com**, variations on the counterfeit slabs, in the holder itself, the label and the hologram, help distinguish the fake slabs from genuine ones. While the enclosed coins were also counterfeit, the label information matches the coin type enclosed. The label information is copied from actual NGC certification labels, and the certification information therefore will match the NGC database. Most frequently, counterfeit Trade dollars and Draped Bust dollars are found in the fake slabs, although Flowing Hair dollars and crown-size foreign coins have also been seen. A range of grades is also represented on the counterfeit slabs, NGC reports.

According to a posting by NGC at its website, the easiest way to identify a fake holder is by the several misspellings on the Professional Numismatists Guild logo on the counterfeit hologram. NGC is the official grading service of the PNG. On the PNG logo on the fake slabs, the word "Knowledge" (from the PNG slogan "Knowledge. Integrity. Responsibility.") is incorrectly spelled with an "R" as "RNOWLEDGE." "Integrity" is incorrectly spelled with an extra "G" as "INTEGRIGY." "Numismatists" is incorrectly spelled as "NUNISMATISTS."

Also, the counterfeit hologram has less rounded corners than the NGC hologram. It is also slightly reflective, while the authentic NGC hologram has a flat brushed finish. The hologram sits higher on the holder on the counterfeit than on the authentic holder. Illustrations of the fake holder show a gap between the bottom of the hologram and the central stabilizing line of the slab.

On the slab, differences include a weld joint that appears as an off-center gap on the top of the counterfeit holder, according to NGC. The authentic NGC holder has a continuous seam, and weld flash (whitish discoloration) will often be visible. The weld flash allows NGC encapsulation technicians to assess the welding pressure and thoroughness of the holder seal, according to the grading service.

A few months later, the appearance of counterfeit U.S., Chinese and Mexican coins in counterfeit Professional Coin Grading Service slabs in online auctions on eBay prompted action in late March on several fronts by PCGS officials.

According to a March 27, 2008, press release from PCGS, company officials said: "All of the counterfeit coins/holders seen so far are coming out of China. Alert members of the PCGS Message Boards were the first to notify PCGS of the counterfeit coins/holders. ... The coins themselves range from poor-quality counterfeits to well-made fakes. The counterfeit PCGS holders are well-executed, but with minor differences from a genuine holder. PCGS anticipates that authentic coins will eventually be placed into counterfeit PCGS holders in the future, perhaps with elevated grades and/or inappropriate designators (Full Bell Lines, Prooflike, etc.), although none have been seen to date."

PCGS identified differences between the counterfeit slabs and the genuine products but would not detail those differences. The firm was "unwilling at this time to point out those differences because that would only provide specific instructions to the counterfeiters on how to improve their fakes," a company spokesman said.

In the Oct. 27, 2008, issue of *Coin World,* photos were published of a fake PCGS encasement along with photos of a genuine slab for comparison and commentary by Scott A. Travers in the 2008 edition of his *Coin Collector's Survival Manual.* Travers found that a primary differentiation between the fake PCGS holders and the genuine holders is how they stack on top of one another. The outside of genuine PCGS holders is designed to lock together with other genuine PCGS holders. The fake holders not only

will not stack with a genuine PCGS holder, but in most cases, won't stack with other fake PCGS holders either.

In the Dec. 12, 2008, issue of *Coin World*, journalist Headley reported one of the counterfeiters provided additional details about the counterfeit PCGS slabs. She reported the following diagnostics:

➤ On the fake holders, you will see a broken line and sometimes an oblong hole or space at the 10:30 and 1:30 clock positions on the obverse of the slab, immediately adjacent to the ring that holds the coin within the slab. On genuine PCGS holders, there are no rectangular spaces or gaps and no breaks in the raised ridge in the same area. This area should appear a solid, uniform color.

For another diagnostic, you must have the holder in hand to make the judgment. There are four little raised L-shaped ridges that fit snugly and precisely into the back frame of another genuine holder placed on top.

➤ On the fake holders, these L-shaped ridges are low, a little too thick and poorly formed compared to the genuine ones. They don't fit snugly, preventing the slabs from stacking properly. On the genuine PCGS holders, these L-shaped ridges are taller, thinner and fit exactly into the back of other genuine holders.

➤ Another diagnostic usually cannot be seen in photos at all, so beware when buying a purported PCGS-slabbed coin from an unknown entity. There should be on genuine PCGS slabs four circles inside the back part of the holder. You may need to tip the holder to the light in various ways to see them. For this diagnostic, fake PCGS slabs are missing these four marks. The back side will be smooth, slightly frosted plastic in these zones. Genuine holders have four little circles, all the same size, each about 3 millimeters in diameter. You cannot feel them on the outside of the holder; they are plastic injection-molding marks inside the back part of the slab.

Although the counterfeiter who provided the diagnostics noted some differences in the size and details of the letters on the blue slab insert, further research indicates that genuine PCGS holders have some variation in letter size and placement. Such lettering variation is not a reliable diagnostic unless the lettering is of a poor, mushy quality.

Keep in mind that the certificate numbers on a fake slab usually check out when verified on the PCGS website. Just because the certificate is valid doesn't mean the holder is genuine.

It is possible that counterfeiters have refined their fake slabs, so do not rely solely on the diagnostics described here.

The parent company of PCGS, Collectors Universe, has taken steps to protect its name and product. It filed a lawsuit on Dec. 7, 2010, in the United States District Court, Central District of California, against a Minnesota coin dealer that CU claimed was selling, over the prior four years, counterfeit rare coins not marked "copy," housed in counterfeit PCGS holders made to order from Chinese manufacturers. The complaint alleged violations of the Hobby Protection Act, the Lanham Act, violation of RICO, common law fraud, conspiracy and violation of California's unfair competition law. It cited an example of a North Carolina collector who purchased two Seated Liberty dollars dated 1851 and 1858 from the defendants in April 2010 for $12,400. The coins were determined to be counterfeit, as were the PCGS holders encapsulating them.

On April 28, 2011, the court issued a default judgment against the dealer, noting that he failed to appear and answer to the complaint. The order also permanently enjoined the dealer and his agents, officers, employees and attorneys from manufacturing and importing counterfeit PCGS holders and from selling any coin, real or counterfeit, in counterfeit PCGS holders. He was also ordered to immediately destroy all counterfeit PCGS holders in his possession, including PCGS coin inserts.

In another potentially dangerous incident, researcher Dubay reported in 2011 that he had recently been offered a roll of "100 (counterfeit) CAC stickers for $200.00." Certified Acceptance Corp. or CAC, is an American firm that independently verifies that a coin graded by NGC or PCGS meets market standards for the grade. The slabs of coins that meet the standards are affixed with a football-shaped CAC sticker. If a counterfeiter is producing rolls of fake CAC stickers, the concern is that a counterfeit coin could be placed into a counterfeit slab that bears a fake CAC sticker.

Owning counterfeits: Is it legal?

As mentioned earlier in this chapter, some collectors like to collect counterfeit coins as an interesting speciality, especially those pieces that are famous or infamous such as the Henning 1944 Jefferson 5-cent coin and the Omega gold counterfeits. Are they breaking the law when they do so?

Armen R. Vartian is an attorney with special knowledge in numismatic law. He is counsel for the Professional Numismatists Guild and writes a monthly column, "Numismatics and Law," for the weekly *Coin World.* Vartian addressed that subject in his column in the Nov. 5, 2001, issue of the publication. The column, with some minor editing for the *Almanac,* follows:

Is it legal for a collector to possess a counterfeit note or coin? This is one of those questions that often don't get asked of the law enforcement officials who can authoritatively answer them, because collectors don't want to hear bad news, and as a rule these officials tend to be expansive in their interpretations of the laws they administer.

The U.S. has an array of anti-counterfeiting laws, most dating back to the early 1900s, with subsequent major revisions in 1948 and again in 1994. These can be found in Title 18, Chapter 25, Sections 470-514 of the United States Code.

Anglo-American law frowns upon crimes based upon mere possession of an illegal substance; possession can come in various ways that do not involve any evil or criminal intent on a person's part.

For example, someone could possess an illegal substance unwittingly, such as when it is slipped into that person's luggage at an airport, or where it is given to the person with the representation that it is a different and legal substance.

Nevertheless, where the U.S. government has felt the compelling need to restrict all ownership of illegal substances, it has done so, and so-called "possession" crimes are commonplace in the war on drugs.

Likewise, the need to eliminate counterfeit coins and currency from possible circulation has resulted in certain "possession" crimes relating to counterfeiting as well. All references that follow are to Title 18 of the U.S. Code Section 470 that makes possession of any counterfeit U.S. currency outside the United States a crime punishable by imprisonment and/or fine, but only if such possession would be a crime under sections 471, 473 or 474 if it occurred within U.S. borders.

Because none of those sections punishes possession of counterfeit money except with intent to sell same, we can assume that it is not a crime simply to possess counterfeit money abroad.

In addition, Section 472, which is not mentioned in Section 470, prohibits "keep[ing] in possession or conceal[ing]" counterfeit money "with intent to defraud," reinforcing the conclusion that counterfeit money may be collected abroad.

As for U.S. collections, the statutes do not criminalize mere possession of counterfeit money, as they do possession of counterfeit dies, rag paper or security devices similar to those used by the United States in manufacturing currency.

Several sections punish possession of "likenesses" of U.S. coins or currency, but only if there is intent to defraud or pass same as genuine, but none punish someone who simply owns a counterfeit coin or note with no intent to sell or use it.

Now for the bad news. Section 492 entitles the government to seize counterfeit notes and/or coins, paraphernalia, etc. wherever found within U.S. borders, and makes it a crime punishable by up to $100 fine and a year in prison to refuse a lawful request from the Treasury Department to forfeit such items. This means that while it may not be a crime in itself to possess counterfeit money, it is a crime to refuse to give them up on proper demand.

The same section entitles persons from whom items have been seized to petition the secretary of the Treasury for remission or mitigation of the forfeiture, which the secretary may grant "if he finds that such forfeiture was incurred without willful negligence or without any intention on the part of the petitioner to violate the law, or finds the existence of such mitigating circumstances as to justify the remission or mitigation of such forfeiture."

But this is highly unlikely to provide any remedy to collectors of counterfeit coins or notes. While mitigation seems appropriate for a company that forfeits its photocopier because an employee surreptitiously made bogus copies of $100 bills as an office prank, it may not be appropriate for a collector who knowingly possesses a counterfeit note, even without any intent on the collector's part to pass it.

The difference is that while the company may get its copier back, it won't get back the counterfeit bills.

Overall, anyone with counterfeit coins or notes should, of course, never offer them for sale or exchange in any manner that could invoke the statutes in Title 18, Chapter 25. But beyond that, collections either should be kept abroad, where they are out of reach of U.S. law, or maintained quietly so as not to prompt forfeiture proceedings, where the coins or notes will surely be lost forever.

Protecting yourself

With counterfeit coins and slabs of various types in the marketplace, it is understandable that collectors might reconsider whether they should be buying coins. Most hobby experts advise that collectors should be cautious in their dealings but not abandon the hobby. Collectors can take some steps to protect themselves.

David Hall, founder of PCGS and a longtime dealer, recommends collectors buy only from trusted sources or coins that have been authenticated and graded by a major authentication and grading service like PCGS or NGC. The major grading services have done a good job of detecting counterfeit coins, and few fakes are believed to have made it into genuine holders from those two firms. Major, trusted dealers will "make right" any transactions if a coin sold as genuine is later judged to be fake, Hall notes.

Following Hall's advice means using care when buying at venues such as eBay, Craig's List, local auctions and flea markets or from someone who stops you on the street and asks if you want to buy some coins. (Don't laugh; the latter situation has occurred.) While these venues can be good places to acquire genuine coins, and many legitimate, honest businesses sell through some of these methods, collectors who lack strong authentication skills may be at risk when buying from such sources. In short, if you cannot authenticate coins yourself, be careful buying unauthenticated coins.

If offered a deal that seems too good to be true, pass on the transaction. *Coin World* has received reports of collectors being offered coins claimed as genuine but at prices that are a fraction of what genuine coins of that type, date and grade are worth. It should not surprise anyone that such deals usually involve counterfeit coins.

Beware of some of the popular techniques used by the unscrupulous. Selling the coins through eBay and other similar sites remains a popular method. Flea markets have proven to be another source for counterfeit coins, with sellers buying fake coins from Chinese minters and then selling the fakes as genuine. Another technique is to salt counterfeit coins among genuine pieces in coin folders and albums, and to then sell the sets of coins to unknowing local dealers and collectors. Rolls of genuine coins salted with fake coins have also entered the marketplace. Techniques like these are why many hobby leaders recommend dealing only with known dealers in coins.

Collectors should learn as much as they can about coins. Students of U.S. coinage have studied the rarer coins extensively. For example, specialists have identified the dies used to strike the 1909-S Lincoln, V.D.B. cent, a classic scarce coin. By carefully examining thousands of coins, specialists know the proper shape of the "S" Mint mark and the letter "B" in the V.D.B. initials. Die gouges and scratches appearing on most examples of certain rare coins have been documented and cataloged. Seek books and information that document such die signatures for rare and scarce numismatic items. They will serve as invaluable reference guides.

Make use of the specifications information for each coin located in the U.S. Coins chapter of this book. We list weight, diameter, metallic content, specific gravity and more for each coin. If the measures of a coin you're offered deviate from the specifications given in the book, beware; they may indicate the piece is counterfeit.

If you intend to collect coins seriously, buy a digital scale to test the weights of coins, and digital calipers to measure their diameter (a good set of scales and calipers can be purchased for about $100 from such sites as **www.amosadvantage.com/**); the minimal expense for these tools will quickly pay for itself if you use the tools to detect possible counterfeits.

Online sites will tell you how to set up a system for measuring the specific gravity of a coin using a digital scale.

Attend a counterfeit detection class such as those offered by the ANA at its annual Summer Seminar and prior to major coin shows. The knowledge you can gain is well worth the expense.

Counterfeit coins have been a problem for mankind for thousands of years, and while it is unlikely Americans will see a counterfeit coin in their change at any time in their lifetime, collectors and dealers risk exposure to buying a fake every time they buy a coin. Don't be afraid to buy coins, just do so wisely.

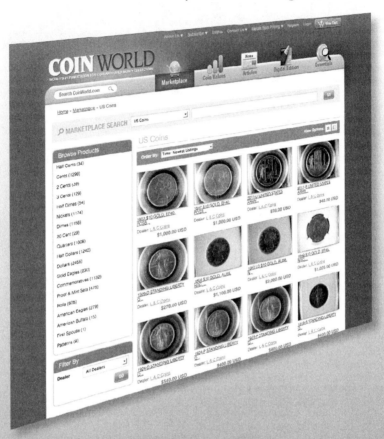

18 Coins as Investments

In the decade since 2000 the rare coin marketplace changed substantially.

The Internet is responsible for the biggest change because it has made coins easier to acquire and sell. Improvements in grading have enhanced consistency in the marketplace in an era when counterfeiters are improving their craft.

Yet, all of the information available about coins and their values can be overwhelming, making the study of coins and the guidance of a trusted adviser as important as ever.

Collectors possess an unquenchable desire to own coins. Many coin collectors also derive much pleasure from the careful study of their coins. When preparation is combined with an exacting eye and an awareness of what is happening in the market, a coin collection can be a vehicle for wealth building and coins can be an interesting diversification in a well-balanced portfolio.

For generations, successful investing in coins has been synonymous with putting together a well-thought-out collection. Many of the greatest collections sold are the result of systematic purchasing over a long period of time, characterized by strong relations with dealers, and a willingness to take advantage of buying opportunities when they present themselves.

Take the example of John Jay Pittman Jr. While financially comfortable, he never had substantial wealth. Yet—over the course of decades of careful collecting—he was able to build a collection that was auctioned in 1997 for more than $30 million.

David W. Akers, who sold Pittman's collection, said it best, writing: "John was not a wealthy man, except in knowledge." With his budget, Pittman purchased rare coins in the best condition he could afford. He took advantage of buying opportunities when they appeared, like when he traveled in 1954 to Cairo, Egypt, to attend the auctions of the grand coin collection of King Farouk of Egypt.

For example, Pittman's Proof 1833 Capped Head gold $5 half eagle realized $467,500 at the Pittman auction in 1997. Pittman had purchased it from the Farouk auction in 1954 for just $635. In January 2005 the same coin—now certified Proof 67—sold for $977,500. While the acquisition price of $635 was a substantial amount of money in 1954, Pittman's willingness to buy the best he could afford and

to "stretch" when acquiring truly rare coins reaped substantial dividends for his heirs.

The rare coin marketplace has shifted in the 21st century because technology makes collecting easier and research more accessible.

The following are some of the key issues affecting investment-grade coins.

Certified versus uncertified

Nearly all investment quality coins in today's marketplace are certified by several major grading services. Coins encapsulated, or "slabbed," by Professional Coin Grading Service and Numismatic Guaranty Corp. enjoy the most liquidity, although coins certified by ANACS and Independent Coin Grading are also very marketable and these two latter services employ consistent grading and excellent counterfeit detection.

For collectors and investors, purchasing certified coins presents several advantages, the most notable of which is the grading guarantee that the services offer. Grading services guarantee the grade and authenticity of the coins that they certify. If a buyer believes that he or she purchased an overgraded, misattributed or counterfeit certified coin, under the grading service guarantee, a coin buyer can send the coin back to the grading service in the original slab. The grading service will then re-examine the coin and work out a remedy in the rare event that a mistake has been made.

An important caveat: clerical or "mechanical" errors are not covered by the guarantee. These include dates on holders that don't match the date on the coin and obviously incorrect designations—PCGS provides an example of a 1945 Winged Liberty Head dime from the Philadelphia Mint (a coin with a notoriously weak strike) with a full bands designation even though "the bands on the reverse were as flat as a pancake and obviously not fully struck," according to an observer. The term "mechanical errors" extends to obviously incorrect variety attributions and clearly misidentified coins. Coins in holders exhibiting tampering generally do not qualify for grading service guarantees.

Another thing that the grading services do not cover is a change in a coin's numismatic status. For example, some numismatists believe that 1856 Flying Eagle cents are Proofs and others consider them circulation strikes. If future research indicates that all 1856 Flying Eagle cents are indeed Proofs, the grading service guarantee would not cover changes in value due to the change in the coin's status.

For copper coins, each service has different standards for guaranteeing color on copper coins, since the color and surfaces of copper coins can change after grading, because of environmental factors.

The guarantees provided by grading services take much of the risk out of coin buying, but it is important for potential coin investors to familiarize themselves with what the guarantees cover along with what they leave out. Guarantees are posted in full on the grading service web sites.

Same coin, different values

Coins certified by different grading services often trade at different values, the result of both perceived and actual differences in the grading standards used by the grading services.

For example, a coin graded by PCGS may trade for more or less than a comparable coin graded by NGC. In some specific series and even in grades within a series, the market has expressed a preference for one grading service over the other, as shown by higher prices realized in auctions when coins graded by both services are offered in a single sale.

When purchasing a coin—especially an expensive one—collectors owe it to themselves to avail themselves of the many different pricing resources accessible online. Auction results from the major coin auction houses are easily found online, and this allows one to track how much coins are actually selling for in the market.

In many ways, auction prices provide the clearest indication of fair market value in that an auction provides a place where a willing buyer and willing seller meet in a transparent public forum. The prices achieved at public auction are good comparables that one can use—along with a dose of common sense and a dash of caution—when figuring out what a coin is worth and how much one should pay for a coin.

While there is surely more consistency in the marketplace today than in 1986 when PCGS was founded, grading is still an art and not a science. As such, the same coin submitted over the course of time to different grading services may be returned with different grades, depending on the graders who examined the coin, and shifting grading standards over time.

Some coins may trade for more than expected because the buyer believes that the coin may upgrade. For example, About Uncirculated 58 coins are often purchased by collectors who intend to resubmit them to the grading services in hopes of getting a Mint State 61 or MS-62 grade.

The difference in price between grades can often be substantial, making the "crack out" game potentially profitable for those confident in their grading skills and having a decent appetite for risk.

Some of the coin types most frequently resubmitted for grading include:

➤ Small sized gold coins, including gold dollars and gold quarter eagles
➤ Indian Head $2.50 quarter eagles and $5 half eagles
➤ Beautifully toned coins
➤ Rare dates
➤ Lightly cleaned coins

If these grading considerations are not enough to make one's head spin, consider that coins can be below-average, average and above-average within any given grade. To make the differentiation of a high-quality coin easier, several new options have emerged in the last few years.

Stickers, pluses and stars

Even within one grade, some coins are nicer than others, and the market has struggled to come up with a way to meaningfully and consistently identify these "PQ"—premium quality—coins.

NGC first began to identify especially nice coins through the use of its Star designation. A ★ on the grading insert on the slab signifies that a coin has exceptional eye appeal for a given grade. NGC describes it as follows: "To receive a star, coins must be free of any obvious planchet irregularities, and display no bothersome spots or blemishes. Toned coins can be of a single color or multicolored but cannot have any areas that are dark brown, approaching black." The coin market responded positively to the NGC Star designation, but by and large, the stars identified coins that were already selling for premiums in the market because of their superior eye appeal.

For years, a gap existed in identifying coins that were simply solid for the grade. Certified Acceptance Corp. began accepting submissions of PCGS- and NGC-certified coins in 2007. The company is not a grading service in a traditional sense, but instead, applies a CAC sticker that signifies that the coin meets CAC standards for a given grade. The marketplace has come to accept a CAC sticker as a signifier of a coin that is premium quality.

Observing collectors and dealer's positive reception of CAC-stickered coins led PCGS and NGC to announce on March 25, 2010, that they were introducing Plus designations to formally signify that a coin is high end for the grade. PCGS also announced that day its new PCGS Secure Plus system, which digitally captures a unique "fingerprint" of each coin and enters it into a permanent database where the system can detect when the same coin is resubmitted.

PCGS President Don Willis stated, "The process can help detect if a previously registered coin has been artificially toned, dipped or processed in some other way in an effort to get a higher grade."

NGC continues to use both the Plus and the Star designation, and while the coin market has accepted that coins with stars, CAC stickers and plus signs are worth more, the degrees of increase in value for each are still being defined. Especially for Plus designated coins, the number of coins evaluated for this designation is small in proportion to the total number of coins on the market.

The absence of a CAC sticker, a plus sign or an NGC Star does not mean that a coin is not superior quality—it could mean only that a coin has not been evaluated for the added designation.

What's a "doctored" coin?

Coin doctoring has been all the buzz of late, although it is a term that defies easy categorization. After exhaustive discussion, the Professional Numismatists Guild defined "coin doctoring" in 2010 as follows: "Coin doctoring is the action of a person, or the enabling of another, to alter a coin's surface or appearance, usually to diminish or conceal defects, and thereby represent the condition or value of a coin as being superior to its actual condition or value."

The PNG definition went on to provide an extensive list of some of the processes that "coin doctoring," includes:

➤ Effacing hairlines by polishing or manipulating the surfaces of Proof coins.

➤ Applying substances to the surface of coins to hide marks and defects.

➤ Hiding marks or otherwise changing the appearance of a coin by adding toning.

➤ Adding chemicals or otherwise manipulating the surfaces to create cameo frost on the devices of Proof coins.

➤ Making a coin appear more fully struck by re-engraving portions of the devices, such as re-engraving bands on the reverse of a Winged Liberty Head dime or adding head detail to a Standing Liberty quarter dollar.

➤ Altering dates or Mint marks or other struck portions of a coin to make it appear to be from a Mint, date or type other than that of origin.

➤ Altering circulation-strike coins to make them resemble Proof issues.

Despite this seemingly all-encompassing list, the definition ended with the caveat: "This definition is not intended to be all-inclusive, but only illustrative of forms of coin doctoring."

Perhaps the definition was too specific, because on Jan. 5, 2011, at the Florida United Numismatists convention in Tampa, the PNG membership voted 45 to 2 to remove the expanded definition. The PNG determined that a sentence in the membership code requiring members "To refrain from knowingly dealing in counterfeit, altered, repaired or 'doctored' numismatic items without fully disclosing their status to my customers" is sufficient.

Unfortunately, coin "doctoring" is a dark area of the rare coin market that defies easy categorization and definition.

The problem of "doctored coins" came to the forefront on May 13, 2010, when Collectors Universe Inc., the parent company of PCGS, filed a lawsuit in a federal district court accusing several coin dealers of various illegal acts related to allegedly submitting "doctored" coins to PCGS for grading on multiple occasions over a period of years.

Both PCGS and NGC have stated in their dealer agreements that dealers will not knowingly submit coins that have been doctored and the PCGS lawsuit sought to establish coin "doctoring" as a federal crime.

The lawsuit brought up a key problem with "doctored" coins: they change over time in the holders. While the coins may defy detection at first, over time the chemicals applied to the coins' surfaces create notable changes in the appearance, revealing their "doctored" nature.

While that lawsuit was dismissed on Dec. 13, 2010, it brought the issue of coin "doctoring" into the open as never before, and both PCGS and NGC have responded with improved detection techniques aimed at helping detect "doctored" coins and fakes. The guarantees offered by the grading services provide an extra layer of protection.

Still, the best protection against buying "doctored" coins is educating oneself on how coins age over time and what genuine coins look like, and working with trusted dealers who can guide potential investors toward high-quality coins that appear to have original surfaces.

Emergence of registry sets

Another development of the past decade has been the increasing popularity of collecting by PCGS and NGC registry sets. These programs allow collectors to record the certified coins in their collections and compete with other collectors, primarily for "bragging rights" of having the finest collection.

Rarity is accounted for by a point system and sets receive a cumulative score. Sets can then be categorized as "Current Finest" and "All-Time Finest," and collectors may browse through collections of other Registry participants online and look at photos and stories posted by collectors about their coins.

Participating in the Registry programs is free and provides collectors with a sense of community. But, perhaps the programs' main success for the grading service is in placing pressure at the very top end of the market, especially for modern coins.

For example, a coin may be common in Proof 69 deep cameo yet be prohibitively rare in Proof 70 deep cameo. In January 2004, Heritage Auctions sold a PCGS Proof 70 deep cameo 1969-S Lincoln cent for $40,250. In contrast, PCGS Proof 69 deep cameo Lincoln cents can be readily found for under $500.

Later, that Proof 70 deep cameo cent developed several small spots and PCGS bought it back under its grading guarantee, as it no longer graded Proof 70.

Even the grading services are beginning to advise collectors to be cautious when purchasing low-population common coins for stratospheric prices. Mark Salzberg, NGC's chairman, warned collectors at the FUN convention on Jan. 8, 2011, that he saw what may be a speculative price bubble forming for such coins.

He cited the example of a 1944 Walking Liberty half dollar graded MS-68 by PCGS that realized $109,250 at an Aug. 10, 2010, Heritage auction. MS-67 examples were routinely trading at the time at the $1,000 to $1,500 level.

His message was that while some coins are truly rare, many extremely high prices achieved in the marketplace for otherwise common 20th century coins of exceptionally high grade may not be fully justified from a value perspective.

When looking at coins for investment purposes, look at rarity both in an absolute sense and a relative sense. Questions to ask when evaluating a coin for investment purposes include:

➤ Is a coin rare because there are few known of the issue or type, or is a coin rare because it is the finest known?

➤ Is this the type of coin that has historically been valued by collectors?

➤ Is this the type of coin that future generations of collectors would likely covet?

➤ Is this price justified from a value perspective and is there room for appreciation in the figure?

Going through this exercise will help a potential buyer identify the marketplace for a given coin in the future, because for coins to be held as an investment, one hopes for price appreciation, which is only possible if demand is sustained for a given coin.

Changes in collectors' buying patterns

Today's collectors and investors are buying coins in different ways as they become more comfortable using the Internet in evaluating coin purchases.

The Internet has led to auctions gaining prominence as collectors are now more at ease bidding online, and online storage and digital photography has made the presentation of coins online much better and easier. The offerings of non-U.S.-based auction houses—once nearly inaccessible to most collectors in the United States—are now easy to find online.

The end result: Collectors have more options than ever before for buying coins.

The Internet has also allowed better research into coin pricing as searching auction records online is now very easy. Auction houses put their prices realized online—often illustrated—allowing would-be bidders to get a better understanding of a coin's price history and place better informed bids.

While this is a boon to collectors, many dealers find they must lower their profit margins when the dealer's acquisition cost of a coin has become transparent. Further, now that collectors can bid online themselves, dealer representation of clients at auctions has decreased over the past decade.

However, loss of dealer representation can be to a buyer's detriment, since, as mentioned earlier, build-ing a good working relationship with a dealer is a key component in putting together a great collection. While many collectors mistakenly think that all coins are offered at auction, the truth is that many more are transacted privately, and a good relationship with a knowledgeable dealer can provide a coin buyer access to further acquisition opportunities and valuable "inside information" on the coins offered at auction.

In an era of collectors connecting with coins and one another online, the role of the coin show has also shifted as more national-level coin shows have emerged.

The largest shows include the Florida United Numismatists convention in January and the summer American Numismatic Association World's Fair of Money, which traditionally rotates but, in 2011 and starting in 2013, will be located in the Chicago area.

The Central States Numismatic Society also hosts a major convention, and starting in 2011 it too will relocate to the Chicago area.

One can add to the list of major shows the three-times-annual Long Beach Coin, Stamp & Collectibles Expo in California, at least four Whitman Coin and Collectibles Expos each year, including three in Baltimore and one in Philadelphia, and two smaller ANA conventions in the spring and fall. These shows are held in addition to regional and local shows taking place across the country each weekend. Collectors and dealers have never had more options in selecting among major coin shows.

The best investments

Q. David Bowers, who wrote the "Coins as Investments" chapter in the Millennium Edition of the *Coin World Almanac,* published in 2000, provided sage advice when he suggested one have a "holistic" relationship with numismatics. On a "holistic" relationship, Bowers wrote:

"By this I mean that the whole is worth more than the sum of the parts. A modest amount of time spent reading and studying coins, plus some intelligent buying, will not only reward you with a nice coin collection but should, over a period of time, give you much collecting enjoyment and the possibility for really super investment."

Bowers suggests that time spent in understanding grading, chatting with other collectors about good dealers, and generally becoming a knowledgeable collector will enable far greater returns on an investment in rare coins. His advice holds as true in 2011 as it did in 2000.

Ultimately, the best coin investments are made when investors are engaged with their coins, when they take a connoisseur's approach to collecting and arm themselves with knowledge about the coins they collect, build relationships with the dealers who make the markets move, and develop a love of numismatics beyond simply the pursuit of good investment returns.

19 Rarities

How a coin becomes rare

Many factors are involved in establishing a coin as a "rare" coin. Total mintage, normal attrition as a result of circulation, official and private meltings, and the level of collector interest for a coin at the time it is being released into circulation are just a few of the factors that can lead to a coin being considered rare.

The total mintage refers to the amount struck at the issuing Mint and presumably released into circulation. The total mintage sets the upper limit of potential collectible examples, barring the production of Mint restrikes. The actual number of examples surviving, especially for coins that are 100 or 200 or more years old, is almost always diminishing. However, the number of collectible examples can never be more than the amount that were originally made, unless restrikes were produced later.

In many instances the total original mintage of a coin may only be approximated. This is especially true of coins struck at the United States Mint when it employed record-keeping methods that today seem quite confusing to rare coin researchers. During its earliest years, the federal Mint's bookkeeping consisted of recording the number of coins turned over to the Treasury during a calendar year. The actual year in which the coins were struck and the date on the coin were not noted separately. For example, the only record possibly available today is that the Treasury Department received 50,000 quarter dollars in April of 1807. Such a shipment could include coins dated 1805, 1806 and 1807. Collectors may never know.

In the earliest years of the Mint's operation, summertime yellow fever outbreaks, spread by mosquitoes, would lead Philadelphia's population to flee the city in justifiable fear for their lives. The Mint was often shut down during the outbreaks, leading to a halt in production.

Once coins are produced and released into circulation, the number of collectible examples rapidly decreases. Coins can become worn beyond recognition, hoarded and melted. Sometimes coins are swallowed, buried by misers never to be found again or placed in cornerstones of historic buildings as mementos.

Although some may logically suggest that disruption to the available supply of collectible examples should occur in equal proportion to the number of coins minted, this is not always the case. Certain coins boasting a very large original mintage are sometimes very difficult to locate in the highest states of preservation. Such coins are considered "condition rarities" and may fetch very large amounts of money at auction, although the coin is relatively common in low grade.

Relatively common coins, such as the 1889 Morgan dollar and the 1916 Winged Liberty Head dime, have experienced an unusual mode of attrition. Many of these coins have been altered in an attempt to disguise them as their more valuable counterparts. As examples, the 1889-CC dollar and the 1916-D dime were issued in much smaller numbers than the Philadelphia Mint strikes that are often altered to mimic those rarer counterparts. Manufacturers of coin jewelry often prefer 1964 Kennedy half dollars over the later years because of the higher silver content. Many 1964 half dollars have been used in pieces of jewelry; others have been melted for the silver content.

The famous $4 gold Stella patterns of 1879 and 1880, minted in small numbers, were holed and made into earrings for presentation to the wives of congressmen in an attempt to influence the husbands into approving the design. The Stella is today an enduring rarity.

Melting

In addition to the occasional destruction of coins by accident or carelessness, coins have often been intentionally melted in large quantities for their precious metal content. A most zealous smelter of U.S. coins has been the U.S. government, although private enterprise has contributed greatly to the demise of many silver and gold coins. Large increases in precious metals prices, especially gold and silver, have led to many millions of coins being melted privately as the intrinsic value of the metal climbed well above the face value of the coin.

Occasionally the government's reasons for melting coins have been aesthetic—not just financial—as in the practice of recoining worn or mutilated coins.

Also, early U.S. silver coins, especially dollars, were often exchanged for worn Spanish colonial coins and the heavier U.S. dollars were then exported and melted.

In 1834, the standard weight of each U.S. gold

denomination was reduced. This resulted in most of the pre-1834 gold coins being melted. A number of pre-1834 gold $5 coins had an original total mintage of 10,000 coins or more, yet today literally only a handful of pieces may survive.

In 1853, the price of silver increased to the point that all silver coins (except for the 3-cent coin) were worth more than face value and were being melted by ambitious entrepreneurs. To combat this problem the government reduced the weight of the half dime, dime, quarter dollar and half dollar by about 7 percent. The silver dollar, which represented a symbolic standard, was minted in limited quantities during this era; its weight remained unchanged. The new lighter weight coins were marked by placing arrows next to the date. This was done, not to inform the public of the weight change, but to assist the Treasury in withdrawing the heavier coins for melting. The government believed it should profit on the deal as well. The arrows were removed from the design after 1855.

In 1873, an otherwise insignificant increase was made in the weight of the dime, quarter dollar and half dollar. Again, arrows were placed at the date to denote the change, even though no withdrawal of the pre-1873 coins was necessary. Some coins had already been struck in 1873 at the lighter weight and without the arrows at the date. Such coins were to be melted, but a few pieces struck at the Carson City Mint survived, resulting in a great rarity. Only five pieces of the 1873-CC Seated Liberty No Arrows quarter dollars are known.

The Morgan silver dollar, struck from 1878 to 1904 and in 1921, was never a necessary or popular coin. Much of the mintage was placed directly into storage in original Mint-sewn bags. More than 270 million of these surplus coins were melted after World War I. Presumably all 1895 Morgan dollars that may have been struck for circulation were melted at this time (Mint records indicate that 12,000 were delivered). However, with the uncertainty about Mint records, people are left wondering whether any circulation-strike 1895 Morgan dollars were struck.

Although large quantities of unwanted and unnecessary silver dollars were melted in 1918, the silver interests (silver miners and barons) in the United States were powerful enough to have yet more unneeded and unnecessary coins struck. The result was the production of tens of millions of Morgan and Peace dollars in 1921 and subsequent years. Most of these coins ended up in the Treasury's vaults, and for years these common-date coins filled the limited demand for gifts and for circulation in the Western states.

This supply of silver dollars might have lasted forever, or at least until the price of silver rose above $1.29 per ounce (the point at which the coins would be worth $1 in precious metal content). However, it was noticed that the Treasury was giving out older silver dollars in addition to the common-date coins

of the 1920s. When it was discovered that a few bags of Seated Liberty dollars, dated 1859 and 1860, had been released at face value, thousands of collectors and speculators rushed to the Treasury to see what else was there. Within months, the stockpile of silver dollars fell from literally hundreds of millions to less than 3 million, and several formerly scarce Morgan silver dollars were instantly quite common.

Most of the 3 million dollars retained by the Treasury were Uncirculated coins struck at the Carson City Mint. Most of these pieces were dated 1882-CC, 1883-CC and 1884-CC. These three dates seemed relatively uncommon when compared to certain other Morgan dollars. After seven successive sales by the General Services Administration beginning in October 1972, even the 1882-CC, 1883-CC and 1884-CC coins had been sold to collectors.

In many instances, the heavy production of one denomination, such as silver dollars, was made at the expense of other denominations. Note the small mintage figures for dimes, quarter dollars and half dollars of 1878 to 1890 and for cents all the way to half dollars for 1921 to 1928, in the U.S. coins chapter.

The production of fractional silver (dimes, quarter dollars and half dollars) increased in 1890 because of the Sherman Silver Purchase Act. The production of dollars declined between 1893 and 1895 because of opposition to them from President Cleveland, not because of the increased production of the other denominations. Cleveland blamed the silver dollar for the business panic of 1893. With a smaller mintage, the 1893-S Morgan dollar therefore is a major rarity.

Collector conservation

Once a coin has been struck for circulation, its chance to survive pristine and Uncirculated is a matter of chance. Occasionally a collector will remove a coin from circulation and preserve it. Prior to the 1820s, there were very few collectors in the United States. Many of the surviving Uncirculated U.S. coins struck before the 1820s are from the collections of Europeans who visited the Philadelphia Mint.

Once collecting became popular in America (early 1860s) and collectors became concerned with a coin's condition, they wanted the best specimens available. This usually meant Proof coins. If the number of Proof coins of an earlier year was insufficient to meet current demand, Mint officials could often be induced to strike a few back-dated coins. In some instances these "semi-official" restrikes have become important collectibles. Similarly, the private restrike 1804 Draped Bust cent (the piece was privately restruck from 1803 and 1820 Mint dies, probably by a pair of early numismatists) is considered important.

Throughout the remainder of the 19th century, the several hundred avid collectors in the United States concentrated on obtaining one example of each date of each denomination in which they were interested. Usually this was taken care of with a Proof coin sent to the collector directly from the Mint. Coins struck for circulation were usually ignored. This was especially true for the Branch Mints, as many coins issued at San Francisco, New Orleans and Carson City are unknown in Uncirculated condition. Nonsilver minor coins (the cent and the 5-cent coins) were the easiest to collect, because they were all struck at the Philadelphia Mint. At this time, most collectors lived on the East Coast between Boston and Washington, D.C.

The national economy greatly affects the number of coins that survive (especially in high grade) from a particular era. During times of recession or depression, few coins are produced and fewer people have the surplus funds to acquire coins for safekeeping and as collectibles. Examples are the Great Depression of 1929 to 1939 and the recessions of 1949 and 1958.

There are always exceptions to the rule. The 1931-S Lincoln cent and Indian Head 5-cent coins, though times were tough, were saved in large quantities. These two coins are more common in Uncirculated condition than one would expect considering their low mintages. It could be that business was so weak during these times that the coins never traveled through the banks into circulation. Or else, some individual hoarded many of them. Other seemingly scarce issues, such as the 1950-D Jefferson 5-cent coin and the 1955 Franklin half dollar, are common in Uncirculated condition because speculators were able to obtain the coins in bag quantities.

The number of collectors is never static. An increased collector base places greater demand on available supply. Generally, prices increase as the number of collectors grows, and prices drop if fewer people are "chasing" the same coins.

Rarities exist by a whim of nature and the greed of man. Mintages rise and fall with the price of gold and the price of wheat. The lowly mosquito and the mighty politician have each been able to restrict production in direct proportion to the venom of their sting.

These things and other factors have led to many numismatic rarities that collectors and investors have searched for high and low.

Famous collections: Coins

Harry W. Bass Jr.

Texas businessman Harry W. Bass Jr. headed his family's oil business in Dallas and was the main developer of the Vail and Beaver Creek ski resorts in Colorado. He left his mark in the numismatic realm by becoming a world-class researcher and collector of U.S. gold coins.

At the time of his death on April 4, 1998, at the age of 71, his collection of more than 6,000 items was acclaimed to include the one of the largest and finest collections of U.S. gold coins from 1795 through 1933 by denomination, Mints, die varieties, die states and die mulings ever assembled. A collector for more than 30 years, he compiled an extensive collection encompassing U.S. gold coins, pattern, experimental and trial pieces, U.S. paper money, medals, numismatic books and catalogs, and many other numismatic-related items.

In 1991 he created the Harry W. Bass Jr. Research Foundation, which holds the core of his collection intact in perpetuity for research and scholarship. The foundation's holdings primarily comprise American gold coins of 1795 to 1834 by die varieties. An exhibit comprising 500 coins from his collection is on long-term loan for exhibit at the American Numismatic Association's museum in Colorado Springs, Colo. When the exhibit opened in July 2001, the coins on display were valued at more than $20 million.

Major holdings from the Bass Collection were sold in a series of four auctions conducted by Bowers and Merena Galleries beginning in May 1999 and culminating in November 2000. Q. David Bowers teamed with Mark Borckardt to write the *Harry W. Bass, Jr., Museum Sylloge*, which details the four auctions and the assemblage of the Bass Core Collection.

Paper money in the Bass Collection offered in the first sale May 7 to 9, 1999, realized $2,986,377.50 for 295 lots or an average of more than $10,000 per lot. The total auction, which also included pattern coinage, realized $6,680,980.

The second auction of the Bass Collection was held Oct. 2 to 4, 1999, posting prices realized of $18,080,388.25, including the buyer's fee. The 1,968 lots offered included U.S. gold in all denominations. The third auction, conducted May 25 to 26, 2000, realized $6,424,838 including the 15 percent buyer's fee, for 920 lots. The fourth auction, offering 981 lots, was conducted Nov 20 to 21, 2000, and realized $6,423,671 including the 15 percent buyer's fee.

Total prices realized for the four auctions were $37,609,877.25.

John Andrew Beck

John A. Beck was born in Chestnut Ridge, Pa., Jan. 5, 1859. After attending St. Vincent's College, he and his brothers went into their father's salt-producing business, drilling for salt on the Ohio River.

When salt was more profitably produced by mining in the West, he sold out his salt and chemical interests and prospected for oil. He continued in this business until his death Jan. 27, 1924.

Beck began collecting coins when he was 10 years old. Important coins in his collection were acquired with the help of prominent Philadelphia coin dealer Henry Chapman.

The Beck collection contained an outstanding array of United States gold coins and other U.S. rarities. Beck considered his collection of pioneer gold coins his most highly prized.

Pioneer gold, a complete set of 1795 to 1804 $10 eagles, commemorative gold, the 1861-D Coronet gold dollar, $4 Stellas and a rare 1900 Indian Head cent struck in gold comprised only a part of this all-encompassing collection. He also "hoarded" 531 1856 Flying Eagle cent patterns.

Beck's collection remained intact until Jan. 27, 1975, when the first of a series of auctions was conducted on behalf of the Trust Division, Pittsburgh National Bank, Pittsburgh, executors of Beck's estate. Abner Kreisberg Corp. conducted three auctions for the bank in Beverly Hills, Calif., that realized $3,232,169.

Virgil M. Brand

Virgil Michael Brand, born in Blue Island, Ill., in 1862, heir to one of the largest brewing businesses in Chicago, began collecting coins in 1889 when he was about 23 years old. His initial recorded purchases were California gold issues. By his death in 1926, Brand had purchased more than 350,000 pieces. Some consider his collection among the greatest ever formed.

Brand purchased everything, refusing to specialize. He bought coins in all areas of numismatics and from nearly every major dealer of the late 19th and early 20th centuries. He did so quietly, preferring to remain an unknown, unlike many prominent collectors of the era.

Following his death, Brand's two brothers, Horace and Armin, fought over the collection after failing to sell it intact. Dealers Henry Chapman and Burdette G. Johnson were hired in 1932 and 1933 to appraise the collection. Parts were sold through consignments and direct sales.

Many coins were given to Armin Brand's daughter, Jane, who kept them in her estate. Bowers and Merena Galleries was selected to sell the Jane Brand Allen estate collection, doing so in two auctions. The first auction, American gold and copper coins plus several foreign pieces, was held Nov. 7 to 8, 1983, and realized $1.9 million. The second, offering American coins and exonumia, was held June 18 to 19, 1984, and realized $1,417,977.

Sotheby Parke Bernet & Co. auctioned the bulk of Brand's estate of ancient and foreign coinage. The Soviet Union, Poland, Germany, Switzerland, France, Austria, Italy, England, Sweden, Finland and Portugal were just some of the countries whose coinage was represented. Ten auctions took place between July 1982 and October 1985 with European sales totaling £4,514,334. The Brand auctions took place in New York, London, Amsterdam and Zurich. Also of note, Brand's collection of numismatic books and literature realized $20,500 when sold at auction by George Frederick Kolbe Aug. 13, 1983, in Los Angeles.

Amon G. Carter Jr.

Paper money collectors invariably think of Amon G. Carter Jr. when they think of great collections. His collection of Texas notes, including national bank notes, was undoubtedly the finest in the world.

Astounding rarities owned by Carter included a Series 1863 $1,000 legal tender note, an 1863 $100 legal tender note, an 1891 $100 "Open Back" Treasury note, and an 1874 $500 United States note. Among the rarer nationals in the collection was an 1875 $100 note from the Desert National Bank of Salt Lake City, Utah Territory. It is possibly the only First Charter $100 territorial national in existence.

Carter's coin collection contained such rarities as the Adams specimen 1804 Draped Bust silver dollar, a Very Fine 1870-S Seated Liberty silver dollar, the 1801, 1802, 1803 dollar restrikes and 1884 and 1885 Trade dollars.

The coins were sold at auction Jan. 18 to 21, 1984, by Stack's of New York. The 1,798 lots brought more than $8 million including a 10 percent buyer's fee. His paper money collection was sold at fixed prices by various dealers.

Carter, publisher of the *Fort Worth Star-Telegram* (founded by his father), died July 24, 1982, at the age of 62.

William Forrester Dunham

William Forrester Dunham was born Oct. 3, 1857, at Barnard, Vt. He was a graduate of Tabor College, Iowa, and the University of Illinois. He died Oct. 12, 1936, at the age of 79.

In early life Dunham was a schoolteacher and later a wholesale and retail grocer. He studied pharmacy and became one of the leading druggists in Chicago. He retired from active business in 1916. Dunham was an ardent numismatist, beginning his collection early in life. He took an active interest in the affairs of the American Numismatic Association and attended conventions regularly. He served as a member of the ANA Board of Governors and as chairman of the board. He was a charter member of the Chicago Coin Club.

His collection included a range of items, for example: an 1804 silver dollar, an 1822 half eagle, an 1852 half cent, an 1802 half dime, a Proof set of the gold coins of 1875, a complete set of quarter eagles, complete set of gold $3 coins, the largest collection of encased postage stamps ever formed, an extensive collection of Hard Times tokens, Canadian coins and medals, 2,500 varieties of Confederate paper currency, and world gold, silver and platinum coins.

The collection was sold by B. Max Mehl on June 3, 1941, with a total of 4,169 lots bringing $83,364.08.

Louis E. Eliasberg Sr.

On April 21, 1976, the Louis Eliasberg memorial exhibition, a complete date and Mint collection of United States coins, plus pattern pieces, paper money, world coins and primitive means of exchange, opened as a Bicentennial exhibit at the Philadelphia Mint.

It was designated as a memorial exhibit in honor of its late owner, who died Feb. 20, 1976. His sons, Louis Eliasberg Jr. and Richard Eliasberg, and his widow, Lucille Eliasberg, officiated at the opening of the exhibit with Acting Mint Director Frank H. MacDonald.

The collection remained on display throughout the Bicentennial year and into America's third century.

Louis Eliasberg Sr. was Life Member No. 169 of the American Numismatic Association and a member of the Baltimore Coin Club. He began his collecting interest in 1925. In the 1930s, comfortably situated as a bank officer and soon to build the Finance Company of America, he realized that President Franklin D. Roosevelt's recall of gold coins and abandoning of the gold standard would start a vast period of inflation. Accordingly, he concentrated on buying as many rare gold coins as he could.

In 1942, he startled the numismatic world by acquiring the famous collection formed by John M. Clapp and his son, John H. Clapp. Eliasberg paid $100,000 for the collection, a transaction that at the time was tied with the 1923 private sale of the James Ellsworth Collection as the all-time high single cash transaction in the history of numismatics.

In 1950, Eliasberg did what no person had ever done before. He completed his collection of at least one each of every known date and Mint mark of United States coin from the 1792 half cent to the 1933 double eagle (though he did not collect by die variety). (Years later, a few coins unknown in Eliasberg's day came to light, including the 1870-S Seated Liberty half dime and the 1797 Capped Bust, 16 Star, Large Eagle $5 half eagles.) By definition he had all of the famous rarities, including the 1913 Liberty Head 5-cent coin, 1804 Draped Bust silver dollar and 1933 Saint-Gaudens $20 double eagle. He turned over his 1933 double eagle to the Treasury Department in 1952, when he heard that the government viewed ownership of this particular coin as illegal.

The Eliasberg gold coin collection was sold Oct. 27 to 29, 1982, by Bowers and Ruddy Galleries Inc., under the sobriquet "The United States Gold Collection" upon the request of one of his two heirs, Louis E. Eliasberg Jr., who specified that the Eliasberg name could be connected with the sale afterward, but not before or during the auction. However, it was widely known throughout the hobby that the coins being sold were from the Eliasberg Collection. The 1,074 lots brought more than $11.4 million, including two coins that each brought the then record price of $625,000—the unique 1870-S Indian Head gold $3 piece and the 1822 Capped Head half eagle.

Nearly 14 years later, on May 20 to 22, 1996, Bowers and Merena Galleries auctioned the smaller denomination copper, copper-nickel and silver coins in the Eliasberg Collection plus pattern pieces and Colonial coins to the tune of nearly $11.6 million. The consignor was the family of Richard Eliasberg. At that auction the Eliasberg specimen of the 1913 Liberty Head 5-cent coin realized $1.485 million, shattering the million dollar barrier and establishing a new world record for an individual United States coin

sold at auction. Q. David Bowers, who had written the book, *Louis E. Eliasberg, Sr., King of Coins*, was the auctioneer at the podium.

On April 6 to 8, 1997, the larger denomination silver coins and some exonumia were sold at auction, again by Bowers and Merena Galleries. This portion of the Eliasberg Collection realized $20.89 million. Star of the auction was the 1804 Draped Bust dollar, which sold for a record $1.815 million.

Selections from the estate of Louise E. Eliasberg Jr. were sold by Stack's in a March 2 and 3, 2008, auction.

Total prices realized from the Eliasberg family's numismatic holdings were $56,917,398.

King Farouk

King Farouk was born in 1919. At age 17, he succeeded his father, King Fuad, as king of Egypt. He ruled Egypt from 1936 to 1952 when he was deposed and forced into exile.

King Farouk assembled one of the largest coin collections in the world. After he was deposed in 1952, his collection was seized by the Egyptian government and sold at public auction in 1954 in Cairo by Sotheby's of London.

An accumulator rather than a student of numismatics, Farouk's collection nevertheless represented one of the finest ever assembled. It included about 8,500 coins and medals in gold and 164 in platinum. In addition it held many copper and silver coins.

Among the pre-19th century items was a group of 19 Brazilian gold bars dating to 1767. Also included were ancient coins struck by the Ptolemys of Egypt, some Roman aureii, and some Roman gold bars of the fourth century A.D. Also represented were extensive selections from Europe and the Far East.

Farouk held an important selection of U.S. gold and patterns. His collection included a 1933 Saint-Gaudens gold $20 double eagle. According to researchers, the U.S. Treasury Department granted an export license to Egyptian officials in 1944 to allow the coin to be transported to Egypt. The coin did not reappear publicly for another decade until Farouk's numismatic rarities were placed up for public sale. Sotheby's withdrew the coin from the sale at the request of the U.S. State Department, but it soon disappeared. According to court records, the coin passed through the hands of a jeweler with ties to a military officer closely aligned with Gen. Gamel Abdel Nasser, who had directed Farouk's ouster and had become Egypt's first president. The coin didn't resurface until Feb. 8, 1996, in New York City when a piece some claim is the Farouk coin was found in the possession of British coin dealer Stephen Fenton by Secret Service agents during a sting operation to buy the coin.

Criminal charges were brought and then dropped against Fenton in pursuit of civil action seeking forfeiture of the coin. In a settlement announced four days before trial was to begin in late January 2001, agreement was reached between Fenton and government attorneys to split the net proceeds from the sale of the coin between the coin dealer and the U.S. Mint.

The 1933 double eagle was sold in single-lot auction, held at Sotheby's New York City galleries in conjunction with Stack's, July 30, 2002, for a record price of $7.59 million. The coin brought a hammer price of $6.6 million after less than 10 minutes of spirited bidding. A 15 percent buyer's fee was added to the total, along with a $20 Federal Reserve note to reimburse the government for officially "monetizing" the double eagle. The coin was accompanied by a bill of sale and transfer of title specially designed and engraved by the Bureau of Engraving and Printing. Government officials have long contended that private citizens cannot legally own any examples of the 1933 double eagle. The buyer has remained anonymous but has allowed the only 1933 double eagle deemed legal for a citizen to own to be placed in the American Numismatic Society's special exhibit at the Federal Reserve Bank of New York.

Many famous U.S. and foreign rarities are pedigreed as "ex Farouk"—that is, from the Farouk Collection.

John J. Ford Jr.

The John J. Ford Jr. Collection of Coins, Medals, and Currency was sold in a series of 21 auctions conducted by Stack's during a five-year period beginning Oct. 23, 2003, with the final sale conducted on Oct. 16, 2007. The 10,885 lots posted a total prices realized of $56,402,744.

Ford's numismatic library, cataloged by George Fredrick Kolbe, was sold by Stack's and Kolbe in two auctions on June 1, 2004, and June 4 and 6, 2005. The 478 lots realized $1,852,604.

Ford died at the age of 81 on July 7, 2005, and was considered at the time the consummate collector, numismatic writer and researcher. He became interested in numismatics at the age of 12, three years after he was introduced to the world of stamp collecting. His first numismatic purchase came in the form of a Confederate $10 note dated Feb. 17, 1864, that he acquired for 10 cents from a Manhattan coin shop.

In his profile of Ford written for the Stack's auction catalogs illustrating the Ford holdings, David T. Alexander wrote that after filling penny boards, "Ford went on to acquire an in-depth knowledge of all areas of U.S. coinage that few could rival. His own personal interests came to focus on the more historical and esoteric areas of American numismatics neglected by many mainstream collectors for whom the penny board-approach sufficed."

The amazing feature of Ford's collection when it was sold is that it contained no regular issue U.S. Mint coinage.

The total prices realized noted do not take into account the many Colonial coins Ford sold in the decade before 2003 under his own name or that of F.C.C. Boyd, from whom Ford obtained many of his rarities in a private transaction during the second half of the 20th century. Among the rarities Stack's sold privately for the Ford family was one of the five original Confederate cents. (At one time Ford owned eight of the possibly 15 pieces known.)

Many suggest the unique set of four Nova Constellatio patterns of 1783 were the greatest rarities in Ford's collection (these were not sold in the Ford auctions). A definite star of the auctions was one of the four struck Confederate half dollars. In addition, in the 1980s and 1990s Bowers and Merena Galleries sold many world coins and patterns, tokens, medals, and Fractional Currency notes anonymously consigned by Ford.

The scope of Ford's collection stunned many veteran collectors. It included Continental dollars; state coppers of New Jersey, Vermont, Massachusetts and Connecticut; coinage and tokens of Virginia, Maryland, and New York; and pieces made in Europe bearing the names of Carolina and Rhode Island. The Ford Collection of Massachusetts silver coins 1652 to 1682 was the largest ever to cross the auction block. Also included were Higley coppers, St. Patrick tokens, Hibernia coinage, Rosa Americana coinage, Voce Populi coppers, Nova Constellatio coppers, French Colonial coins and tokens, Fugio coppers, Indian peace medals, U.S. Hard Times tokens, Confederate coinage, U.S. pioneer and territorial gold coins and assay ingots, U.S. encased postage stamps, Upper Canada tokens, Myddelton tokens, naval and historical medals, United States medals, Betts medals, struck copies of Colonial and early federal coinage, and Western territorial tokens, medals and patterns.

The paper currency portion included: Colonial currency, Continental currency, postage and fractional currency, obsolete currency, U.S. federal interest-bearing notes and bonds, War of 1812 notes, obsolete proof sheets, Mormon currency, John Law notes, Russian-American Co. notes, satirical notes, sutler notes, Southern states and Confederate notes, scrip notes from various eras, and territorial assayers' forms and documents.

Many of the individual collections in the Ford holdings were among the most complete and highest graded specimens ever offered at auction in their series.

Garrett Family collection

T. Harrison Garrett was a student at Princeton in the mid-1860s when he began collecting coins, beginning what was to become one of the landmark collections of U.S. coins and exonumia. Upon his death in 1888, he left the collection to his son Robert, who loaned much of it to Princeton University where it was on display for nearly 20 years. Some medals and tokens remaining in Baltimore were damaged in the 1904 fire that ravaged the city.

Robert Garrett added to the collection until 1919 when he traded it to a brother, Ambassador John Work Garrett, for art objects. J.W. Garrett was able to buy the pick of the Col. James W. Ellsworth Collection when it was sold to him and Wayte Raymond for $100,000 in March 1923, including many 1792 patterns and two Brasher gold doubloons. John Work Garrett died in 1942 having continued his numismatic activity until shortly before then.

The Garrett Collection was bequeathed to Johns Hopkins University in Baltimore, which sold duplicates in March 1976 in a Stack's auction and consigned the bulk to Bowers and Ruddy Galleries, which held a series of four auctions from 1979 to 1981. The coins sold by Bowers and Ruddy included two 1787 Brasher doubloons, many rare Colonial pieces, Washington medals, one of the greatest collections of 1792 pattern coinage assembled, a Proof 1795 silver dollar, an 1804 Draped Bust silver dollar and rare gold coins.

The four auctions were held Nov. 28 and 29, 1979; March 26 and 27, 1980; Oct. 1 and 2, 1980; and March 25 and 26, 1981. Total prices realized were $25,235,360—against a pre-auction estimate of about $8 million. Combined with prices realized from the 1976 Stack's sales, the total prices realized for the Garrett collections was $27,535,360.

The History of United States Coins as Illustrated by the Garrett Collection by Q. David Bowers was published in 1979.

Col. E.H.R. Green

"Texas Colonel" E.H.R. Green was born Aug. 22, 1868, and died June 8, 1936. Before reaching the age of 20, his right leg was amputated 7 inches above the knee. Even so, he stood 6 feet, 4 inches, and weighed 300 pounds.

Green was the eccentric playboy son of the equally eccentric, but miserly, Hetty Green, the famous Wall Street financier and manipulator, known as the "Witch of Wall Street." She died July 3, 1916, and left her entire estate to her son and to a frightened, eremitic daughter, Sylvia Wilks.

Green reputedly spent $3 million a year on yachts, coins, stamps, pornography, orchid culture and Texas politics.

At the time of his death, Green's collection contained some of the finest and rarest numismatic pieces ever assembled by one person, including all known 1913 Liberty Head 5-cent coins plus an example of the 1913 Indian Head 5-cent piece in copper. His collection was dispersed after his death.

Herman Halpern

Herman Halpern was a collector who focused on maintaining quality and rarity. His main interest was large cents. The completeness of his collection was enhanced by rich pedigrees including the names of Harold Bareford, Denis W. Loring and Del Bland.

Stack's auctioned Halpern's collection of large cents March 16 and 17, 1988. The amazing amount of $1.8 million was paid for 774 lots of cents—face value $7.74.

Jimmy Hayes

The Jimmy Hayes Collection of United States Silver Coins demonstrated the ability of one collector to assemble a type collection consisting of the first year of issue of virtually every type of U.S. silver coin from the silver 3-cent piece to silver dollars and commemoratives. The extreme high quality of each coin in the collection heralded a new era in coin collecting, one in which the emphasis was on a narrow focused range of coins, locating the absolutely finest example known of the type.

The 128 coins in the Hayes Collection were sold at auction by Stack's on Oct. 22, 1988. The 128 coins brought nearly $1.2 million, an average of almost $10,000 per lot.

Hayes assembled his collection as a young man. He served as commissioner of financial institutions and as commissioner of securities in his home state of Louisiana before his election to represent Louisiana's 7th District in the U.S. House of Representatives for 10 years, from 1987 through 1997. He is an attorney and chief executive officer of Washington Matters LLC, a consulting and government relations firm in Washington, D.C.

Jascha Heifetz

The Jascha Heifetz Collection of United States coins and patterns was sold by Superior Galleries Oct. 1 to 4, 1989, together with the Albert Hanten Collection of U.S. paper money and the Paul Munson Collection of Bust half dollars. The 6,200 lots in nine sessions realized more than $16 million.

Among the record-breaking highlights were a 1907 Saint-Gaudens, High Relief, Roman Numerals double eagle that brought $200,000 and a Proof 65 Flowing Hair $4 Stella pattern at $270,000.

Dan Holmes

The Dan Holmes Collection of U.S. Large Cents was unique in American numismatics. Formed over 35 years, it was the most complete large cent collection by date and die variety ever assembled. It lacked only two coins: one unique Early Date cent, the 1793 Flowing Hair, Wreath cent described as noncollectible (NC-5) by William H. Sheldon, which resides in the American Numismatic Society's museum in New York City; and one Late Date variety, the unique 1851 Coronet cent, Newcomb 42, discovered in 1986 by Tom R. Wagemaker.

The collection was sold in four auctions, all conducted by Ira & Larry Goldberg Coins & Collectibles, during a two-year span beginning Sept. 6, 2009, and concluding Jan. 30, 2011. Total prices realized, including the 15 percent buyer's fee, was $17,677,230.75.

The Early Date portion of the collection (1793 through 1814) comprising some 572 lots sold in 2009 proved to be the most spectacular. It contained all 302 die varieties that Sheldon identified in *Penny Whimsy,* the definitive reference on the series, and 52 of the 53 known noncollectible die varieties for the series. (Sheldon designated certain of the die varieties as "noncollectible" because they were considered so rare as to be virtually unobtainable by even the most dedicated collector.)

The first auction recorded the first U.S. large cent to break the $1 million mark. The 1795 Liberty Cap, Reeded Edge cent, cataloged as Sheldon 79 and the finest of seven known examples, sold for a winning hammer bid of $1.1 million. With the 15 percent buyer's fee added, the total price was $1,265,000.

The Middle Date cents (1816 to 1839) were sold May 30, 2010; large cent errors on Sept. 19, 2010; and Late Date cents (1840 to 1857) on Jan. 30, 2011.

Holmes, of Cleveland, Ohio, got his start by collecting Lincoln cents at the age of 10. A neighborhood playmate showed him a cent album and explained about dates and Mint marks. For the next 10 years he avidly collected from change, graduating to other denominations and completing many albums. At age 20 he was off to the Army and left coin collecting behind. Later he completed undergraduate and graduate degrees, married and began a family. During that time he also began building a highly successful career in the business world. By age 33 he began to think about collecting and coins again and read about the Early American Coppers club in *Coin World*. He sent in his $10 membership fee in 1973 and began receiving the club's publication, *Penny Wise*, which introduced him to a whole new world and an adventure that has catapulted him to an honored and highly respected status in the numismatic realm.

Holmes had originally intended to begin the sale of his collection sometime in 2011, but moved up the schedule after doctors at the Cleveland Clinic delivered the diagnosis Sept. 23, 2008, that he was afflicted with amyotrophic lateral sclerosis, also known as Lou Gehrig's disease. He stepped down as president of Early American Coppers in April 2009 amid his second term and at age 71 prepared to sell his collection.

Nelson Bunker Hunt and William Herbert Hunt

The collection of ancient coins of Nelson Bunker Hunt may represent a breakthrough in numismatic auction prices. For the first time, coins were sold as art, attracting the heady prices often associated with other areas of the fine arts but rarely seen in the coin field.

A June 19, 1990, Sotheby's session in New York offering just 110 Greek and Roman coins brought a total hammer price of $8.6 million. Another portion of the fabled Hunt Brothers Collection sold at auction in four sessions June 21 and 22, and again Dec. 4 to 7, 1990.

The highest price paid at the June 19 session, and for any non-U.S. coin sold at auction to that date, was $520,000 for a silver decadrachm of Agrigentum, Sicily. Nelson Hunt had purchased the coin from Bruce McNall of Numismatic Fine Arts in a 1980 private transaction for a reported $1 million.

Josiah Kirby Lilly

The Josiah K. Lilly Collection, a specialty collection of United States and foreign gold coins, was transferred to the Smithsonian Institution after an act of Congress in 1968 gave the Lilly estate a tax credit of $5.5 million. Included in the collection of 6,125 gold coins are 1,227 United States gold coins, among them an 1822 Capped Head half eagle (three known) and a 1797 Capped Bust, 16 Star Obverse half eagle; 1,236 Latin American coins; 3,227 European coins; and 243 African, Asian and Far Eastern gold coins.

The only United States gold coin Lilly did not own was the unique 1870-S Coronet $3 coin, which was owned by Louis E. Eliasberg Sr.

Wayne Miller

Wayne Miller, a Helena, Mont., coin dealer and collector, during a span of 16 years starting in the late 1960s completed a set of Morgan and Peace silver dollars.

The quality of the coins in Miller's collection set it apart from others of its type. Included were many finest known examples of rare dates several important branch Mint Proof coins. Branch Mint Morgan dollars are highly prized and rarely seen. Miller sold the 160-piece collection in April 1984 to dealer David Hall, who served as broker for an unnamed collector on the West Coast. The price was believed to be in excess of $1 million.

The coin collection was subsequently sold at public auction by Superior Galleries, Jan. 27 and 28, 1986, in Beverly Hills, Calif., and realized $1,109,375.

Emery May and R. Henry Norweb

Emery May Holden became interested in coins when, at about 9 years old in 1905, she was given a half cent piece. As a young woman she helped her father, Albert Fairchild Holden, attribute Colonial coins to S.S. Crosby's *Early Coins of America* and other references. After her father died a few years later, Emery May continued her interest. She married R. Henry Norweb in 1917.

Ambassador R. Henry Norweb also began collecting, during his long diplomatic career. He died Oct. 1, 1983, and Mrs. Norweb died March 27, 1984.

Mrs. Norweb's collection of English gold coins was believed to be the greatest in the United States, and her collections of American Colonial, United States and Latin American coins were extensive as well.

The Norwebs were philanthropic in nature and donated many rarities to museums. Among them were a 1913 Liberty 5-cent piece, given to the Smithsonian Institution in 1978, and a Brasher doubloon, given to the American Numismatic Society in 1969. A 52-piece collection of Colonial rarities was donated to the Smithsonian in 1982.

Bowers & Merena sold the Norweb family's U.S. material in 1987 and 1988 in three auctions that brought total prices realized of $18,103,365. On Nov. 15, 1996, the same firm sold the Norweb Collection of Canadian and Canadian provincial coins, comprising 741 lots, which realized $2,033,260.90 including a 10 percent buyer's fee.

In 1997, Spink America, then a subsidiary of Christie's, auctioned the Norweb Collection of South American coins. More than half of the 1,200 lots in that collection were coins from Brazil.

Mrs. Norweb's Collection of Washingtoniana, comprising more than 200 pieces, was sold Nov. 7, 2006, by Stack's Rarities LLC. The top price of $391,000 in the sale went to an 1889 Washington inauguration centennial medal in gold by Augustus Saint-Gaudens. The 2006 auction also included Mrs. Norweb's first gold coin—a 1795 Capped Bust gold $10 eagle that her paternal grandfather, Liberty E. Holden, had given her. Holden introduced his granddaughter to numismatics, and specifically to numismatic collectibles related to George Washington, setting into motion a passion for collecting that led to one of most important collections ever built. Holden was the publisher of the *Cleveland Plain Dealer* and the owner of valuable mines in the West. The extremely rare 1799 Washington Skull and Crossbones funeral medal struck in gold and sold in 2006 was among the rarities he passed to his granddaughter.

The lives of the Norwebs and the development of the collection throughout its long history were chronicled by Q. David Bowers and Michael Hodder in *The Norweb Collection: An American Legacy,* published in 1987.

Total prices realized for the Norweb auctions, excluding the South American holdings, was $25,143,977.

John J. Pittman

John J. Pittman has been dubbed "the collector's collector." He came from humble origins, unlike the majority of names in this who's who list of collectors and coin dealers.

Born Feb. 18, 1913, Pittman died Feb. 17, 1996.

He was very active not only as a collector but in the American Numismatic Association and regional coin clubs, and was a familiar face at nearly every major convention over a period of 40 years.

As the collectors' collector, Pittman appreciated 19th century Proof coins in gold, silver and copper and was making prudent acquisitions for his collection as far back as the 1940s. As a collector who knew a bargain when he saw one, Pittman mortgaged his house to be able to attend and make purchases at the King Farouk auction in Cairo in 1954.

Pittman acquired rarities such as the Proof 1833 Capped Head $5 half eagle at the sale for $605. It sold at auction in October 1997 for $467,500. Many such examples appeared in the Pittman auctions. The U.S. coins portion of Pittman's collection, including some important Canadian coins, realized $24,024,020 when sold at auction by David Akers Inc. of Florida.

The world coins portion of the Pittman Collection, also conducted by Akers, brought $5,573,120.80 when it was auctioned Aug. 6 to 8, 1999.

John L. Roper 2nd

Born Sept. 18, 1902, John L. Roper 2nd was an heir to a shipbuilding firm in Norfolk, Va., which allowed him the means to build an important collection of Colonial and early American coinage of the 20th century. Roper died in April 1983.

The Dec. 8 and 9, 1983, auction of Roper's collection by Stack's included a half dozen Sommer Islands pieces, two New England silver pieces, and 34 Massachusetts Tree silver coins. Also included in the auction were copper and silver coins of most American Colonies, the early Confederation and many federal issues. Fifteen Fugio coppers, five 1792 patterns and three 1793 Flowing Hair, Chain cents were also in the collection.

A second Roper auction, held March 20, 1984, offered paper money, Hard Times tokens and other items of numismatic Americana.

Matthew Adams Stickney

Matthew Adams Stickney was born Sept. 23, 1805, at Rowley, Mass., and died Aug. 11, 1894, in Salem, Mass.

He began collecting coins in 1823 and is popularly remembered as the first person in America to form a systematic collection of the various dates in several series.

He assisted Sylvester S. Crosby, who prepared a monumental work on U.S. Colonial, state and Washington coins between 1873 and 1875. Many of Stickney's coins were used as illustrations throughout the Crosby book.

Some of the more famous coins in his collection included: a 1787 New York Brasher doubloon, an 1815 half eagle, an 1804 silver dollar, a 1776 cent of New Hampshire and the unique 1776 "Janus head" halfpenny. Also included were cent series of Massachusetts, Vermont, Connecticut, New York, New Jersey, plus many pattern pieces, world coins, Canadian coins and medals, and pioneer gold coins.

The entire Stickney collection was sold by Henry Chapman June 25 to 29, 1907, with 3,026 lots bringing $37,859.21. That prices realized was considered a huge sum at that time.

George O. Walton

When George Owen Walton's coin collection was sold in 1963, the total hammer price was $874,836.75—then a world record for a single collection of coins offered at public auction. The collection was sold in two auctions—the duplicates were sold in June for $234,735.75 and the primary collection in October for $640,101.

Walton was a prominent collector in the 1940s and 1950s and in some news accounts at the time of his death in 1962, his collection was ranked second only to that of Louis E. Eliasberg Sr. Although his coin collection spanned the entire U.S. federal coinage by date and Mint mark and contained 26 of the 100 greatest American coins as cited by Jeff Garrett and Ron Guth in *100 Greatest U.S. Coins,* Walton's collection of Southern (private Bechtler mint, Charlotte Branch Mint and Dahlonega Branch Mint) gold was considered the best assembled by that time (and possibly even today). It contained 252 Bechtler pieces, including 98 A. Bechtler gold dollars. Walton's primary set contained 25 of the 29 varieties known in the Bechtler gold coins. His collection also included foreign rarities.

Walton was born May 15, 1905, in Franklin County, Va., and spent his boyhood in the hamlet of Gogginsville. He began collecting coins at the age of 12. He told fellow collectors that he worked as an "intelligence agent" during World War II but left government service after the war because of a hearing problem. Shortly after, he parlayed his collecting knowledge into a full-time profession as an appraiser of estates for banks and trust companies. As a "sideline," he said, he acted as a "buyer-agent for several millionaires" in the Carolinas who did not want their collecting interests or identities to become public knowledge. Walton took pride in trading, perhaps more than buying and selling.

He told a number of collectors that he acquired his 1913 Liberty Head 5-cent coin in 1945 from a Winston-Salem millionaire in a trade valued at about $3,750. His good friend and coin collector Dr. Conway A. Bolt of Marshville had purchased the coin in 1943 and then sold it to the collector in Winston-Salem from whom Walton acquired it.

Walton died instantly March 9, 1962, from injuries sustained in a head-on two-car crash. His 1913 Liberty Head 5-cent piece was recovered at the accident scene; however, it was mistakenly identified as an altered date because of a planchet flaw in the date area.

It was returned to his heirs, who kept it in a shoe box in a closet in their home near Roanoke, Va., until 2003 when they were persuaded to have it examined by experts, who declared it to be genuine on July 30. Since 2003 it has been on loan to the American Numismatic Association for exhibit in its museum and at coin shows throughout the nation. The coin is owned jointly by Walton's two nephews and two nieces.

Famous collections: Paper Money

Aubrey and Adeline Bebee

Aubrey and Adeline Bebee began assembling their world class collection of U.S. paper money in 1941 and during the next 40 years it grew to include many spectacular rarities, including a Series 1934 $1,000 Federal Reserve note. Much of the collection was acquired in a single transaction in 1956 when they purchased the James M. Wade Collection. Wade was assistant cashier at the Chase National Bank in New York City.

The Bebees' collection of 905 notes was donated to the American Numismatic Association in two parts, the first portion in late 1987 and the second in early 1988. At the time it was donated the collection was valued at $2 million.

Aubrey died May 5, 1992, at the age of 85, and Adeline died Jan. 10, 1998, but no age was given in her obituary.

The full collection is housed at the American Numismatic Association's Edward C. Rochette Money Museum in Colorado Springs, and can be viewed at **www.ana-museum.org/outstanding.html**.

Albert A. Grinnell

When the Albert A. Grinnell Collection of United States paper money was cataloged and auctioned by Barney Bluestone of Syracuse, N.Y., in the 1940s it was considered the most complete collection of U.S. paper money available at the time. His collection was sold in a series of seven auctions beginning Nov. 25, 1944, through Nov. 30, 1946. The disbursement of Grinnell's collection into the marketplace allowed notes from his collection to form the backbone of many other excellent collections formed in the later half of the 20th century.

Grinnell was born June 12, 1865, in rural New York and died April 18, 1951. He began his business career with the Grinnell Retail Coal and Lumber Yard in Oakfield, N.Y. In 1910 he moved to Detroit and eventually became president of Grinnell Brothers Music House.

Grinnell was a founder and the second president of the Detroit Coin Club. He was Life Member No. 40 of the American Numismatic Association.

In the catalogs, grades for notes were listed as Uncirculated, Extremely Fine, Very Fine and Very Good. Each note was contained in a "heavy transparent envelope, many of which are accompanied with Mr. Grinnell's personal notations," according to the catalog.

Included in the sale were legal tender and United States notes; Treasury/coin notes; demand notes of 1861 including a $5 and a $10 St. Louis note, the rarest of demand notes; interest-bearing notes; compound-interest notes; refunding certificates; California national gold bank notes for all issuing banks; Series 1882 to 1922 gold certificates; Series 1878 to 1923 silver certificates; national bank notes from every state as well as national bank notes from U.S. possessions Alaska, Hawaii and Puerto Rico and former territories Colorado, Montana, New Mexico, Oklahoma, Utah and Indian, plus Washington, D.C.; Federal Reserve Bank notes and Federal Reserve notes as well as low and fancy serial numbered notes, autographed notes, error notes, uncut sheets and other notes. The total prices realized for the seven auctions was $250,457.

Frank Levitan

The Frank Levitan Collection of 400 U.S. type notes was sold by Lyn F. Knight Inc. on Dec. 5, 1998, at the Northeast Paper Money & Historical Artifacts Show in Stamford, Conn. It included an 1890 $1,000 Treasury/coin note, nicknamed a "Grand Watermelon" note because the engraved zeros on the back look like the skin on a watermelon. According to the catalog, it was one of only three known with the "watermelon" design in private collections and one of only two known with a small red Treasury seal. The note sold for $792,000 and the total prices realized for that auction was $6 million.

Levitan was also a collector of Westchester County national bank notes. That collection was also sold by Knight on Dec. 7, 2010, at the firm's auction facility in Kansas. The auction realized more than $500,000.

Levitan died Jan. 22, 2011, at the age of 93.

Herb and Martha Schingoethe

When it came to coins and paper money Herb Schingoethe collected almost everything, but it was obsolete currency that his wife, Martha, liked to collect. She fell in love with the incredible diversity of issuers, and with the artistic quality of the vignettes on the notes. She enjoyed meeting and dealing with the people who bought and sold obsolete currency. Martha had the skills and the energy required to organize and maintain everything they acquired. Her husband, Herb, had the passion to collect on a grand scale.

Together they created what is now known as the Schingoethe Collection.

The collection included more than 30,000 different obsolete notes representing every U.S. state or territory in which paper money was issued. It was considered the largest and most comprehensive collection of obsolete notes ever formed when consigned for auction to R.M. Smythe & Co. in 2004. The collection was sold in a series of 18 auctions, the last of which was held June 25, 2009, during the International Paper Money Show in Memphis, Tenn. The total prices realized for the 18 auctions was $13,103,088.20 (including the buyer's fees).

Martha Schingoethe died Feb. 17, 2005. Herb Schingoethe died March 18, 2005, five days before the second auction.

Pedigrees

Following are pedigrees—or records of owners—of all known examples of three of the most popular rare coins in United States numismatics.

Curiously, none of the three is considered a true issue, but an official restrike, unofficial strike or fantasy piece. However, their histories are legendary. Some of the highest prices ever paid for U.S. coins are for coins appearing on the following lists.

1913 Liberty 5-cent pieces

Apparently struck by or for Samuel W. Brown, one-time storekeeper and later clerk at the Philadelphia Mint.

Specimen 1
Samuel W. Brown
August Wagner
Stephen K. Nagy
Wayte Raymond
Col. E.H.R. Green
Burdette G. Johnson and Eric P. Newman
James F. Kelly
Dr. Conway A. Bolt Sr.
Winston-Salem, N.C., Collector
George O. Walton
Walton Estate
Melva Walton Givens
Heirs of Melva Walton Givens

Specimen 2
Samuel W. Brown
August Wagner
Stephen K. Nagy
Wayte Raymond

Because many collectors (or investors) are reluctant to have their identities known, largely for reasons of security, gaps may appear in some of the pedigrees, but effort has been made to render them as complete as possible. Additions or changes may be sent to *Coin World*, P.O. Box 150, Sidney, OH 45365-0150, or by email to **cweditor@coinworld.com**.

Col. E.H.R. Green
Burdette G. Johnson and Eric P. Newman
Eric P. Newman
James F. Kelly
Fred Olsen
B. Max Mehl
King Farouk
Edwin Hydeman
Abe Kosoff
World-Wide Coin Corp./Bowers & Ruddy
A-Mark Coin Co./Robert L. Hughes Ent.
Superior Stamp & Coin Co.
Dr. Jerry Buss
Reed Hawn
Dwight Manley/Spectrum Numismatics
The Legend Collection
Anonymous Midwest Collector

Specimen 3
Samuel W. Brown
August Wagner
Stephen K. Nagy
Wayte Raymond
Col. E.H.R. Green

Burdette G. Johnson and Eric P. Newman
James F. Kelly
James V. McDermott
Aubrey and Adeline Bebee
American Numismatic Association
Specimen 4
Samuel W. Brown
August Wagner
Stephen K. Nagy
Wayte Raymond
Col. E.H.R. Green
Burdette G. Johnson and Eric P. Newman
Abe Kosoff
Louis E. Eliasberg Sr.
Eliasberg Family
Jay Parrino–The Mint
Dwight Manley/California Gold Group
Edward C. Lee
The Legend Collection
Anonymous California Collector
Specimen 5
Samuel W. Brown
August Wagner
Stephen K. Nagy
Wayte Raymond
Col. E.H.R. Green
Burdette G. Johnson and Eric P. Newman
F.C.C. Boyd
Abe Kosoff
King Farouk
Government of Egypt
Sol Kaplan and Abe Kosoff
Emery May Holden Norweb
Smithsonian Institution/National Numismatic
  Collection

1894-S Barber dime

Twenty-four examples were struck at the San Francisco Mint in 1894, from the remaining silver left over from melted uncurrent coinage turned over to the facility as part of routine business. The rest of the reclaimed coinage silver had been struck into new silver coins of other denominations of current designs. According to contemporary news accounts quoting a San Francisco Mint official, the remaining uncoined silver was sufficient to strike 24 dimes, which had been not scheduled for production because of a surplus of the denomination. Some researchers believe only nine examples can be tracked today.

Specimen 1
Waldo Newcomer
F.C.C. Boyd
Abe Kosoff
Will W. Neil
B. Max Mehl
Edwin Hydeman
Abe Kosoff
Empire Coin Co.
Hazen Hinman
James Kelly, Paramount

Leo A. Young
Rarcoa
Ronald J. Gillio
Unidentified Collector
Specimen 2
John H. Clapp
Stack's
Louis Eliasberg
Eliasberg Family
Anonymous
Specimen 3
John H. Clapp
Louis Eliasberg
H.R. Lee
Stack's
James A. Stack Sr.
Unidentified Collector
Jay Parrino
Bradley Hirst–The Richmond Collection
Daniel Rosenthal
New York City Investor
Specimen 4
J. Daggett
Hallie Daggett
Earl Parker
Dan Brown
Stack's
Chicago Collector
Specimen 5
J. Daggett
Hallie Daggett
Earl Parker
W.R. Johnson
Abner Kreisberg
World-Wide Coin Investment
Midwest Collector
Spectrum Numismatics
Anonymous Collector
Legend Numismatics
Bob R. Simpson
Specimen 6
C.A. Cass
Stack's
James Ruddy
Q. David Bowers
Mr. and Mrs. R. Henry Norweb
Unidentified Collector
Specimen 7
Rappaport
Kagin's
Reuter
Abner Kreisberg
Bowers & Ruddy Galleries Inc.
Eastern Collector
Specimen 8
(Not verified)
California collector
Kagin's
Private Collector

Kagin's
National Coin Co.
Superior Stamp & Coin Co.
Dr. Jerry Buss
Michelle Johnson
Specimen 9
(Circulation find)
Friedberg/Gimbels NYC
Kagin's
New Netherlands Coin Co.
Kagin's
Harmer-Rooke
James G. Johnson Jr.
Old Roman Coin Co.
Robert L. Hughes
Specimen 10
(Circulation find)
Romito-Montesano
Robert Hughes
Laura Sperber
Unidentified Collector

1804 silver dollar

No 1804 Draped Bust dollars bearing that date were actually struck that year. In 1834, the State Department requested Proof sets for diplomatic gifts. Mint Director Samuel Moore interpreted the order to mean 1804-dated dollars should be struck. Sets were presented to the Sultan of Muscat and the King of Siam (specimens 7 and 8). Other coins were kept by the Mint. These are referred to as Class I.

By the 1850s, the 1804 dollar was recognized as a rarity, and the Mint prepared to strike more, using a new reverse die because the original was missing. However, night watchman Theodore Eckfeldt, son of the chief coiner, surreptitiously struck several pieces and sold them to Philadelphia-area coin dealers. Eckfeldt lacked the skill to letter the edges, and the plain-edged coins aroused suspicions at the Mint.

Mint officials, to conceal their own plans to restrike the coins, quietly repurchased all of the plain edge pieces and reported them destroyed. In fact, after lettering was added to their edges the coins went into a Mint vault for 20 years, all but one piece. It been struck over a cut-down 1857 Swiss shooting taler and was left undisturbed. It exists as the sole surviving Class II 1804 dollar and is in the National Numismatic Collection in the Smithsonian Institution.

The pieces with edge lettering added are referred to as Class III 1804 dollars.

The definitive history of the 1804 dollar is *The Fantastic 1804 Dollar* by Eric P. Newman and Kenneth E. Bressett. It was updated in 1987 in the American Numismatic Society's *American Silver Coinage, 1794-1891.*

Class I
Specimen 1
Smithsonian
Specimen 2
United States Mint

Matthew A. Stickney
Stickney Estate
Col. James W. Ellsworth
Wayte Raymond and John Work Garrett
William C. Atwater
Louis Eliasberg
Eliasberg Family
Spectrum Numismatics
Private Collection
Specimen 3
Edward Cohen
Col. M.I. Cohen
H.S. Adams
Lorin G. Parmelee
H.G. Sampson
William B. Wetmore
S.H. and H. Chapman
Thomas L. Elder
James H. Manning
Elmer S. Sears
B. Max Mehl
Lammot du Pont
Lammot du Pont Family
Willis du Pont (stolen 1967, recovered 1993)
American Numismatic Association
Specimen 4
Henry C. Young
Joseph J. Mickley
W.A. Lilliendahl
Edward Cogan
William S. Appleton
Massachusetts Historical Society
Chicago Collector
Reed Hawn
David Queller
Anonymous
Specimen 5
Unknown woman
E. Harrison Sanford
Lorin G. Parmelee
Byron Reed
City of Omaha, Neb.
Durham Western Heritage Museum, Omaha, Neb.
Specimen 6
Adolph Weyl
S.H. and H. Chapman
J.W. Scott
James V. Dexter
Dexter Estate
H.G. Brown
William F. Dunham
B. Max Mehl
C.H. Williams
Sol Kaplan and Abe Kosoff
Harold Bareford
Rarcoa
Leon Hendrickson and George Weingart
American Rare Coin Fund, Hugh Sconyers, manager

California Collector
Harlan White
Unidentified Midwest Collector
Holeceke Family Trust
Anonymous
Specimen 7
Sultan of Muscat
C.A. Watters
Henry Chapman
Virgil Brand
Virgil M. Brand Estate
Armin W. Brand
C.F. Childs
Childs Family
Pogue Family Collection
Anonymous
Specimen 8
King of Siam
David Spink Family
Elvin I. Unterrnan
Elvin I. Unterrnan Family
Continental Rare Coin Fund and
   The Rarities Group
Terry Brand and Iraj Sayah
Spectrum Numismatics
Private Western Collection
Steven L. Contursi
Class II
Specimen 9
Smithsonian
Class III
Specimen 10
Koch and Co.
O.H. Berg
T.H. Garrett
T.H. Garrett Estate and Robert Garrett
John Work Garrett
Johns Hopkins University
Larry Hanks, William Pullen and Sam Colavita
Sam Colavita
Mike Levinson
Pennsylvania Collection
Martin Paul
American Coin Portfolios Inc. for "Mrs. Sommer"
Specimen 11
John Haseltine
Phineas Adams
Henry Ahlborn
John P. Lyman
Waldo Newcomer
Col. E.H.R. Green
A.J. Allen
F.C.C. Boyd
Abe Kosoff and Abner Kreisberg
Percy A. Smith
B. Max Mehl
Amon Carter Sr.
Amon Carter Jr.

L.R. French Jr.
Martin Paul
National Gold Exchange
Heritage Rare Coin Galleries
Midwest Collection
David Liljestrand
National Gold Exchange and Kenneth Goldman
Legend Numismatics Inc.
Private Collection
Phillip Flannagan Collection
Donald Kagin and Martin Paul
Northeast Collector
John Albanese
Specimen 12
J.W. Haseltine
R. Coulton Davis
J.W. Haseltine
George M. Klein
R. Coulton Davis
John N. Hale
Hale Family
H.P. Graves
Ben H. Koenig
Samuel W. Wolfson
Norton Simon
James H.T. McConnell Jr.
Specimen 13
Henry R. Linderman
James Ten Eyck
James Ten Eyck Estate
Lammot du Pont
Lammot du Pont Family
Willis du Pont (stolen 1967, recovered 1982)
ANA, on loan
Smithsonian Institution
Specimen 14
W. Julius Driefus
Isaac Rosenthal
Col. James W. Ellsworth
Wayte Raymond and John Work Garrett
Farran Zerbe
Chase Manhattan Bank
American Numismatic Society
Specimen 15
William Idler
H.O. Granberg
William C. Atwater
William C. Atwater Family
Will W. Neil
Abe Kosoff
Edwin Hydeman
World-Wide Coin Co.
Bowers and Ruddy Galleries
Mark Blackburn
Continental Coin Galleries
Dr. Jerry Buss
Aubrey Bebee
American Numismatic Association

High prices of rare coins

Since the publication of the *Coin World Almanac Millennium Edition* in 2000, much has changed in the values of rare U.S. coins. That edition noted that five-figure bids had become commonplace; in 2011 the same can be said of six-figure bids. By 2000 only four coins had reached the seven-figure mark. Between 2000 and 2011 an average of almost four seven-figure coins changed hands at auction per year.

Some coin series have seen rapid value rises because of the very important collections making their way to the auction block. In early American coinage and other specialty fields, the appearance of items from the John J. Ford Jr. Collection provided for some a once-in-a-lifetime chance to acquire rarities. Much of the Ford collection was originally from the F.C.C. Boyd Collection and many of the items from that collection were from collections that were formed in the late 19th and early 20th centuries.

The large cents series saw important collections come on the market in the last decade. Among the many sales of these big coppers were three very significant sales: the collections of Walter Husak, Dan Holmes, and R.E. "Ted" Naftzger Jr. The Holmes sales contained all but two of the many die varieties of these coins issued from 1793 until 1857.

The Holmes sales gave the collecting public the first million dollar one-cent piece. The Sheldon 79 1795 Liberty Cap, Reeded Edge cent grading only Very Good 10 but the finest known, sold for $1,265,000 in September 2009. The second highest price, for the much more famous 1799 Sheldon 189

cent in Mint State 62, finest known, missed the million mark by $22,500 when it sold for $977,500.

The highest price for a coin sold at public auction came near the beginning of the decade—July of 2002. The single-lot auction featured what the government has proclaimed to be the only 1933 Saint-Gaudens gold $20 double eagle that can be owned by an individual. It sold for $7,590,020. The final $20 in the price represents the face value of the coin, which after the coin was hammered was paid to the U.S. government to "monetize" the coin. Until then the government claimed that no 1933 double eagle had ever been legally released to the public.

The following section lists the 25 top prices for coins by denomination or broad category. In the 2000 edition of the *Almanac* this section listed 600 prices, and 278 or 46 percent were at the six-figure level. In the listing that begins below, 505 of the 600 prices listed are six-figure prices, or 84 percent. Given that two of the categories contain no six-figure prices, it is evident that six-figure prices for rare and high-grade numismatic examples are now commonplace.

The records listed are as reported in official auction prices realized by the individual firms. Later auctions almost certainly include the buyer's fees; earlier sales may not. The listing is as complete as possible, but the sheer volume of coin sales ensures that some sales may be missing. Additions are welcome. Write to *Coin World*, P.O. Box 150, Sidney, OH 45365-0150 or P. Scott Rubin at P.O. Box 6885, Lawrenceville, NJ 08648.

Half Cents

	Price	Coin	Grade	Sale	Lot
1	$506,000.00	1796 No Pole	MS-65 red-brown	1996 Bowers & Merena/Stack's Eliasberg Sale	#407
2	$345,000.00	1796 No Pole	Fine 15+	2008 Goldbergs Rouse Sale	#31
3	$287,500.00	1796 No Pole	MS-64	1999 Stack's Whitney Sale	#1705
4	$253,000.00	1796 With Pole	MS-63 brown	2008 Stack's 7/27 Sale	#1039
5	$218,500.00	1796 With Pole	MS-61 brown	2007 Stack's 8/5 Sale	#226
6	$195,500.00	1793	AU-58	2007 Stack's 1/16 Americana Sale	#5427
7	$195,500.00	1796 With Pole	MS-66	1999 Stack's Whitney Sale	#1706
8	$187,000.00	1796 With Pole	MS-66	1997 Spink America 12/2 Sale	#347
9	$176,000.00	1796 With Pole	Unc.	1997 Spink America 6/3 Sale	#390
10	$165,000.00	1796 With Pole	Unc.	1998 Sotheby's 1/15 Sale	#4
11	$143,750.00	1796 With Pole	MS-66	1999 Stack's Whitney Sale	#1707
12	$138,000.00	1796 With Pole	AU-55	2008 Heritage Ellsworth Sale	#1647
13	$132,250.00	1796 With Pole	MS-65	2000 Stack's 65th Anniversary Sale	#23
14	$130,000.00	1793	MS-64	1990 Auction '90 Sale	#1002
15	$126,500.00	1796 No Pole	Fine 12	2010 Stack's 8/8 Sale	#189
16	$126,500.00	1793	MS-61	2009 Heritage 1/8 Platinum Night 1 Sale	#3567
17	$120,750.00	1793	MS-64	2005 Heritage 1/12 Platinum Night Sale	#30088
18	$115,000.00	1797 1 above 1	MS-65	2006 Heritage 8/14 Platinum Night Sale	#5019
19	$109,250.00	1793	MS-64	2009 Heritage 4/30 Sale	#2016
20	$103,500.00	1794 C-9	MS-65 brown	2009 Heritage 4/30 Sale	#2018
21	$103,500.00	1794 C-9	MS-65 brown	2008 Heritage 1/10 Sale	#2655

Half Cents (continued)

	Price	Coin	Grade	Sale	Lot
22	$103,500.00	1796 With Pole	AU-55	2009 Heritage 4/30 Platinum Night Sale	#2021
23	$86,250.00	1794 C-2	MS-63 brown	2009 Heritage 1/8 Platinum Night 1 Sale	#3568
24	$80,500.00	1831 Original	Proof 58	2006 Heritage 1/24 Sale	#19114
25	$78,100.00	1852 Large Berries	Proof 53	1996 Bowers & Merena/Stack's Eliasberg Sale	#476

Large Cents

	Price	Coin	Grade	Sale	Lot
1	$1,265,000.00	1795 Reeded Edge S-79	VG-10	2009 Goldbergs Holmes Sale	#128
2	$977,500.00	1799 S-189	MS-62 brown	2009 Goldbergs Holmes Sale	#352
3	$862,500.00	1793 Strawberry Leaf NC-3	Fine 12	2009 Stack's 1/5 Sale	#51
4	$690,000.00	1796 Liberty Cap S-84	MS-66 red-brown	2008 Goldbergs Naftzger Sale	#171
5	$661,250.00	1804 S-266c	MS-63 brown	2009 Goldbergs Holmes Sale	#531
6	$632,500.00	1793 Liberty Cap S-13	AU-55	2008 Heritage Husak Sale	#2014
7	$632,500.00	1794 Starred Reverse S-48	AU-50	2008 Heritage Husak Sale	#2050
8	$506,000.00	1794 Liberty Cap S-14	AU-53	2009 Goldbergs Holmes Sale	#24
9	$488,750.00	1794 Head of 95 S-67	MS-67 red-brown	2008 Heritage Husak Sale	#2069
10	$431,250.00	1795 Reeded Edge S-79	Good 5	2011 Heritage 1/11 Platinum Night Sale	#5422
11	$431,250.00	1793 Chain S-2	MS-65 brown	2005 Stack's 1/10 Sale	#69
12	$414,000.00	1793 Strawberry Leaf NC-3	Fine 12	2004 American Numismatic Rarities 11/30 Sale	#130
13	$402,500.00	1793 Chain S-2	MS-63 brown	2009 Goldbergs Holmes Sale	#3
14	$402,500.00	1795 Reeded Edge S-79	Good 4	2008 Bowers & Merena 11/19 Sale	#1143
15	$391,000.00	1793 Chain AMERICA S-4	MS-65 brown	2004 Stack's 7/23 Sale	#69
16	$368,000.00	1793 AMERI. S-1	AU-58	2009 Goldbergs Holmes Sale	#1
17	$368,000.00	1799/8 S-188	EF-45	2009 Goldbergs Holmes Sale	#349
18	$333,500.00	1802 S-234	MS-67 red-brown	2009 Goldbergs Holmes Sale	#455
19	$299,000.00	1823 N-2	MS-66 brown	2009 Goldbergs Naftzger Sale	#140
20	$276,000.00	1793 Wreath S-11c	MS-64 brown	2008 Heritage FUN Sale	#2666
21	$276,000.00	1794 S-59	MS-66 red-brown	2009 Goldbergs Holmes Sale	#95
22	$264,500.00	1793 Strawberry Leaf NC-2	Fair 2	2009 Goldbergs Holmes Sale	#7
23	$264,500.00	1793 Wreath S-5	MS-65 brown	2009 Goldbergs Holmes Sale	#9
24	$264,500.00	1839/6 N-1	MS-65 brown	2009 Goldbergs Naftzger Sale	#437
25	$253,000.00	1793 Chain S-3	MS-62 brown	2008 Heritage Husak Sale	#2002

Small Cents

	Price	Coin	Grade	Sale	Lot
1	$373,750.00	1944-S steel planchet	MS-66	2008 Heritage 7/31 Platinum Night Sale	#1560
2	$253,000.00	1905 struck on $2.50 planchet	MS-64	2010 Heritage 1/6 Platinum Night Sale	#2433
3	$218,500.00	1943 bronze planchet	AU-58	2010 Heritage 1/6 Platinum Night Sale	#2444
4	$212,750.00	1943-D bronze planchet	MS-64 brown	2003 Goldbergs Benson III Sale	#149
5	$207,000.00	1943-S bronze planchet	VF-35	2010 Heritage 2/4 Sale	#178
6	$172,500.00	1856	MS-66	2004 Heritage FUN Sale	#2010
7	$149,500.00	1877	MS-66 red	2009 Heritage 7/31 Platinum Night Sale	#2078
8	$149,500.00	1877	MS-66 red	2007 Heritage 8/9 Platinum Night Sale	#1567
9	$149,500.00	1926-S	MS-65 red	2006 Heritage 1/5 Platinum Night Sale	# 3097
10	$138,000.00	1864 L	Proof 64 red	2002 Heritage FUN Sale	#5202
11	$126,500.00	1872	MS-66 red	2007 Heritage 8/9 Platinum Night Sale	#1565
12	$126,500.00	1914	Proof 68 red	2008 Heritage 4/17 Platinum Night Sale	#2249
13	$126,500.00	1969-S Doubled Die	MS-64 red	2008 Heritage 1/10 Platinum Night Sale	#2718
14	$118,450.00	1864 L	Proof 64 red	2004 Heritage FUN Sale	#4375
15	$115,000.00	1877	MS-66 red	2006 Heritage 8/14 Platinum Night Sale	#5064
16	$115,000.00	1944-D steel planchet	MS-63	2007 Heritage 8/9 Platinum Night Sale	#1583
17	$115,000.00	1943-S bronze planchet	MS-61 brown	2000 Goldbergs Kardatzke I Sale	#257
18	$109,250.00	1864 L	Proof 64 red	2008 Heritage 7/31 Platinum Night Sale	#1544

Small Cents (continued)

	Price	Coin	Grade	Sale	Lot
19	$106,375.00	1926-S	MS-65 red	2006 Heritage FUN Sale	#189
20	$105,800.00	1914-S	MS-66 red	2006 Bowers & Merena ANA Sale	#2028
21	$105,800.00	1944-D steel planchet	MS-62	2006 Bowers & Merena 2/6 Rarities Sale	#41
22	$103,500.00	1856	MS-66	2003 Heritage FUN Sale	#4401
23	$103,500.00	1864 L	Proof 64 red	2007 Heritage 1/3 Platinum Night Sale	#802
24	$97,750.00	1943 bronze planchet	MS-61 brown	2003 Goldbergs Benson III Sale	#148
25	$96,000.00	1864 L	Proof 66 red-brown	1999 Bowers & Merena ANA Sale	#1031

5-cent coins

	Price	Coin	Grade	Sale	Lot
1	$3,737,500.00	1913 Liberty Head	Proof 64	2010 Heritage 1/6 Platinum Night Sale	#2455
2	$1,840,000.00	1913 Liberty Head	Proof 66	2001 Superior 3/8 Sale	#728
3	$1,485,000.00	1913 Liberty Head	Proof 66	1996 Bowers & Merena/Stack's Eliasberg Sale	#807
4	$962,500.00	1913 Liberty Head	Proof	1993 Stack's Hawn Sale	#245
5	$385,000.00	1913 Liberty Head	Proof 63	1985 Superior Buss Sale	#366
6	$350,750.00	1918/7-D	MS-65	2006 Bowers & Merena 8/16 ANA Sale	#512
7	$322,000.00	1926-S	MS-66	2008 Bowers & Merena 4/15 Sale	#218
8	$316,250.00	1916 Doubled Die	MS-64	2007 Bowers & Merena 11/15 Baltimore Sale	#683
9	$276,000.00	1916 Doubled Die	MS-64	2008 Bowers & Merena 4/15 Rarities Sale	#196
10	$264,500.00	1916 Doubled Die	MS-64	2005 Heritage 9/21 Long Beach Sale	#1853
11	$264,500.00	1918/7-D	MS-65	2010 Heritage 1/6 Platinum Night Sale	#2458
12	$253,000.00	1918/7-D	MS-65	2009 Heritage 4/29 Platinum Night Sale	#2136
13	$195,500.00	1916 Doubled Die	MS-64	2009 Heritage 1/8 Platinum Night Sale	#3640
14	$184,000.00	1916 Doubled Die	MS-64	2009 Heritage 4/29 Platinum Night Sale	#2131
15	$163,000.00	1916 Doubled Die	MS-62	2007 Goldbergs 9/23 Pre-Long Beach Sale	#2531
16	$161,000.00	1918/7-D	MS-64	2007 Stack's 11/13 Sale	#391
17	$155,250.00	1918/7-D	MS-64	2008 Bowers & Merena 7/26 Rarities Sale	#384
18	$155,250.00	1918/7-D	MS-65	2002 Heritage Central States Sale	#5374
19	$138,000.00	1917-S	MS-67	2008 Heritage 7/31 Platinum Night Sale	#1568
20	$138,000.00	1920-D	MS-67*	2008 Bowers & Merena 11/22 Baltimore Sale	#1704
21	$132,250.00	1867 Rays	Proof 66 cameo	2004 Heritage 1/29 Long Beach Sale	#5373
22	$132,250.00	1926-S	MS-63	2006 Bowers & Merena 11/9 Baltimore Sale	#760
23	$126,500.00	1918/7-D	MS-64	2007 Heritage 1/3 Platinum Night Sale	#822
24	$126,500.00	1916 Doubled Die	MS-62	2006 American Numismatic Rarities 8/11 Sale	#216
25	$125,350.00	1918-S	MS-66	2008 Bowers & Merena 4/15 Sale	#205

Half Dimes

	Price	Coin	Grade	Sale	Lot
1	$661,250.00	1870-S	MS-63	2004 Bowers & Merena Gray Sale	#2065
2	$345,000.00	1796/5	MS-66	2008 Heritage 1/10 Platinum Night Sale	#2743
3	$299,000.00	1802	EF-45	2006 Heritage 4/26 Sale	#1868
4	$253,000.00	1870-S	Unc.	1986 Auction '86 Sale	#1053
5	$195,500.00	1802	EF-45	2009 Heritage 4/30 Sale	#2186
6	$184,000.00	1795 V-6	MS-67	2007 Stack's Orlando Sale	#352
7	$176,000.00	1870-S	AU-55	1985 Bowers & Merena 9/9 Sale	#174
8	$172,500.00	1796/5	MS-66	2007 Heritage 1/3 Platinum Night I Sale	#842
9	$143,750.00	1794	MS-67	2006 Superior 5/28 Sale	#285
10	$138,000.00	1795	MS-67 prooflike	2005 Heritage 11/3 Sale	#2057
11	$132,250.00	1794	MS-67	2010 Bowers & Merena 8/7 Sale	#1003
12	$126,500.00	1795 V-8	MS-67*	2006 Heritage 8/16 Sale	#5106
13	$115,000.00	1802	VF-30	2008 Stack's 2/26 Sale	#1441
14	$112,500.00	1801 V-1	MS-67	1998 Bowers & Merena 8/3 Sale	#88
15	$104,500.00	1797 15 Stars	Gem Unc.	1997 Akers Pittman I Sale	#426

Half Dimes (continued)

	Price	Coin	Grade	Sale	Lot
16	$97,750.00	1829	Proof 67	2007 Goldbergs September Pre-Long Beach Sale	#2563
17	$94,875.00	1795 V-6	MS-67	2003 Heritage 7/26 Sale	#6408
18	$92,000.00	1842	Proof 68 Ultra Cameo	2008 Heritage Central States Sale	#2378
19	$92,000.00	1845	Proof 68	2008 Heritage FUN Sale	#3028
20	$89,125.00	1797 15 Stars	MS-67	1999 Superior February Pre-Long Beach Sale	#552
21	$86,250.00	1803 Small 8	MS-61	2009 Heritage 4/30 Sale	#2187
22	$86,250.00	1794	Specimen 65	2009 Heritage 4/30 Sale	#2176
23	$86,250.00	1795	MS-67 prooflike	2010 Heritage 1/7 Sale	#2464
24	$83,950.00	1794 V-3	MS-66	2004 Heritage FUN Sale	#6033
25	$80,500.00	1800 LIBERTY V-2	MS-65	2008 Heritage 1/10 Platinum Night Sale	#2745

Dimes

	Price	Coin	Grade	Sale	Lot
1	$1,552,500.00	1894-S	Proof 64	2007 Stack's 10/16 Americana Sale	#4921
2	$1,322,500.00	1894-S	Proof 66	2005 David Lawrence Richmond III Sale	#1295
3	$1,035,000.00	1894-S	Proof 65	2005 Heritage 1/12 Platinum Night Sale	#30164
4	$891,250.00	1873-CC No Arrows	MS-65	2004 Bowers & Merena Gray Sale	#2149
5	$632,500.00	1804 14 Star Reverse JR-2	NGC AU-58	2008 Heritage Price Sale	#1443
6	$632,500.00	1873-CC No Arrows	MS-64	1999 Heritage 4/22 Central States Sale	#5928
7	$550,000.00	1873-CC No Arrows	MS-65	1996 Bowers & Merena/Stack's Eliasberg Sale	#1198
8	$451,000.00	1894-S	Proof 64	1996 Bowers & Merena/Stack's Eliasberg Sale	#1250
9	$431,250.00	1894-S	Proof	2000 Stack's 65th Anniversary Sale	#565
10	$402,500.00	1797 13 Stars JR-2	NGC MS-65	2008 Heritage Price Sale	#1416
11	$322,000.00	1803 JR-3	MS-64	2008 Heritage Price Sale	#1438
12	$299,000.00	1796	MS-67	2008 Heritage Price Sale	#1411
13	$275,000.00	1894-S	Proof	1990 Stack's James A. Stack Sr. Sale	#206
14	$253,000.00	1796	MS-67*	2009 Heritage 4/29 Platinum Night Sale	#2208
15	$253,000.00	1798 Small 8	MS-66	2008 Heritage Price Sale	#1419
16	$230,000.00	1871-CC	MS-65	2005 Bowers & Merena 3/10 Baltimore Sale	#443
17	$230,000.00	1873-CC With Arrows	MS-65	2005 Bowers & Merena 3/10 Baltimore Sale	#445
18	$218,500.00	1919-D	MS-66 full bands	2000 Heritage 8/6 Philadelphia Sale	#6988
19	$195,500.00	1916-D	MS-67 full bands	2010 Heritage ANA Sale	#4490
20	$184,000.00	1804 14 Star Reverse	AU-58	2007 Heritage 8/9 Platinum Night Sale	#1622
21	$165,000.00	1894-S	MS-64	1992 Superior 8/10 Orlando Sale	#104
22	$162,150.00	1874-CC	MS-63	2003 Superior 9/14 Pre-Long Beach Sale	#1490
23	$161,000.00	1796	Specimen Proof	1999 Stack's Walter Sale	#1763
24	$161,000.00	1804 14 Star Reverse	AU-53	2007 Heritage 1/3 Platinum Night Sale	#861
25	$161,000.00	1838 No Drapery	Proof 67 cameo	2008 Heritage 1/10 Platinum Night FUN Sale	#3017

Twenty Cents

	Price	Coin	Grade	Sale	Lot
1	$460,000.00	1876-CC	MS-66	2009 Heritage 4/29 Platinum Night Sale	#2299
2	$350,750.00	1876-CC	MS-64	2007 Stack's 72nd Anniversary Sale	#4941
3	$264,500.00	1876-CC	MS-62	2008 Superior 9/15 Pre-Long Beach Sale	#172
4	$207,000.00	1876-CC	AU-58	2009 Bowers & Merena 6/11 Baltimore Sale	#757
5	$161,000.00	1876-CC	MS-66	2001 Superior ANA National Money Sale	#237
6	$158,125.00	1876-CC	MS-64	2005 David Lawrence Richmond III Sale	#1392
7	$150,600.00	1876-CC	MS-64	2003 Stack's 68th Anniversary Sale	#2599
8	$148,500.00	1876-CC	MS-65	1997 Bowers & Merena/Stack's Eliasberg II Sale	#1353
9	$138,000.00	1876-CC	MS-66	2001 Heritage 10/3 Sale	#6222
10	$115,000.00	1876-CC	Unc.	2002 Stack's ANA National Money Sale	#352
11	$99,000.00	1876-CC	Choice Unc.	1995 Stack's James A. Stack Sr. Sale	#150
12	$85,250.00	1876-CC	MS-65	1988 Auction '88 Sale	#108

Twenty Cents (continued)

	Price	Coin	Grade	Sale	Lot
13	$85,000.00	1876-CC	AU-55	1980 Auction '80 Sale	#110
14	$80,500.00	1875	MS-67	2009 Heritage 4/29 Platinum Night Sale	#2296
15	$80,300.00	1876-CC	MS-64	1994 Bowers & Merena 9/12 Sale	#1181
16	$78,100.00	1876-CC	MS-64	1991 Superior 2/3 Sale	#1291
17	$69,300.00	1876-CC	MS-64 to -65	1987 Bowers & Merena Norweb I Sale	#691
18	$69,000.00	1876-CC	MS-64	2000 Heritage FUN Sale	#5177
19	$66,125.00	1875-S	MS-68	2005 Heritage 11/3 Platinum Night Sale	#2093
20	$66,000.00	1876-CC	Unc.	1983 Auction '83 Sale	#625
21	$66,000.00	1876-CC	MS-65	1984 Bowers & Merena Emery Sale	#492
22	$63,500.00	1876-CC	Unc.	1976 Carlson Sale	#369
23	$63,250.00	1876-CC	Unc.	1988 Stack's 400th Sale	#1405
24	$63,250.00	1875-CC	MS-66	2008 Heritage ANA Platinum Night Sale	#1624
25	$57,750.00	1876-CC	Unc.	1985 Auction '85 Sale	#1653

Quarter dollars

	Price	Coin	Grade	Sale	Lot
1	$550,000.00	1901-S	MS-68	1990 Superior Father Flanagan's Sale	#3701
2	$517,500.00	1838 No Drapery	Proof 65	2008 Heritage Central States Sale	#2375
3	$460,000.00	1850	Proof 68	2008 Heritage Platinum Night FUN Sale	#3035
4	$431,250.00	1873-CC No Arrows	MS-63	2009 Stack's 1/5 Orlando Sale	#338
5	$402,500.00	1805 B-2	MS-66	2008 Heritage Platinum Night FUN Sale	#2775
6	$345,000.00	1804	MS-65	2011 Heritage Platinum Night FUN Sale	#5507
7	$345,000.00	1841	Proof 66	2008 Heritage Platinum Night FUN Sale	#3020
8	$327,750.00	1901-S	MS-68	2010 Bowers & Merena 3/4 Baltimore Sale	#737
9	$322,000.00	1796	MS-65	2010 Heritage 8/11 Platinum Night Sale	#3107
10	$310,500.00	1804	MS-65	2008 Heritage Central States Sale	#2274
11	$310,000.00	1873-CC No Arrows	Unc.	1990 Auction '90 Sale	#659
12	$299,000.00	1841	Proof 66	2009 Heritage Platinum Night FUN Sale	#3762
13	$299,000.00	1844	Proof 66	2009 Heritage Platinum Night FUN Sale	#3764
14	$286,000.00	1873-CC No Arrows	MS-65	1991 Superior 8/11 Chicago Sale	#475
15	$276,000.00	1844	Proof 66	2009 Heritage 7/31 Platinum Night Sale	#1086
16	$276,000.00	1853 Arrows and Rays	Proof 66 cameo	2007 Heritage Platinum Night ANA Sale	#1785
17	$253,000.00	1804	MS-64	2008 Stack's SS New York Sale	#1458
18	$230,000.00	1796	MS-65	2004 American Numismatic Rarities Jung Sale	#46
19	$230,000.00	1853 Arrows and Rays	Proof 66 cameo	2009 Heritage Platinum Night FUN Sale	#3766
20	$218,500.00	1820 B-1	Proof 67	2005 Heritage 9/21 Long Beach Sale	#2639
21	$218,500.00	1831 Large Letters	Proof 66 cameo	2009 Heritage Platinum Night FUN Sale	#3736
22	$209,000.00	1873-CC No Arrows	MS-64	1998 Superior Rasmussen Sale	#2038
23	$207,000.00	1841	Proof 66	2009 Heritage 7/31 Platinum Night Sale	#1084
24	$205,000.00	1873-CC No Arrows	MS-65	1980 New England Met New York Sale	#519
25	$201,250.00	1873-CC No Arrows	MS-63	2005 David Lawrence Richmond III Sale	#1480

Half dollars

	Price	Coin	Grade	Sale	Lot
1	$1,380,000.00	1797 O-101a	MS-66	2008 Stack's SS New York Sale	#4261
2	$966,000.00	1797 O-101a	MS-66	2004 American Numismatic Rarities 3/9 Classics Sale	#76
3	$632,500.00	1838-O	Proof 63	2008 Heritage 2/14 Long Beach Sale	#600
4	$632,500.00	1838-O	Proof 64	2005 Heritage 6/2 Long Beach Sale	#6244
5	$517,000.00	1797 O-102a	Unc.	1995 Stack's Numisma '95 Sale	#1251
6	$460,000.00	1796 16 Stars O-102	Specimen 66	1999 Stack's Whitney Sale	#1778
7	$414,000.00	1796 16 Stars O-102	MS-64	2006 Goldbergs 5/28 Pre-Long Beach Sale	#2908
8	$373,750.00	1796 15 Stars O-101	MS-63	2008 Heritage 2/14 Long Beach Sale	#528
9	$373,750.00	1839-O	Proof 65	2008 Goldbergs 2/10 Pre-Long Beach Sale	#2177

Half Dollars (continued)

	Price	Coin	Grade	Sale	Lot
10	$368,000.00	1853-O No Arrows	Very Fine	2006 Stack's Byers Sale	#1160
11	$356,500.00	1817/4 O-102a	AU-50	2009 Stack's SS New York Sale	#542
12	$333,500.00	1817/4	AU-50	2004 David Lawrence Richmond Part II Sale	#1388
13	$330,000.00	1796 16 Stars	Unc.	1995 Stack's Numisma '95 Sale	#1250
14	$310,500.00	1796 15 Stars	MS-64	2005 American Numismatic Rarities Lee & Park Sale	#388
15	$310,500.00	1796 15 Stars	MS-63	2006 Heritage Platinum Night Denver Sale	#5222
16	$310,500.00	1817/ 4	AU-50	2006 Stack's Byers Sale	#1031
17	$310,500.00	1853-O No Arrows	VF-35	2004 Bowers & Merena Gray Sale	#2332
18	$288,500.00	1794	MS-63	1999 Bowers & Merena 1/5 Rarities Sale	#1
19	$287,000.00	1794 O-105	AU-58	2007 Stack's 11/13 Sale	#2003
20	$276,000.00	1796 16 Stars	MS-64	2004 American Numismatic Rarities 3/9 Classics Sale	#575
21	$276,000.00	1838-O	Proof 45	2008 Heritage 4/17 Platinum Night Sale	#2310
22	$270,250.00	1919-D	MS-66	2004 Heritage 11/4 Palm Beach Sale	#6903
23	$253,000.00	1797	AU-58	2010 Heritage 8/11 Platinum Night Sale	#3137
24	$253,000.00	1919-D	MS-66	2009 Heritage 4//29 Platinum Night Sale	#2504
25	$253,000.00	1838-O	EF	2006 Stack's Byers Sale	#1097

Silver Dollars

	Price	Coin	Grade	Sale	Lot
1	$4,140,000.00	1804 Class I	Proof 68	1999 Bowers & Merena Childs Sale	#458
2	$3,737,500.00	1804 Class I	Proof 62	2008 Heritage Queller Family Sale	#2089
3	$2,300,000.00	1804 Class III	Proof 58	2009 Heritage 4/29 Platinum Night Sale	#2567
4	$1,840,000.00	1804 Class I	Proof 64	2000 Stack's 65th Anniversary Sale	#1167
5	$1,815,000.00	1804 Class I	Proof 63	1997 Bowers & Merena/Stack's Eliasberg Sale	#2199
6	$1,265,000.00	1795 Flowing Hair B-7	Very Choice to Gem Unc.	2005 C.E. Bullowa 12/4 Sale	#393
7	$1,207,500.00	1794	MS-64	2010 Bowers & Merena Boston Rarities 8/7 Sale	#1005
8	$1,207,500.00	1866 No Motto	Proof 63	2004 American Numismatic Rarities 1/10 Classics Sale	#689
9	$1,207,500.00	1804 Class III	Proof 58	2003 Bowers & Merena ANA Sale	#2026
10	$1,150,000.00	1794	MS-64	2005 American Numismatic Rarities Cardinal Sale	#5
11	$1,092,500.00	1870-S	Unc.	2003 Stack's Rodolf Sale	#2136
12	$990,000.00	1804 Class I	Proof	1989 Auction '89 Sale	#247
13	$920,000.00	1802 restrike	Proof 65 cameo	2008 Heritage Queller Family Sale	#2088
14	$874,000.00	1804 Class III	Proof 58	2001 Bowers & Merena Flannagan Sale	#4303
15	$805,000.00	1870-S	EF-40	2008 Heritage Queller Family Sale	#2189
16	$747,500.00	1794	MS-61	2005 Heritage 6/2 Long Beach Sale	#6571
17	$705,698.00	1870-S	VF-25	2008 Bowers & Merena 2/28 Baltimore Sale	#2035
18	$672,750.00	1803 restrike	Proof 66	2007 Bowers & Merena 2/10 Pre-Long Beach Sale	#429
19	$632,500.00	1870-S	EF-40	2010 Bowers & Merena 8/7 Boston Rarities Sale	#1089
20	$577,500.00	1794	Unc.	1995 Stack's Numisma '95 Sale	#1315
21	$575,000.00	1895-O	MS-67	2005 Heritage 11/3 Palm Beach Platinum Night Sale	#2324
22	$552,000.00	1870-S	VF-20	2007 Stack's 72nd Anniversary Sale	#5294
23	$531,875.00	1889-CC	MS-68	2009 Heritage Platinum Night FUN Sale	#4991
24	$529,000.00	1889-CC	MS-68	2001 Bowers & Merena 1/3 Rarities Sale	#336
25	$506,000.00	1794	MS-65	1991 Superior 5/27 Sale	#699

Trade Dollars

	Price	Coin	Grade	Sale	Lot
1	$1,006,250.00	1885	Proof 62	2004 David Lawrence Richmond Part II Sale	#1569
2	$920,000.00	1885	Proof 61	2003 Stack's Rodolf Sale	#2175
3	$907,500.00	1885	Proof 65	1997 Bowers & Merena/Stack's Eliasberg Sale	#2354
4	$603,750.00	1884	Proof 65	2005 Heritage 11/3 Platinum Night Sale	#2281
5	$510,600.00	1884	Proof 67	2000 Goldbergs California Sale	#1784
6	$396,000.00	1884	Proof 66	1997 Bowers & Merena/Stack's Eliasberg Sale	#2353

Trade Dollars (continued)

	Price	Coin	Grade	Sale	Lot
7	$310,500.00	1884	Proof 64 cameo	2004 Bowers & Merena 5/4 Rarities Sale	#328
8	$310,500.00	1884	Proof 64	2004 David Lawrence Richmond Part II Sale	#1568
9	$264,500.00	1884	Proof 65	2000 Superior 10/1 Pre-Long Beach Sale	#3576
10	$258,750.00	1884	Proof 63	2003 Stack's Rodolf Sale	#2174
11	$242,000.00	1885	Proof 61	1993 Superior Worrell Sale	#1325
12	$176,000.00	1884	Proof	1992 Stack's Starr Sale	#844
13	$138,000.00	1884	Proof 63	2002 Heritage Central States Sale	#4131
14	$138,000.00	1884	Proof 63	2003 Bowers & Merena 1/7 Rarities Sale	#569
15	$126,500.00	1884	Proof	2002 Stack's ANA National Money Show Sale	#795
16	$121,000.00	1885	Proof 60-63	1988 Bowers & Merena Norweb Part II Sale	#1848
17	$110,000.00	1885	Proof	1980 Auction '80 Sale	#1626
18	$110,000.00	1885	Proof	1984 Stack's Carter Sale	#441
19	$104,500.00	1885	Proof	1989 Stack's L.R. French Jr. Sale	#202
20	$96,500.00	1885	Proof	1984 Auction '84 Sale	#1810
21	$96,500.00	1885	Proof 65	1987 Superior 2/8 Sale	#1446B
22	$90,750.00	1885	Proof 63	1984 Auction '84 Sale	#192
23	$77,000.00	1884	Proof	1989 Auction '89 Sale	#327
24	$77,000.00	1884	Proof 63	1991 Superior 5/27 Sale	#987
25	$75,000.00	1884	Proof 64	1990 Auction '90 Sale	#1163

Gold Dollars

	Price	Coin	Grade	Sale	Lot
1	$690,000.00	1849-C Open Wreath	MS-63	2004 David Lawrence Richmond I Sale	#1005
2	$373,750.00	1855	Proof 66	2008 Heritage 1/10 Platinum Night Sale	#3051
3	$316,250.00	1855	Proof 66	2007 Heritage 1/3 Platinum Night Sale	#3100
4	$287,500.00	1855	Proof 65	2005 Heritage 1/12 Platinum Night Sale	#30023
5	$218,500.00	1849-C Open Wreath	EF-45	2010 Heritage 2/4 Sale	#1359
6	$176,000.00	1854 Coronet	Proof 65	1997 Akers Pittman I Sale	#864
7	$149,500.00	1855-D	MS-64	2007 Goldbergs 2/11 Pre-Long Beach Sale	#2097
8	$149,500.00	1861-D	MS-65	2008 Heritage 1/10 Platinum Night Sale	#3050
9	$149,500.00	1854 Coronet	MS-68	2008 Heritage 2/14 Long Beach Sale	
10	$143,750.00	1855-D	MS-64	2009 Stack's Orlando Sale	#866
11	$138,000.00	1861-D	MS-65	2006 Heritage Atlanta ANA Sale	#1493
12	$132,250.00	1855-D	MS-64	2006 Heritage Atlanta ANA Sale	#1487
13	$132,000.00	1855 Coronet	Proof 65	1993 Superior 1/31 sale	#1262
14	$126,500.00	1854 Coronet	MS-68	2002 Bowers & Merena 7/31 Rarities Sale	#669
15	$121,000.00	1855	Proof 66	1997 Akers Pittman I Sale	#866
16	$115,000.00	1855-D	MS-64+	2010 Bowers & Merena Boston Rarities Sale	#1441
17	$109,250.00	1855-D	MS-64	2006 Heritage 1/5 Platinum Night Sale 3396	
18	$109,250.00	1875	MS-66	2010 Heritage 2/4 Sale	#1427
19	$97,750.00	1855	MS-67	2007 Heritage 11/29 Sale	#61493
20	$97,750.00	1849-C Open Wreath	Fine 15	2003 Heritage FUN Sale	#4607
21	$92,000.00	1852	MS-69	2006 Heritage 2/9 Long Beach Sale	#2516
22	$92,000.00	1854 Indian, Small Head	MS-67	2003 American Numismatic Rarities 725 Classics Sale	#624
23	$92,000.00	1855-D	MS-62	1999 Bowers & Merena Bass II Sale	#102
24	$90,000.00	1855	MS-67	2005 Heritage 1/12 Platinum Night Sale	#30632
25	$90,000.00	1849-C Open Wreath	EF	1979 Auction '79 Sale	#749

Quarter Eagles

	Price	Coin	Grade	Sale	Lot
1	$1,725,000.00	1796 No Stars	MS-65	2008 Heritage 1/10 Platinum Night Sale	#3058
2	$1,380,000.00	1796 No Stars	MS-65	2005 American Numismatic Rarities Gentleman's Sale	#1002

Quarter Eagles (continued)

	Price	Coin	Grade	Sale	Lot
3	$1,006,250.00	1796 Stars BD-3	MS-65	2008 Heritage 1/10 Platinum Night Sale	#3059
4	$862,500.00	1796 Stars BD-3	MS-65	2007 Heritage 1/4 Platinum Night II Sale	#3382
5	$605,000.00	1796 No Stars	Unc.	1995 Stack's Numisma'95 Sale	#1498
6	$517,500.00	1808 BD-1	MS-63	2008 Stack's 11/18 Sale	#4176
7	$488,750.00	1796 No Stars BD-2	MS-62	2008 Stack's SS New York Sale	#2324
8	$425,500.00	1808 BD-1	MS-63	2007 Stack's Brooklyn Sale	#1441
9	$402,500.00	1848 CAL.	MS-68	2006 Heritage 1/5 Platinum Night Sale	#3419
10	$345,000.00	1796 No Stars	MS-62	2004 American Numismatic Rarities 7/23 Jung Sale	#82
11	$345,000.00	1848 CAL.	MS-68	2008 Heritage 1/10 Platinum Night Sale	#3091
12	$345,000.00	1854-S	EF-45	2007 Heritage Charlotte National Money Sale	#4325
13	$322,000.00	1796 No Stars	MS-61	2006 Heritage 8/14 Platinum Night Sale	#5417
14	$322,000.00	1804 13 Star Reverse	AU-55	2008 Heritage Price Sale	#1459
15	$322,000.00	1804 13 Star Reverse	AU-58	2009 Heritage 7/31 Platinum Night Sale	#1209
16	$322,000.00	1808	MS-63	2008 Heritage 1/10 Platinum Night Sale	#3069
17	$322,000.00	1808	MS-63	2004 American Numismatic Rarities Jung Sale	#84
18	$322,000.00	1848 CAL.	MS-68	2006 American Numismatic Rarities 8/11 Sale	#1201
19	$316,250.00	1829	MS-67	2006 Heritage 8/14 Platinum Night Sale	#5423
20	$299,000.00	1796 No Stars	Unc.	1999 Stack's Whitney Sale	#1787
21	$291,500.00	1798	MS-65	1990 Auction '90 Sale	#664
22	$287,500.00	1796 No Stars	MS-63	2007 Heritage 1/4 Platinum Night II Sale	#3380
23	$287,500.00	1808	MS-63	2007 Heritage 1/4 Platinum Night II Sale	#3392
24	$276,000.00	1796 No Stars	MS-61	2008 Heritage Price Sale	#1451
25	$253,000.00	1836	Proof 66 ultra cameo	2007 Heritage 1/4 Platinum Night Sale	#3104

Three Dollar Gold

	Price	Coin	Grade	Sale	Lot
1	$687,500.00	1870-S	EF-40	1982 Bowers & Ruddy U.S.G.C. Sale	#296
2	$253,000.00	1875	Proof 65	2006 Heritage 11/29 Sale	#2148
3	$253,000.00	1875	Proof 66 ultra cameo	2010 Bowers & Merena 11/4 Sale	#5041
4	$218,500.00	1875	Proof 66 ultra cameo	2007 Heritage Loewinger Sale	#3123
5	$212,750.00	1873 Open 3	Proof 65 ultra cameo	2008 Goldbergs 9/14 Sale	#1239
6	$175,375.00	1875	Proof 64 cameo	2006 Goldbergs 2/5 Sale	#1053
7	$166,750.00	1875	Proof 65	2004 David Lawrence Richmond I Sale	#1288
8	$161,000.00	1873 Open 3	Proof 65	2006 Heritage 11/29 Sale	#2146
9	$161,000.00	1873 Open 3	Proof 65 deep cameo	2007 Goldbergs 2/11 Sale	#2227
10	$159,000.00	1875	Proof 64	1990 Auction '90 Sale	#1775
11	$150,000.00	1875	Proof	1974 Stack's Ullmer Sale	#421
12	$149,500.00	1854-D	MS-62	2006 Heritage 4/6 Sale	#1516
13	$149,500.00	1875	Proof	2005 Stack's 3/15 Sale	#2061
14	$149,500.00	1875	Proof 64 ultra cameo	2007 Heritage 1/4 Platinum Night II Sale	#3479
15	$138,000.00	1875	Proof 64	2005 American Numismatic Rarities 3/8 Sale	#644
16	$135,125.00	1875	Proof	2005 Stack's 10/19 Sale	#1218
17	$132,000.00	1854	MS-67	1990 Superior 1/28 Sale	#4520
18	$126,500.00	1854-D	MS-61	2008 Goldbergs 9/14 Sale	#1232
19	$126,500.00	1875	Proof 65	2004 Heritage Platinum Night Sale	#3014
20	$125,000.00	1875	Proof	1981 Auction '81 Sale	#418
21	$121,000.00	1875	Proof	1984 Stack's Carter Sale	#610
22	$120,750.00	1875	Proof 64	2006 Heritage 11/29 Sale	#2147
23	$120,000.00	1875	Proof	1975 Stack's Clarke Sale	#22
24	$117,875.00	1875	Proof 65	2001 Heritage ANA Sale	#7743
25	$112,125.00	1854	MS-68	2004 Heritage 1/4 Sale	#6219

Four Dollar Gold

	Price	Coin	Grade	Sale	Lot
1	$977,500.00	1880 Coiled Hair	Proof 66	2005 Heritage Gold Rush Collection Sale	#30044
2	$655,500.00	1879 Coiled Hair	Proof 67	2005 Heritage Gold Rush Collection Sale	#30041
3	$618,125.00	1880 Coiled Hair	Proof 63	2005 Superior July Sale	
4	$575,000.00	1880 Coiled Hair	Proof 62	2009 Heritage 1/8 Platinum Night 1 Sale	#4035
5	$546,250.00	1880 Coiled Hair	Proof 62	2009 Heritage 7/31 Platinum Night Sale	#1246
6	$488,750.00	1880 Flowing Hair	Proof 66 cameo	2008 Heritage 3/6 Sale	#1451
7	$440,000.00	1880 Coiled Hair	Proof 66	1991 Superior 8/11 Sale	#707
8	$431,250.00	1880 Flowing Hair	Proof 64	2008 Heritage 6/26 Sale	#1960
9	$414,000.00	1879 Coiled Hair	Proof 63	2007 Goldbergs 5/27 Sale	#1551
10	$402,500.00	1879 Coiled Hair	Proof 63	2006 Heritage 8/14 Platinum Sale	#5468
11	$402,500.00	1879 Flowing Hair	Proof 67	2006 Heritage 8/14 Platinum Sale	#5467
12	$402,500.00	1879 Flowing Hair	Proof 67	2008 Superior 5/26 Sale	#235
13	$402,500.00	1880 Coiled Hair	Proof 62	2004 David Lawrence Richmond I Sale	#1306
14	$379,500.00	1880 Coiled Hair	Proof 61	2004 Bowers & Merena March Sale	
15	$368,000.00	1880 Coiled Hair	Proof	2000 Stack's 65th Anniversary Sale	#1625
16	$345,000.00	1879 Coiled Hair	Proof	2001 Stack's/Sotheby's Dallas Bank Sale	#361
17	$316,250.00	1879 Coiled Hair	Proof 63	2007 Heritage 1/4 Platinum Night II Sale	#3488
18	$316,250.00	1880 Flowing Hair	Proof 65	2007 Heritage 4/9 Sale	#1694
19	$310,500.00	1879 Coiled Hair	Proof	2000 Stack's 65th Anniversary Sale	#1623
20	$310,500.00	1879 Flowing Hair	Proof 67 cameo	2005 Heritage Gold Rush Collection Sale	#30042
21	$308,000.00	1880 Coiled Hair	Proof	1995 Stack's 60th Anniversary Sale	#1548
22	$304,750.00	1879 Coiled Hair	Proof 63	2009 Goldbergs 2/1 Sale	#1433
23	$299,000.00	1879 Coiled Hair	Proof 63	2004 David Lawrence Richmond I Sale	#1304
24	$299,000.00	1879 Flowing Hair	Proof 67 cameo	2010 Heritage 1/6 Platinum Night Sale	#2148
25	$297,000.00	1880 Flowing Hair	Proof 65	1989 Superior 10/1 Sale	#4297

Half Eagles

	Price	Coin	Grade	Sale	Lot
1	$977,500.00	1833 Large Date	Proof 67	2005 Heritage Gold Rush Collection Sale	#30046
2	$690,000.00	1909-O	MS-66	2011 Heritage 1/11 Platinum Night Sale	#5138
3	$690,000.00	1825/4	AU-50	2008 Heritage 7/31 Platinum Night Sale	#1955
4	$690,000.00	1835	Proof 67	2005 Heritage Gold Rush Collection Sale	#30050
5	$687,500.00	1822	VF-30 to EF-40	1982 Bowers & Ruddy U.S.G.C. Sale	#378
6	$586,500.00	1795 Small Eagle BD-1	MS-65	2008 Stack's Husky Sale	#2052
7	$583,000.00	1795 Small Eagle	MS-65 prooflike	2007 Bullowa's 1/20 Sale	#307
8	$467,500.00	1833 Large Date	Proof	1997 Akers Pittman I Sale	#933
9	$460,000.00	1815	MS-64	2009 Heritage 1/11 Platinum Night 1 Sale	#4062
10	$374,000.00	1909-O	Gem Unc.	1998 Akers Price Sale	#21
11	$374,000.00	1829 Small Date	Unc.	1996 Christie's Reed Collection Sale	#118
12	$373,750.00	1795 Small Eagle	MS-64	2008 Heritage 1/10 Platinum Night Sale	#3134
13	$352,000.00	1829 Small Date	Proof 64 to -65	1987 Bowers & Merena Norweb Sale	#779
14	$345,000.00	1795 Small Eagle	MS-65 prooflike	2011 Heritage 1/11 Platinum Night Sale	#5076
15	$345,000.00	1795 Small Eagle	MS-64	2007 Heritage 1/4 Platinum Night II Sale	#3493
16	$345,000.00	1795 Small Eagle	MS-65 prooflike	2009 Heritage 7/31 Platinum Night Sale	#1248
17	$322,000.00	1795 Small Eagle	MS-64	2007 Goldbergs 9/23 Sale	#3276
18	$322,000.00	1795 Small Eagle	MS-64	2008 Stack's 7/27 Sale	#2464
19	$322,000.00	1827	MS-66	2008 Stack's 1/7 Sale	#921
20	$316,250.00	1796/5	MS-64	2008 Stack's Husky Sale	#2055
21	$308,000.00	1835	Gem Proof	1997 Akers Pittman I Sale	#937
22	$299,000.00	1795 Small Eagle	MS-65	2004 Bowers & Merena 5/4 Sale	#407
23	$299,000.00	1797 16 Stars Small Eagle	MS-61	2006 Goldberg 5/28 Sale	#3787
24	$299,000.00	1823	MS-65	2011 Heritage 1/5 Platinum Night Sale	#5096
25	$297,000.00	1832 12 Star Reverse	Unc.	1996 Christie's Reed Collection Sale	#120

Eagles

	Price	Coin	Grade	Sale	Lot
1	$2,185,000.00	1907 Rolled Rim	Proof 67	2011 Heritage 1/6 Platinum Night Sale	#5238
2	$1,725,000.00	1920-S	MS-67	2007 Heritage 3/15 Sale	#2134
3	$1,610,000.00	1839/8 Type of 1838, Large Letters	Proof 67 ultra cameo	2007 Heritage FUN Sale	#3657
4	$718,750.00	1933	Unc.	2004 Stack's 10/13 Sale	#2190
5	$690,000.00	1839/8 Type of 1838, Large Letters	Proof 67	1999 Goldbergs Bloch Sale	#1817
6	$552,000.00	1933	MS-65	2008 Heritage 1/10 Platinum Night Sale	#3291
7	$550,000.00	1838	Choice Proof	1998 Akers Pittman II Sale	#1910
8	$546,250.00	1795 13 Leaves BD-1 T-1	MS-64	2008 Stack's 7/27 Sale	#2564
9	$546,250.00	1933	MS-65	2007 Heritage Kutasi Sale	#3191
10	$517,500.00	1933	MS-65 Premium Quality	2009 Goldbergs 2/1 Sale	#1592
11	$517,500.00	1933	MS-65	2005 Heritage Morse Sale	#6520
12	$506,000.00	1795 13 Leaves T-1	MS-65	2003 Bowers & Merena ANA Sale	#4039
13	$494,500.00	1795 13 Leaves T-1	MS-65	2006 Bowers & Merena ANA Sale	#4296
14	$488,750.00	1933	MS-65	2009 Heritage O'Neal Sale	#3531
15	$460,000.00	1933	MS-65	2009 Heritage 7/31 Platinum Night Sale	#1312
16	$460,000.00	1795 13 Leaves T-5	MS-64	2008 Goldbergs 2/10 Sale	#2432
17	$460,000.00	1907 Rounded Rim	MS-67	2008 Heritage 1/10 Platinum Night Sale	#3271
18	$460,000.00	1933	MS-65	2005 Goldbergs 5/30 Sale	#1065
19	$460,000.00	1795 13 Leaves T-1	MS-64	2005 Heritage Gold Rush Collection Sale	#30054
20	$448,500.00	1795 13 Leaves T-1	MS-64	2007 Goldbergs 9/23 Sale	#3352
21	$448,500.00	1797 Small Eagle	MS-63	2007 Goldbergs 5/27 Sale	#1643
22	$437,000.00	1933	MS-64	2007 Goldbergs 9/23 Sale	#3404
23	$431,250.00	1920-S	MS-66	2009 Heritage O'Neal Sale	#3527
24	$414,000.00	1795 13 Leaves B-1A T-1	MS-64	2005 American Numismatic Rarities Gentleman's Sale	#1014
25	$402,500.00	1795 13 Leaves BD-1 T-1	MS-63	2008 Stack's 5/21 Sale	#4291

Double Eagles

	Price	Coin	Grade	Sale	Lot
1	$7,590,020.00	1933	Unc.	2002 Sotheby's/Stack's 7/30 Sale	
2	$2,990,000.00	MCMVII Ultra HR LE	Proof 69	2005 Heritage Morse Sale	#6522
3	$1,897,500.00	1927-D	MS-67	2005 Heritage Morse Sale	#6697
4	$1,840,000.00	MCMVII Ultra HR LE	Proof 68	2007 Heritage Kutasi Sale	#3258
5	$1,610,000.00	1861 Paquet Reverse	MS-61	2006 Heritage 8/14 Platinum Sale	#5623
6	$1,495,000.00	1921	MS-63	2006 Bowers and Merena ANA Sale	#4504
7	$1,495,000.00	1927-D	MS-66	2010 Heritage 1/6 Platinum Night Sale	#2331
8	$1,437,500.00	1856-O	Specimen 63	2009 Heritage 5/28 Sale	#1989
9	$1,322,500.00	1927-D	MS-65	2006 Heritage 1/5 Platinum Sale	#3624
10	$1,210,000.00	MCMVII Ultra HR LE	Proof 67	1999 Goldberg Coins 5/31 Sale	#885
11	$1,092,500.00	1921	MS-66	2005 Heritage Morse Sale	#6644
12	$1,012,000.00	1921	MS-65	2007 Goldbergs 9/23 Sale	#3524
13	$920,000.00	1907 Small Edge Letters	Proof 68	2005 Heritage Morse Sale	#6535
14	$825,000.00	MCMVII Ultra HR LE	Proof	1996 Sotheby's Bloomfield Collection Sale	#60
15	$805,000.00	1921	MS-65	2005 Heritage Morse Sale	#6645
16	$690,000.00	MCMVII Ultra HR LE of '06	Proof 58	2008 Stack's 7/27 Sale	#4242
17	$690,000.00	MCMVII Ultra HR LE	Proof	2001 Stack's/Sotheby's Dallas Bank Sale	#150
18	$660,000.00	MCMVII Ultra HR LE	Proof 67	1997 Bowers & Merena 1/8 Sale	#353
19	$660,000.00	1861 Paquet Reverse	MS-67	1988 Bowers & Merena Norweb Part III Sale	#3984
20	$603,750.00	1854-O	AU-55	2008 Heritage 10/24 Sale	#3012
21	$577,500.00	1927-D	MS-65	1998 Akers Price Sale	#115
22	$576,150.00	1856-O	AU-58	2008 Heritage 10/24 Sale	#3018
23	$575,000.00	MCMVII HR WR	MS-69	2005 Heritage Morse Sale	#6523

Double Eagles (continued)

	Price	Coin	Grade	Sale	Lot
24	$575,000.00	1927-D	MS-62	2004 David Lawrence Richmond I Sale	#2431
25	$546,250.00	MCMVII HR WR	MS-69	2007 Heritage FUN Sale	#3789

Pioneer Gold

	Price	Coin	Grade	Sale	Lot
1	$747,500.00	1855 Kellogg & Co. $50	Proof 64	2007 Heritage FUN Sale	#3898
2	$690,000.00	1860 Clark, Gruber & Co. $20	MS-64	2006 Heritage FUN Sale	#3673
3	$546,250.00	1851 Humbert Octagon $50	MS-63	2010 Heritage 8/11 Sale	#3677
4	$500,000.00	1851 Humbert Octagon $50	Proof	1980 Bowers & Ruddy Garrett II Sale	#897
5	$434,500.00	1852/1 Humbert $20	Proof 64	1990 Superior October Sale	#2328
6	$431,250.00	1849 Cincinnati Mining $10	EF	2004 Stack's Ford II Sale	#362
7	$374,000.00	1852/1 Humbert $20	Proof 65	1992 Superior Adams, Morley, Pugh	#3111
8	$353,000.00	1849 J.H. Bowie $5	AU-58	2001 Stack's O'Donnell Sale	#1608
9	$345,000.00	1855 Wass, Molitor $50	Gem Proof	2003 Stack's 68th Anniversary Sale	#2289
10	$325,000.00	1852/1 Aug. Humbert $20	Proof	1980 Bowers & Ruddy Garrett II Sale	#890
11	$304,750.00	1855 Kellogg & Co. $50	Gem Proof	2003 Stack's 68th Anniversary Sale	#2292
12	$300,000.00	1855 Kellogg & Co. $50	Proof	1980 Bowers & Ruddy Garrett II Sale	#910
13	$299,000.00	1854 Kellogg & Co. $20	MS-64	2008 Heritage FUN Sale	#3447
14	$287,500.00	1851 Humbert Octagon $50	MS-62	2007 Heritage 8/9 Sale	#2106
15	$287,500.00	1852/1 Humbert $20	Proof 64	2004 Stack's Ford II Sale	#363
16	$275,000.00	1855 Wass, Molitor $50	Unc.	1980 Bowers & Ruddy Garrett II Sale	#947
17	$270,000.00	1849 Cincinnati Mining $10	EF	1980 Bowers & Ruddy Garrett II Sale	#885
18	$264,500.00	1851 Humbert Octagon $50	MS-63	2007 Heritage 8/9 Sale	#2107
19	$241,500.00	1852 Humbert Octagon $50	MS-61	2005 Heritage 7/25 Sale	#10456
20	$230,000.00	1854 Kellogg & Co. $20	Proof	1980 Bowers & Ruddy Garrett II Sale	#908
21	$230,000.00	1849 J.H. Bowie $5	AU-50	2004 Stack's Ford II Sale	#361
22	$212,750.00	1855 Wass, Molitor $50	MS-60	2007 Heritage FUN Sale	#3905
23	$207,000.00	1851 Humbert Octagon $50	MS-62	2007 Heritage 8/9 Sale	#2110
24	$207,000.00	1855 Wass, Molitor $50	MS-61 CAC	2008 Heritage 7/31 Sale	#1864
25	$200,000.00	1830 Templeton Reid $5	EF-40	1979 Bowers & Ruddy Garrett I Sale	#505

Silver Commemoratives

	Price	Coin	Grade	Sale	Lot
1	$86,250.00	1900 Lafayette $1	MS-67 CAC	2008 Heritage 4/17 Sale	#2528
2	$86,250.00	1928 Hawaiian 50¢	Proof 65	2008 Bowers & Merena 9/13 Sale	#619
3	$80,500.00	1900 Lafayette $1	MS-67	2003 Superior 5/25 Sale	#3178
4	$77,625.00	1900 Lafayette $1	MS-67 CAC	2009 Heritage ANA Sale	#1388
5	$71,875.00	1900 Lafayette $1	MS-67	2005 Heritage 2/24 Sale	#4140
6	$69,000.00	1926 Oregon 50¢	MS-67	2004 Superior April Sale	#1787
7	$69,000.00	1925 Lexington 50¢	MS-68	2005 Heritage 2/24 Sale	#4162
8	$69,000.00	1900 Lafayette $1	MS-67	2008 Heritage FUN Sale	#3414
9	$66,700.00	1900 Lafayette $1	MS-67	2004 Heritage FUN Sale	#2233
10	$66,700.00	1900 Lafayette $1	MS-67	2006 Superior 2/5 Pre-Long Beach Sale	#1207
11	$66,125.00	1915-S/S Pan-Pacific 50¢	MS-68	2006 Heritage 10/25 Sale	#1847
12	$65,550.00	1928 Hawaiian 50¢	Proof 66	2006 Bowers & Merena 3/16 Baltimore Sale	#2081
13	$64,400.00	1928 Hawaiian 50¢	Proof 66	2006 Bowers & Merena ANA Sale	#1178
14	$59,800.00	1900 Lafayette $1	MS-67	2002 Heritage 7/27 Sale	#5041
15	$57,500.00	1915-S Pan-Pacific 50¢	MS-68	2005 Heritage 2/24 Sale	#4173
16	$54,625.00	1928 Hawaiian 50¢	MS-67	2007 Heritage 5/10 Sale	#2529
17	$51,750.00	1900 Lafayette $1	MS-67	2007 Heritage 5/10 Sale	#2445
18	$51,750.00	1893 Isabella 25¢	MS-68	2004 Heritage 8/18 ANA Sale	#4198
19	$51,750.00	1915-S Pan-Pacific 50¢	MS-68	2004 Heritage 8/18 ANA Sale	#4306
20	$48,875.00	1936 Gettysburg 50¢	MS-68	2005 Heritage 2/24 Sale	#4156

Silver Commemoratives (continued)

	Price	Coin	Grade	Sale	Lot
21	$48,875.00	1936 Gettysburg 50¢	MS-68	2007 Heritage 5/10 Sale	#2523
22	$46,200.00	1900 Lafayette $1	Gem Unc.	2005 C.E. Bullowa 12/4 Sale	#396
23	$46,000.00	1928 Hawaiian 50¢	MS-67	2005 Heritage 2/24 Sale	#4158
24	$46,000.00	1937 Roanoke 50¢	MS-68	2005 Heritage 2/24 Sale	#4176
25	$46,000.00	1938-D Oregon 50¢	MS-69	2004 Heritage 8/18 ANA Sale	#4300

Gold Commemoratives

	Price	Coin	Grade	Sale	Lot
1	$289,671.20	1915-S Pan-Pacific $50 octagonal	MS-67	2005 Heritage ANA Sale	#10443
2	$230,000.00	1915-S Pan-Pacific $50 octagonal	MS-65	2008 Stack's 6/25 Sale	#2111
3	$207,000.00	1915-S Pan-Pacific $50 octagonal	MS-67	2009 Heritage FUN Sale	#4216
4	$184,000.00	1915-S Pan-Pacific $50 round	MS-66	2008 Stack's 6/25 Sale	#2110
5	$172,500.00	1915-S Pan-Pacific $50 round	MS-66	2006 Heritage ANA Sale	#5739
6	$149,500.00	1915-S Pan-Pacific $50 round	MS-66	2006 Heritage FUN Sale	#3650
7	$149,500.00	1915-S Pan-Pacific $50 round	MS-66	2006 Heritage FUN Sale	#3651
8	$138,000.00	1915-S Pan-Pacific $50 round	MS-66	2009 Heritage FUN Sale	#4212
9	$126,500.00	1915-S Pan-Pacific $50 octagonal	MS-64 CAC	2010 Heritage ANA Sale	#3665
10	$126,500.00	1915-S Pan-Pacific $50 round	MS-65 CAC	2008 Heritage 2/14 Sale	#1039
11	$126,500.00	1915-S Pan-Pacific $50 round	Unc.	1998 Superior Heifetz Sale	#5474
12	$121,325.00	1915-S Pan-Pacific $50 octagonal	MS-65 CAC	2008 Heritage 2/14 Sale	#1046
13	$115,000.00	1915-S Pan-Pacific $50 round	MS-65	2007 Heritage FUN Sale	#3850
14	$115,000.00	1915-S Pan-Pacific $50 round	MS-64	2010 Heritage ANA Sale	#3661
15	$115,000.00	1915-S Pan-Pacific $50 round	MS-65	2010 Heritage 3/26 Sale	#1854
16	$115,000.00	1915-S Pan-Pacific $50 octagonal	MS-65	2006 Heritage 6/3 Sale	#4699
17	$112,750.00	1915-S Pan-Pacific $50 round	MS-66	1993 Superior 7/6 Sale	#798
18	$109,250.00	1915-S Pan-Pacific $50 round	MS-65	2006 Heritage 6/3 Sale	#4697
19	$103,500.00	1915-S Pan-Pacific $50 round	MS-64 CAC	2008 Heritage 9/18 Sale	#1270
20	$103,500.00	1915-S Pan-Pacific $50 octagonal	Choice Unc.	2003 Stack's 68th Anniversary Sale	
21	$100,625.00	1915-S Pan-Pacific $50 octagonal	MS-65	2007 Heritage 7/13 Sale	#2133
22	$100,625.00	1915-S Pan-Pacific $50 octagonal	MS-65	2007 Heritage 6/1 Sale	#1973
23	$100,000.00	1915-S Pan-Pacific $50 octagonal	Unc.	1980 Bowers & Ruddy Garrett II Sale	#876
24	$97,750.00	1915-S Pan-Pacific $50 round	MS-64	2006 Heritage 1/5 Sale	#3649
25	$95,000.00	1915-S Pan-Pacific $50 round	Unc.	1980 Bowers & Ruddy Garrett II Sale	#873

Patterns

	Price	Coin	Grade	Sale	Lot
1	$1,322,500.00	1792 half disme J-7	Specimen 67	2006 Heritage 4/27 Sale	#1860
2	$1,265,000.00	1874 Bickford $10 J-1373	Proof 65 deep cameo	2010 Heritage 1/7 Sale	#2373
3	$862,500.00	1879 Quintuple Stella J-1643	Proof 62	2007 Heritage 1/3 Sale	#1594
4	$690,000.00	1792 copper disme RE J-10	Proof 62 brown	2008 Heritage 7/31 Sale	#1408
5	$603,750.00	1792 No Silver Center cent J-2	VF-30	2008 Heritage 1/10 Sale	#3462
6	$575,000.00	1877 $50 half union copper J-1549	Proof 67 brown	2009 Heritage 1/7 Sale	#1888
7	$529,000.00	1838 Gobrecht $1, copper J-87	Proof 63 red-brown	2008 Stack's 1/7 Sale	#1173
8	$503,125.00	1792 half disme J-7 P-7	MS-63	2008 Heritage FUN Sale	#2741
9	$475,000.00	1907 $20 J-1776	Proof	1981 Bowers & Ruddy ANA Sale	#2434
10	$467,500.00	1907 $20 J-1776	Proof 67	1984 Auction '84 Sale	#542
11	$460,000.00	1915 No S Pan-Pacific 50¢, gold J-1960	Proof 64	2010 Heritage 8/11	#3742
12	$437,000.00	1792 No Silver Center cent J-2	VF-30 PQ	2005 Goldbergs 2/20 Sale	#806
13	$414,000.00	1792 Silver Center cent J-1	Brilliant Unc.	2002 Stack's 1/15 Sale	#724
14	$402,500.00	1792 half disme J-7	MS-63	2007 Stack's Husky Sale	#2007
15	$402,500.00	1878 $5 J-1570	Proof 65	2007 Heritage 1/3 Sale	#1550
16	$402,500.00	1875 20¢ J-1443	Proof 64	2005 Heritage 5/6 Sale	#8337

Patterns (continued)

	Price	Coin	Grade	Sale	Lot
17	$400,000.00	1865 $20 J-452	Proof 64	1990 Auction '90 Sale	#1468
18	$373,750.00	1792 half disme J-7	MS-64	2008 Stack's July Sale	#4148
19	$373,750.00	1879 $4 Coiled Hair, aluminum	Proof 67 cameo	2008 Stack's SS New York Sale	#4228
20	$356,500.00	1836 Gobrecht dollar, copper J-64	Proof 65 red	2009 Stack's SS New York Sale	#813
21	$345,000.00	1915 No S Pan-Pacific 50¢, gold J-1960	Proof 64	2009 Heritage 1/7 Sale	#1962
22	$345,000.00	1878 $10 J-1579	Gem Proof	2003 Stack's 68th Anniversary Sale	#1119
23	$299,000.00	1878 $5 J-1575	Gem Proof	2003 Stack's 68th Anniversary Sale	#1116
24	$294,319.50	1863 $10 J-351	Proof 63	2005 Heritage 1/12 Sale	#30622
25	$287,500.00	1875 $5 J-1438	Proof 65	2005 Heritage 5/6 Sale	#8336

Colonials

	Price	Coin	Grade	Sale	Lot
1	$2,990,000.00	1787 Brasher 'EB' on Breast doubloon, NY	EF-45	2005 Heritage FUN Sale	#30017
2	$2,415,000.00	1787 Brasher doubloon, NY	AU-55	2005 Heritage FUN Sale	#30016
3	$725,000.00	1788 Brasher doubloon, NY	MS-63	1979 Bowers & Ruddy Garrett I Sale	#607
4	$690,000.00	1742 Brasher doubloon, Lima	EF-40	2005 Heritage FUN Sale	#3005
5	$632,500.00	1652 Willow Tree threepence N 1-A	Very Fine	2005 Stack's Ford XII Sale	#12
6	$625,000.00	1787 Brasher doubloon 'EB' on Breast	VF	1981 Bowers & Ruddy Garrett IV Sale	#2340
7	$430,000.00	1788 Brasher doubloon	AU	1979 Auction '79 Sale	#1433
8	$425,500.00	1776 Continental dollar EG FECIT Silver N 3-D	EF	2003 Stack's Ford I Sale	#7
9	$416,875.00	(1652) NE shilling N-III-C	AU-50	2010 Heritage 8/11 Sale	#3002
10	$391,000.00	1792 Getz 50¢, silver circles and squares edge	Gem Brilliant Unc. prooflike	2004 Stack's Ford II Sale	#29
11	$373,750.00	(1652) NE shilling N-III-C	AU-50	2008 Heritage FUN Sale	#624
12	$345,000.00	1776 Continental dollar CURENCY Silver N 1-C	Very Fine	2005 Stack's Ford VII Sale	#159
13	$345,000.00	(1652) NE shilling N-III-B	VF	2005 Stack's Ford XII Sale	#2
14	$322,000.00	(1652) NE shilling N-III-C	EF	2005 Stack's Ford XII Sale	#3
15	$322,000.00	1786 New Jersey, Date Under Plowbeam M-7-E	Choice About Unc.	2003 Stack's Ford I Sale	#76
16	$299,000.00	1776 Continental dollar CURENCY, brass	MS-63 CAC	2009 Heritage 7/31 Sale	#1002
17	$299,000.00	1787 Massachusetts cent Transposed Arrows	Choice Unc.	2004 Stack's Ford V Sale	#85
18	$287,500.00	1776 Continental dollar, CURENCY, silver N-1-C	Very Good-Fine	2003 Stack's Ford I Sale	#2
19	$276,000.00	1776 Continental dollar, CURRENCY, pewter	EF-45 CAC	2009 Heritage 7/31 Sale	#1006
20	$276,000.00	(1652) NE shilling N-III-C	EF	2005 Stack's Ford XII Sale	#4
21	$276,000.00	1652 Willow Tree shilling N-1-A	EF	2005 Stack's Ford XII Sale	#6
22	$253,000.00	(1652) NE shilling N-I-A	Choice VF	2005 Stack's Ford XII Sale	#1
23	$253,000.00	Washington New Jersey copper M-4-C	AU	2003 Stack's Ford I Sale	#73
24	$253,000.00	1652 Willow Tree sixpence N-1-A	Essentially Unc.	2005 Stack's Ford XII Sale	#10
25	$241,500.00	1792 Getz 50¢, silver, Plain Edge	Choice AU prooflike	2004 Stack's Ford II Sale	#28

Fractional Gold

	Price	Coin	Grade	Sale	Lot
1	$80,500.00	1853 $1, round BG-604	MS-62	2003 Bowers & Merena Roe Sale	#137
2	$48,300.00	1854 25¢, round BG-220	MS-62	2003 Bowers & Merena Roe Sale	#34
3	$44,000.00	1854 25¢, round BG-220	Unc.	1998 Superior Lee Sale	#29

Fractional Gold (continued)

	Price	Coin	Grade	Sale	Lot
4	$35,200.00	1853 $1, round BG-604	Unc.	1987 Superior 9/20 Sale	#4487
5	$31,050.00	1853 50¢, round BG-402	MS-63	2003 Bowers & Merena Roe Sale	#60
6	$31,050.00	1853 50¢, round BG-410	MS-64	2003 Bowers & Merena Roe Sale	#68
7	$29,900.00	1853 $1, octagonal BG-503	MS-61	2011 Heritage 2/4 Sale	#4763
8	$25,300.00	1853 $1, octagonal BG-502	AU-58	2003 Bowers & Merena Roe Sale	#100
9	$25,300.00	1854 $1, round BG-602	AU-50	2003 Bowers & Merena Roe Sale	#135
10	$24,150.00	1854 $1, octagonal BG-529	AU-50	2003 Bowers & Merena Roe Sale	#127
11	$24,150.00	1854 $1, round BG-605	AU-55	2003 Bowers & Merena Roe Sale	#138
12	$23,000.00	1853 50¢, round BG-435	MS-63	2003 Bowers & Merena Roe Sale	#97
13	$21,850.00	1852 50¢, round BG-426	MS-62	2003 Bowers & Merena Roe Sale	#86
14	$21,275.00	1853 50¢, round BG-435	MS-64	2008 Heritage 8/24 Sale	#64896
15	$20,700.00	1853 50¢, round BG-411	MS-63	2004 Heritage 1/30 Sale	#6398
16	$20,700.00	1853 $1, octagonal BG-503	AU-58	2003 Bowers & Merena Roe Sale	#101
17	$19,550.00	(1853) 25¢, round BG-204B	AU-58	2011 Heritage 1/7 Sale	#7564
18	$18,975.00	1853 50¢, round BG-435	MS-63	2007 Heritage 6/1 Sale	#2869
19	$18,400.00	1853 50¢, round BG-435	MS-63	2007 Heritage 8/9 Sale	#2173
20	$18,400.00	1854 $1, round BG-602	AU-55	2004 Heritage 6/5 Sale	#10253
21	$17,250.00	1876 25¢, octagonal BG-799GG	MS-65	2009 Heritage 7/31 Sale	#1378
22	$16,675.00	1854 25¢, octagonal BG-103	AU-58	2003 Bowers & Merena Roe Sale	#3
23	$16,100.00	1853 50¢, round BG-411	AU-55	2003 Bowers & Merena Roe Sale	#69
24	$16,100.00	1853 50¢, round BG-413	MS-61	2003 Bowers & Merena Roe Sale	#71
25	$16,000.00	1854 $1, round D-505A	EF	1980 Ivy ANA Sale	#556

20   Potpourri

Ordering from advertisements

Ordering coins, notes, tokens and other numismatic items from an advertiser is a simple matter. We assume the seller has advertised or issued a price list (for tips about ordering online, see the later section). The buyer picks out the item or items desired, then reads the instructions that accompany the price list or advertisement.

The buyer may choose to order by telephone (if a number is given), with payment by credit card or via some other arrangement, or to follow the directions in the advertisement and mail in the order.

If the seller specifies a minimum order amount, the buyer must reach it or not buy from that seller. If the seller requires an added amount for postage, insurance and handling, the order must include it.

The instructions may require payment by a postal money order, or a bank certified check, or warn that payment by personal check will necessitate a delay in shipping to allow the check to clear the bank. The buyer must note of all this, do as instructed and be prepared to wait for the order, from two to four weeks, depending on the distance from the seller and how the payment is made.

Half that time may be due to the check clearing, and the other half to the time it takes for package to transverse the U.S. mail system.

If after three weeks a buyer has not received the shipment, a call to the seller may be in order to inquire about the status of the shipment.

Following are a few more tips for buyers to ensure that transactions go smoothly. Do not forget to include your name and full address including ZIP code when sending an order, both inside and outside the envelope, preferably printed or typed. More disputes have been caused by a buyer's failure to include a legible, or any, return address than all other causes put together. And, strange as it may seem, some buyers have been known to forget to sign their checks.

If the seller says returns will be allowed for three, five or seven days, or any other period, for unsatisfactory merchandise, a buyer must assume the seller means what is said. If the buyer needs more time to get a coin authenticated or graded elsewhere, the buyer should ask the seller.

Most sellers require that all purchased coins be kept in their original holders. If that's the case, removing the coin from the seller's holder voids return privileges, even if the buyer removed the coin to inspect it closer. Sellers impose this restriction to protect themselves from buyers switching coins, i.e., substituting a coin of lower grade for the coin the seller sent, and then claiming the coin doesn't meet their expectations.

The buyer would also be wise to ask for a written guarantee of authenticity with the coin, if it's worth more than a few dollars.

Coin World's advertising policy states that time limits are invalid if a coin is counterfeit. But a buyer must prove the coin was not switched after arrival, if there is any question.

If an advertisement contains the phrase "prices subject to change without notice," in a period of fast-rising markets, a buyer who orders and pays by mail should be prepared to see payment returned. If the coin is one-of-a-kind, a "sold-out" answer to an order should not be unexpected.

In some cases, it is wise for the buyer to phone the seller for confirmation of an order at a given price. The buyer should get the name of the person confirming the order at that price, and how many days will be allowed for forwarding the payment.

Most transactions are simple, and most sellers and buyers are well-meaning and honest. There are a few exceptions on both sides.

If either buyer or seller is "taken" once, suspicion reigns from then on, which makes things harder for everybody involved. If both seller and buyer stick to the "Golden Rule," the hobby and business of numismatics becomes much more pleasant for everyone.

Shipping coins

There are several reasons one may elect to ship coins, paper money or other numismatic items from Point A to Point B.

One reason is to have items graded by a third-party grading service, such as Professional Coin Grading Service, Numismatic Guaranty Corp. or ANACS.

Some grading services will accept coin and paper money submissions directly from a collector, sometimes requiring the submitter to purchase a membership first, although the membership may be waived; others will require the collector to first submit his or her numismatic items through an approved coin dealer. Grading services are very particular about how coins and paper money submitted for grading and authentication should be packaged and shipped. The websites of each of the mentioned grading services provide information on how to accomplish this, or will provide information on how they can be contacted by mail, telephone or email for assistance.

A second reason for shipping could be that the seller has sold an item to a buyer via an Internet auction site, such as eBay. In this instance, it is vital that items be shipped securely and in a manner outlined by the seller in the auction listing. Any buyer who has been the victim of damaged or lost goods because of careless packaging by a seller may likely leave bad feedback and will almost certainly refrain from making further purchases from that seller.

Coins or paper money intended as a gift to a distant family member or friend presents another reason that individuals may find themselves needing to ship. The recipient will certainly appreciate receiving a much-desired set of coins if it arrives at an appropriate time and unscathed.

Additionally, some collectors may wish to mail a numismatic item to *Coin World*, and more specifically, *Coin World's* weekly columns like "Collectors' Clearinghouse" and "Readers Ask." *Coin World* policy requires that potential mailers first call or email a *Coin World* staff member beforehand to ask permission to send any item.

Regardless of the person's reason for shipping, safely shipping the item is essential. For safe shipping, one should be thinking specifically of two things: privacy and packaging.

Privacy

Whether a parcel is sent via the U.S. Postal Service, United Parcel Service, Federal Express, Canada Post or any other delivery company, some possible danger is always present in shipping a valuable item. Physical damage, such as from carrier vehicles suffering a collision—even a plane crash or train wreck—is among potential calamities. One danger to be keenly aware of, however, is human greed.

Every delivery company, large or small, has people in their employ. Unfortunately, in contrast to the thousands of dedicated employees, there always seem to be a few "bad eggs" who allow greed to overcome their employment obligations and their decency.

With the exception of packages carrying contents that must be declared, as, for example, in a shipment heading to a destination outside of the United States, or when the collector wishes to insure the package against theft or damage, under no circumstances should the contents of a package be revealed in great depth. "Fragile," "Handle with Care" and "Do Not Bend" are terms perfectly appropriate for any package in need of careful handling.

Even in circumstances requiring further explanation, a generic term such as "collectible" is often more than satisfactory. Do not say "2009 1-Ounce Gold American Eagle" or "Rare $500 Gold Certificate." Such descriptors most assuredly will tempt the unscrupulous.

Whether the potential danger is unintentional physical damage or intentional theft, purchasing insurance is just a good idea when mailing items of value. However, attempt to make an objective determination of what an item is worth in strict monetary terms. An 1821 Capped Bust half dollar in Very Fine condition handed down to a hobbyist by his or her grandfather may be priceless to the hobbyist, but the Postal Service is not willing to insure it for a million dollars, and attempting that level of insurance would be a real waste of the collector's money. Insuring it for $150 in case of loss or theft is more reasonable.

Over the years, *Coin World* has received numerous coins submitted to Collectors' Clearinghouse that were insured for values well beyond their true value. It is always disheartening to see a collector ship a damaged Lincoln cent worth face value, with an insurance fee attached of $15 to $20 (this is not an exaggeration), and an accompanying personal check of like amount for return postage and insurance fees, all because the owner nurtures unrealistic expectations of the coin's value.

For specific guidelines on how and when numismatic items should be declared, how to send items registered or insured and the associated costs involved, hobbyists should contact in advance the delivery service they plan to use, by telephone, in person or via that company's website.

The labeling of a package is also important, as, for one reason or another, some shipments just don't end up where they're supposed to be. The addressee's information should be correct and clearly typed or written and then securely affixed to the package. It is also a good idea to include a duplicate of the address information on the inside of the package, in case it is inadvertently (or purposely) opened in transit.

If reusing a box or envelope used previously for mailing, remove or black out as completely as possible any previous address information or postal bar codes.

And don't forget to include a clearly typed or written return address, both inside the packaging and on the outside, in case there is a problem.

One more thing to consider: The major delivery companies offer package tracking, by which customers can track the location of their in-transit packages 24 hours a day via the Internet.

Though tracking may entail an added cost, taking advantage of this tool could be worth that cost to the collector, especially for items of great value.

For more information on the policies, procedures and costs of the most commonly used shipping companies in the United States and Canada, visit these websites:

United States Postal Service: **www.usps.com**
United Parcel Service: **www.ups.com**
Federal Express: **fedex.com/us**
Canada Post: **www.canadapost.ca**

Packaging

Maintaining an item's privacy en route to a destination is but one aspect of a successful shipping experience. Equally important is the packaging of that item.

Despite the continuing need for the human element in shipping, package delivery now is largely computerized and mechanized, and the quantities handled are massive. Packages are whisked through sorting areas by conveyor belt, stacked on pallets, thrown onto trucks and flown all across the world. In the process, a machine charged with moving a package is not by itself able to determine when the box contains a rare coin or unique note.

Because a package is at the mercy of any given delivery service once it's beyond the sight of the sender, why not make it as secure as possible before submitting it for delivery?

In her *Coin World* column "Preserving Collectibles," Susan Maltby has touched upon a number of good ideas for those wishing to securely ship coins and paper money. She advises hobbyists to "anticipate the worst-case scenario and pack accordingly."

Maltby states that "if fragile objects can move, they can break," and recommends lightly shaking a packaged item before sealing. If any noise or movement of the object inside the package is detected, she advises opening and repackaging the item or items more securely. Coins, she advises, should be cushioned to prevent abrasion, both from outside dangers and from other coins within the package. Paper money needs to be protected from creasing or tearing. Both collectibles need protection from moisture.

Both coins and notes should be packed in archival-quality holders, and the packaging materials surrounding the holders should be free from acidic substances and other potential contaminants.

Do not simply throw a coin or coins into an envelope without employing a holder first. *Coin World* receives the occasional package in which loose coins were shipped, and in some cases, the shifting coins wore a hole in a corner of the envelope and fell out of the package before the empty envelope's arrival.

Also, do not use the technique practiced by some of directly taping a coin, not in a holder, to a letter. The tape can leave a sticky residue on the surface of the coin and cause chemical damage.

Around any single coin and between multiple amounts of coins, Maltby recommends placing protective cushioning materials, such as bubble wrap or a polyethylene foam. Cellu-cushion, Ethafoam and Volara are foams she recommends.

In addition, supportive outer packaging is important. Maltby recommends Coroplast, which she describes as "a corrugated sheeting made from high impact polypropylene copolymer," or Neutracor, an acid-free cardboard.

(For archival-quality packaging, Maltby recommends contacting these supply houses: Masterpak at **www.masterpak-usa.com**; University Products Inc., found at **www.universityproducts.com**; Gaylord Bros. Inc., found online at **www.gaylord.com**; and Carr McLean, **www.carrmclean.ca**. For Coroplast, collectors can go online to **www.coroplast.com** to locate Coroplast distributors.)

Amos Advantage (**www.amosadvantage.com**) sells various types of holders that will provide archival-quality protection for coin and paper money items for both shipping and storage purposes.

Maltby warns that shipped goods should not be left in their shipping packaging for long-term storage. Those receiving coins or paper money in the mail should move the items immediately to a more suitable environment.

How to buy coins

"How do you buy coins?"

"What's the best way to buy coins?"

"Where do I find coins for my collection?"

Such questions are frequently asked by beginning collectors. They're also being asked more and more by those who once collected and are now reentering the hobby, encountering a marketplace somewhat different from what they remember or experienced years ago.

One fundamental hasn't changed: Know what coin or coins you want to buy. "Knowing" includes understanding how to grade coins and being cognizant of how the grade (state of preservation) relates to a coin's value.

Additionally, the firmer grasp one has of the history of the coin or the series, its characteristics, mintage, survivability rates (rarity) and current value, the more one's chances improve for making good purchases. Therein rests the wisdom of the oft-quoted adage: "Buy the book before the coin."

For our discussion, we'll assume the collector has at least covered the basics of acquiring knowledge, whether from books, educational seminars, videos, coin shows, coin club attendance or information gained from the Internet. The collector has a reliable and up-to-date price guide, and is now ready to venture into buying.

Where does one start?

The most likely place, especially for a true beginner, is nearby: a local bank, a nearby coin shop, or the comfort of one's own home, using various forms of mail order or the Internet.

One of the easiest and most nonthreatening ways to ease into the hobby is to "buy" coins at the bank: That is, exchange paper dollars for rolls of coins—any of the circulating denominations—to search for dates and Mint marks at one's leisure. The out-of-pocket costs can be limited and the fun builds.

To find coins not readily available in circulation, other nearby sources can be tapped.

Although local, retail coin shops and hobby stores with a good selection of collectible coins are not as prevalent as they once were, they do exist in most large metropolitan areas, and some are still to be found in small towns and cities throughout the country. An Internet search, the Yellow Pages of the local telephone directory or the classified ad section of the local newspaper will reveal whether a local dealer or retail shop exists. If so, check the hours the store or dealer is open for business. The smaller the locality, the greater the probability the store is open for a limited number of hours on specified days.

Most coin dealers start out as collectors and many continue to collect though they have elected to become professional numismatists. Coin dealers often have expertise in more than one collecting specialty and are more than willing to provide collecting tips, especially to new collectors. They usually have numismatic reference books and will assist collectors in research. Chances are the local coin dealer may be able to put you in contact with other collectors or provide information about coin clubs in the area.

Absent dealer referral, finding a local or regional coin club may be a matter of checking the community calendar or meeting announcements in the local newspaper, contacting the local public library or the local Chamber of Commerce. In addition to businesses, the chamber usually maintains listings of all clubs and organizations, where they regularly meet and the name of a contact person.

Coin clubs generally provide members opportunities for buying, selling and trading coins and other numismatic collectibles during or after meetings. Many sponsor a coin show annually, affording local collectors the opportunity to purchase from dealers and collectors on a regional or state basis. Large clubs sometimes attract dealers from across the country to their shows. Also, commercial entities sponsor both small and large coin shows.

The big advantage of finding coins at a local coin shop, a local club meeting or during a coin show is the ability to inspect coins first hand, without major travel expense. Because some of the large regional and national coin shows alternate show sites, many collectors have an opportunity to attend a show offering several hundred dealers under one roof on a fairly frequent basis. A good source for finding upcoming coin shows and conventions and their locations is the Events Calendar published in the weekly *Coin World* and at its website **www.coinworld.com.** Many collectors like the convenience of buying coins by mail order. It is especially handy for collectors unable or too busy to travel frequently to shows or attend coin club meetings.

Today's mail-order marketplace offers extensive purchasing opportunities. *Coin World,* as the largest weekly numismatic publication, through its advertising pages and web site is the largest mail-order market by virtue of the number of advertisers and the wide variety of numismatic items available for purchase.

Sometimes the actual coin is pictured in an advertisement. However, the buyer must frequently make his or her decision based on a written description, including the grade, with the quoted price.

As with any buying experience, it pays to comparison shop. Another time-proven adage is especially important to bear in mind: "There are no Santa Clauses in numismatics." A variation on this theme: "If it looks too good to be true, it probably is."

Collectors who expect to purchase coins from advertisements in *Coin World* or any other periodical should seek out and acquaint themselves with the publication's basic mail-order policy. (*Coin World's* policy is published in every issue, and in this chapter of the *Coin World Almanac.*) Such policies are an attempt to ensure equity for both buyers and sellers. A key component of the basic mail-order policy is inspection and return privileges. (Publications differ on the standards and requirements, so before ordering one should become thoroughly acquainted with such policies.)

A cardinal rule of successful buying by mail order is to immediately inspect the ordered coin or other numismatic material upon receipt to verify that it is what was ordered.

Another popular way of acquiring coins is from auctions. Auction lot previewing is generally accorded potential buyers a day or two in advance of public auctions, generally at the site or location at which the sale is to be conducted.

Veteran collectors and dealers who buy coins at auction caution to "never bid blind." That is, they suggest any coin being considered for purchase at auction should be examined. They also suggest if you don't know how to grade coins that you seek the assistance of a professional coin dealer. Often the professional, for a modest fee, will buy coins on your behalf or act as your agent at an auction.

Another important tip veteran buyers offer is to establish a bidding limit before the sale begins, whether you are personally bidding or you have contracted an agent to bid for you. Do price research on the desired coin before the sale begins. Set a maximum price you are willing to pay and stick with it. It is too easy to exceed a coin's value by being caught up in the "heat of the moment." One should also factor in the buyer's fee. Most U.S. auction firms charge a 10 or 15 percent buyer's fee, which is added to the hammer price to arrive at the total price.

Most of the large numismatic auction companies produce descriptive catalogs featuring high-quality photographs of most or all of the coins that will be in the auction. The catalogs are mailed to potential buyers to apprise them of the coins and numismatic collectibles that will be available. Many collectors unable to travel to the auction site and who do not like to use agents to buy for them, prefer to place bids by mail. The sale catalog generally includes a form for placing mail bids and specifies deadlines and terms of the sale. Usually a buyer participating as a mail bidder is accorded inspection and return privileges, if he or she successfully wins the lot with his mail bid.

The Internet has greatly impacted how auctions are conducted. Major auction houses now place their catalogs online and offer online bidding to registered bidders. As with the print editions, these online catalogs will show images of the coins being offered, often providing larger, higher-resolution images than those shown in printed catalogs.

In addition to the long-established auction houses, a number of businesses have formed auction websites that permit collectors, dealers and others to offer any form of collectible, including coins, to a worldwide audience. The impact of online auction companies, such as eBay, is immense.

Some online-only auction sites simply serve as a conduit between sellers and bidders. Unlike established auction houses, which guarantee the authenticity of every coin offered, some online auction firms offer no such guarantees, operating on the concept of "buyer beware." This becomes especially tricky for collectors due to the massive number of counterfeit coins being imported from China and other countries in the Far East.

Since the last edition of the *Coin World Almanac* was published, eBay began offering "Buyer Protec-tion" services. For more information, visit **http://pages.ebay.com/help/policies/buyer-protection.html**.

Ultimately, it is up to the prospective buyer to be aware of the policies of any online auction website before he or she begins placing bids on numismatic items. For more information on buying coins via the Internet, see the "Internet transactions" portion of this chapter.

In addition to auction houses, individual dealers have moved online. Some publish their price lists online and accept online want lists. Collectors can even "subscribe" to a dealer price list, which is auto-matically sent to a collector's email address as soon as it becomes available. As with the online auction sites, collectors should exercise due caution until they become comfortable trading online with a specific dealer or individual.

The largest and most direct sources of new coin issues are the government Mints and sometimes private mints that produce the coins. The U.S. Mint advertises its products in coin periodicals, but it also sells directly to collectors by telephone, by mail order and through its website. For more information on U.S. Mint products, a collector may write the Mint at U.S. Mint, Customer Service, 2799 Reeves Road, Plain-field, IN 20706, call the Mint at (800) 872-6468 or visit the Mint's website at **www.usmint.gov**.

Many foreign mints also sell by mail order, by Internet or through authorized retail establishments within the United States. See the World Coins chapter for a contact information for dozens of world mints.

For the truly adventurous, occasional sources to find coins are estate auctions and flea markets.

Whatever the source, the key to successful coin buying is to know what you are looking for and what you are willing to pay for it.

How to sell coins

"Where can I sell my coins?"

Such a seemingly simple question is not so simply answered, although it is a question frequently asked by beginning collectors, those who have been away from the hobby for a number of years, and by family members who have recently inherited a coin collec-tion.

The first rule of thumb is knowing what you have to sell. Knowing entails identifying the coin or coins in the collection by type, date, Mint mark and variety, if appropriate. Equally important is the state of pres-ervation or grade. Grade is particularly important if one intends to sell U.S. coins, because a coin's "con-dition" or grade is a primary determinant of value. Also important to value is the coin's rarity, that is, the number of like coins that are known to exist.

Beginners and those who have not been involved in collecting sometimes confuse "mintage" and "rarity."

Mintage is the number of coins originally struck. Rar-ity reflects the number of coins that survive. Obvi-ously, if fewer of a certain date were made, the coin may be more difficult to find but it is not necessarily "rare." Conversely, there are years in which large mintages were recorded, but the coins are scare or rare today because the majority of pieces were melted by government decree (many silver dollars and later gold coins) or were sold for melt when the bullion value exceeded face and numismatic value.

Another pitfall common to those not actively involved with coin collecting is to assume that because a coin is "old" it is also "rare," and that it is, therefore, worth lots of money. Age does not neces-sarily equate to high value. Some coins struck nearly 2,000 years ago are in plentiful supply and are inex-pensive (a few dollars each). Other coins struck less than 100 years ago in very small mintages are difficult to locate and are avidly collected. Consequently, a relatively recent coin can command large sums in the marketplace.

Even rarity does not automatically mean that a coin is of great value. Some rare coins can be purchased for modest sums simply because few people are currently interested in collecting or purchasing them.

Ultimately a coin's market value is determined by demand. Demand is determined by the number of buyers desirous of acquiring the coin. Although investors do participate in the coin market, collectors are the ultimate buyers for most coins. Collectors primarily buy a coin because it is "needed" or "fits" in their collections. Sometimes a coin having a tangential relationship to other items in one's collection will be pursued as avidly as the primary collection.

Virtually all of the basics of identifying and grading coins are available in book or video form. Current retail values for U.S. coins can be found in price guides such as *Coin World's Coin Values*, published once a month in the *Coin World Special Edition* and available 24 hours a day to *Coin World* subscribers online at **www.coinvaluesonline.com**. *Coin World's Coin Values* is also published as a paid "app" for the Apple iPad at **www.iTunes.com**.

Additional ways of acquiring information include talking with coin collectors and dealers and attending coin shows, coin club meetings and educational presentations. However, if one is unable or unwilling to spend the time necessary to acquire basic knowledge about coins and their values, he or she may wish to engage the services of a professional numismatist or coin appraiser. Various national organizations provide online listings and contact information for such trained professionals. Professionals, whether dealers or appraisers, usually charge an hourly rate and will provide a preliminary estimate of cost of the appraisal based on the number of coins to be evaluated and the time needed to perform the service. If a dealer is providing an estimate with intent to purchase, he or she may waive the appraisal fee. Under such circumstances, the seller may wish to have more than one prospective buyer provide an estimate of value and submit a proposal to purchase.

If the seller is the person who acquired the coins, he or she likely has some ideas about prospective buyers. The most logical candidates are other collectors or dealers specializing in the coins one has for sale. Often collectors make acquaintances with others in their collecting fields through local coin clubs or regional or national organizations. Many local coin clubs hold club auctions in which members buy and sell coins. Some clubs hold member auctions as often as they meet. Others sponsor bid-boards on which members can list coins for sale or allow members to advertise items for sale in the club's newsletter. Regional and national specialty organizations offer similar venues for members to buy, sell or trade their numismatic collectibles. Clubs and organizations also sponsor shows, inviting members, local coin dealers and dealers from out of state or from various collecting specialties to buy and sell on the coin show's bourse.

"Bourse" is the French word for "exchange." Thus, coin bourse is literally a place to buy and sell coins or numismatic collectibles. Dealers (and sometimes collectors) pay a fee to the show promoter to have a presence on the bourse. Usually this means the show promoter provides a display case, lights, and a table and chairs at an assigned space on the floor where the dealer may transact business. Many shows encourage dealer-to-dealer trading or wholesale purchases during nonpublic hours and retail sales when the show is open to the public. In practice, however, one will find wholesale and retail activity simultaneously on most coin show bourses.

If selling coins is your prime objective at a coin show, the best use of time would be to first identify those dealers who are selling the various types and grades of coins that you may have for sale. The best way to determine this is to spend time going from table to table and looking at what is on display in the dealer's case. After identifying the most likely candidates, the next step is to inquire as to whether the dealer is interested in buying. You will be expected to be able to generally describe your coins by type and grade and have them available for inspection in a reasonably organized and efficient manner. The dealer may not be interested at all. He or she may already be over-stocked and have a large inventory of coins just like yours. If the dealer expresses no interest, thank the merchant politely and move on to the next dealer.

If the dealer looks at your coin or coins and offers a price, you will be expected to respond as to whether the price quoted is agreeable. Sometimes rather than quoting a price, the dealer may ask: "What do you want for this?" When asked, be prepared to give a serious and reasonable answer. It is your responsibility as the seller to know the approximate value of what you are selling and to be able to make a decision as to what price is acceptable.

In general, dealers expect to buy at wholesale. The wholesale market has a rather wide spread, ranging from 30 to 40 percent of retail up to approximately 80 percent of retail, sometimes higher. The price a dealer quotes depends on his individual circumstance. It is not unusual to obtain different bids on the same coin from different dealers. It is up to the seller to decide if his or her price is met and if he or she desires to sell the coin.

Often at shows many people are waiting to talk with a dealer. Although some dealers at the shows will bargain, others are not so inclined, especially if only marginally interested in purchasing the items offered. For best results, have a price in mind for the initial response and a fall-back or bottom line in case bargaining is a possibility, and have those numbers in mind before approaching any prospective buyer.

If you are attempting to sell a collection, determine your strategy—whether to sell it intact or to sell some or all of the coins individually. Sometimes buyers— whether collectors or dealers—will be interested only in certain dates, such as key dates or semi-key dates, or certain grades.

Also, some dealers today buy and sell only coins that have been graded by a third-party grading service and sonically sealed in plastic holders known as "slabs." Upon your initial inquiry, the dealer may ask whether your coin is "raw" or "slabbed." The term "raw" as used in the coin marketplace refers to a coin that is not encapsulated and graded by a third-party grading service.

Many who are ready to sell coins have neither time nor inclination to travel to coin shows or club meetings. Thus, mail-order becomes an option. Seasoned collectors sometimes sell their coins via "fixed-price" lists that they advertise in the classified sections of publications such as *Coin World* or sell to individuals whom they have identified as having an interest in purchasing coins they may have. Classified ads also are a vehicle for selling specific coins. Be sure to check the advertising policies of the publication for how to prepare and place a classified ad.

Many dealers who advertise in publications such as *Coin World* buy as well as sell coins. Often they will list coins that they are interested in obtaining. Usually they provide a toll-free number or email address that can be used to clarify degree of interest or current buy prices. In most cases, the transaction is contingent upon the dealer being able to inspect the coin, to confirm its quality. Whenever sending coins via mail, a cover letter stating terms of sale and an inventory list of what is being offered should be included in the package. Also, coins should be sent by registered mail and insured.

Transactions can be conducted entirely by mail. Before sending any coins, the seller should inquire as to whether the dealer or potential collector-buyer is interested. Again, terms of sale should be stated in a forthright manner and an inventory list presented, listing coin type, date, Mint mark, variety, grade and any other information about the coin. The seller should list a price at which he desires to sell. If he does not list a price, he may ask the dealer to quote a price.

Coins should never be sent on a "blind" inquiry. They should be forwarded only after a prospective buyer has expressed interest in purchasing. If possible, the seller should maintain a photographic record of any coins sent to a prospective buyer. Absent good photographs, detailed inventory records, including grading identification numbers, should be kept by the seller in order to be certain that any coins returned are the same ones he or she sent for possible purchase.

Sometimes dealers or other collectors will take groups of coins or collections on consignment. Consignment agreements should be made in writing and detail the coins, terms of consignment (percentage the consignment agent will receive for selling the coins) and the length of time covered by the agreement.

Public auction is a popular method of selling collectible coins, especially extensive collections and highly collectible coins. Most auction firms that advertise in the weekly and monthly issues of *Coin World* specialize in numismatic collectibles. They have extensive lists of identified customers who have purchased coins in the past, thus providing greater exposure to potential buyers.

Many of the numismatic auction firms have full-time staff that research and prepare descriptions of the coins which they publish in an auction catalog provided to prospective buyers. Most auction houses also extensively advertise forthcoming auctions to the widest possible audiences. Auction preview days are often designated just prior to the sale so that prospective buyers or their agents can inspect the coins. Auction firms charge the seller a fee, usually based on a percentage of the price the coin achieves at auction. Virtually all reputable auction firms require consignors to sign contracts, which state the terms and conditions of the sale. In selecting an auction firm to use to sell your coins, it is important to read and compare consignment contracts.

Depending on the number of coins to be sold in an auction and whether specialized material is being offered, the number of days between consignment and the actual sale date can vary from 30 days up to a year. In traditional auctions, from the date of sale until the consignor receives payment may take an additional 30 to 60 days. Some auctions are conducted electronically and offer faster turnaround, but most deal exclusively in coins graded and authenticated by third-party grading services.

The impact of the Internet on buyers mentioned earlier also holds true for sellers of numismatic materials. Sellers may wish to register with an online auction site and offer their coins directly to collectors worldwide. As with buying coins over the Internet, sellers should also take precaution. A seller may not want to ship coins to a successful bidder until payment has been received. Sellers also should be sure they describe their coins accurately so as to not deceive potential bidders.

Some collectors buy coins with the avowed intent never to sell any. Other collectors buy and sell regularly. Whether a collector sells the coins or passes them on to future generations, good records and inventory lists will assist when the time arrives to evaluate or sell the collection.

Coins can be sold in many ways. Each seller must determine the best method, depending on the time and energy available for the activity.

Internet transactions

Although the majority of transactions that take place on the Internet benefit both the seller and buyer of an item, it's important not to gaze at your computer screen with rose-colored glasses. Some items sold online are sold under fraudulent pretenses—they are either inaccurately (whether intentional or not) described or the seller never intends to provide the item once the fee is collected. The former is the most common problem.

The buyer must always be wary, but particularly wary online. It is best to shop with a trusted dealer or company that is known for its exemplary service either online or in the "real" world. It is also best to shop with a company that is more than just familiar with numismatic items. Remember that part of the price of every coin in a dealer's inventory is the value of his or her expertise.

Some dealers use the Internet as another way to sell their coins—they already advertise in *Coin World* or attend coin shows.

Some dealers operate only on the Internet—they either sell coins at fixed prices or auction the coins at a website designed for auctions.

Before you buy, be aware of the return policy and the amount of time you have to examine an item to see if it is satisfactory to you.

Never provide your credit card number unless using a "secured site," one that encrypts your personal and credit card information for its trip through the information superhighway.

If the page where you submit credit card and personal information is not secure, consider calling in your order instead.

Regardless of how you submit your order, learn the company's physical address and telephone number before you order, if possible.

Online auctions

Before you bid at any online auction site, you will very likely have to register. Always read the user's agreement carefully to know what kind of recourse you will have. Before you bid on an item, pay close attention to the return policies of the seller and any shipping and handling fees. Be sure to contact that person beforehand if you have any questions.

Often online auctions will provide rating information about buyers and sellers. People who have done business with these sellers in the past will rate their attitude, promptness, honesty and so on. Keep this information in mind when buying or selling.

Online auctions are a very popular way to purchase coins. When bidding in an auction, keep your wits about you. If a coin or deal seems too good to be true, perhaps it is.

Don't be too quick to trust a photograph of the lot. Photo quality is often poor and inconsistent. Digital images can be enhanced. Of course, a photo might also be very telling; you may be able to determine the authenticity of a questionable item.

This brings up another important point: Cutting out a dealer or numismatic auctioneer involves a certain amount of risk. You don't get the benefit of their expertise and staff or return policies. Collectors should be wary of the person or company from whom they are buying: Are they selling me a good coin? Will they actually send me the coin after I've paid them? Will they misuse my credit card number?

While a vast number of individuals selling coins on the Internet are honest people, some will either accidentally or intentionally defraud a customer. And while the Internet affords all users a certain amount of anonymity, criminals find they can use this to their advantage.

Auctioneers on the Internet fall into three broad categories: auction venues (middlemen), live auctioneers on the Internet (a company that incorporates online bidding into its live auctions) and Internet auction companies (companies that catalog and auction consigned coins).

A company such as eBay (**www.ebay.com**) acts as a middleman for auctions. On such sites the owners of the coins (who may or may not be coin dealers) post their offerings on the site and pay the site a fee for the service, which is often a percentage of the sale price. If a collector buys a coin on one of these middlemen sites, he and the seller must contact each other to complete the transaction. The seller may be a single individual or a company.

These middlemen sites may indemnify themselves against many potential problems. They may not be involved in the actual transaction between buyers and sellers and have no control over the quality, safety or legality of the items advertised, the truth or accuracy of the listings, the ability of sellers to sell items or the ability of buyers to buy items. In fact, such a site may not confirm that sellers (or buyers) are who they claim to be. Basically, the collector is on his or her own at such sites.

Generally venues try to alert customers to be wary of fraud, warning them in their registration agreements in basically the same verbiage as stated above.

Some limit the kinds of material that may be sold on the site.

Another kind of auction site is one that accepts consignments for auctions and employs a staff of numismatists to catalog the coins before they are posted on the Internet. The buyer does business directly with this company, and the company is responsible for the customer's satisfaction. One such site is Teletrade (**www.teletrade.com**).

When the item arrives at the buyer's door, he or she has an agreed-upon number of days to examine the piece. If it is satisfactory, the money is released to the seller. If not, the item is returned and the buyer gets a refund.

If something should go very wrong with the sale of the item and the two parties cannot come to an agreement, they should seek arbitration through the venue company (if one was used) or from the Better Business Bureau (**www.bbb.org**), which also provides arbitration services for customers.

Incidentally, the Better Business Bureau is a good place to start to determine an ethical track record for any companies with which you may deal. Check to see if the company is a member of BBBOnLine Inc. (**www.bbbonline.org**), which promotes ethics in commerce on the Internet.

As with any coin transaction, be it in a shop or while you are in your pajamas at home, knowledge will do a great deal to protect you.

But in case you have acted to the best of your knowledge, and things still go wrong, know how to protect yourself further.

Coin World's basic advertising policy

Coin World, Amos Hobby Publishing
P.O. Box 150, Sidney, OH 45365-0150

The publisher offers advertising space for the purpose of bringing buyer and seller together for their mutual benefit. Years of publishing experience indicate the reader must be able to expect satisfactory service from the advertiser in order to respond to future advertisements. It is by giving such satisfactory service that advertisers can expect to continue productive advertising. Readers are reminded that in all situations, equity must exist for both parties for a satisfactory transaction.

Advertisements submitted that are not in the best interest of the advertiser specifically, and of the trade generally, in the opinion of the publisher, or that may mislead readers, will be rejected. Customer checks of advertisers are periodically made by the publisher in a practical effort to ensure accuracy and reliability of all advertisements. However, it is impossible to guarantee readers' satisfaction with the advertiser's manner of doing business, and the reader is therefore reminded to exercise common sense in responding to any advertisement. The reader is also urged to exercise patience in awaiting response from an advertiser by making allowances for mail transit time.

Coin World assumes no responsibility for representations made in advertisements.

Inspection and return policy

All individual coins are to be shipped in holders that permit thorough inspection of the coin. Any coin removed from its holder is not returnable. Coins or numismatic material that the buyer finds to be unsatisfactory may be returned to the seller for full refund or replacement unless the advertisement specifies "No returns." (See "No return offerings" section.) Returns must be made within five days of receipt by the buyer, unless other return periods are specified in the advertisement. Refund or replacement will be made by the seller within seven days upon receipt of the returned item. Maximum return period allowed by advertisers is 30 days.

The buyer <u>must</u> verify with seller any extension of return period if coins are to be shipped to a grading or certification service.

Mail order rule

All transactions must be in compliance with the FTC Mail Order Rule regarding delivery of merchandise. For a copy of the FTC Mail Order Rule, write to *Coin World*.

No return offerings

"No Return" offerings must clearly state such and are limited to encapsulated, graded coins. Advertisements that fail to state a return policy will be governed by *Coin World*'s Basic Advertising Policy on Inspection and Return Period as stated above.

Return postage on buy and trade ads

All advertisers who do not state "Write First" in their ads are expected to return merchandise postpaid. Refusal of packages at the post office may be grounds for suspension unless the ad indicates that confirmation is needed before shipping. If overgraded coins are to be returned at the seller's or the trader's expense, advertisement must so state.

Telephone transactions

In the case of telephone transactions when a confirmation number has been issued, both buyer and seller are expected to adhere to the telephonic agreement. Telephone, mail-order and electronic transactions are subject to the same standards.

Liability for contents of ads

Advertiser assumes liability for all contents (including text representation and illustrations) of advertisement printed, and also assumes responsibility for any claims therefrom.

Complaints

All advertisers will be notified of complaints received in writing from the readers, and prompt adjustment by the advertiser, if warranted, and notification to the publisher will be expected as a condition of continued acceptance of advertising. Failure of any advertiser to correct the cause of a complaint or satisfactorily explain the same may result in suspension of advertising privileges at the discretion of *Coin World*.

Verification, inspection, financial statement

Acceptance of advertising for any item or service is subject to investigation and verification of the product or service, and of the claims made for it, in the advertisement submitted for publication.

Coin World will utilize its Customer Checking

Service to verify the accuracy of the specified grade of advertised numismatic items. Collectors living throughout the United States, upon instruction from the publishers, place orders for merchandise advertised. The parcels are forwarded unopened to the publishers for examination of the contents.

Verification by the Customer Checking Service of an advertiser shipping misrepresented merchandise or services may result in suspension of advertising privileges at the discretion of *Coin World*.

The publisher reserves the right to require a current financial statement from any advertiser at any time.

Copy Regulations

All advertisements submitted are subject to copy regulations contained in the rate card. By submitting advertising, the advertiser acknowledges that he is familiar with the advertising contract and copy regulations then in effect. Additional copies will be furnished upon request.

Layaway sales

Advertiser must write *Coin World* for complete policy requirements prior to offering layaways in ads.

Reserve right to reject advertising

All advertising submitted is subject to publisher's approval. The publisher reserves the right to reject advertising, or suspend advertising privileges at their discretion.

Fake, counterfeit or altered coins and paper money

Only genuine numismatic items may be offered for sale. Coins that have been buffed, whizzed, polished, plugged or chemically treated to appear other than their original state must be accurately described as such in *Coin World*.

Altered or counterfeit coins and paper money are not acceptable for advertising in *Coin World*.

Any buyer of a fake or spurious item shall be entitled to a full refund and the normal return period shall be nullified.

The word "coin" may be used only when referring to legal tender.

Coin restrikes

Restrikes are numismatic items reproduced from the original dies or plates, but at a later date than appears on the item; the item must be restruck or reissued by the original issuing government authority, or authorized by decree of proclamation of the issuing government authority.

COINS STRUCK FROM THE ORIGINAL DIES intended for circulation are considered coins rather than tokens and with denominations usually on them: these include pioneer issues, the Confederate half dollar and cent, etc. These are acceptable for advertising, provided they are accurately described and identified as restrikes. Second or later restrikes must be distinguished from earlier restrikes in a permanent manner, such as metal used or appreciable difference

in thickness, to be acceptable.

Any numismatic item created, designed or originally manufactured on or after March 1, 1963, that the owner wishes to advertise in *Coin World* as a restrike, must use the original dies on both obverse and reverse and make the impression transferrable directly from die to planchet without otherwise making transferals to any intermediate materials, dies, hubs, etc. Each piece must be indelibly labeled as a restrike.

It will be incumbent upon the advertiser to verify all facts concerning method and date of production.

Copies

Ads offering reproductions, imitations, replicas or copies of the coins or other numismatic items are acceptable for advertising under the following conditions:

1. That such items are in compliance with the "Hobby Protection Act" and the U.S. Treasury's policy regarding coin replicas.

2. That the advertising copy of offer NOT contain false or misleading statements of the legal tender status of such items.

3. That the items be fully described in ads and samples of such items are submitted to *Coin World* with the initial advertisement.

4. All items falling in this category must be clearly marked "copy."

5. A disclaimer must run in the ad that is selling replicas or reproductions. The disclaimer must appear in close proximity of the image of the replica being sold. For disclaimer sizes and shapes we have available, contact your sales rep.

Cleaned coins

Cleaned coins may be advertised in *Coin World*. Cleaning has become an acceptable practice and in some instances can be beneficial. Light dipping in a mild, nonabrasive solution may actually improve a coin's appearance and may increase its market value.

However, cleaning can also damage a coin. A coin that is dipped improperly or repetitively will have an impaired surface, reducing its market value. Coins that have been damaged by cleaning may be advertised because they still have a collector value, but must be designated in the ad as "cleaned."

Customers are advised of the importance of utilizing the inspection and return period to be sure coins they have purchased meet their standards of acceptability.

Comparative price ads

Coin World will not accept advertising copy that offers to buy or to sell by comparison with any other advertised buying prices. Any such reference will be deleted from the advertiser's copy.

Coin grading and description

Coins and numismatic items offered for sale shall be accurately described. *Coin World* recognizes "The American Numismatic Association Grading Standards for United States Coins," "Photograde," "The

Numismatic Certification Institute Grading Guide" and "A Guide to the Grading of U.S. Coins" by Brown and Dunn as the accepted standard methods of grading U.S. coins. Advertisers who do not use any of these standard grading methods must describe, in each ad, accurately and in detail the method of grading used. Advertisers using any one of the standard methods need to make reference to the grading method(s) used in the ads. *Coin World* reserves the right to reject any ad using methods other than the four methods listed.

Policy for advertising Uncirculated coins

Coin World has adopted the following minimum standards for grading terms used in *Coin World* advertisements in order that buyer and seller can better communicate:

➤ Borderline Uncirculated must be a minimum of AU-55 and cannot be abbreviated as BU.

➤ Uncirculated, Brilliant Uncirculated and Select Uncirculated must be minimum of Mint State 60.

➤ Commercial Graded Uncirculated must be a minimum of Mint State 60.

➤ Choice Uncirculated or Choice Brilliant Uncirculated must be a minimum of Mint State 63.

➤ Gem Uncirculated or Gem Brilliant Uncirculated must be a minimum of Mint State 65.

➤ Superb Brilliant Uncirculated must be a minimum of Mint State 67.

➤ Split grades such as MS-64/65 must fall back into the lowest adjective level.

Any advertiser placing an advertisement in *Coin World* agrees to adhere to these minimum standards. Advertisers found in violation may have their advertising privileges suspended or revoked at the discretion of *Coin World*.

Exonumia

Among the first uses of the word "exonumia" was its use in correspondence between Russell Rulau and James Curto in the 1960s, but the subject matter included in the topic, according to some scholars, harks back to Roman medallions of the second century. Today's definition of exonumia is "numismatic items (as tokens, medals or scrip) other than coins or paper money."

Tokens

Tokens, medals and scrip are given as examples of items an exonumist (a collector of exonumia) might study or collect, but the field of exonumia includes a myriad of subjects. Some are inclusive within the three subjects enumerated, but additional areas of interest do exist. The collection of exonumia lends itself to topical collecting, and it is doubtful that any area of human endeavor is not represented by examples of exonumia. Such diverse fields as photography, politics and popes; lunches, lumber and liquor; sex, slavery and science; buses, bakers and boats; and coal, circuses and calendars have intrigued collectors through the years.

In this brief review of exonumia, tokens, medals and scrip are examined, but no attempt at an exhaustive dissertation is intended. While the main focus is on exonumia of the United States, several major areas of non-U.S. tokens are included as well.

Many of the token specialty categories have collector organizations devoted to the particular field of interest. The names and contact information for these groups can be found in the Organizations chapter.

A token is usually a piece of durable material appropriately marked and unofficially issued for purposes such as monetary use, advertising, or exchange for services.

Early tokens in the United States emanated from England as a principal source but also were occasionally made locally or in other countries. Almost from the outset of colonization they were to be found in America. Sylvester S. Crosby in his book, *The Early Coins of America*, says, "... my intention has been to give ... [information about] ... those coins or tokens which were intended to serve as coins ... in those parts of America which now constitute the United States."

These early tokens were needed because of a shortage of coinage. The tokens looked like and passed for money.

The Coin World Comprehensive Catalog and Encyclopedia of United States Coins is a useful reference for Colonial tokens, as is *Walter Breen's Complete Encyclopedia of U.S. and Colonial Coins*.

One favorite type of token with collectors, the store card, is a token bearing a business name or address, and often intended as a local or ad-hoc medium of exchange as well as an advertisement for the issuer.

The Talbot, Allum & Lee token is generally accepted as the first store card in the United States. In 1794, the company of Talbot, Allum & Lee was an importer of goods from India with offices in New York City. Trade tokens the size of British halfpennies commonly circulated at that time in both countries. The origin of the tokens was not important, only that their content, copper, was pure and that the tokens could be relied upon to not be light or debased. Talbot, Allum & Lee contracted with Kempson & Company of Birmingham, England, to strike at least 2 tons of tokens dated 1794 and 1795 with the intention to circulate them in the United States. This plan backfired and only a small number of the tokens made it into circulation. Talbot, Allum & Lee sold the remaining tokens to the U.S. Mint, who needed the metal. The Mint then overstruck some of the tokens and made them into half cents. Some of the tokens were melted and made into strip for planchets.

Store cards have been popular with U.S. merchants ever since and are still being issued today, but rarely have they passed as money in recent years. However, both in the past and at present, they may be pure advertising pieces, or sometimes called "good fors." They are redeemable and may be exchanged by the issuer for merchandise or a service. "Good fors" bear messages such as "Good for 5 cents in trade," "Good for one drink," "Good for a cup of coffee" and so on.

Tokens designed to pass locally as currency, as previously indicated, have a tendency to appear during times when money is hard to access. It is no surprise that such tokens were found in the Colonies, because of the economic policies of the mother country, Great Britain. Money was in short supply.

Some collectors collect tokens of particular eras or categories. Some of the most popular token specialties are examined in the section that follows.

Conder tokens

In the late 18th century, England's shortage of small denomination copper coinage was tangible. Tavern owners and other merchants who needed something smaller than a silver sixpence for daily commerce ordered them through contractors to make change in their businesses. Within a matter of months, the idea became popular all over the British Isles and eventually thousands of the tokens were struck.

The "Conder token" derives its name from numismatist James Conder, who cataloged them in 1798 and 1799. The title of his book was thoroughly descriptive of its contents: *An Arrangement of Provincial Coins, Tokens and Medalets, issued in Great Britain, Ireland and the Colonies, within the last twenty years; from the farthing to the penny size.* The work was in two volumes, octavo, with three plates of illustrations.

The formal name of the Conder tokens is "British Provincial tokens," which is what numismatists R. Dalton and S.H. Hamer called them. Their book, *Provincial Token Coinage of the 18th Century,* originally published in 1904, remains a comprehensive authority for all 18th century English merchants' tokens. The book does not have a good topical index, though it is arranged geographically by county or "shire."

Hard Times tokens

The period between the end of the Revolutionary War and the beginning of the Civil War was marked by times of economic upheavals, separated by periods of monetary stability. The infant government was attempting to cope with the westward expansion of the country, with animosity directed toward the United States by foreign powers, and with the slow process of learning self-government.

The first U.S. Mint was established in Philadelphia in 1792 but crude equipment and limited experience curtailed production. At the same time, an ever-increasing population required more coins. During periods of economic stability, coin production was able to keep up with use, but during periods of economic upheaval, hard money was taken out of circulation and hoarded.

By the early 1830s, the lack of available coinage had reached almost a critical stage. Although tokens had been issued even before the Revolutionary War, mainly of an advertising nature, they had not been used in commerce to any great degree.

The extreme shortage of small change caused more and more merchants to use tokens in ever greater numbers in lieu of cents in their day-to-day business transactions.

Privately issued token coinage was a preferable alternative to the barter system.

The Hard Times tokens consist of two main types: merchant's advertising tokens (store cards) and political tokens.

The advertising tokens carry information about the location and type of business in which the merchant was engaged. Most are of copper, bronze or brass but some were issued in other metals, such as Dr. Lewis Feuchtwanger's "American silver" composition.

An insight into the practice of issuing token coinage is given in a paper read by Thomas L. Elder to the New York Numismatic Club on Jan. 8, 1915: "It is of interest to read that H.M. & E.I. Richards, of Attleboro, Mass., sold their tokens by the keg-full to their customers for from 60 to 75 cents per hundred."

Elder's statement helps make the practice understandable. Not only was the merchant able to make change for his customers, he bought the tokens at less than one cent each and knew that many would be lost or otherwise unredeemed, reducing his cost per token even more.

The tokens are generally about the size of the large cents of the period in which they were issued. For that reason they were accepted in commerce.

As the economy demanded small change that couldn't be provided in quantity by the Mints and was thus provided by merchants, so too did political actions result in another type of token coinage.

Champions of political causes and detractors of those same causes often issued tokens aimed to advance their particular views. Many of the political tokens centered on President Andrew Jackson's refusal to renew the charter of the Bank of the United States.

Whatever the reasons for issuing Hard Times tokens, the pieces form an interesting and historical segment of numismatics.

Civil War tokens

The Civil War gave rise to numerous forms of emergency money, the variety and ingenuity of which have never been equaled. Early in 1862, all metallic currency was gradually withdrawn from circulation. During the war people feared the total devaluation of currency and started to hoard gold and silver. Finally, even copper currency disappeared from circulation.

The result was chaos for those conducting day-to-day business—there was simply no way to make change.

The first attempted work-around was to use ordinary U.S. postage stamps. However, because of their flimsy nature, stamps had a very short circulating lifespan. Next, the merchants issued small envelopes, generally with some advertising on the back, to afford the postage stamps some degree of protection.

In 1862, John Gault patented a novel brass encasement for the stamps, with a mica cover, so the stamps were easily visible. These encased stamps, made by the Scoville Manufacturing Co. in Waterbury, Conn., with the merchant's advertising on one side, circulated widely. Their main disadvantage was that they cost merchants more than face value to issue because the cost of manufacture of the case had to be added to the face value of the stamp.

Various forms of fractional, privately issued, paper money then appeared, but because it had no intrinsic value (and doubtful backing in many cases) it did not meet with wide acceptance. Cardboard scrip had the same fate.

Finally, the most popular and realistic form of emergency money, in the form of small copper tokens, began circulating extensively throughout the Northeast and Midwest in late 1862. These small coin-like tokens, generally the size and weight of small bronze cents, met with immediate acceptance. The use soon spread to other states and cities.

Two general types of tokens were issued—the so-called "patriotic" tokens and the "tradesmen's" tokens or store cards. The patriotic series, mainly issued in and around New York, have patriotic slogans on the tokens but bear no merchant advertising. Many of the pieces are, in general, an imitation of the Indian Head cent (some bearing the legend NOT ONE CENT on the reverse). The tradesmen's (or merchant's) store cards were widely issued and usually bear the merchant's advertisement on one side and some patriotic symbol on the other.

The issue of Civil War tokens exceeded 25 million pieces, which amply filled the needs of the merchants. The merchants were happy with the arrangement since the tokens not only advertised their business but also cost only 23/100ths of a cent to produce.

The tokens were undoubtedly a source of great relief and convenience, but their irresponsible character soon attracted the attentions of the federal government, when some of the merchants refused to redeem the tokens they had issued. Government attempts at issuing bronze coins and fractional currency were not sufficient, though, to suppress the Civil War tokens then current. Finally, through the Act of April 22, 1864, Congress banned privately produced 1- and 2-cent coins, tokens and "devices" for use as money. Thus ended another era.

For a long time, the authoritative book about the subject of Civil War tokens was Hetrich and Guttag's epic work *Civil War Tokens and Tradesmen's Cards*, published in 1924. They listed some 7,000 varieties, but now more than 11,000 different specimens (different die-metal varieties) are known to exist.

The most comprehensive current works on the subject are the two books, *Patriotic Civil War Tokens* and *U.S. Civil War Store Card Tokens* by George and Melvin Fuld. Both volumes have been revised multiple times since their original publication.

Transportation tokens

A popular and generally more modern token is the transportation token. Transportation tokens—or vectures, as they are sometimes called—include items such as bus and streetcar tokens and tokens for toll roads, bridges and ferries. Tokens for a ride in a carriage, on a carousel or other amusement ride, and in horsecars and taxis also exist and are collected.

Wooden money

Collectors who specialize in wooden money can also be added to the list of exonumists. The science of wooden money collecting is called lignadenarics. While most of the pieces found in such a person's collection are round, and many are labeled "nickel," many are rectangular in shape. Any may be identified with different monetary denominations, such as 50 cents, $1, $10 and even more.

The first known use of wooden tokens in the United States was in Tenino, Wash., in 1931. The Tenino bank had failed, and Don Major, a local publisher, suggested the idea of issuing the wooden money for local use as an emergency measure.

Wooden pieces may be used for any of the purposes of tokens already discussed. Also we find some that are commemorative in nature, and frequently they are used in promotion of an event or person. Politicians often distribute them to promote their cause. For collectors they are inexpensive and are popular with many who have tight budgets.

Scrip

A good definition for scrip is: "tokens and paper currency, often in denominations of less than $1, issued as substitutes for currency to private persons or organizations."

Someone has devised the mnemonic "Substitute Currency Received in Payment"—SCRIP—probably because one often encounters the incorrect spelling "script," an entirely different term. There is no terminal "T" on the term "scrip."

Coal companies, sutlers, lumber companies, prisons and an agency of the United States government (the Alaskan Rural Rehabilitation Corp.) are examples of issuing agencies. Paper scrip was used but often was replaced by metallic scrip that better withstood the damaging effects of hard, daily usage. Denominations issued are usually less than $1, but $5 and $10 pieces are not uncommon. Agencies of the U.S. government have issued scrip. Most notable are military payment certificates provided for the armed forces in certain overseas locations.

Ration tokens

During World War II, rationing was a way of life. Practically all commodities were rationed. The Office of Price Administration was responsible for the program and issued ration stamps and coupons, usually in booklet form. The coupons for meat and processed food were issued in denominations of five points, 10 points and 20 points.

In 1944, tokens good for one point were issued for making change for the meat and processed food coupons. These tokens were produced in red or blue, made of a tough fibrous material, and 16 millimeters in diameter. Each has an outlined number 1 stamped in the center with two small letters on either side of the 1.

The letters are found in various unexplained combinations such as MV, HH, UX, CH and HH. Perhaps this was an attempt to foil counterfeiters.

A complete set requires 30 red tokens and 24 blue tokens. The combinations of WC and WH are the hardest to find. Among all the combinations available, one blue token is scarce and one red token is the key to the series. However, entire sets can often be found already assembled. Most OPA token collectors also collect other ration material.

Community currency

Community scrip is a form of money produced by a community for use in that community. Such money has been around since 1991 when a group in Ithaca, N.Y., created the HOURS local currency program. The idea behind most local scrip systems involves issuing scrip to businesses or individuals with the promise they will use or accept it for part or full payment.

People use this scrip to pay rent, buy groceries, and pay for home repair and improvement services, farm market purchases and so on.

All transactions using local currency are subject to federal, state and local income and sales tax regulations. The main difference between this type of currency and federally issued currency is the "financial" backing of the currency and its limited geographic range of usefulness.

Medals

Medals as collectibles frequently seem to be the province of experienced collectors with a long background in coin collecting. The term medal is defined as "usually a piece of metal marked with a design or inscription made to honor a person, place or event, and is not intended to pass as money."

A medal may be a piece of metal hanging at the end of a ribbon, as commonly imagined, and given as a prize or award for some personal action such as winning a contest or for an act of heroism.

The term medal encompasses much more than this type of award. Collectors of medals often collect them as art objects, and the art medal, so called, undoubtedly represents the zenith of numismatic art. Well-known American sculptors such as Augustus Saint-Gaudens, James Earle Fraser, Victor D. Brenner and Karen Worth are recognized for their work as medallic artists.

Probably the earliest definitive work concerning medals in the United States is C. Wyllys Betts' *American Colonial History Illustrated by Contemporary Medals*. His volume covers the period 1556 to 1786 and remains the basic reference for the era.

When discussing medals, one must reflect on the generalization of the definition and realize that not all medals will be paragons of the medalist's art. Many "lesser" medals exist that, because of their contribution to the recording of historical, parochial or topical subjects, are desired by collectors.

Medals are issued by the various military departments. Though authorized by the federal government or one of its executive branches, they were not designed nor struck at the Mint.

These last mentioned items, while properly categorized under the general heading of medals, usually are listed in the subcategories of "decorations" or "awards." The study of medals includes consideration of at least the following: medalets, medallions, plaques, plaquettes, badges, decorations, awards and orders.

U.S. Mint medals

The United States Mint has been one the biggest issuers of medals in the United States (see section in the U.S. Mint chapter). Congress occasionally honors famous Americans and others by authorizing and presenting to them a national gold medal, the highest award it can present in peacetime.

The U.S. Mint is charged with producing these national gold medals. Usually, Congress authorizes the production of bronze duplicates of the gold medals that can be sold to collectors.

The Mint has been producing national medals since its inception. In his prize-winning book, *Medals of the United States Mint, The First Century, 1792-1892*, R.W. Julian lists, describes, discusses and illustrates United States medals under the following categories: Assay Commission, Indian peace, presidential, military, naval, Mint and Treasury, personal, commemorative, school, agricultural, mechanical, scientific and professional, life saving, marksmanship, religious and fraternal and unclassified. The Mint still produces medals today and sells them through **catalog.usmint.gov**, its online product catalog, or by phone at (800) 872-6468.

Relic medals

Relic medals are composed in part or whole of metal (usually though other substances have been used) taken from historic objects and sites. They provide their owners an inexpensive means of owning a tangible piece of history.

By far, the most commonly encountered relic medals commemorate famous ships. These medals contain metal removed from the vessels (copper sheathing or spikes, propellers and other sources); sometimes, the recovered metal is added to additional metal so that only a portion of the medal's content contains the historic metal, while other medals are composed entirely of the recovered metal.

Some of the famous and historic United States warships represented by relic medals are the USS *Constitution,* USS *Constellation* and USS *Olympia.*

Other relic medals contain metal recovered from spacecraft and historic sites.

Art medals

Art medals are an exonumia collectible that are essentially miniature pieces of art that serve to display the talents and interpretation of the artist who creates them. People collect and treasure these tiny works of art for many reasons, including for their historical, commemorative and artistic qualities.

They are not intended for any practical application; they simply represent sculptural art in miniature. Many collectors delight in the many ways that the medals can be presented, but note that like a painting or a bust, for example, these medals are not paperweights. They are one of the world's many art forms. Some firms issue annual calendar medals. These medals bear the year's calendar on one side and artwork on the other.

Collectors and designers of art medals can contact the American Medallic Sculpture Association at **www.amsamedals.org**. AMSA is primarily for the designers and creators of art medals. It sponsors workshops and exhibitions in the field.

Collectors interested in art and medals may also contact the Medal Collectors of America, which publishes a newsletter, MCA Advisory, and an annual journal, *The Medal Cabinet.* Visit the organization's website at **www.medalcollectors.org**.

Collectible altered coins

Four exonumic categories, properly included in a complete discussion of exonumia, depend on alteration of coins after they have left the Mint—love tokens, elongated coins, counterstamped coins and hobo nickels. See the Organizations chapter for information about clubs for collectors of such pieces.

Counterstamped coins

Counterstamped coins are the simplest alteration, and the title clearly indicates what you might expect—the use of a punch to make a mark or marks on a coin. U.S. collectors of counterstamped coins often direct their efforts toward coins where the counterstamp alters the coin into a presentation piece, a store card or some other use of the piece as a token. Large cents were often used in this fashion.

Love tokens

Love tokens may "mutilate" the coin as a piece of money, but hobbyists collect love tokens because of their intrinsic beauty. A love token is a coin that has been altered by smoothing the obverse, reverse or both surfaces of the coin and engraving initials, scenes, messages and so on thereon. The engraved coins were often given to an individual's loved one, hence the name given them.

Love tokens were especially popular in the 19th century, a time when the engraver's art was pervasive in the United States.

Many of the names, monograms or scenes depicted are beautifully done. Often the engraving appears on the side opposite from the date because the date may have had significance to the originator.

Hobo nickels

Hobo nickels are generally Indian Head 5-cent coins (issued between 1913 and 1938) that have been carved using the design of either the American Indian on the obverse or the bison on the reverse (and sometimes both) as a base.

The Indian, larger than portraits on earlier coinage designs, fills the coin surface, providing artists a large, thick area and a high-relief profile to modify, allowing fine detail work. The Indian has been converted into clowns, a woman, other Indians, bearded men wearing a derby hat, ethnic figures and famous people, and has also been used for self portraits.

The bison has been modified to appear as a donkey, elephant, turtle, boxcar, and hobo with a backpack, among other designs.

Elongated coins

An elongated coin is an oval piece produced by a roller die using a coin, token or medal as a planchet—usually a cent, though higher-denomination coins have been used as planchets. The original design or designs are replaced with new designs formed by the die.

Lee Martin and Dottie Dow in their book, *Yesterday's Elongateds,* discuss the techniques of elongated "rolling." Elongated coins are dated from the World's Columbian Exposition in Chicago during 1892 and 1893.

The typical elongated coin has been rolled with a die that impresses one side of the coin. The die has been engraved with a design, often commemorative, or a message. Subject matter, as Martin and Dow said, is "as wide-ranging as the imagination."

As can be inferred from previous discussion, exonumia lends itself to topical collecting. Geography frequently dictates the direction of a collection—a certain state, county or town of interest to the collector. Many individuals relate their collections to personal interests: business, hobby, a sport or other themes.

Replica coins

Replica coins, as implied, are replicas or reproductions of actual coins and considered exonumia.

Replicas should not be confused with counterfeit or altered coins. A counterfeit or altered coin is generally produced to defraud someone, whether it be a counterfeit of a rare coin produced for sale to an unknowing collector or a copy of a circulating coin designed to pass as genuine. A replica is generally produced for souvenir purposes.

Different forms of replicas exist. They are produced and sold by private companies, generally at prices well below the prices the original numismatic items reap.

Poorly executed cast replicas (which do not ring if tapped on the edge) are found in many tourist locales and should not be confused with high-quality struck replicas. The edges of such pieces often show a raised line from where the two halves of the mold were joined together.

Higher quality replicas are produced to provide collectors with an inexpensive though attractive copy of what is often a rare coin.

Several companies have struck replica coins over the years, including the now-defunct Gallery Mint Museum of Eureka Springs, Ark., which created coin replicas by reproducing the same methods and machinery used to make the original coins. The Royal Oak Mint of Royal Oak, Mich. (**royaloakmint.com**) continues to operate, producing similar-style replica pieces. Dan Carr of the Moonlight Mint, Denver (**www.moonlightmint.com**), is another prominent private issuer of replica/fantasy pieces.

By U.S. federal law, replicas include the word COPY incused on the pieces in accordance with the 1973 Hobby Protection Act. The law was passed to combat those who would seek to use replicas fraudulently.

Problems can arise when an uninformed collector mistakes a replica for the genuine item. In some cases, the word COPY never appeared on the replica. In other instances, the word COPY appears on the replica but the owner fails to recognize the significance of the word. In other cases, COPY has been removed by someone attempting to pass the replica as genuine.

High quality replicas are sometimes fraudulently tampered with in an effort to pass them off as genuine coins. In 1998, an altered Gallery Mint reproduction of a 1793 Liberty Cap cent appeared in the market with the COPY stamp and Gallery Mint edge hallmark nearly obliterated. The surfaces were subjected to acid treatments to make it appear to be a genuine specimen of the rarest collectible 1793 Liberty Cap cent, Sheldon 15 (*Penny Whimsy* by William Sheldon).

In 1999, a Gallery Mint 1796 Draped Bust half dollar replica was submitted to a grading service for authentication, but was detected by the authenticators.

In January 2006, an altered Gallery Mint replica of a rare 1793 Flowing Hair, Chain cent was examined by experts at the Florida United Numismatists show in Orlando, Fla. The reproduction piece had been cleverly aged and the word COPY had been treated with an acid that left only a remnant of the letter Y remaining.

Exonumia organizations

One organization devoted to exonumia not specifically aligned with any of the special areas of exonumia previously discussed is the Token and Medal Society (**www.tokenandmedal.org**). (See the Organizations chapter for a larger listing.)

TAMS caters to all aspects of exonumia and the *TAMS Journal* is professional in aspect and content. In addition to the regular issues of the journal, TAMS publishes supplementary issues which are catalogs of special topics of exonumia and most useful to the collector. As well, TAMS has published several books about various facets of the subject. R.W. Julian's book about the U.S. Mint medals is just one example.

The magnitude and complexity of the study of exonumia eliminates the possibility of a single book covering the subject adequately. As a consequence, many books of specialized interest exist. Books and catalogs in profusion, devoted to special, individual aspects of exonumia are available, many of which are listed in the Books and Periodicals chapter.

Several of the organizations dedicated to exonumia maintain libraries related to the subject. In addition, the American Numismatic Association has many volumes about exonumia. Books can be borrowed by collector members of these organizations, usually at the cost of postage and insurance.

Preserving numismatic collections

Providing a safe and secure environment for numismatic collections will help maintain their value and preserve them for future generations to enjoy. One can provide such security through proper handling, using safe and well-designed enclosures, and providing an appropriate storage environment.

Handling

Improper handling of numismatic collections can cause them considerable harm.

Gloves

From a conservation standpoint, it is important to wear gloves when handling metal coins, tokens or medals. Our hands are acidic and salty—both corrode metals. Handling coins without placing a barrier between your hands and the coin can leave a lasting impression. The acids and salts in our hands eat away the metal leaving the imprint of one's finger. A fingerprint is etched into the metal's surface the same way an artist etches a printing plate.

Gloves are an easy, low-cost way to protect coins and help them to retain their beauty and value. A good glove should provide a barrier between the acid and salts in your hands; be light-weight; place a minimal barrier between you and the coin; and be no harm to the coin (in other words, nonabrasive and noncorrosive).

The type of glove worn will depend on a number of factors. Comfort is a definite issue. Many collectors prefer cotton gloves to latex, vinyl or nitrile, as cotton breathes and is more comfortable to wear. Choose cotton gloves that are thick enough to provide a barrier. Cotton gloves have the advantage of being reusable. However, cotton gloves can be slippery. Because of this, some collectors prefer latex, vinyl or nitrile gloves as they afford a better grip on a coin.

Latex gloves are made from vulcanized natural rubber, which means they contain sulphur. As noted in more detail below, sulphur corrodes silver coins. For this reason, avoid handling silver coins with latex gloves or finger cots. Vinyl gloves, an alternative, although made from vinyl, are not heavily plasticized and appear safe for short-term exposure to your collection.

The following glove guidelines will allow one to handle collections safely:

➤ Choose gloves that are comfortable and fit well to ensure a sure grip.

➤ If wearing cotton gloves, be certain that they are clean and dust-free (dirt and dust embedded in the fibres of a glove will make it abrasive).

➤ Cotton gloves are reusable and can be washed time and time again. Do not bleach them. Residual chlorine bleach can be harmful to your coins.

➤ Buy more than one pair of gloves so that you always have a clean pair ready.

➤ Cotton gloves do not have to be white.

➤ If you do not have a pair of gloves handy, use a clean soft cloth or handkerchief instead.

➤ Vinyl and latex gloves can be uncomfortable if worn for long periods of time. Consider wearing a pair of light-weight cotton gloves underneath to help absorb perspiration and condensation.

➤ When buying latex, vinyl and nitrile gloves, ask for "powder-free" gloves. The powder can be abrasive and scratch your coins.

➤ If one insists on handling metal coins with bare hands, be certain hands are freshly washed and dried, and hold the coin only by its edges. Remove any rings, watches or bracelets that may scratch the surface of the coin.

Paper notes can be safely handled with clean dry hands.

Holders

The holders that you use to house coins or paper notes should be safe and meet the following criteria:

➤ It is see-through: A good holder should allow one to view a coin or bill without removing it from the holder.

➤ It is made of a safe material: Safe materials are stable (nondegradable), acid and lignin-free, and as pure as possible (free of plasticizers and slip agents which can leach out and damage coins and notes).

➤ It is easy to use: You should be able to insert or remove a coin or note easily without risking damage to the piece. Coin holders should not abrade or scratch the surface of the coin.

➤ It holds the coin firmly but gently: A coin should not slide or roll around inside its holder.

Safe plastics

Safe plastics are stable, pure and free of plasticizers. Stable plastics retain their chemical composition over time and do not change. If a plastic changes its properties over time (for example, turns yellow; becomes sticky, brittle or cloudy), it is not a stable material. Pure plastics are free of slip agents, antistatic agents and fire retardants. Slip agents are added to a number of plastics to help them slip through the machinery that makes them. All of these additives are considered unsafe and should not be included in plastics intended for close contact with collections.

Safe plastics do not contain plasticizers. Plasticizers are added to plastics to make them soft and supple. Plasticized polyvinyl chloride (PVC) is probably the best known example of a plasticized plastic. The plasticizer in PVC, a phthalate, is unstable and leaches out of the plastic over time. It causes copper alloy coins and silver coins with sufficient copper content to corrode. The corrosion product is commonly referred to by collectors as "green slime." Leaching phthalates can also stain paper and affect some inks.

Recommended materials include: polyethylene, polypropylene, polystyrene, polyester (polyethylene terephthalate) and polymethyl methacrylate (for example, Plexiglas, a trademarked material).

Cellulose acetate, or acetate as it is commonly called, was once considered safe for archival storage but has fallen out of favour. Both the film and slab forms of cellulose acetate have been found to give off acetic acid during degradation, which will corrode metal coins and degrade paper notes.

Acid and lignin-free

Acids corrode metals and degrade paper. Material in intimate contact with numismatic collections—either coins or notes—should be acid and lignin-free. Archival-quality paper or mat board is acid and lignin-free. It comes from two main sources: rags and purified wood pulp. The best quality paper is rag paper. This paper is made from either cotton or linen rags and is the purest. Paper made from purified wood pulp has been chemically treated to remove lignin. Lignin is found in all vascular plants, including trees, where it provides strength and support to the plant. Unfortunately, lignin breaks down easily to form acidic compounds that in turn attack the cellulose in the paper and cause it to degrade. The presence of lignin in paper automatically makes it nonarchival. Chemically treating wood pulp dissolves and washes away the lignin. Archival-quality paper that is marked "acid and lignin-free" is made from chemically purified wood pulp.

Safe, archival-quality materials should have a pH range of 7 to 8.5. The pH of a material refers to whether it is acidic, basic or neutral. The pH scale is logarithmic and ranges from 0 to 14 with 7 as neutral. Values below pH 7 are acidic and values above are basic or alkaline. The further one goes from the neutral point of 7, the greater the level of acidity or alkalinity. A large number of archival paper products are "buffered." Buffered paper has had an alkaline material—usually calcium carbonate—added to protect the paper against acids found either in the environment or the object itself.

The buffering agent acts like an antacid tablet, neutralizing acids in the vicinity of the object. Archival-quality paper should contain no more than 3 percent of the buffering agent. Archival-quality buffered materials will have a pH higher than 7 but no higher than 8.5. Buffered materials are generally considered safe for numismatic collections. The exception to this is amphoteric metals. Amphoteric metals—lead, tin and zinc—are corroded by both acidic and basic environments. Coins made from these metals should be stored in neutral, nonbuffered materials.

Alum-free

Archival-quality paper should also be free of alum. Many conservation scientists believe that alum is one of the chief sources of acid in paper. Alum reacts with water through a chemical reaction called hydro-lysis to form aluminum sulphate and sulphuric acid. Ambient humidity is sufficient to produce and release small amounts of acid.

Paper coin envelopes

Paper coin envelopes are not recommended because they are not see-through. In addition, many collectors feel these envelopes can abrade the high points of coins as they slide in and out of the envelope. If using paper envelopes for coins or notes, choose ones that are acid and lignin-free.

Glassine

Glassine envelopes and enclosures are not recommended. Glassine eventually becomes acidic even if it is labeled "acid-free."

Sulphur and other pollutants

Sulphur-rich materials in intimate contact with numismatic collection will cause silver coins to corrode and paper notes to degrade. Sulphur is found in poor quality paper and cardboard, in many of the foods we eat and in rubber bands. Sulphur will react with silver to produce the corrosion product silver sulfide. Silver sulfide is often referred to by collectors as toning or tarnish. Silver sulfide can appear in several colors including yellow, red, blue and black. The different colors are the result of a physical phenomenon known as "thin film interference." Essentially, the thickness of the silver sulfide layer on the surface of the coin defines the color we see. A thicker film appears darker in color. Sulphur affects paper by reacting with atmospheric moisture to create sulfuric acid.

Several chemicals used in manufacturing carpets and carpet adhesives can also harm numismatic collections. Such chemicals include acetic acid, ammonia, hydrochloric acid, formaldehyde, hydrogen sulfide and sulphur oxides. They are emitted or "off-gassed" by carpets. Exposing numismatic collections to these chemicals can result in corrosion of coins, metals and tokens and degradation of paper notes.

Storage

Storage is an important consideration. Although many collectors store their most valuable collections in a bank safety deposit box, most keep some of their collection at home. Storage location is key to the long-term preservation of numismatic collections.

In general, metal coins should be stored at or below 35 percent relative humidity (RH). Paper notes, on the other hand, will last longer if stored in a cool (less than 70 degrees Fahrenheit), stable, dark environment at 45 to 50 percent RH.

Paper is hygroscopic, absorbing and desorbing moisture according to the ambient relative humidity. Humidity levels above 70 percent RH can invite mold. Mold is a fungus that feeds by absorbing nutrients from living or dead organisms. Molds prefer starches such as cellulose, the main constitu-ent of paper. Paper kept in a very dry environment, conversely, tends to be brittle and desiccated, making handling without damage difficult.

Areas to avoid

In choosing a storage location for numismatic collections, avoid the following areas:

1) Basements: Basements tend toward dampness and flooding. The high RH levels in many basements can cause coins to corrode and paper notes to mold. Mold is very insidious and difficult to eradicate once established. Mold comes in a wide variety of colors and can irreparably stain a paper note.

2) Exterior walls: Most houses in cold climates have poorly insulated exterior walls. These walls can create moist microclimates. Even when the rest of the house may seem very dry, the area by the wall can

have a higher relative humidity because warm moist air in the room can condense in contact with the cold exterior wall. If one hangs a picture on this wall, or puts a box up against it, the moist air is trapped, creating a bad microclimate. This localized build-up of moisture can cause mold to grow and metals to corrode. Closets against exterior walls, having little or no air circulation, are particularly unsuitable storage areas. Uninsulated concrete floors have the same problems as exterior walls.

3) Attics: Attics are unsuitable storage areas for a number of reasons. An unheated, poorly insulated, attic in colder parts of the country can create a condensing environment where atmospheric moisture condenses on cold surfaces when the temperature drops below the dew point. The "dew" left behind can corrode metals and saturate organic materials such as paper. The colder temperatures will also cause the RH to rise. Daily fluctuations of temperature and RH within an attic are problematic for hygroscopic materials like paper. Cycling hygroscopic materials through drastic RH swings creates stresses. Chemical reactions, such as the degradation of paper, happen faster at higher temperatures such as experienced during the hot summer months. Finally, roofs tend to leak, making an attic space no better than a basement.

Collectors should make the best choices possible balancing the needs of the collection and the rest of the household. The following mitigative steps can be taken to improve less-than-optimal storage areas:

➤ If a collection must be stored in the basement, be certain that it is well up off the floor—avoiding condensation and flood damage—and away from exterior walls. Consider installing a dehumidifier to help control the humidity.

➤ If a closet with an external wall is the only storage space available, make sure there is a space between the storage box and the wall.

➤ Provide extra protection by storing numismatic collections in an archival-quality box. Boxes keep out dust and light and provide a buffer to the external environment, slowing down RH fluctuations.

➤ Daily temperature fluctuations should be minimized. Set the thermostat to a constant temperature, day and night.

Regular inspection of stored collections will help identify problems before they can get out of hand.

Conclusion

The three basic steps to preserving a collection are proper handling, using safe and well-designed enclosures and providing an appropriate storage environment. Making the right choices can help ensure that your collection will maintain its beauty and value for future generations to enjoy.

Cleaning coins

Cleaning coins is a topic hotly debated among many collectors.

"Cleaning" encompasses a broad range of activities ranging from a simple wash in soap and distilled water followed by dewatering with a solvent, to removing corrosion or tarnish from the surface by either physical or chemical means. Washing coins in soap and water removes surface dirt, oils and acids that can accumulate on a coin and that, if not removed, will lead to corrosion. Washing and degreasing is a simple treatment that collectors can carry out safely when warranted. Although degreasing solvents have varying levels of toxicity to the collector—and should be used with great care—they do not harm coins.

Removing corrosion requires physical or chemical treatments. These must be applied cautiously because an inappropriate or improperly executed treatment can cause irreparable damage to a coin. The intervention is best left to a professional conservator.

Coin weights and measures

Weights and measures pertaining to coins are almost as numerous as coin types issued over the centuries. It is only natural that a nation would issue coins based on the weight system recognized by its government.

Ancient weights in many cases became coin denominations. The shekel, a weight mentioned in the Old Testament, became a coin denomination of the ancient Jews.

The British pound and Mexican peso are other examples of denominations named for weights.

The grains-ounces-pounds system of Great Britain was adapted for use by the American Colonies and the United States. The metric system was adopted later by the French and then almost all other countries of the world.

In Europe in the 16th, 17th and 18th centuries, as trade between nations brought coins of many denominations and metals from other countries into a merchant's counting room, special scales were developed to weigh each coin. Instead of a weight representing so many drachma, pennyweights or grams, the weight represented a gold French louis d'or, Spanish pistole or British sovereign. The boxes holding the scales and weights were often inlaid, quite ornate, and are themselves collectibles today.

In Great Britain, three 1-penny coins equaled 1 ounce. Struck to such a fine tolerance were British halfpenny and penny coins that bank clerks counted coins by weighing them. Two hundred and forty 1-penny coins (£1) weighed 80 ounces, and triangular-shaped packages of these coins were prepared for sale to the public on the basis of weight, not counting machines.

An early system used to measure coins in England was to assign a number for each 16th of an inch of a coin; a coin measuring 1 inch in diameter was considered size 16; 1.5 inches, size 24; 2 inches, size 32; and so on. U.S. numismatists adopted this system too, although it is no longer used.

Before the metric system, a Frenchman named Mionnet devised a series of concentric lines emanating from a common plane; whichever number line the coin met, when placed on the plane, such was the size of the coin.

Weights and measures

Included in the following chart are coin weight and measure conversions in grams, grains, millimeters, centimeters and inches.

Gold, silver and platinum coins are usually weighed in grams or grains.

One gram equals:
.001 kilogram
15.43235639 grains
.002204622 pound, avoirdupois
.03527396 ounce, avoirdupois
.002679229 pound, troy
.03215075 ounce, troy

One grain equals:
.00006479 kilogram
.0647989 gram
.000142857 pound, avoirdupois
.002285 ounce, avoirdupois
.000173611 pound, troy
.002083 ounce, troy

One millimeter equals:
.03937 inch

One centimeter equals:
.3937 inch

One inch equals:
25.4 millimeters
2.54 centimeters
.0254 meter

Metric conversion, millimeters to inches

mm	inches	mm	inches	mm	inches	mm	inches	mm	inches
10	.39	21	.83	31	1.22	41	1.61	51	2.01
11	.43	22	.87	32	1.26	42	1.65	52	2.05
12	.47	23	.91	33	1.30	43	1.69	53	2.09
13	.51	24	.95	34	1.34	44	1.73	54	2.13
14	.55	25	.98	35	1.38	45	1.77	55	2.17
15	.59	26	1.02	36	1.42	46	1.81	56	2.21
16	.63	27	1.06	37	1.46	47	1.85	57	2.24
17	.67	28	1.10	38	1.50	48	1.89	58	2.28
18	.71	29	1.14	39	1.54	49	1.93	59	2.32
19	.75	30	1.18	40	1.58	50	1.97	60	2.36
20	.79								

Specific gravity of common elements

Element	Sym.	Sp. Grav.	Element	Sym.	Sp. Grav.	Element	Sym.	Sp. Grav.
Aluminum	Al	2.6989	Iron	Fe	7.874	Silicon	Si	2.33
Antimony	Sb	6.691	Lead	Pb	11.35	Silver	Ag	10.50
Beryllium	Be	1.848	Magnesium	Mg	1.738	Tantalum	Ta	16.654
Bismuth	Bi	9.747	Manganese	Mn	[4]7.3	Tin	Sn	[5]7.298
Cadmium	Cd	8.650	Molybdenum	Mo	10.220	Titanium	Ti	4.5400
Carbon	C	[1]2.250	Nickel	Ni	8.9020	Tungsten	W	19.300
Chromium	Cr	[2]7.19	Palladium	Pd	12.02	Vanadium	V	6.1100
Copper	Cu	8.96	Platinum	Pt	21.45	Zinc	Zn	7.1330
Gold	Au	[3]19.32	Ruthenium	Ru	12.41			

1. Carbon has three distinct ranges of specific gravity, depending upon its form. Amorphous carbon ranges from 1.8 to 2.1; diamonds have the highest, at 3.15 to 3.53.

2. Average in the range of 7.18 to 7.20.

3. At 293k: 19.32 g/cm^3

4. Average in the range of 7.21 to 7.44.

5. Gray tin has a specific gravity of 5.75; white tin has a specific gravity of 7.31. Value given is approximate value of combined white and gray in normally occurring proportions.

Gold and copper

Gold is the one metal that does not lend itself to this method of specific gravity determination. When gold is alloyed with copper there is a molecular interaction with the result that the specific gravity of the two metals in alloy is smaller than the specific gravity of the individual parts that were used to make up the alloy. The following is a table of the specific gravity figures of the most common gold-copper alloys.

Au %	Cu %	Sp. Gr.	Au %	Cu %	Sp. Gr.	Au %	Cu %	Sp. Gr.
99	01	19.099	92	08	17.684	85	15	16.464
98	02	18.883	91	09	17.499	84	16	16.303
97	03	18.672	90	10	17.317	83	17	16.146
96	04	18.465	89	11	17.140	82	18	15.991
95	05	18.264	88	12	16.966	81	19	15.840
94	06	18.066	87	13	16.795	80	20	15.691
93	07	17.873	86	14	16.628			

Submitting articles to *Coin World*

Coin World is a weekly news publication covering many aspects of the numismatic hobby. Articles range from breaking news to analysis to feature material and columns.

Coin World welcomes inquiries from persons interested in writing for the publication, but does not accept unsolicited works. Potential freelance writers should contact the *Coin World* editor and receive permission before submitting any articles or story ideas.

Inquiries regarding articles for *Coin World* should be addressed to Coin World Editor, Amos Hobby Publishing, P.O. Box 150, Sidney, OH 45365-0150, or the *Coin World* editor may be contacted via email at **cweditor@coinworld.com**.

Selecting a magnifying lens

Quality work requires quality tools. It may seem ironic that coins worth thousands of dollars are inspected with pocket lenses that cost less than $10. One reason that this does not usually lead to disaster for the buyer is that most of the processing in vision takes place in the brain. A collector who looks at a coin knows in advance what the coin is supposed to look like. The brain corrects for any distortions or aberrations caused by faulty lenses or bad lighting.

However, there are many times when the brain does not know what to expect. Checking a coin for a repunched date or repunched Mint mark or some other odd flaw is a perfect example of this. Inspecting a toned coin for problems beneath the first molecular layer of coloring is another example.

So, how do you find the right lens?

First of all, you are not looking for a "lens" but for a "comparator." A comparator is a lens mounted for use.

Many collectors use a familiar 5x Bausch and Lomb pocket comparator that has an integral box for holding the magnifier and storing it. These typically sell for less than $10. They are widely used in the hobby because they are cheap and reliable. When you need something more, you can look to other Bausch and Lomb products. In addition, competing products are available from Nikon, Zeiss, Edmund Scientifics and other makers.

"There is a price to performance trade-off," explains Ron De Long, president of Vision Advantage Inc., of Palm Desert, Calif. His company represents Zeiss, Nikon and Coil (CTP Coil Ltd.). "We sell a lot of Nikons to collectors," he said.

However, the Zeiss systems are widely regarded as the top of the line. In 1847, Carl Zeiss was an instrument maker. He built the first compound microscopes. In 1889, the company bought back all of its outstanding stock and became a "foundation." Today, Zeiss makes planetariums and industrial measuring systems as well as telescopes and comparators for the consumer. Zeiss is widely regarded as the world's leading optics company.

According to De Long, a quality optical tool is "AR coated." AR stands for anti-reflective. The physics of optics dictates that about 8 percent of the incident light is reflected from a glass surface. A three-lens system (a "triplet") will allow only about 75 percent of available light to pass through. A triplet that is "AR coated" allows close to 100 percent of the available light to pass through.

Edmund Scientific Co., of Barrington, N.J., got its start after World War II selling military surplus lenses and prisms. Today, its Industrial Optics division still sells comparators, along with lasers and machine vision systems. Its line of comparators includes many with AR coating and reticules. A reticule is a measuring standard, seen as little, regular tics along the side of a frame or on a transparent plane. Precision reticules allow correct measurements of distances under magnification. It is possible to find plastic lenses in the Edmund inventory, but most are glass because glass is less easily scratched and less easily warped by heat.

CTP Coil Ltd. led the way in creation of high quality plastic lenses before World War II. Kodak selected Coil's acrylic optical devices for the Brownie camera of 1959. Today, Coil's lenses are "AR coated."

Most collectors prefer to choose one general purpose "pocket lens." However, owning several kinds of comparators can be useful. The physics of optical systems dictates that the greater the magnification, the smaller the viewing area. A 100x microscope will typically have a viewing area of less than 1 millimeter. Enhancing the resultant image can double that. A 25x microscope will have a viewing area of 3 to 6 millimeters. By comparison, a U.S. silver half dime has a diameter three to five times this size, at 15.5 millimeters. Therefore, it is important to have comparators that let you see the whole coin, as well as those that deliver a large, crisp image.

You can buy lens systems that fit over your glasses. You can buy them to stand on a desk. You can buy them to hold in your hand or hang around your neck.

Dealers and collectors have their own preferences.

As you shop, you need to know whether the lens or lenses in the comparator are glass or plastic. Are they coated for anti-reflective properties? Is the company that makes the lenses well known for its work? What is the warranty period, if any? Is a sales or service center nearby? And last but not least, does the company understand the collector markets?

According to De Long, Zeiss did not market consumer products for many years. Their clients were doctors, optical specialists. On the other hand, Edmund Scientific has a long history of selling to hobbyists and hands-on engineers.

As with any buying decision, knowing as much as you can before you spend your money minimizes your risks and maximizes your profits.

Amos Advantage markets a number of different types of magnifying devices. Collectors will find detailed descriptions at **www.amosadvantage.com**.

Numismatic Crime Information Center

In 2009, Doug Davis, a longtime numismatist and Texas lawman, introduced a Website targeting numismatic crimes, the Numismatic Crime Information Center, found at **www.numismaticcrimes.org**.

The website provides dealers, collectors and law enforcement with a free resource to assist in investigation of crimes related to numismatic materials such as coins, paper money, tokens, medals and related items.

The Numismatic Crime Information Center, a 501(c)(3) nonprofit corporation, assists victims during the investigative process and provides law enforcement agencies with technical and investigative support in order to develop effective case strategies and successful outcomes.

21 Museums

The National Numismatic Collection

The National Numismatic Collection, now housed in the Smithsonian Institution, had its beginnings soon after the United States was formed.

The collection's history begins around 1818, when the Columbian Institute for the Promotion of Arts and Sciences, a literary and science institution in Washington, D.C., was granted a charter from Congress. Located in Washington, D.C., the institute had a small numismatic collection kept in the institute's cabinets and not on display to the public.

In 1841, a few years after the charter for the Columbian Institute expired in 1838, its effects, books and papers in its cabinet were absorbed by the newly formed National Institute for the Promotion of Science, or the National Institute as it was later called. The National Institute for the Promotion of Science was organized on May 15, 1840, under the leadership of Joel Roberts Poinsett. Its purpose was to establish a national museum.

John Varden, however, must be given credit as the first to offer public exhibits featuring numismatic objects. He was an enterprising private citizen of Washington, D.C., who opened a small museum adjoining his home in 1836 with displays consisting of some 500 curiosities. In 1840 Varden sold his collection to the National Institute for the Promotion of Science for $1,500. The curator of the National Institute, Dr. Henry King, had the entire inventory of Varden's museum installed in the National Gallery Hall at the U.S. Patent Office, where the other specimens and items in the organization's collection were maintained under the name of the "National Cabinet of Curiosities." Varden accompanied the collection as an assistant. For four years following its organization in 1840, the National Institute was exceedingly active and prosperous. Its members gathered in rooms made available at the Patent Office Building.

Smithson fortune

In 1846 James Smithson, an English scientist, bequeathed his fortune, including many numismatic items, to the United States for the "increase and diffusion of knowledge." On Aug. 10, 1846, an act of Congress was signed by President Polk establishing the Smithsonian Institution and on May 1, 1847, the cornerstone of its first building was laid on the Mall in Washington, D.C.

Early during the period in which the Smithsonian and the National Institute co-existed, the latter failed to secure public recognition and its collections were neglected; in 1857 the transfer of its collection to the Smithsonian began, but was not completed until 1883.

As the government prepared for the centennial exposition of 1876 to be held in Philadelphia, including the development of government exhibits, an opportunity arose for the expansion of the Smithsonian Institution's physical facilities. The Smithsonian found that it had such an enormous quantity of material in its custody that it became necessary to move to a new building, and the funding for the government exhibits at the Centennial Exposition also including funding for the construction of the U.S. National Museum, now the Arts and Industries Building. George Brown Goode was appointed assistant secretary in charge of the museum.

In 1893 the entire numismatic collection was withdrawn from display and stored, after being crowded out by expanding natural history collections. Even though the numismatic holdings were kept from public view during last few years of the 19th century, an attempt was made to expand the collection by assembling a general collection of currencies of the world, and numismatic acquisitions were both numerous and varied.

During the last decade and a half of the 19th century, the Smithsonian added several important holdings to the collection. One of the most outstanding groups of coins received was a collection of 28 Japanese gold and silver pieces, which came to the museum in 1886 together with other relics once owned by Ulysses S. Grant. Another major accession was a collection of 2,025 Far Eastern coins bequeathed to the Smithsonian by George Bunker Glover in 1897.

Theodore Belote was appointed assistant curator in 1909. This provided a fresh opportunity for the development of numismatic collections in the Smithsonian, for Belote had a particular interest in this subject. Also, in the years from 1910 to 1914, with the addition of a new museum building for natural history, space was gradually regained for the numismatic exhibits. By 1914 Belote had finished selecting, classifying, cleaning and labeling coins and medals for the Smithsonian Institution's numismatic display.

During World War I and the early postwar years, the numismatic acquisitions were heavily weighted toward medals and decorations, including 1,200 Lincoln items covering nearly every phase of his life, assembled by Robert Hewitt.

Mint collection

The most important event of this postwar period was the transfer of the Mint collection in Philadelphia to the Smithsonian. When Dr. T. Louis Comparette, curator, died suddenly in 1922, the Mint collection was closed to the public. At that time it was suggested that it be moved to Washington.

Formal acceptance by the secretary of the Smithsonian Institution followed on Feb. 19, 1923. Exactly 18,291 pieces were included in the transfer, which increased the holdings of the National Numismatic Collection from 21,523 to 39,814 items. In addition to the numismatic items, the Mint transferred 814 books selected by Belote in 1924 from the specialized library at the Philadelphia Mint.

The history of the Mint collection officially started in June 1838, but its actual history goes back to the beginning of the Mint in 1792 and 1793. The chief coiner, Adam Eckfeldt, connected with the Mint since its inception, "led as well by his own taste as by the expectation that a conservatory would some day be established, took pains to preserve master-coins of the different annual issues of the Mint, and to retain some of the finest foreign specimens, as they appeared in deposit for recoinage," according to *New Varieties of Gold and Silver Coins, Counterfeit Coins, and Bullion: With Mint Values,* by Jacob Reese Eckfeldt and William Ewing Du Bois (second edition, 1851).

Among the coins deposited by Adam Eckfeldt was, for instance, the Brasher doubloon.

When Congress instituted a special annual appropriation for this purpose in 1838, the collection took permanent form and grew continuously. The eagerness of the Mint assayers Du Bois and Jacob Eckfeldt to complete the Mint collection contributed to its continued growth. Du Bois in his *Pledges of History* (1846) mentions that after the collection was officially established in June 1838, it "has gone on in a continual augmentation ... specimens of new coinage, domestic or foreign, must be added as they appear."

In the same volume Du Bois also describes the early Mint exhibit, located at that time at 17th and Spring Garden streets in Philadelphia.

Data about the growth of the Philadelphia Mint collection may be gleaned from Mint records preserved in the National Archives as well as from occasional published notes and reports. Some early illustrations of coins from the cabinet are contained in Jacob Eckfeldt and Du Bois' *A Manual of Gold and Silver Coins of All Nations, Struck Within the Past Century* (1842).

The first full catalog of the collection appeared in 1860 under the direction of James Ross Snowden. Titled *A Description of Ancient and Modern-Coins, in the Cabinet Collection at the Mint of the United States* (1860), it was prepared by George Bull, in charge of the cabinet, with the advice and assistance of Du Bois, at that time assistant assayer and curator of the cabinet.

In 1861, Snowden published *The Medallic Memorials of Washington in the Mint of the United States.* He was very much interested in this particular section of the cabinet and made every effort to enlarge it.

Notes about additions to the collections were published by Du Bois in *The United States Mint Cabinet,* where he mentions that "the whole number of coins and medals at this time [1874] is 6,484," and in *Recent Additions to the Mint Cabinet.*

In 1891, R.A. McClure, curator of the Mint collection, prepared *An Index to the Coins and Medals of the Cabinet of the Mint of the United States at Philadelphia,* published by the superintendent of the Philadelphia Mint, O.C. Bosbyshell; and in 1894 the Philadelphia *Telegraph* reported on "Late Additions" to the Mint cabinet: "8,000 coins were on display, the case of current coins stands to the left of the museum door, opposite the curator's desk."

With the completion of a new Philadelphia Mint in 1902, described as "the finest building ever constructed for coinage purposes in the world," the cabinet was moved to the new location. It was reinstalled there in sumptuous surroundings and in new, rather ponderous exhibit cases.

The first and only formally recognized curator of the Mint collection was Dr. Thomas Louis Comparette, appointed to the post in 1905. Various people previously had been delegated to take care of the cabinet but without the curator title. Comparette immediately made plans for expansion and improvement of the Mint collection.

"The most pressing needs appear to be a new catalog and a rearrangement of the coins in the cases," according to his comprehensive report about the numismatic collection.

In the same report he mentions, referring to the past, "An apparent tendency to give undue preference to rather expensive rarities for exhibitions as 'show pieces' has resulted in restricting the numerical development of the collection, in the increase of certain series at the expense of others, and especially in the neglect of the coins of lower denomination, which are much less attractive to the average visitor but necessary in order to gain a proper idea of the complete coinage of a given country or period and highly valued by the better informed.

"The more serious purpose better harmonizes with what is felt to be the worthier function of the collection, for the attitude of the cabinet has been from the first that of an educational institution," he recorded.

The preparation of the catalog took Comparette about seven years; it appeared in 1912 comprising

634 pages and 15 plates. In 1914 a so-called "third edition" catalog followed with the same number of plates but expanded, through additions, to 694 pages. A most useful 106-page *Guide to the Numismatic Collection of the Mint of the United States at Philadelphia, Pa.* was published in 1913. In addition to the catalog Dr. Comparette published various papers, particularly in the field of ancient numismatics.

While in charge of the Mint cabinet Comparette expended considerable time and effort to mobilize support for the improvement of the collection. He attempted to obtain the support of President Theodore Roosevelt to secure for the cabinet the H.C. Hoskier Collection of Greek and Roman coins when the owners who lived in South Orange, N.J., offered it for sale.

Comparette succeeded in obtaining the support of the Assay Commission of 1909; its committee on resolutions passed a motion recommending that the coin collection be improved and suggested the striking of artistic medals with the understanding that the profits from their sale should benefit the Mint Cabinet. Similar resolutions were passed by the annual Assay Commissions meeting in subsequent years.

Reports about the growth of the collection were incorporated in the *Director's Annual Report* from 1910 through 1921 under the title "The State of the Numismatic Collection" (after 1917, "The Progress of the Numismatic Collection"). All these activities ended with Comparette's sudden death on July 3, 1922.

Transferring the collection

The idea of the transfer of the collection to Washington had been proposed as early as 1916 by Dr. George F. Kunz of New York, president of the American Scenic and Historic Preservation Society and one of the most active members of the American Numismatic Society. He discussed the idea with Dr. Charles D. Walcott, secretary of the Smithsonian, and with Director of the Mint Robert W. Wooley on April 4, 1916.

The lack of a curator after the death of Comparette and the closing of the Philadelphia Mint to the public because of a robbery at the Denver Mint (committed after thieves obtained information through a previous visit) were among the factors that persuaded Secretary of the Treasury Andrew W. Mellon to decide to transfer the collection to the Smithsonian Institution in Washington, and he so notified Secretary Walcott in February 1923.

The secretary of the Smithsonian acknowledged Andrew Mellon's letter on Feb. 12 and delegated W. de C. Ravenel, director of the museum, and T.T. Belote, curator of history, to discuss the necessary arrangements for the transfer.

Formal acceptance of the collection by the secretary of the Smithsonian Institution followed on Feb. 19.

On Feb. 28, Theodore T. Belote was authorized to inspect the numismatic collection at the Mint in order to plan for its packing and transportation to the Smithsonian. He spent March 6 and 7 there and reported on March 8 to Miss M.M. O'Reilly, acting director of the Mint, his findings and recommendations.

Pressure, however, built up in Philadelphia against the proposed transfer. The Philadelphia *Ledger* of March 31 expressed great concern "that the Philadelphia Mint's invaluable collections of coins, medals and tokens is being boxed, ready for shipment to the National Museum in Washington. The collection which was begun with the inception of the Philadelphia Mint in 1792, is believed to be one of the finest in the world." Another editorial on the same subject appeared in the *Ledger* on April 1.

Various local organizations, and through them congressmen from the area, were mobilized in an intensive but futile action to reverse the Treasury Department's decision.

On a national level, however, the American Numismatic Association immediately supported the transfer. In an editorial comment that appeared in the May 1923 issue of *The Numismatist*, this position was made very clear:

"Taking a broad view of the matter, the National Museum in Washington is the logical place for the coin collection. It has been termed the Mint collection, though, strictly speaking, it is the national collection. The National Museum already has a collection of medals, and the merging of the two collections will be advantageous.

"The construction of the Mint Cabinet is such that it would be impossible to enlarge the space for the collection without remodeling the entire rotunda. This fact would prevent the material growth of the collection. ... In the national Museum more space will probably be available, and perhaps more money for the purchase of additional specimens can be obtained.

"Washington is the home of our other national collections. ... The Capital City is a Mecca for sightseers and visitors, and the other collections will help to attract a larger number of visitors than a collection of coins alone could command.

"There is one phase of the matter that is worthy of reflection, but which may not have received consideration by the Treasury officials in reaching their decision. The late Dr. Comparette ... is said to have been greatly concerned ... about the apparent deterioration of the condition of the coins in the collection. The cause of this ... was believed to be due to an atmospheric condition ... on The Mall in Washington, all such conditions will be removed."

The editorial concludes that the closing of the Mints to visitors "is to be regretted more than the transfer of the collection from one city to another."

Concerned about the protests from Philadelphia, which multiplied during the month of April, Belote tried to obtain the active support of the national numismatic organizations.

He visited New York where he had a series of meetings on May 7 and 8 with Edward T. Newell, president of the ANS, Moritz Wormser, president of the ANA, and Howland Wood, curator of the ANS collections.

He obtained assurances that efforts would be made to have resolutions passed by the executive bodies of the two societies for presentation to the secretary of the Treasury recommending the proposed transfer without delay.

Because of these conferences, the American Numismatic Society Council passed a resolution favoring the transfer of the Mint Collection to the Smithsonian, and on May 15 a letter to that effect was sent to the secretary of the treasury.

Howland Wood reported to Belote, stating: "Our Council passed a Resolution to write to Secretary Mellon favoring the transfer of the Mint collection to Washington, and a letter was sent to that effect on Saturday last. Also, the N.Y. Numismatic Club on Friday evening passed a similar Resolution. It looks now fairly favorable for the National Museum's getting it."

Similar action was taken by the New York Numismatic Club upon motion brought by Moritz Wormser at its May meeting. After obtaining the unanimous support of the board of governors of the American Numismatic Association as well, Wormser notified Andrew Mellon of this support.

In short sequence, Secretary Walcott informed Mellon on May 16 that "the National Museum has entirely perfected its plans for the acceptance and appropriate installation of the numismatic collection from the United States Mint" and asked whether the Secretary of the Treasury could advise him "of the exact time when transfer ... will be completed."

Actually, all arrangements for the transportation of the collection were completed without further delay. The shipment went forward by registered mail, insured, and was accompanied by Secret Service men. It arrived at the Smithsonian the next morning. It was formally "accessioned" as a transfer on June 13, 1923.

In 1931, the Smithsonian Institution numismatic collection was moved from poorly lighted quarters to a smaller, but much brighter area of the Arts and Industries building where it remained until its transfer to the Museum of History and Technology in 1964.

Belote, curator of the Division of History, remained in charge of the collections until 1948, and by this time the collection had increased to 54,175 pieces.

In 1948, Stuart Mosher was appointed acting curator of the division. He held this position until his death in February 1956. At the time of his death, the collection had a total of 64,522 pieces. This growth included the contribution of Paul Straub consisting of 1,860 gold and 3,886 silver coins.

From February through September 1956, Mendel Peterson served as acting curator of the division until Dr. Vladimir Clain-Stefanelli was appointed curator

in October 1956, and Elvira Clain-Stefanelli was appointed as assistant curator in 1957 and associate curator in 1959.

In October 1964, the Hall of Monetary History and Medallic Art, in the newly built Museum of American History, became the home of the Smithsonian Institution collection after its transfer from the Arts and Industries building.

In 1966, the Smithsonian started acquiring from the Bureau of Engraving and Printing 306,275 "certified proofs" of just about everything the BEP has printed. The certified proofs of paper money, government documents and other inked impressions from new printing plates submitted to BEP officials for approval before the plates went into regular use were transferred to the Smithsonian when the BEP ran out of room to store a century's worth of its printing treasures. This acquisition was completed in July 1984.

In 1968, Congress approved legislation that authorized the Smithsonian to acquire the Josiah K. Lilly Collection of gold coins in exchange for a $5.5 million tax write-off for the Lilly estate. The collection contains 6,125 gold coins and is considered one of the finest gold coin collections in the world. Lilly was heir to the Eli Lilly pharmaceutical company and chairman of its board of directors in the 1960s. The collection arrived at the Smithsonian June 13, 1968.

1972 exhibit

The Smithsonian opened a new exhibit, "The History of Money and Medals," July 12, 1972, showing the history of mankind as it is mirrored in coinage.

The exhibit was compiled in slightly more than six months. Containing more than 10,000 numismatic specimens arranged in 130 units, the display has something for everyone from the most knowledgeable scholars to children (coins for touching were provided for the latter).

Vladimir and Elvira Clain-Stefanelli, co-curators of the Division of Numismatics for more than two decades, used for the central theme of the main display the evolution of the money economy as an integral aspect of the cultural, economic and social development of human society.

Significant contributions to the exhibit were made by private collectors and corporations as well as by government agencies such as the Library of Congress, the Secret Service and the Mints of the United States, Britain and France.

Early in 1974 the Smithsonian and the American Bankers Association announced plans to mount a major Bicentennial exhibit concerning commercial banking in the Smithsonian's National Museum of History and Technology.

The exhibit opened to the public Sept. 18, 1975. It told the story of America's involvement in banking, from Colonial barter systems, when prices were expressed in beaver skins, to the "sophisticated electronic techniques" of the 1970s. The exhibit was supplemented by an illustrated essay, "Two Centuries of

American Banking," written by the Clain-Stefanellis. The exhibit remained in place through the American Bicentennial celebration of 1976.

Important acquisitions

The year 1978 proved one of important acquisitions for the Smithsonian. Formal papers for the transfer of the Chase Manhattan Bank money collection, one of the most famous in the history of the United States, were signed Jan. 16 by S. Dillon Ripley, secretary of the Smithsonian Institution, and David Rockefeller, chairman of the Chase Manhattan Bank in New York. The massive collection of coins, tokens, medals and paper money was formed by the American numismatic immortal, Farran Zerbe. Zerbe began arranging for the transfer of his collection to the Chase Bank in 1926, with completion of the transfer occurring in 1929, the same year Zerbe became the Chase Manhattan Museum's first curator.

On May 17, 1978, in a historic ceremony, the Treasury Department turned over to the Smithsonian a collection of 800 pieces of U.S. paper money with a numismatic value of more than $1 million. The collection, with a face value of $578,365.79, includes nearly one note of every issue of U.S. paper currency between the Civil War period and the early 1960s.

Three months later, in August, R. Henry and Emery May Norweb donated a Proof example of the 1913 Liberty Head 5-cent coin—one of only five such pieces known—to the Smithsonian.

Stack family adds to collection

Starting in the 1950s, Lawrence, Harvey and Norman Stack of the auction firm Stack's in New York began to donate numerous significant items to the National Collection. In 1992, the Stack family donated the personal papers of Charles E. Barber, chief engraver at the U.S. Mint between 1880 and 1917, materials that provide an important record of the day-to-day operations of U.S. die makers and coiners and first-hand evidence of the Proof and regular coinage struck at the Mint during Barber's tenure.

The Stack family gave many significant pieces to the collection in 1993. That year the family donated a unique, reeded edge J.S. Ormsby & Co. $5 pioneer gold piece, one of the extreme rarities never added to the collection's extensive gold coin collection assembled by Josiah Lilly.

Also in 1993, the Stacks donated a 1792 Birch cent, which allowed the museum to complete a denominational set of the first coinage of the U.S. Mint; an 1879 Coiled Hair Stella $4 pattern in gilt aluminum (possibly unique); and a silver 1792 Getz pattern half dollar. The Birch cent was used as a prop by President Clinton March 14, 2000, during a speech about DNA research, in which he compared modern scientific research to a legend on the coin. The cent bears the legend LIBERTY PARENT OF SCIENCE & TECHNOLOGY.

In 1994, the Stack family donated a Proof 1879 quintuple Stella pattern in gold and a second Proof example of the same pattern in copper-gilt. At that time, no other public institution, museum or university coin collection owned or conserved an example of the quintuple Stella in any metal.

Willis H. du Pont donated an Uncirculated Class III 1804 dollar to the Smithsonian in 1994. He gave the Smithsonian the Henry R. Linderman specimen, named after one of the Mint directors who owned it. The Linderman coin and the Edward Cohen specimen of a Class I 1804 dollar were robbed from du Pont and his family at gunpoint in 1967 when their home was burglarized.

The American Numismatic Association recovered the Linderman specimen in 1981 when it was presented for authentication. It was loaned to the ANA by du Pont for display at the ANA Money Museum beginning in 1982. The Cohen specimen was recovered in Switzerland in 1993.

In 1994, du Pont arranged for the Linderman Class III specimen to be donated to the Smithsonian and for the Cohen Class I coin to go to the ANA.

The Smithsonian is the only institution in the world to hold an example of each of the three classes of 1804 Draped Bust silver dollar. The Class II coin in the Smithsonian is unique. (See the chapter Rarities for more information on the 1804 Draped Bust dollar.)

Death ends tenure

On October 19, 1982, Dr. Vladimir Clain-Stefanelli, chairman of the Department of Applied Arts of the Smithsonian Institution and senior historian and curator of the National Numismatic Collection, died at Georgetown University Hospital in Washington, D.C.

During the quarter of a century he was associated with the Smithsonian, Dr. Clain-Stefanelli's acumen and diplomacy were successful in increasing the size of the National Numismatic Collection more than tenfold, building it from a collection of about 64,000 pieces to one of the most outstanding in the world, numbering close to 900,000 pieces.

On Dec. 28, 1982, Emery May Norweb donated a 52-piece collection of U.S. Colonial coins in memory of Dr. Vladimir Clain-Stefanelli.

In September 1983, Elvira Clain-Stefanelli, who had served with her husband as co-curator and carried on the curatorial work they had shared prior to his death, was named to the new title of executive director of the National Numismatic Collection.

At the same time, Cory Gillilland was named curator for the Division of Numismatics, leaving her position as chief of the Bureau of the Mint's consumer affairs staff to assume her new post. She had been associated with the Smithsonian's Division of Numismatics earlier, from 1965 to 1975. Her areas of responsibility included American and foreign medals. She retired in 1993.

In 1986, Dr. Richard G. Doty became the curator of Western Hemisphere Numismatics for the National

Numismatic Collection. Prior to this position, Doty was curator of modern coins and paper money at the American Numismatic Society in New York. He remains chief curator of the NNC in 2011.

In July 1984, the United States Mint transferred 114 Olympic coins, American Arts Gold Medallions, and bronze and pewter national medals to the national collection. This was the largest transaction from the Mint since 1923.

In 1999, the museum acquired a complete set of Greek Demareteion Master coins from a donation by John Whitney Walter. The Smithsonian is the only museum in world with a complete set of these important Greek coins.

In 1999 the museum received a collection of 5,000 obsolete notes. Beginning in 1990, Bradley and Virginia Bennett donated in batches about 8,000 ancient Greek and Greek Imperial coins, almost all bronze.

An era ended in September 2000 when Elvira Clain-Stefanelli retired, after 43 years of service to the Smithsonian and the National Numismatic Collection.

During the last decade, the Smithsonian Institution's National Numismatic Collection has undergone a profound transformation. The collection was removed from public display in 2005 while the building was renovated, in part to showcase the Star Spangled Banner (the flag that flew over Fort McHenry during the siege of Baltimore during the War of 1812). The Smithsonian opened a smaller numismatic gallery June 12, 2009, displaying 187 items from the collection, presented thematically in a 500-square foot area (reduced from the 3,000-square-foot exhibit space of old).

The Smithsonian Institution cooperated with the American Numismatic Association to display items from the National Numismatic Collection at ANA conventions while the collection was inaccessible, a partnership that continues to this day with the commitment to sponsor a traveling exhibit that includes U.S. Mint "heritage assets" in 2011.

In early 2011, Heritage Auction Galleries announced a charity auction to help establish an endowment for the National Numismatic Collection.

In 2011, the collection contained an estimated 1.6 million items.

The Museum of American History, which houses the collection, is located on Constitution Avenue at 14th Street Northwest on the Mall. It is open to the public from 10 a.m. to 5:30 p.m. every day except for Christmas Day. There is no admission charge. Visit **http://americanhistory.si.edu/** for information on the collection.

American Numismatic Association

The American Numismatic Association continually expands its collection of all numismatic items in the museum located at its Colorado Springs, Colo., headquarters. In 2011, the museum holds an estimated 270,000 pieces. The ANA can be accessed via the Internet at **www.money.org**.

Founded in 1891, the ANA received a federal charter from the U.S. Congress in 1912, which was renewed in perpetuity in 1962.

The ANA's Edward C. Rochette Money Museum is one of the most extensive in the world.

The ANA's museum is the largest in the United States dedicated solely to numismatics and uses money as a means to explore culture, art, science and history.

The History Through Money exhibit is the primary interpretive numismatic display in the museum, occupying the entire lower level. The exhibit explores the presence and role of numismatic items in the course of civilization from about 700 B.C. to the present. The galleries include money exhibits of ancient, medieval and modern times as well as colonial money in early America, the history of the U.S. Mint, presidential money-related memorabilia and future money forms.

Significant additions to the Money Museum during the final decades of the 1900s include the Cohen specimen of the Class I 1804 Draped Bust dollar, which was donated by Willis du Pont in 1994 after the ANA helped to recover the coin, and the Idler Specimen of a Class III 1804 dollar, which was donated by longtime ANA members Aubrey and Adeline Bebee in 1991.

In 2001, the museum underwent a renovation to accommodate the Harry W. Bass Jr. Collection, which features a type set of U.S. gold coins plus an extensive collection of U.S. gold varieties and U.S. pattern coins along with a unique display of the series of 1896 silver certificate drawings, designs and proofs.

The permanent or semi-permanent galleries were replaced in 2001 with regularly changing galleries throughout the museum. In 2011, the museum features the following exhibits: "A House Divided: Money of the Civil War" and "The Faces of Money: The Good, the Bad and the Ugly."

Permanent exhibits of certain high-end U.S. rarities include two 1913 Liberty Head 5-cent coins, an 1804 Draped Bust dollar, three 1866 Seated Liberty, No Motto coins from the du Pont holdings and error notes from the Beebe Collection. A steam press was added to the museum in 2000.

The museum is constantly evolving; contact the ANA for details on new exhibits as they replace existing exhibits. Admission is free for ANA members.

The museum is open from 10:30 a.m. to 5 p.m. Tuesday through Saturday. For further information, telephone the ANA at (719) 482-9828, email it at **museum@money.org** or visit **www.money.org**.

American Numismatic Society

The American Numismatic Society Museum, located at 75 Varick St., Floor 11, New York City, N.Y., is unique in being the first museum in the world devoted entirely to numismatics. The ANS may be accessed online at **www.numismatics.org**.

In honor of the society's 125th anniversary celebration in 1983, a new exhibition, "The World of Coins," was mounted with a wholly new approach to the story of money. It showed the use, value and design of money in a cross-cultural story, shedding light on such humanistic issues as economic development, trade patterns, social and political symbolism and the relationship of religion and public life.

The society's extensive holdings are computerized with all of the relevant information available being included for the benefit of the researcher.

The ANS collection is large and representative. All fields are covered, but particularly important are the coins of ancient Greece and Rome, the Far Eastern series, and the Islamic issues. The medieval, modern and American groups are also distinguished.

By far the greater portion of the collection has been received through bequests and gifts both of collections and of single specimens. A relatively small proportion has been acquired by purchase (though sales of duplicate items during the past decade have funded additional acquisitions).

Coinage struck in the 19th and 20th centuries is well represented through the gift of Wayte Raymond of the specimens gathered in preparation of his *Standard Catalogues* of contemporary coins.

The coinage of the United States forms a small section of the society's cabinet. Notable sections have come from the J. Pierpont Morgan, William B. Osgood Field and Elliott Smith collections. The society possesses such treasures as one of the four known examples of the original Confederate half dollar, a gift of J. Sanford Saltus, and the press used by Augustus Bechtler in striking private gold coins in North Carolina, given by Julius Guttag.

One of the richest series is that of the United States copper cents struck between 1793 and 1857, the collection gathered by George H. Clapp and given by him to the society. The Colonial issues of Massachusetts are present as specimens from the Field collection, and the state coinages before the adoption of the Constitution are well represented.

In February 1991, the ANS announced that 129 U.S. cents, part of an extensive collection donated by Clapp, had been switched for identical varieties of coins of lesser quality, according to expert Delmar Bland. Subsequent research findings by the ANS staff in cooperation with Bland demonstrated that the thief was the late William H. Sheldon, who died in 1977. The ANS believes the thefts occurred when Sheldon conducted research in the ANS vaults in 1950. Sheldon was regarded as the preeminent classi-

fier, cataloger and collector of large cents who wrote *Early American Cents* (later called *Penny Whimsy*), which instituted a numbering system for large cents still used today.

Roy E. Naftzger purchased Sheldon's collection in 1972. In a 1997 California Superior Court decision ruling, the court noted that "from as early as 1976 Naftzger was receiving information that Sheldon had switched coins in the Clapp Collection at the ANS ..." and that "Naftzger had sought to conceal from the ANS his possession of the missing coins after the Bland Report was made public [in 1991]."

The court judged the ANS to be the legal owner of 38 large cents dated from 1794 to 1814 in the possession of Naftzger. In addition, the ruling awarded the ANS $229,500 in damages for the value of an additional 20 U.S. cents that belonged to the ANS that Naftzger previously possessed and sold as well as all court costs associated with the case.

Other ANS collections

Tokens, helpmates to coinages in times of stress, offer interesting sidelights to the history of periods of monetary crisis. The richest series of tokens in the collection are those of the Hard Times period in the United States, 1837 to 1841, and the merchants' tokens of the Civil War period of the 1860s, including the Edward Groh Collection of 5,286 pieces donated in 1900.

The collection also includes medals: English medals from the period of Elizabeth I from the Daniel Parish Jr. collection, Indian peace medals from the Stephen H.P. Pell collection, Adm. Vernon medals from the L. McCormick-Goodhart Collection, along with a selection of medals designed by contemporary American and European sculptors. All provide a record of the progress of medallic art.

Paper money is also present in the collection: obsolete bank notes of the "wildcat" bank era of the United States, Continental notes of Revolutionary times, selections of foreign paper currencies and special series such as prisoner of war money, occupational currency, and more.

For details about the ANS Collections, visit **www. numismatics.org/Collections/Collections**.

The ANS has displayed periodic exhibits in conjunction with the Federal Reserve Bank in New York City, including what may be its most successful, "Drachmas, Doubloons and Dollars: The History of Money."

Originally planned for five years, the exhibit made its debut in 2002 after a delay related to the Sept. 11, 2001, terrorist attacks. The period of display has been extended and the exhibit is slated to appear through March 2012. The exhibit at the Federal Reserve Bank includes the Bechtler press mentioned earlier.

United States museums

Any number of museums across the United States have items that are of interest to the coin collector.

The number and scope of collections is always changing, however, and some museums have succumbed to economic pressures, reducing hours of operations or displays, or worse, deaccesioning items.

Although every effort was made to ensure the accuracy of the following listings, readers are encouraged to contact museums before visiting to make certain of both availability and accessibility of numismatic items, museum hours and admission fees.

California

BERKELEY. **Judah L. Magnes Museum**, The Bancroft Library, University of California Berkeley. Jewish American Hall of Fame medal series, modern foreign coins and ancients. In transition and inaccessible in early 2011, its new location was set to open in the fall of 2011 at 2121 Allston Way, 94704. Web: **www.magnes.org**.

LOS ANGELES. **Skirball Cultural Center**, 2071 N. Sepulveda, 90049. Ancient Jewish coins, medals, tokens and numismatic literature. Open only to scholars by appointment. Call: (310) 440-4500. Web: **www.skirball.org**.

SAN FRANCISCO. **Wells Fargo Bank History Museum**, 420 Montgomery St., 94104. Wells Fargo and Company history from 1852 to present. U.S. coins, paper money and modern foreign coins. Open 9 a.m. to 5 p.m. Monday through Friday, closed weekends and national holidays. Call: (415) 396-2619. Web: **www.wellsfargohistory.com/museums/index.html**.

Colorado

COLORADO SPRINGS. **American Numismatic Association**, 818 N. Cascade Ave., 80903. U.S. and foreign coins, medals, tokens, paper money, medieval, ancients and a numismatic library. Open 10:30 a.m. to 5 p.m. Tuesday through Saturday, closed national holidays. Admission: Free. Call: (719) 482-9828. Web: **www.money.org**.

COLORADO SPRINGS. **Pioneers' Museum**, 215 S. Tejon St., 80903. U.S. paper money and medals. Open 10 a.m. to 4 p.m. Tuesday through Saturday, closed national holidays. Admission: Free. Call: (719) 385-5990. Web: **www.springsgov.com/SectionIndex.aspx?SectionID=38**.

DENVER. **Denver Museum of Nature & Science**, 2001 Colorado Blvd., Denver, 80205. Houses "Tom's Baby," 8-pound piece of gold discovered in Colorado. Open 9 a.m. to 5 p.m. daily. Closed Christmas. Call: (303) 370-6000. Web: **www.dmns.org**.

DENVER. **United States Mint**, 320 W. Colfax Ave., 80204. Open 8 a.m. to 2 p.m. daily, closed holidays. Admission: Free. Web: **www.usmint.gov/mint_tours/?action=StartReservation**.

FORT COLLINS. **Fort Collins Museum and Discovery Science Center**, 200 Mathews St., 80524. Coins, medals, tokens and paper money. Open 10 a.m. to 5 p.m. Tuesday through Saturday and noon to 5 p.m. on Sunday. Varied rates of admission. Call: (970) 221-6738. Web: **www.fcmdsc.org**.

Connecticut

HARTFORD. **Museum of Connecticut History**, Connecticut State Library, 231 Capitol Ave., 06106. Joseph C. Mitchelson collection, U.S. coins and medals. Open 9 a.m. to 4 p.m. Monday through Friday, 9 a.m. to 2 p.m., Saturday. Closed Sunday and state holidays. Admission: Free. Call: (860) 757-6535. Web: **www.museumofcthistory.org**.

District of Columbia

WASHINGTON. **B'nai B'rith Museum**, 1640 Rhode Island St. N.W., 20036. Ancient coins (by appointment only). Museum open 10 a.m. to 5 p.m. Sunday through Friday, closed national and Jewish holidays. Admission: Free. Call: (202) 857-6583. Web: **bnaibrith.org**.

WASHINGTON. **Bureau of Engraving and Printing.** Printing facility for U.S. government security documents, including Federal Reserve notes. Both VIP tours (request through senator or congressman) and general tours available. Open 8:30 a.m. to 3:30 p.m. with extended hours during the summer. Closed weekends, federal holidays and the week between Christmas and New Years. Call: (202) 874-2330. Web: **www.bep.treas.gov/tours/washingtondctours.html**.

WASHINGTON. **Smithsonian Institution, National Museum of American History,** Constitution Avenue between 12th and 14th streets Northwest, 20560. "Stories on Money" exhibit. Open 10 a.m. to 5:30 p.m. daily during the winter and 10 a.m. to 7:30 p.m. daily from end of May to early September. Closed Christmas. Admission: Free. Call: (202) 633-1000. Web: **americanhistory.si.edu/collections/subject_detail.cfm?key=32&colkey=9**.

WASHINGTON. **National Archives and Records Administration Exhibition Hall**, 700 Pennsylvania Ave., 20408, where the Declaration of Independence, Constitution and Bill of Rights are permanently displayed. U.S. presidents and Constitution medals. Exhibition Hall open daily 10 a.m. to 7 p.m. March 15 through Labor Day, and 10 a.m. to 5:30 p.m. Labor Day through March 14, except Christmas. Closed Sunday and federal holidays. Web: **www.archives.gov/dc-metro/washington/**.

Florida

KEY WEST. **Mel Fisher Maritime Museum**, 200 Greene St., 33040. Contains the treasures removed from the sunken Spanish treasure ship *Nuestra Senora de Atocha,* including gold and silver bars, ship's artifacts, jewels, etc. Open 8:30 a.m. to 5 p.m., Monday to Friday, 9:30 a.m. to 5 p.m., weekends and holidays. Admission: $12.50 for adults, $10.50 for students, $6.25 for children. Call: (305) 294-2633. Web: www.melfisher.org/.

TALLAHASSEE. Museum of Florida History, 500 S. Bronough St., 32399. 18th century Spanish coins from new world mints, U.S. and foreign coins and paper money. Open 9 a.m. to 4:30 p.m. Monday through Friday; 10 a.m. to 4:30 p.m. Saturday; and 12 p.m. to 4:30 p.m. Sunday and holidays. Closed Thanksgiving and Christmas. Admission: Free. Call: (850) 245-6400. Web: www.museumofflorida history.com.

Georgia

COLUMBUS. National Infantry Museum and Soldier Center, U.S. Army Infantry Center, 1775 Legacy Way, 31903. U.S. and world military medals. Open Tuesday through Friday 9 a.m. to 5 p.m. and Sunday 11 a.m. to 5 p.m. Closed Thanksgiving, Christmas and New Year's. Admission: Free. Call: (706) 545-2958. Web: www.nationalinfantry museum.com.

DAHLONEGA. Dahlonega Gold Museum Historic Site, 1 Public Square, 30533. Georgia's gold mining history, U.S. coins including a set of Dahlonega Mint coinage. Open 9 a.m. to 5 p.m. Monday through Saturday, 10 a.m. to 5 p.m. Sunday. Closed Thanksgiving, Christmas and New Year's Day. $5 adults, $4.50 senior adults (62+), $3.50 for children 6 to 17. Group rates available. Call: (706) 864-2257. Web: www. dahlonega.org/museum/goldmuseum.html.

Idaho

COEUR D'ALENE. Museum of North Idaho, 115 Northwest Blvd., 83816. Idaho medals and tokens. Open 11 a.m. to 5 p.m. Tuesday through Saturday from April 1 to Oct. 31. By appointment only during the winter. Closed holidays. Admission: $3 adults, $1 children, $7 families. Call: (208) 664-3448.

Illinois

CHICAGO. Balzekas Museum of Lithuanian Culture, 6500 S. Pulaski Road, 60629. Lithuanian medals, medieval, ancients and numismatic literature. Open 10 a.m. to 4 p.m. daily. Admission: $5 adults, $2 children under 12. Closed Easter, Christmas and New Year's Day. Call: (312) 582-6500. Web: www. balzekasmuseum.org.

CHICAGO. Field Museum of Natural History, Roosevelt Road at Lake Shore Drive, 60605. Open 9 a.m. to 5 p.m. daily. Closed Christmas Day. Call: (312) 922-9410. Web: www.fieldmuseum.org.

WATSEKA. Iroquois County Genealogy Society, Old Courthouse Museum, 103 W. Cherry St., 60970-1524. Coins, medals, tokens and paper money. Open 10 a.m. to 4 p.m. Monday to Friday, by appointment Saturday and Sunday. Donation Admission: $2 adults, 50 cents children. Call: (815) 432-2215. Web: www.rootsweb.ancestry.com/~ilicgs/.

Indiana

BLOOMINGTON. Indiana University Art Museum, 1133 E. Seventh St., 47405. Ancient and Byzantine coins. Open Tuesday through Saturday 10 a.m. to 5 p.m.; Sunday 12 p.m. to 5 p.m. Closed Monday and major national holidays. Admission: Free. Call: (812) 855-5445. Web: www.indiana. edu/~iuam/iuam_home.php.

NOTRE DAME. Numismatic Collections at the University of Notre Dame Libraries, Department of Rare Books and Special Collections, 102 Hesburgh Library, 46556. Colonial coins and paper currency, U.S. tokens, U.S. and world coins, notgeld. Call: (574) 631-0290. Web: www.coins.nd.edu.

Iowa

MAXWELL. Community Historical Society Museum, Main Street, 50161. U.S. and foreign coins and paper money. Open 1 p.m. to 4 p.m. Sundays and holidays from Memorial Day to Labor Day. Ope by appointment other times. Closed during the winter. Admission: Free. Call: (515) 387-8675.

OKOBOJI. Higgins Museum, 1507 Sanborn Ave., 51355. National bank notes. Open 11 a.m. to 5:30 p.m. Tuesday to Sunday, mid-May until mid-September. Admission: Free. Telephone (712) 332-5859. Web: www.thehigginsmuseum.org.

Kansas

LOGAN. Dane G. Hansen Memorial Museum, 110 W. Main, 67646. Medals, tokens, paper money and other related items. Open 9 a.m. to noon and 1 p.m. to 4 p.m. Monday through Friday, 9 a.m. to noon and 1 p.m. to 5 p.m. Saturday and 1 p.m. to 5 p.m. Sunday and holidays. Closed Thanksgiving, Christmas and New Year's Day. Admission: Free. Call: (785) 689-4846, www.hansenmuseum.org.

LYONS. Coronado-Quivira Museum, 105 W. Lyon, 67554. One of four replicas of the first medal of Catholic missionary Father Juan de Padilla. Open Tuesday through Saturday 9 a.m. to 5 p.m., closed Sunday, Monday and Thanksgiving, Christmas and New Year's Day. Admission: $2 adults; $1 children 6 to 12. Call: (620) 257-2842. Web: skyways.lib.ks.us/ towns/Lyons/museum.

Louisiana

SHREVEPORT. The R.W. Norton Art Gallery, 4747 Creswell Ave., 71106-1899. U.S. coins, medals, paper money and foreign coins available for research by appointment only. Open Tuesday through Friday 10 a.m. to 5 p.m., 1 to 5 p.m. Saturday and Sunday. Closed Mondays and national holidays. Admission: Free. Call: (318) 865-4201. Web: www.rwnaf.org.

NEW ORLEANS. The Louisiana State Museum, housed in the former New Orleans Mint, 400 Esplanade Ave., 70116. Open Tuesday through Sunday 10 a.m. to 4:30 p.m. Closed Monday and state holidays. Admission: Adults $6; students, seniors and active military, $5; children 12 and under, free. Call: (504) 568-6968. Web: http://lsm.crt.state.la.us.

Maine

BRUNSWICK. Bowdoin College Museum of

Art, 9400 College Station, 04011-8494. World medals and ancients. Open Tuesday, Wednesday, Friday and Saturday 10 a.m. to 5 p.m.; Thursday 10 a.m. to 8:30 p.m.; Sunday 1 p.m. to 5 p.m. Closed Mondays and national holidays. Donation accepted. Call: (207) 725-3275. Web: **www.bowdoin.edu/art-museum/**.

Maryland

ANNAPOLIS. **U.S. Naval Academy Museum,** 118 Maryland Ave., 21402-5034. U.S. and world naval medals. Open 9 a.m. to 5 p.m. Monday through Saturday; 11 a.m. to 5 p.m. Sunday. Closed July 4, Thanksgiving, Christmas and New Year's Day. Admission: Free. Call: (410) 293-2108. Web: **www. usna.edu/Museum/homepage.htm**.

BALTIMORE. **Baltimore Museum of Art,** Art Museum Drive, 21218. U.S. medals. Open Wednesday through Friday 10 a.m. to 5 p.m.; Saturday and Sunday 11 a.m. to 6 p.m. Admission: Free, but special exhibits are additional. Call: (443) 573-1700. Web: **www.artbma.org/**.

Massachusetts

BOSTON. **Museum of Fine Arts,** 465 Huntington Ave., 02115-5523. Ancients and medals. Open Saturday through Tuesday 10 a.m. to 4:45 p.m.; Wednesday through Friday, 10 a.m. to 9:45 p.m. Open on all Monday holidays. Closed New Year's Day, Patriots Day, July 4, Thanksgiving and Christmas. Admission: $20 for adults, $18 senior citizens and students; $7.50 for children 7 to 17 before 3 p.m. on schooldays, otherwise free. Call: (617) 267-9300. Web: **www. mfa.org**.

SALEM. **Peabody Essex Museum,** East India Square, 01970. Coins, medals, tokens and paper money. Stored items in Phillips Library are open to scholars only. Tuesday through Sunday (and holiday Mondays) 10 a.m. to 5 p.m. Closed Thanksgiving, Christmas and New Year's Day. Admission: $15 for adults, $13 for seniors, $11 for students, free for youths under 16. Call: (866) 745-1876. Web: **www. pem.org**.

WORCESTER. **American Antiquarian Society,** 185 Salisbury St., 01609-1634. U.S. paper money and numismatic literature. Library open 9 a.m. to 5 p.m. Monday, Tuesday, Thursday and Friday; 10 a.m. to 8 p.m. Wednesday. Closed national holidays. Admission: Free. Call: (508) 755-5221.

Michigan

DETROIT. **Detroit Historical Museum,** 5401 Woodward Ave., 48202. Detroit and Michigan scrip and coins, U.S. coins, medals and paper money. Available to scholars only by appointment. Open Wednesday through Friday 9:30 a.m. to 3 p.m., Saturday 10 a.m. to 5 p.m., Sunday noon to 5 p.m. Closed Monday, Tuesday and national holidays. Admission: $6 adults, $4 seniors (60+) and youths (ages 5 to 17). Call: (313) 833-1805. Web: **www.detroithistorical.org**.

Mississippi

STATE COLLEGE. **Cobb Institute of Archeol-** ogy, Mississippi State University, 39762. Ancient Greek, Roman and Jewish coins, especially those relating to the Bible, medals and numismatic literature. Collection is temporarily inaccessible. Call: (662) 325-3826. Web: **www.cobb.msstate.edu**.

Missouri

COLUMBIA. **Museum of Art and Archeology,** University of Missouri-Columbia, 1 Pickard Hall, 65211. Permanent exhibit of ancient coins. Extensive collection of numismatic literature. Open 9 a.m. to 4 p.m. Tuesday, Wednesday and Friday; 9 a.m. to 8 p.m. Thursday; noon to 4 p.m. Saturday and Sunday. Closed Mondays, holidays and from Dec. 25 to Jan. 1. Admission: Free. Call: (573) 882-3591. Web: **http://maa.missouri.edu/**.

INDEPENDENCE. **Harry S. Truman Library,** U.S. Highway 24 and Delaware St., 64050. U.S. coins and medals on loan to Federal Reserve Bank of Kansas City; U.S. and foreign coins and paper money in study collections only; call for availability. Open to public 9 a.m. to 5 p.m. Monday through Friday; noon to 5 p.m. Sunday; open until 9 p.m. on Thursdays from May to September. Closed Christmas, Thanksgiving and New Year's Day. Admission: $8 for adults, $7 for seniors, $3 for children 6 to 15. Call: (800) 833-1225. Web: **www.trumanlibrary.org**.

ST. LOUIS. **Concordia Historical Institute,** 804 Seminary Place, 63105. Specialized collection of Lutheran and Reformation medals; also medieval and foreign coins, medals, paper money. Shown by appointment only; submit research requests in writing to museum archivist. Call: (314) 505-7900. Web: **www.lutheranhistory.org**.

ST. LOUIS. **Newman Money Museum,** Mildred Lane Kemper Art Museum, Washington University, Eric Newman collection of American Colonial and U.S. coins, paper money and numismatic literature. Research assistance and educational programs by appointment. 11 a.m. to 6 p.m. Tuesday, Wednesday, Thursday; 11 a.m. to 8 p.m. Friday; 11 a.m. to 6 p.m. Saturday and Sunday. Closed Monday and holidays. Call: (314) 935-9595.

ST. LOUIS. **Mildred Lane Kemper Art Museum,** Washington University, Danforth Campus, 63130. More than 1,000 Greek and Roman coins shown by appointment to scholars. Open Monday, Wednesday and Thursday, 11 a.m. to 6 p.m.; Friday, 11 a.m. to 8 p.m.; Saturday and Sunday, 11 a.m. to 6 p.m. Closed Tuesdays and on some national holidays. Call: (314) 935-4523.

Nebraska

HASTINGS. **Hastings Museum of Natural and Cultural History,** 1330 N. Burlington, 68901. U.S. coins, medals, paper money, medieval and ancients. Open 9 a.m. to 5 p.m., Monday through Thursday; 9 a.m. to 8 p.m. Friday and Saturday; noon to 6 p.m. Sunday. Closed Mondays in winter, closed Thanksgiving and Christmas. Admission: $7 adults, $5 children and $6 seniors. Call: (800) 508-4629. Web: www.hastingsmuseum.org.

OMAHA. **Durham Museum,** 801 S. Tenth St. Featuring the Byron Reed Collection, which includes the Parmelee specimen of the 1804 dollar. Open 10 a.m. to 8 p.m. Tuesday; 10 a.m. to 5 p.m. Wednesday through Saturday; 1 to 5 p.m. Sunday. Admission: $7 adults, $6 seniors, $5 children ages 3 to 12. Call: (402) 444-5071. Web: **www.durhammuseum.org/.**

Nevada

CARSON CITY. **Nevada State Museum,** 600 North Carson St., 89710. Exhibit of Carson City Mint mark coins and coin press. Open Wednesday to Saturday, 8:30 a.m. to 4:30 p.m. Closed Thanksgiving, Christmas and New Year's Day. Admission: $8 adults, children 17 and under are free. Call: (775) 687-4810. Web: **www.museums.nevadaculture.org.**

New Hampshire

HANOVER. **Hood Museum of Art,** Dartmouth College, 03755. U.S. coins, paper money, medals, ancients and foreign coins. Open 10 a.m. to 5 p.m. Tuesday through Saturday; Wednesday 10 a.m. to 9 p.m.; Sunday noon to 5 p.m. Numismatic collection shown by appointment only. Call: (603) 646-2900. Web: **http://hoodmuseum.dartmouth.edu.**

New Jersey

NEWARK. **The Newark Museum,** 49 Washington St., 07101. Extensive collection of coins, medals, tokens, paper money and numismatic literature. Open noon to 5 p.m. Wednesday through Sunday. Closed New Year's Day, July 4, Thanksgiving and Christmas. Admission: Free. Call: (973) 596-6550. Web: **www.newarkmuseum.org/.**

New York

NEW YORK. **The American Numismatic Society,** 75 Varick St., Floor 11, 10013. Numismatic library and one of the most extensive numismatic collections in the United States, including more than a million items; U.S. and foreign coins, medals, decorations, paper money, numismatic literature, medieval and ancients. Open 9:30 a.m. to 4:30 p.m. Monday through Friday. Closed weekends and national holidays. Admission: Free. Call: (212) 571-4470. Web: **www.numismatics.org.**

NEW YORK. **The Jewish Museum,** 92nd Street and Fifth Avenue, 11028. Jewish/Israel coins, medals and ancients. Saturday through Tuesday, 11 a.m. to 5:45 p.m.; Thursday 11 a.m. to 8 p.m.; Friday 11 a.m. to 4 p.m. (during winter). Closed Jewish holidays. Adults $12, students $7.50, senior citizens $10. Call: (212) 423-3200. Web: **www.thejewishmuseum.org.**

North Carolina

CHAPEL HILL. **North Carolina Collection,** University of North Carolina, Wilson Library, 27514-8890. Extensive collection of Colonial coins and paper money. Call: (919) 962-1172. Web: **www.lib.unc.edu/ncc/gallery/currency.html.**

CHARLOTTE. **Mint Museum of Art,** 2730 Randolph Road, 28207. Charlotte and Bechtler gold coins, Confederate, North Carolina and state bank notes and bonds. Open Sunday 1 to 5 p.m.; Tuesday, 10 a.m. to 9 p.m.; Wednesday through Saturday, 10 a.m. to 6 p.m. Closed Monday, Easter, July 4, Thanksgiving Day, Christmas Eve, Christmas Day, and New Year's Day. Admission: Tuesdays from 5 p.m. to 9 p.m., free; otherwise $10 adults, $8 senior citizens and students, $5 children 5 to 17, free for children 4 and under. Call: (704) 337-2000. Web: **www.mintmuseum.org.**

RALEIGH. **North Carolina Museum of History,** 5 E. Edenton St., 27601. Bechtler gold, ancient and world coins, military medals, paper money; open to scholars only, call for appointment. Open Monday through Saturday, 9 a.m. to 5 p.m.; Sunday noon to 5 p.m. Closed Christmas and New Year's Day. Admission: Free. Call: (919) 807-7900. Web: **www.ncmuseumofhistory.org**

Ohio

ASHLAND. **Leo & Laura Thomas Numismatic Center, Ashland University Library,** Ashland University, 401 College Ave., 44805. Open 9 to 11:30 a.m. and Wednesday and Friday during classes. Call: (419) 281-2230.

DAYTON. **Air Force Museum, Wright-Patterson Air Force Base,** 45433. U.S. and world Air Force aircraft insignia, decorations, medals and commemorative coins. Open 9 a.m. to 5 p.m. daily. Closed Thanksgiving, Christmas and New Year's Day. Admission: Free. Call: (937) 255-3286. Web: **www.nationalmuseum.af.mil/.**

MARIETTA. **Campus Maritus Museum,** Marietta College, 45750. Coins, medals, paper money. Some items in storage available by appointment. Open Monday, Wednesday through Saturday 9:30 a.m. to 5 p.m.; Sunday, noon to 5 p.m. Closed New Year's Day, Easter, Thanksgiving and Christmas. Admission: adults $7, students $4, children 5 and under free. Call: (740) 373-3750. Web: **http://campusmartiusmuseum.org/.**

OXFORD. **Miami University Art Museum,** Patterson Ave., 45056. Greek and Roman ancients in storage, available for research on request. Open 10 a.m. to 5 p.m. Tuesday through Friday, noon to 5 p.m. Saturday. Closed national and university holidays. Call: (513) 529-2232. Admission: Free. Web: **www.muohio.edu/artmuseum/.**

WAPAKONETA. **Neil Armstrong Museum,** 45895. U.S. and world air and space medals. Open 9:30 a.m. to 5 p.m. Monday through Saturday; noon to 5 p.m. Sunday and holidays. Closed Mondays from October through March. Admission: $8 adults, $4 children 6 to 12. Group rates available. Web: **www.ohiohistory.org/places/armstrong/.**

Pennsylvania

PHILADELPHIA. **Atwater Kent Museum, History Museum of Philadelphia,** 15 S. Seventh St.,

19106. Collection of U.S. coins, medals, tokens and paper money. Exhibition galleries open to general public, storage collections can be seen by appointment with the curators in advance. Museum is open 10 a.m. to 5 p.m. every day except Saturday. Admission: $3 for adults, $2 for seniors; $1.50 for children 3 to 12. Call: (215) 685-4830. Web: **www.philadelphia history.org**.

PHILADELPHIA. **Presbyterian Historical Society**, 425 Lombard St., 19147. Communion tokens collection includes small display and more than 6,000 shown by appointment. Open Monday through Friday, 8:30 a.m. to 4:30 p.m. Closed regular holidays. Admission: Free. Call: (215) 627-1852. Web: **http:// history.pcusa.org/**.

PHILADELPHIA. **U.S. Mint**, 151 North Independence Mall E., 19106-1886. Self-guided tour through production facility. Open 9 a.m. to 4:30 p.m. Monday through Friday, open Saturday 9 a.m. to 4:30 p.m. from May 22 through Labor Day. Call: (215) 408-0112. Web: **www.usmint.gov/mint_tours/?action=philadelphia**.

Rhode Island

PROVIDENCE. **Museum of Art, R.I. School of Design**, 224 Benefit St., 02903. Ancient Greek coins, U.S. and world medals. Open Tuesday through Sunday, 10 a.m. to 5 p.m. Open until 9 p.m. the third Thursday each month. Closed Monday, New Year's Day, Easter, Independence Day, Thanksgiving, Christmas and month of August. Admission: $10 adults, $7 seniors (62+), $3 youth (5 to 18), $3 college students. Call: (401) 454-6500. Web: **www.risdmuseum.org**.

South Carolina

COLUMBIA. **South Carolina Confederate Relic Room and Museum, World War Memorial Building**, Columbia Mills Building, 301 Gervais, 29201. Confederate bonds, U.S. coins, paper money, medals, foreign paper money and medals. Open 10 a.m. to 5 p.m. Tuesday through Saturday, 1 to 5 p.m. first Sunday of the month. Closed national and state holidays (except Confederate Memorial Day and Veterans Day). Admission: $5 adults, $4 seniors (62+) and active duty military, $2 youth (13 to 17), free for children 12 and under. Call: (803) 737-8095. Web: **http://crr.sc.gov**.

FORT JACKSON. **U.S. Army Finance Corps Museum, U.S. Army Finance School**, 10000 Hampton Parkway, Fort Jackson, 29207-7025. Military currency, U.S. and foreign paper money. Open to the public 10 a.m. to 4 p.m. Monday through Friday. Closed federal holidays. Admission: Free. Call: (803) 751-3771. Web: **http://armyfinance.armymilitary museums.org/**.

Tennessee

HARROGATE. **Abraham Lincoln Library and Museum**, Lincoln Memorial University, 37752. Coins, medals, tokens, paper money and historical artifacts of the Lincoln Civil War period. Research collection open for study by appointment only. Open 10 a.m. to 5 p.m. Monday through Friday, noon to 5 p.m. Saturday. Closed academic holidays, Thanksgiving, Christmas and New Year's Day. Admission: $5 for adults, $3.50 for seniors (60+), $3 for children 6-12. Call: (423) 869-6235. Web: **www.lmunet.edu/ Museum/**.

Texas

AUSTIN. **Briscoe Center for American History**, University of Texas, 78705. Swenson collection of coins and medals. U.S. coins, paper money and medals, foreign paper money and medals, medieval and ancients. Open 10 a.m. to 5 p.m. Monday through Friday; 10 p.m. to 2 p.m. Saturday; Closed Sunday. Admission: Free. Call: (512) 495-4532. Web: **www. cah.utexas.edu/**.

NACOGDOCHES. **Stephen F. Austin University**, 75962. Numismatic material, available for research by appointment only. Contact university for public hours. Admission: Free. Call: (936) 468-2408. Web: **www.sfasu.edu/stonefort/**.

Vermont

BENNINGTON. **Bennington Museum, Inc.**, 75 Main St., 05201. Coins and paper money of Vermont. Open 7 days a week in September and October, otherwise open every day except Wednesday from 10 a.m. to 5 p.m. Closed for the month of January, plus Thanksgiving and Christmas. Admission: $10 adults, $9 seniors and students over 18, free to children and students under 18. Call: (802) 447-1571. Web: **www. benningtonmuseum.com**.

Virginia

RICHMOND. **Money Museum, Federal Reserve Bank of Richmond**, 701 E. Byrd St., 23219. History of U.S. coins and paper money, money-related artifacts, primitive, ancients and precious metals. Open 9:30 a.m. to 3:30 p.m. Monday through Friday. Web: **www.rich.frb. org/generalinfo/tourinfo.html**.

RICHMOND. **Museum and White House of the Confederacy**, 1210 E. Clay St., 23219. Paper money of the Confederacy available to scholars by appointment. Admission: Adults $12, seniors (62+) $11, youth (7 to 13) $7. Open Monday through Saturday 10 a.m. to 5 p.m., Sunday noon to 5 p.m. Closed Thanksgiving, Christmas and New Years Day. Call: (804) 649-1861. Web: **www.moc.org**.

WILLIAMSBURG. **Colonial Williamsburg.** Contains numerous archaeological displays of coins recovered from excavations; thousands of Colonial- and Continental-era coins, paper money and tokens, including a 1792 Birch cent and one of five known 1774 Virginia "pattern shillings." Call: (757) 229-1000. Web: **www.history.org**.

Washington

GOLDENDALE. **Maryhill Museum of Art**, 35 Maryhill Museum Drive, 98620. U.S. coins, ancients and U.S. and world medals, research by appointment only. Open daily March 15 to Nov. 15, 10 a.m. to 5 p.m. Admission: Adults $9, senior citizens $8, students 7 to 18 $3. Call: (509) 773-3733. Web: www. maryhillmuseum.org.

West Virginia

CHARLESTON. **West Virginia State Museum, The Cultural Center,** Capitol Complex, 25305. Coal scrip and U.S. and Confederate paper money, including West Virginia issues, accessible by appointment only. Open Tuesday through Saturday 9 a.m. to 5 p.m., Sunday noon to 5 p.m. Closed Christmas. Admission: Free. Call: (304) 558-0220. Web: **www.wvculture. org/museum/State-Museum-Index.html**.

World museums

Australia

HOBART. **Tasmanian Museum and Art Gallery,** 40 Macquarie St., Hobart. Tasmanian tokens and promissory notes, U.S. coins, paper money, ancients, medieval coins, world coins and medals. Open daily 10 a.m. to 5 p.m. Closed Good Friday, ANZAC Day (April 25) and Christmas Day. Admission: Free. Web: **www.tmag.tas.gov. au/**.

Austria

ENNS. **Römer-Museum Lauriacum Enns,** Hauptplatz 19, Enns. About 18,000 ancient Roman coins available to scholars by appointment (some are on display). Open May 1 to Sept. 30: Monday through Friday, 9 a.m. to 6 p.m. Saturday and Sunday 10 a.m. to noon and 2 to 4 p.m. Open April and October, and Nov. 1 to March 31 : Monday to Friday 9 a.m. to 3 p.m., Saturday and Sunday 10 a.m. to noon and 2 to 4 p.m. Admission: €5 adults, €3 seniors and soldiers, €2 young students. Web: **www.museum-lauriacum.at**.

INNSBRUCK. **Das Tirol Panorama,** Museumstrasse 15, 6020 Innsbruck. Historical collection, art from Romanesque to modern, coins, medallions. Open daily, 9 a.m. to 5 p.m. Admission: Contact museum for details. Contact Web: **www.tirolerlandesmuseum.at/**.

KLAGENFURT. **Landesmuseum für Kärnten,** Klagenfurt, A-9021, Museumgasse 2. Ancient and medieval coins. Open Tuesday to Friday 10 a.m. to 6 p.m.; Thursday 10. a.m. to 8 p.m.; Saturday and Sunday 10 a.m. to 5 p.m. Closed Monday. Admission: Contact museum for details. Call: 0043/50/536-30599, fax 0043/50/536-30540. Web: **www.landes museum.ktn.gv.at**.

Belgium

BRUSSELS. Koninklijke Bibliotheek van België/ Bibliothèque royale de Belgique/Royal Library of Belgium, Keizerslaan 4, Brussels. Coins, medals, scales and weights, orders and decorations, books, totaling some 250,000 objects. Open Monday through Friday 9 a.m. to 4:45 p.m. Call for appointment to view numismatic collection. Admission: €2.50/day, €5/week, €20/month. Web: **www.kbr.be/**.

Wisconsin

MADISON. **State Historical Society of Wisconsin,** 816 State St., 53706. U.S. coins, paper money and medals. Open Tuesday to Saturday, 9 a.m. to 4 p.m. Closed Wisconsin state holidays. Admission: $4 for adults, $3 for children under 18, $10 for family. Call: (608) 264-6555. Web: **www.wisconsinhistory. org/museum/**.

STURGEON BAY. **Door County Historical Museum,** 18 North 4th Ave., 54235. U.S. coins, paper money and medals. Admission: Free. Open 10 a.m. to 4:30 p.m. daily from May 1 to Oct. 31. Web: **http:// map.co.door.wi.us/museum/**.

Bermuda

HAMILTON. **Bermuda Monetary Authority,** 4th Floor, 26 Burnaby Street, Hamilton, HM11. Bermuda coins and paper money. Call for appointment. Open Monday through Friday 9 a.m. to 4 p.m. Call: (441) 295-5278. Web: **www.bma.bm/**.

Canada

CALGARY. **University of Calgary Nickle Arts Museum,** 2500 University Drive N.W., Calgary, Alberta T2N 1N4. Ancient Greek, Roman and Byzantine materials. Small collections of medallions and U.S. paper money. Admission: adults, $5; seniors $2. Closed until September 2011. Call: (403) 220-7234. Web: **http://people.ucalgary.ca/~nickle/**.

HALIFAX. **Public Archives of Nova Scotia,** 6016 University Ave., Halifax, Nova Scotia B3H 1W4. Coins, tokens and paper money. Open 8:30 a.m. to 4:30 p.m. Monday through Friday (and until 9 p.m. Wednesday); 9 a.m. to 5 p.m. Saturday. Closed national holidays. Call: (902) 424-6060. Web: **http:// gov.ns.ca/nsarm/**.

KAMLOOPS. **Kamloops Museum and Archives,** 207 Seymour St., Kamloops, British Columbia V2C 2E7. Foreign coins, medals, tokens and paper money. Open Tuesday through Saturday 9:30 to 4:30 p.m. (and until 7:30 p.m. Thursdays, May 24 to Oct. 31). Closed on statutory holidays. Admission: $3 adult, $1 youth and children. Call: (250) 828-3576. Web: **www. kamloops.ca/museum/index.shtml**.

OTTAWA. **Bank of Canada Currency Museum,** 245 Sparks St., Ottawa, Ontario K1A 0G9. National Currency Collection of Canada. U.S. coins and paper money, foreign coins and paper money, medieval, ancients and primitives. Open Monday through Saturday 10:30 a.m. to 5 p.m.; Sunday 1 p.m. to 5 p.m. Closed most Mondays during winter and most statutory holidays. Call: (613) 782-8914. Web: **www.currency museum.ca**.

OTTAWA. **Canadian War Museum,** 1 Vimy Place, Ottawa, Ontario K1A 0M8. Canadian, U.S. and foreign military medals, orders, badges, insignia and scrip. Material on display and in reference collections. Research scholars must query curator. Open daily 9 a.m. to 5 p.m., Thursdays to 8 p.m. Closed Christmas Day. Admission: $12 adults, $10 seniors and students; $8 children 3 to 12; free on Thursdays 4 to 8 p.m. Call: (819) 776-8600. Web: **www.war museum.ca/**.

OTTAWA. Library and Archives of Canada, 395 Wellington St., Ottawa, Ontario K1A 0N3. Medal collection. 12,000 Canadian, British, French, U.S. and other medals. Open 9 a.m. to 4 p.m. Monday, Wednesday and Friday; 10 a.m. to 5 p.m. Tuesday and Thursday, research by appointment. Closed statutory holidays. Admission: Free. Call: (613) 996-5115. Fax: (613) 995-6274. Web: **www.collectionscanada. gc.ca**.

OTTAWA. Royal Canadian Mint, 320 Sussex Drive, Ottawa, Ontario K1N 8V5. Viewing of striking of gold and silver coins, audio and visual presentation on coin production and displays of coins, medals and other products of the RCM, with an emphasis on current issues. Open Monday through Friday 9 a.m. to 6 p.m. Admission: Adults, $5; seniors, $4; children (5 to 17) $3, (lower prices on weekends). Tours are guided and reservations are required. Call: (613) 993-8990. Web: **www.mint.ca/store/mint/about-the-mint/visit-the-mint-1200026**.

PRINCE RUPERT. Museum of Northern British Columbia, Box 669, Prince Rupert, British Columbia V8J 3S1. Ancients, U.S. and foreign coins, medals and paper money. Open 9 a.m. to 5 p.m. Monday through Saturday during the winter; 9 a.m. to 8 p.m. Monday through Saturday and 9 a.m. to 5 p.m. Sunday during the summer. Closed Christmas, New Year's, Easter and Remembrance Day. Call: (250) 624-3207. Web: **www.museumofnorthernbc.com**.

TORONTO. Royal Ontario Museum, Toronto, Canada, 100 Queen's Park, Toronto, Ontario M5S 2C6. Ancient Greek, Roman, Celtic and medieval coins; foreign and Canadian coins and medals. Open 10 a.m. to 5:30 p.m. daily (and to 8:30 Friday). Admission: adults $24; seniors (65+), students (15 to 17) $21; children (4 to 14) $16. Call: (416) 586-8000. Web: **www.rom.on.ca**.

WINNIPEG. Royal Canadian Mint, 520 Lagimodiere, Winnipeg, Manitoba. Viewing of striking of gold and silver coins, audio and visual presentation on coin production and displays of coins, medals and other products of the RCM, with an emphasis on current issues. Open Monday through Friday 9 a.m. to 5 p.m. Admission: adults, $5; seniors, $4; children (5 to 17) $3 (lower prices on weekends). Tours are guided and reservations are required. Call: (204) 983-6405. Web: **www.mint.ca/store/mint/about-the-mint/visit-the-mint-1200026**.

Denmark

COPENHAGEN. National Museum, Royal Collection of Coins and Medals, Ny Vestergade 10 Copenhagen. Open daily 10 a.m. to 5 p.m. Tuesday through Sunday. Closed Monday, Christmas Eve, Christmas Day and New Year's Day. Admission: Free. Web: **www.natmus.dk**.

Finland

HELSINKI. National Museum Kansallismuseo, Mannerheimintie 34, PO Box 913, Helsinki, 00101. Finnish, Swedish and Russian coins, bank notes and medals. Ancient and medieval coins, world coins, medals and paper money. Open Tuesday 11 a.m. to 8 p.m.; Wednesday through Sunday, 11 a.m. to 6 p.m. Closed national holidays. Admission: €7, €5, free for 17 and under, and free Tuesdays from 5:30 to 8 p.m. Web: **www.nba.fi/en/nmf**.

France

PARIS. Cabinet des Médailles, Bibliotheque Nationale, 58 Rue de Richelieu, Paris, F-75084. Coins, medals and antiques. Closed for renovation project through 2013; scholars may access collection by appointment. Web: **www.bnf.fr/**.

PARIS. Musée de la Monnaie, 11, Quai de Conti, 75006 Paris. Ancient and medieval coins, world coins, medals and paper money; French medals and jetons. Minting material since 17th century. Closed for renovation, slated to reopen in 2012. Web: **www. monnaiedeparis.com/musee/index.htm**.

Germany

BERLIN. Staatliche Museen zu Berlin, Münzkabinett, Bodemuseum, Am Kupfergraben 1, 10178 Berlin. Ancient and medieval coins, world coins, medals and paper money. Jetons, seals, shares and bonds. Open daily 10 a.m. to 6 p.m., and Thursdays to 10 p.m. Admission: €8 adults, discounts available and many admitted free. Web: **www.smb.museum/smb/home/index.php**.

BRAUNFELS. Fürstliches Familienmuseum, Schloss, Belzgasse 1, 35619 Braunfels. Medieval, Roman and German coins from 1871 to 1918. Coins and dies of Solms dynasty. Contact museum for public hours and admission fees. Web: **www.schloss-braunfels.de/**.

COLOGNE. Kolnisches Stadtmuseum, Zeughausstrasse 1-3, Cologne, D-50667. Coins of the Bishops of Cologne and city of Cologne. Wednesday to Sunday 10 a.m. to 5 p.m., Tuesday 10 a.m. to 8 p.m. First Thursday each month until 10 p.m. Admission: €5.

DRESDEN. Staatliche Kunstsammlungen Dresden, Münzkabinett, State and public holdings. Open 10 a.m. to 6 p.m. daily; closed Thursday. Admission: Adults, €10; senior citizens and students, €7.50; under 16 years, free. Web: **www.skd.museum**.

FRANKFURT/MAIN. Deutsche Bundesbank, Money Museum, Central Bank of the Federal Republic of Germany, Wilhelm-Epstein-Str. 14, 60431 Frankfurt am Main. More than 230,000 bank notes and 80,000 coins. Sunday through Friday, 10 a.m. to 5 p.m. (Wednesday until 9 p.m.), open public holidays 10 a.m. to 5 p.m. Closed Easter, May

1, Christmas Eve, Christmas, New Years Eve and New Years Day. Admission: Free. Web: **www.geld museum.de**.

KARLSRUHE. Badisches Landesmuseum, Karlsruhe Palace. World coins, medals and paper money. Ancients and coins of South Germany. Open Tuesday to Sunday 10 a.m. to 5 p.m., Friday through Sunday and public holidays, 10 a.m. to 6 p.m. Admission: €4 adults, discounts available and many admitted free. €0.50 students. Call: 49 7621 161 3634. Web: **www.landesmuseum.de**.

MAINZ. Landesmuseum Mainz, Grosse Bleiche 49-51, 55116 Mainz. Ancient, medieval, baroque and world coins. Open Tuesday 10 a.m. to 5 p.m., Wednesday to Sunday 10 a.m. to 5 p.m., closed Monday. Call: (49) 6131 28 570. Web: **www.landes museum-mainz.de**.

MAINZ. Römish-Germanische Zentralmuseum Mainz Forschungsinstitut für Vor- und Frühgeschichte, Ernst-Ludwig-Platz 2, 55116 Mainz. Celtic and Roman republic and imperial coins. Coins of the early Middle Ages. Open by appointment. Web: **http://web.rgzm.de/**.

MÜNSTER. Westfalisches Landesmuseum für Kunst und Kulturgeschichte, Domplatz 10, 48143 Münster. World coins, medals and paper money. German paper money, coins and medals of the region of Westphalia. Open Tuesday to Sunday 10 a.m. to 6 p.m. (Thursday until 9 p.m.) Admission: €2 adults, €1 students, seniors and military. Call: (49) 0251 5907 201. Web: **www.lwl.org/LWL/Kultur/LWL-Landesmuseum-Muenster**.

NÜRNBERG. Germanic National Museum, Kartäusergasse 1, Nuernberg 90402. Coins and medals from German-speaking countries. Open Tuesday to Sunday 10 a.m. to 6 p.m.; Wednesday to 9 p.m. Admission: free after 6 p.m. Wednesday; 6 regular, discounts available and many admitted free. Web: **www.gnm.de/index_en.html**.

SPEYER. Historisches Museum der Pfalz, Domplatz 4, 67346 Speyer. Ancient, medieval and modern material. Open 10 a.m. to 6 p.m., Tuesday through Sunday. Admission: €8 adults; €6 students, children 6 to 17 and military. Web: **www.museum.speyer.de**.

TRIER. Rheinisches Landesmuseum Trier, Weimarer Allee 1 · 54290 Trier. Ancient and medieval coins of Trier. Open Tuesday through Sunday 10 a.m. to 5 p.m. Closed holidays. Admission: €6 regular; €4 students, seniors and military; €3 children 6 to 18. Call: (49) 651 9774-0. Web: **www.landesmuseum-trier.de**.

Greece

ATHENS. Athens Numismatic Museum, Iliou Melathron, El. Venizelou (Panepistimiou) 12, GR-106 71 Athens. Greek, Roman, Byzantine, Medieval, modern coins and medals, Greek and Byzantine weights, Byzantine seals and gems. Open daily 8:30 a.m. to 3 p.m. Closed Mondays, New Year's Day, March 25, Orthodox Easter, May 1, Dec. 25 and 26.

Admission: €3 regular, discounts available and many admitted free. Call: 30210 363 2057. Web: **www.nma.gr/index_en.htm**.

Israel

HAIFA. National Maritime Museum, 198 Allenby Rd., Haifa, 44855. Large collection of coins and medals pertaining to the sea. Extensive collection of Hebrew and Mediterranean maritime history and archaeology. Open Sunday through Thursday 10 a.m. to 4 p.m.; Friday 10 a.m. to 1 p.m. and Saturday 10 a.m. to 3 p.m. Admission: adults, NIS 30; police, military, students, children 5 to 18, NIS 20; seniors, NIS 15. Call: 04-8536622. Web: **www.nmm.org.il**.

JERUSALEM. Israel Museum, POB 71117, Jerusalem 91710. Shrine of the Book (Dead Sea Scrolls), Library of Art & Archaeology, contains collection of ancient Jewish, Greek, Roman Provincial, Islamic and Crusader coins. Open Sunday, Monday, Wednesday and Thursday 10 a.m. to 5 p.m.; Tuesday 4 p.m. to 10 p.m.; Friday 10 a.m. to 2 p.m.; Saturday 10 a.m. to 5 p.m.; some holiday hours. Admission: adult NIS 48, students NIS 36, children 5 to 17 and seniors, NIS 24. Web: **www.english.imjnet.org.il**.

Italy

NAPLES. Museo Archeologico Nazionale di Napoli, Piazza Museo Nazionale 19, 80135 Napoli. Greek, Roman and modern coins and medals. Viewing by appointment only. Web: **http://museoarche ologiconazionale.campaniabeniculturali.it**.

Japan

SAKURA CITY. National Museum of Japanese Culture, 117 Jonai-cho, Sakura City, Chiba Prefecture 285-8502. Closed Monday and Dec. 27 through Jan. 4. Web: **www.rekihaku.ac.jp/english/index.html**.

Luxembourg

LUXEMBOURG. Musée National D'Histoire et D'art, Marche-aux-Poissons, Luxembourg, 2345. More than 80,000 numismatic items from Celtic to modern times. Open Tuesday through Sunday 10 a.m. to 6 p.m. (and Thursday to 8 p.m.). Closed Mondays and Dec. 24, Dec. 25 and Jan. 1. Admission: adults €5, seniors €3. Web: **www.mnha.public.lu/**.

Malaysia

KUALA LUMPUR. Bank Negara Museum and Art Gallery, Level 1, Block A, Jalan Dato' Onn, 50480 Kuala Lumpur. Coins, bank notes and other items with particular emphasis on Malaysian numismatics, as well as exhibits on economics, artwork and finance. Opening October 2011. Web: **http://museum.bnm.gov.my**.

KUALA LUMPUR. Muzium Numismatik Maybank, Kuala Lumpur. Coins from Melaka Kingdom to present day coins and bank notes. Open daily 10 a.m. to 9 p.m. excluding public holidays.

KUALA LUMPUR. National Museum of Malaysia (Muzium Negara), Kuala Lumpur, 50566.

Malaysian and world coins and paper money. 9 a.m. to 6 p.m. daily except certain holidays. Admission: Contact museum for details. Web: **www.muzium negara.gov.my**.

Monaco

Musee des Timbres et des Monnaies (Museum of Stamps and Coins), 11 Terrasse de Fontvieille. Coins and stamps from Monaco, every coin type since 1600s is illustrated. Open daily from 9 a.m. to 5 p.m. Admission: €3 adults, €1.50 seniors and children 12 to 18 years old. Web: **www.oetp-monaco.com/web kit/jsp/index.jsp?langue=EN**.

Netherlands

UTRECHT. **State Museum of Coins and Medals**, Leidseweg 90, 3531 BG Utrecht. The national collection of some 400,000 coins, paper money, medals, and other numismatic items. Open Tuesday through Friday 10 a.m. to 5 p.m.; Saturday and Sunday 12 p.m. to 5 p.m. Admission: adults €9, children 5 to 17 €3.50. Web: **www.geldmuseum.nl**.

Philippines

MANILA. **Central Bank of the Philippines,** Money Museum, Manila, 2801. Philippine coins, bank notes, medals; world coins, bank notes and medals; gold artifacts and potteries. Open Monday through Saturday 9 a.m. to 6 p.m.; closed Sunday and holidays. Admission: Contact museum for details. Web: **www.bsp.gov.ph/about/facilities_money.asp**.

Poland

WARSAW. **The Royal Castle,** Plac Zamkowy 4, 00277. Polish coins and medals, medieval coins, modern world coins and paper money. Open daily Tuesday through Saturday 10 a.m. to 4 p.m.; Sunday 11 a.m. to 4 p.m., by request only. Admission: regular, PLN 13; discounts available. Web: **http://zamek-krolewski.pl/?page=2156**.

Russia

LENINGRAD. **Russian Hermitage Museum.** Extensive collection totaling more than 1.1 million Russian, Oriental, Asian coins and numismatic items. Open daily, except Mondays, 10:30 a.m. to 6 p.m., and Sundays 10:30 a.m. to 5 p.m. Admission: 400 rubles, students free. Web: **www.hermitagemuseum. org**.

Spain

MADRID. **Lazaro Galdiano Museum,** Calle Serrano 122, Madrid, 28006. Medal collection. Open daily 10 a.m. to 4:30 p.m. Closed Monday and certain holidays. Admission: €4 regular, €2 seniors and students, Sundays free. Web: **www.flg.es/museo/ museo.htm**.

MADRID. **Museo del Ejercito, c/o Mendez Nunez,** No. 1, Madrid, 28014. Medals and decorations. Open daily 10 a.m. to 7 p.m. Closed Monday and after 3 p.m. Sundays. Open until 9 p.m. daily from June 1 to Sept. 30. Closed certain holidays. Admission: €5 adults, €2.50 students under 25, free for children under 18. Web: **www.ejercito.mde.es/ en/unidades/Madrid/ihycm/Museos/ejercito/index. html**.

Sweden

MALMO. **Malmo Museums,** Malmohusvagen, Box 406, 20124 Malmo. Ancient, medieval and Scandinavian coins. From June to August, open daily 10 a.m. to 4 p.m. From September through May open 10 a.m. to 4 p.m. weekdays, noon to 4 p.m. Saturday and Sunday. Admission: Free. Web: **www.malmo.se/ museer**.

STOCKHOLM. **Ostasiatiska Museet (Museum of Far Eastern Antiquities),** Skeppsholmen, P.O. Box 16 381, 103 27 Stockholm. Chinese coins, spade and knife money. Coins are not on permanent display. Open daily 11 a.m. to 5 p.m., and Tuesday until 8 p.m. Closed Monday. Admission: 60 crowns adults, free for youths under 19. Web: **www.ostasiatiska.se/**.

Switzerland

GENEVA. **Museum of Art and History,** rue Charles-Galland 2, Geneva, CH-1211. Ancient, medieval and world coins, and coins of Geneva. Open Tuesday through Sunday 10 a.m. to 6 p.m. Closed Monday. Admission: free to permanent exhibits; temporary exhibits: CHF5 adults, discounts available, free 18 and under. Web: **www.ville-ge.ch/ mah/?langue=eng**.

LAUSANNE. **Cabinet des Medailles du Canton de Vaud,** Palais de Rumine, Lausanne, CH-1005. Ancient, medieval and world coins, medals and paper money. Open 7 a.m. to 10 p.m. Web: **www.musees. vd.ch/en/ruminearlaud/palais-de-rumine/**.

LUCERNE. **Historisches Museum Luzern,** Pfistergasse 24, Postfach 7437 6000 Luzern 7. Coins and medals of Lucerne, ancient, medieval and modern world coins. Open Tuesday through Sunday 10 a.m. to 5 p.m. Closed Monday. Admission: adults CHF 10, seniors and students CHF 8. Call: 41 41 228 54 24. Web: **www.historischesmuseum.lu.ch**.

WINTERTHUR. **Munzkabinett der Stadt Winterthur,** Villa Buhler, Lindstrasse 8, Winterthur, CH-8401. Ancient Greek and Roman coins. Tuesday, Wednesday, Saturday, Sunday from 2 to 5 p.m. Web: **www.muenzkabinett.winterthur.ch/**.

ZURICH. **Swiss National Museum,** Museumstrasse 2, 8021 Zurich. Swiss coins and medals, world coins, medals and paper money. A small but representative selection is permanently on view. Open Tuesday to Sunday from 10 a.m. to 5 p.m. (and Thursday to 7 p.m.). Admission: Free. Call: (41) 44 218 65 11. Web: **www.nationalmuseum.ch/e/index.php**.

United Kingdom

BELFAST. **Ulster Museum,** Botanic Gardens, Belfast, BT9 5AB. 50,000 coins, tokens and medals from ancients to modern, plus Irish bank notes. Open Tuesday through Sunday 10 a.m. to 5 p.m. Admission: Free. Web: **www.nmni.com/um**.

BIRMINGHAM. **City Museum and Art Gal-**

lery, Chamberlain Square, Birmingham, B3 3DH. Ancient and medieval coins. Products of the Soho and Birmingham Mints. Open Monday to Thursday and Saturday, 10 a.m. to 5 p.m.; Friday 10:30 a.m. to 5 p.m.; Sunday 12:30 p.m. to 5 p.m. Admission: Free. Web: **www.bmag.org.uk.**

BRISTOL. City of Bristol Museum and Art Gallery, Queens Road, Bristol, BS8 1RL. Local Iron Age; Roman; Bristol Mint, local hoards; trade tokens. Open daily 10:30 a.m. to 5 p.m., and Wednesday to 8 p.m. Reserve collections by appointment only. Admission: Free. Call: 0117 922 3571. Web: **www. bristol.gov.uk/museums.**

CAMBRIDGE. Fitzwilliam Museum, Department of Coins and Medals, Cambridge, CB2 1RB. Collection comprises some 100,000 specimens, of ancient, British Isles, European medieval and Indian coins. Coins department library open by appointment, Monday to Friday, 10 a.m. to 1 p.m. and 2 p.m. to 4:45 p.m. Museum open Tuesday through Saturday 10 a.m. to 5 p.m.; Sunday and bank holidays, noon to 5 p.m. Admission: Free. Web: **www.fitzmuseum. cam.ac.uk/coins.**

EDINBURGH. National Museum of Scotland, Chambers Street, Edinburgh EH1 1JF. Classical, European and Oriental items, modern world coins, totaling about 57,500 pieces; Scottish sections of the collection are of international importance. Open daily 10 a.m. to 5 p.m. Admission: Free. Web: **www.nms. ac.uk**, with some of collection viewable online at **www.scran.ac.uk.**

LONDON. Bank of England Museum, London. Bank notes, token money, regal coinage, silver, documents, books, and photographs relating to social life and economic history of the bank. Open Monday to Friday 10 a.m. to 5 p.m. Admission: Free. Web: **www.bankofengland.co.uk/education/museum/ index.htm.**

LONDON. British Museum, Great Russell Street, London, WC1B 3DG. Hundreds of thousands of numismatic items (including paper money). HSBC Gallery has several thousand items on display. Department open weekdays (except Wednesday) from 10 to 1 p.m. and 2:15 to 4 p.m. Museum open daily 10 a.m. to 5:30 p.m. Galleries open late Fridays. Admission: Free. Web: **www.britishmuseum.org**

OXFORD. University of Oxford, Ashmolean Museum, Heberden Coin Room, Beaumont Street, Oxford, OX1 2PH. Collection of 300,000 coins and medals of all periods and areas. Open Tuesday to Sunday 10 a.m. to 6 p.m. Admission: Free. Web: **www. ashmolean.org/departments/heberdencoinroom.**

NOTES

22 Organizations

American Numismatic Society

Varick Street, between Canal and Watts streets, New York, NY 10013
Mailing address: 75 Varick St., Floor 11, New York, NY 10013
Telephone: (212) 571-4470
Web: www.numismatics.org/
Email: info@numismatics.org

Officers

Kenneth L. Edlow ....Chairman of the Board
Roger S. Siboni..President
Douglass F. Rohrman.. First Vice President
Roger S. Bagnall...Second Vice President
Sydney F. Martin .... Treasurer
Ute Wartenberg Kagan .... Secretary/Executive Director

ANS Board of Trustees

Lawrence Adams	Joel R. Anderson	Jere L. Bacharach
Richard Beleson	Jeffrey D. Benjamin	Jane M. Cody
Richard P. Eidswick	Mike Gasvoda	Daniel Hamelberg
Kenneth W. Harl	Daniel W. Holmes, Jr.	Walter J. Husak
Robert A. Kandel	Charles Paul Karukstis	Thomas Martin
Clifford L. Mishler	Josiah Ober	Stanley DeForest Scott
Peter K. Tompa	Arnold-Peter C. Weiss	

Staff

Andrew Meadows .... Deputy Director
Anna Chang .... Director of Finance & Operations
Joanne Isaac .... Museum Administrator
Robert Wilson Hoge .... Curator of North American Coins and Currency
Peter van Alfen .... Associate Curator of Greek Coins
Gilles Bransbourg .... Assistant Curator of Roman Coins
Sebastian Heath .... Research Scientist
Sylvia Karges ....Curatorial Assistant
Elena Stolyarik .... Collections Manager/Photo Orders and Reproduction Rights
Elizabeth Hahn ....Librarian
Rhonda Yen Kauffman .... Cataloger/Library Assistant
David Hill ....Archivist
Oliver Hoover ....Editor, *American Journal of Numismatics, Colonial Newsletter, Numismatic Literature*

About the ANS

The American Numismatic Society was founded by a group of 12 New Yorkers April 6, 1858. Its objective was "the collection and preservation of coins and medals, with an investigation into their history, and other subjects connected therewith." The American Numismatic Society was incorporated in 1865.

Coins, medals and books were collected from the society's early days. As the collection grew, it became necessary to find quarters to house it. A succession of rented rooms served as meeting-places and headquarters during the first 50 years.

Through contributions by interested officers and members, the society was able to erect its own building in 1907. Since then, its collections and activities have grown progressively.

The ANS Museum houses one of the finest collections of numismatics in the United States. Moved in 2008 to lower Manhattan, New York City, in the same building that houses its offices, collections and libraries, the museum includes coins of all periods from their inception to modern times, and medals and decorations.

Selections from the museum cabinets are on display in an exhibition.

The ANS Library is the most comprehensive numismatic library in the world, consisting of more than 100,000 items. In addition to its excellent book collection, which includes most of the standard references on numismatics, the library holds rare manuscripts, all of the major numismatic periodicals, a special collection of more than 8,000 auction catalogs and six distinct topical pamphlet files.

In all, the ANS houses about a million numismatic items.

The ANS has been active in publishing since its founding. Today it publishes *Numismatic Notes and Monographs,* a series of separately issued publications, each on a single topic. *The American Journal of Numismatics* (formerly *Museum Notes*) is the official journal of the society; it appears annually. *Numismatic Literature,* published infrequently, lists current numismatic publications with abstracts of their content. *Ancient Coins in North American Collections and Numismatic Studies* is a series accommodating works in a larger format.

The ANS has four classes of members: fellows, honorary fellows, associate members and corresponding members. The fellows are limited in number to 225. Persons or organizations who have rendered special service to the society or to numismatics may be elected honorary fellows. Only fellows and honorary fellows may vote at the meetings of the society, and from their number the ANS's governing council is selected.

Persons or organizations not residing in the United States may be elected corresponding members. Associate membership, which is unlimited in number, is open to all with an interest in numismatics.

A summer seminar in numismatics has been held by the society since 1952. Grants-in-aid are offered to university graduate students in humanistic fields such as classics, archaeology, Asian languages, history, economics and art history. The aim of the seminar is to provide the students with an understanding of the contribution numismatics has to make in their own fields of study and to provide them with sufficient training in numismatic techniques to be of use to them in their future careers.

The ANS has offered, since 1958, graduate fellowships to qualified university students in the fields of the humanities or the social sciences.

Applications are accepted annually from students who have completed the general examinations (or the equivalent) for the doctorate, who will be writing dissertations on topics in which the use of numismatics

plays a significant part, and who will have attended one of the society's summer seminars.

In 1998, the ANS established the annual Groves Forum lecture to address topical themes in American numismatics.

The society offers a photographic service, specially equipped for the photography of numismatic objects.

It has two annual awards, the Archer M. Huntington Medal, awarded for outstanding scholarly contributions to numismatics, and the J. Sanford Saltus Medal, honoring sculptors who have achieved merit in the art of the medal.

The first 10 years of the 21st century proved to be a hectic, even tumultuous, decade for the American Numismatic Society.

In 2004, after several years of delays, the ANS moved from its quarters built in 1907 at 155th and Broadway into a new headquarters building that it had purchased at 140 William St. / 96 Fulton St., in lower Manhattan.

A desire to gain more positive exposure for the society motivated the address change from what had become a high-crime area in upper Manhattan.

Previous to the move, the society had become embroiled in controversy involving lack of funding for ongoing operations, plans to slash staff and loss of museum accreditation.

According to ANS Executive Director Ute Wartenberg Kagan, earlier problems with society finances led to the ANS being dropped from accreditation by the American Association of Museums in 1998. The ANS appealed the decision, but its plea was overruled.

The society was faced in 1999 and early 2000 with extreme cost-cutting measures to bring expenses in line with its income, which is derived mainly from dues, publication sales and photography.

Membership benefits were restructured and some educational programs suspended in efforts to reduce a continued operating deficit.

Despite such difficulties, the ANS launched a lengthy exhibit, "Drachmas, Doubloons and Dollars: The History of Money," at the Federal Reserve Bank of New York City. Terrorist attacks Sept. 11, 2001, delayed the exhibit opening by three months, but although the exhibition period was originally planned for five years, it was extended, slated through March 2012.

In continuing efforts to regain financial health, the ANS saw reason to again relocate. Its trustees voted June 16, 2007, to sell the Fulton Street building and move. As of June 14, 2008, the ANS occupied a new, leased, location, the 11th floor of One Hudson Square, in the upscale shopping area of lower Manhattan, where it continues residence.

The move triggered a battle with the Hispanic Society of America, to which the ANS was forced to return a large collection of rare and unique coins connected with Spanish history and culture.

The collection of more than 38,000 coins, worth in excess of $1 million, had been donated by Archer M. Huntington.

Coinage of the Americas Conferences

In 1984, the ANS established the Coinage of the Americas Conference as a forum for numismatic specialists to deliver original research papers on topics related to coinage and currency of the North and South American continents. For many of the confer-

The ANS continues its operations, engaging in numismatic research, publication and education in multiple platforms.

ences, each paper was published in its entirety in a hardcover book that was presented to all participants as part of their registration and offered to the public at a set price. Most COAC references can still be obtained directly from the ANS. COAC topics are:

America's Copper Coinage, 1783-1857... Nov. 30 to Dec. 2, 1984
America's Currency, 1789-1866 ....Oct. 31 to Nov. 2, 1985
America's Silver Coinage ....Nov. 1 to 2, 1986
The Medal in America ....Sept. 26 to 27, 1987
The Coinage of El Perú.. Oct. 29 to 30, 1988
America's Gold Coinage...Nov. 4 to 5, 1989
America's Pre-federal Coins and Currency .... May 4, 1991
Canada's Money... Nov. 7, 1992
America's Silver Dollars...Oct. 30, 1993
The Token: America's Other Money...Oct. 29, 1994
Coinage of the American Confederation Period ....Oct. 28, 1995
America's Large Cent .... Nov. 9, 1996
Circulating Counterfeits of the Americas .... Nov. 7, 1998
Washingtoniana .... Nov. 6, 1999
Money of the Caribbean ....Dec. 4, 1999
Numismatic Errors ....March 17, 2001
Our Nation's Coinages: Varied Origins .... May 17, 2003
Medals Illustrating American Colonial History ....May 14 to 15, 2004
Mark Newby and the Saint Patrick Coinage .... Nov. 11, 2006
Augustus Saint-Gaudens and his Numismatic Legacy.....................................Oct. 10, 2009

American Numismatic Association

Mailing address: 818 N. Cascade Ave., Colorado Springs, CO 80903-3279
Telephone: (719) 632-2646
Web: www.money.org,
Email: ana@money.org

Senior Staff

Larry Shepherd ....Executive Director
A. Ronald Sirna ....General Counsel
Austin M. Sheheen Jr... Treasurer
Kimberly S. Kiick... Senior Administrative Manager
Carol Shuman .... Controller
Rhonda Scurek...Convention Director
Brian Miller...Exposition Manager
Leslie Wigington... Creative Services Director
Susan McMillan..Education Project Manager
Rod Gillis..Numismatic Educator
Tiffanie Bueschel .... Museum Director
Cary Hardy..Membership Director
Jay Beeton.. Marketing and Education Director
Andy Dickes ....Public Relations Specialist
RyAnne Scott... Library Director
Barbara J. Gregory ....Editor-in-Chief
Jerri Raitz..Associate Editor
Marilyn Reback.. Senior Editor
Douglas A. Mudd.. Museum Curator

Elected officials (Two-year term starts August 2011)

Thomas Hallenbeck ....President
Arthur M. Fitts or Walter Ostromecki (results incomplete at press time).......................... Vice President
Gary Adkins .... Governor
Michael L. Ellis .... Governor
Jeff C. Garrett .... Governor
Greg Lyon .... Governor
Clifford Mishler.. Governor
Scott Rottinghaus.. Governor
Wendell A. Wolka .... Governor

The ANA's beginning

Dr. George F. Heath, of Monroe, Mich., a physician, gained knowledge of world history through the study of his collection of coins. Seeking to expand his contact with other collectors and to sell duplicates from his collection, Heath in 1888 published a leaflet titled *The American Numismatist*. After the first issue the periodical was retitled *The Numismatist,* a name in use (except for a brief period in the 21st century when *"The"* was dropped from the title) to the present day.

The little publication found many friends among collectors of the era, especially those in rural areas away from numismatic clubs and societies. As Heath's subscription list increased, a growing need became evident for a society similar to those in the cities, but one that would reach the more isolated and serve the less advanced and the beginner: a national organization of numismatists.

The February 1891 issue of *The Numismatist* printed a question, "What is the matter with having an American Numismatic Association?" Heath added, "There is nothing like the alliance of kindred pursuits to stimulate growth and interest." Aided by Charles T. Tatman, the editor of the coin column in a leading hobby magazine, *Plain Talk,* a campaign was begun to organize such an association. Numismatists from across the United States reacted favorably when they were urged to band together in order to derive greater benefits and pleasure from their avocation.

Founding

On Oct. 7 and 8, 1891, five men—Heath, William G. Jerrems, David Harlow, J.A. Heckelman and John Brydon—holding 26 proxies, met in Chicago and with 61 charter members, founded the American Numismatic Association. Tatman was unable to attend. Heath declined the presidency in favor of his good friend, Jerrems, a collector of ancient coins. He did, however, accept the honor of having No. 1 on the membership roll.

At first, the coin column in *Plain Talk* was selected as the official ANA publication, but soon *The Numismatist* became the official voice of the organization.

Since that meeting in October 1891, the American Numismatic Association, a nonprofit educational association, has grown to become the largest numismatic organization of its kind in the world.

The ANA progressed smoothly for a few years, but an unfavorable national economic climate plus apathy on the part of ANA officers caused the association to become moribund. Many months passed without the officers submitting reports. Heath withdrew *The Numismatist* from the ANA, and it seemed that the organization would disband. In 1898, however, the ANA overcame its difficulties and, due primarily to the efforts of Heath, the ANA experienced growth and expansion.

ANA conventions were held in various cities from 1891 to 1895, in 1901 and in 1904. The 1907 meeting, well publicized, was an outstanding success. Henceforth, it was decided to hold annual meetings. This procedure has continued, with the exception of 1918 when a nationwide influenza epidemic forced the cancellation of public meetings, and 1945, when wartime conditions intervened.

On June 16, 1908, Heath died. Farran Zerbe, then president, assumed the task of editing and publishing *The Numismatist,* and soon purchased the publication from Heath's heirs in a private deal, a transaction that was fraught with controversy, as many ANA members believed that the ANA, not Zerbe, should have been the buyer. By 1911, Zerbe, realizing that he could not turn a profit, decided to sell *The Numismatist.* A Canadian ANA member, W.W.C. Wilson, provided the money to give Zerbe what was described as "a long price," and to present the magazine to the ANA.

Over the years, early copies of *The Numismatist* have become collectors' items in their own right. Today it is believed that fewer than 10 complete sets, from 1888 to date, exist. Particularly rare are issues of the 1888 to 1893 span.

Federal charter and permanent headquarters

On May 9, 1912, through the efforts of Rep. William A. Ashbrook of Ohio, an ANA member, the association was granted a federal charter, signed by President William Howard Taft. Fifty years later, in 1962, Congress granted permanent status to the ANA Charter.

From the early years onward, for a long span, various officials managed the ANA, including General Secretary Lewis M. Reagan. Offices were maintained in cities where officials lived, including Baltimore, Wichita, Kan., and Phoenix. However, some officers and members advocated for a permanent home for the ANA. To achieve that end, an ANA national home and headquarters building fund was established in

1961, and by 1966 the ANA headquarters, in Colorado Springs, Colo., became a reality. Officially opened June 10, 1967, the headquarters building contains business offices, a library, a museum and other facilities. In 1981, construction began on an addition to the facility, to accommodate the growth in staff size from about a dozen to 50. The ANA Museum was expanded to include seven galleries.

As part of its centennial celebration in 1991, the association held its anniversary convention in Rosemont, Ill., a suburb of the city where it all began— Chicago. Two reference books were published: *The ANA Centennial History,* in two volumes, by Q. David Bowers, detailing the growth of the ANA and of the numismatic hobby; and *The ANA Anthology*, edited by then ANA Historian Carl W. Carlson and featuring research articles contributed by more than two dozen prominent numismatic historians.

The 1990s and early 21st century proved challenging for the ANA, as stagnant membership numbers, budgetary and legal problems, plus the controversial hirings of two executive directors from outside the numismatic community, threatened to overshadow the ANA's mission.

ANA services

ANA library

One of the first services, established in the early years for the benefit of its members, was a numismatic library. This library retained a modest status for years, but gained in size and prestige with the growth of membership. Today, housed at ANA headquarters, the Dwight N. Manley Numismatic Library is the largest circulating numismatic library in the world, and comprises more than 60,000 hardcover reference books and other library items that are loaned to members without charge, other than postage and insurance costs.

ANA museum

In 1928, the association, through a fund established by Robert P. King in 1927, deposited a collection of coins and medals in the Smithsonian Institution in Washington, D.C. In the 1960s, the King-funded collection, augmented by further donations since its inception, was moved to ANA headquarters. Many other gifts have been donated by members to the ANA Money Museum, representing collections consisting of coins, paper money and medallic art.

Notable among the benefactors were Aubrey and Adeline Bebee, who donated a superb collection of paper money and a 1913 Liberty Head 5-cent coin, valued in the aggregate at more than $2 million. In 1991, the Bebees made a permanent donation of the Idler specimen of Class III Proof 1804 Draped Bust dollar, which had been on loan the previous six years. In 1994, Willis du Pont donated the Edward Cohen specimen of a Class I 1804 dollar in exchange for the ANA sending du Pont's Linderman Class III 1804 restrike dollar to the National Numismatic Collection at the Smithsonian Institution. The Linderman coin had been on loan to the ANA Museum in gratitude for the ANA's assistance in recovering the coin. Both duPont 1804 dollars had been stolen in 1967. The Linderman coin was recovered in 1982; the Edward Cohen coin was recovered in 1993.

An additional expansion of the museum was completed in 2001 to hold the Harry W. Bass Collection of gold coins, patterns and paper money, which by some estimates is valued at more than $20 million. It is on long-term loan until 2026.

Education, achievements and policies

The annual educational forums were formulated in 1946, moving the ANA closer to adequately fulfilling its credo as stated in the federal charter and constitution "that the objectives of said corporation shall be to advance the knowledge of numismatics along educational, historical and scientific lines in all its various branches."

A new official ANA movement began in 1965 with the establishment of the Young Numismatists Committee. Since its inception, the committee has worked hard to bring the junior movement into its own by sponsoring literary awards, service awards, exhibit awards and other beneficial achievement tributes to those who will, one day, carry on the hobby. In 1965, the ANA lowered the minimum membership age from 17 to 11 and the junior movement really sprang to life. The youth movement, championed by many adult members acting as advisers, now has developed a well-rounded program for the Young Numismatist, reflected in features of the annual conventions and in specialized publications.

By board action in 1965, the ANA Code of Ethics was established, outlining principles of moral conduct that collectors and dealers are required to follow. Any breach of the code is considered cause for disciplinary action by the board.

The District Representatives Committee was established in 1967, through which appointed ANA representatives served the United States, Canada and Mexico through 18 districts. Today, 55 districts are recognized, with one or more representatives (depending on the size of the area involved) for each of the 50 states, Canada, Mexico and certain other nations. Representatives promote good will for ANA, assist in resolving complaints and misunderstandings, visit ANA members at club meetings and conventions, provide information regarding all ANA services and, generally, act as liaisons between the membership and the ANA Board.

In 1969, the ANA initiated the first Summer Seminar (then called the ANA Summer Conference), now an annual numismatic educational opportunity conducted at Colorado Springs and occasionally elsewhere. The program provides instruction on various numismatic subjects and offers tours, food and lodging at a very nominal cost to students. In 2010, the Summer Seminar brought more than 400 numismatists to study in more than a dozen areas of numismatic specialties during two different, consecutive, week-long sessions.

The ANA announced in February 1970 an all-risk coin insurance plan. A continuing ANA offering, the low-cost plan offers participants a broad coverage of theft and fire insurance for their collections.

National Coin Week

An ANA member in 1923 suggested that the association sponsor an annual week-long national celebration of numismatics and collecting. The pitch was made in a letter submitted to the ANA's monthly magazine:

To the Editor of The Numismatist:

It is my opinion that it would be a very good plan to have a "Coin Week" each year. My idea is to have, say, the first week in February set aside as "Coin Week," and I think the dealers throughout the country should form an association, which could obtain funds to carry on an extensive, nationwide advertising campaign in magazines, newspapers, etc., during that week. Dealers and collectors alike would be stimulated, and instead of interesting and starting one collector here and there we would find new collectors by the hundred. In fact, I think such a "drive" would mean a new era for numismatics.

—— *Julius Guttag*

The Numismatist, *November 1923*

ANA officials responded positively to the proposal and in less than a year, had adopted what is known as National Coin Week. The ANA has sponsored National Coin Week since 1924. Its purpose is to bring numismatics into greater public attention and to win new coin collecting devotees.

National Coin Week aims to advance the cultural and artistic aspects of coin collecting, to advance the enjoyment of the hobby through proper education and to advance interest in coin collecting as a science. In 1974, it was acclaimed by presidential proclamation.

Julius Guttag founded the annual effort in 1924 and served as the first chairman.

Awards and prizes

The ANA annually recognizes excellence in numismatic exhibiting, writing, medallic design and more.

The Farran Zerbe Award

The Farran Zerbe Memorial Award, highest American Numismatic Association honor, was established in 1950 by Louis S. Werner of New York, a close friend of Zerbe. Zerbe was at one time the owner and editor of *The Numismatist;* he was often referred to as the dean of American numismatics in the early 20th century.

Zerbe served two terms as president of the American Numismatic Association. He died Dec. 25, 1949, at the age of 78.

The recipient of the Zerbe award each year is selected by the awards committee and approved by the board of governors of the ANA as one considered to have rendered the association distinguished service and to be worthy of the highest honor it can bestow. The traditional plaque was replaced in 1984 by a 2-inch, 10-karat gold medal.

Heath Literary Awards

Numismatic literary awards were initiated in 1924; the name "Heath Literary Awards" was established in 1945 during V. Leon Belt's ANA presidency. The award name honors George Heath. Each year, all papers published in *The Numismatist* are judged on their merits by an impartial committee. First-, second- and third-place medals are presented with as many as five honorable mention awards possible.

Silver and bronze medals, along with cash awards, were presented to Heath Literary Award winners from 1945 through 1954, with honorable mention certificates commencing in 1947. Cash awards were discontinued in 1955, but were resumed in 1973.

Wayte and Olga Raymond Literary Awards

The Wayte and Olga Raymond Literary award, established in 1977, is for distinguished numismatic achievement in the field of United States numismatics. The annual award provides a cash stipend to the authors of outstanding research articles.

ANA Medal of Merit

The ANA Medal of Merit was first awarded in 1948. The silver Medal of Merit is one of the highest awards of the ANA, and is reserved for "those who have shown outstanding devotion to numismatics, the organization and its goals." The medals are given each year in ceremonies generally held at the ANA summer convention.

Medals of Merit are accompanied by special citations that describe in detail the recipients' contributions to the ANA.

ANA Numismatic Art Award for Excellence in Medallic Sculpture

The ANA Numismatic Art Award for Excellence in Medallic Sculpture, popularly known as the Outstanding Sculptor of the Year Award, was brought into existence in 1966 by the ANA, in conjunction with the Franklin Mint. The large gold medal award is presented annually to pay tribute to talented sculptors.

Howland Wood Award

Numismatic displays have been outstanding attractions at ANA conventions since 1904. Thousands of numismatists, as well as curious noncollectors, have viewed these exhibits featuring famous collections and highly publicized rarities.

The Howland Wood Grand Award for "The Best in Show" exhibit is presented at the annual convention of the ANA. A proposal and resolution for the exhibit medal award program was introduced at the

1949 convention in San Francisco. It was continued at the 1950 Milwaukee gathering and established at the 1951 Phoenix convention.

For exhibitors, first-place winners and runners-up in all classifications are presented with memorial award plaques or medals.

ANA Numismatic Hall of Fame

The ANA Numismatic Hall of Fame was established Aug. 18, 1964, and enshrines the names of famous numismatists. Portraits of Hall of Fame members are on view in a special display at ANA Headquarters.

The ANA Numismatic Hall of Fame is open to "persons whose contributions to the field of numismatics have been of the highest excellence and most outstanding." Nominations are accepted between October and December of the year preceding the year of award, and may be made by any ANA member except junior members.

Young Numismatist awards

Thirteen awards in connection with the Young Numismatist program are offered yearly. These awards are given by the ANA, other organizations and individuals interested in encouraging the participation of young collectors in the hobby. See the ANA website, **www.money.org/**, for details on the many awards for YNs.

Membership awards

Two membership awards were established during the 1947 ANA convention. A gold medal is presented to 50-year members of the association, and a silver medal is given to members who have completed 25 consecutive years of membership. Clubs that have completed 25 or 50 years of corporate membership in the ANA receive gold or silver certificates.

ANACS (no longer an ANA service)

The inauguration June 22, 1972, of the ANA Certification Service, popularly known as ANACS, in Washington, D.C., launched one of the association's most popular services. ANACS was initially designed to authenticate coins and to identify counterfeit coins. ANACS became the world's first service designed specifically to give an authoritative answer as to the authenticity of numismatic material submitted by anyone, from any place in the world. Numismatic material was photographed and, if genuine, a certificate was issued to verify same.

In 1977, ANACS was transferred to the headquarters in Colorado Springs.

On March 1, 1979, ANACS began grading coins for a fee and issuing ANACS certificates stating an opinion of grade. Since its inception, the grading service generated controversy. Some collectors and dealers defended the service as an impartial answer to sometimes erroneous grading in the marketplace. Others claimed ANACS grading was inconsistent. In the meantime, Abe Kosoff, Kenneth E. Bressett, and Q. David Bowers wrote *Official ANA Grading Standards for United States Coins,* which uses a numerical grading system and has gone on to be published in several editions.

In 1990, the ANA sold ANACS to Amos Press Inc., parent company of *Coin World,* in Sidney, Ohio. It was the ANA board's decision that a nonprofit organization could not reasonably operate a profit-making enterprise such as ANACS. The decision was made, therefore, to sell the service and concentrate on education and consumer protection. Under terms of the agreement, the ANA retained the right to authenticate coins (with the establishment of the American Numismatic Association Authentication Bureau), and retained copyright to the *Official ANA Grading Standards for United States Coins.* The grading service was relocated to Columbus, Ohio (and eventually again sold in 2005 to Anderson Press Inc., and to Driving Force LLC. in late 2007).

Fédération Internationale de la Médaille

Mailing address for U.S. delegate:
Mashiko, 335 W. 38th St., Fourth Floor,
New York, NY 10018-2916
Web: www.fidem-medals.org
Email: mashiko@medialiagallery.com

The Fédération Internationale de la Médaille, or FIDEM, was founded in the 1930s as an organization representing the major producers of commemorative medals. In the succeeding decades, the scope has been enlarged to emphasize the activity of sculptors and collectors, and the focus is on the art of the medal.

The principal activity of FIDEM is the organization of an international congress and exhibition, usually every two years. At the congress, lectures and workshops explore the aesthetics, production and history of the medal.

The exhibitions feature thousands of medals by artists from dozens of member countries; each country's exhibition is selected by its own delegation.

The membership of FIDEM is organized by participating countries, with each country having an official delegate, which may be an individual or group, responsible for organizing the participation of that country in the congresses and exhibitions.

The central governing body of FIDEM comprises a president, two vice presidents and several additional members as well as the general secretary and treasurer, who are the principal executive officers. All officers are elected in the general assemblies held at the congresses.

FIDEM publishes a journal, *Médailles,* which carries the texts of presentations at the congresses, and supports and distributes the magazine *The Medal,* published four times a year. Membership in FIDEM is open to individual artists, collectors, scholars and producers, as well as institutions and firms.

For convenience in currency transactions, membership fees for Americans and Canadians are collected in U.S. dollars by the American Medallic Sculpture Association.

Professional Numismatists Guild

Mailing address: 28441 Rancho California Road, Suite 106, Temecula, CA 92590
Telephone: (951) 587-8300
Web: www.pngdealers.com/
Email: info@pngdealers.com
Robert Brueggeman, Executive Director

Professional Numismatists Guild Inc. is a non-profit membership corporation founded in the mid-1950s by Abe Kosoff with 33 members represented. The group was incorporated in 1955. Today, PNG comprises the country's top rare coin and paper money experts.

Its motto, "Knowledge, Integrity, Responsibility," continues to reflect the aims of the not-for-profit organization.

For the first decade, membership in the Professional Numismatists Guild was by invitation, and only a few dealers were asked to join. As time passed, the membership rolls were expanded.

Today, the PNG comprises a membership across the United States and abroad of virtually all leading professional numismatists.

All PNG members must adhere to the organization's published strict code of ethics (copies of which can be obtained by writing the executive director), which includes agreement to submit to legally binding arbitration to settle any dispute between a buyer and the PNG member-dealer.

In the late 1990s, the PNG began distributing Pennyboards through its member-dealers and at coins shows around the United States to allow Young Numismatists and new collectors to assemble a collection of Lincoln, Memorial cents from 1959 to the present. The PNG has also been a strong advocate for numismatic education and dissemination of consumer information.

Among the awards presented by the PNG are the Abe Kosoff Founders Award for significant contributions to the PNG or to numismatics in general; the Sol Kaplan Award for assistance in bringing to justice perpetrators of fraud or thievery; and the Robert Friedberg Award for literary achievement. The Kaplan and Friedberg awards are presented through the auspices of the Lewis M. Reagan Memorial Foundation Inc.

To obtain a membership application or information or for a PNG Membership Directory, write to Robert Brueggeman at the mailing address above or visit the PNG website.

Industry Council for Tangible Assets

Mailing address: Box 1365, Severna Park, MD 21146-8635
Telephone for Eloise A. Ullman, Executive Director: (410) 626-7005
Telephone for Diane Piret, Industry Affairs Director: (504) 392-0023
Web: www.ictaonline.org
Email: eloise.ullman@ictaonline.org, dapiret@ictaonline.org

The Industry Council for Tangible Assets is a trade association representing the interests of dealers in tangible assets, including bullion and coins. The members are interested in upholding ethical standards in the industry and working to create a favorable regulatory climate in the federal and state governments for manufacture, distribution and sale of tangible assets. ICTA conducts lobbying in Congress and monitors and advises state organizations regarding the application of state sales taxes on coin and bullion transactions.

Members must uphold a code of ethics and be dealers. The dues vary depending on the size of the company. ICTA was formed in 1983.

Numismatic Literary Guild

Mailing address: 1517 Stewart Drive, Nanticoke, PA 18634
Web: www.numismaticliteraryguild.org

Officials

Ed Reiter ....Executive Director

Kay E. Lenker .... Co-Treasurer
Maurice Rosen .... Co-Treasurer
Michael Sedgwick... Newsletter Editor
John Albanese .... Director
David T. Alexander .... Director
R.W. Julian .... Director
Donn Pearlman .... Director
Will Rossman .... Director

History and function

The Numismatic Literary Guild was founded in August 1969 during the 77th Anniversary Convention of the American Numismatic Association in San Diego.

Membership is open to full-time staff members of numismatic publications, researchers, museum workers, freelance writers, editors and publishers in the field of numismatics.

New members must be sponsored by one NLG member in good standing; dues are $10 per year.

The purposes of NLG are to encourage numismatic writing, provide a central forum for both full-time and part-time writers, and to share conviviality and fellowship at ANA conventions.

NLG recognizes excellence by a series of annual awards for writers and columnists, as well as offering the top "Clemy" award, in honor of Clement F. Bailey, and the Maurice M. Gould award for outstanding literary contributions to numismatics.

Members receive a newsletter, keeping them informed of the activities of fellow writers everywhere and featuring original articles and observations of the members.

New NLG members accepted by the membership committee pay an initial fee of $25, besides the first year's dues.

National and regional associations

Following is a list of national and regional collector associations. Addresses and other details are subject to change without notice.

American Credit Card Collectors Society
P.O. Box 2465
Midland, MI 48640
www.creditcollectibles.com

American Israel Numismatic Association
P.O. Box 20255
Fountain Hills, AZ 85268
Telephone: (818) 225-1348
www.theshekel.org

American Medallic Sculpture Association
P.O. Box 1201
Edmonds, WA 98020
www.amsamedals.org

American Numismatic Association
818 N. Cascade Ave.
Colorado Springs, CO 80903
www.money.org

American Numismatic Society
75 Varick St., Floor 11
New York, NY 10013
www.numismatics.org

American Political Items Collectors
P.O. Box 55
Avon, NY 14414
www.apic.us

American Tax Token Society
569 Diego Rivera Lane
Arroyo Grande, CA 93420
www.taxtoken.org

American Vecturist Association
13927 Wood Duck Circle
Lakewood Ranch, FL 34202-8314
www.vecturist.com

Barber Coin Collectors Society
2053 Edith Place
Merrick, NY 11566
www.barbercoins.org

Blue Ridge Numismatic Association
P.O. Box 56156
Virginia Beach, VA 23456
www.brna.org

Bust Half Nut Club
Glenn R. Peterson
9301 Park West Blvd.
Knoxville, TN 37923-4300
Membership inquiries: herrman102@aol.com

Carson City Coin Collectors of America
P.O. Box 18040
Reno, NV 89511

Casino Chip & Gaming Token Collectors Club
1215 E. Dalton Ave.
Glendora, CA 91741
www.ccgtcc.com

Central States Numismatic Society
P.O. Box 841
Logansport, IN 46947
www.centralstates.info

Civil War Token Society
10616 Ranch Road
Culver City, CA 90230
www.cwtsociety.com

Colorado-Wyoming Numismatic Association
P.O. Box 1423
Canon City, CO 81215
Colonial Coin Collectors Club Inc.
P.O. Box 25
Mountville, PA 17554
www.colonialcoins.org
Combined Organizations of Numismatic Error Collectors of America
101 W. Prairie No. 323
Hayden, ID 83835
http://conecaonline.org
Conder Token Collectors' Club
101 W. Prairie No. 323
Hayden, ID 83835
Dedicated Wooden Money Collectors
P.O. Box 14402
Louisville, KY 40214
Early American Coppers Inc.
9743 Leacrest Road
Cincinnati, OH 45215
www.eacs.org
The Elongated Collectors
P.O. Box 704
Richlandtown, PA 18955-0704
www.tecnews.org
Flying Eagle and Indian Cent Collectors Society
P.O. Box 559
Sandwich, IL 60548
www.fly-inclub.org
Indiana-Kentucky-Ohio Token & Medal Society
3209 Bellacre Ct.
Cincinnati, OH 45248
International Association of Silver Art Collectors
P.O. Box 3987
Clarksville, TN 37043
http://thesilverbugle.com
International Organization of Wooden Money Collectors
9957 W. Margaret Lane
Franklin, WI 53132
Liberty Seated Collectors Club
P.O. Box 6114
Vernon Hills, IL 6061
www.lsccweb.org
Love Token Society
P.O. Box 2351
Denham Springs, LA 70727
www.lovetokensociety.org
Medal Collectors of America
3115 Nestling Pine Court
Ellicott City, MD 21042
www.medalcollectors.org
National Collector's Association of Die Doubling
P.O. Box 15
Lykens, PA 17048-0015
www.ncadd98.org
National Scrip Collectors Association
P.O. Box 922

Skelton, WV 25919
www.nationalscripcollectors.com/
National Silver Dollar Roundtable
P.O. Box 25
Broken Arrow, OK 74013
www.silverdollarroundtable.com
National Token Collectors Association
1425 Cat Mountain Trail
Keller, TX 76248
http://tokencollectors.org
New England Numismatic Association
P.O. Box 2061
Woburn, MA 01888
www.nenacoin.org
Northeast Token & Medal Society
Bob Schopp
16 Sanbert Circle
Hamilton Square, NJ 08690
Northwest Tokens and Medals Society
P.O. Box 1365,
Ocean Shores, WA 98569
www.nwtams.org
Numismatic Bibliomania Society
P.O. Box 82
Littleton, NH 03561
www.coinbooks.com
Email for *E-Sylum*, the NBS electronic newsweekly: **whomren@gmail.com**
Orders & Medals Society of America
P.O. Box 198
San Ramon, CA 94583
www.omsa.org
Original Hobo Nickel Society Inc.
12000 Sunset Ridge Drive
Ozawkie, KS 66070-6045
http://hobonickels.org
Pacific Coast Numismatic Society
P.O. Box 475656
San Francisco, CA 94147
www.pcns.org
Pacific Northwest Numismatic Association
101 W. Prairie Center No. 323
Hayden, ID 83835
www.pnna.org
John Reich Collectors Society
Box 135
Harrison, OH 45030-0135
www.jrcs.org
Society for U.S. Commemorative Coins
P.O. Box 302
Huntington Beach, CA 92647
Society of Lincoln Cent Collectors
P.O. Box 627
Brookline, MO 65619
www.lincolncentsociety.com
Society of Private and Pioneer Numismatics
1550G Tiburon Blvd., No. 201
Tiburon, CA 94920

Society of Ration Token Collectors
18 Wyndhaven Court
Simpsonville, SC 29681-5289
Society of Silver Dollar Collectors
P.O. Box 42112
Greensboro, NC 27425
www.vamlink.com
The Society of U.S. Pattern Collectors
P.O. Box 806
Nyack, NY 10960
http://uspatterns.com
Token and Medal Society
101 W. Prairie Center No. 323
Hayden, ID 83835
www.tokenandmedal.org

U.S. Mexican Numismatic Association
P.O. Box 5270
Carefree, AZ 85377
www.usmex.org
Western States Token Society
P.O. Box 723
Merced, CA 95341-0723
Women in Numismatics
1612 Grandiflora Drive
Leland, NC 28451
www.womeninnumismatics.com
World Bi-Metallic Collectors Club
(Internet-only club based in the Netherlands)
wbcc@hotmail.nl
www.wbcc-online.com

State numismatic associations

Alabama Numismatic Society
P.O. Box 365
Pelham, AL 35124
Arkansas Numismatic Society
P.O. Box 359
Prescott, AR 71857-0359
California Exonumist Society
P.O. Box 6909
San Diego, CA 92154-0909
California State Numismatic Association
P.O. Box 4003
Vallejo, CA 94590-0400
www.calcoin.org
Northern California Numismatic Association
P.O. Box 4104
Vallejo, CA 94590-0410
www.solanocoinclub.com
Numismatic Association of Southern California
P.O. Box 3382
Tustin, CA 92781
www.nasc.net
Washington (D.C.) Numismatic Society Inc.
P.O. Box 9413
Washington, DC 20016
Florida Token Society
1717 Saint Marys Bay Drive
Milton, FL 32583-7343
Florida United Numismatists
P.O. Box 471147
Lake Monroe, FL 32747-1147
www.funtopics.com
Georgia Numismatic Association
P.O. Box 76161
Atlanta, GA 30358-1161
Hawaii State Numismatic Association
P.O. Box 477
Honolulu, HI 96809
www.hawaiicollectibles.org
Illinois Numismatic Association
6455 W. Archer Ave.
Chicago, IL 60638
www.ilnaclub.info

Indiana State Numismatic Association
1123 W. Eighth St.
Anderson, IN 46016-2616
www.indianastatenumismatics.org
Iowa Numismatic Association
615 Central Ave.
Fort Dodge, IA 50501
Kansas Numismatic Association
P.O. Box 11
Derby, KS 67037-0011
http://kansasnumismaticassociation.org/
Kentucky State Numismatic Association
560 Marimon Ave.
Harrodsburg, KY 40330
Maryland State Numismatic Association
P.O. Box 13504
Silver Spring, MD 20911-3504
Maryland Token & Medal Society
P.O. Box 644
Gambrills, MD 21054-0644
Michigan State Numismatic Society
P.O. Box 87931
Canton, MI 48187
www.michigancoinclub.org
Michigan Token and Medal Society
2176 Summerfield Road
Petersburg, MI 49270
Minnesota Organization of Numismatists
P.O. Box 565
Rochester, MN 55903
Mississippi Numismatic Association
P.O. Box 303
Collinsville, MS 39325
Missouri Numismatic Society
P.O. Box 410652
St. Louis, MO 63141-0652
http://missourinumismaticsociety.org
Nebraska Numismatic Association
P.O. Box 5575
Lincoln, NE 68505

New Jersey Numismatic Society
P.O. Box 442
Sparta, NJ 07871
Garden State Numismatic Association
P.O. Box 561
Middlesex, NJ 08846
www.gsna.org
Empire State Numismatic Association
613 W. Fourth St.
Fulton, NY 13069-3104
www.nyscoincollectors.org
North Carolina Numismatic Association
P.O. Box 5846
Statesville, NC 28687
www.ncnaonline.org
Oklahoma Numismatic Association
P.O. Box 277
Jenks, OK 74037-0277
Pennsylvania Association of Numismatists
P.O. Box 10607
Lancaster, PA 17605-0607
www.pancoins.org
South Carolina Numismatic Association
P.O. Box 693

Lugoff, SC 29078
www.sc-na.org/
Tennessee State Numismatic Society
Box 56156
Virginia Beach, VA 23456
www.tsns.org
Texas Numismatic Association
P.O. Box 852165
Richardson, TX 75085-2165
www.tna.org
Utah Numismatic Society
P.O. Box 65064
Salt Lake City, UT 84165
National Utah Token Society
P.O. Box 651071
Salt Lake City, UT 84165
www.utahtokensociety.com/
Virginia Numismatic Association
P.O. Box 16833
Chesapeake, VA 23328
www.vnaonline.org/
Numismatists of Wisconsin
P.O. Box 155
Mazomanie, WI 53560

Paper money and syngraphic organizations

American Society of Check Collectors
Lyman Hensley
473 E. Elm
Sycamore, IL 60178
www.ascheckcollectors.org
Currency Club of Chester County
420 Owen Road
West Chester, PA 19380
www.currencyclubofchestercounty.org
Fractional Currency Collectors Board
Bill Brandimore
1009 Nina
Wausau, WI 54403
International Bank Note Society
U.S. Membership Secretary
Roger Urce
P.O. Box 289
Saint James, NY 11780-0289
www.theibns.org
International Bond and Share Society
Address for U.S. residents:

116 Parklane Drive
San Antonio, TX 78212
www.scripophily.com
Latin American Paper Money Society
3304 Milford Mill Road
Baltimore, MD 21244
www.latinamericanpapermoneysociety.com
Paper Money Collectors of Michigan
P.O. Box 195
Mayville, MI 48744
Society of Paper Money Collectors
P.O. Box 117060
Carrollton, TX 75011-7060
www.spmc.org/
Souvenir Card Collectors Society
P.O. Box 4155
Tulsa, OK 74159-0155
Western Wooden Money Club
P.O. Box 3467
Fairfield, CA 94533-0467

Treasure hunting clubs

The advent and expansion of the Internet has opened up a whole online world for collectors interested in metal detecting and treasure hunting.

At **www.fmdac.org**, the Federation of Metal Detecting and Archaeology provides the names and addresses for nearly 150 specialty interest clubs in the 50 states. Another site, **http://gometaldetecting.com/links-clubs.htm** provides another listing of links for treasure hunting. Another site, **http://metaldetectingworld.com**, offers a personal, step-by-step look at how to begin and enjoy the hobby. Sites like **www.minelabforums.com** allow collectors to share stories and education with each other, adding interaction with fellow humans to the man-and-machine hobby.

North American-based world numismatic organizations

Ancient Coin Collectors Guild
Wayne Sayles
P.O. Box 911
Gainesville, MO 65655
www.accg.us
Armenian Numismatic Society
8511 Beverly Park Place
Pico Rivera, CA 90660-1920
http://armnumsoc.org
Classical and Medieval Numismatic Society
http://home.cogeco.ca/~cmns/
International Coin and Stamp Collectors Society
P.O. Box 854
Van Nuys, CA 91408
International Primitive Money Society
2471 S.W. 37th St.
Ocala, FL 34474
Lithuanian Numismatic Association
P.O. Box 22696
Baltimore, MD 21203

Numismatics International
P.O. Box 570842
Dallas, TX 75357-0842
www.numis.org
Oriental Numismatic Society
ONS Regional Secretary J. Lingen
Lange Stoep 25
2941 AE Lekkerkerk
Netherlands
www.onsnumis.org
Polish American Numismatic Association
P.O. Box 80515
Rochester, MI 48308-0515
www.pans-club.org
Russian Numismatic Society
P.O. Box 3684
Santa Rosa, CA 95402
www.russiannumismaticsociety.org
World Proof Numismatic Association
P.O. Box 4094
Pittsburgh, PA 15201-0094

Royal Canadian Numismatic Association

The Canadian Numismatic Association was established in 1950 and incorporated in 1963. It was granted a name change, to Royal Canadian Numismatic Association, after being granted the use of "Royal" in its title in 2007 by Queen Elizabeth II.

Application for membership in the CNA may be made by any reputable person upon payment to: RCNA, 5694 Highway #7 East, Suite 432, Markham ON Canada L3P 1B4. Web: **www.rcna.ca**

The CNA publishes *The Canadian Numismatic Journal* 10 times a year, which is distributed free to members.

Following is a list of Canadian coin associations that operate on a national or regional scale. A more complete listing, including local and additional regional clubs, is available on the RCNA website.

Canadian Association of Numismatic Dealers
Executive Secretary
Box 10272, Winona PO
Stoney Creek, ON L8E 5R1, Canada
www.cand.org

Canadian Association of Token Collectors
Box 21018 Meadowvale RPO
Mississauga, ON L5N 6A2, Canada
www.nunet.ca/catc.htm

Canadian Association of Wooden Money
Collectors
86 Hamilton Drive
Newmarket, ON L3Y 3E8, Canada
www.nunet.ca/cawmc.htm

Canadian Numismatic Research Society
Harry James
P.O. Box 22022, Elmwood Square PO
2024 First Ave.
St. Thomas, ON N5R 4W1, Canada
www.nunet.ca/cnrs.htm

Canadian Paper Money Society
P.O. Box 562
Pickering, ON L1V 2R7, Canada
www.cpmsonline.ca

Canadian Tire Coupon Collectors Club
Ghislaine Theroux-Memme
1875 ave Raymond
Laval, QC H7S 1R3, Canada
www.ctccc.ca

World coin organizations

Numismatics is popular around the world, and many national collector organizations serve hobbyists in countries across the globe.

Probably many more collector groups exist than are listed here. Contacts at mints and central banks (listed in the World Coins chapter) might be able to direct you to clubs focusing on a specific interest not found here. Some foreign clubs include:

AUSTRALIA
Australian Numismatic Society
P.O. Box 366

Brookvale, NSW 2100, Australia
www.the-ans.com

BRAZIL
Sociedade Numismática de Brasil
Rua 24 de Maio
247 - 2° andar - Centro
São Paulo - SP -
Brasil - CEP 01041-001
www.snb.org.br
GERMANY
Berufsverband des Deutschen Münzenfach-
handels e.V.
Herrn Rechtsanwalt Thomas A. Brückel
Universitätsstr. 5
50937 Köln
Germany
ENGLAND
British Numismatic Society
Membership Secretary
c/o The Warburg Institute
Woburn Square
London
WC1H 0AB
United Kingdom
www.britnumsoc.org
Royal Numismatic Society
c/o The British Museum
Department of Coins and Medals
Great Russell Street
London WC1B 3DG
United Kingdom
www.numismatics.org.uk
FRANCE
Société Française Numismatique
58 rue de Richelieu
75 002 Paris, France
www.sfnum.asso.fr
HUNGARY
Hungarian Numismatic Society
H-1445 Budapest
POB 282, Hungary
www.numizmatika.org
INDIA
Numismatic Society of India
General Secretary
P.O. Banaras Hindu University
Varanasi – 221 005 (U.P.)
India
www.bhu.ac.in/aihc/ins.htm
ISRAEL
Israel Numismatic Society
Haim Gitler

c/o the Israel Museum
P.O. Box 71117
Jerusalem 91710
Israel
www.ins.org.il
ITALY
Societa Numismatica Italiana
Biblioteca e Segreteria
via Orti, 3 - 20122 Milano
www.socnumit.org/e-menu.htm
MALAYSIA
Malaysian Numismatic Society
P.O. Box 12367
50776 Kuala Lumpur
Malaysia
www.money.org.my
MEXICO
Sociedad Numismatica de Mexico
Eugenia 13 Despacho 301
Col. Napoles, C.P. 3810
Mexico 18, D.F., Mexico
www.sonumex.org.mx
NEW ZEALAND
Royal Numismatic Society of New Zealand
P.O. Box 2023
Wellington 6140, New Zealand
www.rnsnz.com
PANAMA
Asociación Numismática de Panamá
Apartado Postal 0834-1931
Panamá, Republica de Panamá
info@asonum.org
PERU
Sociedad Numismatica de Peru
Avenida Pardo 731 Int 1
Miraflores
L-18, Perú
www.dnet.com.pe/webs/usuarios/numismatica
SOUTH AFRICA
South African Numismatic Society
P.O. Box 1689
Cape Town 8000
South Africa
SPAIN
Associacion Numismatica Espanola
Gran Via de les Cortes
Catalanes 627, Pral 1st
080101 Barcelona, Spain
www.numisane.org

International Association of Professional Numismatists

The IAPN states its objective in its charter: "coordination of all efforts and ideas of the development of the numismatic trade, the encouragement of scientific research and the propagation of numismatics, and the creation of lasting and friendly relations among professional numismatists throughout the world."

The IAPN was founded in Geneva, Switzerland, May 12, 1951, and today has members worldwide.

Write to the International Association of Professional Numismatists, General Secretary Jean-Luc Van der Schueren, 14, Rue de la Bourse, BE-1000 Bruxelles Belgium, or visit **www.iapn-coins.org**.

23 Books and Periodicals

First the book

Aaron Feldman (1895 to 1976) was a coin dealer who advised his clients to "buy the book before the coin." In numismatics, knowledge is power. The more you know about the forms and uses of money, the more you will understand and appreciate your collections. The more you know about the many types, varieties, errors and counterfeits, the better you will be at making intelligent—even profitable—purchases and sales.

On the one hand, the classic works by the leading numismatic researchers are important additions to your library. On the other hand, new books by new authorities present the latest information in a modern way, often with charts and pictures.

In fact, books and periodicals are themselves collectible. The Numismatic Bibliomania Society (website at **www.coinbooks.org**) is a collector group dedicated to the study of numismatic books, periodicals, auction catalogs and other printed materials.

If you are a member of the American Numismatic Association (**www.money.org**) or the American Numismatic Society (**www.numismatics.org**), you can use their libraries. Of the two, the ANA's library is the only lending numismatic library; members can borrow books through the mail. Researchers must visit the ANS's library in New York City to use its books and other references. Your local public library can often locate books from other libraries and arrange to borrow them, via "Inter-Library Loan."

If you attend the larger regional or national coin shows, you will meet the dealers who sell new and used books about numismatics. If you look in the *Coin World* classified ads under the heading "1485: Coin Books," you will find contact information for dealers who specialize in numismatic literature.

The bibliographies presented here can only touch the surface. Any collector who specializes will soon assemble a library of resources that is deep and broad.

The standard works of 20 or 30 years ago are often superseded by new references. Sometimes, perhaps often, the more dedicated to a specialty and involved you become, the more you need both the old and the new works.

Some classics can never be replaced. We certainly know more about American coins than did Sylvester S. Crosby (1831 to 1914), but he was a meticulous researcher and his observations in *Early Coins of America* allow us to understand 19th century numismatics from the viewpoint of a 19th century writer. Also, as new books are published, they may tend to ignore or gloss over details that seem not so important today. This is acceptable within limits, but at some level, the collector really wants to know the origins of who, what, when, where, why and how. Only a classic work, sometimes long out of print and collectible in its own right, can provide that knowledge.

It is possible for a numismatic researcher to be an expert in Roman coins, Mexican coins and U.S. pioneer gold. It is less likely that a writer will be an expert in U.S. coins, baseball cards and fighter jets of the world. The fact is that some publishers simply contract out their projects to writers who can make a deadline and who do so by acquiring instant expertise. The bottom line is that not every book about numismatics is worth owning.

The same can be said for resources on the Internet. Since the last edition of the *Coin World Almanac* was published in 2000, there has been an explosion of websites related to numismatics—some are excellent sources of information; others can be misleading or completely incorrect. Proceed with caution.

The *Coin World* staff recommends the following books as being among the titles and authors we depend on for reliable information. Many others that we judge to be excellent and important are not listed due to limitations of space.

U.S. coins

General works

The Coin World Comprehensive Catalog & Encyclopedia of United States Coins. Second edition. Alexander, David T., project editor. Amos Press Inc., 1998. Catalog-style compendium detailing Colonial and early states coins and tokens, federal issues, patterns, Confederate coinage and pioneer gold.

Coin World Almanac. Staff of *Coin World*. Amos Hobby Publishing, 2011. Earlier editions dated 1976, 1977, 1978, 1984, 1987, 1990 and 2000.

Coin World Guide to U.S. Coins, Prices & Value Trends. Staff of *Coin World*. Amos Hobby Publishing.

Published annually since 1989. Price guide plus basic collector and investor information.

The Smart Collector: United States Coins. Staff of *Coin World.* Amos Hobby Publishing, 1997. Half cents to gold $20 coins, information specific to each coin. Essay type presentation. What it would cost to assemble a set, "Fast Facts" and more. Bibliography and Index.

A Guide Book of United States Coins. Yeoman, R.S. Edited by Kenneth Bressett. Whitman Publishing. Published annually since 1947. A basic catalog listing of U.S. Colonial, state, federal, commemorative and pioneer gold coins. Also known as the "Red Book." Published in various formats and editions annually in recent years.

Walter Breen's Complete Encyclopedia of U.S. and Colonial Coins. Doubleday, 1988. Massive volume covering the full range of United States and related coinage.

The History of United States Coinage as Illustrated by the Garrett Collection. Bowers, Q. David. Bowers and Ruddy Galleries Inc., 1979. Covers the history of U.S. coins and collecting, with numerous letters and other documents quoted extensively.

U.S. Mint and Coinage. Taxay, Don. Durst Numismatic Publications, 1983 (reprint of 1966 book). Early history of U.S. Mint and minting processes in detail, plus history from mid-19th century to 1960s coinage.

Numismatic Art in America—Aesthetics of the United States Coinage. Second edition. Vermeule, Cornelius. Whitman Publishing, 2007. A detailed examination of how art influenced United States coinage. The second edition includes an added chapter, "Numismatic Art Into the 21st Century," by David T. Alexander. First edition published in 1971.

Annual Report of the Director of the Mint. United States Mint, Department of the Treasury, issued annually. Until the 1980 edition, an invaluable source for numismatists with mintage figures, photographs of new coins and medals, reports about new coinage programs, reports about technology changes at the Mint, charts about gold and silver deposits to Mint and more. Downsized with 1981 report, less informative since, especially since the mid-1990s. May be ordered from the United States Mint, Treasury Department, Washington, DC 20220.

United States Patterns and Related Issues. Pollack, Andrew W., III. Bowers and Merena Galleries Inc., 1994. An encyclopedic work displaying and describing nonissued United States coin designs with pedigrees, rarity ratings, and recent prices.

United States Pattern Coins. Tenth edition. Judd, J. Hewitt. Edited by Q. David Bowers. Whitman Publishing, 2008. Full-color, updated edition covers the history, rarity and values of the various experimental pieces issued by the U.S. Mint and other entities, from 1792 to 2000.

Encyclopedia of United States and Colonial Proof Coins 1722-1977. Breen, Walter. FCI Press Inc., 1977. Historical information about and pedigrees of U.S. Proofs, with sections covering Branch Mint Proofs and fantasy and restrike pieces.

California Pioneer Fractional Gold. Second edition. Breen, Walter, and Ronald J. Gillio. Bowers and Merena Galleries Inc., 2003. Catalog listing of varieties of California fractional gold, including black and white photos of most coins.

Private Gold Coins and Patterns of the United States. Kagin, Donald H. Arco Publishing Inc., 1981. History and catalog of pioneer gold, excluding fractional parts of a dollar.

America's Copper Coinage 1783-1857. American Numismatic Society, 1985. Features articles about state and federal copper coinage through the demise of the large cent. Reprints of papers presented at the ANS's 1984 Coinage of the Americas Conference.

United States Proof Sets and Mint Sets (1936-2002). Gale, Bill, and Ronald Guth. New York Mint, 2002. A year-by-year guide to United States Proof and Uncirculated Mint sets.

A Guide Book of Modern United States Proof Coin Sets. Second edition. Lange, David W. Whitman Publishing, 2010.

United States Coinage—A Study by Type. Guth, Ron, and Jeff Garrett. Whitman Publishing, 2005. A look at U.S. coins by type, from the half cent to the gold $20 double eagle.

A Guide Book of United States Type Coins. Second edition. Bowers, Q. David. Whitman Publishing, 2008.

Renaissance of American Coinage 1905-1908. Burdette, Roger W. Seneca Mill Press, 2006. A history of the development and striking of the Indian Head gold $2.50 and $5 coins, the Indian Head gold $10 coin and the Saint-Gaudens gold $20 coin.

Renaissance of American Coinage 1909-1915. Burdette, Roger W. Seneca Mill Press, 2007. A history of the development and striking of the Lincoln cent, the Indian Head (Buffalo) 5-cent coin and the Panama-Pacific International Exposition commemorative coinage.

Renaissance of American Coinage 1916-1921. Burdette, Roger W. Seneca Mill Press, 2005. A history of the development and the striking of the Winged Liberty Head (Mercury) dime, the Standing Liberty quarter dollar, the Walking Liberty half dollar and the Peace dollar.

America's Money, America's Story—A Chronicle of American Numismatic History. Second edition. Doty, Richard. Whitman Publishing, 2008. A chronological history of U.S. coins and paper money.

The Mint on Carson Street—A Tribute to the Carson City Mint & A Guide to a Complete Set of "CC" Coins. Goe, Rusty. Southgate Coins and Collectibles, 2003.

James Crawford—Master of the Mint at Carson City—A Short, Full Life. Goe, Rusty. Southgate Coins and Collectibles, 2007. Biographical.

History of the United States Mint and Its Coinage. Lange, David W. Whitman Publishing LLC, 2005.

The Secret History of the First U.S. Mint: How Frank H. Stewart Destroyed—And Then Saved—A National Treasure. Orosz, Joel J., and Leonard D. Augsburger. Whitman Publishing LLC, 2011.

Official Blackbook Price Guide to United States Coins. Forty-eighth edition. Hudgeons, Thomas E., Jr. House of Collectibles, 2009.

100 Greatest U.S. Coins. Third edition. Garrett, Jeff, and Ron Guth. Whitman Publishing, 2008.

Coin Collecting For Dummies. Berman, Neil S., and Ron Guth. Wiley Publishing, 2008. Beginner's guide to coin collecting.

Coin Boards of the 1930s & 1940s—A Complete History, Catalog and Value Guide. Lange, David W. Pennyboard Press, 2007.

Pre-U.S. Mint coins

Money of the American Colonies and Confederation. Mossman, Philip L. American Numismatic Society, 1993. Provides a detailed numismatic, economic and historical study of the coins and paper money of the American Colonies and the United States during the Confederation period.

The Early Coins of America. Crosby, Sylvester S. Kessinger Publishing, 2009 (facsimile reprint of 1873 book). Covers all Colonial, Confederation and state issues, with extracts from authorizing legislation, plus plates.

The Fugio Cents. Kessler, Alan. Colony Coin Co., 1976. A catalog listing of varieties of the United States' first coinage, with historical information.

Whitman Encyclopedia of Colonial and Early American Coins. Bowers, Q. David. Whitman Publishing, 2009. Pre-federal coinage in America.

The 1776 Continental Currency Coinage/Varieties of the Fugio Cent. Newman, Eric P. Sanford J. Durst, publisher, 2005 (reprint of 1952 edition). A valuable resource for collectors of Continental Currency and Fugio coins.

U.S. half cents and cents

Encyclopedia of United States Half Cents 1793-1857. Breen, Walter. American Institute of Numismatic Research, 1983. Historical information and pedigrees, plus catalog listing of all known half cent varieties, with photos accompanying the listings.

Penny Whimsy. Sheldon, William H. Quarterman Publications Inc., 1983 (reprint of 1958 edition, 1976 copyright). Catalog listing of known varieties of large cents from 1793 to 1814, with plates in back.

The Cent Book. 1816-1839. Wright, John D. Self-published, 1992. Covers Middle Date large cents (1816 to 1839) by die variety. Uses photographs to illustrate varieties.

Attribution Guide for United States Large Cents, 1840-1857. Grellman, J.R., and Jules Reiver. Self-published, 1987. Covers Late Date large cents (1840 to 1857) by die variety. Uses line illustrations to depict varieties.

Flying Eagle & Indian Cents. Snow, Richard. Eagle Eye Press, 1992. Descriptive analysis by year and Mint, including patterns.

A Guide Book of Flying Eagle and Indian Head Cents. Second edition. Snow, Richard. Whitman Publishing, 2009. Examines coins by date, mintage, production, survivability, collecting challenges and die varieties.

Flying Eagle and Indian Cent Die Varieties. Steve, Larry R., and Kevin J. Flynn. Nuvista Press, 1995. Descriptive analysis by year and Mint.

The Authoritative Reference on Lincoln Cents. Second edition. Wexler, John, and Kevin Flynn. Kyle Vick, Publisher, 2009. Descriptive analysis by year and Mint, with emphasis on doubled dies, over Mint marks and repunched Mint marks.

The Complete Guide to Lincoln Cents. Lange, David W. Bowers and Merena Galleries Inc., 1996. Descriptive analysis by year and Mint.

The Comprehensive Guide to Lincoln Cent Repunched Mintmark Varieties, Volume 1, Wheat Cents 1909 to 1939. Wexler, John A., Brian Allen and John W. Bordner. John W. Bordner, Publisher, 2003.

The Complete Guide to Lincoln Cents. Lange, David W. Zyrus Press, 2005.

A Guide Book of Lincoln Cents. Bowers, Q. David. Whitman Publishing, 2008.

U.S. 2- and 3-cent coins

The Two-Cent Piece and Varieties. Kliman, Myron M. Sanford J. Durst Numismatic Publications, 1983. Catalog listing of known varieties, with no photos.

The Authoritative Reference on Three Cent Nickels. Third edition. Fletcher, Edward, and Kevin Flynn. Kyle Vick, Publisher, 2009. A complete and comprehensive reference for the copper-nickel 3-cent coin series.

The Authoritative Reference on Three Cent Silver Coins. Flynn, Kevin, and Winston Zack. Self-published, 2010. A complete and comprehensive reference for the silver 3-cent coin series.

U.S. half dimes and 5-cent coins

Federal Half Dimes, 1792-1837. Logan, Russell J., and John W. McCloskey. John Reich Collectors Society, 1998. Descriptive analysis by year and Mint.

Complete Guide to Liberty Seated Half Dimes. Blythe, Al. DLRC Press, 1992. Descriptive analysis by year and Mint.

The Complete Guide to Shield & Liberty Head Nickels. Peters, Gloria, and Cynthia Mohon. DLRC Press, 1995. Descriptive analysis by year and Mint.

The Shield Five Cent Series. Fletcher, Edward L., Jr. Dead End Publishing, 1994. Descriptive analysis by year and Mint.

A Guide Book of Shield and Liberty Head Nickels. Bowers, Q. David. Whitman Publishing, 2006.

The Complete Guide to Buffalo Nickels. Third edition. Lange, David W. DLRC Press, 2006. Descriptive analysis by year and Mint.

The Authoritative Reference on Buffalo Nickels, 2nd Revised Edition. Wexler, John, Ron Pope and Kevin Flynn. Zyrus Press, 2007.

A Guide Book of Buffalo and Jefferson Nickels. Bowers, Q. David. Whitman Publishing, 2007.

U.S. dimes

Early United States Dimes: 1796-1837. Davis, David J., Russell J. Logan, Allen F. Lovejoy, John W. McCloskey, William L. Subjack. John Reich Collectors Society, 1984. Catalog of known varieties for Draped Bust and Capped Bust dimes, with over-sized photos accompanying listings.

Complete Guide to Liberty Seated Dimes. Greer, Brian. DLRC Press, 1992. Descriptive analysis by year and Mint.

Encyclopedia of United States Liberty Seated Dimes. Ahwash, Kamal M. Kamal Press, 1977. Catalog listings of known varieties, with oversized photos accompanying listings.

Complete Guide to Barber Dimes. Lawrence, David. DLRC Press, 1991. Descriptive analysis by year and Mint.

Collecting & Investing Strategies for Barber Dimes. Ambio, Jeff. Zyrus Press, 2009. Provides physical characteristics of each issue, pricing data, and includes mintage figures, rarity ratings and important die varieties.

Complete Guide to Mercury Dimes. Second edition. Lange, David W. DLRC Press, 2005. Descriptive analysis by year and Mint.

The Authoritative Reference on Roosevelt Dimes. Flynn, Kevin. Brooklyn Gallery Coin & Stamp Inc., 2002. Date-by-date analysis includes die varieties, doubled dies, RPM's, scarcity and values.

U.S. quarter dollars

The Early Quarter Dollars of the United States, 1796-1838. Browning, A.W. Sanford J. Durst Numismatic Publications, 1998 (reprint of 1925 book). Catalog listing of known varieties, with plates at back. Updated edition by Walter Breen, 1982.

The Early Quarter Dollars of the United States. Duphorn, R. The Windsor Group and Starline Management Group Ltd. 1975.

Early United States Quarters 1796-1838. Tompkins, Steven M. Catalog listing of all known varieties, 448 pages and more than 500 color photos. Published in 2008.

Early Quarter Dollars of the United States Mint 1796-1838. Rea, Rory R. plus Glenn Peterson, Bradley S. Karoleff and John J. Kovach Jr. Catalog of known varieties, with color photos of each variety and more. Self-published in 2011 by Rea.

The Comprehensive Encyclopedia of United States Liberty Seated Quarters. Briggs, Larry. Larry Briggs Rare Coins, 1991. Descriptive analysis by year and Mint.

The Complete Guide to Barber Quarters. Second edition. Lawrence, David. DLRC Press, 1994.

Standing Liberty Quarters. Fourth edition. Cline, J.H. Zyrus Press, 2007. Historical information, including correspondence between designer and Treasury officials, plus catalog listing and investment advice.

The Complete Guide to Washington Quarters. Feigenbaum, John. DLRC Press, 1994. Descriptive analysis by year and Mint.

A Guide Book of Washington and State Quarter Dollars. Bowers, Q. David. Whitman Publishing, 2008.

U.S. half dollars

Early Half Dollar Varieties 1794-1836. Fourth edition. Overton, Al C., edited by Don Parsley. Self-published, 2006. Catalog listing of all known varieties, with photos accompanying listings.

The Complete Guide to Liberty Seated Half Dollars. Wiley, Randy, and Bill Bugert. DLRC Press, 1993. Descriptive analysis by year and Mint.

The Complete Guide to Barber Halves. Lawrence, David. DLRC Press, 1991. Descriptive analysis by year and Mint.

The Complete Guide to Walking Liberty Half Dollars. Fox, Bruce. DLRC Press, 1993. Listing by Mint and year with a discussion of strikes, errors, and other details.

Collecting & Investing Strategies for Walking Liberty Half Dollars. Ambio, Jeff. Zyrus Press, 2008. Offers information on strike, luster, rarity, pricing data, auction prices realized, significant examples, and insights into how and what to buy.

The Complete Guide to Franklin Half Dollars. Second edition. Tomaska, Rick. DLRC Press, 2002. How to grade Mint State examples, history of the coin, how to grade Proofs, date analysis.

A Guide Book of Franklin & Kennedy Half Dollars. Tomaska, Rick. Whitman Publishing, 2011. Guide to Franklin and Kennedy half dollars.

The Kennedy Half Dollar Book. Wiles, James D. Stanton Printing and Publishing, 1998. Includes, cameo and deep cameo, Mint states, analysis by year and Mint.

U.S. dollars

The United States Early Silver Dollars from 1794 to 1803. Reiver, Jules. Krause Publications, 1999. Catalog listing of dollar varieties, with plates in back. Revision of the classic work by M.H. Bolender.

The Fantastic 1804 Dollar, Tribute Edition. Bressett, Kenneth E., and Eric P. Newman. Whitman Publishing, 2009. A wonderful numismatic mystery is solved in this in-depth study of the 1804 dollar, one of the United States' greatest rarities. 1962 original updated at the ANS Coinage of the Americas Conference, 1986 (update available in book form from ANS).

Silver Dollars & Trade Dollars of the United

States, A Complete Encyclopedia. Bowers, Q. David. Bowers and Merena Galleries Inc., 1993. A two-volume set analyzing each date and Mint mark with historical background and price history information.

The United States Trade Dollar. Willem, John M. Sanford J. Durst Numismatic Publications, 1983 (reprint of 1959 edition). Historical treatment of the Trade dollar, with mintages by month, varieties and rarity levels.

The Comprehensive Catalogue and Encyclopedia of U.S. Morgan and Peace Silver Dollars. Fourth Edition. Van Allen, Leroy C., and A. George Mallis. Worldwide Ventures Inc. and Bob Paul Inc., 1991. Historical information and catalog listing of all known varieties. (Note: VAM varieties of Morgan and Peace dollars were first cataloged in this reference. "VAM" is derived from the initials of the two authors' last names: Van Allen and Mallis.)

Gobrecht Dollars. Van Winkle, Mark, editor, with essays by Michael L. Carboneau, James C. Gray, John Dannreuther and Saul Teichman. Heritage Auction Galleries/Ivy Press, 2009.

A Guide Book of Morgan Silver Dollars. Third edition. Bowers, Q. David. Whitman Publishing, 2007. Full-color guide provides market analysis for each date and Mint mark plus a section on pattern coins.

Top 100 Morgan Dollar Varieties: The VAM Keys. Fourth edition. Fey, Michael S., and Jeff Oxman. Rare Coin Investments, 2009. Covers Morgan dollar varieties. Contains updated rarity and pricing data, census information about deep mirror prooflike and prooflike examples, and additional images, with a new chapter on rotated die varieties.

Carson City Morgan Dollars: Featuring the Coins of the GSA Hoard. Crum, Adam, Selby Ungar and Jeff Oxman. Whitman Publishing, 2009. History, market information, varieties of Carson City Mint Morgan dollars.

A Guide Book of Peace Dollars. Burdette, Roger W., with Barry Lovvorn. Whitman Publishing, 2008. A coin-by-coin analysis that includes market values, certified population data and a discussion of the mysterious 1964-D Peace dollar.

A Buyer's Guide to Silver Dollars & Trade Dollars of the United States. Third edition. Bowers, Q. David, and John Dannreuther, editor. Zyrus Press, 2006. Year-by-year analysis, pricing, mintage figures, estimated surviving examples, auction prices realized, strike characteristics and collecting commentary.

The Authoritative Reference on Eisenhower Dollars. Wexler, John, Bill Crawford and Kevin Flynn. Archive Press Inc., 1998. Descriptive analysis by year and Mint, with emphasis on doubled dies and repunched Mint marks.

U.S. gold coins

America's Gold Coinage. Metcalf, William E., editor. American Numismatic Society, 1990. Publication of papers read during the Coinage of the Americas Conference at the ANS, Nov. 4-5, 1989.

United States Gold Coins, an Illustrated History. Bowers, Q. David. Bowers & Ruddy Galleries, 1982. Overview history of U.S. gold coins.

An Insider's Guide to Collecting Type 1 Double Eagles—A Numismatic History and Analysis. Winter, Douglas, and Adam Crum. Newport Communications, 2002.

U.S. Gold Dollars through U.S. Double Eagles. Akers, David W. Paramount Publications, 1975 to 1982. A series of six books covering gold dollars, quarter eagles, gold $3 and $4 pieces, half eagles, eagles and double eagles; basically it records auction appearances by denomination, date and Mint mark.

United States Gold Patterns. Akers, David W. Paramount International Coin Corp., 1975. Subtitled "A photographic study of the gold patterns struck at the United States Mint from 1836 to 1907."

Encyclopedia of U.S. Gold Coins, 1795-1933. Second edition. Garrett, Jeff, and Ron Guth. Whitman Publishing, 2008. Full-color guide covers U.S. gold coins including proof, circulating, commemoratives and pattern coins with a brief history of each coin.

Collecting & Investing Strategies for United States Gold Coins. Ambio, Jeff. Zyrus Press, 2008. Provides investing and collecting strategies for U.S. gold coins from 1795 to 1933.

A Guide Book of Gold Dollars. Bowers, Q. David. Whitman Publishing, 2008. History and values of U.S. gold $1 coins.

United States Ten Dollar Gold Eagles 1795-1804. Taraszka, Anthony J. Anton's, 1999. List varieties of early gold eagles.

Type Two Double Eagles, 1866-1876. Winter, Douglas, and Michael Fuljenz. UCB/DWN, 1996 and 1999 editions. Analysis of Coronet $20 double eagles from 1866 to 1876.

Type Three Double Eagles, 1877-1907. Fuljenz, Michael. Subterfuge Publishing, 2009. Analysis of Coronet $20 double eagles from 1877 to 1907.

A Guide Book of Double Eagle Gold Coins. Bowers, Q. David. Whitman Publishing, 2004. History and values of U.S. gold double eagles.

Gold Coins of the Dahlonega Mint 1838-1861. Second edition. Winter, Douglas. Zyrus Press, 2003.

Gold Coins of the Carson City Mint 1870-1893. Winter, Douglas. Ivy Press/DWN Publishing, 2001.

Gold Coins of the New Orleans Mint 1839-1909. Second edition. Winter, Douglas. Zyrus Press, 2006.

Charlotte Mint Gold Coins, 1838-1861—A Numismatic History and Analysis. Third edition. Winter, Douglas. Zyrus Press, 2008.

Indian Gold Coins of the 20th Century: The Smart Guide for Rare Acquisitions. Fuljenz, Mike. Subterfuge Publishing, 2010. A history of the popular Indian Head gold $2.50, $5 and $10 coins with expert advice for collecting the coins.

U.S. commemorative coins

Commemorative Coins of the United States Identification and Price Guide. Second edition. Swiatek,

Anthony. *Coin World,* Amos Press Inc., 2001. A complete analysis and history of all U.S. commemorative coins to publication date.

The Encyclopedia of United States Silver & Gold Commemorative Coins, 1892-1989. Breen, Walter, and Anthony Swiatek; updates by Walter Breen. Bowers and Merena Galleries Inc., 1990. Historical and investment information about all U.S. commemorative coinage through 1989.

Commemorative Coins of the United States, A Complete Encyclopedia. Bowers, Q. David. Bowers and Merena Galleries Inc., 1991. A complete analysis and history of all U.S. commemorative coins to 1991.

The Authoritative Reference on Commemorative Coins 1892-1954. Flynn, Kevin. Kyle Vick, Publisher, 2008. Design descriptions, historical facts, origins, striking and wear characteristics, auction prices realized, certified population reports and information gleaned from the annual reports of the director of the U.S. Mint.

A Guide Book of United States Commemorative Coins. Bowers, Q. David. Whitman Publishing, 2007. Covers both early and modern U.S. commemorative coin issues.

U.S. exonumia

The Atwood-Coffee Catalogue of United States and Canadian Transportation Tokens. Sixth edition. Coffee, John M., Jr., and Harold V. Ford. American Vecturist Association, 2007. Catalog of mass transportation tokens and similar items, based on earlier Atwood system and catalog. Other volumes catalog minor die varieties and record the history of the transportation token.

Encyclopedia of the Modern Elongated: A Complete and Authentic Description of All Modern Elongateds, 1960-1978. Rosato, Angelo A. Angros Publishers, 1990. Listing of elongated coins produced from 1960 to 1978.

Supplement to the Encyclopedia of the Modern Elongated: A Complete and Authentic Description of Modern Elongated Coins, 1978-1995. Rosato, Angelo A. Angros Publishers, 1998. Listing of elongated coins produced from 1978 to 1995.

Medallic Portraits of Washington. Rulau, Russell, and George Fuld. Krause Publications, 1999. Revision of William S. Baker catalog of coins, medals and tokens bearing a portrait of Washington.

Medals of the United States Mint—The First Century 1792-1892. Julian, Robert W. Token and Medal Society Inc., 1977. Massive historical work covering all medallic works produced by the Mint during its first 100 years.

Patriotic Civil War Tokens, 5th Revised Edition. Fuld, George, and Melvin Fuld. Civil War Token Society, 2006. Catalog lists all Civil War patriotic tokens, with historical information and chapters on related topics.

So-Called Dollars: An Illustrated Standard Catalog. Second edition. Hibler, Harold E., and Charles V. Kappen. Coin and Currency Institute, 2008. Covers commemorative and exposition medals of near-dollar size in catalog format, listing metal varieties and historical information.

Standard Catalog of United States Tokens, 1700-1900. Fourth edition. Rulau, Russell. Krause Publications, 2004. Omnibus revised edition listing of all U.S. merchant tokens, including Civil War tokens, and related pieces in a soft-cover catalog format.

The True Hard Times Tokens. Schuman, Robert A. M&G Publications, 2010.

U.S. Civil War Store Cards. Second edition. Fuld, George, and Melvin Fuld. Quarterman Publications, 1975. Catalogs all Civil War store cards by city and state, with historical information.

Video Arcade, Pinball, Slot Machine, and Other Amusement Tokens of North America. Alpert, Stephen A., and Kenneth E. Smith. Amusement Token Collectors Association, 1984. The reference book catalogs all amusement tokens known to the date of publication by state, province and miscellaneous categories.

A Guide Book of United States Tokens and Medals. Jaeger, Katherine. Whitman Publishing, 2008. History and values of U.S. tokens and medals.

100 Greatest American Tokens and Medals. Jaeger, Katherine, and Q. David Bowers. Whitman Publishing, 2007.

Alaska and Yukon Tokens: Private Coins of the Territories. Third edition. Benice, Ronald J. McFarland & Co., 2009. A listing and description of all known tokens used from the 1890s Gold Rush through 1959.

Medallic Portraits of Washington. Second edition. Rulau, Russell, and George Fuld. Krause Publications, 1999. Illustrated identification and price guide.

Abraham Lincoln—The Image of His Greatness. Reed, Fred. Whitman Publishing, 2009. Historical overview of Lincoln in photos, film, coins, medals and other collectibles.

Counterfeit detection

Counterfeit Detection. Staff of the American Numismatic Association Certification Service. American Numismatic Association, two volumes, 1983 and 1987. Reprints ANACS's columns appearing in *The Numismatist,* discussing and illustrating counterfeits and genuine specimens of dozens of U.S. coins, plus information about collectible varieties and ANACS procedures.

Detecting Counterfeit and Altered Coins. Martin, J.P. American Numismatic Association, 1996. An ANA correspondence course on counterfeit detection.

Standard Catalog of United States Counterfeit and Altered Coins. Hancock, Virgil, and Laurence Spanbauer. Sanford Durst, 1979. Basic work on techniques of detecting common counterfeits with many illustrations of known examples.

United States Gold Counterfeit Detection Guide. Fivaz, Bill. Whitman Publishing, 2006.

Grading

Making the Grade: A Grading Guide to the Top 50 Most Widely Collected U.S. Coins. Second edition. Deisher, Beth; Michael Fahey, and the staff of *Coin World*. Amos Hobby Publishing, 2008. A collector's guide to grading U.S. coins using large, full-color photographs and detailed grade descriptions.

Grading Coins: A Collection of Readings. Edited by Bagg, Richard, and James J. Jelinski. Essex Publications, 1977. Collection of articles about grading from *The Numismatist, Whitman Numismatic Journal* and *Numismatic Scrapbook Magazine* from 1892 to 1976. Takes a historical approach.

A Guide to the Grading of United States Coins. Brown, Martin R., and John W. Dunn. General Distributors Inc., 1980. Uses line illustrations for U.S. coins in all denominations from half cent to double eagle in all grades.

NCI Grading Guide. Halperin, James L. Ivy Press, 1986. Written by a principal grader of the Numismatic Certification Institute. Provides a step-by-step approach to the grading of Uncirculated and Proof coins. Does not cover circulated grades.

Photograde. Nineteenth edition. Ruddy, James F. Bowers and Merena Galleries Inc., 2005. Photographic guide to the grading of United States coins in all denominations from half cent to $20 double eagle. More than 1,000 photographs.

Official American Numismatic Association Grading Standards for United States Coins. Sixth edition. Bressett, Kenneth, and Abe Kosoff. Whitman Numismatic Products, Western Publishing, 2006. Official ANA guide to grading U.S. coins. Includes unillustrated guide to grading U.S. commemorative coins.

Official Guide to Coin Grading and Counterfeit Detection. Second edition. Professional Coin Grading Service. Dannreuther, John, writer; Scott A. Travers, editor. House of Collectibles, 2004. Illustrated instructional book on all aspects of grading U.S. coins.

Errors, varieties, minting

The Cherrypickers' Guide to Rare Die Varieties of United States Coins: Half Cents to Jefferson Nickels, Vol. I. Fifth edition. Fivaz, Bill, and J.T. Stanton. Whitman Publishing, 2008. Widely used volume illustrating the most popular of U.S. die varieties.

The Cherrypickers' Guide to Rare Die Varieties of

United States Coins: Half Dimes to Modern Dollars, Plus Gold and Commemoratives, Vol. II. Fourth edition. Fivaz, Bill, and J.T. Stanton. Whitman Publishing, 2006. Widely used volume illustrating the most popular of U.S. die varieties.

A Collectors Guide to Misplaced Dates. Flynn, Kevin. KCK Press, 1997. Fully or partially punched into the legend, devices or dentils, or any part of the field not normally associated with the general location of a date on a coin.

The CONECA U.S. Doubled Die Master Listing. Wiles, James, editor. Combined Organizations of Numismatic Error Collectors of America, 1994. Comprehensive listing of hundreds of doubled die varieties discovered to that date. The book has no illustrations, just descriptions.

The Cud Book. Thurman, Sam, and Arnold Margolis. Self-published, 1997. In-depth explanation and photographs of how major die breaks, cuds, occur.

The Encyclopedia of Doubled Dies, Vol. 1 and 2. Wexler, John A. Robert C. Wilharm News Printing Co. Inc., 1978 and 1981. Illustrates and describes doubled dies, and how they occur.

The Error Coin Encyclopedia. Fourth edition. Margolis, Arnold, and Fred Weinberg. Self-published, 2000. Comprehensive guide to the minting process and error coins, including prices.

The Modern Minting Process. Wiles, James. American Numismatic Association, 1997. Book is compiled from a correspondence course by the ANA addressing die-making and coin production processes.

The Lincoln Cent RPM Book. Update: 1997 to 2002. Wiles, James. CONECA, 2003. Listing of repunched Mint marks (RPMs) for the Lincoln cent. Update to the 1997 Lincoln Cent RPM book.

100 Greatest U.S. Error Coins. Brown, Nicholas. Whitman Publishing, 2010.

Error Coins from A to Z: Alphabetical Listings with Prices. Margolis, Arnold. Self-published, 2009. Provides information on the minting process and explanations of error coin types, accompanied by representative photos.

World's Greatest Mint Errors. Byers, Mike. Zyrus Press, 2009. Full-color illustrations and descriptions of major Mint errors. Includes rarity ratings, values and grades.

U.S. paper money

U.S. government issues

Bureau of Engraving and Printing—The First Hundred Years 1862-1962. Sanford J. Durst Numismatic Publications, 1978 (reprint of 1962 book published by the Treasury Department). Government history tracing history of BEP and government-issued paper money, postage stamps and revenue items.

United States Paper Money Errors: A Comprehensive Catalog & Price Guide. Third edition. Bart, Frederick J. Krause Publications, Iola, Wis., 2008. Explains how paper money errors occur. Illustrated and with pricing information.

The Comprehensive Catalog of U.S. Paper Money:

All United States Federal Paper Money Since 1812. Seventh edition. Hessler, Gene, and Carlson Chambliss. BNR Press, 2006. Catalog listings of government issues, with historical information.

Guidebook of United States Currency. Fourth edition. Bowers, Q. David. Whitman Publishing, 2009. Large size, small size, fractional currency.

100 Greatest American Currency Notes. Bowers, Q. David, and David M. Sundman. Whitman Publishing, 2005. A listing of 100 most noteworthy pieces of American paper money.

Comprehensive Catalog of Military Payment Certificates. Fourth edition. Schwan, Fred. BNR Press, 2002. Covers notes issued for use by U.S. military personnel stationed overseas from 1946 to 1973.

Paper Money of the United States. Nineteenth edition. Friedberg, Arthur L. and Ira S. Friedberg. Coin and Currency Institute, 2010. A full-color, illustrated guide with values and a numbering system used throughout the hobby.

Standard Catalog of United States Paper Money. Twenty-ninth edition. Cuhaj, George S., editor and William Brandimore, market analyst. Krause Publications, 2010. Up-to-date market pricing with more than 5,000 listings and 1,400 color images.

National Bank Notes. Sixth edition. Kelly, Don C. Paper Money Institute, 2008. 12,000 banks by state, error notes, uncut sheets, history and economics.

The Engraver's Line: An Encyclopedia of Paper Money and Postage Stamp Art. Hessler, Gene. BNR Press, 1993. Biographies and descriptions of the works of engravers working in the United States.

The International Engraver's Line—Paper Money and Postage Stamp Engravers and Their Work from the 1700s to the Euro. Hessler, Gene. Self-published, 2005. Biographies and descriptions of the works of engravers working outside the United States.

U.S. Essay, Proof and Specimen Notes. Second edition. Hessler, Gene. BNR Press, 2004.

An Illustrated History of U.S. Loans, 1775-1898. Hessler, Gene. BNR, 1988.

The Standard Guide to Small-Size U.S. Paper Money: 1928 to Date. Ninth edition. Schwartz, John, and Scott Linquist. Krause Publications, 2009.

Standard Catalog of United States Obsolete Bank Notes: 1782-1866 (four volumes). Haxby, James A. Krause Publications, 1988.

The Encyclopedia of United States Fractional and Postal Currency. Friedberg, Milton R. NASCA Inc., 1978.

The Alexander Hamilton Web-Fed Press. Kvederas, Bob, Jr., and Bob Kvederas Sr. Self-published, 1998.

The Standard Handbook of $1 Web-Fed Test Notes. Kvederas, Bob, Jr., and Bob Kvederas Sr. Self-published, 1999.

U.S. Error Note Encyclopedia. Second edition. Sullivan, Stephen M. Currency Gallery, 2009.

World War II Remembered—History in your Hands, a Numismatic Study. Schwan, C. Frederick, and Joseph E. Boling. BNR Press, 1995. A guide to coins and currency issued during World War II.

A Guide Book of United States Paper Money. Third edition. Friedberg, Arthur L., and Ira S. Friedberg. Whitman Publishing, 2011.

Obsolete Paper Money Issued by Banks in the United States, 1782-1866. Bowers, Q. David. Whitman Publishing, 2006.

Official Blackbook Price Guide to United States Paper Money. Forty-second edition. Hudgeons, Thomas E., Jr. House of Collectibles, 2009.

Whitman Encyclopedia of U.S. Paper Money. Bowers, Q. David. Whitman Publishing, 2009. All federal notes from 1861 to date, and more.

Nonfederal issues

The Early Paper Money of America. Fifth edition. Newman, Eric P. Krause Publications, 2008. Covers all paper money issued by the Continental Congress, 13 original Colonies.

Confederate and Southern States Currency. Criswell, Grover C. Criswell's Publications, 1992. Covers all CSA issues, plus states issues of the Civil War.

A Guide Book of Southern States Currency. Shull, Hugh. Whitman Publishing, 2006. A full-color, collector-friendly work providing history, rarity and values of Southern state's paper money.

A Guide Book of Counterfeit Confederate Currency. Tremmel, George B. Whitman Publishing, 2007. History, rarity and values of counterfeit Confederate paper money.

Collecting Confederate Paper Money. Fricke, Pierre. Spink Smythe, 2008. An illustrated guide to collecting Confederate notes.

Confederate States Paper Money: Civil War Currency from the South. Eleventh edition. Slabaugh, Arlie R. Krause Publications, 2008. Covers issues of both the Confederacy and the Southern states.

Society of Paper Money Collectors Wismer update series. The SPMC has published a series of catalogs of obsolete notes by state and territory. Books available from the SPMC (see Organizations chapter) include Rhode Island, Florida, Mississippi, Texas, Iowa, Minnesota, Alabama, Maine, Indiana, New Jersey, Vermont, Arkansas, Pennsylvania, Ohio and a volume covering the Indian Territory, Oklahoma and Kansas.

Standard Catalog of United States Obsolete Bank Notes 1782-1866. Four volumes. Haxby, James A. Krause Publications, 1988.

Interesting Notes. Durand, Roger H. Self-published, various years. Multi-volume works on obsolete notes, highlighting portraits, vignettes, history and scrip.

Modern world coins

General works

Standard Catalog of World Coins, 2001-Date. Fifth edition. Cuhaj, George S., editor, Thomas Michael, market analyst. Krause Publications, 2010. All *Standard Catalogs* provide illustrations and prices for world coins using the Krause-Mishler numbering system. All editions of the *Standard Catalog* books listed here are also available in CD-ROM form.

Standard Catalog of World Coins, 1901-2000. Thirty-eighth edition. Cuhaj, George S., editor, Thomas Michael, market analyst. Krause Publications, 2011.

Standard Catalog of World Coins, 1801-1900. Sixth edition. Cuhaj, George S., editor, Thomas Michael, market analyst. Krause Publications, 2009.

Standard Catalog of World Coins, 1701-1800. Fifth edition. Cuhaj, George S., editor, Thomas Michael, market analyst. Krause Publications, 2010.

Standard Catalog of World Coins, 1601-1700. Fourth edition. Bruce, Colin R., II, senior editor, Thomas Michael, market analyst. Krause Publications, 2008.

Collecting World Coins. Twelfth edition. Cuhaj, George S., and Thomas Michael, editors. Krause Publications, 2008. General catalog providing illustrations and prices for circulating issues of world coins from 1901 to the date of publication.

A Catalog of Modern World Coins—1850-1964. Fourteenth edition. Yeoman, R.S. Revised and edited by Arthur L. Friedberg. Whitman Publishing, 2008. Illustrated guide with values.

Unusual World Coins. Fifth edition. Bruce, Colin R., II. Krause Publications, 2007. Catalog providing illustrations and prices for unusual world coins.

Standard Catalog of Modern World Gold Coins, 1801-Present. Fifth edition. Bruce, Colin R., II, senior editor, Thomas Michael, market analyst. Krause Publications, 2007. Catalog providing illustrations and prices for world gold, platinum and palladium coins from 1901 to the present.

Standard Catalog of World Gold Coins, 1600-Present. Sixth edition. Cuhaj, George S., editor, Thomas Michael, market analyst. Krause Publications, 2009. Catalog, with illustrations and prices for world gold, platinum and palladium coins from 1600 to present.

Standard Price Guide to World Crowns & Talers, 1484-1968. Draskovic, Frank, and Stuart Rubenfeld. Krause Publications, 1984. Catalog form.

Money of the World—Coins That Made History. Goldberg, Ira, and Larry Goldberg, editors. Whitman Publishing, 2007. Full-color, illustrated historical guide to coins ranging from Ancient Greece to the 20th century.

Gold Coins of the World, From Ancient Times to the Present. Eighth edition. Friedberg, Arthur L., and Ira S. Friedberg. Coin and Currency Institute Inc., 2009. The 50th anniversary edition, with illustrations and prices.

The Beauty & Lore of Coins, Currency & Medals.

Clain-Stefanelli, E. and V. Riverwood Publications, 1974.

The Art of Coins & Their Photography. Hoberman, Gerald. Spink & Son Ltd., 1982.

Numismatic Bibliography. Clain-Stefanelli, Elvira Eliza. Battenberg, 1985. A comprehensive listing by subject of numismatic books.

Dictionary of Numismatic Names with Addenda. Frey, Albert R. Spink's, 1973. A comprehensive dictionary of numismatic terms, which includes a glossary of equivalent terms in English, French, German, Italian and Swedish.

Biographical Dictionary of Medallists. Forrer, L. A.H. Baldwin & Sons, eight volumes. A comprehensive encyclopedia listing coin and medal engravers and their works from ancient times to modern.

North American Coins & Prices: A Guide to U.S., Canadian and Mexican Coins. Twentieth edition. Harper, David C. Krause Publications, 2010.

Official Blackbook Price Guide to World Coins. Fifteenth edition. Hudgeons, Thomas E., Jr. House of Collectibles, 2011.

Latin American Tokens. Second edition. Rulau, Russell. Krause Publications, 2000. A price and identification guide for tokens of Mexico, Central and South America.

Africa

The Silver Dollars of Africa. Davenport, John S. Whitman Publications Co., 1959. Catalog format with photographs.

Australia

Renniks Australian Coin and Banknote Guide. Skinner, Dion H. Skinner & Warnes, 1976. Catalog form with illustrations, later editions exist.

Coins & Tokens of Tasmania. McNeice, Roger V. Platypus Publications, 1969. Text with some photographs.

Coinage and Currency in New South Wales, 1788-1829. Mira, W.J.D. Wentwork Press, 1981. Text and almanac form with some photographs.

Australian Historical Medals, 1788-1988. Carlisle, Leslie J. Self-published, 2009. Updated version of *Australian Commemorative Medals and Medalets from 1788*.

Austria

Osterreichische Munzpragungen von 1657-1969 (Austrian Money from 1657-1969). Herinek, Ludwig. Herinek, Munzhandlung, 1970. Two volumes. Catalog with illustrations of Austrian coins.

Bolivia

The Coins of Bolivia. Seppa, Dale. Almanzar's, 1970.

Canada

Coins of Canada. Twenty-sixth edition. Haxby, J.A., and R.C. Willey. Unitrade Press, 2011. Spiral-bound price guide for Canadian coins and exonumia.

Canadian Coin Digest. Cuhaj, George S., editor, Thomas Michael, market analyst. Krause Publications, 2010. History and pricing of Canadian coins, including issues of Newfoundland, New Brunswick, Nova Scotia and Prince Edward Island.

Canadian Coins—Volume One, Numismatic Issues. Sixty-fifth edition. Cross, W.K. Charlton Press, 2010. Illustrated, spiral-bound catalog of circulation-strike coins with prices.

Canadian Coins—Volume Two, Collector Issues. First edition. Cross, W.K. Charlton Press, 2010. Illustrated, spiral-bound catalog of collector coins with prices.

Canadian Colonial Tokens. Seventh edition. Cross, W.K. Charlton Press, 2010. Illustrated, spiral-bound catalog of tokens with prices.

Standard Grading Guide for Canadian & Colonial Decimal Coins. Revised edition. Charlton, James E., and Robert C. Willey. Unitrade Press, 1999. Line drawing guide to grading Canadian coins.

Striking Impressions: The Royal Canadian Mint and Canadian Coinage. Haxby, James A. Royal Canadian Mint, 1984. A history of the Royal Canadian Mint and its coinage.

The Canadian Dictionary of Numismatics/Le Dictionnaire Canadien de Numismatique. Pelletier, Serge. Saint Eligius Press, 2008. Lexicon for Canadian coin collectors, but also covers American, British and French coins. In French and English.

China

The Currencies of China. Kann, Eduard. Kelly & Walsh Ltd., 1926 (1978 reprint by Sanford J. Durst of 1926 work). Discussion of the currencies and their effects.

Illustrated Catalog of Chinese Coins, Vols. I-III. Kann, Eduard. Reprint editions. Ishi Press, 2006. Historical, detailed descriptions of Chinese coins from ancient times to the late 1940s.

Chinese Currency. Schoeth, Fredrick, revised by Virgil Hancock. Krause Publications, 1965. Standard reference for all coinage from Chou Dynasty through Chi'ing Dynasty (1100 B.C. to A.D. 1911).

Chinese Cash. Jen, David. Krause Publications, 2000. Catalog and illustrations with values in multiple condition grades for monetary forms issued in Imperial China.

Colombia

Coins of Colombia. Seppa, Dale, and Alcedo Almanzar. Almanzar's Coins of the World, 1973.

Cuba

The Coinage of Cuba, 1870 to Date. Lismore, Thomas. Roy Renderer, 1966.

Czechoslovakia

Czechoslovak Coins. Davis, Dolores H. Numismatics International, 1972. Catalog form with some illustrations.

Dominican Republic

Monedas Dominicanas, (Dominican Money). Gomez, Miguel E. Sociedad Dominicana de Biblofilos, 1979. Text in Spanish.

El Salvador

The Coins and Paper Money of El Salvador. Almanzar, Alcedo. Almanzar's Coins of the World, 1973.

Ethiopia

Ethiopia, Treasure House of Africa. Kohl, Melvin J. The Society for International Numismatics, 1969.

The Coins of Ethiopia, Eritrea and Italian Somalia. Gill, Dennis. Self-published, 1991.

Finland

Suomi, Rahat Ja Setelit (Finland, Coins and Bank Notes 1811-1981). Von Schantz, C. Holmasto Coins & Medals Co., 1982. Catalog form in Finnish and English language.

France

Monnaies Francaises, 1789-2001. Fifteenth edition. Gadoury, Victor. Self-published, 2001. Catalog form, text in French.

Repertoire de la Numismatique Francaise Contemporaine, 1793 a nos jours (Numismatics of Contemporary France from 1793). De Mey, Jean, and Bernard Poindessault. Imprimerie Cultura, 1976. Catalog form, French text.

Les Monnaies Royales Francaises de Hugues Capet a Louis XVI (French Royal Money from Hugh Capet to Louis XVI). Ciani, Louis, 1926. (Reprinted by A.G. Van der Dussen in Maastricht, Netherlands.) Comprehensive catalog of early-modern French coins.

Catalogue General Illustre des Editions de la Monnaie de Paris (General Illustrated Catalog of Issues of the Paris Mint). Monnaie de Paris, four volumes, first volumes published in 1977-78. Illustrated catalog of the medals of the French Mint.

The Talers or Ecus of Alsace-Lorraine. Davenport, John S. American Numismatic Association, 1986.

Germany

Standard Catalog of German Coins, 1501 to present. Third edition. Nicol, Douglas D. Krause Publications, 2011. Catalog providing illustrations and prices for German coins from 1501 to the present, using Krause-Mishler numbering system. Also available in CD-ROM form.

Catalogue of German Coins. Arnold, Paul, Dirk Steinhilber and Harald Kuthmann. Reprinted edition. Ishi Press, 2010. Values of gold, silver and minor coins since 1800. In English, translated from German.

German Talers 1500-1600. Davenport, John S. Schulten, P.N., 1979. Illustrated catalog of taler-size silver coins from 1500 to 1600.

German Secular Talers, 1600-1700. Davenport, John S. Numismatischer Verlag P. N. Schulten, 1976.

German Talers, 1700-1800. Davenport, John S.

Spink & Son, 1979. Illustrated catalog of talers issued from 1700 to 1800.

Silver Gulden, 1559-1763. Davenport, John S. Schulten, P.N., 1982. An illustrated catalog of gulden, a denomination of silver coin smaller than the taler.

Great Britain

Coins of England & the United Kingdom: Standard Catalogue of British Coins. Forty-sixth edition. Spink, 2011. Published annually. Formerly published in multiple volumes by Seaby. Illustrated catalog with prices.

The Token Book: 17th, 18th & 19th Century Tokens and Their Values. Withers, Paul, and Bente R. Withers. Galata Print Ltd., 2010. Illustrated price guide for British tokens.

Coincraft's 1999 Standard Catalogue of English and UK Coins 1066 to Date. Calligas, Eleni. Coincraft, 1999. Excellent layout and presentation of information that overloads most other attempts at encompassing it.

Coincraft's 1999 Standard Catalogue of Scotland, Ireland, Channel Islands, and Isle of Man. Calligas, Eleni, editor. Coincraft 1999. Very accessible and understandable yet objective presentation.

The Standard Guide to Grading British Coins. Allen, Derek Francis. Rotographic Publications, 2009. Grading of British pre-decimal coins from 1797 to 1970.

British Coins Market Values 2011. Thomas, Guy. IPC Media, 2010. Full-color price guide for ancient to modern British coins. Includes pricing for paper money.

British Commemorative Medals and Their Values. Second revised edition. Eimer, Christopher. Spink & Son Ltd., 2010. Detailed price guide with full-color illustrations.

Guatemala

Historia Numismatica de Guatemala (Numismatic History of Guatemala). Prober, Kurt. Bank of Guatemala, 1973. Text and catalog in Spanish language.

Haiti

Coins of Haiti, 1803-1970. Arroyo, Carmen. Almanzar's Coins of the World, 1970.

Hungary

Munzkatalog Ungarn von 1000 bis Heute (Catalog of Hungarian Coins from 1000 Forward). Huszar, Lajos. Battenberg, 1979. Catalog form with illustrations, in German language.

India

Coins. Gupta, Parmeshwari Lal. Natl. Book Trust, 1969. Catalog form, text in English.

Studies in Indian Coins. Sircar, D.C. Motilal Banarsidas, Delhi, India, 1968. Catalog form, text in Indian language.

Iran

Modern Coinage of Iran, 1876-1974. Clarke, Robert L. and A. Mohabat-Ayin. Numismatics Interna-

tional, 1974. Catalog form with some illustrations.

Israel

The History of Modern Israel's Money, 1917-1970. Haffner, Sylvia. Philip J. Matthew, 1970.

Israel's Money & Medals, 1948-1973. Kagan, A.H. A.H. Kagan, Inc., 1974.

AINA Guide Book of Israel Coins & Medals. Schuman, Edward. American Israel Numismatic Association, 1980.

Israel Coins and Medals. Shoham, David. Ben Zvi Printing Enterprises Ltd., 1982.

Israel's 20-year Catalog of Coins and Currency. Bertram, Fred & Weber, Robert. Louis Denberg Foundation Inc., 1968.

Numismatics of the Holocaust, The Shekel. American Israel Numismatic Association, September to October 1982 and March-April 1983, combined reprint.

A Catalog of Holocaust Medals: A History Etched in Metal. Szperling, Severin. Wheatmark Publishing, 2010.

Italy

Super Collezionista di Monete Decimali Italiane, (Comprehensive Manual of Collecting the Decimal Money of Italy). Cesare Bobba, 1977. Catalog form with text in Italian. Later editions exist.

Jamaica

The Coinage of Jamaica. Byrne, Ray, and Jerome H. Remick. Almanzar's Coins of the World, 1966.

Japan

Japanese Coin Catalogue 1985. Oka, M. An illustrated 1985 catalog in the Japanese language of coins and paper money.

Modern Japanese Coinage. Cummings, Michael L. Far East Journal, 1978. Catalog form with illustrations.

Japanese Coinage. Jacobs, Norman, and Cornelius C. Vermeule. Reprint edition. Ishi Press, 2009. Text and illustrated catalog.

Lithuania

Senoves Lietuviu Pinigai (Ancient Lithuanian Currencies). Karys, Jonas K. Immaculata Press, 1959. Identifies and explains coinage, text in English and Lithuanian.

Mexico

A Guidebook of Mexican Coins, 1822 to Date, sixth edition. Buttrey, T.V. and Clyde Hubbard. Krause Publications, 1992. Catalog with prices.

Standard Catalogue of Mexican Coins, Paper Money, Stock, Bonds and Medals. Bruce, Colin R., II. Krause Publications, 1981. Catalog form with text of history, illustrated.

Numismatic History of Mexico. Pradeau, Alberto Francisco. Sanford J. Durst, 1978 (reprint of 1938 edition). A numismatic history of Mexico.

State & Federal Copper and Brass Coinage of Mexico, 1824-1872. Bailey, Don. Self-published, 2008. Numismatic and pricing information.

Morocco

Mondeas de Marruecos, (Moroccan Coins, 1879-1971). Sanchez-Giron, J.M. Self-published, 1972. Catalog format, in Spanish and English languages.

Mozambique

Catalogo Das Moedas De Mocambique (Catalog of Money of Mozambique). Azevedo, Vasco. Livraria Fernando Machado, Portugal, 1969. Catalog with each coin photographed, text in Portuguese.

Netherlands

Nederlandse Munten van 1795-1961 (Dutch Money from 1795-1961). Schulman, Jacques. Jacques Schulman N.V., 1962. Catalog form, well illustrated. Text in Dutch language.

Norway

Norges Mynter, (Coinage of Norway). Ahlstrom, Bjarne, Bernhard F. Brekke and Bengt Hemmingsson. Numismatiska Bokforlaget AB, 1976. Catalog form in Swedish and English language.

Oriental, general works

Oriental Coins and Their Values: The World of Islam. Mitchiner, Michael. Hawkins Publications, 1977. Extensive catalog with essay descriptions.

The Standard Guide to South Asian Coins & Paper Money Since 1556 A.D. Bruce, Colin R., II, John S. Deyell, Nicholas Rhodes and William F. Spengler. Krause Publications, 1981. General catalog of non-Japanese and non-Chinese Oriental coins.

Numismata Orientalia Illustrata, (Oriental Numismatics Illustrated). Album, Stephen. Attic Books Ltd., 1977. Catalog form with some charts.

Panama

Coins & Currency of Panama. Grigore, Julius Jr. Krause Publications, 1972. Illustrated text published in English language.

Paraguay

The Coins of Paraguay. Seppa, Dale, and Alcedo Almanzar. Almanzar's Coins of the World, 1971.

Poland

Hanbuch der Polnischen Numismatik (Handbook of Polish Numismatics). Gumowski, Marian. Akademische Druck-U, Graz, 1960. Identifies and explains coinage in German language.

Rhodesia-Zimbabwe

Keogh On Coins of Rhodesia-Zimbabwe. Keogh, John. Keogh Coins, 1980. Catalog form.

Russia

A Guidebook of Russian Coins, 1725-1982. Harris, Robert P. Mevius Numisbooks Int. B.V., 1983. Catalog form with many illustrations.

Scandinavia, general works

Sieg Montkatalog 1978 (Sieg's Catalog of Money). Sieg, Frovin. Ulbjerg gl. Skole, 1977. Catalog form in Danish language with English summary. Covers all of Scandinavia, revised annually.

South Africa

The South African Coin and Banknote Catalogue. Twelfth edition. Van Rensburg, Cliff. Randburg Coin, 1999. Identification and prices across grades for all issues, including Mint sets.

Money in South Africa. Engelbrecht, C.L. Tafelberg, 1987. Narrative history of Dutch and English communities, commonwealth, and Republic, includes regular issues of coins and bank notes as well as necessity money.

Coins of South Africa. Jacobs, Ken. South African Gold Exchange Company (Pty) Limited, 1983. Lavish catalog organized from farthing through Krugerrand along the historical time line, includes designer, diameter, weight, composition, and other relevant date for each coin.

The Coinage and Counterfeits of the Zuid-Afrikaanische Republiek. Levine, Elias. Purnell, 1974. Close-up photography and detailed descriptions of genuine coins and their forgeries.

Spain

Las Monedas Espanolas Del tremis al euro. Castan, Carlos, and Juan R. Cayon. Artegraf, IGSA, 1998. Authoritative standard reference in catalog form with illustrations, text in Spanish.

Sweden

Sveriges Mynt 1521-1977 (Coinage of Sweden). Ahlstrom, Bjarne, Yngve Almer and Bengt Hemmingsson. Numismatiska Bokforlaget AB, 1976. Catalog form in Swedish and English language.

Switzerland

Die Munzen der Schweiz (The Money of Switzerland). Divo, Jean-Paul, and Edwin Tobler. Bank Leu, 1974. Catalog form in German language. Possible later editions exist.

Uruguay

The Coins of Uruguay, 1840-1971. Seppa, Dale, and Alcedo F. Almanzar. Almanzar's Coins of the World, 1971.

Vatican

Vatican Papal Coins. Berman, Allen. Attic Books, 1991. Complete, one-volume catalog of the circulating coins of the popes.

Vietnam

Socialist Republic of Viet Nam Coins and Currency. Daniel, Howard A., III. Self-published, 2009. Identification and values for coins and paper money issued by Vietnam from 1976 to the present.

Coinage of the Americas

America's Foreign Coins; An Illustrated Standard Catalogue with Valuations of Foreign Coins with Legal Tender Status in the U.S., 1793-1857. Schilke, O.G. Coin & Currency Institute, 1964. (Re-

print available of 1964 edition.)
Coinage of the Americas. Buttrey, Theodore V., Jr. American Numismatic Society, 1973. Discussions of coinage of both continents.
The Coins of Central America, Silver & Copper, 1824-1940. Raymond, Wayte. 1941.
The Coins of South America, Silver & Copper. Raymond, Wayte. 1942.
The Coins of the West Indies, Silver & Copper, Including the Cut & Counterstamped Pieces. Raymond, Wayte. 1942.
The Julius Guttag Collection of Latin American Coins. Adams, Edgar H. Quarterman Publications, 1974.
The Silver Dollars of North & South America; An Illustrated Catalogue of All the Types & an Indication of Their Retail Value. Raymond, Wayte. New York, 1964.
Spanish American Gold Coins; Being a Detailed List of the Gold Coins Struck by the Spanish Kings in America at the Mints of Mexico, Guadalxara, Lima, Potosi, Bogota, Popayan, Guatemala, Santiago. Raymond, Wayte. New York, 1936.

Primitive
Odd and Curious Money: Descriptions and Values. Opitz, Charles J. First Impressions Printing, 1986. Encyclopedic listing of odd and curious moneys.
A Survey of Primitive Money. Quiggin, A. Higston. Methuen & Co. Ltd., Strand, Great Britain, 1963 (Reprint of the 1963 edition by Sanford J. Durst). Text with both line drawings and photographs.
Primitive Money in its Ethnological, Historical and Economic Aspects. Einzig, Paul. Eyre & Spottswood, 1948 (1982 reprint of the 1948 edition by Sanford J. Durst). Text with photographs.
Odd and Curious. Reed, Mort. Fisher Printing Co., 1963 (1980 reprint of the 1963 edition by Sanford J. Durst). Text and line drawings.

Ancient coins

General Works
100 Greatest Ancient Coins. Berk, Harlan J. Whitman Publishing, 2008.
Handbook of Ancient Greek and Roman Coins. Zander, H., and Kenneth Bressett, editors. Western Publishing Co. Inc., 1995. Fundamental yet thorough identifications and explanations of Greek and Roman coinage.
Ancient Coin Collecting. Sayles, Wayne G. Krause Publications, 1996-1999. Six-volume set of stand-alone works. Vol. I *Ancient Coin Collecting*; Vol. II *Numismatic Art of the Greek World*; Vol. III *The Roman World—Politics and Propaganda*; Vol. IV *Roman Provincial Coins*; Vol. V *The Roman/Byzantine Culture*; Vol. VI *Non-Classical Cultures.*

Ancient Greece
Greek Coins & Their Values. Sear, David R. Seaby Publications Ltd., 1978. Two volumes; Europe, and Asia and Africa in catalog form.
Historia Numorum, A Manual of Greek Numismatics. Head, Barclay V. 1911 General Books LLC, Publisher, 2010 (reprint of 1911 work by Sanford J. Durst, New York City). Comprehensive catalog of ancient Greek city-state coinage.
Dictionary of Greek Coin Inscriptions. Icard, Severin. Sanford Durst, 1979. Comprehensive reference for translating Greek coin inscriptions.
A Dictionary of Ancient Greek Coins. Jones, John Melville. Seaby, 1986. People, places, objects, animals and other words and images arranged in alphabetical order, with illustrations as needed.
Greek Imperial Coins and Their Values. Sear, David R. Seaby Publications Ltd., 1982. General catalog of the coins of independent Greek cities within the Roman Empire. "Greek imperial" is synonymous with "Roman Provincial."
Greek Imperial Coins, Vol. I: Dacia, Moesia Supe- rior, Moesia Inferior; Vol. II: Thrace (From Abdera to Pautalia). Varbanov, Ivan. ADICOM, 2005. Vol. I covers Greek Imperial coins struck in the Balkan mints and coins struck in Dacia, Moesia Superior (Viminacium) and Moesia Inferior (Callatis, Dionysopolis, Istrus, Marcianopolis, Nicopolis ad Istrum, Odessus and Tomi). Vol. II covers Roman provincial coins of Abdera, Ainos, Anchialus, Apollonia Pontica, Augusta Traiana, Bizya, Byzantium, Deultum, Hadrianopolis, Maroneia, Mesembria, Nicopolis ad Nestum, and Pautalia. Black and white illustrations.
The Athenian Decadrachm. Fischer-Bossert, Wolfgang. American Numismatic Society, 2009. A die study of 40 genuine Athenian decadrachms in public and private collections augmented with a catalog of more than 90 modern forgeries.

Roman Republic
The Coinage of the Roman Republic. Sydenham, Edward A. Spink & Son Ltd., England. 1952 (1982 reprint of 1952 work by Sanford, J. Durst). Catalog with historical entries on the field in general.
Roman Republic Coinage. Crawford, Michael H. Cambridge University Press, 1974. Two volumes. A comprehensive catalog of Roman Republican coins.
Roman Silver Coins. Seaby, H.A. Seaby, 1978 to 1987. Five volumes. A catalog of Roman silver coins.

Roman Empire
Coinage and History of the Roman Empire. Vagi, David. Fitzroy Dearborn Publishers, 1999. Second edition. Two volumes, Vol. 1 History; Vol. 2 Coinage. Accessible presentation of the huge body of facts about the people and their coins, 82 B.C. to A.D. 480. Scholarly, yet conversational and supported by the best available research.
Roman Coins and Their Values. Volumes I-III. Sear, David R. Spink & Son, Ltd., 2000-2005. Cata-

log form of the field in general. Two further volumes planned.

The Roman Imperial Coinage. Mattingly, Harold, edited by Edward A. Sydenham. Spink & Son. Ltd., 1968 (1968 reprint of the 1884 work). Catalog form, eight volumes, contents: 1. Augustus to Vitellius, 2. Vespasian to Hadrian, 3. Antoninus Pius to Commodus, 4. Pertinax to Geta and Macrinus to Pupienus and Gordian III to Urania Antoninus, 5. Valerian I to Florian, Probus to Amandus, 6. Diocletian's reform to death of Maximinus, 7. Constantine and Licinius, 8. Valentinian I to Theodosius I.

Judaea

Guide to Biblical Coins. Fifth edition. Hendin, David. Amphora, 2010. Comprehensive merger of catalog and historical essays. Includes Persian, Macedonian, Ptolemaic, and Seleucid and City Coins of Old and New Testaments.

Ancient Jewish Coinage. Meshorer, Ya'akov. Amphora Books, 1982. Two volumes in catalog form covering 1. Persian period to Hasmonaeons, and 2. Herod the Great to Bar Cochba.

Catalog of Judaea Capta Coinage. Brin, Howard B. 1986. Complete listing of Judaea Capta coins; illustrated.

The Coinage of the Bar Kokhba War. Mildenberg, Leo. Sauerlander Verlag, 1984. Examines coinage of Jews in Judaea about A.D. 132 to 135.

Other ancient empires

Parthian Coins and History: Ten Dragons Against Rome. Shore, Fred B. CNG, 1993.

An Introduction to the Coinage of Parthia. Sellwood, David. Spink & Son Ltd., 1971. Catalog form of the field in general.

Turkoman figural bronze coins and their iconography. Vol. I: *The Artuqids*; Vol. II: *The Zengids.* Spengler, William F., and Wayne G. Sayles. Clio's Cabinet, 1996. Extensive and intensive presentation of the material.

Imperial Persian Coinage. Hill, George F. Obol International, 1968. Catalog of coins of the Persian Empire.

The Handbook of Syrian Coins: Royal and Civic Issues, Fourth to First Centuries B.C. Hoover, Oliver D. Classic Numismatic Group, 2009. First volume in a planned series of 13 books on Ancient Greek coins.

Medieval coins

General medieval works

Reading Medieval European Coins. Walker, Ralph S. Attic Books Ltd., 1979. Basic book on how to decipher inscriptions on medieval coins.

The Dated European Coinage Prior to 1501. Frey, Albert R. American Journal of Numismatics, 1915 (2000 revised edition of the 1915 work by Sanford J. Durst, New York City). Catalog of all Christian dated coins before 1501.

Medieval Coins in the Christian J. Thomsen Collection. Erslev, Kristian. Allen G. Berman, Publisher, 1992. Reprint catalog of extensive definitive collection. Updated by Alan M. Stahl and Allen G. Berman, with photographs by Alex G. Malloy.

Beschreibung der Bekanntesten Kupfermunzen (Description of Best-known Copper Money). Neumann, Josef. Nabu Press, 2010 (reprint of 1858 edition). Seven volumes, in German. Useful for identifying copper coins of Europe.

Medieval European Coinage: Volume 1, The Early Middle Ages (5th-10th Centuries). Grierson, Philip, and Mark Blackburn. Cambridge University Press, 2007.

Austria

The Coinage of Medieval Austria, 1156-1521. Szego, Alfred A. Sanford J. Durst, Publisher, 1995 reprint. A basic outline on the subject.

Corpus Nummorum: Moser/Tursky, Die Munzen Kaiser Rudolfs II aus der Munzstatte Hall in Tirol 1602-1612. Lanz, Dr. Herbert. Numismatik, 1987. Comprehensive sylloge; illustrated.

Balkans

Medieval Slavic Coinages in the Balkans. Dim-nick, Martin, and Julijan Dobrinic. Spink & Son Ltd., 2008. A catalog and narrative history of the main types of coins from the medieval Slavic Balkan lands and towns.

Byzantine

Byzantine Coins and their Values. Second edition. Sear, David R. Trafalgar Square Publishing, 1987. General catalog on the subject, illustrated.

Byzantine Coins. Grierson, Philip. University of California Press, 1982. Text with charts and tables.

Moneta Imperii Byzantini. Hahn, Wolfgang. 1981. Three-volume illustrated set covering subject from 491-720. Volume I: Anastasius I to Justinian I; Volume II: Justin II to Phocas; Volume III: Heraclius to Leo II.

England

England Hammered Coinage. North, J.J. Spink & Son Ltd., 1960. Two volumes in catalog form, illustrated.

England's Striking History—A Brief History of England and its Silver Hammered Coinage. Perkins, Christopher Henry, editor. Rotographic Publications, 2006. Covers the coinage issued by monarchs from circa A.D. 959 to 1663 using original engravings.

France

Carolingian Coinage of France. Morrison, Karl F. Karl F. Morrison & Henry Grunthal, 1967. Maps, notes and monograms; part of the ANS series.

The Barbaric Tremissis in Spain & Southern France. American Numismatic Society, 1964. Notes and monograms; part of the ANS series.

Catalogue General Illustre et a Prix Marques

en Francs ou de Monnaies Francaises Provinciales (General Illustrated Catalog of the Money of France and the Provinces). Boudeau, E., editor, 1970. Catalog format with illustrations and maps, French text.

The Silver Coins of Medieval France (476-1610 AD). Roberts, James N. Allen G. Berman, Publisher, 1996. Illustrated guide includes related coinages in Flanders, Luxembourg, Alsace-Loraine, Savoy, and the Merovingian coinage of the fifth to eighth centuries.

Germany

Germanic Coinages, Charlemagne Through Wilhelm II. Craig, William D. Wm. D. Craig, 1954. General work with illustrations on the subject.

Altdeutschland 768-1806 (Old Germany). Battenberg, Ernst. Munich, West Germany, circa 1975 (1982 reprint of 1975 work by Sanford Durst). Catalog format of general work in German language.

The Coinage of South Germany in the Thirteen Century. Metcalf, David M. Spink & Son Ltd., 1961. Catalog format.

Islamic countries

Oriental Coins and Their Values, The World of Islam. Mitchiner, Michael. Hawkins Publications, 1977. Catalog form with photographs and some historical facts.

A Catalogue of the Muhammadan Coins in the British Museum. Walker, John. British Museum, 1956. Two volumes: 1. Arab-Sassanian coins, 2. Arab-Byzantine & post-reform Umaiyad coins.

Oriental Coins and Their Values, the Ancient & Classical World 600 B.C.-A.D. 650. Mitchiner, Michael. Hawkins Publications, 1978. Contains much information on ancient coins from this area not found elsewhere.

Islamic History Through Coins: An Analysis and Catalogue of Tenth-Century Ikhshidid Coinage. Bacharach, Jere L. American University in Cairo Press, 2006. Illustrated catalog designed to assist readers to identify coins and their relative rarity.

Italy

The Venetian Tornesello: A Medieval Colonial Coinage. Stahl, Alan. American Numismatic Society, 1985.

Medieval European Coinage: Volume 14, South Italy, Sicily, Sardinia: With a Catalogue of the Coins in the Fitzwilliam Museum, Cambridge. Grierson, Philip, and Lucia Travaini. Cambridge University Press, 2009. Covers coinages of the immediate pre-Norman period and those of the Norman, Hohenstaufen, Angevin and Aragonese dynasties that in turn ruled part or the whole of the Mezzogiorno.

World paper money

General works

Standard Catalog of World Paper Money, Specialized Issues. Eleventh edition. Cuhaj, George S., editor. Krause Publications, 2009. Catalog style, complete listing with photographs of commercial and restricted issues.

Standard Catalog of World Paper Money, General Issues, 1368-1960. Thirteenth edition. Cuhaj, George S., editor. Krause Publications, 2010. Catalog style, complete listing with photographs of commercial and general circulation issues from 230 issuing authorities.

Standard Catalog of World Paper Money, Modern Issues 1961-Present. Sixteenth edition. Cuhaj, George S., editor. Krause Publications, 2010. Catalog style, complete listing with photographs of modern issues in general circulation.

Banknotes & Banking in The Isle of Man, 1788-1970. Second edition. Quarmby, Ernest. Spink & Son Ltd., 1994. Text with photographs.

Canadian Government Paper Money. Twenty-third edition. Graham, R.J. Charlton Press, 2010. Illustrated price guide for Canadian paper money.

English Paper Money. Duggleby, Vincent. Stanley Gibbons Publications Ltd., 1980. Catalog form.

Scottish Banknotes. Douglas, James. Stanley Gibbons Publications Ltd., 1975. Catalog form, later editions may exist.

Notgeld

Das Deutsche Notgeld, (The German Notgeld). Keller, Arnold. Battenberg Verlag, 1976. Catalog in German language in 11 volumes: 1. 1914, 2. Germany, Austria, Hungary 1914-1918, 3. large paper money 1918-1921, 4. small paper money 1916-1922, etc.

A Guide & Checklist of World Notgeld, 1914-1947, and Other Local Issue Emergency Monies. Second edition. Coffing, Courtney L. Krause Publications, 2000. 13,000 entries listed alphabetically by country and city. Includes 16-page color section with more than 100 photos.

Other topics

Dictionaries/Bibliographies

The International Encyclopedic Dictionary of Numismatics. Carlton, R. Scott. Krause Publications, 1996.

The Macmillan Encyclopedic Dictionary of Numismatics. Doty, Richard G. Macmillan Publishing Co. Inc., 1982.

Numismatic Bibliography. Clain-Stefanelli, Elvira E. Battenberg Verlag, 1985. Catalog of known numismatic books.

Investing

It is an axiom of economics that past performance is not an indication of the future. Hundreds of books have been written on investing in rare coins, most published during general price run-ups and obvious "bull" markets. While hobbies such as fishing and reading tend to provide only personal rewards, numismatics is a hobby that involves the buying and selling of money. The following titles are provided as an introductory sampling of the advice available to the collector who considers numismatic material as an investment. These are not recommendations or endorsements by *Coin World* or its staff.

How to Make More Money in Coins Right Now. Second edition. Travers, Scott A. House of Collectibles, 2001. Find the coins that other people want to buy and get them for less than other people are willing to pay.

One-Minute Coin Expert. Fifth edition. Travers, Scott A. Random House, 2004. A guide for finding rare or valuable coins in their pocket change.

The Coin Collector's Survival Guide, 7th edition. Travers, Scott A. House of Collectibles, Random House, 2010. A consumer protection handbook to buying and selling rare and valuable coins.

Precious Metals Investing for Dummies. Mladjenovic, Paul. Wiley Publishing, 2008. A guide to the precious metals market with advice on trading and owning gold, silver, platinum and uranium, as well as base metals such as zinc and copper.

High Profits From Rare Coin Investment. Thirteenth edition. Bowers, Q. David. Bowers and Merena Galleries Inc., 1991. Historical overview of the coin markets since 1940. Closer inspection of the current markets for American numismatics organized by type of product.

The Expert's Guide to Collecting & Investing in Rare Coins, Bowers, Q. David. Whitman Publishing LLC, 2005. Comprehensive examination of collecting and investing based on the author's more than 50 years experience in the rare coin market.

Guide to Coin Investment. Bilinski, Robert. Robert Bilinski, publisher, 1969. Four editions printed. Statistical work on who collects, what they buy and why, written when collecting was only a hobby.

Google Books

Another resource collectors may wish to consider is Google Books (**books.google.com**), which features previews of hobby-related books or books in their entirety, and other publications, for free. The bulk of what is available in full pre-dates the modern copyright cutoff. Copyright has expired for works published before Jan. 1, 1923.

Commercial numismatic publications

Following is a list of commercial numismatic publications published in the United States, with their mailing and Web addresses.

Published weekly

Coin World
Amos Hobby Publishing
P.O. Box 150
Sidney, OH 45365-0150
www.coinworld.com

Numismatic News
Krause Publications Inc.
700 E. State St.
Iola, WI 54945
www.numismaster.com

Published monthly

Bank Note Reporter
Krause Publications Inc.
700 E. State St.
Iola, WI 54945
www.numismaster.com

The Celator
P.O. Box 839
Lancaster, PA 17608
www.celator.com

Coin Prices
Krause Publications Inc.
700 E. State St.
Iola, WI 54945
www.numismaster.com

COINage
Miller Magazines Inc.
290 Maple Court, Suite 232
Ventura, CA 93003
www.coinagemag.com

Coins Magazine
Krause Publications Inc.
700 E. State St.
Iola, WI 54945
www.numismaster.com

Coin World Special Edition
Amos Hobby Publishing
P.O. Box 150
Sidney, OH 45365-0150
www.coinworld.com

Error Trends Coin Magazine
P.O. Box 158
Oceanside, NY 11572
www.etcmmag.com

World Coin News
Krause Publications Inc.
700 E. State St.
Iola, WI 54945
www.numismaster.com

24 Numismatic Terms

Basic numismatic terms likely to cause the most difficulty for both the novice and the advanced collector are included in this guide. Experts in the science of numismatics differ in their interpretation of a number of terms, and reference to a standard dictionary often fails to settle disputes. Terms relating to grading and error coins and notes are more comprehensively defined in their respective chapters.

- A -

accolated, conjoined, jugate—Design with two heads facing the same direction and overlapping.

accumulation—Coins, tokens, etc., unsorted, unclassified and unattributed; not a collection.

adjustment—Filing down the face of an overweight planchet. Filing marks often survive the coining process; common on 18th century coins.

aes grave—Cast bronze issue of the Roman republic; literally "heavy bronze."

aes rude—Large cast rectangular bronze coin, one of the earliest Roman coins.

alloy—Mixture of two or more metals.

altered—A coin or other numismatic item that has been deliberately changed, usually to make it resemble a rare or more valuable piece.

American Arts Gold Medallions—A series of 1-ounce and half-ounce gold bullion medals issued by the U.S. Mint from 1980 to 1984. Medals depict great American artists, writers and actors.

American Bison 5-cent coin—A 2005 Jefferson 5-cent coin issued as one of four circulating commemorative 5-cent pieces in the 2004 and 2005 Westward Journey series celebrating the bicentennial of the Louisiana Purchase and the Lewis and Clark Expedition.

American Buffalo—The name of two different U.S. coin programs with coins bearing designs based on the Indian Head 5-cent coin designs: a 2001 commemorative silver dollar and a series of .9999 fine gold bullion coins issued beginning in 2006.

American Eagle—Bullion coins produced by the U.S. Mint beginning in 1986 (for gold and silver) and 1997 (for platinum). Thirteen coins have been produced: a 1-ounce, .999 fine silver coin with $1 face value; a 1-ounce, .9167 fine gold coin with $50 face value; a half-ounce, .9167 fine gold coin with $25 face value; a quarter-ounce, .9167 fine gold coin with $10 face value; and a tenth-ounce, .9167 fine gold coin with $5 face value; a 1-ounce, .9995 fine platinum coin with $100 face value; a half-ounce, .9995 fine platinum coin with $25 face value; a quarter-ounce, .9995 fine platinum coin with $10 face value; and a tenth-ounce .9995 fine platinum coin with $5 face value. The bullion versions are sold to primary distributors, who in turn sell them to other distributors and customers. Coins sell at prices based on current metal prices plus a markup. The Mint sells collector versions directly to collectors and dealers. The gold coins all contain a full measure of pure gold; the gold is alloyed with other metals (for example, the 1-ounce gold coin has a total weight of 1.09 ounce, with 1 ounce of that being pure gold).

America the Beautiful quarter dollar—A series of commemorative quarter dollars in a program introduced in 2010 recognizing a national park, national forest, national military park or other historic site in each of the 50 states, the District of Columbia and the five U.S. territories of the Commonwealth of Puerto Rico, Guam, American Samoa, the United States Virgin Islands and the Commonwealth of the Northern Mariana Islands. Five different coins are issued each year, in the order in which the selected site for each political entity was federally recognized. The coins are being struck in the standard specifications for circulation and the annual collector sets offered by the U.S., and in 3-inch, 5-ounce .999 fine silver bullion coins (the latter also denominated as quarter dollars). Sometimes promoted as National Parks quarter dollars, although many sites being honored are not national parks. The program follows up the 1999 to 2008 State quarter dollars program and 2009 District of Columbia and U.S. Territories quarter dollar program.

ancient coin—Generally any coin issued before A.D. 500.

anneal—To soften dies, planchets or metal by heat treatment.

ant nose—Primitive copper money of China ca. 600 B.C.

anvil die—The die upon which a planchet rests during striking. See hammer die.

as—(Plural: asses) Bronze or orichalcum coins of the Roman republic.

assay—Analytic test or trial to ascertain the fineness, weight and consistency of precious or other metal in coin or bullion. An assay piece is one that has been assayed.

attribution—The identification of a numismatic item by characteristics such as issuing authority, date or period, Mint, denomination, metal in which struck, and by a standard reference.

auction—Method of selling by which items are presented for sale to the highest bidder.

authentication—Authoritative determination of the genuineness of a numismatic item.

- B -

back—The paper money side opposite the "face"; analogous to the reverse of a coin.

bag marks—See contact marks.

bank note—A promissory note issued by a bank in useful denominations, payable to bearer and intended to circulate as money. The term "bank note" should not be used as a generic term for all forms of paper money since not all notes were issued by banks.

bas-relief—Sculpture style featuring slight differences between the raised design and the field and in which no part of the design is undercut; used to execute models for coins and medals.

base metal—Nonprecious metal; e.g., copper.

Bicentennial coins—The special commemorative quarter dollar, half dollar and dollar struck from mid-1975 to the end of 1976 in honor of the 200th anniversary of American Independence. Coins feature the dual date 1776-1976 and special reverses emblematic of the celebration. Issued in copper-nickel clad versions for circulation. Special silver-copper clad (40 percent silver) versions were sold to collectors.

bid-buy sale—A combination form of fixed-price list and mail-bid sale. Rules may vary from dealer to dealer. However, customers usually may either buy a lot outright at the fixed price or place a bid (higher or lower). It permits buyers to purchase a lot at less than fixed price (in some cases), or by paying more, to ensure a greater chance of obtaining the lot.

bid sheet—A form used by a buyer in an auction or mail-bid sale, on which the buyer lists the item being bid on by the number it is assigned and the price he is willing to pay.

billon—A low-grade alloy used for some minor coin issues consisting usually of a mixture of silver and copper, and sometimes coated with a silver wash.

bison—Species considered typically North American, used on coinage and paper money of the United States; "bison" is a more accurate term than "buffalo," which is a more general term referring to a number of related but different species outside North America.

bit—A popular term for the Spanish-American 1-real piece (also Danish West Indies and other neighboring islands) that formerly circulated in the United States. More often used in the plural, as two bits (25 cents) or four bits (50 cents). A bit is 12½ cents.

blank—See planchet.

block—In paper money collecting, a series of related notes indicated by the same prefix and suffix letters in the serial number. When the suffix letter changes, a new block is created. The suffix currently changes when the serial number reaches 96 000 000.

bourse—Rhymes with "horse," the area at a coin show or convention where dealers set up tables of collectibles for sale.

box coin—A coin, typically of crown or silver dollar size, that has been cut into two halves, each of which has been hollowed out to hold messages or pictures. The two halves can be reassembled.

bracteate—A very thin silver coin, popular in Germany and surrounding areas between about 1100 and 1350, made by striking so that a relief image appears on the obverse and an intaglio image on the reverse side of the coin. The coin is actually struck from the reverse.

brass—Coinage metal alloy containing chiefly copper and zinc.

Britannia—Allegorical representation of Great Britain first found on Roman coinage struck for the occupied British isles and later used on British coinage. Also, a British .917 fine gold and .925 fine silver bullion coin program introduced in 1987 (for gold) and 1997 (silver), with all pieces bearing various Britannia designs.

broadstrike—Coin struck in error outside a restraining collar.

broken bank note—Paper money of a defunct bank or a bank that has failed (broken), but the term is often applied inaccurately to any obsolete bank note.

bronze—Coinage metal alloy containing chiefly copper and tin.

Brown Back—A Brown Back note is a Second Charter, First Issue national bank note. Has brown ink on the back.

buffalo—See bison.

Buffalo nickel—More properly: Indian Head 5-cent coin.

bullion—Uncoined precious metal in the form of bars, plates, ingots, and other items.

bullion coin—A precious metal coin traded at the current bullion price plus a premium to enable seller to make a profit.

buyer's fee—Winning bidders in a public auction in the United States are usually charged a buyer's fee based on a certain percentage of the winning bid. Most U.S. auction houses charge buyer's fees of 15 percent, with some sellers of world coins charging fees of 17 or 18 percent. A buyer placing a $100 hammer bid on a coin would pay an additional $15 buyer's fee, or $115, if charged a 15 percent buyer's fee.

- C -

cabinet friction—Slight surface wear on a coin, token or medal caused by friction between it and the tray or envelope in which it is contained.

cameo—One metal superimposed on a portion of the surface of a coin of another metal, typically gold on silver. The term is also used to describe the contrast between frosted relief devices and mirrored fields on Proof coins, resulting in a cameo effect.

cent—A denomination of coin used in the United States, Canada, Australia and other nations with decimal coinage systems that represents one-hundredth of a dollar. See penny.

Chervonetz—Formal name for the 10-ruble Soviet .900 fine gold trade coin struck in 1923 and again between 1975 and 1982.

chop mark (shroff mark)—A small punched impression applied by Chinese (chop) or Indian (shroff) banks or change offices to attest to the full weight and metallic content of a coin.

Civil War tokens—Privately issued emergency coin-like tokens, the approximate size of current U.S. cents, which circulated during the Civil War because of a scarcity of small change. Two major types were issued: patriotic tokens, with patriotic themes; and store cards, advertising pieces often carrying the issuer's name, address and type of business or services.

clad—Composite coinage metal strip composed of a core, usually of a base metal such as copper, and surface layers of more valuable metal, silver (or sometimes copper-nickel). Cladding is a cost-saving measure, making coins cheaper to produce while maintaining a desired appearance. The U.S. Mint has used three different clad compositions for coins (copper-nickel clad, silver-copper clad and manganese-brass clad).

clashed dies—Dies damaged by being struck against each other and leaving the impression from each die to some degree on the other die due to the absence of a coinage blank, then transferring this ghosting image to coins produced after the damage has occurred.

clip—Term used to denote an incomplete planchet coin; in earlier days, clipping was a process of shaving edges of coins to remove small amounts of metal for illegal gain (which gave rise to lettered or reeded edges).

cob—A 16th to 18th century coin produced at Spanish possessions from blanks sliced from a roll of silver or gold.

coin—Usually a piece of metal, marked with a device, issued by a governing authority and intended to be used as money.

Coin note—See Treasury note.

collar—A retaining ring die within which the coin dies operate. An open collar positions the planchet between the dies but does not form the edge device or completely restrain outward metal flow. A close collar forms the edge design of the piece such as reeding and fully restrains outward metal flow.

Colonial—Refers to coins or paper money issued by the Colonial governments of the 13 British Colonies that became the United States. See state coinages.

commemorative—A coin, note or medal issued to mark, honor or observe an anniversary, other event, place or person, or to preserve its memory. Both circulating and noncirculating commemorative coins and notes exist.

community scrip—Localized paper scrip used to promote a local economy, used in the United States and elsewhere in the world. The methods in which the community scrip works may differ from community to community, but generally participating individuals and businesses agree to accept payment for goods and services in the community scrip, which in turn can be used at other businesses in the community. Such programs are used to promote the use of businesses in the community rather than the use of businesses from other regions. Federal officials recognize community scrip as legal.

compound-interest Treasury note—A type of U.S. paper money authorized in 1863 and 1864; it paid 6 percent interest, and was to be redeemed three years after issue.

condition census—Term introduced by Dr. William H. Sheldon to denote a two-numbered code, representing the finest example and the average condition of next five finest known examples of a given variety of large cent. Catalogers have extending the use of the term to other series, though mostly to note the top-ranked pieces of a particular kind of coin.

conjoined—See accolated.

contact marks—Minor abrasions on an otherwise Uncirculated coin, caused by handling in Mint-sewn bags and contact with other coins' surfaces. Originally called bag marks.

Continental currency—Paper money issued by the authority of the Continental Congress during the Revolutionary War.

Continental dollar—A dollar-sized pattern struck in 1776 as a proposed coinage.

COPE, COPE PAK—Acronyms used at Bureau of Engraving and Printing for Currency Overprinting and Processing Equipment and Currency Overprinting and Processing Equipment, Packaging. Machines used to apply overprinting of seals, serial numbers and Federal Reserve index numbers to 16-note half sheets of paper money; then the COPE cuts the half sheets into single notes, bundles them into 100-note packages with a paper band, and into larger plastic-wrapped packages.

copper-nickel—Coinage alloy composed of copper and nickel in varying amounts.

copy—A reproduction or imitation of an original.

Coronet—Style of Liberty Head design used on U.S. copper and gold coins for much of the 19th century. Liberty wears a coronet (most depicting the word LIBERTY).

counterfeit—An object made to imitate a genuine numismatic piece with intent to deceive or defraud, irrespective of whether the intended fraud is primarily monetary or numismatic.

crown—A general term embracing most silver coins from about 20 to 30 grams in weight and from about 33 to 42 millimeters in diameter. The term has become applicable also to most nickel-alloy coins of the same range of size and weight. Coins of 43 or more millimeters in diameter are said to be multiple crowns.

crack out—A slang term for a coin removed from a third-party certification service encapsulation or "slab," for the purpose of being resubmitted.

cud—A form of die break that leaves a shapeless lump of metal on part of a coin.

cupro-nickel—Copper-nickel; term often employed by the government.

currency—Applies to both coins and paper money. Many use the word "currency" for paper money only. Currency is legal tender.

current—Coins and paper money in circulation.

- D -

Date Back—A Date Back note is a Second Charter, Second Issue national bank note. Refers to the dates 1902-1908 found on the back.

debase—To make less valuable.

decimalization—The changeover from the British pound sterling to a decimal coin system in countries influenced by the British currency system.

demand note—Demand notes, authorized in 1861, were the first paper money issued by the United States federal government for circulation. Nicknamed the "greenback" because of the green ink used on the reverse.

demonetize—The act of declaring a currency no longer legal tender or redeemable.

denarius, denarii (plural)—Roman silver coin, later debased, roughly equal to a Greek drachm. Initiated in 268 B.C., a denarius equaled 16 asses; 25 denarii equal 1 gold aureus.

denomination—The face value of a coin or paper note; the amount of money it is worth.

denticles, dentils—Ornamental device used on rims of coins, often resembling teeth, hence the name; also "beading."

device—The principal element, such as a portrait, shield or heraldic emblem, of the design on the obverse and reverse of a coin, token or medal.

Devil's Face note—On some of Bank of Canada notes, First Issue of 1954, Queen Elizabeth II's hair has a coincidental combination of shading and light that looks like a "devil's" face. Shading was quickly changed under public pressure to remove the "face."

die—A hardened metal punch, the face of which carries an intaglio or incuse mirror-image to be impressed on one side of a planchet.

die scratch—Raised line on the surface of a coin, caused by a scratch in the coinage die.

die variety—Represents a coin struck by a specific pair of dies that can be distinguished from coins of identical design struck from other dies due to differences between the dies. For example, there may be subtle changes in the positions of stars, legends, dates and other design elements unique to one die. Doubled dies, overdates and repunched Mint marks are all

examples of die varieties. The term "die marriage" is synonymous.

disme—Spelling of the word "dime" on U.S. 1792 pattern pieces and name given the 10-cent coin authorized in the Mint Act of April 2, 1792. Probably pronounced like "dime." The "s" was likely silent. The "disme" spelling was used in Mint documents into the 1830s.

District of Columbia and U.S. Territories quarter dollars—One-year program (2009) of circulating commemorative quarter dollars honoring the District of Columbia and the five U.S. territories of the Commonwealth of Puerto Rico, Guam, American Samoa, the United States Virgin Islands and the Commonwealth of the Northern Mariana Islands. Issued for circulation and for the annual collector sets. Follow-up to the State quarter dollars program of 1999 to 2008.

dollar—Unit of money in the United States, Canada, Australia and other nations that use a decimal system of coinage. In the United States, coins and paper money are denominated in dollars, as well as fractional and multiple units of the dollar (quarter dollar, $10). The Act of April 2, 1792, authorizes "dollars."

double eagle—A gold $20 coin of the United States.

doubled die—A die that has a multiple image created during the die-making process. Coins struck from a doubled die show a doubled image. There are many different causes of doubled dies and many doubled die coins. Sometimes mistakenly called "double die."

doubloon—Popular slang name given to Spanish gold 8-escudo pieces of the Conquistador era, often associated with pirate treasure; also, a medal in special circumstances, as in a Mardi Gras doubloon. Name also given to the 1787 Brasher doubloon, a privately struck gold coin.

drachm—An ancient Greek silver coin (pronounced "dram"), plural drachms. Drachma (pronounced "DRAHK-muh") is the modern Greek denomination, plural drachmas.

ducat—Medieval gold coin; also any of a number of modern issues of the Dutch Mint. Pronounced "DUCK-et." Modern slang has spread its use to mean "ticket."

- E -

eagle—A gold $10 coin of the United States.

edge—Often termed the third side of a coin, it is the surface perpendicular to the obverse and reverse. Not to be confused with "rim." Edges can be plain, lettered or milled (reeded or with some other repetitive device).

Educational notes—The Series 1896 $1, $2 and $5 silver certificates are called Educational notes because of the allegorical and educational themes of the vignettes. Replaced in 1899 with a new series.

electrotype—A copy or reproduction of a coin,

token or medal made by the electroplating process.

electrum—Naturally occurring alloy of gold and silver used for early coins of the Mediterranean region.

elongated coin—An oval medalet produced by a roller die using a coin, token or medal as a planchet, usually a cent. The noun form of the coin is "elongate."

encapsulated coin—A coin that has been sealed in a plastic holder, especially by a third-party grading service. Also called slabbed.

encased postage stamp—A postage stamp unofficially encased in a metal, plastic or cardboard frame and intended to be used as small change.

error—A coin, token, medal or paper money item evidencing a mistake made in its manufacture.

essai, essay—In paper money, a print made to test a design; analogous to a trial strike in coinage. See also proof.

euro—A monetary and currency denomination used by countries participating in the European Union currency union.

European Currency Union—An organization of European nations that adopted a common currency, the euro. Participating nations in Europe (the "eurozone") replace their national coinages and paper money with euro-denominated coins and notes. The euro coins and paper money begin circulating in January 2002. See euro.

exergue—(Pronounced "EX-surge") Area on a coin generally below the main design area, often site of date.

exonumia—A broad category of nonmoney, non-legal-tender numismatic items, including tokens, medals and badges. An exonumist is a specialist in exonumia. See also numismatics.

experimental pieces—Struck from any convenient dies to test a new metal, new alloy or new denomination; those testing a new shape; those testing a standard metal for a new denomination; and those representing changes in planchets for the purposes of combating counterfeiting.

eye appeal—The quality of a coin's attractiveness, distinct from any quantifiable measure of condition.

- F -

face—The front of a currency note, generally the side with signatures; analogous to the obverse of a coin.

face value—Refers to the value of a piece of currency; the denomination that appears on the note or coin.

fantasy—An object having the physical characteristics of a coin, issued by an agency other than a governing authority yet purporting to be issued by a real or imaginary governing authority as a coin.

Federal Reserve Bank note—A form of U.S. paper money authorized by the Federal Reserve Acts of Dec. 23, 1913, and April 23, 1918, and by the Act of March 9, 1933. The obligation to pay was by the individual issuing bank, not the federal government or other Federal Reserve Banks. The 1933 notes were an emergency issue to alleviate a shortage of paper money. Not to be confused with Federal Reserve notes.

Federal Reserve note—A form of U.S. paper money authorized by the Federal Reserve Act of February 1913. The obligation to pay is on the United States government and not the issuing banks. This is the only form of paper money currently being printed in the United States.

fiat money—"Unbacked" currency, that which cannot be converted into coin or specie of equal value.

field—The flat part of a surface of a coin surrounding and between the head, legend or other designs.

fineness—Represents the purity of precious metal, either in monetary or bullion form. Most forms of precious metal require an additional metal to provide a durable alloy. Often stated in terms of purity per 1,000 parts: A .925 fine silver coin has 92.5 percent silver and 7.5 percent other metal.

fixed-price list—A price list or catalog of coins, exonumia, paper money or other numismatic items offered at set prices.

flan—A term meaning planchet, generally used for world coins.

flip—A coin holder, usually plastic, that has two pouches, one to hold a coin and the other to hold identification. It is folded over, or "flipped," to close.

flow lines—Microscopic striations in a coin's surface caused by the movement of metal under striking pressures.

follis—A Roman and Byzantine coin denomination; plural is folli.

fractional—Referring to bullion coin, those of less that 1 ounce.

fractional currency—Usually refers to the United States paper money issued from 1862 to 1876 in denominations from 3 to 50 cents.

frost—Crystallized-metal effect caused by striking coin with specially treated dies (where part of die surface is blasted with physical media, pickled in acid or bombarded by computer-guided laser energy) that contrasts with the highly polished, mirrored fields. The "frost" on a coin resembles the frost on a lawn. Often used in reference to Proof coins.

full bell lines—Term is used to describe the lower incused bands on the Liberty Bell on the reverse of the Franklin half dollar when the bands are fully visible, indicative of a sharp strike. Some grading services permit a coin with a slight disturbance to the bands to still receive the "full bell lines" designation. Abbreviated "FBL."

full details—Term coined by numismatist Q. David Bowers to describe an exceptionally well struck coin, with all of the design elements fully struck and formed. Bowers advocates this term over such terms as "full bell lines" and "full head" since some coins bearing those fully struck details still may be weakly struck elsewhere in the design.

full head—Term is used to describe Liberty's head on the Standing Liberty quarter dollar when the figure's cap and head features have full detail. Other areas of a full head coin such as the shield Liberty holds still may be weakly struck.

full split bands, full bands—Term is used to describe the central bands binding the rods that form the fasces on the reverse of the Winged Liberty Head dime when the bands are fully separated. The full split bands generally describe a dime that is well struck. There must be no disturbance to the separation between the bands in order to qualify as full split bands.

full steps—Term is used to describe the steps on Monticello on the reverse of Jefferson 5-cent coins when 5½ or 6 steps are fully defined. There can be no disturbances or interruptions between or crossing the steps.

- G -

galvano—Although no longer used by the United States Mint, a galvano was a metal, larger-than-life model of one side of a coin that was mounted in a reduction engraving machine. The machine traced the design elements of the galvano, reduced them in size through a series of gears, and cut an exact replica into the blank face of a piece of die steel to create the master hub. From this hub, dies were created. The U.S. Mint replaced the galvano with an epoxy model during the latter years of the 20th century, and then in the 21st century replaced the epoxy model with a coin-sized steel model cut by computer-guided laser, making the use of the reduction engraving machine unnecessary. See "master hub."

German silver—An alloy of copper, nickel and zinc but no silver. Also called American silver, Feuchtwanger's composition, nickel silver. Resembles silver in appearance.

gold certificate—A form of U.S. paper money once redeemable in gold coin. Temporarily made illegal for most to hold between 1933 and 1964.

goldine—A gold-colored finish often used for medals or tokens.

grading—The process of determining a coin or note's condition or state of preservation.

- H -

hairlines—Fine scratches in the surface of the coin. Not to be confused with die scratches.

half dime, half disme—A silver 5-cent coin of the United States. The Mint Act of April 2, 1792, authorizes "half dismes."

half dollar—A 50-cent coin of the United States. The Mint Act of April 2, 1792, authorizes "half dollars."

half eagle—A gold $5 coin of the United States.

hammer die—The die that performs the striking

action; see also "anvil die."

hammer price—In an auction, the price the auctioneer calls the winning bid, excluding any additional fees the buyer may have to pay for the lot.

Hard Times token—An unofficial large cent-sized copper token struck in a wide variety of types during 1833 to 1843, serving as de facto currency, and bearing a politically inspired legend; or issued with advertising as a store card.

Helvetia—Gold bullion coins issued by Switzerland; also, the allegorical figure representing Switzerland. From the name given to the area by the Romans.

hoard—Usually a deposit of coins, secreted at some time in the past, discovered accidentally.

hobo nickel—An Indian Head 5-cent coin with Indian bust engraved to resemble a hobo or other individual. Engraving may also alter the bison on the reverse.

hologram—A three-dimensional image on a flat surface, gaining experimental use as a security device on credit cards and printed currency.

hub—A right-reading, positive punch used to impress wrong-reading dies.

- I -

inaugural medal—A medal issued by the official inaugural committee commemorating the inauguration of a U.S. president.

incuse—The opposite of bas-relief; design is recessed rather than raised. Used when referring to coins, medals, tokens and other metallic items.

Indian Head—The preferred name for the 5-cent coin often called "Buffalo nickel." Indian Head cents, gold dollars, gold $3 coins, $5 half eagles and $10 eagles have also been produced.

Indian peace medal—A medal issued by a government agency to an Indian in an attempt to earn goodwill. The U.S. government issued Indian peace medals from the administration of George Washington through the administration of Andrew Johnson.

intaglio—A method of printing using engraved plates. Paper is forced into the ink-filled lines of the plate, leaving a raised line of ink on the paper. U.S. paper money is printed mainly by the intaglio method, although the notes issued since the early 21st century also bear other forms of printing.

intrinsic—As applied to value, the net metallic value as distinguished from face and numismatic value.

irradiated dime—Collectible made by exposing Roosevelt dimes to cesium or other radioactive substance and then placing in a special package; harmless, as any "acquired radioactivity" has dissipated by the time it reaches collectors.

- J -

jugate—Accolated, conjoined.

- K -

Koala—Generic name for a .9995 fine platinum

bullion series of coins of Australia.

Kookaburras—Generic name for a .999 fine silver bullion series of coins of Australia.

Krugerrand—A gold bullion coin of South Africa introduced in 1967. It is composed of .9167 fine gold and has been produced in 1-ounce, half-ounce, quarter-ounce and tenth-ounce sizes, although each coin contains a full measure of pure gold (the gold is alloyed with other metals). For a period starting in 1986, it was illegal to import Krugerrands into the United States and other nations under restrictions imposed on South Africa in reaction to the nation's apartheid policies. Import restrictions were lifted in 1994, following governmental and policy changes in South Africa.

- L -

lamination—Coinage defect consisting of a portion of the metal separating from the rest due to impurities or internal stresses; common with clad or plated coinage.

large cent—Refers to U.S. cents of 1793 to 1857, having a diameter between 26 and 29 millimeters, depending on the year of striking.

large date—A variety of coin on which the date is physically larger than other varieties of the same year.

legal tender—Currency (coins and paper money) explicitly determined by a government to be acceptable in the discharge of debts.

legal tender bullion coin—Government-issued precious metal coins produced for investors, they have legal tender status and usually a nominal face value, even though they are not intended to circulate as currency.

legend—The inscription on a numismatic item.

lepton—Denomination of various values and weights used throughout the ancient Greek world and in modern Greece, generally a small copper or bronze coin.

lettered edge—An incused or raised inscription on the edge of a coin.

Libertad—A silver bullion coin of Mexico, containing 1 ounce of .999 fine silver.

lignadenarist—A collector of wooden nickels and similar items.

Loon dollar—An aureate-nickel composition dollar coin depicting a common loon on the reverse, struck by Canada beginning in 1987 to replace the dollar note. Nickname: "Loonie."

love token—A coin that has been altered by smoothing one or both surfaces and engraving initials, scenes, messages, etc., thereon.

luster—Surface quality of a coin, result of light reflected from the microscopic flow lines. See Mint luster.

- M -

mail-bid sale—Similar to an auction, but all bids and transactions are completed through the mail, by telephone, via e-mail or through other electronic means; no bidding is conducted "in person."

Maple Leaf—A gold, silver or platinum bullion coin of Canada of various sizes and finenesses. Plural, Maple Leafs.

Maria Theresia taler—An Austrian silver trade coin dated 1780, but struck repeatedly since then with the same date.

master die—A metal punch used to produce "working hubs," which are then used to produce "working dies."

master hub—A metal punch used to produce "master dies."

Matte Proof—Especially U.S. gold coins of 1908 to 1916, coins produced from dies entirely sandblasted with no mirror surfaces. (See "frost.")

maverick—An example unidentifiable as to source, generally referring to a token.

medal—Usually a piece of metal, marked with a design or inscription, made to honor a person, place or event, or for artistic purposes; not intended to pass as money.

medalet—Depending on sources, a small medal no larger than 1 inch in diameter or a medal 35 millimeters in diameter or less.

medallion—A large Roman presentation piece of the fifth century. Sometimes used for a large medal, usually 3 or more inches in diameter.

medieval coin—A coin struck from about A.D. 500 to 1500.

Mercury—The unofficial nickname given to the Winged Liberty Head dime of 1916 to 1945. The designer never intended the coin to depict Mercury, a male Greek god. The bust on the dime is an allegorical female Liberty Head figure with a winged cap. Also, some coins have been plated outside the Mint with mercury to give them a "Prooflike" appearance; mercury metal is highly toxic and these coins should not be handled.

microprinting—Extremely small lettering difficult to discern with the naked eye, used as an anti-counterfeiting device on paper money.

milling; milled coin—Milling refers to the devices on the edge of a coin; a milled coin is one struck by machine. The terms are related because the importance of the collar increased with machine-produced coinage.

minor coin—A silver coin of less than crown weight, or any coin struck in base metal.

Mint luster—The sheen or bloom on the surface of an Uncirculated numismatic object resulting from the centrifugal flow of metal caused by striking with dies. Mint luster or bloom is somewhat frosty in appearance as opposed to the mirror-like smoothness of the field of a Proof.

Mint mark—A letter or other symbol, sometimes of a privy nature, indicating the Mint of origin.

Mint set—Common term for an Uncirculated Mint set, an official set containing one of each coin struck during a given year.

mirror—Highly reflective surface or field of a coin; usually mirror field with frosted relief.

model—A clay or plaster three-dimensional design for a coin or medal.

modern coin—Traditionally, a coin struck after about A.D. 1500. However, in reference to U.S. coins (all of which are "modern" under the traditional definition), the term "modern" is reserved for coins struck after the mid-1960s (or later, according to some sources).

money—A medium of exchange.

money tree—A group of coins attached to each other by veins, the result of having been made by casting process through a die into which hot metal was poured. The coins can be removed from these veins and used individually.

mule—A coin, token or medal whose obverse die is not matched with its official or regular reverse die. Among coins, several categories of mules have been produced. A design mule is one where two mismatched designs of the same denomination are used together (for example, a controversial 1959-D Lincoln cent with 1909 to 1958 Wheat reverse instead of the proper Lincoln Memorial reverse). A denominational mule is one where dies for two different denominations are used together (the undated [2000] mule of a State quarter dollar obverse and Sacagawea dollar reverse on Sacagawea planchet). Other mules include a pairing of a Canadian coin die and medal die by the Royal Canadian Mint and a pairing of dies for Canadian 10-cent coins using different finishes. Paper money mules are notes with check numbers of physically different size paired on face and back.

- N -

national bank note—Paper money issued in United States by national banks from 1863 through 1929 and secured by government bonds or other collateral. Also called national currency.

National Coin Week—An annual observance sponsored by American Numismatic Association to acquaint the public with the hobby and science of numismatics, conducted in April.

national gold bank note—National bank notes payable in gold coin by some California banks and one Boston bank pursuant to authorization by Act of July 12, 1870.

nickel—A silver-white metal widely used for coinage, usually alloyed with copper. Also used as a nickname for the copper-nickel 5-cent coin, and in the mid-19th century, as a nickname for copper-nickel cents and 3-cent coins.

noncirculating legal tender coin—A coin made for collector consumption, but not for circulation, that is still redeemable as legal tender money in the country of issue. Abbreviated as NLCT.

novodel—An official restrike of a coin, typically of Russia or the Soviet Union, produced at the Mint of issue using genuine coin dies.

Nugget—Generic name for a .9999 fine series of gold bullion coins of Western Australia, produced by that Australian state's Perth Mint. Produced in various sizes and forms, including under the umbrella name Kangaroo Nugget (for its depictions of kangaroos).

numismatics—The science, study or collecting of coins, tokens, medals, orders and decorations, paper money and similar objects. See also exonumia.

numismatist—A person knowledgeable in numismatics.

- O -

obol—Greek denomination equal to one-sixth drachma.

obsolete bank note—Note of an American bank of issue prior to 1865; a more accurate term than "broken" bank note, since many note-issuing banks converted into national banks or liquidated without failing.

obverse—The side of a numismatic item that bears the principal design or device, often as prescribed by the issuing authority. In paper money, this is called the face. Commonly called the "heads" side of a coin.

offset—Printing method in which a metallic plate places an ink impression on an elastic blanket that then transfers the ink to the paper. Also, a term sometimes used to describe a blanket impression paper money error.

Onza—Generic name for a family of precious metal bullion coins of Mexico.

OPA token—A cardboard fiber token issued in the United States by the Office of Price Administration in 1944 during World War II. OPA tokens were used to make change for meat and processed food coupons (to keep track of ration points awarded each family during periods of rationing). They were issued in red and blue versions. Both sides of an OPA token depict a numeral 1 flanked by two small initials.

overdate—A form of die variety with a date made by a Mint engraver superimposing one or more numbers over the date on a previously dated die (as in 1799/8). Can also be a form of hubbing variety, in which two hubs of different dates were used to produce a die; an example of this kind of overdate is the 1943/2-P Jefferson 5-cent coin.

over Mint mark—A form of die variety with a Mint mark for one Mint punched over the Mint mark for another Mint. Coins struck from a die with an over Mint mark may show a strong primary Mint mark atop a less distinct Mint mark. An example is the 1944-D/S Lincoln cent; it bears a strong D Mint mark punched over a weaker S Mint mark.

- P -

paper money—Printed monetary instruments. Modern collectors may be challenged for a new term as nations experiment with plastics and other materials for their printed currency.

patina—The surface quality that a coin acquires over time as the metal reacts with the environment.

pattern—Coin-like pieces designed to test proposed coin designs, mottoes or denominations proposed for adoption as a regular issue, struck in the metal to be issued for circulation and which were not adopted, at least in year of pattern issue. Sometimes used in a generic sense describing experimental pieces and trial pieces.

penny—A denomination of British coinage. Also, the commonly used though unofficial nickname for the U.S. cent.

pennyweight—A unit of weight, equal to 24 grains or 1/20 ounce troy weight.

peso—A unit of money used in Mexico and various Central American and South American nations.

Philharmonic—A .9999 fine gold bullion coin of Austria struck beginning in 1989 in four sizes: a 1-ounce, 2,000-schilling denomination; a half-ounce, 1,000-schilling coin; a half-ounce, 500-schilling coin; and a quarter-ounce, 200-schilling coin.

pieces of eight—Popular term for silver Spanish 8-real coins; often associated with pirate treasure.

piedfort—An alternative spelling for the word piefort.

piefort—A piece struck on a planchet twice or more the normal thickness. The French spelling used in Europe is piedfort.

pioneer gold coins—Gold coins, often privately produced, struck in areas of the United States to meet the needs of a coin shortage, generally in traditional U.S. denominations. The U.S. Assay Office of Gold coins of California—official coinage struck before the establishment of the San Francisco Mint—are part of the series. Also known as private gold and territorial gold.

planchet—The disc of metal or other material on which the dies of the coin, token or medal are impressed; also called blank, disc, flan. In paper money, a small colored disc embedded in the paper used as an anti-counterfeiting device.

plaster—See model.

plate number—On modern paper money, used as a cross reference for the plate number that appears on the margin of a currency sheet and that is trimmed from the note before it enters circulation, to identify the printing plate from which the note came. Formerly called a check number. On notes printed on a sheet-fed press, the check number is a letter and number combination appearing in the lower right corner on the face; on the back, it is a number only, appearing at the lower right. On experimental $1 notes printed on a web-fed press, the plate or check number appears in the same location on the face as on a note printed on a sheet-fed press, but it lacks the letter found on the sheet-fed notes; the plate number on the back has been moved to above the E in ONE, rather than below it as on the sheet-fed notes.

PNC—Abbreviation of philatelic-numismatic combination (or cover). A combination of a coin, medal, token or other numismatic item inserted into an envelope that is postmarked on a special occasion, such as the release of a new coin. The numismatic item (or numis) is generally visible through a window in the envelope.

polymer—The plastic substrate composition used rather than paper materials in some notes.

postage note—The First Issue fractional note series.

postal note—Forerunner of the postal money order, issued by the U.S. Post Office.

pound—A unit of money (coins and notes) in Great Britain.

premium quality—A coin certified by a third-party grading service as higher than the grade assigned, but not high enough to warrant the next grade increment.

Prestige Proof set—A special U.S. Proof set, containing regular Proof coins plus one or two commemorative coins of that year. It was first offered in 1983 with a 1983-S Olympic silver dollar and offered in subsequent years with commemorative coins of other programs. Production ended in 1997.

privy mark—Small device used on coinage often commemorative in nature, similar to Mint mark in placement, but not indicative of Mint of origin.

probe—A rejected pattern for a coin, typically European or South American, that is struck in quantities for collectors. These typically display the word "probe" as part of their legends.

Proof—A coin struck on specially prepared planchets on special presses to receive the highest quality strike possible, especially for collectors. For paper money, a proof is a print made to test the plate, analogous to a die trial strike in coinage.

prooflike—An Uncirculated coin having received special minting treatment and a mirror surface for the benefit of collectors, with minor imperfections due to the minting process possible and permissible.

Proof set—A set of one Proof coin of each current denomination issued by a recognized Mint for a specific year. See Prestige Proof set.

- Q -

quarter dollar—A 25-cent coin of the United States.

quarter eagle—A gold $2.50 coin of the United States.

- R -

rare—A comparative term denoting a high degree of scarcity. Often modified adverbially, e.g., very rare or extremely rare; or modified by the use of figures, e.g., R-4 or R-7. There is no universally accepted scale of rarity.

"Red Book"—Nickname given to *A Guide Book of United States Coins,* an annually published price guide. The cover of the original editions (all produced in hardcover) was red in color, hence the nickname. Gives retail prices, or what dealers might charge for U.S. coins.

reeded edge—The result of a minting process that

creates vertical serrations on the edge of a coin.

relief—Raised. In coinage and medallic numismatic items, a relief design is raised above the surface of the field. Sometimes called bas-relief. Opposite of incuse and intaglio.

replica—A copy of the original, a facsimile, a reproduction.

repunched Mint mark—A form of die variety with a Mint mark that is punched into a die more than once, with signs of both Mint marks visible on coins struck from that die. The two Mint marks may overlap or be totally separated. For example, the 1960-D/D Lincoln cents have many varieties.

restrike—A numismatic item produced from original dies at a later date; for coins, usually not with a view to meeting monetary requirements but to fill a demand for a numismatic rarity.

reverse—The side opposite to that on which the head or principal figure is impressed. The side opposite the obverse. On paper money this is called the back. Commonly called the "tails" side for coins.

rim—Raised border around the circumference of a coin, not to be confused with the edge.

ringed bimetallic—A coin planchet assembled with two distinctly different metal compositions, one as the outer ring and the other as the center. The two pieces are locked together and jointly depict the images on the coin surfaces.

ringed trimetallic—A coin planchet assembled with three distinctly different metal compositions, one as the outer ring, a second as an inner ring and the third as the center. The three pieces are locked together and jointly depict the images on the coin surfaces.

- S -

scarce—Not common, but not as uncommon as rare.

screw press—Early hand-operated machine for striking coins.

scrip—Paper currency usually of denominations less than $1 issued as substitutes for currency by private persons or organizations. Tokens issued by coal mines and sutlers also are called scrip. See "community scrip."

scripophily—The study and science of collecting financial documents, including stock certificates, shares, government and private bonds, and checks. A student of scripophily is a scripophilist.

seal—A device placed on paper money indicating authority of issue. Modern Federal Reserve notes have two seals—a green Department of Treasury seal and a black Federal Reserve seal.

security thread—A strip inserted into the substrate of paper money and used as an anti-counterfeiting device. Security threads used on Federal Reserve notes bear legends stating the note's denomination and glow when exposed to ultraviolet light, or bear "moving" design elements.

seigniorage—The profits resulting from the difference between the cost to make a coin and its face value, or its worth as money and legal tender. Most coins cost less to make than their face value. See Mint chapter.

serial number—Number used chiefly on paper money and sometimes on limited-issue medals to indicate order of production.

series—Related coinage of the same denomination, design and type, including modifications, or varieties, of design. The Lincoln, Wheat cents of 1909 to 1958 represent a complete series.

sestertius—An ancient Roman coin; plural, sestertii.

shekel, sheqel—Shekel is a silver coin of ancient Judaea of various weights. Sheqel is the modern Israeli denomination; plural, sheqalim.

silver certificate—Authorized by the Acts of Feb. 28, 1878, and Aug. 4, 1886. Was redeemable in silver coin, and in early to mid-1960s, silver bullion. No longer produced, but all silver certificates remain legal tender although the notes can no longer be redeemed in silver.

slab—Popular nickname for certain kinds of coin encapsulation methods, especially those that are permanently sealed and rectangular. Sometimes used in verb form, as in "slabbed." See encapsulated coin.

slug—A term applied to the gold $50 coin issued by various private Mints in California from 1851 to 1855 occurring in both round and octagonal shapes, or to tokens manufactured expressly for use in certain coin-operated machines.

small date—A variety of coin on which the date is physically smaller than other varieties of the same year. Similar varieties include medium date and large date.

so-called dollar—A silver dollar-sized medal commemorating a special event. Cataloged in *So-Called Dollars* (see Chapter 22, Books).

souvenir card—Collectible item, usually well-printed on heavy paper using an engraving used on paper money, stamps or related items. Often also contain historical or commemorative information.

Souvenir Mint sets—An issue of the U.S. Mint, containing the coinage of one Mint. Souvenir Mint sets are generally sold only at the Mint represented by the coins.

Special Mint sets (SMS)—Coins produced under special conditions by the United States Mint at San Francisco during 1965, 1966 and 1967. The coins have no Mint marks. Some 1964 coins are known with a finish the same as or similar to that used on the coins in the Special Mint sets, though the circumstances of their issue are unknown to collectors and dealers.

specie—In the form of coin, especially precious metal coin; paper money redeemable in coin. From Latin meaning "in kind"; see also fiat money.

star notes—Mainly intended as replacements for notes that were damaged or produced with errors or mistakes at the Bureau of Engraving and Printing. On modern Federal Reserve notes, a solid star appears at the end of the serial number; on earlier notes, the star appears at the beginning of the number. Until the 1980s, star notes were also used to represent the 100 millionth note since the serial numbering machinery has only eight digits.

state coinages or notes—Refers to coins issued by one of three state governments (Connecticut, Massachusetts and New Jersey) between the Declaration of Independence and the ratification of the U.S. Constitution when the states' rights to issue coins were suspended, in the period from 1786 to 1788. Vermont issued a copper coinage as an independent republic from 1785 to 1788 before it joined the Union. New York coppers issued in 1786 and 1787 were not authorized by the state. Among paper money, refers to notes issued between Declaration of Independence and Civil War by state governments. See Colonials.

State quarter dollars—Program of 50 commemorative quarter dollars issued from 1999 to 2008, one for each state in the Union. Five coins were issued each year in the order in which the state entered the Union, starting with the Delaware coin and ending with the Hawaii quarter dollar. Issued for circulation and in annual collector sets offered by the U.S. Mint. The program is credited with popularizing coin collecting nationwide, with more than 140 million American adults collecting the coins at the peak of interest.

stater—Greek coin equal to two drachms, a didrachm, or 12 obols.

Stella—A U.S. gold $4 pattern never issued for circulation. Also struck in other metals.

sterling silver—Silver that is .925 fine; in Israel, .935 fine silver. From the British standard "pound sterling."

store card—A token bearing a business name and/or address, and often intended as a local or ad-hoc medium of exchange as well as an advertisement for the issuer.

strike—The act of impressing the image of a die into a planchet, making a coin. The quality of strike is important when determining the amount of wear.

strip—Rolls of coinage metal to be punched into planchets.

surcharge—An extra charge placed on an item, the revenue of which is usually earmarked for a specific fund. Since 1983 it has been the practice of the United States Congress to place a surcharge on commemorative coins, usually to benefit an organization.

syngraphics—The study of printed currency and related items; from "syngraph," a writing signed by all parties to a contract or bond.

- T -

token—Usually a piece of durable material appropriately marked and unofficially issued, used monetarily, in exchange for goods or services specified, as advertising or for other use.

Trade dollar—A silver dollar coin produced for overseas markets. The United States issued a Trade dollar between 1873 and 1885 for use in the Orient. Great Britain also issued a Trade dollar. Also used incorrectly to refer to Canadian trade tokens of $1 nominal value.

Treasury note—Sometimes called a coin note. Issued under the Act of July 14, 1890. Redeemable in silver and gold coins.

tree coinage—Silver coins issued by the Massachusetts Colony in three forms: Willow Tree, Oak Tree, and Pine Tree. Issued between 1652 to 1682 although all but one are dated 1652.

tribute penny—A silver denarius of the Roman emperor Tiberius.

trime—Unofficial nickname given to the silver 3-cent coin. Formed by combining "tri" and the last two letters of "dime."

type set—A collection composed of one of each coin of a given series or period.

- U -

Uncirculated Mint set—Set of coins issued by the U.S. Mint, consisting of one of each coin issued for circulation from each issuing facility. Also called Uncirculated set or a Mint set. The Mint is required by law to issue Uncirculated Mint sets every year.

uncut sheet—Refers to the 32-note (or 32-subject) sheets of Federal Reserve notes sold by the Bureau of Engraving and Printing. The 16-note and four-note sheets sold are cut partial sheets, although they are often referred to as uncut sheets. Earlier sheets of U.S. paper money were produced with different numbers of notes.

uniface—A coin or note having a design on one side only.

unique—Extant in only one known specimen. Very often misused, as in "semi-unique."

U.S. Gold—Marketing name for American Arts Gold Medallions. See Precious Metals and Bullion Coin chapters for more details.

United States note—A specific type of note first authorized in 1862 and called legal tender notes; name officially changed to United States notes in July 1873. The term "United States note" is not a generic term for all forms of U.S. paper money.

upsetting mill—A machine that squeezes planchets so that they have a raised rim, in preparation for striking.

- V -

vectures—Transportation-related tokens, including but not limited to subway and bus tokens, parking tokens and car wash tokens.

vecturist—A collector who specializes in transportation tokens.

vignette—A pictorial element of a note design that shades off gradually into the surrounding unprinted paper or background rather than having sharp outlines or a frame.

Voyageur dollar—A Canadian silver dollar coin between 1936 and 1966 and a nickel composition dollar coin between 1968 and 1987 depicting a trapper and an Indian in a canoe on the reverse. A variation of the design has been used on Canadian commemorative coinage as well.

- W -

wampum—Small beads made of shells used by North American Indians as money and for ornamentation.

want list—A list given by a collector to a dealer listing items the collector desires for a collection. The dealer keeps the want list and attempts to purchase items listed on it for the collector.

watermark—Design formed by creating differing thicknesses of paper during production; often used as security device in paper money. Watermarks were first used on Federal Reserve notes with the Series 1996 $100 note.

web note—A Series 1988A, 1993 or 1995 $1 Federal Reserve note printed on an experimental press that printed notes on a continuous roll ("web") of paper rather than individual sheets. The Bureau of Engraving and Printing operated the press from 1992 to 1995. Development of the press was halted in 1996 by congressional mandate. Web notes were placed into circulation and are prized by collectors. They differ in slight details from notes printed on a conventional sheet-fed press, including lacking the plate position indicator found in the upper left corner of the face (see "check number" for additional details).

whizzing—The severe polishing of a coin in an attempt to improve its appearance and salability to the uninformed. A form of alteration regarded as inappropriate and misleading by the numismatic community, and that actually lowers the value of the coin.

widow's mite—An ancient Jewish lepton denomination coin of the time of Christ.

windowed—A security thread used in notes in which the thread is only partially visible on one side of the note due to the penetration of the thread into the other side.

Winged Liberty Head—The correct terminology for describing the obverse of what is often nicknamed the "Mercury" dime, a dime designed by Adolph A. Weinman and struck between 1916 and 1945.

wire rim—Slight flange on coins or medals caused by heavy striking pressure, often characteristic on Proof coins. The metal is squeezed up the side of the die faces by the collar die. Sometimes called knife rim. Sometimes incorrectly called wire edge.

wooden nickels—Originally, substitute for coins first used in the 1931 to 1935 Depression, having originated in Tenino, Wash. Issued in round or rectangular form and in many denominations. Currently used for advertising and souvenir purposes. Many collectors collect wooden nickels. Also known as wooden money or woods.

working die—A metal punch that is used to impress images into coins; wrong-reading.

working hub—A metal punch used to produce "working dies"; right-reading.

- Y -

year set—A set of coins for any given year, generally containing one specimen of each coin from each Mint issued for circulation, and packaged privately, not by the government.

- Z -

zinc—Metal used in many coinage alloys by mints worldwide. First used for U.S. Mint coinage in 1864 for the bronze Indian Head cent (replacing the copper-nickel alloy used in the cent; the 1864 bronze alloy also featured 95 percent copper and about 1 percent tin) and new 2-cent coins, then in a new application for the 1943 Lincoln zinc-coated steel cent. The alloy of the cent was changed from 95 percent copper and 5 percent zinc to copper-plated zinc.

Zinc is also used in the alloy for Sacagawea, Presidential and Native American dollars.

Index

Tips on using the Index

Researchers seeking information about U.S. coinage will find a general section under the heading of "U.S. coins." In addition, there are individual listings for each denomination. Denominations known primarily by their numeric name—2-cent coin, 3-cent coin, 20-cent coin, for example—are listed at the beginning of the index. All other U.S. denominations are listed alphabetically. We also list all individual series of U.S. coins, such as Indian Head cent, Lincoln cent and State quarter dollars. Those denominations with more than one name—5-cent coin and "nickel," for example—are listed under their "real" name rather than their "common" nickname.

Index of Advertisers